NEPHROLOGY

NOTICE

Medicine is an ever-changing science. As new research and clinical experience broaden our knowledge, changes in treatment and drug therapy are required. The editors and the publisher of this work have checked with sources believed to be reliable in their effort to provide information that is complete and generally in accord with the standards accepted at the time of publication. However, in view of the possibility of human error or changes in medical sciences, neither the editors nor the publishers nor any other party who has been involved in the preparation or publication of this work warrants that the information contained herein is in every respect accurate or complete, and they are not responsible for any errors or omissions or the results obtained from the use of such information. Readers are encouraged to confitm the information contained herein with other sources. For example and in particular, readers are advised to check the product information sheet included in the package of each drug they plan to administer to be certain that the information contained in this book is accurate and that changes have not been made in the recommended dose or in the contraindications for administration. This recommendation is particularly important in connection with new or infrequently used drugs.

NEPHROLOGY

Editor-in-chief
FRANCESCO P. SCHENA
Professor of Nephrology
Department of Nephrology
University of Bari
University Hospital
Bari – Italy

Editors
ALEXANDER M. DAVISON
Professor of Renal Medicine
Department of Renal Medicine
St. James's University Hospital
Leeds – United Kingdom

HEIN A. KOOMANS
Professor of Nephrology
Department of Nephrology and Hypertension
University of Utrecht
University Medical Center Utrecht
Utrecht – The Netherlands

JEAN-PIERRE GRÜNFELD
Professor of Nephrology
Department of Nephrology
René Descartes University of Paris V
Necker Hospital
Paris – France

FERNANDO VALDERRÀBANO
Professor of Medicine
Department of Nephrology
Complutense University
Gregorio Maranon Hospital
Madrid – Spain

FOKKO J. VAN DER WOUDE
Professor of Nephrology
V Medical University Clinic Mannheim
Karl Ruprechts University of Heidelberg
Mannheim Hospital
Mannheim – Germany

Consulting editor
THOMAS E. ANDREOLI
Professor of Internal Medicine
Department of Internal Medicine
University of Arkansas College of Medicine
Little Rock — USA

McGraw-Hill International (UK) Ltd.

London • New York • San Francisco • St. Louis • Auckland • Bogotà • Caracas • Lisbon • Madrid • Mexico City • Milan • Montréal • New Delhi • San Juan • Singapore • Sydney • Tokyo • Toronto

NEPHROLOGY

Shoppenhangers Road
Maidenhead, Berkshire
SL6-2QL England

McGraw-Hill

A Division of the ***McGraw-Hill*** *Companies*

Editor-in-Chief: Francesco P. Schena
Acquisition Editor: Sandra Fabiani
Production Manager: Gino La Rosa
Copyediting and proof-reading: Lorenza Dainese, Faith Voit
Preparation of index: Marji Toensing
Typesetting: Cromographic, Milano, Italy
Printing: CPM, Casarile, Milano, Italy

Cover and page XXI illustration courtesy of: Pascoli Perugino A. *Il Corpo Umano*, Fidenza: Casa Editrice Mattioli, 1991; edition published exclusively for Master Pharma (Parma, Italy), plate II, page 21.

ISBN 007-709525-1
Printed in Italy

Contents

Contributors

Numbers in brackets refer to chapters written or co-written by the cotributor

Dwomoa Adu, MD, FRCP
Doctor
Division of Nephrology
Queen Elisabeth Hospital
Birmingham - United Kingdom [3]

Jean-Michel Achard, MD, PhD
Professor of Physiology
Department of Physiology
University Hospital of Limoges
Limoges - France [12]

Thomas E. Andreoli, MD (HON), MACP, SCD
Professor and The Nolan Chair in Internal Medicine
Department of Internal Medicine
University of Arkansas College of Medicine
Little Rock, Arkansas - USA

Syed M. Alam, MD
Doctor
Department of Nephrology
Fort Sanders Regional Medical Center
Knoxville, Tennessee - USA [25]

Andrew R. Allen, MA, BMBCH, MRCP
Doctor
Renal Section, Division of Medicine
Imperial College School of Medicine
Hammersmith Hospital
London - United Kingdom [21]

Alessandro Amore, MD
Doctor
Department of Nephrology, Dialysis and Transplantation
Regina Margherita Children's Hospital
Torino - Italy [50]

Rashad S. Barsoum, MD, FRCP, FRCPE
Professor of Internal Medicine
Department of Internal Medicine
University of Cairo
Kasr-El-Aini Hospital
Cairo - Egypt [24]

Shanmukham Bhaskaran, MD, DNB (NEPH)
Doctor
The Voluntary Health Services
Ethicare Medical Speciality Centre
Chennai - India [16]

Jo H.M. Berden, MD, PhD
Professor of Nephrology
Division of Nephrology, Department of Medicine
University of Nijmegen
University Hospital St. Radboud
Nijmegen - The Netherlands [22]

Elisabeth W. Boeschoten, MD, PhD
Professor of Medicine
Department of Medicine
University of Amsterdam
Academic Medical Centre
Amsterdam - The Netherlands [45]

Hugh R. Brady, MD, PhD, FRCPI
Professor of Medicine
Department of Medicine and Therapeutics
University College Dublin
Mater Misericordiae Hospital
Dublin - Ireland [43]

Ruth C. Campbell, MD
Doctor
Department of Medicine
University of Alabama
Birmingham, AL - USA [41]

Fernando Carrera, MD
Doctor
Department of Nephrology and Dialysis
SAMS Hospital
Lisbon - Portugal [35]

Daniel C. Cattran, MD, FRCP(C), FACS
Professor of Medicine
Department of Nephrology
University of Toronto
University Health Network - The Toronto General Division
Toronto - Canada [16]

CARLOS CHIURCHIU, MD
Doctor
Renal Service
Catholic University of Cordoba
Centro Medico de Cordoba Private Hospital
Cordoba - Argentina [52]

MICHAEL R. CLARKSON, MRCPI
Doctor
Department of Medicine and Therapeutics
University College Dublin
Mater Misericordiae Hospital
Dublin - Ireland [43]

GIOVANNI CONTI, MD
Doctor
Department of Nephrology, Dialysis and Transplantation
Regina Margherita Children's Hospital
Torino - Italy [50]

ROSANNA COPPO, MD
Doctor
Department of Nephrology, Dialysis and Transplantation
Regina Margherita Children's Hospital
Torino - Italy [50]

DANIEL J. CORDONNIER, MD
Professor of Nephrology
Department of Nephrology
University Hospital CHU
Grenoble - France [38]

JOSÈ MIGUEL CRUZ, MD
Doctor
Department of Nephrology
University of Valencia
La Fe Hospital
Valencia - Spain [37]

ALEXANDER M. DAVISON, MD, FRCP
Professor of Renal Medicine
Department of Renal Medicine
St. James's University Hospital
Leeds - United Kingdom [26]

JOHN M. DAVISON, MD, PhD
Professor of Obstetric Medicine
Department of Obstetrics and Gynaecology
University of Newcastle-upon-Tyne
Royal Victoria Infirmary
Newcastle-upon-Tyne - United Kingdom [49]

PAUL E. DE JONG, MD, PhD
Professor of Nephrology
Division of Nephrology, Department of Internal Medicine
University of Groningen
Hospital of Groningen
Groningen - The Netherlands [48]

THOMAS A. DEPNER, MD
Professor of Medicine
Department of Internal Medicine
University of California
UC Davis Medical Center
Sacramento - USA [46]

DICK DE ZEEUW, MD, PhD
Professor of Clinical Pharmacology
Department of Clinical Pharmacology and Nephrology
University of Groningen
Hospital of Groningen
Groningen - The Netherlands [48]

JEAN-PAUL FERMAND, MD
Professor of Immunology
Department of Immunohematology
University of Paris VII
Saint-Louis Hospital
Paris - France [23]

DANILO FLISER, MD
Professor of Nephrology
Department of Nephrology
Hannover Medical School
Hannover - Germany [11]

JOÃO M. FRAZÃO, MD
Doctor
Department of Nephrology
S. Joâo Hospital
Porto - Portugal [35]

SOLEDAD GARCIA DE VINUESA, MD
Doctor
Department of Nephrology
Complutense University
Gregorio Maranon Hospital
Madrid - Spain [32]

JAMES M. GLOOR, MD
Associate Professor of Nephrology and Transplant
Department of Nephrology and Transplant
Mayo Clinic Rochester Methodist Hospital
Rochester, Minnesota - USA [31]

FRANCISCO J. GÓMEZ-CAMPDERÀ, MD
Visiting Professor of Nephrology
Department of Nephrology
Complutense University
Gregorio Maranon Hospital
Madrid - Spain [51]

JEAN-PIERRE GRÜNFELD, MD
Professor of Nephrology
Department of Nephrology
René Descartes University of Paris V
Necker Hospital
Paris - France [40, 42]

LISA M. GUAY-WOODFORD, MD, PhD
Professor of Medicine and Pediatrics
Department of Medicine
University of Alabama at Birmingham
Birmingham, Alabama - USA [41]

ALI TAHA HASSAN, MD
Doctor
Department of Internal Medicine
South Valley University
Sohag University Hospital
Sohag - Egypt [33]

PASCAL HOUILLIER, MD, PhD
Professor of Physiology
Department of Physiology
University Pierre et Marie Curie
Broussais Hospital
Paris - France [12]

ALEXANDER J. HOWIE, MD, FRCPATH
Doctor
Department of Pathology
University of Birmingham
Birmingham - United Kingdom [3]

MICHEL JADOUL, MD
Doctor
Department of Nephrology
Cliniques St-Luc
Brussels - Belgium [53]

DOMINIQUE A. JOLY, MD
Doctor
Department of Nephrology and INSERM U507
Necker Hospital
Paris - France [40]

PAUL JUNGERS, MD
Professor of Nephrology
Department of Nephrology
University of Paris
Necker Hospital
Paris - France [9, 30]

PAUL L. KIMMEL, MD
Professor of Medicine
Division of Renal Diseases and Hypertension
Department of Medicine
George Washington University Medical Center
George Washington University Hospital
Washington DC - USA [1, 25]

HEIN A. KOOMANS, MD, PhD
Professor of Nephrology
Department of Nephrology and Hypertension
University of Utrecht
University Medical Center Utrecht
Utrecht - The Netherlands

RAYMOND T. KREDIET, MD, PhD
Associate Professor of Medicine
Renal Unit
University of Amsterdam
Academic Medical Centre
Amsterdam - The Netherlands [45]

FADI G. LAKKIS, MD
Professor of Medicine
Department of Nephrology
Emory University
Veterans Affairs Medical Center
Atlanta, Georgia - USA [33]

NORBERT H. LAMEIRE, MD
Professor of Medicine
Department of Internal Medicine
University of Gent
University Hospital
Gent - Belgium [6]

SUSIE Q. LEW, MD
Professor of Medicine
Division of Renal Diseases and Hypertension
Department of Medicine
George Washington University Medical Center
University Hospital
Washington DC - USA [25]

FRIEDRICH C. LUFT, MD, PhD
Professor of Medicine
Department of Nephrology, Hypertension and Genetics
Charité, Humbold University of Berlin
Franz-Volhard Klinik
Berlin - Germany [8]

JOSÉ LUÑO, MD, PhD
Assistant Professor of Medicine
Department of Nephrology
Complutense University
Gregorio Maranon Hospital
Madrid - Spain [32]

MANUEL MARTINEZ-MALDONADO, MD
Professor of Medicine
Department of Research Development and Administration
Oregon Health Sciences University
Portland, Oregon - USA [33]

PABLO U. MASSARI, MD
Professor of Medicine
Renal Service
Catholic University of Cordoba
Centro Medico de Cordoba Private Hospital
Cordoba - Argentina [52]

ALAIN MEYRIER, MD
Professor of Medicine
Department of Nephrology and Immunology
University of Paris VI
University Hospital Broussais
Paris - France [28]

GERJAN NAVIS, MD, PhD
Professor of Experimental Nephrology and Renal Pharmacology
Department of Medicine, Division of Nephrology
Department of Clinical Pharmacology
State University Hospital
Groningen - The Netherlands [48, Appendix]

PATRICK NIAUDET, MD
Professor of Pediatrics
Department of Pediatric Nephrology
University of Paris
Necker-Enfants Malades Hospital
Paris - France [13]

GUY H. NEILD, MD, FRCP, FRCPATH
Professor of Nephrology
Department of Nephrology
University College London
Middlesex Hospital
London - United Kingdom [2]

GIULIO ODONI, MD
Doctor
Department of Nephrology
Ruperto Carola University
Ludwig Krehl Klinic
Heidelberg - Germany [7, 44]

DAVID B.G. OLIVEIRA, PhD, FRCP
Professor of Renal Medicine
Department of Renal Medicine
St. George's Hospital Medical School
London - United Kingdom [18]

PATRIZIA PASSERINI, MD
Doctor
Department of Nephrology and Dyalisis
IRCCS Maggiore Hospital
Milano - Italy [15]

RAFAEL PÉREZ-GARCÍA, MD, PhD
Assistant Professor of Medicine
Department of Nephrology
Complutense University
Gregorio Maranon Hospital
Madrid - Spain [27]

LICIA PERUZZI, MD
Doctor
Department of Nephrology, Dialysis and Transplantation
Regina Margherita Children's Hospital
Torino - Italy [50]

CLAUDIO PONTICELLI, MD
Doctor
Department of Nephrology, Dialysis and Transplantation
Regina Margherita Children's Hospital
Milano - Italy [15]

GABRIELLA PORCELLINI, MD
Doctor
Department of Nephrology, Dialysis and Transplantation
Regina Margherita Children's Hospital
Torino - Italy [50]

CHARLES D. PUSEY, MD, PhD, MSC, FRCP, FRCPATH
Professor of Renal Medicine
Renal Section, Division of Medicine
Imperial College School of Medicine
Hammersmith Hospital
London - United Kingdom [21]

TON J. RABELINK, MD, PhD
Professor of Internal Medicine
Department of Vascular Medicine
University of Utrecht
University Medical Center Utrecht
Utrecht - The Netherlands [10]

SIMONA G.R. RACASAN, MD
Doctor
Department of Nephrology and Clinical Diagnosis
University of Cluj-Napoca
University Hospital Cluj-Napoca
Cluj-Napoca - Rumania [10]

GIUSEPPE REMUZZI, MD
Professor of Nephrology
Unit of Nephrology and Dialysis
Mario Negri Institute for Pharmacological Research
Bergamo - Italy [36]

EBERHARD RITZ, MD
Professor of Nephrology
Department of Nephrology
Ruperto Carola University
Ludwig Krehl Klinic
Heidelberg - Germany [7, 44]

ERIC RONDEAU, MD, PhD
Professor of Nephrology
Department of Nephrology
Pierre et Marie Curie University
Tenon Hospital
Paris - France [19]

MARK E. ROSENBERG, MD
Professor of Medicine
Department of Medicine
University of Minnesota
Minneapolis, Minnesota - USA [5]

PIERO RUGGENENTI, MD
Assistant Professor of Nephrology
Department of Nephrology and Dialysis
Mario Negri Institute for Pharmacological Research
Bergamo - Italy [36]

CAROLINE O.S. SAVAGE, MD
Professor of Nephrology
Division of Medical Sciences
University of Birmingham
Queen Elizabeth Hospital
Birmingham - United Kingdom [20]

FRANCESCO PAOLO SCHENA, MD
Professor of Nephrology
Department of Nephrology
University of Bari
University Hospital
Bari - Italy [17]

MICHAEL W. SCHÖMIG, MD
Doctor
Department of Nephrology
Ruperto Carola University
Ludwig Krehl Klinic
Heidelberg - Germany [7, 44]

GRAHAM C. SMITH, MA, MB, BS, MRCP, FRCPCH
Doctor
Department of Children Health
University of Wales College of Medicine
University Hospital of Wales
Cardiff, Wales - United Kingdom [29]

JUERGEN STREHLAU, MD
Associate Professor of Medicine
Department of Pediatric Nephrology and Metabolic Diseases
Hannover Medical School
Hannover - Germany [14]

AMIR TEJANI, MD
Professor of Pediatrics and Surgery
Department of Pediatrics
New York Medical College
Valhalla, New York - USA [14]

VINCENTE E. TORRES, MD
Professor of Medicine
Department of Internal Medicine
Division of Nephrology
Mayo Foundation
Mayo Clinic
Rochester, Minnesota - USA [31]

MICHAEL TRIMBLE, BMSC, MB, ChB, MRCP
Doctor
Department of Therapeutics and Pharmacology
Belfast City Hospital
Belfast - United Kingdom [54]

WAI Y. TSE, MD, MBCHB, MRCP, BSC, PhD
Consultant Nephrologist
Department of Nephrology
Derriford Hospital
Plymouth - United Kingdom [3]

FERNANDO VALDERRÀBANO, MD, PhD
Professor of Medicine
Department of Nephrology
Complutense University
Gregorio Maranon Hospital
Madrid - Spain [27]

FOKKO J. VAN DER WOUDE, MD, PhD
Professor of Nephrology
V Medical University Clinic Mannheim
Karl Ruprechts University of Heidelberg
Mannheim Hospital
Mannheim - Germany [47]

RAYMOND VANHOLDER, MD, PhD
Professor of Medicine
Renal Division, Department of Nephrology
University of Gent
Gent - Belgium [4]

JOSEPH A. VASSALOTTI, MD
Assistant Professor of Medicine
Department of Medicine
Mount Sinai Medical Center
New York - USA [1]

KATE VERRIER-JONES, MB, BCH, FRCP, FRCPH
Doctor
Department of Child Health
University of Wales College of Medicine
University Hospital of Wales
Cardiff, Wales - United Kingdom [29]

MICHAEL L. WATSON, MD, FRCP
Doctor
Medical Renal Unit
University of Edinburgh
Royal Infirmary
Edinburgh - United Kingdom [39]

ALESSANDRO ZUCCALÀ, MD
Doctor
Department of Nephrology
University of Bologna
University Hospital Sant'Orsola-Malpighi
Bologna - Italy [34]

PIETRO C. ZUCCHELLI, MD
Professor of Medicine
Department of Nephrology
University of Bologna
University Hospital Sant'Orsola-Malpighi
Bologna - Italy [34]

After the introduction of renal biopsy in nephrology in 1951 by Iversen and Brawn the classification of the glomerulonephritides completely changed. Histology, immunofluorescence and electron-microscopy disclosed a new view of diagnosis and therapy.

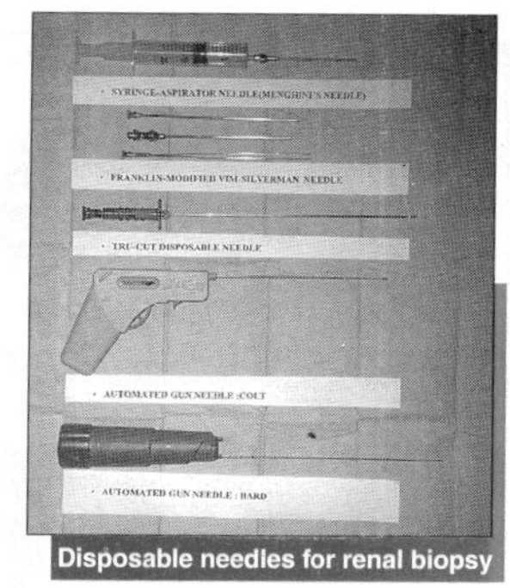

Disposable needles for renal biopsy

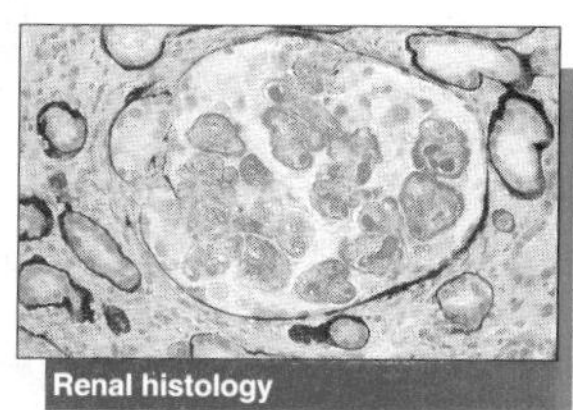

Renal histology

The first renal artificial kidney introduced by Kolff in 1950 has been replaced by modern multifunctional artificial kidneys which have improved the renal replacement therapy in uremic patients.

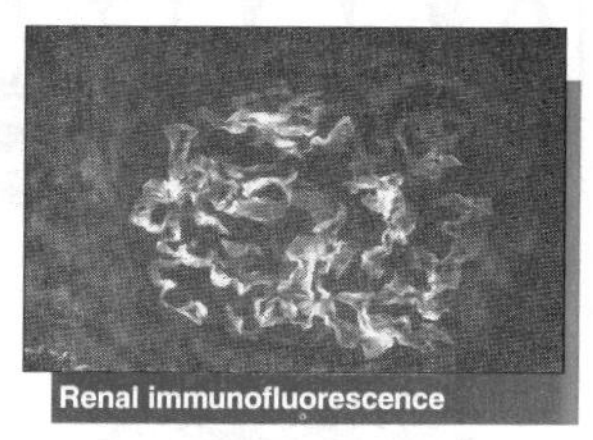

Renal immunofluorescence

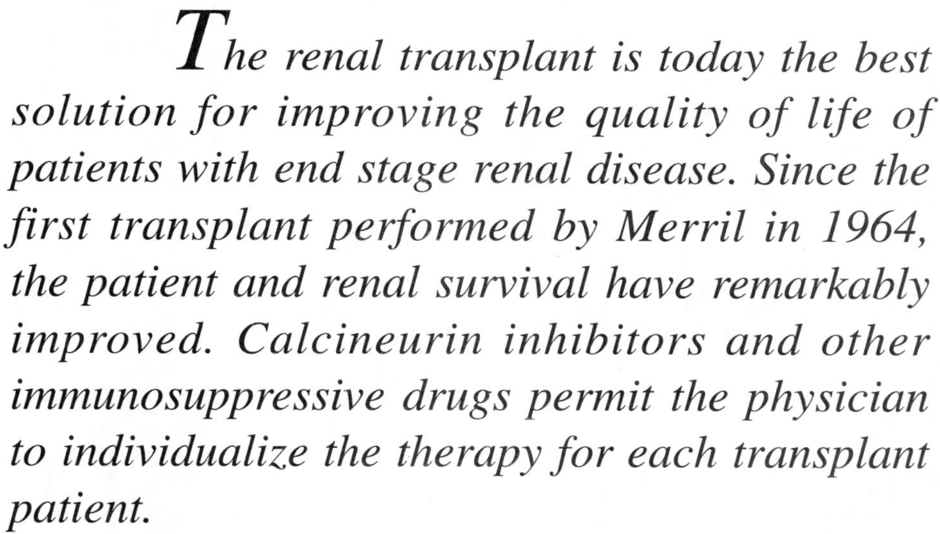

The renal transplant is today the best solution for improving the quality of life of patients with end stage renal disease. Since the first transplant performed by Merril in 1964, the patient and renal survival have remarkably improved. Calcineurin inhibitors and other immunosuppressive drugs permit the physician to individualize the therapy for each transplant patient.

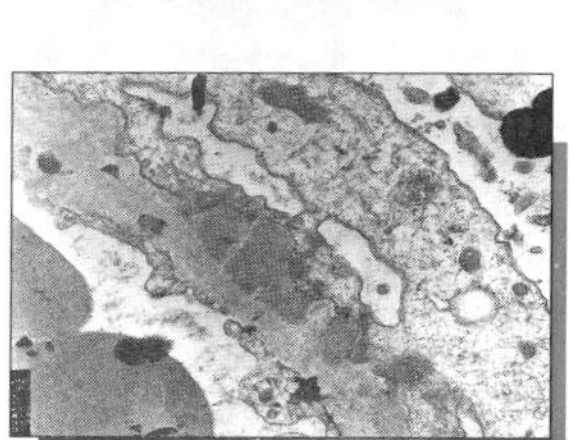

Renal electron-microscopy

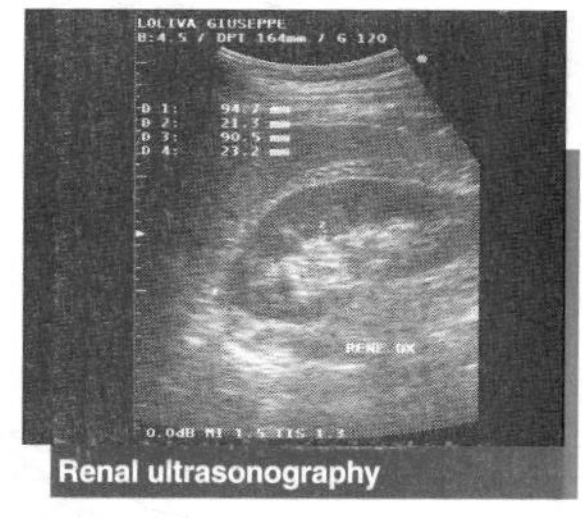

Renal ultrasonography

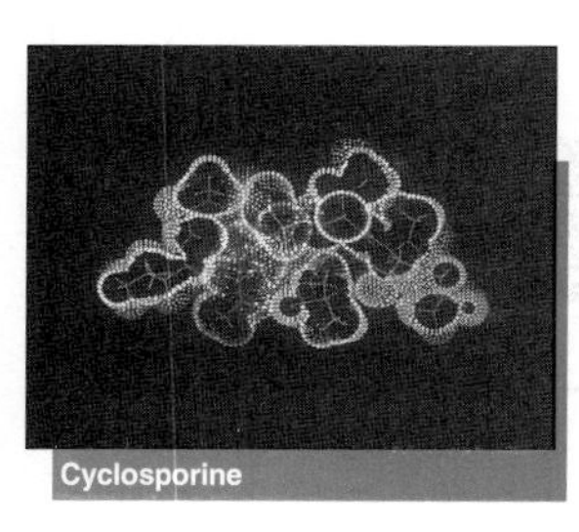

Cyclosporine

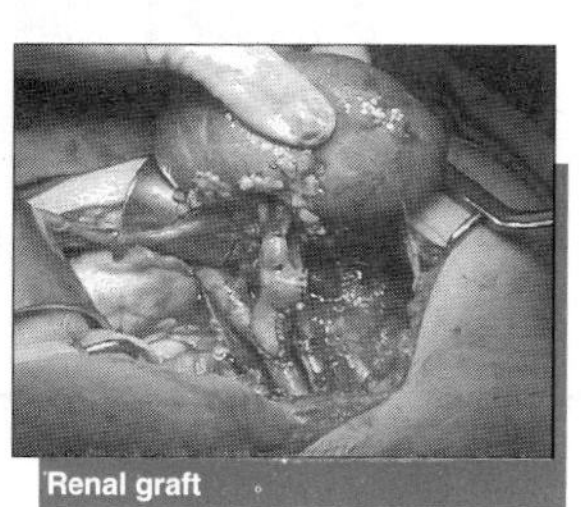

Renal graft

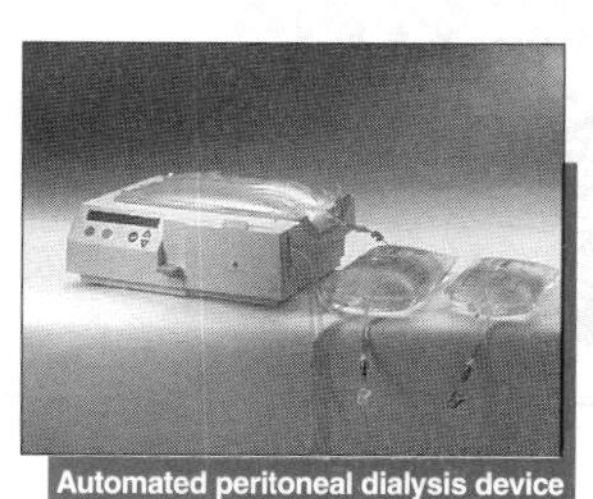

Automated peritoneal dialysis device

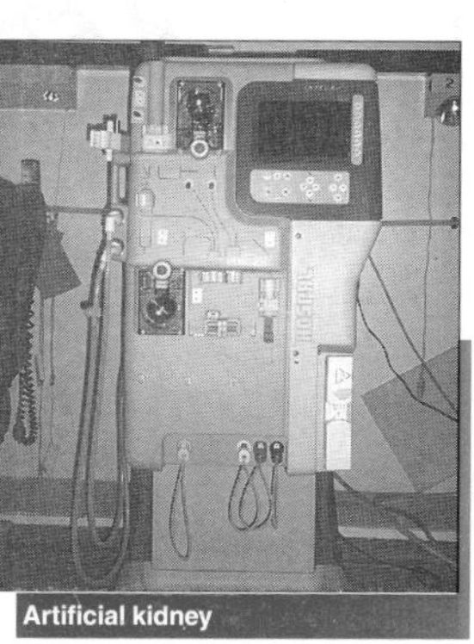

Artificial kidney

SECTION

1

General section

CHAPTER

1

The approach to the patient with renal disease

Paul L. Kimmel, Joseph A. Vassalotti

Patients may be referred to a clinician for evaluation of renal function, perhaps, but not exclusively because of symptoms thought to be related to possible renal disease. Most commonly, this evaluation is within the purview of the internist or nephrologist. However, the most common need for evaluation probably occurs because of the possibility of an abnormality related to renal structure or function, e.g., a laboratory abnormality encountered incidentally. Patients may complain of symptoms related to dysfunction of the genitourinary tract, such as edema or dizziness upon arising; abdominal, flank, or loin pain; gross hematuria; or dysuria (see Chap. 2). Many of the symptoms related to renal disease may, however, be nonspecific, e.g., nausea, anorexia, and confusion. Occasionally, a symptom, such as nocturia, will be relatively specific for the presence of renal disease. Although clues on physical examination, such as hypertension or a flank mass, may point to a renal problem, often the first clue to dysfunction specifically related to the kidneys, comes from the clinical laboratory (see Chap. 3). Such data, and often further focused examinations, allow the clinician to make the provisional diagnosis of a syndrome (see Section 2). The task of the clinician is to determine whether there is indeed an abnormality of kidney structure and/or function, and whether a clinical problem is localized to the kidneys or represents the presentation of a complex systemic disorder. Integrating the history, physical examination, and initial laboratory findings, the clinician can finally establish a syndrome analysis (Tab. 1.1), which is the first step in devising a diagnostic and therapeutic plan.

SYNDROME ANALYSIS IN PATIENTS WITH RENAL DISEASE

Hypertension is often associated with acute and chronic renal disease, and will not be specifically discussed further in this chapter. It is critical, however, that hypertension is controlled in all patients with progressive chronic renal disease. *Electrolyte disorders*, also discussed in another chapter, also may suggest renal disease.

Urinary abnormalities can be defined as abnormal urinary protein excretion, hematuria, pyuria or crystalluria, in the absence of changes in glomerular filtration rate (GFR) or disorders of tubular function. In addition, abnormal findings of urinary dipstick screens in the absence of another syndrome are classified in this category.

Disorders of renal tubular function pertain to the abnormal reabsorption or secretion of substances by the tubules in the presence of a normal GFR and in the absence of another syndrome. Such findings can include nephrogenic diabetes insipidus or isolated glycosuria, aminoaciduria, Fanconi's syndrome, or proximal or distal renal tubular acidosis.

Acute renal failure constitutes a sudden diminution in the GFR, whereas *chronic renal failure* is the slow, often progressive process whereby decrements in renal function progress through characteristic stages to *uremia* and end-stage renal disease, requiring renal replacement therapy with dialysis or transplantation. The stages of chronic progressive renal disease are: loss of renal reserve; renal insufficiency; renal failure; and the final uremic syndrome.

Nephritic syndrome is often defined as the simultaneous presence of proteinuria, decreased GFR, hypertension, edema, and hematuria. The presence of red blood cell (RBC) casts is highly useful in confirming this diagnosis.

Table 1.1 Common renal syndromes

Hypertension
Electrolyte abnormalities
Urinary abnormalities
Disorders of renal tubule function
Acute renal failure
Chronic renal failure
Uremia
Nephritic syndrome
Nephrotic syndrome
Nephrolithiasis

Nephrotic syndrome is variously defined as the presence of proteinuria, edema and hypercholesterolemia, often with lipiduria, but the hallmark is a urinary protein excretion exceeding a fixed level, variably designated as between 3 to 3.5 g/24 hours. Various complications such as abnormalities in coagulation and sodium and lipid metabolism characterize the syndrome.

LABORATORY TESTING IN PATIENTS WITH RENAL DISEASE

Many tests have been designed to assess the status of the kidneys in health and disease. A better understanding of the utility of a test comes from understanding its purposes and limitations and the precise clinical situations in which it is or is not useful. Tests of renal function can be broadly divided into evaluations of glomerular and renal tubular function.

Tests of *glomerular function* assess the kidneys' filtration capacity for water and solutes, the glomerular capillaries' function as a permeability barrier to macromolecular substances of varying sizes, weights and shapes, but most importantly, albumin, and the integrity of the glomerular capillary bed by assessing abnormal red blood cell transit. Tests of *tubular function* assess the ability of the nephron to filter, readsorb, and secrete solutes and water under normal and stress conditions. The finding of these in isolation or with glomerular abnormalities have markedly different diagnostic implications.

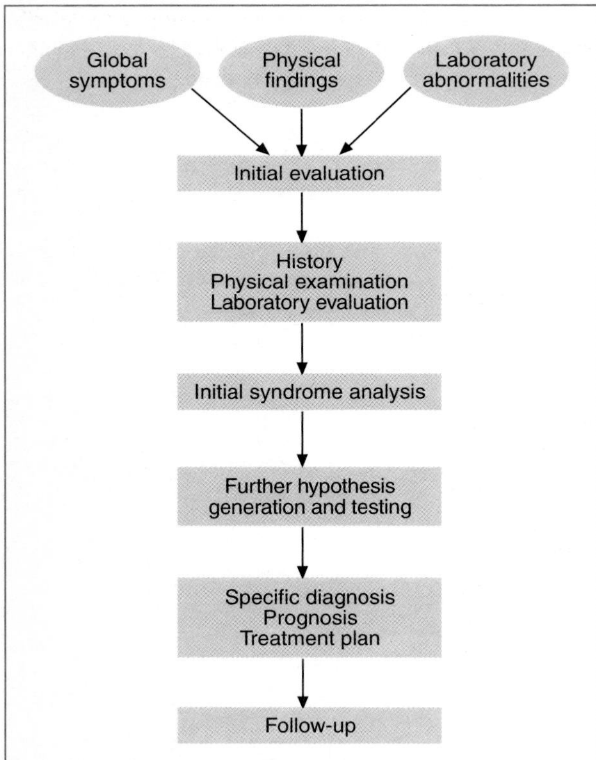

Figure 1.1 Approach to the patient with renal disease.

An initial finding of decreased renal function must be quickly confirmed and analyzed. The first question to be addressed is whether this represents a new, sudden change (acute renal failure) or the discovery of a long-standing process (chronic renal failure) (see Fig. 1.2). A personal or family history of renal disease is indispensable in early decision-making, before laboratory assessment is possible. It is very important to review the licit and illicit medications that the patient may be taking, searching in particular for drugs that can modify glomerular filtration rate (GFR), circulating creatinine (CR) levels, or creatinine metabolism. Assessment of previous measures of circulating creatinine levels may be useful, as are the urinalysis and determinations of renal size, usually by ultrasound, in differentiating acute renal failure and chronic renal failure. If assessment leads to the diagnosis of acute renal failure, evaluation and exclusion of prerenal and postrenal causes must be undertaken expeditiously. These focus on clinical assessment of the patient's volume status, with attention to the presence of edema, ascites, or signs of congestive heart failure, or orthostatic changes in the patients' pulse or blood pressure, and the exclusion of urinary tract obstruction, usually by radiologic methods. If intrinsic renal disease is suspected, a serum and urine protein electrophoresis is important to exclude the diagnosis of a renal disease associated with multiple myeloma or a nephrotoxic gammopathy. The urinalysis will be of extreme importance at this time (see below). A useful way to approach the differential diagnosis of acute renal failure secondary to intrinsic renal disease at the bedside is anatomically, conceptually paralleling the renal blood flow. Diagnostic categories therefore include renal vascular disease, glomerular disease, tubular and interstitial diseases, and renal venous diseases.

The urinalysis is critical. Usually it is the most quickly accessible of tests, and will aid the clinician in determining whether the patient has the nephritic syndrome – in which case diagnostic and therapeutic decisions must often be made expeditiously. Whether in association with investigation of possible decrements in GFR or the presence of tubular dysfunction, the urinary protein: creatinine ratio, or the assessment of 24-hour urinary protein excretion rate (the latter usually performed concomitantly with clearance studies) provides information regarding whether urinary protein excretion is in the range of nonnephrotic proteinuria or, instead, suggests the nephrotic syndrome. These two possibilities lead to widely divergent and usually mutually exclusive diagnostic ramifications (Figs. 1.3 and 1.4). The urinalysis provides data on the specific gravity, or a specimen can be sent to determine urinary osmolality and sodium and creatinine concentration, which can provide important data in patients with acute renal failure and oliguria, differentiating a physiologic response to a hemodynamic stress associated with the diagnosis of prerenal azotemia from an intrinsic renal disease (see Fig. 1.2 and Chap. 5).

In many instances, the performance and analysis of the outlined simple screening diagnostic tests may be sufficient to allow the clinician to care for the patient. An example is a patient with a family history of renal disease, an established diagnosis of long-standing hypertension and chronic renal insufficiency, with an ultrasound showing renal outlines smaller than normal, who has urinary protein excretion less than 2 g/24 hours and a urinalysis without glycosuria, pyuria or hematuria. In such a case, a diagnosis of hypertensive nephropathy is tenable, and treatment with antihypertensive medications is indicated, with serial observation of the outlined clinical renal laboratory tests (see Fig. 1.2). In another example, a patient with acute renal failure after surgery and hypotension, treated with nephrotoxic antibiotics, who has a urinalysis that demonstrates muddy brown casts and tubular casts probably has acute tubular necrosis. It is unusual to perform a renal biopsy in such a patient in the absence of an extremely elevated urinary protein: creatinine ratio or before 3 weeks of observation, because the clinical features point to a common diagnosis with a relatively predictable outcome. In selected cases of patients with acute renal failure, the nephritic and nephrotic syndromes, chronic renal failure (Figs. 1.2, 1.3 and 1.4), and occasionally in patients with tubular dysfunction and urinary abnormalities, initial screening tests evaluating urinalysis, GFR, urinary protein excretion and renal anatomy may not provide specific diagnostic information or adequate information to establish a diagnosis and prognosis, or to formulate a treatment plan. The nephrologist and patient may decide that renal biopsy is needed to establish a precise diagnosis. This is particularly important in patients with the nephrotic syndrome, in the absence of diabetes mellitus and signs of other end-organ dysfunction, or in the absence of an obvious systemic disease. Although the information to be gleaned from a renal biopsy may be of paramount importance in such cases and in cases of progressive renal insufficiency in the presence of urinalyses that suggest the nephritic syndrome, where differentiation of Wegener's granulomatosis from renal vasculitis and other disease entities may have critical therapeutic and prognostic implications, the risks of the procedure should always be considered. For instance, in cases of isolated hematuria (without marked increases in urinary protein excretion or renal insufficiency, or hypertension) the biopsy is likely to be normal or to show thin basement membrane disease or perhaps IgA nephropathy, disease states in which prognostic determinations and treatment imperatives are unclear. Likewise, in patients who have isolated increased urinary protein excretion in the non-nephrotic range, biopsy often is deferred, because the perception is that the benefits of the information to be obtained are outweighed by the possible risks. The finding of hypocomplementemia may add power by narrowing the differential diagnostic possibilities in patients with nephritic or nephrotic syndrome before the biopsy (see Figs. 1.3 and 1.4, and Chap. 5), and this test can be obtained relatively quickly. In addition, many serologic tests (such as anti-glomerular basement membrane antibodies, perinuclear and cytoplasmic antineutrophil cytoplasmic antibodies, anti-double-stranded DNA antibodies, and cryoglobulins) may be obtained before performing a renal biopsy; however, few of them are available on an emergent basis, if decisions must be made immediately. Often, rheumatologists will ask the nephrologist to perform a biopsy in patients with systemic lupus erythematosus in order to grade the activity and chronicity of the disease as a guide in formulating therapy (see Chap. 22).

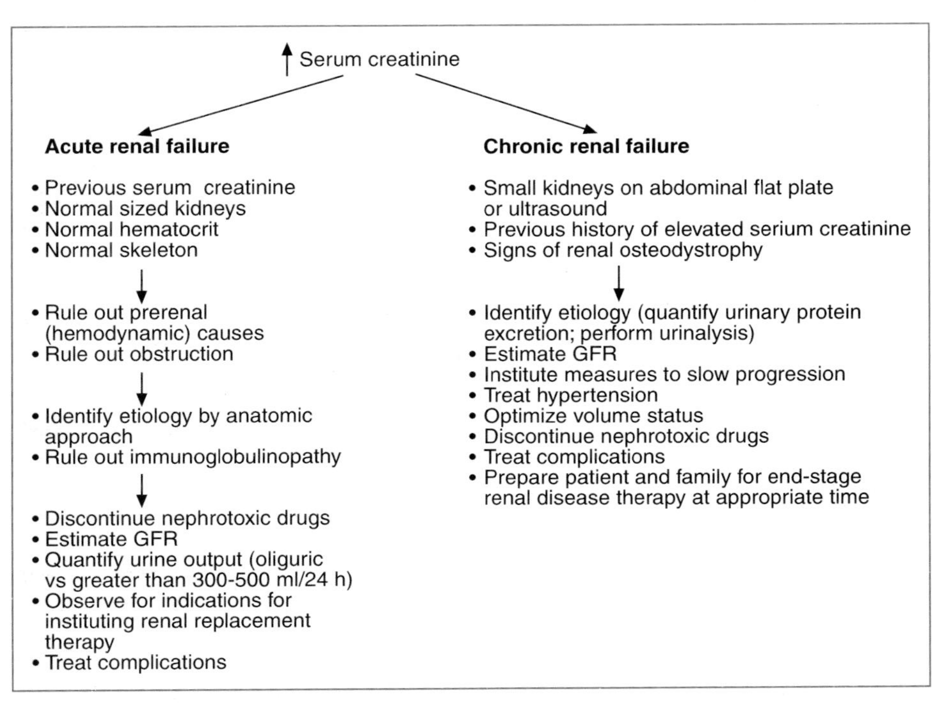

Figure 1.2 Approach to renal insufficiency.

EVALUATION OF RENAL FUNCTION

An overall test of renal mass or total renal function is the GFR. The GFR ultimately depends on renal blood flow (RBF), which in normal humans is approximately one-fifth of the cardiac output, on the glomerular hydraulic permeability and its surface area, and on the absolute values and ratios of the hydrostatic and oncotic pressures and the resistances at the renal afferent and efferent arterioles and along the glomerular capillary beds, which determine the net ultrafiltration pressure. In effect, the ultrafiltration rate of plasma across the glomerular capillary bed is predicated on Starling's forces. Renal plasma flow (RPF), approximately 60% of renal blood flow, is normally in the range of 600 ± 150 ml/min/1.73 m^2 in humans. The necessity of determining renal plasma flow is limited, primarily of interest in calculating the filtration fraction (FF), the ratio of GFR/renal plasma flow, which is of theoretic interest in disorders characterized by diminution of renal plasma flow, increased renal tubular sodium reabsorptive avidity and oliguria. In clinical practice, however, the determination of renal plasma flow is limited primarily to the assessment of renal function by nuclear scanning in the post-transplant setting.

The assessment of total renal GFR depends on measurement of the level in the circulation and in timed collections of urine of a substance freely filtered at the level of the glomerulus, and not reabsorbed, secreted, or metabolized by the tubules. Therefore the amount of the marker filtered in a determined time will equal its excretion in the urine. The exogenous marker, inulin, satisfies this requirement in normal subjects (see Chap. 3).

The use and measurement of inulin or other synthetic and radioactive markers is usually too cumbersome and expensive for the patient and the clinician. The need for a clinically useful test of GFR has culminated in the general use of the circulating creatinine concentration and its clearance (C_{CR}), as markers of GFR (see Chap. 3). There are pitfalls in the use of creatinine as a marker of GFR, however. A variable amount of creatinine is secreted each day by the tubules, and the fractional (but not the absolute) tubular secretion of creatinine as a proportion of the GFR increases in patients with chronic renal insufficiency as its circulating level rises.

The normal GFR, in the range of 125 to 150 ml/min/1.73 m^2 in humans, is somewhat higher in men than in women. The GFR traditionally is normalized for a body surface area of 1.73 m^2, although there is no evidence that GFR varies directly with body surface area in normal subjects. Both the normal GFR and creatinine clearance can be affected by gender, volume status, changes in renal blood flow, various drugs including glucocorticoids and nonsteroidal anti-inflammatory drugs, and acute and habitual dietary protein intake. The normal serum CR (S_{CR}) concentration, ranges between 0.6 to 1.5 mg/dl (to convert to mmol/l, multiply by 88.4), depending on the particular laboratory or the study population, and is usually higher in a male population.

The first sign of the development of renal insufficiency often is an increase in the circulating creatinine concentration. This may be a problematic marker if the patient is slight in body habitus, does not weigh much, is elderly, has decreased muscle mass, ascites, or is extremely obese, or if the decrement in renal function is small and occurs within the normal range.

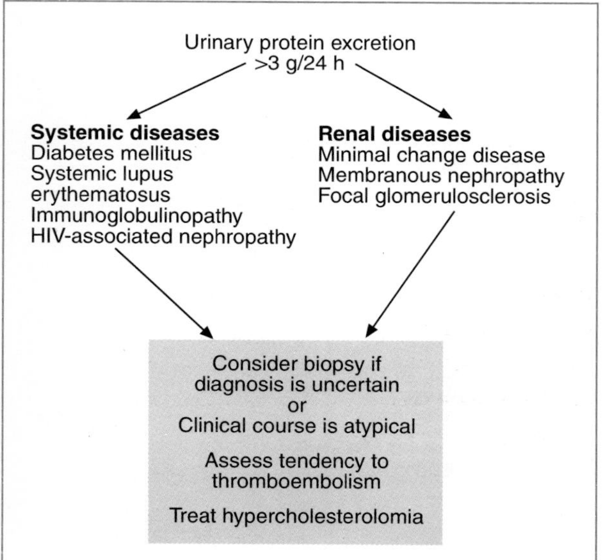

Figure 1.3 Approach to nephrotic syndrome.

UTILITY OF EVALUATION OF GLOMERULAR FILTRATION

It may be useful for various reasons to measure or estimate the GFR (by any means) in patients in whom one wishes: (1) to quantify decrements in GFR in the setting of acute renal failure; (2) to establish the presence or absence of renal insufficiency (determination of normal renal function); (3) to identify the presence of progression in patients with progressive or nonprogressive chronic renal disease in the presence or absence of therapeutic interventions; (4) to assess renal function in the elderly with circulating levels of serum creatinine at the upper limit of normal or above; or (5) to aid in a diagnosis of uremia and to help establish the need to start renal replacement therapy.

Quantifying GFR in patients with acute renal failure Typically it is very difficult to estimate the GFR in patients with acute renal failure. In one careful study, backleak of inulin across the tubules was noted, invalidating the usefulness of the test. Most often patients with acute renal failure are monitored clinically by use of changes in the circulating creatinine, quantitation of rates of urine flow, and among other parameters, observation for signs of congestive heart failure, acidemia, hyperkalemia, pericarditis or encephalopathy, in order to facilitate decision-making regarding dialysis. Simply, if the serum creatinine is rising, GFR is falling; if it is falling, the GFR typically is rising.

Establishing the presence or absence of renal insufficiency (determination of normal renal function) Variation between creatinine clearance in healthy adults of varying ages without renal disease may be a result of differences in muscle mass and/or nutritional protein intake. Values of the serum creatinine in the normal range may be encountered despite diminution in GFR greater than 50% of normal (Fig. 1.5). In a substantial portion of patients with renal insufficiency with GFR in the range of 40-80 ml/min/1.73 m^2, the creatinine clearance overestimates GFR, yielding normal values in the face of renal insufficiency (Fig. 1.5). Because of the hyperbolic relationship between circulating creatinine levels and creatinine clearance, changes at the asymptotes are difficult to evaluate. In effect, circulating creatinine levels and their change over short periods provide very poor estimates of levels of and variations in GFR at normal and at extremely low levels.

This may render the creatinine clearance of doubtful value as a tool for the detection of early renal disease. Low levels of GFR are not necessarily equivalent to a diagnosis of renal disease, especially in patients with low dietary protein intake such as vegetarians, the impoverished, the malnourished, or the elderly. Often the diagnosis of renal disease in the face of a marginally decreased GFR will not be hard to make. The patient will demonstrate clear-cut features of renal disease, such as an abnormal urinalysis, elevated serum creatinine, or proteinuria, which will aid in establishing the diagnosis of a true diminution in GFR. Bosch and colleagues have popularized the notion of diminished "renal reserve" as an early sign of progressive renal disease, during which stage the patient does not respond to a protein load with the typical acute rise in GFR or creatinine clearance. Diet must therefore be considered in the assessment of renal function in patients with estimated GFR in the low normal range before a diagnosis of renal insufficiency can be made. This may be most easily addressed by simultaneous determination of the urinary urea excretion, which is proportional to protein intake. Although some authors have suggested that the mean of the creatinine clearance and the urea clearance is a good clinical measure of GFR, there is little theoretic foundation for this notion. Urea clearance depends on the urea production rate and the urinary flow rate, in addition to any dependence on GFR. However, the urinary urea excretion does vary with creatinine clearance and GFR. Published data allow the determination of whether creatinine clearance is normal for a given urea excretion in young and elderly subjects without renal disease.

Quantifying progression in patients with chronic renal disease Similarly, the hyperbolic relationship between circulating creatinine levels and creatinine clearance renders these poor markers of variation in GFR at low values, consistent with advanced renal failure and uremia. Practically, patients are followed for the progression of renal disease by measurements of serum creatinine, creatinine clearance, and urinary protein excretion over time. Because of

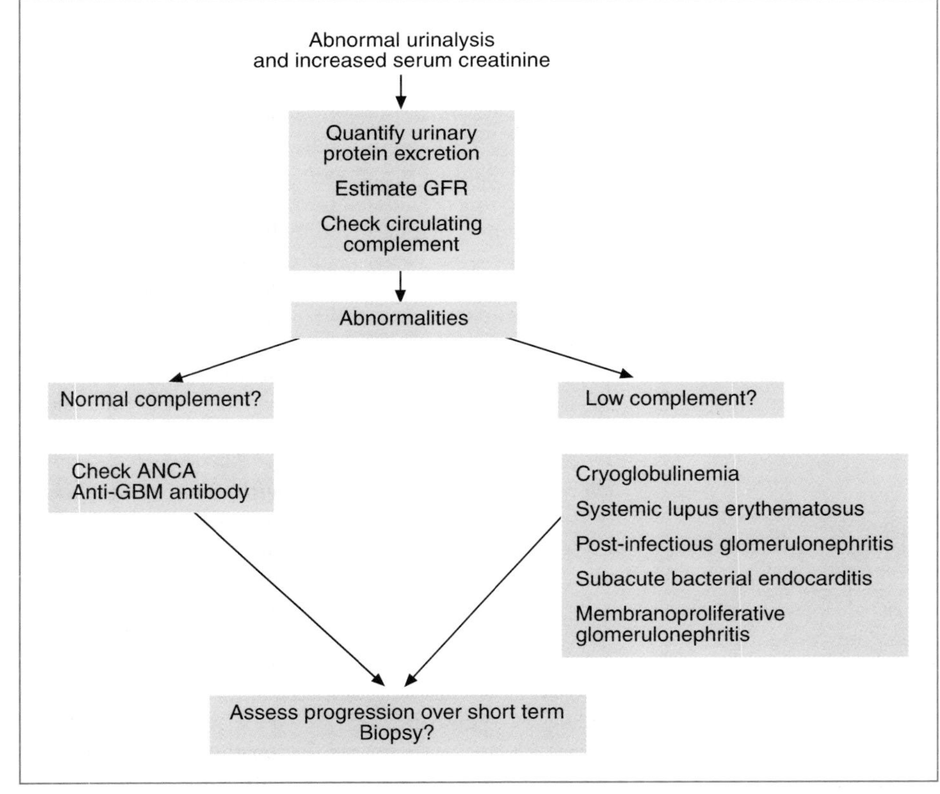

Figure 1.4 Approach to the nephritic syndrome.

the various determinants that can affect the level of serum creatinine in a patient at any time, attempts have been made to quantify the rapidity of progression in a clinically meaningful way by estimating changes in GFR by plotting the reciprocal of patients' serum creatinine over time. A line can often be fit to the serial points. Theoretically, when the line intersects the time axis, the clinician will have to start renal replacement therapy, since creatinine clearance will be zero. Such plots have been advocated as a tool for planning for patients and physicians. One must interpret such findings conservatively, since changes in the magnitude and composition of dietary intake, secondary to uremia or therapeutic interventions, can invalidate the assumption of the existence of a steady state. Such plots may provide useful information regarding changes in renal function, but they have not been shown to be superior to assessment of serum creatinine or creatinine clearance. Such plots may be used to monitor the patient's course on a newly prescribed protein restricted diet, but this has not been shown to be superior to the assessment of urinary urea excretion.

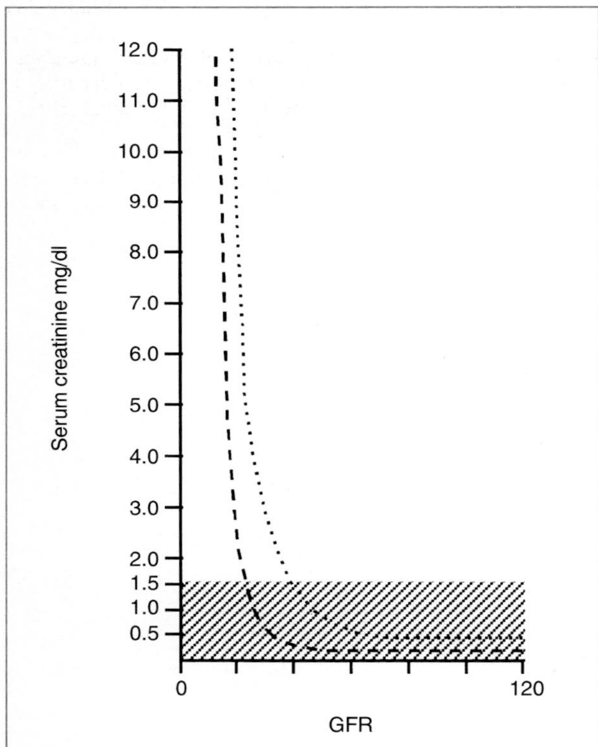

Figure 1.5 Theoretic relationship between serum creatinine concentration and GFR in groups of patients with renal disease. If urinary creatinine excretion is a constant, a hyperbolic relationship exists between the serum creatinine concentration and the creatinine clearance, the clinical marker of GFR. Larger, more muscular patients, men, and younger patients (*dotted line*) will tend to have higher serum creatinine concentrations at any given level of GFR than will smaller, less muscular, women or older adults (*dashed line*). Note, in the latter subjects, a higher proportion of patients will have extremely diminished GFR when the serum creatinine concentration is still relatively low. See text for details.

Assessing renal function in the elderly Similarly, low levels of GFR do not necessarily imply a diagnosis of renal disease in the elderly. Although the diagnosis of renal disease often is obvious because of concomitant abnormalities in laboratory tests, clinical assessments of renal function are problematic in this population because both GFR and urinary creatinine excretion may decrease as aging progresses. The latter may be predicated on changes in exercise, muscle mass, or quality or quantity of diet. Nutritional protein intake often decreases with advancing age, as a physiologic response to aging or as a result of socioeconomic factors, or for other, unknown reasons. Although the level of serum creatinine generally remains stable with age, GFR decreases in patients with increased age, in cross-sectional studies. There exist few longitudinal data, but the Baltimore Longitudinal Study of Aging demonstrated a linear decrease in GFR of 0.75 ml/min/year both across and within populations. Progressive decline in renal function over time was noted in approximately two-thirds of the subjects, but there was no change in GFR over time in one-third of subjects. Lew and Bosch studied 28 healthy older patients without renal disease who were recruited from retirement homes and vegetarian societies. Creatinine clearance was below 120 ml/min/1.73 m^2, in the vast majority of these subjects, but their serum creatinine was not different from that of healthy controls. The mean creatinine excretion/nutritional protein intake, and mean creatinine clearance, however, were significantly lower in older subjects than in younger ones, in spite of similar protein intake.

Because of these relationships, levels of the serum creatinine in the normal range may be encountered despite markedly diminished GFR in older persons (Fig. 1.5). Again, because of the relationship between circulating creatinine levels and creatinine clearance, changes at the extremes of GFR are difficult to evaluate using circulating creatinine levels and their change, making them poor diagnostic tools. The creatinine clearance should be evaluated by measurement or using formulae in elderly patients who are given nephrotoxic drugs, or drugs that must be administered differentially to patients with different levels of GFR. In addition, in such patients it may be useful to assess dietary protein intake by using the urinary urea excretion in order to evaluate level of creatinine clearance.

Diagnosing uremia and timing the need for starting renal replacement therapy The use of serum creatinine and creatinine clearance, in contrast to measurement of GFR, is common in determining the timing of initiation of renal replacement therapy with dialysis or transplantation. Clinical guidelines suggest starting renal replacement therapy when the creatinine clearance is between 3 to 14 ml/min/1.73 m^2 in patients with established chronic renal disease. Although the serum creatinine may not be of great predictive value, only the rare patient will exhibit the uremic syndrome with a creatinine clearance greater than 15 ml/min. Few data exist to aid the clinician in determining whether to start renal replacement early, or as late as possible, managing the patient conservatively, waiting for the onset of uremic symptoms. Late, conservative managment may be difficult when symptoms and complications occur and management of medications and dietary treatments become problematic. In addition, such conservative approaches may cause irreversible worsening of malnutrition, neuropathy, and cardiovascular disease. Some patients may wish to take the risks of a conservative approach in order to enjoy a longer period before beginning treatment with dialysis. The goals of the therapy should be formulated explicitly by physicians and discussed with patients and their families during the early stages of chronic renal disease. Type and timing of renal replacement therapy should be determined after mutual consultation among physicians, patients, and families, after full informed consent and reviewing the risks and benefits of all the options.

Suggested readings

ADDIS T. Glomerular nephritis, diagnosis and treatment. New York: MacMillan, 1948:2.

BOSCH JP. Renal reserve: a functional view of the glomerular filtration rate. Semin Nephrol 1995;15:381-5.

FOGAZZI GB. Crystalluria: a neglected aspect of urinary sediment analysis. Nephrol Dial Transplant 1996;11:379-87.

FOGAZZI GB, CAMERON JS. Urine microscopy from the seventeenth century to the present day. Kidney Int 1996;50:1058-68.

GINSBERG, JM, CHANG BS, MATARESE RA, GARELLA S. Use of single voided urine samples to estimate quantitative proteinuria. N Engl J Med 1983;309:1543-6.

GREGORY MJ, et al. Diagnosis and treatment of renal tubular disorders. Semin Nephrol 1998;18:317-29.

KAYSEN GA, MYERS BD, COUSER WG, et al. Biology of disease: mechanisms and consequences of proteinuria. Lab Invest 1986;54:479-97.

KIMMEL PL, LEW SQ, BOSCH JP. Nutrition, ageing and GFR: is age-associated decline inevitable? Nephrol Dial Transplant 1996;11 (suppl. 9): 85-8.

MILLER SB, KLAHR S. Acute oliguria. N Engl J Med 1998;338:671-5.

MADAIO MP. Renal biopsy. Kidney Int 1990;38:529-43.

MITCH WE, WALSER M, BUFFINGTON GA, LEMANN J JR. A simple method of estimating progression of chronic renal failure. Lancet 1976;2:1325-8.

PARRISH AE. Complications of percutaneous renal biopsy: a review of 37 years' experience. Clin Nephrol 1992;38:135-41.

ORTH SR, RITZ E. The nephrotic syndrome. N Engl J Med 1998;338:1202-11.

WALSER M. Assessing renal function from creatinine measurements in adults with chronic renal failure. Am J Kidney Dis 1998;32:23-31.

WOOLHANDLER S, PELS RJ, BOR DH, et al. Dipstick urinalysis screening of asymptomatic adults for urinary tract disorders I. Hematuria and pyuria. II. Bacteriuria. JAMA 1989;262:1215-24.

CHAPTER

2

Clinical evaluation

Guy H. Neild

KEY POINTS

- All renal failure is due to prerenal factors (renal underperfusion), obstruction, or disease of the renal parenchyma.
- Proper management of renal disease depends on accurate diagnosis and classification of the disease.
- Following clinical evaluation, any renal condition can be categorized with three investigations: ultrasonography, urinalysis, and urine microscopy.

Proper management of renal dysfunction depends on an accurate diagnosis of the underlying problem. For example, a physician is called to see a patient whose creatinine is 1000 μmol/l. It is imperative that a diagnosis be made quickly because early treatment will increase the potential for recovery of function. The most important question is: "Is the problem acute or chronic?" In other words: "Is it reversible?"

All renal failure is due either to prerenal factors (renal underperfusion), obstruction (postrenal), or parenchymal (intrinsic) disease. Prerenal renal failure can be subdivided into *physiologic* (in which the anatomic blood supply is normal) or *pathologic*, when there is anatomic disruption of the blood supply (e.g., in renal artery stenosis).

Renal failure can present as *acute, acute-on-chronic*, or *chronic* renal failure. After a thorough history and clinical examination has been carried out, investigations must establish the cause, chronicity, and complications of the renal problem.

Having taken a history and examined the patient, one can categorize any renal condition with three investigations: **u**ltrasonography, **u**rinalysis, and **u**rine microscopy.

Renal disease can present in only a limited number of ways (Tab. 2.1). The first problem is to recognize it. Impaired renal function (reduced glomerular filtration rate [GFR]) must not be missed.

Parenchymal renal disease

Intrinsic kidney disease is most commonly due to progressive glomerular disease. Glomerular disease is invariably associated with proteinuria, and usually some hematuria, hypertension, and a tendency to retain salt and water.

In contrast, some progressive disease is due predominantly to tubulointerstitial disease, and this typically is seen when there is a primary urologic disease or renal dysplasia. Tubular disease is characterized by minimal proteinuria, early loss of renal concentrating ability, a tendency to salt wasting (therefore no peripheral edema), early onset of acidosis, and normal blood pressure.

Table 2.1 Presentation of renal disease

	Manner of presentation
Asymptomatic	
Hematuria ± proteinuria	Macroscopic hematuria, or dipstick
Proteinuria ± hematuria	Dipstick
Leukocyturia	Microscopy
Hypertension	Routine examination
Reduced GFR	Routine: raised plasma urea, creatinine
Symptomatic	
Edema	Nephrotic syndrome
	Salt and water retention
Renal, ureteric pain	(Mainly urologic causes)
Polyuria	Presents as nocturia
Oliguria	Associated with symptomatic ARF
Anuria	Obstruction

Asymptomatic renal disease

Renal failure developing in the community is often insidious and asymptomatic, and often is noted only by chance at a routine medical examination (Tab. 2.1).

Acute renal failure

With acute renal failure (ARF), the signs and symptoms of the underlying illness usually will dominate the presentation. When ARF develops in hospital the cause often is multifactorial.

Prerenal renal failure is the commonest cause in hospitalized patients. The cause of prerenal failure should be obvious from the history and clinical examination. The patient, who is often elderly, presents with oligo-anuria and deterioration in renal function following an operative procedure. This may be on a background of established renal impairment (Tab. 2.2), and patients often are taking potentially nephrotoxic drugs (Tab. 2.2). Hypovolemia is further exacerbated by preoperative fluid restriction, diuretics, blood loss, inadequate fluid replacement, and increased insensible losses.

Chronic renal failure

Patients with chronic renal failure (CRF) are often asymptomatic, since symptoms of uremia do not arise until the glomerular filtration rate has fallen to 10-15% of normal. Therefore, renal failure often may be found by chance when routine blood tests are done. A detailed history of risk factors for renal disease, family history, past medical and surgical history, and a drug and social history may provide clues to the diagnosis.

Table 2.2 Risk factors for developing acute or chronic renal failure

Causes of decreased renal reserve
- Elderly
- History of CRF
- Hypovolemia
- Cardiac dysfunction
- Sepsis
- Diabetes
- Outflow obstruction

Drugs
- NSAIDs
- ACE inhibitors
- Cyclosporin, tacrolimus
- Nephrotoxic antibiotics
  - aminoglycosides
  - tetracycline
- iv Radio-contrast media
- Diuretics

(NSAIDs = nonsteroidal antiinflammatory drugs; ACE = angiotensin-converting enzyme.)

Obstruction

Complete obstruction causes *anuria* (no urine). Incomplete obstruction often will cause *polyuria*, which usually comes to light as increasing *nocturia*. Polyuria may at first seem paradoxic in the presence of obstruction, but this is due to the progressive tubular injury that causes inability to reabsorb water and concentrate the urine.

Specific renal syndromes

Hematuria and acute nephritic syndrome

Microscopic (asymptomatic) hematuria is common. The presence of blood *and* protein suggests glomerular disease. In all cases a urinary tract infection (UTI) must be excluded.

The characteristic feature of acute nephritic syndrome is abrupt-onset hematuria. Other features of the syndrome, i.e., oliguria, hypertension, renal impairment, and edema may be present, as in postinfectious nephritis, systemic lupus erythematosus (SLE), or hemolytic uremic syndrome (HUS). Not all features occur at the same time. There is glomerular proteinuria, as well as an active urinary sediment. As with other renal causes of renal failure, if the diagnosis is suspected, early referral and renal biopsy are mandatory.

The most severe form of a nephritic syndrome is rapidly progressive glomerulonephritis (RPGN); when it is suspected, a renal biopsy and diagnosis must be made within 24 hours because delay in treatment may result in irreversible loss of function.

Interstitial nephritis

Acute interstitial nephritis is often indistinguishable from acute glomerulonephritis, and both can present with acute loss of renal function and blood and protein in the urine. It can be an acute allergic reaction to a drug (usually an antibiotic), and the patient is systemically unwell, with skin rash and eosinophilia.

More commonly, interstitial nephritis is not associated with symptoms and is due to an immune response to drugs, most commonly nonsteroidal anti-inflammatory drugs (NSAIDs). It may be suspected, but can only be proved by renal biopsy.

HISTORY-TAKING (SYMPTOMS)

There is a logical structure to a medical history. In reaching the diagnosis one is a detective. When renal failure is acquired in a hospital, the clues will all be in the hospital record and the patient's charts. There are often no shortcuts in detective work, but once the entire sequence of events and all the serial results are laid out and charted, the diagnosis will become clear.

History of present complaint

One must establish a chronologic record of the events

leading up to the present. A good starting point is often: "When did you last feel entirely well?" What first took you to the doctor? It is a great help if there are previous records available of blood pressure, proteinuria, or plasma urea and creatinine. One is striving to date the onset of symptoms as accurately as possible.

History

Any previous illnesses and operations are noted. Leading questions would include previous urinary tract infections, enuresis or febrile illnesses as a child; time off school or work for illness; previous gout, hypertension, ankle edema, episodes of hematuria or discolored urine or renal stones?

With women it is vital to take an obstetric history, paying particular attention to miscarriages or problems during pregnancy such as urinary tract infection, hypertension, proteinuria, or pre-eclampsia.

Family and social history

Family

Are any other member of the family or relatives known to have kidney disease? Family history of hypertension, diabetes? Other autoimmune diseases in the family such as rheumatoid arthritis, myxedema, or evidence of atopy such as eczema or hay fever?

One should note the number of siblings, children and the past medical histories of all first-degree relatives.

Social

One should inquire about the patient's work: in particular whether there is any possibility of being exposed to toxic or noxious substances at work, home, or in the local environment. The clinician should make suitable inquiry about the social circumstances of the patient and family, so that one can anticipate how the family can cope with serious illness.

Ethnic

It is always important and relevant to know the ethnicity of the patient. Renal failure, hypertension, and diabetes are all three to six times more common in Indo-Asians and Black populations than in white. Depending on the ethnic origin, some patients will need to be tested for sickle cell disease, glucose-6-phosphate-dehydrogenase deficiency, and thalassaemia.

Systemic lupus erythematosus is more common and often more severe in nonwhite populations, whereas anti-neutrophil cytoplasm antibody (ANCA) positive vasculitides are less common in nonwhites.

Travel

If the patient is febrile and acutely unwell a careful history of foreign travel over the past 12 months is mandatory. Remember, it often is impossible to diagnose a disease you do not think of – such as malaria.

Dietary

Diet and "life-style" often go together. Patients with alternative views on life and diet are more likely to be taking herbal remedies or strange vitamins in excess. Vegetarians may have significant vitamin deficiencies.

Drugs and allergies

It can be surprisingly difficult to ask and find out what drugs the patients are taking. A wide variety of synonyms for "drugs" have to be used such as "medicine," "pills," "tablets," "drugs of any sort, including those bought over the countering". To many people the word *drug* implies something like heroin. Patients may have been taking non-steroidal anti-inflammatory drugs (NSAIDs) for years for pain without thinking of them as any sort of medicine. When appropriate, one must also ask detailed questions about medications that may have either a diuretic or laxative effect. Similarly, one must ask about any known allergies to drugs or environmental factors.

Other systems

Having taken the history as the patient remembers it, one then must double-check by further questions about individual systems.

General

Non-specific With systemic disease, patients often will have such non-specific symptoms as tiredness, lethargy, malaise, and feeling hot and cold. Patients with vasculitis almost invariably have a prodrome of myalgia and arthralgia, anorexia, and weight loss in addition to the above.

Fever If a patient feels hot, have they taken his temperature? A history of rigors is very helpful and important in assessing the severity of an illness and is an indication of a serious problem. Fever, rigors, and weight loss are indicative of occult sepsis, such as a pyelonephritis.

Well-being It sometimes can be difficult to establish just how well someone is, particularly when managing a chronic illness such as systemic lupus. It can be helpful to ask the patient to score their well-being on a scale of 10 (with 0 being worst and 10 best), or out of 100%. Similarly with painful conditions, an objective measure of pain, such as the daily variation in total number of analgesic tablets taken.

Skin Patients with uremia will frequently complain of itching (*pruritus*) and as a consequence develop marked excoriation of the skin (*dermatitis artefacta*) which can masquerade as a primary skin problem. Patients must be asked about any new skin rashes or problems, and whether they have noticed any change to their hair or nails.

Patients should be questioned regarding Raynaud's

phenomenon, particularly if there is a suggestion of an autoimmune disease.

Urinary tract

Because of the importance of urinary tract symptoms in the diagnosis of renal disease a structured approach is necessary.

Frequency The key question concerns the volume passed each time. Is urination frequent and low volume, as in cystitis, or is it large, as in polyuria? The question of polyuria is best approached by leading questions about nocturia. "How often do you get out of bed to pass urine? How long has this been happening? Do you normally require a drink at night? If you do, do you always take a glass or larger container of water to bed with you? A young adult presenting with chronic renal failure and a life-long history of nocturia is going to have a tubular disease – most likely of an urologic nature. When following outpatients, these questions can be best answered by asking for a diary of urine volumes passed (recording time and volume each time).

Dysuria Frequency and small volumes of urine suggest bladder disease, and inquiries about dysuria should follow. Dysuria is a urethral pain or discomfort throughout the urinary stream. Pain at the end of the stream is *strangury*; this occurs with bladder stones. The first thing to establish with dysuria is whether there is inflammation (urine microscopy for white cells) and infection (urine culture for bacteria).

Renal pain Pain is very uncommon with chronic renal disease. Severe pain usually is found only with renal stones or other forms of obstruction, in which case the pain will have a characteristic colicky nature, often with an ureteric component. Pain can occur with acute disease when the kidney is swollen and, presumably, the capsule is stretched. This will present as loin ache or back pain that sometimes is severe – and is found with acute pyelonephritis, acute interstitial nephritis, and acute severe glomerulonephritis. Loin pain is occasionally described with some forms of chronic glomerulonephritis – most commonly IgA disease.

Urine quality Men, for obvious reasons, are able to see much more easily whether there is a change in the quality or color of their urine.

- *Hematuria*: *microscopic* hematuria means that the blood in the urine is not macroscopically visible. It is often a chance finding following a routine urine test. It is vital to know if there is also protein in the urine; if so, the cause is more likely to be renal. If the hematuria is always present over many months, it is also more likely to be renal than urologic in origin (such as a tumor).
  Macroscopic hematuria means that the patient is aware that blood is passing into urine. With women it is important to be certain that the blood is from the urinary tract, not from the reproductive organs. The commonest cause will be a urine infection; but stones and tumors must always be excluded. A good rule of thumb is that hematuria alone should be investigated by urologists, and hematuria with proteinuria by nephrologists. If patients have visible blood, then the urine will be uniformly blood-stained if it is from the kidney or has mixed in the bladder for some time. If the urine starts bloody then becomes clear, it is of urethral origin; if it starts clear and then becomes bloody, it is from the bladder. Is the hematuria painless? Blood clots passing down one ureter can cause ipsilateral ureteric pain.
  Occasionally there may be very heavy microscopic hematuria so that the urine is discolored, but the patient does not recognize it as blood. Patients with persistent microscopic hematuria, as in IgA disease, should be questioned as to whether they have ever noticed discolored urine, particularly with viral infections, sore throats, or after exercise. This kind of urine sometimes is described as "rusty," or "tea colored" (in England, at least). When heavy but hemolyzed it may look like Cola, or even redcurrant juice.
- *Discolored urine*: various pigments and drugs other than blood can cause urine discoloration (Tab. 2.3). Hemoglobinuria and myoglobinuria will both cause discolored urine that tests strongly positive for blood on Stix testing, but by microscopy few or no red cells are seen.
- *Frothy urine*: patients with the nephrotic syndrome will often volunteer that their urine is frothy. They should be asked if this has happened before in the past or if they have ever noticed ankle swelling.
- *Pneumaturia*: frothy urine is not to be confused with pneumaturia (gas bubbles in the urine). This is extremely rare and occurs with a colovesical fistula.

Table 2.3 Discolored urine

Red	Hemolyzed blood Hemoglobinuria	Phenindione Phenolphthalein
Pink	Beetroot Rhubarb	Chloroquine Desferrioxamine
Brown	Myoglobin Rifampicin Jaundice	
Yellow	Nitrofurantoin Fluorescein	
Blue/green	Amitryptyline Methylene blue	
Black	Porphyria* Alkaptonuria* Levodopa*	Melaninuria
White	Phosphates - in alkaline urine	

* on standing.

Urinary tract infection When patients complain of "cystitis," it is very important to establish exactly what they mean by that term and to document their actual symptoms. It is important to learn whether these episodes of symptoms have been associated with positive urine cultures. If it is likely or obvious that the patient is having recurrent episodes of urine infection, then questions related to acute pyelonephritis should be asked.

Patients with pyelonephritis, in contrast, may have no symptoms of cystitis. They should be asked about symptoms suggestive of systemic disease and infection such as fever, hot and cold sweats, malaise, loin pain, and response to antibiotics within 48 hours.

Cardiovascular

Patients should be asked about symptoms suggestive of fluid overload (*hypervolemia*) or heart failure, such as ankle swelling, shortness of breath on exertion, orthopnea, and paroxysmal nocturnal dyspnea. Also, symptoms suggestive of atherosclerosis, such as angina on exertion, and intermittent claudication. Pericarditis can occur with severe uremia, as well as with SLE and the vasculitides.

Respiratory

If patients complain of breathlessness, the history and examination should determine whether this is predominantly due to lung disease, heart failure, or just fluid overload. Patients can be breathless due to alveolar hemorrhage, and careful history for evidence of hemoptysis should be taken when relevant. Patients can loose several pints of blood into their lungs with minimal signs and symptoms.

Gastrointestinal

Anorexia and nausea are non-specific symptoms but common with severe renal failure when the GFR is reduced to around 10% of normal. Diarrhea as a presenting symptom should invite questions as to whether other people are affected, and if blood or abdominal pain is present.

Musculoskeletal

Patients with chronic renal failure can develop non-specific bone and joint pains due to renal osteodystrophy. Osteomalacia, in particular, can lead to spontaneous or inappropriate bone fractures, as well as causing a proximal myopathy. Gout can be a presenting symptom of underlying renal disease and is more common in patients on diuretics. Arthritis can be part of the underlying systemic disease. Myositis, as part of an underlying systemic disease, is often asymptomatic and is detected only by measuring the serum creatinine kinase.

Nervous system

Severe headaches may suggest very high blood pressure, as might recent changes in vision. Changes in power or sensation in the limbs can indicate a peripheral neuropathy. Symptoms of lower limb spasticity might point to a cause for a neuropathic bladder.

Summary

Acute renal failure

With acute renal failure, the symptoms of the underlying illness often will dominate the presentation. When ARF develops in a hospitalized patient, the cause often is multifactorial.

Chronic renal failure

Patients with chronic renal failure may have symptoms relating to uremia, such as anemia and the metabolic and cardiovascular changes of chronic renal failure (Tab. 2.4). Most of the symptoms are attributable to anemia, e.g., malaise, lethargy, and dyspnea. Salt and water retention may lead to weight gain, hypertension, peripheral edema, and breathlessness due to pulmonary edema. Shortness of breath also may be due to metabolic acidosis and anemia.

PHYSICAL EXAMINATION (SIGNS)

General

Skin and periphery

Careful inspection of the *skin* is always necessary. If systemic disease or vasculitis is suspected this must be very thorough, and should include the hands, feet, and *nails* (Fig. 2.1, see Color Atlas). Vasculitic and other immunologic rashes are symmetric (Fig. 2.2, see Color Atlas). Emboli (cholesterol, endocarditis) and focal skin necrosis from septicemia are more random (asymmetric) and may be very discrete (Fig. 2.3, see Color Atlas). The distribution of the rash may give a clue to the diagnosis (Tab. 2.5).

There are few specific signs of uremia. Patients may be pale because of anemia and, if both anemia and renal failure are severe, often have a yellow tinge to their skin. They tan easily in the sun, and the pigmentation fades

Table 2.4 Uremic symptoms

Early (due to anemia)
Malaise, lethargy, tiredness
Shortness of breath on exertion
Late (due to uremic toxins)
Itching (pruritus)
Loss of appetite (anorexia)
Nausea and vomiting
Variable (related to abnormal Ca^{2+}, PO_4^{2-})
Muscle weakness
Bone and joint pain
Severe (after dialysis should have been started)
Pericarditis
Impaired mental performance, drowsiness, stupor, coma
Rapid respiration (tachypnea) due to acidosis

more slowly than normal. There may be excoriation of the skin from scratching. Peripheral lymph nodes must be carefully palpated and noted. The appearance of the eyes, ears, and nose should be noted.

Hypovolemia

Patients with hypovolemia will have a cool or cold periphery, collapsed hand veins, low jugular venous pressure (JVP), and dry skin and mucous membranes. With severe intravascular volume depletion the patient develops a postural drop in blood pressure greater than 10 mm Hg upon standing or sitting up.

Hypervolemia

Fluid overload is associated with peripheral edema, engorged neck and peripheral veins, hyper- or hypotension, tachycardia, pulmonary edema, and hypoxia.

Cardiovascular

There are always two prime considerations. First, assessment of the circulating volume, and second, evidence of end-organ injury. The latter includes assessment of left ventricular hypertrophy, cardiac dilatation, peripheral vascular disease, and retinal pathology. If a pericardial rub is heard, particular consideration must be given to the possibility of a pericardial effusion or even tamponade. The quality and quantity of any edema should be noted.

Table 2.5 Distribution of skin lesions

Symmetric	Asymmetric
Systemic vasculitides	**Other (nonvascular)**
Scleroderma	Amyloid (ecchymoses)
Microscopic polyarteritis	
Systemic lupus erythematosus (SLE)	
Henoch-Schönlein purpura	**Embolic**
Cryoglobulinemia	Septicemia (*ecthyma gangrenosum*)
Livedo reticularis	Endocarditis
	Cholesterol
Other vascular	
Diabetes (*necrobiosis lipoidica*)	
Inherited	
Fabry's disease (*angiokeratomata*)	
Nail patella syndrome (*dystrophic nails*)	
Tuberose sclerosis (*adenoma sebaceum*)	

Respiratory

Respiratory signs and symptoms will draw attention to the possibility of pulmonary edema, infection, pleurisy, pleural effusion, and alveolar hemorrhage. Subsequent investigations will confirm the diagnosis.

Central and peripheral nervous system

Peripheral neuropathies may be diffuse and symmetric (glove and stocking), or multifocal, as seen with a mononeuritis multiplex. Evidence of focal pathology must lead one to determine whether it is due to upper or lower motor neuron disorders. Coma and convulsions have many causes, not least iatrogenic neurotoxicity. Peripheral neuropathy from chronic uremia is now rarely seen, except in chronically underdialyzed patients.

Abdomen

Apart from assessment of liver, spleen, bladder, and exclusion of masses, the aorta and femoral arteries should be palpated and ausculted. To examine the kidneys, they should be ballotted bimanually. The testes should be noted and, when appropriate, the penis examined for evidence of phimosis, epispadias. Striae indicate prolonged treatment with corticosteroids (Fig. 2.4, see Color Atlas), or Cushing's disease, or can be seen in patients who previously were obese but who have lost a substantial amount of weight. The latter can have significant diabetic morbidity, but currently normal blood sugars.

Musculoskeletal

If the renal failure is long-standing since childhood, the patient may be of small stature (in relation to other family members). A long history of "rheumatoid arthritis" but no bony deformity can indicate the underlying diagnosis of vasculitis. Patients with osteomalacia may have a significant proximal myopathy. Tophii indicate prolonged hyperuricemia (Fig. 2.5, see Color Atlas).

Suggested readings

Davison AM, Grunfeld J-P. History and clinical examination of the patient with renal disease. In: Cameron S, Davison AM, Grunfeld J-P, Kerr D, Ritz E, eds. Oxford Textbook of clinical nephrology, 2nd ed. Oxford: Oxford University Press, 1997:3-19.

Roderick PJ, Raleigh VS, Hallam L, Mallick NP. The need and demand for renal replacement therapy in ethnic minorities in England. J Epidemiol Community Health 1996;50:334-9.

CHAPTER

3 Clinical investigation

Dwomoa Adu, Alexander J. Howie, Wai Y. Tse

KEY POINTS

- A detailed history and examination will usually establish the clinical syndrome and guide investigations.
- Dipstick testing and microscopic examination of the urine is mandatory to look for glycosuria, hematuria and/or proteinuria, cells, casts, and bacteria.
- The presence of > 5 red blood cells per high power field and/or persistent proteinuria always requires investigation.
- Precise estimation of renal function requires tests of the glomerular filtration rate.
- Ultrasound examination of the kidneys and bladder is a useful initial investigation procedure for the structure of the urinary tract.
- Renal biopsy is required in selected cases to establish the diagnosis, determine disease activity and severity, and provide prognostic information.

The clinical presentation of renal disease determines the pattern and order in which investigations are performed. A detailed history and clinical examination plus initial urinalysis and biochemistry usually will establish the clinical syndrome under consideration, and this provides a guide to further investigations. Renal disease presents as syndromes that may be idiopathic or secondary to other causes, and a clear understanding of these disorders provides a logical basis for developing protocols for investigations. Most renal diseases are accompanied by proteinuria and/or hematuria often picked up by dipstick testing. Proteinuria picked up on urinalysis should be confirmed by repeated testing of the urine at intervals of at least 1 week on at least two more morning urine samples. All patients in whom persistent proteinuria is confirmed should be investigated. It is important to take a detailed family history, looking for familial diseases such as polycystic kidneys, reflux nephropathy, or hereditary nephritis. A comprehensive drug history should be taken to exclude nephrotoxic drugs that might lead to proteinuria. A full clinical history is also essential in the initial evaluation of hematuria. Initial hematuria suggests prostatic or urethral disease; terminal hematuria may indicate a vesical calculus irritating the trigone as the bladder empties; hematuria throughout the stream is more often vesical or upper tract in origin.

Glomerulonephritis may be suspected from a history of an antecedent infection, the presence of edema or hypertension. Constitutional features such as weight loss, malaise, anorexia, and fever, with or without other features, such as a rash, pulmonary symptoms, arthralgia, and myalgia suggest a multi-system disorder such as systemic lupus erythematosus or vasculitis. Other symptoms such as the passage of stones or prostatic symptoms may point to the cause of hematuria. A thorough review of medications, looking specifically for drugs associated with hematuria, e.g., anticoagulants including aspirin, cyclophosphamide which can lead to a hemorrhagic cystitis, analgesics and antibiotics, which can be associated with an interstitial nephritis must be performed. A careful family history should be taken to look for evidence of hereditary diseases, e.g., polycystic kidneys and Alport's disease. A social history is also important. Urothelial tumors are strongly associated with tobacco smoking. Occupational carcinogen exposure to compounds such as naphthylamine, benzidene, and

4-aminodiphenyl, used often in the rubber or dye industries, predisposes to transitional cell carcinoma. The physical examination includes inspection for hypertension, an irregular cardiac rhythm, splinter hemorrhages, rash, uveitis, hearing loss (Alport's syndrome), heart murmurs, abdominal masses, edema, and lesions of the prostate. The presence of renal tenderness suggests an upper tract cause for the hematuria. A hemoglobin electrophoresis should be performed in black patients to exclude sickle cell disease or trait. Hypertension and renal dysfunction indicate an urgent need for more extensive evaluation. Urine examination can determine the direction of the subsequent work-up and thus avoid unnecessary investigations. Pyuria or white blood cell casts suggest inflammation or infection of the urinary tract, but can also be found in acute glomerulonephritis. Urinary eosinophils are typically found in acute interstitial nephritis. Dysmorphic red blood cells (RBCs) and red cell casts, especially if associated with proteinuria, suggest a glomerular origin for the hematuria. However, proteinuria has been described with gross bleeding into the urinary tract distal to the kidneys. The findings from the initial clinical consultation and urine examination are crucially important in determining the nature of the subsequent investigations.

EXAMINATION OF THE URINE

Examination of the urine forms an essential part of the initial assessment of renal disease. Urinalysis and urine microscopy are simple and inexpensive tests, and evaluation of any abnormalities can lead to the detection of serious underlying diseases.

Appearance (Tab. 3.1)

Fresh normal urine usually is clear. The color may vary from straw, in dilute urine, to yellow in average urine, to slightly amber in a concentrated urine, owing to the presence of the pigment urochrome. Urates (in acid urine) or phosphates (in alkaline urine) may precipitate out in urine, resulting in either a visible sediment or a cloudy appearance. Bacteria, white cells in urinary tract infections, or contamination of the urine with semen or fecal material, can all result in a cloudy appearance. Urine that is milky after meals but clears after an overnight fast suggests chyluria. Red or reddish brown urine usually indicates the presence of blood, and this should be confirmed by urinalysis and microscopy. If red cells are not seen on microscopy, urine should be tested for hemoglobin or myoglobin. Frothy urine usually indicates excessive protein. Yellowish brown urine can be found in patients with liver disease, where the color is due to excessive uroblinogen or bilirubin. Infected urine may emit a fetid ammoniacal odor. Certain metabolic disorders, e.g., maple syrup disease, are associated with a distinctive odor.

Urinalysis

pH Normal urine is slightly acidic but can vary between pH 4.5 to 8 with changes in diet. However a highly alkaline urine suggests infection with urea-splitting organisms, e.g., Proteus species, stones, or renal tubular acidosis. A low urinary pH is sometimes a clue to the presence of uric acid stones.

Glycosuria The stick test for the detection of glucose is based on the enzyme glucose oxidase, which releases hydrogen peroxide from glucose. This test is therefore specific for glucose and will not detect other sugars such as pentose, galactose, or fructose.

Bacteriuria The nitrite test is a useful screening test for infection. Urinary nitrate derived from the diet may be converted to nitrite by urinary pathogens. Nitrites in the urine can be demonstrated by the use of a diazotization reaction. Nitrite reacts with a precursor such as para-arsanilic acid to form a diazonium compound. This diazonium compound then complexes with a suitable colored substrate to form a colored product. False- positives occur if urine has been left standing, thus allowing bacteria overgrowth. Frequent voiding of dilute urine does not allow sufficient time for nitrite to be produced, and the presence of ascorbic acid in the urine can lead to false-negatives.

Leukocyte esterase test Stick tests are now available that are specific for leukocyte esterases, which convert an

Table 3.1 Macroscopic appearance of the urine

Appearance	Cause
Milky/cloudy	Acid urine: urate crystals Alkaline urine: insoluble phosphates Infection: pus Spermatozoa Chyluria
Pink/red	Blood, hemoglobin, myoglobin Porphyrins Aniline dyes in sweets Anthocyanins (beetroot) Drugs (phenindione, phenolphthalein)
Foamy	Proteinuria
Yellow	Conjugated bilirubin Phenacetin Riboflavin
Blue/green	Pseudomonas urinary tract infection Methylene blue
Orange	Drugs (anthraquinone laxatives, rifampicin) Excess urobilinogen
Brown/black	Melanin (on standing) Myoglobin (on standing) Alkaptonuria
Green/black	Phenol Lysol
Brown	Drugs (phenazopyridine, L-dopa, niridazole) Hemoglobin and myoglobin (on standing) Bilirubin

indoxyl ester substrate into indoxyl to produce a blue color in air. The test detects viable leukocyte in the urine and esterases released from degenerated cells.

Microscopic examination of the urinary sediment

White blood cells Up to 2 million white blood cells are excreted in the urine every day. More than four white blood cells per high power field is considered abnormal. The most common cause of pyuria is infection. Sterile pyuria may occur in association with stones, analgesic nephropathy, and renal tuberculosis. Detection of eosinophils suggests the possibility of an allergic interstitial nephritis.

Casts Hyaline casts are formed from Tamm-Horsfall protein in the renal tubule. Occasional hyaline casts may be seen in normal urine, but are increased in renal diseases. Granular casts are thought to be formed by granules of serum proteins trapped in a matrix of Tamm-Horsfall proteins. Granular casts can be found in normal urine, but typically are found in renal diseases. Acute tubular necrosis often leads to the appearance of red-brown granular casts. Red cell casts typically are found in glomerulonephritis. White cell casts are found in acute inflammatory conditions affecting the kidney, such as pyelonephritis, acute proliferative glomerulonephritis, and acute interstitial nephritis. Tubular epithelial cell casts are found in intrarenal inflammation (glomerulonephritis) and tubular damage (acute tubular necrosis). In chronic renal disease, wide casts called broad casts and homogeneous casts with sharp outlines, called waxy casts, are found.

Renal tubular cells Renal tubular cells are one to three times the size of leukocytes and have large round nuclei. Increased numbers of tubular cells reflect active tubular degeneration, and this may be seen in acute tubular necrosis, pyelonephritis or glomerulonephritis. Oval fat bodies are produced when these cells are laden with lipid droplets.

Squamous epithelial cells These cells, shed from the bladder and urethra, are found in normal urine.

Bacteria More than 1 bacterium/high power field in a fresh urine usually indicates the presence of urinary tract infection.

Crystals Crystals are common in urine, and rarely have clinical significance. The presence of crystalline calcium phosphate, calcium oxalate, or urate crystals is not pathologic in itself, and often is a sign of concentrated urine. Cystine crystals are not normally found in urine but, if present, are a sign of cystinuria.

Proteinuria

The stick test strips, such as multistix or dipstix, measure urine protein by altering the color produced by tetrabromphenol blue. At a pH of 3 tetrabromphenol is yellow, but changes to blue-green at pH 4. The reagent strip also contains a citrate buffer that maintains the pH of the paper at about 3. Protein produces a shift in the pH optimum of the indicator, and the blue-green color will appear when protein is present. These commercial stick tests are more sensitive to albumin than to other proteins, and Bence Jones protein and mucoproteins are usually not detected. False-positives can occur with concentrated urine, semen contamination, menstruation, gross hematuria, or with highly alkaline urine, as may occur with some urinary tract infections. False-positives can also result if the strip has been left to soak in urine, or if there is a marked delay in reading the strip. Laboratory testing of proteinuria utilizes a variety of techniques from turbidometric assays to dye binding assays using Ponceau S or Coomassie blue. In addition there are chemical assays using the biuret reaction or folin reagent. These assays all have their drawbacks and give different results. For these reasons we prefer radioimmunoassay for the detection of urinary albumin because of its sensitivity and reproducibility. Conventionally, urine protein is estimated from a 24-hour collection so as to minimize the effects of fluctuation in proteinuria throughout the day. More recently the urine protein:creatinine ratio in a single morning urine sample has been examined as a measure of proteinuria. A recent study showed that the protein:creatinine ratio in a group of patients with nondiabetic chronic renal disease was significantly correlated with absolute 24-hour urine protein values (p=0.0001) and also, importantly, that the urine protein creatinine ratio correlated with the rate of decline of renal function. This method of assessing the degree of proteinuria has attractions because of its simplicity and accuracy.

The incidence of asymptomatic proteinuria has been reported to vary from 0.55% to 5.8% of young army men or freshmen at colleges. The presence of proteinuria may indicate significant renal disease (Tab. 3.2), but many patients with proteinuria will have a benign prognosis. It is therefore important that appropriate investigations be performed to identify those patients with a significant renal lesion. The glomerular ultrafiltrate normally contains a small amount of protein, but the majority of this is reabsorbed by tubular activity. Proteinuria may be categorized as glomerular, tubular, and overload. Glomerular proteinuria occurs because of structural or hemodynamic changes in the glomerulus. Tubular proteinuria occurs when tubular damage causes an inability of tubular cells to catabolize low-molecular weight proteins. Overload proteinuria occurs when there is such overproduction of low-molecular weight proteins that it overwhelms the ability of the tubular cells to remove them. This can occur in the light chain variant of multiple myeloma with overproduction of immunoglobulin light chains, or with myoglobinuria. Proteinuria can also be benign, e.g., functional proteinuria as seen in fever or after exercise, idiopathic transient proteinuria, and orthostatic proteinuria. The physiologic limit of proteinuria in healthy adults has been determined as 80 mg/24 hours. Posture and exercise can increase albumin excretion significantly and, therefore, urinary protein

Table 3.2 Causes of proteinuria

Primary kidney diseases
- Minimal change disease
- Membranous nephropathy
- Focal glomerulosclerosis
- Proliferative glomerulonephritis
- Membranoproliferative glomerulonephritis
- Mesangial proliferative glomerulonephritis
- IgA nephropathy

Systemic diseases
- Malignancies
  - Myeloma, lymphoma
- Drugs
  - Nonsteroidal anti-inflammatory drugs, gold, penicillamine, angiotensin converting enzyme inhibitors
- Infections
  - HIV, hepatitis B, hepatitis C, syphilis, infective endocarditis, shunt nephritis, post-streptococcal glomerulonephritis, malaria
- Collagen vascular diseases
  - Systemic lupus erythematosus, Henoch-Schönlein purpura, vasculitides, cryoglobulinaemia
- Systemic illnesses
  - Diabetes mellitus, sarcoidosis, amyloidosis
- Hereditary disorders
  - Alport's syndrome, polycystic kidney disease, sickle cell disease, congenital nephrotic syndrome, nail-patella syndrome
- Other
  - Preeclampsia, hypothyroidism, renal transplant, renal vein thrombosis, congestive heart failure

excretion of up to 150 mg/24 hours is probably not significant. Normal urinary protein contains about 30% albumin and 70% low-molecular weight globulins, which migrate with the beta-globulins and also the Tamm-Horsfall mucoproteins. Functional proteinuria may occur in the presence of high fever, exertion, heart failure, cold exposure, emotional stress, and hypertension, and will remit with resolution of the underlying cause. Only those patients with persistent proteinuria require further nephrologic investigation. Idiopathic transient proteinuria usually occurs in children and adolescents and resolves with age. It has an excellent long-term prognosis. The distinction between intermittent proteinuria and idiopathic transient proteinuria is ill-defined, as patients with transient proteinuria may continue subsequently to demonstrate intermittent proteinuria. Most of these patients will be free from proteinuria after 5 years, and thus have a good overall prognosis. On renal biopsy, 30% are normal, and the rest have interstitial fibrosis or minor glomerular changes. Orthostatic proteinuria is defined as proteinuria that occurs only in the erect position, resolving completely when the patient is supine. Mild nephritis or anatomic variants are thought to be the cause of such proteinuria. Resolution of proteinuria occurs in about 50% of patients, and the prognosis is generally good. Persistent proteinuria is the presence of at least proteinuria on dipstick testing of two separate early morning samples of urine collected 1 week apart. Persistent proteinuria is associated with a higher incidence of mortality both in general and when specifically associated with renal failure. About 50% of patients with persistent proteinuria will develop hypertension, and 20% will have impaired renal function within 10 years of follow-up. Thus, patients with persistent proteinuria should be investigated to identify any potentially treatable conditions.

The Scottish Intercollegiate Guidelines Network has proposed some guidelines for nephrology referral in patients found to have asymptomatic proteinuria. It is recommended that patients with proteinuria in excess of 500 mg/l or a protein:creatinine ratio >30 mg/mmol, or proteinuria in excess of 250 mg/l, or a protein:creatinine ratio > 20 mg/mmol with coexistent raised creatinine or hypertension should be investigated further, as should patients with coexistent hematuria (Tab. 3.3). Patients with inter-

Table 3.3 Scottish Intercollegiate Guidelines Network (SIGN). Guideline for the investigation of asymptomatic proteinuria in adults

Dipstick testing indicates + protein

Repeat test
- Two morning urine samples, one week apart
- Exclude orthostatic, functional, or idiopathic transient proteinuria
- Intermittent proteinuria. Re-check after 6 months, then monitoring until proteinuria disappears

Persistent proteinuria

Laboratory confirmation
- 24-hour collection or protein: creatinine ratio

Initial assessment and investigation
- History
- Examination
- Urinalysis for hematuria and glycosuria
- Serum urea, electrolytes, creatinine and glucose
- Exclude urinary tract infection

Referral to nephrologist
- If proteinuria >500 mg/l or protein: creatinine >30 mg/mmol
- If proteinuria >250 mg/l or protein: creatinine >20 mg/mmol with either raised serum creatinine or hypertension
- If co-existent haematuria

Nephrologic investigations
- Measurement of glomerular filtration rate
- Immunology (serum and urine electrophoresis, ANCA, ANA, double-stranded DNA antibodies, complement)
- Ultrasound of kidneys and bladder
- Consideration for a renal biopsy

(ANCA = anti-neutrophil cytoplasm antibodies; ANA = anti-nuclear antibodies.)

mittent proteinuria, or patients for whom immediate referral is not appropriate, should receive follow-up at 6 months initially, then annually, to include an assessment of blood pressure, degree of proteinuria, and renal function. Patients with persistent proteinuria should have urine collected for protein or albumin estimation and in addition imaging of the kidneys and bladder, and an immunologic profile should be obtained. Renal biopsy is likely to be required for patients with > 2 g/day of proteinuria, particularly if this is associated with hematuria, hypertension, impaired renal function, or systemic symptoms.

Investigation of hematuria

Cellulose strips impregnated with peroxidase, orthotolidine, and buffers detect the peroxidase activity of heme in urinary red blood cells (RBCs), hemoglobin, or myoglobin with a sensitivity of 91 to 100% and a specificity of 65 to 99%. Some brands of urinary dipsticks can distinguish intact RBCs from hemoglobin or myoglobin. False-negatives will result if the urine contains a reducing agent (e.g., ascorbic acid), is acidic, diluted, or voided after taking fluid. False-positives will occur if the urine contains myoglobin, oxidizing agents, contaminants, bacterial peroxidase, or if the urine is an early-morning concentrated sample. Dipstick tests are highly sensitive and can give a positive result in the presence of a normal number of red cells ($1\text{-}2 \times 10^{12}$/l urine). Therefore a microscopic examination of the urine is mandatory if a dipstick test is positive. If, however, the result of a dipstick test is negative, then further investigation is not necessary.

A number of factors can influence RBC morphology on microscopy. RBCs are better preserved in acidic and concentrated urine, and so the first morning urine sample should be used for urine microscopy. Strenuous exercise can lead to hematuria and should be avoided for 2 to 3 days before the collection of urine for microscopy. To reduce the likelihood of contamination, a midstream urine is used. Hematuria has been differentiated into glomerular and nonglomerular types based on the morphologic differences in urinary RBCs. The presence of dysmorphic RBCs or cells with a low mean corpuscular volume was believed to indicate glomerular bleeding; isomorphic RBCs, or cells with a normal mean corpuscular volume were thought to originate from postglomerular sources. The cause of the distortion that affects RBCs of glomerular origin is not known. Possible explanations are physical disruption of the red-cell membrane during passage through the glomerular basement membrane, osmotic disruption during passage through the distal tubules, and the injurious effects of the tubular enzymes and hemolytic substances. RBC morphology can be readily evaluated using light microscopy, phase contrast microscopy, differential interference microscopy, and scanning electron microscopy. A useful classification of RBC morphology defines ten RBC shapes, five "glomerular" and five "urologic" or "nonglomerular". The finding of at least 15% of glomerular RBCs was indicative of a glomerular source of bleeding, with a sensitivity of 90% and a specificity of 98%. The presence of G1 glomerular cells (doughnut-like cells with one or more blebs) was also suggestive of glomerular disease. It has been proposed that when glomerular hematuria was defined on the basis of 5% or more of G1 cells, the sensitivity, specificity, and efficacy were all 100%. Others have used the presence of 5% or more of acanthocytes (ring-formed cells with one or more protrusions) in the urine as a marker of glomerular hematuria, with a sensitivity of 52-99% and a specificity of 98-100%. Using Coulter counters, RBCs can be readily separated by their mean cell volume. In glomerular bleeding, the mean volume of urine RBCs is about 50 μm^3 or less, whereas in urologic disorders it is about 90-100 μm^3. This method is faster than microscopy, does not require trained personnel, and also avoids subjective variation. Although this method has been validated by a number of investigators, it does, however, have a low sensitivity in cases of mild hematuria. In a meta-analysis appraising the value of urinary red cell shape in the diagnosis of glomerular and nonglomerular hematuria, there was large inter- and intra-observer variability in identifying RBC and disagreement in the proportions of RBC used as a cut-off between glomerular and nonglomerular bleeding (10-80%). Urinary red cell mean corpuscular volume determinations were found to be less affected. The proportion of dysmorphic RBCs and their mean corpuscular volume misclassified 7-20% of those with nonglomerular bleeding. In conclusion, RBC morphology is a useful but not definitive technique for the assessment of a patient with hematuria.

Isolated asymptomatic microscopic hematuria has been found in 4-13% of the general adult population. It may be associated with a wide range of conditions, from transient nondiseases, such as strenuous exercises, rapidly progressive glomerulonephritis, to bladder cancer (Tab. 3.4). In patients with hematuria, the cause should be sought because in 2-22% of cases of asymptomatic microscopic hematuria a serious abnormality is found. The significance of asymptomatic microscopic hematuria is different in men and in women, in young persons and in older adults. In British men, cancers of the urinary tract are fairly common, accounting for more than 15% of all registrations of cancer. In women, with microscopic hematuria, the risk of an underlying cancer is considerably lower. In men aged between 18 and 33 years with microscopic hematuria, the prevalence of cancer is around 0.6%. This rises to 1% in men older than 40 years, and in men older than 50, 13% had neoplasia of the urinary tract.

The commonest causes of glomerular hematuria are IgA nephropathy, thin basement membrane disease, and diffuse proliferative glomerulonephritis. Among 1000 patients with hematuria, the common causes of nonglomerular hematuria were inflammatory conditions of the urethra and prostate (usually trigonitis) (377 cases), benign prostatic hyperplasia (165 cases), cystitis (73 cases), transitional carcinoma of the bladder (65 cases), and stones in the renal pelvis or ureter (34 cases). Altogether 80 patients had some form of cancer. Frank hematuria should always be investigated because the likelihood of urologic cancer averages 23%. In the case of microscopic hematuria, urinalysis should be reevaluated

Table 3.4 Causes of haematuria

Glomerular
- *Primary glomerulonephritis*
  - IgA nephropathy
  - Post-infectious glomerulonephritis
  - Membranoproliferative glomerulonephritis
  - Focal glomerulosclerosis
- *Secondary glomerulonephritis*
  - Systemic lupus erythematosus
  - Vasculitis
  - Essential mixed cryoglobulinaemia
  - Hemolytic-uremic syndrome
- *Familial*
  - Thin basement membrane disease
  - Alport's syndrome

Nonglomerular
- *Renal parenchymal*
  - Renal tumors
    - Hypernephroma
  - Vascular
    - Malignant hypertension
    - Sickle cell disease
    - Loin pain-hematuria syndrome
    - Arteriovenous malformation
  - Metabolic
    - Hypercalciuria
    - Hyperuricosuria
  - Familial
    - Polycystic kidney disease
    - Medullary sponge kidneys
  - Infection
    - Pyelonephritis
    - Tuberculosis
- *Extrarenal*
  - Tumors
    - Pelvis
    - Ureter
    - Bladder
    - Prostate
  - Benign prostatic hyperplasia
  - Stone
  - Infection
  - Other
    - Drugs
      - Heparin
      - Warfarin
      - Aspirin
      - Cyclophosphamide (hemorrhagic cystitis)
    - Systemic bleeding disorders
    - Trauma

once or twice for confirmation. Infection, if present, should be treated, before repeating urinalysis. It is important to note that a subsequent negative test does not obviate the need to investigate in some patients, particularly in older males, because tumors are known to bleed intermittently. In order to exclude false-positives, hematuria should always be confirmed by the demonstration of RBCs in the urine sediment. Our view is that > 5 RBCs/high-power field (12500 RBCs/ml) should be investigated. The number of RBCs excreted is thought not to be related to the severity of the lesion or its cause; hence, there are no criteria to identify patients with microscopic hematuria in which the probability of a significant lesion is low enough to justify exemption from investigation. Cytologic examination of the urine may pick up malignant cells. In a large series from the Mayo Clinic, urinary cytology had a sensitivity of 67% and a specificity of 96% for the detection of uroepithelial cancer, primarily transitional cancer of the bladder. False-positive cytology can occur with nephrolithiasis and urinary tract infections.

In younger patients with hematuria the case can be made for considering a renal biopsy, especially if there is coexistent proteinuria or renal impairment. By contrast, in older patients with a nonglomerular picture or even a mixed pattern on microscopy, a urologic work-up, including cystoscopy, is more appropriate (Tab. 3.5). If the results of investigations are negative, testing for hematuria should be repeated twice at intervals of 6 months, because

Table 3.5 Evaluation of microscopic hematuria in adults

Hematuria on dipstick testing

⇩

Repeat dipstick test looking for hematuria and proteinuria
Urine microscopy to look for erythrocytes, casts and bacteria

⇩

Confirmation of hematuria

⇩

Assessment and investigation
- History
- Examination
- Serum urea, electrolytes and creatinine
- Measurement of glomerular filtration rate
- Immunology (serum and urine electrophoresis, ANCA, ANA, double-stranded DNA antibodies, complements, anti-GBM antibodies, ASO)
- Ultrasound of kidneys and bladder
- Midstream urine to exclude urinary tract infection
- Urine cytology
- Coagulation screen in selected cases
- Hemoglobin electrophoresis in selected cases

⇩ ⇩

Glomerular type (hematuria)	Nonglomerular hematuria
(Dysmorphic RBCs with a low MVC and RBC casts) • Consideration for a renal biopsy	(Isomorphic RBCs with a normal MCV) **Adults > 45** • Urinary calcium excretion • Uric acid excretion • Cystoscopy • Intravenous pyelography • Echocolor Doppler? • CT scan? • Angiography? • Renal biopsy? **Adults < 45** • Urinary calcium excretion • Uric acid excretion • Renal biopsy?

(ANCA = anti-neutrophil cytoplasmic antibodies; ANA = anti-nuclear antibodies; anti-GBM = anti-glomerular basement membrane; ASO = anti-streptolysin titres; MCV = mean corpuscular volume.)

tumors may lead to hematuria on an intermittent basis. Investigations such as ultrasonography, laboratory analysis, and urine cytology should be repeated every 6-12 months for at least 2-3 years, because the cause of microscopic hematuria may be revealed only after many months of follow-up.

LABORATORY INVESTIGATIONS

Renal function

The standard test of overall renal function is the glomerular filtration rate (GFR). This is based on the concept of clearance where the rate of removal of a solute that is solely cleared by the kidney must equal the rate of excretion of that solute into the urine. The GFR is thus the clearance of a substance that is completely filtered at the glomerulus and is neither reabsorbed nor excreted by the renal tubules. The GFR is derived from measurements of urine concentration of the substance (U) multiplied by the urine flow rate (V), with the product being divided by the plasma concentration (P). The gold standard for measuring the GFR is the inulin clearance. Inulin is a polymer of fructose that meets the criteria described above for measuring the GFR. The test, however, requires a constant infusion of inulin together with several blood samples and timed urine collections. For these reasons it is mostly used as a research tool. The GFR as measured is corrected to a body surface area of 1.73 m^2. The normal range for the GFR is 88-174 ml/min in men and 87-147 ml/min in women.

Chromium-51 edetate clearance This is widely used as a single injection method for measuring GFR. Following intravenous injection of Chromium-51 (Cr) edetate, three or more blood samples are taken from the contralateral arm and the fall of concentration plotted against time on semilogarithmic paper. The plasma clearance is determined using compartmental analysis of the disappearance curve, and this correlates well with the GFR as measured by inulin clearance.

Nonradiolabeled contrast media The clearance of iodine containing radiographic contrast media has been used to measure the GFR. Iothalamate was initially widely used but more recently the non-ionic low-osmolality radiographic contrast medium iohexol has been used following intravenous injection to measure the GFR, and a good correlation shown with inulin clearances.

Serum creatinine and creatinine clearance The most widely used measure of renal function is the serum creatinine. Creatinine is formed from muscle creatine and its levels are therefore dependent on muscle mass, being higher in muscular individuals and lower in starvation. The other source of creatine, is of course, dietary meat intake, and it is well recognized that the serum creatinine rises after heavy meat intake. Creatinine is measured by the Jaffe reaction, which, however, also measures noncreatinine chromogens. For this reason, reaction rate analyzers have been developed that are based on a more rapid reaction with creatinine than noncreatinine chromogens. In addition, it is important to recognize that the drugs trimethoprim and cimetidine inhibit renal tubular excretion of creatinine and will therefore lead to a higher serum creatinine and lower creatinine clearance. Creatinine is secreted by the renal tubules; thus, the creatinine clearance exceeds true GFR (inulin clearance) by a factor of 1.1 to 1.2 at high clearances. As renal function deteriorates tubular secretion of creatinine increases and therefore the creatinine clearance increasingly exceeds inulin clearance. For this reason, the creatinine clearance is a useful estimate of GFR at serum creatinines less than 250 µmol/l and above this it is preferable to use the serum creatinine.

Calculated creatinine clearance (The Cockroft Gault formula) This formula is widely used for the calculation of GFR from the serum creatinine but suffers from the limitations inherent in measuring serum creatinine:

$$\text{GFR(ml/min)} = \frac{1.2 \times [140 - \text{age(yrs)}] \times \text{weight}}{\text{plasma creatinine } (\mu\text{mol / l})}$$

In females the result is factored by 0.85 to account for a lower creatinine production.

Immunologic tests

A variety of immunologic tests are used in the diagnosis of renal disease and also in monitoring disease activity in some disorders.

Immunoglobulins and serum and urine immunoelectrophoresis The detection of a serum paraprotein or of monoclonal urine light chain excretion is a pointer to the diagnosis of myeloma in a patient with renal impairment or proteinuria. A serum paraprotein is also often seen in patients with primary (AL) amyloidosis.

Complement Activation of the classic pathway of complement is typically seen in immune complex mediated glomerulonephritis, as in lupus nephritis (see below), and here C3 and C4 levels are low. Low complement levels may also be seen in cryoglobulinemia. Activation of the alternative pathway of complement is seen in patients with dense deposit mesangiocapillary glomerulonephritis (Type II) and here stabilization of C3bBb, the alternative pathway C3 convertase by C3 nephritic factor leads to a low C3 and a normal C4.

Lupus nephritis Patients with lupus almost invariably express antibodies to components of the cell nucleus (ANA). A fluorescent antinuclear test is positive in more than 95% of patients. In this test, various staining patterns (homogeneous, speckled, rim, nucleolar) can be demonstrated depending on the content of different autoantibodies in the serum. A positive fluorescent ANA test is useful because of its sensitivity, although it lacks specificity, and a positive fluorescent ANA test can be found in other connective tissue diseases. More specific, but less sensitive findings, include anti-double-stranded DNA (anti-dsDNA) and anti-Sm autoantibodies. Anti-DNA antibodies bind the helical backbone of native DNA, whereas anti-Sm antibodies bind to proteins on an RNA-protein complex termed snRNP. Antibodies to double-stranded DNA have the highest specificity for SLE, but only about 50% of patients have a positive test. The interpretation of anti-DNA antibodies is also complicated by the lack of standardization, and currently various assays for anti-DNA antibodies are available: the most commonly used are the ELISA, Crithidia immunofluorescence assay, and the Farr radioimmuno assay. These assays differ in the source of DNA and the physical chemical properties of the anti-DNA antibodies detected. Patients with SLE will often have a false-positive response to serologic tests for syphilis such as the Venereal Disease Research Laboratory (VDRL), and rapid plasma reagin (RPR) tests because of antibodies to cardiolipin or other phospholipids. Often, antibodies to phospholipids will also interfere with clotting tests, resulting in prolongation of the partial thromboplastin time. Reduced serum complement concentrations are useful in diagnosis and in assessing disease activity. Many patients with SLE have an activation of the classic component cascade with consumption of the early components C1q, C4, and C3. Persistent C3 or CH50 depression has been associated with progression of renal disease in some, but not all, groups of patients.

Cryoglobulinemia Cold precipitable immunoglobulins are found in association with some types of glomerulonephritis. The phenomenon of cryoprecipitation has been known for more than 50 years. The current classification of cryoglobulins based on their immunochemical characteristics was proposed in 1974, and recognizes three types of cryoglobulins. Type I cryoglobulins are composed of a monoclonal immunoglobulin component only, usually IgM, occasionally IgG, rarely IgA. Type I cryoglobulins are found in association with lymphoproliferative diseases such as myeloma, or Waldenström's macroglobulinemia, or non-Hodgkin's lymphoma. Types II and III cryoglobulins are referred to as mixed cryoglobulins because they consist of a mixture of immunoglobulins of different isotypes. Type II cryoglobulins are composed of a mixture of monoclonal and polyclonal immunoglobulins. Frequently the monoclonal component is an IgM with rheumatoid factor activity, and the second component is a polyclonal IgG which behaves as an antigen for the monoclonal IgM rheumatoid factor. Type II cryoglobulins are found in association with lymphoproliferative disorders, infectious diseases, and autoimmune disorders. Type III cryoglobulins are composed of a mixture of polyclonal immunoglobulins, usually IgM and IgG, and are found in association with a variety of autoimmune disorders and infections. Recently, hepatitis C has emerged as the major pathogenic factor in these patients. Since the initial report of antibodies against hepatitis C virus (HCV) in patients with type II mixed cryoglobulinemia in 1990, other groups have confirmed the presence of anti-HCV antibodies using ELISA and recombinant immunoblot assay in over 80% of patients with mixed cryoglobulinemia.

Microscopic polyangiitis(polyarteritis), classic polyarteritis and Churg-Strauss syndrome Antineutrophil cytoplasmic antibodies (ANCA) were first described in 1982 in patients with a segmental necrotizing glomerulonephritis, some of whom had features consistent with a systemic vasculitis. Subsequently it was shown that antineutrophil cytoplasmic antibodies were commonly found in the sera from patients with Wegener's granulomatosis and microscopic polyangiitis (polyarteritis) (MPA). Two broad patterns of cytoplasmic staining have been recognized. In the first there is granular staining of the cytoplasm of ethanol-fixed neutrophils (c-ANCA). This pattern of staining is commonly seen in the sera of patients with Wegener's granulomatosis. The target antigen for this antibody is a 29 kDa serine proteinase, neutrophil serine proteinase 3. The second pattern is of perinuclear staining (p-ANCA,) which is seen in the sera of patients with MPA and also idiopathic segmental necrotizing glomerulonephritis. A wider range of specificities is seen with p-ANCA, although most of these antibodies are directed against myeloperoxidase and in a few cases against elastase and lactoferrin. Approximately 80% of patients with active systemic Wegener's granulomatosis have c-ANCA antibodies in their sera. p-ANCA are found in the sera of approximately 80% of patients with MPA and about 75% of patients with Churg-Strauss syndrome. p-ANCA is less disease-specific as well as less sensitive. Elevated titers are reported in Kawasaki's syndrome, rheumatoid vasculitis, and idiopathic segmental necrotizing glomerulonephritis. Between 14 and 20% of patients with classic polyarteritis have a positive ANCA, and in patients with a hepatitis B positive classic polyarteritis 11% are reported to have a positive ANCA. It is important to recognize that ANCA have also been described in systemic lupus erythematosus, rheumatoid arthritis, inflammatory bowel disease, and in some infectious diseases.

Imaging investigations

A wide variety of techniques for imaging the kidneys are now available. The choice of the imaging technique is critically dependent on the questions being asked (Tab. 3.6). The optimal imaging technique is one that provides a definitive answer with the minimum of radiation and discomfort or danger for the patient. These choices are best made following consultation with radiologic colleagues, and many centers will have regular reviews of imaging involving radiologists, nephrologists, and urologists.

In investigating a patient with renal disease it is important to know the size of the kidneys, the nature of the renal parenchyma, and the presence and absence of renal cysts, the presence or absence of obstruction to the urinary tract, and the integrity of the renal vasculature. The clinical presentation determines the appropriate imaging investigation.

Table 3.6 Imaging investigations

Clinical problem	Imaging investigation
Hematuria	Intravenous urogram
Proteinuria/nephrotic syndrome	Ultrasound
Renal impairment/renal failure	Ultrasound
Renal artery stenosis	Captopril renography/MR angiography/renal arteriography
Renal vein thrombosis	Doppler ultrasound renal veins/renal venography
Renal tumors	Ultrasound/CT scan/MRI

Ultrasound of the kidneys

This is useful in determining the size of the kidneys, the texture of the renal parenchyma (Fig. 3.1), the presence of renal cysts or renal tumors, and also the presence of renal obstruction (Fig. 3.2). In addition ultrasound scanning is useful for detecting moderate-sized bladder tumors and also the size and structure of the prostate gland. Doppler ultrasound scanning is particularly useful for determining the arterial and venous perfusion of the kidneys (Fig. 3.3). This is helpful in evaluating the perfusion of renal transplants and also for excluding renal vein thrombosis. Some studies have indicated that ultrasound also is useful in detecting renal artery stenosis, but we find this a less reliable technique for this purpose than other investigations.

Intravenous urography A plain abdominal radiography will demonstrate renal calcification, and in this case an intravenous urogram showed the changes of medullary sponge kidney (Fig. 3.4). Intravenous urography remains a reliable initial investigation in patients with hematuria or recurrent urinary infections because it provides good imaging of the renal tract. Renal papillary necrosis and bladder filling defects may be detected (Fig. 3.5). An intravenous urogram also is useful for detecting renal scars, as seen in reflux nephropathy (Fig. 3.6).

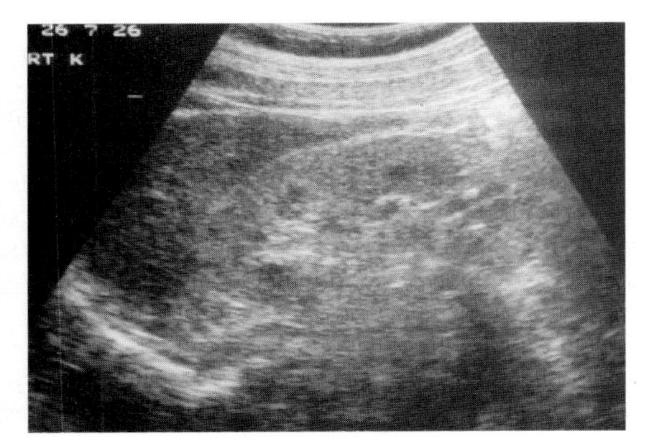

Figure 3.1 Ultrasound of the kidney showing increased echogenicity of the cortex in a patient with chronic renal failure.

Radionuclide scanning

A variety of radionuclides are useful in investigating the structure and function of the kidneys. A DMSA scan is particularly useful for detecting renal scars and filling defects. DTPA and Mag 3 scans provide accurate information on renal perfusion and also of the drainage of the renal tract. The initial concentration curves following renography give good information on arterial perfusion and when coupled with the administration of an angiotensin-converting enzyme inhibitor, e.g., captopril, provide supportive evidence of renal artery stenosis (Fig. 3.7). This test, however, is less useful in patients with advanced renal failure. In patients with a suspected obstruction the administration of intravenous frusemide after a DTPA or Mag 3 scan will confirm or refute this possibility.

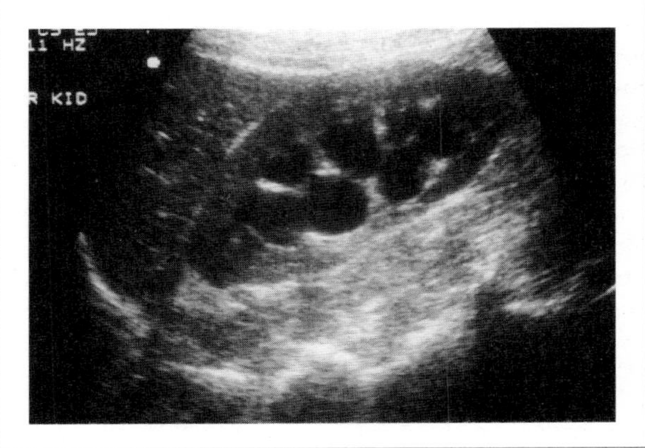

Figure 3.2 Ultrasound scan of the kidney showing a dilated pelvicalyceal system indicating hydronephrosis.

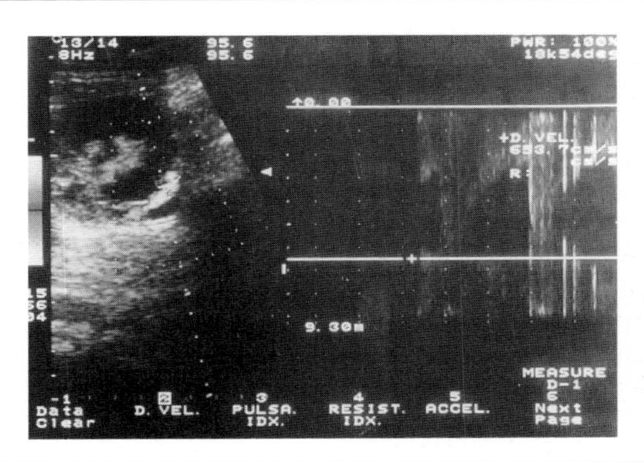

Figure 3.3 Transplant renal artery stenosis as shown by Doppler ultrasound. Image on left shows the Doppler cursor placed in the proximal transplant renal artery (color represented in black or white). The spectral trace on the right shows a very high velocity of 653 cm/s with the turbulent flow. These localized high velocities indicate hemodynamically significant stenosis.

Computed tomographic (CT) scans

This technique is particularly useful in determining the extent of such renal tumors as angiomyolipomata (Fig. 3.8). CT scan will also show the plane of involvement of the renal tumor and also whether the renal veins and vena cava are affected. In addition, a CT scan of the abdomen and

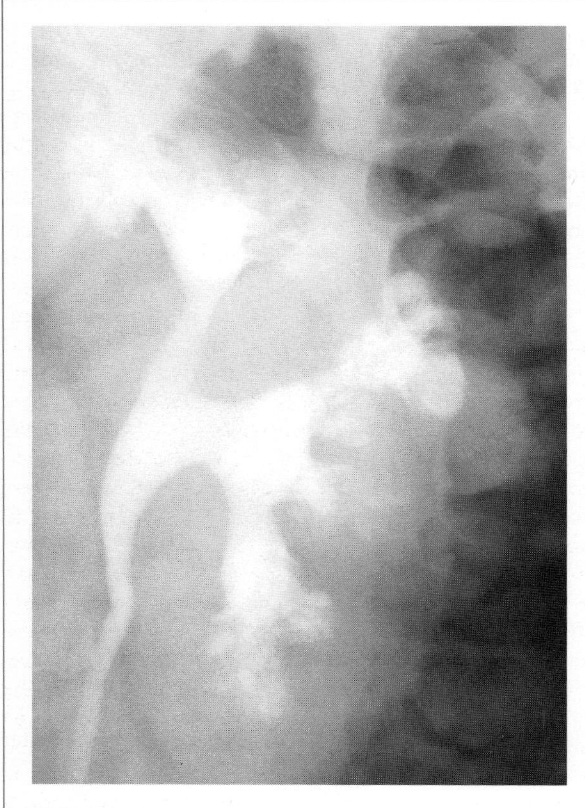

Figure 3.4 IVU film showing ectasic contrast filled tubules in renal medullae. Appearances are those of medullary sponge kidney.

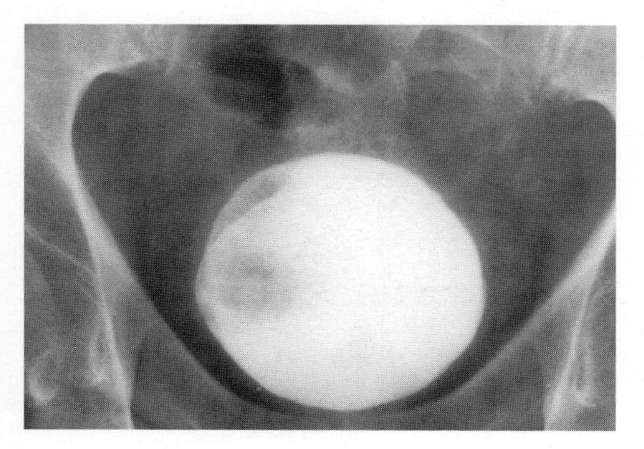

Figure 3.5 Intravenous urogram showing a right bladder filling defect in a patient with bladder cancer.

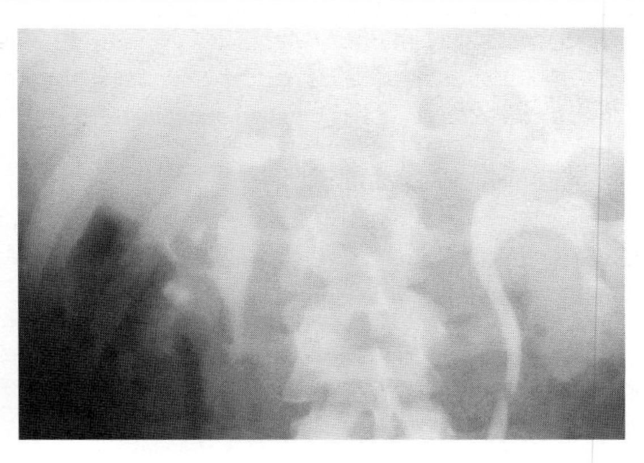

Figure 3.6 Small right kidney with parenchymal loss (note proximity of upper pole calyces to spine compared with left). Dilated abnormal calyces. Appearances are those of reflux nephropathy.

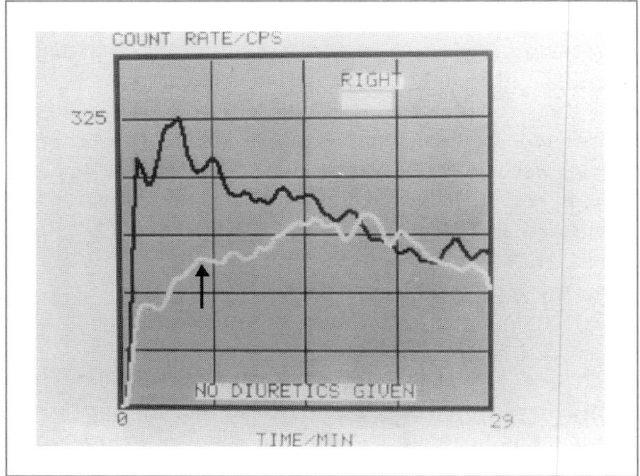

Figure 3.7 MAG3 renogram showing a poor left renogram curve with a delayed peak pre-captopril that further deteriorated following captopril (➧indicative of a left renal artery stenosis. This was confirmed on angiography).

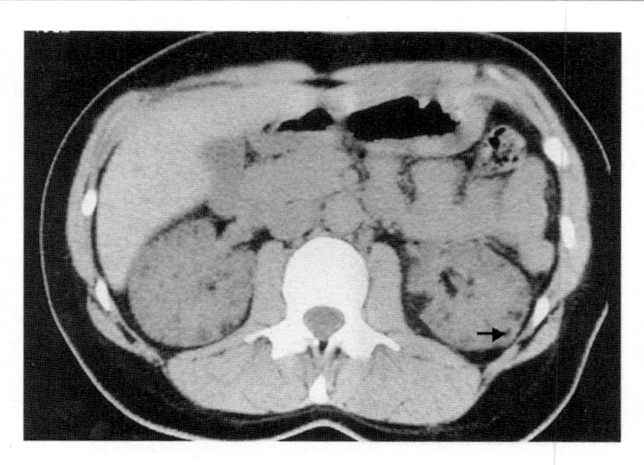

Figure 3.8 Angiomyolipomatosis on a CT scan of the kidneys in a patient with tuberose sclerosis. Unenhanced scan shows multiple cortical low density foci (➧); some of which are undoubtedly fatty.

lungs provides evidence of the extent of the spread of the tumor. Spiral CT scanning is particularly useful in delineating the proximal renal arteries, and this information is useful in deciding whether angioplasty of the lesion is possible.

Magnetic resonance imaging (MRI) scans

As with CT scans, MRI scans with gadolinium imaging are useful in assessing the presence and extent of renal tumors (Fig. 3.9). The technique can also provide good images of the kidneys and collecting systems. We have also found this technique to be useful in delineating the renal arteries (Fig. 3.10), and it does have the advantage of obviating the need for exposure to radiation

Renal angiography

This remains the gold standard investigation for determining the anatomy of the renal vasculature, but it suffers the disadvantages of requiring arterial puncture and also of radiation. Using digital subtraction angiography after intra-arterial injection of contrast, excellent views of the renal arterial circulation are obtained (Fig. 3.11). Renal venography can be used to determine the patency of the proximal renal veins, although this usually can be determined noninvasively by ultrasound.

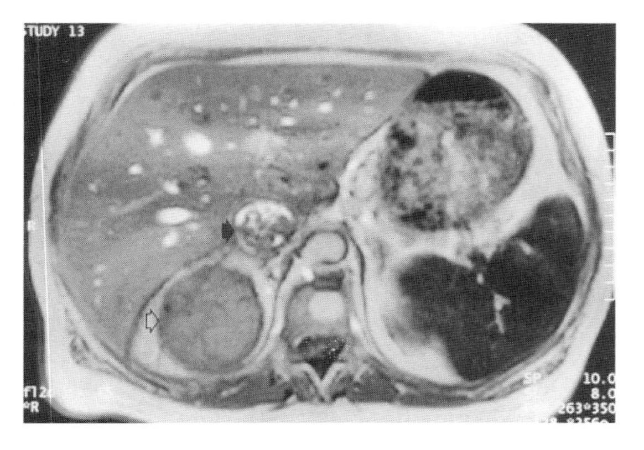

Figure 3.9 Gradient echo T1 weighted axial magnetic resonance images showing a right upper pole renal tumor (⇨) with tumor extension into the IVC. On this sequence flowing blood is white and note therefore the vascularization of the intra-caval tumour (➧).

Renal biopsy

Practical details Our experience is that renal biopsies provide less information and are at the same time more dangerous if the kidneys are less than 8.5 cm in length. Before a renal biopsy, imaging should establish that there are two kidneys, because the risks of major problems after biopsying a single kidney are such as to make this a contraindication in any but exceptional circumstances. It is important to ensure that the patient's coagulation is normal. Thus, all patients should have a platelet count, a partial thromboplastin time, and a prothrombin time. Some also advocate measuring a bleeding time. On empiric grounds our view is that a renal biopsy is contraindicated unless the platelet count is greater than 100×10^9 /l; the partial thromboplastin ratio less than 1.3 and the internationalized normalised ratio for the prothrombin time less than 1.3. Patients who are hypertensive are more likely to bleed after a renal biopsy, and a sustained diastolic blood pressure higher than 100 mmHg is a contraindication for a renal biopsy. Renal biopsies should be performed only after formal training. Most centers now use real-time ultrasound guided biopsies with an automated biopsy device. This does seem safer and is also less painful for the patient. Immediate microscopy of the specimen ensures its adequacy. Following a renal biopsy, the pulse and blood pressure are carefully monitored, and urine passed is examined for blood. Clinically significant complications including frank hematuria occur in about 5-7% of cases,

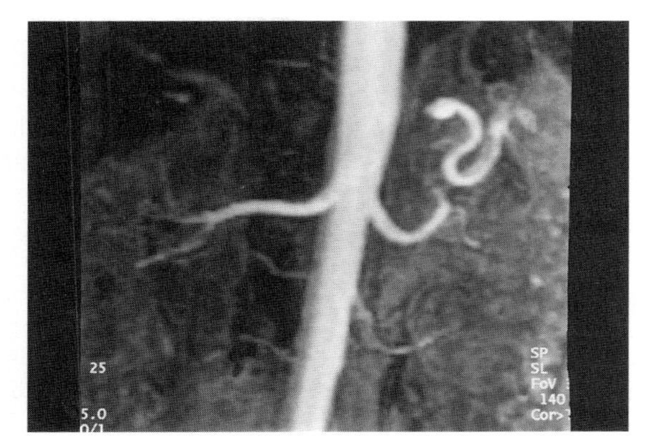

Figure 3.10 MR angiography T1 weighted gradient echo breath hold sequence with a volume acquisition during the first pass of contrast material (gadolinium DTPA) allows a diagnostic MR arteriogram to be displayed.

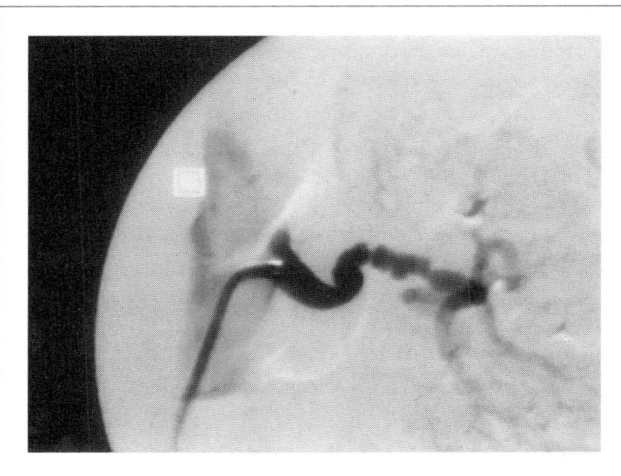

Figure 3.11 Typical corkscrew appearance of the left renal artery in a patient with renal artery stenosis from fibromuscular dysplasia.

but these usually are self-limiting. Major complications including surgery and death have been reported in about 0.12% of cases.

Renal biopsy interpretation Percutaneous needle biopsy of the kidney was probably first performed in 1944, although the first reported series in the literature was described in 1951. Following the description of successful techniques for percutaneous renal biopsy initial reports attested to its usefulness in the diagnosis of renal disease, obtaining prognostic information, and defining the natural history of various forms of renal disease. Despite this there is still great debate, particularly in patients with the nephrotic syndrome, as to whether the risks to the patient from the procedure outweigh the potential benefit. The utility of renal biopsy in adults with an apparently idiopathic nephrotic syndrome has been strongly challenged. Some have questioned the value of renal biopsy in the idiopathic nephrotic syndrome in adults and have advocated, from the use of decision analysis, that blind treatment with short-term alternate-day high-dose steroids was at least as good as biopsy-directed treatment. A very strong argument was put forward that as the prognosis for remission of the nephrotic syndrome and for renal function was determined solely by the patient's responsiveness to steroids and not by the histologic lesion, blind treatment with 2 months of alternate-day high-dose steroids was at least as good as biopsy-based treatment. These analyses were based on several assumptions. First, from the observations of the collaborative study in the USA, in patients with membranous nephropathy, alternate-day prednisolone for 8 weeks was effective in slowing down the progression of renal impairment as compared with placebo. A striking feature of that study was that 50% of all patients with a nephrotic syndrome had membranous nephropathy. If one assumes that a further 25% had minimal change nephropathy, then case for blind treatment with steroids is persuasive. However, in most other studies membranous nephropathy accounts for only 20% of all cases of the nephrotic syndrome in adults. Further, other controlled studies show no benefit of steroids in membranous nephropathy, and the balance of evidence is that steroids are ineffective in this disorder. A further point that is often overlooked is that the nephrotic syndrome in adults with minimal change nephropathy responds to steroids slightly less often than in children, and also more slowly. Only 60% of adults with minimal change nephropathy are in remission at 8 weeks, and this rises to 76% at 16 weeks. There, is thus, good reason to conclude that in these patients, 8 weeks of alternate-day steroids may not lead to remission of the nephrotic syndrome. Similar arguments exist in the case of microscopic hematuria. Opponents of a renal biopsy argue that the results of the biopsy in patients whose hematuria is not accompanied by hypertension, impaired renal function or proteinuria rarely had an impact on therapy or the eventual outcome. On the other hand we have argued that in patients with microscopic hematuria knowledge of renal histology helps in determining the prognosis and may lead to therapy.

Renal biopsy immunohistology The presence or absence of deposits of immunoglobulin and complement within glomeruli is of great value in the interpretation of renal biopsies and also has provided pivotal clues to the immunopathogenetic mechanisms of glomerulonephritis and also to their classification. The classic appearance of linear deposits of IgG on glomerular basement membranes is diagnostic of anti-glomerular basement antibody disease, whereas granular deposits of immunoglobulins and complement in glomeruli indicate an immune complex-mediated glomerulonephritis, as typified by lupus nephritis. Traditionally, immune deposits in glomeruli have been detected by indirect immunofluorescence using monospecific antibodies to the immunoprotein of interest. These include IgG, IgA, IgM, C1q, C4,C3, fibrin, light chains, and amyloid A protein. Recently an immunoperoxidase technique also has been applied, and this offers advantages with stability of the stain and also allows the use of light microscopy for the histologic examination. The main immunofluorescent findings in the more common primary and secondary glomerulonephritides will be reviewed.

Minimal change nephropathy Typically there are no glomerular deposits of immunoglobulin and complement on immunofluorescent microscopy, although rarely minimal amounts of IgM and C3 are found in the mesangium.

Focal segmental glomerulosclerosis This is characterized by deposits of IgM and C3 in sclerosed areas believed to represent nonspecific trapping on these immunoproteins.

Idiopathic membranous nephropathy The specific appearance is of subepithelial deposits of IgG, often with C3 without deposits in the mesangial areas. In about 20% of cases, deposits of IgA and IgM are found.

Mesangiocapillary glomerulonephritis (membranoproliferative glomerulonephritis) In Type I (subendothelial) mesangiocapillary glomerulonephritis (MCGN), immunohistologic examination reveals subendothelial deposits of IgG and less frequently of IgM and IgA and C3. In Type II MCGN (dense-deposit disease), basement membrane and mesangial deposits of C3 are found.

Systemic lupus erythematosus and cryoglobulinemia The typical findings in lupus nephritis on immunofluorescent microscopy are of florid deposition of IgG, IgA, IgM as well as C3, C4, and C1q. This appearance should always raise the possibility of lupus nephritis. In lupus membranous nephropathy there is often mesangial proliferation and C4 and C1q deposits, and this differentiates it from idiopathic membranous nephropathy. In cryoglobulinemia, immunohistology reveals the same class(es) of immunoglobulin in the glomerular deposits as are found in the cryoglobulins, usually IgM and IgG together with C3.

IgA nephropathy and Henoch-Schönlein purpura IgA nephropathy and Henoch-Schönlein purpura are characterized by diffuse mesangial deposits of IgA and C3.

Postinfectious (poststreptococcal) glomerulonephritis Here there are granular subepithelial deposits or humps of C3 and IgG, and these are seen as electron-dense deposits on electron microscopy.

Wegener's granulomatosis and microscopic polyangiitis Frank immune deposits of immunoglobulin and complement are not seen; hence the term "pauci-immune" is often applied to this group of conditions.

Evaluation of renal biopsies Interpretation of a renal biopsy specimen depends on the clinical circumstances, particularly the age and sex of the patient, and the indication for the biopsy. In the original studies of the International Study of Kidney Diseases in Children (ISKDC) the diagnosis of minimal change nephropathy was based on renal biopsies. From these and other studies it was established that in a child aged 1 to 6 years with a nephrotic syndrome and highly selective proteinuria and who did not have microscopic hematuria, hypertension, or renal impairment, the likely diagnosis was minimal change nephropathy. Based on these observations, children aged between 1 and 6 with a nephrotic syndrome and the features summarized above are no longer subjected to renal biopsy and are instead treated with a trial of steroids. This leads to the term "steroid responsive nephrotic syndrome of childhood," and most but not all of such children will have minimal change nephropathy. The diagnosis of minimal change nephropathy should be used only when there is the nephrotic syndrome and no significant abnormality of glomeruli is seen on light microscopy (Fig. 3.12, see Color Atlas). Significant abnormalities include glomerular enlargement, expansion of mesangium, deposition of immunoproteins other than a little IgM in mesangium, and, in particular, any segmental changes.

In adults, three conditions account for two-thirds of cases of the nephrotic syndrome. These are membranous nephropathy, a group of segmental sclerosing glomerular disorders often called focal segmental glomerulosclerosis, and minimal change nephropathy. These and diabetic glomerulonephropathy, lupus glomerulonephritis, and amyloid account for most cases of the nephrotic syndrome in adults. In membranous nephropathy, glomerular basement membranes are uniformly thickened, and often have regular spikes on the epithelial side when stained with periodic acid-methenamine silver, although this feature is not essential for the diagnosis. Immunohistologic study shows uniform granular deposition of IgG and complement on the epithelial side of the glomerular basement membranes (Fig. 3.13, see Color Atlas). The diagnosis of segmental sclerosing glomerular lesions remains difficult. Especially in their late stages, abnormalities are easily noted when part of the glomerular tuft is occupied by solid material stained with periodic acid-methenamine silver, that is sclerosis, or by acellular material stained with eosin, that is hyalinosis (Fig. 3.14, see Color Atlas). A condition affecting part of the tuft is called segmental. Often biopsy specimens with segmental abnormalities appear to have only a proportion of affected glomeruli, and such conditions are called "focal". The term "focal segmental glomerulosclerosis" is applied to many conditions and is accordingly ambiguous, but in the context of the nephrotic syndrome is more straightforward. Early stages of nephrotic-associated segmental sclerosing conditions may be overlooked because glomeruli may have only mild abnormalities, including enlargement, mesangial increase, and segmental changes confined to the part of the tuft next to the opening of the proximal tubule.

Diabetic glomerulonephropathy is characterized in its full blown stage by marked mesangial expansion with the appearance of Kimmelstiel-Wilson nodules (Fig. 3.15, see Color Atlas). The main differential diagnosis is the nodular glomerulopathy of occasional light chain paraproteinaemias, which is diagnosed by immunohistologic study for kappa and lambda light chains. Amyloid is usually easy to diagnose. Glomeruli contain acellular material that stains with Congo red. When the stained section is examined microscopically with crossed polarizing filters, a range of colors is seen, called anomalous colors. This finding is often wrongly called the characteristic apple-green birefringence of amyloid. The amyloid can be characterized further by repeating the Congo red staining after potassium permanganate, and by immunohistologic methods for amyloid A protein and light chains. Secondary amyloid, AA type, does not stain with Congo red after potassium permanganate, but stains immunohistologically for amyloid A protein (Fig. 3.16, see Color Atlas). Primary amyloid, AL type, resists potassium permanganate and stains immunohistologically for light chains.

Clinically apparent nephritis develops in 40-75% of patients with lupus. Renal manifestations and prognosis in lupus nephritis are heterogeneous and reflect the underlying diversity of the histologic lesions. Three major groups of lupus nephritis have been defined based on light microscopy of renal tissue: focal proliferative; diffuse proliferative; and membranous nephropathy. In lupus glomerulonephritis, virtually any glomerular disorder can occur, and so can virtually any combination of disorders in the same glomerulus. The diagnosis is usually obvious clinically in a young woman before biopsy, but if not is suggested by a combination of glomerular abnormalities, which is otherwise unusual, and by heavy deposition of all immunoproteins in glomeruli on immunohistology. Common patterns in lupus glomerulonephritis are membranous nephropathy, segmental abnormalities, and mesangial hypercellularity (Fig. 3.17, see Color Atlas).

In both adults and children, the commonest findings in biopsy specimens taken for hematuria with or without proteinuria are thin glomerular basement membrane disease, IgA nephropathy, and kidneys showing no abnormality. In children, hereditary nephropathy of the Alport type also is important. Thin glomerular basement membrane disease appears to have glomeruli that are normal for the patient's age on light microscopy. Age is a factor in the interpretation because there is progressive loss of glomeruli from ischemia as people get older, and in a biopsy specimen from an older person there may be glomeruli with global sclerosis that would be an indication of other glomerular disorders in children. In thin glomerular basement membrane disease there is no deposition of immunoproteins in glomeruli. Electron microscopy gives the diagnosis and also allows diagnosis of cases showing no abnormality detectable by light or electron microscopy and immunohistology (Fig. 3.18). Hematuria without proteinuria is especially likely to be associated with thin glomerular basement membrane disease. IgA nephropathy can show a range of appearances on light microscopy from normal, through various degrees of mesangial expansion, to late changes with segmental and global sclerosis. The diagnosis is given by immunohistologic finding of IgA in mesangium, often with IgM and complement but rarely with IgG (Fig. 3.19). Hereditary nephropathy of the Alport type also can show a range of appearances on light microscopy, but is usually more severe in boys than in girls or women. Electron microscopy shows glomerular basement membranes of various thicknesses, with an irregular epithelial surface, splitting of the lamina densa and inclusions in the membrane (Fig. 3.20).

Many findings are possible in biopsy specimens taken for acute renal failure, but in all there will be damage to tubules, ranging from slight changes such as loss of brush border in proximal tubules, through more obvious irregularity of cell size, vacuolation and disruption, to necrosis of cells and baring of basement membranes. Usually this damage is called acute tubular necrosis, although frank necrosis is rare. In biopsy specimens, the problem is to determine whether an explanation is evident for the tubular damage. About one-quarter of specimens in acute renal failure show pure tubular damage, and clinical information is needed to

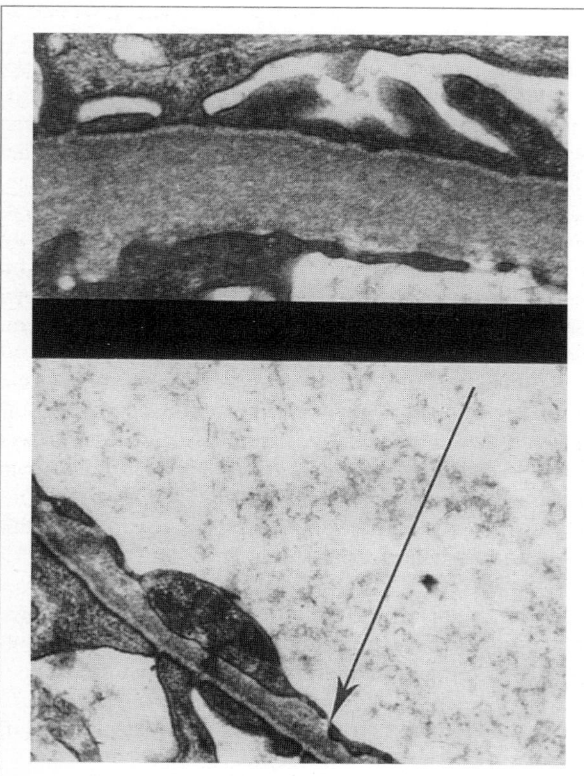

Figure 3.18 Electron micrographs of glomerular basement membranes of normal adult thickness (top) and in thin glomerular basement membrane disease, which is arrowed.

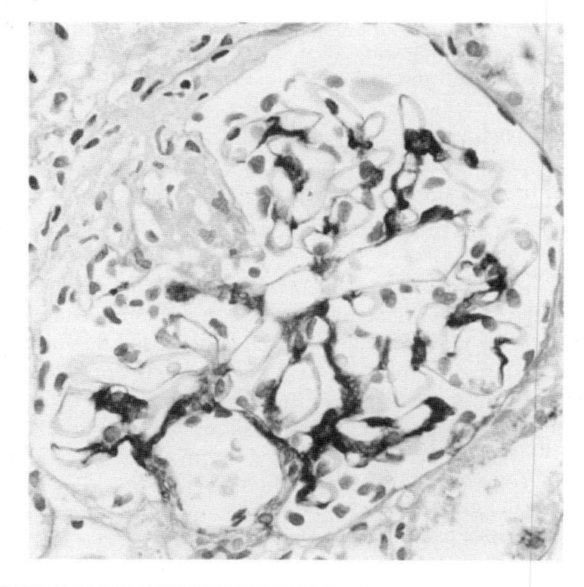

Figure 3.19 Glomerulus in IgA nephropathy, stained by an immunoperoxidase method.

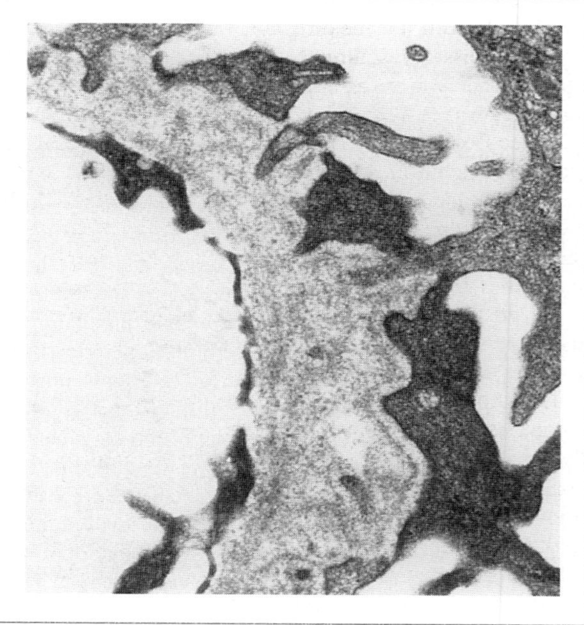

Figure 3.20 Electron micrograph of a glomerular basement membrane in hereditary nephropathy of Alport type. The membrane is of variable thickness with an irregular epithelial surface, split lamina densa and inclusions.

say whether this can be ascribed to ischemia or to a toxin, including such drugs as gentamicin. The commonest findings otherwise, roughly in order from most common to least common, are vasculitic glomerulonephritis, acute interstitial nephritis, small vessel vasculopathy, myeloma kidney, and acute postinfective glomerulonephritis. Vasculitic glomerulonephritis is a useful term for a histologic lesion that has also been called focal segmental thrombosing and necrotizing glomerulonephritis and glomerulonephritis with crescents. In this condition, glomeruli in a biopsy specimen can show changes ranging from a small segmental abnormality in one glomerulus to complete destruction of the tufts in all glomeruli. The earliest detectable change is thrombosis, followed by disruption of basement membranes and accumulation of cells in Bowman's space (Fig. 3.21, see Color Atlas). Usually tubules contain blood, and there is an interstitial infiltrate of inflammatory cells, but inflammation of arterioles and arteries is uncommon in biopsy specimens. Vasculitic glomerular lesions may be seen in IgA nephropathy. In Goodpasture's syndrome, there is a severe glomerulonephritis of vasculitic type, with linear deposition of IgG and complement in glomerular basement membranes (Fig. 3.22, see Color Atlas).

In acute interstitial nephritis, glomeruli appear normal, and there is an infiltrate of inflammatory cells in interstitial tissues, often a mixture of lymphocytes, macrophages, plasma cells, and eosinophils, and often with entry of the inflammatory cells into tubules (Fig. 3.23, see Color Atlas). This is seen most commonly as an allergic response to such drugs as penicillin or nonsteroidal antiinflammatory drugs and in infections, as with hantaviruses, or associated with uveitis, particularly in women, when the condition is called tubulointerstitial nephritis with uveitis. An interstitial infiltrate may also be seen in association with glomerular disorders such as vasculitic glomerulonephritis or lupus glomerulonephritis, but should only be termed acute interstitial nephritis if it is the only abnormality.

Small vessel vasculopathy describes the findings of fibrinoid necrosis of arterioles and loose concentric intimal thickening of the smallest intrarenal arteries (Fig. 3.24, see Color Atlas). These features are seen in accelerated hypertension, systemic sclerosis (which is also called scleroderma), and hemolytic uremic syndrome. In myeloma kidney, the characteristic feature is the presence of casts, meaning intratubular deposits that have a distinctive dry and cracked appearance and are surrounded by giant cells (Fig. 3.25, see Color Atlas). Immunohistology shows restriction of light chains in these casts to either lambda or kappa.

Acute postinfective glomerulonephritis leads to striking changes seen throughout every glomerulus equally. These appear enlarged, solid, and infiltrated by neutrophil polymorphs (Fig. 3.26, see Color Atlas). Periodic acid-methenamine silver staining shows a single basement membrane in capillary loops, and immunohistologic study shows coarse granules of IgG and complement, mainly on the epithelial side of capillary loops. The main differential diagnosis is subendothelial type membranoproliferative (mesangiocapillary) glomerulonephritis. In this, glomerular basement membranes are doubled and there is deposition of immunoproteins on the endothelial side of the original basement membrane (Fig. 3.27, see Color Atlas).

Although there are many causes of chronic renal failure, interpretation of renal biopsy specimens is usually straightforward, and can be simplified to determination of whether or not there is a glomerular disorder. Common glomerular findings in chronic renal failure are late segmental sclerosing conditions, IgA nephropathy and diabetic glomerulonephropathy. Tubules show atrophy – that is, irreversible damage – in all conditions causing chronic renal failure. At times a more precise diagnosis may be impossible, but there may be clinical clues to the cause. Late ischemic damage is suggested by chronic intimal thickening in arteries and particularly by the presence of atherosclerotic or thrombotic embolic material in arteries, although these features could be also seen in late damage due primarily to another cause (Fig. 3.28, see Color Atlas). A problem with urinary drainage, meaning reflux nephropathy or obstruction of the urinary tract, is suggested by a heavy interstitial infiltrate of lymphocytes and the presence of pus cells inside tubules. Other features that may be seen in late nonglomerular conditions include cysts, crystals, and granulomas.

Pure proteinuria without hematuria and without the nephrotic syndrome is often a difficult and unsatisfactory condition to diagnose from a renal biopsy specimen. One of the commonest findings is a segmental sclerosing glomerular condition. Sometimes, despite all investigations, including electron microscopy, no structural abnormality is detected.

Several conditions can account for renal allograft dysfunction, including infarction, pure acute tubular damage, ascending infection, and glomerular disorders. The commonest finding in acute dysfunction is evidence of an immunologic response of the recipient against the graft – that is, rejection. This usually takes the form of an acute interstitial nephritis called acute cellular rejection. This is not all or none, and the line between clinically significant rejection and clinically insignificant rejection is arbitrary. Features that suggest clinically significant rejection are a heavy lymphocytic infiltrate and presence of lymphocytes inside tubular epithelium (Fig. 3.29, see Color Atlas). Acute vascular rejection is diagnosed by endothelial lifting and a lymphocytic infiltrate in the intima of small arteries, and is always clinically significant (Fig. 3.30, see Color Atlas). In chronic graft dysfunction, there may be only areas of tubular atrophy. There are several possible causes that may not be distinguishable in a biopsy specimen. These include chronic vascular rejection, which affects arteries larger than those usually present in biopsy specimens, cyclosporine toxicity, permanent damage following attacks of acute rejection, and damage that was present in the graft before it was transplanted.

Acknowledgment

We are grateful to Dr. P.J. Guest for the radiographs and for their interpretation.

Suggested readings

BRENNER BM, DWORKIN LD, ICHIKAWA I. Glomerular filtration. The Kidney. 3rd ed. W.B. Philadelphia: Saunders Company. 1986; 124-44.

CAMERON JS. The natural history of glomerulonephritis. In: Kincaid-Smith P, D'Apice, SJ, Atkins RW, eds. Progress in glomerulonephritis. New York: John Wiley & Sons, 1979;1-25.

CHANTLER C,S GE, VP, NV. Glomerular filtration rate measurement in man by the single injection method using Cr-EDTA. Clinical Science 1969;37:169-80.

COCKROFT D, GAULT M. Prediction of creatinine clearance from serum creatinine. Nephron 1976;16:31-41.

INTERNATIONAL STUDY OF KIDNEY DISEASE IN CHILDREN. The primary nephrotic syndrome in children. Identification of patients with minimal change nephrotic syndrome from initial response to prednisolone. Journal of Pediatrics 1981;98:561-4.

JENNETTE J, OLSON JL, SCHWARTS MM, SILVA FG. Heptinstalls' pathology of the kidney. 5th ed. Philadelphia: Lippincott Williams & Wilkins Publishers 1998.

KALLENBERG CGM, BROUWER E., WEENING JJ., JW CT. Anti-neutrophil cytoplasmic antibodies: current diagnostic and pathophysiological potential. Kidney International 1994;46:1-15.

LEVEY AS, LAU J, PAUKER SG, KASSIRER JP. Idiopathic nephrotic syndrome. Puncturing the biopsy myth. Annals of Internal Medicine 1987;107:697-713.

MARIANI AJ, MARIANI MC, MACCHIONI C, STAMS UK, HARIHARAN A, MORIERA A. The significance of adult hematuria: 1000 hematuria evaluations including a risk benefit and cost effectiveness analysis. Journal of Urology 1989;141:350-5.

MOHR DN, OFFORD KP, OWEN RA, MELTON LJ.III. Asymptomatic microhematuria and urologic disease: a population-based study. Journal of Urology 1986;256:224-9.

OFFRINGA M, BENBASSAT J. The value of urinary red cell shape in the diagnosis of glomerular and post-glomerular haematuria. A meta-analysis. Postgraduate Medical Journal 1992;68:648-54.

SCOTTISH INTERCOLLEGIATE GUIDELINES NETWORK (SIGN). Investigation of asymptomatic proteinuria in adults. Edinburgh: Scottish Intercollegiate Guidelines Network, 1997.

SMITH H. The kidney: structure and function in health and disease. Oxford University Press, 1951.

VON BORNSDORFF M, KOSKENVUO K, SALMI HA, PASTERNACK A. Pravalence and causes of proteinuria in 20-year-old Finnish men. Scand Journal of Urology and Nephrology 1981;15:285-90.

WOOLHANDLER S, PELS RJ, BOR DH, HIMMELSTEIN DU, LAWRENCE RS. Dipstick urinalysis screening of asymptomatic adults for urinary tract disorders. Journal of the American Medical Association 1989;262:1215-9.

SECTION

2

Clinical syndromes

CHAPTER

4

Asymptomatic urinary abnormalities

Raymond Vanholder

PROTEINURIA

Pathophysiology

Normal urine contains minute amounts of protein (<100-150 mg/24 h). The normal glomerular basement membrane imposes a barrier for large plasma proteins; this effect depends on basement membrane pore size and electrostatic charge and results in the reflection of molecules that are larger and/or negatively charged. Smaller proteins, such as β_2-microglobulin and light-chain immunoglobulin, are filtered freely. Most of the protein normally entering the primitive urine, however, is catabolized by the tubules. Some urinary proteins, such as Tamm-Horsfall protein, immunoglobulin A, and urokinase, originate from the urinary tract itself, albeit in minor amounts.

The most frequent cause of major proteinuria is the functional failure of the glomerular barrier (i.e., *glomerular proteinuria*), in which usually larger proteins (MW > 40 000 Da) are involved. An increase in glomerular capillary pressure (e.g., induced by angiotensin II) may provoke glomerular proteinuria as well. This results in albuminuria and, if resistance is increased further, even globulinuria. If albuminuria is predominant, proteinuria is called *selective proteinuria*. The term *nonselective proteinuria* is used for urine containing immunoglobulins and/or transferrin, in addition to albumin.

In *tubular proteinuria*, functional disturbances of tubules result in a lack of catabolization of smaller proteins that readily can cross the glomerular barrier (e.g., β_2-microglobulin). This is most often the result of intoxication by drugs or environmental agents (e.g., aminoglycosides, trace metals), although congenital disorders (e.g., cystinosis, Lowe's syndrome), light-chain proteinuria, and Sjögren's and Fanconi's syndromes are alternative causes. The shedding of proteins by urinary epithelial cells into the tubule fluid may be an additional cause of tubular proteinuria.

A final variant of proteinuria is caused by the glomerular filtration of compounds that are present in the plasma at higher concentrations in certain diseases than under normal conditions (i.e., *overflow proteinuria*): hemoglobin (in the case of hemolysis), myoglobinuria (rhabdomyolysis), and light chains of immunoglobulins (light-chain disease, multiple myeloma).

If proteinuria becomes important enough, the nephrotic syndrome will develop. In general, this is caused by glomerular proteinuria, since the alternative types of proteinuria are rarely profuse enough. The nephrotic syndrome is defined as proteinuria greater than 3.5 g/24 h in combination with clinical edema, hypoproteinemia or hypoalbuminemia, and hypercholesterolemia. The hypoproteinemia is the consequence of urinary protein losses, insufficiently compensated by hepatic protein synthesis. The subsequent decrease in plasma colloid osmotic pressure results in inadequate retention of plasma water in the blood and leakage of this water into the tissues; as a result, edema may develop despite overt intravascular dehydration. The dyslipidemia is the consequence of shifts in hepatic metabolism, whereby hyperlipoproteinemia is linked to the increased albumin production.

There is still debate about the pathophysiologic importance of proteinuria as such. The degree of proteinuria is proportional to the progression of renal failure. The problem is whether this proteinuria is a reflection of renal damage caused by other mechanisms or the proteinuria *per se* is damaging the kidneys. Recent proof of tubulointerstitial damage provoked by inducing proteinuria after the injection of albumin into the peritoneum of the rat suggests that proteinuria has a pathophysiologic role *per se*. There is no debate about the renal toxicity of hemoglobin and myoglobin, which precipitate in the tubules as casts, causing obstructive renal failure. In addition, light-chain proteinuria may result in renal damage, the so-called light-chain or myeloma kidney.

Loss of immunoglobulins will result in an enhanced susceptibility to infection, which was a major morbid event in the nephrotic syndrome before the introduction of antibiotics, especially related to the development of primary peritonitis in children. This complication still should be suspected in children with the nephrotic syndrome and unexplained abdominal pain.

Clinical findings

In the presence of overt pitting edema, direct quantification of the amount of protein in the urine is done in each patient. Too often patients with edema are submitted to cardiologic, phlebologic, hepatologic, and even rheumatologic investigations, and the simple maneuver of estimating protein in the urine is omitted. Further signs that necessitate the investigation of proteinuria are pulmonary edema, hematuria, hypertension, and foamy urine, as well as the biochemical detection of renal failure and/or hypoproteinemia. Proteinuria should be controlled regularly in any disease potentially related to glomerular damage and/or proteinuria (e.g., diabetes mellitus, amyloidosis, autoimmune disorders).

The fastest and easiest detection method at the bedside, in the outpatient clinic, or in general practice is the use of urinary dipsticks. The disadvantage is that data are semiquantitative. This approach is characterized by a high sensitivity and a low specificity; i.e., the detection limit is low, so a number of subjects with trivial proteinuria also will show a positive test. Sensitivity is high only in those disorders where urinary protein losses are important, such as the nephrotic syndrome. False-positive color changes may occur when the recipient has been cleaned with disinfectants such as chlorhexidine, in the presence of polyvinylpyrrolidone, and in patients with alkaline urine. It is of note that light-chain proteinuria will not be detected by urinary dipsticks. On the other hand, discoloration will occur in the presence of hemoglobinuria, hematuria, and myoglobinuria. In absolute quantities, the degree of proteinuria, however, will be low.

In any instance of a positive dipstick test, quantitative confirmation, preferably by determination of 24-h proteinuria, should be performed. This approach has the advantage of not being influenced by urinary volume or dilution.

Differential diagnosis

An overview of the most current causes of proteinuria and/or the nephrotic syndrome is given in Table 4.1, and a flowchart of the clinical approach to the problem is illustrated in Figure 4.1. Glomerular disease may be idiopathic as well as part of a systemic disorder. In addition, tubular disorders are a cause of proteinuria, although often less pronounced.

Proteinuria may occur as a consequence of resistance to venous outflow, as in orthostatic proteinuria, renal vein thrombosis, and right-sided heart insufficiency. Orthostatic proteinuria occurs mainly as an isolated problem in asymptomatic, young, slim and tall males. The proteinuria disappears in the recumbent position, so the first morning urine may be negative, proteinuria arising only after some hours of quiet standing and walking. This proteinuria is generally benign, although it may be the first sign of underlying renal disease, so yearly follow-up remains advisable. Renal vein thrombosis, although a potential cause of

Table 4.1 Most common causes of proteinuria and/or the nephrotic syndrome

Cause
Glomerular proteinuria
Infectious disorders
Bacterial infections
Poststreptococcal
Endocarditis
Syphilis
Viral infections
Hepatitis B and C
Cytomegaly
Epstein-Barr
Tropical infections
Quartan malaria
Schistosomiasis
Neoplasia
Systemic disorders
Collagen disease, e.g., lupus erythematosus
Cryoglobulinemia
Amyloidosis
Sjögren's syndrome
Rheumatoid arthritis
Metabolic diseases
Diabetes mellitus
Myxedema
Hereditary diseases
Alport's syndrome
Fabry's disease
Sickle cell anemia
Nail-patella syndrome
Congenital nephrotic syndrome (Finnish type)
Drugs and toxins
Mercury derivatives
Organic gold
Penicillamine
ACE inhibitors
Bee sting
Preeclampsia
Rejection of kidney graft
Nephroangiosclerosis
Vesicoureteral reflux
Stenosis of the renal vein
Orthostatic proteinuria
Right-sided heart failure
Idiopathic
Minimal change nephropathy
Membranous nephropathy
Membranoproliferative glomerulonephritis
Focal and segmental glomerulosclerosis
IgA nephropathy
Tubular proteinuria
Intoxication
Drugs (aminoglycosides)
Environmental agents (trace metals)
Congenital disorders
Cystinosis
Lowe's syndrome
Light-chain proteinuria
Sjögren's syndrome
Fanconi's syndrome
Tuberculosis
Overflow proteinuria
Hemoglobinuria
Myoglobinuruia
Light-chain proteinuria

proteinuria, is most often a consequence rather than a cause of the nephrotic syndrome, owing to the concomitant disturbances in coagulation.

The correct diagnosis can only be obtained by renal biopsy. Before renal biopsy, all anticoagulation (including ticlopidine and aspirin) should be withdrawn. In some conditions, the cause may seem obvious, although it is not. Isolated proteinuria in diabetes mellitus in general suggests diabetic nephropathy, but the diabetes must have been present for at least 10 years for diabetic nephropathy to develop. Proteinuria is currently associated with diabetic neuropathy and retinopathy. A disease course shorter than 10 years or the absence of other diabetic complications should incite one to perform a renal biopsy. In non-insulin-dependent diabetes mellitus (NIDDM, or type II), the diabetic history may be shorter because the disease may have been present for several years before diagnosis. In some diseases, renal biopsy may be necessary to allow staging (e.g., in lupus erythematosus disseminatus).

Treatment

The most obvious treatment is direct correction of the cause, mainly by immunosuppression. Dietary protein restriction has an aspecific nephroprotective effect, although the potential for malnutrition, especially in association with severe proteinuria, counterbalances this benefit in part. Aspecific nephroprotection also can be pursued with angiotensin-converting enzyme (ACE) inhibitors, and with these agents, the risk of malnutrition is obviated. Their protective hemodynamic effect is optimal, however, only when their use is associated with restricted salt intake. Moreover, nonsteroidal anti-inflammatory drugs (NSAIDs) also diminish proteinuria, but their use often is associated with a decline in renal function. Edema can be corrected in a first step by salt restriction and diuretic use (e.g., furosemide, spironolactone), which, however, is associated with a decrease in circulating volume.

In severely hypoproteinemic patients, it may become necessary to provide albumin supplementation. This should be done only in symptomatic patients, since most of this protein is readily lost in the urine, whereas the extra protein load may further damage the kidneys. Albumin at best should be associated with diuretics (e.g., furosemide), to achieve as effective a mobilization and removal of tissue fluid as possible.

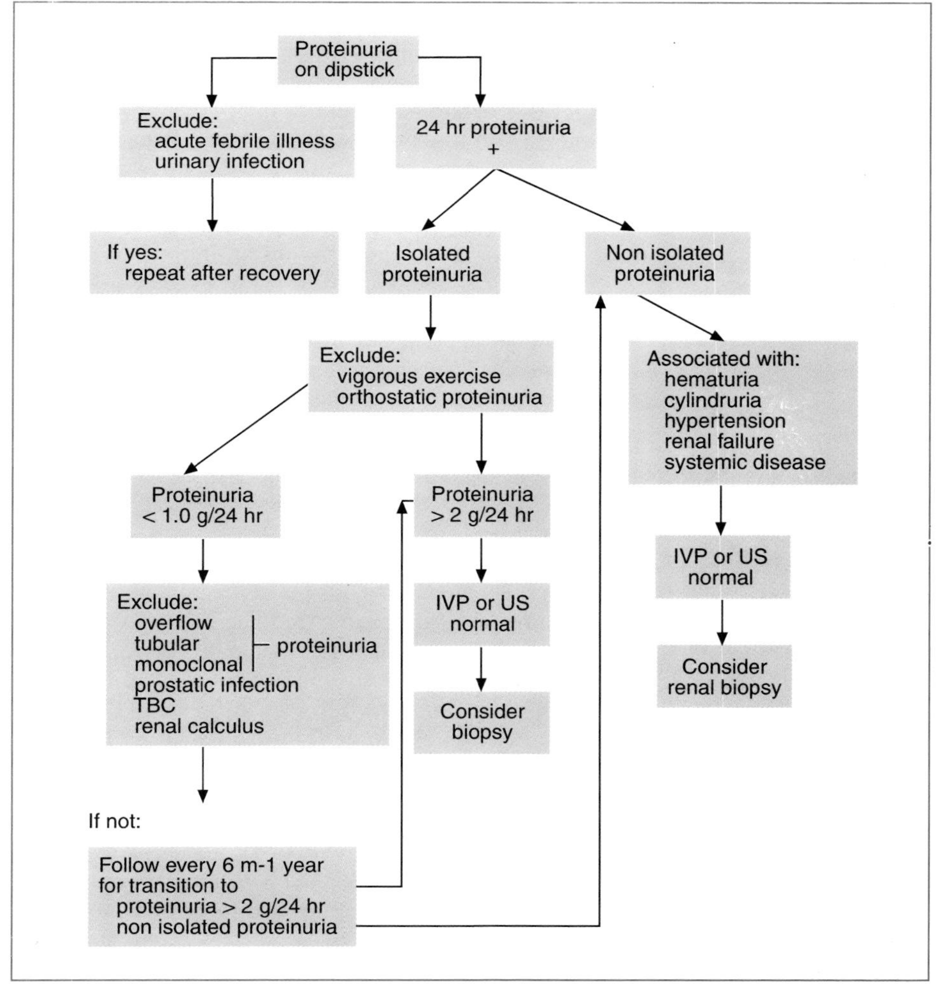

Figure 4.1 Diagnostic approach to proteinuria. (TBC = tuberculosis; IVP = intravenous pyelography; US = ultrasonography.)

MICROALBUMINURIA

Microalbuminuria is a specific form of albuminuria that develops during the early stages of renal damage. It is defined as an elevated urinary albumin excretion (>20-200 μg/min or 30-300 mg/24 h) that is not detectable with the classic registration methods (i.e., dipstick or laboratory determination). Specific dipsticks are available for its determination, but these are relatively costly. Direct laboratory determination, e.g., by nephelometry, is a valuable alternative but offers no immediate result. Microalbuminuria essentially is seen as a first predictive sign for the development of diabetic glomerulosclerosis. However, it also may be present at the onset of diabetes mellitus, together with hyperglycemia, and it may disappear when the glycemia is better controlled. Later, during disease progression, it may reappear in a substantial fraction of the affected population, but then should be persistent to be accepted as a first sign of the deterioration of renal function. In non-insulin dependent diabetes mellitus, microalbuminuria is also related to subsequent cardiovascular disease.

Microalbuminuria shows substantial natural fluctuations. It should be confirmed at least three times consecutively in two or all three samples collected over a 3- to 6-month period before it can be accepted as such. In addition, in other conditions affecting glomerular function, such as hypertension and autoimmune disorders, microalbuminuria can be a sign of subsequent defects of renal function.

HEMATURIA

Pathophysiology

Hematuria is a diagnostic rather than a therapeutic problem. Differentiation between localization in the upper or lower urinary tract is essential.

Hematuria is often the epiphenomenon of serious disease, either glomerular disorders, potentially leading to renal failure if remaining untreated, or malignancies, or infections of the lower urinary tract. Hematuria therefore always should be taken seriously and investigated, even if it has been registered only once. Nevertheless, in a random population, the predictive value of hematuria is rather low, with pathology being found in only 2% of affected subjects. In the 50 years and older age group, however, 26% of affected people will have a urinary tract lesion. Normal urine contains only minute amounts of red blood cells. Under pathologic conditions, an increased number of erythrocytes will appear in the urine following transfer of erythrocytes due to damage either to the glomerular basement membrane or peritubular capillaries (i.e., *nephronal hematuria*) or to the urinary tract itself (i.e., *urologic hematuria*). Hematuria may be readily visible in the urine as a red discoloration and is then called *macroscopic*, or it may be invisible, unless under the microscope, and is then called *microscopic*. Microscopic hematuria is defined as the presence of more than 5 red blood cells(RBCs)/μl, macroscopic as more than 2500 RBCs/μl. The latter amount corresponds to a daily blood loss of 1 ml; hence blood losses from hematuria are rarely important enough to be a cause of anemia. Macroscopic hematuria causes a bright red discoloration of the urine, unless the pH is less than 5, in which case a brownish color appears.

Erythrocytes entering the primitive urine at the glomerular level will cross the entire tubular system before they are seen in the final urine. Passage through the hypertonic medullary tubules causes a structural transformation that is especially apparent under the phase-contrast microscope. Alternatively, cells can be investigated with an automated red cell analyzer. In the case of urologic hematuria, the erythrocytes remain regularly shaped. However, erythrocytes may undergo structural transformation in other conditions, e.g., if they remain too long in hyperosmolar urine. Phase-contrast microscopy therefore preferentially should be performed on freshly voided urine.

Urine should not stand longer than 4 h, and it should not be exposed to sunlight. Even with these precautions, various morphologic changes may be apparent (Figs. 4.1 and 4.2), of which only the acanthocytes are specific for nephronal hematuria. The presence of 80% or more of dysmorphic erythrocytes and the simultaneous presence of marked proteinuria also point to a nephronal origin. It is of note, however, that hemoglobinuria or myoglobinuria will cause minor positivity of urine protein tests. Acanthocyturia and polymorphism should be confirmed at least once. Even with data suggesting nephronal hematuria, an ultrasonography of the kidneys and an intravenous pyelogram (IVP) should be performed to exclude associated anatomic causes.

Another approach to distinguish between nephronal and urologic hematuria is the determination of urinary $\alpha 1$-macroglobulin. This large molecule is unable to pass through the glomerular basement membrane, so its presence in the urine points to urologic hematuria.

Clinical findings

Red discoloration of the urine may occur in the absence of hematuria, e.g., after eating red beets or after treatment with certain drugs, such as vitamin B_{12}, pyrazolone, or phenol-containing laxatives. In such cases, all investigations for true hematuria will remain negative. Blood also can be added to the urine from the female genital tract, e.g., during menstruation. Therefore, urinary investigations for hematuria should be postponed in menstruating women.

The fastest method of detection is the urinary dipstick. False-positive or false-negative results may occur in the presence of ascorbic acid. Recent dipsticks contain a reagent that oxidizes ascorbic acid up to a concentration of 500 mg/dl. False-positive registrations equally occur in the presence of antiseptics or peroxidase-producing microorganisms. The presence of nitrite and protein (>5 g/l) retards the reaction. It is of note that free hemoglobin will cause a similar discoloration as erythrocyturia. Although this may appear as erythrocyturia, it will be homogeneous over the entire surface of the dipstick in the case of hemoglobinuria. It remains difficult, however, to make the distinction. In addition, in urine that has been held a long time, gradual hemolysis will occur, resulting in an appearance similar to hemoglobinuria. This type of hemolysis occurs more readily with hyperosmolar urine or increased pH (as in urinary tract infections). Apart from direct electrophoretic examination, the only method to distinguish between hemoglobinuria and erythrocyturia is the microscopic evaluation. In hemoglobinuria, no erythrocytes will be detected.

The urinary dipstick is highly sensitive and has been developed essentially to detect as many cases of hematuria as possible: discoloration will be seen when as few as 2 erythrocytes per high-power field (HPF) are present. Therefore, microscopic confirmation with direct quantification of the erythrocytes always should be obtained.

It is common practice to quantify hematuria as number of cells per high-power field. This provides no direct quantification of the hematuria, however, since the urine is first centrifuged, and the sediment is then evaluated under the microscope. The number of cells then depends on the volume of urine still present in the sediment. As with proteinuria, a direct quantification of cells per unit of volume or per unit of time is more appropriate. Normal values are less than 8000 RBCs/ml or less than 20 000 RBCs/min.

Differential diagnosis

The origin of hematuria is by far most frequently urologic. This may be important for the choice of the specialist (urologist or nephrologist) if further investigation is needed. In general, a urologist will be the most appropriate choice, unless the patient is younger (<40 years), has combined hematuria and proteinuria, belongs to a family with known hereditary nephropathy, or has a systemic disorder in which glomerular disease is a known complication. In each of these instances, a nephrologist may be the most appropriate first choice.

The cut-off in age for the choice of a specialist is due to the prevalence of malignant urologic tumors in those older than 40 years, although sporadic cases have been reported in younger patients. If the findings by one specialty are nonconclusive, referral to the other specialty should be the next step.

The most current causes of hematuria are listed in Table 4.2, and a flowchart of the clinical approach to the problem is illustrated in Figure 4.2. The most frequent cause is bacterial cystitis. Most affected patients have the classic symptomology of urinary tract infection (urinary urgency), although some patients (e.g., diabetics, patients with neurogenic bladder) may remain asymptomatic. Investigations for urinary tract infection and bacteriuria (see below) always should be performed in patients with hematuria.

Table 4.2 Most common causes of hematuria

Pathologic
Nephronal hematuria
Glomerulonephritis/glomerulopathy
Interstitial nephritis
Vasculitis
Urologic hematuria
Tumors of kidney/urinary tract/prostate
Nephrolithiasis
Papillary necrosis
Urinary tract infection
bacterial
tubercular
yeasts
Prostatitis
Polycystic kidney disease
Trauma to the kidney or the urinary tract
Coagulation disorders
Obstruction of the urinary tract
Nonpathologic
Exercise
Menstruation
Indwelling bladder catheter

Less common but more morbid infections may be caused by mycobacteria or yeasts.

Other trivial causes of hematuria are hyperuricosuria and hypercalciuria. Normal urinary excretion of uric acid and calcium is 750 and 300 mg/24 h. This cause of hematuria should be considered especially in males belonging to families with a history of urolithiasis. When no treatment for uricosuria (e.g., allopurinol) or for hypercalciuria (e.g., thiazide diuretics) is applied, evolution toward kidney stone formation often occurs within 5 years.

Kidney stones can be detected by plain abdominal x-ray (only for radiolucent stones), intravenous pyelogram, or ultrasonography. The detection of tumors of the lower urinary tract is confined to cystoscopic evaluation.

Bleeding at the beginning or end of micturition, in the case of macroscopic hematuria, points to a prostatic or urethral origin. Stains on the underwear point to a lesion of the distal urethra. Total hematuria occurring throughout voiding means that blood has had the opportunity to mix with the urine. Causes of nonpathologic hematuria include exercise and high fever.

It is of note that in some nephrologic disorders, especially hereditary nephropathy (e.g., Alport's syndrome and related syndromes), polycystic kidney disease, cortex necrosis, kidney infarction, interstitial nephritis, and IgA nephropathy, hematuria may occur in the absence of proteinuria. In IgA nephropathy, up to 20% of the erythrocytes may have a nonglomerular appearance.

In the case of negative investigations and a presumed urologic cause, additional examinations of the morpho-

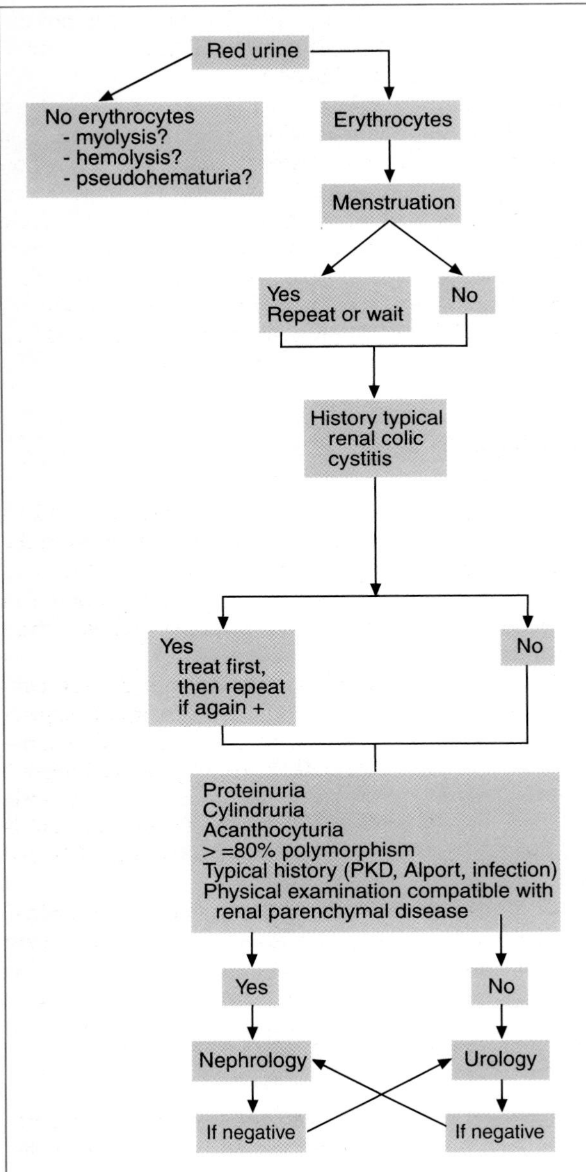

Figure 4.2 Diagnostic approach to hematuria.

logic status of the urinary tract should take place at 6 and 24 months. If all investigations still remain negative at these times, a malignant cause of hematuria becomes highly improbable.

Isolated hematuria in a patient with a coagulation disorder or in an anticoagulated patient may be the consequence of a coagulation disturbance but always should be investigated further because it may be the result of an underlying tumor or another anatomic lesion. Further examples of drug-induced hematuria are hemorrhagic cystitis during treatment with cyclophosphamide and papillary necrosis in association with chronic analgesic intake.

LEUKOCYTURIA

Pathophysiology

Leukocyturia develops in the presence of upper or lower urinary tract inflammation. Fresh urine samples are required because delay in analysis may result in the breakdown of cells. The most common cause is bacterial cystitis, so an evaluation for bacterial infection always should follow the detection of leukocyturia. Contamination of a urine sample by vaginal secretions in females or inflammation of the prostate in males also gives the appearance of leukocyturia. As with hematuria, a quantification on the basis of high-power fields is inaccurate; quantitation with a hemocytometer in leukocytes per milliliter is more precise. The upper limit of normal leukocyturia is 1 to 2 white blood cells (WBCs)/high-power field or 2000 to 8000 WBCs/ml. More than 5 WBCs/high-power field or 25 WBCs/μl is clearly pathologic. Values in between need to be reevaluated. Pyuria develops in 96% of symptomatic patients with bacteriuria. The presence of symptoms that are compatible with urinary tract infection, of course, increases suspicion. If no current bacterial agents can be cultured from the urine, one should consider the presence of infection with yeast, tuberculosis, or protozoa (e.g., *Chlamydia*), genital infection, or urinary tract infection in which antibiotic treatment has already been started.

If these causes also have been excluded, sterile leukocyturia is a final potential cause. This finding points to a noninfectious inflammatory disorder of the kidneys, mainly acute or chronic tubulointerstitial nephritis, kidney stones, papillary necrosis, or diabetes mellitus.

Clinical findings

Leukocyturia can be detected by urinary dipsticks, in which the operating principle is based on registration of the esterase activity of leukocytes in the urine. This activity is still present even after lysis of the leukocytes, which is in contrast with microscopic registration, which becomes impossible after lysis. Registration by dipstick is disturbed in the presence of vitamin C and proteins. Moreover, the presence of formaldehyde antiseptic may cause false-positive results. A more direct estimation can be obtained from light microscopic evaluation. Neutrophils are predominant in infection. Eosinophiluria points to allergic interstitial nephritis but is not specific and can occur as well in other conditions such as acute glomerulonephritis, prostatitis, and urinary tract infection.

BACTERIURIA

Pathophysiology

Bacteria enter the urine in infections but also can be mixed with the urine due to contamination from the skin or the genital tract. To avoid this contamination, only midstream urine should be collected or, even better, urine from a bladder puncture. Urine also can be obtained via catheterization, but this brings with it risk of infection. If urine is voided through natural pathways (even midstream), bacteriologic culturing techniques should be started as soon as possible. An elegant way to do this is to use dip-slides, which are plastic paddles containing an agar that is selective for gram-negative organisms on one side and has a nonselective medium on the other. After an overnight incubation, positive slides can be sent to a reference laboratory for species identification and antibiogram. The rule of Kass, which states that at least 100 000 organisms should be present to accept a culture as positive, has been applied incorrectly to bacteriologically positive urine. The rule of Kass, in fact, only applies to asymptomatic women if organisms are detected in midstream urine. This means that the rule does not apply to any other condition, e.g., symptomatic patients, males, or urine obtained by bladder puncture or catheterization; in such cases, the cut-off limit can be relaxed to below 10^5 organisms. Especially with bladder puncture urine and midstream urine from men, any concentration of organisms, even corresponding to only 100 colony-forming units (CFUs)/ml, should be considered significant. Bacteriuria in the presence of leukocyturia should be considered to be the hallmark of lower and upper urinary tract infection. The clinical presentation (more fever, flank pain, and signs of bacteremia in upper urinary tract infection) allows one to distinguish between both conditions, although there may be some overlap. The presence of bacteriuria without leukocyturia suggests bladder colonization rather than real infection. Unless one is examining a patient with a bladder catheter or a neurogenic bladder, the occurrence of a positive culture for two or more different organisms suggests contamination.

Clinical findings

Most polyvalent dipstick tests contain an indirect system for the detection of bacteriuria, based on the bacterial reduction of nitrate in the urine to nitrite, in which nitrites are measured. These dipsticks are most reliable on first morning urines and are accurate for the detection of Enterobacteriaceae but not gram-positive organisms or Pseudomonas. False-negative results occur in the presence of vitamin C, proteinuria, gentamicin, or cephalexin or if no nitrite is present in the urine (e.g., malnutrition, parenteral nutrition, or a diet containing no vegetables) and when the urine remained in the bladder for a too short a time for transformation into nitrite. False-positive results occur due to vaginal contamination or if the urine is not fresh (maximum 4 h between voiding and investigation). Here also the first investigation should be confirmed by a second one or preferably by a classic culture.

Treatment

Bacteriuria should be accompanied by leukocyturia and symptomology before treatment is undertaken. An absence of complaints with a positive infection may occur, however, in diabetes mellitus, pregnancy, old age, immunosuppression, and neurogenic bladder.

If the bacteriuria is considered pathologic (i.e., related to infection, not to colonization), one cán take hygienic measures and treat the patient with antibiotics for a short interval if only cystitis is present. In the case of pyelonephritis, antibiotics should be administered for a longer time course, first intravenously until fever has subsided for 48 to 72 h and then orally for at least 2 to 3 weeks. Treatment of asymptomatic bacteriuria always should be performed in pregnant women, who should be screened regularly throughout the pregnancy.

GLUCOSURIA

Normally, glucose is filtered by the glomerulus, and its concentration is the same in the primitive urine as in the blood. All this glucose, however, is reabsorbed later in the tubular system, unless the glucose concentration in the primitive urine exceeds the tubular reabsorption threshold.

Thus, glucosuria occurs when the serum glucose concentration exceeds the normal tubular reabsorption capacity (e.g., in diabetes mellitus) and exceptionally when tubular reabsorption capacity is decreased (e.g., in nephrogenic diabetes mellitus). Moreover, the absence of glucosuria does not exclude the presence of diabetes mellitus and is not reliable for guiding the administration of hypoglycemic agents.

Glucosuria can best be detected by dipsticks. Vitamin C can give rise to false-negative results, whereas oxidant antiseptics can cause false-positive results.

KETONURIA

Ketonuria is present in most conditions where diabetes mellitus decompensates, apart from hyperosmolar coma. Ketonuria also appears in any condition where the caloric intake fails (e.g., with vomiting or prolonged fasting). These latter conditions, in contrast to diabetes mellitus, are not associated with glucosuria.

The diagnosis can be made by dipstick. False-positive results are found in the presence of phenylketonuria, low pH, highly concentrated urine, and in association with the administration of phthaleine (e.g., after the bromsulphalein test for cirrhosis) or metabolites of L-dopa.

UROBILINOGENURIA

Urobilinogen appears in the urine when liver function fails, as well as when the liver is "overloaded," e.g., in the case of hemolysis. Its practical use is in the differentiation between bile duct and liver disease, since it is absent from the urine when the bile duct is completely occluded. However, it also remains absent from the urine in terminal liver failure and in the absence of intestinal flora, as seen in neonates and patients under extensive antibiotic treatment. Detection is most easy by dipstick. Contact with light oxidizes urobilinogen so that it disappears from the urine.

BILIRUBINURIA

Bilirubin appears in the urine when liver disease or bile duct obstruction is present. Nonconjugated bilirubin, which is increased in the blood when hemolysis is present, is not water soluble and does not appear in the urine. Detection is by dipstick. Large quantities of ascorbic acid give rise to false-positive results. Contact with light causes false-negative results.

CHAPTER

5

Symptomatic urinary abnormalities: nephrotic and nephritic syndrome

Mark E. Rosenberg

KEY POINTS

- The nephrotic syndrome consists of proteinuria (>3.5 g/24 h), edema, hypoalbuminemia, and hyperlipidemia.
- The nephritic syndrome comprises a spectrum of presentations based on the temporal course of the disease. Clinical features include an active urine sediment, often with red blood cell casts, variable amounts of proteinuria, renal failure, hypertension, and edema.
- The etiology of the nephrotic and nephritic syndromes can be idiopathic or due to a large number of systemic diseases, and there may be significant overlap between these syndromes. A renal biopsy often is needed for a definitive diagnosis.
- Treatment of the nephrotic and nephritic syndromes is directed at the underlying cause, with some specific therapies available for diseases limited to the kidney.

Symptomatic urinary abnormalities are the hallmark of glomerulonephritis (GN). Glomerular diseases can be classified in a number of ways based on etiology (primary vs secondary), pathogenesis, morphology, or clinical presentation. For example, the glomerulonephritis associated with systemic lupus erythematosus (SLE) is an example of a secondary glomerular disease caused by SLE; it is an immune complex mediated-disease; has a number of morphologic patterns (e.g., diffuse proliferative GN); and usually presents with the nephritic syndrome. Because of these different classification schemes, the terminology used to describe glomerular disorders can become confusing. Some of the more commonly used terms are listed in Table 5.1. These are based on morphologic or clinical criteria; however, many of the morphologic terms have clinical connotations. For example, the terms "crescentic glomerulonephritis" and "rapidly progressive glomerulonephritis" are often used interchangeably.

A glomerular disease is suspected when there are clinical findings such as edema or systemic manifestations of another disease; urinary abnormalities including proteinuria, hematuria, or urinary casts particularly red blood cell casts; and often but not always when there is an increase in serum creatinine. This chapter will focus on general aspects of the clinical presentation, diagnostic approach, and management of glomerular diseases. The two broad categories of these symptomatic urinary abnormalities are the nephrotic syndrome and the nephritic syndrome. As the eponym "syndrome" implies, this clinical classification is based on a constellation of clinical findings summarized in Table 5.2. There is an overlap between these syndromes, and some glomerular diseases may present with either nephrotic or nephritic features, combinations of both syndromes, or with milder urinary abnormalities such as isolated proteinuria or hematuria.

NEPHROTIC SYNDROME

The nephrotic syndrome comprises the following clinical findings: proteinuria (>3.5 g/24 h), hypoalbuminemia, edema, and hyperlipidemia. The urinary sediment is classically bland or inactive with few red blood cells or casts, suggesting a lack of inflammation in the glomerulus. Lipiduria is a common feature and correlates with the degree of albuminuria. The lipid can be present in degenerating tubular epithelial cells (oval fat bodies) or can occur as fatty casts. The serum creatinine often is normal but can be increased. These clinical findings represent the classic features of the nephrotic syndrome. However, a spectrum of abnormalities is often present, particularly variations in the absolute amount of protein excretion, which can vary for a given disease in different patients. In the absence of the other manifestations of the nephrotic syndrome, patients excreting more than 3.5 g/24 h of protein are referred to as having "nephrotic range proteinuria".

Proteinuria is the hallmark of these disorders and results from disruption of the glomerular capillary barrier, which under normal conditions, has size and charge selective properties that limit the loss of plasma proteins. With disease of this barrier, plasma proteins enter Bowman's space and overwhelm the reabsorptive capacity of the renal tubules, resulting in the loss of proteins into the urine. The most abundant urinary protein in these circumstances is albumin. In most primary renal diseases the degree of proteinuria is a good predictor of renal prognosis, with the worst prognosis being seen in patients with the greatest proteinuria.

Etiology

The nephrotic syndrome may be due to a primary renal disease (also known as idiopathic) or it can be secondary to another disease process. The most common causes of primary nephrotic syndrome are listed in Table 5.3. The individual disorders are discussed in more detail in Chapters 13-19.

Table 5.1 Terminology of glomerular disorders

Primary	Pathology limited to the kidney
Secondary	Renal pathology secondary to another disease
Focal	< 50% of glomeruli involved
Diffuse	> 50% glomeruli involved
Global	Involvement of the whole glomerulus
Segmental	Involvement of part of the glomerulus
Rapidly progressive GN	Acute nephritis with progressive renal failure occurring over weeks to months
Crescentic GN	Crescent shaped collections of cells in Bowman's space associated with rapidly progressive GN as defined above
Proliferative GN	Increased glomerular cell number (resident or infiltrating cells)
Sclerosis	Lesion consists of fibrillar material and associated with capillary collapse

Table 5.2 Clinical syndromes

Nephrotic syndrome	Nephritic syndrome
Proteinuria >3.5 g/24 h	Proteinuria
Hypoalbuminemia	Hematuria
Edema	Hypertension
Hyperlipidemia	Edema
	Oliguria
	Elevated serum creatinine

The most common cause of nephrotic syndrome in adults is membranous GN, which accounts for 40% of cases. This disorder is more common in men and has a peak age incidence of 30 to 50 years. Membranous GN is due to immune complex deposition in the subepithelial space with subsequent complement activation. On light microscopy, there is diffuse thickening of the glomerular basement membrane.

Minimal change disease, so named for the lack of renal histologic abnormalities on light microscopy, accounts for 20% of adult nephrotic syndrome – but up to 80% of childhood nephrotic syndrome. Morphologic changes can be seen only by electron microscopy, and consist of diffuse fusion of glomerular epithelial cell foot processes.

Focal and segmental glomerulosclerosis, as the name implies, affects only certain portions of some glomeruli. On a light microscopic level, areas of sclerosis are seen in portions of the glomerulus and often are associated with trapping of hyaline material in the sclerotic areas. About two-thirds of patients present with nephrotic syndrome, and one-third with lesser degrees of proteinuria. In addition to being a primary cause of nephrotic syndrome, focal sclerosis is a common secondary lesion in a number of other disorders.

Membranoproliferative GN accounts for 10% of adult nephrotic syndrome. The morphologic features of this disorder comprise a membranous component with thickening of the glomerular basement, and a proliferative component with an increase in mesangial cells. Type I membranoproliferative GN is characterized by deposits of C3 and IgG

Table 5.3 Causes of idiopathic nephrotic syndrome in adults

Disease	Incidence
Membranous	40%
Minimal change disease	20%
Focal and segmental glomerulosclerosis	20%
Membranoproliferative	10%
Other	10%

in the mesangium and subendothelial space. It is a common lesion in a number of secondary glomerular diseases including hepatitis C and other infections, mixed cryoglobulinemia, and certain neoplasms. Serum C3 levels are often low. Type II membranoproliferative GN is characterized by diffuse deposition of electron-dense material in the glomerular basement, which stains for C3 but not immunoglobulin. Many cases are due to an autoantibody called C3 nephritic factor, which leads to activation of C3. Although patients with type II membranoproliferative GN can present with nephrotic syndrome, they can also have nephritic features.

Other causes of idiopathic nephrotic syndrome are fibrillary-immunotactoid glomerulopathy and mesangial proliferative GN. Secondary causes are frequent and are listed in Table 5.4. The most common secondary cause is diabetic nephropathy. Other metabolic causes are primary amyloidosis and mixed cryoglobulinemia, the latter often associated with hepatitis C infection. Neoplasms can be associated with nephrotic syndrome. In solid tumors the most common pathologic finding is membranous nephropathy secondary to an immunologic reaction to tumor antigens. Lymphomas are associated with minimal change disease. Many of these secondary causes are discussed in more detail in Chapters 20-26.

Table 5.4 Secondary causes of nephrotic syndrome in adults

Metabolic
Diabetes mellitus *
Cryoglobulinemia
Amyloidosis *
Hypothyroidism
Infectious
Hepatitis *
Syphilis
Other bacterial (poststreptococcal endocarditis)
HIV infection
Epstein-Barr virus
TB
Malaria
Schistosomiasis
Toxoplasmosis
Vasculitis
SLE *
Scleroderma
Mixed connective tissue disease
Neoplasms
Solid tumors
Multiple myeloma
Lymphomas
Leukemia
Drugs
Penicillamine
Heavy metals (mercury, gold)
Intravenous drug use (heroin)
Nonsteroidal antiinflammatory agents
Genetic
Alport's syndrome
Congenital nephrotic syndrome of the Finnish type
Nail patella syndrome
Fabry disease
Sickle cell anemia
Renal vascular
Renal artery stenosis
Malignant hypertension
Other
Chronic transplant glomerulopathy
Vesicoureteral reflux
Massive obesity
Preeclampsia

* most common causes.

Differential diagnosis

The general approach to diagnosing the etiology of the nephrotic syndrome is to search for potential secondary causes by using the history, physical examination, and laboratory tests. If these are unrevealing, the diagnosis most likely is a primary renal disorder. The gold standard for the diagnosis of nephrotic syndrome is the renal biopsy, but the biopsy may not differentiate between primary versus secondary causes because the pathologic findings may be similar. For example, membranous GN can be a primary glomerular disease or secondary to neoplasms or hepatitis B infection.

A careful history should include the presence of preexisting disease (e.g., hepatitis or diabetes), medications (e.g., NSAIDs, gold, intravenous drug abuse), recent travel (e.g., exposure to malaria or schistosomiasis), HIV risk factors, or recent infections (e.g., streptococcal). A careful review of systems should be performed to look for other manifestations of a systemic disease (e.g., rash and arthritis in SLE; congestive heart failure in amyloidosis). A positive family history of kidney disease suggests a genetic disorder such as Fabry disease.

The physical examination should include a careful assessment of volume status, including orthostatic hypotension, which could predispose to renal insufficiency. Hypertension is less common in nephrotic syndrome than in nephritic syndrome, but is possible. Fundoscopic exam may reveal diabetic retinopathy. A careful skin and joint exam should be performed to rule out underlying vasculitis or connective tissue disorders. The presence of hepatomegaly suggests underlying liver disease. An underlying malignancy may become apparent on examination of the prostrate, breast, lymph nodes, or stool for occult blood.

Basic laboratory tests such as serum glucose and liver function tests often can point to a specific secondary cause. Additional tests can be helpful, but none is absolutely diagnostic. A serum and urine protein electrophoresis and immunoelectrophoresis is performed to detect a monoclonal protein, suggesting multiple myeloma, amyloidosis, or light chain nephropathy. Other tests and their clinical associations are listed in Table 5.5. Hepatitis or HIV serology, serum cryoglobulins, or anti-DNA antibodies can lead to specific diagnoses. The laboratory assessment of the consequences of the proteinuria should include serum albumin, calcium, and a lipid profile.

Renal biopsy

A renal biopsy will provide a definitive morphologic diagnosis of the nephrotic syndrome and is recommended by most nephrologists for the adult patient with nephrotic syndrome. In children, minimal change disease is so common that many pediatric nephrologists will give a trial course of prednisone before deciding on a biopsy for the patient. The biopsy is important for deciding on appropriate therapy, but also may provide prognostic information based on the degree of glomerular sclerosis and tubulointerstitial disease. In most diseases the amount of tubulointerstitial disease correlates with prognosis.

Renal biopsy usually is done under ultrasound guidance and is followed by overnight observation in the hospital. The most common complications and their frequency are gross hematuria (5 to 10%), need for blood transfusion (1%), need for radiologic or surgical procedure to stop the bleeding (0.1%), arteriovenous fistula requiring intervention (1%), need for nephrectomy (0.5%). The specimen is evaluated by light and electron microscopy, and immunoflourescent studies are performed to determine the final renal diagnosis.

Complications

The many consequences of heavy proteinuria are listed in Table 5.6. Three of these, hypoalbuminemia, edema, and hyperlipidemia, are included in the definition of the nephrotic syndrome.

Hypoalbuminemia

Decreased serum albumin plays a critical role in the clinical manifestations of the nephrotic syndrome. The major factors responsible for the hypoalbuminemia seen in nephrotic patients are increased urinary losses and enhanced catabolism of albumin. Albumin synthesis is increased, but is unable to keep up with losses. The serum albumin level correlates with the amount of proteinuria. The low serum albumin decreases drug binding and can lead to toxicity unless doses are adjusted.

Edema

This is a common presenting complaint of nephrotic patients. It can range from mild periorbital and pedal edema to anasarca. Fluid movement across capillaries is determined by the imbalance of hydrostatic and oncotic pressures – the Starling forces. Under normal conditions fluid moves from the capillary space to the interstitium and is returned to the circulation via lymphatic drainage when the hydraulic pressure difference exceeds the oncotic pressure difference. Traditionally, the explanation for edema formation in nephrotic syndrome is based on lower serum albumin concentration resulting in lower plasma oncotic pressure, thus altering Starling forces in favor of fluid movement into the interstitium. The decrease in plasma volume that occurs as fluid moves into the interstitial space activates vascular volume sensors, leading to

Table 5.5 Laboratory evaluation of nephrotic and nephritic syndrome

Test	Clinical association
Serum and urine electrophoresis and immunoelectrophoresis	Multiple myeloma, light chain deposition disease, amyloidosis
C3, C4, CH50	Decreased in immune complex disease with complement activation (SLE, cryoglobulinemia, membranoproliferative GN, postinfectious)
C3 nephritic factor	Membranoproliferative GN type II
Antinuclear antibodies	SLE or other connective tissue diseases
- anti-double stranded DNA	SLE
- anti-Sm	SLE
- anti-RNP	SLE, mixed connective tissue disease
- anti-SSA/Ro	SLE, Sjögren's syndrome
- anti-SSB/La/Ma	SLE, Sjögren's syndrome
- anti-histone	Drug-induced SLE
- anti-Scl-70	Scleroderma, CREST syndrome
Rheumatoid factor	Rheumatoid arthritis
ANCA	Wegener's granulomatosis, microscopic polyangiitis, pauci-immune rapidly progressive GN
Anti-GBM antibodies	Anti-GBM nephritis, Goodpasture's syndrome
Hepatitis serology	Membranoproliferative GN, membranous, cryoglobulinemia
Cryoglobulins	Cryoglobulinemia
Anti-streptolysin O, anti-DNAase B, anti-hyaluronidase	Poststreptococcal (anti-streptolysin O elevated in only 50% of patients with impetigo)
Platelets	HUS/TTP
HIV serology	HIV nephropathy
Syphilis serology	Syphilis

Table 5.6 Complications of proteinuria

Complications
Secondary to urinary protein loss
Hypoalbuminemia
Edema
Hyperlipidemia
Thromboembolism
– renal vein thrombosis
Infection
Serum protein abnormalities
– iron deficiency
– copper deficiency
– hypocalcemia
Malnutrition
Secondary to hemodynamic factors
Hyponatremia
Acute renal failure

increased renal sodium reabsorption as compensation to restore the depleted circulation. This increased sodium reabsorption completes a vicious cycle in which expansion of the extracellular volume leads to further edema formation. However, more recent experimental evidence suggests that primary sodium retention by the kidney may be the most important factor in the development of edema.

Hyperlipidemia

Increases in cholesterol and phospholipids occur early in the course of nephrotic syndrome and worsen with increased severity of the disease, whereas elevations of triglycerides are mainly seen in severe disease. In general, hyperlipidemia correlates with the degree of hypoalbuminemia. The etiology of the hyperlipidemia involves both increased lipoprotein synthesis and decreased lipoprotein catabolism. Along with the increased hepatic synthesis of albumin, which occurs as a consequence of hypoalbuminemia, the production of lipoproteins is also elevated. The stimulus for the increased synthesis appears, at least in part, to be a decrease in oncotic pressure rather than the hypoalbuminemia per se. The increased cholesterol in the setting of increased LDL/HDL cholesterol ratios should put nephrotic patients in the high-risk category for cardiovascular disease. However, several studies examining age-adjusted risk for coronary disease in nephrotic syndrome differ in their findings, with some noting increased cardiovascular mortality while others do not.

Hypercoagulable state

Patients with nephrotic syndrome are at risk of thromboembolic disease. Both arterial and venous thrombosis can develop. Thrombosis of the renal vein can occur in as many as 35% of patients and is associated with sudden onset of flank pain and hematuria, but can be asymptomatic. The highest incidence of renal vein thrombosis is seen in membranous glomerulonephritis. The gold standard for diagnosis of renal vein thrombosis is venography; however, a high proportion of patients can be diagnosed by magnetic resonance imaging (MRI). Pulmonary emboli are the most devastating consequence of venous thrombosis. The higher risk of thromboembolic complications in nephrotic patients is multifactorial, and includes loss of the thrombolytic protein antithrombin III in the urine, decreased levels of protein C and S, hyperfibrinogenemia secondary to increased hepatic synthesis, increase in the coagulation factors V, VII, VIII and X, and platelet hyperaggregability.

Other complications

Table 5.6 summarizes other complications seen in the nephrotic syndrome. Some complications are secondary to the loss of specific proteins in the urine, such as iron deficiency due to transferrin loss, copper deficiency due to loss of ceruloplasmin, and vitamin D deficiency with hypocalcemia secondary to loss of the vitamin D carrier protein. Other complications such as an increased risk of infection are most likely multifactorial due to a loss of immunoglobulins in the urine, malnutrition, and decreased cell-mediated immunity. Hemodynamic alterations may be responsible for some of the other complications such as hyponatremia and acute renal failure.

Treatment

Decisions regarding specific therapy of the nephrotic syndrome depend on making the correct diagnosis (Fig. 5.1). The treatment of the specific types of glomerulonephritis is discussed in Chapters 13-19. Effective therapy is available for minimal change disease; most patients are steroid-responsive. Treatment of membranous GN is more controversial. One-third of patients have a spontaneous remission and one-third will not progress. Therapy with steroids combined with cytotoxics is beneficial either as primary therapy or as salvage treatment once the serum creatinine begins to increase. Focal sclerosis was once considered unresponsive to treatment, but more recent evidence supports a trial of steroids to improve the long-term renal prognosis. No effective therapy is available for membranoproliferative GN

Supportive management of all patients with nephrotic syndrome is directed primarily at reducing edema, controlling BP, maintaining nutrition, and reducing secondary complications (Tab. 5.6). The edema can be treated effectively by sodium restriction and diuretics. For BP control, agents directed at blocking the action of angiotensin II are particularly beneficial, not only in reducing the amount of proteinuria but also in slowing the progression of renal failure. The best evidence for a renal protective effect has been seen in diabetic nephropathy. Proteinuria can be reduced in refractory cases by the use of nonsteroidal anti-inflammatory agents. However, the cost is a reduction in GFR.

The goal of nutritional therapy should be to maintain nitrogen balance. The more traditional view has been to place these patients on a high-protein diet in view of their hypoalbuminuria and urinary protein losses. However, more recent evidence supports cautious restriction of dietary protein, which can reduce proteinuria and consequently increase serum protein levels. The degree of protein restriction should never be less than 0.6 grams of protein/kg body weight/day supplemented gram for gram by the amount of urine protein loss. Careful attention to nutritional parameters is critical. The mechanism by which dietary protein restriction lowers proteinuria may be through improvement in glomerular hemodynamics. Dietary protein restriction may also slow the progression of renal failure in nephrotic patients. In the large trial of dietary protein restriction in progressive renal disease known as the MDRD study, urinary protein excretion greater than 3 g/day predicted a beneficial response to a low-protein diet in slowing progression. No consistent beneficial effect was seen in patients with less severe proteinuria.

A reduction in cholesterol and saturated fat intake is warranted. Although definitive proof is lacking, most nephrologists would use lipid-lowering drugs for treatment of the hyperlipidemia to reduce the risk of atherosclerotic complications. The most effective agents are the HMG-CoA reductase inhibitors. Treatment with angiotensin converting enzyme inhibitors has been associated with a decrease in lipid levels, most likely secondary to a decrease in proteinuria.

Other aspects of therapy include administering pneumococcal vaccine to reduce the incidence of infection with this organism. Unfortunately, pneumococcal peritonitis has been observed in vaccinated patients due either to inadequate response to the vaccine or infection with serotypes not covered by the vaccine. Prolonged immobilization should be avoided to reduce the risks for thromboembolic disease. Anticoagulation therapy for established thromboembolic disease needs to be continued for as long as the patient is nephrotic.

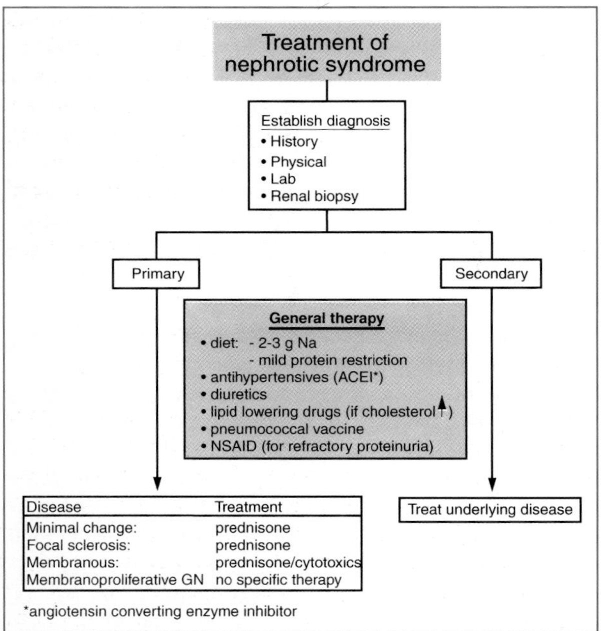

Figure 5.1 The approach to the management and treatment of the nephrotic syndrome. Establishing the diagnosis is critical before any therapeutic decisions are made. General therapy applies to all patients with the nephrotic syndrome. Specific therapies are directed at the underlying disease in secondary forms of the nephrotic syndrome and depend on the underlying renal pathology in primary forms.

NEPHRITIC SYNDROME

A number of clinical syndromes comprise the nephritic syndrome. The classic presentation of acute nephritis is exemplified by poststreptococcal GN characterized by rapid onset of hematuria, proteinuria, and hypertension, with or without an increase in serum creatinine. Another clinical presentation is rapidly progressive glomerulonephritis, which is acute nephritis associated with a rapid deterioration in renal function leading to renal failure in weeks to months. Persistent or recurrent hematuria is another way the nephritic syndrome can present. Finally, the nephritic syndrome can be a slowly progressive deterioration in renal function leading to end-stage renal disease.

The classic urinary findings in the nephritic syndrome are an "active" urinary sediment consisting of red blood cells, particularly dysmorphic-appearing ones; cellular casts with red blood cell casts being pathognomonic of GN; and varying amounts of proteinuria ranging from minimal increases to nephrotic range. Gross hematuria may be present in some patients, giving rise to red-to-brown urine that often appears "tea-colored." For maximal diagnostic value a fresh urine specimen should be examined because casts often degenerate over time. Possible systemic manifestations of the nephritic syndrome include hypertension, edema, and in many cases impairment of glomerular filtration with an increase in serum creatinine.

Etiology

The initial classification of nephritic syndrome is based on whether the pathology is limited to the kidney (primary renal disease) or whether renal pathologic changes are part of a multisystem disease (secondary renal disease). The most common causes of nephritic syndrome in adults are IgA nephropathy, membranoproliferative GN (can present with both nephritic and nephrotic features), postinfectious GN, SLE and other vasculitides, and hereditary nephritis (Alport's syndrome) (Tab. 5.7).

The pathogenesis of the nephritic syndrome is varied, but the most common pathophysiologic mechanisms involve circulating antibodies to the glomerular basement membrane (anti-glomerular basement membrane disease or Goodpasture's syndrome), immune complex deposition in the kidney with complement activation in the subendothelial space or mesangium (e.g., SLE or IgA nephropathy), or circulating antibodies to neutrophil cytoplasmic antigens (e.g., Wegener's granulomatosis).

Table 5.7 Causes of nephritic syndrome in adults

Primary renal disease
IgA nephritis
Anti-GBM disease
Membranoproliferative GN, type I and II
Idiopathic crescentic
Alport's syndrome (hereditary nephritis)
Secondary renal disease
Poststreptoccal
Other postinfectious (endocarditis, shunt, viral, other)
SLE
Wegener's granulomatosis
Henoch-Schönlein purpura
Microscopic polyarteritis nodosa
Cryoglobulinemia
Churg-Strauss syndrome

Differential diagnosis

In the patient presenting with acute nephritic syndrome it is important to make a timely and definitive diagnosis because many of these disorders respond to therapy. The history and physical exam frequently will provide clues about the presence of a multisystem disease. For example, a recent skin infection or pharyngitis suggests poststreptococcal GN. The presence of alopecia, photosensitivity and arthritis suggests lupus nephritis. Specific laboratory evaluation looking for secondary causes can be extensive, and is summarized in Table 5.5. A few tests are highlighted below.

Serum complement levels can give a clue to the underlying renal disease. The most common tests are C3, which is the most abundant complement component and an indicator of activation of the alternative complement pathway; C4, which is an indicator of activation of the classic complement pathway; and CH50 or total hemolytic complement which represents activation of the whole complement cascade. Low serum complement usually means complement activation by immune complexes and is found in membranoproliferative GN, SLE, cryoglobulinemia, and in postinfectious GN. An example of how these measurements of the complement system may be useful in the differential diagnosis of the nephritic syndrome is in membranoproliferative GN. In membranoproliferative GN type I, both complement pathways are activated with C3 levels being lower than C4 levels. In membranoproliferative GN type II, complement activation is mainly through the alternative pathway so that C3 is low but C4 is normal. Many patients with membranoproliferative GN type II have an IgG autoantibody, named C3 nephritic factor, which promotes complement activation by binding to the C3 convertase, preventing its inactivation and resulting in continued C3 breakdown and activation of the alternative pathway. Certain hereditary complement deficiencies can lead to glomerulonephritis, e.g., C2 deficiency, and are suspected when CH50 is decreased but C3 and C4 are normal. Serial measurement of complement levels can correlate with disease activity in some settings. Low complement levels can be found in such nonimmune complex diseases as hemolytic uremic syndrome and atheroembolic disease.

Measurement of antineutrophil cytoplasmic antibody (ANCA) by immunofluorescence and ELISA can provide important diagnostic clues. The main diseases associated with ANCA are Wegener's granulomatosis, microscopic polyangiitis, and idiopathic necrotizing GN (pauci-immune rapidly progressive GN). Elevated titers also can be seen in such disorders as Churg-Strauss syndrome, antiglomerular basement disease and SLE. There are two main patterns of staining, diffuse cytoplasmic staining of cytoplasmic serine proteinase 3 (C-ANCA) or perinuclear staining predominantly against lysosomal myeloperoxidase (P-ANCA). C-ANCA is increased in Wegener's granulomatosis with a specificity of over 95%. In microscopic polyangiitis about one-half of patients have C-ANCA and one half P-ANCA. About 75% of patients with idiopathic necrotizing GN have P-ANCA.

Antiglomerular basement antibodies (anti-GBM) are directed against the $\alpha3$ chain of type IV collagen. These antibodies can be detected by immunofluorescent staining and more sensitive RIA or ELISA assays. The diseases associated with anti-GBM antibodies are Goodpasture's syndrome, which consists of rapidly progressive glomerulonephritis and pulmonary hemorrhage, or a renal limited form known as anti-GBM nephritis. Linear staining of the glomerular basement membrane is seen on immunofluorescent studies of kidney biopsies in patients with anti-GBM antibodies.

Other serologic tests useful in the diagnosis of acute nephritic syndrome are listed in Table 5.5 and include the spectrum of antinuclear antibodies, cryoglobulins, and various serologic tests for such infections as hepatitis B and C, HIV, and syphilis. Renal biopsy is used for definitive diagnosis, although the morphologic response of the kidney may be similar in some of the disorders, highlighting the importance of the serologic evaluation. For example, the renal appearance of many of the vasculitic syndromes resembles focal necrotizing GN.

Treatment

The treatment of many of the secondary causes of acute nephritis are reviewed under the specific etiologies in Chapters 20-26. The cornerstone of therapy in these disorders is some form of immunosuppressive treatment, including combinations of steroids, cytotoxic agents, and plasmapheresis. It is important for the clinician to realize that therapy is available and that often can save the kidneys, even though it may not be life-saving. In postinfectious GN treatment of the underlying infection with appropriate antimicrobial agents is critical. Rapidly progressive glomerulonephritis is treated with steroids and cytotoxic agents, often in combination with plasma exchange – particularly if the renal disease is secondary to antiglomerular basement membrane antibodies.

Treatment of IgA nephropathy is controversial. Most nephrologists would not treat with steroids, except in a variant of IgA nephropathy associated with diffuse foot process fusion. Conflicting results have been obtained with fish oil (omega-3 fatty acids) treatment; however, a recent meta-analysis failed to show a beneficial effect.

Suggested readings

Bernard DB. Extrarenal complications of the nephrotic syndrome. Kidney Int 1988;33:1184.

Churg J, Bernstein J, Glassock RJ. Renal disease. Classification and atlas of glomerular diseases. 2nd ed. New York: Igaku-Shoin, 1995.

Couser WG. Rapidly progressive glomerulonephritis: classification, pathogenetic mechanisms, and therapy. Am J Kidney Dis 1988;11:449.

Dillon J. Fish oil therapy for IgA nephropathy: efficacy and interstudy variability. J Am Soc Nephrol 1997;8:1739.

Falk RJ. ANCA-associated renal disease. Kidney Int 1990; 38:998.

Heeg JE, de Jong PE, van der Hem GK, de Zeeuw D. Efficacy and variability of the antiproteinuric effect of ACE inhibition by lisinopril. Kidney Int 1989;6:272.

Howard AD, Moore J Jr, Gouge SF, et al. Routine serologic tests in the differential diagnosis of the adult nephrotic syndrome. Am J Kidney Dis 1990;15:24.

Joven J, Villabona C, Vilella E, et al. Abnormalities of lipoprotein metabolism in patients with the nephrotic syndrome. N Engl J Med 1990;323:579.

Keilai T, Schlueter WA, Levin ML, Batlle DC. Improvement of lipid abnormalities associated with proteinuria using fosinopril, an angiotensin-converting enzyme inhibitor. Ann Int Med 1993;118:246.

Klahr S, Levey AS, Beck GJ, et al. The effects of dietary protein restriction and blood pressure control on the progression of chronic renal disease. N Engl J Med 1994;330:877.

Llach F. Hypercoagulability, renal vein thrombosis, and other thrombotic complications of nephrotic syndrome. Kidney Int 1985;28:429.

Madio MP. Renal biopsy. Kidney Int 1990;38:529.

Ponticelli C, Passerini P. Treatment of the nephrotic syndrome associated with primary glomerulonephritis. Kidney Int 1994;46:595.

Rosenberg ME, Swanson JE, Thomas BL, Hostetter TH. Glomerular and hormonal responses to dietary protein intake in human renal disease. Am J Phys 1987;253:1083.

Wheeler DC, Bernard DB. Lipid abnormalities in the nephrotic syndrome: causes, consequences, and treatment. Am J Kidney Dis 1994;23:331.

CHAPTER

6

Acute renal failure

Norbert H. Lameire

KEY POINTS

- Three factors play an important pathophysiologic role in the acute fall in glomerular filtration rate: renal ischemia, nephrotoxicity, and pigmenturia.
- Acute renal failure (ARF) is traditionnally classified as prerenal, renal, and postrenal (obstructive).
- The clinical presentation of ARF is by: (1) an unexpected elevation in blood urea and serum creatinine; (2) an alteration in urine flow rate, whereby one-third of acute tubular necrosis cases are nonoliguric; (3) features of the underlying precipitating cause; (4) clinical/biochemical complications of uremia.
- A stepwise diagnostic approach to a patient with ARF is needed.
- Important and inexpensive laboratory tests include an adequate examination of the urinary sediment and determination of the urinary indices.
- The prognosis in ARF is determined largely by the clinical setting of the patient (community-acquired versus critical illness-associated ARF).

Acute renal failure (ARF) can be defined as a sudden, potentially reversible deterioration of renal function that results in the retention in the body of nitrogenous waste products and in failure to maintain fluid and electrolyte homeostasis. In this definition, the presence of oligo-anuria is not required, since nonoliguric ARF increasingly is being recognized and may account for up to 50% of total cases. This is due to a more frequent biochemical monitoring of critically ill patients and the more widespread use of agents that typically induce milder degrees of renal injury.

Specific quantification of the decline in renal function, which is necessary in the diagnosis of ARF, is variable. Commonly used definitions of ARF include an increase in serum creatinine of > 0.5 mg/dl (44 μmol/l) over the baseline value, a reduction in the calculated creatinine clearance of 50%, or a decrease in renal function that necessitates dialysis.

In the clinical setting, the terms ARF and acute tubular necrosis (ATN) have become synonymous. ATN is a histopathologic diagnosis, and although patients with ischemic or toxic insults to their kidneys may be expected to have tubular necrosis, these lesions are not consistently detectable. In the strictest sense, the terms ARF and ATN should not be used interchangeably. ARF due to ATN is commonly encountered in contemporary medicine but its prevalence is highly dependent on the setting and clinical circumstances.

Community-acquired ARF has an incidence of 1% of all hospital admissions in the USA and occurs at an annual incidence of 172.5 cases per million population in the UK. *In a tertiary care hospital*, ARF accounts for 5% of admissions. In critically ill, *intensive care unit* patients, the incidence of ARF ranges from 7 to 23% of all ICU admissions. The development of hospital-acquired ARF increases the mortality by six- to eightfold. The large majority of patients presenting with a syndrome of ARF suffer from acute prerenal failure and ATN.

Pathophysiology

Three major factors predispose to the acute fall in glomerular filtration rate (GFR) in ATN, including renal ischemia (prolonged prerenal azotemia), nephrotoxins, and pigmenturia (hemoglobinuria and myoglobinuria).

Early in ischemic ATN, a decrease in renal perfusion pressure and afferent arteriolar vasoconstriction initiate a reduction in GFR. Later, a decrease in glomerular capillary permeability, an increase in intratubular hydrostatic pressure due to obstructing casts and debris, shed from ischemic tubular brush border epithelium, and "back-leak" of filtered fluid through leaky tubular epithelium further maintain a reduced GFR in ischemic ATN.

Vascular factors

A number of factors can cause afferent arteriolar constriction, thereby reducing glomerular capillary hydrostatic pressure. These include enhanced renal adrenergic neural tone and either locally produced or circulating humoral substances such as norepinephrine, several peptides (angiotensin II, endothelins), and selected lipid-derived substances (endotoxin, thromboxane A2 , leukotrienes, and prostaglandin F_2 alpha-like compounds). The kidneys possess a unique capacity to counteract the local effects of systemic vasoconstrictors and enhanced sympathetic tone, all of which tend to reduce the RBF.

One of the major protective adaptations of the kidney toward hypotension, volume depletion, or reductions in cardiac output is the ability to autoregulate renal blood flow (RBF) and GFR to a relatively constant level over a wide range of renal perfusion pressures. As cardiac output decreases or when blood pressure falls, this autoregulation is seen as a gradual vasodilatation, maintaining RBF. This vasodilatation is mediated primarily by an intrinsic myogenic mechanism at the level of the preglomerular afferent arteriole, but the release of prostanoids like PGI_2, PGE_2 and cytochrome 450 derived arachidonic acid metabolites plays a major role.

Ischemia increases the cytosolic calcium concentration in the endothelial and vascular smooth muscle cells, which results in vasoconstriction, loss of renal autoregulation, increased sensitivity of renal blood flow to renal nerve stimulation, and injury to endothelial cells. The loss of RBF autoregulation may have important clinical implications. A modest arterial pressure reduction during the course of the disease, such as frequently occurs with hemodialysis treatment, can result in recurrent ischemic injury and prolongation of ARF.

In ischemic tissue, extravasated neutrophils adhere to the vascular endothelium. After adherence and chemotaxis, the neutrophils release oxygen species and enzymes that damage the tissue. Intracellular adhesion molecule 1 (ICAM-1) on endothelial cells promotes the adhesion of neutrophils to these cells and the administration of monoclonal antibodies directed against ICAM-1 protects animals from ischemic ATN

Tubular factors

At the level of the renal tubular epithelial cell, depletion of adenosine triphosphate (ATP) is the initial step in cellular damage. This depletion leads to disruption of the cytoskeleton, which maintains tight junctions. Loss of polarity of the ischemic cell results in displacement of enzymes such as the sodium pump (Na-K-ATPase) and of integrins (adhesion molecules) from their normal basolateral position to an apical (brush border) position. The translocation of the Na-K-ATPase may explain the high fractional urinary excretion of sodium, characteristic of postischemic ATN.

Since viable tubular cells have been found in the urine of patients with ATN, it is highly probable that, besides necrotic tubular cells, exfoliation of viable cells also contributes to the tubular obstruction. The reorientation of the integrins toward the apical membrane can mediate cell-cell adhesion via an arginine-glycine-aspartic (RGD) inhibitable mechanism. The RGD domain is the most common domain contained in a variety of matrix proteins and serves as the recognition site for various integrin receptors.

Following ischemia, and antedating evidence of membrane damage, a significant rise in free cytosolic calcium is observed in the tubule cell. This calcium overload may activate several enzyme systems, leading to membrane and organelle disruption and dysfunction. One of the activated enzyme systems in ischemia is phospholipase A_2, a family of enzymes that hydrolyze phospholipids to free fatty acids and lysophospholipids. One of the products of phospholipase A_2 is arachidonic acid that is converted to vasoconstrictive and chemotactive active eicosanoids. Two other potential activated enzymes are calpain, a calcium-dependent cysteine protease, and nitric oxide synthase (NOS), which has calcium-dependent constitutive isoforms, neuronal nNOS and endothelial eNOS, and a calcium-independent inducible form, iNOS. Selective iNOS inhibition with oligodeoxynucleotides protects the rat against ischemic ATN.

In the later stages of renal ischemia, when reflow is established, generation of oxygen free radicals causes lipid peroxidation, leading to further destruction of tubular cell and organelle membranes.

As with ischemic ATN, nephrotoxins impair GFR by causing intrarenal vasoconstriction (e.g., cyclosporine, radiocontrast compounds), direct tubular injury (aminoglycosides, amphotericin B), or tubular obstruction (myeloma light chains).

Classification of acute renal failure

Traditionnally, ARF has been divided in three categories: prerenal, postrenal, and renal.

Prerenal causes They lead to renal failure by decreasing the perfusion of the kidney parenchyma; recovery of renal function occurs after correction of the hemodynamic disturbance. In prerenal ARF, the kidney is structurally normal but functionally compromised. An absolute decrease in extracellular fluid volume (hypovolemia) is the most common prerenal disorder in any clinical setting, and is certainly the most frequent cause of community-acquired ARF.

In some conditions of extracellular or plasma volume sequestration, e.g., sepsis or severe congestive heart failure, the kidneys respond as though the "effective" circulating blood volume were decreased, when in fact the measured volume is normal or even increased.

Particularly common are the *hemodynamically-induced forms of ARF* by nonsteroidal antiinflammatory drugs

(NSAIDs), angiotensin converting enzyme (ACE) inhibitors, or, more recently, angiotensin II receptor blockers.

- *Nonsteroidal antiinflammatory drugs (NSAIDs)*: whereas prostaglandins do not appear to moderate renal hemodynamics and glomerular filtration in healthy subjects, they do play a role in the maintenance of RBF and GFR in diseases associated with activation of the renin-angiotensin system, sympathetic nerve stimulation, and catecholamine release. These vasoconstricting factors stimulate renal synthesis of PGI_2 and PGE_2, which act to preserve GFR in situations such as sodium depletion, surgical stress, and reduced cardiac output. It is well known that cyclooxygenase (COX_1)-inhibition reduces the GFR and RBF in these conditions. It is the hope that NSAIDs, which selectively block the inducible COX_2 enzymes, will not be associated with this form of ARF in the future.
- *ACE-inhibitors*: in the lower zone of GFR and RBF autoregulation, concomitant vasoconstriction at the post-glomerular arteriole occurs, mainly under the influence of angiotensin II. This vasoconstriction maintains a constant glomerular capillary hydrostatic pressure. Impairment of this vasoconstriction by ACE inhibition or administration of angiotensin II blockers when renal vascular stenosis is present may lead to an abrupt fall in GFR. However, autoregulation may also be overcome under conditions of low cardiac output or extracellular volume depletion. These situations are characterized by high circulating levels of systemic vasoconstrictors (catecholamines, angiotensin II, ADH, endothelins) and an enhanced sympathetic tone. The fall in GFR induced by ACE inhibition in these patients is due primarily to failure to increase the postglomerular resistance.

Postrenal ARF It may be caused by either extra- or intrarenal obstruction. Concomitant bilateral ureteral obstruction is quite rare; more common in bilateral ureteral obstruction is that one kidney is blocked for several days or weeks before obstruction of the contralateral kidney causes complete obstruction. Much more common is postrenal ARF by urethral obstruction due to a bladder outlet syndrome, often caused by prostatic hypertrophy, cancers, or iatrogenic causes.

Renal causes They can be classified according to the anatomic compartments of the renal tissue. First, this includes the extra- and intrarenal large and small vasculature, with, as typical examples, the renal artery thrombosis or renal emboli; and the involvement of the renal arterial and arteriolar vessels in diseases such as systemic or renal vasculitis, malignant hypertension, eclampsia, and the thrombotic microangiopathies, e.g., hemolytic uremic syndrome and thrombotic thrombocytopenic purpura.

Atheroemboli These are the most frequent cause of this type of ARF and are usually dislodged from the atheromatous aorta during arteriography, angioplasty, or aortic surgery.

Second are the acute *glomerular* inflammatory syndromes, causing ARF by sharp reduction of the glomerular blood flow and GFR. In general two categories of glomerular diseases provoke ARF de novo: the diffuse proliferative glomerulonephritis, of which postinfectious streptococcal or staphylococcal glomerulonephritis is a prototype, and the crescentic rapidly progressive glomerulonephritis forms.

Third, *acute interstitial nephritis* (AIN) is a term that denotes a group of diseases characterized by acute interstitial inflammation of either allergic or postinfectious origin. They include allergic AIN, allograft rejection, severe acute pyelonephritis, or infiltrative disorders (e.g., sarcoidosis, lymphoma).

Finally, the most frequent form of hospital- or ICU-acquired ARF is the *acute tubular necrosis* (ATN). ATN is broadly subdivided into *ischemic* and *nephrotoxic* causes. In many cases of ATN, more than one cause can be found, and combinations of ischemic and toxic aggressions to the kidney are not exceptional.

In many instances, the *ischemic* forms of ATN have been preceded by a prerenal phase of ARF that has gone unrecognized or treated inadequately. Hypovolemia, severe hypotension, shock, and sepsis are nowadays the most frequent initiating ischemic renal insults. Ischemic ATN is common in the hospitalized patient undergoing cardiac surgery or in patients requiring prolonged clamping of the aorta above the level of the renal vessels, as in emergent repairs of abdominal aortic aneurysms. The risk of ATN increases with the time of cardiopulmonary bypass or of aortic cross-clamp. However, 50% of cases of postoperative ATN develop despite the lack of documented hypotension.

Among the *exogenous toxins*, aminoglycoside antibiotics, immunosuppressive agents such as cyclosporine and FK506, heavy metals and radiocontrast agents are the most frequent causes of posttoxic ATN. The most important risk factors for radiocontrast nephropathy are preexisting renal failure, advanced age, volume depletion, diabetes mellitus and multiple myeloma.

The most common endogenous toxins causing ATN are myo- and hemoglobin, immunoglobulin light chains, and a combination of hyperuricemia and hyperphosphatemia as seen in the *tumor cell lysis syndrome*.

Although the spectrum of causes of ARF is the same in developing and developed countries, the quantitative contribution of each cause is different. For example, postobstetric and postobstructive ARF are more frequent in developing than in developed countries.

Clinical findings

Acute renal failure can present in one of four ways: (1) with an unexpected elevation in blood urea and serum creatinine; (2) with an alteration in urine flow rate; (3) with the clinical features of the underlying precipitating cause; and (4) with the clinical/biochemical complications of uremia.

1. Although a rising serum creatinine is a more reliable marker of a reduction in GFR than a rise in blood urea, it is not always associated with a decline in GFR. This is the case when massive release of creatinine from injured muscle, as in traumatic or nontraumatic rhabdomyolysis, occurs or by interference with the tubular secretion of creatinine by drugs such as cimetidine or trimethoprim. A disproportionate increase in blood urea is seen in conditions of prerenal failure or in obstructive uropathy due to the slow fluid flow in the distal tubule. In most cases however, the rates of increase in blood urea and creatinine are comparable, with urea rising by 20 to 40 mg/dl/day and serum creatinine by 0.5 to 1.0 mg/dl/day.
2. Oliguria is arbitrarily defined as a urine volume of less than 400 ml per 24 hours, because this is the minimum volume required to excrete the daily nitrogenous waste products when the urine is maximally concentrated. Nonoliguric ARF is more common after aminoglycoside nephrotoxicity, burns, and the administration of radiocontrast dye, but may occur after any cause of ARF. Oliguric ARF may be converted to nonoliguric ARF by the administration of fluids in combination with high doses of potent diuretics. Anuria, the passage of less than 50 ml of urine per day, occurs less commonly and indicates a diagnosis of urinary tract obstruction intrarenal or extrarenal), although occasionally it is observed in cases of severe rapidly progressive glomerulonephritis, bilateral cortex necrosis, and renal infarction. Alternating oliguria with polyuria is suggestive for incomplete urinary tract obstruction.
3. Because ARF has many causes, both extrinsic and intrinsic to the kidney, it is not surprising that ARF may present with the clinical features of the underlying cause of renal injury. The most important ones will be considered in the discussion on the clinical approach of the patient.
4. The severity and frequency of the clinical and biochemical complications of ARF will depend on the precipitating cause of the renal failure, the duration of the illness before detection, the rapidity of development of ARF, and the degree of residual renal function. ARF is often complicated by hypervolemia, hyperkalemia and other electrolyte disturbances, bleeding diathesis, or the gastrointestinal or neurologic manifestations of uremia.

Figure 6.1 presents an algorhithm of the stepwise diagnostic approach to a patient with ARF.

This approach starts with a careful *clinical history and physical examination*. Careful tabulation and recording of data such as current symptoms and past illnesses, vital signs, evolution of daily body weight, records of fluid intake and output, past and current laboratory data. A care-

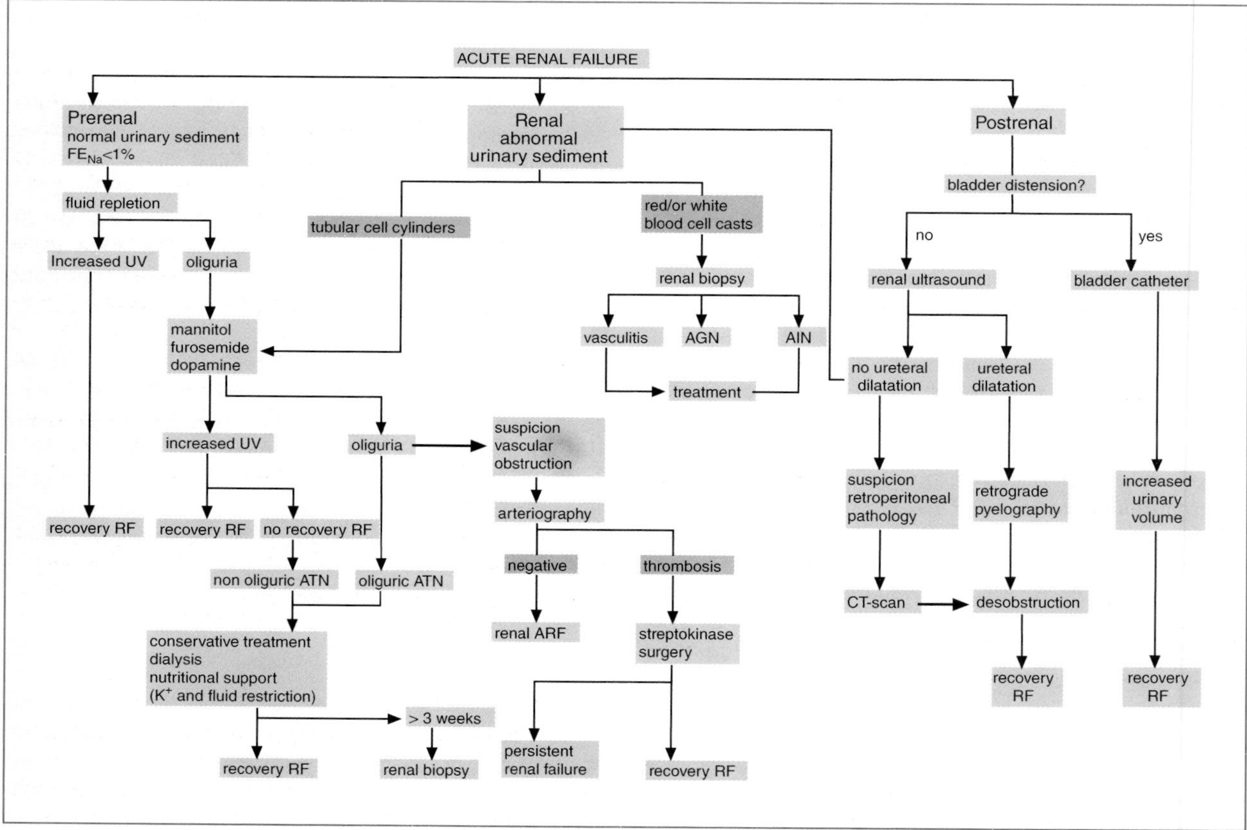

Figure 6.1 An algorhithm of the stepwise diagnostic approach to a patient with ARF. (ATN = acute tubular necrosis; AIN = acute interstitial nephritis; AGN = acute glomerulonephritis; RF = renal function; UV = urinary volume.)

ful history of medication intake should be obtained, and it should not be forgotten that drug-induced ARF can present under various forms of ARF. For example, NSAID-induced nephrotoxicity can present as prerenal azotemia (in those whose RBF is prostaglandin-dependent), allergic AIN, ATN, or nephrotic syndrome.

Symptoms and signs

Although the clinical examination of the ARF patient should be complete, attention should be given to three important points: the assessment of the circulating volume status; the exclusion of any possibility of urinary tract obstruction (a rectal and/or pelvic examination should always be performed!); the search for any physical sign of a possible systemic disease, such as a skin rash, petechiae, purpura, splinter hemorrhages, or arthralgia. The clinical determination of the circulating volume status is crucial but is not always easy. Invasive hemodynamic monitoring with measurement of the pulmonary capillary wedge pressure can be helpful and can also serve to monitor the response to fluid therapy. One single example of a finding at clinical examination that gives a clue to a correct diagnosis of renal cholesterol emboli is the presence of cutaneous livedo reticularis or a "black toe or finger" in a patient who develops ARF after an aortographic examination.

Diagnostic procedures

Urinary sediment This examination is of great value in the differential diagnosis of ARF. A normal or scant sediment is found more frequently in a prerenal or postrenal cause of ARF, but also may be found in large vessel vasculitis and renal atheroemboli.

Red blood cells and/or red blood cell casts together with significant proteinuria suggest glomerulonephritis and /or small vessel vasculitis. A dipstick positive for blood in the absence of red blood cells in the sediment suggests either myo- or hemoglobinuria. White blood cell casts or eosinopils are indicative of AIN, although eosinophiluria can also be found in atheroembolic disease. Pigmented granular casts or renal epithelial cell casts are compatible with ATN. The presence of eosinophils in a urinary sediment of a patient who develops ARF during the treatment with drugs such as NSAIDs, antibiotics, or allopurinol suggests the diagnosis of AIN. In the search for eosinophils the Hansen staining is preferred over the Giemsa technique.

The significance of crystalluria in ARF is confined to oxalate and uric acid. The former is seen in ethylene glycol intoxication, where the presence of uric acid crystals is suggestive of acute uric acid nephropathy, commonly associated with the tumor lysis syndrome. Intraleukocyte crystals have been observed in patients with acyclovir nephropathy.

Urinary indices Analysis of the electrolyte composition of the urine is sometimes helpful in the differential diagnosis between prerenal ARF and established ATN. Since tubular function is preserved and the renal concentrating mechanisms are stimulated in prerenal azotemia, the urine osmolality exceeds the plasma osmolality, spot urine sodium (U_{Na}) are usually less than 30 mmol/l, and the fractional excretion of sodium (FE_{Na}) is less than 1%. However, low U_{Na} concentrations are also observed in some of the renal forms of ARF, e.g., states of intense renal vasoconstiction like sepsis, hepatorenal syndrome, therapy with NSAIDs, acute glomerulonephritis, early postrenal obstructions and intrarenal tubular obstructions by myoglobin or contrast agents.

In contrast, in established ATN, the damaged renal tubule cells fail to reabsorb the filtered sodium normally, perhaps because of altered cell polarity, resulting in a spot U_{Na} concentration of greater than 50 mmol/l and a FE_{Na} of more than 1%. However, a number of situations decrease the diagnostic value of these tests, such as fluid replacement, the use of diuretics and/or vasodilators like dopamine and the presence of preexisting chronic renal failure, among others. It should be emphasized that no single test is reliable and that all tests give only hints about the diagnosis.

Blood chemistry A complete blood chemistry should include parameters of hemolysis, of organ infarction like LDH and transaminases, and the presence of schistocytes in the peripheral blood count. Immunologic parameters should be determined like antistreptolysin titers, complement, cryoglobulins, antiDNA, and the ant-neutrophil anticytoplasmatic antibody (ANCA) titers.

Imaging studies Among all diagnostic imaging procedures renal ultrasonography remains the single most important examination. Ultrasound, at least in experienced hands, gives information on renal size, the presence of renal calculi, and, most important, it is helpful in the exclusion of hydronephrosis. Once hydronephrosis is detected, a urologic consult should be asked, and in presence of a dilated pyelum, a percutaneous pyelostomy with antegrade pyelography will provide localization and release of the level of obstruction. It should however be remembered that (sub)-obstruction may be present in the presence of polyuria, that it may be painless, that it may take several days for the pelvis and calyces to dilate, especially in the presence of volume depletion, and that obstruction may be caused by radiolucent stones such as uric acid stones.

Renal arteriography is performed when noninvasive tests such as radionuclide scans or duplex sonography are suggestive of diminished renal blood flow. It is in general reserved for patients with suspected renal artery thrombosis or renal periarteritis nodosa.

Renal biopsy When AIN, glomerulonephritis, or vasculitis is suspected, there should be no hesitation to perform a renal biopsy to establish the correct diagnosis. At least some of these diseases have a favorable prognosis with prompt but sometimes aggressive treatment. We also believe that a renal biopsy should be performed when a diagnosis of ATN cannot be made with certainty after

1 week, and in case of an unusually protracted course of ARF.

Acute glomerular diseases, especially crescentic glomerulonephritis, contribute significantly to the diagnostic spectrum of ARF, in elderly patients.

NSAID-induced AIN differs significantly from AIN associated with other drugs, because it occurs after longer periods of use, in the absence of hypersensitivity features, and it may be associated with nephrotic proteinuria. Prompt recognition of this disease by renal biopsy may lead to early intervention with steroids and more rapid recovery of the renal function.

Prognosis

One of the major frustrations in nephrology is that despite advances in supportive care, renal replacement therapy, and better knowledge of the pathophysiology of the disease, the mortality rate of patients suffering from ATN still exceeds 50% in many studies and remains unchanged over the last 30 to 40 years. This is due to a major change in the case mix of patients in whom ATN occurs in the setting of extrarenal critical illness. The prognosis of community-acquired ATN, characterized by isolated failure of the kidneys has undoubtedly improved over the years (mortality rates now as low as 10%). On the other hand, critically ill patients suffering from ATN caused by prolonged hypotension, sepsis, or developing ATN as part of a multiple organ failure syndrome and needing vasopressors and prolonged artificial ventilation have a somber prognosis, with mortalities up to 70 to 80%. However, even these forms of ARF show considerable improvement over recent years.

Infectious complications account for much of the morbidity and mortality of ATN. The most frequent sites involved are chest, urinary tract, and wounds. A major predispong factor to infections is the frequent use of indwelling urinary catheters and peripheral and central intravenous lines, needed in these critically ill patients.

Another important prognostic factor is the malnutrition often seen in these patients. Hypercatabolism is present in as many as 35% of patients, especially those suffering from tissue necrosis, sepsis, trauma, and burns.

Suggested readings

Badr KF, Ichikawa I. Prerenal failure: a deleterious shift from renal compensation to decompensation. N Engl J Med 1988; 319:623-9.

Brady HR, Singer GG. Acute renal failure. The Lancet 1995; 346:1533-40.

Conger J. Hemodynamic factors in acute renal failure. Adv Ren Replac Therapy 1997;4:(suppl. 1)25-37.

Conlon PJ, Schwab SJ. Renal failure in the intensive-care unit: an old tale gets better. Mayo Clin Proc 1996;71:205-7.

Faber MD, Kupin WL, Krishna GG, Narins RG. The differential diagnosis of acute renal failure. In: Lazarus JM, Brenner BM, eds. Acute renal failure. 3rd ed. New York: Churchill-Livingstone, 1993;133-92.

Lameire N, Hoste E, Van Loo A, et al. Pathophysiology, causes, and prognosis of acute renal failure in the elderly. Renal Failure 1996;18:333-46.

Lameire N, Verbeke M, Vanholder R. Prevention of clinical acute tubular necrosis with drug therapy. Nephrol Dial Transplant 1995;10:1992-2000.

Lieberthal W. Biology of acute renal failure: therapeutic implications. Kidney Int 1997;52:1102-15.

McCarthy JT. Prognosis of patients with acute renal failure in the intensive-care unit: a tale of two eras. Mayo Clin Proc 1996;71:117-26.

Mindell JA, Chertow GM. A practical approach to acute renal failure. Med Clin North Am 1997;81:731-48.

Sponsel H, Conger JD. Is parenteral nutrition therapy of value in acute renal failure patients? Am K Kidney Dis 1995;25:96-102.

Thadhani R, Pascual M, Bonventre JV. Acute renal failure. New Engl J Med 1996;334:1448-60.

Verbeke M, Van De Voorde J, Lameire N. Prevention of experimental acute tubular necrosis: clinical applications and perspectives. Adv Nephrol 1995;25:177-216.

CHAPTER

7

Chronic renal failure

Michael Schömig, Giulio Odoni, Eberhard Ritz

KEY POINTS

- Chronic renal failure is likely to progress because of maladaptive features of increased function of residual nephrons. The main factors in the process are blood pressure and dietary protein.
- Reduction of nephron numbers leads to impaired exocrine function (sodium/water retention with hypertension and edema, phosphate retention) and endocrine function of the kidney (reduced synthesis of erythropoietin and calcitriol).
- Chronic renal failure ends in a syndrome of intoxication (uremia), characterized mainly by CNS dysfunction and gastrointestinal signs.
- The most common causes of chronic renal failure are: diabetic nephropathy, glomerulonephritis, interstitial renal disease, polycystic kidney disease and vasculitis.
- Renal function can be assessed by measuring serum creatinine and creatinine clearance.

Chronic renal failure (CRF) can be defined as permanent impairment of exocrine and endocrine renal function caused by irreversible loss of functioning nephrons. The type of renal functional disturbance depends more on the fraction of nephrons lost than on the underlying primary renal disease.

Etiopathogenesis

The kidney adapts to nephron loss by an increase in the function of residual nephrons. Although this mechanism increases the function of the remaining nephrons in the short term, such overwork is maladaptive in the long term and causes progressive loss of renal function. Progression is perpetuated by all factors that contribute to the increase in single nephron GFR and glomerular pressure, particularly by hypertension and high dietary protein load. The damaged kidney is particularly susceptible to elevated blood pressure because preglomerular arterial vessels are dilated and autoregulation is lost. As a result, a higher proportion of systemic pressure is transmitted into the glomerular microcirculation.

Reduction of nephron numbers leads to impaired exocrine and endocrine function of the kidney. Impaired excretion of solute leads to sodium retention (thus predisposing to edema formation and hypertension) and to cumulation of nitrogenous substances (thus leading to symptoms of uremic intoxication). Impairment of endocrine function of the kidney is responsible for hyporegeneratory anemia (because of reduced production of erythropoietin) and disturbed calcium/phosphate metabolism and secondary hyperparathyroidism [because of the diminished renal synthesis of the active vitamin D metabolite 1,25 $(OH)_2D_3$].

CRF culminates in a syndrome of intoxication that mainly affects central nervous system (CNS) function and ends in uremic coma. CNS dysfunction is accompanied by signs and symptoms in the gastrointestinal tract (nausea, vomiting, gastrointestinal hemorrhage) and the heart (pericarditis, left ventricular failure), but if one looks hard enough the function of all organ systems is deranged – e.g., polyneuropathy, impaired immune response, impaired leukocyte function, impaired sexual function, etc.

Currently, the most frequent causes of endstage renal failure are (Tab. 7.1):

- diabetic nephropathy (mostly Type 2 diabetes);
- glomerulonephritis;
- interstitial renal disease, i.e., obstructive uropathy, vesicoureteral reflux, urolithiasis, malformation, neurogenic bladder, analgesic nephropathy;
- polycystic kidney disease;
- systemic disease (systemic lupus erythematosus, Wegener's granulomatosis, microscopic polyangiitis);
- other hereditary renal diseases (e.g., Alport's disease).

Less frequent causes include amyloidosis (AA or AL type), myeloma kidney, light chain deposit disease, malignant hypertension, hemolytic uremic syndrome, ischemic nephropathy (particularly atherosclerotic renal artery disease and cholesterol microembolism), renal vein thrombosis, interstitial nephritis, Balkan nephropathy, nephronophthisis, chronic tubular syndromes, nephrocalcinosis (primary oxalosis, secondary oxalosis in intestinal disease, renal tubular acidosis) and several hereditary disorders, e.g., Bartter's syndrome, Fabry's disease, lecithin-cholesterol acyltransferase deficiency, Refsum syndrome.

Clinical findings

Symptoms and signs

In the evolution from early renal dysfunction to end-stage renal failure, chronic renal failure is characterized by the progressive appearance of ever more clinical signs and symptoms. The presentation is highly variable, however, because of (1) interindividual differences and (2) comorbidity, particularly hypertension and diabetes mellitus.

The first abnormality to be noted by the patient is usually nycturia and polyuria. Patients complain of asthenia and loss of performance (beginning at approximately plasma creatinine 2-3 mg/dl). This may be accompanied by hypertension and its sequelae (headache, dyspnea, left heart failure, coronary heart disease) and by edema (particularly in patients with the nephrotic syndrome and diabetic nephropathy).

When GFR has decreased to approximately 30 ml/min, patients develop anemia; hyperpigmented, dry, scaling skin; sexual dysfunction; loss of appetite, and a number of metabolic abnormalities, e.g., hyperphosphatemia (leading to extraosseous calcification and hyperparathyroidism), metabolic acidosis (causing catabolism and cardiovascular malfunction), etc.

The final stage of intoxication is heralded by headache, change of personality, apathy, confusion, nausea and vomiting. Fetor uremicus is unreliable because it depends not only on plasma urea concentration, but also on oral hygiene and other factors. The terminal stage, infrequently observed today, is characterized by hiccups, muscular twitches, lethargy, somnolence, and coma. Depending on the state of hydration and left ventricular function, patients may develop pulmonary edema and/or hypertensive encephalopathy, i.e., cerebral edema with headache, amaurosis, hemiplegia, and fits.

Table 7.1 Frequency of major causes of end-stage renal failure among patients admitted for renal replacement therapy (annual report German Renal Registry 1998; Frei U. et al., Nephrol Dial Transplant, 1999)

Cause	%	
Diabetes, Type 2	24%	31%
Diabetes, Type 1	7%	
Glomerulonephritis	16%	
Interstitial renal disease	13%	
Cystic renal disease	6%	
Systemic disease	4%	
Various hereditary renal diseases	1%	
Unknown, vascular, various	29%	

Diagnostic procedures

In Chapter 44 the necessary steps to establish the diagnosis will be discussed in detail. Table 7.2 lists the recommended investigations in a patient with chronic renal failure. Table 7.3 gives a brief summary of the rationale for and results of laboratory investigations.

The most important index of renal function is glomerular filtration rate (GFR). Although accurate measurements of this parameter are available only for investigational purposes, clinically useful approximations are obtained by measuring plasma creatinine or endogenous creatinine clearance. Creatinine is the anhydride of creatine. A constant amount (approximately 1000-1500 mg/24 h) is produced in the muscles and is excreted almost exclusively via the kidneys. The exact amount of creatinine synthesized depends on muscle mass; it is higher in males than in females. There is an inverse hyperbolic relationship between GFR and plasma creatinine, as indicated in Figure 7.1. This implies that a given absolute reduction in GFR leads to much smaller changes in plasma creatinine concentration in early as compared with advanced renal failure (the same is true for the plasma concentration of other substances excreted via the kidney, particularly drugs and their metabolites).

Plasma urea concentration is also elevated in CRF, but it is less specific as an index of GFR. It depends not only on GFR, but also on the rate of urine excretion and the rate of formation of urea in the intermediary metabolism. As a consequence, despite no change in GFR, plasma urea concentrations may decrease when patients drink more water, or may increase when (1) dietary consumption of proteins is increased, (2) gastrointestinal hemorrhage occurs, or (3) endogenous proteins are broken down in catabolic patients.

Table 7.2 Investigation of the patient with chronic renal failure

Obligatory

Family history

Patient's history

Physical examination

Urinalysis: sediment, cell count, proteinuria (quantitative), microbiology, immunelectrophoresis

Laboratory examination: creatinine, urea, uric acid, Na, K, Cl, Ca, P, blood gas analysis, hematology

Ultrasonography (in selected cases CT, NMR, angiography)

Further investigations, depending on clinical circumstances

Renal biopsy

Rectal mucosa biopsy (amyloid)

Serologic investigation (ANA; dsDNA; antibasement membrane antibodies; anticytoplasmic antibodies [ANCA], complement, cryoglobulins, hepatitis serology)

Blood glucose, oral glucose tolerance test, funduscopy, fluorescence angiography of retina

Audiometry (familial glomerulonephritis)

Search for complications of uremia

Anemia

Hemorrhagic diathesis (bleeding time)

Bone disease (Ca, P, alkaline phosphatase [bone isoenzyme], PTH, 25-OH-D_3, skeletal X-ray, plasma aluminium concentration, bone biopsy)

Soft tissue calcification (vascular, periarticular, visceral), X-ray

Polyneuropathy (vibration sensation, reflexes, sensory and motor nerve conduction velocity)

Gout, pseudogout (clinical examinations, uric acid, X-ray)

Sexual function (impotence, amenorrhea)

Skin changes (xerosis, pruritus, prurigo, hyperkeratosis)

Sequelae of hypertension (ECG, stress-ECG, cardiac transversal diameter [thoracic X-ray], echocardiography, funduscopy, duplex sonography of carotid artery, investigation for peripheral arterioocclusive disease)

Hyperkalemia

Metabolic acidosis

Dyslipidemia, hyperlipidemia

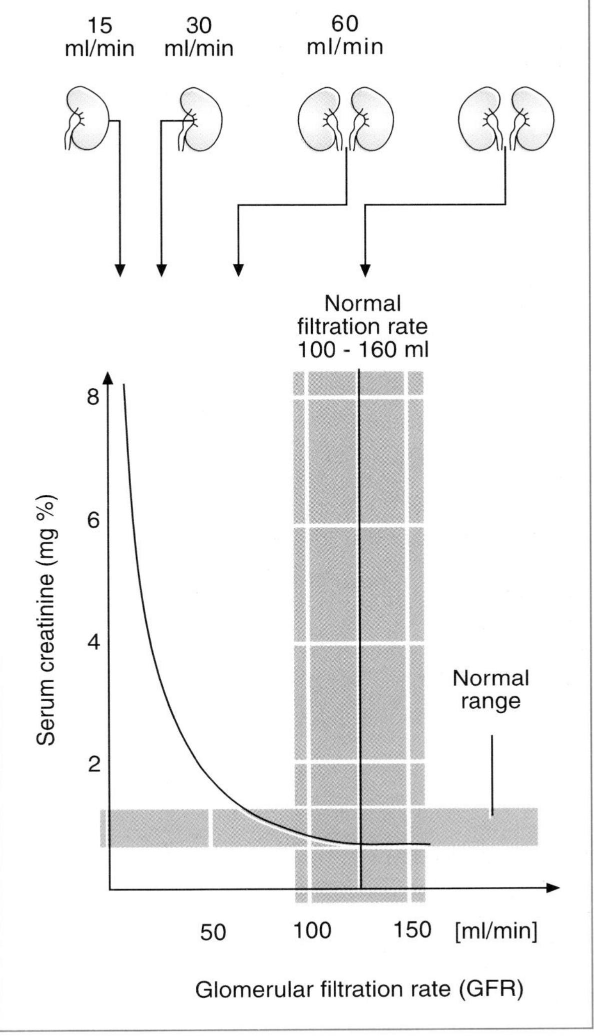

Figure 7.1 Hyperbolic relationship between creatinine clearance as an index of glomerular filtration rate (abscissa) and plasma creatinine concentration (ordinate). The graph illustrates that because of the underlying mathematics (hyperbolic function) in the range 30-150 ml/min/1.73 m^2 GFR, large changes in GFR lead to only modest changes in plasma creatinine concentration. In contrast, below GFR 30 ml/min/1.73 m^2 minute changes of GFR cause major changes in plasma creatinine concentration.

Imaging

Today, evaluation of the CRF patient is incomplete without imaging of the kidneys. As shown in Table 7.4, presence of nephrocalcinosis or lithiasis points to a specific set of diagnoses. Primary glomerular disease usually leads to symmetric changes of the kidneys (enlarged, normal or reduced size), whereas urologic disease often causes asymmetric renal lesions. Recognition of urinary tract obstruction at a supravesical or infravesical level is of paramount importance. Additional investigations are necessary if ischemic nephropathy is suspected, e.g., atherosclerotic renal artery stenosis, cholesterol microembolism, dissection of the abdominal aorta.

Table 7.3 Laboratory investigations in the patient with chronic renal failure

Measurement	Interpretation
Urine	
Excretion rate of:	
Protein	> 1 g/d pointing to glomerular disease, > 3.5 g/d conventionally designated nephrotic syndrome. Confounder: orthostatic proteinuria (measure protein excretion during nighttime). If problems with urine collection: measure protein/creatinine ratio in spot urine. Urine protein excretion a valuable index to assess response to antihypertensive treatment, particularly ACE inhibitors and response to immunotherapy, e.g., minimal change GN or membranous GN
Urea	Index of dietary protein intake (e.g., to assess compliance with dietary recommendations) or catabolism (in patients with intercurrent disease)
Sodium	Control of compliance with dietary sodium restriction, important in antihypertensive treatment of CRF patients
Plasma concentration of:	
Creatinine	Index of GFR. Confounding factor: muscle mass (see above)
Urea	Index of GFR, but also of protein intake or protein breakdown (confounders, see text)
Uric acid	Variably elevated in CRF. Does not contribute to progression. Routine allopurinol treatment not advisable, but at concentration 9-10 mg/100 ml high risk of gout. Hyperuricemia frequent in lead intoxication
K	Hyperkalemia usually seen only in terminal oliguric CRF (in earlier stages dietary potassium restriction not necessary). Hyperkalemia may be seen before the terminal stage in patients on K-sparing diuretics, or other drugs (ACE inhibitors, beta blockers, NSAIDs), metabolic acidosis (particularly in interstitial renal disease e.g., analgesic nephropathy) or hyporeninemic states (Schambelan syndrome)
Na	Until the preterminal stage of CRF Na concentration is usually normal. Hyponatremia may occur with excessive water intake (more than approximately 4-6 l/day) or with aggressive diuretic treatment. Hyponatremia is common in terminal renal failure because of inability of kidney to excrete osmotically free water
Ca (total calcium)	In preterminal CRF tendency of hypocalcemia (low total calcium, in cases of doubt measure ionized calcium). High normal or elevated calcium points to myeloma, vitamin D intoxication, administration of excessive calcium containing oral phosphate binders, metastatic bone disease, immobilisation, occasionally severe osteitis fibrosa or use of thiazides
P	At approximately GFR 30 ml/min tendency for hyperphosphatemia. Concentration very much dependent on dietary intake, release of P from bone (e.g. in severe osteitis fibrosa) and degree of hyperparathyroidism
1,84 iPTH	Tendency to increase in early CRF, but great interindividual differences. Because of PTH resistance of skeleton and/or measurement of inactive fragments by the 1,84 iPTH assay, concentrations 2-3 times above normal range advisable. Main causes of hyperparathyroidism failing renal production of active vitamin D and hyperphosphatemia
25(OH)D_3	Decreases with diminished sun exposure (common in renal patients). Biologically relevant because renal synthesis of active vitamin D (1,25$[OH]_2D_3$) dependent on substrate concentration, i.e. 25(OH)D_3
Hb	Tendency for decrease of Hb at approximately GFR 30 ml/min. Usually normochromic, hyporegeneratory anemia. In preterminal renal failure aggravated by intestinal blood loss (gastric and colonic bleeding). Some renal diseases associated with hemolysis
Ferritin	Index of iron deficiency (note normal range in uremic patients different from non-renal individuals). Iron repletion indispensible for full effect of rhEPO treatment
HBV (hepatitis B)	Rarely associated with renal disease (e.g. membranous GN). If protective antibodies not present, prophylactic vaccination advised by some authors (because of insufficient immune response in terminal CRF)
HCV (hepatitis C)	Associated with cryoglobulinemia and mesangial capillary GN
Serology	ANA, dsDNS, antibasement membrane ab, ANCA; if necessary complement, cryoglobulins to recognize systemic disease
HbA1c	To recognize diabetes mellitus. Only HPLC methods reliable in CRF. HbA1c may normalize if patients are anorectic (funduscopy helpful to recognize microvascular disease from past hyperglycemia)

Table 7.4 Ultrasonographic investigation of the patient with chronic renal failure

Calcification demonstrable

- nephrolithiasis
- primary hyperparathyroidism
- hypercalcemia syndrome
- analgesic nephropathy with calcified papillary necrosis
- urotuberculosis
- renal tubular acidosis, oxalosis, sponge kidney

No calcification demonstrable

Shrunken kidney symmetrical	*Shrunken kidney asymmetrical*	*Kidney normal size or enlarged*
• glomerulonephritis • benign and malignant hypertension • recurrent embolism • analgesic nephropathy (rare) • hereditary renal disease • amyloidosis • interstitial nephritis • final stage of tubular syndrome	• urologic disease (reflux, nephrolithiasis, obstruction, tumor) • analgesic nephropathy	• diabetic glomerulosclerosis • glomerulonephritis • systemic diseases • amyloidosis • myeloma kidney • interstitital nephritis • obstruction (acute stage) • polycystic kidney disease (important: must be differentiated against multiple acquired renal cysts in patient with longstanding renal disease)

Renal biopsy

Renal biopsy is rarely required in the patient with CRF. It should be considered only if the result presumably will impact on patient management. In patients with diabetes it is indicated only if there are reasonable doubts that CRF is due to causes other than Kimmelstiel Wilson glomerulosclerosis. It is indicated when a nephritic sediment points to glomerulonephritis or vasculitis, if amyloidosis is a strong possibility, etc.

Suggested readings

Brenner BM, Meyer TW, Hostetter TH. Dietary protein intake and the progressive nature of kidney disease: the role of hemodynamically mediated glomerular injury in the pathogenesis of progressive glomerular sclerosis in aging, renal ablation, and intrinsic renal disease. N Engl J Med 1982;307:652-9.

Eckardt KU. Pathophysiology of renal anemia. Clin Nephrol 2000;53:S2-8.Falk RJ, Jennette JC. ANCA small-vessel vasculitis. J Am Soc Nephrol 1997;8:314-22.

Feest TG, Mistry CD, Grimes DS, Mallick NP. Incidence of advanced chronic renal failure and the need for end stage renal replacement treatment. BMJ 1990;301:897-900.

Frei U, Schober-Halstenberg HJ. Annual Report of the German Renal Registry 1998. QuaSi-Niere Task Group for Quality Assurance in Renal Replacement Therapy. Nephrol Dial Transplant 1999;14:1085-90.

Mogensen CE. Microalbuminuria, blood pressure and diabetic renal disease: origin and development of ideas. Diabetologia 1999;42:263-85.

Remuzzi G, Bertani T. Pathophysiology of progressive nephropathies. N Engl J Med 1998;339:1448-56.

Ritz E, Orth SR. Nephropathy in patients with type 2 diabetes mellitus. N Engl J Med 1999;341:1127-33.

Ritz E, Schomig M, Bommer J. Osteodystrophy in the millennium. Kidney Int Suppl 1999;73:S94-8.

Ritz E, Rychlik I, Locatelli F, Halimi S. End-stage renal failure in type 2 diabetes: a medical catastrophe of worldwide dimensions. Am J Kidney Dis 1999;34:795-808.

CHAPTER

8 Hypertension

Friedrich C. Luft

KEY POINTS

- The relationship between blood pressure and risk for stroke or cardiovascular disease is linear and becomes manifest at pressure values still in the normal range.
- Twenty-four-hour blood pressure monitoring permits the assessment of blood pressure load, which is particularly helpful if the diagnosis of hypertension is in doubt.
- A number of monogenic forms of hypertension have been identified, and these may be diagnosed by molecular genetic tests. Furthermore, the angiotensinogen gene, the adducin gene, a G-protein subunit gene, and the beta-2 adrenoceptor gene have been shown to be relevant to essential hypertension.
- The use of sublingual nifedipine in the treatment of hypertensive emergencies should be reconsidered.
- Systolic and diastolic function must be considered separately in patients with hypertensive heart disease.
- Hypertension in children must be considered secondary until proved otherwise.

The clinical definition of hypertension is a systolic blood pressure of 140 mmHg or greater, and a diastolic blood pressure of 90 mmHg or greater. The term also is used in connection with patients taking antihypertensive medications.

Hypertension is the primary risk factor for cardiovascular disease, which in turn is the most common cause of death worldwide; therefore, the topic is of considerable medical importance. The objective of identifying and treating high blood pressure is to reduce the risk of cardiovascular diseases and their associated morbidity and mortality. The risks inherent in increases in systolic blood pressure and diastolic blood pressure are not different. In fact, the risk presented by increased systolic blood pressure may be greater than that for diastolic blood pressure although hypertension awareness, treatment, and control rates have steadily increased, this increase has leveled off in recent years. Age-adjusted mortality rates for stroke and coronary heart disease have declined, whereas the incidence of end-stage renal disease and the prevalence of heart failure are increasing.

Secondary hypertension

Hypertension may have identifiable causes. Additional diagnostic procedures are warranted in patients whose age, history, physical examination, severity of hypertension, or initial laboratory findings suggest such causes. Furthermore, patients whose blood pressure responds poorly to medication warrant further evaluation, as do those with well controlled hypertension whose blood pressure suddenly increases, or those patients who abruptly develop hypertension but have no family history of the condition.

Labile hypertension or paroxysms accompanied by headache, palpitations, pallor, and perspiration suggest pheochromocytoma. Abdominal bruits radiating to the flanks, bruits with a diastolic component, and abrupt episodes of pulmonary edema suggest renal vascular hypertension. Abdominal or flank masses suggest autosomal-dominant polycystic kidney disease. Absent femoral arterial pulses and decreased blood pressure in the lower extremities suggest aortic coarctation. Truncal obesity with purple striae may indicate Cushing's syndrome. Clues from the laboratory include unprovoked hypokalemia, suggesting primary aldosteronism (Conn's syndrome), hypercalcemia, suggesting hyperparathyroidism, or elevated creatinine levels, suggesting underlying renal disease. Appropriate investigations should be made when a high index of suspicion for an identifiable cause exists. Such an evaluation need not require hospitalization or great expense.

Genetic hypertension

Blood pressure levels are correlated in family members, and a genetic influence has been recognized since the early twentieth century. High blood pressure is a complex genetic trait that does not follow classic mendelian inheritance. However, rare, monogenic forms of hypertension exist, including the chimeric 11-β-hydroxylase/aldosterone synthase gene, the mutated gene for the β or γ subunit of the epithelial, amiloride-sensitive sodium channel (ENaC), and the mutated gene for 11-β-hydroxysteroid dehydrogenase. An additional monogenic form of hypertension cosegregates with type E brachydactyly and neurovascular anomalies impinging on the ventrolateral medulla. These anomalies have also been described in essential hypertension, although their significance is currently uncertain. Genes relevant to essential hypertension are of great interest. The angiotensinogen gene, the adducin gene, a gene encoding for a G-protein subunit, and the beta-2 adrenergic receptor gene have been implicated fairly convincingly thus for. The relevance of these and other genes is the topic of much ongoing research.

Essential hypertension

The vast majority of patients have essential hypertension, a relatively heterogeneous, polygenic condition of unknown cause. Risk stratification is important and is accomplished by considering other major risk factors. The presence of these risk factors makes antihypertensive treatment all the more mandatory. The major risk factors are smoking, dyslipidemia, diabetes mellitus, left ventricular hypertrophy, male gender, age, and a family history of hypertension with onset <65 years in women or <55 years in men. The major target organ damage involves the heart, in the form of left ventricular hypertrophy, coronary heart disease, and congestive heart failure, the brain in the form of stroke or transient ischemic attacks, the kidneys in the form of nephropathy, the central and peripheral arteries, and the retina.

The goal for blood pressure reduction is to reduce morbidity and mortality by the least intrusive means possible. This goal may be accomplished by achieving and maintaining systolic blood pressure below 140 mmHg and diastolic blood pressure below 90 mmHg – and lower if tolerated – while controlling other modifiable risk factors for cardiovascular disease. Particular concern should be extended to those at highest risk: older patients, patients with diabetes mellitus or hypercholesterolemia, patients with left ventricular hypertrophy or decreased renal function, or patients who smoke (and for whatever reason will not or cannot stop). In older patients, a tolerated reduction in blood pressure is advisable (ideally below 140/90 mmHg). Isolated elevated systolic blood pressure in older patients should be reduced below 160 mmHg.

Treatment

Nonpharmacologic treatments Nonpharmacologic treatment should be advised for all patients with hypertension. Weight reduction – as little as 4.5 kg – reduces blood pressure in a large proportion of overweight persons with hypertension. Excessive alcohol intake (>30 ml ethanol day) is an important risk factor for high blood pressure. Regular aerobic physical activity – adequate to achieve at least a moderate level of physical fitness – can enhance weight loss and functional health status and reduce the risk for cardiovascular disease and all-cause mortality. Moderation of sodium chloride intake (Na 75 to 100 mmol/day) lowers blood pressure over periods of several weeks to years. High dietary potassium intake may protect against developing hypertension and improves blood pressure control in patients with hypertension. The risk of stroke may be reduced independent of blood pressure. Other factors such as calcium intake, magnesium intake, and measures of stress reduction have less well documented benefits. The issue of dietary fat intake as risk factor in the development of vascular disease is also important and may require consideration. Finally, cigarette smoking is a powerful risk factor for cardiovascular disease, and avoidance of tobacco in any form is essential.

Drug therapy Pharmacologic treatment requires the consideration of several factors: the degree of blood pressure elevation, the presence of target organ damage, and the presence of clinical cardiovascular disease or other risk factors. A low dose of the initial drug of choice should be given; the dose should then slowly be titrated upward at a schedule determined by the patient's age, needs, and responses. The optimal therapy should provide 24-hour efficacy with a once-daily dose, with at least 50% of the peak effect remaining at the end of 24 hours.

Although five classes of drugs are acceptable for first-line treatment of hypertension (Fig. 8.1), on the basis of outcomes data from currently available randomized, controlled trials, the preferred starting pharmacologic therapy for patients with uncomplicated hypertension consists of thiazide diuretics and beta-blockers.

Thiazide diuretic use is supported by clinical trial evidence of reduced cardiovascular morbidity and mortality. Low doses of thiazide diuretics successfully potentiate the effect of other agents without producing adverse metabolic effects. Low-dose thiazide diuretics were highly effective in older hypertensive patients and in older patients with isolated systolic hypertension. The risk of hypokalemia can be reduced by using thiazides in conjunction with potassium-sparing agents (amiloride and triamterene) and by relying on low doses (≤25 mg/day).

Beta-blockers have been extensively tested in mortality

and morbidity clinical trials. In addition, beta-blockers are the drugs of choice for patients with coronary artery disease or prior myocardial infarction. They decrease cardiovascular risk in older patients undergoing major operations for any reasons and decrease the risk of atrial fibrillation in patients undergoing bypass surgery. Beta-blockers are of proven value in patients with congestive heart failure. Thus, these drugs should not be withheld in patients with decreased left ventricular function. Although beta-blockers may cause diabetic patients to be less aware of hypoglycemia, and although both thiazides and beta-blockers may unfavorably alter lipid profiles, randomized, controlled trials suggest that these agents are highly effective in hypertensive patients with diabetes.

ACE-inhibitors are indicated in patients with reduced left ventricular function (ejection fraction <40%) and/or heart failure. Furthermore, randomized trials suggest that ACE-inhibitors retard the development of diabetic nephropathy (microalbuminuria or greater) even in diabetic patients without hypertension. Hypertensive patients with reduced renal function from any cause may benefit from ACE inhibitors, particularly if they have heavy proteinuria. Blockade of the angiotension II (AT1) receptor presents a new avenue of treatment. AT1 receptor blockers are remarkably free of side-effects, notably cough. Whether or not the drugs have other advantages over ACE inhibitors or provide an additive benefit is currently being tested in randomized trials. Both ACE inhibitors and AT1 receptor blockers are contraindicated in pregnancy.

Calcium channel blockers are generally well tolerated when long-acting formulations are given. In a recently completed randomized trial of systolic hypertension in older patients, a long-acting dihydropyridine calcium channel blocker was the initial therapy. The trial showed a reduction in stroke and cardiovascular mortality in the treated group. Calcium channel blockers exert no adverse metabolic effects. Immediate-release nifedipine has precip-

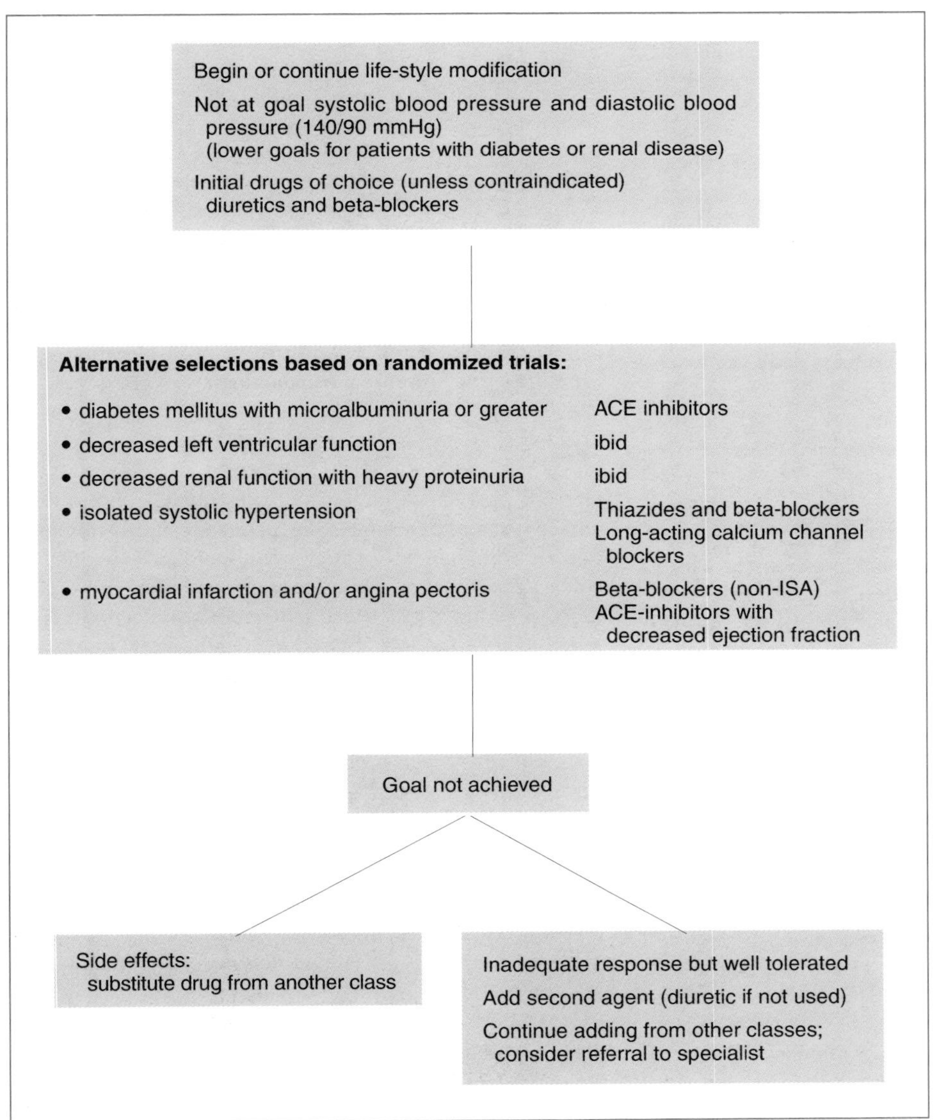

Figura 8.1 Treatment algorithm.

itated ischemic events and, in large doses, may increase coronary mortality in patients who have had a myocardial infarction. Therefore, this agent should be used with caution.

Alpha-blockers are effective, generally well tolerated (occasional postural hypotension after the first dose), and are particularly helpful in older male patients with prostatic hypertrophy. Alpha blockers may decrease serum cholesterol and increase HDL-cholesterol.

Hypertension with dyslipidemia

Dyslipidemia and hypertension commonly coexist. Because life-style modifications are the first approach to both conditions, great emphasis must be placed on controlling overweight and on reduced intake of saturated fat, cholesterol, salt, and alcohol. Recent trials have shown that HMG-CoA reductase inhibitors provide both primary and secondary protection against coronary heart disease. Fenofibrates also have been shown to be effective in secondary prevention. Life-style changes and hypolipidemic agents should be used to achieve appropriate goals in hyperlipidemic hypertensive patients.

In high doses, thiazide diuretics may increase total cholesterol, LDL-cholesterol, and triglyceride values. These effects have not been documented with low-dose thiazides. Beta-blockers may transiently increase triglycerides and reduce HDL-cholesterol values. Nevertheless, in the Systolic Hypertension in the Elderly Program (SHEP) study, the combination of these agents reduced risk for stroke and coronary events equally in patients with normal or elevated lipid values. Alpha-blockers may decrease serum cholesterol and increase HDL-cholesterol. ACE-inhibitors, calcium channel blockers and centrally acting agents are neutral with respect to plasma lipid values.

Hypertensive urgencies and emergencies

Hypertensive emergencies are unusual situations in which immediate blood pressure reduction is necessary. This reduction does not necessarily need to be in the normal range. Examples include hypertensive encephalopathy, intracranial hemorrhage, unstable angina pectoris or acute myocardial infarction, acute pulmonary edema, dissecting aortic aneurysm, and eclampsia. Parenteral drugs such as nitroglycerin, sodium nitroprusside, hydralazine hydrochloride, enalaprilat, labetalol, or phentolamine may be necessary. Hypertensive urgencies are defined as severely hypertensive patients not requiring intensive care but warranting hospitalization. These patients can be treated with oral agents, including loop diuretics, beta-blockers, ACE-inhibitors, α_2-agonists, or calcium channel blockers. Absolutely mandatory is examination of the eye. Figure 8.2 (see Color Atlas) shows retinal photographs from a young patient with initial blood pressure values of 300/200 mmHg. His complaint was sudden, progressive blindness. Bilateral retinal detachment had occurred. With parenteral therapy and adequate blood pressure control, his retinas reattached, revealing bilateral papilledema and cotton wool exudates representing retinal infarction. Surprisingly, these changes were reversible, and 1 year later with good blood pressure control his optic fundi were almost normal. An underlying chronic renal disease was responsible for the hypertension.

As this patient illustrates, important conclusions about the severity of hypertension and particularly the risk of end-organ damage can be obtained by examining the eyes. The eyes permit a noninvasive inspection of the body's small blood vessels. Unfortunately, internists in some European countries are not routinely trained in the use of the ophthalmoscope.

Most clinicians follow the grading proposed years ago by Keith and Wagner. In general, this grading scale takes into account the degree of hypertensive change in the vessels without independently grading the degree of the arteriolar sclerotic changes. For the purposes of uniformity, it is wise to follow this classification. The cases are divided into four groups, increasing in severity:

- stage I: the caliber of the arterioles is definitely reduced to three-quarters to one-half the caliber of the corresponding vein. An occasional focal constriction in an arteriole may be seen. No hemorrhages or exudates are present;
- stage II: there is a further reduction in the average caliber to one-half or one-third that of the corresponding vein. Several focal constrictions may be present in the arterial tree. No hemorrhages or exudates are present;
- stage III: in addition to the changes just given, there are flame-shaped hemorrhages or cotton wool patches. Edema residues may be present. The optic disc shows no changes;
- stage IV: in addition to the stage III picture, the disk now shows edema, ranging from mild blurring of its outlines to a full-blown choked disk.

Compliance with the regimen

General pharmacologic considerations suggest that long-acting formulations are preferred for many reasons. Patient compliance is better with once-daily dosing; for some agents, fewer tablets mean lower costs; control of blood pressure is persistent and smooth; protection is provided against the risk for sudden death, heart attack, and stroke, that may be caused by the abrupt increase in blood pressure after arising from overnight sleep. Furthermore, the duration of action is generally such that missing a dose does not result in a prompt, dangerous increase in blood pressure. The manufacturers claim does not always coincide with the clinical data in that regard. This may particularly true for ACE inhibitors. Physicians should modify their prescribing practices accordingly.

Finally, step-down therapy is indicated in some patients. An effort to decrease the dosage and number of antihypertensive drugs should be considered after hypertension has been controlled effectively for at least 1 year. The reduction should be made in a deliberate, slow, and progressive manner. Step-down therapy is particularly successful in patients who were able to make life-style modifications.

Suggested readings

Appel LJ, Moore TJ, Obarzanek E, et al., (DASH Collaborative Research Group). A clinical trial of the effects of dietary patterns on blood pressure. N Engl J Med 1997;157:657-67.

Curb JD, Pressel SL, Cutler JA, et al. Effect of diuretic-based antihypertensive treatment on cardiovascular disease risk in older diabetic patients with isolated systolic hypertension: Systolic Hypertension in the Elderly Program Cooperative Research Group. JAMA 1996;276:1886-92.

The EUCLID Study Group. Randomised placebo-controlled trial of lisinopril in normotensive patients with insulin-dependent diabetes and normoalbuminuria or microalbuminuria. Lancet 1997;349:1787-92.

Frost PH, Davis BR, Burlando AJ, et al., for the Systolic Hypertension in the Elderly Research Group. Serum lipids and incidence of coronary heart disease: findings from the Systolic Hypertension in the Elderly Program (SHEP). Circulation 1996;94:2381-88.

The GISEN Group. Randomised placebo-controlled trial of effect of ramipril on decline in glomerular filtration rate and risk of terminal renal failure in proteinuric, non-diabetic nephropathy. Lancet 1997;349:1857-63.

Grossman E, Messerli FH, Grodzicki T, Kowey P. Should a moratorium be placed on sublingual nifedipine capsules given for hypertensive emergenecies and pseudoemergencies? JAMA 1996;276:1328-31.

Gueyffier FL, Boutitie F, Boissel JP, et al. (INDANA Investigators). Effect of antihypertensive drug treatment on cardiovascular outcomes in women and men: a meta-analysis of individual patient data from randomized, controlled trials. Ann Intern Med 1997;126:761-7.

Kaplan NM, Gifford RW Jr. Choice of initial therapy for hypertension. JAMA 1996;275:1577-80.

Linjer E, Hansson L. Underestimation of the true benefits of antihypertensive treatment: an assessment of some important sources of error. J Hypertens 1997;15:221-5.

Luft FC. Molecular genetics of hypertension. J Hypertens 1998; 16:1871-78.

Psaty BM, Smith NL, Siscovick DS, et al. Health outcomes associated with antihypertensive therapies used as first-line agents: a systematic review and meta-analysis. JAMA 1997;277:739-45.

The Sixth Report of the Joint National Committee on Prevention, Detection, Evaluation, and Treatment of High Blood Pressure. Arch Intern Med 1997;157:2413-46.

Staessen JA, Fagard R, Thijs L, et al. Randomised double-blind comparison of placebo and active treatment for older patients with isolated systolic hypertension. The Systolic Hypertension in Europe (Syst-Eur) Trail. Lancet 1997;350:757-64.

CHAPTER

9

Renal stone disease

Paul Jungers

Urolithiasis is now the most frequent of all renal diseases. Renal colic is the most common presenting symptom, reflecting acute obstruction of the urinary tract by a calculus lodged in the ureter. Urolithiasis is usually a painful but otherwise benign condition. However, some peculiar forms of stone disease, in relation to inborn errors of metabolism, may result in bilateral recurrent stones and crystal infiltration of the renal parenchyma, ultimately leading to loss of renal function.

Biochemical composition of stones

The chemical composition of stones is multiple. Calcium-containing stones are the preponderant type, with a cumulative prevalence of nearly 80%. Calcium oxalate is the main component (i.e., accounting for 50% of stone content) in more than 75% of cases, more frequently in male patients. Uric acid accounts for about 10%, being twice as frequent in males. Struvite (magnesium-ammonium phosphate, MAP) stones are now very infrequent (2%) in industrialized countries, whereas cystine stones represent about 1% of cases.

Calcium and uric acid stones are either secondary to an underlying pathologic condition or idiopathic (the most frequent situation). Proper identification of the chemical nature of stones and careful evaluation of the stone-forming patient are needed to provide a rational basis for preventive therapy.

Clinical findings

Signs and symptoms

Renal stones may be revealed by lumbar pain and/or gross hematuria (very suggestive if occurring after physical exercise) or discovered on incidental abdominal radiography or echography. Ureteral obstruction occurring in a patient with a solitary kidney may be revealed by sudden anuria. Silent, painless stones (such as large infection stones or uric acid stones) may cause insidious parenchymal alteration and may be revealed by chronic renal insufficiency. The most common presenting symptom of urolithiasis, however, is renal colic. Renal colic presents as an extremely intense, acute unilateral lumbar pain starting in the costovertebral angle and typically radiating downward to the inguinal ligament and testis. Pain often coexists with hematuria and frequency, as well as with such gastrointestinal symptoms as nausea, vomiting, and intestinal paresis that may falsely orient the diagnosis. When the stone has reached the terminal, juxtavesicular part of the ureter, urinary frequency and dysuria occur, possibly being mistaken for cystitis or prostatitis.

Diagnosis

Pain of renal colic must be differentiated from a number of other causes of abdominal or pelvic pain, as shown in Table 9.1.

Renal colic is the consequence of the distention of the renal capsule due to the increased pressure in the renal pelvis and calices above the obstructive stone. This enhances intrarenal production of prostaglandin E_2, resulting in a further increase in glomerular filtration pressure, often associated with a rise in systemic blood pressure. This explains why nonsteroidal anti-inflammatory drugs (NSAIDs) are effective in relieving the pain of acute urinary obstruction, inasmuch as they simultaneously contribute to reducing the inflammatory cushion formed in the ureteric wall in front of the obstructive stone.

Evaluation of the patient during renal colic aims to confirm the diagnosis of ureteric stone obstruction and to relieve pain.

Table 9.1 Differential diagnosis of renal colic

Appendicitis	Cystitis
Biliary colic	Prostatitis
Intestinal colic	Epididymitis
Gastric or duodenal ulcer	Orchitis
Cholecystitis	Testis torsion
Diverticulitis	Ovarian cyst torsion
Colitis, sigmoiditis	Ectopic pregnancy

If the patient has a known history of stones, plain x-ray and/or ultrasound usually suffices to establish the diagnosis. If renal colic is the first stone episode, intravenous pyelography (IVP) or spiral computed tomography is often required to ascertain the diagnosis and identify the size and location of the stone, either radiopaque or radiolucent. Evaluation also includes urinary dipstick (in a search for hematuria and infection), serum creatinine determination, and a blood count (to evaluative leukocytosis), urinary pH determination, and urine culture.

Radiodensity of urinary stones, on plain x-ray, based on their chemical composition, is given in Tables 9.2 and 9.3.

The major sign of renal colic on intravenous pyelography is retardation of radiocontrast filling in the affected kidney, with distention of the pyelocaliceal cavities and ureter above the obstructive stone. Small stones lodged in the juxtavesicular part of the ureter are poorly apparent but may be seen as an abnormally dense filling of the ureter. Echography may reveal a dilated pelvis and/or calices, but in the first hours following ureteric obstruction, pelvicaliceal distention may not be apparent.

A peculiar plain x-ray finding is medullary nephrocalcinosis, characterized by multiple small calcareous nodules clustered in the renal pyramids. Such a finding is suggestive of a metabolic disease associated with hypercalcemia (e.g., primary hyperparathyroidism or vitamin D excess) or with a distal tubular acidification defect (e.g., primary or secondary distal tubular acidosis or medullary sponge kidney) or papillary necrosis or calcified tuberculous lesions.

Treatment

The medical treatment of renal colic due to ureteric stone obstruction is based on parenteral administration of analgesics and NSAIDs, which rapidly decrease intrapyelic pressure. They should be used only in the presence of a functioning contralateral kidney (to avoid acute oliguria in the case of a solitary kidney) and in the absence of infection (since NSAIDs may promote pyelonephritic diffusion of urinary tract infection).

More than 80% of ureteric stones are passed spontaneously, especially if the stone diameter is less than 6 mm, whereas the probability of passage is virtually null when the stone exceeds 10 mm in diameter. When renal colic has ended, one should always verify that the stone has been passed and is not still lodged in the ureter with the risk of silent chronic obstruction.

Intervention of a urologist is needed to relieve ureteric obstruction in the case of intractable pain, severe pyelocaliceal distention, or superimposed urinary tract infection by means of palliative emergent placement of a ureteral stent or percutaneous nephrostomy. If not passed spontaneously, ureteric stones may be removed by means of extracorporeal shock-wave lithotripsy (ESWL) or, if this fails, ureteroscopy or (rarely now) open uroterolithotomy.

Table 9.2 Radiodensity of stones on plain x-ray on the basis of chemical composition

Radiopaque
- Calcium phosphate
- Calcium oxalate
- Magnesium-ammonium phosphate

Weakly radiopaque
- Cystine

Radiolucent
- Uric acid
- 2,8-Dihydroxyadenine
- Xanthine
- Triamterene
- Indinavir and other drugs
- Protein calculi

Table 9.3 Prevalence and x-ray opacity of urinary calculi

Chemical composition	Frequency	Opacity
Calcium oxalate	70%	Dense
Monohydrate (whewellite)		(Regular)
Dihydrate (weddellite)		(Radiate strippling)
Calcium phosphate	15%	Dense
Struvite + carbonate apatite	3%	Moderate
Cystine	1-2%	Faint to moderate
Uric acid, urates	10%	Radiolucent
Xanthine, 2,8-DHA, drugs	< 1%	Radiolucent

Surveillance of stone-forming patients

When properly evaluated and treated, renal stone disease is usually a benign condition, a part of painful episodes due to ureteric obstruction. Secondary forms of calcium urolithiasis respond only to etiologic treatment, such as removal of a parathyroid adenoma. In idiopathic forms of calcium nephrolithiasis, identification of lithogenic risk factors allows effective prevention of recurrence in the majority of cases (see Chap. 30).

However, when neglected or misdiagnosed, a prolonged ureteric obstruction may lead to renal atrophy and loss of function, especially if a urinary tract infection is superimposed. Large "staghorn" calculi, either infection stones or large cystine or uric acid stones, when left untreated or improperly managed, are especially prone to result in altered function of the affected kidney. In addition, some severe (fortunately infrequent) inborn metabolic diseases entail the risk of relentless crystal deposition in the renal parenchyma of both kidneys, resulting in progressive loss of renal function.

This is especially of concern in the case of 2,8-dihydroxyadenine lithiasis, primary hyperoxaluria type 1, congenital tubular acidosis, and Dent disease (or X-linked recessive nephrolithiasis). Such potentially severe forms of nephrolithiasis require full evaluation, adapted therapy, and regular follow-up to prevent the development of end-stage renal failure.

Suggested readings

GUPTA M, STOLLER ML. Acute and chronic renal pain. In: Coe FL, Favus MJ, Pak CYC, et al, eds. Kidney stones: medical and surgical management. Philadelphia: Lippincott-Raven, 1996;463-500.

JUNGERS P, DAUDON M, CONORT P. Lithiase rénale: diagnostic et traitement. Paris: Flammarion Médecine-Sciences, 1999.

RAMCHANDANI P, POLLACK HM. Radiologic evaluation of patients with urolithiasis. In: Coe FL, Favus MJ, Pak CYC, et al, eds. Kidney stones: medical and surgical management. Philadelphia: Lippincott-Raven 1996;369-435.

SECTION

3

Metabolic disorders

CHAPTER

10

Regulation and disturbances of sodium and water, and potassium homeostasis

Simona G.R. Racasan, Ton J. Rabelink

REGULATION AND DISTURBANCES OF SODIUM AND WATER BALANCE

The water and solute composition of the internal milieu is tightly regulated so as to maintain a constant internal balance that is essential for normal cellular function and adequate tissue perfusion. Total-body water is distributed between three body compartments: the intracellular volume, the interstitial space, and the intravascular space (the last two compartments form the extracellular volume). The total-body water averages 60% of lean body weight in men and 50% in women. On average, 60% of body water is confined to the intracellular compartment and 40% to the extracellular space, of which one-third constitutes the intravascular volume.

Water freely crosses the cell membranes that separate these compartments, its movement being driven by osmotic forces. The osmotic forces are determined by the solute composition, which is different for each of the body compartments; most solutes cannot freely cross the cell membranes, and cells accumulate or exclude specific solutes by active transport systems. Na^+ and Cl^- principally account for extracellular osmoles, and K^+, Mg^{2+}, organic acids and phosphates are largely confined to the intracellular space. Glucose crosses membranes through an insulin-activated transport system and is rapidly metabolized to glycogen or other compounds, so it is found only in the extracellular space. Urea freely crosses most cell membranes. If an osmotic gradient is generated by a difference in the concentrations of solutes, water will flow from the compartment of low osmolality to that of high osmolality in order to equalize the osmotic pressure so that the extracellular and intracellular fluids are in osmotic equilibrium.

Osmolality and tonicity *Osmolality* is a measure of the physical properties of the solutes. It can be measured using the freezing point or vapor pressure of a solution relative to a standard and is expressed in units of osmolality (milliosmoles of solute per kilogram of water, mosmol/kg) or osmolarity (milliosmoles of solute per liter of water, mosmol/l).

Tonicity is an expression of the forces that determine water movement across membranes that are permeable to water but impermeable to solutes. Measured osmolality (by the methods mentioned earlier, which are used in laboratories) does not give a real image of the solutes that drive water movement through membranes. This difference between measured osmolality and tonicity has lead to the term *effective osmolality*, which refers only to tonicity (the contribution to osmolality of only those solutes which cannot freely cross the cell membranes). These parameters can be calculated from the measured concentrations of the major solutes.

Plasma osmolality (P_{osmol}) can be calculated by the formula:

$$P_{osmol} = 2 \times \text{ plasma } [Na^+] + \text{plasma glucose} + \text{plasma urea}$$

where 2 reflects the osmotic contribution of the anions (assuming that each Na^+ is balanced by one anion), and all concentrations are expressed in millimoles per liter of water. Multiplying serum [Na^+] by 2 approximates the osmotic effect of Na^+ and its accompanying anions because NaCl is only 75% dissociated at the ionic strength of extracellular fluid, and only 93% of plasma is water (the rest is composed of lipids and proteins); these two factors would give an osmotic coefficient for NaCl of 1.86 × [Na^+]. Using factor 2 accounts for the contribution of other cationic components of plasma (K^+, Ca^{2+}, and Mg^{2+}).

Effective plasma osmolality (effective P_{osmol}) does not take into account plasma urea, which can cross most cell membranes freely, so it is not "osmotically effective":

$$\text{effective } P_{osmol} = 2 \times \text{ plasma [Na}^+\text{] + plasma glucose}$$

Under normal circumstances, plasma glucose represents only 5 mosmol/kg, so

$$\text{effective } P_{osmol} = 2 \times \text{ plasma [Na}^+\text{]}$$

This equation reflects the fact that Na^+ is the main determinant of plasma osmolality.

Normal values in humans for these parameters are P_{osmol} = 275 to 290 mosmol/kg, effective P_{osmol} = 270 to 285 mosmol/kg, and plasma [Na^+] = 135 to 145 mmol/l.

Total-body osmolality Since there is an equilibrium in osmolality between body water compartments owing to the free movement of water through cell membranes,

$$\text{effective } P_{osmol} = \text{effective osmolality of total-body water}$$
$$= \text{(extracellular + intracellular solutes)/(total-body water)}$$

The primary intracellular and extracellular solutes are Na^+ and K^+, so

$$\text{effective osmolality of total-body water} =$$
$$= (2 \times [Na_e^+ + K_e^+])/\text{(total-body water)}$$

where Na_e^+ and K_e^+ represent the "exchangeable" portions of these two ions (30% of Na^+ and a small part of K^+ are bond in tissues such as bone, where they are osmotically inactive), and 2 reflects the osmotic contribution of the anions accompanying Na^+ and K^+.

Combining the two equations, we have

$$\text{effective } P_{osmol} = 2 \times \text{ plasma [Na}^+\text{]} =$$
$$= (2 \times [Na_e^+ + K_e^+])/\text{(total-body water)}$$

Under normal conditions, the water content and solute content of the body are maintained within narrow limits by altering urinary excretion to match the variations in dietary intake.

Daily water loss is represented by insensible losses (through evaporation from skin and the respiratory tract, which can vary with exercise, climate, and such pathologic conditions as fever and hyperthyroidism), stool water, and renal water excretion. There is an obligatory renal water loss, which depends on solute excretion (ions and urea resulting from metabolism). A normal human has to excrete approximately 700 to 800 mosmol per day, which at the maximum urine concentration of 1200 mosmol/kg requires a minimum quantity of urine of 600 ml.

The water intake comes from drinking, water content of food, and metabolic oxidative processes. In order to maintain the balance, an obligatory intake of drinking water of 400 ml is necessary. Humans drink a higher volume of water than that induced by thirst, due mostly to social habits (Tab. 10.1).

The normal water balance has the purpose of maintaining plasma osmolality within normal values. When deviations from these limits occur, the body has homeostatic mechanisms that alter the rate of water intake or excretion. Water intake is influenced by thirst, and water excretion is regulated by antidiuretic hormone (ADH), which affects water reabsorption in the renal collecting tubules.

Thirst

Thirst can be defined as the conscious desire to ingest water. The most potent stimulus for thirst is an increase in osmolality. A rise of 2 to 3% of plasma osmolality above the osmotic threshold for thirst (the value of plasma osmolality above which an individual senses the desire to drink, a value that varies from person to person around 295 mosmol/kg) determines the sensation of thirst. The thirst threshold is about 10 mosmol/kg higher than the level of plasma osmolality that induces ADH secretion. Thirst is induced by stimulation of specific osmoreceptors in the anterolateral thalamus, which are localized near (but are not the same as) those which regulate ADH release. Besides osmolality, thirst is stimulated by hypovolemia and hypotension. The mechanisms by which those nonosmotic stimuli induce thirst are not known precisely but may involve the renin-angiotensin system.

The decline in plasma osmolality apparently suppresses water intake via a satiety mechanism. Stimulation of oropharyngeal receptors by drinking also suppresses thirst, but only for a short period of time. Thirst also has a component of central regulation (which influences drinking not related to plasma osmolality increase, i.e., social drinking).

Table 10.1 Normal human daily water balance

Source	Water intake (ml/day)	Source	Water output (ml/day)
Ingested water	1400	Urine	1500
Water content of food	850	Skin	500
Water of oxidation	350	Respiratory tract	400
		Stool	200
Total	2600	Total	2600

Antidiuretic hormone

Antidiuretic hormone (ADH), or arginine vasopressin, in humans is a nonapeptide produced by supraoptic and paraventricular nuclei in the hypothalamus as a prohormone; the granules containing the prohormone are transported down the axons into the posterior pituitary. The prohormone is cleaved into vasopressin and neurophysin (the vasopressin-binding protein) and stored in the neurohypophysis. Specific stimuli determine release of the hormone into circulation and an increase in prohormone synthesis.

Control of ADH release

The release of ADH is stimulated mainly by an increase in effective plasma osmolality and a reduction in blood volume and pressure. In addition, several other factors may influence ADH release (Tab. 10.2).

Osmotic regulation

Osmoreceptors situated in the region of anterolateral hypothalamus sense the variations of effective plasma osmolality. At levels lower than the threshold for ADH release (which is variable from individual to individual between 275 and 290 mosmol/kg, with an average of 280 mosmol/kg, and appears to be genetically determined), the plasma level of ADH is very low or undetectable. Minor (as low as 1-2%) variations of plasma osmolality increase levels of ADH enough to alter urinary flow and concentration (the osmoregulatory mechanism functions as a "set-point" receptor; see Fig. 10.1). Osmoreceptors are probably stimulated by volume variations of receptor neurons induced by water movement down a concentration gradient produced by the rise in extracellular solute concentration. The major osmotic stimulus for ADH release is plasma [Na^+]. Variations in plasma urea (a solute that crosses most cell membranes freely) or glucose (which enters cells by an insulin-mediated transport system and is there metabolized quickly) do not create the osmotic gradient and have a small effect on ADH release. However, in states of insulin deficiency, hyperglycemia leads to increased ADH release because its transport across the cell membrane is slower in the absence of insulin, and the osmotic gradient becomes effective. Infusing mannitol or sucrose, osmotic substances that do not equilibrate across cell membranes, induces ADH release as effectively as a rise in plasma [Na^+].

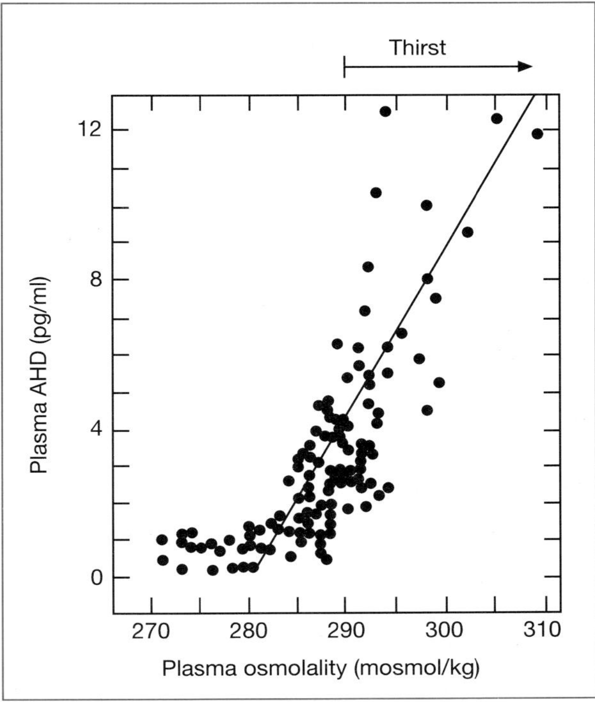

Figure 10.1 Relationship of plasma ADH and plasma osmolality in healthy subjects. Plasma osmolality was changed by varying the state of hydration. (Adapted with permission from Robertson GL, Aycinena P, Zerbe RL. Am J Med 1982;72:339.)

Table 10.2 Factors that influence ADH secretion

Stimulation	Inhibition
Hyperosmolality	Hypoosmolality
Hypovolemia (total or effective)	Hypovolemia
Hypotension	Increase in blood pressure
Nausea/emesis	Ethanol
Hypoglycemia	Drugs hormones:
Angiotensin II	Norepinephrine
Stress, pain	Promethazine
Hypoxia and hypercapnia	Morphine (low doses)
Temperature	Carbamazepine
Pregnancy	Glucocorticoids
Drugs hormones:	Phenytoin
Nicotine	Clonidine
Morphine (high doses)	
Epinephrine	
Isoproterenol	
Histamine	
Bradykinin	
Prostaglandins	
Cyclophosphamide	
Vincristine	
Insulin	
Chlorpropamide	
Clofibrate	
Naloxone	
Colecystokinin	

Hemodynamic regulation

Reduction in blood volume or/and pressure determines also ADH release; these changes are sensed by pressure receptors in the left side of the heart, aorta, and carotid sinus. The ADH response is different from that induced by osmotic stimuli; a reduction in blood pressure or volume of 5 to 10% does not increase ADH levels (or increases them very little), but at higher variations there is an exponential rise in plasma ADH, resulting in levels much higher than those induced by osmotic variations (Fig. 10.2).

Many pharmacologic or pathologic influences on ADH

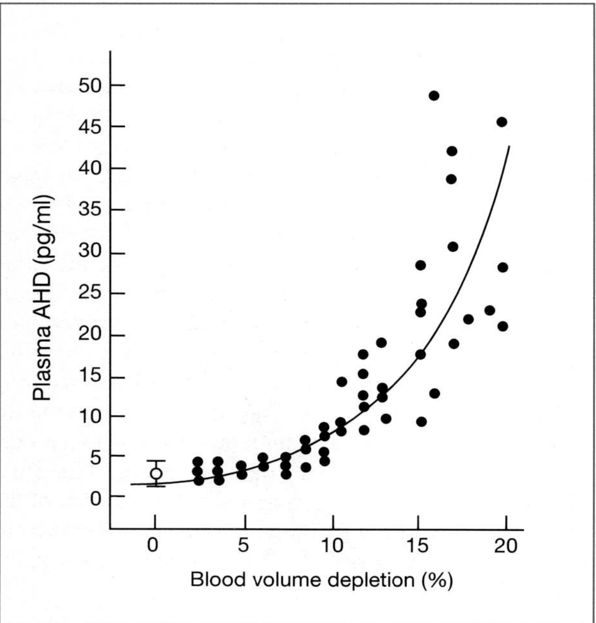

Figure 10.2 Relationship of plasma ADH to blood volume in the rat. (Adapted with permission from Dunn FL, Brennan TJ, Nelson AE, Robertson GL. J Clin Invest 1973;52:3212.)

release are mediated through baroreceptors. A reduction in blood pressure and/or volume is determined by diuretics, isoproterenol, prostaglandins, nitroprusside, histamine, morphine, and bradykinin; norepinephrine raises blood pressure. Upright posture, hemorrhage, congestive heart failure, cirrhosis, nephrosis, reduced total or effective blood volume, orthostatic hypotension, and vasovagal reactions lower blood pressure.

The influence of hemodynamic regulating mechanisms

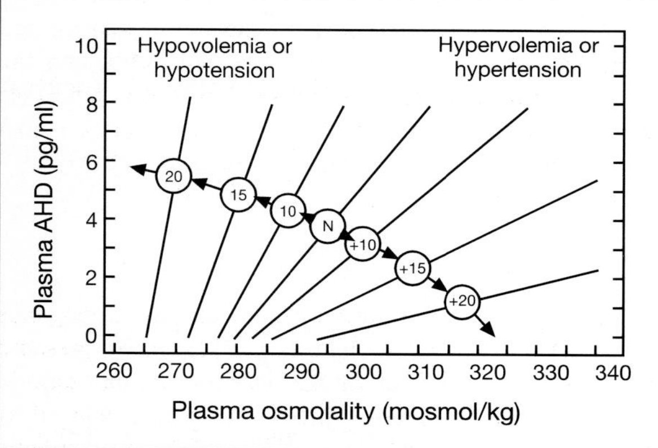

Figure 10.3 Influence of effective circulating volume on osmoregulation of plasma ADH in healthy subjects. The numbers in the circles refer to the percentage change in circulating volume from normal (N). (Adapted with permission from Robertson GL, Shelton RL, Athar S. The osmoregulation of vasopressin. Kidney Int 1976;10:25.)

does not alter the osmoregulation of the hormone. Variation in hemodynamic stimuli modifies the "setpoint" for osmotic regulation of ADH secretion; an increase in blood pressure or volume elevates the osmotic threshold, and a reduction lowers it (Fig. 10.3).

Other influences

Nausea is a strong stimulus for ADH release, but its effect is short and disappears immediately after the relief of symptoms; morphine, nicotine, alcohol, and colecystokinin act through the same mechanism.

Angiotensin II administered centrally into the ventricles of the brain or intravenously induces increased ADH release and water intake in animal experiments; thus angiotensin regulates not only sodium excretion by aldosterone release but also water intake and excretion by influencing thirst and ADH. The brain renin-angiotensin system is one of the mechanisms that regulate thirst and ADH release, and it acts synergistically with osmotic and hemodynamic stimuli. Vasopressin release in response to angiotensin is also a major pressor mechanism of central angiotensin II, besides activation of the sympathetic nervous system.

Pain, stress, emotion, experimental manipulation of the abdominal viscera, and fever have been shown to induce ADH release, but it is not proved that they have different pathways and do not act through their influence on blood volume and pressure and nausea. Due to the high incidence of the syndrome of inappropriate secretion of ADH in conditions that imply these factors (e.g., surgery, trauma, febrile illnesses), clarification of their role is important.

Hypoxia and hypercapnia induce ADH release. Moreover, a large number of drugs influence ADH secretion, most of them acting on the regulatory mechanisms already mentioned. Chlorpropamide seems to stimulate the secretion of ADH, and alcohol seems to inhibit it directly.

The physiologic role of ADH

The main role of ADH is regulation of free-water excretion. This effect is mediated through the V2 receptors on the basolateral membrane of the principal cells of the cortical and medullary collecting tubule. The interaction of ADH with V2 receptors induces the activation of adenylate cyclase, cAMP being the second messenger that initiates insertion of water channels (aquaporins) into the apical membrane of the collecting tubule cells that are otherwise impermeable to water. The water channels allow water to move down an osmotic gradient into the hypertonic medullary interstitium.

The interaction of ADH with V1 receptors on vascular smooth muscle cells, white cells, platelets, and endothelium has other effects (i.e., proliferation, vasoconstriction, enhanced coagulation) through a different second messenger, phosphatidylinositol.

The countercurrent mechanism

The capacity of the kidney to vary the osmolality of final urine is essential for water balance. The kidney can excrete urine with an osmolality ranging from 50 mosmol/kg to a maximum that averages 1200 mosmol/kg (between 900 and 1400 mosmol/kg) in humans. The kidney is able to excrete the obligatory 700 to 800 mosmol/day of solutes in a quantity of urine that varies from a minimum of 600 ml to many liters.

Besides the action of ADH on the collecting tubules, the countercurrent mechanism determines the capacity of the kidneys to concentrate or dilute the urine. The proximal tubule reabsorbs NaCl and water isoosmotically. The rest of the filtrate (35-40%) reaches the loop of Henle; in the thick ascending limb of the loop of Henle, which is impermeable for water, NaCl is reabsorbed in excess of water. The result is a diluted fluid that leaves the loop of Henle and an increased osmolality of the interstitium that has received solute but no water from this process. The descending loop of Henle is permeable to water, so water leaves the tubule in this segment of the nephron, equilibrating the intratubular fluid with the interstitium. This process goes on by continuously transporting NaCl from the fluid in the thick ascending limb of the loop of Henle to the interstitium so that the osmolality is highest at the hairpin of the loop and in interstitium at the tip of the papilla (900-1400 mosmol/kg).

The hypoosmolar fluid that leaves this diluting segment of the nephron (with an osmolality of about 100 mosmol/kg) reaches the collecting tubules that descend through the hyperosmolar medulla. The collecting tubule is impermeable to water and NaCl, so if no ADH reaches the collecting tubules, the kidney will produce a diluted urine. Osmolality in the urine is even lower (50-75 mosmol/kg) than in the fluid leaving the loop of Henle (100 mosmol/kg) because active NaCl reabsorption continues in the distal tubule. In the presence of ADH, collecting tubules allow water to leave the intratubular fluid and equilibrate with the high osmolality of the medullary interstitium. The final urine will have the maximum osmolality of the interstitium (around 1200 mosmol/kg). The effect of ADH in the cortical collecting tubules is essential for this concentrating ability; a high influx of water in the medullary interstitium will dilute the high interstitial osmolality and also the maximum concentration of urine. ADH acting in the cortical collecting tubules determines the reabsorption of about two-thirds of the water that enters the collecting tubule by allowing equilibration of the luminal fluid with the cortical interstitium, which is isoosmolar with plasma.

Urea also has an important role in determining the high osmolality of the medullary interstitium. The cortical and outer medullary collecting tubules are impermeable to urea; in the presence of ADH, as water leaves the tubular fluid, urea concentration increases. The collecting tubule becomes permeable to urea in the inner medulla (the presence of ADH increases the permeability of medullary collecting tubule for urea); there, urea leaves the intratubular fluid down a concentration gradient, and then a fraction of the urea reaching the interstitium reenters the tubular fluid in the descending and ascending limbs of the loop of Henle. The final effect is that urea concentration is highest in the collecting tubule downward to the inner medulla, which allows a greater quantity to be excreted in the final urine without water loss, and on the other hand, this recirculation of urea adds to the countercurrent mechanism, enhancing medullary osmolality.

The capillaries of the renal medulla, which have the same hairpin configuration as the loops of Henle, function as a countercurrent exchanger, maintaining the gradient of osmolality of the medulla that otherwise would dissipate. As the descending vasa recta enter the progressively more hypertonic medullary interstitium, water leaves and solutes enter the blood. In the ascending vasa recta, the inverse phenomenon takes place: water enters the vessels and solutes leave it, "trapping" in this way the hypertonicity in the medulla. On the other hand, vasa recta have the role to remove the NaCl and water reabsorbed in the loop of Henle and collecting tubules so that the volume of blood that leaves the ascending vasa recta is twice than that entering the descending vasa recta. The slow medullary blood flow (which accounts for only 6% of the renal blood flow) contributes to this countercurrent exchange; an accelerated blood flow would induce solute washout.

Free-water clearance C_{H_2O}

The concept of free-water clearance was developed in order to measure water handling by the kidney. When plasma tonicity is high, the kidneys should adapt by reabsorbing an excess of free water. In hypotonic states, the kidneys should excrete the excess free water. The free-water clearance measures the amount of solute-free water that can be excreted by the kidneys per unit of time. A volume of urine (V) that is not isoosmotic with plasma can be described as being composed by a volume that has the same osmolality as plasma and contains all the urinary solutes (equal to osmolal clearance C_{osmol}) and a volume of free water-the free-water clearance (C_{H_2O}):

$$V = C_{osmol} + C_{H_2O}$$

C_{H_2O} can be calculated by the usual formula for clearances:

$$C_{osmol} = (U_{osmol} \times V)/P_{osmol}$$

so

$$C_{H_2O} = V - C_{osmol} = V - [(U_{osmol} \times V)/P_{osmol}] = \\ = V[1 - (U_{osmol}/P_{osmol})]$$

When the urine is hypoosmolar to plasma, then C_{H_2O} has a positive value, indicating excretion of excess free water (positive free-water clearance). If the urine is hyperosmolar to plasma, C_{H_2O} has a negative value, indicating reabsorption of free water (negative free-water clearance).

HYPONATREMIA

Hyponatremia is defined as a reduction of plasma [Na^+] below 135 mmol/l and represents one of the disorders of osmolality.

Pathophysiology

Hyponatremia can be generated either by loss of solutes (Na^+ or K^+) or by excessive water retention. Solute depletion can occur by renal or nonrenal loss of fluids; usually excreted or secreted body fluids are isotonic or hypotonic in relation to plasma, so hypoosmolality occurs in these situations by replacement of lost fluid by more hypotonic solutions. One conclusion is that hyponatremia cannot occur without water intake. The physiologic response to a reduction in plasma osmolality, as produced by a water load, is diminished release and synthesis of ADH and excretion of a dilute urine. The kidney has the capacity to excrete large quantities of dilute urine, so water retention that results in hyponatremia can appear only when renal excretion of water is impaired.

Plasma [Na^+] also can be reduced by the presence in the extracellular fluid of a solute that is totally or partially excluded from the cells and that drives water out of the intracellular space, a situation that appears in hyperglycemia, after intravenous administration of mannitol, or after transurethral resection of the prostate or bladder when irrigant solutions of glycine, sorbitol, or mannitol are used. In these situations, there is a real hyponatremia because of increased water content of the extracellular fluid; the osmolality may be normal or, more frequently, elevated, showing an increased osmolal gap (the *osmolal gap* is defined as the difference between measured and calculated plasma osmolality; in normal subjects, the osmolal gap is close to 0 or arbitrarily said to be normal when it is less than 10 mosmol/kg).

There are also situations in which plasma [Na^+] is falsely lowered; plasma is composed of 93% water and 7% lipids and proteins; if plasma lipid or protein content increases severely, the methods that measure plasma [Na^+] in the total volume of plasma (such as flame photometry or indirect electrode techniques that involve dilution of the sample) but not techniques that sense [Na^+] in the aqueous phase (such as ion-specific electrode measurements) will give falsely low values of [Na^+]. This situation is called *pseudohyponatremia.*

Etiology

"True" hyponatremia can be classified on the basis of the effective circulating volume (as in Fig. 10.4) as (1)

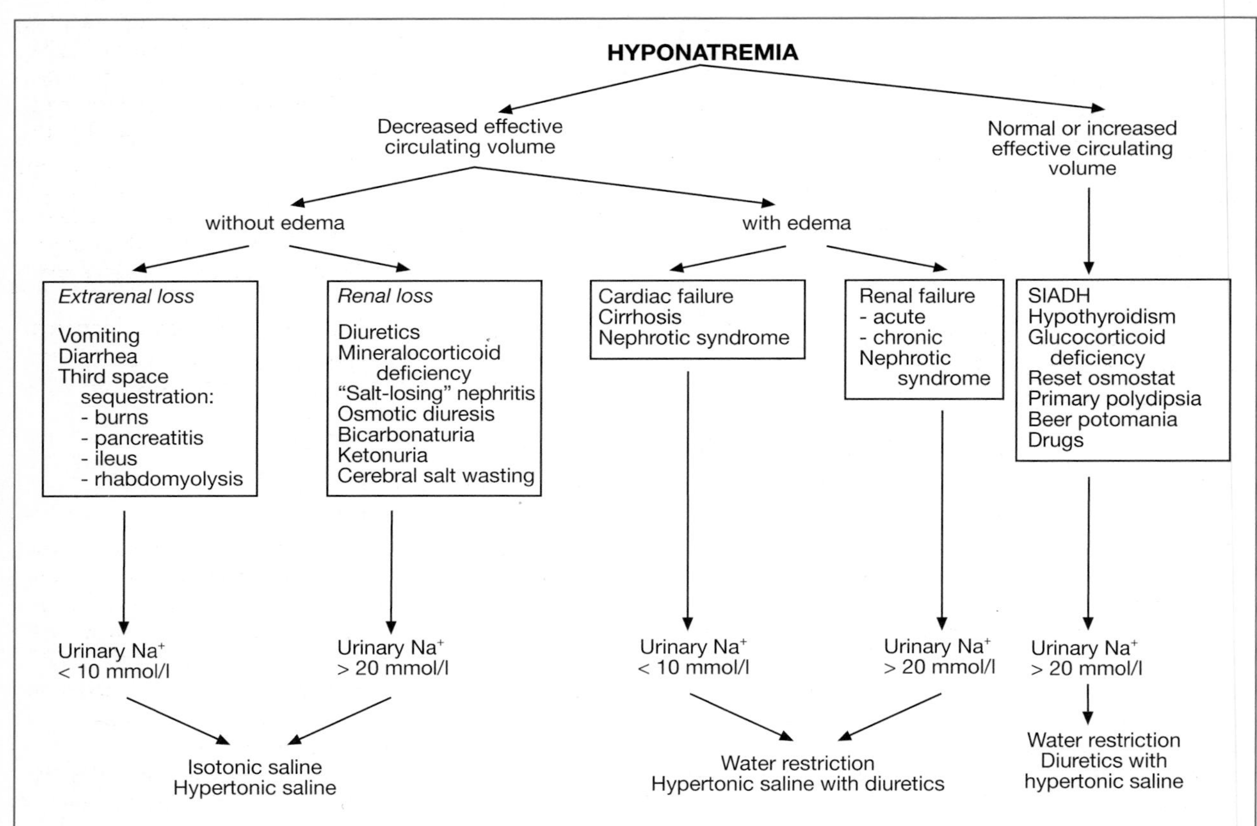

Figure 10.4 Diagnostic and therapeutic approach to the hyponatremic patient. (Adapted with permission from Berl T, Anderson RJ, McDonald KM, Schrier RW, Clinical disorders of water metabolism. Kidney Int 1076;10:117.)

hyponatremia with decreased effective circulating volume (with or without edema) or (2) hyponatremia with normal or increased effective circulating volume.

Hyponatremia with decreased effective circulating volume

This form of hyponatremia is characterized by a reduction in effective circulating volume caused either by loss of solutes and water, a situation in which total extracellular fluid volume is reduced, or by arterial underfilling, with increased total extracellular volume and edema formation. In both settings, the reduction in effective vascular volume is the stimulus for ADH release, and it resets the threshold for osmotic stimulation of ADH release to a lower point, and water is retained with the purpose of avoiding vascular collapse (the body is "sacrificing tonicity for volume").

Hyponatremia with decreased effective circulating volume without edema

This situation is characterized by a loss of total body Na^+ or K^+ in excess of the loss in body water. Patients are clinically hypovolemic, apparent from orthostatic hypotension and tachycardia, dry mucous membranes, decreased skin turgor, and flat jugular veins.

The source of sodium loss may be renal or extrarenal. Urinary Na^+ excretion helps differentiate between these two sources (see Fig.10.4). A low urinary Na^+ (<10 mmol/l) is found when extrarenal loss of solute leads to hypovolemia, and the kidney is responding by conserving Na^+. When urinary Na^+ is above 20 mmol/l, the kidney is the source of sodium loss.

Extrarenal volume depletion is due most commonly to gastrointestinal loss (e.g., vomiting, diarrhea, or gastrointestinal bleeding). Excessive sweating is less likely to be so important as to cause hyponatremia. Sequestration of fluids in the "third space" may appear in patients with burns, pancreatitis, ileus, and rhabdomyolysis.

Renal volume depletion may occur in a number of situations. Hyponatremia is a common complication of diuretics use. Women and old patients have a higher risk. The main mechanisms by which diuretics induce hyponatremia are (1) volume depletion, which will induce ADH release and decreased fluid delivery to the diluting segment of the nephron, (2) K^+ depletion, which will lower plasma K^+ and induce a shift of K^+ from the cells to extracellular space (as a consequence, Na^+ will enter the cells to maintain the electroneutrality), and (3) a direct lowering of NaCl reabsorption in the loop of Henle and distal tubule.

Diuretic-induced hyponatremia appears mainly with the use of thiazides and less with loop diuretics because they have different mechanisms of action (i.e., impaired Na^+ and Cl^- reabsorption in the thick ascending limb of the loop of Henle determined by loop diuretics reduces the osmolality of the medullary interstitium and limits water reabsorption in the collecting tubule under the action of ADH). Thiazides, which influence the distal tubule in the cortical segment, have no action on the concentrating mechanism in the medulla, so ADH stimulation can result in more water reabsorption.

Adrenal insufficiency leads to loss of Na^+ and Cl^- in the urine with volume depletion that will induce ADH secretion and water retention; hyponatremia with extracellular fluid contraction is associated in this setting with raised serum K^+, urea, and creatinine. Besides the lack of mineralocorticoid, the lack of cortisol plays a crucial role, since cortisol mediates a negative feedback for ADH release.

In hypothyroidism, impaired water excretion and hyponatremia are due to reduced delivery of fluid to the diluting segment because of the reduced renal plasma flow and glomerular filtration rate (GFR) and to secretion of ADH. Thyroid hormone therapy promptly reverses the diluting defect.

Tubular salt wasting appears in renal diseases that affect primarily the tubules, such as interstitial nephritis, medullary cystic disease, polycystic kidney disease, obstructive uropathy, and analgesic nephropathy. The marked and generalized injury to the distal tubule impairs reabsorption of Na^+ and Cl^- and secretion of K^+ and H^+. The result is inappropriately high sodium excretion with hyponatremia and potassium retention with hyperkalemia. The distal tubule is resistant to aldosterone, which is (secondarily) elevated.

Osmotic diuresis is induced by the presence in the urine of an osmotically active substance such as glucose in diabetes mellitus, mannitol administered intravenously, or urea after relief of an obstruction of the urinary tract or renal recovery after tubular necrosis. The osmotic substance (which must be nonreabsorbable or poorly reabsorbable) induces water loss in excess of Na^+ loss, and hyponatremia develops when lost fluid is replaced with more hypotonic solutions. The same effect is observed when a nonreabsorbable anion, such as bicarbonate, is eliminated in excess in the urine, as is the case in metabolic alkalosis and type II renal tubular acidosis. Ketonuria (in diabetes, starvation, or alcoholic ketoacidosis) also induces renal Na^+ wasting.

Cerebral salt wasting has been described in patients with subarachnoid hemorrhage; it has been suggested that the release of brain natriuretic peptide is the cause of sodium loss and volume contraction.

Hyponatremia with decreased effective circulating volume with edema

A reduction in effective circulating volume, sensed by baroreceptors, induces thirst, Na^+ retention, and ADH release. Avid Na^+ retention appears, with urinary Na^+ concentrations below 10 mmol/l; patients have an increased total-body Na^+ and a rise in total-body water that exceeds that of Na^+. Diuretics, commonly used in the treatment of these disorders, mask the reduced Na^+ excretion and further impair solute-free water excretion.

Congestive heart failure is frequently accompanied by hyponatremia. The delivery of fluid to the distal tubule is decreased because of reduced cardiac output and associated hormonal changes, such as stimulation of the renin-angiotensin system and catecholamine release.

Hepatic cirrhosis with ascites is also a common setting for hyponatremia. Reduced effective intraarterial volume is determined by hypoalbuminemia, splanchnic venous pooling, and lower peripheral resistance. Hyponatremia is a strong negative prognostic factor in both heart and liver failure.

Nephrotic syndrome is not so frequently associated with hyponatremia as the precedent diseases. In some patients (mainly children and adults with minimal-change nephropathy and with normal GFR), a reduction in effective circulating volume due to hypoalbuminemia increases ADH secretion. Other patients (mostly when a reduction in GFR occurs) have normal ADH secretion, and Na^+ retention is determined by an intrinsic intrarenal mechanism. The inadequate water excretion is correlated with the impairment of GFR.

Hyponatremia with normal or increased effective circulating volume

There are several causes of this type of hyponatremia (see Fig. 10.4); the most important is the syndrome of inappropriate antidiuretic hormone secretion (SIADH), which is the most common cause of hyponatremia in hospitalized patients. SIADH is characterized by nonphysiologic sustained release of ADH. The consequence is water retention, increased total-body water (intracellular and extracellular), and hypoosmolality. Volume receptors sense expansion of extracellular fluid and an increase in Na^+ excretion, and GFR is induced so that detectable edema does not occur. With continuous secretion of ADH, a new steady state is attained, with low plasma [Na^+], and Na^+ and water excretion equal intake. If water ingestion is restricted, SIADH cannot develop. The secretion of ADH in SIADH has been found to have four patterns: in 40% of patients there is no relationship between plasma osmolality and ADH secretion; in 33% the pattern is that of "reset osmostat" (ADH secretion responds to changes in plasma osmolality, but the threshold for ADH release is reduced); in about 16% there is a normal ADH release when plasma osmolality is increased, but a reduction in plasma osmolality fails to suppress ADH secretion; and in the remaining 14% normal levels of ADH are seen, and the cause of the hyponatremia is unknown, possibly resulting from an increased sensitivity to ADH or another antidiuretic factor. These patterns of ADH secretion show no relation to the etiology.

The conditions associated with persistent ADH secretion can be classified into three categories of diseases: malignancies, pulmonary disorders, and central nervous system diseases (Tab. 10.3). Central nervous system diseases cause SIADH by excessive release of ADH. Tumors are the source of ectopic production of ADH. AIDS patients are particularly at risk to develop SIADH (35% of hospitalized AIDS patients have this disorder) because of complications of the disease, namely, *Pneumocystis* pneumonia, central nervous system infections, and malignancies.

Such patients are clinically slightly hypervolemic; the increase in GFR reduces plasma urea, creatinine, and uric acid concentrations. The reduction in plasma [Na^+] depends on the balance between ADH and the amount of water intake but is usually lower than 130 mmol/l. Urinary [Na^+] varies with the intake and is usually higher than 40 mmol/l. Urinary osmolality is inappropriately high (>100 mosmol/kg).

Other causes of hyponatremia with normal or increased effective circulating volume are as follows: in reset osmostat, there is a normal response of osmoreceptors to variations of plasma osmolality, but with a lower threshold for ADH release and thirst. Plasma Na^+ has a lower but stable value. It may appear in SIADH, volume depletion, quadriplegia (due to the pooling of blood in the legs with reduction in effective blood volume), psychosis (associated with antipsychotic medication, but it also has been reported in patients off medication), and chronic malnutrition. Pregnancy is accompanied by a lowering of the threshold for ADH release due to the secretion of human chorionic gonadotropin, which contributes to systemic vasodilata-

Table 10.3 The etiology of the syndrome of inappropriate secretion of ADH

CNS diseases	Pulmonary diseases	Tumors
Infection	Pneumonias	Lung (small cell)
Encephalitis	Viral	Duodenum
Meningitis	Bacterial	Pancreas
Brain abscess	Fungal	Ureter
Head trauma	Tuberculosis	Bladder
Vascular thrombosis	Cystic fibrosis	Prostate
Subarachnoid/subdural hemorrhage	Pulmonary abscess	Thymoma
Hypoxic injury	Aspergillosis	Lymphoma
Multiple sclerosis	Respiratory insufficiency	Sarcoma
Brain tumors	Asthma	Mesothelioma
Guillain-Barré syndrome	Pneumothorax	Olfactory neuroblastoma
Autonomous neuropathy	Atelectasia	
Hypothalamic granulomas		
Acute psychosis		

tion and possibly affects the osmoreceptors. Renal failure, acute or chronic, may be associated with hyponatremia, when the reduction in GFR is severe.

Primary polydipsia occurs in psychotic patients, some of whom compulsively ingest large amounts of water daily, or in neurologic diseases such as multiple sclerosis, tuberculous meningitis, and sarcoidosis that may affect the hypothalamus. Most of these patients would drink about 3 to 5 liters of water a day, a quantity that can be readily eliminated by normal kidneys in the presence of normal food intake (e.g., given a daily solute excretion of 600 mosmol and a minimal urine osmolality of 50 mosmol/kg, a person can excrete 12 liters daily in the absence of significant hyponatremia). Hyponatremia develops only if ADH release is suppressed insufficiently, such as caused by antipsychotic drugs or when diuretics are used.

Drinking excessive amounts of beer can cause hyponatremia if it is associated with a low dietary intake, with reduction of solute excretion and hence also of water excretion. A patient who ingests high quantities of beer that is low in sodium and almost no other food will eliminate a lower quantity of solutes in the urine daily (around 200-300 mosmol/d), so at the maximum diluting capacity of the kidneys (50 mosmol/kg), the maximum quantity of water that can be eliminated is $250 \div 50 = 5$ liters. A higher fluid intake, not unusual for beer drinkers, can lead to water retention and hyponatremia. A similar syndrome has been described in individuals who have unbalanced diets (i.e., vegetarians, those on slimming diets) and ingest high quantities of fluids daily. Hyponatremia associated with both the two last conditions abates promptly with limited water intake and refeeding in the last setting.

Table 10.4 lists the drugs that are commonly associated with impaired water handling: (1) chlorpropamide potentiates the action of ADH and enhances solute reabsorption in the medullary ascending limb with increased interstitial osmolality, (2) anticonvulsants (carbamazepine) increase the release of ADH and potentiate the renal effect of the hormone, (3) antipsychotic drugs have been implicated in the etiology of hyponatremia in psychotic patients, although there is no clear evidence that they directly influence ADH release or its actions (these drugs also have an anticholinergic action leading to dryness of the mucous membranes and thirst stimulation), (4) antineoplastic drugs also may be associated with hyponatremia (vincristine has a neurotoxic effect on the hypothalamus, which increases the sensitivity of the osmoreceptors; cyclophosphamide enhances the tubular action of ADH and is particularly prone to cause hyponatremia because cyclophosphamide-treated patients are vigorously hydrated to avoid bladder complications), (5) narcotics reduce diuresis by an antidiuretic effect, and (6) angiotensin-converting enzyme inhibitors have been associated with a few cases of hyponatremia. The mechanism may involve increased ADH release induced through effective circulating volume reduction.

Table 10.4 Drugs associated with hyponatremia

- Hypoglycemic drugs
  - Chlorpropamide
- Anticonvulsants
  - Carbamazepine
  - Oxcarbazepine
- Antipsychotic agents
  - Phenothiazines
  - Tricyclic antidepressants
  - Haloperidol
  - Fluoxetine
  - "Ecstasy"
- Antineoplastic drugs
  - Vincristine
  - Vinblastine
  - Cyclophosphamide
  - Ifosfamide
- Narcotics
- Angiotensin-converting enzyme inhibitors

Clinical findings

Symptoms are mainly related to CNS dysfunction and are manifested by headache, nausea, and vomiting, progressing to disorientation, lethargy, seizures, and coma. Patients with a plasma [Na^+] higher than 125 mmol/l are usually asymptomatic; symptoms develop at a plasma [Na^+] below 120 mmol/l. The intensity of clinical manifestations is related to the severity of hyponatremia and the speed of its onset. Cerebral symptoms are due to brain swelling by water movement into brain cells. Brain cells adapt to hyponatremia by extrusion of, first, inorganic ions and, later, organic osmolytes (i.e., inositol, taurine, betaine, and glutamine). This response, which limits the increase in cell volume, is complete in 72 hours, so patients can tolerate severe hyponatremia much better if it develops gradually.

Diagnostic procedures

Plasma [Na^+] and osmolality confirm hyponatremia and hypoosmolality. If the measured osmolality is normal or elevated, causes of pseudohyponatremia should be investigated for. History, clinical examination, and further tests (e.g., determinations of plasma K^+, Cl^-, HCO_3^-, pH, urea, uric acid, and glucose concentrations and determinations of urinary Na^+, K^+, Cl^-, and osmolality) help the diagnosis. These tests allow differentiation between hyponatremia associated with low, increased, or normal effective circulating volume. Urinary [Na^+] is low (<10 mmol/l) in hyponatremia due to extrarenal loss of solute and in cardiac and hepatic failure. In SIADH, renal loss of solute, and reduced GFR, urinary [Na^+] is higher than 20 mmol/l. Observing the effect of an NaCl load on urinary osmolality and [Na^+] contributes to the diagnosis. If the patient is volume-depleted, urinary [Na^+] will remain low and urinary osmolality high because of volume-regulated ADH release. In SIADH, urinary [Na^+] will be high, and urinary osmolality remains high because of sustained ADH release. If excessive water intake is the cause of hyponatremia, urinary osmolality is low. Plasma uric acid is low in SIADH. Plasma $[K^+]$ and $[HCO_3^-]$ add information also: hypokalemia associated with metabolic alkalosis suggests vomiting or diuretics; hyperkalemia associated with metabolic acidosis appears in renal failure or mineralocorticoid deficiency; and hypokalemia associated with metabolic acidosis suggests loss of solutes by diarrhea. Primary polydipsia is associated to hypokalemia because of obligate loss of K^+ in the high urinary volume.

Treatment

The treatment of hyponatremia is addressed toward correcting the low plasma sodium concentration and the underlying cause. The therapeutic attitude is different in symptomatic hyponatremia, where the electrolyte disorder is life-threatening, and in asymptomatic hyponatremia, where there is no immediate danger, as well as in acute (more recent than 48 h) versus chronic hyponatremia. In chronic hyponatremia, brain adaptation to hypoosmolality has had time to develop, and rapid or excessive correction could lead to central pontine myelinolysis. This demyelinization syndrome is characterized clinically by tetraplegia, pseudobulbar palsy, and altered consciousness; it is often fatal or results in permanent brain damage. It is thought to be caused by brain cell dehydration due to overzealous correction, but it also can be caused by the hyponatremia itself. Besides postmortem diagnosis, lesions can be seen by computed tomographic (CT) scanning and by magnetic resonance imaging (which is more sensitive).

It is often difficult to determine the duration of hyponatremia, and the degree of clinical manifestations is variable. It is probably safe to correct hyponatremia at a rate of 0.5 to 1.0 mmol/l per hour (maximum, 20 mmol/l/d). Complete correction is not necessary, a level of 120 to 125 mmol/l being safe. Another recommendation is to use only water restriction whenever possible, because this treatment has the lowest rate of complications.

The management of hyponatremia depends also on effective circulating volume status. Hyponatremia with reduced effective circulating volume without edema, induced by extrarenal or renal solute and water loss, is treated by salt supplements, as isotonic saline (0.9%) in mild asymptomatic cases or hypertonic (3%) saline in symptomatic patients or if the plasma $[Na^+]$ is below 120 mmol/l. The Na^+ deficit can be calculated as follows: a 60-kg woman with a plasma $[Na^+]$ of 110 mmol/l, who has a total-body water of 50% of her body weight, has an $[Na^+]$ deficit of

$$Na^+ \text{ deficit} = 0.5 \times 60 \times (140 - 110) = \\ = 900 \text{ mmol } Na^+$$

For the initial therapy, the goal would be to raise the plasma $[Na^+]$ to 120 to 125 mmol/l in 24 hours, so

$$\text{initial } Na^+ \text{ deficit} = 0.5 \times 60 \times (125 - 110) = \\ = 450 \text{ mmol } Na^+$$

One thousand milliliters of hypertonic saline has 513 mmol Na^+, so about 900 ml of 3% saline contains the necessary amount of solute. After this first correction, isotonic saline can be used. These calculations are only an estimate, and repeated measurements of electrolytes and osmolality should be performed during the treatment. Special attention must be paid to thiazide-induced hyponatremic patients, in whom after the initial slow rise of Na^+ during volume correction the stimulus for ADH secretion disappears and a high quantity of dilute urine is produced, with the risk of a too rapid correction of hyponatremia.

Frequently, hyponatremia due to diuretics or gastrointestinal loss of fluids is accompanied by hypokalemia. Correction of hypokalemia is as effective as Na^+ administration in raising plasma $[Na^+]$ because the transcellular shift of K^+ into the cells after K+ supplementation drives Na^+ out of the cells. Excessive K^+ and Na^+ combined can overcorrect hyponatremia, however.

Hyponatremia with normal or increased effective circulating volume is produced by excess water retention in relation to solute and has SIADH as the most frequent cause. The best choice for treatment in this condition is water restriction associated with a normal Na^+ intake.

The excess water that has to be excreted can be calculated: a 70-kg man with a plasma Na^+ of 110 mmol/l, a plasma osmolality of 225 mosmol/kg, and a total-body water of 60% of his lean body weight (42 kg) has an excess water of

$$\text{excess water} = 0.6 \times 70 \times [(140 - 110)/140] = 9 \text{ liters}$$

His total-body osmoles are $42 \times 225 = 9450$ mosmol.

With water restriction, the excess water will be eliminated in several days. In symptomatic patients, this may be too long, so NaCl can be administered. Giving 2000 ml of isotonic saline (Na^+ and Cl^- content, 154 mmol/l; osmolality, 308 mosmol/kg) to the patient means an initial increase in plasma osmolality, because the solution infused has a higher osmolality. However, persistent ADH secretion maintains a high urinary osmolality, and the infused solute will be excreted in an amount of urine that depends on urinary osmolality. If the patient has a urinary osmolality of 775 mosmol/kg, the solutes will be excreted in

$$308 \times 2/775 = 616/775 = 0.8 \text{ liter of urine}$$

Thus total-body water will increase by 1.2 liters, and the patient's total-body osmoles will be distributed in 43.2 liters of water. The plasma osmolality will be even lower than in the beginning:

$$\text{plasma osmolality} = 9450/43.2 = 219 \text{ mosmol/kg} = \\ = 2 \times \text{ plasma } [Na^+] \\ \text{plasma } [Na^+] = 219/2 = 109.5 \text{ mmol/l}$$

Giving 1000 ml of 3% saline will do little better. The solute contained in it will be excreted in 1026/775 = 1.3 liters of urine, and only a 0.3-liter negative water balance is obtained. The way to improve this is to lower urinary osmolality through the use of a loop diuretic (furosemide 20 mg once or twice a day). This lowers urinary osmolality to about 300 mosmol/kg, and the solutes in the 3% saline will be eliminated in 1026/300 = 3400 ml of urine, which reduces total-body water by 2.4 liters. Plasma osmolality is 9450/39.6 = 238.6 mosmol/kg, and plasma [Na^+] is 119 mmol/l.

Chronic SIADH can be treated with water restriction, to which a high-salt, high-protein diet may be added (or 30-60 g urea per day orally); this will increase solute excretion as well as water excretion. An alternative is a loop diuretic together with NaCl supplements. Drugs that interfere with ADH action in the distal tubule (e.g., lithium or demeclocycline) can be used in patients who do not respond to or do not tolerate the diet and loop diuretic. Demeclocycline is better tolerated than lithium. Antagonists of the ADH receptor are not yet available for human use.

Patients with reduced effective circulating volume with edema (e.g., patients with congestive heart failure, cirrhosis, or renal failure) benefit from water restriction, but the reduction in circulating volume produces an intense thirst. A loop diuretic promotes [Na^+] and water loss, and then, in the same way as described above, plasma [Na^+] can be replaced by hypertonic saline.

HYPERNATREMIA

Hypernatremia is defined as a plasma [Na^+] higher than 145 mmol/l and represents one of the disorders of osmolality.

Pathophysiology

Hypernatremia is always an expression of hyperosmolality. It may be produced by water loss in excess of solute or Na^+ retention. The physiologic response to hyperosmolality is thirst and ADH release. Thirst is a potent stimulus, and hypernatremia appears only if water ingestion is impossible, because there is no water available (a rare situation), the individual is unable to search for water or communicate thirst (confused, comatose, old disabled patients, infants) or unable to ingest enough fluid to match losses (severe gastrointestinal loss), or thirst perception is reduced. The hyperosmolality of extracellular fluid induces water shift from the intracellular space, including brain cells, with cell dehydration.

Hyperosmolality also may result from the presence in plasma of other substances that are osmotically active (such as glucose, which cannot penetrate cell membranes in the absence of insulin) or osmotically inactive (such as urea or ethanol) and cross cell membranes but do not induce cellular dehydration.

Etiology

Similar to hyponatremia, hypernatremia can be classified according to the status of effective circulating volume into (1) hypernatremia with normal effective circulating volume (excess water loss), (2) hypernatremia with increased effective circulating volume (excess solute intake), and (3) hypernatremia with reduced effective circulating volume (excess solute and water losses) (Fig. 10.5).

Hypernatremia with normal effective circulating volume

This type of hypernatremia is induced by water loss in excess of solutes by renal or extrarenal routes. Total-body water is reduced, but patients appear euvolemic because overt volume contraction does not occur in the absence of Na^+ deficit.

Extrarenal losses occur through the lungs or skin in pathologic states such as burns, febrile illnesses, exercise at high altitude, exposure to high temperatures, and respiratory infections. Hypernatremia develops only if the patient does not have access to water or is unable to search for it. Urine osmolality is high (due to normal ADH release in response to the osmotic stimulus), and Na^+ excretion is variable, matching the intake (see Fig. 10.5).

Renal loss of water in excess of solute appears when there is an impairment in ADH production and/or release (e.g., central diabetes insipidus), renal response to ADH is impaired (e.g., nephrogenic diabetes insipidus), or in essential hypernatremia.

Diabetes insipidus

Impaired secretion of ADH or renal resistance to ADH induces elimination of high quantities of dilute urine (more than 3 l/d). Most patients do not develop hypernatremia because their thirst mechanism is intact; if diabetes insipidus is present in the postoperative or comatose patient, severe hypernatremia may occur. Causes of central diabetes insipidus are listed in Table 10.5.

Central diabetes insipidus is common after neurosurgery involving the hypothalamus, in children most frequently for craniopharyngiomas. Head trauma and brain tumors are also common causes. Lesions of the hypophyseal stalk may produce a transient reversible defect, or if the damage is more severe, the disturbance has a triphasic pattern: an initial polyuric phase, followed by a transient recovery and then by permanent central diabetes insipidus when the neurohypophyseal stores are depleted. Ethanol ingestion induces a transient inhibition of ADH secretion.

Nephrogenic diabetes insipidus is caused by the failure of the collecting tubules to respond to otherwise normal ADH release; the etiology is listed in Table 10.5. Familial nephrogenic diabetes insipidus is a rare condition; the defect is in most cases a mutation of V2 receptor gene on the X chromosome. Men express the disease, and women have various degrees of penetrance. An autosomal recessive form has been described, involving a mutation on chromosome 12, with an inactive tubular water channel.

The acquired form of nephrogenic diabetes insipidus is mostly due to lithium therapy, which inhibits cAMP generated by V2 receptor activation by ADH. The defect is usually (partially) reversible after cessation of treatment but may be permanent. The tetracycline-related drug demeclocycline has a similar mechanism. Hypercalcemia reduces the responsiveness of tubules to ADH and injures tubules by calcium deposition in the medulla. Severe hypokalemia interferes with NaCl transport in the thick ascending limb of the loop of Henle because sodium entry in the tubular cells of this segment of the nephron is realized by an Na^+-K^+-$2Cl^-$ carrier that is situated in the luminal membrane. All sites of the carrier must be occupied in order to make it functional, so when not enough K^+ reaches the distal tubule, NaCl reabsorption is impaired. Acute and chronic renal failure is accompanied by reduced concentrating ability due to osmotic diuresis (increased solute excretion in the remaining nephrons) and disturbed architecture of the medulla. Some kidney diseases, such as polycystic kidney, chronic obstructive nephropathy, analgesic nephropathy, renal amyloidosis, and sickle cell disease, that affect the renal medulla more in the initial stages may produce a reduction in concentrating ability that is disproportionate to the reduction in GFR, leading to hypernatremia.

Table 10.5 Causes of diabetes insipidus

Central	Nephrogenic
Head trauma	Familial: X-linked (V_2 receptor)
Postoperative	Autosomal (aquaporin)
Hypophysectomy	Acquired
Craniopharyngioma	Drugs:
Hypothalamic tumors	Lithium
Infections	Demeclocycline
Encephalitis	Loop diuretic
Meningitis	Osmotic diuretics
Brain tumors	Amphotericine
Primary	Vasopressin antagonists
Metastatic	Polycystic kidney disease
Hypoxia	Medullary cystic disease
Aneurysms	Obstructive uropathy
Granulomas	Analgesic nephropathy
Tuberculosis	Multiple myeloma
Sarcoidosis	Renal amyloidosis
Wegener granulomatosis	Sickle cell disease
Histiocytosis	Electrolyte disorders
Guillain-Barré syndrome	Hypokalemia
Idiopathic	Hypercalcemia
Familial	Acute and chronic renal failure
Isolated cases	
Ethanol ingestion (transient)	

Primary hypodipsia

Hypodipsia may appear secondary to a lesion affecting the osmoreceptors that regulate thirst. Reduced thirst perception severe enough to induce hypernatremia is rare; the patients do not replace the daily obligatory water loss. The same causes that produce diabetes insipidus can affect the osmoreceptors that regulate thirst, situated close by (tumors, surgery, trauma of the hypothalamic region).

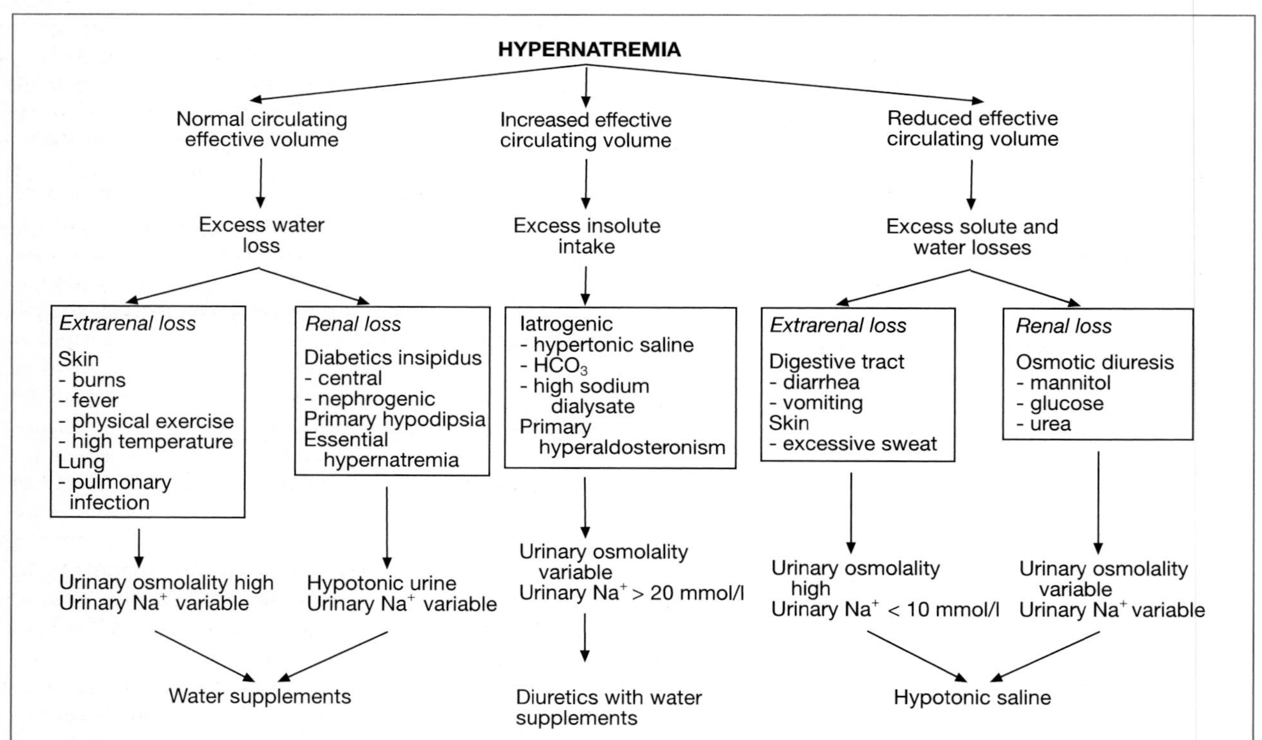

Figure 10.5 Diagnostic and therapeutic approach to the hypernatremic patient. (Adapted with permission from Berl T, Anderson RJ, McDonald KM, Schrier RW, Clinical disorders of water metabolism. Kidney Int 1076;10:117.)

Frequently there is also a degree of impairment of ADH release.

Essential hypernatremia refers to hypernatremia that results because of the resetting of osmostat for ADH secretion in an upward direction. It seems that in this setting, osmoreceptors are rather insensitive to plasma osmolality, more than being reset, because they fail to maintain a constant level of plasma Na^+, and plasma ADH regulation is realized through volume receptors.

Hypernatremia with increased effective circulating volume

This is a rare form of hypernatremia; it can result from accidental, deliberate, or (mostly) iatrogenic excessive Na^+ intake. Deliberate or accidental ingestion of high amounts of salt is extremely rare, but instillation of NaCl in the uterus for abortion has been described, and parenteral infusion of hypertonic NaCl or $NaHCO_3^-$ for the treatment of metabolic acidosis, hypoosmolality, or cardiac arrest and the use of high Na^+ content dialysate may induce severe hypernatremia. Patients are hyperhydrated and have high plasma and urinary [Na^+]. The moderate hypervolemia associated with primary hyperaldosteronism resets the osmoreceptors for ADH secretion at a higher value (145-150 mmol/l usually).

Hypernatremia with reduced effective circulating volume

This form of hypernatremia is produced by renal or extrarenal loss of water in excess of solutes (loss of hypotonic fluids). The causes (listed in Fig. 10.5) of this kind of hypernatremia more frequently result in hyponatremia because thirst and ADH stimulation by volume contraction determine water intake and dilution of the ECF. However, if the patient cannot ingest water or signal thirst, hypernatremia appears. Volume contraction is apparent by orthostatic hypotension, tachycardia, flat neck veins, dryness of mucous membranes, and altered mental status.

Extrarenal losses are mostly gastrointestinal (e.g., diarrhea, vomiting, or use of osmotic agents that induce diarrhea, such as lactulose or charcoal-sorbitol). Excessive skin loss through sweat acts in the same way. Patients have low urinary [Na^+] and high urinary osmolality.

Renal loss appears in osmotic diuresis, which promotes water excretion in excess of solutes (glucose, mannitol). Urinary [Na^+] and osmolality are variable in this form of hypernatremia.

Clinical findings

Clinical findings are mainly related to the neurologic consequences of the disturbance. The hyperosmolality of the extracellular space drives water out of cells. Cell shrinkage induces a decrease in brain volume and rupture of cerebral veins with focal intracerebral and subarachnoid hemorrhages. Brain cells defend themselves from cellular dehydration by water movement from the cerebrospinal fluid into the brain due to the pressure difference, by electrolyte entry into the cells, and by increased cellular content of organic osmolytes.

These mechanisms diminish symptoms but must be taken into account in the treatment of hypernatremia because a too rapid correction of plasma [Na^+] can induce cerebral edema. Clinical manifestations of hypernatremia are severe thirst, sensation of dry mucous membranes, nausea, weakness, somnolence, seizures, and coma. Because most patients with severe hypernatremia have some degree of neurologic dysfunction, it is often difficult to assess impairment due to hypernatremia itself. Signs of volume expansion (peripheral or pulmonary edema) or dehydration may be present. Polyuria, polydipsia, and nocturia are the main complaints of patients with diabetes insipidus.

Diagnostic procedures

History is usually difficult due to neurologic symptoms. Urine [Na^+] and osmolality are of great help in the etiologic diagnosis of hypernatremia (see Fig. 10.5). A low urinary [Na^+] and high urinary osmolality are features of extrarenal loss of water or hypotonic fluids. A high (>20 mmol/l) urinary [Na^+] and normal or high urinary osmolality are found in Na^+ overload and primary hyperaldosteronism.

The polyuric patient may have renal water loss due to osmotic diuresis or diuretics (situations that may be excluded easily), diabetes insipidus (central or nephrogenic), or primary polydipsia. A water restriction test can be used to differentiate between these causes. Patients are submitted to complete water restriction until urinary osmolality reaches a plateau or plasma osmolality rises to 295 to 300 mosmol/kg. Urinary osmolality remains below 300 mosmol/kg in "complete" central or nephrogenic diabetes insipidus, and urine output remains high; urinary osmolality rises to a value of 300 to 600 mosmol/kg in "partial" central or nephrogenic diabetes insipidus; in primary polydipsia, urinary osmolality reaches 500 to 800 mosmol/kg. The administration of exogenous ADH after the water restriction differentiates between central (positive response, with an increase in urinary osmolality by at least 100 mosmol/kg) and nephrogenic diabetes insipidus (no response).

Treatment

The purpose of the treatment is restoration of plasma osmolality. A similar problem as in hyponatremia appears: if brain cells have had time to adapt to ECF hyperosmolality, then a rapid correction of plasma osmolality will induce water shift into the cells and cerebral edema. The rate of correction needs to be slow (0.5 mmol/l/h), unless the patient is symptomatic.

The treatment differs according to the effective circulating volume status: for the patient with apparently normal effective circulating volume who has water loss as the cause of hyponatremia, replacement of the water deficit is indicated. The water deficit can be calculated as follows:

$$\text{total-body osmoles} = \text{total-body water (TBW)} \times P_{osmol} = \\ = \text{TBW} \times (2 \times \text{plasma [Na}^+])$$

If the hyponatremia is due to water loss only, then

$$\text{current body osmoles} = \text{normal body osmoles}$$

Normal plasma [Na^+] is 140 mmol/l, so

$$\text{current body water (CBW)} \times \text{plasma [Na}^+] = \\ = \text{normal body water (NBW)} \times 140$$

$$\text{NBW} = \text{CBW} \times \text{plasma [Na}^+]/140$$

$$\text{water deficit} = \text{NBW} - \text{CBW}$$

$$\text{water deficit} = [\text{CBW} \times (\text{plasma [Na}^+]/140)] - \text{CBW}$$

$$\text{water deficit} = \text{CBW} \times [(\text{plasma [Na}^+]/140) - 1]$$

For instance, for a 60-kg woman with a plasma [Na^+] of 160 mmol/l and a total-body water of 50% of the lean body weight (but in states of volume depletion, total-body water is estimated as being 10% lower):

$$\text{water deficit} = 0.4 \times 60 \times [(160/140) - 1] = \\ = 3.4 \text{ liters}$$

This amount of fluid could be administered as 5% glucose in water over the next 40 hours to achieve a rate of correction of 0.5 mmol/l per hour. At the same time, urinary and insensible water losses (30-50 ml/h) also should be replaced, as well as, if present, gastrointestinal losses. Frequent monitoring of plasma electrolytes and osmolality is required.

For the patient with *reduced effective circulating volume*, quarter-isotonic saline can be used, but if the patient is hypotensive because of hypovolemia, the treatment should begin with isotonic saline in order to restore tissue perfusion, and then more hypotonic solutions may be used. The cause should be addressed.

Patients with *increased effective circulating volume* should be treated by stopping the source of Na^+; if renal function is normal, the kidneys will eliminate rapidly the excess Na^+, and adding a loop diuretic with replacement of urine output only with water lowers the plasma osmolality further. Attention must be paid to the fact that these patients are volume-expanded, so there is a high risk of pulmonary edema. When renal function is impaired, hemodialysis or peritoneal dialysis is indicated.

Treatment of diabetes insipidus Central diabetes insipidus is treated with ADH hormone replacement in the form of aqueous vasopressin subcutaneously (5-10 units every 4-6 h), as tannate vasopressin intramuscularly (2-5 units every 24-48 h), or as nasal spray (lysine vasopressin). These preparations have been replaced largely by desmopressin (10-20 µg intranasally every 12-24 h). The main complication of the treatment is water intoxication; there is no risk of hypernatremia without treatment because of the thirst mechanism, but after the initiation of treatment, ADH has no mechanism of regulation. Therefore, the minimum dosage that reduces urine output should be used, and patients should be instructed to observe their water intake and body weight.

Non-ADH drugs can be used, such as:

- chlorpropamide, which promotes the renal action of ADH, in doses of 125 to 250 mg once or twice daily;
- carbamazepine (100-300 mg twice daily), which increases the effect of ADH, and clofibrate (500 mg every 6 h), which increases ADH release;
- thiazide diuretics, which may reduce the urine output of diabetes insipidus patients even without ADH supplements by inducing a mild volume depletion, which enhances proximal tubular reabsorption (less water reaches the site of ADH action).

The association of a low-sodium, low-protein diet will further lower urine output, and a potassium-sparing diuretic (amiloride) enhances the effect.

Nephrogenic diabetes insipidus does not respond to ADH or drugs that act through increased ADH secretion or action. Treatment can be accomplished by allowing enough water intake and using thiazide diuretics along with a low-sodium, low-protein diet. Amiloride, besides increasing the effect of thiazide diuretics, is specifically indicated in lithium-induced nephrogenic diabetes insipidus because it prevents accumulation of lithium in collecting tubule cells. Nonsteroidal anti-inflammatory drugs (NSAIDs), by inhibiting prostaglandin synthesis, antagonize their effects on water and sodium handling in the kidneys, the result being a reduced volume of urine due to an increase in the medullary osmolality (by enhanced Na^+ and Cl^- transport in the thick ascending limb of the loop of Henle and increased urea transport from the collecting tubule) and by reducing medullary blood flow. In some cases of nephrogenic diabetes insipidus, the combination of a thiazide diuretic with a NSAID gives the best results.

HYPEROSMOLALITY DUE TO HYPERGLYCEMIA

This is the final type of disorder of osmolality.

Pathophysiology

Hyperglycemia is a commonly encountered form of hyperosmolality. Insulin deficiency and/or resistance increases the level of glucose in plasma, with high osmolality. Besides hyperosmolality, there are various other life-threatening disturbances that may accompany hyperglycemia. Plasma [Na^+] may be reduced, normal, or increased. Hyperglycemia drives water out of cells, with dilutional hyponatremia; a 3.5 mmol/l increase in plasma glucose corresponds to a 1 mmol/l lowering of plasma [Na^+]. Osmotic diuresis by glucosuria and ketonuria implies water loss in excess of Na^+ and promotes hypernatremia but also causes Na^+ loss. Hypovolemia due to osmotic diuresis is a common feature. Low water intake may contribute in elderly, confused hyperglycemic patients. Plasma [K^+] also may be high, normal, or reduced. Osmotic diuresis implies K^+ loss, but ketoacidosis and hyponatremia drive K^+ out of cells and increase the plasma [K^+]. This explains why plasma [K^+] at presentation is usually normal to high, even though patients frequently have a total-body potassium deficit of several hundreds millimoles due to urinary loss. Acidosis is also dangerous, and other acid-base disorders may occur. Renal function frequently is moderately impaired, especially due to hypovolemia.

Etiology

There are two types of severe hyperglycemia in diabetic patients: diabetic ketoacidosis (which appears mostly in patients with insulin-dependent diabetes mellitus) and nonketotic hyperglycemia (which is more frequent in patients with non-insulin-dependent diabetes mellitus). Diabetic patients may develop these conditions in certain situations, such as omission of therapy, infections, surgery, or dehydration. It is not well known why some patients develop impressive hyperglycemia without ketoacidosis. Non-insulin-dependent diabetes mellitus patients seem to have higher levels of insulin in the portal system than insulin-dependent diabetic patients, so liver ketogenesis is inhibited.

Clinical findings

Patients have symptoms related to hyperglycemia and glucosuria (e.g., polyuria, polydipsia, and weight loss), related to hypovolemia (e.g., increased thirst, orthostatic hypotension, and tachycardia), and to hyperosmolality, with the same consequences for neurologic function as in hypernatremia. The hyperosmolality of the ECF drives water out of brain cells, and the same defense mechanisms develop as in hypernatremia. Brain dehydration is manifest as lethargy, motor or sensory defects, seizures, and coma. A too rapid correction of the hyperosmolality is associated with similar risks of cerebral edema as the hypercorrection of hypernatremia. In ketoacidosis, the symptoms of metabolic acidosis are additive (i.e., hyperventilation).

Diagnostic procedures

Hyperglycemia is diagnostic. Before starting treatment, information must be obtained about plasma electrolytes, osmolality and acid-base status, urinary glucose, electrolytes, and ketones. Serum urea and creatinine may be elevated because of renal impairment by hypovolemia.

Treatment

Treatment should be supported by frequent monitoring of plasma and urinary parameters. Insulin and rehydration are the most important measures. Insulin lowers the plasma glucose level, reduces ketone production, and promotes ketone use. Crystalline insulin is used in the acute phase, intravenously, subcutaneously, or intramuscularly. Doses of 15 to 20 units are used at first, and then around 10 to 15 units per hour are usually enough. If the patient is hypovolemic, volume supplementation should precede insulin.

For example, a patient with a plasma glucose concentration of 33.5 mmol/l, [Na^+] of 133 mmol/l, [K^+] of 2.9 mmol/l, [HCO_3^-] of 15 mmol/l, arterial pH of 7.30, urea concentration of 8 mmol/l, creatinine concentration of 140 μmol/l, plasma ketones positive, and overt signs of hypovolemia should be treated initially with isotonic saline with 40 mmol K^+ added in each liter of saline. Starting insulin first would have two deleterious effects: by driving glucose into cells and lowering plasma osmolality, it induces water entry into the cells with accentuation of the hypovolemia. Also, it drives K^+ into cells, exacerbating the hypokalemia. After about 2 liters of this fluid replacement, a reevaluation of the patient's clinical status and laboratory data leads the treatment.

Rehydration Fluid lost due to osmotic diuresis is hypotonic. Rehydration is started with isotonic saline, which restores the ECF and lowers plasma osmolality and glucose concentration. Hypotonic saline can be used after the patient is rehydrated, but rapid lowering of plasma osmolality is dangerous.

Potassium is added to the fluids infused as soon as the plasma [K^+] falls below 4.5 mmol/l, and if it is low, from the beginning. The normal or high [K^+] value is false in these patients because of the transcellular shift of K^+ due to insulin deficiency. Treatment results in an opposite movement of K^+ and possible severe hypokalemia.

Bicarbonate therapy is indicated only if plasma pH is below 7.10, because of possible cardiac depression, or if there is a normal anion gap, which means that no ketoacids are available for bicarbonate regeneration. An overcorrection of acidemia by bicarbonate may, by reducing the stimulus for hyperventilation, increase P_{CO_2} rapidly. CO_2 crosses the blood-brain barrier and paradoxically decreases brain pH.

REGULATION AND DISTURBANCES OF POTASSIUM HOMEOSTASIS

Ton J. Rabelink, Kim Edwards-Teunissen, Hein A. Koomans

The normal, dietary intake of potassium for an adult is 80 to 100 mmol per day (all the following absolute values given refer to healthy adults). This potassium is almost entirely absorbed by the intestines. Under normal conditions, 90% is eliminated through the kidneys and 10% through the intestines. The only cause of potassium retention is kidney disease. However, both the kidneys and the intestines can be sites of potassium loss.

The normal potassium stores amount to about 3000 to 4000 mmol, or 50 to 55 mmol/kg of body weight. Most of the potassium by far is found intracellularly (i.e., muscle, bone, liver, and erythrocytes) at a concentration of 150 mmol/l. The concentration in ECF is much lower, about 4.0 to 4.5 mmol/l. This means that given a total extracellular volume of 14 liters, only about 65 mmol K^+ (2% of the total-body potassium at most) is found extracellularly. This large difference between intra- and extracellular [K^+] means that two components are involved in potassium balance regulation: regulation of total-body potassium through potassium excretion (external K^+ balance) and regulation of the distribution of potassium between intra- and extracellular compartments, which depends on the external balance (internal balance).

Potassium plays an important role in the formation of the resting potential across the cell membrane. The resting membrane potential is largely based on the relationship between intra- and extracellular [K^+]. Because the resting membrane potential is essential for the development of an action potential, potassium is extremely important for the proper functioning of excitable tissues (e.g., muscle strength, heart rate and contractility). Potassium is also important for cell metabolism; during K^+ deficiency, many cellular functions can no longer be carried out (e.g., disturbances in renal concentration).

Internal K^+ balance

Two factors, namely, Na^+,K^+-ATPase pump activity and cell membrane potassium permeability, determine the steady-state transmembrane K^+ gradient and in so doing the plasma [K^+]. All factors that, acutely or chronically, regulate or influence the plasma [K^+] do so by influencing either Na^+,K^+-ATPase activity or K^+ permeability or both.

Na^+,K^+-ATPase and K^+ permeability

Na^+,K^+-ATPase is the motor that maintains differences in Na^+ and K^+ concentrations across the membrane. It promotes cellular Na^+ efflux and K^+ influx at a ratio of Na^+_{eff}:K^+_{in} = 3:2. Na^+ leaks into the cell along the thus created gradient; however, this occurs very slowly due to the low membrane permeability to sodium. Membrane permeability is also low for K^+, but 100 times higher than that for Na^+. Consequently, K^+ leaks more easily out of the cell and causes an electrical gradient across the membrane (outside more positive than inside) of about 90 mV cell negative resting membrane potential. This results in an intracellular to extracellular K^+ gradient of approximately 150:4. This gradient, and thus the K^+ distribution over intra- and extracellular spaces, can be influenced acutely or chronically.

The need for rapid regulation becomes apparent by examining what happens when a single dose of potassium is given. When a healthy adult consumes 75 mmol K^+ (approximately the normal consumption for an entire day) at once, not only have the intestines absorbed the entire amount, but the plasma [K^+] also has already reached its peak within 2 hours (Fig. 10.6). At this point, about 35 mmol is excreted via the urine. If the remaining 40 mmol were to stay in the extracellular compartment (• 4 liters), then the plasma [K^+] would rise a worrisome 3 mmol/l. In reality, plasma [K^+] rises only 0.7 to 1.0 mmol/l; this means that the larger portion of the absorbed K^+ is stored in the cell. Cell storage is temporary; the rise in plasma [K^+] stimulates renal potassium excretion, causing the plasma [K^+] to fall and the intracellular stored K^+ to be mobilized out of the cell. The entire K^+ dose is excreted within 6 to 8 hours.

This cycle repeats itself at every meal. The temporary K^+ storage in the cell that occurs after every meal protects against life-threatening hyperkalemia. This process occurs primarily in muscle cells, where most of the K^+ is found. The rise in plasma [K^+] is assumed to be the most important force driving this intracellular uptake. Insulin, catecholamines, and aldosterone all play a role in this process as well.

Insulin

Administration of insulin causes a rapid fall in plasma [K^+] by stimulating cellular uptake. This uptake concerns liver cells initially and later is followed by muscle cells. The mechanism is not completely understood. Insulin stimulates Na^+/glucose transport into the cell, which results in a higher intracellular [Na^+] and activation of the Na^+,K^+-ATPase pump. Insulin stimulates Na^+,K^+-ATPase and cell K^+ uptake, however, independent from glucose; the effect occurs earlier and at lower insulin concentrations than that of glucose uptake. Insulin also has an effect on the above-mentioned (temporary) cellular storage of K^+ intake; the rise in plasma [K^+] after K^+ intake is higher in the absence of insulin. Administration of K^+ alone does not increase the plasma insulin concentration. Under these conditions, insulin only facilitates the cellular storage of ingested K^+. However, potassium is usually ingested together with glucose (e.g., by a meal), a situation in which insulin plays more than only a facilitating role.

Catecholamines

β_2-adrenergic signals stimulate Na^+,K^+-ATPase and therefore the K^+ intake by the cell. This is also an acute phenomenon, as becomes apparent by the administration of β_2-selective sympathomimetics. Just as is the case with insulin, β_2-adrenergic tone facilitates the cellular uptake of acutely ingested K^+; the rise in plasma [K^+] after a meal or exercise is higher during β_2-blockade. A K^+ load, however, has no influence on sympathetic tone. Strong adrenergic stimulation (stress, administration of epinephrine or β_2-sympathomimetics) can easily lead to a fall in the plasma [K^+] on the order of 0.5 to 1.0 mmol. β-Receptor stimulation, on the other hand, lowers the cellular K^+ uptake and strengthens the hyperkalemic effect of K^+ administration. The physiologic explanation and the receptor subtype concerned (1 or 2) are not known.

Mineralocorticoids

Although mineralocorticoid involvement in intra- and extracellular K^+ distribution is not completely supported

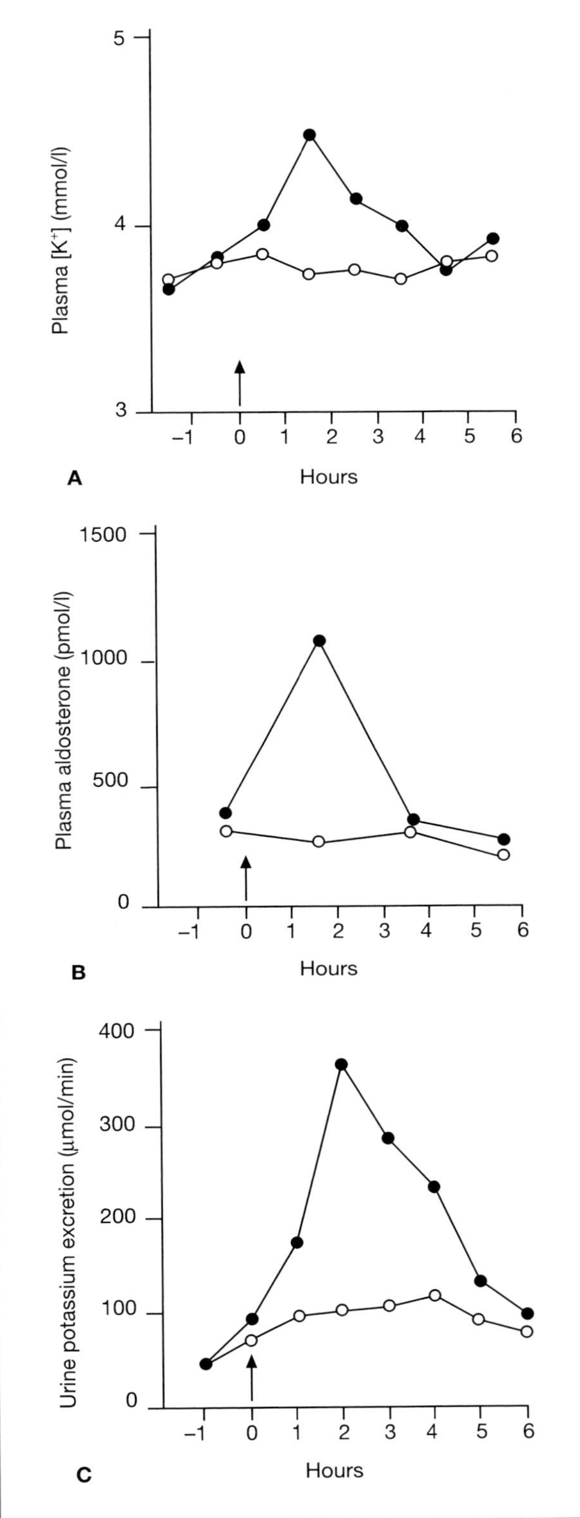

Figure 10.6 Changes in plasma potassium and aldosterone levels and urine potassium excretion after a single oral potassium load (75 mmol KCl; *arrow*) in healthy subjects (*closed circles*). Data are compared with a time-control study (*open circles*). (Adapted with permission from van Buren M, Rabelink TJ, van Rijn HJM, Koomans HA: Effects of acute NaCl, KCl and $KHCO_3$ loads on renal electrolyte excretion in humans.Clin Sci 1992;83:567-574.)

by in vitro experiments, it is quite probable in vivo. Similar to insulin and the β_2-sympathetic tone, aldosterone also appears to facilitate cellular K^+ uptake after a K^+ load. In addition, K^+ ingestion stimulates an acute release of aldosterone from the adrenal glands (see Fig. 10.6), resulting in an even stronger facilitation of cellular uptake. Aldosterone probably stimulates chronic cellular uptake of K^+ as well. Hyper- and hypokalemia occurring with hypoadrenocorticism (Addison's disease) and hyperaldosteronism, respectively, are at least in part to be accounted for by deviations in the K^+ distribution.

Plasma osmolality

Increases in plasma osmolality by increases in concentrations of strictly extracellular species such as Na^+, mannitol, or glucose (in the absence of insulin) extract water from the cell compartment. Since the intracellular [K^+] is high, some of the K^+ leaves the cell with the water, and plasma [K^+] increases. Every 10 mosmol/kg increase can raise the plasma [K^+] by 0.5 mmol/l. This is a rapid phenomenon, especially important in diabetes mellitus, in which large changes in blood sugar levels can be accompanied by large changes in plasma [K^+].

Acid-base balance

Changes in the plasma [H^+] are accompanied by parallel changes in plasma [K^+]. By increasing the [H^+] (lowering of pH) with, for example, HCl, some of the H^+ ions will be taken up by the cell (buffering). Electroneutrality theoretically can be maintained in two ways: Cl^- also flows into the cell, or K^+ leaves the cell. The first is not possible because permeability for Cl^- is low. Therefore, the second is what happens, and plasma [K^+] rises (Fig. 10.7 A). The reverse is true for alkalosis. Cellular buffering of acid-base variations is (in part) a rapid phenomenon; this is the reason that the reciprocal variations in plasma [K^+] also occur so rapidly (in minutes to hours). The reverse is also true: in the event of K^+ loss, decreases in plasma [K^+] are limited by releasing K^+ from the

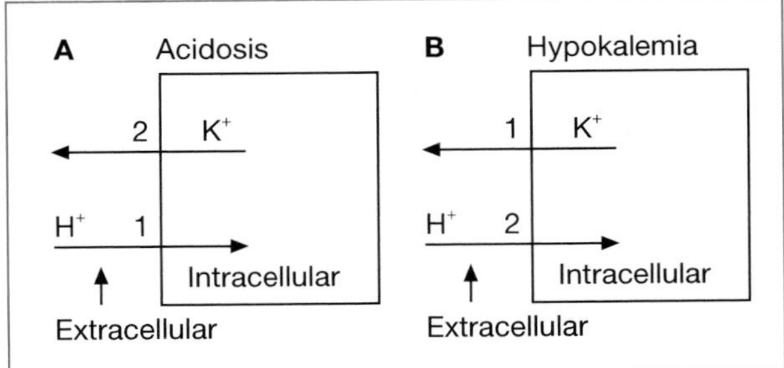

Figure 10.7 Relationship of transcellular distribution of K^+ and H^+. **A.** During acidosis, cells take up H^+ in exchange for K^+, which shifts to the extracellular fluid. **B.** During hypokalemia, K^+ shifts out of the cells into the extracellular fluid in exchange for H^+, which shifts into the cells.

intracellular to the extracellular compartment. Electroneutrality is achieved by H^+ ion influx into the cell (see Fig. 10.7 B). Hyperkalemia is thus accompanied by acidosis, acidosis by hyperkalemia, hypokalemia by alkalosis, and alkalosis by hypokalemia.

External K^+ balance

The average daily K^+ intake amounts to 80 to 100 mmol. However, day-to-day variation can be much larger (40-200 mmol). If the daily excretion were not adjusted to these variations, the plasma [K^+] would greatly vary despite the buffering capacity of the cell. Efficient and direct regulation of K^+ excretion takes place exclusively in the kidney. Approximately 10% of the daily K^+ intake is excreted through the intestinal tract; however, this process cannot be well regulated.

The high efficiency with which the kidney can regulate K^+ excretion is best illustrated by the rapid excretion of a single K^+ dose (see Fig. 10.6). The kidney also works efficiently during chronic increases in K^+ intake. When the K^+ intake in healthy adults is raised from one day to another from 100 to 400 mmol/day, 300 mmol is excreted already on the first day of the new diet and 360 mmol on the third day (this is the normal, maximum capacity; 90% of the K^+ excretion takes place in the kidney) (Fig. 10.8 B).

The plasma [K^+] increases on average by only 0.4 mmol/l. A less efficient excretion would result in hyperkalemia. Chronic hyperkalemia therefore is always due to a disturbance in the renal K^+ excretion. Lowering the K^+ intake to below the daily requirements interferes with the efficiency. When switching to a 10 mmol K^+ per day diet, renal K^+ excretion requires about a week before it is completely adjusted (see Fig. 10.8 A). This is accompanied by a fall in the plasma [K^+] to about 3.0 mmol/l.

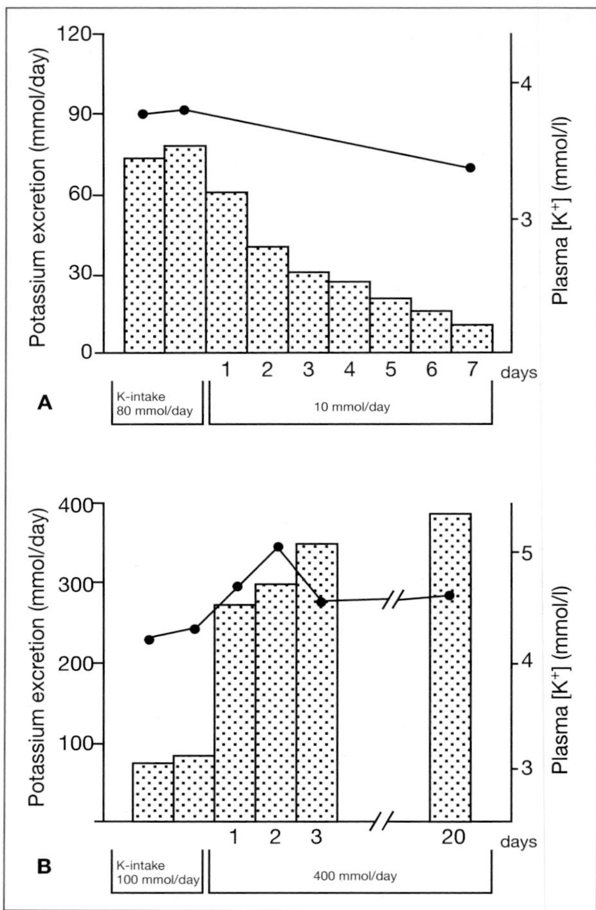

Figure 10.8 **A.** Effect of a reduction in potassium intake from 80 to 100 mmol per day in healthy humans. The adaptation is slow and accompanied by a negative potassium balance and hypokalemia. **B.** Effect of an increase in potassium intake from 100 to 400 mmol per day in healthy humans. Renal excretion adapts quickly and the final increase in plasma potassium concentration is modest.

Tubular K^+ handling

In the proximal tubule, 60 to 70% of the filtered K^+ is reabsorbed. This is passive reabsorption, in other words, parallel to Na^+ and water reabsorption in this segment. The [K^+] in the tubular fluid remains equal to the concentration in the plasma. Potassium is actively reabsorbed in Henle's loop. Only 7 to 10% of the filtered K^+ reaches the distal tubule (~50 mmol/d in the healthy adult). Regulation of K^+ excretion takes place in the remainder of the nephron, namely, the connecting tubules and collecting ducts. Depending on the need, potassium can be either further reabsorbed or secreted here.

K^+ secretion takes place in the principal cells of the connecting tubule and the cortical collecting duct. These cells reabsorb Na^+ and secrete K^+. The amount of transport is determined by:

- *the plasma [K^+].* Increases in plasma [K^+] promote K^+ secretion directly by stimulating the Na^+ pump (Na^+,K^+-ATPase) in the basolateral membrane and K^+ permeability at the luminal membrane and indirectly by stimulating aldosterone release and Na^+ and water delivery to this segment (see below);
- *the plasma aldosterone concentration.* Aldosterone stimulates the basolateral Na^+ pump and the luminal K^+ permeability, as well as the luminal Na^+ permeability;
- *the Na^+ flow in the lumen (the "distal" Na^+ delivery).* The more Na^+ that reaches this part of the nephron (the less Na^+ is reabsorbed by the proximal tubule and Henle's loop), the more Na^+ there is to be reabsorbed and thus the more K^+ can be secreted;
- *the water flow rate.* Greater flow rates of water in this part of the nephron also stimulate the K^+ secretion by keeping luminal K^+ low; this maintains a favorable K^+ gradient across the luminal membrane;
- *the Na^+ to Cl^- proportion in the lumen.* Chloride can be reabsorbed by the principal cells more easily than any other type of ion such as sulfate or bicarbonate. The more Na^+ that arrives in this part of the nephron without Cl^-, the more Na^+ reabsorption must be matched by K^+ secretion (and H^+ secretion);

- *the plasma [H^+].* Increases in the plasma [H^+] decrease the intracellular [K^+] (see Fig. 10.7 B) and the K^+ secretion accordingly; alkalosis has the reverse effect;
- *the plasma ADH concentration.* ADH inhibits K^+ secretion.

K^+ reabsorption takes place in the intercalated cells of the connecting tubule and the cortical and medullary collecting ducts. Net K^+ reabsorption takes place in these cells together with either Cl^- reabsorption or in exchange for H^+ secretion and is aided by (1) high luminal [K^+], (2) low plasma [K^+], (3) high plasma [H^+] (this lowers cellular [K^+] and thus stimulates the luminal K^+ uptake), and (4) high plasma aldosterone concentrations (this stimulates the luminal H^+ secretion in particular and therefore K^+ reabsorption).

Regulation of the renal K^+ excretion

The above-mentioned regulation process will be illustrated by the following two physiologically relevant situations (Fig. 10.9): (1) variation in K^+ intake and (2) variation in Na^+ intake. In the first instance, K^+ intake raises the plasma [K^+]. This directly promotes tubular K^+ secretion (see above). Furthermore, this increase in plasma [K^+] (via processes that are not completely understood) increases the water and Na^+ delivered distally. An increased plasma [K^+] also stimulates adrenal aldosterone release. All in all, these three factors allow kaliuresis following acute or chronic increases of potassium intake. Because the increased tubular Na^+ flow is almost totally nullified by increased Na^+ reabsorption in the distal nephron, net Na^+ excretion remains relatively stable. Indeed, by affecting the delivery of Na^+ to the distal tubules and aldosterone similarly, variations in K^+ intake greatly influence K^+ excretion. The body therefore can make adjustments to a large range in K^+ intake and excretion while keeping Na^+ in balance.

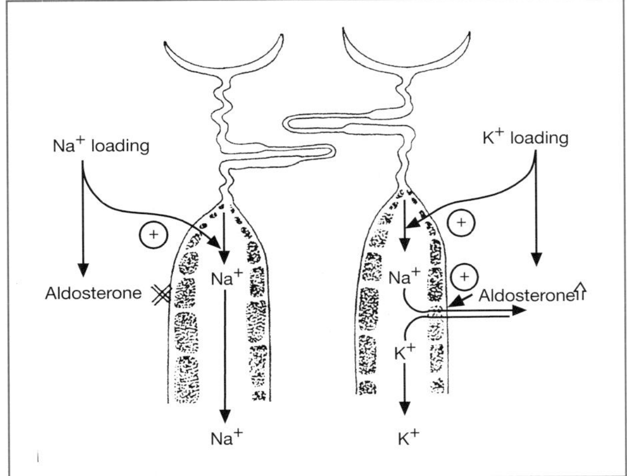

Figure 10.9 Effects of a Na^+ load and of a K^+ load on distal tubular Na^+ delivery and plasma aldosterone level. Both the Na^+ load and the K^+ load stimulate distal delivery, but the effects on aldosterone are in opposite directions. This different response in aldosterone determines whether the increased distal Na^+ delivery leads to excretion of Na^+ or of K^+.

In the second instance, increases in Na^+ intake must be compensated by proportional increases in renal Na^+ excretion. This requires a decrease in tubular Na^+ reabsorption by which more Na^+ and water are presented to the distal nephron. This would lead to an increase in K^+ excretion if not for the fact that a rise in Na^+ intake decreases renin and aldosterone release. Aldosterone suppression inhibits K^+ secretion. These opposite effects balance each other so that variations in Na^+ intake normally have little or no effect on the K^+ balance. Changes in Na^+ intake affect aldosterone and distal Na^+ delivery oppositely, resulting in no net change in the K^+ excretion. The body therefore can make adjustments to large ranges in Na^+ intake and excretion without affecting K^+ excretion.

This system is almost but not entirely perfect. Extremely limited Na^+ intake is accompanied by some K^+ retention, and extremely high Na^+ intake is accompanied by some K^+ loss. Variations in K^+ intake are accompanied by small, brief (similar) changes in Na^+ excretion.

HYPOKALEMIA

Pathophysiology

From the preceding paragraphs, it can be concluded that hypokalemia (plasma [K^+] < 3.5 mmol/l) is caused by either a K^+ shift or a K^+ deficiency.

Hypokalemia through cell inward K^+ shift

H^+ loss causes a flux of H^+ toward the extracellular compartment and, as a consequence, a cell influx of K^+. A rise in pH of only 0.1 units is already accompanied by a plasma [K^+] fall of about 0.4 mmol/l. During metabolic alkalosis, there is not only K^+ influx but also an actual K^+ shortage, since causes of metabolic alkalosis (e.g., vomiting, diuretics, hyperaldosteronism) generally cause loss of K^+ as well. Moreover, metabolic alkalosis in itself stimulates renal K^+ loss (see below).

Hypokalemia through insulin administration is seen most often during correction of preexisting hyperglycemia. In this situation, despite an often large K^+ deficit (through osmotic diuresis), the plasma [K^+] is normal owing to the hyperosmolality (hyperglycemia). Hypokalemia starts nevertheless as soon as insulin is administered. The plasma [K^+] can fall rapidly (within an hour). A large fall in plasma [K^+] also can occur in patients receiving concentrated glucose solution (see "Treatment"). Increased sympathetic tone plays a major role in hypokalemia during stress situations. The plasma [K^+] decrease is acute, with a peak of minus 1 mmol/l, and, like stress itself, transitory. As a rule, it does not cause problems. An exemption to this are patients with coronary ischemia or a recent myocardial infarction; the combination of hypokalemia and ischemia promotes the initiation of ventricular fibrillation. This is even more likely when these patients have prior K^+ depletion induced by diuretics. Administration of β_2-sympathomimetics (e.g., bronchial dilators and uteral spasmolytics) always results in some drop of plasma [K^+]. Problems (i.e., ventricular fibrillation) also can arise under these circumstances especially if they occur together with myocardial ischemia and preexistent K^+ depletion (use of diuretics); this combination is not uncommon in patients with chronic obstructive pulmonary disease (COPD).

In periodic paralysis, the normal cell K^+ influx, such as during exercise and glucose intake, is amplified (plasma [K^+] decreases to 2.5 mmol/l or lower). The cause is unknown. This condition is characterized by acute attacks of (local or generalized) muscle weakness or even flaccid paralysis. The attacks disappear spontaneously (within minutes to hours) but are not completely harmless (breathing paralysis). This condition occurs as a rare (autosomal dominant) hereditary disorder or during thyrotoxicosis. Hypokalemia through accelerated cell division is seen at the start of treatment for anemia caused by vitamin B_{12} or folic acid deficiency (plasma [K^+] falls sometimes by 1 mmol/l).

Hypokalemia through renal K^+ loss

Hypokalemia caused by K^+ deficiency can only exist when the daily loss exceeds the daily intake (normally 80-100 mmol/d). A diet low in K^+ lowers the plasma [K^+], as illustrated when healthy adults are placed on a 10 mmol/day potassium diet (see Fig. 10.8 A). The kidney adjusts to the excretion in about 7 days, but in the meantime, the K^+ balance is negative (>130 mmol), and hypokalemia ensues. In almost every case, renal K^+ loss is based on the simultaneous increased delivery of Na^+ (and water) to the (K^+-secreting part of the) distal nephron and a stimulated (at least not suppressed) plasma aldosterone; this is the case in primary hyperaldosteronism and a few forms of secondary hyperaldosteronism that will be discussed below.

Hypersecretion of aldosterone occurs spontaneously in primary hyperaldosteronism. This amplifies the Na^+ reabsorption in the distal nephron. The resulting volume retention suppresses the Na^+ reabsorption in the proximal tubule, causing even more Na^+ to reach the distal nephron. In this manner, the combination of an increased distal Na^+ delivery and a stimulated release of aldosterone is created and thus the ideal conditions for renal K^+ and H^+ loss. The Na^+ retention causes hypertension but rarely edema. Metabolic alkalosis, a high aldosterone concentration, and a low renin concentration are present. The plasma [Na^+] is often slightly elevated (145-150 mmol/l) as a result of volume-regulated ADH suppression. Primary hyperaldosteronism can be caused by adrenal gland hyperplasia (60%) or a unilateral adenoma (40%). The clinical presentation of hyperaldosteronism can be imitated by an overproduction of another mineralocorticoid (deoxycorticosterone by β- or 17β-hydroxylase deficiency), cortisol (by Cushing's disease), and excessive licorice intake. Licorice contains glycyrrhizic acid, which inhibits cortisol breakdown and thus acts like a mineralocorticoid. In contrast to primary hyperaldosteronism, these causes are characterized not only by a low plasma renin concentration but also by a low plasma aldosterone concentration.

Hypokalemia as a result of secondary hyperaldosteronism occurs as a result of diuretic use, Bartter's syndrome, metabolic alkalosis, magnesium deficiency, and renal tubular acidosis. Every diuretic that blocks Na^+ reabsorption in the proximal tubule, Henle's loop, or early distal nephron (the principle site of action of carbonic anhydrase inhibitors, loop diuretics, and thiazides, respectively) automatically increases distal Na^+ delivery. Aldosterone is stimulated by Na^+ loss, and optimal conditions are created for K^+ loss. The half-life of the diuretic and the degree of aldosterone stimulation determine the severity of K^+ loss and hypokalemia: K^+ loss occurs less by short-acting diuretics (such as the loop diuretics) because the K^+ (and Na^+) balance is restored between doses (unless dosing is frequent). Chronic K^+ loss is seen more often by the longer-acting thiazide diuretics. When thiazides are taken daily, a stable minimum plasma [K^+] is reached in about 2 weeks. Strict limitations in NaCl intake (<3 g/d) often lower plasma [K^+] even further (by stronger aldosterone stimulation). In secondary hyperaldosteronism, there is often mild hyponatremia. This is due both to an intracellular Na^+ shift (in exchange for K^+, just like the intracellular H^+ shift) and to volume-regulated ADH secretion.

Bartter's syndrome is a rare cause of spontaneous hypokalemia. The mechanism is deficient NaCl reabsorption in Henle's loop. The patient has, as it were, a built-in loop diuretic. The most common characteristics besides hypokalemia are (low) normal blood pressure, metabolic alkalosis, mild hypomagnesemia, and a stimulated renin-aldosterone. Clinical presentation varies greatly. The syndrome occurs both in young children, who are also mentally retarded and suffer from growth retardation, and occasionally in asymptomatic adults (accidentally as a result of preoperative electrolyte screening). Gitelman syndrome presents with similar biochemical characteristics but more profound hypomagnesemia. In this case, the NaCl reabsorption defect is probably in the cortical thick ascending limb or distal tubule, where magnesium is also reabsorbed.

In the case of metabolic alkalosis, the plasma [HCO_3^-] is raised above the absorption maximum in the proximal tubule, thus increasing the $NaHCO_3^-$ delivery to the distal nephron. This Na^+ is in part reabsorbed distally in exchange for K^+ secretion (HCO_3^- is after all an anion that is difficult to reabsorb). Part of the $NaHCO_3^-$ is excreted, resulting is aldosterone stimulation and further loss of K^+. This is in fact the major cause of K^+ and Na^+ loss by vomiting; gastric juice in itself contains very little K^+ and Na^+.

Mg^+ loss often exists in combination with K^+ loss (thiazides, Gitelman syndrome). Shortage of Mg^+ maintains a low renal K^+ and H^+ threshold in part through stimulating aldosterone release. Renal K^+ loss also occurs in renal tubular acidosis of the proximal type and as a result of distal renal tubular acidosis caused by an H^+-ATPase defect. In both cases, the mechanism is once again based on a high distal Na^+ delivery ("Na^+ loss") in combination with aldosterone stimulation.

Hypokalemia through gastrointestinal K^+ loss

Gastric juice contains 10 mmol potassium per liter. Even maximum loss of gastric juice (about 2 liters/d) causes only little direct K^+ loss. This is accompanied by alkalosis, however, and thus increased renal K^+ excretion; the K^+ deficiency as a result of vomiting can be ascribed mainly to renal K^+ loss. Intestinal fluids also contain approximately 10 mmol K^+ per liter. The $[K^+]$, however, can be higher during diarrhea (20-30 mmol/l). Intestinal fluid is alkaline. This explains hypokalemia and acidosis by lengthy drainage of the small intestine, severe diarrhea caused by infection (cholera), chronic laxative abuse, villous adenoma of the colon, and the Verner-Morrison syndrome.

Clinical findings

Muscle weakness

Hypokalemia causes muscle weakness, cramps, and paresthesia. Complaints usually start at a plasma $[K^+]$ of less than 3.0 mmol/l. The increased intra-/extracellular K^+ ratio and thereby the altered resting membrane potential (hyperpolarization) explain these symptoms. This resting potential lies even further from the activation threshold needed to be reached to develop an action potential.

Hyperpolarization only exists when hypokalemia is caused by a K^+ redistribution; if intracellular K^+ stores are also decreased, the resting membrane potential can be normal despite the hypokalemia. This explains why hypokalemia through chronic K^+ loss is better tolerated than acute hypokalemia. Severe hypokalemia can cause rhabdomyolysis.

Arrhythmia

Hypokalemia accelerates depolarization and increases the automaticity of the conductance system. The mechanism is unclear, but the result is atrial and ventricular extrasytoles and sometimes ventricular fibrillation. Hypokalemia also delays ventricular repolarization, as illustrated by flat T waves and amplified U waves on the ECG. Arrhythmias usually do not occur until the plasma $[K^+]$ is less than 2.5 mmol/l. The risk is higher during use of digitalis (which acts by inhibiting Na^+,K^+-ATPase-dependent cellular K^+ uptake), exercise, and acute ischemia. In the latter case, plasma $[K^+]$ can fall even further due to sympathetic activation.

Disturbances in renal function

K^+ deficiency is accompanied by metabolic alkalosis; an H^+ shift into cells is caused by the cell efflux K^+ shift (see Fig. 10.7 B). The $[H^+]$ also increases in the renal tubular cells, by which both proximal and distal H^+ secretion are increased. Moreover, the proximal tubules will produce more NH_3. This is significant for patients with cirrhosis of the liver, in whom hypokalemia can promote hepatic coma. K^+ deficiency decreases the ability of the kidney to concentrate urine by impairing the creation of an osmolar gradient in the medulla. This concentration disturbance is ADH-resistant, but the polyuria is mild and usually remains unnoticed. The maximum urine osmolality never falls below 300 mosmol/kg, and no more than 2 to 3 liters of urine will be needed to excrete the normal daily output of 600 to 900 mosmol. During hypokalemia, the ability of the kidney to vary NaCl excretion becomes impaired; a diet high in NaCl will sooner cause edema, and a diet too low in NaCl will sooner cause volume depletion. Chronic hypokalemia is accompanied by interstitial nephritis and, eventually, loss of renal function. This problem occurs mainly as a result of chronic diuretic use. Furthermore, hypokalemia often occurs together with hyponatremia (see above).

Diagnostic procedures

Important parameters for the differential diagnosis of plasma $[K^+]$ disturbances are the plasma concentrations of HCO_3^-, Na^+, Cl^-, Ca^{2+}, Mg^{2+}, glucose, and creatinine and the urinary excretions of K^+, Na^+, and Cl^-. Patient history should include past medical history and medications; physical examination should concentrate on the patient's volume state.

Figure 10.10 presents a flow chart for the analysis of hypokalemia. The diagnostic process is usually concerned with finding the cause of chronic hypokalemia (acute hypokalemia through K^+ shift is, after all, easy to exclude through the patient history, e.g., recent administration of insulin or sympathomimetics, angina, familial periodic paralysis). There is always a shortage of K^+. Measurement of urine K^+ is extremely important for uncovering the source of K^+ loss. If this is nonrenal, the kidney will try to conserve K^+. For example, renal excretion should be less than 30 mmol per day or less than about 3 mmol K^+ per millimole of creatinine if plasma K^+ is about 3 mmol/l or less. Higher urinary potassium excretion will indicate renal loss. The flowchart is schematic, and one must keep in mind that the cause of hypokalemia can be quite complex, e.g., alkalosis and hyperaldosteronism. In the subgroup "hypokalemia through renal loss and metabolic alkalosis," the urinary $[Cl^-]$ can help to differentiate between nonrenal causes (the urinary $[Cl^-]$ is low, <20 mmol/l, in the case of vomiting) and renal causes (urinary $[Cl^-] > 20$ mmol/l). It is essential to measure the plasma renin and aldosterone levels to differentiate between excessive licorice and the various forms of steroid "overproduction." Furthermore, laxative abuse also can be accompanied by metabolic alkalosis (Cl^- loss).

Sometimes its appropriate to speak of "pseudohypokalemia." This occurs when the cellular K^+ uptake by leukocytes continues to take place in the test tube used to draw the blood sample. This is seen in case of leukocytosis with leukemia.

Treatment

Severe, symptomatic hypokalemia

Symptomatic hypokalemia (paralysis or life-threatening

arrhythmia) demands acute treatment. Rapid, complete correction of the deficiency, however, is dangerous. Increasing the plasma [K^+] by only 0.7 to 1.0 mmol/l is often enough to bring the patient into a safe range. This is achieved by administering about 60 mmol potassium in, for example, 2 hours (more rapid administration by exception). The rate of administration thereafter can be decreased to 10 mmol per hour. Important guidelines are:

- potassium preferably should not be administered in glucose (chance of further lowering the plasma [K^+]); rather, in NaCl;
- to prevent iatrogenic hyperkalemia, the infusion fluid should contain no more than 40 mmol K^+ per liter, and the infusion rate should not be higher than indicated earlier. Plasma [K^+] must be measured every 1 or 2 hours;
- oral administration is less dangerous (less chance of hyperkalemia) and just as effective (see Fig. 10.6). This is the preferred method for the conscious patient, given, of course, that an unobstructed oral route is available;
- when hypokalemia occurs together with acidosis or hyperglycemia, one must always administer potassium first before correcting the acidosis or hyperglycemia.

Chronic hypokalemia

This usually concerns prevention of chronic hypokalemia caused by long-term use of diuretics. When does the plasma [K^+] need to be corrected? A general cutoff point of about 3.5 mmol/l or less is used for patients at risk, e.g., patients using digitalis or sympathomimetics or those with ischemic heart disease, glucose intolerance, or cirrhosis of the liver (NH_3 production). The cutoff point for patients without such risk factors is 3.0 mmol/l. Experts do not agree on these points. Keeping all the metabolic consequences in mind, one can defend the cutoff point of 3.5 mmol/l for all patients. In fact, modern diuretics do not need to lower the plasma [K^+] below this level anyway.

In case of intestinal K^+ loss, the plasma [K^+] can be corrected by increasing the daily K^+ intake by the amount lost, e.g., 60 mmol per day. Such a treatment is not effective for renal K^+ loss; the kidney will excrete more potassium as a result of even a very small rise in the plasma [K^+]. The only effective measure is raising the K^+ excretion threshold. Spirolactone, amiloride, and triamterene are given to do just this. NSAIDs and ACE inhibitors sometimes are used (e.g., in Bartter's syndrome). Hypokalemia through renal K^+ loss is sometimes accompanied by severe Mg^{2+} deficiency. This maintains hypokalemia and must be supplemented accordingly.

KCl or $KHCO_3$?

Because K^+ shortage is often accompanied by alkalosis or acidosis, it is important to choose the right anion; it is not

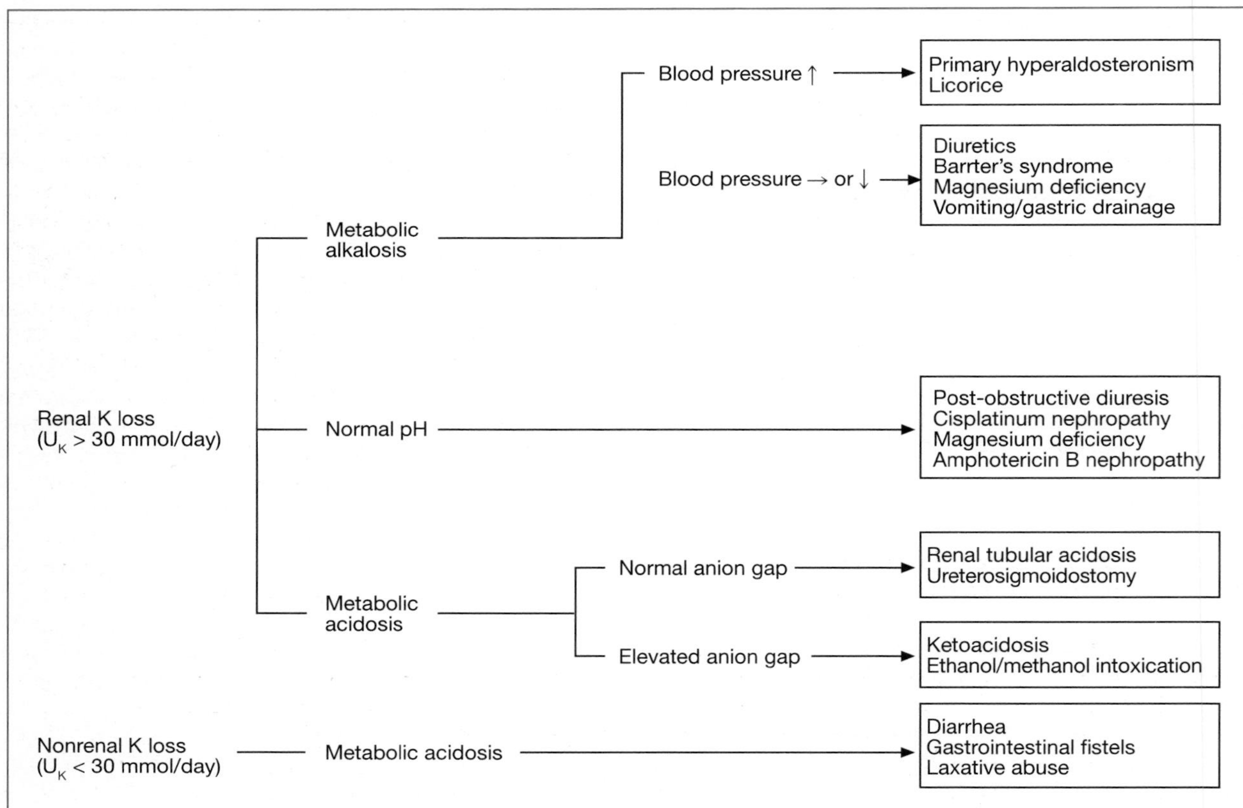

Figure 10.10 Diagram to analyze the cause of hypokalemia.

advisable to give $KHCO_3$ (or potassium citrate) in alkalosis. Uncorrected alkalosis maintains the hypokalemia (K^+ shift) and the renal K^+ loss. It is essential to give KCl in order to replace HCO_3^- by Cl^-. $KHCO_3$ is given in case of acidosis.

HYPERKALEMIA

Pathophysiology

Hyperkalemia through efflux of K^+ from the cells

Intracellular buffering of the H^+ ions in metabolic acidosis causes an efflux of K^+, resulting in hyperkalemia (plasma $[K^+] > 5.5$ mmol/l; see Fig. 10.7 A). This occurs particularly in hyperchloremic acidosis, since the associated anion (Cl^-) cannot accompany H^+ into the cells. It does not occur or occurs much less in ketoacidosis or lactacidemia, where the associated anions are taken up by the cells. Respiratory acidosis also influences the plasma $[K^+]$ to a much lesser degree. The hyperkalemic effect of acidosis is determined in part by total-body K^+ stores and is difficult to predict (0.2-1.5 mmol/l of plasma $[K^+]$ increase per 0.1 units of pH decrease). Insulin deficiency is accompanied by hyperkalemia, unless the total-body K^+ stores are depleted, as in prolonged glucosuria. The rise in plasma $[K^+]$ can be both rapid and severe (e.g., IDDM patients are completely dependent on exogenous insulin). Plasma hyperosmolality (hyperglycemia) also plays a role in this process. This is even more so when the kidney fails to correct the hyperkalemia (renal insufficiency in IDDM). β_2-Sympatholytics often cause some rise in the plasma $[K^+]$ (about 0.2 mmol/l). Moreover, β_2-blockers amplify the physiologic rise in plasma $[K^+]$ during exercise (usually < 1.0 mmol/l). Digitalis inhibits the cellular K^+ uptake by the Na^+,K^+-ATPase pump in the cell membrane. Hyperkalemia is thus a characteristic of digitalis intoxication. Tissue injury also mobilizes K^+ from the cells. Other characteristics of this form of hyperkalemia are the elevated plasma concentrations of phosphate and uric acid. This is seen in rhabdomyolysis and rapid tumor lysis after cytostatics.

Hyperkalemia through disturbances in K^+ excretion

The renal K^+ excretory capacity far exceeds the normal physiologic demand. Hyperkalemia (chronic) is thus always caused by impaired renal K^+ excretion. Impairment can be caused by either a decreased GFR or by a discrepancy in the distal Na^+ delivery and the plasma aldosterone level. In order to maintain K^+ homeostasis during renal insufficiency, the K^+ excretion per (remaining) nephron (fractional K^+ excretion) must be increased. Three factors are involved in the stimulation of tubular K^+ secretion: (1) the rise in plasma $[K^+]$, (2) the corresponding rise in plasma aldosterone, and (3) a decrease in the NaCl reabsorption (and thus high distal delivery) per nephron. Gradual decreases in GFR lead initially to slight increases in the plasma $[K^+]$, which are needed to maintain K^+ homeostasis. True hyperkalemia does not develop until GFR is severely reduced, unless, of course, the K^+ intake is drastically

reduced. In two situations the tendency for hyperkalemia is increased: the first is a primary tubular disease, because of the associated disturbances in distal tubular function (e.g., polycystic kidney disease, analgesic-induced renal insufficiency, interstitial nephritis). In such patients, the raised plasma $[K^+]$ raises the plasma aldosterone even more, which serves in part to compensate the tubular disturbances. The second is a relatively suppressed aldosterone (e.g., hyporeninemic hypoaldosteronism; see below).

In mineralocorticoid deficiency, one of the most important stimuli of K^+ secretion is absent, and at the same time, there is a tendency toward Na^+ loss. The latter stimulates proximal NaCl resorption (through the usual mechanisms, such as lowering blood pressure and stimulating renin-angiotensin and sympathetic tone). K^+ retention is thus the result of both a lack of aldosterone and a low distal Na^+ delivery. K^+ balance can only be maintained at the cost of often strong increases in plasma $[K^+]$ (~6 mmol/l). There is also a tendency toward acidosis, which amplifies the hyperkalemia. Mineralocortoicoid deficiency is usually accompanied by glucocorticoid deficiency (e.g., acquired adrenal insufficiency, congenital 21-hydroxylase deficiency). This amplifies the tendency toward Na^+ loss; the kidney cannot limit the Na^+ excretion to below a value of about 30 mmol per day. Dietary restrictions in Na^+ below this level automatically cause a negative Na^+ balance. Pharmacologic inhibition of the aldosterone effect also causes hyperkalemia. Amiloride and triamterene inhibit the Na^+ permeability of the luminal membrane in the collecting duct (Na^+ channel blockers) and, in so doing, the Na^+ reabsorption and the K^+ secretion. Spirolactone is an aldosterone receptor antagonist, and ACE inhibitors reduce alsdosterone secretion. The rise in plasma $[K^+]$ induced by these agents is mostly limited (0.5 mmol/l) but can become severe if there is a predisposition to K^+ retention (e.g., renal insufficiency, diabetes mellitus, use of NSAIDs) or if K^+ intake is high. In hyporeninemic hypoaldosteronism, the renin secretion is less than that expected for a given volume status. This results in a lower aldosterone level than is appropriate for the corresponding distal Na^+ delivery. This situation is seen in diabetes mellitus (decreased renal sympathetic tone), during use of NSAIDs (prostaglandins stimulate renin release), in chronic interstitial nephritis (mechanism unknown), and sometimes in cyclosporine use. Such patients have the characteristic of becoming severely hyperkalemic and acidotic by no or only slight decreases in renal function. Unlike patients with adrenal insufficiency, these patients usually exhibit Na^+ retention, hypertension, and slight edema. This forms the basis of treatment (see below). Diabetics and patients with interstitial nephritis are prone to develop hyperkalemia and acidosis if they use NSAIDs, ACE inhibitors, or aldosterone antagonists.

Clinical findings

Muscle weakness This complaint only occurs in severe

hyperkalemia (plasma [K+] > 7.5 mmol/l) because only then may the resting membrane potential drop below the level of the threshold potential.

Arrhythmia Hyperkalemia is associated with rapid repolarization and slow depolarization. Rapid repolarization shows by the shortening of the QT time and the pointed T wave (plasma [K+] > 6.0 mmol/l) on the ECG. Slow depolarization causes wide QRS complexes (plasma [K+] > 7.0 mmol/l). Asystole eventually can occur. The sensitivity to hyperkalemia is increased by acidosis, hypocalcemia, and hyponatremia, as well as if its genesis is fast.

Diagnostic procedures

The same information as in hypokalemia is useful in the diagnosis of hyperkalemia (see "Hyopkalemia"). Figure 10.11 illustrates how the cause of hyperkalemia can be defined. As in the case of hypokalemia, the pathogenesis of hyperkalemia is often complex, e.g., use of an NSAID or aldosterone antagonist in patients with diabetes mellitus, renal failure, or heart failure. Despite the disturbance in renal K+ excretion, the 24-hour K+ excretion is generally normal. The excretion defect appears because this "normal" excretion can only be achieved when the plasma [K+] is high. In order to diagnose hyporeninemic hypoaldosteronism and adrenal insufficiency correctly, determination of plasma renin and aldosterone levels is important. However, a differential diagnosis and treatment strategy can be set up even without this information.

"Pseudohyperkalemia" sometimes can occur; a high plasma [K+] is caused by hemolysis in the blood sample tube. One should keep this cause in mind when severe hyperkalemia fails to be accompanied by any symptoms (ECG). The solution to this dilemma is to take a fresh blood sample for plasma [K+] determination.

Treatment

Treatment depends on the severity and etiology of the hyperkalemia. Concomitant metabolic acidosis or hyperglycemia should be treated first. Medication that raises the plasma [K+] and K+ supplementation must be discontinued.

Severe, symptomatic hyperkalemia The most rapid, effective treatment of severe or symptomatic hyperkalemia is the administration of calcium (10% calcium gluconate intravenously; 10 ml in a few minutes; repeat if necessary or use continuous infusion). Calcium has no effect on the plasma [K+] but acts by lowering the threshold potential of excitable cells. This neutralizes the decrease in the resting membrane potential caused by the hyperkalemia. Administration of glucose (50-100 ml 50% intravenously) stimulates endogenous insulin secretion, thus accelerating cellular glucose and K+ uptake. This causes a substantial decrease in the plasma [K+] within an hour; however, the effect is temporary. Insulin, of course, should be coadministered with the glucose in patients with IDDM. A K+ surplus is almost always the case in hyperkalemia, and thus a definite correction of the plasma [K+] can only be made by depleting K+ accordingly. This is the rationale behind treatment with the Na+/K+ exchange resins (e.g., 50 g sodium polystyrene sulfate in 100 ml mannitol given by enema). This resin binds potassium in the intestine (1-1.5 mmol/g). By remaining in the intestine for 2 hours, approximately 50 to 75 mmol potassium can be removed; this is a very effective treatment. Hemodialysis is a good alternative, however, but it is not necessarily more effective; 30 to 60 mmol potassium can be removed per hour.

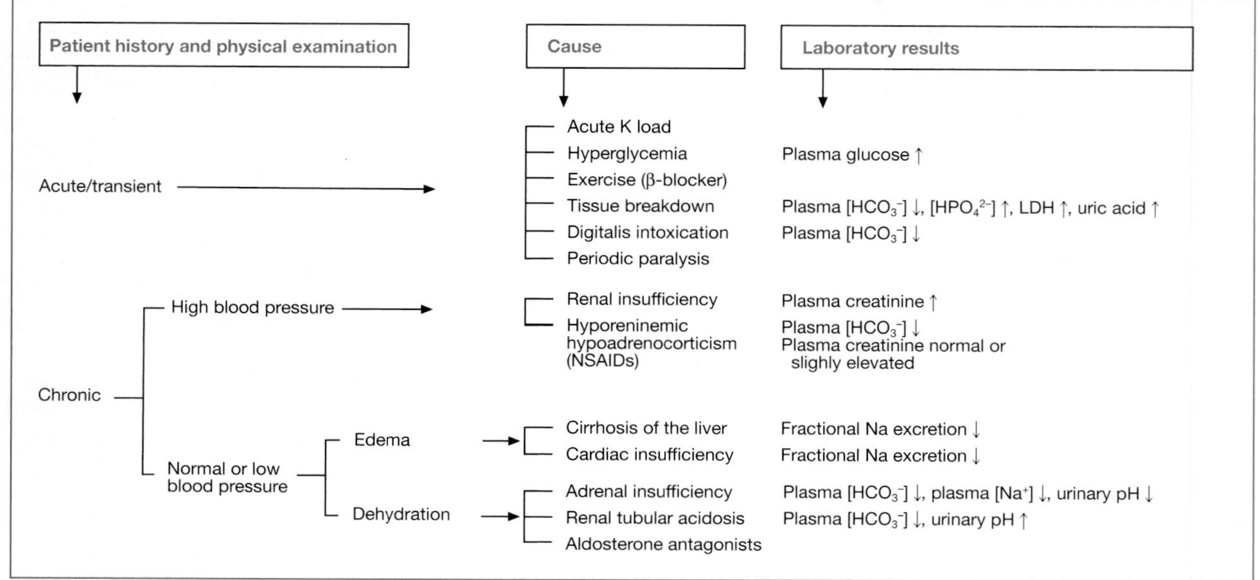

Figure 10.11 Diagram to diagnose the cause of hyperkalemia.

Peritoneal dialysis has little effect; 10 to 15 mmol potassium at most is removed per exchange.

Chronic hyperkalemia In this case, the treatment is directed primarily at increasing renal K^+ excretion by either increasing the distal Na^+ delivery and/or stimulating aldosterone secretion. Important determinants in making a treatment strategy are the effective circulating volume and the renal function.

- *(Almost) normal renal function, (slight or extreme) high blood pressure.* There is a strong possibility of hyporeninemic hypoaldosteronism; administration of a loop or a thiazide diuretic is almost always enough to correct all the symptoms (hypertension, edema, acidosis, hyperkalemia).
- *(Almost) normal renal function, low blood pressure.* There is either primary hypoadrenocorticism (mineralocorticoid administration is the only treatment option), reduced effective circulating volume due to NaCl loss (replete!), or some other cause, e.g., heart failure. In the latter case, treatment of the edema (diuretic) also corrects the plasma $[K^+]$.
- *Decreased renal function.* If there is volume excess, diuretics will lower the plasma $[K^+]$ by increasing distal NaCl delivery and plasma aldosterone. If there is volume depletion, NaCl (or, in case of acidosis, $NaHCO_3$) administration will increase renal K^+ excretion again by increasing distal NaCl delivery. If loss of renal function is severe (<10% of normal function), renal K^+ excretion will always remain below the level of normal K^+ intake. The K^+ supply must be lowered by dietary measures and administration of resins (e.g., 15 g/d sodium polystyrene sulfate orally).

Suggested readings

Berl T. Nephrology forum: treating hyponatremia: damned if we do and damned if we don't. Kidney Int 1990;37:1006-18.

DeFronzo RA. Clinical disorders of hyperkalemia. In: Seldin DW, Giebisch G, eds. The kidney: physiology and pathophysiology. 2nd ed. New York: Raven Press, 1992;2279-338.

Gennari FJ. Hypo-hypernatremia: disorders of water balance. In: Davison AM, Cameron JS, Granfeld JP, Kerr DMS, Ritz E, Winnearls CG, eds. Oxford Textbook of clinical nephrology. 2nd ed. Oxford, England: Oxford University Press, 1998;175-224.

Gonzales-Campoy JM, Knox FG. Integrated responses of the kidney to alterations in extracellular fluid volume. In: Seldin DW, Giebisch G, eds. The kidney: physiology and pathophysiology. 2nd ed. New York: Raven Press, 1992;241-97.

Hogarthy DC, Tran DN, Phillips MI. Involvement of angiotensin receptor subtypes in osmotically induced release of vasopressin. Brain Res 1994;637:126-32.

Höjer J. Management of symptomatic hyponatremia: dependence on the duration of development. J Int Med 1994;235:497-501.

Kumar S, Berl T. Electrolyte quintet: sodium. Lancet 1998;352:220-8.

Mujais SK, Katz AI. Potassium deficiency. In: Seldin DW, Giebisch G, eds. The kidney: physiology and pathophysiology. 2nd ed. New York: Raven Press, 1992;2249-78.

Neal A, Snyder MD, David W, et al. Hypernatremia in elderly patients. Ann Intern Med 1987;107:309-19.

Robertson GL. Regulation of vasopressin secretion. In: Seldin DW, Giebisch G, eds. The kidney: physiology and pathophysiology. 2nd ed. New York: Raven Press, 1992;1595-613.

Robertson GL, Berl T. Pathophysiology of water metabolism. In: Brenner BM, Levine SA, eds. The kidney. 5th ed. Philadelphia: Saunders, 1996;873-928.

Rose BD. Clinical physiology of acid-base and electrolyte disorders, 4th ed. New York: McGraw-Hill, 1994;219-34, 261-73, 638-762.

Shoker AS. Application of the clearance concept to hyponatremic and hypernatremic disorders: a phenomenological analysis. Clin Chem 1994;40:1220-7.

Smithline N, Gardner KD. Gaps: anionic and osmolar. JAMA 1976;236:1594-7.

Strange K. Regulation of solute and water balance and cell volume in the central nervous system. J Am Soc Nephrol 1992;3:12-27.

Verbalis JG. Adaptation to acute and chronic hyponatremia: implications for symptomatology, diagnosis, and therapy. Semin Nephrol 1998;18:3-19.

Weisberg LS. Pseudohyponatremia: a reappraisal. Am J Med 1989;86:315-8.

Wright FS, Giebisch G. Regulation of potassium excretion. In: Seldin DW, Giebisch G, eds. The kidney: physiology and pathophysiology. 2nd ed. New York: Raven Press, 1992;2209-48.

CHAPTER

11 Acid-base physiology and clinical disorders

Danilo Fliser

REGULATION OF ACID-BASE EQUILIBRIUM

Maintenance of steady-state free hydrogen ion concentration within body fluids

Aerobic metabolism continuously produces a preponderance of acid substances (the word oxygen means *generator of acid*). The principal product of metabolism, *carbon dioxide* (CO_2) is continually in reversible equillibrium with *carbonic acid* (H_2CO_3), which in turn dissociates into *bicarbonate* (HCO_3^-). and into *hydrogen ion* (H^+), a proton donor. Protons are chemically so reactive that even minute changes in their concentration markedly influence intracellular metabolic reactions and physiologic processes. As a consequence, the *steady-state free hydrogen ion concentration $[H^+]$* in body fluids must be maintained within a narrow range. This is accomplished through a series of reversible chemical buffers and physiologic pulmonary and renal compensations.

Because normal blood $[H^+]$ is very small, the term *pH* was introduced in order to obviate the need for expressing $[H^+]$ in terms of 10^{-7}, etc. The pH notation uses a logarithmic scale, so that $pH = \log 1/[H^+]$, or $pH = -\log [H^+]$. Thus, a solution with a $[H^+]$ of 1×10^{-7} moles per liter (i.e., 100 nmol/l) is the same as one with pH 7.0. In most laboratories the normal range of pH in arterial blood (measured at 37°C using glass electrodes) is between 7.35 and 7.45, i.e., 7.40 ± 0.05, or a $[H^+]$ of about 40 nmol/l. A decrease in arterial blood pH below 7.35 is defined as *acidemia*, whereas an increase in pH above 7.45 is called *alkalemia*. The pH of venous blood and of interstitial fluid is less (about 7.35), and the intracellular pH is thought to be about 6.90. In general, a disease process that adds acid to or removes alkali from body fluids is defined as *acidosis* – if left unopposed, it will result in *acidemia*. Conversely, *alkalosis* is the manifestation of a disease process that removes acid from or adds base to body fluids – if left unopposed it will cause *alkalemia*.

Body buffers with special reference to the bicarbonate buffer system

Some 15 000 mmol of volatile CO_2 is expelled from the lungs. In addition, a surplus of about 80 mmol of nonvolatile ("fixed") acids are formed daily from the oxidation of protein-contained amino acids, commonly referred as "endogenous acid production." In strenuous exercise, lactic acid temporarily may appear from the muscles, and under abnormal conditions organic acids like acetoacetic and ß-hydroxybutyric acid may accumulate. The excess of nonvolatile acids, whether normal or pathologic, can only be excreted in the urine. Both CO_2 and nonvolatile acids must gain access to the blood before they can be removed by the lungs or the kidney; however, pH remains stable owing to the presence of *buffers*, which can take up or release protons instantaneously. Most buffers of biologic fluids are composed of a weak acid (HA) and its conjugated base (NaA). The dissociation of the acid component can be expressed by an equation derived from the *law of mass action*:

$$K_A = [H^+][A^-] / [HA]$$

where K_A is the dissociation constant. The formula can be rewritten as:

$$[H^+] = K_A \times [HA] / [A^-] \text{ (Henderson)}$$

or in its negative logarithmic form

$$pH = pK_A + \log [A^-] / [HA] \text{ (Hasselbach)}$$

It follows that the ability of the buffer system to resist changes in pH (i.e., *buffering power*) is maximal when the pH of the solution is identical to that of the pK value of the buffer system. The buffering power of course also depends on the molar concentration of the buffer system components.

Although all body buffers such as intracellular proteins

(e.g., hemoglobin), bone carbonates, and extracellular bicarbonate and phosphate, participate in acid-base regulation, it is convenient to think in terms of the *bicarbonate buffer system*, because (1) all (extracellular) buffer systems are essentially in equilibrium (*isohydric principle*) and (2) the concentration of each of the two elements of the bicarbonate system, and hence pH, can be regulated by the lungs and the kidneys. Applying the law of mass action to this buffer system gives:

$$K = [H^+]\,[HCO_3^-] / [H_2CO_3]$$

Carbonic acid dissolves rapidly and is in continuous equilibrium with CO_2, so that the above equation can be rewritten as:

$$K = [H^+]\,[HCO_3^-] / [CO_2], \text{ or } [H^+] = K\,[CO_2] / [HCO_3^-]$$

and in its negative logarithmic form

$$-\log [H^+] = -\log K + \log [HCO_3^-] / [CO_2]$$

Since $-\log [H^+]$ = pH and $-\log K$ = pK (which for the bicarbonate buffer system is 6.1), it follows

$$pH = 6.1 + \log [HCO_3^-] / [CO_2]$$
(= Henderson-Hasselbach equation)

The concentration of carbon dioxide in blood (pCO_2) can be measured; hence

$$pH = 6.1 + \log [HCO_3^-] / [pCO_2 \times 0.03]$$

A primary increase in plasma bicarbonate concentration will cause a rise in pH (i.e., decrease of $[H^+]$), whereas a primary increase in pCO_2 will decrease pH (i.e., increase $[H^+]$), and vice versa. It is convenient to describe acid-base disorders as *respiratory* when pCO_2 of body fluids (regulated by the lungs) is primarily changed, whereas acid-base disorders with a primary perturbation in plasma bicarbonate concentration (regulated by the kidneys) are called *metabolic*. According to the Henderson-Hasselbach equation, secondary adjustments of plasma bicarbonate concentration or pCO_2 must be in the same direction as the primary change in order to keep pH constant. For example, to resist a change in pH, an increase in pCO_2 is followed by an increase in plasma bicarbonate concentration, and vice versa. Physiologic compensation to primary metabolic acid-base disorders involves adjustments in alveolar ventilation, whereas the secondary response to primary respiratory acid-base disturbances involves adjustments of renal bicarbonate reabsorption, respectively acid excretion.

Respiratory adjustment of acid-base homeostasis

Although CO_2 reacts with water and body buffers, mainly hemoglobin, during transport from cells to pulmonary alveoli, no net change in body fluid composition results, since the CO_2 excreted by the lungs is equal to the CO_2 produced by the cells. However, it takes several minutes for the respiratory system to readjust the hydrogen ion concentration after changes of pH, so that the normal concentration of carbon dioxide in body fluids is fixed around 1.2 mmol/l (pCO_2 = 5.3 kPa = 40 mmHg). At this concentration pulmonary excretion equals metabolic production. Doubling the rate of alveolar ventilation will raise pH by about 0.23, and halving it will decrease pH for about 0.2 units. On the other hand, pH respectively pCO_2 affects the ventilation rate by a direct action on the respiratory center in the medulla oblongata. The power of this physiologic buffer system to adjust blood hydrogen ion concentration is limited, however, because as the pH returns toward normal, the stimulus that has been causing either increased or decreased respiration will itself begin to be lost. Thus, respiratory compensation of metabolic acid-base disorders is almost never complete. Because the lungs daily expel an amount of volatile acids about 200-fold larger than the amount of nonvolatile acids excreted by the kidneys, severe acidemia resulting from acute respiratory arrest may develop within minutes. In contrast, it may takes days to reach a comparable deviation of blood acidity as a result of retention of fixed acids when renal function is compromised.

Renal handling of hydrogen and bicarbonate

Some 170 l of glomerular filtrate, containing about 25 mmol/l bicarbonate, are filtered daily in man; this amounts to a total load of about 4250 mmol of bicarbonate. At a pH of 6.1, 1.0 l of urine formed per day contains about 1.25 mmol of bicarbonate – reabsorption is thus almost complete under normal circumstances. The process by which the proximal tubule reclaims the filtered bicarbonate load is shown in Figure 11.1. The tubule cells form H_2CO_3 from CO_2 and H_2O under the influence of the enzyme *car-*

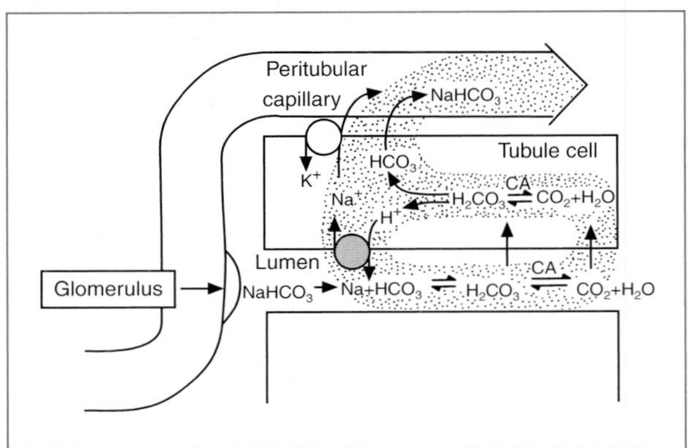

Figure 11.1 Schematic presentation of renal bicarbonate reabsorption. The proximal tubule cells form carbonic acid (H_2CO_3) from carbon dioxide (CO_2) and water (H_2O) under the influence of the enzyme carbonic anhydrase (CA). H_2CO_3 ionizes to yield hydrogen (H^+) and bicarbonate (HCO_3^-). H^+ formed in the cell exchanges with sodium (Na^+) in the tubular fluid (dashed circle). As a net effect, sodium bicarbonate ($NaHCO_3$) is reabsorbed, and the H^+ secreted into the tubule is buffered by filtered bicarbonate.

bonic anhydrase. H_2CO_3 ionizes to yield H^+ and HCO_3^-. H^+ formed in the cell exchanges with Na^+ in the tubular fluid; effectively $NaHCO_3$ is reabsorbed into the blood. The H^+ secreted into the tubule can be buffered by filtered bicarbonate, and as a net effect of the process, bicarbonate body stores are conserved. When the secreted protons are buffered by other buffers present in the tubular fluid, a net gain of bicarbonate is achieved. Since the kidney cannot produce a urine more acid than pH ~ 4.5, the presence of buffer salts in the tubular fluid is therefore vital for the excretion of maximal amounts of H^+ and, correspondingly, for the reabsorption of the maximal amount of bicarbonate and sodium. The phosphates are the most important buffers in the urine (HPO_4^{2-} accepts H^+ to form $H_2PO_4^-$), although in acid urine the formation of ammonium helps to keep H^+ concentration lower than it would otherwise be. In addition to proximal tubular bicarbonate reabsorption, bicarbonate can be secreted into urine in the cortical collecting duct via a chloride-bicarbonate exchanger on the apical membrane of type B intercalated cells. Further, hydrogen secretion takes place in more distal parts of the nephron as well.

Several factors influence renal acid-base regulatory mechanisms, such as extracellular fluid volume, pH and pCO_2, luminal pH, bicarbonate concentration and flow rate, angiotensin II, body chloride, and potassium stores, etc. For example, overbreathing decreases tissue pCO_2, bicarbonate reabsorption is reduced, and bicarbonate is excreted (accompanied inevitably by sodium) in the urine. Conversely, an increase in pCO_2 enhances reabsorption of HCO_3^-. If pCO_2 is chronically raised (e.g., in emphysema), bicarbonate reabsorption is complete. At an arterial pCO_2 of 40 mmHg, bicarbonate reabsorption normally stabilizes at a value between 2.6 and 2.8 mmol – above this concentration bicarbonate is excreted in the urine. Effective extracellular volume also importantly influences bicarbonate reabsorption. In volume-depleted states, proximal tubular bicarbonate reabsorption is increased, possibly mediated by angiotensin II. In addition, distal tubular proton secretion is increased by aldosterone; volume depletion therefore induces metabolic alkalosis. Further, chloride depletion also limits bicarbonate excretion, because less chloride is available for NaCl reabsorption; hence bicarbonate is reabsorbed with sodium. On the other hand, a sodium-deficient subject cannot produce an alkaline urine because his sodium absorption is complete; as a result most of the bicarbonate as well as the chloride ions are absorbed passively along with the sodium, for there is little H^+ formed to exchange with sodium. Alkalosis superimposed on sodium deficiency therefore leads to a conflict between two regulatory functions of the kidney, and the regulation of acid-base balance is sacrificed to the conservation of sodium.

Renal ammonium mechanism

The renally excreted nonvolatile (fixed) acids such as phosphates or sulfates must be accompanied by an equivalent amount of cations for maintenance of eletrical neutrality. Usually their amount exceeds the amount of metallic cations (Na^+, K^+, Ca^{++}) ingested in the average diet. Consequently, if these anions were fully covered by metallic cations, an equivalent amount of cation (mainly Na^+) would be drained out of the body, with disastrous results. The kidney has solved the problem by manufacture of H^+ and ammonium (NH_3), which "cover" the excreted anions. More than 60% of NH_3 is formed in the proximal tubular epithelium from blood glutamine by the action of the enzyme glutaminase. The remainder is derived mainly from glycine, alanine, leucine, and aspartic acid by the action of amino-acid oxidase. Dissolved NH_3 is a proton acceptor, appropriating H^+ from an aqueous environment to become NH_4^+. The cell membrane is permeable to NH_3 but not to NH_4^+, hence NH_3 can diffuse from the tubule cell into the tubular fluid, where it captures H^+. The higher the hydrogen ion concentration, the larger the formation of nondiffusible NH_4^+ excreted. The formation and excretion of NH_4^+ allows the excretion of anions which otherwise would require the accompaniment of metallic cations. The ammonium mechanism thus assists the body sodium conservation. The ammonium content of the urine is negligible until the pH falls below 6.0. Ammonium excretion then increases linearly as the urinary pH falls below this value. Both chronic acidosis and chronic potassium depletion can markedly increase ammonium production by tubular cells.

Titratable acidity is referred to as the amount of alkali (in mmol/l) required to adjust the pH of a urine sample to 7.4. Multiplied by the daily volume of urine (in liters), it gives the total amount of sodium conserved by the renal mechanism of H^+ secretion. In a healthy man this is normally 20-30 mmol per day, but it may increase to 150 mmol per day in severe acidosis. Actually, the total daily renal secretion of H^+ is equal to the titratable acid of the urine plus the ammonium excreted, for NH_3 accepts H^+; the whole amount of sodium conserved by the kidneys is given by the sum of these two.

DIAGNOSTIC APPROACH TO ACID-BASE DISTURBANCES

Acid-base homeostasis exerts a major influence on cellular function, thereby critically affecting tissue and organ performance, and deviations of blood acidity in either direction can be life-threatening when severe. Yet it is the nature of the pathologic condition responsible for acidemia or alkalemia that often determines the prognosis. For example, the presence of an unexplained respiratory alkalosis may lead to a diagnosis of pulmonary embolism. Thus, the principal reason that one seeks an accurate assessment of acid-base equilibrium is not only to obtain an appropriate guide for (immediate) therapy to combat the acid-base deviation, but in addition, to identify the underlying cause(s) of the acid-base disorder. In view of the potential complexitiy of acid-base disorders, it is desirable to have a systematic approach, centering around a sequential analysis of the following questions: (1) is an acid-base disorder present? (2) is it a simple or a mixed disturbance, and what is the primary or dominant disorder? and (3) what is (are) the cause(s) of the disorder?

Clues to the diagnosis of an acid-base disorder

It is not practical to obtain an analysis of acid-base equilibrium in every patient, and judgments about the possible presence of an acid-base abnormality must be based on knowledge of the patient´s history and clinical presentation. Table 11.1 lists a number of common clinical settings in which acid-base disorders occur often enough to warrant laboratory testing. Occasionally, one first suspects an acid-base disturbance on the basis of clinical signs: acidemia may present as hyperventilation, and alkalemia as paresthesias or tetany. The presence of an acid-base disturbance never can be established solely on clinical grounds, however, and appropriate laboratory confirmation is mandatory. This includes examination of the blood acid-base status, measurement of urine pH, plasma and urine electrolyte concentrations, and of ancillary laboratory data (e.g., lactate concentration, etc.).

Evaluation of the acid-base status

Acid-base parameters can be measured either in arterial or venous blood; the former provides useful information on pulmonary gas exchange, whereas the latter better reflects tissue hypercapnia and acidemia in the presence of severe hypoperfusion. Thus, in some clinical settings both arterial and venous blood samples are needed for correct assessment of acid-base status. Blood samples must be collected with anticoagulant (heparin), anaerobically, and promptly evaluated or stored at 4 °C for later analysis. Normal values for acid-base laboratory studies are shown in Table 11.2. As with all laboratory testing, slight differences with respect to reference values may exist between laboratories. Factors that can influence acid-base status include age, altitude (hyperventilation develops at high altitudes), diet (changes in endogenous acid production), body position, and pregnancy.

Standard bicarbonate is the plasma HCO_3^- concentration present in an arterial blood sample that is fully saturated with oxygen and equilibrated in vitro at 38 °C with pCO_2 equal to 40 mmHg. In a patient with normal pCO_2 standard bicarbonate is identical to actual plasma bicarbonate concentration; the relationship is disrupted during acute severe hypercapnia, however. In venous blood, total CO_2 concentration provides a reasonable approximation of bicarbonate concentration. The blood *base excess* concentration is the amount of buffer required to adjust the pH of a fully oxygenated blood sample exposed in vitro to a pCO_2 of 40 mmHg at 38 °C to achieve a normal pH of 7.40. It is negative when pH is lower than 7.40, and alkali must be added to achieve a normal pH; the base excess is positive when pH is higher than 7.40, and acid must be added to titrate blood to normal pH. The base excess mirrors changes in the "metabolic component" of the bicarbonate buffer system. It is therefore closely interrelated and changes in parallel with both standard and actual bicarbonate concentration in most clinical conditions associated with acid-base disorders – for practical purposes the relationship can be taken as 1:1:1 (except in the first hours after a major change in pCO_2). A positive base excess characterizes clinical conditions with an increased "metabolic component" such as metabolic alkalosis or chronic respiratoy acidosis. On the other hand, a negative base excess is observed in conditions with a decreased "metabolic component" such as metabolic acidosis or chronic respiratory alkalosis. The *anion gap* represents the amount of nonmeasurable plasma anions (Fig. 11.2), and can be calculated using a simple equation, provided that the plasma protein concentration is normal. For simplicity, plasma potassium concentration is omitted from the calculation:

$$\text{anion gap} = \text{plasma}\ [\text{sodium} - (\text{chloride} + \text{bicarbonate})\ \text{concentration}]$$

The anion gap is particularly helpful in the diagnostic approach to primary metabolic acidoses and to mixed metabolic acid-base disorders. In metabolic acidoses with increased anion gap the rise in the anion gap (i.e., Δ anion

Table 11.1 Common clinical settings associated with acid-base disorders

Clinical setting	Metabolic		Respiratory	
	acidosis	alkalosis	acidosis	alkalosis
Cardiopulmonary arrest	x		x	
Chronic obstructive pulmonary disease			x	
Pulmonary embolism				x
Gastric suction/vomiting		x		
Diarrhea	x			
Renal failure	x			
Hepatic insufficiency	x			x
Sepsis	x			x
Coma	x		x	
Diuretic therapy		x		

Table 11.2 Normal values of laboratory tests for diagnosis of acid-base disorders

Arterial blood
pH = 7.36-7.44([H^+]=36-44 nmol/l)
pCO_2 = 36-44 mmHg
Actual bicarbonate = 22-26 mmol/l
Standard bicarbonate = 22-26 mmol/l
Base excess = 0(±2 mmol/l)
Anion gap = 12±4 mmol/l

Venous blood
pH = 7.34-7.42([H^+] = 38-46 nmol/l)
pCO_2 = 42-50 mmHg
Total CO_2 = 23-30 mmol/l

gap) is usually in close reciprocal relationship with the fall in plasma HCO_3^- (i.e., Δ bicarbonate).

The accuracy of acid-base measurements can be checked using the nonlogarithmic form of the Henderson-Hasselbach equation, i.e., $[H^+] = 24\ [pCO_2]\ /\ [HCO_3^-]$, because the components of the bicarbonate buffer system are always at equilibrium and therefore must adhere to the mathematical constraints of the equation. For this purpose pH must be converted into [H^+] (Tab. 11.3). The measurements should be repeated if the actual acid-base values do not fit in the equation.

Which is the primary acid-base disturbance?

As a general rule, the finding of an abnormal plasma bicarbonate concentration provides the first indication of disordered acid-base equilibrium, because compensatory mechanisms may keep pH within the normal range. One must be aware of the fact, however, that a normal or nearly normal value for plasma bicarbonate concentration does not exclude the presence of an acute respiratory abnormality, nor of certain mixed disturbances. Having established the presence of an acid-base disturbance, one must identify the primary disturbance by application of guidelines shown in Tables 11.4 and 11.5. Accurate assessment of simple acid-base disorders requires knowledge of both the time course and the magnitude of the secondary (adaptive) response. As a rule, a simple metabolic disorder is present when pH, plasma bicarbonate concentration, and pCO_2 are decreased (metabolic acidosis) or increased (metabolic alkalosis) in the same direction (Tab. 11.5). In clinical practice, the confidence band technique can also be applied in order to "visualize" uncomplicated acid-base disorders (Fig. 11.3). This technique does not permit automatic identification of acid-base disorders, however, because the range of physiologic response for any simple disturbance is wide enough to allow the superimposition of another primary disturbance to cause a mixed acid-base disorder without shifting the acid-base equilibrium beyond the expected limits.

In addition to these guidelines, some empiric observations may be helpful. For example, if the plasma bicarbonate concentration is less than 10 mmol/l, primary metabolic acidosis must be present, because secondary hypobicarbonatemia alone never reaches this level. Similarly, if plasma bicarbonate is greater than 40 mmol/l, metabolic alkalosis is almost certainly present, because the secondary response to chronic hypercapnia only rarely causes such a large increment in plasma bicarbonate concentration. Sometimes one needs information on the patient´s history and the clinical setting to establish the nature of the primary process. For example, in a patient with no history of pulmonary disease, the finding of even a moderately increased plasma bicarbonate following treatment with a potent diuretic reflects metabolic alkalosis rather than respiratory acidosis.

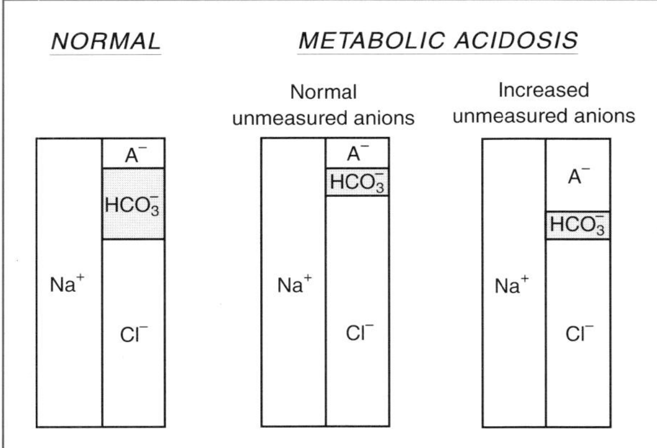

Figure 11.2 The anion gap. In the extracellular fluid, sodium ions account for the bulk of cation equivalents, whereas chloride and bicarbonate account for most of the anion equivalents, under all conditions. The difference between sodium concentration and the sum of chloride and bicarbonate concentrations in plasma is defined as the "unmeasured anion" concentration (anion gap = A^-). It is composed of anionic groups of proteins as well as other organic and inorganic anions.

Table 11.3 Interconversion of pH and hydrogen ion concentration

pH	Hydrogen ion concentration (nmol/l)		
	derived values		actual values
	I	II	
7.80	-	16	16
7.70	-	20	20
7.60	-	26	25
7.50	30	32	32
7.40	40	40	40
7.30	50	50	50
7.20	60	63	63
7.10	-	78	79
7.00	-	98	100
6.90	-	122	126

I - between pH 7.20 and 7.50, with every 0.1 unit change in pH, [H^+] changes by 10 nmol/l in the opposite direction.
II - with every 0.1 unit rise in pH, multiply preceding [H^+] by 0.8. With every fall in pH, multiply preceding [H^+] by 1.25.

Table 11.4 Simple (compensated) acid-base disorders and predicted compensations

Acid-base disorder	Primary/secondary change	Expected range of secondary response	Maximal limits of compensation	Time to completion
Metabolic acidosis	$\downarrow[HCO_3^-]$ / $\downarrow pCO_2$	$pCO_2 = 1.5 \times [HCO_3^-] + 8\ (\pm 2)$ = last two digits of pH	pCO_2 = 10 mmHg	12-24 h
Metabolic alkalosis	$\uparrow[HCO_3^-]$ / $\uparrow pCO_2$	$pCO_2 = 0.9 \times [HCO_3^-] + 16\ (\pm 5)$ = last two digits of pH	pCO_2 = 55 mmHg	24-36 h
Respiratory acidosis				
acute	$\uparrow pCO_2$ / $\uparrow[HCO_3^-]$	$[H^+] = 0.75 \times pCO_2 + 9\ (\pm 4)$ $\Delta[HCO_3^-] = 0.1 \times \Delta pCO_2$	$[HCO_3^-]$ = 30 nmol/l	5-10 min
chronic	$\uparrow pCO_2$ / $\uparrow[HCO_3^-]$	$[H^+] = 0.3 \times pCO_2 + 28\ (\pm 3)$ $\Delta[HCO_3^-] = 0.4 \times \Delta pCO_2$	$[HCO_3^-]$ = 45 nmol/l	72-96 h
Respiratory alkalosis				
acute	$\downarrow pCO_2$ / $\downarrow[HCO_3^-]$	$[H^+] = 0.75 \times pCO_2 + 9\ (\pm 4)$ $\Delta[HCO_3^-] = 0.2 \times \Delta pCO_2$	$[HCO_3^-]$ = 18 nmol/l	5-10 min
chronic	$\downarrow pCO_2$ / $\downarrow[HCO_3^-]$	$[H^+] = 0.3 \times pCO_2 + 28\ (\pm 4)$ $\Delta[HCO_3^-] = 0.5 \times \Delta pCO_2$	$[HCO_3^-]$ = 15 nmol/l	48-72 h

Is a mixed acid-base disorder present?

Examining this possibility represents the next step in evaluating acid-base disturbances. First one must define the primary disorder and the renal or pulmonary compensation – the confidence band technique and/or the guidelines in Table 11.4 may be helpful. Laboratory values that do not fit within the expected range of laboratory data for the appropriate simple acid-base disturbance strongly indicate the existence of a mixed acid-base disorder. Even when pH, pCO_2, and bicarbonate concentration are normal, mixed metabolic acidosis and alkalosis may be present. Critical evaluation of the clinical setting is therefore unavoidable, and may give clues to the correct diagnosis. The most common clinical conditions associated with mixed acid-base disorders are summarized in Table 11.6.

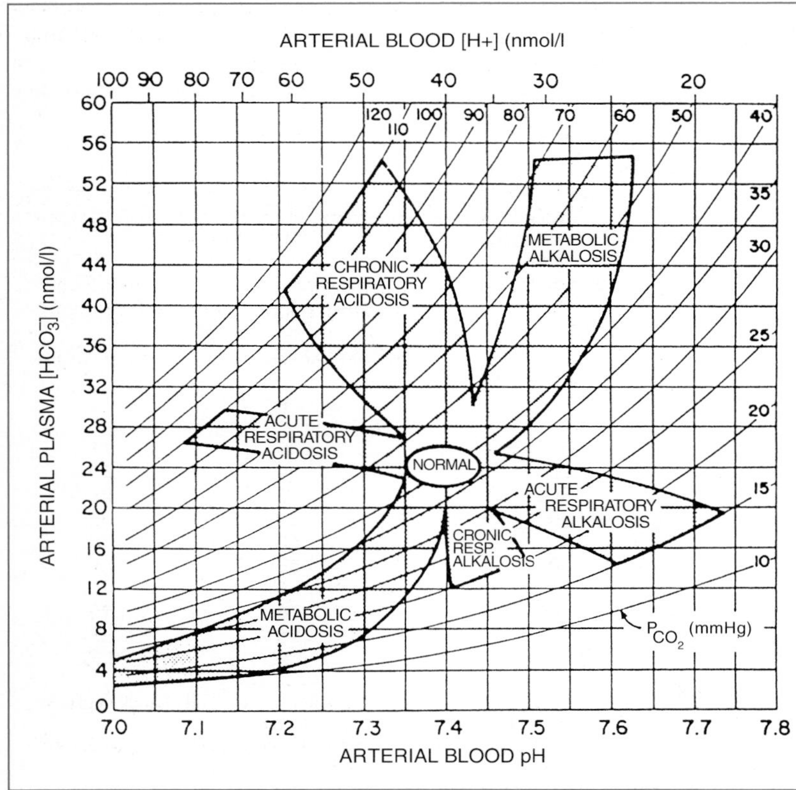

Figure 11.3 Confidence band technique (acid-base nomogram). The nomogram depicts the 95% confidence limits of the normal metabolic and respiratory adaptation to each of the four primary acid-base disorders. Acid-base parameters falling within the expected range of a simple acid-base disorder are consistent with, but not diagnostic of, the particular disturbance, whereas acid-base data falling outside the expected range signify the presence of a mixed acid-base disorder. (From Cogan MG, Rector FC. Acid-base disorders. In: Brenner B, Rector FC, eds. The kidney. Philadelphia: WB Saunders, 1991;753.)

Table 11.5 Patterns of laboratory values in simple decompensated acid-base disorders

Acid-base disorder	pH	pCO_2	HCO_3
Metabolic acidosis	↓	↓	↓
Respiratory acidosis	↓	↑	↑
Metabolic alkalosis	↑	↑	↑
Respiratory alkalosis	↑	↓	↓

ACIDOSIS

Clinical findings

Whereas mild acidemia usually does not cause complaints, especially when present chronically, severe acidemia (*blood pH < 7.20*) critically affects the function of several organs and can be life-threatening. Symptoms and signs occur independently of whether acidemia (acidosis) is of metabolic, respiratory, or mixed origin (Tab. 11.7). Most symptoms are not specific, however, and the diagnosis depends on recognition of the clinical setting and laboratory studies.

The effects of acidemia on the cardiovascular system are particularly pernicious and include decreased myocardial contractility and cardiac output, resulting in cardiac failure, hypotension, decreased hepatic and renal blood flow, centralization of effective blood volume, tissue hypoxia, and pulmonary edema. Re-entrant arrhythmias and a reduction in the threshold for ventricular fibrillation can occur. Acidemia progressively attenuates the effect of catecholamines on the heart and the vasculature; therefore, increasingly larger doses of catecholamines must be given in order to maintain organ perfusion. Brain cell metabolism and volume regulation are impaired by severe acidemia as well. Acidemia also has important metabolic consequences – it decreases insulin sensitivity and inhibits anaerobic glycolysis. The uptake of lactate by the liver is reduced, and the liver can even be converted to a net lactate producer. In patients with severe acidosis development of a catabolic state also occur. Because cellular potassium exchanges for hydrogen ions, acidemia usually causes hyperkalemia; the effect is more prominent in inorganic acidosis than in organic and respiratory acidosis.

Metabolic acidosis

Pathophysiology and diagnosis

Metabolic acidosis can result from: (1) an increase in net acid production or net acid intake above net renal excretion (e.g., ketoacidosis, lactic acidosis, ammonium chloride loading); (2) failure of renal net excretion to match net acid production plus net acid intake (e.g., renal tubular acidosis); (3) bicarbonate loss via the gastrointestinal tract (e.g., diarrhea, gastrointestinal fistula); and (4) extracellular fluid dilution by a nonbicarbonate-containing solution (e.g., rapid saline administration). The compensatory response to metabolic acidosis is an increase in ventilation that returns blood pH toward normal; complete compensation does not occur, however. In addition, with normal kidney function net acid excretion increases promptly owing to increased titration of urinary phosphate, but over several days ammonium production becomes the most impor-

Table 11.6 Common causes of mixed acid-base disorders

Clinical setting	Metabolic		Respiratory	
	acidosis	alkalosis	acidosis	alkalosis
Cardiopulmonary arrest	x		x	
Severe pulmonary edema	x		x	
Pulmonary disease with				
renal failure	x		x	
diuretic therapy		x	x	
steroid therapy		x	x	
Sepsis	x			x
Vomiting superimposed on				
renal failure	x	x		
diabetic ketoacidosis	x	x		
pregnancy	x			x
Chronic liver disease with diuretic therapy		x		x
Salicylate overdose	x			x
Combined hepatic and renal insufficiency	x			x

tant renal mechanism of proton excretion. When the metabolic acidosis is compensated, the pCO_2 approximates the last two digits of the blood pH. If this is not the case, a mixed acid-base disorder should be considered.

The plasma anion gap (see Fig. 11.2) helps in determining the etiology of a metabolic acidosis (Tab. 11.8). The majority of clinical conditions resulting in *increased anion gap* acidosis with normal plasma chloride concentration are characterized by overproduction of organic acids, e.g., ketones and lactic acid. A *normal anion gap* acidosis with increased serum chloride concentration (i.e., hyperchloremic metabolic acidosis) generally is due to gastrointestinal tract or renal bicarbonate wasting, because chloride must replace the lost plasma bicarbonate in order to maintain electroneutrality. Calculating the *urine anion gap* (= *urine* $[Na^+ + K^+] - Cl^-$) is the next diagnostic step in the differentiation of a normal gap metabolic acidosis. If the acidosis is due to an extrarenal disorder such as diarrhea, there will be considerably more chloride than sodium plus potassium in the urine, resulting in a large negative urine anion gap. The missing cation is ammonium, indicating preserved renal acidification in response to systemic acidosis. In contrast, if a defect in renal acidification is the major contributing factor to acidosis, a positive urine anion gap can be expected, because ammonium excretion is low. This is found in syndromes of distal *renal tubular acidosis (RTA)*. The urine anion gap can be applied only if no unusual anions (e.g., ketone bodies) are present in the urine and bicarbonate excretion is low, however. Finally, normo- or hypokalemia may be a clue to pathologic conditions in which concomitant acidosis and potassium depletion are present, such as diarrhea, administration of acetazolamide, and proximal or classic distal renal tubular acidosis. An urine pH above 5.5 will disclose the latter form of renal tubular acidosis, whereas in proximal renal tubular acidosis an urine pH below 5.5 usually is observed.

Table 11.7 Major adverse consequences of severe acidemia

Cardiovascular
- Impairment of cardiac contractility with reduction in cardiac output
- Decreased arterial blood pressure and reduction of organ blood flow
- Arteriolar dilation, venoconstriction and centralization of blood volume
- Increased pulmonary vascular resistance
- Sensitization to re-entrant arrhythmias and reduction in threshold of ventricular fibrillation
- Attenuation of cardiovascular responsiveness to catecholamines

Respiratory
- Hyperventilation (Kussmaul respiration) and dyspnea
- Decreased strength of respiratory muscles and promotion of muscle fatigue
- Pulmonary edema

Metabolic
- Increased metabolic demands
- Insulin resistance (i.e., reduced insulin-mediated glucose uptake)
- Inhibition of anaerobic glycolysis
- Reduction in ATP synthesis
- Inhibition of metabolism and cell-volume regulation
- Hyperkalemia
- Increased protein degradation (hyperkatabolic state)

Central nervous system
- Vasodilation and signs of increased intracranial pressure (due to increased pCO_2 with respiratory acidosis)
- Progressive fatigue, confusion, stupor and coma

Treatment

General principles of alkali therapy

In certain organic acidoses (e.g., ketoacidosis, lactic acidosis), effective treatment of the underlying disease can foster conversion of the accumulated organic anions to bicarbonate within hours. By contrast, in hyperchloremic acidosis such an endogenous regeneration of bicarbonate cannot occur. Therefore, even if the cause of the acidosis can be reversed, alkali administration often is required for treatment of severe acidemia. Currently, intravenous *sodium bicarbonate* is the cornerstone of acute alkali therapy. Other alkalizing salts, such as sodium lactate, citrate, or acetate, are not reliable substitutes, since their alkalizing effect depends on oxidation to bicarbonate, a process that can be seriously impaired in several clinical conditions (e.g., liver disease and circulatory failure). Because the administration of sodium bicarbonate entails certain risks, it should be given judiciously in amounts that will return blood pH to a safer level, i.e., about 7.20. To accomplish this goal, plasma bicarbonate must be increased to about 8 to 12 mmol/l. There is no simple prescription for reaching this target, partly because the apparent space of distribution of infused bicarbonate may be very variable in accordance to the patient´s acid-base status. The normal value is thought to be close to 50% of body weight, but it may be

Table 11.8 Differential diagnosis of metabolic acidosis using the anion gap

Increased anion gap	Normal anion gap
Ketoacidosis (diabetic)	Loss of bicarbonate
Uremia (renal failure)	diarrhea, small bowel disease
Salicylate intoxication	ureterosigmoidostomy, ileostomy
Starvation ketoacidosis	pancreatic or biliary fistulas
Methanol intoxication	post hypocapnia
Alkohol ketoacidosis	Renal tubular acidosis
Unmeasured osmoles (intoxication)	Dilution
Lactic acidosis	Acid loads
	lysine and arginine hydrochloride
	NH_4Cl, hyperalimentation

as much as 80% in severe metabolic acidosis. Being mindful of overtreatment, it is advisable to take the bicarbonate space to be 50% of body weight, and to calculate the bicarbonate load as follows:

$$NaHCO_3 \text{ in mmol} = (\text{desired - actual plasma bicarbonate}) \times \times \text{ kg body weight} \times 0.5$$

Thus, to increase plasma bicarbonate from 10 to 18 mmol/l in a 80-kg patient, the estimated amount of sodium bicarbonate required is 8 × 80 × 0.5, or 320 mmol. Sodium bicarbonate should be infused slowly rather than given as a bolus, because too rapid administration may induce cardiac arrhythmias. Another risk of the administration of sizable amounts of undiluted sodium bicarbonate preparation are hypernatremia and hyperosmolality. These complications can be avoided by adding 100 mmol of sodium bicarbonate to 1 liter of a 0.9% NaCl solution or 150 mmol to 1 liter of a 5% glucose solution. Further, alkali therapy can lead to extracellular-fluid volume overload, especially in patients with congestive heart failure or renal failure. If adequate diuresis cannot be established with loop diuretics, hemofiltration or dialysis with a bicarbonate-buffered fluid may be required. Last but not least, *"overshoot" alkalosis*, an abrupt transition from severe acidemia to alkalemia, can result from overly aggressive alkali loading. Follow-up monitoring of the patient´s acid-base status is therefore mandatory to determine additional alkali requirements; at least 30 minutes must elapse after the infusion of bicarbonate is completed, however, before its clinical effect can be judged.

Carbicarb, an alternative source of alkali, consists of equimolar concentrations of sodium bicarbonate and sodium carbonate. Because carbonate is a stronger base, it is used in preference to bicarbonate for buffering H^+, generating bicarbonate rather than carbon dioxide. In addition, the carbonate ion can react with carbonic acid, thereby consuming carbon dioxide. Thus, Carbicarb limits but does not eliminate the generation of CO_2. Clinical experience with the substance is still limited, however. As with sodium bicarbonate, treatment with Carbicarb confers the risks of hypervolemia and hypertonicity. *THAM* is another carbon dioxide-consuming alkalinizing agent. This sodium-free solution of 0.3 N-tromethamine buffers both metabolic acids and respiratory acids. Nevertheless, serious side effects, including hyperkalemia, hypoglycemia, ventilatory depression, and local injury in case of extravasation limit its usefulness.

Alkali stimulates anaerobic glycolysis and organic acid production – effects that must be considered in the management of lactic acidosis and ketoacidosis. Such effects can be nonsalutary, since they limit the alkalizing action of bicarbonate. In contrast, in cases of tissue hypoperfusion and hypoxemia, alkali-induced stimulation of 6-phosphofructokinase acitivity may allow the partial regeneration of depleted ATP stores in vital organs. Buffering of protons by bicarbonate releases carbon dioxide and can raise the prevailing pCO_2 in body fluids. This effect can be consequential in patients with limited ventilatory reserve, those in advanced circulatory failure, or those undergoing cardiopulmonary resuscitation. Under these circumstances, paradoxic worsening of intracellular (and even extracellular) acidosis can occur. This counterproductive effect may be evident only in mixed venous blood, which better reflects the tissue acid-base status.

In clinical situations that do not necessitate acute treatment, such as chronic renal failure or renal tubular acidosis, oral sodium bicarbonate can be administered. Treatment usually should begin with 0.5 g three times daily, and should be increased to maintain the desired plasma bicarbonate level. Alternative sources of bicarbonate may be used (e.g., sodium citrate or acetate), but have no advantage over sodium bicarbonate.

Common causes of metabolic acidosis and their treatment

Lactic acidosis Under basal metabolic conditions production and degradation of lactate are in balance because of liver and kidney lactate consumption. With tissue hypoxia of any cause, both overproduction and underuse of lactic acid lead to its accumulation; this type of lactic acidosis is sometimes referred as *type A lactic acidosis* (Tab. 11.9). Reduced oxygen tissue delivery decreases intracellular ATP formation, shifts the cell redox pairs such as NADH/NAD toward the reduced state, increases ADP and AMP concentrations within cells, and activates phosphofructokinase, the key enzyme of glycolysis. Consequently, glycolysis is accelerated, increasing the production of pyruvate and lactate, because lactate is in near-equilibrium with pyruvate ($pyruvate + NADH + H^+ \Leftrightarrow lactate + NAD$). The reaction is catalyzed by lactic dehydrogenase. The overall process of glycolysis generates one H^+ for each lactate molecule produced – acid production therefore increases proportionately with lactate production. The resultant acidemia further suppresses liver and kidney consumption of lactate, thereby establishing an ominous vicious circle. Lactic acidosis also can be present in clinical conditions whitout apparent tissue hypoxia (*type B lactic acidosis*), including leukemia, lymphoma, solid tumors, severe hepatic failure, diabetic coma, a variey of intoxications, etc. (Tab. 11.9). The diagnosis of lactic acidosis (i.e., increased anion gap acidosis) is confirmed with measurement of blood lactate concentration.

Therapy should focus primarily on identifying and treating the underlying cause of lactic acidosis, because this will correct the acidosis by metabolism of lactate. Cause-specific measures should therefore be instituted promptly, including operative intervention in severe intestinal ischemia due to embolism, neutralization and removal of toxins, discontinuation of biguanide and nitroprusside therapy, administration of insulin in patients with diabetes mellitus, low-carbohydrate diet and antibiotics in *D-lactic acidosis* due to short-bowel syndrome, etc. Administration of oxygen or even ventilator support may be necessary when improvement of tissue oxygenation is mandatory. Repletion of extracellular fluid volume, afterload-reducing agents, and inotropic compounds such as dopamine and dobutamine, should be administreted when

Table 11.9 Causes of lactic acidosis

Type A

Increased oxygen demand
- Vigorous voluntary exercise
- Generalized convulsions
- Hypothermia

Reduced oxygen delivery
- Shock
- Low cardiac output
- Mesenterial embolism
- Severe hypoxemia or anemia

Type B

Sytemic disorders
- Diabetes mellitus
- Malignancy
- Pheochromocytoma
- Thiamine deficiency
- Liver disease

Drugs and toxins
- Salicylates, paracetamol
- Ethylene glycol, ethanol, methanol
- Sorbitol, xylitol
- Sodium nitroprusside, cyanide
- Isoniazid, nalidixic acid
- Biguanides
- Epinephrine, norepinephrine

Congenital enzymatic defects
- Glucose-6-phosphatase
- Pyruvate carboxylase
- Pyruvate dehydrogenase
- Fructose-1,6-diphosphatase

indicated. Vasoconstricting agents such as norepinephrine should be avoided, if possible, since they can worsen tissue hypoxia. Results of experimental studies have suggested that alkali therapy in lactic acidosis may be counterproductive because correction of acidosis appears to increase lactate production. However, acidemia may contribute to circulatory collapse, thereby perpetuating the underlying cause of lactic acidosis. Hence, in the presence of severe acidemia, cause-specific measures can be supplemented by cautious administration of intravenous bicarbonate at a rate sufficient to maintain plasma bicarbonate at about 10 mmol/l and pH above 7.2. Restraint should be exercised during cardiopulmonary resuscitation, however, because the markeldy reduced pulmonary blood flow can lead to retention of CO_2 generated in the process of buffering, potentially exacerbating the prevailing acidosis. Removal of lactic acid using extracorporeal devices has not been proved effective in the treatment of acidemia.

The prognosis of patients with lactic acidosis remains poor, because the underlying disease frequently cannot be managed effectively. As a consequence, particular attention should be paid to preventive measures (e.g., maintaining adequate fluid balance, treating infections, cautiously prescribing drugs that promote lactic acidosis), especially in patients at high risk for lactic acidosis, such as those with diabetes mellitus or advanced cardiac, respiratory, renal, or hepatic disease.

Ketoacidosis In *diabetic ketoacidosis* acetoacetic and ß-hydroxybutyric acids are produced more rapidly than they can be metabolized. Nausea, vomiting, and abdominal pain are frequent complaints in patients with diabetic ketoacidosis. Insulin administration is the cornerstone of treatment; fluid and electrolyte deficits should also be replaced. Alkali should not be administered routinely, since the metabolism of the retained ketoacids in response to insulin therapy results in swift regeneration of bicarbonate with resolution of acidemia. Nonetheless, in patients with marked acidemia (pH < 7.10 or plasma bicarbonate < 8 mmol/l), intravenous alkali should be administered. *Alcoholic ketoacidosis* usually corrects itself spontaneously with the provision of nutrients, thiamine, multivitamin preparations, and interruption of alcohol intake. *Starvation* by itself can sometimes promote a mild ketoacidosis, but when combined with prolonged alcohol abuse severe acidemia may ensue. The infusion of glucose stimulates insulin secretion, which in turn promotes the regeneration of bicarbonate from the metabolism of ketoacids. An extracellular-fluid volume deficit can be repaired with saline administration.

Intoxications *Methanol and ethylene glycol* intoxications can produce severe, high anion gap metabolic acidoses. These intoxications can be suspected when the measured plasma osmolality exceeds calculated plasma osmolality (osmolal gap). Plasma osmolality can be calculated as following:

$$\text{plasma osmolality} = [2 \times \text{Na (in mmol/l)}] + \text{glucose} / 18 \text{ (in mg/dl)} + \text{BUN} / 2.8 \text{ (in mg/dl)}$$

Detection of a large osmolal gap in patients with suspected intoxication permits immediate treatment while awaiting confirmation of diagnosis with specific tests for toxins. Large amounts of alkali often are required to combat the severe acidemia; additional therapeutic measures include oral charcoal, intravenous or oral ethanol (which inhibits the generation of toxic metabolites due to its higher affinity for liver alcohol dehydrogenase), and in severe cases hemodialysis. Forced diuresis can prevent acute renal failure due to intratubular calcium oxalate crystal deposition in cases of ethylene glycol intoxication. 4-Methylpyrazole, a potent inhibitor of alcohol dehydrogenase, can reduce the generation of toxic metabolites.

Aspirin intoxication is confirmed by measuring plasma salicylate concentration (toxic range > 2.9 mmol/l or > 40 mg/dl). It can cause several acid-base disorders, e.g., respiratory alkalosis, mixed respiratory alkalosis and metabolic acidosis, or (less commonly) simple metabolic acidosis. Respiratory alkalosis is caused by a direct stimulation of the respiratory center by salicylate, whereas the accumulation of lactic acid and ketoacids largely acounts for metabolic acidosis. Because the risk of death and the severity of neurologic manifestations depend on the concentration of salicylate in the central nervous system, drug absorption should be limited with activated charcoal. In addition, blood pH should be raised to about 7.45 to 7.50 using alkali (unless the blood is already alkalinized by respiratory alkalosis) in order to promote the exit of the toxin from the cerebral tissue. In turn, the resultant alkalinization of the urine facilitates the excretion of salicylate. Establishing a high urinary flow rate also enhances salicylate excretion. Hemodialysis is reserved for severe cases, especially those involving renal dysfunction.

Renal failure The metabolic acidosis accompaning *chronic renal failure* develops progressively when the glomerular filtration rate falls below 60 ml/min. It has an increased anion gap due to accumulation of endogenous organic acids. The renal ammonium mechanism usually is compromised as well, whereas acidification of the urine is normal. Plasma bicarbonate decreases progressively, but usually stabilizes between 12 and 18 mmol/l owing to increased stimulation of acid excretion and buffering by bone carbonate and phosphate. In order to prevent the undesirable effects of the latter process, oral sodium bicarbonate therapy is recommended to stabilize plasma bicarbonate concentration above 20 mmol/l. *Acute renal failure* in a catabolic patient can cause severe metabolic acidosis. In this clinical setting plasma bicarbonate concentration usually decreases by approximately 1 to 2 mmol/l per day if reduced renal excretion is the only cause of metabolic acidosis. Alkali should be administrated to combat the acidosis; in severe therapy-resistant cases, hemodialysis with bicarbonate-rich solutions is indicated.

Renal tubular acidosis (RTA) Proximal renal tubular acidosis (type 2 renal tubular acidosis) is characterized by excessive proximal tubule bicarbonate loss resulting in profound bicarbonaturia, which can be accompanied by other defects of proximal tubule function, e.g., glucosuria, aminoaciduria, phosphaturia. Proximal renal tubular acidosis is observed in primary Fanconi syndrome, renal transplants, tubulointerstitial diseases, nephrotic syndrome, or multiple myeloma; it can be induced by certain drugs or toxins (e.g., gentamicin, mercury, lead, acetazolamide). In some patients with proximal renal tubular acidosis, plasma bicarbonate concentration decreases sufficiently to limit the filtered load of bicarbonate, so that most of it is reabsorbed. This permits acidification of the distal tubule; hence the patients are able to reduce urine pH below 5.5 in severe acidemia. As a consequence, patients with proximal renal tubular acidosis typically have only mild to moderate acidemia with a plasma bicarbonate concentration above 15 mmol/l. In children it presents as failure to thrive, growth retardation, vomiting, volume depletion, and rickets; in adults osteomalacia is common. The diagnosis is confirmed by measuring fractional excretion of bicarbonate, which exceeds 15%. The treatment can be difficult, often requiring more than 15 mmol/kg/day of oral bicarbonate.

Classic distal renal tubular acidosis (type 1 renal tubular acidosis) is characterized by a defective collecting duct urine acidification (proton pump failure) leading to a normal anion gap metabolic acidosis accompanied by normo- or hypokalemia. Even in the presence of profound acidemia, these patients cannot maximally acidify their urine (i.e., below pH 5.5). The disease can occur as an autosomal dominant inherited disorder or can be aquired in tubulointerstitial diseases, autoimmune diseases, diseases associated with nephrocalcinosis, or produced by certain drugs or toxins (e.g., amphotericin B, analgesics). Patients may present with profound acidemia, but incomplete classic distal renal tubular acidosis with even (sub)normal plasma bicarbonate concentration may exist – it can be detected only by a formal test of urine acidification. Given a standardized load of ammonium chloride (0.1 g/kg daily for 3 to 5 days) these patients fail to reduce urine pH below 5.5 despite a decrease in plasma bicarbonate concentration. Small amounts of oral bicarbonate (less than 3 mmol/kg/day) usually are sufficient to treat the acidosis. Correction should be complete, however, in order to prevent such complications as osteomalacia, hypercalciuria, nephrocalcinosis, and nephrolithiasis.

Hyperkalemic distal renal tubular acidosis (type 4) is the consequence of reduced aldosterone production or resistance to the action of aldosterone. The former type can be observed in Addison's disease, in patients with the *syndrome of hyporeninemic hypoaldosteronism*, and in patients treated with ACE inhibitors and potassium-sparing diuretics. Such individuals can reduce urine pH below 5.5. Impaired aldosterone production responds well to mineralocorticoid replacement therapy (e.g., fludrocortisone acetate 0.1 to 0.2 mg/day). Hyperkalemic renal tubular acidosis is common in diabetic nephropathy, tubulointerstitial nephropathies, and after renal transplantation; most patients are best treated with loop diuretics and sodium alkali therapy, if necessary.

Gastrointestinal bicarbonate loss Loss of bicarbonate from the digestive tract due to diarrhea or intestinal malabsorption of any cause can lead to marked metabolic acidosis that requires exogenous replenishment of body alkali stores, in addition to administration of water, sodium, and potassium. These patients typically present with a hyperchloremic metabolic acidosis accompanied by hypokalemia, although a high anion gap can develop when fluid losses are profuse. Patients with severe diarrhea and those with pancreatic allografts, in whom the exocrine pancreas drains into the urinary bladder, have this type of acidosis.

Respiratory acidosis

Pathogenesis and diagnosis

Respiratory acidosis is observed whenever CO_2 excretion by the lungs lags behind metabolic CO_2 production, resulting in positive CO_2 balance. An acute increase in pCO_2 results in an increased carbonic acid concentration that is buffered primarily by intracellular buffers, resulting in a small increase in plasma bicarbonate concentration. When hypercapnia is sustained (chronic), the kidneys compensate by increasing net acid excretion, but the renal adaptation usually takes longer than 48 hours to develop fully, generating the hypochloremic hyperbicarbonatemia characteristic of chronic hypercapnia. The increment in plasma bicarbonate attributable to renal compensation is represented by the difference between the curves marked chronic respiratory acidosis and acute respiratory acidosis using the confidence band technique (see Fig 11.3). Life-threatening acidemia of respiratory origin can occur during severe acute respiratory acidosis or during respiratory decompensation in patients with chronic hypercapnia.

Respiratory acidosis is frequently encountered in diseases involving the central nervous system, lungs, and heart (Tab. 11.10). Sedatives and opiates that depress the respiratory center are common iatrogenic causes of respiratory acidosis. In *acute respiratory acidosis* the rise in pCO_2 will cause obligatory hypoxemia in patients breathing room air. The resultant fall in pO_2 limits hypercapnia to approximately 80 to 90 mmHg; a higher pCO_2 imposes a pO_2 that is incompatible with life. Under these circumstances, it is hypoxemia, not hypercapnia or acidemia, that poses the principal threat to life. Consequently, oxygen administration represents a critical element in the management of acute respiratory acidosis. In chronic hypercapnia, progressive narcosis and coma, known as *hypercapnic encephalopathy*, can ensue when pCO_2 exceeds 70 mmHg. Asterixis and even papilledema may occur, because of increased intracranial pressure due to cerebral vasodilatation. Avoidance of tranquilizers and sedatives, gradual reduction of supplemental oxygen (aiming at pO_2 of about 60 mmHg), and treatment of a superimposed element of metabolic alkalosis will optimize the ventilatory drive.

Table 11.10 Common causes of respiratory acidosis

Alveolar hypoventilation (decreased CO_2 removal)

Depression of respiratory center:

- drugs (e.g., opiates, benzodiazepines, barbiturates, alcohol)
- CNS lesions (e.g., trauma, cerebrovascular accidents, meningitis, encephalitis, brain tumor, multiple sclerosis)

Decreased stimulation of respiratory center (e.g., sleep apnea)

Neuromuscular diseases (e.g., Guillain-Barrè syndrome, spinal cord injury, myasthenia gravis, muscular dystrophy, myositis, hypokalemia, hypophosphatemia)

Drugs and toxins (e.g., succinylcholine, curare, botulism, tetanus)

Ventilation-perfusion mismatch

Obstruction (e.g., laryngospasm, bronchospasm, aspiration of foreign body, emphysema)

Ventilatory restriction (e.g., pneumothorax, hemothorax, hydrothorax, adult respiratory distress syndrome, massive pulmonary embolism, severe pneumonia, Pickwickian syndrome, kyphoscoliosis, obesity, ascites, interstitial fibrosis, radiation pneumonitis)

Decreased capillary exchange of CO_2

Cardiac arrest, circulatory shock, severe pulmonary edema

Treatment

Management of respiratory decompensation depends on the cause, severity, and rate of progression of carbon dioxide retention. Whenever possible, treatment must be directed at removing or ameliorating the underlying cause (e.g., administration of naloxone to reverse the suppressive effect of narcotic agents on ventilation). In addition, conservative measures such as treatment of pulmonary infections, bronchodilator therapy, and removal of secretions can offer considerable benefit. Efforts should focus on securing a patent airway and restoring adequate oxygenation by delivering an oxygen-rich inspired mixture. Noninvasive mechanical ventilation with a nasal or facial mask can be tried to avert the possible complications of endotracheal intubation. Mechanical ventilation must be initiated in the presence of apnea, severe hypoxemia unresponsive to conservative measures, or progressive respiratory acidosis, i.e., at a pCO_2 above 70 mmHg.

Whereas an aggressive approach that favors the early use of ventilator assistance is most appropriate for patients with acute respiratory acidosis, a more conservative approach is advisable in those with chronic disease that limit pulmonary reserve, because of the great difficulty in weaning such patients from ventilators. However, if the patient is obtunded or unable to cough, and if hypercapnia and acidemia are worsening, mechanical ventilation should be initiated. Minute ventilation should be raised so that the pCO_2 gradually returns to near its long-term base line and excretion of excess bicarbonate by the kidneys is accomplished. Overly aggressive pCO_2 reduction can lead to *posthypercapnic alkalosis*. This complication can be ameliorated by providing potassium chloride and administering acetazolamide at doses of 250 to 500 mg once or twice daily.

It has been standard practice to prescribe tidal volumes two to three times normal (i.e., 10 to 15 ml/kg) when instituting mechanical ventilation for patients with acute respiratory failure. This approach can cause tissue injury as a result of alveolar overdistention, culminating in lung rupture. An alternative approach is to achieve a plateau airway pressure no higher than 35 cm of water using tidal volumes of 5 to 7 ml/kg or less. This strategy is referred to as *permissive hypercapnia* or controlled hypoventilation, because a high pCO_2 may ensue. The increased respiratory drive due to the high pCO_2 causes discomfort, however, making sedation and often also neuromuscular blockade necessary. Contraindications to the use of permissive hypercapnia include cerebrovascular disease, brain edema, increased intracranial pressure, convulsions, depressed cardiac function, arrhythmias, and severe pulmonary hypertension. Importantly, most of these conditions can develop as adverse effects of permissive hypercapnia itself, especially when substantial acidemia is present. It therefore appears prudent to keep the blood pH at approximately 7.30 by cautious administration of intravenous alkali during controlled hypoventilation.

ALKALOSIS

Clinical findings

The symptoms and signs of alkalemia are summarized in Table 11.11. Severe alkalemia (*blood pH > 7.60*) compromises cerebral and myocardial perfusion by causing arteriolar constriction, an effect that is more pronounced in respiratory than in metabolic alkalosis. Neurologic abnormalities may ensue, including headache, tetany, seizures, lethargy, delirium, and stupor. Alkalemia predisposes to refractory cardiac arrhythmias; this action is accentuated in patients with underlying heart disease. Further, alkalemia depresses respiration – an effect that can be significant in patients with compromised ventilation. In addition, even mild alkalemia can frustrate efforts to wean patients from mechanical ventilation. Hypokalemia is an almost constant feature of alkalemic disorders, but it is more prominent in those of metabolic origin. Hypokalemia (and decreased ionized calcium) may contribute to muscle cramps, weakness, and hyperreflexia.

Metabolic alkalosis

Pathophysiology

Metabolic alkalosis is due to a primary increase in plasma bicarbonate concentration, resulting in an increase in blood pH. Alveolar hypoventilation is the compensatory respiratory response to metabolic alkalosis, but it is usually limited to a rise in pCO_2 of 50 to 60 mmHg. The increase in plasma bicarbonate concentration can result from addition of bicarbonate or its precursors (e.g., lactate, citrate, acetate) to the extracellular fluid, or loss of fluid with a chloride-to-bicarbonate ratio greater than that of plasma. The latter leads to extracellular volume contraction and an increase in plasma bicarbonate concentration (*contraction alkalosis*). Volume depletion increases renal bicarbonate retention by decreasing the glomerular filtration rate, increasing the proximal and distal tubule proton secretion and reducing the luminal chloride delivery to the collecting duct, which limits chloride-bicarbonate exchange. As a consequence, despite elevation of plasma bicarbonate concentration, the urine pH usually is less than 7.0 in patients with sustained metabolic alkalosis due to volume depletion ("*paradoxic aciduria*"). Metabolic alkalosis can also result from potassium depletion, but uncomplicated potassium depletion usually produces only a mild metabolic alkalosis unless there is concomitant hyperaldosteronism. In this condition the increase in plasma bicarbonate reflects the generation and retention of bicarbonate by the kidney as a consequence of increased net acid excretion.

Table 11.11 Major adverse consequences of severe alkalemia

Cardiovascular
- Arteriolar constriction
- Reduction in coronary blood flow
- Reduction in angina treshold
- Predisposition to refractory arrhythmias

Respiratory
- Hypoventilation with attendant hypercapnia and hypoxemia

Metabolic
- Stimulation of anaerobic glycolysis and lactic acid production
- Hypokalemia, hypomagnesia, and hypophosphatemia
- Decreased plasma ionized calcium concentration

Cerebral
- Reduction of cerebral blood flow
- Tetany, seizures, lethargy, delirium, and stupor

Diagnosis

For practical purpose, the clinical conditions associated with metabolic alkalosis can be divided into those with and those without volume depletion, if one eliminates alkali ingestion or administration from consideration (Tab. 11.12). Patients from the first group are characterized by volume-contraction invariably due to chloride depletion, their kidneys are sodium- and chloride-avid, and alkalosis is chloride-responsive (that is, readily corrected by chloride administration). Such individuals often exhibit other features of reduced effective circulating volume, e.g., orthostatic hypotension, tachycardia, etc. Unless a renal mechanism is responsible for the volume and chloride depletion (e.g., diuretics), these patients will exhibit intense chloride conservation – as a rule, urinary chloride concentration will be below 10 mmol/l. The most common causes of severe chloride-responsive metabolic alkalosis are due to loss of gastric secretions and administration of loop or thiazide diuretics. The characteristic hypochloremic hyperbicarbonatemia results from the loss of hydrochloric acid or

Table 11.12 Common causes of metabolic alkalosis

Chloride-responsive (U_{Cl} < 10 mmol/l)	Chloride-resistant (U_{Cl} > 20 mmol/l)
Gastric fluid loses	Primary aldosteronism
vomiting, bulimia	Drugs (e.g., licorice)
drainage	Renin-secreting tumor
Stool loses	Bartter´s syndrome
villous adenoma	Gitelman´s syndrome
congenital chloridorrhea	Cushing´s syndrome
Diuretic therapy	Renovascular hypertension
Posthypercapnic state	

(U_{Cl} = urine chloride concentration.)

from urinary excretion of excess ammonium chloride caused by these chloruretic diuretics. Substantial contraction of the extracellular fluid volume can further amplify the resulting hyperbicarbonatemia by limiting the space of distribution of bicarbonate. This is often observed in patients with massive edema treated with a combination of loop and distal tubular diuretics. Maintenance of chloride-responsive metabolic alkalosis is then effected by increased renal bicarbonate reabsorption, frequently coupled with a reduced glomerular filtration rate. The volume deficit and consequent hyperaldosteronism with concomitant hypokalemia, stimulate proton secretion, generating and maintaining the alkalosis. Large amounts of chloride appear in the urine of patients during the action of the diuretic, but urine chloride concentration falls to low levels after the diuretic action has dissipated. Thus, if diuretic abuse is suspected, measurement of chloride in sequential urine specimens or measurement of drug concentration in the urine portion with the greatest chloride concentration may prove diagnostic.

In the second group of patients, metabolic alkalosis is euvolemic or volume-expanded; their kidneys excrete all ingested sodium and chloride. The most common causes are syndromes of excessive mineralocorticoid production and action (Tab. 11.12). Mineralocorticoids stimulate renal hydrogen secretion, which in turn stimulates bicarbonate reabsorption, thereby sustaining the metabolic alkalosis. In these patients blood pressure is usually increased as well. This type of metabolic alkalosis does not respond to NaCl administration. Urinary chloride excretion typically exceeds 20 mmol/l. Hypokalemia is a consistent feature of this type of metabolic alkalosis unless frank renal insufficiency is present. Hypokalemia stimulates tubular acid secretion as well, and may help to sustain metabolic alkalosis in hypermineralocorticoidism. Assessment of urinary potassium excretion, blood pressure status, and plasma renin activity (or plasma concentration of active renin) can be helpful in the differentiation of disorders associated with chloride-resistant metabolic alkalosis (Tab. 11.13).

Table 11.13 Diagnostic algorithm for chloride-resistant metabolic alkalosis

Urine $K^+ < 10$ mmol/l
Laxative abuse
Severe K^+ depletion

Urine $K^+ > 10$ mmol/l
Blood pressure
- normal: Bartter´s syndrome
- high⇒ plasma renin activity
  - low: primary aldosteronism, licorice abuse, carbenoxolone
  - high: renin secreting tumor, Cushing´s syndrome, malignant hypertension, renovascular hypertension

Treatment

If the processes that generate metabolic alkalosis are still ongoing, every effort should be made to moderate or stop them. Vomiting should be countered with antiemetics. If continuation of gastric drainage is required, the loss of gastric acid can be reduced by administering inhibitors of the gastric H^+/K^+-ATPase. Decreasing the dose of loop and/or thiazide diuretics can be coupled with the addition of a potassium-sparing diuretic that curtails potassium excretion and decreases distal tubular acidification. Sometimes, absorbable alkali is not a complicating factor but the very cause of the metabolic alkalosis, as in patients ingesting inordinate amounts of calcium carbonate and milk (*milk-alkali syndrome*); severe metabolic alkalosis coupled with hypercalcemia and renal impairment can occur. If drugs with mineralocorticoid activity (e.g., fludrocortisone) or glucocorticoid compounds are being administered, their indications and dose should be reassessed. Having addressed the factors that cause or aggravate the alkalosis, one must then focus on ameliorating the existing hyperbicarbonatemia. Just as in severe metabolic acidosis, the immediate goal of therapy of metabolic alkalosis is moderation but not full correction of the alkalemia. Reducing plasma bicarbonate to less than 40 mmol/l is an appropriate short-term goal, since the corresponding pH is on the order of about 7.55 or lower.

Chloride-responsive metabolic alkalosis will correct with provision of both sodium chloride and potassium chloride. This will repair the often-present functional azotemia and promote bicarbonaturia. Treatment of severe chloride-responsive metabolic alkalosis is considerably more challenging in patients with cardiac or renal dysfunction. Downgrading the diuretic regimen, adding the carbonic anhydrase inhibitor acetazolamide (250 to 500 mg once or twice daily), and cautiously administering NaCl sometimes may suffice. Acetazolamide fosters bicarbonaturia but promotes kaliuresis as well. Infusion of hydrochloric acid can be efficacious, but the associated fluid load is often problematic. Under these circumstances, use of hemodialysis and ultrafiltration with reduced bicarbonate concentration of the standard dialysate can rapidly correct severe alkalemia and volume overload. In patients with unstable hemodynamics, the same goals can be achieved with continuous venovenous hemofiltration with sodium chloride as the replacement solution.

Life-treathening alkalemia is a very rare occurrence in chloride-resistant metabolic alkalosis. Aggressive potassium repletion usually will correct or ameliorate moderate chloride-resistant alkalosis. When the cause of the mineralocorticoid excess cannot be reversed, potassium-sparing diuretics coupled with moderate restriction of dietary salt intake can provide symptomatic relief. Potassium-sparing diuretics, nonsteroidal antiinflammatory drugs, or ACE inhibitors can ameliorate Bartter's or Gitelman's syndrome. If the pace of correction of the alkalemia must be accelerated, alkali stores can be titrated by infusing hydrochloric acid. Because of its sclerosing properties, hydrochloric acid should be added to amino acid or glucose solutions containing electrolytes and administered through a central venous line at an infusion rate of no more than 0.2 mmol/kg/h. However, it can also be administered through a peripheral vein cannula if it is mixed with a fat emulsion. Calculation of the amount of hydrochloric acid solution to be infused is based on the bicarbonate distribution space (i.e., about 50% of body weight). Thus, to reduce plasma bicarbonate from 50 to 40 mmol/l in a 80-kg patient, the estimated amount of hydrochloric acid required is $10 \times 80 \times 0.5$, or 400 mmol. Precursors of hydrochloric acid, such as ammonium chloride and arginine monohydrochloride can be used, but both of these preparations are hyperosmotic solutions. In addition, ammonium chloride can raise serum ammonium concentration in patients with liver failure, and arginine monohydrochloride can induce serious hyperkalemia in patients with renal failure, especially when there is coexisting liver disease.

Respiratory alkalosis

Pathophysiology and diagnosis

Respiratory alkalosis is the most frequently encountered acid-base disorder, since it occurs in normal pregnancy and with high-altitude residence. The pathologic causes of respiratory alkalosis are shown in Table 11.14. Respiratory alkalosis is particularly prevalent among critically ill patients; its presence is a bad prognostic sign, because mortality increases in direct proportion to the severity of the hypocapnia.

Hypocapnia elicits a secondary change in plasma bicarbonate that has two components. A moderate acute decrease in plasma bicarbonate originates from tissue buffering. A larger decrease accompanies chronic hypocapnia as a result of down-regulation of renal acidification and inhibition of tubular reabsorption and generation of bicarbonate – it requires at least 2 days to reach completion. As in respiratory acidosis, compensation for the chronic state is much more complete than for the acute (see Fig. 11.3). Because blood pH does not exceed 7.55 in most cases of respiratory alkalosis, severe manifestations of alkalemia usually are absent. Marked alkalemia can be observed, however, with inappropriately set ventilators, some psychiatric disorders, and lesions of the central nervous system. Obviously, clinical manifestations of severe alkalemia are more likely to occur in the acute, rather than the chronic, phase of respiratory alkalosis. Patients often present with hyperventilation, perioral and extremity paresthesias, light-headness, muscle cramps, hyperreflexia, seizures, or cardiac arrhythmias. In patients with the anxiety-hyperventilation syndrome, alkalemia directly enhances neuromusclar excitability and, in addition, decreases ionized plasma calcium concentration – both effects can provoke tetany.

Arterial blood hypocapnia can be also observed in an atypical form of respiratory acidosis, which has been termed *pseudorespiratory alkalosis*. It occurs in patients with profound depression of cardiac function and pulmonary perfusion, but with relative preservation of alveolar ventilation (e.g., patients undergoing cardiopulmonary resuscitation). The severely reduced pulmonary blood flow limits CO_2 delivery to the lungs, thereby increasing the mixed venous blood pCO_2. By contrast, the increased ventilation-perfusion ratio causes the removal of a larger-than-normal amount of CO_2 per unit blood traversing the pulmonary circulation, thereby creating arterial eucapnia or frank hypocapnia. Nonetheless, absolute excretion of CO_2 is reduced, and the carbon dioxide balance of the body is positive – the hallmark of respiratory acidosis. Such patients may have severe venous acidemia accompanied by an arterial pH that ranges from the mildly acidic to the frankly alkaline. Thus, to rule out pseudorespiratory alkalosis, blood gas monitoring must include sampling of mixed venous blood. Management of pseudorespiratory alkalosis is directed toward optiminzing systemic hemodynamics.

Table 11.14 Common causes of respiratory alkalosis

Hypoxia (compensatory hyperventilation)
- Acute (e.g., pulmonary edema or emboli, pneumonia, hemodialysis)
- Chronic (e.g., severe anemia, high altitude, asthma, hypotension)

Respiratory center stimulation
- Pregnancy
- Anxiety (hyperventilation syndrome)
- Fever, heat stroke
- Sepsis (especially gram-negative sepsis)
- Salicylate intoxication
- Cerebral disease (infection, trauma, tumor, infarction)
- Hepatic cirrhosis
- Overcorrection of metabolic acidosis
- Catecholamines

Increased mechanical ventilation

Treatment

Correcting the underlying cause, whenever possible, is the treatment of choice. Because most cases of respiratory alkalosis pose little risk to health and produce few or no symptoms, treatment of the deranged acid-base equilibrium is not required. The anxiety-hyperventilation syndrome is an exception – an active therapeutic approach that provides reassurance, and ultimately psychotherapy, is most helpful in these cases. Rebreathing into a closed system (e.g., paper bag) provides prompt, but only short-lived symptomatic relief. If alkalemia is severe and persistent, sedation may be required.

MIXED ACID-BASE DISORDERS

Mixed acidoses

Coexistent respiratory acidosis and metabolic acidosis can be observed in several clinical conditions (see Tab. 11.6). The additive effects on blood acidity of primary hypercapnia and bicarbonate deficit can produce profound acidemia requiring prompt therapy. The pH can be substantially lowered even though pCO_2 and plasma bicarbonate concentration may not be markedly changed, so that the laboratory values definitely do not fit on the confidence band for either metabolic or respiratory acidosis (Fig. 11.3). In most cases, the acid-base parameters will fall between the bands for metabolic acidosis and acute respiratory acidosis on the nomogram, but the bicarbonate/pCO_2 ratio will be inappropriate for either disorder. Whenever possible, both components of the mixed acidosis must be treated.

Mixed alkaloses

Extreme alkalemia can occur in patients with combined metabolic and respiratory alkalosis, even with only moderate changes in plasma bicarbonate and pCO_2. A mixed disorder can be suspected if a respiratory alkalosis is not accompanied by the appropriate change in pCO_2. This combination occurs frequently in critically ill patients owing to excessive mechanical ventilation and diuretic use. Mixed alkalosis also can occur in patients with primary hypocapnia associated with chronic liver disease, in whom metabolic alkalosis develops because of vomiting, nasogastric drainage, diuretics, profound hypokalemia, or alkali administration, especially in the context of renal insufficiency. Further, mixed alkalosis can be observed in patients with end-stage renal disease on maintenance hemodialysis in whom primary hypocapnia develops; the inappropriately high plasma bicarbonate level reflects the absence of the renal response to the prevailing hypocapnia and the dialysis-induced alkali load. Patients undergoing peritoneal dialysis are even more vulnerable, because peritoneal dialysis maintains plasma bicarbonate at higher level. Reducing the base concentration of the dialysate or switching the patient from peritoneal dialysis to hemodialysis will ameliorate the situation.

Complex acid-base disorders

In *mixed metabolic acidosis and respiratory alkalosis* the bicarbonate concentration and pCO_2 are both reduced, but pCO_2 will be lower than predicted for the respiratory compensation of the metabolic acidosis (Tab. 11.4). A *mixed metabolic acidosis and metabolic alkalosis* can be difficult to diagnose because both disorders primarily affect the plasma bicarbonate concentration. The pH and bicarbonate concentration can be increased, decreased, or normal. An elevated anion gap with normal or even increased plasma bicarbonate concentration suggests the presence of a metabolic acidosis with increased anion gap and a metabolic alkalosis, because these two variables usually are in reciprocal relationship (i.e., a rise of the anion gap is accompanied by a fall in the plasma bicarbonate concentration of approximately the same magnitude). Coexisting *metabolic alkalosis and respiratory acidosis* are characterized by an increased bicarbonate concentration and increased pCO_2. By applying the equations in Table 11.4 (or the acid-base nomogram), the elevation in bicarbonate concentration will be greater than predicted for compensation caused by respiratory acidosis. Finally, a *triple acid-base disorder* can exist, due to combined metabolic acidosis and metabolic alkalosis accompanied by either respiratory acidosis or respiratory alkalosis. It frequently occurs in an alcoholic or diabetic patient with vomiting, lactic acidosis or ketoacidosis, and superimposed sepsis. The underlying causes of the acid-base disorders must be treated in such patients.

Suggested readings

ANDROGUE HJ, MADIAS NE. Management of life-threatening acid-base disorders. First of two parts. N Engl J Med 1998;338:26-34.

ANDROGUE HJ, MADIAS NE. Management of life-threatening acid-base disorders. Second of two parts. N Engl J Med 1998;338:107-11.

ANDROGUE HJ, RASHAD MN, GORIN AB, et al. Assessing acid-base status in circulatory failure: differences between arterial and venous blood. N Engl J Med 1989;320:1312-6.

COHEN RD. Lactic acidosis: new perspectives on origin and treatment. Diabetes Rev 1994;2:86-97.

FABER MD, KUPIN WL, HEILIG CW, NARINS RG. Common fluid, electrolyte and acid-base problems in the intensive care unit: selected issues. Semin Nephrol 1994;14:8-22.

FEIHL F, PERRET C. Permissive hypercapnia: how permissive should we be? Am J Respir Crit Care Med 1994;150:1722-37.

GABOW PA. Disorders associated with an altered anion gap. Kidney Intern 1985;27:472-81.

HOOD VL, TANNEN RI. Maintenance of acid-base homeostasis during ketoacidosis and lactic acidosis: implications for therapy. Diabet Rev 1994;2:177-94.

KRAPF R, BEELER, HERTNER D, HULTER HN. Chronic respiratory alkalosis: the effect of sustained hyperventilation on renal regulation of acid-base equilibrium. N Engl J Med 1991;324:1394-401.

LEBOVITZ HE. Diabetic ketoacidosis. Lancet 1995;345:767-72.

MADIAS NE, ANDROGUE HJ. Acid-base disturbances in pulmonary medicine. In: Arieff AI, DeFronzo RA, eds. Fluid, electrolyte, and acid-base disorders. 2nd ed. New York: Churchill Livingstone, 1995:223-53.

NARINS RG, COHEN JJ. Bicarbonate therapy for organic acidosis: the case for its continued use. Ann Intern Med 1987;106:615-8.

RIMMER JM, GENNARI FJ. Metabolic alkalosis. J Intensive Care Med 1987;2:137-50.

CHAPTER

12

Calcium, phosphate, and magnesium disorders

Pascal Houillier, Jean-Michel Achard

DISORDERS OF CALCIUM METABOLISM

NORMAL HOMEOSTASIS

Total-body calcium content in a healthy 70-kg adult is about 33 000 mmol (1300 g), 99% of which is contained in bone and 1% in soft tissues, whereas only 0.1% is present in the extracellular fluid (ECF). Serum calcium concentration in normal subjects ranges from 2.2 to 2.6 mmol/l. Total serum calcium is composed of different fractions: the ionized, free calcium is the biologically active and regulated fraction, which normally represents about 55% of total serum calcium; the remaining 45% is biologically inert, mostly bound to serum proteins (chiefly albumin) or complexed to serum anions. In hypoalbuminemia, total calcium is low, and in hyperalbuminemia, it is high, but free calcium is normal. Total calcium can be "corrected" knowing that each gram of albumin binds 0.02 mmol calcium.

Serum calcium is maintained remarkably constant thanks to integrated regulation of calcium fluxes between the extracellular fluid and the kidneys and bone. Normal intestinal calcium absorption is critical for the stability of body calcium content and the maintenance of bone calcium stores. During fasting, extracellular fluid calcium concentration depends on bone calcium release that balances the urinary calcium loss (Fig. 12.1). In the absence of an appropriate calcium intake (usually 20-25 mmol/d) or adequate intestinal calcium absorption, extracellular fluid calcium concentration is maintained at the expense of a sustained bone calcium mobilization that results in a progressive decrease in bone calcium content. In a normal individual with a diet that is adequate for calcium and a normal intestinal absorption (about 20% of the amount of ingested calcium), 24-h urine calcium excretion equals net intestinal calcium absorption. About 500 mg of calcium leaves the bone daily, but an equal amount is deposited back in the skeleton by a process called *bone remodeling* that relies on the coupled activities of two different bone

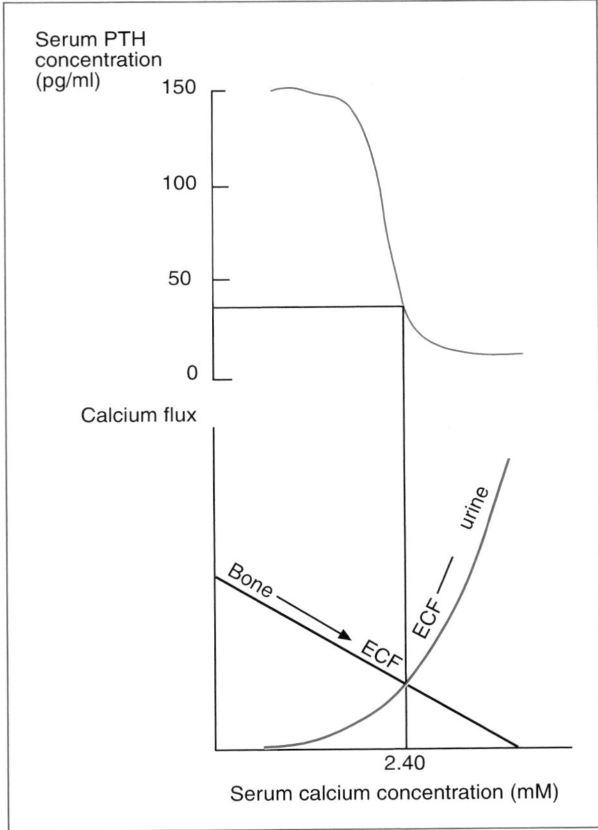

Figure 12.1 Relationships between fasting serum calcium concentration and parathyroid hormone concentration (*upper panel*) and bone-extracellular fluid and extracellular fluid-urine calcium fluxes (*lower panel*). In the fasting state, serum calcium concentration is maintained constant because the urine loss of calcium is balanced by bone calcium release. A decrease in serum calcium concentration results in an increase in parathyroid hormone secretion that enhances bone calcium release and decreases urine calcium excretion, thereby restoring a normal serum calcium concentration. This equilibrium requires the presence of a plasma membrane calcium-sensing receptor in parathyroid cells and adequate blood concentrations of both parathyroid hormone and calcitriol.

cell types: osteoblasts and osteoclasts. Under normal conditions, the net flux is zero.

The kidney is the main excretory organ for calcium. Per day, about 250 mmol calcium is filtered, of which normally only 1 to 3% appears in the urine. Given a daily intake of 25 mmol, renal excretion averages 5 mmol/d. Most reabsorption takes place in the proximal tubule along an electrochemical gradient and a sodium-dependent active transport mechanism. Therefore, dehydration impairs calcium excretion, whereas (saline) expansion enhances calcium excretion. About 20% is reabsorbed in the ascending limb of Henle's loop, and the remainder is reabsorbed in the distal convoluted tubule. The latter is under the control of parathyroid hormone (PTH), which stimulates calcium reabsorption.

The precise regulation of the plasma calcium concentration is controlled by PTH and $1{,}25(OH)_2$ vitamin D_3 (calcitriol). PTH is a peptide hormone that acts on bone and kidney through a G protein-coupled plasma membrane receptor. Calcitriol is a steroid hormone that binds to a specific cytosolic receptor present in numerous cell types, including renal tubular, intestinal epithelial, and bone cells; calcitriol-receptor complex acts in the nucleus by modulating transcription in areas of chromatin called *vitamin D-responsive elements*. PTH stimulates bone calcium reabsorption and increases extracellular fluid calcium. PTH also increases renal tubular reabsorption of calcium and stimulates α-hydroxylase-dependent conversion of 25(OH) vitamin D_3 into calcitriol; this latter hormone markedly increases intestinal calcium absorption and is required for a full end-organ action of PTH.

An acute decrease in extracellular fluid calcium concentration activates a calcium-sensing receptor expressed in the cell membrane of parathyroid cells and produces an immediate increase in PTH secretion. The parathyroid glands of mammals are remarkably sensitive to extracellular fluid calcium and a steep, immediate (seconds) inverse sigmoidal relationship between extracellular fluid calcium and PTH secretion has been demonstrated both in vitro and in vivo.

HYPERCALCEMIA

Pathophysiology

Two conditions may be responsible for persistent hypercalcemia. Besides the clinical data described below, the main criterion to distinguish between these conditions is the serum PTH concentration. The first condition occurs when the relationships between serum calcium and PTH secretion, bone-extracellular fluid calcium flux, and extracellular fluid-urine calcium flux are all shifted to a higher serum calcium level. In such a situation, a normal extracellular fluid calcium level is associated with a high PTH secretion. Consequently, the PTH-dependent net calcium flux from bone into extracellular fluid is increased, and urine calcium excretion is low. Extracellular fluid calcium level increases, and a new steady state is reached when urine calcium excretion equals net bone calcium release. Minimal net flux of calcium occurs in the new steady state, and bone mass and calcium balance both remain unaltered. Therefore, fasting and 24-h urine calcium excretions may well be normal; in fact, 24-h urine calcium excretion increases only when net intestinal calcium absorption is elevated because of the PTH-induced increase in calcitriol excretion. The resulting stable hypercalcemia is called *equilibrium hypercalcemia*. Primary hyperparathyroidism in its usual presentation is a typical example of equilibrium hypercalcemia.

The second condition is a disturbance of the bone-remodeling system resulting in a dramatically increased net bone resorption, a decrease in bone mass, and a negative calcium balance. This is observed when an increased osteoclastic bone resorption is associated with an uncoupled (i.e., not increased, or even depressed) osteoblastic bone formation. Despite the inhibition of PTH, the net influx of calcium into the extracellular fluid may exceed the capacity of the kidney to excrete the excess calcium, inducing progressive hypercalcemia called *disequilibrium hypercalcemia*. In fact, because an extracellular fluid volume decrease frequently occurs (due to vomiting and hypercalcemia-induced decrease in renal tubular NaCl reabsorption), glomerular filtration rate also decreases and renal calcium reabsorption increases, worsening hypercalcemia. Hypercalcemia of malignancies is the prototype of disequilibrium hypercalcemia. In this condition, at variance with what is observed in equilibrium hypercalcemia, fasting as well as 24-h urine calcium excretions are always higher than normal.

Whatever its mechanism, hypercalcemia is tolerated least well if it is of greater magnitude and/or rapidly increasing. Hypercalcemia causes gastrointestinal, neurologic, cardiac, and renal derangements (Tab. 12.1). A major and early complication is renal concentration disturbance (polyuria) and NaCl loss. The latter is particularly impor-

Table 12.1 Manifestations of hypercalcemia

Gastrointestinal
Anorexia
Nausea, vomiting
Acute pancreatitis
Neuropsychiatric
Asthenia
Confusion, disorientation
Irritability, depression
Stupor, coma
Cardiovascular
Shortening of QT interval
Increased toxicity of cardiac glycosides
Arrhythmias
Renal
Polyuria, polydipsia
NaCl wasting
Nephrolithiasis, nephrocalcinosis
Renal failure
Metastatic calcifications

tant in acute situations, since hypovolemia impairs renal calcium excretion and worsens hypercalcemia. In addition, dehydration of some other cause may quickly evoke serious symptomatic hypercalcemia in patients with preexisting mild asymptomatic hypercalcemia. Therefore, NaCl supplementation is a first indispensable step in the treatment of hypercalcemia.

Etiology (Tab. 12.2)

Parathyroid hypercalcemia

Primary hyperparathyroidism (PHPT) is the most frequent cause of hypercalcemia. PHPT predominantly affects females over age 40. It results from a primary and inappropriate excess of PTH secretion that is usually moderate, yielding to a mild and stable increase in extracellular fluid calcium. Today, 80% of primary hyperparathyroidism is diagnosed in symptomless patients. Only about 20% of patients have a recurrent calcium stone disease, and less than 1% have osteitis fibrosa cystica. Hypercalcemia is usually mild (serum calcium = 2.8-3 mM) and remains relatively constant for many years. Plasma PTH and urine cyclic AMP levels are high. Renal tubular reabsorption of phosphate is low, often yielding hypophosphatemia. Hypercalciuria occurs in 50% of patients due to the PTH-induced increase in calcitriol synthesis and intestinal calcium absorption. Plasma acid-base status is usually normal, and metabolic acidosis occurs only occasionally when nephrocalcinosis, renal failure, or severe phosphate depletion is present. That bone mass is lost is still debated. An excess in PTH stimulates osteoclastic bone resorption, but osteoblastic bone formation is increased as well. Biochemical indexes of bone resorption (such as deoxypyridinoline) and bone formation (such as osteocalcin or bone-specific alkaline phosphatase) are both increased. No increased rate of bone loss or fracture risk was found in patients with asymptomatic mild primary hyperparathyroidism.

Table 12.2 Principal causes of hypercalcemia

Parathyroid hypercalcemia
Primary hyperparathyroidism
Familial benign hypercalcemia
Lithium therapy
Extraparathyroid hypercalcemia
Hypercalcemia of malignancies
Humoral hypercalcemia of malignancies
Local osteolytic hypercalcemia
Thyrotoxicosis
Granulomatous diseases (e.g., sarcoidosis, coccidioidomyosis, histoplasmosis, tuberculosis)
Vitamin D intoxication
Immobilization hypercalcemia
Vitamin A intoxication
Adrenal insufficiency
Milk-alkali syndrome
Idiopathic hypercalcemia of infancy

Familial benign hypercalcemia

This disorder, also referred to as *familial hypocalciuric hypercalcemia* (FBH), is inherited as an autosomal dominant pattern with complete penetrance. It is characterized by a stable, usually asymptomatic hypercalcemia present from early childhood. The course may be complicated by acute pancreatitis, or pseudogout. Familial hypocalciuric hypercalcemia is mostly due to a heterozygous loss-of-function mutation of the calcium-sensing receptor. Consequently, a steady state is achieved with normal PTH but increased extracellular fluid calcium values. Renal calcium excretion is low, despite a high filtered calcium load; the same calcium receptor is involved in the control of calcium reabsorption in the thick ascending limb of the loop of Henle. The diagnosis relies on the combination of asymptomatic hypercalcemia, low renal excretion of calcium and magnesium, and an autosomal pattern of inheritance or the demonstration of a mutation of the calcium-sensing receptor gene, located on chromosome 3. This condition should not be misdiagnosed as primary hyperparathyroidism because parathyroidectomy is to be avoided.

Lithium therapy decreases renal calcium and magnesium clearance and can increase secretion of PTH, thereby causing hypercalcemia that is reversible when lithium is withdrawn.

Extraparathyroid hypercalcemia

Hypercalcemia of malignancies

The annual incidence is approximately 150 new cases per million. Lung cancer and breast cancer are the most common solid malignancies associated with hypercalcemia. The main factor is dramatic bone reabsorption uncoupled from bone formation. The calcium release overwhelms the ability of the kidney to clear calcium, especially when renal failure is present. The osteolysis may be due to local tumor effects or to humoral tumor products. Local osteolytic hypercalcemia occurs in 20 to 30% of patients with malignancy-associated hypercalcemia. These patients have extensive skeletal tumor involvement and mostly suffer from myeloma, breast cancer, or lymphoma. The mechanism is tumor cell secretion of paracrine factors (interleukin-1α, interleukin-1β, interleukin-6, tumor necrosis factors α and β, and transforming growth factor α) that stimulate nearby osteoclasts. Plasma phosphate is usually normal. Plasma PTH, nephrogenous cAMP, and plasma calcitriol are reduced. Urinary calcium excretion is high, due to the high filtered calcium load and decreased distal tubular calcium reabsorption, and intestinal calcium absorption is decreased. Humoral hypercalcemia of malignancy is due to tumor secretion of a parathyroid hormone–related protein (PTH-rP). It is most frequently associated with squamous cell carcinomas of the lung, neck, and head, but it occasionally has been observed in almost all kinds of cancers, including hematologic malignancies. These patients may or may not have bone metastases.

PTH-rP is secreted as a 139-, 141-, or 173-amino-acid molecule that is highly homologous to PTH at its N-terminal end. PTH-rP binds to bone and kidney PTH receptors with the same affinity as PTH and induces hypercalcemia, hypophosphatemia, and elevated nephrogenous cAMP production when infused in vivo. However, different from primary hyperparathyroidism, bone turnover is uncoupled, and 1,25$(OH)_2$ vitamin D_3 production is inhibited, perhaps by cosecretion of other factors such as transforming growth factor a (TGF-α). Plasma PTH is suppressed.

Others causes of extraparathyroid hypercalcemia

Thyrotoxicosis About 10 to 20% of patients with thyrotoxicosis develop mild hypercalcemia (2.75 mM) at some time during the disease. Thyroid hormones increase bone turnover with a predominant stimulation of osteoclast activity that accounts for hypercalciuria. Moderate hyperphosphatemia is common, due to stimulation of renal phosphate reabsorption by thyroid hormones. PTH secretion is suppressed, and PTH-dependent tubular calcium reabsorption is decreased, explaining the mildness of the hypercalcemia. PTH-dependent calcitriol synthesis and, accordingly, gut calcium absorption are low.

Sarcoidosis and other granulomatous diseases A majority of patients with sarcoidosis have hypercalciuria, and about 10 to 15% develop hypercalcemia at some stage. Hypercalcemia is due to both an increased intestinal uptake and an increased bone resorption. The mechanism is an unregulated synthesis of calcitriol by granuloma tissue and by alveolar macrophages. Accordingly, circulating PTH level is low, 25(OH) vitamin D_3 concentration is normal, and 1,25$(OH)_2$ vitamin D_3 concentration is higher than normal. Hypercalcemia is worsened by sunlight exposure or vitamin D therapy and may be reduced by limiting the calcium intake and exposure to sunlight. Hypercalcemia responds within 7 days to daily administration of prednisone that limits calcitriol synthesis in the granuloma tissue. Chloroquine is an alternative treatment. Hypercalcemia also may occur in patients with other granulomatous diseases such as coccidioidomycosis, histoplasmosis, and tuberculosis.

Vitamin D intoxication generally occurs in patients treated for chronic renal failure or chronic hypocalcemic conditions with pharmacologic amounts of vitamin D. Patients vary considerably in their tolerance of vitamin D, but most adults probably require at least 50 000 units per day. Hypercalcemia may be severe and often is associated with hyperphosphatemia and impaired renal function due to nephrocalcinosis. It is due to both enhanced intestinal calcium absorption and net bone resorption, together with the reduced ability of the kidney to excrete calcium. Plasma 25(OH) vitamin D_3 may be increased for several weeks once vitamin D is discontinued, whereas calcitriol remains normal or moderately increased, and PTH is suppressed. With vitamin D derivatives with shorter half-lives (e.g., alfacalcidol or calcitriol), toxicity is of shorter duration. Corticosteroids may be used to inhibit gut calcium absorption and impair the conversion of vitamin D to its active metabolites.

Immobilization hypercalcemia Patients who are completely immobilized develop hypercalciuria because the lack of mechanical stress uncouples bone remodeling. In particular, patients with a high prior bone turnover (e.g., adolescents and patients with Paget's disease, thyrotoxicosis, or primary hyperparathyroidism) may develop severe hypercalcemia. The serum PTH is suppressed. Fluid treatment is useful to prevent renal calculi and nephrocalcinosis. Bisphosphonates, an osteoclast-inhibiting agent, have been used with success. The milk-alkali syndrome is characterized by hypercalcemia, hyperphosphatemia, and alkalosis and historically was described in patients taking the Sippy regimen for peptic ulcers. It may still be observed in patients ingesting large amounts of calcium carbonate. Hypercalcemia is explained by the high calcium intake (>4 g elemental calcium per day), the metabolic alkalosis (which enhances tubular calcium reabsorption), and renal impairment due to nephrocalcinosis. Hypercalcemia vanishes once calcium intake is reduced.

Treatment

Symptomatic treatment of extraparathyroid hypercalcemia

Patients who are symptomatic or have a plasma calcium level that is greater than 3.25 mM require immediate therapy. The idea is to correct dehydration, enhance renal excretion of calcium, and inhibit increased calcium input into the extracellular fluid. The first step is administration of isotonic saline. A moderate (0.5 mM) decrease in plasma calcium concentration is to be expected because the correction of extracellular fluid increases the amount of filtered calcium and decreases proximal tubular calcium reabsorption. This may be combined with a calciuretic loop diuretic. Calcitonin inhibits bone reabsorpion and increases renal calcium excretion and is a very efficient means to decrease extracellular fluid calcium, especially in malignancy-associated hypercalcemia. Plasma calcium concentration begins to decline within a few hours of initiation of therapy, and a nadir is reached within 12 to 24 hours. The expected decrease in plasma calcium concentration is approximately 0.5 mM. Its effect is short, unless combined with bisphosphonates or glucocorticoids. Bisphosphonates are synthetic, stable analogues of pyrophosphate that inhibit osteoclastic bone resorption. When administrated intravenously (intestinal uptake is poor), etidronate, clodronate, and pamidronate (in increasing order of potency) efficiently lower plasma calcium concentration. Usually, the plasma calcium level begins to decrease within 24 to 48 hours of the onset of treatment, and a nadir is reached within 7 days. Glucocorticoids can be effective in patients with hematologic cancer-associated hypercalcemia, as well as in hypercalcemia caused by vitamin intoxication and granulomatosis.

Treatment of primary hyperparathyroidism

To date, there is no specific pharmacologic treatment for primary hyperparathyroidism. Bisphosphonates and calcitonin are effective in acute hypercalcemia but are of little benefit for the long-term treatment. Surgery remains the only treatment available for patients with complications of primary hyperparathyroidism such as osteitis fibrosa cystica, nephrolithiasis, severe gastrointestinal complications, or neuromuscular manifestations. Surgery is also recommended in patients with asymptomatic disease who meet the criteria for severe primary hyperparathyroidism (i.e., serum calcium >0.25 mM above the upper limit of normal for the laboratory, an episode of serious hypercalcemia, a greater than 30% decrease in creatinine clearance, urinary calcium >10 mmol/day, and a decrease in bone mass greater than 2 SD when expressed in Z-score). About 50% of patients do not meet the criteria for surgical therapy at the time of diagnosis. They should be evaluated every 6 months for 1 to 3 years to determine that their condition is stable, with specific attention paid to neurologic impairment, muscle weakness, depression, and gastrointestinal, bone, or renal disease, as well as hypertension and serum and urinary calcium levels.

HYPOCALCEMIA

Pathophysiology

PTH plays a central role in the defense against hypocalcemia, and persistent hypocalcemia may occur only if PTH secretion is absent or decreased, if there is a resistance of target organs to the action of PTH, or if a net flux of calcium into bone occurs despite PTH. In the first condition, in the case of a normal serum calcium concentration, urinary calcium excretion is higher than normal, and net bone calcium release is lower than normal. The plasma calcium level falls until urinary calcium excretion is equal to net bone calcium release. In the new steady state, extracellular fluid calcium concentration is low, serum PTH concentration is low or normal, and fasting and 24-h urinary calcium excretion is low to normal. In the second condition, hypocalcemia supervenes because both bone and kidney become resistant to the biologic action of PTH. A higher than normal PTH secretion therefore is required to eventually restore a normal end-organ action of PTH. The occurrence of clinical symptoms (Tab. 12.3) depends on both the magnitude and the rate of fall in extracellular fluid calcium concentration. The main complication is tetany, which may be overt or subclinical.

Etiology (Tab. 12.4)

Hypoparathyroid hypocalcemia

Hypoparathyroidism

Hypoparathyroidism results from an impaired synthesis or secretion of PTH. The plasma calcium concentration may be as low as 1.2 mM. The plasma PTH level varies from indetectable to low normal. Hyperphosphatemia develops because of increased renal phosphate reabsorption. Intestinal tract calcium absorption is reduced because calcitriol synthesis is inhibited by high phosphate and low PTH concentrations, and 24-h calciuria is reduced. Hypoparathyroidism may be due to acquired disease, such as from gland removal during extensive cervical surgery, infiltrative disease of the parathyroids (e.g., Wilson's disease, hemochromatosis, thalassemia), or irradiation to the neck. Reversibly impaired PTH secretion occurs in severe

Table 12.3 Manifestations of hypocalcemia

Neurologic
- Tetany
- Seizures
- Intracranial calcifications (long-standing hypocalcemia)
- Papilledema
- Mental changes

Cardiovascular
- Prolonged QT interval
- Arrhythmia
- Heart failure

Miscellaneous
- Dry skin, hair loss
- Brittle nails
- Abnormal dentition
- Cataracts

Table 12.4 Principal causes of hypocalcemia

Hypoparathyroid hypocalcemia
- Hypoparathyroidism
- Inherited
  - Branchial dysembryogenesis
  - Polyglandular autoimmune disorders (HAM syndrome)
- Acquired
  - Cervical surgery
  - Infiltrative diseases (e.g., Wilson's disease, hemochromatosis, thalassemia)
  - External irradiation to the neck
  - Severe magnesium deficiency
- Autosomic dominant hypocalcemia

Extraparathyroid hypocalcemia
- Pseudohypoparathyroidisms (PHPs)
  - Albright's hereditary osteodystrophy (PHP-Ia)
  - PHP-Ib
  - PHP-II
- Vitamin D disorders
  - Vitamin D deficiency
  - Vitamin D-dependent rickets
- Chronic renal failure
- Miscellaneous
  - Osteoblastic metastases (prostate and breast cancer)
  - Tumor lysis
  - Drugs (e.g., bisphosphonates, plicamycin, calcitonin, citrated blood, foscarnet)

magnesium deficiency and alcoholism. Hypoparathyroidism is called *idiopathic* if it is due to branchial dysembryogenesis or congenital absence of parathyroid glands or is associated with polyglandular autoimmune disorders.

Autosomal dominant hypocalcemia

This disorder, also known as *familial hypercalciuric hypocalcemia*, is due to a gain-of-function mutation of the calcium-sensing receptor gene and has as an autosomal dominant pattern of inheritance. PTH concentration is inappropriately normal, and calcium excretion is normal or elevated. Treatment with calcium or vitamin D results in frank hypercalciuria, inducing nephrocalcinosis, nephrolithiasis, and renal insufficiency.

Extraparathyroid hypocalcemia

In this case, PTH secretion is appropriately elevated. Hypocalcemia occurs because of end-organ resistance to PTH action or because the underlying pathophysiologic process overwhelms the ability of PTH to restore a normal serum calcium concentration.

Pseudohypoparathyroidism (PHP)

This describes a heterogeneous syndrome characterized by hypocalcemia, hyperphosphatemia, high serum PTH concentration, and unresponsiveness of target tissues to the biologic actions of PTH. PHP is classified on the basis of the renal cAMP response to exogenous PTH infusion. In PHP types Ia and Ib, the nephrogenous cAMP response to PTH is decreased. PHP type Ia patients have a decreased amount of stimulatory G-proteins, which explains the associated resistance to other hormones (such as thyroid-stimulating hormone and gonadotropins). PHP type Ib patients have normal G-protein activity but a defect in the receptor for PTH. These patients often manifest bone lesions similar to those of patients with primary hyperparathyroidism. Patients with PHP type II have a normal renal cAMP response to PTH and probably a post-adenylyl cyclase defect.

Vitamin D disorders

Deficiency of vitamin D can occur in patients with minimal exposure to sunlight, poor nutritional status, and malabsorption (e.g., celiac disease, cystic fibrosis, chronic pancreatitis, primary biliary cirrhosis, and short-bowel syndrome, since vitamin D is a fat-soluble vitamin), as well as during anticonvulsant use (i.e., phenobarbital and phenytoin). Vitamin D-dependent rickets refers to a group of syndromes with either inborn errors in the conversion of 25(OH) vitamin D_3 to $1,25(OH)_2$ vitamin D_3 or resistance of target organs to active vitamin D metabolites because of a mutation in the vitamin D receptor. Vitamin D deficiency is characterized by bone mineralization defects, which manifest as bone pain and bowing deformities. In moderate vitamin D deficiency, hypocalciuria is present, but the secondary hypersecretion of PTH allows ECF calcium to be maintained in the normal range. In more severe vitamin D deficiency, hypocalcemia occurs because of bone and kidney resistance to PTH. Circulating 25(OH) vitamin D_3 concentration is severely reduced in absolute vitamin D deficiency but normal in vitamin D-dependent rickets.

Chronic renal failure

As renal function declines, a secondary hyperparathyroidism appears and steadily worsens. In fact, chronic renal failure is responsible for an impaired conversion of 25(OH) vitamin D_3 to $1,25(OH)_2$ vitamin D_3 and a decrease in PTH receptor expression in target organs. The secondary hyperparathyroidism allows the maintenance of extracellular fluid calcium and phosphate concentrations within the normal range until renal insufficiency becomes very severe; at that time, both hypocalcemia and hyperphosphatemia are commonly observed.

Other causes of extraparathyroid hypocalcemia

Hypocalcemia also may be observed in various circumstances such as osteoblastic metastases (e.g., prostate and breast cancer); tumor lysis that leads to release of intracellular ions and subsequent hyperphosphatemia, hypercalciuria, hyperuricemia, and hypocalcemia; and the use of a variety of drugs (e.g., bisphosphonates, plicamycin, calcitonin, citrated blood, and foscarnet).

Treatment

Acute, symptomatic hypocalcemia requires prompt oral or intravenous calcium supplement, according to the severity of hypocalcemia and the presence of tetany. The aim of treatment is to maintain the serum Ca^{2+} concentration within 1.0 to 1.2 mmol/l without (latent) tetany. Treatment of chronic hypocalcemia depends on the cause of hypocalcemia but, in most instances, relies on the combination of oral calcium (25-50 mmol/d elemental calcium) and vitamin D derivatives. In the case of true vitamin D deficiency, the treatment of choice is vitamin D_2 itself (2.5-10 μg/d). In other disorders, the most appropriate vitamin D derivative is either alfacalcidol (1α-OH vitamin D) or calcitriol [$1,25(OH)_2$ vitamin D_3] at a daily dose of 0.25 to 2 μg. During chronic calcium supplementation, one should keep in mind that renal calcium excretion should be below approximately 7 mmol/day because a higher excretion increases the risk of nephrolithiasis, nephrocalcinosis, and chronic renal insufficiency.

DISORDERS OF PHOSPHATE METABOLISM

NORMAL HOMEOSTASIS

Total-body phosphorus content in a healthy 70-kg adult is about 23 mol (700 g), 80% of which is contained in bone and 9% in skeletal muscle; the remainder is in viscera and the extracellular fluid. Plasma phosphorus concentration is determined as the inorganic phosphate (P_i) and is present as monohydrogen phosphate in equilibrium with dihydrogen phosphate. Undissociated phosphoric acid and fully dissociated trivalent phosphate ions are virtually absent from plasma at physiologic pH. The ratio of HPO_4^{2-} to $H_2PO_4^-$ at pH 7.4 is about 4:1, so the average valence of inorganic phosphate in plasma (P_i), is 1.8. The normal range of plasma concentration of P_i is 0.9 to 1.4 mM. Plasma P_i varies with a circadian rhythm, influenced by dietary intakes of phosphates and carbohydrates. Plasma P_i decreases progressively during childhood. Most intracellular phosphate exists as organic phosphate. The intracellular P_i concentration is estimated to about 1 mM.

Phosphorus is largely present in cereals, meat, eggs, and dairy products. The dietary intake in European countries (30-70 mmol/d) exceeds the Recommended Dietary Allowances (RDAs) of the American National Research Council (40 mmol/d for teenagers and during lactation and 30 mmol/d for adults and children 1-10 years of age). Roughly 70% of ingested phosphate is absorbed, mainly in duodenum and jejunum. Net phosphate transport across intestinal epithelium results from absorption and secretion. Both transports occur through transcellular apical sodium-dependent cotransport and paracellular passive diffusion. The main homeostatic control of intestinal absorption of phosphate (and calcium) is by the active metabolites of vitamin D, mainly calcitriol [1,25$(OH)_2$ vitamin D_3]. Calcitriol stimulates apical Na/Pi cotransport and inhibits the secretory system. PTH has no direct effect on phosphate absorption but indirectly stimulates calcium and phosphate absorption by stimulating renal synthesis of calcitriol.

Plasma phosphorus is present almost entirely as inorganic phosphate. The kidney plays a major role in regulating plasma P_i. About 95% of plasma P_i is filtered in the glomerulus, and normally about 20% is excreted in the urine. The proximal tubule is the major site of reabsorption. At low plasma concentrations, nearly all filtered phosphate is reabsorbed. At higher concentrations, the amount that is reabsorbed reaches a maximal value. This constant value of reabsorbed phosphate, expressed as amount per minute, is known as the *transport maximum* (T_m) (Fig. 12.2). This T_m is related to the number of apical carriers for phosphate. Normally plasma P_i is at a level where slightly more phosphate is filtered than the tubules can reabsorb. This fact enables the kidney to regulate phosphate balance. If intake increases and plasma P_i rises, the surcharge is excreted; conversely, if intake decreases and plasma P_i falls, the filtered load is conserved. This feedback mechanism is a direct consequence of the saturation kinetics of the phosphate carrier independent of hormonal regulation. However, PTH can reset P_i reabsorption in the proximal tubule to a lower rate.

PHOSPHATE DEPLETION AND HYPOPHOSPHATEMIA

Pathophysiology

Modest hypophosphatemia (0.3-0.8 mmol/l) does not produce adverse clinical effects. Severe acute hypophosphatemia (<0.3 mmol/l) can interfere with cell function or cause cell injury. The critical factor is cytoplasmic P_i. Below a critical level, glycolysis and oxygen consumption are compromised, and ATP level falls. This affects the Na^+,K^+-ATPase and Ca^{2+}-ATPase activities, impairing Na-dependent transport activities. These changes result in profound changes in cell function and eventually in cell death.

P_i concentration is critical for synthesis of 2,3,-diphosphoglyceride (2,3-DPG) in erythrocytes. A decrease in 2,3-DPG impairs tissue oxygen delivery, which compromises mitochondrial respiration-dependent ATP production further. Strong intracellular P_i deficiency may cause rhabdomyolysis. Long-term phosphorus deficiency results in proximal myopathy, respiratory failure, and paralytic ileus, and occasionally impairs cardiac function.

Phosphate depletion decreases erythrocyte half-life and, if severe, may cause acute hemolysis. Leukocyte dysfunction may result in increased vulnerability to infection, and thrombocytopenia increases the risk of gastrointestinal bleeding. Nervous system dysfunction includes numbness, paresthesias, visual and auditory hallucinations, confusion, obtundation, convulsive seizures, and coma. Brainstem dysfunction and peripheral neuropathy also may be present.

Sustained phosphate depletion inhibits proximal bicarbonate reclamation and ammonium production and impairs active distal proton excretion, resulting in a decreased net excretion of protons and development of metabolic acido-

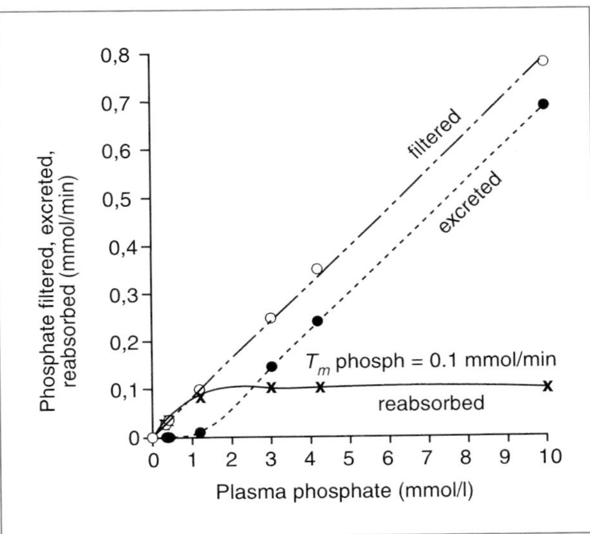

Figure 12.2 Transport maximum (T_m) of phosphates. Renal filtration, excretion, and reabsorption of phosphates are plotted as a function of plasma phosphate concentration in dogs. T_m phosphate represents the maximal amount of phopshate that the tubules can reabsorb per unit time. All filtered phosphate beyond this limit is excreted in the urine. T_m phosphate is decreased by parathormone. (Adapted with permission from Pitts RF, Alexander RS. The renal reabsorptive mechanism for inorganic phosphate in normal and acidotic dogs. Am J Physiol 1944;142:248-53.)

sis. Hypophosphatemia increases renal calcitriol production, thereby stimulating intestinal calcium absorption and PTH-independent osteolysis. This also increases calcium influx into the extracellular compartment. Nonetheless, since P_i depletion also inhibits tubular calcium reabsorption and induces hypercalciuria, hypercalcemia is rare.

Etiology

Hypophosphatemia may be due to inadequate dietary intake, impaired intestinal absorption, or increased renal excretion or may result from phosphate shift from the extracellular to the intracellular compartment (Tab. 12.5).

Insufficient dietary intake

Hypophosphatemia due to intake deficiency is rare because phosphate is widely available in nutrients. An exception is chronic alcoholism. Starvation alone usually does not induce hypophosphatemia, since fecal loss is minimal, phosphaturia is blunted, and bone and accelerated cell catabolism release phosphates, maintaining a normal plasma phosphate level. In adults, hypophosphatemia may occur on refeeding after prolonged starvation, unmasking the depletion of cell P_i. Significant hypophosphatemia may occur rapidly in starving children, in whom a positive phosphate balance is mandatory for growth.

Table 12.5 Principal causes of hypophosphatemia

Insufficient dietary intake and intestinal loss
- Chronic alcoholism
- Starvation (children)
- Phosphate binding antacides.
- Vitamin D deficiency
- Cushing's syndrome and steroid therapy
- Malabsorption, steatorrhea, secretory diarrhea

Increased urinary loss
- Primary hyperparathyroidism
- Secondary hyperparathyroidism
- Malignant neoplasms
- Paraneoplastic production of PTH-related peptide
- Tumor-induced osteomalacia associated with mesenchymal tumors, hepatocellular carcinoma, and breast, prostate, and lung tumors
- Impaired tubular function
  - Fanconi's syndrome
  - X-linked hypophosphatemic rickets
  - X-linked hypercalciuric nephrolithiasis
- Drugs
  - Foscarnet
  - Antineoplastic drugs (e.g., ifosfamide and cisplatin)
  - Antibiotics (e.g., aminoglycosides)
  - Diuretics (acetazolamide> thiazides> furosemide)

Phosphate shift
- Respiratory alkalosis
- Correction of diabetic ketoacidosis
- Nutritional recovery syndrome, hyperalimentation
- Hematologic cancer
- Correction of anemia with erythropoietin or vitamin B_{12}
- Hungry bone syndrome
- Treatment of osteomalacia and hyperresorptive bone diseases
- Recovery from severe hypothermia, severe hyperthermia, exercise

Mixed hypophosphatemia
- Chronic alcoholism
- Kidney transplant patients
- ICU patients

Intestinal loss of phosphate

The main cause of phosphate malabsorption is the use of aluminum-based phosphate-binding antacids. These compounds bind not only the phosphate from the diet but also that excreted into the intestinal lumen, and thus they induce a negative phosphate balance. Vitamin D deficiency can lead to hypophosphatemia with osteomalacia. Calcium uptake is also impaired, and the secondary rise in PTH further aggravates the phosphate depletion. Corticosteroids reduce intestinal phosphate absorption and cause phosphaturia. Hypophosphatemia is seen commonly in patients receiving corticosteroids or in Cushing's syndrome. Rare hereditary diseases are responsible for vitamin D-dependent hypophosphatemic rickets. Type I is due to an abnormality in 1,α-hydroxylase activity, with a low $1,25(OH)_2$ vitamin D_3 concentration, and therefore is remediable with calcitriol. Type II is characterized by a high circulating level of $1,25(OH)_2$ vitamin D_3, which is ineffective because of a receptor defect (see under "Hypocalcemia").

Increased urinary loss of phospate

Hyperparathyroidism

Hypophosphatemia occurs often in hyperparathyroidism, whether primary or secondary to vitamin D deficiency.

Hypophosphatemia and malignant neoplasms

Hypophosphatemia may occur in as many as 30% of patients with malignant neoplasms. It depends on the production of PTH-rP, causing pseudohyperparathyroidism with downregulation of PTH. Tumor-induced osteomalacia is a paraneoplastic disorder associated with mesenchymal tumors, hepatocellular carcinoma, and breast, prostate, and lung tumors. In this condition, the T_m phosphates/glomerular filtration rate Co (Fig. 12.2) (GFR) is also low, but the PTH level is normal. Removal of the tumor results in resolution of the abnormalities, suggesting production of some unidentified phosphaturic factor.

X-linked hypophosphatemic rickets

This is a familial disorder characterized by hypophosphatemia, retarded growth, and typical rachitic skeletal abnormality in children. The serum $1,25(OH)_2$ vitamin D_3 and PTH concentrations are normal. Inappropriate phosphaturia is caused by a gene defect-related insufficient breakdown of some natural phosphaturic factor.

X-linked hypercalciuric nephrolithiasis

This comprises several familial syndromes characterized by hypercalciuria, low-molecular-weight proteinuria, and a proximal tubular dysfunction responsible for renal wasting of phosphate, uric acid, glucose, and amino acids. Nephrolithiasis, nephrocalcinosis, progressive renal insufficiency, and eventually rickets have been described. The molecular basis is a defective gene encoding for a renal chloride channel. Renal loss of phosphate also may be due to generalized impaired proximal tubule function as occurs in Fanconi's syndrome.

Drugs

The antiviral agent foscarnet is a potent inhibitor of the Na/P_i cotransporter in the proximal tubule and the intestine and can cause hypophosphatemia. Antineoplastic drugs such as ifosfamide and cisplatin or antibiotics such as aminoglycosides are prone to cause proximal tubule damage, impairing phosphate reabsorption. However, their propensity to cause acute renal failure makes them more frequently responsible for hyperphosphatemia. Use of diuretics, in particular acetazolamide, followed by thiazides and furosemide also may be associated with hypophosphatemia.

Hypophosphatemia due to phosphate shift

Respiratory alkalosis can cause hypophosphatemia by quickly increasing cell pH, resulting in a marked stimulation of glycolysis and intermediary metabolism. Correction of diabetic ketoacidosis is another well-known condition associated with a marked redistribution hypophosphatemia. During the development of ketoacidosis, phosphate compounds are decomposed, and P_i is wasted in the urine. Plasma P_i level is usually normal, even elevated, in the setting of renal failure. Starting insulin therapy rapidly restores cell phosphorylation, resulting in a massive uptake of P_i from the extracellular fluid. This need prompt recognition and correction before cellular P_i use becomes jeopardized. A similar mechanism is responsible for hypophosphatemia during nutrition after starvation. Phosphate uptake by proliferating malignant cells in lymphoma and leukemia and by erythroblasts after stimulation by erythropoietin or correction of pernicious anemia with vitamin B_{12} occasionally can cause hypophosphatemia.

A rapid transfer of phosphate from plasma to bone, known as the *hungry bone syndrome*, is characterized by severe hypocalcemia and hypohosphatemia occurring after surgical treatment for hyperparathyroidsm or during the treatment of osteomalacia or neoplasia with bone metastasis, or after calcitonin treatment for an hyperresorptive bone disease. Recovery from severe hypothermia, severe hyperthermia, and exhausting exercise have been reported to cause hypophosphatemia, likely by the sustained high cell metabolic needs for P_i. Redistribution hypophosphatemia has been reported with infusion of interleukin-2 and during tumor necrosis factor infusion into the hepatic artery.

Treatment

Intravenous infusion of phosphorus may induce severe hypocalcemia, and its use should be restricted to intensive care unit patients with severe symptomatic phosphate depletion. Even in such a setting, replacement therapy preferably should be continued orally whenever possible. Phosphate replacement therapy is advised if moderate hypophosphatemia (<0.5 mmol/l) is associated with symptomatic phosphate depletion or if the serum phosphate concentration is below 0.3 mmol/l, since such severe hypophosphatemia is always indicative of intracellular phosphate depletion. Usually, 1 g/day (35 mmol) of elemental phosphorus as long as plasma phosphate is not normalized is sufficient.

HYPERPHOSPHATEMIA

Hyperphosphatemia is defined by a fasting plasma P_i concentration of greater than 1.45 mmol/l in adults. Upper normal values in children are listed in Table 12.6. No specific clinical manifestation is imputable to hyperphosphatemia *per se*. However, as the plasma phosphate concentration increases, a rise in the calcium phosphate product may result in calcium deposition in soft tissue responsible for pruritus and skin lesions, and hypocalcemia with tetany may ensue.

Etiology

Hyperphosphatemia can result from an excessive phosphate load, a transcellular phosphate shift, a reduced urinary excretion, or more frequently, a combination of these (Tab. 12.7).

Phosphate load

Hyperphosphatemia may occur during intravenous repletion therapy for hypophosphatemia because of persistent tubular phosphate reabsorption as a result of P_i depletion. Hyperphosphatemia due to excessive digestive absorption

Table 12.6 Normal range of plasma phosphates in children

Age	Plasma phosphate mmol/l	mg/l
Premature	1.92-2.88	60-90
First week	1.6-2.4	50-75
1-12 months	1.76-2.24	55-70
1-2 years	1.6-2.08	50-65
2-12 years	1.44-1.76	45-55
12-16 years	1.12-1.44	35-45

Table 12.7 Principal causes of hyperphosphatemia

Phosphate load
Intravenous repletion therapy of hypophosphatemia
Vitamin D intoxication
Phosphate-rich laxative abuse
Phosphate shift
Organic metabolic acidosis
Respiratory acidosis
Tumor-lysis syndrome
Severe hemolysis, rhabdomyolysis, bowel infarction
Malignant hyperthermia
Reduced urinary excretion
Renal failure (acute and chronic)
Primary hypoparathyroidism
Acromegaly
Thyrotoxicosis

is rare in the absence of vitamin D intoxication. Unless renal function is impaired, hyperphosphatemia usually requires massive amounts of exogenous phosphate but may occur in children in the setting of phosphate-rich laxative abuse. In premature neonates, cow's milk may cause hyperphosphatemia and induce tetany.

Phosphate shift

Acid-base disorders may result in hyperphosphatemia secondary to the release of Pi from the cells. Organic metabolic acidosis such as diabetic ketoacidosis or lactic acidosis, as well as respiratory acidosis, can cause serum phosphates levels to increase. Hyperphosphatemia also may occur as a consequence of extensive cell lysis in the tumor-lysis syndrome, severe hemolysis, rhabdomyolysis, bowel infarction, or malignant hyperthermia. Hyperphosphatemia is usually accompanied by a rise in plasma potassium and urate concentrations, and acute renal failure is frequent in these circumstances and contributes to the increase of plasma phosphate level.

Reduced urinary excretion

Reduction of glomerular filtration is by far the most common cause of hyperphosphatemia. In patients with mild to moderate renal failure, the secondary increase in PTH concentration inhibits renal tubular reabsorption of phosphate and balances the renal phosphate retention so that plasma levels remains within the normal range. With overt renal failure, acute or chronic, hyperphosphatemia is an almost constant finding. The abnormalities of calcium-phosphate homeostasis and their consequence for the bones in chronic renal failure are discussed elsewhere. Primary hypoparathyroidism, acromegaly, and thyrotoxicosis are also associated with a decrease in renal phosphate excretion, although GFR is normal.

Treatment

Acute and severe hyperphosphatemia as seen in rhabdomyolysis are usually associated with renal function impairment, and renal replacement therapy is indicated to decrease plasma phosphate concentration but also to correct the usually associated hyperkalemia and acidosis. Otherwise, a moderately restricted protein diet associated with administration together with the meal of phosphate-binding salts of calcium, magnesium, or aluminum is usually efficient. The prevention and treatment of renal osteodystrophy in chronic renal failure are discussed in detail in Chapter 44. In these patients, the chronic use of aluminum phosphate binders is contraindicated because of the risk of aluminum accumulation in bone (a dynamic bone disease) and brain (aluminum encephalopathy).

DISORDERS OF MAGNESIUM METABOLISM

NORMAL HOMEOSTASIS

Magnesium is the fourth most abundant cation in vertebrates and critical for a number of biologic processes such as oxidative phosphorylation, glycolysis, DNA transcription, and protein synthesis. Bone and soft tissue each contain about 50% of the total-body magnesium content (1000 mmol, 2000 mEq, or 24 g in an adult human). Bone magnesium is mainly deposited on the bone crystal surfaces and therefore rapidly exchangeable. Extracellular magnesium represents only 1% of the total-body content. The normal plasma magnesium concentration is 0.75 to 1 mmol/l; 60% is free, and the remainder is bound to protein or complexed with HCO_3^-, phosphate, or citrate. Cell magnesium concentration is 5 to 20 mmol/l, of which only 1 to 2% is ionized. Most cell magnesium is bound to metalloenzymes and phosphates and highly compartmentalized in microsomes and mitochondria.

The average daily intake of magnesium is 5 to 15 mmol, equally absorbed in the jejunum and ileum through both active transport and facilitated diffusion. The fraction of dietary magnesium absorption is poorly defined (20-60%), and the role of Ca^{2+} and vitamin D metabolites on its regulation is disputed. Optimal dietary intake has been estimated to 0.25 to 0.5 mmol/kg per day. In the steady state, the magnesium absorbed by the gastrointestinal tract is entirely eliminated in the urine. The concentration of magnesium in the extracellular fluid is determined by the kidney, and the contribution of bone and the cellular pool to the maintenance of extracellular magnesium concentration in states of deficiency is unclear.

Renal magnesium handling is a filtration-reabsorption process. Of the filtered load, 20 to 30% is reabsorbed in the proximal convoluted tubule, 65% is reabsorbed in the cortical thick ascending limb of the loop of Henle (CTAL), and less than 10% is reabsorbed in the more distal parts of the renal tubule. The tubular site primarily involved in the regulation of magnesium reabsorption is the CTAL. Hypercalcemia and hypermagnesemia decrease magnesium transport in the CTAL because both cations activate the basolateral calcium-sensing receptor and decrease magnesium (and calcium) reabsorption. Conversely, during magnesium deprivation, magnesium virtually disappears from urine (<1 mmol/d) because the CTAL's capacity to reabsorb magnesium is enhanced in this situation.

Extracellular fluid volume expansion, phosphate depletion, metabolic acidosis, diuretics, and abnormalities in potassium balance decrease magnesium reabsorption within CTAL. However, except for acidosis and diuretics, the physiologic significance of these observations remains unknown. Numerous peptide hormones (e.g., PTH, calcitonin, glucagon, and antidiuretic hormone) have been shown to enhance magnesium transport in the CTAL. Again, the physiologic relevance of these observations is uncertain, because no change in serum magnesium concentration has been observed in patients with hyper- or hypoparathyroidism or disorders in calcitonin, glucagon, or antidiuretic hormone (ADH) secretion.

MAGNESIUM DEPLETION AND HYPOMAGNESEMIA

Magnesium is mainly an intracellular cation, and the serum magnesium concentration may not reflect the intracellular magnesium content. Therefore, depletion also may be present in patients with a normal serum magnesium level. For this reason, and because a simple and reliable measurement of intracellular magnesium concentration is not available, a magnesium loading test has been developed that allows calculation of the retention of a parenterally administered magnesium load. This retention is increased in patients with true magnesium deficiency, even if the plasma magnesium concentration is normal. Of course, the test is useless in patients with renal magnesium leak.

Mild hypomagnesemia or depletion is usually asymptomatic. The possible clinical consequences of moderate to severe magnesium deficiency are shown in Table 12.8.

Physiopathology and etiology

Magnesium depletion is rare in healthy individuals with normal caloric intake because magnesium is ubiquitous in food. Thus, clinically apparent hypomagnesemia usually results from either gastrointestinal or renal losses.

Extrarenal magnesium loss

Extrarenal magnesium depletion is easy to diagnose. Because of an appropriate renal tubular adaptation to magnesium depletion, daily urinary magnesium excretion is less than 1 mmol. Magnesium depletion is common in intestinal disorders because intestinal fluid magnesium content is high (up to 7.5 mmol/l). It is frequent in acute and chronic diarrhea, regional enteritis, ulcerative colitis, and intestinal and biliary fistulas. It also may be encountered in malabsorption syndromes (e.g., nontropical sprue, radiation injury, and extensive bowel resection) and acute pancreatitis.

Renal magnesium loss

In this situation, renal magnesium excretion is maintained despite magnesium depletion and hypomagnesemia. A 24-h magnesium excretion in excess of 1 mmol, in the presence of hypomagnesemia, indicates renal magnesium loss. Renal magnesium wasting can be observed in a great variety of disorders, such as osmotic diuresis (diabetes mellitus) and hypercalcemia, which decreases magnesium reabsorption in the CTAL. It is also common during treatment with loop diuretics, aminoglycosides, amphotericin B, pentamidine, cisplatin, and cyclosporine. Although renal magnesium depletion vanishes rapidly after withdrawal of loop diuretics, it may persist for months or even years after treatment with cisplatin.

Alcohol-induced renal magnesium wasting may contribute to magnesium depletion in chronic alcoholism. Similarly, acidosis induces a renal magnesium loss that may contribute to the hypomagnesemia in acidosis associated with diabetic ketoacidosis, starvation, or alcoholism. Primary defects in renal Na reabsorption located either in the CTAL (Bartter's syndrome) or in the distal convoluted tubule (Gitelman's syndrome) are associated with secondary hyperaldosteronism, renal potassium leak and hypokalemia, metabolic alkalosis, and in many patients, renal magnesium wasting and hypomagnesemia. Uncommon syndromes of primary renal magnesium wasting, distinct from Bartter's and Gitelman's syndromes, have been described, but their pathophysiology is unknown.

Treatment

Patients with signs and symptoms of magnesium deficiency should be treated with magnesium supplementation. A continuous intravenous infusion of 25 mmol magnesium (as magnesium sulfate) over 24 hours usually results in a

Table 12.8 Manifestations of hypomagnesemia

Neuromuscular
Tetany, tremor, muscular weakness, fasciculations
Seizures
Irritability, depression
Cardiovascular
Prolonged PR and QT intervals, U waves
Atrial, junctional, and ventricular arrhythmias
Increased toxicity of cardiac glycosides
Myocardial ischemia and infarction
Potassium homeostasis
Renal potassium wasting
Mineral metabolism
Hypocalcemia, impaired PTH secretion, renal and skeletal resistance to PTH
Osteoporosis and osteomalacia
Nephrocalcinosis, chondrocalcinosis

normal serum magnesium concentration. The repletion of body magnesium stores is achieved within 3 to 7 days. Once repletion has been obtained, a normal magnesium status usually can be maintained by a regular diet, provided that the cause for magnesium depletion has been corrected. In ongoing intestinal or renal magnesium loss, oral magnesium supplementation is indicated (10-25 mmol elemental magnesium daily).

HYPERMAGNESEMIA

Patients with magnesium concentrations up to 2 mmol/l are usually asymptomatic; more severe hypermagnesemia can cause neuromuscular transmission depression, resulting from inhibition of acetylcholine release. In hypermagnesemic patients, nausea and vomiting, lethargy and confusion, hypotension and bradycardia, and loss of tendon reflexes occur progressively. At levels of about 9 mmol/l, complete paralysis of skeletal muscles induces respiratory depression, while cardiac conduction impairment causes heart block and ultimately cardiac arrest. It is important to notice that the neuromuscular and cardiac effects of hypermagnesemia are both antagonized by calcium and that hypocalcemia may occur with hypermagnesemia because magnesium mimics the effect of calcium on the parathyroid calcium sensor receptor, thereby suppressing PTH secretion.

Severe hypermagnesemia is rare and most often due to an excessive administration of magnesium salts, especially when renal failure is present and decreases the ability of the kidney to rapidly excrete the excess magnesium. Modest elevations in serum magnesium concentration are observed in familial benign hypercalcemia, treatment with lithium carbonate, diabetic ketoacidosis, and hypothyroidism. Most cases of magnesium intoxication can be prevented by monitoring the serum magnesium concentration, especially in patients with parenteral infusion and/or renal failure.

Treatment

In patients with normal renal function, treatment is based on discontinuation of magnesium; in patients with severe symptomatic magnesium intoxication, intravenous calcium, which antagonizes the toxic effects of magnesium, has an immediate, albeit transient, effect. Finally, in patients with severe renal failure, peritoneal dialysis or hemodialysis is a rapid and efficient method to lower serum magnesium concentration.

Suggested readings

BARRI YM, KNOCHEL JP. Hypercalcemia and electrolyte disturbances in malignancy. Hematol Oncol Clin North Am 1996;10:775-90.

CROOK M, SVAMINATHAN R. Disorders of plasma phosphate and indications for its measurement. Ann Clin Biochem 1996;33:376-96.

GUISE TA, MUNDY GR. Evaluation of hypocalcemia in children and adults. J Clin Endocrinol Metab 1995;80:1473-8.

HEBERT SC. Extracellular calcium-sensing receptor: implications for calcium and magnesium handling in the kidney. Kidney Int 1996;50:2129-39.

KUROKAWA H. The kidney and calcium homeostasis. Kidney Int 1994; 45:S97-S105.

PARFITT AM. Equilibrium and disequilibrium hypercalcemia: new light on an old concept. Metab Bone Dis Rel Res 1979;13:279-93.

PAYNE RB. Renal tubular reabsorption of phosphate (TmP/GFR): indications and interpretation. Ann Clin Biochem 1998;35:201-6.

QUAMME GA. Renal magnesium handling: new insights in understanding old problems. Kidney Int 1997;52:1180-95.

RUDE RK. Magnesium deficiency: a cause of heterogeneous disease in humans. J Bone Miner Res 1998;13:749-58.

SECTION

4

Primary glomerular disorders

CHAPTER

13

Minimal change disease

Patrick Niaudet

KEY POINTS

- Minimal change disease is the most frequent cause of the nephrotic syndrome in childhood.
- The main complications of the nephrotic syndrome are infections, thrombosis, hypovolemia with collapse, acute renal failure, malnutrition, and complications related to the drugs used to maintain the remission of the disease.
- More than 90% of children respond to prednisone. The duration of initial treatment influences the risk of relapse. Steroid-dependent patients or frequent relapsers should be treated with low-dose alternate-day prednisone for several months or years.
- Levamisole has a weak steroid-sparing effect.
- Patients who relapse on high-dose alternate-day prednisone and develop serious steroid side effects may receive a course of alkylating agents. Cyclosporine should be reserved for patients who experience further relapses despite a course of alkylating agents.
- A few patients with minimal change disease do not respond to steroids and may progress to chronic renal failure, a complication not observed in patients who are steroid-responsive.

Minimal change disease is the commonest form of primary nephrotic syndrome, at least in children. Other descriptive terms also have been used in the literature, e.g., nil disease, minimal change nephrotic syndrome, minimal change nephropathy, childhood nephrosis, lipoid nephrosis. Minimal change disease is defined by the association of a nephrotic syndrome and minimal changes on renal biopsy with electron microscopic findings of foot process fusion of epithelial cells. No immunoglobulin or complement fraction deposits are seen on immunofluorescence examination in most cases. Patients with minimal change disease most often respond to corticosteroids with a complete remission and have a favorable long-term prognosis. As there is a strong correlation between minimal changes on renal biopsy and steroid responsiveness, a renal biopsy usually is not performed when the patient – particularly pediatric patients – respond to corticosteroids. Further, for many authors, minimal change disease has become synonymous with "steroid-sensitive nephrotic syndrome."

However, some patients with diffuse mesangial proliferation and/or focal and segmental glomerular sclerosis (FSGS) also respond to steroid therapy, as do some patients who show IgM deposits on immunofluorescence examination. This raises questions about the classification of patients with idiopathic nephrotic syndrome. Several authors believe that minimal change disease is a distinct disease and that diffuse mesangial proliferation, FSGS, and IgM nephropathy are distinct entities. There is no doubt that patients with diffuse mesangial proliferation or FSGS are more frequently resistant to corticosteroids and have a significant propensity for progression to renal failure. However, there is an overlap between these histologic variants, and a significant proportion of patients with FSGS respond to corticosteroids, whereas some patients with minimal change disease are resistant to corticosteroids and may ultimately progress to end-stage renal failure. As the histopathologic features in most children with idiopathic nephrotic syndrome – particularly those who are steroid-responsive – have not been determined, many authors classify the patients according to their response to steroids: "steroid-responsive idiopathic nephrotic syndrome" or "steroid-resistant idiopathic nephrotic syndrome." Moreover, experience has shown that response to steroid therapy has more impact on the prognosis than do the histologic features seen on the initial biopsy.

Epidemiology

Minimal change disease is more frequent in children than in adults. The annual incidence in children is two to three cases per 100 000 according to the geographic area, with a prevalence of 16 cases for 100 000. Conversely, the annual incidence in adults is only three cases per 1 million. The incidence of minimal change disease is higher in children from Asia than in children from Europe or North America, whereas the disease is much less common in Africa. A six-fold increased incidence of steroid-responsive nephrotic syndrome has been found in children from Bangladesh, India, or Pakistan, compared with children from Europe. Minimal change disease is the most common cause of nephrotic syndrome in children, representing 60 to 90% of all nephrotic syndromes in pediatric patients. In children between 3 and 6 years of age, minimal change disease represents almost all cases of nephrotic syndrome. The International Study of Kidney Disease in Children found minimal change disease in 76.6% of children with primary nephrotic syndrome. In the United States, minimal change disease is more common in white children than in black or Hispanic children, in whom focal and segmental glomerular sclerosis frequently is observed. In adults, idiopathic nephrotic syndrome accounts for only 25% of patients with nephrotic syndrome. In children, minimal change disease is more frequent in boys than in girls, with a male:female ratio of 3:2. Both sexes are equally affected in adult life.

Genetic factors

A familial occurrence of minimal change disease has been reported by several authors. A survey performed in 24 European pediatric nephrology centers showed that 3.4% of 1877 children with idiopathic nephrotic syndrome had a familial history of nephrotic syndrome. Nineteen of the 63 children had minimal change disease, and 18 of them had affected siblings. The remaining child's father was affected with the disease. The response to therapy was identical within members of individual families.

Histocompatibility antigens and minimal change disease

There is an association between minimal change disease and certain antigens of the major histocompatibility complex. An increased incidence of HLA-DR7 has been reported in France, in Spain and in Australia. In these studies, HLA-DR7 was three to four times more frequent in children with the disease compared with controls, and the relative risk of having the disease was between 4.5 and 6.8. An association with HLA-B8 was reported in England. In the same study children with atopy and HLA-B12 had a 13-fold increased risk of developing idiopathic nephrotic syndrome. An association with HLA-B8 was also found in Ireland and in Germany. Other studies have not confirmed these associations. These differences may be explained if the disease segregates with different alleles in different populations.

Apart from single allele associations, possible associations with certain haplotypes have been studied. Clark et al. investigated the frequencies of the major histocompatibility complex class II alleles using analysis of restriction fragment length polymorphism DNA. They found a strong association between HLA-DR7 and the DQB1 gene of HLA-DQW2 and steroid-sensitive nephrotic syndrome. These authors suggested that the beta chains of DR7 and DQW2 contribute to disease susceptibility. A strong association with DQW2 and steroid-responsive nephrotic syndrome was also found. Two extended haplotypes HLA-A1, B8, DR3, DRW52, SCO1 and HLA-B44, DR7, DRW53, FC31 occur with a significantly increased incidence in these patients. It should be remembered that class I and class II glycoproteins play a key role in the presentation of the antigen to the T-cell receptor. Some antigens reacting with particular class II glycoproteins and not with others may play a role in the disease.

Etiopathogenesis

Minimal change disease has been reported to occur in association with atopy (Tab. 13.1). Indeed, in some series, 30 to 60% of the patients have a history of allergic reactions, and improvement of the renal disease may be observed following desensitization or exclusion ot the allergen. Different allergens including wheat flower, egg, cow's milk, and tree or grass pollen have been identified in patients as being responsible for relapses, and their withdrawal was shown to improve the course of the disease. However, the allergen is most often not known.

Minimal change disease also has been reported in association with malignancies, particularly Hodgkin's disease and non-Hodgkin's lymphomas. The nephrotic syndrome, which may be the first symptom of the disease, usually responds with a complete remission after successful treatment of the malignancy. Minimal change disease has also been observed in patients with bronchial, colon, pancreatic, or prostatic carcinoma, and may remit following chemotherapy. Finally, an association of minimal change disease and diabetes mellitus has been reported in a few cases.

The mechanisms of proteinuria in the absence of histologic alterations on light microscopy have been the subject of numerous studies. In normal individuals, the clearance of albumin is about 1% of that of neutral proteins with similar molecular weight, such as polyvinylpyrrolidone or dextran. Similarly, the clearance of neutral dextran is higher than that of anionic sulfate dextran of similar molecular weight. These data indicate that the permeability of the glomerular basement membrane is determined not only by the size but also by the charge of the protein. It is believed that the anionic charge of the glomerular basement membrane is responsible for the charge selectivity of filtration. The anionic (negative) charge of the glomerular basement membrane repulses the negatively charged albumin molecules.

In children with minimal change disease, the clearance of neutral macromolecules with the same molecular weight as albumin is paradoxically decreased, indicating that the "pore" size of the glomerular basement membrane is smaller than in normal individuals. It was postulated that massive proteinuria in these patients may be secondary to the loss of charge selectivity of filtration, which could be the result of a loss of anionic charges of the glomerular basement membrane or a neutralization of these anionic charges (Tab. 13.1). A decrease in the anionic charges of the glomerular basement membrane in patients with minimal change disease was demonstrated using polyethylamine as a cationic probe.

A mouse monoclonal antibody to partially purified heparan sulfate proteoglycan isolated from rat glomeruli was produced. This monoclonal antibody, directed against the glucosaminoglycan side of the molecule, was specific for heparan sulfate and did not react with other components of the glomerular basement membrane. By indirect immunofluorescence on rat kidney sections, the monoclonal antibody bound to the glomerular basement membrane with a fine granular to linear staining pattern, whereas, by electron microscopy, a diffuse staining of the whole width of the glomerular basement membrane was observed. After intravenous injection, the monoclonal antibody localized immediately along the glomerular basement membrane with a granular staining, and one day later, the antibody was localized in the mesangium with a parallel decreased staining along the glomerular basement membrane. Precise localization of the antibody was evaluated by electron microscopy. One hour after intravenous injection, the antibody bound mainly to the inner side of the glomerular basement membrane. Intravenous injection of this anti-heparan sulfate proteoglycan monoclonal antibody to rats resulted in selective proteinuria. The degree of proteinuria was dependent on the dose of monoclonal antibody injected. The proteinuria was maximal at day 1 and decreased thereafter. The quick disappearance of proteinuria may be due to the IgM isotype of the antibody whose high molecular weight prevents penetration in the glomerular basement membrane. This model shows that antibodies against heparan sulfate are nephritogenic and produce proteinuria when injected to the rat.

Proteinuria may be secondary to a neutralization of the anionic charge of heparan sulfate. A neutralization of the anionic charge of the glomerular basement membrane may occur via cationic proteins. A highly cationic protein has been found in the plasma and the urine of children with steroid-responsive nephrotic syndrome. This cationic factor, which may arise from cells of the immune system, could bind and neutralize the anionic charges of the glomerular basement membrane.

Shalhoub in 1974 postulated that lymphokines might be responsible for the increased permeability of the glomerular basement membrane. Lagrue et al. first described the vascular permeability factor, a lymphokine found in the supernatant of concanavalin A-activated lymphocytes from patients with minimal change disease that enhances vascular permeability when injected intradermally in the guinea pig. The vascular permeability factor is produced by T lymphocytes and is distinct from interleukin-2. Cyclosporine at concentrations ranging from 100 to 250 ng/ml is able to suppress the in vitro production of the vascular permeability factor by mononuclear cells from patients with minimal change disease. It should be noted that the vascular permeability factor has also been found in patients with other diseases, such as IgA nephropathy.

The supernatants of peripheral blood mononuclear cells stimulated with concanavalin A have been tested for their ability to induce proteinuria when injected in the renal artery of the rats. It was shown that the supernatants derived from patients with minimal change disease induced a marked proteinuria and a reduction of the anionic charges of the glomerular basement membrane. When lymphocyte culture supernatants are infused into the renal artery of rats, colloidal iron staining in the kidneys is reduced, suggesting a loss of negative charges of the glomerular basement membrane. Similarly, the infusion of plasma from nephrotic patients to rabbits induces proteinuria and a reduction in the number of anionic sites on the glomerular basement membrane.

Koyama et al. identified a glomerular permeability factor in the supernatant of T-cell hybridoma derived from peripheral T lymphocytes of a patient with minimal change disease. The hybridoma was obtained by fusion of peripheral T lymphocytes with CCRF-HSB2 cells. The

Table 13.1 Etiology and pathogenesis of minimal change disease

Associations
- Atopy
- Hodgkin's disease
- Carcinoma in adult patients

Genetic factors
- Familial occurrence
- Association with certain histocompatibility complex antigens

Mechanism of proteinuria
- Loss of the anionic charge of the glomerular basement membrane
- Presence of cationic proteins

Immunologic abnormalities
- Vascular permeability factor, inhibited by cyclosporine
- Supernatants from mononuclear cells or plasma from patients induce proteinuria after injection to/in animals
- Glomerular permeability factor produced by T lymphocytes
- High soluble IL-2 receptor levels
- Increased T-suppressor cell activity
- Impaired response of lymphocytes to mitogens

glomerular permeability factor was identified by the ability of the supernatant to induce proteinuria when injected intravenously in the rat. The supernatant containing the glomerular permeability factor was able significantly to enhance the concanavalin-A-induced lymphocyte blastogenesis. The authors showed that the glomerular permeability factor was different from the main known lymphokines. The molecular weight of the glomerular permeability factor was estimated to be between 60 and 160 kD. In rats injected with the supernatants, the authors found a partial fusion of foot processes of epithelial cells of the glomerular basement membrane with minor histologic changes and no immune deposit. Electron microscopy studies showed a decreased interspacing and a decreased density and diameters of injected polyethylenimide particles suggesting changes in the negative charges of the glomerular basement membrane induced by the glomerular permeability factor.

Other authors have looked for T lymphocyte abnormalities. The soluble form of the interleukin-2 receptor (sIL-2 R) has been measured in patients with minimal change disease. High sIL-2 R levels were found in the plasma and the urine during the proteinuric phase, whereas the levels were normal during the remission, suggesting that sIL-2 R may be one of the inhibitory serum factors, since a high sIL-2 R level is strongly correlated to the decreased response to mitogens seen in these patients. T lymphocyte subsets from children with steroid-responsive nephrotic syndrome were studied by flow cytometry. Patients in relapse demonstrated a significant increase in the percentage of activated T8 lymphocytes and a decrease of T4 lymphocytes. The decrease of T4 lymphocytes may be related to steroid therapy, whereas the increase of activated T8 lymphocyte was also found in untreated patients. Altered T lymphocyte function is also suggested by the suppression of in vitro lymphocyte response to phytohemagglutinin induced by prednisolone. The prednisolone dose that suppresses PHA-induced blastogenesis was significantly higher in patients with minimal change disease. However, the pattern of response was no help in predicting the steroid responsiveness.

Other lymphokines may play a pathogenic role. Increased interleukin 2 levels have been found in lymphocyte culture supernatants from patients with minimal change disease, and interleukin-2 can induce proteinuria and a reduction of the anionic sites of the glomerular basement membrane when injected into the rat kidney. A nephrotic syndrome has been described in several patients treated with recombinant IL-2 and alpha-interferon.

Clinical findings

Symptoms and signs

Minimal change disease is characterized by sudden onset, edema being the major symptom. Initially, periorbital edema may be mistaken for an allergic reaction. Edema localizes to the lower extremities in the upright position and to the dorsal part of the body in the reclining position. The edematous areas are white, soft and pitting, retaining marks after finger pressure. Anasarca may develop with ascites and pleural and pericardial effusion. Periorbital edema may limit eye opening, and edema of the scrotum, penis, or labia may be seen. A rapid formation of ascites is often associated with abdominal pain and malaise: these symptoms may also be related to concomitant hypovolemia. Abdominal pain is occasionally due to a complication such as peritonitis, thrombosis or, rarely, pancreatitis. Cardiovascular shock may occur secondary to the sudden fall of plasma albumin, with abdominal pain and symptoms of peripheral circulatory failure with cold extremities and hypotension. Emergency symptomatic treatment is needed. Blood pressure is usually normal but sometimes transiently elevated.

The nephrotic syndrome occasionally is discovered during routine urinalysis. Macroscopic hematuria is observed in rare cases. The disease also may be revealed by a complication, particularly infectious or thrombotic.

Relapses often occur following an episode of upper respiratory tract infection.

Laboratory findings

Proteinuria is important over 50 mg/kg/day or 40 mg/h/m^2. It is higher at onset and decreases as plasma albumin concentration falls. In young children it may be difficult to obtain a 24-hour urine collection, and urinary protein/creatinine ratio or albumin/creatinine ratio in untimed urine specimens are useful. For these two indices the nephrotic range is 200-400 mg/mmol. In most cases, proteinuria is highly selective, consisting of albumin and lower molecular weight proteins. The selectivity of proteinuria may be appreciated by polyacrilamide gel electrophoresis or by the evaluation of the Cameron index, which is the ratio of IgG to transferrin clearances. Microscopic hematuria is present in 20% of cases, and this symptom has no influence on the response to steroid therapy. The urine sediment often contains fat bodies. Hyaline casts are also usually found in patients with massive proteinuria, but granular casts are not present unless there is associated acute renal failure and acute tubular necrosis. Urinary sodium is low, 1-2 mmol/day, resulting in sodium retention and edema.

Plasma protein levels are markedly reduced, <50 g/l, due to hypoalbuminemia. Plasma albumin level is usually lower than 25 g/l. Electrophoresis also shows an increase of alpha2 globulins and a decrease of gammaglobulins due to low IgG levels. Lipid abnormalities include high levels of cholesterol, triglyceride, and lipoproteins. Total cholesterol and LDL cholesterol are elevated, whereas HDL cholesterol remains unchanged or low, particularly HDL2, leading to an increased LDL/HDL cholesterol ratio. Patients with severe hypoalbuminemia have increased triglycerides and VLDL. Apoproteins, apo B, apo CII, apo CIII are also elevated. The levels of lipoprotein Lp(a) are elevated in nephrotic patients, which further contributes to an increased risk of cardiovascular and thrombotic complications.

Serum sodium is often reduced, due in part to hyperlipemia and in part to the dilution from renal retention of water due to hypovolemia and inappropriate antidiuretic hormone secretion. Hyperkalemia may be observed in renal insufficiency. Hypocalcemia is related to hypoalbuminemia, but the level of ionized calcium is normal. Plasma creatinine is elevated in one-third of cases and returns to normal when the remission occurs. Severe impairment of renal function may be seen in severe hypovolemia. Hemoglobin levels and hematocrit are increased in patients with plasma volume contraction. Thrombocytosis is common, and may reach 5×10^8 or 10^9/l. Fibrinogen, factors V, VII, VIII, and X are increased, whereas antithrombin III, heparin cofactor, and factors XI and XII are decreased. These abnormalities contribute to a hypercoagulable state.

Renal biopsy

Minimal change disease is defined by histologic criteria. In fact, the indications for a renal biopsy depend on age and clinical features. Renal biopsy is not performed in children aged 1 to 8 years with typical symptoms, and in these patients treatment with corticosteroids is started. A complete remission is a major argument for the diagnosis. Renal biopsy is indicated at onset when another type of glomerular disease is suspected (macroscopic hematuria, marked hypertension, renal insufficiency, decreased plasma C3 fraction, patients older than 10 years). However, in children, the main indication is the failure to respond to a 4-week course of prednisone.

Renal biopsy is also proposed for steroid-responders who relapse frequently and in whom cyclosporine treatment is started in order to allow nephrotoxicity to be assessed on a later biopsy.

Since idiopathic nephrotic syndrome is much less common in adults, a renal biopsy usually is performed before starting treatment, although this remains controversial.

On light microscopy, the glomeruli may be normal, with normal capillary walls and normal cellularity. Swelling and vacuolation of epithelial cells and a slight increase in mesangial matrix are often observed. Mild mesangial hypercellularity may be noted as well as scattered foci of tubular lesions and interstitial fibrosis.

Ultrastructural changes are always present, involving podocytes and mesangial stalks. Podocyte foot process fusion is generalized and constant; its extent is closely related to the degree of proteinuria. Other epithelial changes consist of microvillus formation and the presence of numerous protein reabsorption droplets. The glomerular basement membranes are normal with no parietal deposits. The endothelial cells often are swollen. Mesangial alterations include mesangial cell hyperactivity, increased mesangial matrix, and occasionally finely granular, osmiophilic deposits located along the internal side of the basement membrane. These ultrastructural alterations are nonspecific and probably are related to massive proteinuria.

Complications

Renal function is usually within normal limits. A reduction of the glomerular filtration rate secondary to hypovolemia is frequent and may be observed in patients with normal effective plasma flow. This reduction is transitory. Acute renal failure may be secondary to bilateral renal vein thrombosis. Interstitial nephritis is another possible cause of acute renal failure, especially in association with furosemide administration.

Bacterial infections are frequent in nephrotic children. Sepsis may occur at the onset of the disease. The most common infection is peritonitis, often with *Streptococcus pneumoniae*. Other organisms may be responsible: *E. coli, Streptococcus B, Hemophilus influenzae*, and other gram-negative organisms. Apart from peritonitis, children may develop meningitis, pneumonitis, or cellulitis. Several factors explain the propensity of nephrotic children to develop bacterial infections: low IgG levels due to an impaired synthesis; urinary loss of factor B; and impaired T lymphocyte function. Factor B is a cofactor of C3b in the alternative pathway of complement which has an important role in opsonization of bacteria such as *Streptococcus pneumoniae*. Viral infections may be observed in patients given immunosuppressive agents.

Nephrotic patients are at risk of developing thromboembolic complications. Several factors contribute to the increased risk of thrombosis: a hypercoagulability state, hypovolemia, immobilization, and infection. A number of hemostatic abnormalities have been described in nephrotic patients: an increase in platelet aggregability; an increase in fibrinogen, factors V, VII, VIII, X, and XIII, while the levels of anti-thrombin III, heparin cofactor, protein C, protein S, factors XI and XII are decreased; and an increase in fibrinolytic system components such as tPA and PAI-1. The incidence of thromboembolic complications in nephrotic children is close to 3%. However this percentage may be underestimated, as shown by systematic ventilation-perfusion scans, showing defects consistent with pulmonary embolism in 28% of patients with steroid-dependent minimal change disease. Pulmonary embolism should be suspected in patients with pulmonary or cardiovascular symptoms, and may be confirmed by angiography or angioscintigraphy. Renal vein thrombosis should be suspected when there is sudden macroscopic hematuria or acute renal failure. Doppler ultrasound shows an increase in kidney size and the absence of blood flow in the renal vein. Thrombosis may also affect arteries such as pulmonary arteries or it may affect other deep veins.

Treatment

Symptomatic treatment

A child with nephrotic syndrome should be kept mobile; bed rest is avoided because of the increased risk of thrombosis. Dietary therapy should include a protein intake of around 130 to 140% of the recommended daily allowance according to statural age (1 to 2 g/kg body weight). High-protein intake has no significant effect on albumin plasma levels (Tab. 13.2). Salt restriction is advised for the prevention and the treatment of edema. A very low-salt diet is necessary only in cases of severe edema. Fluid restriction is recommended for moderate to severe hyponatremia (plasma sodium concentration less than 125 mEq/l).

Hypovolemia occurs as a consequence of rapid loss of protein, and is sometimes aggravated by the use of diuretics. This complication needs emergency treatment by rapid infusion of plasma (20 ml/kg) or albumin 20% (1 g/kg) together with strict control of blood pressure. Diuretics should be used only in severe edema, after hypovolemia has been corrected. Furosemide is administered at a dose of 1 to 2 mg/kg. Spironolactone may also be used at a dose of 2 to 10 mg/kg, provided the plasma creatinine concentration is normal. Patients with severe edema may be treated with furosemide and albumin to increase the rate of diuretic delivery to the kidney. This approach is not long-lasting, and pulmonary edema with congestive heart failure has been observed in some patients following albumin infusion when the volume status has not been well evaluated.

Nephrotic patients with severe hypoalbuminemia are at risk of thromboembolic complications. Prevention of these includes mobilization, avoidance of hematoconcentration due to hypovolemia, and early treatment of sepsis or volume depletion. Prophylactic vitamin K antagonist treatment may be given to high-risk patients with a plasma albumin concentration below 20 g/l, a fibrinogen level over 6 g/l, or an antithrombin III level below 70% of normal. Patients at risk may also be treated with low-dose aspirin and dipyridamole. Heparin is given initially if thrombi do occur, either alone or with thrombolytic agents. The heparin dose necessary to obtain a therapeutic effect is often greater than normal owing to decreased antithrombin III level.

Prophylactic antibiotics are not recommended, but bacterial infections should be promptly treated. If the child presents signs suggestive of peritonitis, abdominal paracentesis allows Gram staining of ascites and rapid differentiation of pneumococcal infection or gram-negative peritonitis. Many centers recommend polyvalent pneumococcal vaccine, but it does not prevent all cases of *S. pneumoniae* infection. Chicken pox and measles may be life-threatening in patients receiving immunosuppressants. Varicella antibodies should be checked; in case of exposure, children receiving high doses of steroids or alkylating agents should be treated with zoster immunoglobulins and acyclovir in case the disease occurs.

Calcium and vitamin D supplements are often prescribed with steroid therapy.

Table 13.2 Symptomatic treatment

Protein intake: 1-2 g/kg Low-salt diet
Hypovolemia: albumin infusion 1 g/kg BW
Severe edema Furosemide: 1-2 mg/kg Spironolactone: 2-10 mg/kg

Steroid therapy

Steroid therapy should not be started too early because spontaneous remission may occur in 5% of cases. When the diagnosis of idiopathic nephrotic syndrome is most likely or after a renal biopsy has been performed, steroid therapy is started. In France, prednisone is prefered to prednisolone, although both agents have been widely used worldwide. It is given at a dose of 60 mg/m^2/day with a maximum of 60 mg/day (Fig. 13.1). Proteinuria usually disappears between the eighth and fifteenth days of treatment. Prednisone at the same dosage is continued for 30 days and switched to alternate days for 2 months. Thereafter, the dose is decreased every 2 weeks by 15 mg/m^2. The total duration of treatment for the first attack is thus 4.5 months.

The initial course recommended by the International Study of Kidney Disease in Children consists of prednisone, 60 mg/m^2 for 4 weeks, followed by 40 mg/m^2 given 3 consecutive days out of 7 for 4 weeks. The Arbeitsgemeinschaft für Pädiatrische Nephrologie showed that an alternate-day regimen (40 mg/m^2 on alternate days for 4 weeks) resulted in a significantly lower number of patients with relapses and a significantly lower number of relapses per patient.

Several studies have addressed the question of the optimal duration of treatment for the initial attack to prevent subsequent relapses. The Arbeitsgemeinschaft für Pädiatrische Nephrologie compared three regimens. The short regimen consists of continuous prednisone given until the urine is protein-free for 3 days, followed by alternate-day prednisone until plasma albumin returns to normal values. The percentage of patients with relapses was significantly higher (81%) than for the patients receiving the standard regimen (61%). Interestingly, a longer regimen of 12 weeks of prednisone, starting with daily prednisone, 60 mg/m^2 for 6 weeks followed by alternate day prednisone, 40 mg/m^2 for 6 weeks, resulted in only 36% patients with relapses within the first year of the disease. The French Society of Pediatric Nephrology also showed in a randomized trial that the relapse rate of patients receiving a 8-week treatment for the initial attack was significantly higher than that of patients treated for 4.5 months.

If proteinuria persists at the end of the first month, corticosteroid dosage may be increased. We favor a series of three methylprednisolone pulses (1000 mg/1.73 m^2) every other day, because the side effects of such treatment are less important than an increase of the prednisone daily dose (Fig. 13.2). The persistence of proteinuria after this treatment defines steroid-resistant nephrotic syndrome.

In most cases, at least in children, minimal change disease is steroid-responsive. About 30% of patients have only one attack and are definitively cured after the course of corticosteroids. Ten to 20% of patients relapse several months after stopping the treatment, and a cure takes place after three or four episodes that respond to a standard course of corticosteroids. The remaining 40 to 50% of patients experience frequent relapses either as soon as steroid therapy is stopped or when the dosage is decreased. These patients often raise difficult therapeutic problems.

Steroid-dependent patients may be given repeated courses of treatment consisting of prednisone 60 mg/m²/day continued 3 days after the urine has become protein-free, followed by alternate-day prednisone, 40 mg/m², for 4 weeks, as proposed by the International Study of Kidney Disease in Children. Another approach recommends treatment of relapses with daily prednisone, 40 to 60 mg/m², until proteinuria has disappeared for 4 to 5 days. Thereafter, prednisone is switched to alternate days and the dosage is tapered to 15 to 20 mg/m² every other day, according to the steroid threshold, i.e., the dose at which the relapse has occurred. The treatment is then continued for 12 to 18 months. The first approach allows better definition in terms of relapses but is associated with more relapses. The latter regimen is associated with fewer steroid side effects because the cumulative steroid dosage is lower. Prolonged alternate-day steroid therapy usually is well tolerated by young children, and rate of growth is not affected. This may not be true in adolescents, in whom steroid therapy is often accompanied by a decreased growth rate.

Whereas the initial steroid dosage prescribed in children is rather uniform among pediatricians, adult nephrologists often use lower doses, with extremes between 0.33 to 2 mg/kg/day. The duration of treatment also varies in the literature from 2 weeks to 6 months. Unlike children, adult patients appear to need a longer course of prednisone in order to achieve equally good results. Many nephrologists use a protocol consisting of prednisone, 1 mg/kg/day, with a maximum of 80 mg/day, for 8 to 12 weeks followed by 0.5 mg/kg/day for another 6 to 8 weeks and a tapering phase of 8 weeks.

Levamisole

During the past 10 years, levamisole, which stimulates the immune system, has been shown to have a steroid-sparing effect in children with steroid-responsive nephrotic syndrome with steroid dependency or frequent relapses. The British Association for Paediatric Nephrology performed a

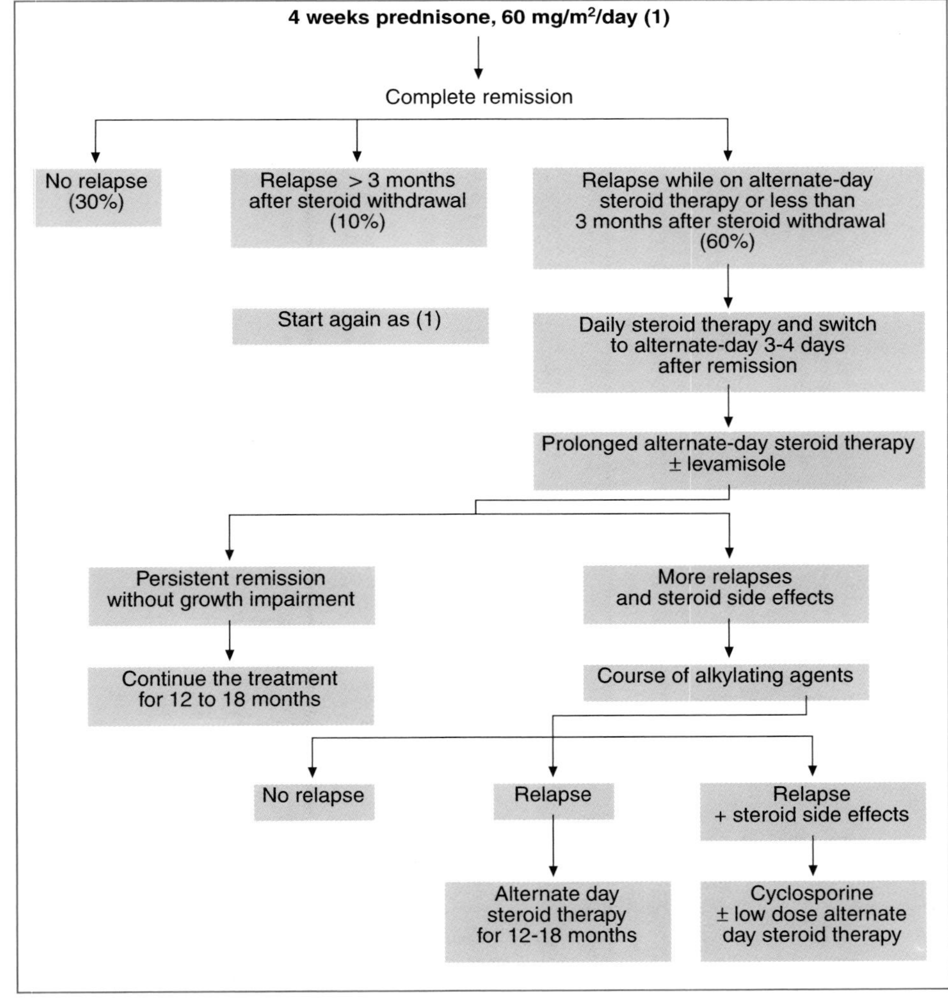

Figure 13.1 Therapy of steroid-sensitive MCD.

multicenter randomized study where 61 children received either levamisole (2.5 mg/kg on alternate days) or placebo. Fourteen patients in the levamisole group and four in the control group were still in remission after 112 days, despite prednisone withdrawal. Most patients relapsed within 3 months after cessation of treatment. Although no episode of neutropenia or agranulocytosis was reported, regular blood counts should be performed as the most serious side effect is neutropenia, which has been reported in 2% of children and is reversible after discontinuation of levamisole.

Immunosuppressive agents

Steroid-dependent patients may develop symptoms of steroid toxicity, including statural growth impairment, obesity, osteoporosis, cataract, and psychologic disturbances. In such cases, corticosteroids should be withdrawn. It has been known for many years that alkylating agents, cyclophosphamide or chlorambucil, are effective in such situations.

The efficacy of cyclophosphamide for preventing further relapse of idiopathic nephrotic syndrome was reported more than 30 years ago, and proved by a prospective study that compared an 8-week course of cyclophosphamide with prednisone alone. Identical results were observed in a trial conducted by the International Study of Kidney Disease in Children. However, it soon became apparent that the duration of remission induced by cyclophosphamide varies from patient to patient and may be very short. Data from the literature show a remission rate of 67 to 93% at 1 year and 36 to 66% at 5 years following a course of cyclophosphamide. The therapeutic effect is related to the duration of treatment. In a study from the Arbeitsgemeinschaft für Pädiatrische Nephrologie, 67% of steroid-dependent patients were still in remission 2 years after a 12-week course of cyclophosphamide at a daily dose of 2 mg/kg, compared with only 30% after an 8-week course. The daily dose of cyclophosphamide should not exceed 2.5 mg/kg. The response to cyclophosphamide is also related to the pattern of response to steroids. Seventy per cent of children with frequent relapses remained in remission after an 8-week course of cyclophosphamide, whereas only 30% of steroid-dependent patients had prolonged remissions.

Remissions also may be obtained with chlorambucil. The recommended dose is 0.2 mg/kg for 2 months. Higher daily doses give similar results. Frequently relapsing patients have more prolonged remissions than do steroid-dependent children.

Mechloretamine can be useful because it induces a rapid remission within an average of 7 days. Following a course of mechloretamine (0.8 mg/kg iv in two courses of four injections, 1 month apart), most children remain in remission without steroids, but the remission rate is only 15% after 3 years for steroid-dependent patients.

Side effects of alkylating agents limit their use. Bone marrow toxicity requires regular blood cell counts. If white blood cells fall below 3000/mm^3, the drug should be withdrawn until the count rises. The treatment also should be discontinued in case of infection. The risks of varicella should be explained to the parents so that acyclovir treatment may be started quickly. Alopecia and hemorrhagic

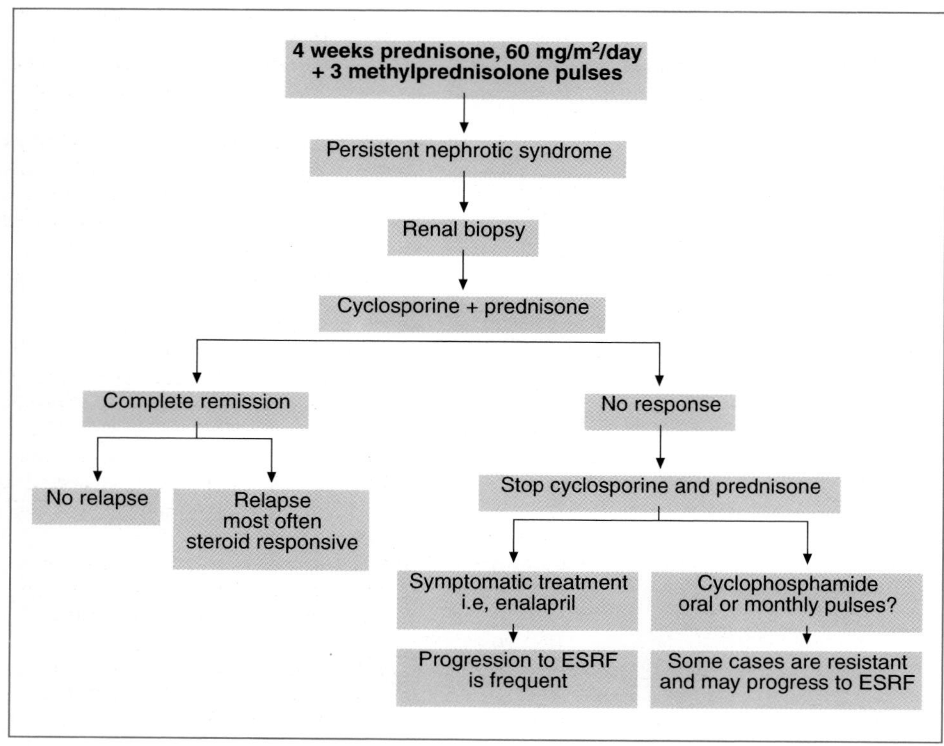

Figure 13.2 Therapy of steroid-resistant MCD.

cystitis rarely occur with the dosage used in these patients. Long-term toxic effects include the risk of developing cancer. Gonadal toxicity is well established, and the risk is greater in boys than in girls. The gonadal toxicity threshold is between 200 and 300 mg/kg for cyclophosphamide and 8 to 10 mg/kg for chlorambucil.

Cyclosporine

Cyclosporine has been shown to be effective in more than 80% of patients with steroid-dependent nephrotic syndrome. Cyclosporine treatment may induce a remission if the patient is treated while in relapse, or it may maintain a remission, thus allowing withdrawal of prednisone. The recommended dosage is 5 mg/kg/day in two oral doses. The dose may be adjusted to maintain trough blood levels between 100 and 200 ng/ml, but it should not exceed 200 mg/day. Cyclosporine-induced remission is not long-lasting, and most patients relapse when cyclosporine treatment is tapered or within a few months following cessation of treatment. Patients who were steroid-dependent become cyclosporine-dependent. Therefore, cyclosporine may have to be administered for long periods, thus running the risk of nephrotoxicity. Consequently, renal function should be monitored frequently, although our results on serial renal biopsies indicate that lesions of nephrotoxicity may arise in the absence of any sign of renal function impairment. The most prominent histologic feature of chronic cyclosporine nephrotoxicity is tubulointerstitial lesions, characterized by stripes of interstitial fibrosis containing groups of atrophic tubules. The so-called cyclosporine-associated arteriolopathy is rare; therefore, renal biopsy appears to be the surest method of detecting patients with cyclosporine nephrotoxicity. We currently propose it after 18 months of treatment. It has been our experience that patients who relapse on cyclosporine or after cyclosporine withdrawal often respond poorly to a second or third course of treatment. Low-dose alternate-day prednisone in combination with cyclosporine may be a better approach in these patients.

The French Society of Pediatric Nephrology conducted a randomized controlled trial comparing the efficacy of chlorambucil at a cumulative dose of 8 mg/kgBW with cyclosporine in inducing sustained remission. Of the 20 patients treated with cyclosporine, only one remained in remission 16 months after the end of treatment, whereas, of the 20 patients who received chlorambucil, six were still in remission 27 to 49 months after the end of the treatment. Thus, we believe that children with minimal change steroid-dependent nephrotic syndrome and steroid toxicity should first be treated with alkylating agents at a nongonadotoxic dose before resorting to cyclosporine.

Treatment of steroid-resistant minimal change disease

Approximately 7% of patients with minimal change disease are steroid-resistant, either primary non-responders or late non-responders. These patients may develop in the long term lesions of focal and segmental glomerular sclerosis and progress to end-stage renal failure. The treatment of these patients remains difficult. Several therapeutic protocols have been proposed, but there are no controlled studies available. The results of these trials are difficult to analyze because a significant proportion of the patients, up to 40%, progress to cure gradually, with slowly decreasing proteinuria, and in such cases relapse is rare.

A recent study suggests that intravenous pulse cyclophosphamide is more effective than oral cyclophosphamide. In that trial, patients receiving cyclophosphamide pulses had a higher frequency of remission, a lower cumulative dose of cyclophosphamide, and fewer side effects. The French Society of Pediatric Nephrology reported the results of a prospective trial in which children with steroid-resistant idiopathic nephrotic syndrome were treated with cyclosporine, 150-200 mg/m^2, and prednisone, 30 mg/m^2/day for 1 month and on alternate days for 5 months thereafter. Complete remission was observed in 21 of the 45 patients with minimal change disease. None of the 21 patients who responded to the treatment progressed to renal failure. Six patients relapsed after cyclosporine was stopped, and they responded to a second course of prednisone. Therefore, a combined treatment of cyclosporine and prednisone may induce a remission in steroid-resistant minimal change disease.

Suggested readings

Arbeitsgemeinschaft für Pädiatrische Nephrologie. Cyclophosphamide treatment of steroid-dependent nephrotic syndrome: Comparison of eight weeks with 12 weeks course. Arch Dis Child 1987;62:1102-6.

British Association for Paediatric nephrology. Levamisole for corticosteroid-dependent nephrotic syndrome in childhood. Lancet 1991;337:1555-7.

Brodehl J. The treatment of minimal change nephrotic syndrome: lessons learned from multicenter co-operative studies. Eur J Pediatr 1991;150:380-7.

Broyer M, Meyrier A, Niaudet P, Habib R. Minimal changes and focal and segmental glomerular sclerosis. In: Davison AM, Cameron JS, Grünfeld JP, Kerr D, Ritz E, Winearls CG, eds. Oxford Textbook of Clinical Nephrology. Oxford: Oxford Medical Publications 1998:493-535.

Churg J, Habib R, White RHR. Pathology of the nephrotic syndrome in children. Lancet 1970;i:1299-302.

Clark AGB, Vaughan RW, Stephens HAF, Chantler C, Williams DG, Welsh KI. Genes encoding the chains of HLA-DR7 and HLA-DQW2 define major susceptibility determinants for idiopathic nephrotic syndrome. Clin Science 1990;78:391-7.

Habib R, Churg J. Minimal change disease, mesangial proliferation glomerulonephritis and focal sclerosis: Individual entities or a spectrum. In: Robinson RR, ed. Nephrology, New York, Springer Verlag, 1984:634-44.

International Study of Kidney Disease in Childhood. Clinical significance of histologic variants of minimal change and of diffuse mesangial hypercellularity. Kidney Int 1981:20:765-71.

Koyama A, Fujisaki M, Kobayashi M, Igarashi M, Narita M. A glomerular permeability factor produced by human T cell hybridoma. Kidney Int 1991;40:453-60.

LAGRUE G, XHENEUMONT S, BRANELLEC A, HIRBEC C, WEIL B. Vascular permeability factor elaborated from lymphocytes. I Demonstration in patients with nephrotic syndrome. Biomedecine 1975;23:37-40.

NIAUDET P, HABIB R. Cyclosporine in the treatment of idiopathic nephrosis. J Am Soc Nephrol 1994;5:1049-56.

NIAUDET P AND THE FRENCH SOCIETY OF PEDIATRIC NEPHROLOGY. Treatment of childhood steroid resistant idiopathic nephrosis with a combination of cyclosporine and prednisone. J Pediatr 1994;125:981-5.

ROBSON AM, GIANGIACOMO J, KIENSTRA RA, NAQUI ST, INGELFINGER JR. Normal glomerular permeability and its modification by minimal change nephrotic syndrome. J Clin Invest 1974;54:1190-9.

TROMPETER RS. Immunosuppressive therapy in the nephrotic syndrome in children. Pediatr Nephrol 1989;3:194-200.

WHITE RHR. The familial nephrotic syndrome. A European survey. Clin Nephrol 1973;1:215-9.

CHAPTER 14

Focal segmental glomerulosclerosis

Amir Tejani, Juergen Strehlau

KEY POINTS

- Among glomerular disorders that affect children and young adults, focal segmental glomerulosclerosis is the most common disorder leading to end-stage renal disease. The lesion is more frequent and the severity of the disease is greater in patients of African-American origin.
- Clinically, the lesion of focal segmental glomerulosclerosis can be observed in a wide variety of disorders. In the idiopathic variety there is proteinuria, hypoalbuminemia, and generalized edema, together with varying degrees of hypertriglyceridemia and hypercholesterolemia.
- Since focal segmental glomerulosclerosis is a histologic diagnosis, a renal biopsy is necessary. The characteristic light microscopic lesion consists of glomerular sclerosis affecting some but not all glomeruli in a segmental manner, together with varying degrees of deposition of C3 in the sclerosed area.
- The pathogenesis of this disease continues to be elusive; however, in recent years studies point to the role of transforming growth factor beta (TGF-β) in inducing the sclerosis.
- Most cases of focal segmental glomerulosclerosis tend to be resistant to steroid therapy as well as to therapy with alkylating agents such as cyclophosphamide. Controlled trials have documented the efficacy of cyclosporine in inducing a remission of the proteinuria, particularly in children; however, relapses tend to occur upon withdrawal of cyclosporine. In severe edema intravenous furosemide often is necessary. Antihypertensive therapy should consist of ACE inhibitors and calcium channel blockers.

Epidemiology

Focal segmental glomerulosclerosis (FSGS) is not a disease, but a pathologic lesion first described by Rich in autopsy studies of the kidneys of children with nephrotic syndrome. As the term "focal" suggests, the lesion is not present in all glomeruli. The sclerotic process is defined by glomerular capillary collapse with an increase in mesangial matrix. The scarring affects only a portion of the glomerular tuft – hence, the qualifying term "segmental." Before the lesion was defined, it was always a mystery why some patients with nephrotic syndrome developed progressive renal insufficiency, whereas others continued to have a benign course. Glomerulosclerosis is seen in a variety of settings and is the glomerular end-point in such diseases as obesity, hypertension, diabetic nephropathy, and human immunodeficiency virus (HIV) infection. The same lesion is also seen in very late stages of other diseases that affect the glomeruli, such as IgA nephropathy, membranoproliferative glomerulonephritis, lupus nephritis, Henoch Shonlein's purpura, and malignant nephrosclerosis. The broad spectrum of underlying diseases associated with the histologic lesion of focal sclerosis reflects the presence of diverse pathogenic mechanisms leading to the development of sclerosis. The most common and the most important lesion is the one seen in association with a full-blown nephrotic syndrome. This lesion, discussed in this chapter, often is referred to as idiopathic focal segmental glomerulosclerosis.

Since the diagnosis is tissue-based, it is difficult to estimate the frequency of the lesion. Among glomerular disorders in children, nephrotic syndrome due to focal segmental glomerulosclerosis accounts for the largest percentage of patients who reach end-stage renal disease. The 1995 North American Pediatric Renal Transplant Cooperative Study (NAPRTCS) report shows an incidence of 12%, with hemolytic uremic syndrome and lupus nephritis accounting for 2.7% and 5%, respectively. The importance of focal segmental glomerulosclerosis as a cause of end-stage renal disease is vividly brought out in the pediatric dialysis population, where it accounts for 15%, second only to dysplastic kidney disorders. What is also clear, but not well known, is that the frequency of the lesion differs by racial groups. The lesion is seen more frequently in African-American patients, and the severity of the disease is greater in patients of African-American descent. Data from the United States Renal Data Systems (USRDS) show that among glomerular disorders that lead to end-stage renal disease in children, focal segmental glomerulosclerosis is three times more frequent in African-American children than in Caucasian children. These data are shown in Table 14.1. Data from the NAPRTCS show the differential distribution even more vividly. Non-Caucasian children form 38% of all transplant recipients; however, when transplantation by disease category is reviewed, non-Caucasian children form 46% of all recipients transplanted for focal segmental glomerulosclerosis. This preponderance is further revealed in the dialysis report of the NAPRTCS, where African-American and Hispanic children account for 52% of all cases of end-stage renal disease due to focal segmental glomerulosclerosis, leaving Caucasian children in the minority. The higher frequency of the lesion in African-American adult patients is seen in studies from Buffalo, where, of 100 patients studied, 30% of the African-American subjects had focal segmental glomerulosclerosis compared with 10-15% in all races. We have shown in a single center experience that the disease progresses to end-stage renal disease status faster in African-American and Hispanic children in the US than reported in Caucasian children in Europe and Canada.

In order to understand why the lesion progresses relentlessly, insight into the pathogenesis of the disease is essential. A histologic abnormality common to minimal change disease (MCD) and focal segmental glomerulosclerosis is the effacement of the foot processes of the podocytes. Whereas most patients with minimal change disease have a benign course, those who have multiple relapses tend to undergo a morphologic transition from minimal change disease to focal segmental glomerulosclerosis. Such transition has been described in both adults and children. Whether the two diseases are two ends of a common spectrum or two different disorders is a controversy that has persisted for a long time. The frequency with which reported morphologic transition occurs varies with the diligence with which repeat biopsies are performed. In a recent review we studied 49 patients over a 10-year period whose disease pattern was characterized by frequent relapses. These patients underwent repeat biopsies for diagnostic or therapeutic purposes. We observed that 25 of the patients had minimal change disease at the onset as confirmed by a renal biopsy. Of these 25, upon repeat biopsy the disease had evolved into IgM nephropathy in seven patients, and in 14 patients the histologic lesion had evolved into focal segmental glomerulosclerosis. We also noted that of 12 patients with an initial biopsy diagnosis of IgM nephropathy, 50% had evolved into focal segmental glomerulosclerosis. As our review points out, the three lesions appear to be part of the same spectrum in that at presentation they manifest common clinical features and a common histologic lesion.

Pathogenesis

The glomerulus is the target for many types of injury. Some of the injury can be immunologic, such as immune complex mediated injury; other injuries could be hemodynamically mediated, such as hypertensive injury. Certain basic responses are common to all forms of glomerular injury and consist of cell proliferation and hypertrophy, together with extracellular matrix deposition.

It has been suggested that components of the mesangium may be critical to the pathogenesis of human glomerular disease. The mesangium is the connective tissue lying between the glomerular capillaries, and an

Table 14.1 Incidence of end-stage renal disease in children due to glomerulonephritis*

	Total patients	Incidence %	Median age	Male %	White %	African-American %
Glomerulonephritis	1381	36.1	16	54.1	61.9	30.6
Goodpasture's syndrome*	20	0.5	17	40.0	85.0	15.0
Focal glomerulosclerosis*	365	9.5	16	57.0	47.4	48.2
Membranous nephropathy*	23	0.6	16	56.5	65.2	34.8
Membranoproliferative GN*	121	3.2	15	50.4	67.8	23.1
All other glomerulonephritis*	852	22.3	16	53.6	66.7	24.4

* Adapted from the USRDS 1996 Annual Report.

experimental model of a proliferative glomerulonephritis confined to the mesangium has been described. A prominent function of mesangial cells is the synthesis and maintenance of the mesangial extracellular matrix. Mesangial cells in culture secrete collagen types 1, 3, 4 and 5, as well as myosin, fibronectin, laminin, intactin, and proteoglycans. The mesangial extracellular matrix has been suggested to be the key to the pathogenesis of glomerulosclerosis.

The tendency of the nephrotic syndrome to manifest and relapse after viral infections or an allergic diathesis, the association with HLA antigens, and the therapeutic response to steroids and immunosuppressives such as cyclosporine suggest a possible immunologic role in its pathogenesis. Neither circulating nor in situ complexes have been consistently demonstrated in patients with nephrotic syndrome, but evidence of intrarenal T-cell infiltration has been shown. Lymphocyte-mediated immune mechanisms have been implicated in the genesis of nephrotic syndrome. Recently it has been shown that while peripheral blood counts of CD4 and CD8 lymphocytes remain unaltered, both CD4 and CD8 lymphocytes infiltrate kidneys of patients with focal segmental glomerulosclerosis, and the intrarenal CD4/CD8 ratio declines as compared to normal kidneys. More recently elevated levels of circulating cytokines have been observed in patients with both minimal change and focal segmental glomerulosclerosis.

We prospectively studied interleukin2 receptor in 70 children during active disease using an ELISA. IL-2r levels were elevated in 32 of the 70 patients (range 227-919 U/ml). Non-white patients had a higher mean IL-2r level of 1042±22 U/ml, compared with white patients, who had a mean level of 737±23 U/ml (p= 0.034). Repeat IL-2r levels measured in 14 patients after treatment with cyclosporine demonstrated a decrease in their IL-2r level from a mean of 1583±44 to a mean of 8904±36 U/ ml (p= 0.002). More interestingly there was a significant decrease in the individual IL-2r levels in 13 of the 14 patients, and the only patient who did not show a drop in the level following cyclosporine had a relapse of the disease a week later.

Similar data of the rise of IL-2 levels with the onset of the disease, and fall with cyclosporine induced remission have been presented by others. The mechanism of cytokine-induced injury is obscure. It has been suggested that IL-2 induces a vascular leak syndrome by altering the permselectivity of the glomerular basement membrane. In the animal model, injected recombinant IL-2 has been shown to reduce the number and density of anionic sites of the glomerular basement membrane, which is associated histologically with fusion of epithelial foot processes and massive proteinuria. In the rat model, administration of recombinant IL-2 induces proteinuria in a dose-dependent manner, and the administration of human IL-2 for cancer chemotherapy has led to the development of a nephrotic range proteinuria that resolves after treatment is discontinued. The studies presented so far indicate a role for IL-2 in the pathogenesis of the nephrotic syndrome patient, but do not establish a role as an effector, suppressor, or mediator of the altered glomerular permeability. Assigning a role to the cytokine IL-2 in the induction of proteinuria necessitates determining its presence in the renal parenchyma during an episode of relapse.

To ascertain whether interleukin-2 is present intrarenally, we recently studied renal biopsy tissue from children with a variety of histologic lesions, all of which manifest with nephrotic range of proteinuria. Renal tissue was obtained by percutaneous biopsy in all patients. Renal biopsy was performed for either diagnostic or therapeutic purposes. All biopsies were performed using either a 15- or 18-gauge needle. Two cores of tissue were obtained; one core was placed into a 1 ml nunc cryo tube and sealed. The nunc tube was then immediately snap frozen in liquid nitrogen and the frozen tube stored in a -70° C freezer. When an adequate number of samples had been collected, we studied mRNA for IL-2 and the alpha chain of IL-2 receptor by using a reverse transcription polymerase chain reaction.

We did not detect IL-2 mRNA in any of the biopsy specimens; however, IL-2r was detected in 30/53 biopsy specimens. The distribution of IL-2r mRNA did not help in distinguishing its role in the pathogenesis of any of the histologic lesions. We detected IL-2r mRNA in 24/42 patients in relapse of their nephrotic syndrome, but the gene transcript for IL-2r was also present in 6/11 patients whose nephrotic syndrome was in remission at the time of biopsy. We observed that the gene transcript for IL-2r was detected in the majority of patients with focal segmental glomerulosclerosis, but the gene transcript was also present in patients with other histologic lesions. Specifically, IL-2r mRNA was detected in 14/20 patients with focal segmental glomerulosclerosis, in 5/7 minimal change disease patients, and in 5/7 IgM nephropathy patients. The presence of IL-2r mRNA in nephrotic patients with a variety of histologic lesions suggests that it may have a role in the pathogenesis of the disease; however, it is more likely that its action in the proliferation and differentiation of T-lymphocytes to release other cytokines and growth factors may be more relevant.

In a large study we have measured mRNA gene transcripts in 20 focal segmental glomerulosclerosis patients, 7 patients with minimal change disease, 7 patients with IgM nephropathy, 10 patients with lupus nephritis, and 9 patients with a mixed bag of glomerular disorders. We compared the intrarenal gene expression of T-cell related cytokines, (IL-2, IL-4, IL-15), chemokines (RANTES, IL-8), and CTL effector molecules (Fas-ligand, granzyme B, perforin) utilizing quantitative competitive template RT-PCR. TGF-β transcripts were detectable in 18/20 focal segmental glomerulosclerosis patients. In contrast, TGF-β transcripts were detected in only 2/14 patients with either minimal change disease or IgM nephropathy, and both these patients evolved into focal segmental glomerulosclerosis on repeat biopsy.

The data presented here would suggest that for both minimal change disease and focal segmental glomerulosclerosis similar stimuli, as yet undefined, damage the permeability of the basement membrane. However it is the mesangial matrix proliferation and the accumulation of extracellular matrix under the stimulus of growth promoting factors, primarily TGF-β, that lead to the development of focal segmental glomerulosclerosis and, relentlessly, to end-stage renal disease status.

Clinical findings

Clinically minimal change disease, IgM nephropathy and focal segmental glomerulosclerosis present with nephrotic syndrome. Nephrotic syndrome is defined as: (1) proteinuria greater than 40 mg/m^2/hour in the child, or greater than 3 g/24 hours in the adult; (2) hypoalbuminemia less than 2.5 g/dl; and (3) generalized edema. The disease also is accompanied by hypertriglyceridemia and hypercholesterolemia. Clinically it is impossible to distinguish between the three lesions by looking at these parameters quantitatively, although in general minimal change disease tends to exhibit greater edema and a more profound degree of hypoalbuminemia, particularly in children. In fact, degrees of hypoalbuminemia where the serum albumin is less then 1 g/dl are rarely observed in focal segmental glomerulosclerosis, but are a common feature in minimal change disease in infants and children.

Hematuria Microscopic hematuria is a common finding in minimal change disease, and it is present in as many as 50% of the patients, whereas gross hematuria is rare in minimal change disease, being present in fewer then 10%. The presence of gross hematuria should alert the clinician to the possibility of a more severe lesion, such as IgM nephropathy or focal segmental glomerulosclerosis. The distinction is particularly important in children, since many pediatric nephrologists are reluctant to resort to performing a renal biopsy at presentation, preferring to await the result of a course of steroid therapy.

Hypertension At presentation hypertension is rarely observed in minimal change disease, IgM nephropathy, or focal segmental glomerulosclerosis, and persistent hypertension points to other disorders. Although hypertension invariably appears in patients with focal segmental glomerulosclerosis during the course of the disease, this event is a late finding and suggests that the lesion has been present for a while. As pointed out in the section on therapy, the distinction between long-standing and recent-onset lesions has prognostic implications. The possible lesions in the setting of hypertension are discussed under differential diagnosis.

Renal function At presentation and thereafter, renal function, as reflected by the serum creatinine, is always normal in patients with minimal change disease. Unfortunately, at presentation renal function as reflected by serum creatinine very often is normal in patients with IgM nephropathy and focal segmental glomerulosclerosis as well, and an elevated serum creatinine at presentation should suggest a long-standing disorder.

Diagnostic procedures

In an adult patient the need to perform a renal biopsy in the presence of the triad of nephrotic range proteinuria, hypoalbuminemia, and edema, with or without hematuria, hypertension, and decreased renal function, is quite clear. In the past in children there was a reluctance to perform a biopsy before giving a course of steroid therapy. However, with the availability of safer biopsy needles, such as the 18-gauge Biopsy gun, and the awareness that diseases, such as focal segmental glomerulosclerosis, which are refractory to steroid therapy do respond to alternative therapy if started early, pediatric nephrologists now perform preliminary biopsies. Currently most academic centers will perform a renal biopsy in a child over 6 years old who presents with the triad of nephrotic range proteinuria, hypoalbuminemia, and edema, particularly if there is associated hematuria or decreased renal function.

The glomerulus in minimal change disease is essentially normal by light microscopy but may exhibit slight increase in mesangial matrix or cellularity. Immunofluorescence usually is negative, although some pathologists may consider the presence of small amounts of IgM or C3 as still consistent with minimal change. Electron microscopy in patients with minimal change will reveal a diffuse effacement of the foot processes, with a normal glomerular basement membrane and absence of electron-dense deposits. In contrast, serial studies in recurrent focal segmental glomerulosclerosis after transplantation have shown that the earliest lesion arises in the visceral epithelial cell. Whereas in minimal change disease only podocyte effacement occurs, in focal sclerosis epithelial cells proliferate and extracellular matrix accumulates, inducing sclerosis. Different variants of primary focal segmental glomerulosclerosis lesions have been described with varying prognosis, and distribution of the lesions, whether diffuse or focal, may have pathogenic implications. Variants of primary focal segmental glomerulosclerosis in adults, including vascular pole lesions, and glomerular tip lesions with or without mesangial hypercellularity, have been described. Tip lesions are thought to be early lesions with a good prognosis. Multiple segmental lesions are presumed to be late occurring and thought to carry a poor prognosis. A recently described variant of focal segmental glomerulosclerosis is characterized by widespread collapse of the capillary loops and has a rapid progression with a poor prognosis.

Differences have been noted in the histologic lesions seen in children compared with those in adults. Serial sections of biopsy tissue reveal greater increase in sclerosis in children than in adults, reflecting the predominance of peripheral and more segmental lesions in children. More glomeruli are involved in the sclerotic process in adults than in children, a finding that may have implications in the outcome of therapy in the two groups.

Diagnosis

The renal response to a variety of toxic, metabolic, or immunologic insults or injuries is stereotypically exhibited as proteinuria, hematuria, and edema, with or without hypertension and elevated serum creatinine. When a patient presents with the triad of edema, hypoalbuminemia, and proteinuria in the nephrotic range, and there is no secondary cause for nephrotic syndrome, the age of the patient helps in making an intelligent guess. In children under 6 years of age, the most likely diagnosis is minimal change disease. This is confirmed by the International Study of Kidney Disease in Children (ISKDC), a study of over 600 children biopsied at the onset of disease, wherein the lesion was minimal change disease in 98% of those under 6 years of age. Single-center data have shown that after 6 years of age the incidence of minimal change disease in children drops significantly. We looked at a population of adolescents, all biopsied at presentation, and observed that the incidence of minimal change disease dropped below 50%, whereas other mesangioproliferative disorders, such as IgA nephropathy, IgM nephropathy, and focal segmental glomerulosclerosis begin to be seen more frequently. When the clinical presentation in children includes hypertension, a differential diagnosis requires consideration of poststreptococcal glomerulonephritis or membranoproliferative glomerulonephritis, and if the clinical presentation includes a decrease in renal function, as exhibited by an elevated serum creatinine, a diagnosis of rapidly progressive glomerulonephritis should be entertained.

In adult patients the diagnosis is more difficult. In the presence of the triad of nephrotic range proteinuria, hypoalbuminemia, and edema, the most common lesion observed is membranous nephropathy, whereas minimal change disease and focal segmental glomerulosclerosis account for about 10-15% of the lesions. It has been shown repeatedly that in adults, unlike children, idiopathic nephrotic syndrome is uncommon, and a host of diseases that produce a nephrotic range of proteinuria enter into the differential diagnosis. Frequent clues to the presence of focal segmental glomerulosclerosis in an adult patient are hypertension and decreased renal function, both of which are unlikely in either minimal change disease or membranous nephropathy. The possibility of focal segmental glomerulosclerosis secondary to either drug addiction (heroin) or HIV disease must also be entertained in adult patients, since clinical findings are similar but the histology may be varied.

Treatment

Specific therapy

Corticosteroids In children there have been numerous attempts to use a course of steroid therapy; however, with a better understanding of the disease and as other therapeutic modalities have become available, some centers now eschew a prolonged course of steroid therapy and proceed with the alternative course after a month of steroids. When steroids are used, dosing in children is by the ISKDC regimen, a method popularized by the International Study of Kidney Disease in Children in the early 1960s. Prednisone is administered in a dose of 60 mg/m^2 daily for 4 weeks, then reduced to 40 mg/m^2 every other day for 4 more weeks, and then abruptly discontinued (the maximum daily dose permitted under this regimen is 80 mg/day.) In adults much larger doses are used, and the duration of therapy is much longer as well. A popular regimen in adults consists of daily or alternate-day prednisone at 2 mg/kg, the dose being maintained for 3 months if a remission is achieved. A slow stepwise taper is then started, with each step maintained for 2 weeks, and the therapy eventually discontinued at the end of 1 year. The total dose and duration of the therapy described is very high, and there is reluctance to use such doses in children because it invariably leads to toxicity, particularly growth retardation. These side effects are particularly distressing when one recognizes that even with such high doses and duration lasting a whole year, the rate of remission in adults, based on an analysis of 153 patients collected over a 16-year period from 1961 to 1986, was only 25%. In children the remission rate following a standard course of therapy has been said to be anywhere from 0-50%. A judicious reading of the literature would show that the response rate with either a standard or more extended course of steroid therapy is about 20%. What is not well appreciated is the fact that the response varies according to the ethnic background of the patient, with African-American children being particularly unresponsive to steroid therapy.

Alkylating agents Neither cyclophosphamide nor chlorambucil alone has much efficacy in patients with steroid-resistant nephrotic syndrome, but, cyclophosphamide has been used in conjunction with pulse methylprednisolone therapy. It has been suggested that the concurrent use of alkylating agents and steroids increases the probability of remission, although no controlled study has shown this. Since both cyclophosphamide and chlorambucil have a significant gonadal toxicity, their isolated use in children is fraught with danger. In a controlled clinical trial in children with steroid-resistant focal segmental glomerulosclerosis, the addition of a 90-day course of cyclophosphamide to alternate-day prednisone therapy achieved no better response than prednisone alone, and it was concluded that children with focal segmental glomerulosclerosis should not be treated with cyclophosphamide. The cumulative dose for gonadal toxicity in the male is 300 mg/kg, and in the female the dose is 500 mg/kg. Thus, the drug should not be administered in doses greater than 2-3 mg/kg, and the total duration of therapy should not exceed 90 days. Similar gonadal toxic dose for chlorambucil in the male adolescent is 10 mg/kg cumulative dose. Because of the diminished risk of gonadal toxicity, the alkylating agents find greater acceptance in adults; however, there are eminent nephrologists who would not use these drugs at all because of unproved efficacy.

Cyclosporine therapy Cyclosporine is a fungal decapeptide that initially was used in transplantation for grafting solid organs, where it improved graft survival for kidney, heart, and liver significantly over historical controls. The mechanism of action of this drug is complex. Cyclosporine is a specific modulator of T-cell function. The drug suppresses the proliferative response of mitogen-stimulated cells, and is effective in the early stages of T lymphocyte activation. Specifically, it inhibits induction of T-helper cells and the generation of T-cytotoxic effector cells. On a molecular level, the drug selectively inhibits both the production and the release of interleukin2 from activated T-helper cells, which is essential for the proliferation of T-lymphocytes, and it also reduces the release of interleukin1, another cytokine from the macrophages. IL-1 is essential for helper T-cell activation and IL-2 release.

The efficacy of cyclosporine in treating patients with nephrotic syndrome was first reported in 1985. At the 18th Annual Meeting of the American Society of Nephrology in New Orleans, we reported on 20 children who had either steroid-dependant or steroid-resistant nephrotic syndrome and whose mean duration of illness was 5 years. Cyclosporine was started at a dosage of 7 mg/kg, given orally in a single dose, and was then titrated to maintain a trough blood level between 100-200 ng/ml. The drug was administered for 8 weeks and then abruptly discontinued. Of the 20 patients, 14 achieved a remission, defined as disappearance of edema and proteinuria, and normalization of serum albumin. Of the 20 patients, 10 had the lesion of focal segmental glomerulosclerosis, and 6 of these responded to cyclosporine therapy.

Since that original report there have been over 50 published reports of the efficacy of cyclosporine in patients with nephrotic syndrome, with varying results. Unfortunately all the studies were uncontrolled – a phenomenon that is all too common since practicing nephrologists are loathe to subject patients destined for end-stage renal disease to a controlled study. Recently we reported on the only controlled trial of cyclosporine in children with steroid-resistant focal segmental glomerulosclerosis. In a prospective randomized double-blind placebo-controlled trial of cyclosporine, the NewYork/NewJersey Pediatric Nephrology Study Group undertook to test the efficacy and safety of a 6-month course of cyclosporine.

Biopsies from 38 patients from eight centers were submitted for tissue evaluation. Of these, 31 patients satisfied the inclusion criteria. Sixteen patients were randomized to receive cyclosporine, whereas 15 were randomized to the placebo arm. The mean proteinuria of the cyclosporine-treated patients diminished significantly when compared to the placebo-treated group at the end of the treatment period. The individual proteinuria in these patient also showed a dramatic drop when compared with the placebo-treated group. Overall, four of the cyclosporine-treated patients had a complete remission and eight exhibited a partial remission; in contrast none of the placebo-treated patients had any reduction in proteinuria and none achieved a remission. A special purpose of this study was to evaluate the nephrotoxicity of the drug, since administration of cyclosporine on a long-term basis has been associated with a reduction in renal plasma flow and GFR. This functional form of nephrotoxicity is mediated by renal vasoconstrictor mechanisms. The vasoconstriction is mediated in part by neural mechanisms and in part by activation of the renin angiotensin axis. Another factor implicated is the role of eicosanoids.

Routine measurements of renal function, such as serum creatinine, are frequently inaccurate in estimating the degree of damage; therefore, a more sophisticated method was used to determine renal function. We measured the GFR with technetium-99m-DTPA as the filtration marker, using a two-plasma sample method for calculation.

The GFR of the groups, obtained before initiation and after discontinuation of the study drug, as measured by DTPA, showed interesting data. For the cyclosporine-treated group the GFR marginally, but significantly declined from 103 ± 36 to 82 ± 19 (p=0.05), and insignificantly declined for the placebo group from 86 ± 31 to 75 ± 30 (p=0.06). However, the fractional decline in GFR, expressed as the percentage change of the post-study value from the pre-study value, was not significantly different between the two groups (15% in the cyclosporine group and 11% in the placebo group [p=ns]). Based on this study it was reassuring to note that a short (6- month) course of cyclosporine did induce a remission and did not lead to marked toxicity. Since both the cyclosporine-treated and the placebo-treated patients showed a decrease in the calculated GFR, we postulated that this was a reflection of the natural course of the disease of focal segmental glomerulosclerosis. In this instance it is worthwhile to point out that children usually exhibit less nephrotoxicity when exposed to cyclosporine than adults do, and that the GFR of a group of children receiving long-term cyclosporine remained stable after an initial drop.

On the grounds of our experience we would recommend that, in pediatric patients with steroid-resistant focal segmental glomerulosclerosis, cyclosporine be started at 8 mg/kg/day, together with 20 mg of prednisone daily. If after 4 weeks of cyclosporine therapy there is no significant reduction in proteinuria and the cholesterol level is >300 mg/dl, the cyclosporine dose should be increased by 2 mg/kg/day until a remission is achieved. While the cyclosporine dose is being increased the serum creatinine must be measured twice weekly, and if it rises by more than 0.3 mg/dl the cyclosporine dose should be reduced by one-third and not raised again for 2 weeks. When the increase in cyclosporine dose results in a serum creatinine rise of more then 0.3 mg/dl on two consecutive occasions, the drug should be discontinued. When remission is achieved the cyclosporine dose should be gradually reduced every 2 weeks until a baseline dose of 8 mg/kg is reached. For patients who remain in remission our policy is to maintain the 8 mg/kg dose for at least 6 months before attempting further tapering of the drug. Cyclosporine blood levels are generally low in the presence of marked hypercholestrolemia, and it has been our experience that, even with whole blood trough levels >200 ng by monoclonal RIA, cyclosporine nephrotoxicity, as determined by a rise in serum creatinine, is unlikely. In patients who achieve remission, the prednisone dose should be reduced gradually every 2 weeks until a dose of 5 mg/day is reached, and this dose should be maintained.

We define remission as reduction in the daily proteinuria to <500 mg/day. When remission has been maintained for 6 months we would reduce the cyclosporine further, striving to maintain the patient on the lowest possible dose. Cyclosporine as low as 2 mg/kg/day, together with 5 mg/day of prednisone, has been shown to maintain patients free of proteinuria for as long as 8 years. It has been our experience that discontinuation of cyclosporine leads to a relapse in many cases, and therefore we have opted to continue low-dose therapy indefinitely. In patients who develop a relapse (proteinuria >1 g/24 hours) cyclosporine is reintroduced at 8 mg/kg/day and titrated to cholesterol levels as described.

Whereas cyclosporine is effective in controlling proteinuria, the question arises whether cyclosporine therapy prevents progression to end-stage renal disease. As described previously there is a correlation between the degree of proteinuria and progression to end-stage, and it has been shown that massive proteinuria will accelerate the disease process.

Long-term studies of cyclosporine are difficult to carry out because the drug has inherent nephrotoxicity; however, we conducted a study that begins to answer the question. We treated 21 African-American and Hispanic children who had steroid-resistant focal segmental glomerulosclerosis with cyclosporine, starting at a dose of 6 mg/kg daily, titrating the dose to serum cholesterol level to achieve a response. The dose range varied from 6-20 mg/kg/day, and the mean duration of therapy was 27 months. Five of the 21 patients reached end-stage renal disease status despite cyclosporine therapy. Seven children continue to receive CSA, and the rest are in remission. We compared this patient group to a historical group of patients with similar age and similar duration of follow-up. These data are shown in Table 14.2. The frequency of end-stage renal disease in the historical group (78%) was significantly higher than the frequency noted in the cyclosporine treated group (25%).

There are no long-term studies of cyclosporine therapy in adults, but current recommendations are to initiate cyclosporine at 5 mg/kg/day together with a small dose (10-15 mg/day) of prednisone. Attempts should be made to maintain whole blood trough levels at 200 ng/dl using a specific monoclonal antibody. Cyclosporine dose should be reduced by 25% if there is a rise in serum creatinine over 30%, which should be measured every week. If the serum creatinine continues to remain elevated despite two attempts at dose reduction, cyclosporine therapy should be discontinued. In patients who respond with a remission, cyclosporine should not be continued beyond 12 months without a renal biopsy. Continuation of cyclosporine therapy is recommended only if the characteristic lesion of stripe interstitial fibrosis is absent. In patients who respond to therapy, attempts to reduce the cyclosporine dose to a level of 2-3 mg/kg/day often are successful, and nephrotoxicity is less likely at such low doses.

Table 14.2 Comparative data of children treated with steroids and cyclophosphamides (historical controls) and patients treated with cyclosporine (current study)

	Historical controls	Current study
African-American N (%)	38/57 (70)	13/21 (62)
Age at diagnosis (years)	7.3 ± 4.6	8.4 ± 4.5
Follow-up (years)	8.3 ± 4.3	8.5 ± 4.7
End-stage renal disease N (%)	42/54 (78)	5/21 (21)*

* $p<0.05$.

General measures

Diet Since most patients with focal segmental glomerulosclerosis present with edema, low sodium intake is recommended; however, this is often difficult in children. Restriction of protein intake is advised for adult patients, but should not be recommended for children.

Diuretics Recent studies on the pathogenesis of edema in nephrotic syndrome have shown that most nephrotic patients have either normal or increased blood volume, and that the sodium retention is not humoraly mediated. Furosemide is well tolerated by both adults and children. The initial dose for adults is one 40 mg tablet per day, whereas in children the dose should be 3-4 mg/kg/day in two divided doses. In severe edema intravenous furosemide is often necessary. It has been our policy to use intravenous furosemide in association with albumin. For intractable edema, generally seen in patients resistant to all specific drugs including cyclosporine, we use 0.5 g/kg of albumin followed by 5 mg/kg of furosemide, given twice daily. When this potent combination is utilized most patients will undergo a diuresis, but the combination therapy requires careful monitoring and should be done in a hospital setting. A side effect of the albumin/furosemide therapy is kaliuria, and a potassium-sparing diuretic, such as amyloride, given in a dose of 2.5 mg twice a day in children and 5 mg twice a day in adults, is necessary. The use of albumin and furosemide can be done only for a short period because persistent use will lead to metabolic alkalosis, even with a potassium-sparing diuretic. Most patients who are specific therapy-resistant will progress to end-stage renal disease status because of progressive glomerular sclerosis and tubular disruption. In these patients glomerular destruction often diminishes the basement membrane surface area available for protein leakage. A decrease in proteinuria appearing in such a patient is not a reflection of stabilization or improvement in the patient's condition, but more ominously a transition to end-stage renal disease.

Hypertension With progressing glomerular sclerosis, hypertension invariably develops in most patients. Angiotensin-converting enzyme inhibitors and calcium channel blockers are currently recommended for both adults and children; however, noncompliance in adolescent patients is often better controlled by a clonidine patch.

Prevention of infection In the preantibiotic era, steroid-resistant nephrotic patients invariably died of infection. The most common infection is pneumococcal peritonitis and, in infants, pneumococcal sepsis. Unfortunately vaccination against *Streptococcus pneumoniae* is not effective because the urinary protein loss in patients with focal segmental glomerulosclerosis includes such large molecular proteins as gamma globulins, and we have demonstrated that the antibody titer following vaccination against the pneumocous is lost within a few months. We, therefore, do not recommend vaccination, but would suggest that any child or adult nephrotic patient with fever and abdominal pain be investigated for peritonitis and covered with appropriate antibiotics.

Preventing thrombosis Nephrotic patients are at an increased risk for the development of thrombosis. However, the risk for patients with focal segmental glomerulosclerosis appears to be less than that seen in patients with membranous nephropathy. Thus, we do not recommend routine treatment with systemic anticoagulation unless the patient has had a previous episode of thrombosis.

Suggested readings

BORDER WA, OKUDA S, LANGUINE LR, RUOSLAHTI E. Transforming growth factor-b regulates production of proteoglycans by mesangial cells. Kidney Int 1990;37:689-95.

CORTES L, TEJANI A. Dilemma of focal segmental glomerular sclerosis. Kidney Int 1996;49:53:S57-S63.

FEUTREN G, MIHATSCH MJ. Risk factors for cyclosporine-induced nephropathy in patients with autoimmune diseases. N Engl J Med 1992;326:1654-60.

FOGO A, GLICK AD, HORN SL, HORN RG. Is focal segmental glomerulosclerosis really focal? Distribution of lesions in adults and children. Kidney Int 1995;47:1690-6.

ICHIKAWAI, FOGO A. Focal segmental glomerulosclerosis. Pediatr Nephrol 1996;10:374-91.

INGULLI E, SINGH A, BAQI N, et al. Aggressive long-term cyclosporine therapy for steroid resistant focal segmental glomerulosclerosis. JASN 1995;5:1820-5.

INGULLI E, TEJANI A. Severe hypercholesterolemia inhibits cyclosporin A efficacy in a dose-dependent manner in children with nephrotic syndrome. J Am Soc Nephrol 1992;3:254-9.

INGULLI E, TEJANI A. Racial differences in the incidence and outcome of idiopathic focal segmental glomerulosclerosis in children. Pediatr Nephrol 1995;5:393-7.

LIEBERMAN KV, TEJANI A. Double-blind placebo-controlled trial of cyclosporine in steroid-resistant idiopathic focal segmental glomerulosclerosis in children. J Am Soc Nephrol 1996;7:56-63.

MEYRIER A, CONDAMIN MC, BRONEER D. Treatment of adult idiopathic nephrotic syndrome with cyclosporin A: Minimal change disease and focal segmental glomerulosclerosis. Clin Nephrol 1991;35:S37-S40.

NIAUDET P, BROYER M, HABIB R. Treatment of idiopathic nephrotic syndrome with cyclosporin A in children. Clin Nephrol 1991;35:S31-S34.

NIAUDET P, AND THE FRENCH SOCIETY OF PEDIATRIC NEPHROLOGY. Treatment of childhood steroid resistant idiopathic nephrosis with a combination of cyclosporine and prednisone. J Pediatr 1994;125:981-6.

PONTICELLI C, RIZZONI G, EDEFONTI A, et al. A randomized trial of cyclosporine in steroid-resistant idiopathic nephrotic syndrome. Kidney Int 1993;43:1377-84.

TEJANI A, BUTT KMH, TRACHTMAN H, et al. Cyclosporine induced remission of childhood nephrotic syndrome. Kidney Int 1988;33:729-34.

TEJANI A, BUTT KMH, TRACHTMAN H, et al. Cyclosporine-induced remission of relapsing nephrotic syndrome in children. J Pediatr 1987;3:1056-62.

CHAPTER

15

Membranous nephropathy

Patrizia Passerini, Claudio Ponticelli

KEY POINTS

- Membranous nephropathy is the most common cause of nephrotic syndrome in adults.
- Histologically, it is characterized by a diffuse thickening of the glomerular basement membrane.
- If untreated the disease progresses to end-stage renal failure within 10 years from clinical onset in 50% of patients.
- Treatment with corticosteroids plus cytotoxic agents favors remission of the nephrotic syndrome and protects renal function in the long term.

The term membranous nephropathy (MN) describes a glomerular disease clinically characterized by proteinuria and slow progression to renal insufficiency, although spontaneous remission may occur in some patients. The name of the disease derives from its histologic features, showing a diffuse thickening of the glomerular capillary wall due to a subepithelial deposition of immune complexes. The synonyms for this disorder, epimembranous, perimembranous, or extramembranous glomerulonephritis emphasize the particular location of these deposits.

In most cases the disease is not associated with any known etiologic factor, and is called idiopathic MN. However, in about one-third to one-fifth of cases MN can be associated with other diseases, such as infections, neoplasms, and autoimmune disorders, or with exposure to drugs or toxins (Tab. 15.1). The term "secondary membranous nephropathy" is applied to these cases.

Epidemiology

Membranous nephropathy is the commonest cause of adult-onset nephrotic syndrome, accounting for 25 to 40% of all cases. The true incidence and prevalence of MN are unknown because a number of patients do not see a nephrologist. Moreover, the indications for renal biopsy are variable. For example, many older patients with proteinuria, who probably have an underlying MN, are not subjected to renal biopsy because of concerns over potential complications following this invasive procedure. At any rate, an analysis of the Italian Registry of Renal Biopsies showed that among 13 835 renal biopsies performed in native kidneys over a period of 7 years, more than 20% were cases of MN.

Males are affected more often than females, usually in a ratio of 2:1. Membranous nephropathy most often occurs in adults, with a peak incidence around the fourth and the fifth decades, but the disease also is frequent in older persons, although rare in childhood. When MN occurs outside the usual age group, the possibility that it may be secondary should be taken into account.

Etiopathogenesis

Although a variety of antigens have been implicated as possible causative factors of the secondary forms of membranous nephropathy, the etiology of idiopathic disease is still unknown. However, in idiopathic MN a genetic basis of predisposition is likely. A strong association between idiopathic MN and the major histocompatibility complex antigens has been extensively described. HLA DR3 is found in 65 to 75% of Caucasian patients compared with 20 to 25% in controls. The incidence of HLA B8 is also increased. On the other hand, Japanese patients show a strong association with HLA DR-2.

The pathogenesis of human membranous nephropathy has not been completely elucidated, but there is today agreement that MN is an immunologically mediated disorder, as demonstrated by the finding of immune complex deposition along the glomerular basement membrane. For many years it was thought that MN resulted by the trapping of circulating immune complexes within the glomeruli. Further studies showed that this mechanism might be operating in some cases of secondary MN, but not in the idiopathic form of the disease. In fact, circulating immune complexes can be found in MN secondary to systemic lupus erythematosus, viral hepatitis, or neoplasia, but they are rare in idiopathic MN. Experimental studies tend to support the hypothesis that in idiopathic MN there is an "in situ" formation of immune complexes as a consequence of a reaction between an antibody and an antigen either intrinsic to the glomerulus or "planted" in the subepithelial position.

The Heymann nephritis represents the paradigm of the *in situ* formation of immune complexes in the glomeruli. There are two models of Heymann nephritis. In the first model or active Heymann nephritis, the renal damage is induced by immunizing a rat with a crude proximal tubular brush border extract. In the passive model, Heymann nephritis is induced into a normal animal by injecting preformed antibodies against this extract. With both models, subepithelial glomerular immune-deposits appear within a few minutes, followed by proteinuria 5 or 6 days later.

A number of studies have now identified the antigen involved in Heymann nephritis. It is a glycoprotein, now named megalin, located both at the base of the microvilli in the proximal tubular brush border and along the sides and the base of the podocyte foot processes. This double location explains why a glomerular disease can develop after the injection of crude proximal tubular brush border extract. More recently, a second protein (44-kd), that binds to megalin, also was shown to be a target antigen. It appears to function as its intracellular chaperone, assisting in the folding of megalin in the endoplasmic reticulum and its transport to the cell surface.

For the pathogenesis of immune deposit-formation it is relevant that megalin is present on the bases of foot processes of podocytes where initial immune-complexes are formed. In passive Heymann nephritis circulating anti-megalin IgG crosses the glomerular basement membrane and approaches megalin located in clathrin-coated pits of glomerular epithelia. Then anti-megalin IgG binds its antigen megalin in the coated pits, forming an initial immune complex. The immune deposit then grows in size by repeated cycles of in situ immune complex formation and shedding into the lamina rara externa of the glomerular basement membrane; eventually it encroaches on the area of the slit diaphragm. By repeated cycles of this process,

Table 15.1 Associated conditions that have been linked to membranous nephropathy (secondary MN)

Infections
- Enterococcal endocarditis
- Filariasis
- Hepatitis B or C
- Hydatid disease
- Leprosy
- Quartan malaria
- Schistosomiasis
- Streptococcal infection
- Syphilis

Neoplasia
- Benign tumors
- Carcinomas
- Hodgkin's disease
- Melanoma
- Mesothelioma
- Non-Hodgkin's lymphoma
- Pheochromocytoma
- Retroperitoneal sarcoma

Rheumatologic disorders
- Alkylosing spondylitis
- Dermatomyositis
- Mixed connective tissue disease
- Rheumatoid arthritis
- Systemic lupus erythematosus
- Systemic sclerosis

Drugs or toxic agents
- Captopril
- Diclofenac
- Fenoprofen
- Formaldehyde
- Gold
- Hydrocarbons
- Ketoprofen
- Lithium
- Mercury componds
- Penicillamine
- Probenecid
- Sulindac
- Thiola
- Trimethadione

Miscellaneous conditions
- Adult polycystic kidney disease
- α_1-Antitrypsin deficiency
- Crohn's disease
- Dermatitis herpetiformis
- Diabetes mellitus
- Guillan-Barré syndrome
- Hemolytic-uremic syndrome
- Kimura's disease
- Miller Fisher syndrome
- Multiple sclerosis
- Myastenia gravis
- Myelodysplasia
- Periaortic fibrosis
- Primary biliary cirrhosis
- Renal transplantation
- Sarcoidosis
- Sickle cell disease
- Sjögren's syndrome
- Systemic mastocytosis
- Temporal arteritis
- Thyroid disease
- Urticarial vasculitis
- Weber-Christian disease

more immune complexes can accumulate at the same spot, and eventually the immune deposits become morphologically apparent.

Soon after the identification of megalin as the antigen responsible for inducing immune deposits, it became apparent that antimegalin antibodies were inefficient in inducing proteinuria. In passive Heymann nephritis proteinuria was demonstrated to depend on activation of complement and formation of the late components of complement C5b-9, also called membrane attack complex. C5b-9 causes increased local production of reactive oxigen species, which flood the entire glomerular basement membrane and its matrix proteins. Here the formation of lipid peroxidation adducts triggers structural changes within the glomerular basement membrane matrix proteins, thus causing proteinuria.

This sequence of pathogenetic events of Heymann nephritis is thought to operate in human membranous nephropathy, although there are still some unanswered questions. The target antigen in human MN, for example, has yet to be identified, and it is not clear whether a single antigen provides the target for all cases of human MN or whether different antigens are involved in different circumstances. These data raise the possibility that the term "idiopathic" will remain unchanged in the near future for most cases of MN.

Pathophysiology

Membranous nephropathy is characterized by the typical alterations of the glomerular basement membrane, caused by subepithelial deposition of immune deposits. This process produces a diffuse and uniform thickening of the glomerular basement membrane, which is the typical finding of a well developed MN at light microscopy. Instead, at least in the idiopathic form, there is little or no associated cellular proliferation. The morphologic details of glomerular changes in MN were first described by Ehrenreich and Churg. They introduced a staging system based on the changes in the glomerular basement membrane that develop during the evolution of a single generation of deposits. The earliest phase (stage I) is characterized by the presence of small subepithelial electron-dense deposits along the capillary walls. In stage II, the basement membrane-like material projects between and around the enlarging deposits, forming the so-called spikes. In stage III, the spikes fuse over the deposits, incorporating them into a markedly thickened basement membrane, while some of the deposits become rarified. In stage IV, most of the deposits disappear, leaving an irregularly thickened basement membrane variously described as "moth-eaten" or "Swiss cheeselike" (Fig. 15.1). Quite often more than one stage is seen in the same biopsy. Varying degreees of glomerular sclerosis, tubular atrophy, interstitial fibrosis, and vascular changes also may be found, reflecting the severity of the disease at renal biopsy.

Immunofluorescent techniques reveal the deposition of IgG in a uniform granular distribution outlining all of the capillary loops, but sparing the mesangium. The distribution of immunoglobulin corresponds to that of the electron-dense deposits seen on electron microscopy. C3 usually is present, showing a pattern and intensity similar to IgG.

Atypical features, such as mesangial proliferation and/or a wide spectrum of different immunoglobulins and complement components deposits at immunofluorescence suggest that the disease may be secondary to lupus, cancer, drug reaction, or infectious disease.

Clinical findings

Symptoms and signs

The onset of the disease usually is insidious. In a few cases, however, idiopathic membranous nephropathy may be preceded by infections or vaccinations. Proteinuria and edema are hallmarks of the disease. At presentation some 70 to 90% of patients have a nephrotic syndrome. Asymptomatic proteinuria may be present in the remaining minority, but some of these patients may become nephrotic subsequently. Hypertension (25-40% of cases) and renal dysfunction may be associated with the nephrotic syndrome at clinical onset, but more often these complications develop later in the course of the disease.

Diagnostic procedures

Laboratory abnormalities reflect some or all of the metabolic consequences of the nephrotic syndrome, such as hypoproteinemia and hypoalbuminemia, hyperlipidemia, abnormalities of immunoglobulins, circulating hormones, and vitamins. The serum levels of the C3 and C4 complement components are always normal in the idiopathic form, but may be lowered in membranous nephropathy secondary to systemic lupus erythematosus or viral hepatitis. The amount of proteinuria is usually greater than 3.5 g per day, and it may exceed 20 g per day. Most commonly proteinuria is nonselective and is associated with microhematuria, whereas gross hematuria is rare. Dysmorphic ery-

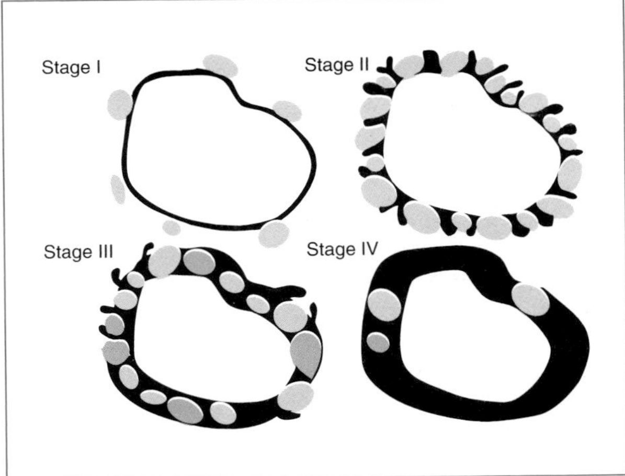

Figure 15.1 Schematic representation of four stages of membranous nephropathy.

throcytes, casts, and oval fat bodies may be seen in the urinary sediment.

When membranous nephropathy is associated with a systemic disease, such as systemic lupus erythematosus, infection, or neoplasia, the nephrotic syndrome may develop before, coincident with, or after the underlying disorder has been diagnosed. In these cases, laboratory abnormalities will reflect the specific underlying cause. Thus, positive B or C virus, reduced levels of C3 and C4, anti-DNA antibodies, rheumatoid factors, or cryoglobulins will point to a secondary cause of MN, as will abnormal thyroid or liver function tests, and the positivity for neoplastic-specific antigens.

The natural course of idiopathic membranous nephropathy

Idiopathic MN may have a variable outcome. Spontaneous remission of the nephrotic syndrome may occur in some, and these patients usually will maintain normal kidney function over time. Remission usually develops after 3 or more years from clinical onset, and it can be followed by relapses of the nephrotic syndrome. In other patients the nephrotic syndrome persists. Usually renal function deteriorates slowly in these cases, but sometimes patients progress to end-stage renal failure in a few years. A few patients may even die of complications caused by the nephrotic syndrome.

The proportions of these different outcomes are difficult to assess because most of the available data come from retrospective studies in which the criteria for inclusion of patients varied, the follow-ups were usually short, and the analysis often included treated and untreated patients or nephrotic and nonnephrotic patients. Limiting the analysis of the actuarial survival rate to a selected population of adult untreated patients with MN and nephrotic syndrome, it appears that 40 to 50% of these patients either died or progressed to end-stage renal failure within 10 years of clinical onset. It is possible, however, that an adequate control of blood pressure and of hyperlipemia, as well as the use of anticoagulants when appropriate may contribute to improved prognosis.

Several studies have been performed to identify which factors can influence the long-term prognosis in membranous nephropathy. Women usually follow a more benign course than men. Younger patients seem to do better than older ones. However, once adulthood is reached there is no further worsening of prognosis with increased age. Genetic markers may also influence prognosis. Caucasian patients with HLA DR3 and B8 have been found to have a worse clinical outcome. The amount and duration of proteinuria also are correlated with the renal prognosis. Patients with heavy proteinuria, particularly those with a urinary protein excretion exceeding 10 g/day are particularly likely to develop renal failure. Even more predictive of renal outcome is a long duration of elevated proteinuria. Also important is the severity of hypoalbuminemia, which has been found to predict a bad prognosis, not only for the kidney. As a matter of fact, the lower the serum albumin levels, the higher the risk of death from cardiovascular disorders. There is a general consensus that impaired renal function at diagnosis presages terminal renal failure. Some studies found a correlation between arterial hypertension and development of renal insufficiency, but this was not confirmed by others. The complete disappearance of proteinuria, either spontaneously or after treatment, usually heralds a fair outcome. Data from the literature show that only 1 of 157 patients who attained complete remission had to be submitted to dialysis in the long term.

Some histologic features can be considered as useful markers of prognosis. Many analyses reported a good correlation between the severity of tubulointerstitial lesions at renal biopsy and the development of renal insufficiency. An unfavorable prognostic role also has been attributed to the finding of a superimposed focal glomerulosclerosis. Indeed, there is not agreement about the significance of glomerular staging at renal biopsy. Some authors reported that patients with stage 1-2 glomerular lesions are unlikely to progress to uremia, but others have found no correlation between staging and eventual outcome.

In summary, many factors may influence the renal outcome of patients with idiopathic MN. Among the clinical factors, severe and persistent proteinuria, low levels of serum albumin, initial abnormal serum creatinine, and male sex were those more frequently associated with renal failure, while the presence of severe tubulointerstitial lesions at renal biopsy was the strongest predictor of renal insufficiency among histologic factors. On the other hand, a complete remission of proteinuria probably represents the most reliable clinical predictor of a favorable outcome in the long term.

Complications

Patients with membranous nephropathy are exposed to renal complications that may lead to sudden renal function deterioration. Patients with severe hypoalbuminemia and/or massive use of diuretics may have an acute hypovolemia with consequent oligoanuria. The diagnosis is usually easy because of the concomitant hypotension and tachycardia that are aggravated by the orthostatic posture. In doubtful cases it is helpful to measure the central venous pressure. A careful test with 100 ml of 20% mannitol and infusion of albumin or other plasma-expanders also may be tried. These agents may restore volemia and diuresis in most cases.

Rarely, a superimposed interstitial nephritis may occur. This may be triggered by diuretics, antibiotics, anticoagulants, nonsteroidal anti-inflammatory drugs or other agents. The diagnosis rests on the classic symptomatic triad of fever-eosinophilia-rash associated with a rapidly declining renal function. In many cases, however, one or more of the typical signs or symptoms may be lacking. In the most difficult cases renal biopsy is irreplaceable. The removal of the offending agent and an early course with high-dose prednisone (1 mg/kg/day) may achieve recovery in most cases. If undiagnosed or untreated, interstitial nephritis may eventually lead to irreversible lesions.

Exceptionally a superimposed extracapillary glomerulonephritis may develop. The diagnosis may be suspected whenever there is a rapidly progressive renal function deterioration, associated with an increase in urine erythrocytes and leukocytes, not explained by other causes. However, only renal biopsy can allow a final diagnosis. The prognosis for this complication is poor. However, prompt treatment with high-dose intravenous methylprednisolone pulses followed by high-dose oral prednisone associated with oral cyclophosphamide may rescue renal function in several patients.

Finally, although chronic renal vein thrombosis does not affect renal function, the onset of an acute renal vein thrombosis may lead to a sudden renal insufficiency. Flank pain and macroscopic hematuria should raise the suspicion, which can be confirmed by echo-color Doppler, renal venography, or MRI. Fibrinolytic agents may achieve recovery of renal function if promptly administered.

Membranous nephropathy may also expose the patient to several extrarenal complications. Nephrotic patients are at greater risk for coronary heart disease than are sex- and age-matched controls. Moreover the risk of thrombotic events is increased. The thrombotic complications are probably the consequence of the typical coagulation abnormalities caused by the nephrotic syndrome. Intravascular thrombosis is particularly frequent and severe in older patients. In addition to older age factors such as hypertension, hypoalbuminemia, and hyperfibrinogenemia, hypercholesterolemia may contribute to thrombotic complications. Deep vein thrombosis, which develops in about 10% of patients, and, more rarely, arterial occlusion may complicate the course of the disease. Renal vein thrombosis is particularly frequent in MN, affecting up to 50% of nephrotic patients. It is still unclear why renal vein thrombosis is more frequent in MN than in other glomerular diseases. As recalled above, chronic insidious renal vein thrombosis seems to exert only a minimal impact on renal function or on the degree of proteinuria. However, it does predispose patients to pulmonary embolism. Finally the nephrotic status increases the risk of infection, hydroelectrolyte disorders, malnutrition, and pulmonary or cerebral edema.

Secondary membranous nephropathy

As shown in Table 15.1 a number of pathologic conditions may be associated with MN. However, the vast majority of cases of secondary MN are due to systemic lupus erythematosus, hepatitis viral infection, malignancy, or drugs.

The prevalence of a secondary disease varies from 20 to 40% among biopsy-proven cases of MN. It is somewhat higher in children, in whom MN is more frequently secondary to infections, particularly hepatitis B or C, and in older adults in whom MN is more frequently secondary to neoplasia or to the use of nonsteroidal anti-inflammatory drugs. Secondary MN may be suspected on the basis of those subtle histopathologic atypical features at renal biopsy previously described, although these are by no means essential or pathognomonic.

In patients with systemic lupus erythematosus, membranous nephropathy is found in approximately 8-15% of cases. The etiologic diagnosis may be difficult because the nephrotic syndrome can antedate the clinical and biologic features of lupus even by years. Although the presence of atypical features at light microscopy or immunofluorescence may suggest the diagnosis, only the finding of virus-like particles on electron microscopy is considered to be specific for lupus.

A wide variety of infections may be associated with MN. Hepatitis B viral infection is by far the most common. Usually patients with membranous nephropathy have no history of acute hepatitis, and liver function tests are normal or mildly abnormal. Patients have HBs antigenemia at the time of diagnosis, and core or antibody may or may not be detected. Hepatitis B viral DNA is also frequently found in the circulation. Using monoclonal and polyclonal antibodies, a number of investigators have demonstrated viral antigenic proteins in the glomerular immune deposits. Hepatitis B e antigen has been the most common antigen detected along the glomerular basement membrane. More recently the association of hepatitis C with MN also has been well documented.

Another frequent condition associated with membranous nephropathy is malignancy. Among patients with cancer-associated nephrotic syndrome, 70% have MN. The prevalence of malignancy in patients with MN was reported to vary from 5 to 11%. This percentage increases with age, reaching 20% in patients aged 60 years or older, whereas the association is uncommon in younger populations. The most common neoplasm associated with MN is carcinoma. The incidence of carcinoma in MN has been estimated to be more than tenfold higher than that expected for an age-matched normal population. In several cases the nephrotic syndrome precedes the discovery of malignancy. The most frequent carcinomas associated with MN are lung cancers, the great majority of which are bronchogenic rather than small cell tumors. Next, in order of frequency, are carcinomas of the colon and rectum, kidney, breast, and stomach. Less frequently MN can complicate Hodgkin's disease, chronic lymphocytic leukemia, and non-Hodgkin's lymphoma. Very rarely MN can also be associated with benign neoplasms. In several cases nephrotic syndrome may recede with tumor removal or successful chemotherapy. Recurrence of clinical manifestations of the nephrotic syndrome often appear contemporaneously with relapse or metastatic disease.

Drug-associated MN probably accounts for between 5-10% of cases. The agents most frequently associated with MN include nonsteroidal anti-inflammatory drugs, captopril, gold, and penicillamine. The last two drugs have been widely studied and seem to induce MN in HLA-restricted patients. Typically the nephropathy develops relatively soon after exposure to the involved drug. Withdrawal of the drug usually is associated with resolution of MN, although remission of the disease may take many months, being related roughly to the duration of the exposure.

Special mention is due to two other pathologic conditions that may be associated with MN, namely diabetes and rheumatoid arthritis. Patients with MN may show an abnormal glucose tolerance or an overt diabetes mellitus more commonly than might be expected by chance alone. The association of MN with diabetes mellitus is variably reported, depending on the indications for renal biopsy. Although abnormality in glucose metabolism may be a manifestation of previously latent diabetes mellitus or may represent a complication of MN, it seems likely that this association between MN and diabetes mellitus is related to a common HLA phenotype, making the individual susceptible to both diabetes and MN.

Membranous nephropathy may also develop in patients with rheumatoid arthritis. This association usually is related to the use of agents that may trigger MN such as gold, penicillamine, or nonsteroidal antiinflammatory drugs. However, MN may also develop in a number of patients not exposed to any of these drugs. Once again it seems possible that the association between rheumatoid arthritis and MN is related to a common genetic basis of susceptibility to both the diseases.

Diagnosis

Since the clinical presentation and biochemical finding are similar in MN and in other glomerular diseases, renal biopsy is required for a correct diagnosis. Once the histologic diagnosis is obtained, the next step in the clinical work-up is to determine whether the disease is idiopathic or secondary to an underlying cause. In some cases a thorough clinical history and examination, together with some laboratory investigations, will be sufficient to recognize whether a secondary condition exists.

The discovery of an underlying condition may have clinical, prognostic and therapeutic significance because appropriate interventions may resolve both the precipitating cause and the nephropathy. Thus, in all patients the clinical history should include a review of drug administration (including the use of topical agents). Physical examination should pay attention to skin lesions, lymph nodes, breasts, and prostate. Laboratory investigations should include anti-double-stranded DNA antibody, C3 and C4 components of complement, hepatitis B and C viral infection markers, and neoplasia markers. Selected patients may need hemoglobin electrophoresis, serologic tests for syphilis, and antithyroglobulin or antimicrosomal antibodies.

Among the various possible underlying diseases, neoplasms can pose major diagnostic problems. The discovery of a neoplasm-associated MN obviously will have extremely important prognostic as well as therapeutic significance. In approximately 50 to 60% of patients, cancer is recognized before or at the time of renal biopsy, but in other cases proteinuria may antedate the initial manifestations of an underlying neoplasm by months or even years. From the morphologic point of view it is almost impossible to differentiate the idiopathic form from cancer-associated-MN on the basis of light-immunofluorescence and electron microscopy. Extensive mesangial and/or subendothelial deposits may evoke a secondary form, but are seen only infrequently. It is still debated how extensive the investigation for an underlying cancer should be. At least in older patients with MN, however, an extensive investigation is recommended, because of the greater probability that these patients have underlying malignant disease. Thus, appropriate cancer screening tests should be performed as part of the diagnostic evaluation. These patients should have at least a stool examination for occult blood, a chest X-ray examination, and kidney ultrasound. Women should undergo mammography. Furthermore, selected patients could undergo colonscopy and CT of the abdomen.

Treatment

The clinical management of nephrotic patients with MN should take into account both symptomatic measures aimed at reducing proteinuria and preventing the extrarenal complications of nephrotic syndrome and the so-called specific therapy for MN.

Symptomatic therapy

Symptomatic therapy includes treatment of edemas, proteinuria, hypertension, hyperlipidemia, and hypercoagulability. The combination of dietary sodium restriction, diuretics, angiotensin inhibitors, and hypolipidemic drugs may maintain some patients with nephrotic syndrome almost without symptoms.

Angiotensin-converting enzyme (ACE)inhibitors and/or antagonists of angiotensin receptors can be particularly useful, since these agents may reduce proteinuria by altering the glomerular permeability to macromolecules and/or by modifying glomerular hemodynamics. In order to maximize the antiproteinuric effect, these drugs should be given at the highest tolerated doses while the patient is salt-restricted. If all these conditions are respected, proteinuria may reduce by 60% or more. The effect may require several weeks of treatment to be complete. These drugs usually are well tolerated, except in patients with renal artery stenosis, who are at risk for developing a severe, although reversible, renal failure.

Many lipid-lowering drugs have been used in nephrotic patients. Among these, hydroxymethylglutaryl coenzyme A reductase inhibitors are the preferred agents for handling hyperlipidemia. The reduction of serum cholesterol is dose-dependent. These agents usually are well tolerated. A mild increase in serum transaminase may occur initially, but this increase usually is transient. Myopathy is rare, but may occur when high doses are given. In order to recognize early signs of a drug-induced myopathy, regular control of muscle enzyme levels is recommended, particularly in the first period of therapy.

Whether or not nephrotic patients should be treated with anticoagulants is still debated. However, using decision analyses, some authors have found that in nephrotic patients with MN who are particularly exposed to the risk of intravascular thrombosis, the benefits of prophylactic anticoagulants significantly outweigh the risk of hemorrhagic complications. At any rate there is a general consensus that patients at higher risk for thrombosis such as those with more severe nephrotic syndrome (serum albumin lower than 2.5 g/dl, proteinuria more than 10 g/day), and/or antithrombin III levels lower than 75%, as well as during prolonged bed rest, surgery, episodes of dehydration, appropriate anticoagulation should be given. In patients who have had thrombotic events, a life-long prophylaxis with oral anticoagulant agents may be recommended (Tab. 15.2).

Specific therapy

Before considering any specific treatment for membranous nephropathy, one must recognize whether the disease is idiopathic or secondary in order to reserve specific treatment to the idiopathic disease and to cure appropriately any underlying disorder in the secondary form. Moreover, there is a general consensus that patients with nonnephrotic proteinuria do not need specific therapy, because they are not exposed to the complications of the nephrotic syndrome and run a minimal risk of developing renal failure.

There is much controversy about the treatment of the nephrotic patient. Some clinicians think that MN is a benign disease and prefer not to expose their patients to potentially toxic drugs unless renal insufficiency develops; others suggest an early specific treatment that may favor remission of the nephrotic syndrome and may prevent renal function deterioration.

Glucocortocoids and immunosuppressive agents, given either alone or in combination, have been widely studied in MN. Controlled studies with glucocorticoids did not show a clear benefit of these agents, either in improving the chances of remission of the nephrotic syndrome or in decreasing the risk of renal failure. In those trials, however, prednisone usually was given either for short periods (8 weeks) or at moderate doses (20-30 mg/day). Other studies have reported that higher dosage and/or more prolonged treatment may improve the natural course of MN.

Another therapeutic approach in membranous nephropathy is based on the use of cytotoxic drugs. Some trials reported that chlorambucil or cyclophosphamide given for 1-2 years can significantly reduce proteinuria. However, such a long treatment with alkylating agents exposed patients to severe side effects. Moreover, it is difficult to assess the efficacy of these drugs in protecting renal function because the follow-ups of the available studies were too short. Even less defined is the role of azathioprine, which has been tested in only a few patients followed for short periods.

Because prolonged administration of glucocorticoids or cytotoxic agents can lead to a disquieting morbidity, a treatment based on alternation of glucocorticoids and cytotoxic agents has been devised in Italy in order to reduce the risk of side effects. Treatment consisted of 1 month of glucocorticoids-methylprednisolone, 1 g intravenously daily for 3 consecutive days, followed by oral prednisone 0.5 mg/kg/day for the rest of the month, followed by 1 month with oral chlorambucil at a dose of 0.2 mg/kg/day. This 2-month cycle was repeated three times until a total of 6 months of therapy had been given. With such a treatment the probability of having a remission of the nephrotic syndrome as a first event was significantly higher in treated (83%) than in untreated patients (38%). It is important to point out that the remission of the nephrotic syndrome tended to occur toward the end of the treatment or even some months later. About 10% of treated patients experienced relapses of the nephrotic syndrome that responded to a new course of therapy. The actual probability of surviving without developing end-stage renal failure at 10 years was 92% for treated patients versus 60% for untreated patients. In another controlled trial comparing methylprednisolone plus chlorambucil with methylprednisolone alone, the probability of remission of the nephrotic syndrome at 4 years was 62% for the combined therapy versus 42% for patients given steroids alone. The reciprocal of plasma creatinine declined of 5% at 4 years in patients given combined treatment and 15% in patients given steroids alone. Finally, a recent controlled trial showed that, when combined with methylprednisolone, either chlorambucil or cyclophosphamide (2.5 mg/kg/day) may offer similar results in terms of remission (more than 80% as a first event), relapse of proteinuria, and renal function. Severe but reversible side effects were observed in less than 10% of patients treated with steroids alternated with a cytotoxic agent. Since the most frequent side effects are leukopenia and infection, blood cell count should be checked at least every 7-10 days during the

Table 15.2 Symptomatic therapy in patients with nephrotic syndrome due to membranous nephropathy

Management of edema	Management of proteinuria
I Step Dietary salt restriction to 3-4 g/day	Moderate protein intake restriction (1 g/kg/day)
II Step Hydrochlorothiazide 12.5-50 mg/day plus amiloride 5-10 mg/day (or triamterene or spironolactone)	ACEi and/or angiotensin receptor antagonists at the highest dose tolerated together with a low salt intake
III Step Oral furosemide 40-80 mg/day	**Management of hypercoagulability** (In the case of severe hypoalbuminemia or immobilization or previous thrombosis) Intravenous or subcutaneous heparin at anticoagulant doses, followed by long-term oral coumadin or warfarin at a dosage adjusted to keep the INR between 2 and 3
IV Step Oral furosemide 160-480 mg/day or bumetamide 1-5 mg/day or torasemide 40-160/day	
V Step Intravenous furosemide up to 2 g/day (or bumetamide or torsemide) plus metalozone 2.5-10 mg/day plus hydrochlorothiazide	**Management of hyperlipidemia** HGM coA-reductase inhibitors, 20-40 mg/day

cytotoxic drug cycle. The dose of the cytotoxic agent must be halved when leukocytes fall below 5000 and should be stopped if they fall below 3000/mm^3. Cytotoxic drugs also can cause azoospermia, and young males should be encouraged to deposit their semen in a sperm bank before starting therapy. A main concern about the use of cytotoxic drugs is the possible development of cancer. However, there is little if any oncogenic risk with a cumulative treatment of 3 months' duration with either chlorambucil or cyclophosphamide.

Other therapeutic options, alternative to glucocorticoids or cytotoxic agents, are cyclosporine or intravenous high-dose immunoglobulins. Cyclosporine may reduce proteinuria to less than 3 g per day in 60 to 70% of nephrotic patients. The effects are dose-dependent and rapid in onset. Unfortunately most responders relapse when the drug is stopped, but a few patients can maintain remission if cyclosporine is tapered off very gradually. Since cyclosporine is a potentially nephrotoxic drug, it should not be used in patients with renal insufficiency, severe hypertension, and/or interstitial fibrosis at renal biopsy. Moreover, the initial dose should not exceed 5 mg/kg/day with the old formulation or 4 mg/kg/day with the new microemulsion. In patients treated with cyclosporine renal function must be carefully monitored. Cyclosporine should be stopped whenever plasma creatinine increases 30% or more over the basal value. In most responders proteinuria decreases within 3 months of cyclosporine therapy. Thus, the drug may be stopped if no change in proteinuria is seen in the first 3 months. Finally, since cyclosporine may have a thrombophylic effect, its prolonged use might be of particular risk to patients already exposed to thromboembolic complications.

High-dose intravenous immunoglobulins (0.4 g/kg three times a week every 21 days repeated for three cycles, then 1 pulse every 3 weeks for 10 months) may also reduce proteinuria to nonnephrotic levels in about two-thirds of patients. Although usually well tolerated, this treatment may cause some side effects, such as renal function impairment and respiratory distress. Moreover the treatment is quite expensive (Tab. 15.3).

In summary, there is evidence that MN is a treatable disease. The probability of remission of the nephrotic syndrome is better for patients given immunosuppressive therapy than for those given glucocorticoids alone.

On the basis of the available data it seems that a 6-month course alternating methylprednisolone and an alkylating agent (chlorambucil or cyclophosphamide) every other month has the highest therapeutic index among the various regimens suggested. This treatment not only favors remission of the nephrotic syndrome but also can protect renal function in the long term.

When to start treatment is also a matter of discussion. There are at present two different attitudes among those clinicians who favor treatment. Some authors recommend an early treatment in order to prevent the complications of the nephrotic syndrome and the development of irreversible histologic lesions. This policy may expose patients with a benign course to the risk of a 6-month treatment with glucocorticoids and cytotoxic agents. Thus, other physicians prefer not to start treatment unless renal function deteriorates or a disabling nephrotic syndrome develops. This latter approach, however, leaves the patient exposed to the complications of the nephrotic syndrome. Moreover, waiting to treat until renal insufficiency appears may be too late, since the development of renal insufficiency and tubulointerstitial lesions can reduce the probability of a complete response to treatment and can increase the toxicity of cytotoxic drugs.

A compromise between these two diverging approaches could be an immediate treatment for patients with severe, symptomatic nephrotic syndrome, while postponing treatment in relatively asymptomatic patients.

If specific treatment is requested, we suggest the following algorithm (Fig. 15.2): if there are no specific contraindications, the physician can start with methylprednisolone alternated with a cytotoxic drug for 6 months. For patients who show remission and then have a relapse of the nephrotic syndrome, a second course of treatment can be given, since the probability of response is similar to that observed after the first course. For patients who have contraindications to corticosteroids, a 6-month treatment with cyclophosphamide (2 mg/kg/day) plus prednisone 5-10 mg/day may be tried. On the other hand, if the patient has contraindications to cytotoxic drugs, alternate-day prednisone (0.5 mg/kg) for 6 months plus three methylprednisolone pulses at the beginning of months 1, 3, and 5 may be given. In the case of persisting severe nephrotic syndrome 6-12 months after the end of the therapeutic cycle (the response may be delayed in many cases), a trial with cyclosporine may be done. Intravenous immunoglob-

Table 15.3 Possible therapeutic options for a patient with membranous nephropathy

1. A. MONTH 1, 3, 5: intravenous methylprednisolone, 1 g for 3 consecutive days, followed by oral prednisone 0.5 mg/kg/day for 27 days
   B. MONTH 2, 4, 6: chlorambucil, 0.2 mg/kg/day for 30 days or cyclophosphamide, 2.5 mg/kg/day for 30 days
2. Intravenous methylprednisolone, 1 g for 3 days at the beginning of month 1, 3, 5. Oral prednisone 0.5 mg/kg every other day for 6 months
3. Oral cyclophosphamide, 2 mg/kg/day for 6 months (plus prednisone 5-10 mg/day)
4. Cyclosporin (Neoral): 4 mg/kg/day. When remission is obtained, taper cyclosporin very gradually to the lowest effective maintenance dose
5. Intravenous immunoglobulins, 0.4 g/kg for 3 consecutive days every 3 weeks for 3 times, followed by 0.4 g/kg every 3 weeks for a further 10-month period

(Intravenous methylprednisolone pulse may be reduced to 0.5 g in patients under 50 kg body weight. The dose of chlorambucil and of cyclophosphamide should be halved if WBC count falls below 5000 per mm^3, and should be stopped if WBC falls below 3000 per mm^3. Chlorambucil and cyclophosphamide may be halved in young males in order to prevent azoospermia. Cyclosporin should not be given in patients with renal insufficiency and/or severe hypertension.)

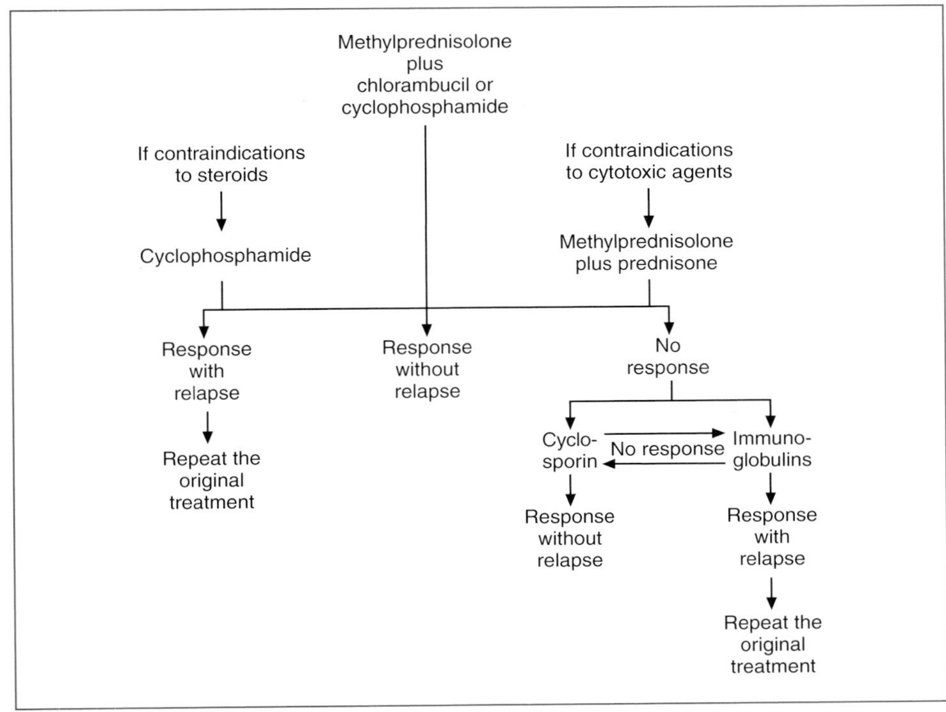

Figure 15.2 Suggested therapeutic steps in patients with membranous nephropathy and severe nephrotic syndrome.

ulins may be reserved for patients with severe nephrotic syndrome who failed to respond to any previous treatment.

Treatment in patients with declining renal function

In patients with no superimposed cause for renal failure, the progression usually is slow and the decrease in renal function is often linear. Thus, in the case of a sudden increase in plasma creatinine, an effort should be made to recognize and treat appropriately any superimposed complications.

In patients with slow progression not due to superimposed complications, treatment should be limited to those who have a real chance of improving. In fact the therapeutic results depend not only on the regimen used but also on the severity of the underlying histologic lesions. Thus, renal biopsy may be useful in deciding whether or not to treat a patient. In severe glomerular sclerosis and severe tubulointerstitial lesions, any form of treatment probably is useless.

Good results have been reported with cytotoxic drugs, often associated with glucocorticoids, but side effects were more frequent and more severe in these patients. Prolonged treatment (2 years) with oral cyclophosphamide associated with low-dose prednisone, and the 6-month regimen with methylprednisolone alternated with chlorambucil or cyclophosphamide obtained improvement of renal function and reduction of proteinuria in several cases. In order to reduce iatrogenic morbidity the daily dose should not exceed 1.5 mg/kg per day for cyclophosphamide and 0.1 mg/kg per day for chlorambucil, and the doses of intravenous methylprednisolone pulses should not exceed 0.5 g each.

Suggested readings

CAMERON JS, HEALY MJR, ADU D. The Medical Research Council trial of short-term high dose alternate day prednisone in idiopathic membranous nephropathy with a nephrotic syndrome in adults. Q J Med 1990;74:1313-56.

CATTRAN DC, DELMORE T, ROSCOE J, et al. A randomized controlled trial of prednisone in patients with idiopathic membranous nephropathy. N Eng J Med 1989;320:8-13.

EHRENREICH T, CHURG J. Pathology of membranous nephropathy. In: S.C. Sommers ed., Pathology Annual. New York: Appleton-Century-Crofts, 1968.

HOGAN SL, MULLER KE, JENNETTE JC, FALK RJ. A review of therapeutic studies of idiopathic membranous glomerulopathy. Am J Kidney Dis 1995;6:862-75.

KERJASCHKI D. Molecular pathogenesis of membranous nephropathy. Kidney Int 1992;41:1090-105.

PALLA R, CIRAMI C, PANICHI V, et al. Intravenous immunoglobulin therapy of membranous nephropathy: efficacy and safety. Clin Nephrol 1991;35:98-104.

PONTICELLI C, ZUCCHELLI P, PASSERINI P, CESANA B, AND THE ITALIAN IDIOPATHIC MEMBRANOUS TREATMENT STUDY GROUP. Methylprednisolone plus chlorambucil as compared with methylprednisolone alone for the treatment of idiopathic membranous nephropathy. N Eng J Med 1992;327:599-603.

PONTICELLI C, ZUCCHELLI P, PASSERINI P, et al. A 10-year follow-up of a randomized study with methylprednisolone and chlorambucil in membranous nephropathy. Kidney Int 1995;48:1600-4.

PONTICELLI C, ALTIERI P, SCOLARI F, et al. A randomized study comparing methylprednisolone plus chlorambucil versus methylprednisolone plus cyclophosphamide in idiopathic membranous nephropathy. JASN 1998;9:444-50.

CHAPTER

16 Membranoproliferative glomerulonephritis

Shanmukham Bhaskaran, Daniel C. Cattran

KEY POINTS

- The incidence of primary type I membranoproliferative glomerulonephritis has decreased substantially over the past two decades, except for that of the type II variant, which has remained unchanged.
- Although the complement abnormalities and their relationship to the nephritic factors in the serum has been clarified, their role in the pathogenesis of the disease is still debated.
- Type I is still the most common variant and predominantly affects young adults. Long-term treatment with corticosteroids seems to influence the outcome favorably in children with type I disease, but the risks are substantial.
- There is no proven treatment for types II and III. All types commonly recur post-transplant, but rarely destroy graft.

Membranoproliferative glomerulonephritis (MPGN) is characterized histologically by prominent glomerular hypercellularity, accompanied by an increase of mesangial matrix, thickening of the peripheral capillary walls, and mesangial interposition into the capillary walls, producing the appearance of splitting of the glomerular basement membrane. Other names used for this entity have included lobular glomerulonephritis, mesangiocapillary glomerulonephritis and chronic hypocomplementemic glomerulonephritis.

Epidemiology

The prevalence of the disease is decreasing worldwide. During the 1970s, it represented in most series 16-20% of the annual total primary glomerulonephritis, but in recent epidemiologic surveys it has decreased to less than 5%. This decrease seems limited to type I MPGN, since the frequency of type II MPGN, although always a small percentage of the total, has remained unchanged. In France, the decrease was observed among resident people but was not seen in patients referred from other parts of the world. The incidence was 0.9 per 100 000 during 1976-80, 0.5 per 100 000 during 1981-85, and 0.15 per 100 000 during 1986-90. Similar trends were reported from Italy (21% of primary glomerulonephritis during the period 1972-75 to 6.6% during 1987-93) and Spain (17% of primary glomerulonephritis during 1977-81 to 8% during 1981-85)

Etiopathogenesis

A genetic marker or link of the disorder to a particular major histocompatibility complex has been described, i.e., the extended haplotype HLA B8, DR3, SCO1, GLO2 with a relative risk score of 15 to 1. How this gene variant is related to the increased susceptibility to this disease is unknown.

Complement abnormalities and nephritic factors

MPGN is associated with unique complement profiles (Fig. 16.1). Considerable heterogeneity is seen in MPGN type I, and the abnormalities are as follows: (1) predominant activation of terminal components, resulting in depression of one or more of the terminal components (C6, C7 and C9); (2) classic activation alone with normal terminal components (depressed C1q, C2, C4). Hypocomplementemia accompanied by low C4 level indicates classic pathway activation, presumably by circulating immune complexes; (3) predominantly C3 activation with normal early and terminal components.

All groups have depressed properdin, factor B and C8.

MPGN type II is associated with a complement profile characterized mainly by C3 depression, slightly depressed factor B in some, with normal C5. In contrast, in type III MPGN, there may be severe hypocomplementemia associated with depressed C5, properdin, and terminal components, or moderate hypocomplementemia associated with depressed C3 alone.

The cause of the perturbation is that circulating C3 convertase is combined with its autoantibodies, making it resistant to inactivation. Convertase can be designated in its simplest form as C3bBb. Convertase is continually being formed by hydration of C3 and reactions involving factors B and D. These convertases would rapidly deplete the serum of C3, unless controlled by factors H (serum protein which promotes the dissociation of Bb from C3b and acts as a cofactor to factor I) and factor I (which mediates proteolysis of C3b) (Fig. 16.1). Moreover, since the alternative pathway uses a positive feedback mechanism, regulation of the amplification mechanism is important for the host and unless regulated it will cycle until all C3 is completely cleaved.

Nephritic factors are immunoglobulin G autoantibodies that stabilize convertase by inhibiting the binding of factor H to the C3b. In their presence, active convertase circulates and produces hypocomplementemia, the hallmark of the presence of nephritic factor in MPGN types II and III and, in some cases, in type I. Two different nephritic factors have been delineated. Nfa, or the nephritic factor of the amplification loop, first recognized as C3NeF, is found in MPGN type II and/or in partial lipodystrophy. It activates only the amplification loop, essentially affecting the level of C3 only, producing a marked depression of C3, with usually normal C5. When serum containing Nfa is added to normal serum, conversion of C3 is complete in 20 to 30 minutes, and the reaction is not properdin-dependent. The stabilized convertase has the configuration C3b,Bb,Nfa. The structural basis of C3NeF formations was recently studied in a monoclonal cell line established by EBV transformation of mononuclear cells from a patient with type II disease. The complete nucleotide sequences of the heavy and light chain variable regions of an IgG autoantibody were determined. The conclusion suggested that the nephritic factor is antigen driven and is a part of a normal immune response. The peripheral control however must fail in individuals that go on to excess C3NeF production and disease.

The other nephritic factor has been designated as Nft. because it is related to the terminal pathway. Nft was noted to convert C3 very slowly and to activate the terminal pathway of complement. It has been found in all patients with type III and in some patients with type I. The reaction is properdin-dependent and the complement profile it produces is markedly depressed levels of C3 accompanied by markedly depressed levels of C5. In addition, one or more of the terminal components, especially C7, C8, and C9 are also very low. Properdin levels usually are also low, and those of factor B occasionally are low, but classic pathway components are unaffected. The stabilized convertase is thought to have the configuration C3b,Bb,P, Nft, in which P is properdin.

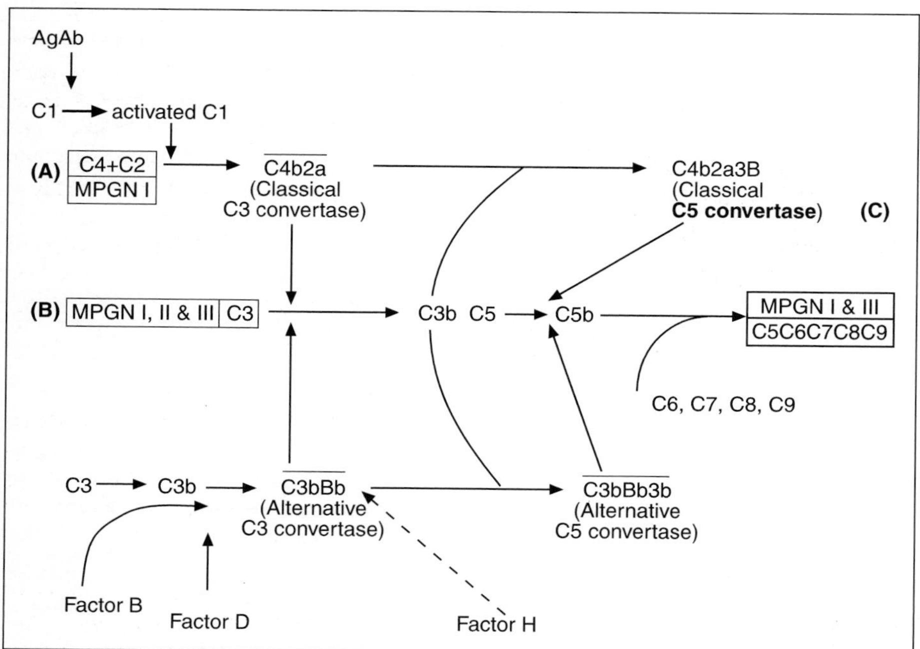

Figure 16.1 The complement cascade with the classic and alternate pathways of activation. **(A)** Classic pathway activation with low C2, C4 seen in type I. This is commonly associated with immune complexes in the serum. **(B)** Low C3 seen in type I, II and III. The C3 is lowest in type II and in these cases Nfa is commonly found in the circulation. **(C)** Low terminal components C5 to C9 seen in type I and III. In these cases Nft is often found in the circulation.

Evidence favoring the hypothesis that convertase in the circulation predisposes to glomerulonephritis is provided by three described abnormalities that cause dysfunction of factor H (a) homozygous factor H deficiency, (b) a circulating factor H inhibitor, and (c) heterozygous absence of a factor H binding site on C3b (Marder disease) which result in nephritis in approximately 50% of the human subjects associated with decreased levels of C3. Moreover, it has been shown that pigs genetically deficient in factor H consistently develop a lethal membranoproliferative glomerulonephritis type II characterized by massive glomerular deposits of complement, intramembranous deposits and mesangial hypercellularity. In these animals, in situ glomerular complement activation occurs in utero before the appearance of intramembranous deposits or mesangial proliferation, and kidney failure coincides with the secondary morphologic phenomenon of pronounced mesangial cell proliferation that causes loss of glomerular capillary patency.

Assuming that circulating convertase is nephritogenic, the differences in the glomerular morphology and in the severity of the convertase nephritides may be explained by the differences in composition and reactivity of the convertases. In Marder disease and factor H deficiency, it is native convertase, C3bBb, that circulates in excess, and nephritis develops in only half of the cases and is usually mild. Native convertase has a half-life of 3 minutes, a molecular weight of 240 kd, and activates only C3. On the other hand, the convertase that circulates in MPGN type II, which also activates only C3, is stabilized by the nephritic factor of the amplification loop, has a half-life of 52 minutes, and a molecular weight of 400 kd. Few escape the development of severe nephritis. In MPGN type III, properdin is required for the formation of convertase stabilized by the nephritic factor of the terminal pathway. It activates the terminal pathway as well as C3, and has a molecular weight of 980 kd. When native convertase circulates, paramesangial deposits predominate. With the larger and more stable convertase in type II, deposits are both paramesangial and subepithelial but subendothelial deposits are absent. In type III, with the largest and perhaps most stable convertase circulating, deposits are more abundant and can be present in all three locations. Interestingly, CR1 which is an integral membrane protein expressed on glomerular podocytes and erythrocytes, a receptor for C3b, promotes dissociation of C2a from C4b (which together constitute classic pathway C3 convertase) and acts as a cofactor for the catabolism of C4b and C3b by Factor I. In MPGN type I CR1 expression on podocytes was more severely defective and was not recoverable in patients with persistent massive proteinuria and hypocomplementemia. Moreover, CR1 expression at the time of first biopsy is a significant predictor for prognosis of MPGN type 1.

Although the circulation factors are designated nephritic and are measurable, their nephritogenicity is still debated. Findings of MPGN with normal C3, hypocomplementemia without nephritis, lack of correlation of C3 levels with renal function, clinical and histologic improvement in spite of persistent hypocomplementemia, and recurrence of dense deposits after renal transplantation in the absence of hypocomplementemia have contributed to this debate of their relevance. Potential reasons for this lack of correlation include the possible requirement of another factor or factors, persistence of nephritic factor-stabilized convertase for a long period before manifestation of nephritis, and glomerular injury secondary to hyperfiltration despite normocomplementemia.

The role of cell-mediated immunity remains poorly defined. Marked intraglomerular infiltration of leukocytes is sometimes observed in MPGN and LFA-1/ICAM-3 interaction as well as leukocyte adhesion Mac-1/complement interaction may be involved in MPGN type 1. LFA-1/ICAM-3 interaction could promote cell-cell adhesion between granulocytes/monocytes and migrating macrophages in glomeruli. All of these could contribute to the inflammatory component often observed in types I and sometimes in type III.

It has been recognized that platelet survival is significantly reduced in patients with active MPGN. Although this abnormality may not be of primary pathogenetic importance, it has been the rationale for several different treatment protocols.

Pathophysiology

The pathologic characteristics of the three types of MPGN are given in Table 16.1.

Type 1 MPGN

Light microscopy The "classic" pattern is characterized by mesangial cell proliferation, mesangial matrix increase and diffuse GBM thickening with a double contour appearance due to the progressive encroachment of the extracellular matrix into the paramesangial and loop areas (Fig. 16.2 A). Sometimes more marked mesangial expansion occludes the capillary lumina of some loops and produces the "lobular" pattern. "Nodular" MPGN is characterized by centrilobular sclerosis of the expanded mesangium and is always associated with microaneurysmatic dilatation of glomerular capillaries.

Using trichrome staining, large subendothelial deposits may be identified, although they are better demonstrated by immunofluorescence and electron microscopy. Most commonly there is a moderate glomerular infiltration of neutrophils and monocytes. In approximately 20% of cases a more severe influx of monocytes is observed. Other variants include only focal and segmental changes, diffuse glomerular disease with massive deposits, and occasionally crescentic involvement. Tubulointerstitial damage is quite variable and, as in other glomerular based diseases, is the best guide to prognosis.

Immunofluorescence There is almost always granular staining for C3, with two major patterns; one with capillary deposits only and the other with both mesangial and capillary deposits. Other complement components activated early in the cascade are present in about 50% of cases (C4 and C1q), whereas properdin is almost always present. In two-thirds of cases, IgG and IgM are found in the same location as C3 but with less intensity.

Electron microscopy Electron microscopy shows increased mesangial cells and matrix, a dominance of subendothelial electron-dense deposits and thickened GBM with a double-contour appearance due to the expanded matrix pushing out from the stalk into the paramesangial and loop areas (Fig. 16.2 B).

Type II MPGN (Dense-deposit disease)

Light microscopy The characteristic lesion is thickened GBM caused by irregular intramembranous lesions that are ribbon-like, brightly eosinophilic, and sometimes refractile. They are intensely periodic acid-Schiff (PAS) positive, and appear fuchsinophilic with trichrome stain. This lesion also may be present in the basal lamina of Bowman's capsule and in the tubular basement membrane (Fig. 16.2 C). Mesangial involvement varies from minimal to diffuse proliferative lesions, with or without crescents. The degree of paramesangial deposits correlates closely with the level of complement.

Immunofluorescence The characteristic finding is intense staining for C3 along the glomerular capillary walls and in the glomerular mesangial regions. The C3 is often along the capillary walls in a double-contour, linear-looking configuration, giving a "railroad track" appearance, and in the mesangial region, ringlike staining is seen. C3 also is frequently present in Bowman's capsule and along the tubular basement membrane. The dense deposit itself does not stain with antisera to any of the immunoglobulins or complement components. They do stain brightly with thioflavine-T, and glycoprotein material has been demonstrated to accumulate within the basement membranes.

Electron microscopy Diffuse thickening of GBM due to the presence of electron-dense material within the lamina densa is the characteristic lesion (Fig. 16.2 D). This corresponds to the area between the "tracks" seen on immunofluorescence. Similar electron-dense material is usually present in mesangial areas, and these correspond to the central nonstaining part of the mesangial rings seen on immunofluorescence. Electron-dense deposits also may be seen along the basal lamina of Bowman's capsule, along the tubular basement membrane, and in capillaries, arterioles, and small arteries.

Type III MPGN

This type is best distinguished by electron microscopy of silver-impregnated tissue. Deposits are usually both subendothelial and subepithelial, and the latter are most often covered by basement membrane material, so the deposits appear to be intramembranous. Silver impregnation reveals frequent disruption and duplication of the basement membrane, resulting in a frayed and fenestrated appearance.

Clinical findings

MPGN affects all age groups. Type I MPGN can be seen in patients of any age, although it is most common between the ages of 5 and 40 years. Type II, on the other hand is almost always seen in patients 3 to 20 years of age. Sex distribution is equal for all types of MPGN, and whites are the most commonly affected racial group. Patients with type III MPGN are rare and tend to be older and to have a more silent, insidious onset and progression compared with those with type I disease.

Eighty percent of patients with MPGN have the type I variant, 10 to 20 5 have type II, and less than 5% type III. The mode of presentation is extremely variable and

Table 16.1 Pathologic characteristics of the three types of MPGN

	Type I	Type II	Type III
Light microscopy	Mesangial cell proliferation and increased mesangial matrix, subendothelial invasion of peripheral capillary wall, classic double contouring of basement membrane	Mesangial cell proliferation, replacement of lamina densa with electron dense material, apparent basement membrane thickening	Mesangial cell proliferation less severe
Immunofluorescence	Peripheral C3 often with IgG, C1q, C4	Linear and mesangial C3, mesangial rings	Like type I but usually C4 not present
Electron microscopy	Subendothelial deposits basement membrane normal appearance	Linear intramembranous electron dense material	Subendothelial and subepithelial deposits basement membrane disrupted and fragmented

includes the acute nephritic syndrome (10-20%), asymptomatic proteinuria (20-40%), and the nephrotic syndrome (10-30%). Other findings at onset include gross hematuria (5-10%), hypertension (up to 20%), and asymptomatic elevations of serum creatinine values (10-20%).

Type II MPGN has been associated with fundus changes with drusen-like deposits and mottled pigmentation. Electron-dense deposits have been described in choriocapillaries and along the inner collagenous layer of Bruch's membrane. Mild changes are easily detected with fluorescein angiography. Changes worsen with time, and choroidal neovascularization may occur, resulting in loss of vision.

Treatment

Medical treatment

The following comments about drug therapy are limited to type I MPGN because there have been no series large enough to permit valid conclusions relative to types II or III.

Anticoagulants

One therapeutic trial used the combination of aspirin (975 mg per day) and dipyridamole (325 mg per day). The study was a well-designed, randomized, 1-year trial. The rate of change in renal function was measured not only by creatinine clearance but also by the more precise radioisotope iothalamate method. An additional interesting feature of this study was the monitoring of the patient's platelet survival times. At follow-up there was better preservation of glomerular filtration rate and better platelet survival in the drug-treated group, but no improvement in the urine sediment activity, the complement profile, or the severity of proteinuria. The majority of the treated patients continued to receive the medication, and after an average of 4 years of follow-up had a lower percentage of end-stage renal failure than did the control group. This drug combination can produce problems, however, especially in patients with more advanced renal failure, and three of the treated patients (15%) had

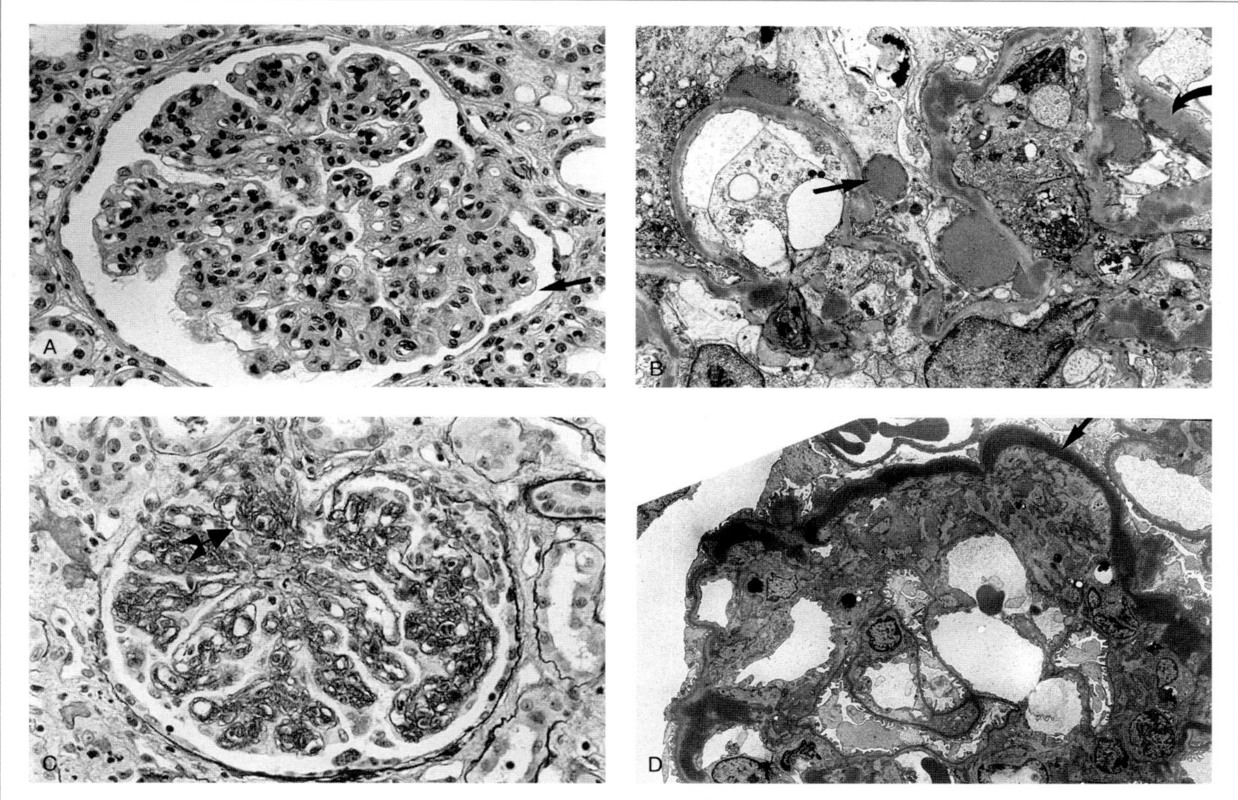

Figure 16.2 (**A**) Typical appearance of membranoproliferative lesion type I on light microscopy. Lobular segmental accentuation with mesangial cell and matrix proliferaton is evident. The double contouring of the peripheral capillary loops is also seen (*arrow*) (Hematoxylin-eosin x 250). (**B**) Electron micrograph of type I MPGN showing mesangial matrix interposition along with variable size subendothelial deposits and new basement membrane like material (*curved arrow*). Scattered subepithelial lumps are also evident (*straight arrow*) (Hematoxylin-eosin x 2500). (**C**) Light microscopic appearance of type II, membranoproliferative lesion lobulation is evident. The intramembranous lesions are PAS positive and often have a hard refractile quality (*arrow*) (Periodic-acid Schiff x 250). (**D**) Type II MPNG with electron dense ribbon like material within the basement membrane (*arrow*). The variability of the involvement of BM is evident (Hematoxylin-eosin x 2000).

to discontinue the medication because of bleeding complications.

Another trial used a regimen of warfarin combined with dipyridamole, which also was shown to have a beneficial effect. These results were much less convincing considering the sample size and the higher complication rate; the trial was designed to be a randomized, cross-over prospective study of 22 patients, but because of problems only 13 completed the study. Significant side effects included one death due to a cerebrovascular accident, two significant hemorrhagic episodes (in two patients) and one duodenal ulcer.

The introduction of anticoagulant therapy and antiplatelet agents was based on the observation that platelet survival time is reduced in patients with MPGN. These drugs may work by reducing platelet-derived growth factor release, decreasing smooth muscle cell proliferation, and/or reducing chemotaxis of monocytes and neutrophils to the area, thereby helping to limit the severity of injury. The aspirin and dipyridamole may also act via inhibition of intrarenal prostaglandin synthesis and/or through a change in the balance between thromboxane production and endothelial cell prostacyclin release. Despite these positive findings, the known variation in the natural history of the disease, the lack of homogeneity in these study populations and the risks of therapy have resulted in quite limited use of these agents for treatment in this disease.

Anticoagulant plus cytotoxic agents

An uncontrolled study done in the early 1970s that combined a cytotoxic agent with an oral anticoagulant and dipyridamole showed dramatic improvement in patients with MPGN. Unfortunately a more rigorous, prospective study done by our group using this therapy showed no benefit.

Corticosteroids

Another therapeutic approach has been prednisone treatment. Studies of this therapy have been confined to children, and although the studies have been performed over the long term, they have been uncontrolled. The results have suggested that steroid treatment for patients with type I MPGN results in a significant improvement in both renal survival and severity of proteinuria. It is interesting to note that this beneficial effect was demonstrated only after 3 years of treatment and only if the prednisone was initiated within 12 months of the initial presentation. The dose is substantial; alternate-day prednisone is begun at 2 to 2.5 mg/kg and is reduced to 1.5 to 2.5 mg/kg after 1 year, to 1 to 1.5 mg/kg after 2 years, and to 0.8 to 1.5 mg/kg after 3 years. These patients are still receiving significant prednisone in a dose between 0.2 and 1 mg/kg at 4 years. The International Study of Kidney Disease in Children (ISKDC) carried out a prospective randomized trial to test this regimen. In MPGN patients with a glomerular filtration rate of greater than or equal to 70 ml/min/m^2 and proteinuria greater than or equal to 40 mg/h/m^2, they compared the effects of prednisone, 40 mg/m^2 given on alternate days, with those of placebo. Patients excluded from the study were those with any evidence of systemic disease and those previously treated with steroids or immunosuppressive drugs. There were 80 patients entered into the study, 47 received the active drug and 33 received placebo. The mean duration of treatment was 41 months. Treatment failure was defined as an increase from baseline of 30% or more in serum creatinine, or an absolute increase of 35 μmol/l. There was better preservation of creatinine clearance in the prednisone group; with a treatment failure rate of 55% in placebo patients, compared with 40% in the prednisone group. Life-table analysis showed a renal survival rate at 130 months of 61% among patients receiving prednisone and 12% among patients receiving placebo, although the numbers were quite small by this time point. In the patients with type I or III MPGN, 33% of the treatment group failed, compared with 58% in the placebo group. However, statistical significance of less than 0.05 was not achieved in any type, probably due to the small sample size, and significant side effects did occur in the treated patients. These included hypertension, hypertensive encephalopathy, osteoporosis, mild diabetes mellitus, and obesity. Although the authors concluded that long-term treatment with prednisone appears to improve the renal outcome of children with MPGN, the risk/benefit ratio was high and the actual number of patients at the end of the follow-up period was small.

Other therapeutic approaches

These have included the long-term use of nonsteroidal anti-inflammatory drugs (NSAIDs). They are associated with a significant reduction in the glomerular filtration rate, although uncontrolled trials have suggested that the improvement in proteinuria is greater than expected by these changes alone. This reduction in the glomerular filtration may be acceptable, especially if the patient is rescued from severe hypoalbuminemia and the associated debilitating edema.

Cyclosporine also has been used, and may act through its suppression of T-cell activity and/or have an effect similar to that of the NSAIDs, with the improvement in proteinuria being related to a reduction in the glomerular filtration rate. This drug does have other significant side effects and its use must be considered experimental since no well-designed studies have been published in this area using this agent.

Surgical treatment

Renal transplantation

Biopsies of renal allografts will reveal up to a 30% recurrence of type I lesion and up to 35% of type II lesions. However failure of the renal graft due to recurrence is uncommon in either type and is estimated to occur in only 5-10% of cases. Recurrence of type III MPGN also has been reported. Despite this, transplantation is still recommended in all types.

Prognosis

The natural history in patients with MPGN often fluctuates spontaneously. This variability includes periods of acute deterioration and rapid improvement in both the glomerular filtration rate and proteinuria in as many as one-third of patients. However, there are certain clinical features associated with a poor prognosis, including persistent nephrotic range proteinuria for greater than 6 months and/or a progressive decline in creatinine clearance over a similar time frame. Unfavorable histologic features include glomerulosclerosis and crescent formation as well as moderate to severe tubular-interstitial pathology. By contrast, isolated focal and segmental MPGN lesions rather than diffuse involvement carry a much more benign prognosis.

Features of no prognostic importance include the age at onset, gender, nephritic presentation, the initial creatinine and proteinuria values, and the complement profile at any time during the disease.

Ten-year renal survival rates in both adults and children vary, but are in the range of 60 to 75%.

Suggested readings

Belgiojoso GBD, Baroni M, Pagliari B, et al. Is membranoproliferative glomerulonephritis really decreasing? Nephron 1985;40:380-1.

Cameron JS, Turner DR, Heaton J, et al. Idiopathic mesangiocapillary glomerulonephritis: comparison of types I and II in children and adults and long-term prognosis. Am J Med 1983;74:175-92.

Cattran DC, Cardella CJ, Roscoe JM, et al. Results of a controlled drug trial in membranoproliferative glomerulonephritis. Kidney Int 1985;27:436-41.

Cattran DC. Current status of cyclosporin A in the treatment of membranous, Ig A and membranoproliferative glomerulonephritis. Clin Nephrol 1991;35:S43-7.

Coppo R, Gianoglio B, Porcellini Mg, Maringhini S. Frequency of renal diseases and clinical indications for renal biopsy in children (Report of the Italian National Registry of Renal Biopsies in Children). Nephrol Dial Transplant 1998;13:293-7.

D'Amico G, Ferrario F. Mesangiocapillary glomerulonephritis. J Am Soc Nephrol 1992;2:S159-66.

Donadio JV, Anderson CF, Mitchell JC, Holley KE, Ilstrup DM, Fuster V, Chesebro JH. Membranoproliferative glomerulonephritis. A prospective clinical trial of platelet-inhibitor therapy. N Engl J Med 1984;310:1421-6.

Donadio JV, Offord KP. Reassessment of treatment results in membranoproliferative glomerulonephritis, with emphasis on life-table analysis. Am J Kidney Dis 1989;14:445-51.

Jansen JH, Hogasen K, Harboe M, Hovig T. In situ complement activation in porcine membranoproliferative glomerulonephritis type II. Kidney Int 1998;53:331-49.

Penina T, Jay B, Jonathan NT, Chester MEJ. Treatment of mesangiocapillary glomerulonephritis with alternate-day prednisone - report of the International Study of Kidney Disease in Children. Pediatr Nephrol 1992;6:123-30.

Simon P, Ramee Mp, Autuly V, et al. Epidemiology of primary glomerular diseases in a French region. Variations according to period and age. Kidney Int 1994;46:1192-8.

Soma J, Saito T, Seino J, Sato H, Ootaka T, Yusa A, Abe K. Participation of CR1(CD35), CR3(CD11b/CD18) and CR4(CD11c/CD18) in membranoproliferative glomerulonephritis type I. Clin Exp Immunol 1995;100:269-76.

Varade WS, Forrestal J, West CD. Patterns of complement activation in idiopathic membranoproliferative glomerulonephritis, type I, II, and III. Am J Kidney Dis 1990;16:196-206.

West CD, McAdams J. Glomerular paramesangial deposits: association with hypocomplementemia in membranoproliferative glomerulonephritis types I and III. Am J Kidney Dis 1998;31:427-34.

West CD, McAdams J. Membranoproliferative glomerulonephritis type III: association of glomerular deposits with circulating nephritic factor-stabilized convertase. Am J Kidney Dis 1998;32:56-63.

CHAPTER

17

IgA nephropathy

Francesco Paolo Schena

KEY POINTS

- IgA nephropathy is the most common glomerulonephritis worldwide in children and adults, with a low incidence in Afro-Americans and black-skinned Africans. Familial clustering of IgAN patients has been observed worldwide.
- Clinically IgAN is characterized by recurrent intrainfectious episodes of macroscopic hematuria in association with mucosal infections, e.g., tonsillitis, bronchitis, and gastroenteritis, or by persistent microscopic hematuria and/or chance proteinuria. In a few cases, nephrotic syndrome, acute renal failure, or rapidly progressive deterioration of the renal function can occur.
- The grading of histologic lesions is based principally on the severity of cellular proliferation and glomerulosclerosis, on the number of crescents and/or the presence or absence of tubular atrophy, interstitial cellular infiltrates, and fibrosis.
- The gold standard method of diagnosis remains the renal biopsy, which clearly reveals mesangial deposits of IgA.
- It is advisable to treat patients exhibiting nephrotic syndrome and minimal change lesions, patients with moderate lesions, patients with acute renal failure, and patients with rapid deterioration of renal function. Different regimens of therapy have been used, but it is evident that not every patient who is treated reaches stabilized renal function.

IgA nephropathy (IgAN), or Berger's disease, is the most common glomerular disease worldwide. It is characterized by recurrent intrainfectious episodes of gross hematuria and persistent microscopic hematuria and/or proteinuria in the absence of any recognizable systemic disease, e.g., Schönlein-Henoch purpura, lupus erythematosus or cryoglobulinemia, liver disease or lower urinary tract infection. The dominance or codominance of IgA-IgG or IgA deposits, especially in the mesangium, characterizes Berger's disease and a group of diseases known as IgA-associated nephritides.

Epidemiology

The high prevalence rate of IgAN is expressed in terms of the percentage of primary glomerulonephritis or the total biopsy series originating in national renal registries. The frequency of the disease varies considerably in different geographic areas because each area has its own local standards for performing renal biopsies on patients exhibiting symptoms of a nephritic disorder or persistence of urinary abnormalities. Also, each area has different standards for screening urine samples. These two factors strongly influence statistics. The highest prevalence rates are found in Asia, Australia, and southern Europe. The lowest prevalence rates are found in North America and the United Kingdom. In Asia, the prevalence rate approaches 30-50% of the patient population with primary glomerulonephritis. In Europe there seems to be a difference between the northern and southern parts of the continent; the prevalence rate in southern Europe is 20-35%, whereas the rate is 10-20% in northern Europe. A low prevalence rate has been reported in the United States (5-10%); nonetheless, Native Americans living in the Southwest exhibit a prevalence rate of over 25%. Moreover, males express a much greater incidence of IgAN worldwide, except for Japan, where the male prevalence is only 2:1. Only a few cases of

IgAN have been documented within the Afro-American population, and the disease remains virtually nonexsistent among black-skinned Africans. Once again, these remarkable differences are naturally influenced by the conservative approach taken by some nephrologists who do not perform renal biopsies on patients demonstrating an episode of macroscopic hematuria, persistent isolated microscopic hematuria, or mild proteinuria.

Genetically influenced IgAN also has been observed in different geographic areas of the world. After detailed reports of families exhibiting genetic IgAN, serologic markers were investigated without receiving much positive data. It is interesting to note that urinary abnormalities are more frequent in family members of an IgAN patient than in the population at large. However, the invasive nature of the renal biopsy necessary to define the immunohistologic pattern of IgAN discourages nephrologists from performing this technique on a patient's relative who exhibits only minimal urinary findings, persistent microhematuria, or sporadic episodes of macrohematuria. Nonetheless, the urine of family members should be monitored systematically, and if possible a renal biopsy should be performed on family members with persistent microscopic hematuria.

In order to understand the genetic influences of this disease, the frequency of HL-A antigens in IgAN patients was studied. At present, no consistent associations between IgAN and HLA antigens have been noted; even the association between polymorphisms of the immunoglobulin heavy chain region on chromosone 14 and IgAN is at the moment uncertain. Many obstacles need to be overcome in order to evaluate and design genetic studies on IgAN. First, the occurrence of multiple pathogenetic mechanisms, which indicates a polygenic disease. Second, environmental factors may play a major role in the pathogenesis and may interact with several genes in different loci, since the disease is clinically evident only in some family members and appears at various stages of life. However, epidemologic investigations have not revealed a common environmental factor involved in IgAN, since occupation, type of residence, and diet varied for each patient. Third, the correct diagnosis requires a renal biopsy, which is an invasive procedure in apparently healthy subjects who exhibit only microscopic hematuria and/or proteinuria.

Etiopathogenesis

The classic immunofluorescent pattern characterized by mesangial deposits of IgA, mainly the IgA1 subclass, provides several theories in the pathogenesis of IgAN. Despite intensive investigation by several research groups, a widely accepted hypothesis has not yet emerged.

Immunologic abnormalities in the mucosa and the bone marrow in IgAN patients are shown in Table 17.1. It is evident that tonsillitis, pharyngitis, bronchitis, gastroenteritis, and other infections of the mucosas commonly precipitate an episode of hematuria in an IgAN patient. It can be suggested that viral, bacterial, or food antigens can enhance the production of dimeric and polymeric IgA by lymphoid cells present in the mucosal lamina propria. Normally IgA acts as an immunologic barrier in the secretions and in the cells by neutralizing the pathogenes through a specific receptor. Individuals with insufficient function of the polymeric immunoglobin receptor and with persistent mucosal infections have more viral antigens being shed in the lamina propria. Thus, dimeric and polymeric IgA and IgA immune complexes spill over into the circulation. The excessive presence of circulating IgA immune complexes and their impaired clearance contribute to their deposition in the kidney.

Table 17.1 Immunologic abnormalities at the mucosa and bone marrow levels of IgA nephropathy patients

Mucosas
Increased number of IgA producing cells in tonsils
Abnormal production of IgA by pokeweed mitogen-stimulated tonsillar lymphocytes
High concentration of IgA in pharyngeal and nasal secretions
Bone marrow
Increased percentage of plasma cells containing IgA1
Increased synthesis of IgA1 after influenza virus vaccine stimulation

Nevertheless, in IgAN patients, the increased precentage of bone marrow plasma cells containing IgA1 contingent with increased synthesis of IgA1 suggests the participation of the bone marrow in the pathogenesis of the disease. These data propose a possible relationship between the mucosa and the bone marrow in IgAN. Hypothetically, after precursor B cells have been stimulated by the antigen and helper T-cells, the lymphocytes migrate via regional lymphonodes to the circulation. Most of these cells return to the mucosal sites. Some B cells localize in the bone marrow and transform themselves into IgA-producing plasma cells. Many investigators have witnessed an abnormal production of IgA antibodies to different antigens such as subcutaneous, oral vaccines, or food challenge in IgAN patients – thus, demonstrating an upregulation of both the systemic and mucosal IgA systems following systemic immunization.

Chronic and persistent exposure to unknown antigens determines a persistent depletion of suppressor/inducer T-cells and a persistent elevation of helper/inducer T-cells – thus, promoting an increased number of circulating IgA-bearing cells, IgA-specific switch T-cells, and serum IgA and IgA1-containing immune complexes.

The characteristics of serum IgA1 are represented by its multimeric form as well as the presence of a J-chain, suggesting its prevalent anionic charge (pI= 4.5 to 6.8) and reduced terminal galactose residues or inaccessible galactose residues on the heavy chain. The overproduction of polyclonal or antigen-specific polymeric IgA1 with the above normalities and/or its defective clearance may explain the permanent deposition of IgA in the mesangial area of IgAN patients' glomeruli. Recently it has been demonstrated that a small population of IgA1 molecules, Gal deficient in O-linked glycans of the hinge region, are responsible for the abnormal formation of IgA1-IgG complexes in IgAN patients; this may induce a reduced rate of its elimination and catabolic degradation by the liver. The undergalactosylated IgA1 complexes are formed owing to a deficiency or a structural modification in the β1,3 galactosyltransferase enzyme that mediates the transfer of UPD-Gal to an acceptor such as Gal Nac-Ser in IgA1 producing cells. Defective galactosylation reduces IgA1 affinity for the hepatic and extrahepatic asialoglycoprotein receptor (mesangial cells in the kidney), resulting in failure of the normal catabolic route. Therefore, the defective clearance of IgA1 contributes to the persistence of circulating IgA1 immune complexes and their deposition in the kidney. In addition, the elevated serum levels of IgA downregulate Fca receptor expression on monocytes – another receptor involved in IgA catabolism and the clearance of IgA1 immune complexes from the circulation. This defect contributes to the permanence of IgA1 and IgA1 complexes in IgAN patients' blood circulation.

Clinical findings

IgAN occurs at all ages, but it is seen most frequently in children and in young adults (second and third decades of life). The onset of the disease is characterized by one of two common presentations. First, the abrupt appearance of macroscopic hematuria may occur in association with a febrile infectious illness, e.g., pharyngitis or tonsillitis, or, less often, pneumonia, gastroenteritis, urinary tract infections, or other current general infections – and rarely after vaccination or heavy physical exercise. Second, asymptomatic microscopic hematuria and/or mild proteinuria may be detected accidentally as a result of a preemployment health exam, blood donor screening, or investigative testing. In the first case, the interval between a febrile infectious disease and the appearance of macroscopic hematuria is very short, 24-72 hours, compared with 1 or 2 weeks of postinfectious acute glomerulonephritis. In our studies about 56% of patients demonstrating macroscopic hematuria fall into this category. The episode of macroscopic hematuria usually is brief and lasts for 1-3 days, but may continue for a week. It is more frequent in children and becomes less common with age. Loin pain is present in approximately one-third of the patients, and the color of the urine is red or brown ("Coke"-colored) and rarely contains blood clots. In the second case, persistent microscopic hematuria occurs in 39% of patients; sometimes it is intermittent. This pattern usually is found more frequently in patients from Asia and Europe where urinary screening procedures employed in schools and communities increase the precentage of patients found exhibiting microscopic hematuria or chance proteinuria. Unfortunately, urinary abnormalities may be overlooked or intentionally ignored by further testing until renal function has deteriorated. It is imperative to pursue urine sediment changes when first detected so as not to delay making an accurate diagnosis. This raises the controversial issue that plagues nephrologists: when and when *not* to perform a renal biopsy. This matter will be discussed further in the diagnosis section of this chapter.

However, in all patients the presence of mesangial IgA deposits in the kidney occurs in association with clinical signs, except for a few cases in which IgA deposition affects the patients months or years after the clinical onset of the disease.

Acute renal failure occurs in 3% of IgAN patients and is not common in association with an episode of microscopic hematuria. Twenty to twenty-five percent of this subgroup exhibiting acute renal failure may require dialysis. Two possibilities may induce acute renal failure: the benign constitution of red blood cell casts in tubules may interefere with the passage of urine with concomitant anuria; or there may be severe crescentic glomerulonephritis in which hypertension, edema, and oliguria are present. The former is more frequent in children and young adults, and the latter occurs in older patients and is known as rapidly progressive glomerulonephritis or malignant IgAN.

Finally, IgAN may induce nephrotic syndrome in 3% of patients, more frequently children and adolescents. In nephrotic syndrome, renal lesions may be minimal; however, severe renal lesions may occur during the natural course of the disease. The onset of the disease may be spontaneous in some patients, mainly children, in whom a renal biopsy revealed minimal change disease along with IgA mesangial deposits. The presence of mild or minimal glomerular lesions, normal renal function, a positive response to corticosteroids, and a tendency to relapse characterize minimal change disease. In some cases, it is possible that IgAN is superimposed on a previous undiagnosed minimal change disease. This hypothesis is supported by the occurrence of nephrotic syndrome in children whose first renal biopsy failed to reveal mesangial IgA deposits subsequently detected in a renal biopsy. Alternative explanations for this particular form of IgAN may be the possible intermittent appearance of IgA deposits, the failure to identify IgA deposits in the initial biopsy, or the presence of IgAN with IgA deposits in a focal distribution, affecting only some glomeruli.

IgAN may be associated with several diseases, but most of these associations appear to be random, with no hint of pathogenesis. However, the most frequent associations have been made with coeliac diseasae and dermatitis herpertiformis, in which symptomatic or asymptomatic gluten-sensitive enteropathy is present.

Diagnostic procedures

High serum levels of IgA are present is 30-50% of patients. This observation may indicate the possible presence of an IgAN in conjunction with urinary abnormalities (persistent microscopic hematuria and/or proteinuria). IgA serum levels change during the clinical course of the disease. Therefore, intial high levels may persist in some patients, whereas they may decline to normal in others. In most cases IgA1 subclass is particulary predominant, while in Afro-American patients the serum concentration of IgA2 is also elevated. Immunofluorescent studies demonstrate a deposition of IgA2 in the mesangial area of glomeruli in 56% of Afro-American IgAN patients.

High serum levels of polymeric IgA have also been found in 25% of patients; they may have an anti-IgG activity (rheumatoid factor) or an anti-IgA activity. High serum levels of IgA immune complexes and a low frequency of IgG immune complexes have been detected in the blood of IgAN patients by a variety of techniques. These immune complexes may contain antibodies against bacterial, viral, and food antigens. Even though high serum levels of IgA-IgG have been demonstrated in patients with an acute phase of the disease, e.g., fever, upper respiratory tract infection, and macroscopic hematuria, and in those containing food antigens after food challenge, no relationship between the occurrence of increased immune complex levels and the clinical course of the disease has been found.

High titers of antistreptolysin O, cryoglobulin, and anti-neutrophil cytoplasmic autoantibodies, rarely IgA class, have been detected in a small number of patients. Serum complement components and their control proteins remain normal. Several deficiencies of complement proteins associated to IgAN have been described. Urinary abnormalities, characterized by persistent microscopic hematuria and/or proteinuria, are the most frequent markers of IgAN. Direct examination of the urine sediment, so called Addis count, using a phase-contrast microscope, allows for the identification of red blood cells, leukocytes, casts, and, in particular, dysmorphic red blood cells, which indicate that bleeding in the urinary tract is of a glomerular origin. This should then spare the patient from such urologic procedures as cystoscopy and retrograde pyelography.

In addition, quantitative proteinuria can be assessed by measuring the 24-hour total urine protein in adults and the protein-creatinine ratio or the protein level in mg/h/m^2 in the first morning- voided urine sample in children, since it may be difficult to obtain a 24-hour urine collection in these patients. Proteinuria may be mild (<1 g/day), moderate (1-3 g/day), or heavy (>3 g/day). In asymptomatic patients during a routine medical examination, the associated proteinuria detected is usually less than 1g/day and exceeds 3g/day in only a few cases. The amount of proteinuria when it is mild or moderate tends to remain fairly stable. A slight increase occurs in patients in association with an episode of macroscopic hematuria.

The presence of urinary abnormalities and moderate or severe proteinuria requires the measurement of renal function, since it is essential to the long-term outcome of patients with mild renal insufficiency. Serum creatinine and its clearance are currently used as a marker for renal function. It is preferable to use a clearance technique to estimate the glomerular filtration rate. A small group of patients may have high serum levels of creatinine and azotemia, signifying that they have an aggressive form of IgAN.

Outcome

In IgAN, episodes of macroscopic hematuria are more frequent during the first years of disease and then tend to disappear in older patients – more than in children and young adults. After considering the medical history of a patient there are three possible indicators for the onset of disease (1) a single episode of macroscopic hematuria, followed by persistent microscopic hematuria; (2) recurrent episodes of macroscopic hematuria that reduce gradually over years, along with persistent microscopic hematuria; (3) persistent microscopic hematuria that remains consistent throughout the patient's medical history. In a small percentage of cases, approximately 4%, a spontaneous regression of all clinical signs has been reported. However, the simultaneous disappearance of IgA deposits and histologic lesions is an exceptional phenomenon. In most patients, microscopic hematuria and/or proteinuria are found persistently or intermittently for years. Occasionally infectious diseases involving the mucosal surfaces may precipitate an episode of gross hematuria or an increase in the urinary excretion of red blood cells. Except for such temporary exacerbations, the amount of proteinuria remains low for years, frequently below 1g/day.

IgAN may have a completely benign outcome if renal function is well monitored throughout the patient's life. Nonetheless, many patients – a variable percentage depending on when the disease is diagnosed – may demonstrate a chronically slow progressive decline in renal function over 10-20 years. Several studies performed in a large series of patients on the long-term prognosis of IgAN have analyzed the various clinical and histologic predictions of an unfavorable outcome. They are documented in Tables 17.2 and 17.3. In this section, we will discuss further the clinical risk factors.

Table 17.2 Clincal risk factors in IgA nephropathy

Male sex
Adult onset of disease (older age at the onset)
Absence of medical history of recurrent macroscopic hematuria
Hypertension at presentation
Elevated serum creatinine at time of diagnosis
Severe proteinuria

Table 17.3 Immunohistologic risk factors in IgA nephropathy

Global and segmental glomerular sclerosis
Marked extracapillary proliferation
Marked intracapillary proliferation
Interstitial infiltrates and/or fibrosis
Marked arteriolar hyalinosis
Extensive IgA deposition in the capillary wall

CHAPTER

18

Endocapillary glomerulonephritis

David B.G. Oliveira

KEY POINTS

- Poststreptococcal glomerulonephritis remains a significant public health problem in some communities.
- In other areas, endocapillary glomerulonephritis in association with other infections (endocarditis, infected ventriculo atrial shunts) is more prevalent.
- Poststreptococcal glomerulonephritis usually presents with the abrupt onset of hematuria, edema, oliguria, and hypertension (the nephritic syndrome). Other forms of infection-related glomerulonephritis may have a more varied presentation.
- The diagnosis is suggested by the presence of hypocomplementemia.
- Treatment involves elimination of the associated infection and management of edema, hypertension, and renal failure as required.
- The prognosis of poststreptococcal glomerulonephritis (with respect to recovery and long-term preservation of renal function) is excellent in children, but less good in adults.

Endocapillary glomerulonephritis is a histopathologic diagnosis: it refers to a proliferative glomerular lesion characterized by increased numbers of native glomerular cells together with an inflammatory infiltrate. Although strictly a histologic entity, this condition is exemplified by poststreptococcal glomerulonephritis, which usually presents clinically as an acute nephritic syndrome; this disease will form the main focus of this chapter.

Epidemiology

The introduction of antibiotics and the developments in public health over the last few decades have led to a decline in the incidence of streptococcal infections in developed countries. As a consequence, sequelae of acute streptococcal infections such as rheumatic fever and poststreptococcal glomerulonephritis have become rarities. Thus, poststreptococcal glomerulonephritis made up only 1.8% of 20074 renal biopsies reported to the Italian Registry of Renal Biopsies for the years 1987-1995, with other infection-related glomerulonephritides contributing a further 0.77%.

This optimistic picture must be tempered by a number of considerations. First, Lancefield group A streptococcal infections and subsequent nephritis are still very prevalent in some societies, such as the aboriginal communities in Australia; the disease may indeed occur a epidemic in such settings. Second, even in more developed countries there has been a resurgence of streptococcal infections in recent years. For example, deterioration in living conditions in Armenia has been associated with a tenfold rise in the number of cases of poststreptococcal glomerulonephritis over the period 1992/3 to 1995. Third, with the decrease in streptococcal infections, staphylococci and gram-negative bacteria have been found to be a commoner cause of endocapillary glomerulonephritis, at least in one report from France, and in both this report and another from Germany this glomerular lesion was found particularly among alcoholics.

The site of the initiating infection also varies. Originally, poststreptococcal glomerulonephritis was seen most typically after pharyngeal infection, and this remains an important association. However, streptococcal skin infections are more prevalent in some situations, such as the Australian aboriginal communities. In France, skin infections and visceral abscesses, with or without endocarditis, are commoner associations with renal lesions than are pharyngeal infections. The lesion found in association with acute endocarditis is very similar to that of poststreptococcal glomerulonephritis, including the presence on electron microscopy of subepithelial humps. An endocapillary glomerulonephritis may also be seen in infected atrioventricular shunts (shunt nephritis), although a mesangiocapillary pattern is more usual.

The disease is seen most commonly in younger persons between the ages of 2 and 12, but may occur at any age. Overt disease is approximately twofold commoner in males, but when subclinical disease is taken into account the sexes are probably equally affected. The possibility of a genetic component to susceptibility is supported by an increased attack rate among siblings compared with the general population. The proportion of affected siblings is compatible with an autosomal recessive trait, but no genetic markers have been identified that might support this hypothesis; there probably are no consistent associations, for instance, with alleles of the major histocompatibility complex.

Etiopathogenesis

Poststreptococcal glomerulonephritis typically occurs 2 to 3 weeks after infection with a nephritogenic strain of Lancefield Group A streptococcus. Such strains are defined on the basis of their M protein, with type 12, among others, being particularly nephritogenic. Although there is still a degree of uncertainty, the generally accepted mechanism is that of a planted antigen: a streptococcal component(s), released into the blood stream during the initiating infection, deposits in the kidney due to a particular affinity for glomerular structures. With the onset of the host immune response 10-14 days later, antibodies bind to the planted streptococcal antigen(s) and, via fixation of complement and attraction of polymorphonuclear leukocytes, cause the characteristic endocapillary glomerulonephritis. This acute inflammatory response usually successfully clears the streptococcal antigen(s), leading to resolution of the glomerulonephritis and a subsequent good prognosis (see below). Occasionally, the inflammation during the acute phase is sufficiently severe to cause breaks in the glomerular basement membrane and leakage of fibrin into Bowman's space. This probably represents the main stimulus to crescent formation, which is seen in a small proportion of cases of poststreptococcal glomerulonephritis.

There are, inevitably, a number of issues that complicate this basic pathogenic mechanism. First, there is still uncertainty as to the nature of the nephritogenic antigen(s). Although an obvious candidate, the nephritogenic strain defining M protein does not seem to be involved: one episode of poststreptococcal glomerulonephritis provides lasting immunity against a second, suggesting that there is a common nephritogenic antigen other than the variable M protein. A variety of more plausible candidate antigens have been proposed. These include an extract from disrupted streptococci named endostreptosin, a derivative from the endostreptosin complex named preabsorbing antigen, a nephritogenic strain-associated protein (NSAP), a nephritis plasmin binding protein, a series of cationic proteins produced from culture supernatants, and a protein identified by its heparin-inhibitable binding to basement membrane. The position is confused: it seems likely that several of these species are closely related. In particular, endostreptosin, preabsorbing antigen, and NSAP have similar physicochemical properties. In addition, the latter two are able to activate complement and cause a proliferative glomerulonephritis in experimental animals. This (probably single) species, therefore, represents the best candidate for the nephritogenic antigen, although more detailed molecular characterization is needed.

Second, other pathogenic mechanisms in addition to that of a planted antigen may be involved. It is difficult to exclude a contribution from the deposition of circulating immune complexes. Although concentrations of these do not correlate with the degree of nephritis, they could contribute to the build-up of in situ complexes once these have been formed by the planted antigen mechanism. There is evidence that autoantibodies are present in poststreptococcal sera, including some with reactivity for basement membrane collagen and laminin; whether these are involved in pathogenesis or simply represent epiphenomena is uncertain. The M protein has the ability to act as a superantigen, that is, it is capable of activating a relatively high proportion of T-cells in a non antigen-specific way. The relative contribution of T-cells to pathogenesis, however, is unclear, although they certainly are present in the glomerulus in poststreptococcal glomerulonephritis. The in vitro T-cell responsiveness to glomerular basement membrane antigens found in some cases is almost certainly nonspecific, because it is also seen in a range of other glomerulonephritides. The depressed cellular immune response to streptococcal antigens, found in some cases years after the acute event, is similarly of uncertain significance.

Finally, far less is known concerning the other presumably closely related forms of endocapillary glomerulonephritis seen in the context of nonstreptococcal infections. As mentioned above in the section on epidemiology, in some situations such infections are a much more common cause of endocapillary glomerulonephritis than streptococcal infections. Although not as well defined as for streptococci, bacterial antigens and corresponding antibody can be found in the glomeruli of patients with infective endocarditis. Similarly located antigens, usually from coagulase-negative staphylococci, may be found in shunt nephritis. The circumstantial evidence that the glomerulonephritis in these conditions is mediated by immune complexes is strong, but again the same question arises as to whether these complexes deposit preformed from the circulation or are formed in situ. The lack of a correlation between amount of circulating immune complexes and the severity of glomerulonephritis in infective endocarditis is perhaps some evidence for an in situ mechanism, but, as discussed above, the two processes are not mutually exclusive.

Pathophysiology

Light microscopy of a renal biopsy from a case of poststreptococcal glomerulonephritis shows proliferative glomerular lesions characterized by increased numbers of native glomerular cells (mesangial and endothelial cells) together with an inflammatory infiltrate, composed principally, at least in earlier lesions, of polymorphonuclear leukocytes. Crescent formation (extracapillary proliferation) is rare. By electron microscopy the most characteristic lesion is the subepithelial "hump," an electron-dense deposit projecting outward from the basement membrane. A number of immunofluorescence patterns (principally for C3, IgG and/or IgM) have been defined, with varying degrees of deposition in the mesangium and capillary walls.

The lesions found in other forms of infection-related glomerulonephritis may be similar to those found with poststreptococcal glomerulonephritis, particularly in acute endocarditis. In subacute endocarditis and infected ventriculoatrial shunts the usual pattern is of a type I mesangiocapillary glomerulonephritis, with immune deposits, seen by immunofluorescence and electron microscopy, predominantly in the capillary walls but also in the mesangium. A focal glomerulonephritis with areas of necrosis also may be seen, although again immunofluorescence and electron microscopy usually demonstrate diffuse deposits of IgG, IgM, and complement.

Clinical findings

Symptoms and signs

The classic presentation of poststreptococcal glomerulonephritis is with an acute nephritic syndrome: the relatively sudden onset of edema, hematuria (which is often macroscopic), oliguria, and hypertension. This typically occurs 1-2 weeks after a streptococcal pharyngitis, whereas the timing when it is secondary to a streptococcal skin infection is more variable. The full syndrome is seen in just under half of symptomatic cases. The most frequent individual symptom is edema, characteristically periorbital in children, which is found in 90% of cases. Hypertension is another very common feature. When severe, this may results in the clinical syndrome of accelerated hypertension, culminating in hypertensive encephalopathy.

The symptoms usually start to resolve within 1 week and are gone within 1 month, although urinary abnormalities may persist for up to 1 year. In some cases, particularly in adults and in nonstreptococcal-associated endocapillary glomerulonephritis, there is more severe renal involvement, which may be associated with a crescentic nephritis on renal biopsy (see below). In this situation the clinical picture may resemble that of the rapidly progressive glomerulonephritis seen in other forms of crescentic nephritis. The nephrotic syndrome occasionally may be seen, particularly in shunt nephritis.

Diagnostic procedures

The abnormalities found in poststreptococcal glomerulonephritis can be divided into those common to a variety of glomerular diseases (impairment of renal excretory function, hematuria, variable degrees of proteinuria) and those reflecting the more specific immunologic upset induced by the infection.

Significant rises in the serum concentration of urea and creatinine are found in one-quarter to one-half of children with poststreptococcal glomerulonephritis. In adults the impairment of renal function is usually more severe, occurring in over 80% of older patients. Hematuria is universal in symptomatic individuals, although microscopic in two-thirds. Indeed, microscopic hematuria may be detected in a significant proportion of asymptomatic individuals when evaluated in an epidemic situation. Examination of the urinary sediment will show the characteristics of glomerular bleeding, with dysmorphic red cells and red cell casts. Heavy proteinuria is unusual in children, with nephrotic range proteinuria being found in less than 5% of cases. Again, adults are more severely affected and heavy proteinuria is more common, as it is in forms of infection-related endocapillary glomerulonephritis other than poststreptococcal glomerulonephritis.

The laboratory findings that are more specific to poststreptococcal glomerulonephritis are essentially serologic. These include polyclonal increases in IgG and IgM as well as the development of antibodies to a number of streptococcal components (e.g., streptolysin O, DNAse B, hyaluronidase). Immune complexes, rheumatoid factors and cryoglobulins also may be detected. These latter abnormalities probably are a reflection of polyclonal B cell activation, although there has been some interest in the possibility that streptococcal neuraminidase could alter the carbohydrate composition of IgG, rendering it immunogenic and predisposing to the formation of rheumatoid factors.

Hypocomplementemia is a particular serologic feature of poststreptococcal glomerulonephritis: reduced serum concentrations of C3 are found in almost 90% of cases. Activation of complement appears to be mainly via the alternative pathway, but in some cases there is also evidence of a degree of classic pathway activation. The hypocomplementemia characteristically resolves within 1 to 2 months; persisting hypocomplementemia beyond this time suggests the presence of another condition, such as mesangiocapillary glomerulonephritis.

The serologic abnormalities found in endocapillary glomerulonephritis in infective endocarditis, shunt nephritis, and other infections are very similar to those found in post-streptococcal glomerulonephritis. They include polyclonal increases in immunoglobulins, the presence of antibodies to the infecting organism, increased amounts of immune complexes, the presence of rheumatoid factors and cryoglobulins, and hypocomplementemia. In contrast to poststreptococcal glomerulonephritis, however, the hypocomplementemia, at least in infective endocarditis, usually appears to be due to classic pathway activation, with depression of C4 in addition to C3.

Diagnosis

In an area in which poststreptococcal glomerulonephritis is common, or in an epidemic, the diagnosis may be made on clinical grounds: a history of a preceding infection characteristic of the streptococcus followed, after the appropriate time interval, by the onset of the nephritic syndrome. The most helpful laboratory finding is that of hypocomplementemia, as its presence, and whether there is classic and/or alternative pathway activation, produces a relatively narrow differential diagnosis (Tab. 18.1). The presence of antibodies to streptococcal components (most commonly antistreptolysin O in postpharyngitic cases, and antiDNAse B or antihyaluronidase after skin infections) provides supportive evidence, but may only be found in 50-80% of cases.

In areas in which poststreptococcal glomerulonephritis is uncommon, an argument can be made for a diagnostic renal biopsy in most cases. In such a situation other conditions such as IgA nephropathy or small vessel vasculitis may be commoner causes of an acute or subacute nephritic syndrome, and differentiation is important on both therapeutic and prognostic grounds. In other cases, a biopsy would be indicated only if there were atypical features. Examples would be absence of hypocomplementemia or, conversely, persistent (greater than 4-5 weeks) hypocomplementemia, heavy proteinuria, or progressive deterioration in renal function.

Table 18.1 Renal disease and hypocomplementemia

Disease	Complement abnormalities
Poststreptococcal glomerulonephritis	↓C3
Glomerulonephritis secondary to infective endocarditis, infected ventriculoatrial shunts, visceral abscesses	↓C4 ↓C3
Mesangiocapillary glomerulonephritis type I	(↓C4) ↓C3
Mesangiocapillary glomerulonephritis type II	↓C3
Systemic lupus erythematosus	↓C4 ↓C3
Cryoglobulinemia	↓C4 ↓C3

Treatment

This may be divided into treatment of the associated infection on the one hand, and management of the glomerulonephritis and its consequences on the other.

It is important to eliminate any residual infection which could contribute to an ongoing endocapillary glomerulonephritis. Although in many cases of poststreptococcal glomerulonephritis the initiating infection will have resolved, and there is no evidence that it alters the natural history, a course of phenoxymethylpenicillin is recommended; erythromycin may be used in patients allergic to penicillin (see Table 18.2 for drug dosages). Managing the associated infection in other forms of endocapillary glomerulonephritis may be much more problematic. Infected ventriculoatrial shunts will need to be replaced. Infective endocarditis will require the appropriate prolonged course of antibiotics (4-6 weeks), possibly combined with valve replacement. The choice of antibiotics and duration of use depends crucially on the nature and sensitivity of the infecting organism; close liaison with a microbiologist is required. Dosage of some appropriate antibiotics are given in Table 18.2; a combination of benzylpenicillin and gentamicin would be suitable for a streptococcal infection, flucloxacillin and fusidic acid for a staphylococcal, and benzylpenicillin, gentamicin and flucloxacillin if the organism is unknown. Localization and drainage of visceral abscesses may be challenging. Although treatment of the infection may be more difficult, it is particularly important in these nonstreptococcal cases: persistence of the infection with ongoing release of bacterial antigens will continue to drive the glomerulonephritis, with a real danger of progression to end-stage renal failure.

Management of the glomerulonephritis in straightforward cases of poststreptococcal glomerulonephritis is supportive. Edema is treated by fluid and salt restriction, together with loop diuretics such as furosemide (Tab. 18.2), if necessary. If severe, hypertension will also require treatment with conventional agents (Tab. 18.2). Dialysis may be needed for more severe cases, but this is unusual in the absence of crescentic changes on the renal biopsy (see below). The rare cases with persistent nephrotic syndrome may require the general management appropriate to this state (see Chapter 5).

Management of the more severe cases associated with a crescentic nephritis is problematic. The importance of elimination of the source of microbial antigen has been mentioned above. If, despite this, there is continuing glomerulonephritis with progressive renal impairment, it would be reasonable to give high-dose corticosteroids. Further therapeutic maneuvers that could be considered if there is an inadequate response to the above measures include the addition of plasma exchange and/or cytotoxic therapy. It should very rarely be necessary to contemplate these more extreme forms of treatment, which is fortunate because there is no adequate evidence base to support their

Table 18.2 Drug dosages

Drug	Dose	
Phenoxymethylpenicillin	Age: < 1 yr:	62.5 mg
	1-4 yr	125 mg
	5-12 yr	250 mg
	> 12 yr	500 mg
Erythromycin	Age: 1 month-1 yr:	125 mg
	2 - 8 yr	250 mg
	> 8 yr	500 mg
Benzylpenicillin	Total daily dose: 180 mg/kg, to 6 g	
Gentamicin	Total daily dose: 6 mg/kg, to 240 mg	
Flucloxacillin	Total daily dose: 200-400 mg/kg, to 12 g	
Fusidic acid	Total daily dose: 20 mg/kg sodium fusidate, up to 1.5 g	
Furosemide	0.5-2 mg/kg	
Atenolol	1-2 mg/kg	
Nifedipine LA	0.25-1 mg/kg	
Captopril	0.3-5 mg/kg	

use. One possible exception is the rarely described development of a necrotizing glomerulonephritis associated with antineutrophil cytoplasm antibodies (ANCA) on the background of an endocapillary glomerulonephritis, typically in infective endocarditis. It would seem reasonable to treat this in the same way as other forms of ANCA-associated necrotizing glomerulonephritis (see Chap. 20).

Prognosis

There is general agreement that the prognosis of poststreptococcal glomerulonephritis in children is excellent: the mortality in the acute nephritic phase is less than 1%, and the vast majority (greater than 80%) will do well in the long term. The subset that have a poorer renal prognosis with respect to the ultimate development of chronic renal failure may be associated with the presence of crescentic change on the renal biopsy, or particular patterns of immune deposits as identified by immunofluorescence.

In adults with poststreptococcal glomerulonephritis the prognosis is less certain, but almost certainly worse — particularly with respect to the development of chronic renal failure. However, even in adults it is likely that at least 60-80% will make a full recovery.

The prognosis of other forms of postinfectious endocapillary glomerulonephritis will depend to a large extent on that of the associated infection, and the ease with which it can be eliminated. Because the associated infection may itself carry a serious prognosis (e.g., 50% mortality rate in infectious endocarditis), and may not be as self-limiting as a streptococcal infection, the overall outlook is worse.

Acknowledgment

I would like to thank Prof. David Turner, Histopathology Department, St George's Hospital, for the photomicrograph.

Suggested readings

BACH JF, CHALONS S, FORIER E, et al. 10-year educational programme aimed at rheumatic fever in two French Caribbean islands. Lancet 1996;347:644-8.

EDELSTEIN CL, BATES WD. Subtypes of acute postinfectious glomerulonephritis: a clinico-pathological correlation. Clin Nephrol 1992;38:311-7.

MONTSENY JJ, MEYRIER A, KLEINKNECHT D, CALLARD P. The current spectrum of infectious glomerulonephritis: experience with 76 patients and review of the literature. Medicine (Baltimore) 1995;74:63-73.

OLIVEIRA DBG. Poststreptococcal glomerulonephritis: getting to know an old enemy. Clin Exp Immunol 1997;107:8-10.

POPOVICROLOVIC M, KOSTIC M, ANTICPECO A, JOVANOVIC O, POPOVIC D. Medium- and long-term prognosis of patients with acute poststreptococcal glomerulonephritis. Nephron 1991;58:393-9.

RICHMOND DE, DOAK PB. The prognosis of acute post infectious glomerulonephritis in adults: a long-term prospective. Aust N Z J Med 1990;20:215-9.

SARKISSIAN A, PAPAZIAN M, AZATIAN G, ARIKIANTS N, BABLOYAN A, LEUMANN E. An epidemic of acute postinfectious glomerulonephritis in Armenia. Arch Dis Child 1997;77:342-4.

SCHENA FP. Survey of the Italian Registry of Renal Biopsies. Frequency of the renal diseases for 7 consecutive years. Nephrol Dial Transplant 1997;12:418-26.

SORGER K, GESSLER U, HÜBNER FK, et al. Subtypes of acute postinfectious glomerulonephritis. Synopsis of clinical and pathological features. Clin Nephrol 1983;17:114-28.

VELLA J, CARMODY M, CAMPBELL E, BROWNE O, DOYLE G, DONOHOE J. Glomerulonephritis after ventriculo-atrial shunt. QJM 1995;88:911-8.

WASHIO M, OH Y, OKUDA S, et al. Clinicopathological study of poststreptococcal glomerulonephritis in the elderly. Clin Nephrol 1994;41:265-70.

WATANABEOHNISHI R, AELION J, LEGROS L, et al. Characterization of unique human TCR Vbeta specificities for a family of streptococcal superantigens represented by rheumatogenic serotypes of M protein. J Immunol 1994;152:2066-73.

CHAPTER

19

Primary crescentic glomerulonephritis

Eric Rondeau

KEY POINTS

- Primary crescentic glomerulonephritis usually has a rapidly progressive course and requires early and aggressive immunosuppressive treatment.
- At least three different pathophysiologic mechanisms of glomerular injury have been identified in crescentic glomerulonephritis: anti-GBM antibody deposition, immune complex accumulation, and ANCA-associated angiitis.
- Renal biopsy is required to make the diagnosis, evaluate the prognosis, and plan treatments.
- Aggressive immunosuppression is effective on cellular inflammatory glomerular lesions of recent onset and may lead to complete or partial recovery of renal function.
- Life-threatening complications may occur because of renal failure and immunosuppression, especially in patients older than 70.

Crescentic glomerulonephritis (CGN), also named extracapillary proliferative glomerulonephritis, usually is a severe form of glomerular disease, characterized by the development of an extracapillary cell proliferation within the urinary chamber of the glomeruli. Frequently it expresses a rapidly progressive course leading to severe renal failure, and there is a significant correlation between the percentage of glomeruli with crescents and the decrease in renal function. Crescentic glomerulonephritis can be classified into five different types according to immunologic markers that are detected both in the blood stream and in the renal biopsy (Tab. 19.1). The extracapillary proliferation may be superimposed on another primary glomerular disease such as mesangiocapillary glomerulonephritis (especially type II), membranous nephropathy, fibrillary and immunotactoid glomerulonephritis, and, more rarely, focal sclerosis. These forms will not be discussed in this section.

Interestingly, primary forms of crescentic glomerulonephritis share similar pathogenetic mechanisms and immune abnormalities with crescentic glomerulonephritis secondary to autoimmune multisystem diseases, infection, and drug reaction (Tab. 19.2). In addition, mild extrarenal symptoms are not infrequent during primary crescentic glomerulonephritis. Thus, it is likely that several primary crescentic glomerulonephritis actually correspond to manifestations of multisystem diseases whose organ involvement is limited to the kidney. During the last 20 years, a dramatic improvement in the outcome of crescentic glomerulonephritis has been achieved, owing to both earlier diagnosis and better treatment. However, crescentic glomerulonephritis is still an important disease that frequently leads to chronic renal failure. In addition, life-threatening complications related to therapeutic immunosuppression may occur, especially in the elderly.

Epidemiology and prognosis

The incidence of crescentic glomerulonephritis ranges from 5 to 30% in all biopsy-proven glomerulonephritis, depending on whether or not rapidly progressive forms with crescents affecting more than 50% of glomeruli or milder forms with a lower percentage of crescents are taken into account. In Western Europe and the USA its estimated incidence is 7 cases per million per year, and crescentic glomerulonephritis is responsible for fewer than 5% of all cases of chronic renal failure leading to chronic dialysis and transplantation. Crescentic glomerulonephritis is found more frequently in underdeveloped countries, where postinfectious forms usually are encountered.

Without treatment, the prognosis in crescentic glomerulonephritis is very poor; in the late 60s a 90% mortality rate frequently was reported. It is hoped that both the renal and the vital prognosis have improved during recent years. Depending on the severity of the initial renal injury, complete or partial recovery of renal function is now obtained in more than 70 to 80% of cases. Thus, chronic renal failure requiring dialysis and transplantation complicates only 20 to 30% of cases. In parallel, a dramatic improvement in patient survival has been achieved, and now a mortality rate lower than 10% per year is reported.

Pathophysiology

Several immunologic mechanisms may be implicated in the pathophysiology of crescentic glomerulonephritis (Tab. 19.2).

The prototypic form corresponds to the anti-glomerular basement membrane (anti-GBM) glomerulonephritis or type I primary crescentic glomerulonephritis. In this case, an autoantibody, usually of the IgG class, directed against a defined epitope of the GBM binds to the GBM, inducing a local activation of the complement cascade, and subsequently a severe inflammatory reaction with disruption of the glomerular capillary wall. The main epitope recognized by anti-GBM antibodies has been characterized recently, and corresponds to a peptide sequence located on the noncollagenic domain (NC1) of the α3(IV) collagen chain. This epitope also may be expressed by the alveolar basement membrane, explaining the possible association with pulmonary hemorrhages which, when combined with anti-GBM crescentic glomerulonephritis, constitutes the Goodpasture's syndrome. The causes of this syndrome are still obscure, although some toxic factors altering the basement membrane antigenicity may play a role. The anti-GBM crescentic glomerulonephritis can be reproduced experimentally in animals. Recent studies indicate that several genetic determinants control both the ability to form crescents and the association with pulmonary hemorrhages. In addition, not only B cells, which produce the anti-GBM antibody, but also T lymphocytes seem to play a critical role in the development of this autoimmune disease. Mice lacking the ability to produce antibodies still develop an extracapillary glomerulonephritis in the anti-GBM model.

The type II form of primary crescentic glomerulonephritis corresponds to the other classic mechanisms of glomerular injury in crescentic glomerulonephritis: (1) the local deposition of immune complexes, with secondary activation of the complement cascade; (2) inflammatory reaction and necrosis of the glomerular capillary wall. It may result from circulating immune complexes, which are entrapped in small vessels of the renal circulation. Deposition of these immune complexes in other organs may induce extrarenal manifestations, which can be observed in these forms. The in situ formation of immune complexes within the glomeruli also may occur when a circulating antibody recognizes a "planted" antigen. Experimental models of immune complex-mediated cres-

Table 19.1 Immunologic mechanisms of glomerular injury in experimental and human crescentic glomerulonephritis

Type	Effector in the circulating blood	Immune deposits in fluorescence analysis	Auto/alloantigen	Experimental model	Genetic predisposition
I	Anti-GBM antibody (IgG subclass, less frequently IgA)	Linear deposition of IgG along the GBM, few C3, C1q deposits	NC1 domain of α3 (IV) collagen chain antibody	IV injection of anti-GBM	Yes
II	Immune complexes cryoglobulins	Mesangial and sub-endothelial deposit	DNA IgM, bacterial antigens	IV injection of immune complexes	Yes
III	Antineutrophil cytoplasmic antibody (ANCA), IgG subclass, less frequently IgA	No deposit or few IgG and C3	Myeloperoxydase proteinase 3, less frequently lactoferrin, cathepsin G	Immunization against myeloperoxydase	Not reported
IV	Association of anti-GBM antibody and ANCA	Linear deposition of IgG (GBM) and necrotizing angitis	Same as type I and type III	Not reported	Not reported
V	No anti-GBM antibody No ANCA	No deposit	Unknown	Not reported	Not reported

centic glomerulonephritis such as serum sickness disease or injection of cryoglobulins are useful for the study of the pathogenesis of the disease. Spontaneous lupus-like diseases with renal immune complex deposition also are encountered in specific strains of mice, indicating again a role for genetic factors in the development of such nephropathies.

Finally, the other classic mechanism of injury corresponds to the type III primary crescentic glomerulonephritis or pauci-immune crescentic glomerulonephritis without evidence of anti-GBM antibody or immune complex deposition. In these forms, 75 to 90% of the affected patients exhibit autoantibodies directed against cytoplasmic antigens of the polymorphonuclear neutrophil (ANCA). By indirect immunofluorescence on fixed and permeabilized polymorphonuclears, the antibodies produce a perinuclear or a diffuse cytoplasmic staining. The main antigens involved are two enzymes: myeloperoxidase and proteinase 3. In an estimated 10% of cases, other antigens also may be involved, such as cathepsin G and lactoferrin. In most cases, the perinuclear staining corresponds to anti-myeloperoxidase antibodies, whereas the cytoplasmic staining corresponds to anti-proteinase 3 antibodies. The ANCA are able to activate neutrophils in vitro and to induce endothelial cell damage in coculture experiments. In vivo they are associated with angiitis and necrosis of the vascular wall, from the medium-size arterioles to the glomerular capillaries with an extracapillary proliferation. Actually, type III primary crescentic glomerulonephritis corresponds to a renal-limited form of a systemic ANCA-associated vasculitis, e.g., microscopic polyangiitis.

Type IV primary crescentic glomerulonephritis is characterized by the combination of circulating anti-GBM antibody and ANCA. In this form, the renal biopsy reveals a crescentic glomerulonephritis, frequently associated with a necrotizing angiitis, and a linear deposit of IgG along the GBM. These cases may represent 10 to 30% of anti-GBM associated crescentic glomerulonephritis. The pathogenesis is still debated, but it has been proposed that ANCA-associated GBM lesions unmask the NC1 domain of $\alpha3$(IV)collagen chain which secondarily induces autoantibody production.

Type V primary crescentic glomerulonephritis could correspond to another rare form of crescentic glomerulonephritis without any evidence of anti-GBM antibody, ANCA, or circulating immune complexes, and with no or few immune deposits in the kidney. The existence of this form, also known as true idiopathic crescentic glomerulonephritis, is still debated. It is thought to correspond to a type III-like form and to require similar treatment.

Table 19.2 Clinicopathologic classification of crescentic glomerulonephritis

Primary crescentic glomerulonephritis
- Type I: anti-GBM crescentic glomerulonephritis without pulmonary hemorrhage
- Type II: immune complex-mediated crescentic glomerulonephritis
- Type III: pauci-immune crescentic glomerulonephritis associated with ANCA
- Type IV: crescentic glomerulonephritis with the association of anti-GBM antibody and ANCA
- Type V: pauci-immune crescentic glomerulonephritis (without anti-GBM nor ANCA)

Crescentic glomerulonephritis associated with multisystem diseases
- Goodpasture's syndrome (anti-GBM crescentic glomerulonephritis with pulmonary hemorrhages)
- Systemic lupus erythematosus
- Mixed IgG/IgM cryoglobuminemia (hepatitis C)
- Schönlein-Henoch purpura
- Systemic polyangiitis (with ANCA)
  - Microscopic polyangiitis
  - Wegener's granulomatosis
  - Churg-Strauss disease
- Carcinoma, lymphoma
- Relapsing polychondritis

Crescentic glomerulonephritis associated with infectious diseases
- Poststreptococcal glomerulonephritis
- Bacterial endocarditis
- Visceral abcess
- Hepatitis B and C
- Others

Crescentic glomerulonephritis associated with medications
- D-Penicillamine
- Allopurinol
- Hydralazine
- Rifampicin
- Others

Composition of the crescent

Renal biopsy is required to identify the crescentic glomerulonephritis. Light microscopy and immunofluorescence studies must be performed in any case to make the diagnosis, to evaluate the severity and extension of the renal disease, and to demonstrate local deposition of immunoglobulins, complement components, and fibrin. Recent breakthroughs have been made by immunohistochemical and in situ hybridization techniques that are able to identify specific markers of the various cell types involved in crescent formation. At the very early stage of the disease, polymorphonuclear leukocytes infiltrate the glomeruli, but later the monocytes-macrophages predominate. After disruption of the GBM, an inflammatory reaction develops in the urinary chamber with fibrin formation, macrophage accumulation, and epithelial cell proliferation. This lesion can be associated with the delayed-type hypersensitivity reaction and granuloma formation. The parietal epithelial cell rather than the visceral epithelial cell is thought to proliferate during crescent formation. The cells contained in the crescents expressed cytokeratin in their cytoskeleton, similar to the parietal but not the visceral epithelial cells. T lymphocytes and macrophages have been shown to accumulate in the crescents and in the periglomerular interstitium, suggesting a role for potent chemotactic factors. In the most severe cases, a large crescent formation may occupy all the urinary chamber space and may extend out of Bowman's capsule. Rupture of the capsule allows interstitial fibroblasts to migrate within the crescent where they proliferate and produce collagen. At this stage, the crescent becomes fibrocellular and seems irreversible.

Mediators involved in crescent formation

Several mediators have been known to play a role in crescent formation. At the early stages, complement activation may induce a diffuse cell activation involving endothelial cells and circulating inflammatory cells. Upregulation of cell adhesion molecules, such as ICAM1 and LFA1, promote the infiltration of glomeruli by inflammatory cells. Oxygen free radicals, arachidonic acid derivatives, and nitric oxide produced by inflammatory cells and by activated resident glomerular cells have potent vasoactive and proinflammatory effects. Recently the role of various cytokines has been demonstrated. Interleukin 1 and TNFα have the main proinflammatory role, inducing the expression of cell adhesion molecules, cytokines, and tissue factor. It has been demonstrated that crescent formation depends on T lymphocytes, and especially on a Th1-type response, which is characterized by a predominant IL-2 and γ interferon release. On the other hand, IL-4 and IL-10 secreted by Th2 lymphocytes seem to have an inhibitory effect. The local release of proteolytic enzymes and of oxidants by activated leukocytes lead to GBM degradation and to extracapillary extension of the inflammatory reaction. Most of all, the exudation of fibrinogen and the activation of coagulation in the urinary chamber of the glomeruli induce fibrin formation. The extrinsic pathway of coagulation seems to be activated predominantly through an increased expression of tissue factor by infiltrating macrophages and by resident glomerular cells. Thrombin, which cleaves fibrinogen into fibrin, can also induce a chemotactic effect on inflammatory cells and a proliferative effect on glomerular cells and fibroblasts. In addition, thrombin is a potent stimulus of the plasminogen activator inhibitor type 1 (PAI-1), which is the main inhibitor of fibrinolysis. The fibrin matrix seems to facilitate fibroblast accumulation and subsequent fibronectin and collagen deposition. In addition, an accumulation of PAI-1 and other protease inhibitors such as tissue inhibitor of metalloproteinase type 1 (TIMP1) has been demonstrated and may explain the persistence of fibrin and the progression of these lesions to glomerulosclerosis.

Recovery or progression to glomerulosclerosis

Early treatment of crescentic glomerulonephritis may be associated with an almost complete functional recovery, indicating that cells which constitute the crescent may be eliminated, presumably by apoptosis. In addition, the fibrin matrix can be degraded due to the local release of plasminogen activators. However, it is well established that the later the treatment, the lower the chance of recovery. Myofibroblast infiltration and proliferation in and around the crescent, as shown by immunohistochemistry with an antibody against smooth-muscle cell actin, is associated with an accumulation of extracellular matrix proteins. The local release of PAI-1 and TIMP-1 may also prevent any degradation of fibrin and other matrix proteins. With time, the cellular crescents progress to fibrocellular lesions and irreversible glomerulosclerosis.

Clinical findings

Hematuria (which is always observed and which may be macroscopic), proteinuria (sometimes in the nephrotic range), and renal failure are the main characteristics of crescentic glomerulonephritis. The blood pressure usually is normal, but may be elevated in some patients, and edema of the lower limbs, indicating sodium retention, also may be present. The rapidly progressive course of the renal failure within days or weeks is strongly suggestive of so-called rapidly progressive glomerulonephritis (RPGN) associated with an extensive crescent formation. Besides these manifestations of renal involvement, it is important to look for extrarenal symptoms, which, if present, indicate a secondary rather than a primary form of crescentic glomerulonephritis: pulmonary hemorrhage, cutaneous eruption or purpura, central or peripheral neurologic deficits, arthritis, and abdominal pain. Asthenia, low-grade fever and anorexia are general symptoms not infrequently encountered in patients with crescentic glomerulonephritis that reflect the inflammatory syndrome.

A complete biochemical, bacteriologic, and immunologic evaluation is required to determine the intensity of the inflammatory syndrome (blood fibrinogenic sedimentation rate, C-reactive protein, fibrinemia), to detect a potential underlying infectious disease, especially endocarditis (blood culture, urine culture), which can be either the cause of or fortuitously associated with the crescentic glomerulonephritis, and to identify the immune mechanisms of crescentic glomerulonephritis: serum complement, anti-GBM antibodies, ANCA, antinuclear antibodies and anti-DNA antibodies, circulating immune complexes, and cryoglobulinemia.

Diagnostic procedures

Renal biopsy The renal biopsy provides important data about the diagnosis and the prognosis of the crescentic glomerulonephritis. It must be performed in every patient immediately after the diagnosis is suspected. Repeated biopsies usually are required in a given patient along the course of a crescentic glomerulonephritis to determine the response to treatment, the disease activity, or the occurrence of a relapse.

Light microscopy By light microscopy (Fig. 19.1), the extracapillary proliferation can be evaluated by the percentage of affected glomeruli, the size of the crescents (which may be segmental or circumferential), the inflammatory infiltrates, and the degree of fibrosis of the crescents themselves and of the interstitium. Severe tubulointerstitial lesions and fibrocellular crescents have a poor functional prognosis. The rupture of Bowman's capsule also indicates a severe glomerular injury and responds poorly to treatment. The cellular composition of the crescents varies with time, as discussed earlier. As shown in Figure 19.1, at the very early stage, small crescent formation is seen only in association with glomerular basement membrane rupture. At a later stage, all of the urinary chamber can be filled with cells; later, fibrosis can progress in crescentic lesions. An endocapillary proliferation of mesangial and/or endothelial cells, combined with infiltration by inflammatory cells, is associated with extracapillary proliferation in type II crescentic glomerulonephritis, whereas it is unusual in types I or III. In contrast, necrotic lesions of the glomerular tuft frequently are found in type III crescentic glomerulonephritis, less frequently in type I, and are very unusual in type II CGN.

Immunofluorescence This rapid test for fibrin deposition in the kidney is useful and may be obtained in less than a few hours. It has a strong diagnostic value for crescentic glomerulonephritis when glomerular fibrin can be seen in the urinary chamber of the glomeruli. Immunofluorescence analysis is also very helpful for classifying crescentic glomerulonephritis. Three different forms can be distinguished:

- linear deposition of IgG along the GBM indicates the

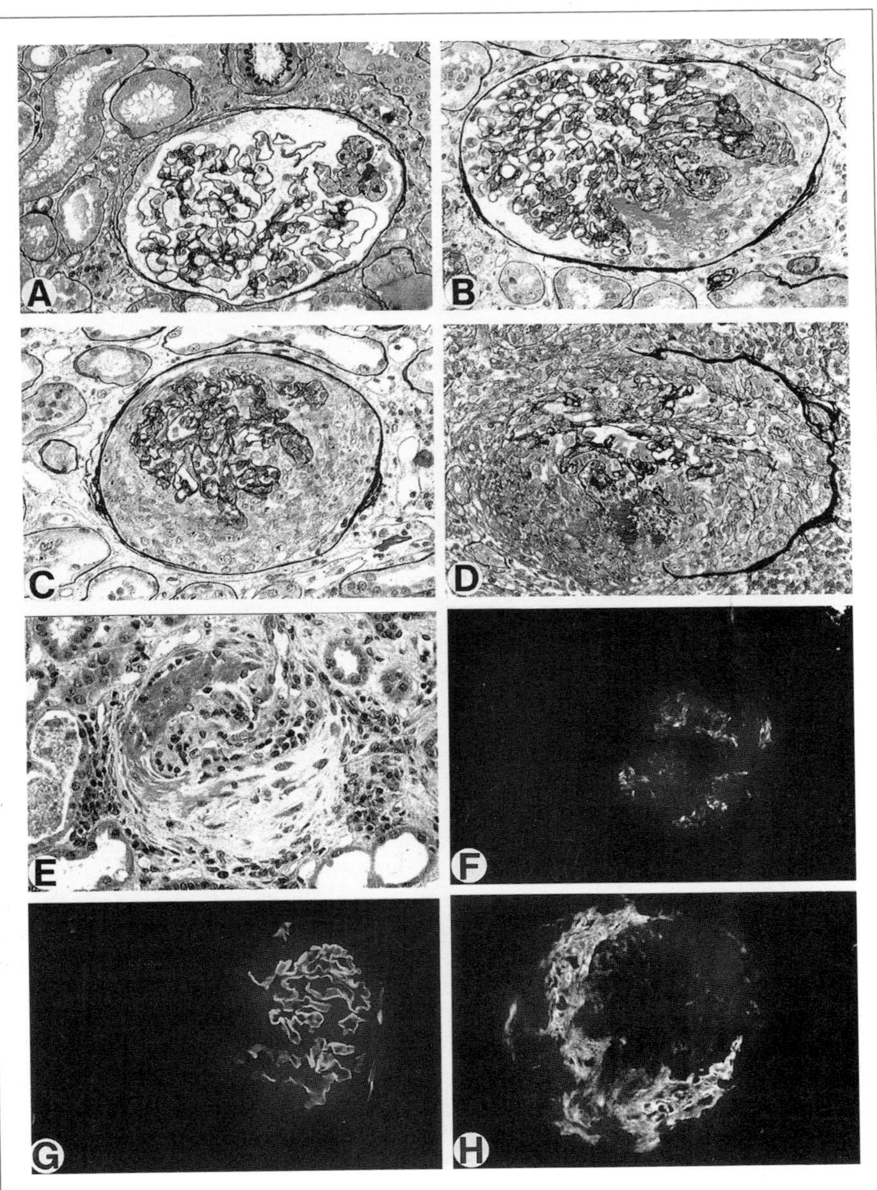

Figure 19.1 (**A**) Very early stage: small necrotic lesion of a single capillary loop, mixed with few cells (PASM x 300). (**B**) The cellular crescent partly covers glomerular tuft. Fibrin deposits are noted toward 6 o'clock (PASM x 300). (**C**) Circular crescent compressing glomerular tuft. (**D**) Advanced stage. Large crescent with breaks in the Bowman's capsule and glomerular basement membrane. The infiltration by inflammatory cells is obvious. (**E**) Late stage. Fibrous crescent (6 o'clock) and collapsed capillary tuft. (**F**) Immunofluorescence microscopy. Deposits of IgA along the mesangial stalk. (**G**) Immunofluorescence microscopy. Linear deposition of IgG along the GBM. (**H**) Immunofluorescence microscopy. Deposition of fibrin in the crescent (by courtesy of Prof. Callard, Hopital Tenon, Paris).

presence of an anti-GBM antibody, which is also found in the circulating blood in more than 90% of the cases. Few C3 and C1q deposits are seen in the glomeruli;

- granular deposits of IgG, IgM, and C3 within the mesangial and subendothelial areas indicate an immune complex-mediated crescentic glomerulonephritis. A combined endocapillary proliferation usually is observed with a segmental or diffuse distribution. Predominant mesangial IgA deposition is the hallmark of IgA nephritis (Berger disease) and of rheumatoid purpura (Schönlen-Henoch purpura). Monotypic IgM κ or λ deposition and intraglomerular thrombi are observed in mixed cryoglobulinemia;
- the absence of significant immune deposition is the rule in ANCA-associated crescentic glomerulonephritis, although in some cases faint deposits of IgG and complement components are observed. Actually, the term pauci-immune is subjective, and, in some series, only 30% of the patients have no deposit of IgG and complement, whereas 70% have some IgG and/or C3 deposition.

Electron microscopy The analysis of the renal biopsy of crescentic glomerulonephritis by electron microscopy is not useful on a routine basis. The ultrastructural alterations that can be demonstrated in crescentic glomerulonephritis include large discontinuities in the GBM and Bowman's capsule through which fibrin and monocytes are supposed to reach the urinary space, focal detachment of endothelial cells, and fibrin deposition. In type II crescentic glomerulonephritis, electron-dense deposits are found in the mesangium and in subendothelial areas. Subepithelial deposits with a humplike aspect are observed in infection-related crescentic glomerulonephritis, and large subendothelial deposits are seen in mixed cryoglobulinemia. Finally, ultrastructural analysis of renal biopsies may show GBM alterations or organized light chain deposits, indicating that the extracapillary proliferation is not primary but rather complicates the course of a mesangioproliferative glomerulonephritis or of an immunotactoid glomerulopathy.

Diagnosis

As summarized in Table 19.1, crescentic glomerulonephritis can be classified according to the mechanism of glomerular immune injury and the immunofluorescence analysis of the renal biopsy. In addition to this pathophysiologic classification, it is important to note that four different types of crescentic glomerulonephritis can be distinguished according to the clinical presentation: the primary forms of crescentic glomerulonephritis, with no extrarenal involvement; crescentic glomerulonephritis occurring in the context of multisystem diseases; crescentic glomerulonephritis complicating infectious diseases; and drug-associated forms. As shown in Table 19.2, the primary forms of crescentic glomerulonephritis and the crescentic glomerulonephritis secondary to systemic diseases have several similarities suggesting, as already mentioned, that they may represent different presentations of the same disease. The infection-associated crescentic glomerulonephritis are mediated usually via an immune complex deposition, except in hepatitis B antigenemic-associated polyarteritis, where ANCA are found in 2 to 40% of the cases. The drug-induced crescentic glomerulonephritis may be related to the formation of anti-GBM antibodies (D-penicillamine), to immune complex deposition (penicillin), or to ANCA generation (hydralazine).

Anti-GBM related crescentic glomerulonephritis

This may occur as a rapidly progressive glomerulonephritis without any pulmonary symptom or may be part of a Goodpasture syndrome with pulmonary hemorrhages. Primary type I crescentic glomerulonephritis should not be associated with hemoptysis, pulmonary infiltrates, hypoxia, and microcytic anemia. There is no extrarenal symptom unless an ANCA-related vasculitis is associated with anti-GBM crescentic glomerulonephritis. The serum level of complement components is normal, and circulating anti-GBM antibodies are detected in more than 90% of cases. Anti-GBM crescentic glomerulonephritis is a rare primitive autoimmune disease, presumably with a genetic predisposition, as indicated by the high prevalence of HLA class II antigen DR2 found in more than 85% of the affected patients, and the DRB1*1501 and DRB1*0602 alleles. In rare cases, it may also be observed after treatment with D-penicillamine or after toxic inhalation of hydrocarbons.

Immune complex-mediated crescentic glomerulonephritis

In the presence of low serum levels of complement components, the most frequent causes of these primary crescentic glomerulonephritis are postinfectious crescentic glomerulonephritis and mesangiocapillary glomerulonephritis. Extrarenal manifestations may indicate a secondary form of crescentic glomerulonephritis, such as diffuse proliferative lupus nephritis, endocarditis- or shunt-associated nephritis, and mixed cryoglobulinemia. Specific clinical presentation and immunologic markers of each of these diseases, such as ANA and cryoglobulinemia, are available, so that the diagnosis can be made. In primary crescentic glomerulonephritis, circulating immune complexes, positive latex reaction, and hypocomplementemia can be encountered.

With normal complement levels, the most frequent causes of immune complex-mediated crescentic glomerulonephritis are IgA nephropathies, and visceral abcess-associated crescentic glomerulonephritis. Primary IgA nephritis or Berger disease is infrequently responsible for rapidly progressive glomerulonephritis, but has a poor renal prognosis. Crescentic glomerulonephritis with IgA deposits may occur as an isolated disease or in the context of hepatic cirrhosis, Crohn disease, celiac disease, or spondylarthritis. It also may be observed as a Schönlen-Henoch disease with the combination of IgA crescentic glomerulonephritis, cutaneous purpura, arthritis, and abdominal symptoms. High serum levels of polyclonal IgA can be found.

Visceral abscess-associated crescentic glomerulonephritis was first described in critically ill patients with intrathoracic or intraabdominal abscess. Several nonspecific immunologic abnormalities may be encountered, but serum complement levels usually are normal. In a recent retrospective study of 41 cases of "idiopathic" crescentic glomerulonephritis, Ferrario et al. reported that nonnecrotizing crescentic glomerulonephritis must be distinguished from necrotizing crescentic glomerulonephritis, since, as compared with these latter, they are usually associated with a marked mesangial proliferation, scarce interstitial infiltrates, lack of rupture in Bowman's capsule, and a marked degree of glomerulosclerosis and interstitial fibrosis. All patients in this group had immune deposits of IgG and/or C3, and none of them had detectable circulating ANCA. Unlike necrotizing crescentic glomerulonephritis, these forms have a poor response to treament. It has been suggested that these forms may correspond to a superimposed extracapillary proliferation on a preexisting chronic nephropathy. More recently, various forms of glomerulonephritis, including crescentic glomerulonephritis, have been reported in methicillin-resistant *Staphylococcus aureus* infection. In these cases, it appears that bacterial enterotoxins could act as superantigens and induce polyclonal increases of IgG and IgA and massive T-cell activation, with subsequent immune complex formation and deposition of IgG, IgA, and C3 in the kidney.

Pauci-immune crescentic glomerulonephritis

These forms may appear as primitive crescentic glomerulonephritis without extrarenal manifestations. They are however closely related to the crescentic glomerulonephritis that may be observed during vasculitis, such as microscopic polyangiitis and Wegener granulomatosis and, less frequently, macroscopic polyarteritis (Kusmall-Maier disease), and Churg-Strauss disease. In a retrospective study conducted in 40 cases of pauci-immune crescentic glomerulonephritis selected only on pathological criteria, Bindi et al. reported that 14 patients could be classified as having Wegener granulomatosis, 15 as having micropolyangiitis, and 11 as having primary necrotizing crescentic glomerulonephritis, including 5 with evidence of renal vasculitis. Among the patients with so-called primary necrotizing crescentic glomerulonephritis, all but one had at least mild general symptoms or extrarenal manifestations. In addition, this study and other reports indicate that in more than 90% of the primary pauci-immune crescentic glomerulonephritis, ANCA, mainly of the antimyeloperoxidase type, are present in the sera of patients, indicating that these forms correspond to microscopic polyarteritis affecting the kidney exclusively or predominantly. In addition to the crescents, necrotizing lesions of the glomerular tuft and of small arterioles are found on the renal biopsy. The endocapillary proliferation is absent or minimal; the interstitial infiltrates are intense, with a prominent periglomerular localization and frequent loss of integrity of Bowman's capsule. Granuloma formation, especially in the perivascular and periglomerular areas, indicates Wegener disease. Immunologic tests are needed to distinguish between anti-GBM crescentic glomerulonephritis and ANCA-associated crescentic glomerulonephritis or to demonstrate the association of these two autoantibodies in the same patient. Rare forms of pauci-immune crescentic glomerulonephritis – less than 10% – appear idiopathic without detectable circulating ANCA or anti-GBM antibody. Their pathogenesis may be similar to that of ANCA-mediated vasculitis or, on the other hand, they may constitute a distinct group whose pathogenesis remains to be elucidated.

Treatment

Medical treatment

Drugs and plasma exchange

As discussed earlier, the pathogenesis of crescentic glomerulonephritis includes the combination of an autoimmune or alloimmune disease with a severe inflammatory reaction. These two processes are limited to the glomeruli at the early stages, but frequently extend to the surrounding interstitium in the most severe forms. The aim of current treatments is to block both the immune process and the inflammatory reaction. Various methods have been used in the treatment of crescentic glomerulonephritis. The infection-associated crescentic glomerulonephritis usually is reversible, at least in part, after treatment of the causative infectious disease. Similarly, but not always, drug-induced crescentic glomerulonephritis resolve after drug withdrawal. The same immunosuppressive treatment can be used for the primary crescentic glomerulonephritis and for the counterparts secondary to autoimmune multisystem disease.

Corticosteroids have profound anti-inflammatory and immunosuppressive effects, inhibiting mainly chemotactism of polymorphonuclear leukocytes and macrophages, arachidonic acid metabolite synthesis, and T-cell functions. They have a potent anti-inflammatory action that also explains their efficacy in the context of crescentic glomerulonephritis. The combination of short-term high-dose pulses of intravenous methylprednisolone and prolonged oral prednisone therapy is now commonly used. The steroid pulses initially used for the treatment of acute renal transplant rejection have a marked effect on cytokine production by monocytes-macrophages and can induce lymphocyte depletion.

The most commonly used cytotoxic agent is cyclophosphamide. It is an alkalyting agent that must be hydroxylated in the liver to be effective. It is cytotoxic on tumor cells and hematopoietic cells, which proliferate rapidly. Owing to its mechanism of action, e.g., inhibition of DNA synthesis by DNA cross-linking, depurination and/or chain scission, it has also carcinogenic and mutagenic actions. Other main side effects include alopecia, hematuric cystitis, and gonadal dysfunction. The estimated incidence of bladder cancer after the first exposure to cyclophosphamide has been reported to reach 5% 10 years after treatment and 16% after 15 years. During the last 10 years, the daily low doses of cyclophosphamide have been replaced by monthly intravenous injections of 500 to 700 mg/m^2 in many forms of crescentic glomerulonephritis. This pulse therapy seems to be as effective as the daily dose regimen and is far less toxic.

Azathioprine is an antimetabolite also used in organ transplantation. Its metabolite, 6 mercaptopurine, inhibits DNA synthesis of rapidly proliferating cells. It mainly affects T lymphocyte proliferation, but also may affect hematopoietic cells and can induce leukothrombopenia. However it exhibits no teratogenic effects. Other immunosuppressive drugs such as cyclosporine or, more recently, mycophenolate mofetil have been proposed. No significant benefit has been reported with cyclosporine. In contrast, recent preliminary studies reported the effectiveness of mycophenolate mofetil in lupus-associated crescentic glomerulonephritis.

Since fibrin deposition is a component of crescent formation, various methods have been used to prevent or limit fibrin formation. However, despite several encouraging experimental studies, neither anticoagulant therapy nor fibrinolytic treatment has been shown to improve the outcome of crescentic glomerulonephritis in humans. Whether or not thrombin receptor antagonists may be useful in these cases remains to be investigated.

Plasma exchanges by centrifugation or by filtration induce a rapid decrease in various circulating factors, including mediators, coagulation factors, immune complexes, and autoantibodies. Fluid replacement can be accomplished with normal plasma to prevent hemorrhagic complications and/or albumin and macromolecules. A rebound synthesis of autoantibodies usually occurs after cessation of plasma exchanges unless immunosuppressive drugs are administered concomitantly.

Polyvalent immunoglobulins, when administered at very high doses (0.4 mg/kg/day for 5 days) have been shown to be effective for the treatment of such autoimmune diseases as hemolytic anemia, idiopathic thrombocytopenic purpura, and acquired autoimmune hemophilia. Although many mechanisms have been proposed, an anti-idiotypic effect of polyvalent immunoglobulins was demonstrated in vitro and suggested to be relevant to the in vivo effect. They may be associated with plasma exchanges.

Adjunctive treatments are also of major importance for the management of these patients, especially for the prevention of life-threatening complications due to renal failure itself or to immunosuppressive drugs. Hemodialysis and antihypertensive drugs are useful in this context. Prevention and treatment of infection, usually with cotrimoxazole, is of particular importance, since many studies reported relapses of systemic disease after or during infection. Infection itself can induce crescentic glomerulopathies. Finally, infectious complications represent a significant cause of mortality in these patients, especially in older persons. Cotrimoxazole is an effective drug for the prevention of *Pneumocystis carinii* infection. In addition, it has been proposed as the sole treatment of limited forms of Wegener granulomatosis.

Specific indications and evolution

Many studies have reported on treatment and prognosis of crescentic glomerulonephritis in humans. However interpretation of the results remains difficult in most cases because of: (1) the heterogeneity of underlying diseases and mechanisms; (2) the report of essentially retrospective analysis with different immunosuppressive regimens and adjunctive treatments; and (3) the small numbers of patients included in these retrospective or prospective studies. Nevertheless treatment must be considered in each patient with biopsy-proven crescentic glomerulonephritis of recent onset (Tab. 19.3). It is a medical emergency because treatment must be started before severe renal failure and extensive crescentic lesions are established. Refraining from therapy is justified in patients with fibrocellular crescents and sclerotic glomerular and interstitial lesions.

Antiglomerular basement membrane glomerulonephritis

In most reported studies, treatment of this form includes methylprednisolone pulses, usually 500 to 1000 mg for 3 days, oral steroid therapy, 0.5 to 1 or even 1.5 mg/kgbw/day, cyclophosphamide, 50 to 100 mg/day, and plasma exchanges, 2 to 4 liters being exchanged every day or every other day. Six to more than twenty plasma exchanges have been performed. Beneficial effects of this treatment can be demonstrated in most patients with Goodpasture's syndrome. In addition, improvement in the detection of circulating anti-GBM antibodies allows an earlier diagnosis than in the past, and less severe diseases are now recognized. The less severe forms respond well to conventional immunosuppression (steroid and cyclophosphamide) and plasma exchanges. However the most severe diseases with a high percentage of glomerular crescents (more than 50%) and severe renal failure (anuria and/or plasma creatinine greater than 500 μmol/l) do not respond to this treatment. Pulse methylprednisolone therapy has been shown to improve pulmonary hemorrhage, but its effect on renal function was less evident. A decrease of circulating anti-GBM antibodies is induced by immunosuppressive treatment, and an earlier decrease is achieved when plasma exchanges are combined with immunosuppression. Maintenance immunosuppression for at least 8 to 12 weeks is required to prevent further resynthesis of anti-GBM antibodies. Overall, 60 to 70% of patients with mild-to-moderate renal failure will be improved by conventional immunosuppression and plasma exchanges. Goodpasture's syndrome leads to chronic renal failure and dialysis in about 40 to 60% of cases and to patient death in 6 to 30%. Infection and uncontrolled pulmonary hemorrhage are major causes of death in these patients, indicating that pulmonary manifestations have to be carefully monitored. Recurrence of the crescentic glomerulonephritis on a renal graft has been reported in 10 to 30% of cases, especially when grafting is performed shortly after the initial disease and when circulating anti-GBM antibodies are still detectable.

Type II crescentic glomerulonephritis: IgA nephritis IgA crescentic glomerulonephritis is assumed to have a grave prognosis, and some physicians do not recommand any treatment for patients who are diagnosed with this disease. Spontaneous remission of IgA crescentic glomerulonephritis has been reported when less than 30% of the glomeruli exhibited an extracapillary lesion. For those with a larger percentage of affected glomeruli, aggressive immunosuppressive treatment has been proposed, with variable efficacy. High doses of methylprednisolone, prolonged steroid therapy, cyclophosphamide, and plasma exchanges were reported recently to result in a significant but transient improvement in clinical parameters, whereas florid crescents were still observed on a second renal biopsy. Thus, in contrast to vasculitis-associated crescentic glomerulonephritis, IgA crescentic glomerulonephritis is less responsive to immunosuppressive therapy.

Other type II primary crescentic glomerulonephritis These forms appear to be quite uncommon, and may represent, in some cases, severe post-infectious glomerulonephritis. Spontaneous improvement is possible, especially when the extracapillary proliferation involves less than 30% of the glomeruli and is associated with a massive endocapillary proliferation. In the more severe cases, methylprednisolone pulses and oral steroid therapy are currently recommended, sometimes in association with cyclophosphamide when vasculitis-like lesions are present. In 60 to 80% of patients this treatment may induce an improvement in renal function and in histologic parameters. As reported for lupus nephritis, plasma exchanges do not seem to add any benefit to this conventional immunosuppression.

Fauci-immune crescentic glomerulonephritis Without treatment, more than 80% of these patients died or had terminal renal failure. Spontaneous improvement was observed in fewer than 20%. Retrospective studies demonstrated a beneficial effect of methylprednisolone pulse therapy or plasma exchanges combined with conventional immunosuppression achieving a 75% immediate success rate. For both pulse therapy and plasma exchanges, the greater efficacy was found in the most severe cases, where patients were dialysis-dependent and had a high percentage of crescents, whereas there was no long-term difference with conventional immunosuppression for milder diseases. In several prospective studies, plasma exchanges were not found to increase the success rate over conventional immunosuppression except possibly in anuric patients.

In the recent years, rapid detection of circulating ANCA has also improved the management of these patients. An earlier diagnosis is now possible, and patients are referred for treatment with a less severe disease than before. A good response to treatment is now achieved in 75 to 100% of cases, as shown in several prospective studies. Methylprednisolone pulses and conventional immunosuppression are effective in most cases. Plasma exchanges have no advantage over methylprednisolone pulses, except perhaps in dialysis-dependent patients or in patients with severe pulmonary hemorrhage. Cyclophosphamide, which is required in the treatment of vasculitis can be administered by intravenous pulses monthly (700 mg/m^2, adjusted for renal function). These pulses have been shown to have therapeutic effects similar to continuous oral cyclophosphamide, with a decrease in the total dosage administered and fewer adverse effects. However the incidence of relapses is much greater in patients given pulses of cyclophosphamide than in those who receive continuous oral cyclophosphamide. The immunosuppressive treatment must be given for 12 to 24 months to prevent relapses, and long-term treatments with alkylant agents are associated with carcinogenesis and gonadal dysfunction. Some authors also use

Table 19.3 Therapeutic regimens for primary crescentic glomerulonephritis

	Anti-GBM	ANCA-associated glomerulonephritis	Type II crescentic glomerulonephritis
Steroid pulses (10-20 mg/kg/day for 3 days)	+++	++++	+++
Oral steroid therapy (1 mg/kg/day for 6-8 weeks, progressively tapered to 0.5 mg/kg/ day at 6 months and 0.1-0.2 mg/kg/day at 12 months)	+++	+++	+++
Oral cyclophosphamide (1 to 2 mg/kg/day for 6 to 24 months)	+++	+++	++
Cyclophosphamide pulses* 700 mg/m^2 every 3 to 4 weeks for 6 to 12 months	?	++	++
Plasma exchanges (2-4 l every day or every other day for 6 to 12 times)	+++	±	±
Azathioprine (1-2 mg/kg, day for 1 to 2 years)**	?	++	?

* Cyclophosphamide pulses may be used at the beginning of the treatment, then followed by continuous oral cyclophosphamide.
** Azathioprine is administered after a remission has been obtained with cyclophosphamide, and is given to prevent the relapses.
(+++ = certainly good indication; ++ = presumably useful; ± = unproven and debated indication; ? = effect unknown or not reported.)

azathioprine in combination with cyclophosphamide or in patients who are in remission after cyclophosphamide treatment. Azathioprine inhibits mainly T-cell-mediated immunity and its usefulness in the treatment of crescentic glomerulonephritis has not been clearly demonstrated. However long-term treatment with azathioprine seems less toxic than with cyclophosphamide. About 50% of patients with Wegener's granulomatosis experience at least one clinical relapse within 5 years, and this may be preceded by an increase in ANCA titer. However some patients exhibit ANCA titer variations without clinical manifestations. The treatment of the relapse is identical to the induction therapy.

Suggested readings

ANDRASSY K, KÜSTER S, WALDHERR R, RITZ E. Rapidly progressive glomerulonephritis: analysis of prevalence and clinical course. Nephron 1991;59:206-12.

ATKINS RC, NIKOLIC-PATERSON DJ, SONG Q, LAN HY. Modulators of crescentic glomerulonephritis. J Am Soc Nephrol 1996; 7:2271-78.

BINDI P, MOUGENOT B, MENTRE F, et al. Necrotizing crescentic glomerulonephritis without significant immune deposits: a clinical and serological study. Q J Med 1993;86:55-68.

BOLTON WK. Rapidly progressive glomerulonephritis. Semin Nephrol 1996;16:517-26.

CALABRESI P, PARKS RE JR. Antiproliferative agents and drugs used for immunosuppression. In: Goodman and Gilman's. The pharmacological basis of therapeutics. New York: McGraw-Hill. 7th ed. 1985.

COLE E, CATTRAN D, MAGIL A, et al, AND THE CANADIAN APHERESIS STUDY GROUP. A prospective randomized trial of plasma exchange as additive therapy in idiopathic crescentic glomerulonephritis. Am J Kidney Dis 1992;20:261-9.

FALK RJ. ANCA-associated renal disease. Kidney Int 1990; 38:998-1010.

FERRARIO F, TADROS MT, NAPODANO P, SINICO RA, FELLIN G, D'AMICO G. Critical re-evaluation of 41 cases of "idiopathic" crescentic glomerulonephritis. Clin Nephrol 1994; 41:1-9.

GLASSOCK RJ, ADLER SG, WARD HJ, COHEN AH. Primary glomerular diseases. In: Brenner and Rector, eds. The Kidney. Philadelphia: WB Saunders, 1991.

JOHNSON JP, MOORE J JR, AUSTIN HA, BALOW JE, ANTONOVYCH TT, WILSON CB. Therapy of anti-glomerular basement membrane antibody disease: analysis of prognostic significance of clinical, pathologic and treatment factors. Medicine 1985;64: 219-27.

KITCHING AR, TIPPING PG, HUANG XR, MUTCH DA, HOLDSWORTH SR. Interleukin-4 and interleukin-10 attenuate established crescentic glomerulonephritis in mice. Kidney Int 1997;52:52-9.

NACHMAN PH, HOGAN SL, FALK RJ. Treatment response and relapse in antineutrophil cytoplasmic autoantibody-associated microscopic polyangiitis and glomerulonephritis. J Am Soc Nephrol 1996;7:33-9.

ROCCATELLO D, FERRO M, COPPO R, GIRAUDO G, QUATTROCCHIO G, PICCOLI G. Report on intensive treatment of extracapillary glomerulonephritis with focus on crescentic IgA nephropathy. Nephrol Dial Transplant 1995;10:2054-9.

RONDEAU E, KOURILSKY O, PERALDI MN, ALBERTI C, KANFER A, SRAER JD. Methylprednisolone and cyclophosphamide pulse therapy in crescentic glomerulonephritis: safety and effectiveness. Renal Fail 1993;15:495-501.

RONDEAU E, LEVY M, DOSQUET P, et al. Plasma exchange and immunosuppression for rapidly progressive glomerulonephritis: prognosis and complications. Nephrol Dial Transplant 1989;4:196-200.

SECTION

5

Secondary glomerular disorders

CHAPTER 20

Vasculitis

Caroline O.S. Savage

KEY POINTS

- Vasculitis comprises a collection of disorders that cause inflammation and necrosis of blood vessel walls.
- The incidence of vasculitis appears to be increasing; this can be attributed both to improved awareness and to a true increase.
- The clinical features of each form of vasculitis reflect the size of vessel affected and the pattern of organ involvement.
- Forms of vasculitis that involve small vessels of the size of capillaries, arterioles, or venules often are associated with glomerulonephritis.
- The gold standard for confirmation of diagnosis remains tissue biopsy, but typical clinical features and serologic markers (e.g., presence of antineutrophil cytoplasm autoantibodies) often allow diagnosis in individual patients.
- Threatened major organ function, (e.g., of kidneys by rapidly progressing glomerulonephritis, lungs by pulmonary hemorrhage, eyes in the presence of giant cell arteritis) is a medical emergency requiring urgent assessment and treatment.
- Cyclophosphamide has dramatically improved patient and organ survival in those vasculitides associated with antineutrophil cytoplasm autoantibodies.

"Vasculitis" is a pathologic term meaning the presence of fibrinoid necrosis and inflammation of blood vessel walls. It characterizes a group of disorders, often referred to as the "primary systemic vasculitides", where fibrinoid necrosis and inflammation of blood vessel walls is the central feature leading to clinical symptoms and signs. In addition, vasculitis may be associated with other well-defined conditions, such as malignancy, systemic lupus erythematosus, or rheumatoid arthritis, when it said to be a secondary feature. This chapter will focus on the primary systemic vasculitides, particularly those that affect the kidney.

Classification can be confusing for the nonspecialist because there is no single agreed classification system for the systemic vasculitides. The situation has been further complicated by the fact that clinical features of different vasculitic syndromes overlap, and specialists have disagreed over what clinical features may constitute particular syndromes. The Chapel Hill Consensus Conference that met in 1994 went some way toward resolving these problems by suggesting definitions for primary systemic vasculitides. The recommended definitions are shown in Table. 20.1.

The multi-organ nature of many of the vasculitic syndromes is worth emphasizing because this affects the care and management of patients. The generalist needs to appreciate the potential for disorders to affect not only the kidneys but other organs as well. Conversely, vasculitis may be localized to a single organ and may or may not become systemic.

Epidemiology

Systemic vasculitis has been considered a rare disorder, and this has discouraged the collection of accurate epidemiologic data. Early data from the west of England in the 1970s suggested an overall annual incidence for systemic vasculitis of 10 per million. Data collected in Leicester, United Kingdom, in the 1980-86 and 1987-89 periods suggested the combined annual incidence of Wegener's granulomatosis and microscopic polyangiitis to be 1.5 per million and 6.1 per million, respectively. Over a similar period (1979-1988) the prevalence of Wegener's granulomatosis was approximately 30 per million in the

United States. During 1988-94, incidences of 8.5 per million for Wegener's granulomatosus were being reported from the Norwich area of the United Kingdom, with an overall annual incidence of systemic vasculitis (excluding giant cell arteritis) of 42 per million. Accurate incidence/prevalence figures are not available to allow comparison between countries. However, from the data cited, there appears to be an increased incidence of vasculitis. This probably reflects improved awareness and diagnosis as well as a real increase.

Etiopathogenesis

In most patients the etiology is unknown. Viral infections have been implicated, and there is a close association between hepatitis B virus and polyarteritis nodosa in some patients and between hepatitis C virus and essential cryoglobulinemia. Arboviruses were associated with an outbreak of a microscopic polyangiitis-like syndrome in Australia, but such infection is not present in most patients with microscopic polyangiitis. Immune stimulation by bacteria capable of producing superantigens that can stimulate cells of the immune system by binding antigens of the major histocompatibility antigen system and engaging

Table 20.1 Classification of vasculitis as adopted by the consensus conference on the nomenclature of systemic vasculitis

Large vessel vasculitis[1]		
Giant cell arteritis	Granulomatous arteritis of the aorta and its major branches, with a predilection for the extracranial branches of the carotid artery	Often involves the temporal artery Usually occurs in patients over 50 years of age Often associated with polymyalgia rheumatica
Takayasu arteritis	Granulomatous inflammation of the aorta and its major branches	Usually affects individuals less than 50 years of age
Predominantly medium-sized vessel vasculitis[1]		
Polyarteritis nodosa	Necrotizing inflammation of medium-sized or small arteries, without glomerulonephritis, pulmonary capillaritis or vasculitis in arterioles, capillaries or venules	
Kawasaki disease	Arteritis involving large, medium-sized and small arteries, and associated with mucocutaneous lymph node syndrome	Coronary arteries are often involved Aorta and veins may be involved Usually occurs in children
Predominantly small vessel vasculitis[1]		
Wegener's granulomatosis[2,3]	Granulomatous inflammation involving the respiratory tract, and necrotizing vasculitis affecting small to medium-sized vessels (e.g. capillaries, venules, arterioles, and arteries)	Necrotizing glomerulonephritis is common
Microscopic polyangiitis[2,3]	Necrotizing vasculitis with few or no immune deposits affecting small vessels (i.e., capillaries, venules, or arterioles)	Necrotizing arteritis involving small and medium-sized arteries may be present Necrotizing glomerulonephritis is very common Pulmonary capillaritis often occurs
Churg-Strauss syndrome[2,3]	Eosinophil-rich and granulomatous inflammation involving the respiratory tract and necrotizing vasculitis affecting small to medium-sized vessels, and associated with blood eosinophilia and usually asthma	
Henoch-Schönlein purpura[3]	Vasculitis with IgA-dominant immune deposits affecting small vessels (i.e., capillaries, venules, or arterioles)	Typically involves skin, gut and glomeruli, and is associated with arthralgias or arthritis
Cryoglobulinemic vasculitis[3]	Vasculitis with cryoglobulin immune deposits affecting small vessels (i.e., capillaries, venules, or arterioles) and associated with cryoglobulins in serum	Skin and glomeruli are often involved

[1] Large artery indicates aorta and the largest branches directed toward major body regions; medium-sized artery indicates main visceral arteries; small artery indicates distal arterial radicals that connect with arterioles. Small and large vessel vasculitides may involve medium-sized arteries, but large and medium-sized vessel vasculitides do not involve vessels smaller than arteries.
[2] Often but not always associated with antineutrophil cytoplasm autoantibodies (ANCA). Usually with specificity for proteinase 3 or myeloperoxidase.
[3] Glomerulonephritis may develop in these disorders and be manifest as nephritis or pulmonary-renal vasculitic syndrome.
(Modified from Jennette JC, Falk RJ, Andrassy K, et al. Nomenclature of systemic vasculitides: the proposal of an international consensus conference. Arth Rheum, 1994;37:187-9.)

certain T lymphocytereceptor Vβ chains, have been implicated in the childhood form of vasculitis known as Kawasaki disease. However, the initiating agent is unknown in most patients with systemic vasculitis.

The etiologic factors that cause vasculitis may not be known, but the resultant pathogenic mechanisms that cause the vascular damage are believed to be inflammatory and immune-mediated. The response of many vasculitides to corticosteroids and other therapies that modulate the immune responses would support this. Some vasculitides are associated with development of autoantibodies, suggesting a loss of tolerance to constitutive body molecules. The best characterized of these are the antineutrophil cytoplasm antibodies (ANCA). These are associated most consistently with three vasculitides: Wegener's granulomatosis, microscopic polyangiitis, and Churg-Strauss syndrome.

Antineutrophil cytoplasm antibodies

These antibodies are useful diagnostically, may be helpful in monitoring disease activity, and may contribute to causing the vascular lesions, although this remains unproved. Two major types of ANCA can be distinguished by their binding pattern to ethanol-fixed normal neutrophils in indirect immunoflourescence studies. The C-ANCA pattern denotes a cytoplasmic, granular pattern, and the antigenic target usually is the enzyme proteinase-3, which is present in neutrophil azurophil granules. The P-ANCA pattern denotes a perinuclear pattern, and the antigenic target is often, but not always, the enzyme myeloperoxidase. Myeloperoxidase also resides within neutrophil azurophil granules, but its strong cationicity allows it to migrate to the nuclear membrane in ethanol-fixed neutrophils, an artefact that allows the broad distinction into C-ANCA and P-ANCA subtypes. P-ANCA patterns associated with vasculitis may rarely be due to antibodies that are directed against other neutrophil constituents such as lactoferrin, elastase, or lysozyme.

WEGENER'S GRANULOMATOSIS

The disease owes its name to Friedrich Wegener, who described the disorder in 1936. Generalized Wegener's granulomatosis is characterized by granulomatous inflammation of the upper and lower respiratory tract and necrotizing vasculitis affecting small to medium-sized vessels. Renal involvement is common, occurring in >80% of patients, and is characterized by necrotizing glomerulonephritis. Wegener's granulomatosis most commonly occurs in middle age, peaking at around 50 years, but no age group is exempt. Men are affected slightly more frequently than women.

Pathophysiology

The renal changes caused by vasculitis are very typical, particularly within the glomeruli. The glomerular changes comprise focal (some glomeruli affected), segmental (part of the glomerular capillary tuft affected), necrotizing lesions that frequently contain neutrophils; with progression, there may be rupture of the glomerular basement membrane with exudation of plasma and cells causing development of crescentic lesions composed of macrophages and fibroblasts within Bowman's space (Fig. 20.1). As parts of glomeruli or whole glomeruli heal, they are replaced by fibrotic scars. Elsewhere in the kidney, there may be inflammatory infiltrates within the tubulo-interstitium, and small vessels may contain inflammatory infiltrates and fibrinoid necrosis of the vascular wall (Fig. 20.2). There is usually little deposition of immunoproteins such as complement components or immunoglobulins in the glomeruli which has led to the use of the descriptive word "pauci-immune" glomerulonephritis. Nonrenal tissues that are affected by vasculitis typically show an inflammatory exudate dominated by polymorphonuclear leukocytes, but to characterize the lesion at least one of the following must also be present: necrotizing vasculitis affecting small to medium-sized vessels, epithelioid granulomata, or presence of giant cells.

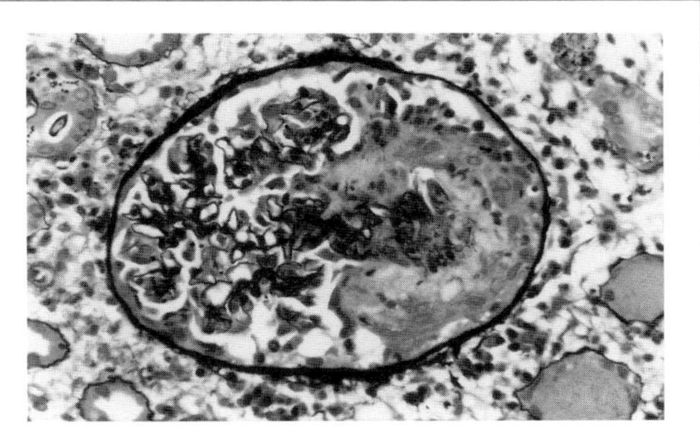

Figure 20.1 Acute vasculitic glomerulonephritis. Periodic acid-methenamine silver x 200.

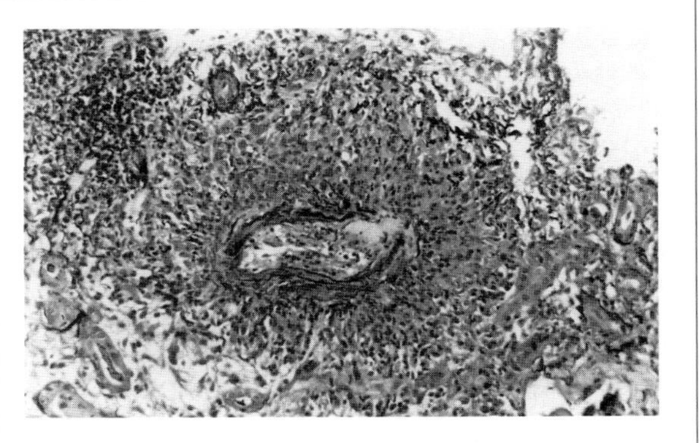

Figure 20.2 Acute renal arteritis. Periodic acid-methenamine silver x 100.

Clinical findings

The classic triad of organ involvement in Wegener's granulomatosis comprises upper airways, lungs, and kidneys, but not all patients have obvious symptoms referable to all three compartments. Often the disease begins with malaise and profound fatigue. Fevers, arthralgia, myalgia (often of calf muscles), and weight loss may follow. Typical upper airway features include nasal stuffiness, nasal crusting or bleeding, deafness, and sinusitis. Involvement of the trachea may cause a hoarse voice. Purpuric rash or conjunctival injection may develop. Involvement of the lungs or kidneys may be symptom-free initially, although the aim is to detect and diagnose disease before extensive organ damage has developed. Thus, involvement of the lungs may cause nodules that are detectable radiologically; while renal disease is initially manifest as proteinuria and/or hematuria. The most serious form of lung involvement is hemorrhage, causing breathlessness, hemoptysis, and hypoxia; renal disease will progress to overt renal failure if untreated. As disease progresses, damage to other organs may accumulate, including tracheal stenosis, ocular proptosis, collapse of the nasal bridge, and such neuropathies as mononeuritis multiplex of cranial or peripheral nerves.

The term "limited Wegener's granulomatosis" is sometimes used to describe patients whose disease is restricted to the respiratory tract; such patients may be ANCA-negative at the outset. In time, many patients develop systemic features, and the disease phenotype changes from being predominantly granulomatous to systemic and vasculitic in nature.

Clinical assessment of disease activity and damage

Wegener's granulomatosis, as with other forms of vasculitis, is characterized by acute lesions and development of tissue damage due to nonhealing scars, which may result either from the disease itself or from treatment. It is important to distinguish the two, since only acute disease is amenable to immunosuppressive therapy. Tools have been designed to help the clinician with the assessment of acute disease and tissue damage.

The Birmingham Vasculitis Activity Score (BVAS) is a validated and internationally recognized scoring system for assessment of disease activity solely due to vasculitis. It can be used to monitor patients, evaluate their responses to therapy, and screen for relapse. Other scoring systems have been described, such as the Vasculitis Activity Index, which, like the BVAS, consists ofa number of rating scales, but suffers from the disadvantage that it does not differentiate chronic damage from acute damage. Other indices include the Disease Extent Index (ELK) which has now been extended to include organs in addition to the ear, nose and throat, liver, and kidneys. The Groningen Vasculitis Score was designed for use only in Wegener's granuomatosis and has the disadvantage that the assessment requires a biopsy, thus limiting its use.

The Vasculitis Damage Index (VDI) aims to provide information on chronic damage and scores the accumulation of nonhealing scars due to effects of disease (e.g., end-stage renal failure) or therapy (e.g., infertility due to cyclophosphamide). Over time, the Vasculitis Damage Index score will stay the same (if there is no further damage events) or increase (if the patient continues to suffer further tissue damaging events). The BVAS, VDI, and Short-Form-36 (a validated functional assessment tool) have been incorporated into a uniform index in order to provide the ability to assess disease activity, distinguish the difference between new symptoms and chronic damage, and provide information on functional status and prognosis. The overall index is called the Vasculitis Integrated Assessment Log (VITAL).

Symptoms and signs

Consideration of the diagnosis depends first on a high index of clinical suspicion in an individual with a suggestive pattern of symptoms and signs. Often, patients present to the generalist with nonspecific symptoms suggestive of a flu-like illness; antibiotics or nonsteroidal anti-inflammatory drugs are frequently prescribed. The challenge is to recognize those patients with systemic symptoms who have a serious underlying illness; finding hematuria on simple dipstix testing should be an alerting feature and, indeed, all patients with hematuria warrant referral to a specialist. Once suspected, serology is helpful because 90% of individuals have a positive ANCA test by indirect immunoflourescence and/or specific ELISA. In most patients with Wegener's granulomatosis, the ANCA is of the C-ANCA type by indirect immunoflourescence and PR3-ANCA by ELISA. About 5-10% of patients have a negative ANCA; some of these develop a positive ANCA at a later stage, and others have ANCA directed against unusual neutrophil antigens. A few appear to be genuinely negative.

Tissue biopsy is required for a firm diagnosis. In patients with proteinuria or hematuria, a renal biopsy may show the typical focal segmental necrotizing glomerulonephritis that is specific to vasculitis as it affects renal glomeruli. If the biopsy specimen contains an arteriole, this may show acute vasculitis with fibrinoid necrosis and peri-vascular inflammation. Other tissues frequently biopsied include nasal mucosa and lungs; these typically contain inflammatory infiltrates compatible with, but not diagnostic of, Wegener's granulomatosis. For diagnostic confirmation, such biopsies must contain epithelioid granulomata, giant cells or vasculitic vessels.

Diagnostic procedures

Laboratory investigations are a necessary adjunct to clinical assessment. Acute active vasculitis usually is associated with an acute phase response resulting in elevated erythrocyte sedimentation rate and C-reactive protein levels. Renal involvement will cause proteinuria (usually less than 3 g/24 hours), hematuria and cellular casts in the urine sediment. Renal function must be measured using plasma urea and creatinine, supplemented as necessary by creatinine clearance or isotopic measurements of glomerular filtration rate; in vasculitis with developing crescentic glomerulonephritis; renal function may deteriorate over days, so patients with hematuria or a slightly raised plasma creatinine need daily measurements. Renal ultrasound and renal biopsy generally will be required in patients with evidence of renal involvement, both to confirm the diagnosis and to assess prognosis.

Pulmonary assessment in the acute patient is aimed at determining the presence or absence of granulomata (requiring radiologic imaging by chest radiography and often by CT scanning) and assessment for lung hemorrhage (by chest X-ray studies and measurement of arterial blood gases and of lung transfer factor).Other parameters of lung function usually are not needed in the acute phase, but may be required later to assess damage. However, in the acutely ill patient, it may be difficult to determine whether pulmonary involvement is due to vasculitis or infection. Then it may be necessary to proceed to bronchoscopy or open lung biopsy. In this group of patients bronchial biopsies rarely provide useful diagnostic information, and therefore open lung biopsy is the investigation of choice. Other investigations that may be needed to assess the patient with acute Wegener's granulomatosis include nasal swabs to detect *Staphylococcus aureus* (which may be associated with increased risk of relapse, see below), specialist ENT review with nasal endoscopy and biopsy, specialist opthalmologic review with fluorescein angiography, or nerve conduction studies if neuropathy is present.

Differential diagnosis

This is wide, given the range of symptoms and signs that may be encountered and the multiple organs that may be involved. The differential includes infection, particularly tuberculosis; neoplasia, particularly lung carcinoma, and paraneoplastic syndromes; connective tissue disorders, including systemic lupus erythematosus; and antiglomerular basement membrane disease (which can occur concurrently with ANCA-associated vasculitis).

Treatment

Untreated, systemic Wegener's granulomatosis follows a progressive course, with death due to vital organ failure. The use of corticosteroids and cyclophosphamide therapy improved 5-year survival for Wegener's granulomatosis with renal or other life-threatening organ involvement from less than 20% to better than 60% in uncontrolled studies. Nowadays, there are numerous variations between centers as to dose, route of administration, and length of therapy, particularly with respect to cyclophosphamide. Results of conclusive controlled trials to guide use of these drugs are lacking, although a number of trials are in progress in Europe under the auspices of the European Union Vasculitis Study Group (EUVAS). One outline regimen is shown in Table 20.2.

Some general comments that need consideration when treating patients with generalized Wegener's granulomatosis are as follows. Patients preferably should be treated by a specialist with experience in vasculitis. Toxicity of therapy is a major issue. Corticosteroids have many well-known side effects. Toxicity from cyclophosphamide (which is a prodrug that is converted to active alkylating agents in the liver) includes alopecia, increased risk of intercurrent infections, bone marrow suppression and leukopenia, infertility, hemorrhagic cystitis, carcinoma of the bladder, and a tenfold increased risk of leukemia and lymphoma. Infrequent side effects include pulmonary fibrosis, hepatitis, and the syndrome of inappropriate ADH secretion. Toxicity with cyclophosphamide is related to the total cumulative dosage; some regimens such as the original one described by the National Institutes of Health have recommended using cyclophosphamide and corticosteroids to both induce and maintain remission, continuing with cyclophosphamide for 12 months before slowly tapering the dose; however, such regimens have resulted in huge morbidity and mortality. There have been attempts to

Table 20.2 Treatment of vasculitis

	Cytotoxic agent	Corticosteroids
Induction therapy 4-6 months	Cyclophosphamide 2 mg/kg/day orally (max 150 mg) lower dose by 25 mg if >60 yrs WBC must be >4.0x10^9/l	Prednisolone 1 mg/kg/day (max 80 mg) Reduce weekly to 10 mg/day by 6 months
Maintenance therapy 6-24 months	Azathioprine 2 mg/kg/day	Prednisolone 5-10 mg/day
Escalation therapy	*Acute severe disease with creatinine >500 mmol/l or pulmonary hemorrhage*: consider 7-10 plasma exchange treatments over 14 days such that 60 ml/kg of plasma is exchanged for 4.5% or 5% human albumin solution or consider 3 pulses of methylprednisolone, 15 mg/kg/day for 3 days. These patients (if under 60 years) may also require 2.5 mg/kg daily of cyclophosphamide	

reduce toxicity by using shorter courses or intravenous pulse therapy. One approach is to use cyclophosphamide for induction of remission for 4-6 months and then to switch to a less toxic agent (e.g., azathioprine) in order to maintain remission (as suggested in Table 20.2). There are concerns that intermittent therapy with pulses of intravenous or oral cyclophosphamide may be less effective and may be associated with an increased risk of relapse compared with daily oral cyclophosphamide (but this needs to be tested directly in a controlled trial). The dose of cyclophosphamide needs to be reduced in the elderly, in those with reduced renal function, and it must be reduced or discontinued commensurate with a fall in the peripheral white blood cell count. It should always be stopped completely if the white cell count is approaching or falls below 4×10^9/l. Rescue therapy with G-CSF may be needed for patients who are severely neutropenic. Patients with severe disease (e.g., a plasma creatinine greater than 500 μmol/l or presence of lung hemorrhage) may benefit from additional therapy; the choice lies between three pulses of methylprednisolone (15 mg/kg/day; maximum daily dose 1 g) and a course of plasma exchanges (at least seven treatments within the initial 2 weeks where 60 ml/kg of plasma is exchanged for 4.5% or 5% human albumin solution).

Patients treated with prednisolone and cyclophosphamide usually require a range of additional prophylactic medications, including gastric protection (e.g., once-daily ranitidine), fungal infections (e.g., amphotericin lozenges), and pneumocystis carnii prophylaxis (e.g., three times-weekly co-trimoxazole). Patients who have previously suffered from tuberculosis should be offered prophylaxis with isoniazid. Mesna may help to reduce bladder toxicity, particularly when pulses of cyclophosphamide are used. Finally, it is important to offer sperm or oocyte storage to young patients, along with appropriate counseling.

Following induction of remission (which implies the complete absence of clinical disease activity as, for example, assessed using the item list of BVAS), many specialists discontinue cyclophosphamide after 4-6 months total therapy to avoid serious long-term toxicity. The choice lies between reducing and discontinuing all therapy (cyclophosphamide and prednisolone) within a year or replacing cyclophosphamide with a less toxic therapy for maintenance . Azathioprine has been successfully used in this regard. Unfortunately many patients will experience a relapse, and around 30-50% of patients will have relapsed by 2 years following diagnosis. Some relapse within the first year, and others relapse while therapy is reduced or after it has been withdrawn. Thus, there is a need to try to reduce or prevent relapse, whilst avoiding long-term toxicity. The policy of discontinuing all therapy as soon as possible has the advantage that toxic drugs are withdrawn, but relapses need to be identified and therapy reinstituted quickly to prevent further organ damage. There is the risk that much larger doses of drugs will be needed to control the relapse. The potential benefit of continuing therapy long-term with low-dose prednisolone and/or azathioprine is the prevention of relapse or reduced severity of relapse, but this needs to be established, as does the question of how long such treatment should be continued. It would be useful to have clinical and serologic markers to identify those patients at high risk of relapse; unfortunately such markers are not available, although continuing presence of ANCA is associated with increased risk of relapse. Similarly, a rising ANCA titer or recurrence of ANCA after its initial disappearance from the circulation, may predict impending relapse. Such patients should be monitored closely for clinical symptoms or signs of relapse (as measured by a rising BVAS); if there is evidence of increased vasculitic disease activity, therapy should be adjusted accordingly. Mild disease activity occurring after induction of remission may be managed with an increased dose of steroids or azathioprine. Development of more severe disease activity that threatens organ function, may require reintroduction of cyclophosphamide and, if very severe, supplementary therapy with pulse methylprednisolone or plasma exchange.

Another approach to prevention of relapse is the use of sulfamethoxazole/trimethoprim treatment, which appeared to prevent relapses and to reduce intercurrent infections in a prospective placebo controlled study. The mechanism of this effect was unknown, although there is a possibility that sulfamethoxazole/trimethoprim treatment eradicates *Staphylococcus aureus* carriage from the nose as chronic nasal carriage of *S. aureus* appears to identify a group of patients with Wegener's granulomatosis at increased risk of relapse. The antistaphylococcal nasal ointment, mupirocin, has been suggested as a useful adjunct to therapy for prevention of relapse, and its effectiveness will be tested in a controlled trial by EUVAS.

Risk of relapse, even years after the initial episode, means that patients with Wegener's granulomatosis require regular follow-up every 3-6 months for life.This should be undertaken by practitioners experienced in the care of patients with vasculitis who can distinguish problems associated with tissue damage from those of vasculitis activity.

Limited Wegener's granulomatosis may be responsive to lesser degrees of immunosuppression than is required when renal disease or other life-threatening manifestations are present, but controlled trials are lacking. EUVAS are currently conducting a trial to compare the use of cyclophosphamide with methotrexate in patients with non-renal Wegener's granulomatosus. Septrin has been advocated as monotherapy for Wegener's limited to the upper airways but has met with variable success.

In addition to the therapies just described, others have been used in small numbers of patients or are under evaluation. These include intravenous immunoglobulin, methotrexate, mycophenolate mofetil, cyclosporine A, and anti-T cell monoclonal antibodies.

MICROSCOPIC POLYANGIITIS

Microscopic polyangiitis is characterized by a vasculitis that predominantly affects small vessels, although medium-sized vessels may be affected. Renal involvement is usual and is caused by a necrotizing glomerulonephritis. Granulomata are absent.

The annual incidence of microscopic polyangiitis and Wegener's granulomatosus probably exceeds 20-30 per million per year (if accurate figures could be predicted), and together they account for at least 5% of end-stage renal failure. The two diseases have many similarities, including age and sex distribution. Clinically, a similar range of symptoms and signs due to similar organ involvement is seen, except that microscopic polyangiitis lacks the granulomatous involvement of the respiratory tract and the particular symptoms and signs that can accompany this.

Serologically, microscopic polyangiitis and Wegener's granulomatosis are both ANCA-associated disorders. However, the ANCA pattern and specificity differ between the two. Although over 90% of patients with Wegener's are C-ANCA /PR3-ANCA, in microscopic polyangiitis there is a 50-50 split between patients with P-ANCA/MPO-ANCA and those with C-ANCA/PR3-ANCA.

The shared properties of microscopic polyangiitis and Wegener's granulomatosus have allowed a common approach to therapy, and patients are treated along the lines already outlined for Wegener's. Response to therapy is similar in the two disorders, although relapse rates may be slightly higher in Wegener's granulomatosus than in microscopic polyangiitis.

RENAL-LIMITED VASCULITIS

An apparently renal limited form of vasculitis is recognized that demonstrates the same histologic findings as seen with microscopic polyangiitis and Wegener's granulomatosus. Again, it may be ANCA-associated, usually of the P-ANCA pattern and MPO-ANCA specificity. On occasion such patients develop more widespread systemic features, evolving into full-blown microscopic polyangiitis or occasionally Wegener's granulomatosus. Therapy for the renal-limited disease follows that for more generalized forms.

CHURG-STRAUSS SYNDROME

The Churg-Strauss syndrome is a distinct clinical syndrome, described in 1951 by Drs Churg and Strauss. It is characterized by the triad of:

- an eosinophil-rich and granulomatous inflammation involving the respiratory tract and necrotizing vasculitis affecting small to medium-sized vessels;
- peripheral blood eosinophilia ($>1.5 \times 10^9$/l);
- asthma (usually), allergic rhinitis or other allergic manifestations. The mean age of onset of asthma is 35 years and the interval between the onset of asthma and vasculitis is variable but may be as long as 30 years.

Other features may include rashes (purpura, urticaria, subcutaneous nodules), cardiac disease (myocarditis with eosinophilic infiltration, coronary arteritis, cardiac failure, myocardial infarction), pulmonary infiltrates, pulmonary hemorrhage, peripheral neuropathy (typically mononeuritis multiplex), cerebral involvement (cerebral hemorrhage or infarction), and gastrointestinal features (eosinophilic gastritis, gut vasculitis with diarrhea, abdominal pain, bleeding, perforation, infarction). Renal disease with a focal segmental necrotizing glomerulonephritis similar to that seen with Wegener's granulomatosus and microscopic polyangiitis may develop, but renal failure is not a major feature of Churg-Strauss syndrome.

Like Wegener's granulomatosus and microscopic polyangiitis, the Churg-Strauss syndrome is an ANCA-associated vasculitis. About three-quarters of patients with Churg-Strauss syndrome test ANCA-positive, usually with a P-ANCA/MPO-ANCA pattern and specificity, although C-ANCA/PR3-ANCA may also occur. In Churg-Strauss syndrome a differential white cell count will reveal the typical eosinophilia, although this feature is not specific to Churg-Strauss syndrome (it may also occur in Wegener's granulomatosus). As in Wegener's granulomatosus and microscopic polyangiitis, there is usually an elevation of the erythrocyte sedimentation rate and the C-reactive protein levels.

Pathologic examination of tissue biopsy specimens (e.g., skin, lung, kidney) shows three cardinal features: (1) infiltration by eosinophils; (2) formation of granulomas; (3) and necrotising vasculitis. Within the kidney, the typical focal segmental necrotising glomerulonephritis may develop.

Treatment

The approach to therapy for Churg-Strauus syndrome varies, and there are few reported controlled trials with this disorder alone. In patients with severe disease (e.g., focal segmental necrotizing glomerulonephritis and renal impairment, severe gastrointestinal involvement, cardiomyopathy, or central nervous system disease), therapy may be administered as for Wegener's granulomatosis and microscopic polyangiitis. Guillevain et al. have run combined trials of therapy for patients with Churg-Strauss syndrome and polyarteritis nodosa (see below); in patients with mild disease, high-dose prednisolone may be sufficient, but, again, cyclophosphamide is recommended for serious disease. Asthma will require therapy of its own.

The 5-year survival rate is now in excess of 80% with appropriate therapy. These patients should be followed over the long term because of their propensity for relapse.

HENOCH-SCHÖNLEIN PURPURA

This vasculitis is characterized by IgA-containing immune deposits affecting small vessels (capillaries, venules, arterioles). It is a distinct syndrome that usually occurs in children, although adults may be affected. The typical clinical features comprise purpuric rashes on the buttocks and lower limbs, usually around the ankles; these may coalesce to form areas of large necrotic ulceration. Arthralgia affecting large joints is usual. Gastrointestinal features develop, including colicky abdominal pains and bloody diarrhea; occasionally there is life-threatening gastrointestinal hemorrhage. Renal involvement may develop when there is hematuria and proteinuria, sometimes of nephrotic range. Of those with renal involvement, functional impairment develops in about one-third, with around 10% progressing to end-stage renal failure Adults appear to be more susceptible to severe renal involvement than do children.

The diagnosis is confirmed by skin biopsy showing a leukocytoclastic vasculitis with deposition of vascular IgA or by renal biopsy showing a focal segmental necrotizing glomerulonephritis with mesangial deposition of IgA. The serum levels of IgA often are elevated. Isolated IgA nephropathy with evidence of focal segmental necrotizing lesions, may be a renal-limited form of Henoch-Schonlein purpura.

Treatment depends on severity. In mild cases, symptomatic therapy alone may suffice. Moderately severe involvement of the skin and arthralgia – but without renal impairment – may be treated with corticosteroids, commencing at 0.5 mg/kg/day and reducing the dose every 1 to 2 weeks, depending on the clinical response. Henoch-Schonlein purpura patients, usually adults, who develop severe gastrointestinal hemorrhage and/or renal impairment, require treatment along the lines described for Wegener's granulomatosis and microscopic polyangiitis, although there are no prospective, controlled clinical trials to confirm the benefit of this approach.

Henoch-Schönlein purpura may relapse one or more times following the inital episode, sometimes following an upper respiratory tract infection. In unselected populations of patients, over 90% show complete recovery. Patients who have had renal involvement, particularly those with residual functional impairment, require long-term follow-up to monitor renal function and blood pressure.

CRYOGLOBULINEMIC VASCULITIS

Cryoglobulinemic vasculitis (sometimes called essential cryoglobulinemic vasculitis) is characterized by cold-precipitating immunoglobulins of at least two immunoglobulin classes. Usually one will be polyclonal IgG and the other will be an IgM rheumatoid factor. Where the rheumatoid factor component is monoclonal, cryoglobulinemic vasculitis may be referred to as type II; if it is polyclonal, it is referred to as type III. There is a strong association with presence of the hepatitis C virus, and antibodies to hepatitis C virus or viral RNA have been detected in more than 80% of patients with cryoglobulinemic vasculitis; cryoglobulinemia may develop in association with other illnesses, including connective tissue diseases and lymphoproliferative disorders, where it is considered as "secondary mixed cryoglobulinemia."

The original clinical description of "essential cryoglobulinemic vasculitis" by Meltzer et al. in 1996 drew attention to the presence of purpura, arthralgia, and weakness. Presence of a monoclonal IgM kappa component often is associated with cryoglobulinemic glomerulonephritis, which is a special form of membranoproliferative glomerulonephritis (also known as mesangiocapillary glomerulonephritis) with subendothelial deposits in which there may be intracapillary thrombi, marked leukocyte infiltration, and vasculitis in small or medium-sized renal arteries. A segmental necrotizing glomerulonephritis is not seen even when there are vasculitis arterial lesions in the renal biopsy. Cryoglobulinemic glomerulonephritis is almost always associated with hepatitis C virus. Membranoproliferative glomerulonephritis associated with hepatitis C virus but without cryoglobulinemia has also been reported. The renal lesions of cryoglobulinemic glomeruelonephritis present most frequently with isolated proteinuria and hematuria; about one-half of patients have evidence of renal impairment, and one-quarter have nephrotic syndrome, although this usually is not severe clinically.

Laboratory tests useful in cryoglobulinemic vasculitis include measurement and characterization of the cryoglobulins, measurement of serum complement levels (C4 is very low, with normal or slightly reduced C3 levels), detection of antibodies to hepatitis C virus and viral RNA, and tests of organ function. Tissue biopsy of kidney is diagnostic in patients with renal involvement. Skin or liver biopsy may be useful in some patients.

Treatment

Steroids and/or cyclophosphamide have been used extensively to treat cryoglobulinemic vasculitis, particularly when associated with cryoglobulinemic glomerulonephritis. Pulses of methylprednisolone or plasma exchange have been added for severe acute renal disease or systemic disease with vasculitis. This approach seems to have reduced the risk of progression to end-stage renal disease in susceptible patients, although there is a risk that hepatitis C viremia may persist or worsen as a direct result of immunosuppression. Recognition that cryoglobulinemia may be associated with hepatitis C virus infection provides a rationale for treating with interferon-alpha. Beneficial effects of interferon-alpha have been reported on clinical features, biochemical markers, and viral load in type II mixed cryoglobulinemia in both uncontrolled and controlled studies. However, recurrent disease manifestations are frequent after discontinuation of therapy. In a randomized control study by Lauta and Desangro using 33 patients with type II mixed cryoglobulinemia, combination of prednisolone with interferon-alpha-2β, administered as induction therapy (3 Mu/day) and then as maintenance therapy (3 Mu three times a week) was more effective than corticosteroids alone, with 83% responding to the combined medication and 27% to prednisolone-only treatment.

About one-quarter of patients present initially with an acute nephritic syndrome that is due to massive deposition of cryoglobulins in glomerular capillaries, which may cause acute oliguric renal failure. About one-third of patients go into partial or complete remission following therapy; others run an indolent course for many years or experience multiple acute relapses. End-stage renal failure develops in only 10%, usually after several years. The presence of hepatitis C virus may also cause liver damage.

ANTIGLOMERULAR BASEMENT MEMBRANE DISEASE (GOODPASTURE'S DISEASE)

Vasculitis occurs also in antiglomerular basement membrane disease, which is discussed in the chapter on pulmonary-renal syndromes.

POLYARTERITIS NODOSA

The first major postmortem macroscopic description of polyarteritis nodosa is attributed to Kussmaul and Maier (1866). They described thickened, cordlike arteries with nodular protrusions in a 27-year-old male patient with abdominal pain, and muscle and nerve involvement. Polyarteritis nodosa frequently has been confused with the entity now known as microscopic polyangiitis, despite the fact that Davson, Ball, and Platt in 1948 clearly distinguished between the two diseases. Thus polyarteritis nodosa comprises a nongranulomatous necrotizing vasculitis of medium-sized or small vessels without glomerulonephritis, pulmonary capillaritis, or involvement of other arterioles, capillaries, or venules. The vasculitic lesions frequently affect branch points and may lead to aneurysmal dilatation of the vessel wall. Histologic sttudy reveals fibrinoid necrosis and inflammatory infiltration within and around the vessel; initially this is neutrophil-rich, and later it is mononuclear cell-rich. Lesions heal by fibrosis.

Polyarteritis nodosa is uncommon in the UK; an incidence of 2.4 per million recently was quoted in a study from East Anglia. The incidence of classic PAN may differ around the world. This may in part reflect the incidence of hepatitis B virus infection, which undoubtedly is associated with a proportion of cases. In patients with hepatitis B virus infection, viral antigen has been detected in vasculitic sites. The pathogenic mechanisms operating in cases without hepatitis virus are unclear, but these also may involve immune complex formation.

Polyarteritis nodosa may develop at any age but is most common around 50 years. Both males and females may be affected. Fever, malaise, weight loss, arthralgias, and myalgias may develop. Peripheral neuropathy (mononeuritis multiplex), gastrointestinal involvement (hemorrhage, perforation, infarction), cardiac involvement (angina, myocardial infarction), and renal involvement (renal infarcts leading to severe hypertension and renal failure) can develop. Intraperitoneal or retroperitoneal rupture of an aneurysm is life-threatening. Hepatitis may reflect the presence of hepatitis B virus.

As in many other vasculitides, an acute phase response with elevated erythrocyte sedimentation rates and C-reactive protein levels develops. Tests of organ function reflect hepatitis or renal impairment. A proportion of patients will test positive for hepatitis B virus. Antineutrophil cytoplasmic antibody test is generally negative, occurring in around 10%; when positive, it is usually of the P-ANCA/MPO-ANCA type. Angiography will show aneurysmal dilatations and other vessel irregularities in the renal, hepatic, splenic, or splanchnic circulations.

Biopsy of muscle or nerve tissue may be diagnostic, revealing vasculitic lesions. In patients with known aneurysmal lesions in the kidneys, renal biopsy is best avoided to avoid precipitating hemorrhage.

Treatment

Patients with hepatitis B virus-associated polyarteritis nodosa appear to benefit from the use of an antiviral agent such as interferon-alpha-2β, given in conjunction with short-term immunosuppression; one regimen uses prednisolone at 1 mg/kg, tapering rapidly over 2 weeks, combined with intensive plasma exchange over 10 weeks or more. Patients with non-hepatitis B virus-associated polyarteritis nodosa benefit from high-dose steroids, initially at 1 mg/kg, with gradual tapering as disease improves for a year or longer. Sometimes methylprednisolone is given to patients with severe disease as pulses of 15 mg/kg for 3 days, although there are no controlled trials to support its greater efficacy. Cyclophosphamide may be helpful in non-hepatitis B virus-associated disease. As with Wegener's granulomatosis and microscopic polyangiitis, there is debate about whether cyclophospohamide, when used, should be administered as daily oral or intermittent pulses of therapy. A regimen devised by Guillevin et al. recommends pulse intravenous cyclophosphamide given as 0.6 g/m^2 monthly for 1 year. However, the direct comparison of daily oral versus pulse cyclophosphamide awaits a formal controlled trial. It is possible that only patients with severe disease require cyclophosphamide; again this awaits formal testing as well as the identification of reliable features associated with a poorer prognosis. In the French series, patients presenting with proteinuria, renal insufficiency, gastrointestinal involvement, cardiomyopathy, or central nervous system involvement appeared to have a worse prognosis, but this series of patients may have included some with microscopic polyangiitis. Plasma exchange does not appear to offer any additional advantage over the use of prednisolone and cyclophosphamide in patients with non-hepatitis B virus-associated polyarteritis nodosa. It is notable that the 5-year survival rate for polyarteritis nodosa increased from around 10% to around 55% with use of steroids alone.

KAWASAKI DISEASE

The disease that is now commonly referred to as Kawasaki disease was originally described by Tomisaku

Kawasaki in 1967 in Japanese children. It comprises an arteritis involving medium-sized and small arteries that is associated with a mucocutaneous lymph node syndrome. The coronary arteries usually are involved, and the aorta and veins also may be involved.

Kawasaki disease occurs worldwide, but is most frequent in Japan, where both endemic and epidemic patterns are seen. An infectious agent is suspected. Recent data implicate staphylococcal and streptococcal toxins (superantigens) in the pathogenesis. A number of different toxins are known, including staphylococcal enterotoxins (SE) A , B and C1; toxic shock syndrome toxin (TSST); and streptococcal erythrogenic toxins A, B and C. Superantigens stimulate a large proportion of T-cells in a HLA-DR-dependent but unrestricted manner. The toxins bind to conserved amino acid residues outside the antigen-binding groove on class II MHC molecules and selectively stimulate T-cells expressing specific T-cell receptor β-chain variable gene segments. Superantigens stimulate T-cells to divide and produce inflammatory cytokines. There is evidence for T-cell activation and for enhanced cytokine production in Kawasaki disease Most evidence points toward T-cell activation during the acute phase of Kawasaki disease being mediated by a superantigen that induces Vβ2 expansion.

Pathophysiology

Arteritis of the coronary arteries is always a feature of Kawasaki disease. Initially there is a mixed infiltrate of lymphoid cells and neutrophils through all layers of the arterial wall and in the periarterial tissue. This form of arteritis differs from other necrotizing arteritides because it involves the larger epicardial arteries from their ostia along their whole course and very rarely produces fibrinoid necrosis. Aneurysms resulting from the vascular damage may be diffuse and cylindric or localized and saccular. Thrombosis of the aneurysms is the major cause of death in acute disease. Healing of the lesions is associated with thickening of the arterial wall and luminal narrowing. Narrowing may contribute to late myocardial infarctions in survivors.

Aneurysm formation is much less frequent in other systemic vessels. Systemic artery aneurysms are detectable in less than 5% of patients. Aneurysms of the renal arteries are rare. Glomerulonephritis is not a feature.

Clinical findings

Kawasaki disease affects children, primarily those between 6 months and 8 years of age. Criteria for making a clinical diagnosis of Kawasaki disease have been proposed. Five out of the following six must be fulfilled: (1) fever lasting for 5 days or more; (2) conjunctival congestion; (3) changes of lips and oral cavity (dry, red, fissured lips; strawberry tongue; reddening of oral and pharyngeal mucosa); (4) changes of peripheral extremities (red palms and soles; indurative edema; membranous desquamation of fingertips during convalescent stage); (5) macular polymorphous rash of body trunk; (6) swollen cervical lymph nodes.

The most serious consequences of Kawasaki disease relate to the coronary artery involvement, which may cause echocardiographically demonstrable aneurysms, thrombosis, and areas of narrowing. In atypical cases, patients with fewer than five criteria may be diagnosed as Kawasaki disease if coronary aneurysms are present. Aneurysms occur in about 20% of untreated patients, usually 3 to 4 weeks into the illness. Myocardial infarction can occur acutely, and there is an increased risk of infarction during the year following the acute episode. Myocarditis, acute mitral valve prolapse, or pericarditis develop in some children.

Other noncardiac features include pyuria and urethritis, aseptic meningitis, tympanitis, arthralgia and arthritis, and abdominal organ involvement (with diarrhea and abdominal pain, obstructive jaundice or cholecystitis).

Laboratory findings are largely nonspecific. Marked thrombocytosis may develop. Cardiac aneurysms may be detected by echocardiography. Positive tests for ANCA are seen in a proportion of patients; the pattern is usually atypical.

Treatment

Several controlled studies have demonstrated that early treatment with high-dose intravenous immunoglobulin (IVIG) reduces the prevalence of coronary artery aneurysms, from about 20% to 6-10% in acute Kawasaki disease. IVIG, 400 mg/kg/day intravenously for 4 days, and aspirin, 100 mg/kg/day for 14 days, should be given within 10 days of onset. Prednisolone is contraindicated because it has an adverse effect on coronary artery aneurysms. The mechanisms of action of IVIG are poorly understood, but may include inhibition of T-cell responses to staphylococcal superantigens. Aspirin is recommended in low dose when thrombocythemia is present. The reduction in incidence of coronary artery aneurysms has been associated with a reduction in early and late morbidity and mortality.

LARGE VESSEL VASCULITIS

Giant cell arteritis (also known as temporal arteritis) is a granulomatous arteritis of the aorta and its major branches, with a predilection for the extracranial branches of the carotid artery and often involving the temporal artery. It most frequently affects patients older than 50 years, and may be associated with polymyalgia rheumatica. Takayasu arteritis is also a granulomatous inflammatory vasculitis of the aorta and its major branches, but it usually affects patients younger than 50 years, often women.

Histologically, both giant cell arteritis and Takayasu arteritis are characterized by focal granulomatous inflammation of the vessel wall. The lesions often contain multinucleate giant cells. With time, the lesions heal by fibrosis, causing scarring and narrowing of the arterial wall. As with most other primary vasculitides, the etiologic factor is unknown, but both giant cell arteritis and Takayasu arteritis have been regarded as having a strong cell-mediated element to their pathogenesis owing to the presence of T-cells, macrophages and mulnucleate giant cells. Weyand has undertaken studies using human temporal arteries from patients with giant cell arteritis implanted into severe combined immunodeficiency (SCID) mice. Following implantation of the inflamed temporal artery, the inflammation persists, indicating that all the elements are present to enable the inflamed focus to persist as an independent inflammatory unit. Selective proliferation of T-cells bearing particular T-cell receptor Vβ chains occurred in the xenografts, suggesting recognition of a locally expressed antigen. Reconstitution of diseased artery-derived T-cells into engrafted mice, themselves depleted of T-cells, restored the transcription of IL-2 and IFN-γ in the implanted arteries.

Clinically, fever, arthralgia, myalgia, and weight loss attest to the inflammatory nature of these vasculitides. Involvement of major arteries leads to ischemia of the supplied tissue. Typically Takayasu arteritis affects arteries supplying the upper limbs, leading to claudication and signs of vessel narrowing, such as bruits or absent pulses. Indeed, Takayasu arteritis has been called "pulseless disease." Involvement of vessels supplying the heart and lungs may lead to congestive cardiac failure, ischemic heart disease, aortic regurgitation, and pulmonary hypertension. Involvement of the abdominal aorta and its branches may lead to bowel ischemia, renal artery stenosis, and renovascular hypertension, which is seen in 30-40% of patients.

Giant cell arteritis is associated with polymyalgia rheumatica in over one-half of patients; this syndrome causes morning stiffness and painful muscles around the shoulder girdle, neck, and pelvic girdle. The vasculitis of giant cell arteritis can attack any artery in the body, but it selects the extracranial arteries of the head and neck in over 90% of patients. The alternative name "temporal arteritis" reflects the fact that the temporal arteries are often tender and swollen, but involvement of the temporal arteries is not invariable in giant cell arteritis. Arteritis of the retinal artery may threaten vision, and giant cell arteritis should be considered in any older patient who presents with headache in order to permit early diagnosis and avoid visual loss. Other symptoms include amaurosis fugax (due to involvement of the posterior ciliary arteries), diplopia due to ischemia of ocular muscles, vertigo, facial pain, and claudication of the jaw. In 10-15% of cases, there is involvement of the aorta and its branches, giving rise to the aortic arch syndrome with arm claudication and absent pulses, or Raynaud's phenomenon. Cardiac disease, renal artery disease, and hypertension are rare.

In both giant cell arteritis and Takayasu arteritis, there is a pronounced acute phase response, with elevated erythrocyte sedimentation rate and C-reactive protein. Temporal artery biopsy, performed within 24 hours of starting corticosteroids, is the best way of confirming the diagnosis in giant cell arteritis. In Takayasu arteritis, diagnosis depends on careful clinical evaluation (particularly loss of major pulses) and angiography (conventional or magnetic resonance angiography).

Treatment

In patients with suspected giant cell arteritis, prednisolone must be started immediately in high dose (e.g., 1 mg/kg/day) to avert any loss of vision. The dose may gradually be reduced, using the erythrocyte sedimentation rate as a guide, but a maintenance dose of 5-10 mg/day may be required for a year or longer. Occasional patients with severe or resistant disease, may require additional therapy with cyclophosphamide along the lines described above under Wegener's granulomatosis.

Takayasu arteritis may likewise respond to prednisolone, with additional cyclopohosphamide for severe disease or in the presence of steroid toxicity. Immunosuppression will do little for stenosis due to fibrosed scars, where reconstructive surgery may be required, provided the disease is quiescent. Hypertension and cardiac failure require therapy of their own.

Suggested readings

Brack A, Geisler A, Martinez-Taboada VM, Younge BR, Goronzy JJ, Weyand CM. Giant cell vasculitis is a T cell-dependent disease. Molecular Med 1997;8:530-43.

Churg A, Churg J. Systemic vasculitides. New York: Igaku-Shoin, 1991.

D'Amico G, Fornasieri A. Cryoglobulinemic glomerulonephritis: a membranoproliferative glomerulonephritis induced by Hepatitis C virus. Am J Kidney Dis 1995;25:361-9.

Gaskin G, Pusey CD. Systemic vasculitis. In: Cameron JS, Davison AM, Grunfeld J, Kerr DNS, eds. Oxford Textbook of Clinical Nephrology. Oxford: Oxford University Press, 1992;612-36.

Guillevin L, Lhote F, Gayraud M, et al. Prognostic factors in polyarteritis nodosa and Churg-Strauss syndrome. Medicine 1996;75:17-28.

Hagen EC, Daha MR, Hermans J, et al. Diagnostic value of standardized assays for anti-neutrophil cytoplasmic antibodies in idiopathic systemic vasculitis. Kidney Int 1998;53:743-53.

Hoffman GS, Kerr GS, Leavitt RY, et al. Wegener's granulomatosis: an analysis of 158 patients. Ann Int Med 1992;116:488-98.

Jayne DRW, Rasmussen N. Treatment of ANCA-associated vasculitis: Initiatives of the European Community Systemic Vasculitis Clinical Trials Study group. Mayo Clin Proc 1997;72:737-47.

Jennette JC, Falk RJ, Andrassy K, et al. Nomenclature of systemic vasculitides: the proposal of an International Consensus Conference. Arth Rheum 1994;37:187-92.

Lauta VM, Desangro MA. Long-term results regarding the use of recombinant interferon-alpha-2β in the treatent of II-type mixed essential cryoglobulinemia. Med Oncol 1995;12:223-30.

Leung DYM, Meissner HC, Fulton DR, Quimby F, Schlievert PM. Superantigens in Kawasaki syndrome. Clin Immunol Immunopathol 1995;77:119-26.

LUQMANI RA, BACON PA, MOOTS RJ, et al. Birmingham Vasculitis Activity Score (BVAS) in systemic necrotising vasculitis. Q J M 1994;87:671-8.

ROWLEY AH, SHULMAN ST. Current therapy for acute Kawasaki syndrome. J Pediatr 1991;118:987-91.

SAVAGE COS, HARPER L, ADU D. Primary systemic vasculitis. Lancet 1997;349:553-8.

STEGEMAN CA, COHEN TERVAERT JW, DE JONG PE, KALLENBERG CGM, for the Dutch Co-trimoxazole Wegener Study Group. Trimethoprim-sulfamethoxazole for prevention of relapses of Wegener's granulomatosis. N Engl J Med 1996;335:16-20.

CHAPTER

21

The pulmonary renal syndrome

Andrew R. Allen, Charles D. Pusey

KEY POINTS

- Pulmonary renal syndrome may be rapidly fatal, and patients should be stabilized with ventilation and dialysis as required, prior to establishing etiology.
- If alveolar hemorrhage is present, ANCA and anti-GBM antibody assays should be performed urgently.
- Immune complex disease of infective etiology, most commonly infective endocarditis, should be excluded.
- Aggressive immunosuppression is indicated in autoimmune pulmonary renal syndrome, with the addition of plasma exchange or intravenous pulse methylprednisolone likely to be beneficial.

The pulmonary renal syndrome (PRS) refers to the clinical picture of acute renal failure (ARF) combined with acute respiratory failure, the latter often being associated with a "white-out" of the lung fields on the plain chest radiograph (Fig. 21.1, see Color Atlas). It is important that an accurate diagnosis be established promptly, since the condition can be rapidly fatal and has various etiologies, the treatments of which are quite distinct. The major causes of PRS are listed in Table 21.1, and specific features of the major disorders will be discussed below.

ANTI-GLOMERULAR BASEMENT MEMBRANE (GBM) DISEASE

The development of autoantibodies to the α3 chain of type IV collagen, present within the normal GBM, can result in a severe glomerulonephritis (GN), swiftly leading to destruction of the kidneys. All such severe forms of GN are grouped under the heading of rapidly progressive glomerulonephritis or RPGN (Tab. 21.2). Because the same collagen antigen is present in the alveolar basement membrane, lung injury also can result from autoantibody deposition, particularly in smokers, leading to alveolar hemorrhage. The combination of RPGN and alveolar hemorrhage is referred to as Goodpasture's syndrome, of which anti-GBM disease, also known as Goodpasture's disease, is an important cause.

Epidemiology

Anti-GBM disease is rare, with an estimated UK incidence of 0.5-1.0 cases per million population per year. It is commoner in caucasians and males, and case clusters are reported, although no clear association with a particular infection has been established. Lung hemorrhage is rare in nonsmokers, although hydrocarbon exposure, infection, and fluid overload may all precipitate alveolar bleeding, possibly by damaging the endothelium in such a way as to expose the antigen to circulating antibody.

Etiopathogenesis

A role for T-cells in the etiology of anti-GBM disease is suggested by HLA associations with disease (susceptibility is linked to HLA-DR2), together with the observed proliferation of patients' T-cells in response to purified GBM antigen. The exact role of T-cells remains unclear, however, and the best characterized immune pathology is the development of autoantibodies to the α_3 chain of type IV

Table 21.1 The major causes of pulmonary renal syndrome. These can be divided according to whether the pulmonary lesion is alveolar hemorrhage, alveolar edema, or another process such as embolic disease

Alveolar hemorrhage
- Antiglomerular basement membrane disease (Goodpasture's disease)
- ANCA-associated systemic vasculitis (e.g., Wegener's granulomatosis, microscopic polyangiitis, Churg Strauss syndrome)
- Systemic lupus erythematosus
- Mixed cryoglobulinemia
- Henoch-Schönlein purpura
- Behcet's syndrome
- Drug-induced vasculitis
- Cholesterol emboli syndrome (rare)

Pulmonary edema
- Any case of acute renal failure with oligoanuria and secondary pulmonary edema
- Severe cardiac failure with "prerenal" renal failure
- Bilateral renal artery stenosis with "flash" pulmonary edema

Other
- Severe pneumonia (e.g., Legionnaire's disease)
- Acute renal failure with secondary pneumonia (patient may be immunosuppressed)
- Hantavirus infection
- Renal vein/inferior vena cava thrombosis with pulmonary emboli
- Pulmonary malignancy with paraneoplastic renal disease

collagen in all patients with the disorder. Transfer experiments demonstrated that such antibodies are pathogenic in monkeys, and disease activity in humans correlates with autoantibody titer. Autoantibodies are believed to bind their antigen in the basement membranes of kidney and lung, and to initiate an inflammatory reaction with complement fixation, leukocyte attraction, and, in the kidney, glomerular necrosis with crescent formation.

Table 21.2 Rapidly progressive glomerulonephritis (RPGN). The causes of RPGN (and PRS) can be grouped under three headings according to the pattern of immunoglobulin (Ig) deposition seen on renal biopsy

Linear IgG (and C3) deposition along GBM
- Antiglomerular basement membrane disease (Goodpasture's disease)

Pauci-immune – i.e., no significant Ig deposition
- ANCA-associated systemic vasculitis (e.g., Wegener's granulomatosis, microscopic polyangiitis, Churg-Strauss syndrome)

Granular Ig/complement deposition within glomerulus
- Systemic lupus erythematosus
- Mixed cryoglobulinemia
- Henoch-Schönlein purpura
- Drug ingestion (e.g., penicillamine)

Clinical findings

There is little prodrome with anti-GBM disease, although symptoms of iron-deficiency anemia from occult lung hemorrhage may predate acute presentation. Typically, patients present with dyspnea and hemoptysis, and clinical examination reveals cyanosis, tachypnea and inspiratory lung crackles with areas of bronchial breathing. One-third of patients have no lung symptoms at presentation, however, and complain of nonspecific features of acute renal failure or develop macroscopic hematuria and loin pain.

Diagnosis

Assay of the circulating titer of anti-GBM antibody, typically with an ELISA, is a simple test of high specificity and sensitivity. Some patients also have antineutrophil cytoplasmic antibody (ANCA) in their serum, although such "double positives" tend to behave more as ANCA-associated systemic vasculitis patients (see below). Table 21.3 shows the probable etiology of PRS with alveolar hemorrhage in patients presenting to North American and Swedish hospitals. A renal biopsy is diagnostic, with light microscopy showing an initial focal and segmental proliferative GN that progresses to severe glomerular necrosis and crescent formation (Fig. 21.1, see Color Atlas). Critically, immunofluorescence demonstrates linear deposition of IgG and often C3 along the GBM (Fig. 21.1, see Color Atlas). The chest radiograph in patients with alveolar hemorrhage shows dense airspace shadowing, often sparing apices and bases. Serial monitoring of alveolar hemorrhage can be performed by measurement of the Kco (see Tab. 21.6). Occasionally, bronchoalveolar lavage is required to confirm alveolar hemorrhage and exclude infection.

Treatment

Full supportive measures are necessary for all patients with PRS – close monitoring of oxygenation with supple-

Table 21.3 The etiology of pulmonary renal syndrome in two large series

Disorder	Niles et al. (%, n = 88)	Saxena et al. (%, n = 40)
Wegener's granulomatosis	17	17.5
Other vasculitis (mainly ANCA +ve)	39	60
Anti-GBM disease	12.5	17.5
Connective tissue disease	4.5	2.5
Other, e.g., cancer, infection, PE	27	2.5

mental oxygen and ventilation as required, and optimal fluid balance management with dialysis used early to avoid fluid overload (which can precipitate lung hemorrhage). Early therapies for anti-GBM disease typically comprised immunosuppressive drugs such as cyclophosphamide (to inhibit antibody synthesis) and corticosteroids (for an anti-inflammatory effect). In the mid-1970s, plasma exchange was added to the drug regimen to remove pathogenic anti-GBM antibody. Such a protocol is now standard, and has reduced the mortality of the condition to 10-20% at one year (from over 90% if untreated). Lung hemorrhage, in particular, appears to be effectively controlled by plasma exchange within 72 hours in most cases, although randomized trial data concerning efficacy is scant. Typically 10-14 exchanges are performed on a daily basis. Some units use pulses of high-dose intravenous methylprednisolone (e.g., 3×1g) in place of plasma exchange, although this is not widely supported and carries its own risks. Typical doses of the drugs used are shown in Table 21.5, although, unlike vasculitis, cyclophosphamide is often stopped after 3 months without substitution of azathioprine if the patient has no circulating anti-GBM antibodies.

For patients whose plasma creatinine is <600 μmol/l at the start of therapy, 80-90% can expect to have independent renal function at 1 year. Unfortunately, patients who are on dialysis at the start of therapy for anti-GBM disease have a very small chance of regaining dialysis independence. Once a full remission has been induced, relapse or recurrence of anti-GBM disease is rare, although recurrent pulmonary disease (with circulating anti-GBM antibody), with little renal involvement, is well described. Immunosuppression can usually be weaned off within the first year. Renal transplant recipients are at-risk for recurrent renal disease, and transplants usually are not performed until the anti-GBM antibody titer has declined after the acute episode.

ANCA-ASSOCIATED SYSTEMIC VASCULITIS

The discovery of ANCA in the serum of some patients with RPGN and systemic vasculitis has accelerated the diagnostic process and is casting light on pathogenic mechanisms. Such ANCA-positive patients all exhibit histologic evidence of vasculitis, but different diseases affect blood vessels of particular sizes, and some are associated with granulomata on biopsy of affected organs. A consensus meeting was held in Chapel Hill, USA, to standardize the nomenclature of systemic vasculitis, and the resulting classification divides diseases according to the size of vessels affected (Tab. 21.4). Involvement of small vessels (arterioles, capillaries and postcapillary venules) can result in both necrotizing glomerulonephritis and alveolar capillaritis, leading to a PRS. The forms of systemic vasculitis with a predilection for small vessels, Wegener's granulomatosis (WG), and microscopic polyangiitis (MP) will therefore be the focus of this section. These two disorders are characteristically associated with ANCA, and sometimes are termed ANCA-associated systemic vasculitis (AASV).

Epidemiology

True incidences of WG and MP are hard to establish because their multisystem nature means that patients gather in different speciality clinics according to the major organ system affected. A recent study suggests an incidence of around 15 cases per million population per year, but this may be an underestimate. There is a slight male preponderance, and the disease incidence is maximum in middle age, although it can occur at either extreme of the age spectrum.

Etiopathogenesis

Wegener's granulomatosis is defined as the presence of small-vessel necrotizing inflammation together with granuloma formation in any part of the respiratory tract. MP patients exhibit similar necrotizing vasculitis of small vessels, but granulomata are absent, and the only pulmonary lesion seen is an alveolar capillaritis. The vasculitis is notable for the lack of Ig and complement deposition (termed pauci-immune), despite often severe necrotizing inflammation with fibrinoid necrosis, neutrophil influx, and karyorrhexis (leukocytoclasia). The inciting event is unknown, and HLA associations with disease susceptibility are weak, leading to an emphasis on humoral immunity and, in particular, ANCA as a possible pathogenic factor. Current work suggests that ANCA may activate neu-

Table 21.4 Small vessel systemic vasculitis causing pulmonary renal syndrome

Disorder	Characteristics
Wegener's granulomatosis	Granulomatous inflammation involving respiratory tract and small-medium vessel necrotizing vasculitis
Microscopic polyangiitis	Necrotizing vasculitis of small vessels
Churg-Strauss syndrome	Eosinophil-rich granulomatous inflammation involving respiratory tract and small-medium vessel necrotizing vasculitis plus asthma and eosinophilia
Henoch-Schönlein purpura	Small vessel vasculitis with IgA-rich immune deposits
Mixed cryoglobulinemia	Small vessel vasculitis with cryoglobulin immune deposits and detectable serum cryoglobulin

(Modified, from Jennette JC, Falk RJ, Andrassy K, et al. Nomenclature of systemic vasculitides. Proposal of an international consensus conference. Arthr Rheum 1994;37:187-92.)

trophils, which then mediate the vessel injury. ANCA are autoantibodies specific for neutrophil granule proteins, and these proteins can be displayed on the neutrophil surface, where they would be accessible to circulating autoantibodies. There are two main patterns of ANCA binding to human neutrophils fixed on a slide in an immunofluorescence assay: cytoplasmic ANCA (cANCA), where antibody binds (usually) to the granular enzyme proteinase 3 (PR3) distributed throughout the cytoplasm; and perinuclear ANCA (pANCA), where the antigen is often, but not always, myeloperoxidase (MPO), which clusters around the neutrophil nucleus after fixation and gives rise to a perinuclear staining pattern (Fig. 21.1, see Color Atlas).

Clinical findings

Typically, AASV presents with a prodrome that can last for several months, comprising malaise, arthralgia, myalgia, fever, and weight loss. Patients with WG and upper airway granulomata may complain of nasal stuffiness, sinusitis, or epistaxis. In view of their systemic nature, both WG and MP can present with involvement of any organ, including purpuric skin rash, abdominal pain and gastrointestinal bleeding (from gut vasculitis), pulmonary hemorrhage (and cavitating lung granulomata in WG), mononeuritis multiplex (vasculitis of vasa nervorum), and nephritis (hematuria, proteinuria and renal impairment). A full PRS is a not uncommon presentation of these disorders.

Diagnosis

The PRS patient with a history of the prodromal illness described above must have AASV high on the differential diagnosis. Clinical features are sought, as described above, and routine blood tests usually disclose a normochromic and normocytic anemia, neutrophilia, thrombocytosis, elevated acute phase markers (including ESR, CRP, alkaline phosphatase) and renal impairment of variable degree. It should be noted that profound urinary abnormalities (dysmorphic erythrocytes and red cell casts) can be seen in a patient with preserved creatinine clearance, a consequence of the difference between glomerular inflammation and functional renal impairment. Of note, immune complex disease related to bacteremia (particularly infective endocarditis) should be specifically excluded, since many of the clinical features are similar. Blood should be sent urgently for ANCA assay since a positive result is very helpful in establishing the diagnosis. The cANCA is highly sensitive for WG in the appropriate clinical setting, but MP can be associated with either p- or cANCA, the latter group tending to have a more difficult relapsing and remitting course than the former. Churg Strauss syndrome is also associated with the presence of p- or cANCA. In general, pANCA is less specific than cANCA, since it may also be found in patients with other disorders such as rheumatoid arthritis and ulcerative colitis, in which pANCA reactivity is often not to MPO. Histology is important in confirming the diagnosis of AASV, biopsies of involved organs revealing the features described above, although actual granulomata are not always seen in biopsy specimens from patients with WG. The presence of cavitating lung lesions on radiology, or necrotizing upper airway vasculitis in association with a focal necrotizing pauci-immune GN, is usually deemed sufficient to establish the diagnosis of WG.

Treatment

Specific induction treatment for acute PRS is the same for both WG and MP, comprising corticosteroids and cyclophosphamide, as shown in Table 21.5. A small randomized trial suggested additional benefit from plasma exchange if patients were dialysis-dependent, although some groups use high-dose intravenous methylprednisolone instead. These additional treatments also are used for lung hemorrhage or other life-threatening organ involvement. Most PRS patients respond well to therapy, although common adverse effects include leukopenia, infection, steroid-induced diabetes mellitus, peptic ulceration, and hypertension. Close monitoring of full blood count and blood glucose is therefore mandatory, and prophylaxis with oral amphotericin and nystatin (for oral Candida) and co-trimoxazole (for *Pneumocystis carinii* pneumonia) is given while the patient receives cyclophosphamide. Oral H_2 antagonists or proton pump inhibitors also may be used if gastric inflammation or ulceration is anticipated. After about 3 months of induction therapy, maintenance therapy in the form of prednisolone and azathioprine is substituted. If the patient remains in remission, the doses of both drugs are tapered over 1-2 years and may be stopped after 2 years in some patients. Many patients relapse, however, particularly those with cANCA-positive disease or a persistent ANCA despite treatment, and such patients are weaned from immunosuppression more gradually, some requiring continuous low-dose immunosuppression to maintain remission. Serial assessment of circulating ANCA is particularly helpful in those patients in whom a rising autoantibody titer precedes clinical features of relapse.

Table 21.5. Common treatment for autoimmune rapidly progressive glomerulonephritis and alveolar hemorrhage

Drug/treatment	Dose	Duration
Prednisolone	1 mg/kg/day	1-2 weeks and slow taper
Cyclophosphamide	2.0-3.0 mg/kg/day	3 months and substitute azathioprine
Plasma exchange	3-4 l on 5-10 occasions (for albumin or plasma)	Performed daily if possible
or		
Methylprednisolone	10 mg/kg iv	Daily for 3 days

In contrast to anti-GBM disease, patients with AASV who require dialysis at or soon after presentation, often can regain independent renal function, and therefore active therapy is warranted in nearly all cases. The renal biopsy can guide management to some degree, extensive scarring making a successful renal outcome less likely, but the disease is patchy, and biopsy sampling error limits the conclusions that can be drawn from a single tissue sample. With alveolar hemorrhage, immunosuppression is necessary, irrespective of renal disease.

SYSTEMIC LUPUS ERYTHEMATOSUS (SLE)

Both SLE and mixed cryoglobulinemia (see below) are regarded as examples of immune complex (IC) disease. (SLE nephritis is considered in detail in Chapter 22). This can result in IC deposition in both glomerular and alveolar capillary walls, leading to complement fixation via the classic pathway, and leukocyte chemoattraction with resultant tissue injury. In SLE, autoantibodies can form ICs both in the circulation, and in situ when antibody binds antigen which has already deposited in the basement membrane. Most SLE patients experience mild disease with predominant skin, joint, and hematologic involvement, but a substantial subset develop significant renal disease, with proliferative GN of variable severity.

The diagnosis of SLE relies on clinical features (rash, arthropathy, vasculitis), with hematologic and serologic abnormalities, particularly autoimmune hemolytic anemia, lymphopenia, thrombocytopenia and the presence of positive autoantibodies (ANA, anti-DNA, and antiextractable nuclear antigens [ENA] such as nucleosome and histone). Serum complement levels are often low, particularly C4, and anti-C1q autoantibodies are strongly associated with lupus nephritis. It should be remembered that lupus nephritis may precede other features of SLE, but the renal biopsy is usually characteristic with a proliferative nephritis and deposition of immune complexes containing all Ig subclasses and complement components (so-called "full-house" immunofluorescence).

Oral corticosteroids and cyclophosphamide are often used in the therapy of SLE PRS, at the doses outlined in Table 21.5. SLE usually has a chronic, relapsing course, such that cytotoxic drugs may be given continuously for prolonged periods. The cumulative dose of cyclophosphamide can therefore rise above 10g when concerns about infertility (SLE is common in young women) and secondary malignancy (particularly bladder cancer) assume major proportions. For this reason, a regimen of monthly intravenous cyclophosphamide, at doses of 0.5-1.0 g/m^2 body surface area, combined with oral corticosteroids, has been adopted widely and appears to be effective. Pulsed intravenous methylprednisolone (typically 0.5-1 g on three consecutive days) appears to add benefit if a rapid response is needed, and there is little evidence that plasma exchange is superior to this protocol. Once a patient is in remission, a combination of low-dose prednisolone and azathioprine usually is effective as maintenance therapy.

CRYOGLOBULINEMIA

Cryoglobulinemia is defined as the presence of circulating immunoglobulins that reversibly precipitate on cooling. The culprit antibody(s) may be a monoclonal paraprotein (type I cryoglobulinaemia), a monoclonal Ig which acts as a rheumatoid factor (type II, the nephropathic variant), or a polyclonal mix of Ig (type III). These immunoglobulins can deposit around the circulation, typically causing a peripheral cutaneous purpuric rash, mononeuritis multiplex, mild hepatitis, mesangiocapillary GN (type I) and, occasionally, alveolar capillaritis. As in SLE, immunoglobulins deposited within the GBM excite an inflammatory response with mesangial cell proliferation and capillary wall thickening – hence the histologic description of the resulting nephritis, most commonly seen in type II cryoglobulinemia. It has become apparent that many patients with type II disease have chronic hepatitis C virus (HCV) infection, and the previously large pool of idiopathic type II cryoglobulinemia patients (termed mixed essential cryoglobulinemia) has shrunk substantially. Diagnosis of cryoglobulinemia is simple, requiring the demonstration in serum of a precipitating cryoglobulin, although blood must be taken into a warmed flask to prevent loss of cryoglobulin in the blood clot.

Acute cryoglobulinemia with nephritis or PRS is typically treated as shown in Table 21.5, with plasma exchange particularly helpful in removing the pathogenic immune complexes. For those with HCV-associated disease, recombinant interferon-α reduces circulating viral RNA, and many of the symptoms, but such therapy is too slow to be effective in the emergency setting of PRS.

PULMONARY EDEMA AND ACUTE RENAL FAILURE

Any cause of oligoanuric renal failure can lead to fluid overload and pulmonary edema, making this a relatively common cause of PRS. The patient will be sweaty, clammy, anxious, cyanotic, and often confused. Tachypnea, tachycardia, peripheral circulatory constriction, and diffuse inspiratory lung crepitations will be found, and arterial blood gases show type I respiratory failure, often with lactic acidosis. Early pulmonary edema adopts an interstitial pattern on chest radiography, but this becomes diffuse alveolar shadowing as the condition worsens. Oxygen, venodilatation (with intravenous nitrates), morphine (as anxiolytic and vasodilator), and potent diuretic therapy (intravenous loop diuretics plus dopamine) are often ineffective if ARF is established, and dialysis or ultrafiltration may be urgently required. In extremis, venesection can buy a little time while dialysis is arranged. The etiology of ARF can be determined once the life-threatening hypoxemia has been corrected.

In patients with either unilateral or bilateral renal artery stenosis, the phenomenon of sudden or "flash" pulmonary edema has been described. It is believed to represent the circulatory response to a surge in systemic vascular resistance as a consequence of renal ischemia and renin release. Such patients do not experience the phenomenon after renal revascularization, eliminating the heart as a primary cause. The frequency of this disorder is unknown, and it is often recorded in single case reports.

OTHER CAUSES OF PULMONARY RENAL SYNDROME

Alveolar hemorrhage and RPGN can be seen in non-ANCA-associated forms of vasculitis such as Behcet's syndrome or Henoch-Schonlein purpura. Treatment is usually along the same lines as for primary systemic vasculitis. Drug-induced vasculitis is well described, particularly with propylthiouracil, and responds to withdrawal of the offending drug. The cholesterol emboli syndrome is another rare cause of PRS, and is seen in suitable clinical contexts, e.g., following cardiac catheterization of an elderly man with widespread vascular disease. This disorder has no effective therapy and carries high mortality, although precipitating events, such as intraarterial procedures, thrombolysis and anticoagulation, should be avoided.

Severe pneumonic illness can also lead to ARF, either through profound sepsis and multi-organ failure, or as a consequence of infection-related interstitial nephritis, such as that seen with Legionnaire's disease. In some parts of the world, PRS related to Hantavirus infection is increasingly recognized. Of note, patients with RPGN often receive immunosuppressive treatment, and this can lead to opportunistic respiratory infection with consequent PRS.

It is clear that many different disorders can lead to potentially fatal PRS, and a rapid diagnosis of the etiology is both feasible and has important therapeutic implications. A useful approach to any patient with suspected PRS is shown in Table 21.6.

Table 21.6 The approach to the patient with suspected pulmonary renal syndrome

Organ	Test	Explanation
Blood	Full blood count/clotting/cross match	Identify and treat anemia
	Blood cultures	Identify infection
	Anti-glomerular basement membrane (GBM) antibody	Serologic test for anti-GBM disease
	Antineutrophil cytoplasmic antibody (ANCA)	Serologic test for ANCA-associated systemic vasculitis
	Antinuclear antibody, rheumatoid factor, anti-double-stranded DNA, complement levels, antibodies to extractable nuclear antigens, anti-C1q antibody, anti-cardiolipin antibody	Identify connective tissue diseases, particularly SLE
	Cryoglobulins	Diagnose cryoglobulinemia (send blood in warm flask)
Lung	Sputum/bronchoalveolar lavage (BAL) fluid examination – culture and cytology	Microorganisms, leukocytes, neoplastic cells, hemosiderin-laden macrophages (if chronic alveolar hemorrhage)
	Chest X-ray	Pulmonary infiltrates (classically apical and basal sparing with hemorrhage) and cardiac abnormalities
	Pulmonary function tests	Transfer factor (Kco) will rise if alveolar hemorrhage since free Hb binds CO avidly – can be used to monitor hemorrhage
	Fiberoptic bronchoscopy	Visualize airways and collect cytology/microbiology specimens, including BAL
	Lung biopsy (usually open)	Confirm diagnosis and allow immunofluorescence, e.g., for anti-basement membrane antibody
Kidney	Urea, creatinine and electrolytes	Assess renal function
	Urine analysis and microscopy	Red cell casts diagnostic of glomerulonephritis or interstitial nephritis
	Urine culture	Urinary infection
	24-hour urine	Determine proteinuria and creatinine clearance
	Renal ultrasound	Assess renal size (should be normal to large in ARF)
	Renal biopsy	Histologic features often diagnostic

Suggested readings

AGNELLO V, CHUNG RT, KAPLAN LM. A role for hepatitis C virus in type II cryoglobulinaemia. New Eng J Med 1992;327:1490-5.

BALOW JE, BOUMPAS DT, FESSLER BJ, AUSTIN HA. Management of lupus nephritis. Kidney Int 1996;49 (suppl. 53):88-92.

BOUMPAS DT, et al. Controlled trial of pulse methylprednisolone with 2 regimens of pulse cyclophosphamide in severe lupus nephritis. Lancet 1992;ii:41-5.

GASKIN G, PUSEY CD. Systemic vasculitis. In: Davison AM, Cameron JS, Grünfeld J-P, Kerr DNS, Ritz E, Winearls CG, eds. Oxford Textbook of Clinical Nephrology. 2nd ed. Oxford: Oxford University Press, 1998;877-910.

JENNETTE JC, FALK RJ, ANDRASSY K, et al. Nomenclature of systemic vasculitides. Proposal of an international consensus conference. Arthr Rheum 1994;37:187-92.

JOHNSON JP, MOORE J, AUSTIN HA, BALOW JE, ANTONOVYCH TT, WILSON CB. Therapy of anti-glomerular basement membrane antibody disease: analysis of prognostic significance of clinical, pathologic and treatment factors. Medicine (Baltimore) 1985;64:219-27.

NILES JL, BOTTINGER EP, SAURINA GR, et al. The syndrome of lung hemorrhage and nephritis is usually an ANCA-associated condition. Arch Int Med 1996;156:440-5.

SAVAGE COS, PUSEY CD, BOWMAN C, REES AJ, LOCKWOOD CM. Antiglomerular basement membrane disease in the British Isles 1980-4. Brit Med J 1986;292:301-4.

SAXENA R, BYGREN P, ARVASTON B, WIESLANDER J. Circulating autoantibodies as serological markers in the differential diagnosis of pulmonary renal syndrome. J Int Med 1995;238:143-52.

TURNER AN, REES AJ. Antiglomerular basement membrane disease. In: Davison AM, Cameron JS, Grünfeld J-P, Kerr DNS, Ritz E, Winearls CG, eds. Oxford Textbook of Clinical Nephrology. 2nd ed. Oxford: Oxford University Press, 1998;877-910.

VAN DER WOUDE FJ, et al. Autoantibodies against neutrophils and monocytes: tool for diagnosis and marker of disease activity in Wegener's granulomatosis. Lancet 1985;i:425-9.

CHAPTER

22

Lupus nephritis

Jo H.M. Berden

KEY POINTS

- Systemic lupus erythematosus mainly affects women between the ages of 20 and 40.
- In every lupus patient measurement of serum creatinine and blood pressure and urinalysis should be performed every 3 months.
- Onset or flares of lupus nephritis are preceded in 90% of patients by an increase in titer of anti-dsDNA antibodies; therefore, these titers should be monitored every 3 months.
- Prompt treatment of lupus nephritis decreases the risk of end-stage renal failure.
- Proliferative forms of lupus nephritis should be treated with cytotoxic immunosuppressives (azathioprine or cyclophosphamide), since prednisone monotherapy is insufficient in patients with such renal involvement.
- After development of end-stage renal failure, lupus disease activity decreases.
- Results of renal replacement therapy (dialysis, transplantation) in lupus patients are as good as in patients with non lupus renal diseases.
- Recurrence of lupus nephritis after renal transplantation is rare.
- Pregnancy is contraindicated in patients with active lupus nephritis, and/or a nephrotic syndrome, uncontrolled hypertension, impaired renal function (serum creatinine ≥ 150 μmol/l).
- Lupus patients who want to become pregnant should be analyzed for the presence of antiphospholipid antibodies, lupus anticoagulant, and anti-SS-A antibodies.

Systemic lupus erythematosus (SLE) is an autoimmune disease characterized by the formation of autoantibodies directed against a number of nuclear and intracytoplasmic autoantigens. Antibodies against doublestranded (ds)DNA are regarded as a serologic hallmark of the disease. It is truly a systemic disease, since all tissues and organ systems can be involved. The disease is very heterogeneous in its manifestations, severity, and course. Because of this pleiotropic nature, SLE is one of the great mimics in clinical medicine.

Epidemiology

Depending on racial and geographic factors, the prevalence of the disease varies between 15 and 200 per 100 000 individuals, being more prevalent in Asians and Afro-Americans. The annual incidence ranges from 1.8 to 7.6, with an average of about four cases per 100 000 persons. In most patients onset of the disease occurs between the ages of 20 and 40 years. At this age women are primarily affected, with a female to male ratio of 9:1; at younger and older ages, this gender ratio is less. This suggests an estrogen effect on the pathogenesis of SLE. The genetic influence on disease development is illustrated by the high concordancy of the disease in monozygotic twins (60%), the familial aggregation of SLE in 5-10% of the patients, and the association with certain MHC alleles (HLA-A1, B8, DR2, DR3), complement factor polymorphisms, and deficiency of the early complement factors (C1q, C4 and C2).

Etiopathogenesis

The etiology of SLE is still unknown. Genetic and epidemiologic studies suggest a polygenic and multifactorial etiology. It is assumed that, on a basis of a genetic susceptibility, environmental factors (viral infections, drugs, UV radiation) induce an abnormal immune response leading to the formation of many auto-antibodies directed mainly against nuclear antigens. Initially, it was thought that this autoantibody formation was due to a polyclonal B-cell activation. More recently, however, it has become clear that the abnormal immune response is T-cell-dependent and (auto-) antigen driven. During the last decade evidence has emerged that a major, not to say the principal, driving auto-antigen in SLE is the nucleosome, a macromolecular complex within the nucleus consisting of dsDNA and histones. T-helper cells specific for nucleosomes have been identified, and these T-cells were able to induce antibodies to nucleosomes, dsDNA, and histones. The only way to generate nucleosomes in vivo is by the process of apoptosis, a form of programmed cell death. There is now increasing evidence that apoptosis is disturbed both in experimental models of lupus as well as in SLE patients. During apoptosis several autoantigens are clustered in apoptotic blebs (like nucleosomes, spliceosomal protein complexes like Sm, RNP, SS-A, SS-B) or expressed on the surface (like anionic phospholipids and β_2-glycoprotein I) of apoptotic cells. During abnormal apoptosis these autoantigens can be modified through different mechanisms, making them more immunogenic and revealing cryptic epitopes to which no tolerance has been induced. These phenomena could explain why in lupus autoantibodies are formed against so many different intranuclear and intracytoplasmic auto-antigens. Besides their role as a major autoantigen, nucleosomes also are important for the development of glomerulonephritis in lupus. They are able to target antinuclear autoantibodies complexed to nucleosomes to the glomerular basement membrane (GBM). This occurs because the cationic histones within the nucleosome can mediate binding to the intrinsic anionic GBM component, heparan sulfate, a molecule responsible for the charge-dependent permeability of the GBM. Indeed in lupus nephritis nucleosomes, antinucleosome and anti-dsDNA autoantibodies and nucleosome/antinuclear autoantibody complexes have been identified in the GBM. Since molecules similar to heparan sulfate (glycosaminoglycans) are present in the vessel wall, in joints and in the skin, a binding mechanism comparable to that in the glomerulus could ensue in these tissues, leading to vasculitis, arthritis, and dermatitis.

Pathophysiology

The variability in clinical manifestations is reflected by the broad spectrum of histologic abnormalities that can be found in kidney biopsies of lupus patients with nephritis. These abnormalities can be categorized according to the WHO classification of lupus nephritis shown in Table 22.1. A central feature of lupus nephritis is the presence on immunofluorescence of deposits in the glomerulus of immune complexes consisting of all immunoglobulin classes and the early complement factors (C1q and C3). The different forms of lupus nephritis are related to the site where these immune complexes localize or are formed and their capacity to incite an inflammatory response. Very rarely, no histologic abnormalities or deposits are seen in conjunction with clinical symptoms (class I). The mildest form of lupus nephritis (class II) is characterized by mesangial deposits, which may be accompanied by mesangial proliferation. In the more severe forms of lupus nephritis (classes III and IV) not only mesangial deposits are found, but also in the glomerular capillary loops. On light microscopy a glomerular influx of granulocytes and monocytes is seen, together with proliferation of endothelial cells and sometimes crescent formation. In addition segmental capillary loop necrosis, hyalin thrombi, and duplication of the glomerular basement membrane can be present. On electron microscopy most of the deposits are localized subendothelially. In WHO class IV lupus nephritis, almost all glomeruli show diffuse lesions, whereas in class III fewer glomeruli are affected and the lesions are more segmental. However, the differentiation between classes III and IV is difficult and arbitrary and may be influenced by sampling error. Also, in terms of prognosis, there are no great differences between these two classes. Morphologically, membranous lupus nephritis (class V) is hard to distinguish from idiopathic membranous glomerulonephritis, although in lupus mesangial

Table 22.1 World Health Organization morphologic classification of lupus nephritis (1995 revised version)

Class	Description
I	Normal glomeruli A. Nil (by all techniques) B. Normal by light microscopy but deposits seen by electron or immunofluorescence microscopy
II	Pure mesangial alterations (mesangiopathy) A. Mesangial widening and/or mild hypercellularity (+) B. Moderate hypercellularity (++)
III	Focal segmental glomerulonephritis (associated with mild or moderate mesangial alterations) A. Active necrotizing lesions B. Active and sclerosing lesions C. Sclerosing lesions
IV	Diffuse glomerulonephritis (severe mesangial, endocapillary or mesangiocapillary proliferation and/or extensive subendothelial deposits). Mesangial deposits are present invariably and subepithelial deposits often, and may be numerous) A. Without segmental lesions B. With active necrotizing lesions C. With active and sclerosing lesions D. With sclerosing lesions
V	Diffuse membranous glomerulonephritis A. Pure membranous glomerulonephritis B. Associated with lesions of Class II (a or b)
VI	Advanced sclerosing glomerulonephritis

abnormalities are more prevalent and the deposits contain more classes of immunoglobulins and more frequently C1q. Very often a membranous component is present together with proliferative abnormalities, as described for class III and IV. These cases are categorized as class III or IV, since their prognosis is different from the pure membranous form. Advanced or end-stage forms of proliferative lupus nephritis, characterized by pronounced sclerosis and hyalinosis are classified as class VI lupus nephritis.

The prognostic value of the WHO classification of the renal lesion can be increased by including indices for activity and chronicity as proposed in the so-called NIH index given in Table 22.2. The assessment of lupus nephritis according to these two classification systems is important, since it has been shown that the risk for development of end-stage renal failure is significantly greater in patients with WHO class IV lupus nephritis, a chronicity index ≥ 3, or an activity index ≥ 12. The estimation of the incidence of the various forms of lupus nephritis is obviously influenced by various factors, such as ethnic background, geographic area, and type of referral hospital. Therefore, the incidence figures in Table 22.4 are a gross average of the reported data, but nevertheless give an impression about the relative frequencies.

The renal manifestations of primary APS are characterized by non-inflammatory occlusion of glomeruli and vessels, lesions akin to those observed in the hemolytic uremic syndrome and scleroderma. In the glomerulus these thrombi may induce mesangiolysis, while in the arterioles they may induce intimal fibrosis and medial hyperplasia.

Clinical findings

General features The clinical manifestations of SLE at onset and cumulatively during follow-up are listed in Table 22.3. These data represent a gross average of a number of cohorts studied in the USA, Canada, and Europe. These frequencies obviously are influenced by the ethnic background of the population studied and the specialty of the reporting investigators, and should therefore be regarded as relative frequencies. Nevertheless, they illustrate the systemic character of the disease. A discussion of the extra-renal manifestations of SLE is beyond the scope of this chapter. Certain SLE patients can present a typical cluster of clinical features, including recurrent arterial and venous thrombosis, habitual abortion, and thrombocytopenia. It is associated with the presence of a particular autoantibody specificity directed against anionic phospholipids (like cardiolipin) and/or proteins (like β_2-glycoprotein I) bound to these phospholipids. This spectrum of abnormalities is known as the anti-phospholipid antibody syndrome (APS). It can occur alone (primary APS) or in conjunction with an autoimmune disease like SLE (secondary APS).

Renal symptoms Clinically, glomerulonephritis develops in 50 to 60% of lupus patients during their disease; however, in approximately 10-20% of the patients nephritis is the presenting symptom. Renal biopsies, however, show some glomerular abnormalities in virtually all lupus patients. In general lupus nephritis develops in patients with otherwise active disease, mostly characterized by facial rash and arthritis. In most patients renal flares are preceded by an increase in anti-dsDNA titers and a reduction in complement levels, mainly C4. Such changes should alert the clinician for the development of renal manifestations. Like the disease itself, the renal symptoms are highly variable, ranging from mild proteinuria to rapidly progressive renal failure. In fact, every

Table 22.2 The National Institute of Health histologic scoring system for activity and chronicity in lupus nephritis

	Activity index	Chronicity index
Glomerular	Endocapillary hypercellularity Leukocyte infiltration Fibrinoid necrosis/karyorhexis* Cellular crescents* Hyalin deposits/wire loops	Glomerular sclerosis Fibrous crescents
Tubulointerstitial	Mononuclear cell infiltration	Fibrosis Tubular atrophy
Maximal score	24	12

(Scoring per item from 0-3; for parameters with asterisks the score is doubled.)

Table 22.3 Mean frequency and ranges in percentages of the various disease manifestations of SLE at disease onset or cumulatively during the disease course (adapted from several studies)

Disease manifestations	At onset (n = 1376)*	Cumulative incidence (n = 2214)*
Constitutional symptoms (fever, fatigue, weight loss)	41 (36-53)	58 (41-77)
Skin lesions	53	69 (55-78)
Arthritis	59 (44-69)	78 (63-91)
Pleurisy	17 (16-17)	33 (30-36)
Pericarditis	13	19 (12-23)
Raynaud's syndrome	22 (18-33)	41 (24-60)
Renal involvement	22 (16-38)	49 (28-74)
CNS involvement	15 (12-24)	33 (11-53)
Cytopenias		
anemia		50 (30-78)
leukopenia		49 (35-66)
thrombocytopenia		18 (7-30)

* Number of patients studied.

renal syndrome can be caused by SLE. The renal manifestations of lupus nephritis are not different from those in other glomerular diseases and include a microscopic hematuria with a nephritic urinary sediment (dysmorphic erythrocytes and erythrocyte casts), proteinuria or nephrotic syndrome, impaired renal function, and hypertension. The frequencies of these symptoms in the various forms of lupus nephritis are given in Table 22.4. Although certain renal manifestations are more prevalent in certain forms of lupus nephritis, it is clear that on the basis of clinical symptoms, it is impossible to classify correctly the type and severity of lupus nephritis. This makes a kidney biopsy almost mandatory, since the treatment regimen is tailored mainly according to the classification of the type of renal lesion (see below). Measurement of serum creatinine and blood pressure and urinalysis should be performed routinely and regularly in every lupus patient, since early diagnosis and prompt treatment of lupus nephritis will reduce the risk of developing end-stage renal failure (ESRF). Also, after diagnosis of lupus nephritis these parameters should be followed regularly, since a transition to a more severe form of lupus nephritis or a relapse of nephritis is heralded by worsening of renal symptoms.

Diagnostic procedures

Because of the kaleidoscopic clinical manifestations of SLE, a large number of laboratory abnormalities can be present, depending on the tissue or organ affected by the disease. It is beyond the scope of this chapter to discuss all these abnormalities. This part will be confined to the serologic diagnosis of SLE and the identification of the major autoantibody specificities, since lupus nephritis generally develops in patients with active disease. Monitoring lupus activity serologically can be helpful to anticipate onset or flares of renal disease.

Table 22.4 Frequency (in percentages) of the various forms of lupus nephritis (classified according to the WHO classification), incidence of clinical renal symptoms, and incidence of the "typical" autoantibody/complement profile in patients with lupus nephritis (data derived from different sources)

Parameter	WHO class lupus nephritis			
	II	III	IV	V
Frequency	10-15	10-20	50-60	10-20
Nephritic sediment	9	53	78	40
Proteinuria	36	67	89	100
Nephrotic syndrome	0	27	56	90
Impaired renal function	13	20	22	10
Hypertension	22	40	56	50
High anti-dsDNA/low C3	36	63	80	33

Autoantibodies

Antinuclear antibodies The occurrence of antinuclear antibodies is a characteristic feature of SLE. Their presence can be identified by the Anti-Nuclear Antibody (ANA) test, in which serum is incubated with sections of tissues or cultured cells. Because this test has a high sensitivity but a low specificity, it can be used only as a screening procedure. Antibody binding from the serum to the nucleus is detected by subsequent incubation with fluorescinated anti-human immunoglobulin antibodies. The nuclear staining pattern can already give an indication of the specificity of the antinuclear antibody: a homogeneous or peripheral rim pattern is caused mainly by autoantibodies directed against the nucleosome (histone/DNA complex) or dsDNA, whereas a speckled pattern is observed with antibodies against nuclear/spliceosomal proteins like Sm, RNP, SS-A (Ro), or SS-B (La). To further define the antinuclear antibody specificity, additional tests are necessary. Specificity for anti-dsDNA can be identified with the Crithidia luciliae test or the Farr assay in which pure dsDNA is used as substrate. The Farr assay allows furthermore an estimation of the anti-DNA titer, which can be used to monitor disease activity in conjunction with complement C3 and C4 levels, since disease onset or flares are in 80-90% associated with rises in anti-dsDNA titers. Specificity for nuclear or spliceosomal proteins can be documented by using western blotting on nuclear extracts. For this immunoblotting technique nuclear proteins are extracted from cells, separated on polyacrylamide gels, and transferred to nitrocellulose blots. Identical strips of this blot are incubated with test serum samples and reference sera. Binding of autoantibodies is visualized with enzyme-linked secondary antibodies. The position(s) and composition of the staining pattern allows identification of the specificity like anti-histone, anti-RNP, anti-Sm, anti-SS-A (Ro) or anti-SS-B. If this western blot technique is not available, an alternative approach is the Ouchterlony immunodiffusion technique using extractable nuclear antigens (ENA), which allows identification of anti-Sm and/or anti-RNP. Since the RNP antigen is sensitive to digestion by ribonuclease in contrast to the Sm antigen-complex, the two reactivities can be differentiated. Both anti-dsDNA and anti-Sm are almost pathognomonic for SLE and can be regarded as marker-antibodies. Both specificities are incorporated in the ARA criteria (Tab. 22.6). However, unlike anti-dsDNA, anti-Sm antibodies cannot be used to monitor disease activity. The frequencies of the various autoantibodies in SLE are listed in Table 22.5. In addition, association with certain disease manifestations are given. For the analysis of antinuclear antibodies the next algorithm is proposed: (1) for screening purposes the ANA test can be used; (2) if negative: no further analysis unless strong clinical suspicion; (3) if positive: the Crithidiae assay can be used as a screening procedure for the presence of anti-dsDNA; (4) if positive: Farr assay which allows quantification; (5) if negative: Western blot on nuclear extracts to determine whether antibodies against nuclear proteins are present.

Antiphospholipid antibodies In certain lupus patients autoantibodies can be present against negatively charged phospholipids, which includes anticardiolipin and the lupus anticoagulant activity (LAC). Anticardiolipin antibodies can be detected by either an ELISA or radioimmunoassay using cardiolipin and β_2- glycoprotein I as antigen. IgG anticardiolipin antibodies show a better correlation with the APS than do IgM antibodies. Lupus anticoagulant activity can be demonstrated by a prolongation of the partial thromboplastin time that cannot be corrected by addition of normal, platelet-free, plasma. Since the results of both tests (anticardiolipin and LAC) are not fully overlapping, both tests should be performed if there is clinical suspicion for the APS.

Additional autoantibody specificities Hematologic abnormalities are frequent in SLE, and include hemolytic anemia, leukopenia, and thrombocytopenia. They are included in the ARA criteria for the diagnosis of SLE. There are many potential causes for anemia in SLE, but frequently it is due to the formation of autoantibodies against red blood cells, which can be detected by the Coombs test. Leukopenia, after exclusion of other causes (drugs, infections) might be due to antileukocyte antibodies that can be detected by indirect immunofluorescent techniques. Also, thrombopenia can be the result of autoantibodies either directed against thrombocytes or against cardiolipin as a feature of the APS. Therefore, in most hematologic cytopenias, the reduction in cell numbers is due to peripheral autoantibody-mediated sequestration. To distinguish between reduced production or increased cell turnover, a bone marrow aspirate can be helpful.

Complement levels Active lupus disease is in general accompanied by activation of the classic pathway of the complement system. This can be identified by a lower overall activity of the lytic complement cascade from C1 to C9 by measuring the CH50 titer. If the CH50 titer is 0, one should consider a deficiency of one of the early complement factors. In addition, plasma levels of C1q, C4, and C3 can be measured. The most sensitive in this respect is the C4 level, which decreases earlier and to a greater extent than do the other complement factors. An alternative approach is the identification of increased levels of C3d, indicating an enhanced activition of C3. Especially in patients with lupus nephritis complement levels can be used to monitor disease activity in conjunction with anti-dsDNA antibody titers. In 90% disease flares are preceded by significant rises of anti-dsDNA and/or decreases of complement levels.

Renal parameters Renal signs of disease activity are a nephritic urinary sediment, increased urinary protein excretion, and a decreased GFR. As is known, the use of the creatinine clearance underestimates the GFR, especially in lupus nephritis. Dysmorphic red blood cells and/or red cell casts in the urinary sediment are indicators of glomerular pathology and should therefore be looked for with care. However, the only reliable procedure to document and classify renal involvement in lupus is the renal biopsy.

Diagnosis

Because of the variability in clinical disease manifestations, criteria were developed for the diagnosis of SLE. These criteria were revised in 1982, and are listed in Table 22.6. They were selected for their sensitivity and specificity for SLE by comparing the prevalence of these features in SLE patients with that in patients with nontraumatic, nondegenerative connective tissue diseases, mainly rheumatoid arthritis. If a patient has any four or more of

Table 22.5 Prevalence of autoantibodies in SLE, specificity for the disease, and association with certain disease manifestations

Antibody specificity	Frequency (%)	Specificity	Associated disease manifestations
ANA	95	–	
dsDNA	60-90	++	Nephritis
Histones	50-70	+	Drug-induced SLE
Nucleosomes	50-80	?	Nephritis ?
Sm	10-30	++	?
RNP	30-50	+	Raynaud, myositis, MCTD, frequently in conjunction with negative anti-dsDNA
SS-A (Ro)	25-40	+	Discoid lupus? Sjögren syndrome Previously ANA-neg patients Neonatal lupus Congenital heart block
SS-B (La)	10-20	+	Mostly in conjunction with SS-A
Cardiolipin	10-30	–	Recurrent thrombosis, fetal loss, thrombopenia

++ = marker antibody for SLE.
\+ = also present in other autoimmune diseases.
– = also present in other nonautoimmune diseases.

these criteria, simultaneously or serially, SLE can be diagnosed with a specificity and a sensitivity of 96%. Three positive criteria make the diagnosis of SLE probable, whereas two positive criteria make it possible.

Treatment

The discussion here will be confined to an overview of immunosuppressive treatment. Additional therapeutic measures, such as antihypertensive treatment, management of electrolyte disturbances, and impaired renal function are not discussed.

The options for immunosuppressive treatment of the different forms of lupus nephritis are summarized in Table 22.7. Only for classes III, IV, and V are a limited number of prospective studies available. For the other forms, a balanced compilation is made from the literature and from personal experience.

For class I lupus nephritis, no specific "renal" therapy is necessary; treatment is dictated by the presence of extrarenal symptoms. Patients with class II lupus nephritis in general respond satisfactorily to monotherapy with oral corticosteroids. However, the patient should be monitored for transition to a more severe form, which is in general heralded by worsening of the clinical renal symptoms. Corticosteroid monotherapy is not sufficient for classes III and IV, since it will lead in a greater proportion of the patients to end-stage renal disease. Cytotoxic immunosuppressives, either cyclophosphamide (CPM) or azathioprine (AZA) should be added to the regimen. The use of these cytotoxic drugs for the treatment of patients with WHO class III or IV lupus nephritis clearly improved renal and patient survival, as revealed by a number of meta-analyses and prospective trials carried out at the NIH. The pathophysiologic basis for this beneficial effect is that these drugs could prevent an increase in chronicity index over time, as found between the first and second kidney biopsy, whereas during prednisone monotherapy a clear increase of this chronicity index was observed. It has been shown in various studies that this chronicity index is the strongest predictor for development of end-stage renal failure. In the prospective NIH trials two other important observations were made. First, although the therapeutic efficacy was equal for oral and monthly intravenous pulses of CPM, there were fewer side effects when CPM was given intravenously. Second, there was no significant difference between the therapeutic efficacy of CPM and AZA. However, the side effects of these drugs are not identical. CPM has a greater bone marrow toxicity, leads to amenorrhea in a substantial proportion of patients, can induce azospermia, is teratogenic, and displays an unique urothelial toxicity (hemor-

Table 22.6 The 1982 revised ARA criteria for classification of systemic lupus erythematosus

Criterion	Sensitivity (%)	Specificity (%)
Malar rash	57	96
Discoid rash	18	99
Photosensitivity	43	96
Oral ulcers	27	96
Arthritis (two or more joints)	86	37
Serositis pleuritis *or* pericarditis	56	86
Renal disorder proteinuria > 0.5 g/24 h *or* cellular casts (red, hemoglobin, granular, tubular or mixed)	51	94
Neurologic disorder seizures *or* psychosis	20	98
Hematologic disorder hemolytic anemia *or* leukopenia ($<4x10^9/l$) *or* lymphopenia ($<1.5x10^9/l$) *or* thrombopenia ($<100x10^9/l$)	59	89
Immunologic disorder positive LE cell test *or* positive anti-dsDNA *or* positive anti-Sm *or* false positive TPI/VDRL	85	93
Antinuclear antibody	99	49

(These criteria were selected for their sensitivity and specificity to classify SLE patients by analyzing these criteria in 177 SLE and 162 control patients, who were matched for age, sex and race. The control patients had a nontraumatic, nondegenerative connective tissue disease, mainly rheumatoid arthritis (n = 95). For each criterion the sensitivity and specificity are given. The sensitivity was calculated as a percentage from the number of lupus patients positive for this criterion over the number of lupus patients in whom this criterion was analyzed. The specificity was calculated from the number of control patients who were negative or normal for that criterion over the number of control patients analyzed.)

Table 22.7 Summary of treatment of the different forms of lupus nephritis

WHO class	Treatment option
I	Treatment guided by extrarenal lesions
II	Corticosteroids
III/IV	iv cyclophosphamide pulses/oral prednisone
	iv methylprednisolone pulses/azathioprine/low doses of oral prednisone
V	Corticosteroids initially
	If failure: either azathioprine or oral cyclophosphamide for 6 months, eventually followed by azathioprine
VI	In general no further immunosuppression Supportive treatment

rhagic cystitis, bladder carcinoma). Therefore, prospective studies comparing CPM with AZA are warranted, but not available. If the results of the NIH trial for CPM are compared with those reported in the literature for AZA, there is no significant difference in efficacy between both drugs.

Besides cytotoxic drugs, intravenous pulses of methylprednisolone (MP) also are frequently used in the treatment of lupus nephritis. Mainly from uncontrolled studies, it has become clear that this treatment generally induces a rapid improvement of renal symptoms and autoimmune serology. Also, the side effects of MP seem to be less than those of high oral doses of prednisone. However, its long-term efficacy on preserving renal function is largely unknown. A recent prospective trial carried out at the NIH showed that six monthly iv pulses of MP were associated with a significantly higher frequency of deterioration of renal function and relapses than 6 or 30 monthly iv pulses of CPM. On the basis of the results discussed so far, one can conclude that: (1) it has not been proved that AZA is less effective than CPM; (2) AZA is less toxic than CPM; and (3) iv MP pulses are as good as high doses of oral prednisone with fewer side effects. Therefore, a combination of AZA (which prevents progression of chronic lesions) with iv MP (which reduces acute lesions) might be an ideal combination, combining efficacy with lower toxicity. Based on these conclusions, the Dutch Working Party on SLE is currently comparing CPM and the AZA/iv MP combination prospectively. For practical purposes both treatment arms are detailed in Tables 22.8 and 22.9. A recent large scale prospective trial revealed that the addition of plasmapheresis to cytotoxic immunosuppressives did not confer a significant therapeutic benefit. Based on this observation, plasmapheresis does not seem any longer to have a place in the treatment of lupus nephritis.

Patients with a pure membranous lupus nephritis without a proliferative component (class V according to the 1995 revised WHO classification) in general respond satisfactorily to corticosteroid monotherapy. Patients with a membranous nephropathy with a proliferative component (formerly classified as WHO class VC or VD) have a much worse prognosis and should be treated as patients with a class IV lupus nephritis. If a patient with class V (A or B) lupus nephritis does not respond to corticosteroids, one should consider addition of AZA or CPM (as in idiopathic membranous glomerulonephritis, where oral treatment seems to be superior to monthly intravenous pulses). If CPM treatment is initiated, the therapeutic response should be evaluated after 6 months and the drug should be discontinued if no improvement has occurred. It remains to be determined whether cyclosporine A is useful for the treatment of membranous lupus nephritis; however, its use is associated with nephrotoxicity and an increased risk of hypertension.

Treatment of WHO class VI nephritis should be balanced upon weighing the risks of intensivation of

Table 22.8 Treatment options for proliferative lupus nephritis (WHO class III or IV) consisting of either intravenous pulses of cyclophosphamide (iv CPM) in conjunction with high oral doses of prednisone (PRED), or intravenous pulses of methylprednisolone (ivMP), together with azathioprine (AZA) and low oral doses of prednisone (treatment protocols of the Dutch Working Party on SLE)

Phase	iv CPM/high oral PRED	iv MP/AZA/low oral PRED
Induction week 0-20	Cyclophosphamide 6 times every 4 weeks 750 mg/m² iv	Methylprednisolone 1 g iv on: day 0,1,2 day 14, 15, 16 day 42, 43, 44
	Prednisone 4 weeks 1.0 mg/kg/day 4 weeks 0.75 mg/kg/day 4 weeks 0.5 mg/kg/day daily dose to be decreased with 5 mg every 4 weeks until 10 mg/day	Azathioprine 2 mg/kg/day Prednisone 20 mg/day
Maintenance week 21-104	Cyclophosphamide 3-monthly 750 mg/m² iv	Azathioprine 2 mg/kg/day
	Prednisone Daily dose to be decreased with 5 mg every 4 weeks Until 10 mg/day	Prednisone week 21-28: 15 mg/day week 28-104: 10 mg/day
Maintenance week 105-208	Azathioprine 2 mg/kg/day (start at week 108)	Azathioprine 2 mg/kg/day
	Prednisone 10 mg/day	Prednisone 10 mg/day

immunosuppressive treatment and the benefits to be expected from this treatment. If renal function already is greatly impaired and the renal biopsy shows predominantly chronic, irreversible lesions, one should consider not increasing immunosuppressive treatment and accepting further deterioration of renal function. This approach is strengthened by the fact that results of renal replacement therapy in lupus patients are good.

Patients with renal disease associated with APS sometimes present with acute renal failure often accompanied by malignant hypertension (the so-called "catastrophic APS"). Plasmapheresis combined with adequate anticoagulation with heparin is probably the treatment of choice in this severe, life-threatening condition.

Table 22.9 Protocol for the administration of intravenous pulses of cyclophosphamide or methylprednisolone

Cyclophosphamide infusion
(preferably during a 24-hour hospitalization)

0 hour	8 mg ondansetron dissolved in 50-100 ml saline in 15-30 min iv
30 min	iv MESNA (2-mercaptoethanesulfonate): 20% of the required cyclophosphamide dose in 50-100 ml saline in 15-30 min
	iv cyclophosphamide (standard dose 750 mg/m^2, for creatinine clearances below 40 ml/min the dose is reduced to 500 mg/m^2) in 100 ml saline in 30-60 min
	start of posthydration: 3 liters 2.5% glucose/0.45% NaCl infused over 24 hours
4 hour	iv MESNA: 20% of the cyclophosphamide dose in 50-100 ml saline in 15-30 min
8 hour	iv MESNA: 20% of the cyclophosphamide dose in 50-100 ml saline in 15-30 min

1) When cyclophosphamide is given on an outpatient basis, administer MESNA at 1/2, 3 and 6 hours, give 1 liter of glucose/saline as posthydration, and instruct the patient to drink at least 2 liters at home
2) Do not administer a glucose 5% solution, as this may lead to hyponatremia secondary to inappropriate ADH secretion induced by cyclophosphamide
3) In case of fluid retention, administer furosemide
4) In case of persistent or recurrent vomiting, repeat the administration of ondansetron, or administer metoclopramide (10-20 mg iv or 20 mg as suppository)

Methylprednisolone infusion

Check before administration serum potassium which should be > 3.5 mmol/l, if below, correct this before starting the infusion

Methyl-prednisolone (MP) has to be dissolved in the available solvent, and diluted in 50-100 ml saline. The infusion is given slowly iv over 1 hour

Blood pressure should be measured before and after infusion

1) Advise the patient to restrict salt intake on the day of infusion and the days thereafter
2) Fluid retention during the MP pulse therapy resolves spontaneously within a few days. It is seldom necessary to prescribe diuretics

End-stage renal failure

End-stage renal failure (ESRF) develops in approximately 20% of patients with lupus nephritis, mainly in patients with a proliferative form of lupus nephritis (WHO class III or IV). The mean interval between reaching ESRF and onset of renal symptoms is 5 years. A number of factors have been identified that increase the risk of developing ESRF. The major factors are elevated serum creatinine at onset, a histologic activity index of ≥ 12, chronicity index ≥ 3, and persistent disease activity. The results of dialysis treatment in lupus patients for both hemodialysis and peritoneal dialysis are as good as those for other patients, with a 5-year patient survival between 80 and 90%. In general, lupus disease activity declines significantly during dialysis treatment, even with minimized immunosuppression. Also, the results of kidney transplantation are good – comparable to those seen in patients with nonlupus glomerular disease. Lupus disease activity declines further after renal transplantation, and lupus nephritis seldom recurs in the renal transplant.

Oral contraception

Epidemiologic and experimental animal studies suggest that estrogens may unmask or activate lupus disease activity. Also, estrogen replacement therapy in postmenopausal women is associated with a small increase in the incidence of SLE. Therefore, concerns have been raised about prescribing oral contraceptives (OC) to women with SLE. Indeed, in anecdotal reports activation of SLE has been described during the use of estrogen-containing OC, especially in patients with lupus nephritis. However, this risk is lower with the currently used OCs containing progesterone and low doses of estrogens (mainly ethinyl-estradiol). Although prospective data are lacking, it seems prudent if oral contraception is requested, to prescribe an OC with a low dose of estrogens (≤ 30 μg/day). In a limited number of retrospective and prospective case-control studies the flare rate was in general identical in women taking OC and in controls. Therefore, it seems safe to prescribe low-estrogen OCs to women with inactive or clinically stable SLE, without a history of venous or arterial thrombosis. For patients with a history of thrombosis, with antiphopholipid antibodies in high titers, or with a nephrotic syndrome, the risks should be balanced against the benefits, and other forms of contraception should be considered. Finally, it has been suggested, but not proved, that OCs may protect against the development of avascular osteonecrosis and osteoporosis and may preserve ovarian function during CPM therapy.

Pregnancy

Fertility in lupus patients may be reduced, either due to autoimmune ovarian failure or to previous use of CPM. Depending on the cumulative dose and age, permanent amenorrhea may develop in up to 60% of the patients over 30 treated with CPM. The consequences of lupus during pregnancy for mother and fetus and the effects of pregnancy on lupus disease activity are rather complex and heterogeneous. It is therefore very difficult to formulate guidelines that will be applicable for individual patients. Therefore, in this section only general guidelines are given. Because of space limitations, the therapeutic options for the different conditions associated with pregnancy in lupus patients, are not discussed.

Pregnancy in SLE patients can lead to a number of problems: (1) exacerbation of the disease; (2) fetal loss; and (3) neonatal lupus.

Lupus disease flares during pregnancy

It is difficult to draw a definite conclusion on the impact of pregnancy on lupus disease activity since the available data do not present a consistent picture. In some studies the rate of exacerbation is not higher than in nonpregnant control patients, while others observed increased disease activity in 60% of the pregnant patients. As for patients with nonrenal lupus, the frequency of disease exacerbations in patients with lupus nephritis seems to depend on the activity of the disease at the time of conception. For those with inactive disease for at least 6 months, the flare rate ranges from 10-30%, while for those with active disease renal exacerbations may occur in up to 60%. More severe renal exacerbations may occur in patients with proliferative lupus nephritis (WHO class III or IV). Apart from disease exacerbations, patients with lupus nephritis have an increased risk of developing hypertension (40-60%) or preeclampsia (30%). These risks are even higher if the patient has an active renal disease and/or impaired renal function at conception and/or preexisting hypertension and/or antiphospholipid antibodies. Sometimes it is difficult to differentiate an exacerbation of lupus nephritis from preeclampsia. In general a flare of lupus nephritis is associated with an active urinary sediment (dysmorphic erythrocytes, erythrocyt casts), decreased levels of complement factors C3 and C4, and a rise in anti-dsDNA titer. These findings are in general not present in preeclampsia. The latter condition generally is accompanied by thrombocytopenia and elevated liver enzymes.

Fetal loss

The overall prevalence of fetal loss in SLE patients is two to three times higher than in the general population. Although initially an increased fetal loss was noted in patients with active lupus, this was not confirmed in more recent studies. In patients with active lupus nephritis, and especially in patients with antiphosphilipid antibodies or lupus anticoagulant, the risk of fetal loss is higher. In a recent analysis the overall incidence of fetal loss in SLE patients was 20%, while in SLE patients with antiphopholipid antibodies it was 59%. As expected, an impaired renal function (serum creatinine ≥ 150 μmol/l) and/or hypertension increases the risk of fetal loss, as in patients with other non-SLE renal diseases.

Neonatal lupus

This syndrome, which may develop in children of mothers with SLE, consists of cutaneous lupus manifestations, congenital heart block, and sometimes other systemic manifestations of lupus. It is associated with the presence of anti-SS-A (Ro) with or without anti-SS-B (La) antibodies. The overall prevalence of congenital heart block in children from anti-SS-A-positive mothers is 7.2%, while in the general population this figure is very low (0.005%). Therefore, lupus patients who want to become pregnant should be analyzed for anti-SS-A antibodies to anticipate frequent fetal surveillance during pregnancy and placement of a pacemaker in the newborn child.

Based on the above data it can be concluded that pregnancy is contraindicated in patients with active SLE nephritis, and/or a nephrotic syndrome, and/or uncontrolled hypertension, and/or a serum creatinine above 150 mmol/l. In lupus patients who want to become pregnant, the presence of antiphospholipid antibodies (anticardiolipin, anti-β_2-glycoprotein I), LAC, and anti-SS-A antibodies should be analyzed.

Suggested readings

Austin III HA, Muenz LR, Joyce KM, Antonovych TT, Balow JE. Diffuse proliferative lupus nephritis: identification of specific pathologic features affecting renal outcome. Kidney Int 1984;25:689-95.

Balow JE, Austin III HA, Muenz LR, et al. Effect of treatment of the evolution of renal abnormalities in lupus nephritis. N Engl J Med 1984;311:491-5.

Bansal VK, Beto JA. Treatment of lupus nephritis: a meta-analysis of clinical trials. Am J Kidney Dis 1997;29:193-9.

Berden JHM. Lupus nephritis. Nephrology Forum. Kidney Int 1997;52:538-58.

Berden JHM, Assmann KJM. Renal involvement in collagen vascular diseases and dysproteinemias. In: Schrier RW, ed. Atlas of kidney diseases. Philadelphia: Current Medicine, 1998, volume IV: chap.11, 11.1-11.31.

Boumpas DT, Austin III HA, Vaughan EmM, et al. Controlled trial of pulse methylprednisolone versus two regimens of pulse cyclophosphamide in severe lupus nephritis. Lancet 1992;340:741-5.

Churg J, Bernstein J, Glassock RJ. Lupus nephritis. In: Churg J, Bernstein J, Glassock RJ, eds. Renal diseases. Classification and atlas of glomerular diseases. 2nd ed. New York: Igaku-Shoin, 1995;151-80.

Gladman DD, Urowitz MB. Systemic lupus erythematosus, clinical features. In: Klippel JH, Dieppe PA, eds. Rheumatology. 2nd ed. London: Mosby, 1998;1.1-1.17.

Lewis EJ, Hunsicker LG, Shuäping LAN Ma, Rohde RD, Lachin JM. A controlled trial of plasmapheresis therapy in severe lupus nephritis. N Engl J Med 1992;326:1373-8.

Mojcik CF, Klippel JH. End-stage renal disease and systemic lupus erythematosus. Am J Med 1996;101:100-7.

Nossent JC, Swaak AJG, Berden JHM. Systemic lupus erythematosus: Analysis of disease activity in 55 patients with end-stage renal failure treated with hemodialysis or continous ambulatory peritoneal dialysis. Am J Med 1990;89:169-74.

Nossent JC, Swaak AJG, Berden JHM Systemic lupus erythematosus after renal transplantation: patient and graft survival and disease activity. Ann Int Med 1991;114:183-8.

Petri M, Robinson C. Oral contraceptives and systemic lupus erythematosus. Arthr Rheum 1997;40:797-803.

Tax WJM, Kramers C, van Bruggen MCJ, Berden JHM. Apoptosis, nucleosomes, and nephritis in systemic lupus erythematosus. Editorial review. Kidney Int 1995;48:666-73.

Ter Borg EJ, Horst G, Hummel EJ, Limburg PC, Kallenberg CGM. Predictive value of rises in anti-double-stranded DNA antibody levels for disease exacerbations in systemic lupus erythematosus: a long term prospective study. Arthr Rheum 1990;33:634-43.

CHAPTER

23

Amyloidosis

Jean-Paul Fermand

KEY POINTS

- Amyloidosis is not a single disease but a general term related to a group of disorders characterized by the extracellular deposition of protein in a unique fibrillar form.
- Several different proteins can be involved in the formation of amyloid fibrils; the present classification is based on the predominant protein in the structure of the amyloid. These can derive from normal proteins (such as serum amyloid A or β_2-microglobulin), from monoclonal immunoglobulins, or from variants of normal proteins (as in most hereditary amyloidosis).
- The different amyloid proteins are related to distinct clinical forms of amyloidosis. These are often characterized by a particular distribution of amyloid deposits in tissues and organs and by diverse associated disorders:
  - AL amyloidosis has fibrils derived from the light chain of immunoglobulins and can complicate most clonal B-cell diseases such as multiple myeloma;
  - AA amyloidosis derives from the acute phase reactant serum amyloid A protein and is associated with such long-standing inflammatory diseases as rheumatoid arthritis, especially the seronegative juvenile form, and chronic pyogenic infections;
  - β_2-microglobulin amyloidosis is most commonly seen as a long-term complication of hemodialysis, and is due to a greatly increased serum concentration of β_2-microglobulin of which the kidney is the only route of excretion, and current hemodialysis techniques remove only inadequate amounts.
- Diagnosis of amyloidosis relies on biopsy and the demonstration of particular staining characteristics with Congo red dye.
- The treatment of amyloidosis aims to reduce the supply of the respective fibril precursor in an attempt to prevent further amyloid deposition and to induce regression of existing deposits, thereby leading to an improvement of organ function. These objectives are presently achieved in only a few patients.
- Prognosis is poor, with a median survival in untreated AA amyloidosis of 5 years; there is a worse outcome in patients with AL amyloidosis. Renal failure and cardiac failure are the most common causes of death. If the underlying disease can be controlled, dialysis and/or transplantation may be beneficial.

Amyloidosis is the general term for a morphologic entity defined by visceral, extracellular deposition of a peculiar fibrillar protein material, the amyloid substance. First descriptions were made in the middle of the nineteenth century, notably by Rokitansky and Wirchow. Because of its relevant resistance to solution in physiologic solvents and to proteolytic digestion, amyloid remained poorly characterized until recently. The demonstration of solubility in distilled water has opened the way to the characterization of several (currently 18) different types. Amyloidosis may be either inherited or acquired, and the deposits may be widespread or localized. Clinical manifestations depend on the amount and distribution of the amyloid deposits and their effect on organ function.

Pathophysiology

Properties common to all amyloidoses

All amyloid substances have unique tinctorial and ultrastructural characteristics. On light microscopy, deposits have a homogeneous, amorphous, hyaline appearance, identification of which requires specific stains such as Congo red which stains faintly red and shows a characteristic apple-green birefringence under polarized light. Metachromasia is also observed with methyl and crystal violet.

Ultrastructural examination reveals amyloid to have a highly ordered and stable molecular organization composed of rigid, linear, nonbranching, aggregated fibrils consisting of two 3 nm wide filaments with a regular antiparallel β-pleated configuration perpendicular to the filament axis.

Several components of amyloid are common to all forms, notably amyloid P component, glycosaminoglycan, and apolipoprotein. Amyloid P component is derived from a serum glycoprotein (SAP). It is probably bound to the fibrils directly, and this accounts for the resistance of the fibrils to proteolysis. Glycosaminoglycans, particularly the basement membrane heparan sulfate proteoglycan, may be important for inducing and stabilizing the ß-pleated structure. Several apolipoproteins may be involved in amyloid fibrillogenesis, notably apoE which in its allelic form, apoE4, is a risk factor for Alzheimer's disease.

Classification

In spite of similarities in appearance and staining characteristics, amyloid is biochemically a very heterogeneous material. The fibrils differ in protein composition according to clinical type, and the different amyloidoses should be regarded as a group of "protein folding diseases." The present classification is based on the nature of the amyloid proteins which are either mutant, as in most familial forms, or of wild type (Tab. 23.1).

AL amyloid fibrils are derived from the N-terminal region of the monoclonal immunoglobulin (Ig) light chains, and consist of the whole or part of the variable (V_L) domain, although occasionally intact light chains are present. In contrast, the involvement of Ig heavy chains in AH amyloidosis is exceptional. AL amyloid light chains are most often of the λ isotype with a ratio of κ to λ of 1:3 (as compared to 3:2 in the normal state). In vitro, the proteolytic digestion of most light chains yields fibrils resembling amyloid, but, experimentally, light chains produce only typical fibrillar deposits if they have been derived from patients with amyloidosis. This suggests that important pathogenic factors, such as structure and/or specific affinity for extracellular structures, are intrinsic to the light chains involved in amyloidosis.

AL amyloid results from a complex process involving the initial formation of a pseudocrystalline nucleus followed by the addition of monomers leading to elongation of the fibrils. This contrasts with other forms of tissue deposition of immunoglobulins, notably monoclonal Ig deposition disease, where there is a disorganized amor-

Table 23.1 Classification of amyloidoses

Type	Precursor protein	Variant	Associated clinical syndrome
AA	SAA		Systemic secondary amyloidosis Familial Mediterranean fever Muckle Wells syndrome
AL	Ig light chain	Ak, Aλ	Immunoglobulinic, primary systemic amyloidosis Some localized amyloidosis
AH	Ig heavy chain		Idem
ATTR	Transthyretin	 Met 30 Ile 122	Senile amyloidosis Familial amyloid neuropathy (FAP) Familial amyloid cardiopathy
AApoAI	Apolipoprotein AI	Arg 26	Familial neuropathy (Iowa)
AGel	Gelsolin	Asn 187	Finnish hereditary amyloidosis
Acys	Cystatin C	GPn 688	Iceland-type hereditary amyloid angiopathy
Aβ	β-Amyloid-precursor protein (β-APP)	Gln 618	Alzheimer's disease Down's syndrome
$A\beta_2m$	β_2-Microglobulin		Uremic amyloidosis
AprP	Prion P (PrP)	Scrapie's protein	Prion diseases, Creutzfeld-Jacob disease and other spongiform encephalopathies
	Polypeptidic hormones:		
Cal	Procalcitonin		Localized amyloidosis (thyroid medullary carcinoma, heart, pancreas)
AANF	Natriuretic atrial factor		
AIAPP	Islet polypeptide		

(Adapted from Husby G. Nomenclature and classification of amyloid and amyloidoses. J Intern Med 1992;232:511-2.)

phous precipitation of monoclonal immunoglobulins, particularly along basement membranes. It is worthy of note that, the coexistence of the two types of deposits in a single patient is not rare.

AA amyloid derives from serum amyloid A (SAA) protein, which is associated with circulating high density lipoproteins (HDL3). It is an acute phase protein synthesized by hepatocytes in response to inflammation and mediated by cytokines such as interleukin-1, interleukin-6, and tumor necrosis factor. The function of serum amyloid A has not been identified. It is highly conserved among vertebrates and in most species is polymorphic. Susceptibility to AA amyloidosis might be related to particular highly "amyloidogenic" serum amyloid A amino acid sequences. Macrophages appear to play a key role in the processing of serum amyloid A to amyloid.

AA familial amyloidosis occurs in familial Mediterranean fever (FMF) and the Muckle Wells syndrome. The gene responsible for familial Mediterranean fever has been localized to chromosome 16 and encodes for a protein, marenostrin, which may be involved in the regulation of the expression of inflammatory related proteins.

The other hereditary amyloidoses are due to autosomal dominant inheritance of variant amylodogenic proteins (Tab. 23.1). Mutations in the protein transthyretin (TTR), a transport protein for thyroid hormone and vitamin A, are responsible for a number of familial amyloidoses. More than 50 mutations result in familial amyloidotic polyneuropathy, whereas substitution of isoleucine for valine at position 122 has been associated with a form of late-onset cardiac amyloid.

Aβ amyloid is found in the walls of cerebral vessels and in the core of senile plaques in patients with Alzheimer's disease. The β-protein derives from an amyloid precursor protein (β-APP), which is encoded on chromosome 21. Mutations of the gene cause Alzheimer's disease, but most familial cases are due to mutations of the genes coding for two other proteins, presenilin 1 and 2, which are associated with an increased production of a very amyloidogenic form of β-protein. These data suggest a close link between cerebral amyloidosis and the pathogenesis of the common sporadic form of Alzheimer's disease.

Uremic amyloidosis is associated with the deposition of β_2-microglobulin, the light chain of class 1 MHC antigens. β_2-microglobulin is only excreted by the kidney, and in renal failure the plasma concentration increases. It is not excreted to any extent by conventional hemodialysis, and the increased concentration results in deposition, particularly around joints and in synovial sheaths, giving rise to characteristic joint stiffness and carpal tunnel syndrome. The repeated exposure of blood to bioincompatible dialysis membranes may result in increased β_2-microglobulin production and therefore increased deposition in tissues such that nearly all hemodialysis patients receiving treatment for more than 10 years are symptomatic.

Several other types of amyloid are recognized, such as senile amyloidosis, but none are significantly more common in patients with renal disease.

Clinical findings

Amyloid deposits, whatever their composition, exert similar pathologic effects because of their physical presence, which causes disruption of normal tissue structure and function. The different forms of amyloidosis occur in various circumstances, and have characteristic tissue tropism that can cause protean clinical features.

Renal amyloidosis is usually manifest as urinary protein loss, often resulting in the nephrotic syndrome and associated with renal insufficiency. Even in advanced renal failure the kidney size usually is normal, frequently providing a clue to the underlying diagnosis. The proteinuria is commonly massive, with hypoproteinemia and edema even when renal function is severely impaired. Hematuria is rare, and hypertension is uncommon.

Amyloid deposition also occurs in the myocardium, commonly presenting with a rapid onset of congestive cardiac failure that responds poorly to therapy. There may be a dilated cardiomyopathy with impaired systolic function, or a constrictive cardiomyopathy. Less commonly there is involvement of the pericardium, valves, and coronary arteries. Echocardiography usually reveals asymmetric thickening of the interventricular septum with concentric thickening of the ventricular walls. An almost pathognomonic finding is increased myocardial echogenicity with a "granular sparkling" appearance.

Gastrointestinal involvement is often asymptomatic, but parenchymal and vascular deposits may result in obstruction, pseudotumors, perforation, bleeding, and malabsorption. Infiltration of the tongue may lead to macroglossia. Other intestinal symptoms such as dysphagia, gastroparesis, constipation, or diarrhea are most often due to amyloid involving the autonomic nervous system. Liver involvement is common and results in hepatomegaly but little impairment of function. Splenic amyloid rarely causes functional impairment.

Cutaneous manifestations result from infiltration of blood vessel walls or direct infiltration of the skin. Purpura and spontaneous ecchymoses, especially of the eyelids and flexural regions, are common and may be a result of increased fragility of cutaneous blood vessels, but also may be due to impaired coagulation as a consequence of the binding of calcium dependent clotting factors to amyloid. Dystrophic nails and alopecia have been reported.

Neurologic involvement occurs in both motor and sensory nerves as well as in the autonomic system. Clinical manifestations include a distal, symmetric, and progressive sensorimotor neuropathy that involves the lower limbs earlier and more severely than the upper limbs. Autonomic dysfunction includes disordered gastrointestinal motility, bladder dysfunction, impotence, abnormalities of sweating, and postural hypotension. Cranial nerve involvement is rare.

Many other organs may be involved, such as the respiratory tract, endocrine glands, synovial tissue, and para-articular structures (producing notably the carpal tunnel syndrome).

Clinical amyloidosis syndromes

The systemic amyloidoses characterized by multivisceral deposition of amyloid material exist in many forms, both inherited and acquired. Renal involvement occurs in both AL and AA amyloidosis, and patients with long-standing renal functional impairment develop a particular form of amyloidosis that frequently is referred to as "dialysis-related amyloidosis," but should more correctly be labelled uremic amyloidosis. It is due to the deposition of β_2-microglobulin in particular anatomic sites.

AL amyloidosis AL amyloidosis can complicate most clonal B-cell diseases, including up to 15% of patients with multiple myeloma and a much smaller proportion of those with Waldenstrom's macroglobulinemia, other lymphomas, and benign monoclonal gammopathies. Conversely, a minority of patients presenting with AL amyloidosis have an overt immunoproliferative disorder. Calculations of the incidence of myeloma depend on the criteria used for diagnosis and differentiation of AL amyloidosis on the basis of the presence or absence of myeloma which is frequently difficult and indeed artificial because the two disorders are both of plasma cell proliferation and have much overlap. From a practical point of view, AL amyloidosis without overt myeloma, in which the amyloid is almost exclusively responsible for the symptoms, usually is referred to as primary systemic amyloidosis.

A monoclonal immunoglobulin and/or light chain can be detected by immunoelectrophoresis and/or immunofixation in the serum or urine in about 90% of patients with AL amyloidosis. Moreover, a monoclonal plasma cell population synthesizing large amounts of free light chains can be demonstrated by immunofluorescence and by biosynthetic or immunoglobulin gene rearrangement studies in bone marrow samples of all patients, even if no monoclonal immunoglobulin can be detected in urine or serum, and the bone marrow reveals a normal percentage of plasma cells. This would suggest that "primary" amyloidosis is a plasma cell dyscrasia.

The median age at diagnosis of systemic AL amyloidosis is similar to that of myeloma, approximately 60 years. Men are more frequently affected than women. The initial symptoms frequently are weakness and weight loss, but the diagnosis usually is made only on investigation of specific organ dysfunction. Early recognition may become more frequent with the increased screening of urine and serum by electrophoresis.

The clinical manifestations of systemic AL amyloidosis are extremely polymorphic because virtually every organ except the brain can be involved. The kidney and the heart are predominantly affected. At the time of diagnosis approximately 50% of patients have a nephrotic syndrome, and 30% have symptomatic cardiac involvement. Autonomic and sensory neuropathy are also common findings. These and other presenting manifestations (such as easy bruising and macroglossia, which is almost pathognomonic) should prompt immunochemical investigation of serum and urine to detect monoclonal immunoglobulins or light chains.

AA amyloidosis Systemic AA amyloidosis can occur as a consequence of any inflammation resulting in a long-term sustained acute phase response. It was the first recognized form of amyloidosis, but is now relatively rare in the developed world. Currently the most common causes are inflammatory rheumatic diseases, such as rheumatoid arthritis, especially the seronegative juvenile form, and chronic inflammatory bowel diseases such as Crohn's disease. Commonly such chronic inflammatory processes have been present for 10 to 15 years before there is any clinical indication of a complicating amyloidosis.

The development of antibiotic and antituberculosis therapy has resulted in a marked reduction in chronic pyogenic infections such as bronchiectasis, osteomyelitis, and tuberculosis, and consequently there has been a parallel reduction in associated AA amyloidosis. This is true even in patients with a high risk of chronic infection, such as those with paraplegia and cystic fibrosis, because of the recognition of the need for prompt and effective treatment of any associated infection. AA amyloidosis with malignancy is rare but is a recognized complication of renal cell carcinoma.

The most common mode of presentation of AA amyloidosis is with nonselective proteinuria or renal insufficiency, and even in those who present with other manifestations, renal involvement is almost universal, and renal failure is the most common cause of death. Surprisingly, extensive deposits can be present without causing symptoms. Deposits in the thyroid and adrenal glands are well recognized and may cause functional impairment of these organs. Peripheral neuropathy, carpal tunnel syndrome, and macroglossia are frequent. Cardiac involvement is rarely extensive and almost never results in cardiac failure. AA amyloidosis, particularly if renal failure is present, has a poor prognosis; 50% of patients die within 5 years of diagnosis. Effective treatment of the underlying cause may lead to regression of the amyloid deposits.

Uremic amyloidosis This has been described most commonly, but not exclusively, in patients who have been treated by hemodialysis longer than 5 years. It most commonly presents as a carpal tunnel syndrome, which differs from the idiopathic form in that there is no predilection for females, those aged over 40 years, or the dominant hand. Patients may complain of arthralgia, particularly of the shoulders, hips, and knees, a destructive spondylarthropathy of the spine leading to compression fractures and paraplegia, subchondral bone cysts, trigger fingers, and subcutaneous tumors.

The main component of the amyloid deposits is β_2-microglobulin, which is significantly increased in renal failure and may be further increased by dialysis with a bioincompatible membrane.

Predisposing factors seem to be the duration of the uremia, duration of the dialysis, the age of the patient (elderly patients being more affected), and the membrane used in the artificial kidney. There is no evidence that any particular underlying renal disease predisposes to the condition.

Symptomatic improvement occurs following renal transplantation, but, as yet, there is no convincing evidence that there is significant reduction in the deposits of β_2-microglobulin amyloid.

Other forms of amyloidosis Renal involvement with amyloidosis of the AA type occurs in familial Mediterranean fever, an inherited disease of Sephardic Jews and Armenians. There are two recognized presentations. In the first, brief, episodic, febrile attacks of peritonitis, pleuritis, or synovitis associated with a dramatic increase in serum amyloid A protein and all acute phase reactants precede renal symptoms; in the second, renal involvement occurs first and may be the only manifestation. Colchicine is an effective treatment for this form of amyloidosis.

The Muckle Wells syndrome, characterized by progressive perceptive deafness, episodes of chills and fever, and urticaria, is associated with amyloidosis of the AA type mainly involving the kidney. Other hereditary systemic amyloidoses and senile amyloidosis rarely involve the kidney.

Diagnostic procedures

The diagnosis of amyloidosis can be made only after tissue biopsy. The most appropriate biopsy is of an affected organ, but this is not without risk, particularly from bleeding. This has prompted alternatives, such as fine needle aspiration of subcutaneous fat, or biopsy of rectum, gum, labia, or salivary gland. To be successful these biopsies must contain submucosal vessels in which early deposits are localized. These samples may produce positive results in up to 80% of patients with systemic amyloidosis.

The histologic diagnosis depends most commonly on pathognomonic red-green birefringence on polarization microscopy following Congo red staining. Small deposits may be missed, and electron microscopy may be necessary. Immunohistochemical identification of amyloid protein can be used as a marker for deposition. Treatment of sections with permanganate prior to Congo red staining may allow discrimination of AL from AA amyloid. Determination of type is, however, more commonly performed by immunohistochemistry. After a positive biopsy result is obtained, the type of amyloidosis frequently is suspected from the clinical context. Otherwise, since AL amyloidosis is the most common type, a search for a clonal B-cell disorder is mandatory, at least by performing immunochemical studies of serum and urine.

Radiolabeled serum amyloid protein rapidly and specifically localizes to amyloid deposits in vivo in proportion to the quantity of amyloid present, thereby allowing an evaluation of the extent of deposition by scintigraphy. This technique may be particularly useful in the evaluation of the response to treatment.

Renal amyloidosis Amyloid usually is detected in the glomeruli, small arteries, and arterioles, and only rarely is peritubular. In the glomeruli the mesangium is most commonly involved, and deposits may be present to such an extent as to result in a differential diagnosis of nodular diabetic glomerulosclerosis or mesangiocapillary glomerulonephritis. Congo red staining produces a characteristic apple-green birefringence when viewed under crossed polarized light. Immunohistochemistry may be helpful in patients with AA and β_2-microglobulin amyloidosis, but fewer than 50% of patients with AL amyloidosis will demonstrate the presence of λ chains. Electronmicroscopy characteristically shows irregularly oriented, nonbranching fibrils 7-10 nm in diameter.

Treatment

In general current treatment regimens for patients with amyloidosis have been disappointing. Three possibilities exist: reduction in the production in amyloid precursors; inhibition of aggregation of the amyloid proteins; and dissolution of formed amyloid. At present there is some success with reducing amyloid precursors in AA amyloidosis, particularly in familial Mediterranean fever, and following transplantation there is certainly clinical improvement in β_2-microglobulin amyloidosis, although there is as yet no convincing evidence for the reabsorption of formed amyloid deposits. The treatment of AL amyloidosis remains disappointing. In most patients treatment remains supportive because no specific therapy is available.

In AL amyloidosis, cytotoxic therapy directed at the plasma cell clone to reduce light chain production is logical in patients with myeloma but is questionable in patients in whom the malignant nature of the underlying proliferation is uncertain. However, therapy with melphalan and prednisolone has been shown to prolong survival in patients with primary amyloidosis. In such patients prognosis is related to the main clinical syndrome at presentation; the median survival was shortest for those with obvious cardiac involvement (5 months), longer for those with a presentation of nephrotic syndrome (16 months), and for those presenting with peripheral neuropathy survival was 34 months. On treatment with melphalan and prednisolone a significant reduction in the concentration of monoclonal immunoglobulin is the most favorable prognostic indicator and is achieved in about one-third of patients, usually within 1 year. The total duration of treatment should not exceed 2 years because of the risk of developing leukemia with prolonged exposure to alkylating agents. High-dose melphalan followed by peripheral blood stem-cell rescue frequently produces good, even complete, immunochemical remission, but this must be balanced against the risk of mortality and morbidity which, at present, limits this therapy to selected young patients. In addition, it is too soon to assess the long-term effects and the effect on amyloid-related organ dysfunction.

The AA amyloidosis of familial Mediterranean fever responds to colchicine. The prophylactic administration of colchicine, at a minimal daily dose of 1 mg, not only prevents the occurrence of febrile attacks, it also can prevent the appearance and/or worsening of renal amyloid deposition. In some patients the nephrotic syndrome has regressed following the introduction of colchicine. This has prompted the introduction of colchicine in the management of patients with other forms of AA amyloidosis, notably rheumatoid disease, but as yet there are only anecdotal reports of a beneficial effect. The treatment of secondary AA amyloidosis is directed at the underlying cause. Successful treatments of chronic infection and immunosuppression for rheumatic diseases have been associated with regression of amyloid deposits in a few patients, but in general the response is disappointing.

In patients with β_2-microglobulin associated amyloidosis there may be a beneficial effect of altering the dialysis regimen by the introduction of a more biocompatible membrane, such as polysulfone or by high-flux hemodiafiltration. The results, however, are disappointing. There is no evidence that either will result in an efficient and complete removal of the daily production of β_2-microglobulin (approximately 20 mg) although there may be symptomatic improvement. Similarly, following transplantation there is a prompt reduction in symptoms but, as yet, no convincing evidence for significant removal of deposited amyloid. It is possible that the beneficial effect is due to the effect of prednisolone reducing the inflammation which surrounds the deposits together with the reduction in plasma concentration of β_2-microglobulin, which occurs promptly following the restoration of satisfactory renal function.

Whatever the amyloid type, new therapeutic strategies are required to prevent the synthesis of amyloid precursors, prevent the deposition of amyloid fibrils, and dissolve deposits. The results with dimethyl sulphoxide (DMSO), an amyloid solvent, have been disappointing. However, a new novel agent, 4'-iodo-4'deoxydoxorubicin (I-DOX), which can interfere with heparan sulfate-stimulated fibril aggregation may prove promising. It is to be hoped that with increased understanding of the mechanism of amyloid fibril deposition new more specific therapeutic interventions will develop.

Prognosis

In AA amyloidosis the median survival is about 5 years in untreated patients. If the underlying inflammatory condition can be eradicated or controlled, the outlook improves. The plasma concentration of serum amyloid A protein provides a useful marker to the degree of inflammation present.

AL amyloidosis has a worse prognosis than the AA form with a median survival which is between 12 and 15 months. In patients presenting with cardiac failure the median survival is only approximately 6 months. Cytotoxic therapy improves the outlook, but therapeutic regimens are still being refined and evaluated.

Renal replacement therapy by dialysis and/or transplantation can prolong survival in patients with either AA or AL amyloidosis. Prognosis depends on the extent of extrarenal amyloid deposition, particularly in the myocardium. In myeloma-associated amyloidosis, the myeloma may be sustained in remission, and the patient may survive for a prolonged period. Exact statistics are not available owing to the small number of patients and the heterogeneity of the condition. Following transplantation, prolonged survival may occur in AA amyloidosis, particularly if the underlying disease is controlled. The transplanted kidney may itself become involved in amyloid deposition; again; experience is limited, and therefore the overall prognosis is, as yet, undetermined.

Suggested readings

Bergethon PR, Sabin TD, Lewis D, et al. Improvement in the polyneuropathy associated with familial amyloidotic polyneuropathy after liver transplantation. Neurology 1996;47:944-51.

Comenzo RL, Vosburg E, Simms RW, et al. Dose intensive melphalan with blood stem cell support for the treatment of AL amyloidosis: one year follow-up in five patients. Blood 1996;88:2801-6.

Falk RH, Comenzo RL, Skinner M. The systemic amyloidoses. N Eng J Med 1997;337:898-909.

Gertz MA, Kyle RA. Secondary systemic amyloidosis: response and survival in 64 patients. Medicine 1991;70:246-56.

Geygo F, Arakawa M. β_2-microglobulin-associated amyloidosis. J Intern Med 1992;232:531-2.

Gianni L, Bellotti V, Gianni AM, Merlini G. New drug therapy of amyloidosis: resorption of AL-type deposits with 4'-iodo-4'-deoxydoxorubicin with amyloid fibrils. Blood 1995;86:855-61.

Gillmore JD, Hawkins PN, Pepys MB. Amyloidosis: a review of recent diagnostic and therapeutic developments. Brit J Haematol 1997;99:245-56.

Glenner CG. Amyloid deposits and amyloidosis: the β-fibrilloses. New Eng J Med 1980;302:1283-92 and 1333-43.

Hawkins PN, Vigushin DM, Richardson S, et al. Evaluation of 100 cases of systemic AL amyloidosis by serum amyloid P component scintigraphy. In: Kisilevesky R, Benson MD, Frangione B, Gauldie J, Muckle TJ, Young ID, eds. Amyloid and amyloidosis, Pearl River, New York: Parthenon Publishing, 1993:209-11.

Kisilevsky R, Lemieux LJ, Fraser PE, et al. Arresting amyloidosis in vitro using small-molecule anionic sulphonates or sulphates: implications for Alzheimer's disease. Nature Medicine 1995;1:143-8.

Kyle RA, Gertz MA. Primary systemic amyloidosis: clinical and laboratory features in 474 cases. Semin Hematol 1995;32:45-59.

Kyle RA, Gertz MA, Greipp PR, et al. A trial of three regimens for primary amyloidosis: Colchicine alone, Melphalan and Prednisolone, and Melphalan, Prednisolone and Colchicine. New Eng J Med 1997;336:1202-7.

Livneh A, Zemer D, Langevitz P, et al. Colchicine in the treatment of AA and AL amyloidosis. Semin Arthritis Rheum 1993;23:206-14.

Pascali E. Diagnosis and treatment of primary amyloidosis. CRC Crit Rev Oncol Hematol 1995;19:149-81.

Scheuner D, Eckman C, Jensen M, et al. Secreted amyloid beta-protein similar to that in the senile plaques of Alzheimer's disease is increased in vivo by the presenilin 1 and 2 mutations linked to familial Alzheimer's diaease. Nature Medicine 1996;2:864-70.

CHAPTER

24

Infection-related glomerular diseases

Rashad S. Barsoum

KEY POINTS

- We now know that pratically every known glomerular pathologic process may be induced by infection, depending on its nature, site, duration, and severity as well as on the host's age, gender, ethnic and genetic backgrounds, immune responsiveness and comorbid conditions.
- Although some viral glomerulopathies have been attributed to a direct cytopathic effect on glomerular cells, the overwhelming majority of infection-induced glomerulophaties are due to immune reactions. Four principal mechanisms may be incriminated: immune-complex depositions; direct complement-lymphocyte and endothelial-activation.
- The more common clinical profiles are: occult glomerulopathy, acute glomerulopathies (including acute nephritic syndrome, renal vasculitis, hemolytic-uremic syndrome, and rapidly progressive glomerulonephritis), and chronic glomerulopathies.
- Almost all forms of primary glomerulonephritis are reproduced by infection. Chronicity and progression of glomerular pathology are usually the exception rather than the rule. It is often possible to identify compounding pathogenetic factors that lead to chronicity.
- Modern medical and surgical technology can eradicate most infections that cause glomerular disease; a few challenges remain with viral infections as HIV, HCV, and HBV. Control of infection cures most of the glomerular complications.

Modern techniques have made it possible to interpret ancient scripts in the Hippocratic collections as a typical portrayal of malarial nephropathy, and this sets the starting point in the history of infection-related glomerulopathies at about the year 400 BC. More than 20 centuries later, a similar signal was made in the clinical synopsis of scarletina, providing the first notion about the relation of glomerulonephritis to a streptococcal infection. These two infections remain as prototypes of infection-related glomerulopathy in the southern and northern hemispheres, respectively.

More concrete global information became available during the later half of the nineteenth century, shortly after Richard Bright had made his classic description of glomerulonephritis. Working in the tropics, Atkinson (1884) provided convincing clinical evidence that malaria might be a potential cause of Bright's disease in Africa, and contemporary observations in Europe by Rokitanski, based on over 30 000 autopsies, showed that bacterial endocarditis was associated with distinct glomerular lesions. It took another half-century to establish the epidemiologic significance of streptococcal infections as being the principal cause of nephritic syndrome, and of malaria as the major cause of secondary nephrotic syndrome worldwide. The northern and southern lines continued to expand over the years, ending with long lists of biologic agents that may cause glomerular disease. We now know that practically every known glomerular pathologic process may be induced by infection, depending on its nature, site, duration, and severity as well as on the host's age, gender, ethnic and genetic backgrounds, immune responsiveness and comorbid conditions. With the wide spectrum of glomerular diseases caused by infection as it is, and in order to avoid unnecessary repetition, the reader is referred to other chapters in this text for detailed clinical and laboratory descriptions of the individual glomerular syndromes.

Etiopathogenesis

Although some viral glomerulopathies have been attributed to a direct cytopathic effect on glomerular cells, the overwhelming majority of infection-induced glomerulopathies are due to immune reactions. Four principal mechanisms may be incriminated: immune-complex deposition; direct complement-; lymphocyte -; and endothelial-activation.

Immune complexes

Several antigens may be involved in initiating the immune response:

- *intrinsic microbial antigens*, which may be parts of the core, envelope, or nonstructural viral protein, bacterial cytoplasmic or cell wall protein, or a parasitic tegument, gut-, or egg-antigen;
- endogenous host antigens released as a result of infection-mediated tissue injury;
- combination of the above, where microbial structures combine with host's proteins to form the offending antigens;
- idiotypic antigens, the outcome of changes in the configuration of the variable portions of immunoglobulin molecules that no longer remain recognized as "self".

The immune response to all these antigenic challenges is fairly standard. They are recognized first by the antigen presenting cells (APCs), which vary according to the site of infection. Many of these have a phagocytic potential, which leads to internalization of the antigen, which is subsequently catabolized by lysozymes. This mechanism is of fundamental importance in the clearance of large particulate antigens as those of fungal and parasitic infections. Certain small parasites (e.g., *Leishmania*) can override this mechanism as their means of survival.

Many APCs are also able to produce toxic cytokines that help in the elimination of infection, e.g., interferons with viral diseases. However, the major role of the antigen presenting cell is to process the antigen, expressing it on its surface along with the major histocompatibility complex (MHC) in a way that makes it readable by the T lymphocytes. The CD8 cytotoxic cells recognize antigens presented with Class I while the CD4 T-helper cells read antigens presented with Class II MHC markers. Quiescent T-helper cells, called Th0, are activated by this contact, and are under the strong influence of the antigen-presenting cell cytokines. They subsequently proliferate and differentiate into either Th1 or Th2 cells, depending on the predominant initial cytokine released by the antigen presenting cell – IL-1 or IL-12, respectively. The latter also activates the natural killer cells (NKC) as a part of the innate system of immunity.

Th1 cells further proliferate under the influence of IL-2 released by active Th0 cells, as well as by their own activity (autocrine secretion). They also secrete TNF-α, which upregulates the antigen-presenting cell, and IL-6, which further propagates the effects of IL-1. Interleukin 2 upregulates the already active CD8 cells, as well as certain B-lymphocyte clones, thus promoting the secretion of immunoglobulins, mainly IgM, IgG_2, and IgG_3. Thus, Th1 cells are proinflammatory, representing the angry side of the immune reaction.

Th2 cells, on the other hand, tend to be immune-modulatory. Their role is more prominent in the later phases of immune activation, leading to either cure, on one hand, or chronic infection on the other. Their main cytokines are IL-4, IL-5, and IL-10, which switch the B-lymphocyte proliferation in the direction of clones that preferentially secrete blocking antibodies as IgG_1 and IgG_4, or low-complement affinity antibodies as IgA. Interleukin-10 provides a negative feedback to the antigen-presenting cell as a part of Th2 immune modulating role (Fig. 24.1).

Infection-associated immune complexes are usually formed in the circulation. They tend to be trapped in different tissues, depending on their physical properties and the presence of specific receptors. In the kidney, the latter are located on all glomerular cells, particularly the mesangial – hence the localization of most immune-complex glomerulopathies associated with infection. However, under specific conditions, the immune complexes may be formed in situ, because the antigens and antibodies combine only while in the subepithelial plane, leading to membranous nephropathy. The injury induced by circulating immune complexes is attributed mainly to complement activation via the classic pathway, ultimately leading to the formation of the terminal complex C5-9 (membrane attack complex, MAC). Although the latter often is cited as inducing T-cell membrane injury, this is seen mostly in the red cells rather than in the capillary endothelium. To the latter, it is a potent activator leading to the release of proinflammatory cytokines and growth factors known to be associated with

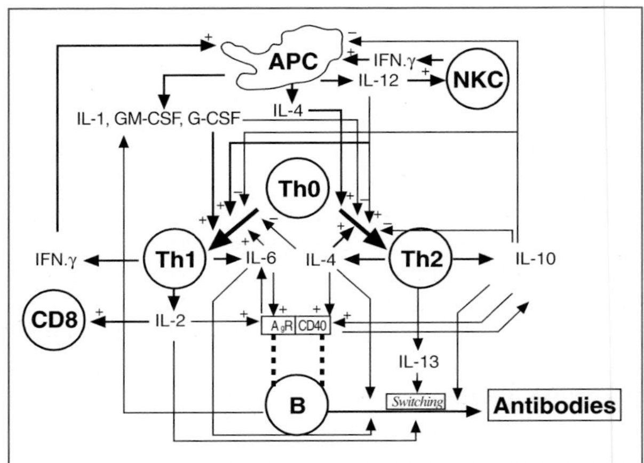

Figure 24.1 Broad lines of the immune response to infection. (APC = antigen presenting cell; Th = T-helper lymphocyte; B= B-lymphocyte, dotted lines indicate relevant receptors for antigen [AgR] or interleukins [CD40]; NKC = natural killer cell; CD8= cytotoxic lymphocyte; IL = interleukin; IFN = interferon; G- and GM-CSF = granulocyte- and granulocyte-monocyte colony stimulating factors respectively.)

glomerulonephritis. The mechanism of glomerular injury in membranous nephropathy is less well understood, but it is also associated with the formation of membrane attack complex, probably due to local complement activation.

Direct complement activation

Some bacteria, e.g., *Streptococci*, *Staphylococci*, and *Salmonella* are innately able to activate the alternate complement pathway directly, leading to consumption of C_3 without involvement of the early complement components as C_4 and C_{1q}. These conditions often are associated with subendothelial glomerular immune deposits, formed mainly of C_3 with little or no immunoglobulins. The histopathologic response usually is florid, with diffuse glomerular proliferation and infiltration with transit inflammatory cells as monocytes, lymphocytes, eosinophils, and neutrophils. When the latter predominate, the glomerular lesion is often described as being "exudative". Electron microscopy shows the subendothelial deposits, as well as large subepithelial "humps" sitting over cracks in the basement membrane.

Direct lymphocyte activation

Several viral agents are known to be lymphotropic, leading to immune deficiency (e.g., HIV, CMV), oncogenic (e.g., EBV, HTLV), or to cause persistent upregulation (e.g., HCV). The latter generates a clone of hyperactive lymphocytes that may be expressed in many ways, including the formation of immune complexes with viral antigens or with antiidiotypic antibodies, cryoglobulinemia, and ultimately lymphoproliferative disorders.

A similar scenario may be generated by infection with bacteria, e.g., certain strains of streptococci and pneumococci, which produce "superantigens" that directly activate the T-cells by combining with MHC Class II antigens and other non-antigen-binding receptors. The resulting glomerular injury is typical of mesangial immune complex deposition, yet without (or with minimal) complement activation.

Direct endothelial activation

Certain bacterial antigens are able to attach and activate endothelial receptors without any antibody formation or complement activation. This leads to massive endothelial injury, release of proinflammatory and vasoactive mediators, activation of coagulation and secondary microangiopathic hemolytic anemia. Notorious bacterial antigens associated with this syndrome are the Shiga-like verocytotoxins released from *E. coli* strains 0157:H7, 103:H2, 0111, *Shigella dysenteriae* type 1, *Salmonella typhi, Campylobacter jejuni, Streptococcus pneumoniae, and Yersinia pseudotuberculosis.*

Clinical findings

The clinical spectrum of infection-associated glomerulopathies is very broad, extending all the way from mild or subclinical disease at one end to acute and chronic renal failure at the other. In between, there are different acute

and chronic presentations that often overlap, and that vary in severity according to agent and host factors, some of which have been outlined above. The following is a brief account of the more common clinical profiles.

Occult glomerulopathy

This is undoubtedly the most common pattern of glomerular injury associated with infection (Tab. 24.1). An insignificant mesangial proliferative lesion, often with immune deposits including microbial antigens, may be the only expression of renal involvement. This may be associated with variable tubulointerstitial disease that usually dominates the clinical picture and determines the prognosis.

Patients with isolated mesangial proliferation often are entirely asymptomatic. The renal complication usually is spotted by routine urinalysis that may show microhematuria, mild proteinuria, and cylindruria. Renal function is preserved. In the occasional cases where renal biopsy was obtained, or autopsy done, the glomerular lesions were mostly focal or axial, with immune complex deposits comprising IgM, little IgG, and complement. Spontaneous clearance of the urinary abnormality is the rule upon control of the infection. However, little is known about the fate of the histologic lesions because longitudinal studies are not available and, indeed, may be ethically unjustified.

Glomerular involvement is also silent in patients with predominant tubulointerstitial disease; its faint tune is lost within the noise of the primary infection and acute interstitial nephritis. It is rarely identified clinically, needs no treatment, and does not seem to alter the prognosis.

Table 24.1 Infections associated with occult glomerulopathy

Viral	BK papovirus, Coxsackie B4, Dengue**, Echovirus, Hantavirus**, herpes simplex*, JC virus, measles*, mumps, Parvo B19*, varicella, Yellow fever
Mycoplasma	*M. pneumoniae**
Bacterial	*Brucella**, Gonococci, *Klebsiella***, *Leptospira***, *Legionella*, *Listeria*, Meningococci, *M. tuberculosis*** and *lepri**, Pneumococci*, *P. pyoceaneus*** and *pseudomallei***, *Salmonella**, *Yersinia*
Fungal	*Candida***, *Histoplasma***
Parasitic	*Echinococcus**, *Filaria**, *Leishmania***, *Schistosoma hematobium***, *Strongyloides*, *Toxoplasma*, *Trichinella**, *Trypanosoma*

* Overt glomerular syndromes have occasionally been described.
** Tubulointerstitial lesions usually supervene.

Acute glomerulopathies

There are four notorious acute clinical presentations of infection-associated glomerulopathy: the acute nephritic, the vasculitic, the hemolytic uremic, and the rapidly progressive glomerulonephritis syndromes.

Acute nephritic syndrome

This is the most classic presentation of postinfectious glomerulonephritis, initially and most extensively studied in relation to group A hemolytic streptococcal infections of the pharynx in the north, or of the skin in the tropics. Only certain streptococcal strains that contain an "M" protein in their cell walls can induce glomerular pathology – hence the name "nephritogenic strains." Of many candidate antigens studied, the "pre-absorbing antigen" (PAAg), the "nephritis strain-associated protein" (NSAP), and the closely related "nephritis-plasmin-binding protein" (NPBP) are most likely incriminated. When combined with their respective antibodies, these antigens form immune complexes with the right physical properties that favor their glomerular deposition. In addition, some of these antigens may lead to the formation of antibodies that cross-react with the glomerular basement membrane proteins or cells. The antibodies they provoke may initiate an idiotype-antiidiotype cascade that leads to glomerular injury. In addition, streptococcal antigens may directly activate lymphocytes (as superantigens) or the alternative complement pathway.

The acute nephritic syndrome can complicate other bacterial (Tab. 24.2) and viral infections. Of the latter, EBV (infectious mononucleosis), measles and mumps have been most often reported. Acute nephritis has also been described with *Mycoplasma pneumoniae* infection, falciparum malaria, trichinosis, urinary schistosomiasis and bancroftian filariasis.

The clinical syndrome is characterized by the triad of typical urinary changes, salt and water retention, and constitutional manifestations. The patient is usually ill, with low-grade pyrexia, headaches, back and loin aches, shortness of breath, and poor appetite. Salt and water retention manifests by facial puffiness and generalised edema, volume-dependent hypertension and mostly dilutional anemia. The urine volume is reduced, and it becomes typically "smoky." It keeps a fairly high specific gravity, contains mild to moderate amounts of protein, of the order of 1-3 g/24 hours, and the sediment shows many dysmorphic red cells, leucocytes and red cell casts. Mild to moderate azotemia mirror the impairment of glomerular filtration, and serum electrolytes may reflect an acute renal insufficiency. Serum complement, particularly C_3, is moderately reduced, and may be taken as a clinical indicator of continued immune complex deposition.

Renal biopsy shows a diffuse proliferative glomerulonephritis in which mesangial, endothelial and epithelial cells usually participate (Fig. 24.2, see Color Atlas). Transit inflammatory cells, including neutrophils, monocytes (and eosinophils, particularly in certain parasitic infections as filariasis) infiltrate the mesangium, and spill into the Bowman's capsule as well as the periglomerular interstitium. Electron microscopy usually shows typical subepithelial "humps" often overlying cracks in the basement membrane. Deposits are also seen in the mesangium or underneath the endothelium.

Acute renal failure, hypertensive encephalopathy and left ventricular failure are the major complications which happen in 5% of patients during the peak of glomerular inflammation. These occur mostly in patients whose renal lesion shows a prominent vasculitic component (fibrinoid necrosis) or those who progress to crescentic glomerulonephritis.

Otherwise, the disease is fairly benign, with spontaneous recovery in 95% of the children and 80% of adults. Parameters of follow-up include resolution of signs and symptoms, regression of proteinuria and hematuria, and restoration of normal serum C3 concentration. At least in the majority of children, there is no evidence of significant long-term consequences. This may not be the case in adults, where persistent mesangial hyperplasia may be associated with chronic renal disease many years later.

Renal vasculitis

Infections may be associated with vasculitis in several ways:

Table 24.2 Bacterial infections causing the acute nephritic syndrome

Clinical syndrome	Causative agents
Pharyngitis	Group A beta-haemolytic streptococci
Pneumonia	Streptococci, pneumococci
Osteomyelitis	Streptococci, *Staph. aureus*
Impetigo	Group A beta-haemolytic streptococci
Infected scabies	Group A beta-haemolytic streptococci
Bacterial endocarditis	
Acute	*Staph. aureus*
Subacute	*Strept. viridans, mitis, mutans, beta-* and *alpha- hemolyticus; Staph. albus* and *epidermidis; Enterococcus, Gonococcus, Ps. aeruginosa, Coxiella burnetii*
Ventriculo-atrial shunts[1]	*Staph. albus, epidermidis, aureus, Diphtheroids, L. monocytogenes, Serratia, B. subilitis, Peptococcus, B. cereus, P. acnes, Ps. aeruginosa*
Visceral abscess[2]	*Staph. aureus, Ps. aeruginosa, E. coli, Proteus mirabilis*
Tropical fevers	
Enterica	*S. typhi, S. paratyphi A, C*
Weil's disease	*L. icterohemorrhagica*
Infected wounds	MRS strains

[1] Also ventriculovenous and ventriculoperitoneal shunts for the treatment of obstructive hydrocephalus.
[2] Intra-abdominal, intrathoracic and also dental, maxillary sinus abscesses.

- *direct invasion of the vascular walls*. Examples include *salmonella, leptospira* and *rickettsia*, which can be recovered in cultures obtained from the typical skin eruptions. *Salmonella* antigens can be recovered from the exudative glomerular lesions, and leptospires can be seen in the renal interstitium and peritubular capillaries. Hepatitis B core antigen has been demonstrated in the walls of intermediate and small arteries in patients with polyarteritis nodosa as a complication of this infection;
- *immune complex associated vasculitis*. This occurs with many exanthematous bacterial and viral diseases. Of particular importance in this respect are the cryoglobulin-associated infections (Tab. 24.3) which lead to typical purple papular lesions noticed mostly in the lower limbs. Raynaud's phenomenon and mononeuritis multiplex are often associated in severe cases. Distinctive of this type is the remarkable consumption of the early serum complement components (measured as C_4 and C_{1q}), that may be reported as "undetectable" by routine laboratory techniques;
- *ANCA (anti-neutrophil cytoplasmic antibody)-associated vasculitis. Staphylococcus* aureus sinus infection is known to precipitate Wegener's granulomatosis (cANCA positive), while several other infections (e.g. beta-hemolytic streptococci, HBV, falciparum malaria) may precipitate pANCA-positive vasculitis. The exact role of infection as a neutrophil activator in the presence of anti-neutrophil antibodies is uncertain, but it seems to involve an exaggerated release of reactive oxygen radicals.

The clinicopathologic expression of vasculitis is described in more detail elsewhere (Chap. 20). One important feature of infection-associated vasculitis is that it cannot be renal-limited. A skin eruption, myalgias, arthralgias, pyrexia and/or a flu like illness usually hallmarks the onset of the renal lesion. Bloody sputum or a nasal bleed may be the clue to the diagnosis of Wegener's granulomatosis. Pulmonary vasculitis may be misdiagnosed as a nonspecific concomitant chest infection. Severe anemia may suggest a thrombotic microangiopathy.

Hematuria is invariable, though often microscopic. Mild to moderate proteinuria; red and granular casts are usually seen in the urinary sediment. Renal function may be impaired; acute renal failure may occur in severe cases, when there is massive glomerular fibrinoid necrosis or extensive crescent formation. Serum complement is reduced in the immune-complex mediated types, normal in ANCA-associated forms and variable according to the causative agent with direct vascular invasion.

Table 24.3 Main infections associated with cryoglobulinemic nephropathy

Viral	HCV, HBV, HIV
Bacterial	Bacterial endocarditis, "shunt nephritis", visceral abscess, leprosy
Parasitic	Schistosomiasis

The distinctive histologic feature is focal glomerular necrosis (Fig. 24.2, see Color Atlas), which may be associated with perivascular infiltration, capillary thrombosis and/or crescent formation, depending on the etiology. Patients with cryoglobulinemia may show characteristic casts in their renal tubules. Immunofluorescence shows a plethora of immunoglobulins, complement and fibrin in the immune-complex mediated types, while only fibrin may be seen in the ANCA-associated forms.

Hemolytic-uremic syndrome

The endothelial injury characteristic of the hemolytic uremic syndrome (HUS) is dominated by a widely spread thrombotic microangiopathy that combines hemolytic anemia with thrombocytopenia and acute renal failure. The infection-associated form of this disease usually follows an acute infective bloody diarrhoeal illness (hence the term D+, which carries a better prognosis). The diagnosis is confirmed by finding fragmented forms of red cells in the peripheral blood, together with moderate thrombocytopenia.

The renal lesions in hemolytic uremic syndrome are mostly glomerular in children and arterial in adolescents. The former are dominated by endothelial swelling, widening of the subendothelial space which gives a double contour appearance, and the formation of intralumenal thrombi. Mesangial broadening and proliferation may occur. The arterial lesions are mostly seen in the interlobular arteries which exhibit intimal edema and myointimal cell proliferation. This process may result in acute tubular or cortical necrosis. The salient feature by immunofluorescence is the deposition of fibrin along the glomerular capillary walls and in the arterial thrombi. Granular deposits of C3 and immunoglobulin M may be observed.

Rapidly progressive glomerulonephritis

Two forms of rapidly progressive glomerulonephritis may be associated with infection: the exudative and the crescentic.

Exudative glomerulonephritis This is a form of proliferative glomerulonephritis characterized by excessive infiltration by polymorphonuclear leucocytes, mainly neutrophils (Fig. 24.2, see Color Atlas). The exudative features may be superimposed on several other glomerular lesions when the causative infection directly activates complement, as with salmonellosis, filariasis, falciparum malaria or certain streptococcal infections. They can also result from lymphocyte activation by superantigens as with certain streptococcal and pneumococcal infections. The mechanisms underlying the pathogenesis of exudative glomerulonephritis in AIDS are not understood.

The clinical synopsis is usually dominated by pyrexia, severe anemia, a vasculitic skin rash associated with a rapidly developing nephrotic syndrome. Hypertension is uncommon; renal function is moderately impaired, but acute renal failure is rare. Urinalysis shows gross proteinuria with a rich urinary sediment including red and white cells and casts. Serum C3 is usually very low with complement-activating infections, but not with superantigen-producing ones. Early complement components are not affected.

Crescentic glomerulonephritis Many infections may be complicated by crescent formation. In accordance with the general classification, these may be categorised into:

- *type I: antiglomerular basement membrane (AGBM) disease*. This has been rarely described following infection with influenza A_2 virus, where the typical features of Goodpasture's syndrome were described. The latter include pulmonary hemorrhage, hematuria, nephrotic range proteinuria, hypertension and rapidly developing renal failure. Renal biopsy shows extensive epithelial proliferation with crescent formation, and linear deposition of IgG along the capillary walls. Circulating anti-GBM antibodies correlate with viral activity. Such antibodies have also been described with other infections as Hanta virus, malaria and schistosomiasis yet without clinical sequelae. They may be an epiphenomenon resulting from antigenic mimicry. Prognosis of this form of glomerulonephritis is generally gloomy; renal survival rarely exceeding 20% in 2 years;
- *type II: immune complex-associated crescentic glomerulonephritis*. This has been described with HIV, HAV, HCV, mycoplasma pneumoniae lung infection, post-streptococcal glomerulonephritis, staphylococcal and other bacterial infections of the endocardium, ventriculoatrial shunts or sinus, dental or visceral abscess. It may occur with secondary syphilis and lepromatous leprosy. As described earlier, many of these infections are associated with mixed type III essential cryoglobulinemia. The prognosis of this type of glomerulonephritis is generally poor, though complete recovery was reported in more than 80% cases of complicating post-streptococcal glomerulonephritis;
- *type III: pauci-immune crescentic glomerulonephritis*. This usually occurs with ANCA-associated vasculitis (vide supra). Prognosis is generally favorable under intensive therapy, though recurrence is common.

As described in more detail elsewhere (Chap. 19), the salient feature of crescentic glomerulonephritis is rapid progression, ending up with renal failure in less than 6 months. Edema, hypertension and progressive anemia are typical. The urine volume is reduced, with proteinuria that often spills into the nephrotic range, with plenty of red and white cells and granular and cellular casts.

Chronic glomerulopathies

Almost all forms of primary glomerulonephritis are reproduced by infection. However, chronicity and progression of glomerular pathology are usually the exception rather than the rule. It is often possible to identify compounding pathogenetic factors that lead to chronicity such as persistence of antigenemia (e.g., HBV, leprosy), provocation of an auto-immune response (e.g., HCV, onchocercosis), Th_2 predominance (e.g., helminthic infections), suppression of the host's immune response (e.g., HIV, EBV-associated malaria), or a co-morbid condition (e.g., hepatic fibrosis in schistosomiasis). More than one pathogenetic factor may be involved with a particular infection.

The following are the main glomerular lesions encountered with infection.

Mesangioproliferative glomerulonephritis:

This is only quantitatively different from the usually subclinical axial proliferation described earlier. Mesangial proliferation is more remarkable (Fig. 24.2), but without significant mesangial matrix expansion, and no interposition. Immune complexes are deposited in the mesangium, rarely spilling into subendothelial locations. IgM and C_3 are most often detected, IgG appearing at a later stage. Microbial antigens are also detected in a variable proportion of cases. They represent the most conclusive evidence of the secondary nature of the renal pathology.

Typical nephrotic syndrome is the usual presentation. Hypertension is unusual. Proteinuria is fairly gross, and is unselective. The sediment is rich, with microhematuria, leucocyturia and cylindruria. Renal function is usually preserved. Recovery is the rule after control of the infection.

Mesangiocapillary glomerulonephritis

In addition to cellular proliferation, the mesangial matrix is expanded, with subendothelial interposition that gives the impression of a tram-track. Immune complex deposits, usually IgG and C_3, occasionally IgA or IgM, are deposited mostly subendothelially and in the basement membrane itself. Subepithelial deposits are often seen in infection-related mesangiocapillary glomerulonephritis, thereby superimposing considerable basement membrane thickening on classic pathology (mesangiocapillary type III, Fig. 24.2, see Color Atlas). Microbial antigens are only rarely seen with this pattern of glomerular response, reflecting the significance of co-pathogenetic mechanisms.

Many infections are associated with this lesion, most distinctive being hepatitis C, with or without cryoglobulinemia. Other viral infections include HBV in adults, CMV (usually post-transplant), HIV (usually in Caucasians), and EBV (when associated with Burkitt's lymphoma). It also occurs with *staphylococcus aureus* infections in shunt-, heroin- and visceral abscess nephropathies. In the tropics, it is commonly seen with parasitic infections as schistosomiasis, quartan malaria and hydatid disease, and rarely with extrapulmonary tuberculosis.

The clinical presentation is similar to that associated with mesangioproliferative glomerulonephritis, but hypertension and impairment of renal function are often observed. Response to treatment is generally poor, even with the complete eradication of the initial infection.

IgA nephropathy

Insignificant IgA deposits are often detected among other immunoglobulins in many forms of infection-related proliferative glomerulonephritis. In a few infections, on the other hand, IgA may be predominant, thereby categorizing the lesion as secondary IgA nephropathy. Such infections include HIV, HBV (usually with persistent anti-HBs antibodies), HCV and occasionally CMV and EBV. IgA nephropathy is also encountered with *mycoplasma pneumoniae* infection salmonellosis, and *staph aureus*-induced bacterial endocarditis.

The pathogenetic and prognostic significance of IgA deposits in these conditions is unclear. However, it seems to be of crucial importance in schistosoma-mansoni associated glomerulopathy. In this condition, IgA mucosal synthesis is augmented owing to the presence of intestinal granulomata, while its clearance is impaired due to associated hepatic fibrosis. IgA glomerular deposits in schistosomiasis correlate with proteinuria, mesangial proliferation and disease progression.

Most patients with infection-associated IgA nephropathy present with gross hematuria. This diagnosis should be considered in any patient with systemic infection who passes red urine. Treatment of infection usually leads to resolution of symptoms.

Membranous nephropathy

Only a few infections may be associated with subepithelial (extramembranous) deposits leading to a membranous nephropathy. These include HBV in black children (usually with persistent anti-HBe antibodies), HCV and possibly CMV in renal transplant recipients, congenital and secondary acquired syphilis, schistosomiasis mansoni, loasis, echinococcosis, and rarely AIDS. In many of these, mesangial cellular proliferation and matrix expansion may also occur (i.e., type III mesangiocapillary glomerulonephritis).

The distinctive feature of those infections is the ability of their antigens, by virtue of their size, configuration or charge, to cross the glomerular basement membrane, to react with their specific antibodies in situ underneath the epithelial foot processes. It has also been suggested that the microbial antigens may lead to local injury of the epithelial cells themselves, ultimately leading to the local deposition of autoantigens.

Patients with infection-associated membranous nephropathy usually present with the nephrotic syndrome. Hypertension is uncommon. The urinary sediment is benign. Renal survival is fairly long unless transformation to secondary crescentic glomerulonephritis occurs. Response to antimicrobial treatment is poor.

Focal and segmental sclerosis

This is most often secondary to other forms of glomerulonephritis, or to healing of necrotic glomerular segments resulting from vasculitis. The scarred segments may exhibit immune complex deposits similar to those observed in the uncomplicated pattern of glomerular response. Classic focal and segmental sclerosis may be the primary renal lesion in certain viral infections as HCV, HBV, HIV and parvovirus B19. It is also encountered with bacterial endocarditis and in African children with hepatosplenic schistosomiasis.

A special type of infection-associated focal and segmental sclerosis that has a notoriously poor prognosis is collapsing glomerulopathy (Fig. 24.2), often encountered in patients with HIV or HCV infection. The renal survival of those patients may not exceed a couple of years after the diagnosis has been established.

Amyloidosis

Chronic infections characterized by ambivalent effects on the monocytes (Fig. 24.3) are often associated with amyloidosis. These include tuberculosis, leprosy, leishmaniasis, schistosomiasis, echinococcosis and filariasis. Prolonged suppuration by any bacterial infection can also lead to amyloidosis, classic examples being osteomyelitis and intrathoracic suppuration.

In addition to the kidneys, amyloid deposits may be detected in the liver, spleen, gums, rectal submucosa and abdominal subcutaneous fat. Biopsy from any of these sites makes the diagnosis and confirms that the amyloid fibrils are of the AA type.

While amyloid deposits are often mixed with proliferative glomerular lesions, some patients have a purely amyloid glomerulopathy. These cannot be clinically distinguished from other forms of chronic infection-associated glomerulonephritis, though they tend to have selective proteinuria, and their blood cholesterol levels are not elevated owing to the associated hepatic pathology. The disease is generally progressive.

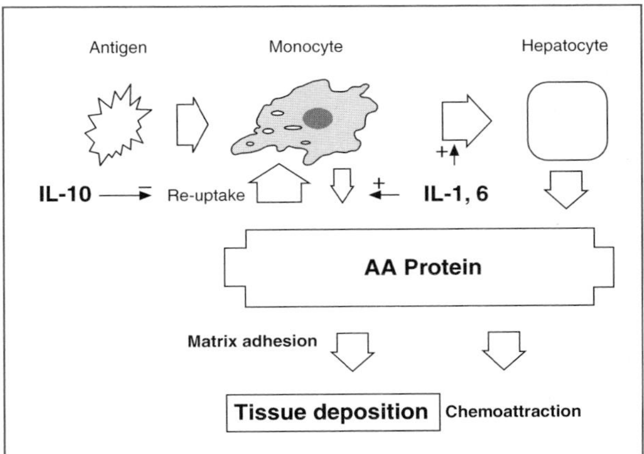

Figure 24.3 The mechanism of glomerular amyloidosis complicating infection. Persistent antigenic stimulation of the monocytes leads to the continued release of IL-1 and IL-6, which augment the secretion of AA protein from the hepatocytes as well as the monocytes themselves. AA protein is a useful chemoattractant, that is normally catabolized, again in the monocyte. IL-10, a major Th_2 cytokine inhibits this function leading to AA protein accumulation. Preexisting, even subclinical, glomerular pathology provides the adequate soil for the tissue deposition of AA protein.

Treatment

Epidemiologic studies show that glomerulonephritis is much more common in under-developed communities, with poor hygienic standards and high prevalence of infections. This emphasizes the importance of adequate prevention both at community and individual levels. It has been shown that the application of effective malaria eradication programs in Uganda, and schistosomiasis control in Egypt, have resulted in a remarkable drop in the prevalence of glomerulonephritis. There is still a lot to do in this direction in the developing world. The importance of early diagnosis and management of infection at an individual level is a global issue, that does not necessitate any further elaboration.

With modern medical and surgical technology, it is possible to eradicate most infections that cause glomerular disease. A few challenges remain with viral infections as HIV, HCV and HBV, which may persist, lead to progressive renal damage and pose important problems when corticosteroids or other immunosuppressive agents are considered.

They can also be an important barrier against successful transplantation if end-stage renal disease sets in. Such infections also constitute an important risk of transmission in dialysis units, although the risk has been minimized by the adoption of standard hygienic criteria.

Control of infection cures most of the glomerular complications, particularly the occult. Acute nephritic presentations are usually self limited, also regressing upon the control of infection, unless they have progressed to more serious pathology. Exudative glomerulonephritis and the vasculitic syndromes associated with direct tissue invasion are also cured by adequate antibiotics.

Immune-mediated vasculitis and crescentic glomerulonephritis necessitate aggressive treatment with corticosteroids, immunosuppressive agents, plasmapheresis, intravenous immunoglobulin and other measures detailed elsewhere (see Chap. 20). This may result in a considerable conflict when the original infection cannot be eradicated as with hepatitis viral infections. Several protocols have been proposed for this dilemma, including the combined, alternating or sequential use of anti-viral and immunosuppressive agents.

Symptomatizing mesangio-proliferative glomerulonephritis is the only of many chronic infection-related glomerulopathies that generally responds well to treatment. Most cases resolve upon the control of infection, while an occasional patient may need a short (3-6 months) course of corticosteroids with or without azathioprine or cyclophosphamide.

Although some improvement may be noticed in patients with IgA, membranous and mesangiocapillary glomerulonephritis upon the eradication of infection, significant renal pathology persists, and the majority of patients pursue the natural course of the primary forms of these glomerulopathies. Focal segmental sclerosis does not seem to be affected at all by anti-microbial chemotherapy.

Regression of renal amyloidosis has been described after successful treatment of tuberculosis, leprosy and schistosomiasis. Life-long treatment with colchicine has been advocated to slow down the progression. However, all these observations have been made on small series without adequate control.

Suggested readings

Barsoum R, Sitprija V. Tropical Nephrology. In: Schrier RW, Gottaschalk CW, eds. Diseases of the kidney. 6th ed. Boston, New York, Toronto, London: Little Brown & Co. 1996;2221-68.

Barsoum RS. Schistosomiasis. In: Davison AM, Cameron JS, Grunfeld JP, Kerr DNS, Ritz E, Winearls CG, eds. Oxford Textbook of clinical nephrology. 2nd ed. Oxford, New York, Tokyo: Oxford University Press 1997;1287-302.

Barsoum RS. Schistosomal glomerulopathies. Kidney International, 1993;44:1-12.

Barsoum R. Malaria nephropathies. Nephrol Dial Transplant 1988;13:1588-97.

Chugh KS, Sakhuja V. Glomerular disease in the tropics. In: Davison AM, Cameron JS, Grunfeld JP, Kerr DNS, Ritz E, Winearls CG, eds. Oxford Textbook of clinical nephrology. 2nd ed. Oxford, New York, Tokyo: Oxford University Press 1997;703-19.

Cohen AH. HIV-associated nephropathy: current concepts. Nephrol Dial Transplant 1998;13:540-2.

Coutinho A. The network theory: 21 years later. Scand J Immunol 1995;42:3-8.

Dahlberg PJ, Kurtz SB, Donadio JV, et al. Recurrent Goodpasture's syndrome. Mayo Clin Proc 1978;53:533-7.

D'Amico G. Renal involvement in hepatitis C infection: cryoglobulinemic glomerulonephritis. Kidney Int 1998;54:650-71.

Davison A. Infection-related glomerulonephritis. In Davison AM, Cameron JS, Grunfeld JP, Kerr DNS, Ritz E, Winearls CG, eds. Oxford Textbook of clinical nephrology. 2nd ed. Oxford, New York, Tokyo: Oxford University Press 1997;668-88.

Glassock RJ. Immune complex-induced glomerular injury in viral diseases. An overview. Kidney Int 1991;40(suppl 35):S1-5.

Johnson RJ, Couser WG. Hepatitis B infection and renal disease: clinical, immunopathogenetic and therapeutic considerations. Kidney Int 1990;37:663-76.

Michie CA, Cohen J. The clinical significance of T-cell superantigens. Trends Microbiol 1998;6:61-5.

Sansonno D, Cornacchiulo V, Iacobelli AR, et al. Hepatitis C virus infection and clonal B-cell expansion. Clin Exp Rheumatol 1996, 14(suppl. 14):S45-S50.

CHAPTER

25

Renal disease in patients with substance abuse

Paul L. Kimmel, Syed M. Alam, Susie Q. Lew

KEY POINTS

- The use of various different prescription and nonprescription drugs that may lead to dependency or that may have recreational or psychologic effects can cause renal disease.
- A syndrome analytic approach is the easiest first step in differentiating these renal diseases.
- Patients who use alcohol or cocaine may develop acute renal failure from rhabdomyolysis and myoglobinuria, which may be traumatic or nontraumatic, the latter often a direct effect of muscle injury caused by alcohol.
- Any drug that causes central nervous system depression may be critical in the pathogenesis of rhabdomyolysis, since muscular compression and seizures may be associated with the outpouring of intracellular contents that causes the nephropathy. Compression of muscles may be the critical factor in producing rhabdomyolysis in patients with drug-related coma or stupor.

Various prescription and nonprescription drugs may lead to dependency or may have recreational or psychologic effects that predispose a person to drug-seeking behavior and the continued, dangerous, and surreptitious use of the drug. Substance abuse is common. It may involve alcohol, opiates, sedatives, hypnotics, cocaine, cannabis, hallucinogens, psychedelic drugs, psychotropic stimulants, anxiolytic medications, analgesics, and amphetamines. The spectrum of renal dysfunction associated with the use of these agents is vast, and may present a diagnostic challenge. A history of substance abuse is often hidden or denied, and may involve several substances with different pharmacologic properties and potential idiosyncratic interactions. Patients with renal disease related to substance abuse can present with acute or chronic renal disease and nephritic or nephrotic syndromes (Tab. 25.1).

ACUTE RENAL FAILURE

Rhabdomyolysis

Rhabdomyolysis, a syndrome resulting from skeletal muscle injury and release of muscle cell contents to the circulation, may present with weakness and myalgia, nausea and vomiting, disorientation, stupor or coma, and hard swollen muscles; weakness may progress to paralysis. Findings of increased serum creatine phosphokinase (CPK), aldolase and myoglobin, and myoglobinuria support the diagnosis. Myoglobinuria, producing a red or brown urine, usually occurs, but often is missed.

Disseminated intravascular coagulation (DIC), hyperkalemia, hypocalcemia, hyperphosphatemia, hyperuricemia, increased anion gap, and a low ratio of BUN to creatinine are typical of acute rhabdomyolysis. Hyperkalemia, from the release of intracellular potassium, often is exacerbated by acidemia and oliguria. Hypocalcemia results in part from the deposition of calcium in injured skeletal muscle and sometimes in soft tissues, blood vessels, and eyes. Urinary findings include a positive dipstick test for heme in the absence of red blood cells on microscopy. Myoglobinuria is variable because it may be rapidly and completely cleared by the kidney before the diagnosis becomes a clinical consideration.

Rhabdomyolysis may occur after muscle injury, including excessive exercise, after trauma or crush injury, and following seizures. Staphylococcal toxin is the most common infectious agent associated with rhabdomyolysis, and its presence must be suspected in intravenous drug users who present with fever, hypotension, and rhabdomyolysis. Alcohol, heroin, cocaine, and central nervous system (CNS) depressants are leading causes of rhabdomyolysis, and the CNS depression may be critical in the pathogenesis because of associated muscular compression or seizures. Muscle compression may be a critical factor in drug-related coma or stupor, but alcohol may also be a direct cause of muscle damage.

Table 25.1 Renal syndromes associated with substance abuse

Acute renal failure
- Prerenal azotemia
  - Vomiting
  - Gastrointestinal bleeding
  - Nonsteroidal anti-inflammatory drugs
- Rhabdomyolysis
  - Alcohol
  - Cocaine
  - Heroin
  - Central nervous system depressants
- HIV infection
  - Acute tubular necrosis
  - Thrombotic microangiopathies

Nephrotic syndrome - intravenous drug use
- Infective endocarditis
- Vasculitis
- HBV infection
  - Membranoproliferative GN
  - Membranous nephropathy
  - Vasculitis
- HCV infection
  - Membranoproliferative GN
- HIV infection
  - Immune complex renal disease
  - IgA nephropathy

Chronic renal disease
- Nephrotic syndrome
  - Amyloidosis
  - Nonsteroidal anti-inflammatory drugs
  - Heroin nephropathy
  - HIV-associated nephropathy
- Nonnephrotic renal insufficiency
  - Lead nephropathy

Cocaine has been associated with rhabdomyolysis, and those who use cocaine commonly have elevated CPK and dystonic muscular reactions. Cocaine may have direct effects on renal cells, modifying the handling of immune complexes and their interaction with circulating and resident macrophages. Acute renal failure has been reported after inhalation of cocaine with no signs of rhabdomyolysis.

Renal failure in rhabdomyolysis may be due to a combination of intracellular events affecting renal tubule physiology. There may be direct toxic effects of myoglobin on intracellular metabolism, in addition to the tubule obstruction from cell debris seen in acute tubular necrosis of any etiology. At or below a urine pH of 6.5, myoglobin dissociates into ferrihemate and globin. Ferrihemate is nephrotoxic in a dose-dependent manner because it can deplete intracellular ATP, inhibiting tubular cell function. In addition, iron released after catabolism of myoglobin may generate reactive superoxide radicals. In turn, nitric oxide metabolism may be affected, leading to renal vasoconstriction. Renal injury from myoglobin usually is associated with volume depletion and low intratubular pH. Renal failure typically presents with a classic oliguric phase followed by a diuretic phase, lasting a total of 1 to 3 weeks. If the patient is hypotensive and tachycardic or in shock – common findings in patients with rhabdomyolysis – volume replacement with normal saline to restore circulation should be administered. Alkalinization of the urine should be induced with either intravenous sodium bicarbonate or sodium lactate. Diuretic administration may be needed to correct volume overload or oliguria, but the efficacy of loop diuretics in such cases has not been established. The infusion of mannitol to decrease tubular cell swelling and increase urine flow has been advocated. The development of uremia, volume overload, and hyperkalemia associated with acute renal failure requires dialysis. The acute renal failure is generally transient and reversible, and carries a relatively good prognosis.

Human immunodeficiency virus (HIV) infected patients

Acute tubular necrosis and acute interstitial nephritis

Acute renal failure is a prevalent problem in patients with HIV infection, and this is associated with complications of the viral illness and their treatment. The most common causes are volume depletion, sepsis and its complications, and the use of nephrotoxic drugs. Urinary tract obstruction must be considered when the urinary findings do not suggest a specific diagnosis such as acute tubular necrosis. Potential nephrotoxins such as aminoglycosides, foscarnet, sulfamethoxazole, trimethoprim, amphotericin, and pentamidine have been associated with acute renal failure, commonly due to either acute tubular necrosis or interstitial nephritis. The latter is usually differentiated from acute tubular necrosis by the finding of sterile pyuria and white blood cell casts. Recently, the use of the HIV-protease inhibitors indinavir and ritonavir has been associated with the development of reversible acute renal failure.

Thrombotic microangiopathies

Hemolytic-uremic syndrome (HUS) and thrombotic thrombocytopenic purpura (TTP) in HIV-infected patients may present as acute or chronic renal failure. The diagnostic features of HIV-associated hemolytic-uremic syndrome/thrombocytopenic purpura, the pentad of fever, CNS disease, renal insufficiency, thrombocytopenia, and microangiopathic hemolytic anemia, may not occur simultaneously. This syndrome may be the first manifestation of HIV infection. The etiology is poorly understood, but endothelial cell dysfunction is central to pathogenesis. Patients have been treated with plasmapheresis with replacement with fresh-frozen plasma, or exchange transfusions, as well as with corticosteroids, aspirin, intravenous IgG, dipyridamole, and vincristine with variable outcomes. There is a lack of controlled therapeutic trials in this patient population.

NEPHRITIC SYNDROME

Infective endocarditis

Infective endocarditis due to *Staphylococcus aureus*, fungi, and gram-negative bacilli associated with intravenous drug abuse has increased in incidence. Postinfectious immune complex-mediated glomerulonephritis can occur in patients with bacterial endocarditis, and clinical manifestations include hematuria, red blood cell casts, proteinuria, and renal insufficiency. Hypocomplementemia is usual, suggesting activation of the classic pathway. Histologic findings include glomerular hypercellularity and subendothelial and subepithelial electron-dense deposits within the glomerular capillaries. Occasionally patients with renal embolic disease will present with loin pain. In such cases, intravenous pyelography or renal nuclear scanning will highlight unilateral or, less commonly, bilateral abnormalities. Glomerulonephritis is common at the time symptoms of cardiac or infectious disease present. Renal functional impairment may progress to require dialysis. Successful treatment of the infectious disease often is accompanied by prompt resolution of the renal dysfunction. Recovery of renal function occurs less frequently, however, in patients with severely impaired renal function.

Vasculitis

Vasculitis has been linked to intravenous amphetamine use. However, there have been few subsequent large series corroborating these findings. Several reports have also associated use of cocaine with the development of vasculitis. The pathogenic association is controversial. Most reports were published before serologic tests for many viruses were in clinical use, and before the availability of tests for vasculitic syndromes.

Hepatitis B virus infection

The association between HBV infection, common in intravenous drug users, and renal disease was first reported in 1971. HBV infection is associated with a variety of renal diseases, such as membranous nephropathy, membranoproliferative glomerulonephritis, a serum sickness-like syndrome, vasculitis, and IgA nephropathy, but a causal link is often tenuous. The incidence of HBV-related renal disease is low in the US and Western Europe. The pathogenic role of viral infection has been established by the demonstration of HBV antigen-antibody complexes and deposition of HBV antigens in renal lesions. HBV nucleic acid has been localized in glomerular and tubular cells.

HBV-associated membranous nephropathy

Membranous nephropathy is the most common renal disease linked with HBV infection. The deposition of HBe antigen (HBeAg) and cationic anti-HBe antibody is associated with the formation of subepithelial immune deposits. HBsAg and anti-HBc are demonstrated in most cases. More than half of patients with membranous nephropathy have circulating HBeAg, and serum C3 and C4 often are depressed. In HBV-associated membranous nephropathy, subendothelial and/or mesangial deposits are frequently encountered, in addition to subepithelial immune deposits, in contrast to idiopathic membranous nephropathy, where deposits are subepithelial. Patients usually have proteinuria, often in the nephrotic range, and may have renal insufficiency, but few progress to end-stage renal disease (ESRD). In children, spontaneous remission is seen in many cases, but resolution is uncommon in adults.

Treatment options include glucocorticoids and interferon alpha. It has not been demonstrated that corticosteroids confer distinct advantages, and such therapy might enhance viral replication. Therapy with interferon has been associated with diminution in urinary protein excretion, but this may be limited to the duration of treatment. The risk of side effects may exceed the long-term benefits. Randomized, controlled trials of therapy are needed in well-documented adult patients with HBV-associated membranous nephropathy, especially in areas where HBV infection is not endemic but, rather, associated with substance use.

HBV-associated membranoproliferative glomerulonephritis and polyarteritis nodosa

Membranoproliferative glomerulonephritis has been reported in both adults and children with chronic HBV infection. In some patients this may be associated with mixed cryoglobulinemia due to concurrent but undetected HCV infection. Patients commonly manifest nephrotic syndrome, microscopic hematuria, hypertension, renal insufficiency and hypocomplementemia. There usually is serologic evidence of HBV infection in the absence of a history or signs or symptoms of hepatic disease.

Mesangial proliferative disease is less common and has a clinical spectrum including proteinuria and renal insufficiency. The pathogenesis may be similar to that invoked for other HBV-associated renal diseases.

Lamivudine, a nucleoside analog that inhibits viral DNA replication, has been promising in preliminary studies. Its therapeutic role in patients with HBV-associated renal diseases is uncertain at present.

A serum sickness-like syndrome occurs in 10 to 25% of patients in the early prodrome of HBV infection, and is characterized by fever, maculopapular rash, and arthralgia. Renal manifestations include variable degrees of proteinuria, hematuria and renal insufficiency, but seem to be relatively uncommon. The syndrome often is accompanied by hypocomplementemia, suggesting an immune-mediated pathogenesis. It is typically self-limiting.

Polyarteritis nodosa was reported concomitant with hepatitis more than 50 years ago in association with vaccinations. A link with HBV infection was made later. This complication has been reported more often in Europe and the United States, where HBV disease is not endemic and infection is acquired through parenteral routes. In addition, there is wide geographic variation in the US, with a greater prevalence of HBV-associated polyarteritis in New York compared with northern midwestern cities. In Asia and Africa, where the infection is endemic and occurs in children, often through vertical or horizontal transmission, the complication is less common. These epidemiologic findings suggest substance abuse may be important in the pathogenesis of the polyarteritis.

Polyarteritis nodosa is a multisystem disease with a clinical presentation similar to that of the serum sickness syndrome. The associated renal syndromes are varied, but serologic evidence of HBV infection usually is present. The diagnosis may be made by demonstrating arteritis on biopsy, or from angiographic evidence of vascular abnormalities. Patients often do not have detectable antineutrophil cytoplasmic antibodies. The disease has a poor prognosis if it is untreated. Steroids, cytotoxic and antiviral drugs, as well as dapsone and plasmapheresis have been used in uncontrolled studies. Antiviral therapy, such as interferon or vidarabine, may be beneficial in patients (particularly young children and patients from nonendemic areas) with vasculitis.

Hepatitis C virus-associated renal diseases

Risk factors for HCV infection include direct exposure, such as transfusion of blood or blood products, transplantation of organs or tissues from infected donors, and sharing of contaminated needles among injection drug users. Although in the latter group the incidence of HCV infection is rapidly declining, almost half of newly acquired infections result from drug use in the 6 months before onset of disease.

Fifty to eighty per cent of new users test positive for anti-HCV antibodies 6 to 12 months after beginning intravenous drug abuse.

The mechanisms of replication of HCV and its chronic persistence, and the mediators of hepatic cellular injury are not well characterized. Glomerular deposition of circulating immune complexes is thought to be critical in the pathogenesis of several HCV-associated renal diseases. The immunochemical characteristics of the pathogenic immune complexes, such as type, size, charge, and the presence of idiotypic antibody responses may be important.

Patients with HCV infection may present with acute or chronic renal disease, the nephritic or nephrotic syndromes, vasculitis, or with urinary abnormalities such as proteinuria or hematuria. A variety of extrahepatic syndromes have been reported with chronic HCV infection, including mixed cryoglobulinemia, membranoproliferative glomerulonephritis (in the presence and absence of cryoglobulinemia), a Sjögren's-like sicca syndrome, and membranous nephropathy.

Membranoproliferative glomerulonephritis is the most common finding in studies of HCV infection and renal disease. HCV infection may be responsible for 10 to 30% of membranoproliferative glomerulonephritis in the United States, but may be associated with up to 60% of those in Japan.

Some patients with membranoproliferative glomerulonephritis may present with manifestations of cryoglobulinemia, such as rash, arthritis, or neuropathy. In many cases, however, no extrarenal manifestations are present. Patients often have hypertension and edema. Investigations reveal hematuria and proteinuria, renal insufficiency, anemia, hypoalbuminemia, hypocomplementemia, and the presence of circulating immune complexes and rheumatoid factors. Patients with HCV-associated renal disease and cryoglobulinemia often do not progress to end-stage renal disease.

Renal pathologic studies show a lobular increase in mesangial cellularity and matrix with a variable degree of sclerosis and foci of tubular atrophy with interstitial mononuclear cell infiltration. Immunofluorescence may demonstrate IgG, IgM, and C3. It has been shown that most patients in widely disparate geographic settings who have "essential mixed cryoglobulinemia" have chronic infection with HCV; however, pathophysiologic and pathogenic causal questions remain regarding the relationships of the infection to the immune dysregulation.

Membranous nephropathy has also been associated with HCV infection in a few cases. Patients have presented with nephrotic syndrome, but unlike HCV-infected patients with membranoproliferative glomerulonephritis, they had normal complement and no detectable cryoglobulinemia or rheumatoid factors.

Treatment of HCV-associated membranoproliferative glomerulonephritis with interferon-alpha has demonstrated suppression of viremia, improvement in serum transaminase, and reduction in proteinuria, but no clinically important effect on renal function. Clearance of circulating HCV-related nucleic acid may be a good prognostic sign. The long-term effects of this therapy remain to be determined.

Interferon-alpha has been used for the treatment of HIV-associated essential mixed cryoglobulinemia. This may result in suppression of viremia and improvement in parameters of hepatic disease, but disease markers often recur after discontinuation of therapy. Ribavirin has also been used in such patients.

HIV-associated immune-complex renal disease

Circulating immune complexes are common at any stage in HIV infection, and immune-mediated renal disease has been reported since the beginning of the epidemic in the 1980s. Membranoproliferative and diffuse proliferative glomerulonephritis, IgA nephropathy, and membranous nephropathy have all been described. These are much less common than the classic HIV-associated nephropathy. However, the ethnic background of the patient may determine the type of renal disease that may occur with HIV infection.

Glomerulonephritis may be only indirectly related to the HIV infection, because patients may have coinfection with HBV or HCV, or may have cryoglobulinemia or postinfectious glomerulonephritis. The rate of coinfection with HBV in patients in the US is extremely high. Typically there is microscopic hematuria and nephrotic range proteinuria, hypoalbuminemia, and disordered liver function. Cryoglobulinemia and renal insufficiency may be present. Membranoproliferative and mesangial proliferative glomerulonephritis, membranous nephropathy, and mixed inflammatory and sclerotic lesions are found.

There is no evidence-based treatment for patients with HIV infection and glomerulonephritis. The role of antiretroviral therapy has not been rigorously evaluated.

HIV-associated IgA nephropathy

HIV-associated IgA nephropathy is a relatively common renal disease in a specific population of patients: young Caucasian, Hispanic, or Asian men with hematuria, proteinuria, and mild renal insufficiency. IgA nephropathy in the absence of HIV infection is rare in patients of African descent. The prognosis seems in general to be good, but there are few long-term studies. Limited data exist about treatment with antiretroviral drugs. Patients with HIV-associated IgA nephropathy and rapidly progressive renal failure have been treated with glucocorticoids, but the outcomes are unclear.

CHRONIC RENAL FAILURE

In general, the diagnostic possibilities for patients with chronic renal failure related to substance abuse will be better delineated by categorization into groups with urinary protein excretion in excess of 3 g/24 h (nephrotic patients) and those with lesser degrees of proteinuria (non-nephrotic).

Nephrotic syndrome and renal insufficiency

Amyloidosis

Amyloidosis occurs with an increased frequency in drug users, as noted in several studies of patients with renal disease who used heroin. Prolonged inflammation from skin infections due to skin popping may be important in pathogenesis. The inflammatory process need not be present for a long period. The average duration of abuse in one study was approximately 3 years. Renal amyloid secondary to drug abuse is relatively frequent. Biopsy-proved renal amyloidosis among drug abusers with systemic amyloidosis and proteinuria varies between 25 and 67%, whereas autopsies of drug addicts show an incidence of approximately 5%. Colchicine alone or in combination appears to be somewhat effective in patients with secondary amyloidosis, whereas melphalan in combination with prednisone seems to be beneficial in patients with primary amyloidosis. Although therapy with colchicine has been used most frequently in patients with renal amyloidosis associated with substance use, the outcome tends to be poor. Patients with an elevated serum creatinine at the time of diagnosis or with a high degree of proteinuria are more likely to progress to end-stage renal disease.

Heroin-associated nephropathy (HAN)

Renal disease associated with the use of heroin was first suggested in the 1970s. Focal and segmental glomerulosclerosis (FGS) is the most common finding, although there is a low prevalence of imflammatory lesions. The disease is characterized clinically by nephrotic range proteinuria in the presence or absence of renal insufficiency. Patients who exhibit both pathologic findings progress relatively rapidly to end-stage renal disease. It is generally found to be disproportionately present in African-Americans, and is unexplained by the epidemiology of drug-use in the reporting areas. There is a male preponderance.

The different renal diseases reported in series of patients who used heroin raises questions regarding a causal relationship. Renal disease may be a direct response to the opiate, or to an immune response to adulterants used in the processing of illicitly purchased drugs. It is not clear whether the sclerosing glomerular diseases are a result of the heroin use, or merely represent the coexistence of renal disease that may be present or overrepresented in the populations of drug users. It is also difficult to verify the history of single drug use, or heroin use, in patients admitted to the care of physicians with whom they do not have an ongoing, trusting relationship. Since reports of heroin-associated nephropathy predated the surveillance of HCV and HIV infection with serologic and molecular biologic testing, it is conceivable that some of the variation in histologic findings might be related to the spectrum of viral illnesses encountered in injection drug users.

A recent report from Brooklyn, New York, suggested that the incidence of heroin-associated nephropathy is decreasing markedly in contrast to the increasing prevalence of renal diseases associated with HIV infection in this population (see below).

Although few direct effects of heroin on renal structure and function have been reported, studies suggest that morphine, a metabolite of heroin, has direct effects on kidney cells and their interaction with circulating and resident macrophages.

Markers of the severity of the renal disease improve in some patients who discontinue the use of heroin, suggesting that the drug might be directly related to the nephropathy. Approximately 0.2% of end-stage renal disease in the US has been attributed to heroin-associated nephropathy. Transplantation has been successfully performed in patients with heroin-associated nephropathy, although many centers limit this modality of renal replacement therapy to patients who have demonstrated abstinence, since the disease may recur after transplantation.

HIV-associated nephropathy (HIVAN)

HIV-associated nephropathy is the most common type of kidney disease in biopsies and autopsies of patients with HIV infection. Renal disease affects up to 10% of HIV-infected patients, but the vast majority are males of African descent. Patients with HIV-associated nephropathy often have hypoalbuminemia, but hypertension, edema, and hyperlipidemia are less common, possibly depending on nutritional status and the stage of the viral illness. Renal ultrasound yields characteristic findings of large echogenic kidneys in the absence of obstruction. Renal biopsy demonstrates focal and segmental glomerulosclerosis with glomerular collapse, glomerular epithelial cell abnormalities, tubular interstitial infiltration and fibrosis, and such tubular abnormalities as atrophy and microcystic dilatation. Tubular reticular structures, perhaps a result of cytokine stimulation, are typically encountered, usually within endothelial cells. The disease may be rapidly progressive, and it is uncertain whether the prognosis has changed in the era of potent antiretroviral therapies. Renal biopsy is necessary to make a precise diagnosis, but in many cases it is not necessary for patient management. The role of biopsy may be increased if specific therapies evolve. The treatment of patients with HIV-associated nephropathy prior to the onset of end-stage renal disease is unclear, and has only recently been a focus of study. Cyclosporine, glucocorticoids, and angiotensin-converting enzyme inhibitors have all been used in small numbers of patients in poorly controlled trials.

A lower incidence or improved outcome of nephropathy has been suggested in HIV-infected patients treated with antiretroviral agents, compared with untreated patients. Most studies involved treatment with zidovudine. Further studies are needed in patients treated with protease inhibitors. Uncontrolled studies suggest glucocorticoids might ameliorate renal insufficiency in patients with HIV-associated nephropathy. Decreased urinary protein excretion and improved renal function were demonstrated in patients treated with high-dose prednisone tapered over a 2- to 11-week course in a nonrandomized, uncontrolled trial. Long-term follow-up was limited, and the development of opportunistic infections, steroid-induced psychoses, and upper gastrointestinal bleeding were common, as were relapses, including progression to end-stage renal disease after tapering of the steroids.

In one study, mean renal survival time to the development of end-stage renal disease or death in patients with biopsy-proved HIV-associated nephropathy treated with captopril was approximately 5 months, significantly longer than the controls. In a multiple regression analysis, treatment with captopril and antiretroviral medications, but not age, renal function, or CD4 count, were associated with maintenance of kidney function. A second study reported similar findings in patients treated with another angiotensin-converting enzyme inhibitor. In contrast to the results of treatment with glucocorticoids, there were few complications in either of these studies. Renal function and serum potassium should be regularly assessed in patients treated with angiotensin-converting enzyme inhibitors. Further randomized, prospective controlled studies are needed to assess the value of these therapies.

Although both hemodialysis and peritoneal dialysis have been used as treatment for patients with HIV-associated end-stage renal disease, the prognosis for patients is poorer than that of patients without viral infection. Renal transplantation is generally not advised for patients with HIV infection because of the unknown effect of immunosuppressive therapy on the prognosis in such patients.

Non-nephrotic proteinuria and renal insufficiency

Lead nephropathy

Whiskey produced in illegal stills (moonshine) remains an important and underappreciated source of lead toxicity in rural areas of the southeastern US. The source of the metal in moonshine is the soldered lead leached from radiators or the adjoining copper pipes of the still during distillation of the liquor.

A blood lead concentration of greater than 80 μg/dl may cause renal tubule damage. Lead poisoning should be considered in patients with a history of moonshine ingestion, especially if the clinical presentation includes non-nephrotic proteinuria and renal insufficiency associated with abdominal pain, microcytic anemia, muscle weakness or encephalopathy. "Saturnine" gout occurs frequently in patients who drink moonshine. Decreased clearance of uric acid in patients with chronic lead intoxication may be a direct effect on tubular function, or may be caused by renal failure.

Miscellaneous complications of electrolyte homeostasis and renal function in patients with alcohol dependence

Decreased nutritional intake, intestinal malabsorption of phosphate and magnesium, inappropriate renal phosphate or magnesium excretion, or shifts of phosphate from the extracellular into the intracellular space may cause hypocalcemia, hypophosphatemia, and hypomagnesemia in patients who use alcohol chronically. These abnormalities may be reversible after abstinence and resumption of normal nutritional intake. Hypocalcemia and hypomagnesemia may also be manifestations of insufficient parathyroid hormone production, secretion, and action, seen in patients with magnesium depletion. Hypokalemia, associated with abnormally increased urinary potassium excretion, may result from hyperaldosteronism in patients after vomiting, or from hypomagnesemia and magnesium depletion.

Phosphate depletion may result in a catastrophic syndrome in patients who abuse alcohol. Patients with a plasma phosphate of less than 1 mg/dl may have hematologic abnormalities, including hemolytic anemia, abnormal white blood cell and platelet function, and CNS disorders. Rhabdomyolysis and acute renal failure may be seen. The effects may be due to decreased red blood cell 2,3 diphosphoglycerate and depletion of intracellular ATP stores. Refeeding, intravenous saline, or the provision of glucose may precipitate the syndrome if phosphorus is not also administered. Alkalemia may aggravate hypophosphatemia. Treatment with skim milk or oral phosphate supplements often cannot be tolerated, or cannot be given in sufficient quantities to bring plasma phosphate to normal. Intravenous therapy with phosphate salts may be technically difficult owing to such complications as hypocalcemia, calcium phosphate deposition syndromes, and acute renal failure.

Alcoholic patients may present with the full gamut of acid-base abnormalities. Metabolic acidosis can result from alcoholic ketoacidosis, a result of the metabolism of alcohol, exacerbated in the presence of malnutrition, or may be associated with the ingestion of isopropyl alcohol or methanol. Lactic acidosis can occur because of changes in tissue oxidation/reduction capacities associated with the metabolism of alcohol. Volume depletion, potassium losses, and hyperaldosteronism can result in metabolic alkalosis. Respiratory alkalosis is associated with alcohol withdrawal. Respiratory acidosis may be seen with the CNS depression encountered during alcohol intoxication.

Suggested readings

Arruda JA, Kurtzman NA, Pillary VK. Prevalence of renal disease in asymptomatic addicts. Arch Intern Med 1975;135: 535-7.

Bakir AA, Dunea G. Drugs of abuse in renal disease. Curr Opin Nephrol Hypertension 1996;5:122-6.

Cohen AH. HIV-associated nephropathy: current concepts. Nephrol Dial Transpl 1998;12:540-2.

De Broe ME, Elseviers MM. Analgesic nephropathy. N Engl J Med 1998;339:446-52.

Emmerson BT. Chronic lead nephropathy. Kidney Int 1973;4:1-5.

Enriquez R, Palacios FO, Gonzalez CM, et al. Analgesic nephropathy. Am J Kidney Dis 1998;332:351-60.

Jacob H, Charytan C, Rascoff JH, et al. Amyloidosis secondary to drug abuse and skin suppuration. Arch Intern Med 1978;138:1150-1.

Levine OS, Vlahov D, Koehler J, et al. Seroepidemiology of hepatitis B virus in a population of injection drug users: Association with drug injection patterns. Am J Epidem 1995;142:331-41.

Mannof SB, Vlahov D, Herskowitz A, et al. Human immunodeficiency virus infection and endocarditis among injecting drug users. Epidemiol 1996;7:566-70.

Menchel S, Cohen D, Gross E, et al. AA protein-related renal amyloidosis in drug addicts. Am J Pathol 1983;112:195-9.

Neugarten J, Gallow GR, Buxbaum J, et al. Amyloidosis in subcutaneous heroin abusers ("skin poppers amyloidosis"). Am J Med 1986;81:635.

Rao TK, Nicastri AD, Friedman EA. Natural history of heroin-associated nephropathy. N Engl J Med 1974;290:19-23.

Weeden RP, D'Haese P, Van de Vyver FL, et al. Lead nephropathy. Am J Kidney Dis 1986;8:380-3.

Weisbord SD, Soule JB, Kimmel PL. Poison on line: Acute renal failure caused by oil of wormwood purchased through the internet. N Engl J Med 1997;337:825-7.

CHAPTER

26

Malignancy associated glomerular disease

Alexander M. Davison

KEY POINTS

- Renal involvement in malignancy may represent a direct or indirect effect of the tumor or its treatment, or it may be an immunologic consequence of the cancer.
- Glomerular lesions are most commonly produced by tumor antigen-associated immune complexes.
- Electrolyte disorders include hypercalcemia, hypokalemia, and hyponatremia.
- Radiation nephritis has become uncommon owing to effective shielding of the kidney during radiotherapy.
- Membranous nephropathy is the most common histologic finding associated with solid tumors.
- Minimal change nephropathy is a recognized association of Hodgkin's disease.
- Plasma cell dyscrasias (myeloma) are associated with cast nephropathy, Fanconi syndrome, and amyloidosis.

Patients with malignancy may have renal involvement for a number of reasons (Tab. 26.1). There may be direct effects if the kidney is the site of a primary tumor or, less commonly, a secondary tumor. In spite of the kidney's high blood flow metastatic tumors are relatively uncommon. Lymphomatous or leukemic infiltrates may occur, and frequently result in renal failure. Tumor mass at the hilum may compress the renal artery or vein, and urinary outflow obstruction can be caused from retroperitoneal or pelvic malignancies. Transitional cell tumors of the urothelium may cause an obstructive uropathy.

There are many indirect effects. Electrolyte disorders can arise – hypokalemia and/or hyponatremia from prolonged vomiting, hypercalcemia from marrow infiltration (especially in myeloma), prolonged immobilization, secretion of PTH-like substances, or hormonal therapy, and hyponatremia from the inappropriate secretion of ADH. In a number of instances it is the metabolic abnormality that is the first manifestation of an underlying malignancy.

Renal disease may also arise as a complication of therapy. Radiation nephritis is now rare since the recognition that the kidney is particularly sensitive to radiation, which has led to effective shielding of the kidneys during radiotherapy. Drug nephrotoxicity remains a problem, particularly with cisplatin and occasionally with analgesics.

MALIGNANCY-ASSOCIATED NEPHROPATHY

Malignancy associated glomerulopathy was first reported over 70 years ago, but only relatively recently has the relationship been clarified. There are a number of series, none large, and many anecdotal reports that confirm the association between malignancy, nephrotic syndrome, and membranous nephropathy and between Hodgkin's disease, nephrotic syndrome, and minimal change nephropathy. There is, however, no relationship between the site of the tumor and the histologic type and either the mode of presentation or the pathologic nature of the renal disease. This chapter is specifically devoted to the glomerular consequences of malignancies.

Table 26.1 Renal involvement in malignancy

Direct effects
Primary tumors
Metastatic tumors
Tumor infiltration
Obstruction
Indirect effects
Electrolyte disorders
Intravascular coagulation
Renal vein thrombosis
Amyloidosis
Glomerulopathy
Nephrocalcinosis/lithiasis
Treatment effects
Drug nephrotoxicity (interstitial nephritis)
Tumor lysis syndrome (crystal formation)
Radiation (fibrosis)

Etiopathogenesis

Glomerular changes in patients with malignancy may be immunologically mediated, may result from intravascular coagulation, or may be due to amyloidosis (Tab. 26.2). Immune deposits may be the result of the systemic release of tumor-associated antigens or from reexpressed fetal antigens. Antigens deriving from bronchogenic, colonic, gastric, and prostatic carcinoma have been described in glomerular deposits, supporting the concept of tumor-derived immune complex involvement in the pathogenesis of the glomerular lesions. In some tumors, particularly lymphoproliferative diseases, there may be causally related viruses and the consequent formation of immune complexes comprising viral antigen and antibody. Intravascular coagulation may be initiated by the release of coagulant proteins from tumor cells. Amyloidosis has been described, particularly in association with renal cell carcinoma, possibly because of the secretion of an amyloid precursor by the tumor.

Clinical findings

Symptoms and signs

Clinically malignancy associated glomerular disease most commonly occurs in adults, presenting as a nephrotic syndrome. In about 40% of cases the nephrotic syndrome presents before the diagnosis of malignancy. The true incidence of glomerulopathy in malignancy is not known, because many patients have only minor urinary abnormalities, microscopic hematuria and/or minor hematuria, and many are never referred for renal investigation because of their poor prognosis and the belief that it is unlikely that the renal involvement will be the ultimate cause of death. The nephrotic syndrome in patients with malignancy is rarely accompanied by any significant reduction in renal function.

Table 26.2 Pathogenesis of malignancy-associated nephropathy

Tumor associated antigen
Reexpressed fetal antigen
Viral antigens
Intravascular coagulation
Amyloidosis

The prevalence of malignancy-associated nephropathy is not known. In view of the frequency of malignant disease in the general population and the relative paucity of reported cases of associated nephropathy, it must be rare – although subclinical nephropathy probably is common. Patients with advanced malignancy are unlikely to be subjected to invasive renal investigations, such as renal biopsy, and the detection of minor urinary abnormalities may be attributed to other causes, such as urinary tract infection. Studies have suggested that glomerular immune deposits are detectable in 17 to 30% of patients with malignancy coming to autopsy, although histologically obvious glomerular lesions are less frequent. In clinical studies, urinary abnormalities, hematuria and/or proteinuria, have been detected in 12 to 58% of patients with tumors. Although the autopsy and clinical studies are at some variance, it is likely that mild glomerulopathy without marked urinary abnormalities is relatively common in patients with solid tumors. The reported incidence and prevalence of nephropathy will to a large extent depend on whether the series is published by an oncologist or a nephrologist.

Electrolyte disorders occur frequently. Hypokalemia may arise from potassium loss, as occurs in prolonged vomiting, or from diarrhea associated with a villous adenoma of the rectum. Hyponatremia may occur from prolonged vomiting but is also seen in patients with inappropriate ADH secretion, as may occur in oat cell carcinoma of the lung. Hypercalcemia most commonly is seen in patients with myeloma but it also occurs following prolonged immobilization, from bone metastases, and rarely in association with hormonal therapy for breast carcinoma. The hypercalcemia may result in nephrocalcinosis with consequent impairment of urinary concentration, clinically manifest as polyuria and thirst, with the risk of dehydration if vomiting is prolonged.

Diagnostic procedures

Hematuria, most frequently microscopic, is common in patients with malignancy and may be due to interstitial nephritis as a consequence of chemotherapy, analgesics, or antibiotic therapy. In addition, stone formation, a result of hypercalcemia, may cause hematuria. Macroscopic hematuria is uncommon except in primary malignancies of the renal tract. Asymptomatic proteinuria is common, but in some patients is sufficient to produce the nephrotic syndrome. Significant impairment of renal function is rare except in those few patients who develop intravascular coagulation or rapidly progressive glomerulonephritis.

There may be progressive deterioration in renal function, but in most patients the malignancy is advanced before renal manifestations become clinically obvious, and the tumor tends to progress faster than the associated glomerulopathy.

If renal biopsy is performed, the most common finding is a membranous nephropathy although many other appearances, including IgA nephropathy, mesangiocapillary, proliferative and crescentic glomerulonephritis, and minimal lesion nephropathy, have been described. There is no consistent link between the site and nature of the malignancy and the glomerular histopathologic findings. The only exception to this appears to be the association of renal cell carcinoma and glomerular amyloidosis. There does not seem to be a relationship between the mass of the tumor and the risk of developing malignancy.

Diagnosis

This can be difficult, and it is likely that in many patients the glomerular involvement will remain undetected owing to the understandable reluctance of clinicians to undertake invasive investigations in patients with terminal disease. In many patients the diagnosis can only be inferred, as it is not possible to demonstrate the presence of tumor or tumor-associated antigens in glomeruli. It is reasonable to assume that the development of nephrotic range proteinuria within 6 months (either before or after) of the diagnosis of a malignancy suggests a causal relationship. This can only be proved following renal biopsy, and, as discussed, this may not be clinically indicated.

Treatment

The management of patients with malignancy-associated renal disease involves:

- symptomatic treatment of nephrotic syndrome by diuretic therapy;
- detailed investigation of electrolyte abnormalities to institute appropriate therapy;
- evaluation of the extent of the malignancy to determine whether tumor removal can be undertaken;
- careful evaluation of all drug therapy to avoid any potential nephrotoxicity.

In most patients the nephrotic syndrome can be controlled by diuretic therapy. The diuretic regimen used will depend on the severity of the edema. Most patients will be rendered edema free if an agent acting on the distal tubule is used, such as bendrofluazide (5-10 mg daily orally) or metalozone (5-10 mg daily orally). Loop diuretics such as furosemide and bumetanide should be reserved for severe edema that cannot be controlled by less "powerful" agents. The disadvantages of loop diuretics are that they produce a prompt, but short-lasting, marked diuresis that may render the patient housebound for several hours after administration. On occasions patients will appear "resistant" to the effect of diuretics, and this is because the compensatory mechanisms that arise lead to the avid retention of sodium and, as a result, water that cannot be overcome by a single diuretic. In such patients it is often possible to establish a satisfactory diuresis by using combined diuretic therapy with a loop diuretic, either furosemide or bumetanide, and a distal tubule diuretic, either bendrofluazide, metolazone, or chlorthalidone. Occasionally triple therapy including a late distal tubule diuretic such as spironolactone or amiloride will be required. It is only rarely necessary to use albumin infusions to initiate a diuresis. Frequently the therapy required to maintain a patient edema free is significantly less than that required to establish the initial diuresis, and therefore there is a need for constant review of the diuretic requirement to avoid overtreatment. "Dehydration" can be avoided if the patient is left at the end of the day with a small amount of edema at the ankle.

Electrolyte disorders frequently cause the patient significant distress. Hypokalemia results in muscle weakness and lethargy. Hyponatremia, particularly if severe, may cause muscle pain and disordered thought processes. Hppercalcemia produces thirst because of interference with the ability of the kidney to concentrate urine. In addition, it may, if prolonged, result in nephrocalcinosis and nephrolithiasis. It is important to determine the cause of any electrolyte derangement and to institute appropriate corrective measures. Control of vomiting and the use of supplements usually will promptly correct the metabolic consequences of prolonged gastric fluid loss. In these circumstances if potassium supplements are required, potassium chloride should be used, not the effeverscent forms of potassium, which contain a mixture of potassium chloride and bicarbonate. Most patients with significant potassium loss develop a metabolic alkalosis, and therefore it is inappropriate to give alkali in the form of bicarbonate salts.

It should be remembered that there may be associated magnesium depletion, and clinical improvement will not occur unless this is corrected. Hypercalcemia, if greater than 3 mmol/l, should be treated. Bisphosphonates, such as pamidronate or clondronate, are effective and should be given initially by mouth, although maintenance therapy can be achieved by oral clondronate. There is some evidence that hypercalcemia can influence pain threshold, and so there may be additional benefit to be gained from reduction of elevated concentrations.

A number of anecdotal reports have recorded remission of the nephrotic syndrome after removal or adequate treatment of the tumor. There may even be improvement following reduction in tumor mass, even when complete resection is not possible. Relapse of the malignancy after treatment has been reported to be associated with a relapse of the nephropathy.

In patients with malignancy-associated renal disease it is important to avoid any additional renal insult. Thus careful watch needs to be maintained on any drug therapy to avoid nephrotoxicity. On occasions it is necessary to use potentially nephrotoxic drugs, e.g., cisplatin, and this usually is without problems as long as the patient is suitably hydrated and monitored. If there is reduction in renal function there may need to be an alteration in drug dose to ensure that toxic plasma concentrations are avoided. In pain control it is important to avoid any preparation that might be associated with the development of analgesic nephropathy. Thus, all drug therapy needs to be carefully reviewed to prevent harmful effects, but it is seldom necessary not to use an essential drug on the grounds of potential renal damage. It is a case of carefully weighing the risks and benefits and making an informed decision in the best interests of the patient and then monitoring effect and plasma concentrations.

Prevention

There are no effective preventive measures that can be introduced clinically. Good clinical care of the patient with malignancy is paramount, with prompt intervention to control pain, nausea, and vomiting.

LYMPHOMA

Renal involvement in lymphoma includes obstructive uropathy from enlarged lymph nodes, renal infiltration (which only rarely leads to functional impairment), glomerulopathy, amyloidosis (rare), and, as a consequence of therapy, the development of the tumor lysis syndrome. This arises when effective chemotherapy increases the breakdown of tumor cells with the release of nucleic acids that are metabolized to uric acid. The recognition of this syndrome has resulted in careful clinical control of hydration during the initiation of chemotherapy. As a consequence this is now rarely encountered.

The most common nephropathy associated with Hodgkin's lymphoma is minimal change nephropathy, possibly due to disordered T-cell function. Nephropathy seems to be very rare in association with non-Hodgkin's lymphoma.

LEUKEMIA

There are a few reports of glomerulopathy in association with leukemia, mesangiocapillary glomerulonephritis being the most common lesion described. Interestingly, renal functional impairment is more commonly found in patients with nephropathy associated with leukemia than in patients with solid tumors. The cause for this is not known.

PLASMA CELL DYSCRASIAS

Plasma cell dyscrasias are characterized by the uncontrolled proliferation of B-cells and are associated with the secretion of a monoclonal immunoglobulin product. Such proteins may become deposited in tissues and result in impairment of function. In the kidney the deposits may form as intratubular casts (cast nephropathy), crystals (in myeloma-associated Fanconi's syndrome), or fibrils (in myeloma-associated amyloidosis). The prevalence of these myeloma-associated renal lesions is unknown because many patients do not undergo detailed investigations such as renal biopsy.

Myeloma cast nephropathy

This is the most common renal lesion in patients with myeloma and is the major cause of renal failure that usually presents acutely. Most of these patients have a high tumor mass, and most commonly a light-chain myeloma. The risk of developing cast nephropathy increases with increasing light-chain proteinuria. Clinically, patients present with symptoms and signs of the myeloma such as weakness, weight loss, bone pain, and infections rather than with symptoms of renal impairment. On investigation, monoclonal light-chain proteinuria (Bence Jones proteinuria) is present, but it must be remembered that this will not be detected by conventional urinary stik testing. Urinary protein electrophoresis is required for diagnosis.

A number of clinical situations may precipitate light-chain deposition in the renal tubule. Dehydration is particularly recognized as precipitating renal failure. This may arise from a hypercalcemia-associated diabetes insipidus state or may follow a period of vomiting. It has also been reported in patients undergoing fluid deprivation as preparation for intravenous urography. It has been suggested that contrast agents promote precipitation of light chains, but this has not been proved, and IVU can be performed if care is taken to maintain adequate hydration. Some drugs, particularly aminoglycosides and NSAIDs, have been implicated in precipitating cast nephropathy and must be used with caution in patients with myeloma.

Myeloma cast nephropathy is characterized by large casts, particularly in the distal tubule and collecting duct. Typically the casts appear "fractured". Frequently the casts are surrounded by mononuclear cells and multinucleated giant cells. Considerable tubular disruption is present, and commonly the glomeruli appear remarkably normal. Immunofluorescence studies of the casts indicate that they are composed of the same monoclonal light chains that are excreted in the urine.

Management is primarily symptomatic treatment followed by measures to control renal failure and chemotherapy to the tumor. Attempts should be made to limit further light chain precipitation by maintaining hydration and avoiding potentially harmful medications such as NSAIDs. Urinary alkalinization is recommended in an effort to reduce the potential for interaction between light chains and Tamm-Horsfall protein resulting in the formation of more casts. Light chains may be removed from the circulation by plasma exchange, but this remains controversial. The chemotherapy regimen is best discussed with local oncologists and is beyond the scope of this chapter.

The prognosis is changing with the development of greater understanding of the underlying pathologic process and more effective chemotherapy. In patients with widespread interstitial damage, there is less chance of renal recovery. After effective tumor chemotherapy, renal recovery may take place after several months. If renal function does not return, the results of long-term dialysis is not as bleak as was once thought, with some patients surviving more than 2 years. In general, survival depends more on the results of tumor control than on the effectiveness of dialysis.

Myeloma associated Fanconi's syndrome

The Fanconi's syndrome (glycosuria, aminoaciduria, hypophosphatemia, acidosis, hypouricemia, and hypokalemia) is an uncommon but recognized association with plasma cell dyscrasias, usually a kappa light chain secreting myeloma. Most patients present with symptoms consequent to the Fanconi's syndrome: bone pain and pseudofractures from osteomalacia. Renal failure occurs in about 50% of patients. The renal lesion consists of crystal formation in the proximal tubular cells associated with interstitial cellular infiltration and fibrosis, and patchy tubular atrophy. It is thought that the intracellular crystal deposits result in impairment of cellular function and the consequent biochemical derangements as noted above. Management is by treatment of the underlying myeloma and correction, where possible, of the disordered plasma potassium, phosphate, urate, and acidosis.

Monoclonal immunoglobulin deposition disease

Monoclonal immunoglobulin deposition disease is a rare complication of plasma cell dyscrasias in which heavy and/or light chains are deposited in glomerular capillary walls and tubular basement membranes. Impaired renal

function is common at presentation and progresses rapidly to failure. Management is by treatment of the underlying myeloma and appropriate intervention for renal failure. Prognosis is uncertain owing to the few reported cases.

Suggested readings

Alexanian R, Barlogie B, Dixon D. Renal failure in multiple myeloma Arch Intern Med. 1990;150:1693-5.

Cameron JS, Ogg CS. Neoplastic disease and the nephrotic disease. Quart J Med 1975;44:630-1.

Coward RA, Mallick NP, Delamore IW. Tubular function in multiple myeloma. Clin Science 1984;66:229-32.

Dabbs DJ, Morel-Maroger SL, Mignon F, Striker G. Glomerular lesions in lymphomas and leukemias. Am J Med 1986;80:63-7.

Egen JW, Lewis EJ. Glomerulopathies in neoplasia. Kid Intern 1977;11:297-306.

Lee JC, Yamauchi H, Hopper J. The association of cancer and the nephrotic syndrome. Ann Intern Med 1966;64:41-51.

McLigeyo SO, Notghi A, Thomson D, Anderton JL. Nephrotic syndrome associated with chronic lymphatic leukaemia. Nephrol Dial Transpl 1993;8:461-3.

Pai P, Bone JM, McDicken I, Bell GM. Solid tumour and glomerulopathy. Quart J Med 1996;89:361-7.

Pascal RR. Renal manifestations of extra-renal neoplasms. Human Pathol 1980;11:7-17.

Sawyer N, Wadsworth J, Winnen M, Gabriel R. Prevalence, concentration and prognostic importance of proteinuria in patients with malignancies. Brit Med J 1988;296:295-8.

Yamauchi M, Linsey MS, Biava CG, Hopper J. Cure of membranous nephropathy after resection of carcinoma. Arch Intern Med 1985;145:2063-3.

SECTION 6

Interstitial disorders

CHAPTER

27

Tubulointerstitial nephritis

Rafael Pérez-García, Fernando Valderrábano

Tubulointerstitial nephritis (TIN) comprises a heterogeneous group of diseases that mainly and initially affect the renal interstitium and tubules. The term *tubulointerstitial nephritis*, more appropriate than *interstitial nephritis*, originates from the fact that both the tubules and the interstitium are affected together in the majority of these diseases, which better explains the pathogenesis and clinical findings. Normal interstitial volume has been estimated to amount to 13% of kidney volume, and it comprises the extravascular intertubular spaces. In many of the pathologies that fundamentally affect the vessels and glomerulus there are associated tubulointerstitial lesions that significantly influence prognosis and contribute important data regarding the acuteness or chronicity and other characteristics of the renal pathology. This type of tubulointerstitial involvement is referred to as *secondary* (i.e., *secondary TIN*). The name *primary TIN* is usually reserved for those renal diseases in which involvement of the tubules and interstitium predominates at the histologic and functional levels, and initiation of the inflammatory or cytotoxic process occurs at that level. This division is partially arbitrary, since, for example, in chronic primary tubulointerstitial nephropathies, glomerulosclerotic lesions with severe proteinuria can appear. The etiologic factors that can influence these diseases are many, basically enumerated in the Table 27.1, making up a heterogeneous group of renal pathologies (see "Classification", below). It is now apparent that only a small proportion of these lesions results directly from infection. Two pathogenic forms of these diseases are fundamental, the first due to immunologic mechanisms that provoke an acute and/or chronic inflammatory situation and the second direct nephrotoxicity of the renal (mainly tubular) cells (see "Mechanism", below). Some of these diseases, because of their importance, constitute the subject matter of other chapters in this book. The rest are described in this chapter.

These diseases can be recognized clinically by the symptoms and signs that appear with malfunctioning of the renal tubules and interstitium, and the majority of these pathologies affect glomerular filtration (GF) through a variety of mechanisms that will be described later by showing a closer relation between ultrastructural damage and decrease in GF than in the case of glomerular pathology. The diagnostic scheme and treatment of some of these diseases, such as acute interstitial nephritis (AIN), constitute a subject that is presently being reconsidered and which requires the performance of a renal biopsy as a fundamental diagnostic step. A few years ago, these diseases were diagnosed by exclusion or were included within the "chronic pyelonephritides." Nowadays, through clinical and occupational background, analytical, audiovisual, and histologic studies, a specific diagnosis is possible (see "Diagnosis", below). The TINs are important because they constitute a group of renal diseases that most often lead to both acute and chronic renal failure. Some of these diseases are specific geographically, such as Balkan nephropathy, or are influenced by social situations, such as analgesic nephropathy.

EPIDEMIOLOGY

It is difficult to offer epidemiologic data about all the TINs because different diseases are grouped within this definition. There are epidemiologic studies based on some of the signs that give rise to these diseases, such as proteinuria plus hematuria, chronic renal failure (CRF), and acute renal failure (ARF).

In a Finnish study carried out on 314 000 soldiers, renal biopsies were performed on 174 of those who showed hematuria or persistent proteinuria; TIN was found in 2 patients, which would give a prevalence of 0.7 per 100 000. This study is not representative of real prevalence because it included only generally healthy males of a certain age without infection who were not taking any medication.

The data from the European Dialysis and Transplant Association (EDTA-ERA) regarding the causes of renal failure that require replacement therapy contribute information on TINs as a cause of terminal renal failure. In the years between 1980 and 1983, the cause of renal failure in 24% of the children who started replacement therapy was "pyelonephritis/interstitial nephritis." Of these, 60% suffered from congenital obstructive uropathy or reflux nephropathy. With age comes a greater increase in the proportion of patients with a diagnosis of "pyelonephritis/non-cause-specific TIN," which ranges from 10% in patients of under age 15 years to over 60% in patients between the ages of 40 and 70 years. At these ages,

Table 27.1 Classification of tubulointerstitial nephritis

1. Acute tubulointerstitial nephritis (AIN)
   a. Drug-related AINs (hypersensitivity)
   b. AINs associated with infections (reactive)
   c. Idiopathic AINs
2. Acute tubular necrosis (ATN)
3. Chronic tubulointerstitial nephritis (CIN)
   a. Analgesic nephropathy
   b. Lithium nephropathy
   c. Cisplatin nephropathy
   d. CIN caused by other medications (methyl-CCNU, gentamicin, cyclosporin A)
   e. Lead nephropathy
   f. Nephropathy caused by other metals (mercury, cadmium, gold, iron)
   g. TIN caused by other toxins
4. Metabolic tubulointerstitial nephritis
   a. Acute and chronic nephropathy caused by uric acid
   b. Oxalate nephropathy
   c. Hypercalcemic nephropathy
   d. Hypokaliemic nephropathy
   e. Other TIN caused by various metabolic toxins: cystinosis, Fabry disease
5. Tubulointerstitial nephritis (TIN) in systemic and immunologic diseases
   a. TIN in primary glomerulonephritis
   b. Systemic diseases: systemic lupus erythematosus; Sjögren's syndrome, cryoglobulinemia, vasculitis
   c. Amyloidosis
   d. Transplant rejection
   e. TIN mediated by anti-TBM antibodies
   f. TIN associated with uveitis
6. TIN in malignancy (induced by cancer)
   a. Lymphomas
   b. Leukemia
   c. Multiple myeloma
   d. Monoclonal gammapathies
7. TIN in urinary tract infection and reflux nephropathy and urinary tract obstruction
   a. Acute pyelonephritis
   b. Chronic pyelonephritis
   c. Acute and chronic obstructive uropathy
   d. Vesicoureteral reflux
8. TIN in vascular and hematologic diseases
   a. Nephroangiosclerosis
   b. Atheroembolic disease
   c. Renal infarctions
   d. Acute tubular necrosis
   e. TIN in hematologic diseases: sickle cell disease
9. Hereditary diseases and TIN
   a. Renal cystic diseases
   b. Sponge kidney
   c. Hereditary nephropathies: Alport's syndrome, others
10. Idiopathic and familial TIN: miscellaneous
    a. Radiation nephropathy
    b. Balkan nephropathy
    c. Idiopathic interstitial nephropathies
       (1) Idiopathic TIN caused by anti-TBM antibodies
          (a) Idiopathic
          (b) Familial and nonfamilial associated with membranous GN
       (2) Idiopathic TIN caused by immune-complex deposits
          (a) IgE
          (b) Familial
       (3) Idiopathic granulomatous TIN
       (4) TIN with uveitis
       (5) Familial TIN linked to HLA and hypokalemia
       (6) Systemic karyomegaly (megakaryocytic TIN)

pyelonephritis/TIN represents approximately 20% of the total number of patients. In Spain, 17% of the patients who started dialysis in 1986-1987 (n = 3716) were diagnosed with pyelonephritis/TIN, without including cystic nephropathies, which alone account for 10.4%. In the United States, the frequency of TINs that cause terminal CRF, including adult polycystic disease, is 26%, similar to that mentioned in Europe. At all ages, the female sex predominates among patients with TINs.

The majority of ARF episodes, excluding prerenal and postrenal episodes, are caused by ischemic-nephrotoxic tubular necrosis and a minority by AINs. The proportion of AINs to ARF is between 0.8 and 8% but reaches between 11 and 24% in biopsied patients. We must remember that the diagnosis of AIN is established according to clinical and histologic criteria, and few ARF patients are biopsied; the rest are simply considered to have tubular necrosis. Furthermore, many AINs develop subclinically and are undetected, such as some nonoliguric ARFs, in general, due to nephrotoxic tubular necrosis or rhabdomyolysis. Cases of ARF associated with the ingestion of medication, the cause of most nephrotoxic tubular necroses and AINs, have increased in the last 20 years from 5% to 16 to 25%.

With regard to the total number of renal biopsies performed in hospitals, between 1.1 and 3.4% correspond to TINs. In 25 000 autopsies, 1.7% acute TINs, excluding pyelonephritis, and 0.2% chronic TINs were found.

The geographic distribution of TIN is not uniform and depends on the different incidences of the diseases included in this group. For example, the incidence of analgesic nephropathy varies from one country to another, even from one region to another. Within the United States, this varies from 2 to 2.8% of the patients starting dialysis in California and Washington, D.C., to 20% in Philadelphia. In Europe, there is a variation from 1% in Great Britain to 44% in Belgium, with a prevalence of 2.2% for all of Europe (that is, 1488/67 412 patients). These differences can be explained by the magnitude of the consumption of analgesics, since the relationship between the incidence of this disease and the consumption of analgesics per capita is well founded; the composition of the analgesics most often consumed; and the greater susceptibility of the population, including racial and environmental factors such as climate. There are some very interesting epidemiologic studies on many TINs that help to better explain their causes and prevention.

CLASSIFICATION

Table 27.1 shows a clinicoetiopathogenic classification, which is useful on a clinical level. The classification of TINs into acute and chronic is of use because these data, in general, are easily checked and separates two large groups of TINs. Table 27.2 enumerates some of the causes of TINs according to the types of predominant tubular involvement to which they give rise.

In histologic studies of the kidney in TIN, we find four basic types of lesions: (1) inflammatory infiltration, (2)

Table 27.2 Tubulointerstitial nephropathies according to the predominant form of functional tubular alteration

Proximal tubule

Complete or incomplete Fanconi's syndrome: aminoaciduria, glycosuria, phosphaturia, uricosuria, bicarbonaturia, proximal or type II RTA, hypokalemia, salt wasting, hypovolemia

Hereditary disorders (cystinosis, Lowe's syndrome)
TIN induced by metals (lead, cadmium, mercury)
Drug-induced toxicity (Azathioprin, streptozocin, out-of-date tetracyclin, lithium)
Idiopathic TIN
Chronic hypocalcemia
Nephrotic syndrome
Multiple myeloma
Hemoglobinuria paroxysmal nocturnal

Distal tubule

Distal tubular acidosis, hyperkalemia, salt loss nephropathy, hypostenuria

Acute tubulointerstitial nephritis, drug-related
Hypercalcemic TIN (nephrocalcinosis)
TIN in immunologic diseases (Sjögren's syndrome, SLE, lupoid hepatitis)
Amyloidosis, multiple myeloma
Obstructive uropathy
Medullar cystic nephropathy
Balkan nephropathy

Medullar and papillary structures

Diminished urine concentrating capacity (nocturia and polyuria)

Analgesic nephropathy
Drug toxicity (lithium, amphotericin B, cyclamate)
Acute TIN caused by hyperuricosuria or hyperoxaluria
Sarcoidosis
Acute pyelonephritis
Medullary sponge kidney
Adult polycystic disease
Sickle cell disease (falciform syndromes)
Eliptocytosis

interstitial edema and flattening of the tubular cells, (3) Necrosis-apoptosis of the tubular cells, and (4) fibrosis. The first type of lesion is typical of immunoallergic and infectious interstitial nephritis, the second of ischemic diseases, the third of nephrotoxic syndromes, and the fourth may be associated to any of the preceding three. The four types of lesions tend to overlap, with three of them appearing in a kidney as a result of the same disease. When the histologic lesions become chronic, fibrosis, tubular atrophy, and small lymphocytes appear.

CLINICAL MANIFESTATIONS AND FUNCTIONAL ABNORMALITIES

A number of syndromes and symptoms appear as a result of tubular lesions. Functional damage depends on the segment of the tubule and the type of nephron affected. Lesions of the proximal tubule give rise to complete or noncomplete Fanconi's syndrome, consistent with generalized aminoaciduria, glycosuria, and phosphaturia increased with hypophosphatemia, hypercalciuria, hypokalemia, increased proximal natriuresis, uricosuria with hypouricemia, bicarbonaturia with proximal tubular acidosis, or type II and tubular proteinuria.

Alteration of the distal tubule produces different forms of distal tubular acidosis: traditionally, type I or classic; type III, associated with bicarbonaturia (nonclear); and type IV, associated with hyperkalemia. A physiopathologic classification shows alterations of the hydrogen ion pump and of the electrical gradient facilitator for secretion and increased tubular permeability for hydrogen ions with retrograde flow and lack of proton acceptor ions, basically ammonia, in the urine. Another alteration that appears with lesions of the distal tubule is hyperkalemia, without renal failure, and this frequently is associated with metabolic acidosis, which may due to primary or hyporeninemic hypoaldosteronism but also can be caused by tubular resistance to mineralocorticoids in their different forms. Finally, salt-loss situations also can be produced by distal lesions, with a negative Na balance not justified by other causes.

Predominantly medullar and deep nephron lesions produce alterations in urine-concentrating capacity, giving rise to nephrogenic diabetes insipidus with polyuria, nocturia, and polydipsia. This is frequently the earliest symptomology of chronic TIN. Many TINs predominantly affect a segment of the tubule, and therefore, we can establish a classification of TINs according to the type of functional involvement (see Tab. 27.3).

A decrease in GF is a frequent sign of TIN, both acute and chronic forms. Approximately 15% of ARFs and between 17 and 25% of CRFs biopsied are due to TIN. As we have already mentioned, there is a significant correlation between the number of ultrastructural tubulointerstitial lesions and the deterioration of GF. The mechanisms responsible for this decrease in GF are obstruction of the damaged tubules, which impedes GF, and obstruction of the peritubular capillaries, which increases postglomerular vascular resistance and decreases glomerular blood flow. Tubular malfunction also produces a hyperflow of water

Table 27.3 Forms of acute renal failure

1. Prerenal
2. Vasculorenal: occlusion of the large vessels
3. Intrarenal or intrinsic alteration
   a. Intrarenal vascular occlusion (microembolisms, atheroembolisms, intravascular coagulation, cortical necrosis, microangiopathies, etc.)
   b. Ischemic tubular necrosis
   c. Nephrotoxic tubular necrosis
   d. Acute glomerulonephritis
   e. Acute tubulointerstitial nephritis
4. Postrenal or obstructive

and ions at the distal tubular level, which through tubuloglomerular control and the juxtaglomerular apparatus decreases GF.

Some clinical data are helpful in the diagnosis of TIN when a differential diagnosis with a vasculoglomerular nephropathy is done. In early stages, it is unusual to find proteinurias of over 1.5 to 2 g/day in TINs. Proteinuria in TIN tends to be very slight and corresponds to low-molecular-weight proteins, which, when filtered, are normally reabsorbed in the tubules, such as β_2-microglobulin (11 600 Da), immunoglobulin light chains (22 000 Da), lysozyme (14 000 Da), complement proteins, etc., or those formed in the tubules, such as the mucoprotein called *Tamm-Horsfall protein*. The majority of these proteins appear normally in the urine in small quantities of less than 150 mg/day, or 100 μg/min. These increase in TIN because reabsorption or tubular metabolization is decreased. Although some degree of glomerular proteinuria frequently is associated because of direct or hemodynamic effects on the glomerulus, this is usually slight. In more advanced stages, with GF reduction, significant proteinuria may appear, even in the nephrotic range. The possible mechanisms in cases of significant proteinuria are hyperfiltration and vascular and immunologic involvement, with the presence of antibodies due to common tubuloglomerular antigens. Glomerulosclerotic lesions are observed frequently in these cases, most commonly in patients with chronic pyelonephritis or reflux nephropathy.

Drug-induced functional renal failure

Renal function disorders caused by medication are common in clinical experience. Renal functions affected most frequently are glomerular filtration (GF), capacity for urine concentration or dilution, and capacity to eliminate potassium. The groups of medications most commonly involved are angiotensin converting enzyme (ACE) inhibitors, nonsteroidal anti-inflammatory drugs (NSAIDs), and diuretics. The most common disturbances produced are disturbances of juxtaglomerular apparatus function and pre- and postglomerular arteriolar tone balance, regulation of ADH effect at the distal and collecting tubule levels, and distal potassium secretion mechanisms.

Tubulointerstitial disease in the pathogenesis of salt-dependent hypertension

Recently, the hypothesis that acquired tubulointerstitial diseases play a part in the pathogenesis of essential salt-dependent hypertension has been established. There is evidence of this clinical association, particularly in elderly, black, and obese patients.

DIAGNOSIS

TIN should be suspected when the physician is confronted with a patient with a series of the following syndromes or symptoms. First, TIN should be a part of the differential diagnosis for acute or chronic renal failure. In a patient with normal or slightly reduced renal function, TIN should be suspected in the presence of (1) polyuria, nocturia, and polydipsia, (2) hyperchloremic metabolic acidosis, (3) hyperkalemia, (4) salt-losing nephropathies, and (5) Fanconi's syndrome. All these symptoms and signs have specific functional tests that permit diagnosis. Tubular alterations found through functional tests allow the differential diagnosis of the tubulointerstitial lesions in diverse renal diseases such as glomerulonephritis (GN), pyelonephritis, and diabetic nephropathy. TINs may appear as a complication in numerous systemic diseases that should be ruled out at diagnosis or during evaluation. In the diagnosis of chronic interstitial nephritis, and especially in the diagnosis of analgesic nephropathy, ultrasound is useful because it is capable of showing the papillary calcifications in a garland pattern around the central sinus, and thus it can be used to detect previously unknown analgesic abuse. Computed tomographic (CT) scanning without contrast material is the best method for detecting papillary calcifications. CT scan is indicated in all patients with chronic renal failure of unknown etiology.

Special mention should be made of acute interstitial nephritis (AIN). The cardinal indicator of these diseases is a sudden decrease in GF, generally expressed as a decrease in creatinine clearance of more than 10 to 20 ml/min or as an increase in serum creatinine of 0.4 to 1 mg/dl. In the presence of these data, possible diagnoses are enumerated in Table 27.3. In the presence of intrarenal acute renal failure, differentiating between acute tubular necrosis, acute glomerulonephritis (GN), and AIN can be difficult. AINs should be suspected in a patient with a history of hypersensitivity to drugs or infection, previous exposure to a drug, fever of noninfectious origin, cutaneous rash, pain in the lumbar region, arterial hypertension, eosinophilia, Na excretion fraction of greater than 1%, isosthenuria with Na concentration in the urine of more than 40 mEq/l, microscopic hematuria, slight proteinuria (<1.5 g/d), leukocyturia and leukocyte cylinders with a negative urine culture, and eosinophiluria that can be better detected with Hansel stain than with conventional ones (Tab. 27.4). Some of these findings are common to other causes of ARF, and TIN can develop practically symptomlessly. A gammagraphy with gallium-67 can be useful in the differential diagnosis between AIN and tubular necrosis.

When AIN is suspected, all potentially causative medications should be suspended, the infection treated, and the metabolic disorder corrected. When there is no response in a few days, there is no evident cause of the acute tubular necrosis, and as long as the urine analyses show abnormalities – proteinuria and/or alterations in sediment – renal biopsy is indicated and, if it is examined using the proper techniques by experienced personnel, will define diagnosis. There also will be signs, such as the degree of fibrosis, that orient the physician with regard to the reversibility of the lesions and the usefulness of immunosuppressant treatment. Immunologic findings in blood, urine, or the biopsy itself, such as the discovery of anti-basal tubular membrane antibodies or cell markers, also orient the physician

Table 27.4 Diagnostic features in acute tubulointerstitial nephritis

1. Acute renal failure (acute increase in serum creatinine)
2. Fever, skin rash, and arthralgias
3. Previous history of drug ingestion or systemic infection
4. Blood eosinophilia
5. Signs of hepatocellular damage
6. Tubular proteinuria, usually < 1 g/day
7. Increase urinary leukocytes without pyuria
8. Eosinophiluria (Hansel stain)
9. Macroscopic or microscopic hematuria
10. Fractional excretion of sodium, of > 1%
11. Thrombocytopenia, hemolysis
12. Positive bilateral gallium uptake
13. Predominantly interstitial inflammation in renal biopsy

with regard to diagnosis and treatment to be used. A renal biopsy can correctly diagnose 77% of AINs, helping to determine prognosis and choice of treatment.

PATHOGENIC MECHANISM: INTERSTITIAL INFLAMMATION, NEPHRITOGENIC IMMUNE RESPONSE, INTERSTITIAL FIBROSIS, CHEMICAL AND PHYSICAL NEPHROTOXICITY

Renal pathology induced by medications and other toxic substances is very frequent nowadays. The kidney has specific physiologic characteristics that make it susceptible to toxic agents. Among these, the most significant include the fact that renal blood flow is very high, corresponding to 25% of cardiac output; the contact surface of vessels and nephrons is very extensive; renal metabolism energy necessary to deal with renal transport functions is very high; in many cases the kidney is responsible for metabolizing and/or eliminating toxic substances; some of its functions, such as urine concentration, can determine the concentration and accumulation of toxic agents; and renal hemodynamics and glomerular filtration depend on a balance of vasoactive substances, such as renin-angiotensin and the prostaglandins. Selective interference in any of these systems can cause, in some cases, functional disorders and even structural damage.

Exposure to toxic substances, both in the environment and in the workplace, is at present a frequent cause of renal pathology. Today's industrially developed society exposes workers to a higher number and concentration of toxic substances. A good example is environmental lead contamination, the concentration of which in Greenland has increased by 20 times in the last 200 years.

On the other hand, the use of medications has increased considerably, and although this may be rationalized and nephrotoxicity is prevented where possible, such as in the case of anticancer drugs and iodine contrast agents, the frequency of clinical symptoms due to nephrotoxicity secondary to medications is steadily increasing.

The degree of exposure to the toxic substances, individual susceptibility, the presence of other concurrent factors, and individual fibrogenic capacity indicate the intensity of the clinical situation and its chronic or acute expression. In this type of pathology, prevention is fundamental and is intimately involved in environmental conservation and the rational use of medications.

TINs globally respond to two types of pathogenic mechanisms. In the first, a series of factors induce interstitial inflammation, which, in some cases, can lead to fibrosis; in the second, there is cellular damage due to direct toxicity that can produce cellular necrosis, apoptosis, or reversible functional alterations. The two mechanisms are probably interrelated. The tubuloepithelial cells, the fibroblasts, and the cells of the interstitial vessels are the target for the etiologic factors involved in interstitial nephritis. Lesions in these cells unleash the following: functional disorders, secretion of inflammation mediators, and expression of neoantigens and cellular immune response amplifier molecules. Obstruction of the tubules by cellular remains and proteins, edema, and interstitial infiltration contribute to the lesion process in TIN. Various etiologic factors can stimulate the fibroblasts directly and cause chronic fibrosis in some cases. The effect on the interstitial vessels can produce tubular ischemia, thereby contributing to direct cellular damage. The endothelial cells also contribute with the secretion of inflammation mediators. Therefore, it is important to have an overview of tubulointerstitial lesions that accommodates the various pathogenetic mechanisms. Table 27.5 lists the principal mechanisms by which ARF due to medications occurs, indicating the most common medications responsible for each one.

Interstitial inflammation and nephritogenic immune response

The inflammatory process in the renal interstitium may appear as a consequence of an altered immune response or

Table 27.5 Mechanisms of drug-induced acute renal failure

1. Hemodynamic effect, ischemia, prerenal failure: NSAIDs, ACE inhibitors, norepinephrine, cyclosporine
2. Acute tubular necrosis (ATN), ischemic and nephrotoxic: aminoglycosides, cephaloridine, cephalothin, amphotericin B, NSAIDs, glafenin, contrast media, cisplatin, cyclosporine
3. Tubular obstruction: sulfonamides, methotrexate, triamterene, acyclovir
4. Acute interstitial nephritis (AIN): antibiotics, NSAIDs, glafenin, allopurinol, sulfonamides
5. Hypersensitivity vasculitis: penicillin, ampicillin, sulfonamides
6. Thrombotic microangiopathy: oral contraceptives, mitomycin C, cyclosporine

direct infection of the interstitium (Tab. 27.6). The forms mediated by immune mechanisms are based on the presence of antigens, antibodies, cytotoxic T cells, and rarely antigen-antibody complexes. In both humoral and cellular response forms, the presence of CD4+ nephritogenic T-helper cells, type Th-1 secretors of interleukin 2 (IL-2) and interferon-γ is of vital importance. Loss of control by the T-cell suppressers in the afferent phase of the nephritogenic response may be another of the factors involved. The presence of antigen-antibody complexes is rare in TINs, probably because the glomerulus acts as a filter. In the efferent immune phase, antibodies on tubulointerstitial structures may cause inflammation through direct cytotoxic effects, activation of complement, chemotaxis, and induction of a cell-mediated cytotoxic response. The direct cytotoxic response mediated by CD8+ restricted MHC class 1 cells, accompanied by CD4+ cells and macrophages, is the most typical. Cytotoxic action is mediated by the perphorins or by a delayed-type hypersensitivity reaction with the release of cytokines. In each of the TINs, the most characteristic immune mediators are commented on. Infectious tubulointerstitial nephritis is principally caused by organisms that reach the kidney from the lower urinary tract. The most common of these are the *Enterobacteriaceae*, but other causative organisms are listed in Table 27.6. Their presence alone can cause inflammation. The cytokines play an essential role as mediators. Nonspecific factors are able to induce an inflammatory response in the kidney, such as, for example, ammonium, which can activate complement by the alternate pathway.

Table 27.6 Acute tubulointerstitial nephritis related to infections

1. Bacterial infections
   - Streptococci
   - Staphylococci
   - Diphtheria (*Corynebacterium diphtheriae*)
   - Brucellosis
   - Typhoid fever (*Salmonella*)
   - Enterobacteriacea
   - *Yersinia pseudotuberculosis*
   - *Legionella pneumophila*
   - Tuberculosis
   - Pneumococci
   - Tularemia (*Francisella tularensis*)
   - Syphilis (*Treponema*)
   - Leptospirosis
   - *Campylobacter*
2. Rickettsial infections
   - Rocky Mountain fever (*R. rickettsii*)
3. Mycoplasmal infections
   - *Mycoplasma pneumoniae*
4. Parasitic infections
   - Schistosomiasis
   - Toxoplasmosis
   - Leishmaniasis (*L. donovani*)
5. Viral infections
   - Epstein-Barr virus
   - Human immunodeficiency virus
   - Mumps
   - Cytomegalovirus
   - Hepatitis B virus
   - Kawasaki disease virus
   - Rubeola
   - Hantaan virus
   - Hepatitis A and B

In secondary TINs, a series of factors can provoke tubulointerstitial inflammation and the progression of renal fibrosis. Some of these are listed in Table 27.7. As the table shows, these factors coincide with those which influence the progression of renal failure in diseases with vasculoglomerular lesions. It is probably the secondary tubulointersitital lesion that principally causes evolution toward chronic renal failure. Among these factors, it is important to emphasize the role of proteinuria, i.e., the amount of some proteins in the tubular liquid, such as the transferrin-iron complex and albumin, that are capable of producing tubulointerstitial lesions. Holotransferrin induces cytotoxicity in proximal tubule cells via a mechanism that involves cell uptake of holotransferrin, intracellular iron accumulation, and lipid peroxidation. Actions taken to lower the degree of proteinuria, such as the administration of ACE inhibitors, may have a significant role in slowing the progression of the tubulointerstitial lesions in the vasculoglomerular pathology.

Renal interstitial fibrosis

The development of renal interstitial fibrosis in association with the inflammatory process greatly influences the evolution to renal failure. This fibrous response depends on the inflammatory stimuli to which the kidney is exposed and individual susceptibility. The normal balance between interstitial cell protein synthesis and degradation is disrupted in renal fibrosis; upregulation of protein synthesis and downregulation of proteolytic enzymes cause cellular hypertrophy and expansion of the extracellular matrix.

The progression to fibrosis can be divided into three phases: induction, production of a protein matrix, and its deposit and resolution. Fibrosis can be a reparative and self-controlled phenomenon, but when uncontrolled, it leads to the fibrosis of the organ. There are various types of fibroblasts at the renal level. In kidneys that develop fibrosis, the normal proportion of fibroblasts is altered so that 39% are mitotic MF1 cell types, whereas in the normal kidney there is only 2%. The phenotypic expression of fibroblasts in kidneys with fibrosis is also altered. The interstitial cells involved in this type of injurious process may show a phenotypic state similar to that of the fetal kidney. In chronic inflammation of the kidney, the heterogeneity is accentuated by the selection of highly proliferative subsets. The production of collagen by these fibroblasts is also increased.

However, it is not just the renal fibroblasts that contribute to the fibrosis. The tubuloepithelial cells can change their phenotype, go through the interstitium, and participate in synthesis of the extracellular matrix. The extracellular matrix is made up of type I and III collagen,

Table 27.7 Mediators involved in interstitial inflammation

1. Cellular and humoral immunity
2. Monocytes, cytokines, and chemokines
3. Proteinuria: albumin and Fe-transferrin
4. Lipids: hyperlipidemia and lipid peroxidation
5. Calcium-phosphorus deposits
6. Metabolic acidosis
7. Tubular epithelial cells and fibroblasts

fibronectine, and various proteoglycans. The fibronectine is chemotactic for the fibroblasts. The initial tubulointerstitial fibrosis induced by the inflammation is reversible. Reversibility depends on the presence of proteolytic enzymes, especially the metalloproteases; downregulation of matrix metalloproteases is usually found in renal fibrosis. The activating enzymes of these proteases may be inhibited in certain circumstances. The endothelial and mononuclear cells may be the greatest source of metalloprotease inhibitors. Many of these inhibitors are upregulated during fibrogenesis. Among the humoral factors, transforming growth factor β1 (TGF-1) is the most important cytokine, and it favors fibrosis by stimulating the synthesis of extracellular matrix molecules. In such cases, resolution is only partial. Interstitial fibrosis and tubular atrophy are the common route of almost all the chronic diseases with progressive renal failure.

Cytotoxic mechanisms

Lesions of the tubular cells are another key element in these nephropathies, on the one hand, because they cause loss of function and, on the other, because they are able to provoke or contribute to the inflammatory process. Knowledge of the forms of cytotoxicity is important because frequently it is the association of two or more toxic effects, a hemodynamic and/or functional renal situation that finally provokes the lesion. Avoidance of these situations is the best treatment – i.e., prevention.

Oxidative stress Toxins that interfere with mitochondrial function cause an increased generation of reactive oxygen species (ROS). ROS also can arise from the cyclooxygenase function if hydroperoxides are present. Other ROS-forming systems are leukocyte membrane oxidating enzymes, microsomes, and xanthine oxidase. The increase in free radicals, together with a possible decrease in the antioxidating reducing systems, may influence the oxidation of vital cell structures, fundamentally through lipid peroxidation and proteolysis. Scavengers of ROS, glutathione, vitamin E, xanthine oxidase inhibitors, and iron chelators protect against ischemic injury.

Covalent binding The covalent binding of activated metabolites of drugs and other toxins to cell macromolecules can induce significant changes in cellular function. Glutathione and cysteine conjugates can result in toxic activation.

ATP deficit: cell energy depletion, oxygen deprivation The cell needs energy to preserve cellular functions. The production of energy requires, first, a sufficient amount of substrates reaching their place of metabolization in the cell. The main renal cellular substrates are glutamine, glucose, lactate, and triglycerides. Some of these substances need membrane transporters to reach organelles such as the mitochondria. Substances that interfere with this transport impede the use of these substrates. At a later step, and principally at the mitochondrial level, the respiratory chain can be hampered. Another point of toxicity affects the oxide-reduction system and its place in the energy chain. Cellular ATP deficit also can be caused by a lack of oxygen, as in ischemia. Certain renal areas are particularly susceptible to ischemia, such as the renal medulla. Medullar oxygen delivery is specific, and there are factors that regulate medullar blood flow. There is an equilibrium between medullar vasoconstrictors, vasodilators, and the mechanism that regulates tubular transport. The principal medullar vasoconstrictors are endothelin, angiotensin, and vasopressin. The principal medullar vasodilators are the prostaglandins (PGE_2), nitric oxide, urodilatin, and adenosine. Another factor that influences this balance is tubuloglomerular feedback, which, through a decrease in GF, protects the thick ascending limb from ischemia. The other aspect that determines ATP deficit besides level of production is consumption. Tubular functions are principally responsible for renal energy consumption and especially for membrane transport functions. A decrease in the transport of solutes or the presence of inhibitors of membrane transport decreases energy needs and may reduce the effects of ischemia. The administration of ATP precursors in experimental renal ischemia models has produced an improvement in functional recuperation.

Cell calcium disruption and intracellular acidosis An ATP deficit inhibits the exit of calcium and modifies its destination toward intracellular calcium deposits. These intracellular calcium disorders are related to cell damage. The cell calcium overload that occurs in ischemic cells means that the mitochondrial electrochemical gradient will be used to support calcium translocation at the expense of ATP generation. In the final phase of this process, mitochondrial destruction occurs. Lowering of extracellular calcium levels and calcium channel blockers are protective against hypoxic cell damage. Calcium-mediated mechanisms of cell damage involve activation of phospholipases, nitric oxide, and proteases. Cellular ischemia produces intracellular acidosis, partially because it inhibits the exit of hydrogen ions from the cell and partially due to an increase in its formation. The degree of intracellular acidosis is essential with regard to the protection-aggravation of the other cellular mechanisms that produce ischemia. Severe acidosis can cause cell death.

Membrane phospholipids These are the principal components of the cellular membrane. Their normal structure is key in the preservation of membrane integrity. The membrane phospholipids regulate permeability and modulate the activity of the enzymes integrated in the membrane, such as ATPase. Membrane phospholipids undergo continuous change; phospholipids are formed to replace lysophospholipids. Various enzymes regulate this physiologic replacement, such as phospholipase A_1 and A_2 and glycerophospholipid acyltransferase. Certain factors favor the formation of lysophospholipids; free radicals, phospholipase A_2 activation and others, such as sulfhydryl binding, alter the lipid structure of the membrane (lipoperoxidation). On the other hand, factors such as intracellular calcium or ATP deficit may affect the function of the phospholipases. Ischemia results in increased phospholipase A_2 activity with generation of lysophospholipids. The increase in lipid peroxidation of the membrane may cause an increase in permeability and cellular lysis.

Once cellular damage occurs, a process of regeneration-recuperation is set in motion. This is a preestablished program involving the expression of immediate-response genes and the production of growth factors. The proper coordination of this program leads to *restitutium ad integrum*; if this is not so, chronic lesions will remain.

ACUTE INTERSTITIAL NEPHRITIS

Acute interstitial nephritis (AIN) usually is defined as an ARF with predominantly interstitial inflammation. The kidney is especially susceptible to the adverse effects of drugs and other toxic substances. Although all the structures that make up the kidney are affected, this process in particular applies to the tubules and the interstitium. There are two fundamental types of involvement, although other mechanisms cannot be excluded. The first is direct toxic action of the substance on the tubular and interstitial cells, produced basically by aminoglycosides, other antibiotics, radiographic contrast agents, nonsteroidal anti-inflammatory drugs (NSAIDs), etc. The second is mediated by immunoallergic mechanisms responding to neoantigens or autoantigens, such as occurs with penicillin and its derivatives, rifampicin, sulfonamides, phenindione, etc. The number of substances that can produce this type of adverse reaction increases continually, making this type of pathology more and more frequent.

The first physiopathologic group is usually called *nephrotoxic tubular necrosis* (NTN). The frequency of NTN has increased in the last decade, together with an increase in nonoliguric ARF and that associated with medications. The group of immunoallergic drug-induced ARFs clearly falls within the TIN group and makes up a fairly well defined entity, AIN, which will be discussed later. Apart from medications, other factors can be associated with this type of tubulointersitital pathology, such as infections and systemic diseases, fundamentally due to immunologic disorders. Other cases, in which other causes associated with AINs are not found, fall within the idiopathic forms. The following sections will discuss the immunoallergic or unclear AINs. The factors that are associated most frequently with this pathology are drugs, infections, and other toxins.

DRUG-RELATED AINs (HYPERSENSITIVITY)

Immunologic reactions to drugs often affect the renal tubules and interstitium; this is known as *drug-induced AIN* or *hypersensitivity*. The majority of the cases described are due to methicillin and other beta-lactam derivatives, phenindione, and NSAIDs, although the number of medications involved is slowly increasing with the description of new cases. Table 27.8 enumerates some of the drugs that have been referred to as possible causes of this pathology; it is still usual, as can be seen from the references, to find the description of isolated cases in published literature.

Despite the fact that this pathology is increasing, most probably in relation to the increase in consumption of medications, it is still rare. In general, it represents no more than 1 to 2% of the renal biopsies performed, although in many hospitals renal biopsy is not normally indicated for ARF. In patients biopsied for ARF, AINs accounted for 15% of the lesions found.

Clinical findings

The acute deterioration, in days, of renal function or, more explicitly, of glomerular filtration in a patient in whom pre- and postrenal causes have been ruled out and with no predisposing causes of tubular necrosis should make us suspect the existence of an AIN. Table 27.4 mentions the characteristic clinical data in this entity. Urinalysis and renal biopsy will be the most helpful in the differential diagnosis between AIN and vasculoglomerular lesions. The onset of a progressive rise of serum creatinine concentration may occur after 2 to 20 days of drug therapy. It can occur with the first exposure to a drug or also can occur *de novo* in response to a drug previously tolerated by the patient. The antecedent of exposure to a medication or other substance, together with the existence of signs of a reaction to the same, is another fundamental fact. These signs are (1) fever, which appears in approximately 75% of patients, more frequently with some medications than others, (2) eosinophilia, which may appear in up to 80% of patients, above all in cases involving antibiotics (it is usually temporary and not always an objective sign), (3) cutaneous rash, which is present in at least 50% of patients and even can be unnoticed (the presence of this triad, although very suggestive of drug-induced AIN, appears in less than 30% of patients, and is even rarer in patients affected by NSAIDs), (4) pain in the lumbar region, generally produced by distension of the renal capsule, (5) alteration of hepatic function due to associated effects of the same process on this organ, and (6) arterial hypertension that did not exist previously.

Urinalyses are among the most useful analytical tests apart from checking for possible eosinophilia. The AIN may appear with conserved diuresis or with oliguria.

Table 27.8 Drugs associated with actue tubulointersitial nephritis

Beta-lactam antibiotics	Other antibiotics and chemotherapy	Nonsteroidal anti-inflammatory drugs
Penicillin G	Cotrimoxazole	Indomethacin
Methicillin*	Sulfonamides*	Phenylbutazone
Ampicillin	Rifampicin*	Ketoprofen
Cloxacillin	Ethambutol	Naproxen
Nafcillin	Pyrazinamide	Tolmetin
Oxacillin	Tetracycline	Diclofenac
Carbenicillin	Vancomycin	Piroxicam
Piperacilina	Erythromycin	Fenoprofen*
Cephalothin	Kanamycin	Meclofenamate*
Cephalexin	Gentamicin	Ibuprofen
Cephazolin	Amikacin	
Cefoxitin	Chloranphenicol	**Other drugs**
Cephradin	Ciprofloxacin	Contrast media
Ceftazidima	Lincomycin	Phenindiona*
	Acyclovir	Diphenylhydantoin*
Analgesics and antipiretics	Indinavir	Phenobarbital and other barbiturates
Acetaminophen		
Phenacetin	**Diuretics**	Carbamazepine
Sulphinpirazone	Thiazides*	Sodium valproate
Aspirin	Chlorthalidone	Diazepam
Glafenin*	Furosemide*	Allopurinol*
Antipirin	Tielinic acid	Cimetidine*
	Triamterene	Omeprazol
		Clofibrate
	Other substances	Captopril
	Glue inhalation	Alpha methyl dopa
		Azathioprine
		Alpha interferon
		Gold salts and bismuth
		D-Penicillamine
		Chlorprothixene
		Heroin
		Codeine

* These drugs indicated have been described as causing AINs with more frequency.

Oliguria is present in less than 20% of AIN patients. The elimination of Na from urine may be increased, maintaining a concentration of more than 40 mmol/ml despite minimal ingestion; the patient may even have water and Na depletion, with an Na excretion factor higher than 1%. The presence of specific tubular alterations is not common in this AIN as they are in chronic TIN. Proteinuria is frequently present but rarely exceeds 1.5 to 2 g/day. Nephrotic syndrome may appear rarely, caused by the association of glomerular lesions, such as the minimal glomerular lesions that appear in some cases caused by NSAIDs. Proteinuria generally has tubular characteristics, with a predominance of low-molecular-weight proteins (see above). Macroscopic hematuria is observed occasionally, although more frequent and practically a constant is the presence of microhematuria and leukocyturia. The presence of leukocyte cylinders in fresh sediment is frequent. Eosinophilia is fairly suggestive of AIN and can be identified in more than 80% of patients, above all if special stain techniques are used. In the cases caused by NSAIDs, the presence of eosinophilia is less constant. Eosinophiluria is not specific to the AINs, since it also can be seen in rapidly progressive GN, bladder carcinoma, renal atheroembolic disease, and lower urinary tract infections, such as prostatitis. In some cases, high elevations of total IgE may be found in serum, and there may be a positive skin test for the drug.

Radiologic and ultrasound studies do not show differential features, since renal size is increased or normal. The diagnostic value of gammagraphy with gallium-67 citrate for diagnosis of AINs has been mentioned. The increased reception of the isotope in this pathology is a replica of the existing inflammatory process and therefore nonspecific, since it also appears in acute pyelonephritis (usually unilateral uptake only), TIN due to sarcoidosis, renal transplant rejection, and even in nephrotic syndrome due to minimal glomerular lesions. This is useful in the differential diagnosis with tubular necrosis, in which reception is not increased. There is the possibility of false-positive results in patients with iron overload or cirrhosis.

In the presence of a clinical situation as described, a differential diagnosis should be effected, for which the performance of a renal biopsy is frequently indicated (see above), especially when renal function fails to improve after drug discontinuation.

Histopatology

The basic characteristic of the immunoallergic AINs is the presence of edema and focal or diffuse cellular infiltrates in the renal interstitium, particularly in the corticomedullar joint, the subcapsular cortex, and around the glomerulus. In contrast to these lesions, the glomerulus and vessels are usually well conserved. The absence of glomerular lesions and of significant glomerular deposits by direct immunofluorescence (IF) is required for differential diagnosis of primary AINs.

In drug-induced AINs, the presence of eosinophils, sometimes in accumulations, is observed frequently. The finding of leukocytes is more common in the AINs associated with infections. The majority of the infiltrate cells are mononuclear, fundamentally T-lymphocytes, although there are also monocyte-macrophages that may appear as epithelial cells, sometimes even forming granulomas. The number of plasma cells, usually slight, is variable.

At present, a sample of renal tissue in which AIN is suspected should be studied by optic microscope, analysis of the infiltrate cells by staining and of immunoperoxidase using monoclonal antibodies, direct immunofluorescence, and even electron microscopy. With these data, the results may be classified as:

1. *classic form*: (a) only mononuclear cells, IF negative (the most frequent histologic findings); (b) mononuclear cells and deposits of immune complexes in IF; (c) mononuclear cells and anti-tubular basement membrane antibodies (anti-TBM Abs);
2. *granulomatous form*;
3. *glomerular form*: frequently with minimal glomerular lesions;
4. *other associated lesions*: vasculitis, fibrosis.

Form 1a This is the most frequent form, and together with the signs already mentioned of cellular infiltrate and interstitial edema, we also may observe loss of continuity of the tubule basement membrane (TBM) and tubules infiltrated with lymphocytes, generally CD4+ and CD8+, a lesion known as tubulitis. Necrosis of the tubular cells is not frequent, but when present, it should make us think about a nephrotoxic cause. In the most severe cases, the destructurization of the interstitium occurs.

Form 1b This form shows the same characteristics as the preceding but also includes the appearance of immune complexes in the form of discontinuous granular deposits along the TBM, which is sometimes associated with complement. This is the rarest form.

Form 1c This histologic pattern shows, together with the findings described in form 1a, the presence of anti-TBM antibodies in linear deposits generally composed of IgG and complement. It is difficult to know precisely what percentage of lesions show this pattern, although it is estimated at between 9.5 and 17%.

Form 2 Granulomatous reactions are frequent in drug-induced AINs, appearing in up to 36% of patients. The granulomas are found in the interstitium; the presence of giant cells is unusual, as is the presence of necrosis. The cells of which they are composed are similar in appearance to that of activated macrophages in retarded hypersensitivity reactions. The appearance of this type of lesion implies the need to make a differential diagnosis with the diseases that produce granulomatous interstitial nephritis, enumerated in Table 27.9.

Form 3 The glomerular involvement associated with the interstitial lesions is more frequent with certain drugs, such as NSAIDs (Tab. 27.10). Most cases correspond to minimal glomerular lesions and membranous GN. AINs accompanying acute GN typically are present in any patient with acute GN and ARF.

Form 4 Vasculitic lesions have been observed in patients with AIN induced by penicillin, allopurinol, clofibrate, barbiturates, methicillin, and penicillamine. It is difficult to establish causal relations among these clinical associations.

The inflammation of the urinary tract at other levels may be present in drug-induced AINs. There is a histologic continuity between the acute and chronic forms of TIN, which ranges from the initial inflammatory process mediated by cells to fibrogenesis that finally destroys the interstitial structure. This transition may occur sooner or later, taking from a week to years. More or less fibrogenesis is highly related to the type of inflammation mediated by the cells.

Etiopathogenesis

Both the clinical appearance and histology of drug-related

Table 27.9 Granulomatous interstital nephritis

1. Infectious: *Mycobacterium, Brucella, Salmonella, Histoplasma, Candida, Toxoplasma, Schistosoma*, Epstein-Barr, cytomegalovirus
2. Acute tubulointersitial neprhtitis: drug-induced immunoallergic: allopurinol, ampicillin, fenoprofen, glafenin, methicillin, sulfonamide, cotrimoxazole, thiazides
3. Vasculitis: Wegener's granulomatosis, Churg-Strauss granulomatosis
4. Granulomas caused by foreign bodies: oxalosis, gout, heroin contaminants
5. Hematologic: granuloma lymphoid
6. Others: sarcoidosis, associated with uveitis, Crohn's disease
7. Idiopathic granulomatosis

Table 27.10 Renal alterations related to the use of NSAIDs

Functional
Retention of NaCl
Water retention, hyponatremia
Hyporeninism, hyperkalemia
Decrease of renal plasma flow and glomerular filtration
Flank pain syndrome
Acute renal failure by tubular necrosis
Acute tubulointerstitial nephritis
Nephrotic syndrome, minimal glomerular lesions
Chronic renal failure, papillary necrosis

AIN suggest that we are seeing a disease provoked by a drug or other substance that, through immunoallergic mechanisms, is going to produce predominantly renal interstitial lesions. Most of the data regarding the immunopathogenesis of AIN come from the study of animal models. This type of abnormal immune response to drugs may be qualified as nephritogenic and implies three phases: (1) recognition of the antigen, (2) the immune-regulating mechanisms of the immune response to this antigen, and (3) the lesion or effective phase.

1. Medications can act as haptens, joining the tubulointerstitial structures or modifying them, thereby acquiring immunogenic capacity. They also can produce a toxic effect on the renal interstitial structures with the appearance of nephritogenic neoantigens. Another mechanism is the presence in germs or complex drugs of a structure similar to that of an interstitial antigen, producing a crossed reaction.

   The precipitating factor of the abnormal nephritogenic response is not always the appearance of a new antigen associated with the drug, since the effect may be caused by the loss of immunologic tolerance to potentially nephritogenic endogenous tubulointerstitial antigens, such as 3M-1 of the TBM, which is an antigen of the anti-TBM Ab. There is speculation regarding various mechanisms through which an organism reacts or does not in a self-controlled, noninjurious manner to its own antigens; when these mechanisms are altered, an immune reaction may be caused, which can be local, with activation of lymphocytes at that level, or general. The fact that certain individuals of a certain species provoke a response in the T-helper lymphocytes to a certain antigen depends, in part, on the genes that determine the immune response related to the major histocompatibility complex (MHC). These genes determine, to a large degree, the susceptibility to development of autoimmune diseases and the balance of the immune response. The drugs behave like haptens, which may bind to serum or cellular proteins and subsequently are processed and presented by major histocompatibility complex molecules as hapten-modified peptides.
2. The AINs are an infrequent form of immune reaction, perhaps because the immune response through the nephritogenic T- and B-lymphocytes is limited by negative control mechanisms. The genes that control the immune response play an important part in the fact that some people develop AINs and others do not. The regulating phenomena of the immune response are also important in the type of response provoked and its intensity.
3. The possible effects of the immune response, caused by the determinants in the two preceding phases are multiple. They can be classified according to experiences with animal models in (a) formation and deposition of immune complexes with soluble or fixed (trapped) exogenous or endogenous antigens, (b) reactive antibodies to the antigens of the tubular cells or their products (Heymann type), (c) antibodies to structural antigens, anti-TBM Ab (70, 48, and 58 kDa, associated with transplantation), (d) anti-glomerular basement membrane antibodies (anti-GBM Ab) and anti-TBM Ab, (e) retarded hypersensitivity reaction, (f) cell reaction to homologous TBM antigens, (g) cellular reaction to tubular cell antigens, and (h) non-immune-specific inflammatory mechanisms. Usually, effector cells in TIN are either CD8+ cytotoxic cells or B cells.

The deposition of circulating immune complexes is one form of tubulointerstitial effect. When this occurs, it usually affects, with time and predominantly, the preglomerular vessels or the glomerulus, although the effect also can be local in the tubular interstitium only. This effect is typical of systemic autoimmune diseases such as systemic lupus erythematosus (SLE). The AINs with deposition of immune complexes have been classified experimentally by the source of the antigen, whether autologous or exogenous.

The majority of the antibodies that appear in the interstitium are due to a process of union in situ more than a precipitation of circulating immune complexes. Locally, these immunoproteins are capable of provoking inflammatory processes through diverse mediators: direct cellular cytotoxicity, complement, chemotaxis of diverse leukocytes, and the production and liberalization of their mediators (cytokines, class II MHC, VCAM, and ICAM 1).

Another immune response consists of the production of anti-TBM Ab that is deposited along the same, in linear fashion. The determinants of susceptibility to the development of disease due to anti-TBM Abs are (a) expression of 3M-1 antigen (membrane glycoprotein), (b) abolition of immunologic tolerance, (c) presence of immune-response contrasuppression genes, and (d) visibility of MHC parenchymatous antigens.

On some occasions, the immune response is produced through IgE antibodies that are induced fundamentally by certain antigens such as parasites, certain bacterial products, and substances that act as haptens. The IgE response is regulated by different types of T-lymphocytes that segregate lymphokines causing the proliferation of IgE secretor B cells. These antibodies are capable of attracting and releasing basophil mediators (degranulation) [interleukin 3 (IL-3) and IL-4; high-affinity receptor for IgE] and eosinophils (IL-5; low-affinity receptors).

As mentioned in the histopathology section, the cells that predominate in the infiltrates of AIN lesions are mononuclear, normally corresponding to T-lymphocytes and, rarely, B-lymphocytes. These lymphocytes usually belong to the CD4+ and CD8+ subpopulations. T cells of the interstitium express some cytokines, including γ-interferon, IL-2, IL-4 and TNF-α. The effector cells are usually CD8+ and class I restricted and are capable of producing lesions through two mechanisms. The first is a response of the retarded cutaneous hypersensitive type, through the release of inflammatory lymphokines and other mediators, and the second is by direct cellular cytotoxicity, through the proteases (e.g., granzymes and perphorins).

The facilitating and cytotoxic lymphocytes produce others besides the lymphokines mentioned, which are responsible for the increase in extracellular matrix, in the form of fibrosis, through stimulation of production by fibroblasts and epithelial cells. This phase of immune response is generally slower, although it can appear as early as the first week, and its severity marks the difference between acute or cellular lesions and chronic or fibrotic lesions.

Diagnosis

The diagnosis of this disease is clinical and histopathologic. In some cases with clear amanuensis and symptomatology that recedes with the suspension of the medication, the performance of a renal biopsy is not necessary, although it should be performed in the rest. Diagnostic guidelines for AIN are outlined above.

Prognosis

On suspension of the medication, most patients recover renal function completely or to a major degree when evaluated at the end of 1 year. Other patients, however, still show a certain deterioration of renal function; some of them, when biopsied again, show interstitial fibrosis with tubular atrophy. The persistence of renal failure for more than 3 weeks, oliguria, and advanced age of the patient are some of the factors involved in a negative prognosis for AIN. The extension of cellular infiltrates, becoming diffused, correlates with a higher level of serum creatinine at the moment of biopsy and during follow-up and, for some authors, a more negative prognosis evaluated at 6 to 8 weeks. The degree of tubular involvement also could be another prognostic factor.

Treatment

Many cases of drug-induced AIN do not require any treatment other than the suspension of the provoking medication. In patients in whom renal function has not returned within a week after suspension of the medication, steroid treatment could be indicated, which, according to some authors, should be given early if a clear response is to be obtained. Prednisone in an oral dose of 1 mg/kg daily for a period of 4 weeks is used. Patients treated at 3 weeks of evolution show a worse prognosis. Early treatment is clearly indicated, given the rapidity with which fibrogenesis can develop, from 7 to 14 days, since if fibroid lesions already exists at biopsy, the patient not only will not benefit from steroid treatment, but it may even be harmful. There are patients who remit spontaneously and others who do not respond to steroids, and therefore, given the lack of wide, controlled studies regarding their efficiency, the use of steroids is still debatable, although some evidence exists in favor of this treatment.

Immunosuppressive drugs such as cyclophosphamide (1-2 mg/kg daily) also have been tried in AIN, although the majority of studies have been carried out on animal models. The importance of rapid treatment is also true with these drugs. Renal biopsy should be performed before the initiation of immunosuppressive drugs other than steroids. Cyclosporin A also has shown positive results in diseases due to anti-TBM Abs. This drug could be indicated in patients with AIN and progressive or persistent renal failure with acute histologic lesions who do not respond to steroids in 2 weeks of treatment. If there is no response in 5 or 6 weeks of treatment, this should not continue because of both collateral toxic effects and possible direct adverse responses. In these patients, along with treatment, protein ingestion should be strictly reduced because the response to immunosuppressors could be more effective with the nonspecific decrease in T-lymphocyte functions. Plasmapheresis may be considered adjunctive therapy in the case of anti-TBM Abs.

Together with these nonspecific immunosuppressive treatments, at present, tests are being conducted on animals for specific treatment through the induction of anti-idiotype antibodies against anti-TBM Abs.

Specific characteristics of AINs caused by specific drugs

Penicillin and beta-lactam antibiotics This group of medications represents the most frequent cause of hypersensitivity AINs. The frequency with which methicillin provokes the disease is significant; up to 17% of the patients treated show renal failure. With the appearance and use of other antibiotics for the treatment of Staphylococcus (i.e., cloxacillin and vancomycin), the consumption of methicillin has decreased. Despite the fact that AINs have been described with the medications mentioned, frequency is much lower than with methicillin. The incidence of AINs induced by these drugs is three times more frequent in males than in females. It can appear at any age but is most usual in young adults.

Renewed contact with these medications causes worsening of the condition or relapses, and therefore all beta-lactam antibiotics should be avoided. Most patients recover on suspension of the drug, although some may show permanent renal damage. The use of steroids is doubtful, since studies in favor of their use are either based on isolated cases, retrospective, or experimental (using animals).

Rifampicin Most cases of AINs described as due to

rifampicin appeared in the treatment of tuberculosis. Although it is usually mentioned as associated with the intermittence in treatment, there have been some cases described during continuous daily treatment. The incidence in both sexes is the same. The clinical manifestations in patients with AIN induced by rifampicin in discontinuous therapy include chills, fever, myalgia, dark urine, cephalea, and cutaneous rash. Most patients also show oliguria, and two-thirds of them require dialysis. In the patients undergoing continuous treatment, there are no significant clinical manifestations, aside from the frequent presence of tubular alterations such as insipid nephrogenic diabetes and others. In some patients with TIN due to rifampicin, this is associated with the nephrotic syndrome (NS) by minimal glomerular lesions. AINs associated with rapidly progressively GN also have been described. Recuperation on suspension of the drug is the rule, although there are exceptions in the short and long term. The pathogenesis is similar to that of the other AINs induced by drugs, although with some peculiarities such as the presence in some biopsies of predominant tubular necrosis lesions and negative direct IF. It is wise to prevent interruptions in the treatment of tuberculosis with rifampicin and other drugs and to periodically control serum creatinine, especially in the first 3 months, when these situations are most frequent.

NSAIDs These drugs are used widely and often affect renal function through various mechanisms (see Tab. 27.10):

1. Functional renal disorders, basically produced by the inhibition of prostaglandins with reduction of renal blood flow and an increase in NaCl reabsorption; salt and water retention; a tendency to hyporeninemic hypoaldosteronism with hyperkalemia.
2. Acute renal failure caused by tubular necrosis, in which, although possibly appearing in healthy persons, the NSAIDs usually act as coadjutants, together with a series of predisposing factors (e.g., advanced age, contraction of extracellular volume, cardiac failure, cirrhosis, NS, previous renal disease, and other nephrotoxic drugs).
3. Acute tubulointerstitial nephritis. Some of the NSAIDs that have been described as producing AINs are described in Table 27.8. The nonsalicylate AINs belong to six families of molecules: propionic acid, indolacetic acid, phenylacetic acid, oxicams, pyrazolones, and mefenamic acid (fenamates). Those which most frequently provoke AINs are fenoprofen, from the first group, and meclofenamate, from the last. In renal histologic study, focal lymphocyte infiltrates and interstitial edema are found, as in the case of other drugs, but it is rare to find eosinophils and usual to find B-lymphocytes and plasma cells. The majority of the T cells belong to the CD8+ subgroup, more than the CD4+, as occurs with AINs caused by beta-lactam antibiotics. It is not infrequent to find associated NS that corresponds histologically to LGM. It is also not unusual to find the clinical symptoms and signs of hypersensitivity absent, although there are exceptions. As mentioned earlier, NS can be associated. Once the medication is suspended, renal function gradually recovers, and steroids could accelerate this process.
4. Nephrotic syndrome. This basically appears in association with the administration of two groups of NSAIDs: propionic acid and indolacetic acid. The NS and AIN are generally associated, but patients have been described with only NS, associated with sulindac, tolmetin, and ibuprofen. The relationship between two types of renal manifestation is clearly established, both of which recede on suspension of the medication. Histologic findings include glomerular lesions that are indistinguishable from those of idiopathic NS (Tab. 27.11).
5. Chronic renal failure. This is usually associated with prolonged use of these drugs and implies papillary necrosis.

NSAIDs with longer half-lives may be associated more frequently with renal toxicity. It is not clear that sulindac is associated with less renal toxicity.

Diuretics Despite the wide use of these drugs, very few cases of AIN induced by diuretics have been described. The thiazides and furosemide are most frequently associated with this pathology, although patients have been described with AIN associated with chlorthalidone, tri-

Table 27.11 Glomerulonephritis associated with drugs and other substances

On occasion accompanied by AINs

1. Minimal glomerular lesions
   - NSAIDs
   - Ampicillin
   - Rifampicin
   - Penicillamine
   - Diphenylhydantoin
   - Alpha interferon
   - Lithium
2. Membranous nephropathy
   - Metals: gold, mercury, bismuth
   - Penicillamine
   - Captopril
   - Anticonvulsives: trimethadione, messantoin
   - Chlorometiazol
   - Hydrocarbons
3. GN caused by anti-GBM antibodies
   - Hydrocarbons: organic solvents
4. Variable morphologic pattern
   - Heroin (focal segmental glomerulosclerosis, membranous-proliferative GN, others)
   - Rifampicin: proliferate GN, MGL
   - Mercury: membranous GN, proliferate GN, MGL
   - Sickle cell diseases: membranous-proliferative GN, poststreptococcal GN, membranous GN and focal segmental glomerulosclerosis
5. Vasculitis
   - Amphetamines

amterene, and tienilic acid. Clinically, the majority of cases are classic, with renal function recovered on suppression of the medication. If there is an adverse reaction of this type with a diuretic, bumetanide is recommended as a substitute.

AINs ASSOCIATED WITH INFECTIONS (REACTIVE)

The terms *reactive* or *nonspecific* are used to differentiate this from pyelonephritis. The AIN is produced by a germ that is capable of inducing a nephritogenic immune response that alters the renal tubules and interstitium. Pyelonephritis is caused directly by infection at the renal level and is dealt with in Chapters 4 and 9. Its mechanism, therefore, is similar to that described in drug-induced AIN, varying basically in the pathogenic factor.

The first descriptions of AIN were in patients with infections caused by *Streptococcus* and *Corynebacterium diphtheriae* in the last century. Klein concluded that interstitial nephritis was the rule, more than the exception, with scarlet fever. Councilman found histologic changes that, for the first time, classified acute interstitial nephritis in 25% of the autopsies of children who died of scarlet fever and 23% of those who died of diphtheria. With new preventive possibilities, including vaccination, and the use of effective antibiotics, these infectious diseases have become less frequent, at least in the "developed" countries, and cases of associated AIN are very rare. In children, however, these are still the most frequent causes of AIN, together with immunologic disorders. The infections that are most frequently related to AINs are shown in Table 27.6.

Clinical findings

Clinical presentation is similar to that described in drug-induced AIN and usually appears a week or two after the infection, although some of the symptoms may be masked by the infection and the complication is suspected in only half of patients. Many times it is the detection of deteriorating renal function or anomalies in the urine (e.g., cylindruria) with a negative urine culture that warns of the presence of this pathology. For this reason, the incidence of AIN at the histologic level in necropsies on patients with certain infections is much higher than that described at a clinical level.

Histopathology

In general, histologic findings are similar to those in drug-induced AIN, described previously. The typical lesions with edema and infiltrates of mononuclear cells are usually focal and are found basically around the veins and in the cortical medullar joint. Plasma cells and lymphocytes predominate. Tubular involvement correlates with the presence of granulocytes more than lymphocytes. There may be loss of the brush border in the proximal tubular cells and fragmentation and lamination of the TBM. Eosinophils may be observed at times.

Etiopathogenesis

The fact that the infection itself is capable of provoking an AIN is clearly proven by the possibility of developing the disease through virus inoculation and leptospires (spirochetes) in animals.

In the majority of patients, there is an immunologic reaction, caused by the infectious organism, that damages the tubulointerstitial structures. The organisms only invade the kidney in infections by viruses and rickettsias, and all phases of the immunologic reaction are produced at the local level. It is significant to note that the majority of the microorganisms implicated are intracellular pathogens (see Tab. 27.6). Various hypotheses have been proposed to explain this pathology. The first only implicates the existence of a factor released by the germ that has a chemotactic effect on lymphocytes. These substances, such as lymphokines and monokines, released at the systemic level, accumulate at the kidney, are filtered, and then are reabsorbed in the tubules. The second possibility is that this is an immune reaction produced by an antigen of the microorganism. This theory is supported by the possibility of developing an AIN through a chronic serum disease in rabbits.

Even in direct renal infections by the pathogenic organism, the alterations could be due to immune reactions together with the direct toxic effect of the germ. In leptospire infections, the hematogenic arrival route and their presence in renal tissue are conditions that favor the development of lesions, although this mechanism is not clear. The difference between TIN due to direct infections and infectious "reactive" TIN is not clear in some cases.

Diagnosis

Diagnosis is based on the same principles as those mentioned in the section on drug-induced AIN. It is important to emphasize two aspects of diagnosis of AINs associated with infections. First of all, we must rule out the possibility that the infection has directly affected the kidney to be able to speak of a reactive AIN, which is not always easy. It is sometimes necessary to use special histologic study techniques, in an attempt to show the antigens or DNA/RNA of the germ, although antigenic material of the microorganism at the interstitial level can be found in reactive AINs. The second aspect is that patients with infections who develop an AIN are often receiving medication that could potentially provoke the AIN, and therefore their physicians tend to support an adverse reaction to this medication more than the infection as the cause.

Prognosis and treatment

Most infections associated with AIN are self-limiting in relation to treatment of the infection. Renal recuperation is generally complete, although it may take 3 months or more. Some authors feel that steroids do not offer any benefits to treatment. Others feel that they do.

Special characteristics of AINs associated with particular infections

Streptococcus At the end of the nineteenth century and the beginning of the twentieth century, scarlet fever was the most frequent cause of AIN. AINs are one of the most frequent complications of this disease – significantly more than acute GN – 25 to 77% versus 2%. These percentages are valid today in children with scarlet fever studied with renal biopsies. Logically, incidence in many countries has decreased with the decrease in the number of untreated infections with beta-hemolytic Streptococcus. The histologic alterations have been described already; there may be areas of tubular necrosis regeneration. In the children studied, renal function had recovered at 2 to 3 months.

Brucella Brucellosis can cause other complications, including direct granulomatous infection of the urinary tract and an AIN with no evidence of renal invasion by the germ, the same way it seems to appear in brucellotic endocarditis. Some of the patients described had indications of a typical histology for this affectation. There are frequent references in the literature to the presence of ARF due to brucellosis.

Enterobacteriacea A case of AIN during sepsis caused by enterobacteria has been described, which is an example that warns of the possibility of not diagnosing an ARF due to AIN, since this clinical association seems to indicate tubular necrosis. The clinical presentation, with cutaneous rash, eosinophilia, and high serum IgE levels, together with gammagraphy with gallium, indicated the need for renal biopsy, with which the AIN was diagnosed. The ARF appeared together with a relapse of the infection by enterobacteria and was prolonged, with only partial renal recuperation. AIN also has been described with Yersinia and Salmonella.

Legionella Cases of AIN in patients with Legionnaire's disease have been described. The clinical presentation is similar to that of Goodpasture's syndrome because of the pulmonary effects of the infection together with AIN. In a communal outbreak of this disease in Barcelona that affected 56 patients, 21.4% showed ARF, which was an independent variable of prognosis, although the publication does not analyze the causes of the ARF.

Leishmania and Toxoplasma Tubulointerstitial histologic manifestations are frequent in kala-azar, whereas at the clinical level, TIN is rare in toxoplasmosis.

Epstein-Barr virus Between 2 and 18% of patients with mononucleosis showed proteinuria and/or hematuria, which could be due to a GN or an AIN; in the majority of patients, the process is subclinical, except on rare occasions. The appearance of ARF in infectious mononucleosis is less frequent (between 1 and 2%), corresponding to cases of AIN. Histologically, the patients described show an intense mononuclear infiltrate, mainly composed of lymphocytes that can be atypical, plasma cells, and macrophages. Granulomatous lesions may appear. In some cases, deposits of antibodies of doubtful significance have been observed. It is difficult to establish whether, in the patients described, there was or was not direct renal involvement by the virus. Recovery of renal function, although the rule, is sometimes partial.

Human immunodeficiency virus (HIV) Involvement tends to be more renal than glomerular, with segmentary and focal sclerohyalinotic lesions, although TIN lesions also have been described, but within the context of other concurrent infections, and the use of medications makes it very difficult to establish a causal relationship. The renal histopathologic data most characteristic of this infection are "globally" collapsed glomeruli, less glomerular hyalinosis than in heroin-induced nephropathy, more changes in the visceral epithelial cells, degenerative changes in the tubular cells, tubuloreticular inclusions in the glomerulus and interstitium, and large amounts of CD8+ lymphocytes, macrophages, and plasma cells in the interstitium. There are no specific renal histologic data for this infection, but the group is quite indicative.

Kawasaki disease This is a viral infection caused by a retrovirus, which appears with arteritis and inflammatory changes at multiple organ levels, with an acute and generally shortened clinical course. It affects children at approximately 1 year of age. Renal involvement is usually at the renal artery and its main branch level. TIN appears in 31% of patients, with mononuclear cell infiltrates and focal tubular alterations.

ACUTE IDIOPATHIC TUBULOINTERSTITIAL NEPHRITIS (AIN)

This group includes the cases of AIN for which no cause has been found, although this does not mean that one does not exist. Other cases have a high family incidence, which makes us suspect congenital causes. Many of these patients are chronic, although the clinical beginning may appear acute, developing with Fanconi's syndrome or slow-evolution renal failure. These will be discussed below. Table 27.12 classifies the idiopathic TINs.

In some series, one third of the AINs are labeled idiopathic, since no cause is found, and there are no immunoglobulin deposits. In some patients, this is the beginning of a sarcoidosis or an association with other diseases such as active chronic hepatitis, primary biliary cirrhosis, or retroperitoneal fibrosis.

Table 27.12 Idiopathic tubulointerstitial nephritis

1. Idiopathic TIN caused by anti-TBM antibodies
   a. Nonfamilial
   b. Familial
   c. Familial and nonfamilial associated with membranous GN
2. Idiopathic TIN caused by immune-complex deposits
   a. IgE
   b. Familial
3. Idiopathic granulomatous TIN
4. TIN with uveitis
5. Familial TIN linked to HLA with hypokalemia
6. Systemic karyomegaly

TIN syndrome with idiopathic uveitis is discussed below, together with the TIN in immunologic diseases, the majority of the cases corresponding to AINs that remit spontaneously or with steroids, although relapses can occur and chronicity is also possible. Steroids also can be useful in idiopathic AINs, at least in shortening the evolution, and relapses have been described on discontinuation.

ACUTE TUBULAR NECROSIS (ATN)

This is discussed in Chapters 2 and 6.

CHRONIC TUBULOINTERSTITIAL NEPHRITIS (CIN)

Earlier, in the introduction and under epidemiology, the importance of CIN as a cause of terminal renal failure was emphasized, since it represents approximately 20% of the patients on dialysis. While in patients under age 15 the most frequent CINs are congenital obstructive uropathies or reflux nephropathy, in adults, the most frequent are *nonspecific*, and among these, especially in certain countries, is analgesic nephropathy. This is the principal entity in the group because of both its frequency and its gravity, although many medications and toxins can cause CIN. The mechanisms that produce tubulointerstitial lesions in these diseases are direct toxicity or the result of an immune mechanism. At other times, the physiopathology is unclear.

This section discusses TINs with chronic evolution caused by substances foreign to the organism, generally medications and certain metals. The TINs of this source may be classified as in Table 27.1. Many of these substances give rise to ARF by "tubular necrosis," and some patients, generally with the most serious intoxications, may retain a certain degree of renal failure as a consequence; other patients with prolonged exposure to these toxins develop chronic renal failure (CRF) through CIN.

ANALGESIC NEPHROPATHY (AN)

Analgesics, antipyretics, and in general, NSAIDs can cause both acute and chronic renal pathology. Among the chronic forms, classic AN stands out with clear characteristics. Knowledge of the condition has allowed its prevention in many countries where it was highly prevalent.

The association between CIN, papillary necrosis, and a history of excessive consumption of certain analgesics was described at the beginning of the 1950s. AN is a slowly progressive disease that causes chronic renal failure resulting from the daily use for many years of mixtures containing two or more analgesics.

Epidemiology

This pathology shows a peculiar epidemiology and was one of the most frequent causes of terminal CRF in countries such as Australia and New Zealand, Switzerland, Belgium, Sweden, and South Africa. The geographic distribution of AN is not uniform and varies even from one region to another. Within the United States, it oscillates between 2 and 2.8% of the patients starting dialysis in California and Washington, D.C., and 20% of those in Philadelphia. In Europe, it varies from 1% in the United Kingdom to 44% in Belgium, with a prevalence of 2.2% for all of Europe, 1488 of 67412 patients. These differences can be explained by the magnitude of consumption of analgesics, since the relationship between the incidence of the disease and consumption per capita is well proven; the composition of the most frequently consumed analgesics (acetaminophen or phenacetin + aspirin + codeine-caffeine); and the higher susceptibility of the population, including racial and environmental factors, such as climate. Fuller knowledge of this pathology has made its prevention possible, including laws that prohibit the unrestricted sale of analgesic mixtures, and its incidence has decreased in the countries mentioned. Taking acetaminophen off the market alone does not seem to be the reason for the decrease in this pathology, which more likely is the regulation or prohibition of the sale of analgesic mixtures in some countries.

Clinical findings

The clinical presentation of this disease is discreet and generally limited to sterile polyuria and occasional nephritic colics associated, or not, with hematuria and rarely with bilateral renal obstruction. Nocturia seems to be the earliest symptom. AN is frequently asymptomatic for years.

A fundamental fact in a patient with analgesic CIN is the antecedent of analgesic ingestion. This continuous ingestion is often denied or underestimated by patients. The social causes that tend to induce excessive ingestion of certain analgesics include socioeconomic problems, psychoneurotic disorders, and certain types of work, which implies that the patients frequently are women, in a proportion of 4 or 5:1, from lower socioeconomic groups in developed countries. These patients often have problems with their spouses or are frequently divorced and also consume an excess of alcohol and cigarettes. AN is rare in patients less than 30 years old.

The basic clinical problem of these patients is renal, frequently lower urinary tract symptomatology with polyuria, nocturia, and dysuria. The appearance of hematuria and lower back pain, sometimes accompanied by nephritic colic, is also common. The first symptoms are those of a urinary infection and incapacity to concentrate urine. The secondary symptoms correspond to papillary necrosis, which may even give rise to an obstructive uropathy that may or may not be associated with sepsis. Diffuse papillary necrosis can give rise to a bilateral obstruction and therefore acute renal failure.

In many patients, the initial phase remains undetected, and the patient is studied for the first time for renal failure. Renal function may stabilize for long periods, especially if the ingestion of analgesics stops, since this is the main determinant in the progressive deterioration of renal function. Arterial hypertension is very frequent among patients with CRF due to analgesic nephropathy. In Australia this figure is approximately 78%. It is not infrequent to find that the hypertension is vasculorenal, secondary to atheromatosis of the renal artery. Up to 20% of the patients suffer crises of gout and hyperuricemia. The appearance of malignant uroepithelial carcinoma is more frequent in these patients than in those who suffer from other nephropathies.

Urinalysis shows (in sediment) sterile pyuria and hematuria and discreet tubular proteinuria. The thirst test illustrates the incapacity to concentrate urine and is resistant to vasopressin. Urinary acidification disorders also can be associated. The presence of hypocytraturia may favor the appearance of nephrocalcinosis.

The extrarenal clinical symptoms includes the existence of peptic ulcer in up to one-third of the patients in some series, more frequent in patients in whom aspirin was part of the analgesic ingested. Multifactorial-source anemia may be present. The most important of these factors are the ARF, digestive hematic losses, hemolysis, and even medullar alterations. Mild hemolysis, splenomegaly, and methemoglobinemia may be associated with acetaminophen.

The appearance of early arteriosclerosis is frequent, and the most common cause of death in these patients is acute myocardial infarction. Psychoneurotic disorders are frequent because of both the excessive use of analgesics and induced by them, since organic psychiatric disorders have been described in these patients.

Histopathology

The kidneys are usually reduced in size, with adherence on the capsule and irregular "bumpy" contours. The renal surface is pallid, with no scars. The papillae vary depending on the type of mixture of analgesics ingested. They usually show brown striations, and deformations range from swelling to defects of various degrees. The sequestered papillae may have black pigmentation. When the papillae are recently separated, there may be necrotic remains with lymphocyte infiltrates at the edges.

In more advanced or chronic cases, the kidneys are reduced in size, the papillae are grayish and atrophied, and there is no clear delineation between the necrotic and viable parenchyma. The cortex is decreased in relation to the papillary lesions. Calcium deposits are frequent on the necrotic lesions.

Another type of lesion affects the vasa recta, with concentric thickening of the vessels in the internal medullar area. Segmentary lesions in the urothelial capillaries of the urinary tract also have been described.

Classic AN histology can be obscured by complications such as pyelonephritis, hydronephrosis, pyonephrosis, and hypertension.

Etiopathogenesis

This disorder is caused by the excessive ingestion of mixtures of analgesics and antipyretics, fundamentally containing phenacetin, acetaminophen, and aspirin, frequently together with caffeine and codeine. Although aspirin and acetaminophen separately are capable of provoking papillary necrosis (PN), this is not seen frequently. Therefore, the factors for ARF secondary to this pathology are ingestion of a mixture of these analgesics, dosage, and length of exposure.

Phenacetin undergoes a metabolic transformation in the liver, generating acetaminophen. Renal concentration of phenacetin, as opposed to acetaminophen, is very low and has no corticopapillary gradient. Acetaminophen is filtered at the glomerular level and is passively reabsorbed in the tubules. It concentrates five to seven times in the renal medulla in situations of antidiuresis. Aspirin and salicylates are eliminated at the proximal tubule level by the anionic secretor system and are reabsorbed in the distal nephron by anionic diffusion, concentrating in the medulla. The combination of salicylate and acetaminophen has a synergetic effect, increasing the covalent unions and thereby acting as a cellular toxin.

The papillary necrosis mechanisms are, on the one hand, ischemic and, on the other, directly nephrotoxic. The ischemia is secondary to the vasa recta lesions, with a diminishing of capillary lumen. Prostaglandin inhibition is another factor that diminishes medullar blood flow. The vasodilator-producing medullar cells may be destroyed by the analgesics, and therefore, these vasodilators also will be lacking. The direct toxicity of these analgesics on the tubular cells is due, in part, to the decrease in glutathione and other reducers and to the cellular incorporation of amino acids. In the tubule cells of the rat in culture, acetaminophen in high concentrations causes the death of the cells by apoptosis. These analgesics generate free radicals in their metabolism. In vivo, high concentrations of these analgesics are capable of causing cell death through irreversible oxidative alterations. Therefore, dehydration-antidiuresis is one of the fundamental coadjutant factors in this pathology.

Diagnosis

The presence of anemia, moderate arterial hypertension, and renal failure with a tubular urinary syndrome in a female should make one suspect AN. The antecedent of excessive ingestion of analgesics is fundamental. Proof that analgesics are the cause of CRF is more difficult and can only be effected practically if the existence of papillary necrosis is shown, given that there are other causes of the papillary necrosis, some of which are shown in Table 27.13. A diagnosis of papillary necrosis implies the presence of necrotic papillary material in the urine after expulsion. Radiology can help in this diagnosis by showing the papillary cavities and the presence of ring-shaped calcifications around the papillae.

Until a short time ago, the diagnosis of AN was based on the clinical and biochemical data mentioned earlier, which are very nonspecific. The universal use of analgesics and NSAIDs by the population in general implies that it is the quantity over a long period of time that defines abuse. The limit of this pathology is not clear and varies from one patient to another. We have noted that to diagnose AN, one would need an accumulated consumption of 3 kg of analgesics, or more than 1 g/day for more than 3 years. This difficulty has led to wide case-control studies to determine the sensitivity and specificity of the symptoms and clinical signs for diagnosis of this disease. Findings of a decrease in the length of the kidneys, irregular "bumpy" contours, and papillary calcifications on sonography, conventional tomography, or computed tomography (CT) were the most specific. In another study, CT scanning without contrast medium was the best method for detecting papillary calcifications. In this study, the CT scan finding of papillary calcifications had a sensitivity of 92% and a specificity of 100%. Calcifications also may be found in other causes of papillary necrosis (see Tab. 27.13). Patients with renal tubular acidosis or primary hyperparathyroidism also have renal calcification, but not discreetly localized on the papillary line. CT scanning may be indicated in all patients with CRF of unknown etiology. Ultrasound also can be useful in defining papillary calcifications.

Vascular lesions characteristic of this disease, which can be found even in the bladder, have been described and demonstrated in biopsy material at this level.

Table 27.13 Causes of renal papillary necrosis

Analgesic nephropathy
Diabetes mellitus
NSAIDs
Sickle cell disease
Obstructive uropathy + pyelonephritis (pyonephritis)
Shock, dehydration, renal ischemia
Sepsis in children, disseminated intravascular coagulation
Renal vein thrombosis
Vasculitis
Alcoholism

Prognosis and treatment

The fundamental factor that defines the evolution to terminal CRF is the continued ingestion of analgesics. When this ingestion is interrupted, the majority of patients remain the same or improve. There are some patients who evolve unfavorably, which can be explained by other factors such as urinary infection, arterial hypertension, kidney stones, hyperalimentation, papillary necrosis, or obstructive uropathy. All these complications should be diagnosed and treated properly.

One of the factors in the improvement of these patients is hydrosaline repletion, with careful monitoring of hydration and the sodium balance. Recuperation of renal function in the long term is usual if analgesic ingestion is stopped.

Recommendations of the National Kidney Foundation on analgesics and the kidney

On June 9 to 11, 1995, the National Kidney Foundation convened an expert group of investigators and clinicians to consider and develop recommendations on the issue of analgesic-related kidney disease. The following recommendations were published in the January 1996 issue of the *American Journal of Kidney Disease* (G. R. Aronoff wrote this résumé).

Aspirin as a single analgesic In patients with normal renal function, aspirin should not be taken within 48 hours of ingestion of any nonnarcotic NSAID, and vice versa.

In patients with impaired renal function, acute GN, sodium depletion, or cirrhosis with ascites and in children with congestive heart failure, aspirin should be avoided. If its use is necessary, careful monitoring of renal function should be undertaken. This would consist at least of serum creatinine determinations at baseline and at regular intervals.

Acetaminophen as a single analgesic Acetaminophen remains the nonnarcotic analgesic of choice for episodic use in patients with underlying renal disease.

The habitual consumption of acetaminophen should be discouraged.

Aspirin-acetaminophen combinations The availability of analgesic mixtures as an over-the-counter produce should cease. Analgesic mixtures as prescription products should have a label warning of the increased prevalence of kidney injury and CRF associated with habitual use.

NSAIDs There should be an explicit label warning patients taking over-the-counter NSAIDs of the potential renal risks of consuming the drugs. The use of NSAIDs during pregnancy should be avoided. The prolonged regular use of NSAIDs also should be discouraged. Combinations of NSAIDs with other analgesics or caffeine should be prospectively evaluated for renal safety before the release of any such combination.

LITHIUM NEPHROPATHY

Lithium salts have become one of the most useful medications in the long-term treatment of chronic affective/depressive disorders. Lithium is filtered at the glomerular level, and 65% is reabsorbed at the proximal tubule level. Various renal alterations associated with its use have been described: defects in urine concentrating capacity, reversible or not; CIN and CRF; nephrotic syndrome; and hyperparathyroidism.

Diabetes insipidus

The development of a discreet disorder in urine concentrating capacity at the outset of medication with lithium salts is frequent, commonly polyuria and polydipsia. This is generally temporary and is corrected at 4 to 6 weeks after suspension of the treatment. Some patients develop a more severe disorder that can give rise to dehydration. The concentrating defect is of the nephrogenic diabetes insipidus type, since it does not respond to antidiuretic hormone. The impairment of urinary concentrating ability is not always reversible.

Concentrating capacity diminishes with age and the total dose of lithium received, even in patients not intoxicated. The psychotropic medication associated with the treatment could play a role in this functional defect. Lithium decreases the level of vasopressin-sensitive adenylcyclase activity.

A renal biopsy in these patients shows ballooning, swelling, and vacuolation of the epithelial cells at the distal tubule and the collecting duct, as well as the deposit of a material that is positive to periodic-acid Schiff (PAS-positive) staining. These cells can separate at the tubular lumen, forming cylinders. There are also changes in cell nuclei. These lesions usually are reversible with longer or shorter periods after suspension of the lithium. This type of lesion appears in rats treated with lithium carbonate. The lesions do not depend on the polyuria and imply a direct toxic effect.

Thiazides and amiloride, as well as indomethacin, recently have been used in treatment to decrease polyuria in lithium diabetes insipidus. If possible, diuretics should be avoided because of the resulting volume contraction. Lithium toxicity is increased with the simultaneous use of NSAIDs.

Chronic TIN and CRF

This is less usual than the concentrating defect, since proven cases of chronic TIN evolving to CRF are rare. In these patients, there is tubular atrophy, flattening of the epithelial cells of the distal tubule, interstitial medullar fibrosis with mononuclear infiltrates, and sclerotic glomeruli; in some cases, cystic lesions can be observed. The specific role of lithium in these patients is not clear. It may only act as a predisposing factor for the action of other toxins. To prevent chronic evolution, it is necessary to avoid episodes of acute lithium toxicity, maintaining blood levels at less than 0.4 to 0.6 mmol/liter.

Nephrotic syndrome

The appearance of NS in patients on lithium treatment has been described, corresponding to the histology of minimal glomerular lesions. The process is reversible at 2 to 12 weeks after discontinuation of lithium and relapses if it is used again. This lesion is not related to the TIN described (see Tab. 27.11).

Hyperparathyroidism

Hyperparathyroidism may appear due to an imbalance in parathormone secretion.

CISPLATIN NEPHROPATHY

Cisplatin (*cis*-dichlorodiamine platinum, CDDP) is an antineoplasic medication that contains platinum and is used in the treatment of various carcinomas, particularly those of the testicle. Its principal toxic effects appear at the renal, ear, and gastrointestinal levels. Its nephrotoxicity has been well known since the beginning of its use and includes ARF, CRF, hyperuricemia, and magnesium depletion.

This medication generally is administered intravenously in the form of isolated doses for various days in cycles of various weeks. Its fundamental elimination route is renal. After administration, renal concentration at the external medullar level is three times that of plasma and lasts for 12 days.

The appearance of ARF during treatment with cisplatin is frequent and shows the characteristics of a nephrotoxic "tubular necrosis." The incidence depends on the dosage used and certain patient circumstances before administration. In adequate hydration conditions and with doses of less than 3 mg/kg, it appears in 25% of the patients treated; with higher doses, it appears even more frequently.

The lack of recovery of renal function after ARF or the development of insidious CRF usually corresponds to chronic tubulointerstitial lesions. The cases of evolution to CRF seem to be the minority, although incidence is difficult to establish, and such cases could be more frequent. The loss of renal function is partial and stable at medium term. Histologically, the condition corresponds to chronic TIN with fibrosis. The initial lesions are at the distal tubule and collector, with focal necrosis and hyaline cylin ders, together with interstitial edema and mitochondrial alterations of the tubular cells.

A study in rats shows that the urine concentrating defect produced by cisplatin is due, at least in part, to a decrease in NaCl transport in the proximal tubule and the ascending limb of the loop of Henle. The toxicity of this drug is due to its platinum content and is similar to that described for other heavy metals. Like cadmium, it has inhibitory effects on the tubular ATPases.

Treatment consists of prophylaxis of the renal toxicity. The methods that seem to be the most useful are slow intravenous infusion of the medication, less than 1 mg/kg per hour; administration of each cycle's dosage distributed in various doses; and previous hydration, generally intravenously with sodium chloride or mannitol, to achieve an increase in urinary volume at the moment of administration of 100 ml/hour. This is the most often used system and probably the most effective, achieving the desired effect without increasing the urinary elimination of the drug, probably through its dilution at the tubular level, decreasing its renal concentration. It is not clear if furosemide offers any benefits over the former method. When the total dose is higher than 200 mg/m^2, the simultaneous administration of sodium thiosulfate is useful.

NEPHROPATHY INDUCED BY OTHER MEDICATIONS

Methyl-CCNU [1-(2-chloroethyl)-3-(4-methyl cyclo hexyl)-1 nitrosourea] is an antineoplasic drug used fundamentally in the treatment of certain carcinomas, glyomas, and melanomas. It is a liposoluble nitrosourea. It does not produce ARF but rather CRF through CIN. It has long been well known that this drug was nephrotoxic in rats. The first time its nephrotoxicity was described in humans was in CRF in direct relation to the dosage. Renal biopsy in these patients showed chronic interstitial nephritis lesions. Renal symptoms appear in those patients who receive more than 1200 mg/m^2.

NSAIDs NSAIDs can cause irreversible CRF, generally with papillary necrosis. This complication has been little described but occurs with the majority of the NSAIDs (e.g., indomethacin, phenylbutazone, ibuprofen, and fenoprofen).

Gentamicin Some of the nephrotoxic substances incriminated in ARF by nephrotoxic TN can produce chronic TIN. Through low, continuous dosages of gentamicin in animals, CIN can be produced. The toxicity of the aminoglycosides in 10 to 15% of the patients treated with adequate serum levels is produced by renal factors independent of the pharmacokinetics of the drug.

Cyclosporin A (CsA) This nephrotoxic substance is used as an immunosuppressive drug, fundamentally in the preventive treatment for rejection in organ transplant. Its nephrotoxicity affects the blood vessels, tubules, and even the glomeruli. Its effects on the kidney may be functional or structural, reversible or irreversible. Since this drug is described in the chapters dealing with renal transplantation, here we will only mention, briefly, interstitial changes (Chaps. 3 and 47).

At the histologic level, the lesions caused by CsA are:

1. *acute*. (a) Appearance of giant mitochondria and vacuoles in the proximal tubular cells (CsA is joined to the vacuolated cells), (b) glomerular intracapillary thrombosis, (c) absence of tubular necrosis;
2. *chronic* (involvement is usually focal). (a) Atrophy of the tubular cells and thickening of the TBM, (b) interstitial fibrosis, (c) glomerular sclerosis, (d) focal hyalinosis of the arterioles and small arteries.

Clinically, chronic toxicity gives rise to a decrease in glomerular filtration, renal failure, hypertension, low-range proteinuria, and functional tubular alterations. The majority of these effects are irreversible.

Today, many precautions are taken to avoid these harmful effects, including : suspension of CsA while there is tubular necrosis, substitution of the drug after 3 or 6 months (the time within which most renal lesions are still reversible), and use of lower doses (triple association). As long as there is no other similar immunosuppressor drug for organ transplantation, its use is justified despite its nephrotoxicity. Treatment of type I diabetes, SLE, minimal glomerular lesions and other GNs, and AIN should take into account that this is a drug that potentially leads to chronic renal failure, by CIN, with significant fibrosis.

TIN INDUCED BY HEAVY METALS

Diverse toxins, among which metals clearly stand out, have been known to produce various types of renal disorders. In cases of acute intoxication, there is ARF with tubular necrosis, but in others, there are true chronic tubulointerstitial lesions as a result of the acute lesion or chronic exposure to the toxin.

Nowadays, there is evidence that when another renal pathology is associated with subclinical metal intoxications that affect glomerular filtration or tubular functions implying greater passage of these metals to the tubule, interstitial nephritis may be induced by accumulation at this level, either by direct toxic mechanisms or by immunologic mechanisms.

Lead nephropathy

Although lead poisoning is generally occupational or accidental, there are studies of the general population that show a relationship between plasma creatinine concentration, blood pressure, and lead concentration in the blood. The meaning of this type of subclinical poisoning and whether or not it acts as a coadjutant with other nephropathies causing interstitial fibrosis are a controversial subject. Low-level lead exposure contributes to hypertension in the general population.

According to the type of poisoning, lead enters the

organism through the digestive tract, skin, or respiratory tract; two-thirds is eliminated by the kidney and one-third by the intestine. Lead is filtered at the glomerular level and is secreted and reabsorbed at the tubular level. It accumulates fundamentally in the bones, liver, and kidney.

Lead nephropathies may be acute or chronic. Acute lead intoxication produces digestive, neurologic, and renal disorders. Renal involvement, depending on its intensity, may go from Fanconi's syndrome to tubular necrosis with ARF. The appearance of acute hemolysis with hemoglobinuria may complicate matters even more. In these patients, the following can be determined from the urinalysis: increased excretion of lead, delta-aminobrumilinic acid, coproporphyrines, urobilinogen, and urobilin. Acute lead poisoning in children may cause encephalopathy and seizures.

The most characteristic histologic changes appear in the tubular cells, concretely in the nuclei, which tend to be larger in size, with acid-fast intranuclear inclusion bodies in the proximal tubules, corresponding to protein-lead complexes. An increase in the number of mitoses also can be observed. Tubular necrosis lesions without cylinder cells may be found focally.

On occasion, chronic exposure to lead does not give rise to a clinical problem, despite the existence of high levels of lead in the organism; other patients, however, show a decrease in GF, which, in the most marked cases, enters into CRF range. Histologically, signs of chronic TIN in evolution to fibrosis and tubular atrophy are found. Initially, the proximal tubular lesions predominate, with tubular atrophy, dilatation, interstitial fibrosis, and periglomerular and vascular lesions. The nuclear lesions described in acute cases may or may not be found in chronic cases. Granular deposits of IgG and C3 and linear deposits of IgM at the glomerular level and the TBM have been described in some patients.

Clinically, the appearance of signs of tubular lesions with more or less complete Fanconi's syndrome stands out. Saturnine nephropathy is frequently associated to uric gout (50% of cases) that is due to a defect in tubular urate secretion, although there also may be an excess of reabsorption. The appearance of hypertension in these patients is also common, even in those intoxicated without clinical nephropathy. The existence of chronic uric nephropathy may be doubtful because in many cases the hyperuricemia is a consequence of a tubular disorder rather than the cause, including subclinical lead poisoning. The existence of other nephropathies or hypertension facilitates the tubulointerstitial toxicity of metals, as we shall see with regard to iron. Gout is rare in renal hypertension disease with renal failure unrelated to lead exposure. Evolution to terminal CRF is rare, unless there are other associated factors.

When diagnosing this type of intoxication, it is useful to perform a mobilization test with EDTA to evaluate the lead deposits in the tissues. We administer 2 doses of 1 g intramuscularly or intravenously over an interval of 8 to 12 hours, collecting the 24-hour urine to determine lead concentration. The test is positive if the quantity measured is higher than 650 μg/24 hours, implying that there is an increase in lead deposited in the tissues that is undetectable with simple plasma level analysis. Bone lead concentration, as determined by direct measurement in bone in vivo or by in vivo tibial K x-ray fluorescence, shows correlation with chelatable lead. Lead chelate excretion over 3 days after the intramuscular injection of 2 g EDTA results in moderate exposure when higher than 660 μg/3 days and high chronic exposure when higher than 1000 μg/3 days. Urinary markers in chronic exposure to lead are thromboxane B_2 and *N*-acetyl-β-D-glucosaminidase; no changes are observed in intestine alkaline phosphatase, β_2-microglobulin, and microalbuminuria, as with other metals.

Although the appearance of clinical renal problems with the use of quelantes to treat saturnine intoxication has been described, this is the chosen treatment, together with the avoidance of new exposure to the metal. The dose is 1 g of $CaNa_2$ EDTA three times a week, which should even improve glomerular filtration.

NEPHROPATHY INDUCED BY OTHER METALS

Mercury

Mercury poisoning is also usually occupational or accidental, appearing on occasion in epidemic form because of food contamination. The inorganic compounds of mercury are much more nephrotoxic than the organic compounds. When mercury diuretic use was more common, this was one of the sources of this nephropathy.

Mercury intake routes are digestive, cutaneous, and respiratory, fundamentally affecting the kidney, nervous system, and liver. The inorganic compounds are principally excreted by the kidneys. Compounds of the alquil mercury type are fundamentally eliminated in feces. Their effect is directly toxic, since there is an affinity for a series of chemical groups in the organism such as sulphydryls, metallothionein, and amino, carboxyl, and phosphonil groups, inhibiting enzymes and other vital functions of the organism.

Mercury poisoning is usually discussed in chapters on tubular necrosis ARF, since this is its principal effect on the kidney, although as a consequence of tubular necrosis and in chronic intoxications, CIN and renal failure may develop. There is selective accumulation in the *pars recta* of the proximal tubules.

Acute intoxication produces both symptoms derived from the caustic action on the tissues of the entrance route and nephrotoxic ARF with tubular necrosis. This is one of the experimental models of nephrotoxic ARF most often used in animals. Since tubular necrosis is the subject of another chapter (Chap. 43), it will not be discussed here. Chronic intoxications may give rise to various renal syndromes such as more or less complete Fanconi's syndrome, CIN, minimum-change GN, or membranous or proliferative GN. Anti-GBM antibody disease also has been reported. The CRF generally associated with these pathologies may occur with diffuse fibrous interstitial nephritis.

Blood mercury concentration is a helpful indicator of the body burden of methyl mercury but is inappropriate for monitoring inorganic mercury. In this nephritis, the excretion of urinary proteins such us intestinal alkaline phosphatase and Tamm-Horsfall protein is increased.

In acute episodes especially, BAL (2,3-dimercapto-propanol) is used as quelante, 2 or 3 mg/kg every 4 hours in about six doses. It is also important to remember that the majority of the complexes formed with mercury are dialyzable. The minimal glomerular lesions associated with mercury poisoning responded well to treatment with steroids.

Cadmium

Occupational poisoning with this metal usually appears in those who work with electric batteries and other components that employ cadmium. There are also accidental exposures, fundamentally due to water and food contamination, especially rice and fish. This is a metal with a great affinity for mammalian cells. Functional disorders are produced in the tubular cells, especially at the proximal level, with Fanconi's syndrome. Tubular characteristic proteinuria of low molecular weight may become significant and is present in up to 82% of the people exposed, serving as discriminator of the intoxication at the population level. Urinary protein markers of cadmium toxic nephritis are intestinal alkaline phosphatase, Tamm-Horsfall glycoprotein, *N*-acetyl-β-D-glucosaminidase, retinol-binding protein, β_2-microglobulin, and microalbuminuria.

In advanced stages, there is high urinary excretion of uric acid, phosphorus, and calcium, giving rise to hypouricemia due to hyperuricosuria, which in turn may give rise to renal uric acid lithiasis and osteomalacia, with intense bone pain and pathologic fractures, caused by the latter plus the osteodystrophy typical of renal failure and the deposition of cadmium in the bones. The persistent hypercalciuria of cadmium nephritis is responsible for kidney stones and osteomalacia. Hypertension is also very frequent in these patients, as in lead poisoning.

Histologically, there is chronic TIN, with an increase of lysosomes and mitochondrial swelling in the tubular cells, and later tubular atrophy and interstitial fibrosis. The pathogenesis seems to occur through direct cellular toxicity as the cadmium interferes with the function of various ATPases of the membrane.

Clinically, abnormalities of proximal tubular function are associated with urinary cadmium excretion of more than 30 μg/day. Measurement of liver and kidney cadmium content by neutron γ-ray analysis is accurate .There is no effective treatment for cadmium nephritis.

Gold salts

These are used in the treatment of the more serious forms of rheumatoid arthritis, generally when there is no response to NSAIDs. They may provoke ARF with tubular necrosis or membranous GN. The appearance of CIN with renal failure is rare, associated with high doses.

Iron

Patients with hemochromatosis may present CRF with interstitial fibrosis. The proper techniques can show iron deposits at this level. It has been commented that the presence of iron in high concentrations in the tubular liquid in the experimental model of GN and TIN called serum nephrotoxic nephritis is the principal determinant of the tubulointerstitial lesions in this nephropathy. This alteration is the main cause of progressive deterioration of the renal function. Some metals, either because they reach high levels in the blood or because their glomerular filtration is increased, may determine some of the tubulointerstitial lesions in numerous nephropathies. Earlier, the relationship between proteinuria, holotransferrin, and renal fibrosis was discussed.

CHRONIC TIN INDUCED BY OTHER TOXINS

Beryllium

This rare intoxication gives rise to a granulomatous TIN and kidney stones of beryllium oxalate. The most typical manifestation is granulomatous disease. Beryllium also induces pulmonary fibrosis, hypercalcemia, and hypercalciuria.

Arsenic

These are usually occupational or accidental poisonings. Ingestion as a form of suicide is rare in present times. Arsenic is used in many industries, such as coloring, dyes, paint, ceramics, insecticides, raticides, etc.

Both acute and chronic arsenic intoxications have renal effects. The acute forms show ARF, together with gastrointestinal symptoms, principally diarrhea. The histologic lesions are similar to those caused by mercury, with frequent areas of tubular necrosis. When the intoxication is by arsine (AsH_3), hemolysis is produced, and the hemoglobinuria factor is a coadjutant of the TIN.

Chronic forms are usually the consequence of the acute forms, which may take months to recover from or may be due directly to TIN with fibrosis and renal atrophy. Despite the high incidence of hepatic, pulmonary, skin, and other neoplasias in chronic arsenic intoxication, they are not more frequent at the renal level.

Other substances

TIN in cases of bismuth, chromium, germanium, and antimony poisonings has been described. These substances are used in medications or in industry.

METABOLIC TUBULOINTERSTITIAL NEPHRITIS

Tubulointerstitial involvement in renal metabolic diseases is discussed in Chapters 2, 3, 9 and 31.

TUBULOINTERSTITIAL NEPHRITIS IN GN AND SYSTEMIC IMMUNOLOGIC DISEASES

Tubulointerstitial damage is also reported in amyloidosis and transplantation (Chapters 23 and 47), and in Sections 4 and 5. This section discusses only TIN mediated by anti-TBM antibodies and TIN associated with uveitis.

TIN MEDIATED BY TBM ANTIBODIES

This section describes a group of TINs produced by anti-TBM antibodies, which may appear idiopathically or associated with other pathologies (Tab. 27.14). Demonstration of anti-TBM Abs in the blood of a patient with TIN is not frequent, nor is it common to find linear deposits of IgG along the TBM (these appeared in 0.8% of a series of renal biopsies). These are the data that define this group of pathologies. In drug-induced AINs, this histologic pattern appears in 9.5 to 17% of patients. In another series of children with TIN, 14% showed anti-TBM Abs.

Some of the cases described in literature are well documented, demonstrating the presence of anti-TBM Abs in blood or tissue using IF techniques on the healthy kidney or ELISA. In others, it is only possible to document the linear deposits of IgG, which are only suggestive of this pathology. Linear deposits of IgG without accompanying anti-TBM Abs have been described in diabetic patients. These are produced by nonspecific apposition on the TBM, accompanied by albumin and other proteins, demonstrable by using serum antialbumin as control.

Table 27.14 Tubulointerstitial nephritis with anti-TBM antibodies

1. Idiopathic TIN with anti-TBM antibodies
2. Familial and nonfamilial TIN associated with membranous nephropathy
3. Associated with anti-GBM antibodies (Goodpasture's syndrome and variants)
4. Associated with other glomerulonephritides
5. Drug-related AINs with anti-TBM antibodies
6. TIN with anti-TBM antibodies in renal transplantation
7. TIN with anti-TBM antibodies associated with other diseases

Clinical findings

This pathology is either idiopathic or associated with other diseases enumerated in Table 27.14. In some of these diseases, the TIN at clinical level is of secondary importance and therefore may not be diagnosed or may be underestimated. The forms listed under numbers 3, 4, 6, and 7 in Table 27.14 are the most frequent.

1. *Idiopathic TIN with anti-TBM Abs.* These are rare cases of idiopathic TIN with anti-TBM Abs described in children and in adults with Fanconi's syndrome and/or renal failure. More than 50% evolve to chronic renal failure.
2. *Familial and nonfamilial TIN associated with membranous nephropathy.* There are various families in which there is more than one member with nephrotic syndrome and associated Fanconi's syndrome. Renal biopsy defines membranous nephropathy and linear deposits of IgG along the TBM, together with TIN. In those studied, anti-TBM Ab was shown. The majority are children, aged between 3 and 12 years when diagnosed, who evolve to terminal renal failure. There are also nonfamilial cases with this clinical association. On occasion, these cases are associated with the presence of autoantibodies to tissues such as jejunum or basal alveolar membrane, which would suggest that these patients have a special predisposition to react to their own epithelial antigens.
3. *Nonfamilial TIN with anti-TBM Abs associated with anti-GBM Ab.* This association is the most frequent clinical form of anti-TBM Ab. In Goodpasture's syndrome, up to 84% of the patients had anti-TBM Abs. The anti-TBM Abs are of the IgG type in all cases. In some cases, IgA or IgM was associated. The linear deposits on the tubules tend to be focal and less intense than the glomerular deposits. The intensity of the TIN associated with the glomerular nephropathy is related to the presence of the deposit on the TBM. The anti-GBM Abs are of two types according to studies with IF, and those of the second type are the ones that present a crossed reaction with the TBM.
4. *Anti-TBM Abs associated with other GNs.* Publications refer to a patient with poststreptococcal GN who showed anti-TBM Abs. The demonstration of linear deposits of IgG on the tubular membranes is frequent in various GNs.
5. *Drug-induced AIN with anti-TBM Abs.* As mentioned regarding the pathogenesis of this TIN earlier, this histologic pattern is presented by between 9.5 and 17% of all drug-induced AINs. In these patients, males are five times predominant over females, while in the rest, without tubular deposits, they are only double. This immunologic form is less frequent in methicillin-induced AINs.
6. *TIN with anti-TBM Abs in renal transplantation.* It is not infrequent that patients with a renal transplant develop anti-TBM Abs. In some of these patients, other manifestations of immunologic alterations are associated, such as *de novo* membranous GN, GN with anti-GBM Abs, and even the recurrence of linear tubular deposits after renal transplantation. The linear deposits of IgG appear 3 to 13 months after kidney transplantation and may exist not only at the proximal tubular level, as is usual, but also in the distal tubule and even in the collector tubule. The production of anti-TBM Ab *in situ* by the lymphocytes of the transplanted patient has been described. These deposits frequently disappear with time. There is no evidence that the appearance of anti-TBM Abs or lin-

ear tubular deposits imply worse survival of the transplant or significant clinical consequences.

7. *TIN with anti-TBM Abs associated with other diseases.* Patients with SLE with anti-TBM Abs have been described, some even with prominent interstitial lesions. The presence of anti-TBM Abs in nephronophthisis and medullary cystic disease is not infrequent, although its clinicopathogenic significance is not clear.

Histopathology

As we have mentioned, this pathology is recognizable by the presence of linear deposits of IgG along the TBM and is rarely accompanied by other immunoglobulins. C3 usually accompanies the IgG but is nonspecific, unless some of the antigens of the molecule are shown to be uncovered after activation. Not all the tubules habitually present these deposits, and even in the areas with deposits, there may be interruptions due to fragmentation of the TBM, which can make diagnosis difficult.

Etiopathogenesis

In the majority of cases, there is a pathologic process that modifies the TBM antigens or that discovers or makes already existing antigenic structures and provokes an immune response through the formation of anti-TBM Abs. This pathologic process may be an interstitial inflammatory reaction to different toxins such as germs, crystalline deposits (oxalic), etc. The cases of pure or primary immunologic deregulation are few. In the majority of cases, these antibodies are pathogenic, giving rise to TIN, with functional tubular alterations and a decrease in GF, as demonstrated in experimental models. The deposition of antibodies can recruit nonspecific cytotoxic effector cells to the site. Earlier, we mentioned the factors which, for Neilson, give rise to this type of immune reaction.

Various types of autoantigens have been isolated by digestion of TBM, which are classified by Colvin and Fang as antigen 1 (48-54 kDa), which is the most frequent in idiopathic cases and is not present in the GBM; antigen 2 (70 kDa), which appears in cases associated with glomerular affectation, anti-GBM Abs, or SLE (it is present in the GBM); and antigen 3 (40-50 kDa), which is the most extensive antigen of the GBM and appears in cases of Alport's syndrome, anti-GBM Abs, and cases with involvement of the epithelial cells and their basal membrane (it is the hidden antigen of the "specific" anti-GBM Ab that appears on denaturalization).

Prognosis and treatment

The evolution to CRF is not infrequent in familial and idiopathic cases. In secondary cases, prognosis is associated with the primary disease.

UVEITIS-ASSOCIATED TIN

This rare association of TIN and uveitis, in some cases together with bone marrow or lymph node granulomas, may appear as (1) an idiopathic primary form or (2) within the framework of other diseases or syndromes as a secondary form. These are usually infections such as toxoplasmosis, brucellosis, tuberculosis, infectious mononucleosis, and histoplasmosis. In sarcoidosis, Sjögren's syndrome, and Behçet's syndrome also may appear.

At present, there is still no clear pathogenic explanation, but this appears to be an autoimmune disease, fundamentally mediated by cellular immunity. For this reason, it is classified in this group, although we also mention it within the idiopathic TINs.

The first case described, in a 10-year-old child with toxoplasmosis, showed TIN and uveitis and atypical evolution for an infectious AIN. The next description corresponds to two idiopathic cases, mentioning the name of this syndrome for the first time. This syndrome is more frequent in adolescents, approximately 14 years of age, but also appears in adults, in whom medullar and lymphatic granulomas are more frequent, appearing in half the patients.

Clinical findings

In adolescents, this syndrome predominantly affects females, in a proportion of 8:1 or more. The symptomatology at onset is nonspecific, with asthenia, anorexia, weight loss, and fever. The appearance of the TIN and uveitis tends to occur at the same time, although either one can precede the other, even by up to 3 months. The TIN tends to present a proximal tubular syndrome; sterile leukocyturia is habitual, and on rare occasions, a transitory hematuria appears. There also may be polyuria and polydipsia, as expressions of the urinary concentrating disorder. Except in isolated cases, there is usually a greater or lesser deterioration of GF. The anterior uvea is most frequently affected, although the posterior also can be affected; there also can be bilateral involvement.

Analytically, the frequent existence of anemia, high globular sedimentation rate, and hypergammaglobulinemia stands out. Eosinophilia may appear in one third of patients. In many cases, circulating immune complexes were detected, although the complement components are usually normal. Differential diagnosis with initial stages of collagenosis may be difficult in some patients, since there may be anti-DNA, ANCA, or anti-smooth muscle Abs. Various cellular immunity disorders have been described in these patients.

Females also predominate in adult patients, but in a lower proportion of 3:1. Clinical presentation is similar but is differentiated by the frequent finding of granulomas in the bone marrow and lymph nodes, together with an evolution that, on occasion, is more insidious.

Examination of these patients with gallium-67 is useful, allowing the diagnosis of the TIN and the uveitis even before the symptoms appear.

Histopathology

At the renal level, there are interstitial infiltrates composed of lymphocytes, eosinophils, and plasma cells, the proportion of which varies from one patient to another. The proximal tubule is the most affected, with areas of flattened epithelium and necrosis together with regenerative forms. Granulomas may be found in the kidney, although they are more frequent in the bone marrow and lymph nodes. Direct IF is negative in all patients, except for a few described with linear fixation of IgG and C1Q. In the later stages there may be interstitial fibrosis and tubular atrophy.

Etiopathogenesis

As mentioned earlier, a similar clinical situation appears associated with a series of infectious diseases, sarcoidosis, etc., and there are cases in which differentiation from collagenosis may be difficult. In all the primary cases mentioned here, logically there was no associated pathology found. The most popular hypothesis in these cases is that this is an autoimmune disease. The same process affects the uvea as the kidney, since parallel activity in the two processes has been demonstrated in some patients.

This does not seem to be a disease produced by immune complexes despite their presence in the blood and in the uvea in quite a few patients, since they do not appear as deposits on renal lesions. It is probably a deregulation of cell immunity and T-lymphocytes in response to tubular autoantigens or to modified antigens with a cross-reaction to the uvea. The immunohistochemical analysis of five patients revealed a predominance of memory T-lymphocytes (CD45TO+) in the tubulointerstitial infiltration, which could be the result of T-cell activation at sites of inflammation.

Prognosis and treatment

In children and adolescents, total remission is the rule, with recovery of renal function occurring either spontaneously or with steroid treatment. The response to steroids may be dramatic. In adults, total recovery is less frequent, often leaving renal failure. Relapses are infrequent, on occasion on reduction of the steroids. The uveitis usually responds to topical steroids, although it may persist or recur. Few of these patients are controlled at the long term, so it is difficult to judge later evolution.

TIN IN MALIGNANCY (INDUCED BY CANCER)

The TINs that appear in dysproteinemias, generally through renal protein deposits, are explained in Chapters 4 and 26. The following are TINs that may appear in lymphomas or leukemias, generally due to renal infiltration.

TIN AND LYMPHOMAS

Lymphomas may affect the kidney through various mechanisms, giving rise to a different pathologies, among which are (1) obstructive uropathy caused by involvement of the urinary tract, (2) thrombosis of the renal vein, (3) nephrotic syndrome with minimal glomerular lesions (this is more frequent in mixed cell Hodgkin's disease), (4) other GNs, e.g., mesangial IgA, extracapillary, membranous, and membranous-proliferative, (5) hypercalcemia, (6) dysproteinemia and amyloidosis, and (7) direct renal invasion.

This section will only review this last group. Direct invasion of the kidney by malignant cells of lymphocyte type is a frequent finding in the autopsies of these patients. These infiltrates tend to be diffuse, sometimes forming lymphoid nodules, and appear in 6 to 60% of patients. In some lymphomas, such as mycosis fungoides, the renal histologic involvement is between 28 and 50%.

Most patients are asymptomatic. The increase in renal size or renal failure can be demonstrated in 4 to 14% of patients. The latter is usually due to obstructive uropathy secondary to retroperitoneal infiltration or other enumerated causes. Significant renal failure only appears in 0.5% of patients. In any case, there are cases of terminal renal failure due to renal interstitial infiltration.

TIN AND LEUKEMIA

In both acute and chronic leukemias, half of patients necropsied showed renal infiltration, although as we mentioned in regard to lymphomas, symptomatology is rare. The infiltration is generally diffuse, more of the nodular type than in lymphomas. Some patients show an increase in the size of the kidney, although less frequently than in lymphomas. There may be tubular disorders with loss of potassium and magnesium and tubular acidosis in patients with myelogenic leukemia, especially in the monocyte type.

TIN IN URINARY TRACT INFECTION AND REFLUX NEPHROPATHY

Obstructive uropathy Each of the TINs included in this section are discussed in Chapters 6 and 31.

TIN IN VASCULAR AND HEMATOLOGIC DISEASES

The TINs secondary to ischemia in vascular diseases and acute tubular necrosis are discussed in Chapters 3 and 6.

TIN IN HEMATOLOGIC DISEASES

Sickle cell diseases

Sickle cell diseases are a group of hemolytic anemias caused by genetic hemoglobin disorders and are included with the drepanocytic syndromes. There are three types: (1) drepanocytic type, (2) drepanocytic anemia, and (3) double heterozygous states.

Group 1 includes heterozygotes for hemoglobin S (HbAS), which, for example, includes 8% of the black population in the United States. Group 2 is made up of homozygotes for this trait (HbSS), and group 3 includes those in which another abnormal hemoglobin associates with the drepanocytic allele (Hb SC, S-Thal).

The renal medulla is especially susceptible to these diseases because drepanocytic transformation takes place in these vessels, which gives rise to microinfarctions. These changes are favored by the special physiologic circumstances of the renal medulla, such as hyperosmolarity and low pH.

Clinical findings

The most frequent alteration of renal function in these patients is the incapacity to concentrate urine, which is due to the existence of more or less intense nephrogenic diabetes insipidus, shown even by some of the patients in group 1. This facilitates dehydration and increases the injurious medullar environment. The mechanism that gives rise to this alteration is not clear, although it has been suggested that these patients had a functional papillectomy even before the possible necrosis. At present, there is a tendency to implicate more cortical areas of the kidney in the pathophysiology of the renal involvement in this disease. Other functional tubular alterations also have been described. Proximal and distal tubular abnormalities are also present in this disease.

In group 2 patients, there is frequent presence of frank, painless hematuria or ureteral colic due to papillary necrosis. Hematuria may become a significant problem for these patients, with significant iron loss, which increases the anemia. Papillary necrosis is one of the most frequent complications in the sickle cell diseases. It is often associated with urinary infection. Another possible complication is the appearance of more or less extensive renal infarctions, which can even give rise to perirenal hemorrhages.

Intravenous urography may show defects around the calyx, which appear in 50% of patients in group 1. By sonography, conventional tomography, or computer tomography, papillary necrosis or papillary calcifications can be demonstrated, with the typical garland pattern of calcified renal papillae..

The appearance of nephrotic syndrome of unknown cause has been described in these patients. This generally corresponds to a membranous-proliferative GN at the histologic level, but poststreptococcal GN, membranous GN, and focal segmental glomerulosclerosis also have been described.

Despite all the renal involvements described, there are few patients who develop terminal renal failure in the sickle cell diseases. Renal failure was diagnosed in only 4.2% of the sickle cell anemia patients after 25 years in a longitudinal study.

Histopathology

The most characteristic lesions are observed at the medullar renal level, where the capillaries are usually thickened, with intracapillary falciform hematies. The juxtamedullary glomerulus increases in size in relation to the age of the patient and the degree of anemia. At the glomerular level, other nonspecific alterations may be observed. A frequent finding is that of focal interstitial fibrosis at the medullar level.

Treatment of the renal complications

Hematuria should be prevented and treated in these patients, using any of the various methods available. The use of mannitol infusion, water ingestion, thiazides, or loop diuretics to decrease medullar osmolarity has proven useful. Alkalinisation with sodium bicarbonate also may be effective. Drugs capable of causing hyperkalemia should be used with caution. -Amino-caproic acid should be reserved for serious cases, given its high risk. In some cases it has been necessary to resort to nephrectomy when urinary hemorrhage persists despite treatment. This nephrotic syndrome has been treated with steroids with contradictory results.

HEREDITARY DISEASES AND TIN

Hereditary renal diseases are discussed in Chapters 39, 40, 41 and 42.

IDIOPATHIC AND FAMILIAR TIN: MISCELLANEOUS

RADIATION NEPHRITIS

Radiation nephritis (RN) generally is associated with the use of high doses of radiotherapy applied over short periods of time. This nephropathy is rare nowadays, since protective measures are taken during radiotherapy.

This type of pathology has been seen since the beginning of the twentieth century, but in the 1940s, the moderate sensitivity of the kidneys to radiation, as well as lymph tissue, skin, lungs, and liver, became more well known.

The cases described at present come from the treatment of renal or pararenal tumors such as Wilms' tumor, seminoma, ovarian tumor, and retroperitoneal infiltrates. RN also may develop following the combined use of total-body radiation and chemotherapeutic agents in preparation for bone marrow transplantation.

RN is mentioned in some pathology books in chapters that discuss vascular nephropathies, since although, histologically, the lesions affect all the renal structures, at the functional level they behave like malignant arterial hypertension with deterioration of renal function, which supports the idea of an ischemic pathogenesis.

Clinical findings

The clinical presentation of RN is arbitrarily divided into acute and chronic, more a function of intensity and type of symptoms than of time. The acute form usually appears 6 to 12 months after radiation. There is usually arterial hypertension, often with malignant criteria, deterioration of renal function, and marked saline retention. This situation could be due to glomerulotubular ischemia secondary to the vascular lesions, with an intense increase of the renin-angiotensin system. The clinical presentation may be similar to nephritic syndrome and can be aggravated by cardiac failure or encephalopathy.

Anemia is frequent, with multiple causes (e.g., hemolytic, hyporegenerative because of renal failure). Microangiopathy, with anemia, thrombocytopenia, and evidence of intravascular coagulation, may develop. In some series, the acute form shows high mortality due to arterial hypertension. Prognosis depends on the proper control of arterial pressure. The chronic form corresponds to chronic TIN, with proteinuria (rarely above 2 g/day), microhematuria, and hyaline-granule cylinders. Hypertension is frequent. The kidneys tend to be small and scarred. The clinical situation can evolve to chronic renal failure.

Histopathology

Vascular lesions are frequent and consist of fibrinoid necrosis and intimal proliferation of the arterioles. These typical radiation lesions may be complicated by those of nephroangiosclerosis secondary to the hypertension which these patients develop. The glomerular lesions vary from fibrinoid necrosis in segments of the glomerular capillary loops to its complete hyalinization. Both at this level and in the arterioles, the lesions may be superimposed on those caused by the hypertension. Radiation can cause edema of the endothelial cells, mesangial proliferation, and an increase in the mesangial matrix, lesions that are similar to the double-contour image characteristic of membranoproliferative GN.

At the tubular and interstitial levels, there is often tubular atrophy, together with interstitial edema and capillary congestion. In the later phases, interstitial fibrosis may predominate. Direct IF is negative.

BALKAN NEPHROPATHY

This is an endemic disease of the Balkans which, through chronic TIN, leads to terminal chronic renal failure. The geographic area where it appears includes defined endemic areas in the Danube basin and the Balkan mountain system that corresponds to Bulgaria, Yugoslavia, and Rumania. It is a wet region with high annual rainfall.

Clinical findings

The disease begins clinically at between 30 and 60 years of age. Women are affected earlier than men. It is more frequent within the rural population, with up to 30% affected in some areas. Those who emigrate young to other areas are not affected, whereas immigrants may be affected after spending an average of 15 years in the endemic region, which supports the idea of an environmental cause.

The onset is insidious, with symptoms of progressive renal failure. In the early, subclinical phases, there are urinary abnormalities common to alteration of tubular function (e.g., low-range proteinuria with tubular characteristics, tubular acidosis, and proximal tubular syndrome). The population of this area, even those not affected, tends to show an increased urinary elimination of β_2-microglobulin. The measurement of this protein in urine, together with that of Tamm-Horsfall protein, has been used as a marker of this disease in subclincal phases. The appearance of transitional papilloma and carcinoma of the renal pelvis and urethra, often bilateral and multifocal, is frequent in these patients.

Histopathology

The kidneys tend to diminish in size. Histologically, the kidneys show tubular atrophy and interstitial fibrosis; it is unusual to find cellular infiltrates. The glomeruli are not normally affected, although they may hyalinize in later phases, probably as a consequence of the tubulointerstitial involvement. Early changes in the interstitial capillaries have been described.

Etiopathogenesis

Given the epidemiologic characteristics of the disease, researchers have looked for the presence of an environmental toxin or microorganism, including a virus, to explain this disease, with inconclusive results. At present, the most widely accepted causative factor is environmental contamination by fungi of the *Aurantiogriseum penicillium* type, which has been shown to be nephritogenic. These fungi also could be responsible for the high incidence of urologic carcinomas in these patients. The lesion mechanism is unclear, although the toxic role of certain micotic derivatives such as ochratoxin A has been mentioned. *Aristolochia clematitis* is a plant native to the endemic area that contains the nephrotoxin aristolochic acid. This is another pathogenetic factor common in Chinese herb nephropathy. The fact that some people develop the disease and others do not depends on the degree of exposure to the injurious agent and individual susceptibility, which could be genetic in part.

Prognosis and treatment

The usual evolution of the disease is that of terminal renal failure in 50% of patients at 2 years after the onset of symptoms and practically 100% at 10 years. Effective prevention of Balkan nephropathy is not yet possible. Treatment of Balkan nephropathy includes general measures to prevent the progression of renal failure. With longer survival on dialysis, many patients develop tumors of the urinary tract.

IDIOPATHIC INTERSTITIAL NEPHRITIS

Idiopathic TIN caused by anti-TBM Abs

These TINs were discussed earlier.

Idiopathic TIN caused by immune-complex deposits

TINs with immune-complex deposits of granular appearance in the interstitium and along the TBM are often found in association with a series of diseases and occasionally are described in isolated or idiopathic cases. The diseases to which this form of TIN is usually associated include (1) drug-related AINs (see above), (2) those associated with infections (see above), (3) glomerulonephritis (see above), and (4) autoimmune diseases (see above).

Two primary forms have been described: TIN with IgE immune complexes and familial TIN with immune complexes.

TIN with IgE immune complexes Two cases of acute TIN with granular deposits of IgE on the TBM have been described. The first was in a 54-year-old woman with anemia, diverticulitis, hypergammaglobulinemia, hypocomplementemia, eosinofilia, renal failure, and proteinuria. There was no evidence of an associated disease. The renal biopsy showed granular deposits of IgE on the TBM and not on the glomerulus. Another similar case was described in a 72-year-old man with antinuclear antibodies but without other stigmata of SLE.

Familial TIN with immune complexes A syndrome appearing in infancy has been described as including chronic TIN with immune-complex deposits on the TBM, diarrhea, dermatitis, and autoantibodies. This is on occasion associated with membranous nephropathy.

Idiopathic granulamatous TIN

The granulomatous TINs are classified in Table 27.9, and some have been described in earlier sections. There are idiopathic and primary cases. Of significance in these patients is the existence of drugs or infections that potentially could give rise to the TIN, sarcoidosis, forms associated with uveitis, and Still disease. On occasion, the cause of these cellular immunity responses that give rise to the formation of granuloma is the deposition of microstructures or crystals on the interstitium. An example of this is granulomatous TIN that appears after derivations such as jejunoileostomy, probably caused by oxalate crystals.

TIN with uveitis (see above)

Familial TIN linked to HLA with hypokalemia

There are some families in which chronic TIN with hypokalemia associated with HLA has been described. This disease is diagnosed at between 10 and 39 years of age and develops with chronic renal failure. Histologically, at the renal level there is a chronic nonspecific TIN with lymphocytic infiltrates, tubular atrophy, and fibrosis. The mitochondria are large, with an increase in electrodensity. The TBM is thickened, and there are drops of lipid osmiofils in the tubular cells.

The disease is hereditary, with an autosomal recessive pattern of inheritance, and is linked to HLA. This association with HLA is probably due to the fact that the genes responsible are also located on the short arm of chromosome 6; some genes at this location are implicated in the reabsorption of potassium.

Systemic karyomegalia (megakaryocytic TIN)

Alteration of the nuclei of tubular cells is frequent in TIN induced by lead and other heavy metals, busulfan, and radiation nephritis. A similar involvement has been described without finding a clear associated cause. This interstitial nephritis with focal tubular necrosis, mononuclear cell infiltrates, tubular atrophy, and fibrosis shows the fundamental trait of an increase in nuclear size of the tubular cells of up to 30 μm, as well as less frequently cells in other organs. The nucleoli are large and multiple. Clinical presentation is progressive chronic renal failure. It is not known whether this disease is caused by a toxin that interferes with the reduplication of DNA.

Suggested readings

CHEN L, WANG Y, TAY YCH, HARRIS CH. Proteinuria and tubulointerstitial injury. Kidney Int 1997;52(suppl 61):S60-2.

COWLEY A, ROMAN R. The role of the kidney in hypertension. JAMA 1996;275:1581-9.

DE BROE ME, ELSEVIERS MM. Analgesic nephropathy. N Engl J Med 1998;338:446-52.

ELSEVIERS MM, DE SCHEPPER I, CORTHOUTS R, et al. High diagnostic performance of CT scan for analgesic nephropathy in patients with incipient to severe renal failure. Kidney Int 1995;48:1316-26.

HENRICH WL, AGODOA LE, BARRETT R, et al. Analgesics and the kidney: summary and recommendations to the Scientific Advisory Board of the NKF from an Ad Hoc Committee of the NKF. Am J Kidney Dis 1996;27:162-4.

may also be signs of septicemia, including low blood pressure and sometimes hypothermia. Such severe clinical manifestations occur in case of obstruction, often in acute prostatitis, and in immunodepressed patients, especially diabetics.

Laboratory criteria Tissue infection is always accompanied by inflammation, reflected by erythrocyte sedimentation rate (ESR) above 20 mm at the first hour and C reactive protein (CRP) over 20 mg/l. Whether the infection involves the kidney (pyelonephritis) or the prostate (prostatitis), bacteria enter the circulation, and the severity of laboratory results ranges from bacteremia to septicemia.

Imaging Ultrasound examination and tomodensitometry can confirm infection of the renal and/or prostate tissue. Renal scintigraphy, using ^{99m}Technetium-dimercaptosuccinic acid, is an excellent means of diagnosing acute pyelonephritis, although it can hardly be envisaged outside a specialized hospital setting. However, some pediatricians recently stated that isotopic imaging of the kidney should now be the first-line investigation to diagnose renal infection in children.

Intravenous pyelography (IVP) does not show the tissue lesions but can detect an abnormality of the urinary tract responsible for the infection. An abnormal upper urinary tract is indicative of upper UTI. This is also true in case of vesicoureteral reflux.

Primary versus secondary infections

The term "primary" denotes an infection occurring in a urinary tract that is anatomically normal, without obstruction, without lithiasis and without reflux. This is the case in most simple urinary tract infections in the female, in whom primary infection has two causes. The first is anatomic, due to a short urethra that tends to open during sexual intercourse. The second is the uropathogenicity of *E. coli* endowed with attachment factors (fimbrial or nonfimbrial adhesins). These bacteria progress along the perineal mucosa from the anus to the urethra and gain entry into the bladder. They subsequently ascend along the ureter to contaminate the pelvocalyceal system and the renal tissue.

In the male and the child (especially boys), primary infections are rare. In most cases, they are due to a urinary tract abnormality. Work-up requires IVP followed if necessary by urethrocystography by suprapubic bladder puncture.

Given the above considerations, several methods can be used to classify urinary tract infections. They can be differentiated as affecting the male or the female, as upper or lower infections (taking into account the limitations above), or as primary or secondary infections.

It is, however, easier to adopt a classification based on the infected organ, that is, cystitis, pyelonephritis, or prostatitis. These are subdivided into clinical forms that vary according to gender, immune status (including pregnancy) and age.

URINARY INFECTION IN THE FEMALE

CYSTITIS

Cystitis is very common, and the denomination should be reserved to the female. In the male, cystitis is almost always accompanied by prostatitis. Signs and symptoms of cystitis are well known: burning on micturition, frequency, sometimes hematuria due to purpura of the bladder mucosa, normal body temperature, normal ESR and CRP, and presence of bacteria (usually *E. coli*) and of leukocytes in the urine. Absence of pathogens can result from factors described above. Absence of leukocytes is most often an indication that sampling was inadequate with contamination by nonurinary pathogens, aside from some cases seen early in the course of the infection.

Two types of cystitis should be distinguished: those that occur as a solitary episode or at lengthy intervals, and those relapsing three or four times a year.

Acute, occasional cystitis is very common. It is almost always due to a community-acquired *E. coli* sensitive to most antibiotics specific for the urinary tract (except ampicillin and trimethoprim/sulfamethoxazole [TMP/SMX])] and requires only urine culture and cytology along with antibiotic sensitivity tests. Treatment should be started before receiving these results. It can be brief, limited to 4 days (either 4 days of an antibiotic with a short half-life, or a single dose of an antibiotic with slow urinary elimination). Short-term recurrence of infection after 4-day treatment of cystitis with low-grade fever can reflect previously undetected pyelonephritis that was insufficiently treated.

Relapsing cystitis Cystitis can recur rapidly (within a few days) because the antibiotic treatment was not well adapted, as soon confirmed by the results of the antibiotic sensitivity test. Some women suffer multiple relapses, ranging from two or three a year to as many as one a month. The cause may be an anomaly of the urinary tract, requiring careful examination of the genitalia and of the urethral outlet, especially if the episodes appear to be associated with sexual intercourse. This may disclose hymeneal scars favoring urethral opening during intercourse. In some cases lateral pressure on the urethra induces oozing of pus, indicating infection within a suburethral gland. Such minor anomalies can be easily cured by a simple local surgical procedure. Conversely, if this physical examination is normal, an IVP focusing on the bladder and the urethra on micturition should be performed. In an older woman, relapsing cystitis may indicate presence of bladder tumor, justifying bladder ultrasound examination and cystoscopy.

URETHRAL SYNDROME

The urethral syndrome is characterized by urgency, burning on micturition, and pelvic pain, without bacteriuria or leukocyturia. Such manifestations that indicate urethral inflamation but not cystitis can have a gynecologic origin or occasionally may be due to *Chlamydia* infection. When such etiologies have been ruled out, it is occasionally tempting to suggest a psychogenic origin. However, the physician should be careful not to overlook an organic cause, especially when urinalysis finds sterile leukocyturia. The causes of sterile leukocyturia are listed in Table 29.1. Again, before retaining the diagnosis of "urethral syndrome", bladder ultrasonography and cystoscopy should be carried out.

ACUTE PYELONEPHRITIS

Acute pyelonephritis consists of microbial inflammation of the renal pelvis along with infection of the renal tissue. The term *pyelitis* is inappropriate because it has been demonstrated that when the pelvocalyceal cavities are infected the renal tissue is also involved. *Renal abscess* should be considered a form of development of pyelonephritis with liquefaction leading to a walled-off cavity. *Pyonephrosis* refers to infection of renal cavities and renal tissue above urinary tract obstruction with rapid destruction of the renal tissue. Finally, *primary* pyelonephritis, that is, renal infection in the absence of urologic anomalies should be distinguished from *secondary* pyelonephritis, a complication of uropathy or obstruction.

Pathophysiology

All forms of pyelonephritis, primary or secondary, are characterized by acute suppuration of the renal tissue. At histology, the lesions consist of extensive inflammatory edema, infiltration with polymorphonuclear leukocytes, hemorrhagic streaks, and severe tubule cell injury with presence of leukocyte casts in the tubular lumina. In some areas these lesions develop to necrosis and abscess formation. Papillary necrosis is not a common finding in simple pyelonephritis. It usually complicates renal infection in the diabetic and infected hydronephrosis with increased pressure in the renal cavities.

Simple, uncomplicated pyelonephritis in the young female

Primary pyelonephritis in the absence of urologic anomaly, renal stone, and vesicoureteral reflux is extremely frequent in young females. Pathophysiologic factors pertain both to the host and to the parasite.

The host Concerning the host, two questions must be answered. The first is to ascertain that pyelonephritis does not complicate some overlooked urinary tract abnormality, essentially migration of a renal stone or vesicoureteral reflux. Normal plain abdominal film and ultrasound examination argue against an obstacle. Normal retrograde cystography rules out VUR. The second is to determine whether the patient is affected by an impairment of her defenses against infection. Diabetes and pregnancy will be considered below.

The parasite With regard to the bacteria, the principal element to consider is how the urinary pathogens gain access from the bladder to the kidney. Most likely, uropathogenic strains progress along the perineal mucosa, gain access to the bladder, without necessarily eliciting signs and symptoms of cystitis, and ascend along the ureter to the renal pelvis. It has been established that some strains of Enterobacteriaceae, essentially *E. coli*, are uropathogenic owing to adhesins on the bacterial fimbriae (pili) or on the surface of the bacterial cell. The great majority of primary pyelonephritis in the young female is due to community-acquired *E. coli* with a uropathogenic phenotype. It should be stressed that uropathogenicity and sensitivity to antibiotics have nothing in common. Most community-acquired uropathogenic strains usually are sensitive to most antibiotics.

Clinical findings

Pyelonephritis is characterized by the abrupt appearance of severe infection with high fever, well over 38 °C, chills and unilateral abdominal pain resembling renal colic, accompanied with nausea and sometimes vomiting. On palpation, the loin is tender and the kidney swollen. Signs and symptoms of cystitis are evocative but inconstant. ESR and CRP levels are elevated. Urinalysis discloses pyuria and bacteriuria. Blood cultures may grow to the same strain as found in the urine. In case of primary, noniatrogenic pyelonephritis, more than 90% of cases are due to *E. coli*.

Diagnosis

Imaging studies A first, pyelonephritis in a young female with no history of renal infection does not require an IVP. As stated above, a plain abdominal film and ultrasound examination suffice.

Tomodensitometry (CT scan) has raised considerable interest since 1979 because, for the first time, imaging showed the exact appearance of infectious renal tissue lesions. However, CT scan should not now be considered a routine investigation in common forms of pyelonephritis.

The CT scan images of acute pyelonephritis must be studied before and after contrast medium injection. Before injection the kidney appears swollen and occasionally surrounded by edema. After injection the lesions consist of hypodensities that correspond to zones of vasoconstriction within the suppurative areas. (For a thorough description, see Talner et al. in "Suggested readings".) Hypodensities are triangular with a hilar summit and a cortical base, or round-shaped with a lobar situation, or more diffuse. CT scan often discovers small abscesses that are overlooked by ultrasound examination. The finding of a large abscess indicates liquefaction of a suppurative area. This represents massive bacterial inoculum, which would suggest pursuing treatment for a longer period than in the usual, nonexcavated forms.

Treatment

Acute pyelonephritis in a young, nonimmunocompromised female is a benign condition. After beginning antibiotic therapy, urine is sterile within hours, fever and pain abate within 2 to 4 days, and laboratory indices of inflammation wane within 1 to 2 weeks. Persistence of aseptic leukocyturia for 2 or 3 weeks is common and does not indicate treatment failure. In some studies based on repeat CT scan imaging, it has been shown that hypodensities and/or small abscesses can be followed by cortical scars.

Pyelonephritis and pregnancy

Pyelonephritis in pregnancy, usually a complication of previous occult asymptomatic bacteriuria, is found in 3.5 to 7.1% of pregnant women. Asymptomatic bacteriuria should therefore be systematically sought and treated during pregnancy.

In case of pyelonephritis in a pregnant woman, imaging usually is restricted to ultrasonography. Ultrasound examination can be difficult to interpret owing to the physiologic dilatation of the urinary tract during pregnancy. In case of severe pyelonephritis where a urologic cause is suspected, it is acceptable to carry out IVP with a minimum of films. Pyelonephritis of pregnancy can be a severe condition, leading to uterine contractions and premature labor.

Complicated pyelonephritis

Any abnormality of the urinary tract that entails urinary tract distention and slowing of the urinary flow leads to complicated pyelonephritis. Although *E. coli* is the predominant strain, it may lack the uropathogenic phenotype. Infection due to *Proteus mirabilis* can be complicated with build-up of staghorn stones made of struvite. Thereafter the infectious calculus increases stasis, and stasis maintains infection.

All urinary malformations, including vesicoureteral reflux, renal stones, prostate hypertrophy, and neurogenic bladder can be complicated with acute pyelonephritis, especially after catheterization or endoscopy. Pyelonephritis can be bilateral, and suppuration of urine under pressure entails a hazard of gram-negative strain septicemia, shock, disseminated intravascular coagulation, and anuria. Surgical drainage of the urinary tract is an emergency, along with affirmative antibiotic treatment.

URINARY TRACT INFECTION IN THE MALE

In the male, UTI rarely occurs within a normal urinary tract. In addition, it virtually always involves a solid organ, that is, the prostate, the kidney, or both. Male UTI is an indication for thorough uroradiologic investigation.

ACUTE PROSTATITIS

Acute prostatitis is common in adult males. However, it is often misdiagnosed.

Prostatitis usually follows *E. coli* infection ascending from the urethra to the bladder. *E. coli* is the most common strain. However, prostatitis can also be hematogenous following remote infection, in particular staphylococcal infection.

The typical picture of prostatitis is observed in the young male with an acute condition comprising rigors, spiking fever and malaise.

Diagnosis is rapidly made on the basis of bladder irritation, burning on urination and cloudy urine. Orchiepididymitis can be associated with prostatitis. Dysuria can be complicated by complete bladder retention.

Drainage should never be done by the urethral route, but by suprapubic percutaneous catheterization.

Not infrequently, acute prostatitis lacks lower urinary tract manifestations and is mistaken for a viral febrile episode.

Delayed treatment opens the door to severe complications such as gram-negative sepsis followed by metastatic infection with a predilection for intervertebral disk localization.

In fact, rectal digital examination should be systematic in a male with febrile infection.

The prostate is swollen and tender. Palpation must be gentle to avoid flushing pathogens into the circulation. Diagnosis of prostatitis rests on identification of pathogens in the urine, or in urethral discharge, along with laboratory evidence of inflammation. Chills indicate bacteremia and the necessity of blood cultures.

Acute prostatitis requires thorough uroradiologic imaging of the whole urinary tract, including prostate ultrasound examination by endorectal probe. Following a few days of treatment, an IVP must be carried out, including study of the urethra on micturition.

CHRONIC PROSTATITIS

Chronic prostatitis follows acute prostatitis, or develops progressively without a clear-cut date of onset. This form usually is associated with chronic infection of the urethra and of the spermatic duct, such as epididymitis and deferentitis. Rectal palpation discloses a hypertrophic, or edematous, or pseudoadenomatous prostatic gland.

The prostate is tender, which is abnormal. Urine culture does not always grow a pathogen, and identification of prostate infection may require prostatic massage.

Chronic complaints of dysuria, burning on micturition and perineal discomfort, in a patient whose urine cultures are stubbornly negative, are difficult to interpret. Such "prostatodynia" may stem more from psychologic reasons than from an organic cause.

URINARY TRACT INFECTION IN CHILDREN

Childhood urinary tract infection can occur at any age. *E. coli* is the major pathogen in girls. In boys it represents only 40% of the urinary strains, as the foreskin is a source of various gram-negative bacteria, and especially *Proteus*. It has been established that circumcision clearly diminishes the incidence of UTI.

URINARY TRACT INFECTION IN THE NEWBORN

Neonatal UTI is not necessarily explained by an anomaly of the urinary tract. It occurs especially in males and manifests as fever or hypothermia, poor feeding, vomiting, diarrhea, failure to thrive, cyanosis, liver enlargement, and sometimes meningitis. Blood cultures grow in one-third of the cases. Such septicemic forms are severe and require early diagnosis and treatment.

URINARY TRACT INFECTION IN THE TODDLER AND THE CHILD

Lower, afebrile cystitis is a possibility in young girls, owing to perineal fecal contamination.

A single episode does not necessarily require thorough uroradiologic investigations, and treatment can be short and simple.

In young children febrile UTI often presents with poorly localizing signs, such as vomiting or abdominal pain. Unexplained fever, irrespective of the accompanying signs, should include urine cultures in the diagnostic work-up. Renal infection in this age group is essentially the consequence of some urinary tract malformation, especially vesicoureteral reflux (VUR). VUR is a common malformation and there is a trend for familial occurrence. VUR has been classified in four stages of increasing severity, stage IV being characterized by massive intrarenal reflux. The risk of noninfected refluxing urine is limited.

On the other hand, the first episode of pyelonephritis can lead to cortical scars. Neglected reflux with chronic UTI leads to cortical scars, arrest in kidney growth and later to chronic pyelonephritis. Other common urinary tract malformations are ureteropelvic junction stenosis, megaureter, and posterior urethral valves that, when overlooked, can lead to silent, progressive dilatation of the urinary tract.

Any febrile UTI in a child is a mandatory indication for thorough uroradiologic imaging, including ultrasound examination, IVP, and retrograde cystography. The last can also be carried out by isotopic methods that entail very little irradiation and have the advantage of better detecting intermittent reflux.

PARTICULAR FORMS OF URINARY TRACT INFECTION

Acute pyelonephritis in the immunocompromised patient

Pregnancy

Pregnancy is a state of acquired immunodepression characterized by reduced cytotoxic and increased suppressor T-cell activity. The frequency of bacteriuria and the attending risk of developing acute pyelonephritis are related to impaired response to urinary pathogens. There is significant difference in host response in nonpregnant and pregnant women. In the latter serum and urine antibody response is lower, and this is also true for urine IgG and IgA antibody activity. Finally, the immunodepression of pregnancy impairs the mucosal IL-6 response to acute pyelonephritis caused by *E. coli*.

Pyelonephritis in the diabetic

Asymptomatic bacteriuria is common in the diabetic. It proceeds from glycosuria, poor bladder contractility, and impairment of granulocyte function. In the diabetic, pyelonephritis can be painless and afebrile. This is a serious condition, and hospitalization is mandatory. A special complication of pyelonephritis in the diabetic is papillary necrosis. The clinical picture comprises severe pyelonephritis, macroscopic hematuria and shedding of tissue fragments, that can be obstructive, along the urinary tract. Following papillary necrosis, the appearance of the IVP is evocative. Calyxes are eroded and club-shaped. Occasionally, the sloughed papilla remains in the calyx and can undergo calcification. Papillary necrosis is followed by cortical scars. Multiple necroses lead to chronic renal failure with early urinary concentration defect.

Pyelonephritis in the renal transplant recipient

Acute pyelonephritis in a transplant recipient is usually an early event, occurring within 2 months following transplantation. It can be painless and may favor transplant rejection.

Pyelonephritis in the older patient

Acute pyelonephritis is a common complication in older, bedridden patients. Thirty percent of cases of sepsis in older hospitalized patients proceed from acute urinary tract infection, and this represents a significant cause of mortality in such patients. Diagnosis can be delayed, as loin pain is inconstant, or owing to patient unresponsiveness. Any febrile episode in a bedridden elderly patient should indicate, among other investigations, a urine culture.

Renal abscess

Renal abscess was a common complication of staphylococcal sepsis. It is still a possibility, especially in intravenous illicit drug users with staphylococcal endocarditis. In fact, most renal abscesses are ascending in nature. The clinical picture is that of acute pyelonephritis due to gram-negative organisms, that can be primary or that may complicate some urologic lesions such as renal stones. The course of renal abscess differs from that of uncomplicated pyelonephritis in that despite appropriate antibiotic treatment, fever and high leukocyte counts persist for more than 5 days. The diagnosis rests on ultrasound and CT scan examination. The abscess consists of a walled-off cavity containing fluid. After contrast medium injection, CT scan examination shows contrast reinforcement around the abscess. The prognosis of renal abscess depends on its cause, its size and its background. Small abscesses are common in acute pyelonephritis and resolve with medical treatment. Conversely, a large abscess in a diabetic can be severe enough to require rescue nephrectomy.

Urinary tract infection and chronic bladder catheterization

Patients with long-term indwelling bladder catheters, such as those with neurologic bladders, always have infected urine. The urinary strains are diverse and change constantly. Chronic pyuria must not be treated when asymptomatic. This would only lead to selection of resistant strains. Intercurrent acute febrile episodes require short, high-dose treatment with bactericidal antibiotics.

Xanthogranulomatous pyelonephritis

Xanthogranulomatous pyelonephritis is usually unilateral. This is a rare complication of chronically infected renal stones. The typical picture is that of a woman in her 50s suffering from weight loss, fatigue, fever, and renal pain. Palpation discloses a tumoral kidney. IVP shows absence of contrast medium secretion. CT scan examination rules out renal cancer because lesions are poorly vascularized. Tomodensitometry may show extension of the inflammatory process to the perirenal space and to the neighboring organs, and occasionally fistulization to the colon or the duodenum. Treatment consists of nephrectomy and cure of fistulae. The appearance of the lesion is particular. The calyxes are surrounded with a yellowish inflammatory zone that consists of a three-layer granulomatous reaction. The lesion shows lipid-laden macrophages and often cholesterol crystals.

Malacoplakia

Similar to xanthogranulomatous pyelonephritis, malacoplakia is the consequence of an abnormal response of macrophages to *E. coli.* The inflammatory lesion involves the bladder mucosa the urethra and the renal pelvis. It is composed of submucosal infiltration with lymphocytes, polymorphs and histocytes. Michaelis-Gutmann bodies (calcospherite) are characteristic.

Treatment

Drugs Treatment of urinary tract infection requires antibiotics with the five following properties. (1) They must be bactericidal (2) with rapid absorption, early plasma peak, predominant urinary excretion and high concentration in kidney and urine. (3) They must span the spectrum of the majority of usual uropathogens. (4) They should not rapidly select resistant strains, and (5) they must have good tolerance.

Their prescription should also consider the route of administration (oral or parenteral), their availability (which varies from country to country), and their cost. The main antibiotics used in urinary tract infections are listed in Table 28.3.

Indications Simple cystitis in a young female requires a short 4-day treatment with an appropriate oral antibiotic. Another mode of treatment consists of a single absorption of an antibiotic with prolonged urinary elimination. This is the case for pefloxacin and fosfomycin-trometamol. Relapsing cystitis, defined by four or more episodes per year, once a urologic cause has been ruled out, is an indication for prophylactic treatment. This regimen is based on absorption, three times per week at bedtime, of a small dose of antibiotic. Several drugs have been successfully tried in this indication, including quinolones, nitrofurantoin and TMP/SMX. This small dosage is insufficient to obtain bactericidal levels in the bladder urine, but sufficient to impede bacterial replication. As long as treatment is pursued, no relapse occurs, with the exception of occasional infectious episodes due to nonsensitive strains, such as *Staphylococcus saprophyticus*, or other occasional gram-positive strains.

Treatment of simple acute pyelonephritis must be started after sampling of urine and blood, for adapting antibiotic treatment according to antibiotic sensitivity tests. Before results are available, antibiotic treatment usually consists of the association of intramuscular aminoglycoside and another, oral, antibiotic. Several drugs are appropriate for treating pyelonephritis. They include fluorinated quinolones, but also third-generation cephalosporins, or the association of amoxicilin plus clavulanic acid, or ticarcillin plus clavulanic acid, or aztreonam. After 4 days of drug association, the patient is continued on oral monotherapy for 10 days, for a total of 14 days of treatment. It is mandatory to carry out urine culture 1 month after ending treatment, to detect possible recurrence of bacteriuria that would require new investigation and treatment.

Acute prostatitis Initial treatment requires the association of two intravenous antibiotics, usually an aminoglycoside plus another bactericidal antibiotic with good penetration into the prostatic tissue, such as TMP/SMX or a fluorinated quinolone. A course of a nonsteroidal anti-inflammatory drug helps reduce inflammation. After the acute phase, oral treatment must be pursued for a long period, on the order

Table 28.3 Appropriate antibiotics for the treatment of urinary tract infections

	General indications	Pregnancy	Children	Prophylaxis
Aminoglycosides	+	+[1]	+	-
Aminopenicillins	+[2]	+	+	-
Carboxypenicillins	+	+	+	-
Ureidopenicillins	+	+	+	-
Quinolones	+[3]	-	+[4]	+
Fluoroquinolones	+[5]	-	-	+
Cephalosporins, 1st generation	+[6]	+	+	+[7]
Cephalosporins, 2nd generation	+	+	+	-
Cephalosporins, 3rd generation	+	+	+	-
Monobactams	+	+	+	-
Carbapenem	+	+	+	-
TMP/SMX	+	-	+	+[8]
Fosfomycin-trometamol	+[9]	-	-	-

1 Aminoglycosides should not be prescribed during pregnancy except in case of very severe infection, and for the shortest possible duration.
2 With the exception of amoxicillin + clavulanic acid, aminopenicillins should not be prescribed as first-line treatment owing to frequency of primary resistance to this class of antibiotics.
3 According to antibiotic sensitivity tests.
4 Nalidixic acid only.
5 Fluoroquinolones entail a risk of tendon rupture (especially Achilles' tendon).
6 Oral administration only.
7 According to antibiotic sensitivity tests.
8 According to antibiotic sensitivity tests.
9 Single-dose treatment of cystitis.

of 1 to 2 months, because prostatic tissue sterilization is obtained slowly. Too short a treatment course entails risks of flare-ups and development to chronic prostatitis.

Chronic prostatitis Rules for the treatment of chronic prostatitis are difficult to establish In many cases urine culture identifies no pathogens that might orient treatment. Any possible urologic abnormality, such as urethral stricture, should be treated by the urologist. Medical management rests on long-term treatment with an antibiotic with good prostatic penetration, such as TMP/SMX.

Childhood urinary tract infection In the child, treatment must be oriented by antibiotics and sensitivity tests. Table 29.3 shows that not all antibiotics used in adults are allowed in children. Fluoroquinolones are contraindicated before completion of growth, owing to possible cartilage toxicity. Nalidixic acid can be complicated with pseudotumor cerebri (brain edema) in young children.

Schematically, the treatment schedule, as in the adult, depends on the site of infection (cystitis versus pyelonephritis), the existence of an anatomic anomaly of the urinary tract, and age. In all cases, the goal of treatment is the same, that is, rapid and durable urine sterilization.

Simple cystitis in a young girl is the indication for a short treatment with amoxicillin + clavulanic acid, or nitrofurantoin, or TMP/SMX. The family must be instructed to verify local hygiene and to teach the child to avoid wiping from anus to perineum after the stool, a commonly overlooked cause of lower UTI. Simple but relapsing cystitis in the young girl is managed by oral prophylactic treatment, as in the adult, using nitroxoline, nitrofurantoin, or TMP/SMX.

In case of renal infection (pyelonephritis), first-line treatment requires a 3-day IV combination of aminoglycoside and betalactamine, the latter being preferably a cephalosporin. Treatment is continued orally for 10 additional days. Neonatal infection, or sepsis, is an indication for combined therapy using two antibiotics for at least 2 weeks. Urine should be cultured after 3 days of treatment to assess sterility, and recultured 7 to 10 days after stopping antibiotics to detect relapse. Relapse may be due to a urologic cause or to poor compliance.

In cases of pyelonephritis complicating urinary tract abnormality, such as VUR, treatment of the acute phase must be followed by maintenance treatment in order to maintain urine sterility until surgery is carried out.

Suggested readings

Case records of the Massachusetts General Hospital. N Engl J Med 1995;332:174-179.

Childs SJ. Current concepts in the treatment of urinary tract infections and prostatitis. Am J Med 1991;91:120S-3S.

Gratacos E, Torres PJ, Vila J, Alonso PL, Cararach V. Screening and treatment of asymptomatic bacteriuria in pregnancy prevent pyelonephritis. J Infect Dis 1994; 169:1390-2.

HOOTON TM, STAMM WE. Management of acute uncomplicated urinary tract infection in adults. Med Clin North Am 1991;75:339-57.

JOHNSON JR, STAMM WE. Urinary tract infections in women: diagnosis and treatment. Ann Intern Med 1989;111:906-17.

KUNIN CM, VANARSDALE WHITE L, TONG HH. A reassessment of the importance of "low-count" bacteriuria in young women with acute urinary symptoms. Ann Intern Med 1993;119:454-460.

LINSHAW M. Asymptomatic bacteriuria and vesicoureteral reflux in children (Nephrology Forum). Kidney Int 1996;50:312-29.

LIPSKY BA. Urinary tract infections in men. Epidemiology, pathophysiology, diagnosis and treatment. Ann Intern Med 1989;110:138-50.

MEYRIER A. Diagnosis and management of renal infections. Curr Opin Nephrol Hypertens 1996;5:151-7.

MEYRIER A, GUIBERT J. Diagnosis and drug treatment of acute pyelonephritis. Drugs 1992;44:356-67.

PAPPAS PG. Laboratory in the diagnosis and management of urinary tract infections. Med Clin North Am 1991;75:313-25.

PETERSSON C, HEDGES S, STENQVIST K, SANDBERG T, CONNELL H, SVANBORG C.: Suppressed antibody and interleukin-6 responses to acute pyelonephritis in pregnancy. Kidney Int 1994;45:571-7.

TALNER LB, DAVIDSON AJ, LEBOWITZ RL, DALLA-PALMA L, GOLDMAN SM. Acute pyelonephritis: can we agree on terminology? Radiology 1994;192:297-306.

WILKIE ME, ALMOND MK, MARSH FP. Diagnosis and management of urinary tract infection in adults. Br Med J 1992;305:1137-41.

ZHANEL JJ, HARDING JKM, NICOLLE LE. Symptomatic bacteriuria in patients with diabetes mellitus. Reviews of Infectious Diseases 1991;13:150-4.

SECTION

7

Obstruction and stone disease

CHAPTER

29 Reflux nephropathy

Graham C. Smith, Kate Verrier-Jones

KEY POINTS

- Efforts to reduce the incidence of reflux nephropathy should concentrate on improving the recognition and prompt treatment of urinary tract infection in infants and young children.
- Families with history of reflux nephropathy should be counselled on benefits of screening neonates for vesicoureteric reflux and on the symptoms of urinary tract infection in infancy.
- Antibiotic prophylaxis against urinary tract infection remains the first-line management for children with vesicoureteric reflux.
- Patients with reflux nephropathy require annual measurement of blood pressure and measurement of urinary protein excretion to detect progressive renal disease. The greatest risk is in children with bilateral renal scarring.
- Reflux nephropathy is an important cause of hypertension and chronic renal failure.

The term reflux nephropathy (RN) refers to areas of renal scarring secondary to urinary tract infection occurring in association with vesicoureteric reflux (vesicoureteric reflux). Other terms for this condition include "chronic pyelonephritis" and "chronic atrophic pyelonephritis." Vesicoureteric reflux describes the flow of urine retrograde from the bladder to the kidneys, either spontaneously or during micturition. Vesicoureteric reflux often is not recognized in children with reflux nephropathy if cystography is not performed or if the reflux resolves before the investigation is made, or it may be missed on cystography, which has a false-negative rate of 15%. Defects identified on Technetium-99m (^{99m}Tc) dimercaptosuccinic acid scans (DMSA) may occur in the absence of vesicoureteric reflux, but it is not clear whether these are identical to the focal scars seen using intravenous urography.

Vesicoureteric reflux may occur in isolation (primary vesicoureteric reflux) or in association with distal obstructive lesions secondary to posterior urethral valves, neuropathic bladder, or dysfunctional voiding. Obstructive (secondary) vesicoureteric reflux can cause renal damage without infection, owing to the high voiding pressures encountered. Nonobstructive, low-pressure reflux, in the absence of infection, is rarely associated with scarring.

Epidemiology

The prevalence of vesicoureteric reflux in the general population has been estimated to be 0.4 to 1.8% of healthy children, but vesicoureteric reflux is found in one-third of children with urinary tract infections. Primary vesicoureteric reflux is present from birth and appears to be familial. There is an association with other anomalies of the urinary tract, e.g., duplex systems and multicystic dysplastic kidneys. The prevalence of vesicoureteric reflux decreases with age, and it has been estimated that it resolves in 10% of cases per year.

Reflux nephropathy carries with it a significant morbidity, accounting for 25% of children entering the European Dialysis and Transplant Programme. It also causes a significant number of cases of childhood hypertension and is associated with hypertension and proteinuria, particularly in pregnancy.

Etiopathogenesis

Vesicoureteric reflux

Primary vesicoureteric reflux is thought to be due to delayed maturation of the vesicoureteric junction, sometimes with lateral displacement of the ureteric orifice and a shortened intramural ureter segment. A familial basis for primary vesicoureteric reflux has long been recognized, and evidence suggests an autosomal dominant mode of inheritance. Studies have shown a 30 to 35% occurrence rate in asymptomatic siblings and a higher incidence in neonates and in the children of individuals with a history of vesicoureteric reflux.

The severity of the reflux can vary from a small amount of urine passing into the distal ureter during micturition, to urine passing back through the renal papillae into the collecting ducts (intrarenal reflux). This is best described using the International Grading system (Fig. 29.1).

Vesicoureteric reflux leads to residual urine in the bladder following micturition, and this in turn acts as a culture medium for bacteria, particularly bowel organisms that ascend the urethra. Infected urine then refluxes to the kidneys and may enter the renal papillae in intrarenal reflux, causing acute pyelonephritis and renal scarring. The development of acute pyelonephritis puts the kidney at risk of scarring (Fig. 29.2).

In the presence of reflux, organisms normally of low pathogenicity may cause infection. The lower virulence characteristics of these organisms leads to a less marked host response, resulting in delayed diagnosis and treatment. Paradoxically this may increase the risk of renal damage. This compares with nephropathogenic P-fimbriated *E.coli*, which produce a more aggressive inflammatory response and, consequently, earlier treatment. As a result, both pyelonephritis and renal scarring are more frequently due to infection with non-P-fimbriated *E.coli* in children with reflux.

Sterile vesicoureteric reflux

Scars have been observed in areas of the kidney drained by refluxing papillae in the absence of urinary tract infection (UTI). It is not clear whether this is due to failure to detect urinary tract infection clinically or whether these scars have been acquired following vesicoureteric reflux and intrarenal reflux alone. Animal models have been used on both sides of the argument, but the results of these studies indicate that obstruction is required for scarring to occur if there is no infection. There is no doubt that damage occurs when the pressure inside the renal pelvis exceeds 35 mm Hg, but the question remains whether vesicoureteric reflux in children is associated with such pressures, other than in the presence of distal obstructive lesions. One situation where this might occur is in children with detrusor-sphincter dyssynergia. These children present with infrequent micturition, diurnal enuresis, difficulty initiating and maintaining a urinary stream, and suprapubic pain. Recurrent urinary tract infections are common. Koff et al measured pressures over 150 mm Hg in such uninhibited bladders. Therefore, in the toddler age-group, when sphincter control is being achieved, it is possible that high intravesical pressures may be generated and may lead directly to renal damage or may exacerbate the effect of refluxing infected urine.

Clinical findings

Reflux nephropathy is a silent condition with no clearly defined symptoms and no outward signs. It is detected only by renal imaging techniques usually undertaken following urinary tract infection, when between 5 and 20% of children will be found to already have renal scarring at the time of their first urinary tract infection. Some children with scars detected during screening programs have a history of recurrent urinary tract infections and give symptoms of acute pyelonephritis, but in many there is no clear history, although children with renal scarring visit their doctors more often than do controls in early childhood. In a small number of children, particularly neonates screened because of a family history of vesicoureteric reflux, scarring is identified despite the absence of evidence of a previous urinary tract infection, suggesting that damage has occurred in utero or that there is renal dysplasia in association with vesicoureteric reflux.

In some cases older children and adults present with complications of renal scarring: hypertension; proteinuria; chronic renal failure; during pregnancy.

Diagnosis

Reflux nephropathy is detected when imaging techniques are carried out in at-risk patients such as children with urinary tract infections, antenatal hydronephrosis, or a family

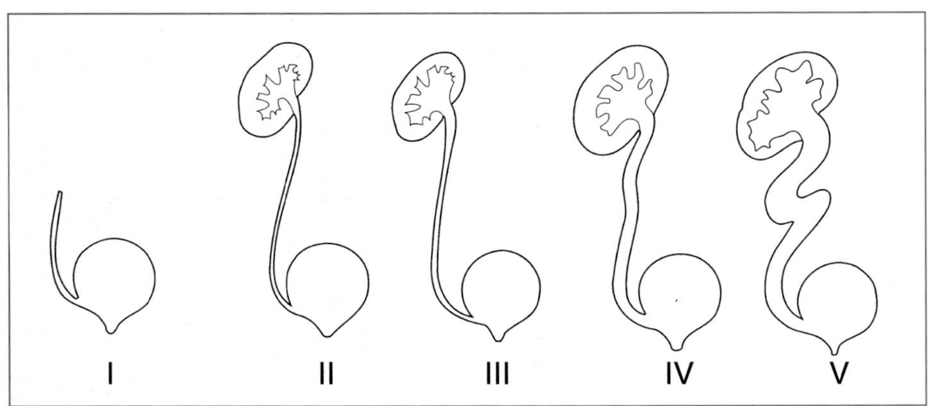

Figure 29.1 International grading system for vesicoureteric reflux.

history of vesicoureteric reflux. In the classic studies of Hodson and Edwards, renal scarring was diagnosed on intravenous urography in children with recurrent urinary tract infection and vesicoureteric reflux. This technique is now rarely used in children with straightforward urinary tract infection and has been replaced by dimercaptosuccinic acid scan scintigraphy, which is safer, more sensitive, and involves less radiation. Scars may be seen on ultrasound in older children and adults, but new scars in young children cannot be seen when the standard equipment is used. Recent studies using power Doppler have shown promising results, and this may become the method of choice for identification of both acute pyelonephritis and renal scarring as skills and equipment improve.

The aim of management is to prevent renal scarring by the early detection and treatment of urinary tract infection and to prevent acute pyelonephritis in high-risk cases by using antibiotic prophylaxis or surgery to correct vesicoureteric reflux (Fig. 29.3). Unfortunately, a significant number of children will have scarring by the time they are first investigated. Possible strategies for reducing the number of children with reflux nephropathy include: prompt recognition and treatment of urinary tract infection, particularly in the vulnerable population under 2 years of age; identification of children with vesicoureteric reflux at risk of developing reflux nephropathy following acute pyelonephritis by appropriate imaging techniques; effective management of vesicoureteric reflux by antibiotic prophylaxis or surgery; counselling and screening of first-degree relatives of patients with vesicoureteric reflux and reflux nephropathy.

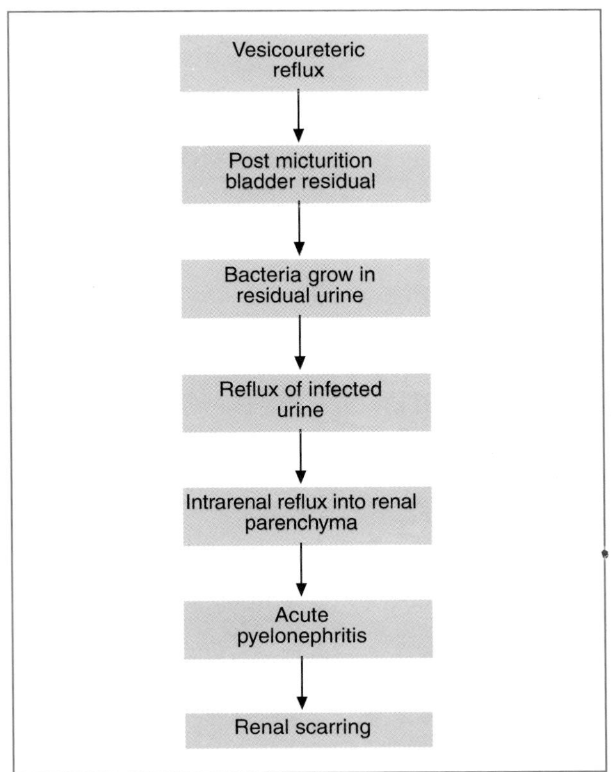

Figure 29.2 Mechanism for the development of reflux nephropathy.

Recognition and treatment of urinary tract infections

Evidence from clinical studies indicates that renal scarring is acquired very early in infancy and childhood following upper tract urinary tract infection. Scarring is more likely if there is a delay in diagnosis and treatment, particularly in young children with vesicoureteric reflux. In children under 2 years, symptoms of urinary tract infection are nonspecific, and there are concerns that urinary tract infections are frequently not identified. It is therefore important that urinary tract infection is considered in the differential diagnosis of a sick, febrile infant, and the urine examined. The development of urine sticks capable of detecting the presence of leukocyte esterase and nitrite can aid in the identification of urinary tract infections. However, these are screening tests, and they do not remove the need for microscopy and culture of a properly collected urine specimen. Once urine has been collected, a suitable antibiotic can be given for 5-10 days, depending on the severity of the illness. In sick children, particularly under 1 year of age, intravenous antibiotics should be used. Failure to respond within 48 hours is an indication for urgent ultrasound to exclude obstruction and a review of the antibiotic sensitivity of the organism. Once the treatment course has been completed, children under 5 years should be placed on night-time antibiotic prophylaxis while awaiting further investigations.

Identification of children at risk of developing reflux nephropathy

Investigation of children with urinary tract infection is aimed at identifying children who have scarred kidneys and those who have vesicoureteric reflux and are at risk of developing scars. As the youngest children are most at-risk for renal damage, more invasive investigations are reserved for this group. Our policy is outlined in Table 29.1 and reflects the guidelines of the Royal College of Physicians.

Renal ultrasound Renal ultrasound is a simple, safe, painless, noninvasive investigation and is most useful in identifying dilatation and obstructive lesions. It will also show the presence or absence, size and position of the kidneys as well as larger scars. Vesicoureteric reflux may

Table 29.1 Investigation of urinary tract infection in children

Age (yrs)	Investigation
0 - 1	Renal ultrasound ^{99m}Tc-dimercaptosuccinic acid (DMSA) scan Micturating cystourethrogram (MCUG)
1 - 7	Renal ultrasound DMSA scan +/- Abdominal X-ray
Over 7	Renal ultrasound +/- Abdominal X-ray

manifest itself on ultrasound as ureteral dilatation, but this is unreliable because vesicoureteric reflux can be present without dilatation and dilatation may be due to conditions other than vesicoureteric reflux.

Abdominal radiographs An abdominal X-ray examination is useful in the assessment of constipation, a well-described contributing factor to the development of urinary tract infection. It is also indicated in the case of *Proteus* urinary tract infection, to exclude the presence of renal calculi. Spinal dysraphism occasionally is detected in children with occult lesions.

Micturating cystourethrogram (MCUG) Diagnosis of vesicoureteric reflux is based on cystography; in boys, this examination also can identify posterior urethral valves. Cystography can be carried out either via a bladder catheter using standard contrast fluid or a radioisotope, or indirectly during radioisotope renography. A standard micturating cystourethrogram is required to establish the precise anatomy, but this can be an unpleasant investigation

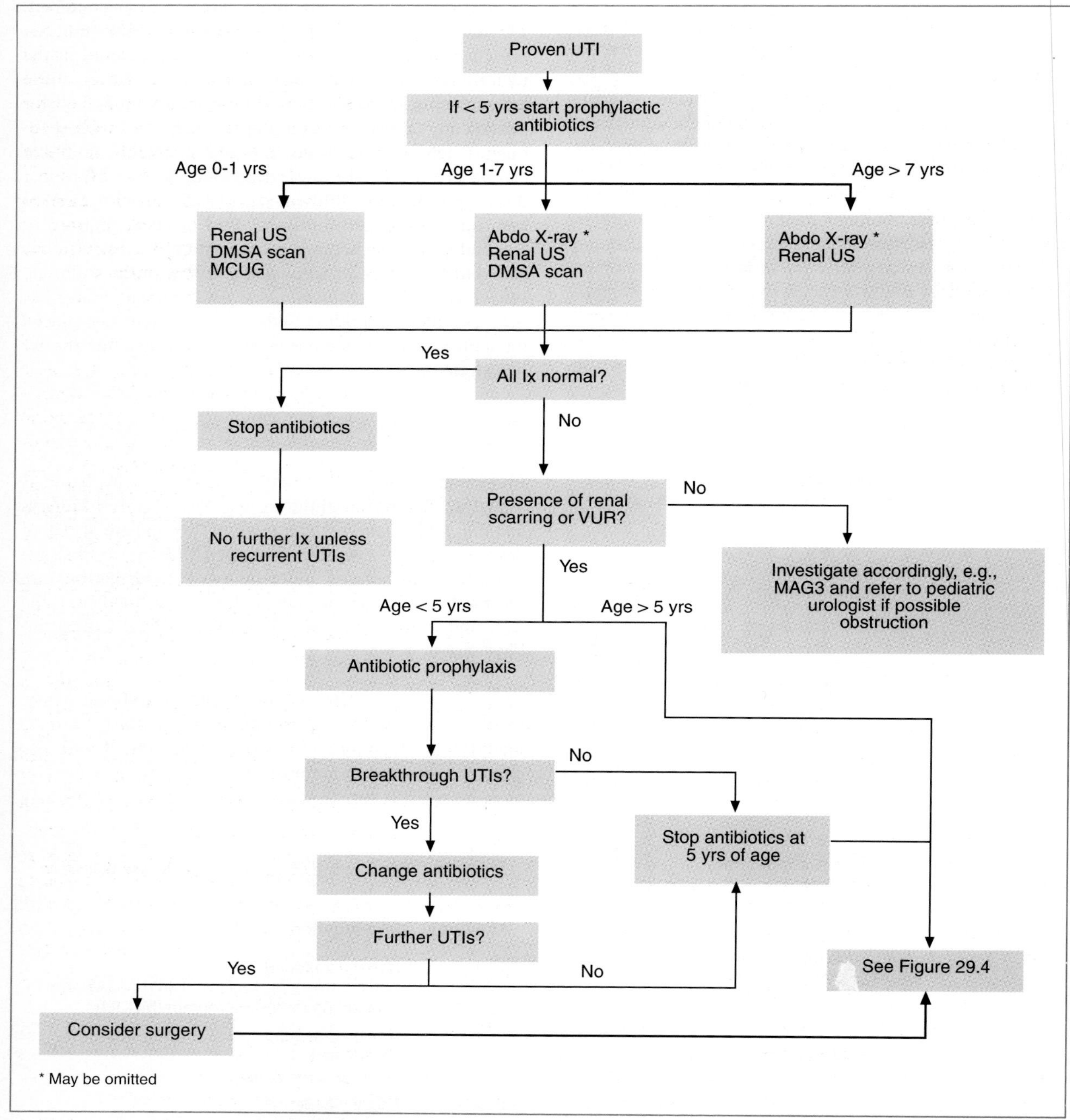

Figure 29.3 Management and investigation of urinary tract infections and vesicoureteric reflux.

in older children and exposes the pelvic organs to a relatively high radiation dose. It is therefore reserved as a routine investigation for children under 1 year and is carried out in older children only when specifically indicated.

Technetium-99 (^{99}Tc) dimercaptosuccinic acid (DMSA) scan Dimercaptosuccinic acid scans have now replaced intravenous pyelograms as the means of identifying renal scars. If performed in the immediate period following a urinary tract infection, areas of decreased uptake may be found, reflecting an acute inflammatory process, which can resolve over subsequent months. This has led many units to delay dimercaptosuccinic acid scans for 3 months following the presenting urinary tract infection. However, the finding of these acute changes on dimercaptosuccinic acid scan may identify children at risk of scarring who need antibiotic prophylaxis and appropriate follow-up. If an abnormal dimercaptosuccinic acid scan is found, this may prompt the performance of a micturating cystourethrogram in older children. However, an abnormal acute dimercaptosuccinic acid scan indicates the risk of possible scar formation regardless of whether vesicoureteric reflux is present, and, unless specific information is required with regard to the anatomy of the lower urinary tract, a micturating cystourethrogram can be avoided. A normal dimercaptosuccinic acid scans scan in most instances precludes any need for further investigation or review. A recent study has shown that children with normal kidneys on dimercaptosuccinic acid scan after the third birthday have only a 1 in 40 risk of developing a scar subsequently, and a normal scan after the fourth birthday indicates a very low or zero risk.

Treatment

Medical treatment

Although surgery is essential in the management of obstruction, a number of studies have shown that the results of nonsurgical management of nonobstructive vesicoureteric reflux, match those of surgical intervention. Breakthrough infection, renal function, renal growth, and fresh scars were identical in medically and surgically managed children in two large studies. Therefore, in the UK, antibiotic prophylaxis has been the main therapy for the prevention of progressive renal scarring in infants and children with vesicoureteric reflux. It is recommended that urine cultures be checked periodically, and attention is paid to the maintenance of a regular bowel habit and good fluid intake. In children managed medically, development of breakthrough infections, not controlled by switching antibiotics, or poor compliance, may be an indication for surgical repair of the refluxing ureter, particularly in children under 5 years and those with more severe grades of reflux.

The antibiotics used for prophylaxis need to have a number of characteristics: effective against organisms causing urinary tract infections; excreted in an active form in the urine; low levels of bacterial resistance; free of side effects; able to be used from birth; well tolerated and palatable; sugar-free preparation available.

The antibiotics currently favoured are trimethoprim or nitrofurantoin at a dose of 1 mg/kg taken before bedtime. The daily dose is given at night because, in toilet-trained children, the antibiotic will remain in the bladder for several hours overnight.

Compliance Compliance is often poor, particularly when parents are asked to administer prophylactic antibiotics from birth up to at least 5 years of age in apparently healthy children. In trials in which parents have voluntarily enlisted, compliance rates greater than 90% have been achieved, but in other studies compliance rates as low as 12% have been reported. A study looking at factors affecting compliance found no relationship with socioeconomic factors such as income, level of education, social class, and distance from the hospital-based specialists. The only positive finding was that mothers over 36 years of age were more reliable in bringing their children for follow-up. In this group of patients one-third remained untreated, despite an educational program consisting of written materials and computerized mailings. This mirrors compliance in other settings, such as hypertension, where the patient is generally asymptomatic and there is no noticeable morbidity or discomfort.

Surgical treatment

Observations of poor compliance in medically managed children suggest that surgical treatment might be beneficial, particularly in more severe degrees of vesicoureteric reflux. Ureteric reimplantation via either an extravesical or intravesical approach has a high success rate for correcting vesicoureteric reflux and a low morbidity, although this generally requires admission to the hospital for at least 2 days. This has led to the development of minimally invasive surgical and cystoscopic techniques to reduce morbidity and length of hospital stay. These techniques have many failings. The first cystoscopic procedures used Teflon paste, but migration of particles via the submucosal venous circulation to distant organs, including the brain, and granulomatous reactions at the injection site and in regional lymph nodes raised concerns. As a result the Food and Drug Administration in the United States has not licensed this product, and many urologists do not like to use it. An alternative is bovine collagen paste, which is nonparticulate but forms a mesh of cross-linked collagen fibers at the injection site. In a study comparing subureteral collagen injection with standard surgical techniques in the treatment of grade III reflux, only 59% of the collagen group were free of reflux at 12 months, compared with 96% in the surgical group. The incidence of urinary tract infection after 12 months was comparable, 14 versus 8%. This should be compared with success rates using Teflon in the treatment of grade II-IV reflux of up to 94%. Endoscopic reimplantation techniques also have been developed to reduce hospital stay and patient discomfort, but they too have had only modest success rates, and various technical difficulties need to be overcome.

Against the use of surgery, it can still be argued that the outcomes in the studies carried out have been the same for medical and surgical groups, even when compliance with medical management may have been poor and surgery was carried out in specialist centers. In practice, many of these children may not need any intervention, but would benefit from good practical advice given to parents and GPs on how to diagnose and treat further infections promptly and how to reduce the risk of urinary tract infections. With further progress, particularly in the development of safer materials for cystoscopic intervention, the performance of a one-off procedure, rather than prolonged antibiotic prophylaxis, may become more attractive.

Follow-up of children with reflux nephropathy

The long-term outlook for children with refux nephropathy depends on the degree of scarring, whether it is unilateral or bilateral, and on the presence of any underlying abnormality that may have led to the development of vesicoureteric reflux and might contribute to further renal damage (Fig. 29.4).

Patients with primary vesicoureteric reflux and unilateral scarring have a good outlook. There is a spontaneous resolution of milder degrees of vesicoureteric reflux as children get older, with 20-30% of lower-grade vesicoureteric reflux resolving each year. The overall resolution rate is 80% of grade I, 60% of grade II, and 50% of grade III, although this may not occur until adolescence. The presence of renal scarring is a risk for later development of hypertension. In a long-term follow-up study of 294 reflux nephropathy patients over 15 years of age, 38% were hypertensive or receiving antihypertensive medication, hypertension occurring more commonly in patients with bilateral scarring. Therefore, long-term follow-up should incorporate annual blood pressure monitoring, and particular care should be taken during pregnancy.

Patients with bilateral scarring, as well as being at risk of hypertension, are also liable to the development of renal failure. As has already been stated, they represent a significant number of adults and children entering dialysis and transplant programs. Bilateral scarring can initiate a series of events that can lead to renal failure. The initial feature is proteinuria, which can be assessed by measuring the early morning protein: creatinine ratio (normal <20 mg / mmol). Worsening proteinuria usually precedes any measured deterioration of renal function as indicated by serum creatinine measurement. Initially the falling glomerular filtration rate (GFR) is obscured because of the large renal reserve. Hypertension may develop at any time. The underlying mechanism for deterioration in renal function is thought to be one of hyperfiltration injury with nephron loss leading to the remaining nephrons having to compensate by increasing their individual filtration rates. This leads to glomerulosclerosis and further nephron loss, increasing further still the workload of the remaining nephrons.

Efforts to slow down this process have centered on trying to reduce proteinuria, which has been shown in diabetic nephropathy to be associated with improved renal survival. Similarly, in children with refux nephropathy it seems sensible to ensure that their diet does not have an excessive protein content. Angiotensin converting-enzyme (ACE) inhibitors have potential benefits and should be the first-line antihypertensive agent in these patients. They produce dilatation of the efferent glomerular arteriole and thus reduce the intraglomerular capillary blood pressure, which is raised in models of hyperfiltration injury. This in turn reduces proteinuria. ACE inhibitors may also have beneficial effects on the levels of inflammatory cytokines within the glomerulus, which may play a role in promoting

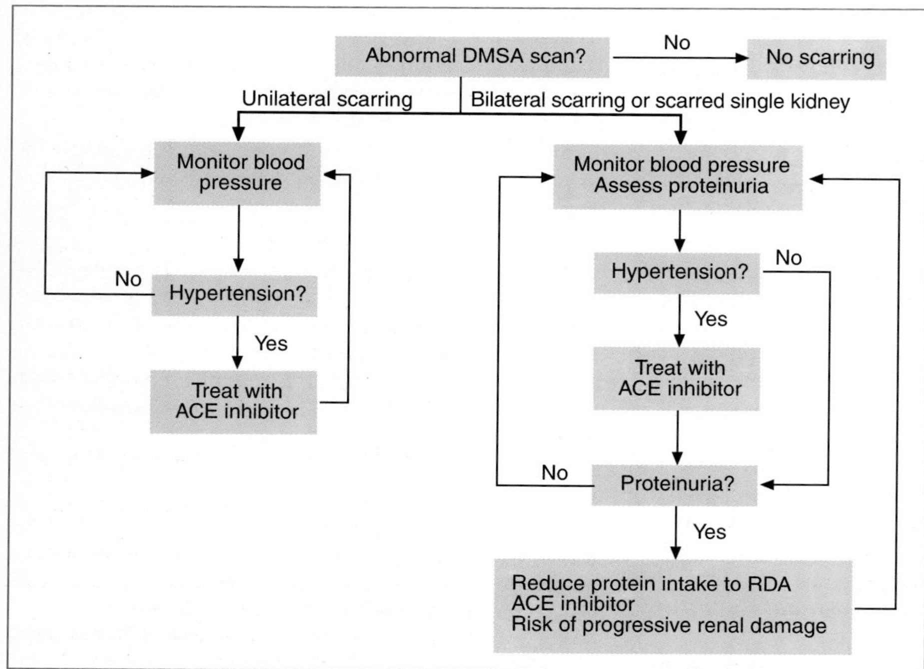

Figure 29.4 Management of reflux nephropathy.

glomerulosclerosis. The ACE gene also has been found to exhibit an insertion/deletion polymorphism in intron 16 and the presence of the deletion allele (D) is associated with higher levels of ACE. An adverse prognosis in diabetic nephropathy has been associated with the DD genotype, and there is some indication that this also may be true in reflux nephropathy. Patients with reflux nephropathy plus proteinuria can be treated with ACE inhibitors, even if they are normotensive, after dietary protein intake has been assessed and modified appropriately.

Management during pregnancy

Pregnancy is a period of concern for patients with vesicoureteric reflux, with or without reflux nephropathy. During pregnancy, the overall incidence of urinary tract infection is up to 8%; in women with a history of vesicoureteric reflux, even when this has been surgically corrected, this rises to 40%. Treated urinary tract infection does not appear to have a detrimental effect on pregnancy or fetal outcome if renal function is normal, but women with reflux nephropathy have an increased risk of preeclampsia and hypertension. Surgical correction of vesicoureteric reflux does not protect against urinary tract infection, and one study identified bacteruria of pregnancy in 40% with surgical correction against only 15% in women who had persisting reflux at their last evaluation. Eighteen percent of the surgical group went on to develop pyelonephritis, against 1.5% of the nonoperated group, although this may reflect the choice of cases for surgical rather than medical treatment.

Prevention

Screening of first-degree relatives

It is now recognized that vesicoureteric reflux has an autosomal dominant mode of inheritance. On the basis that urinary tract infection in the presence of vesicoureteric reflux in babies can lead to renal scarring, it seems reasonable to screen neonates whose parents or siblings have been diagnosed as having vesicoureteric reflux, particularly if they have reflux nephropathy. This requires a micturating cystourethrogram, and, if vesicoureteric reflux is demonstrated, antibiotic prophylaxis can be offered in order to minimize the risk of urinary tract infection until 5 years of age. A dimercaptosuccinic acid scan is also advised, because some of these infants will have abnormal scans even in the absence of previous urinary tract infections. This is presumed to be secondary to renal dysplasia.

Preventing renal scarring

The most important means by which the incidence of reflux nephropathy can be reduced is by prompt recognition and treatment of urinary tract infections in the at-risk age group of infants and young children. Education programs to increase the awareness of parents and health care professionals have a valuable role in changing practice in this area.

The inflammatory response to infection is important in the development of reflux nephropathy, and strategies to control this process may offer benefits. The addition of allopurinol to antibiotic therapy for acute pyelonephritis in monkeys, gave additional protection, presumably through its effect on reperfusion events.

The optimal management regimen for children with urinary tract infection, with respect to investigation and treatment, has yet to be identified, and this is reflected in the differences worldwide, particularly between Europe and the United States. Further refinements will continue to be made as more information becomes available.

Suggested readings

Birmingham Reflux Study Group. Prospective trial of operative versus non-operative treatment of severe vesicoureteric reflux in children: five years observation. BMJ 1987;295:237-41.

Brenner BM. Hemodynamically mediated glomerular injury and the progressive nature of kidney disease. Kidney Int 1983;23:647-55.

Gorjani N, Frankenschmidt A, Zimmerhackl LB, Brandis M. Subureteral collagen injection versus antireflux surgery in primary vesico-ureteral reflux grade III. Nephrol Urol 1996;155:491-4.

Hodson CJ. Vesicoureteral reflux and renal damage. In: Robinson RR, ed. Nephrology, vol 2. New York: Springer-Verlag, 1984.

International Reflux Study Group in Children European Group. Five-year study of medical or surgical treatment in children with severe reflux: radiological findings. Pediatr Nephrol 1992;6:223-30.

International Reflux Study in Children. International system of radiographic grading of vesicoureteric reflux. Pediatr Radiol 1985;15:105-9.

Koff SA, Lapides J, Piazza DH. Association of urinary tract infection and reflux with uninhibited bladder contractions and voluntary sphincteric obstruction. J Urol 1979;122:373-6.

Mansfield JT, Snow BW, Cartwright PC, Wadsworth K. Complications of pregnancy in women after childhood reimplantation for vesicoureteral reflux: An update with 25 years of followup. J Urol 1995;154:787-90.

Ransley PG, Risdon RA, Godley ML. High pressure sterile vesicoureteral reflux and renal scarring: an experimental study in the pig and minipig. Contrib Nephrol 1984;39:320-43.

Report of a working group of the research unit, Royal College Of Physicians. Guidelines for the management of acute urinary tract infection in childhood. J R Col Phys Lond 1991;25:36-42.

Roberts JA, Kaack MB, Baskin G. Treatment of experimental nephritis in the monkey. J Urol 1990;143:150-4.

van der Voort J, Edwards A, Roberts R, Verrier Jones K. The struggle to diagnose urinary tract infection in children under two in primary care. Family Practice 1997;14:44-8.

Vernon SJ, Coultard MG, Lambert HJ, Keir MJ, Matthews JNS. New renal scarring in children who at age 3 and 4 years had normal scans with dimercaptosuccinic acid: follow up study. BMJ 1997;315:905-8.

Wan J, Greenfield SP, Talley M, Ng M. An analysis of social and economic factors associated with follow-up in patients with vesicoureteral reflux. J Urol 1996;148:1688-92.

Zhang Y, Bailey RR. A long term follow up of adults with reflux nephropathy. N Z Med J 1995;108:142-4.

CHAPTER

30

Renal stone disease

Paul Jungers

KEY POINTS

- Prevalence of calcium oxalate urolithiasis dramatically increased in industrialized countries in the last half-century.
- Extracorporeal shock wave lithotripsy, ureteroscopy, and percutaneous surgery now provide simple, rapid, and noninvasive means of stone removal.
- Stone removal procedures in no way prevent some recurrences and should never lead to neglect of proper etiologic evaluation of patients who have had stones.
- Secondary forms of calcium or uric urolithiasis, as well as such inherited lithogenic conditions as cystinuria or primary hyperoxaluria require specific therapy based on etiologic factors.
- Idiopathic calcium urolithiasis often is associated with hypercalciuria, which itself depends on calcium, protein, and salt intake.
- Readjustment of dietary habits is therefore the basis of prophylactic medical treatment, making it possible for the clinician to stop or significantly reduce stone production in virtually all patients.

Urolithiasis is at present the most common renal disorder. Nearly 10% of men and 5% of women will experience renal colic at some time in their lives, and stone episodes will recur in almost all patients not properly treated.

The incidence of urolithiasis has increased dramatically since the end of World War II in all industrialized countries, especially in the form of calcium oxalate stones, which now represent more that 70% of all urinary stones. Such increased incidence in calcium oxalate stones parallels the marked modifications in dietary habits that took place in affluent countries during the past half-century, reinforcing the significance of nutritional factors in lithogenesis – in addition to endogenous factors.

Extracorporeal shock wave lithotripsy, ureteroscopy, and percutaneous surgery now provide simple, rapid, noninvasive means of stone removal. However, such methods in no way prevent stone recurrence, and they should never lead one to neglect evaluation of etiologic factors in these patients.

Epidemiology

Renal stones are classified on the basis of their chemical composition . A century ago, phosphate and uric acid stones were the most prevalent. Today, calcium stones largely predominate, and calcium oxalate is found in 80% of stones, constituting the main component (i.e., accounting for 50% or more of the total stone content) of more than 70% of stones, especially in males. Various types of calcium phosphate are the main component of about 15% of stones, especially in females. Uric acid urolithiasis accounts for nearly 10% of stones in western countries, and is more frequent in males than in females. Stones made of magnesium-ammonium phosphate (struvite), or infection stones, now represent less than 2% of all stones in industrialized countries. Cystine stones account for 1-2% of stones in adult patients, whereas various types of infrequent stones, mainly related to inborn metabolic disorders, and drug-induced stones, account for the remainder. Table

30.1 shows the relative prevalence of stones according to their main component, as observed in France in the Paris area over the past 5 years.

Pathophysiology

Kidney stones initially form as a result of urinary supersaturation, which induces solute crystallization followed by growth, aggregation, and retention of crystals to form calculi.

The mechanism of lithogenesis is monofactorial in some specific forms of urolithiasis (mostly hereditary), e.g., stones made of cystine, 2,8-dihydroxyadenine (2,8-DHA), or magnesium-ammonium-phosphate (MAP). Here, formation of crystals results from the excessive concentration of the respective compounds in urine. Formation of uric acid stones relies mainly on permanent acidity of urine (pH <5.5).

By contrast, the lithogenic process is more complex and multifactorial in calcium oxalate stones, the most prevalent type of urinary stones. Stone formation here depends on an imbalance between an excessive concentration of promoters (calcium and oxalate) and a defective concentration of crystallization inhibitors.

When urine is supersaturated with calcium oxalate, formation of crystals by homogeneous nucleation occurs. At a lower saturation level preexisting crystals may grow through further deposition of calcium oxalate. In addition, the presence in urine of particles (such as cell debris) or other preformed crystals (such as uric acid or calcium phosphate) may induce heterogeneous nucleation of calcium oxalate crystals. Urinary pH has little effect on calcium oxalate crystallization, but markedly influences calcium phosphate crystallization, which is favored by a urine pH > 6.2.

Once formed, crystal nuclei grow and aggregate. Crystal aggregation is an important process because it may lead within as little as 1 minute to the formation of particles 50 μm or more in diameter that can attach to the wall of the collecting duct, the inner diameter of which is 60-100 μm, or to the tip of the papilla during the transit time (5-7 min) of urine along the tubule.

Crystallization inhibitors

Urine contains natural inhibitors of crystal formation and aggregation. Evidence of the role of inhibitors is provided by the observation that a higher calcium and/or oxalate urine concentration is needed in non stone-formers than in stone-formers to induce crystal precipitation, and that spontaneous calcium oxalate crystallization occurs at a lower calcium oxalate product level in stone formers than in healthy subjects. Low molecular weight inhibitors, such as citrate, magnesium, and pyrophosphate act mainly in complexing calcium ions, whereas macromolecular inhibitors such as nephrocalcin, glycosaminoglycans, and non-polymerized Tamm-Horsfall protein act at low concentration by adsorbing on the crystal surface and blocking growing sites of crystals ("crystal poisoning"). Such proteins are secreted in the lumina of renal tubules in order to overlay the epithelium of distal parts, where urine is the most concentrated and where crystal aggregation is more likely to occur.

Low citrate concentration relative to calcium concentration frequently is found in calcium oxalate stone-formers. Quantitative and/or qualitative defects in macromolecular inhibitors probably play a role in calcium stone-formers, but their evaluation is not possible in routine practice and none, natural or synthetic, is presently available for therapeutic use.

The main steps of crystal formation and the corresponding inhibitors are summarized in Figure 30.1.

Influence of hypercalciuria and hyperoxaluria

It has long been debated whether hypercalciuria or hyperoxaluria is more important in inducing CaOx crystal formation. A small increase in oxalate concentration is more potent that an equimolar increase in calcium concentration to induce CaOx crystal precipitation. However, both ions are important to consider, especially because molar concentration of calcium usually is about 10 times that of oxalate. We observed that the CaOx molar product corre-

Table 30.1 Distribution of renal stone disease: main component of 11 735 stones analyzed at Necker Hospital from 1993 to 1997

Main component (≥50% of stone content)	Percent prevalence		
	Males (n=8,369)	Females (n=3,365)	Total (n=11,734)
Calcium oxalate	76.6	62.1	72.5
Calcium phosphate	9.6	24.5	13.9
Uric acid	11.1	7.2	10
Struvite (MAP)	1.3	4	2.1
Cystine	1	1.3	1.1
Other	< 0.5	< 1	< 0.5

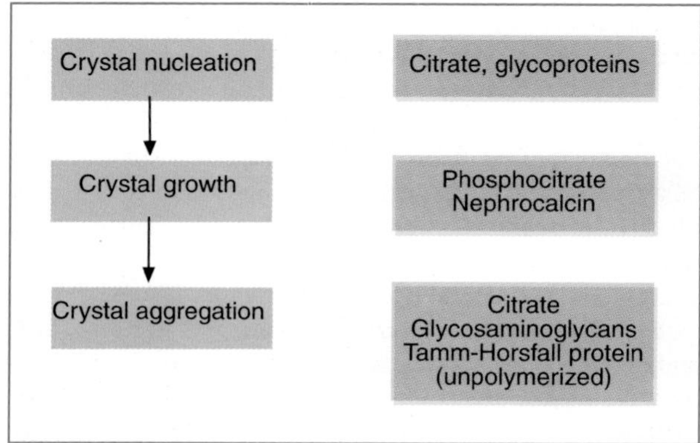

Figure 30.1 Steps of crystal formation and corresponding inhibitors in calcium oxalate urolithiasis.

lates with the formation of CaOx crystals, whereas the Ca/Ox molar ratio determines the type of CaOx crystals. A low Ca/Ox ratio, as occurs in hyperoxaluric states, preferentially induces the formation of CaOx monohydrate crystals, whereas a high Ca/Ox ratio, as occurs in hypercalciuric states, predominantly favors formation of CaOx dihydrate crystals.

It is worthy of note that, daily excretion of such stone-promoters as calcium and oxalate defines the *metabolic* risk, whereas the concentration of the same molecules, which depends both on 24-hour excretion and urine volume, best accounts for the *lithogenic* risk.

Clinical findings

Careful history, accurate stone composition analysis, and appropriate radiologic and laboratory procedures make it possible to identifiy the chemical type and cause of nephrolithiasis, if secondary to a definite pathologic condition, or the risk factors responsible for stone formation in the case of idiopathic calcium or uric acid lithiasis.

History is of primary interest in the stone-forming patient. The patient's age at onset of stone disease is important to consider, because stones that start in childhood suggest an inherited disease, such as cystinuria, primary hyperoxaluria, or severe idiopathic hypercalciuria. Family history is often positive in patients with idiopathic hypercalciuria, cystinuria, gout, renal tubular acidosis, or other genetically transmitted disorders.

The number of stone episodes followed by spontaneous passage, and of urologic procedures (extracorporeal shock wave lithotripsy, ureteroscopy, percutaneous nephrolithotomy, open surgery, nephrectomy), should be carefully recorded in chronologic order. The number of stones produced until referral is an index of stone disease activity. A stone index $\geq$ 0.6 stones/year is indicative of a metabolically active disease, as well as the presence of bilateral and/or multiple stones, or nephrocalcinosis at presentation. Attention should be paid to a history of bowel disease or surgery, and to signs or symptoms suggestive of systemic disease. All drugs taken by the patient should be recorded, e.g., vitamin D, antacids, triamterene, diuretics, carbonic anhydrase inhibitors, or the antiproteases now used for the treatment of HIV-positive patients.

Past and present dietary habits are of primary importance, especially fluid, protein, purine, carbohydrate, fiber, and salt intake, as well as usual consumption of dairy products and oxalate-rich foods. The assistance of a skilled dietician, when available, is of great help in evaluating nutritional intake.

Diagnostic procedures

Stone and crystals analysis Spontaneously passed or surgically removed stones, as well as fragments extracted by percutaneous nephrolithotomy or passed following extracorporeal shock wave lithotripsy, should always be analyzed. Classic chemical methods are often inaccurate and even misleading. X-ray diffraction or, better, infrared spectroscopy offer the best identification and quantification of stone components.

In the case of specific stone diseases, stone analysis itself immediately provides the etiologic diagnosis when revealing calculi made of cystine, 2,8-DHA, xanthine, MAP (pathognomonic of urinary tract infection with urea-splitting microorganisms such as *Proteus* species), or ammonium acid urate (suggestive of chronic diarrhea or laxative abuse). A peculiar morphology of calcium phosphate stones is associated with distal tubular acidosis. An unusual morphology of calculi made entirely of CaOx monohydrate (COM) is, in our experience, virtually pathognomonic of massive hyperoxaluria as encountered in primary hyperoxalurias or enteric hyperoxaluria. Such calculi are whitish in color, contrasting with the dark-brown, umbilicated, smooth, and spheric appearance of usual CaOx monohydrate calculi and the light-brown, spiculated appearance of common CaOx dihydrate (COD) calculi. Stones with a high proportion of calcium phosphate (carbapatite or hydroxyapatite) are compatible with a tubular acidification defect or hyperparathyroidism, whereas presence of CaOx monohydrate renders the latter diagnosis unlikely. Among usual CaOx stones, calculi predominantly made of CaOx monohydrate (whewellite) are mainly associated with hyperoxaluria, whereas those made of CaOx dihydrate (weddellite) are essentially associated with hypercalciuria.

Study of urinary crystals provides the same information as stone analysis, and may allow rapid identification of the type of urolithiasis, even if no stone or fragment is available, especially when revealing cystine, uric acid, 2,8-DHA or MAP crystals.

Radiologic examination If an intravenous pyelogram (IVP) was not obtained during an acute renal colic episode, it should be obtained as part of basal evaluation of any stone-former in order to identify abnormalities of the kidney and urinary tract that cause urine stasis, such as horseshoe kidney or hydronephrosis.

However, the most commonly encountered is medullary sponge kidney (MSK), a very frequent, often underdiagnosed, cause of recurrent calcium stone disease. The plain abdominal film (KUB) is very suggestive of medullary sponge kidney when it shows multiple calcareous images at the corticomedullary junction.

Laboratory evaluation The type and extent of laboratory evaluation depends on the chemical type of stones, age of patient at onset, and the severity of stone disease. However, especially if no stone is available for analysis, initial evaluation should cover all usually encountered types of urolithiasis.

As recommended by the NIH Consensus Conference on Stone Disease, a limited approach may be sufficient in the case of first-time adult stone former. However, a more complete evaluation is needed in patients with recurrent, bilateral, or multiple stones, and in children.

Metabolic evaluation (especially 24-hour urine analysis) should not be performed during an acute renal colic episode or during hospitalization, but ideally should be deferred for at least 1 month after a stone episode, or 3 months after extracorporeal shock wave lithotripsy, because transient tubular alterations result from obstruction, use of NSAIDs, or the extracorporeal shock wave lithotripsy procedure itself, and these may falsely lower calcium excretion. Initial laboratory testing should be performed in an ambulatory patient, on usual diet and having normal activity.

Table 30.2 lists blood and urine tests included in the first-intent metabolic evaluation. Many authors still ask for two or three 24-hour urine collections, because diet varies from day to day. We prefer to instruct our patients to collect carefully a 24-hour urine sample only once, usually during the weekend, because, at least in Europe, food intake and recreational physical activity frequently are higher during that time. Also, when previously using two consecutive 24-hour collections, we observed that the second one exhibited less marked abnormalities than did the first in more than 90% of cases. Alternatively, a reasonable approach would be to have one collection during a weekend day and another during a working day. In addition to the 24-hour collection, the patient should collect in a separate container the first voided morning urine for evaluation of crystalluria, pH, and specific gravity. A test for cystinuria should be performed if no stone is available for analysis.

It is worthy of note that the cost of such laboratory investigation is modest, and in any case far lower than the direct cost of urologic procedures or the indirect cost of worktime loss during episodes of renal colic.

Combining data from history, dietary habits, radiology, stone analysis, and blood and urine biochemistry allows one to identify specific forms of urolithiasis (requiring specific therapy) and secondary forms of calcium or uric acid urolithiasis that require etiologic treatment. In idiopathic, primary calcium or uric acid stone disease, identification of lithogenic factors makes it possible to plan an adapted prophylactic treatment.

Table 30.2 Basic laboratory investigation in the stone-former patient

Blood biochemistry (serum)
Calcium, phosphate, uric acid
Total proteins, glucose
Creatinine, urea
Sodium, potassium, chloride, bicarbonate

24-hour urine
Calcium, phosphate, uric acid
Creatinine, urea, sodium
Oxalate, citrate, magnesium

First-voided morning urine
Specific gravity, pH
Crystalluria

Treatment

At the present time, extracorporeal shock wave lithotripsy (extracorporeal shock wave lithotripsy) is the treatment of first intent for stones of ≤ 2 cm in diameter when lodged in the renal pelvis or calyces. Stones lodged in the upper extremity of the ureter may be pushed upward into the renal pelvis before being disrupted by extracorporeal shock wave lithotripsy. A double-J stent is often placed in the ureter in the case of large stones to allow passage of stone fragments without inducing ureteric obstruction. Stones located in the middle or lower part of the ureter may be disrupted by extracorporeal shock wave lithotripsy or extracted by ureteroscopy. Large kidney stones (especially staghorn calculi) most often are removed by percutaneous nephrolithotomy (PCNL) or a combination of percutaneous nephrolithotomy and complementary extracorporeal shock wave lithotripsy. Conventional open surgery is now required in fewer than 5% of patients, mainly in the case of large infected stones. The success rate of percutaneous nephrolithotomy is virtually 100%, whereas it is about 80% for stones of ≤ 2 cm in diameter located in the kidney pelvis or upper calyces, and only about 60% for calculi lodged in the lower calyces. Blood pressure should be monitored in patients who undergo repeated shock wave procedures, because extracorporeal shock wave lithotripsy, through renal parenchyma alteration, may favor permanent hypertension.

Techniques that permit rapid and noninvasive removal of calculi should not in any way preclude proper etiologic evaluation of the stone-former patient and adapted prophylactic treatment aimed at preventing stone recurrence.

SECONDARY CALCIUM UROLITHIASIS

The main pathologic conditions associated with the formation of calcium stones are listed in Table 30.3. They will be described with respect to the principal etiologic condition, either hypercalciuria (with or without hypercalcemia), hyperoxaluria, or renal tubular acidosis with hypocitraturia.

Hypercalcemia with hypercalciuria

The most frequent cause of urolithiasis associated with hypercalcemia is primary hyperparathyroidism, found in 3-5% of calcium stone-formers. The main lithogenic factors are hypercalciuria, hyperphosphaturia, and alkaline urine, thus explaining that stones are a mixture of CaOx dihydrate and calcium phosphate (carbapatite and/or brushite), but almost never contain CaOx monohydrate.

Parathyroid hormone (PTH) enhances the synthesis of calcitriol, resulting in increased intestinal calcium absorption, hypercalcemia, and finally hypercalciuria, when the increased filtered load of calcium outweighs the PTH-stimulated tubular reabsorption. PTH simultaneously reduces tubular reabsorption of phosphate, thus inducing hyperphosphaturia, hypophosphatemia, and inhibition of proximal tubular reabsorption of bicarbonates, the latter resulting in alkaline urine.

The diagnosis is based on the simultaneous presence of hypercalcemia and of an inappropriately elevated level of PTH. Usually total calcium is slightly raised (between 2.6 and 3.0 mmol/l) as is ionized calcium. Intact PTH level is above the upper limit of normal (normal range, 10-65 pg/ml) and does not significantly decrease following an oral calcium load. Hypophosphatemia is frequently, but not constantly observed.

Noninvasive localization of hyperactive parathyroid gland(s) may be made by echography, isotopic imaging, tomodensitometry or magnetic resonance imaging. However, in a symptomatic patient with active stone disease, most authors agree that attempts at preoperative localization is not justified in first intent, and should be reserved for recurrent hypercalcemia following previous neck surgery. The operation should be performed by an experienced surgeon, who will either remove a solitary adenoma (about 95% of cases) or perform subtotal parathyroidectomy in the case of diffuse hyperplasia, which is especially to be sought in familial cases. Hypercalcemia and hypercalciuria rapidly normalize following removal of hyperactive parathyroid tissue, but in some cases hypercalciuria persists or reappears, suggesting that underlying idiopathic hypercalciuria is present and probably was the initial stimulus for parathyroid cell hyperactivity.

An important differential diagnosis of hyperparathyroidism is familial hypocalciuric hypercalcemia, which in fact is very rarely responsible for stones. This autosomal dominant disorder is characterized by impaired tissue response to PTH. Parathyroidectomy would be ineffective here and even deleterious. Lithium salt therapy may also mimic parathyroid hyperplasia.

Sarcoidosis (or other types of granulomatosis) results in excess ectopic production of calcitriol, thus leading to hypercalcemia, hypercalciuria, and stone formation, but PTH level is normal or low; the disease rapidly responds to a moderate dose of corticosteroids. Long-term immobilization, in a growing adolescent or in a subject with active Paget's disease may result in stone formation in the absence of appropriate prophylactic high fluid intake.

Table 30.3 Main causes of calcium urolithiasis

Metabolic factor	Etiologic conditions
Hypercalcemia with hypercalciuria	Primary hyperparathyroidism[1] Sarcoidosis Vitamin D intoxication Paget's disease, immobilization Malignancy-associated osteolysis Hyperthyroidism, acromegaly
Hypercalciuria without hypercalcemia	High calcium intake Phosphate depletion (phosphate-binding antacids) Hereditary distal tubular acidosis[1, 2] Acquired distal tubular acidosis[1, 2] (Sjögren's syndrome, hypergammaglobulinemia, chronic active hepatitis) Acetazolamide[1, 2] Loop diuretics, lithium salts Cushing's syndrome Primary hyperaldosteronism[2] Glucocorticoid therapy Medullary sponge kidney Idiopathic hypercalciuria
Massive hyperoxaluria (≥1 mmol/day)	Primary hyperoxalurias Enteric hyperoxaluria
Moderate oxaluria (0.5-0.9 mmol/day)	Oxalate-rich food gluttony Low dietary calcium intake Mild metabolic hyperoxaluria Pydoxine deficiency Ascorbic acid abuse Idiopathic hyperoxaluria
Moderate hypocitraturia (<1.5 mmol/day)	Chronic diarrheal states Chronic potassium depletion (laxatives, diuretics) High animal protein intake Idiopathic hypocitraturia

[1] Significant amounts of calcium phosphate in stone.
[2] Associated with marked hypocitraturia (<0.5 mmol/day).

Hypercalciuria without hypercalcemia

High dietary calcium intake (≥1 g/day) may itself induce hypercalciuria in the absence of any underlying calcium metabolic disorder. Prolonged use of phosphate-chelating antacids induces phosphate depletion and hypophosphatemia, which stimulates calcitriol secretion, resulting in hypercalciuria. Acetazolamide, or other carbohydrate inhibitors used orally for treatment of glaucoma, induces hypercalciuria, hypocitraturia and alkaline urine, thus resulting in the formation of phosphate stones, especially in patients with underlying hypercalciuria. A new acetazolamide preparation for local use now offers a valuable alternative for such patients. Furosemide increases in parallel renal sodium and calcium excretion. Corticosteroids, through increased bone resorption, increase urinary calcium excretion.

Medullary sponge kidney (MSK), when associated with hypercalciuria, is a very frequent cause of recurrent calcium nephrolithiasis. Lithogenic factors are slowing flux of urine in ectatic portions of collecting ducts, which favors precipitation of calcium, oxalate and phosphate, and local tubular acidification defects, which result in hypocitraturia. These factors in conjunction with hypercalciuria provoke the relentless formation of stones of mixed composition, made of CaOx monohydrate, CaOx dihydrate, and carbapatite in variable proportions. On plain X-ray examination, multiple small calculi appear just behind the tips of papillae. On intravenous pyelogram, tubular ectasia appears as linear striations in the concavity of calyces and, in florid cases, have the aspect of "bunches of grapes". However, the most frequent cause of excess urinary calcium excretion is idiopathic, primary hypercalciuria, which will be considered below.

Hyperoxaluric states

Massive hyperoxaluria (up to 1 mmol/day or more) is observed in two different diseases: enteric hyperoxaluria, an acquired condition, and primary hyperoxaluria, an inherited disease.

The term "enteric hyperoxaluria" defines increased urinary oxalate excretion that occurs in patients with inflammatory ileal disease (such as Crohn's disease), ileal resection, or jejunoileal by-pass for obesity, in the presence of an intact colon. Hyperoxaluria results from increased free oxalate content in the intestinal lumen, because calcium and magnesium are bound to malabsorbed fatty acids, thus reducing the luminal content of free calcium and, therefore, the complexation of oxalate ions. In addition, colonic permeability to oxalate is enhanced due to the increased content of bile acids. Lithogenic factors include marked hyperoxaluria, reduced urine volume, hypomagnesuria, and hypocitraturia, thus resulting in the formation of stones predominantly made of CaOx monohydrate. The resulting urinary profile thus characteristically combines hyperoxaluria and hypocalciuria. Treatment is based on calcium, magnesium and citrate supplementation (the latter optimally provided in the form of magnesium-potassium citrate), oxalate-poor diet, increased diuresis, medium-chain triglycerides, and cholestyramine to bind biliary salts.

Primary hyperoxaluria type 1 (PH1) is the most severe condition responsible for massive hyperoxaluria and recurrent stone disease. It is transmitted as autosomal recessive, so that only homozygous subjects are affected. The metabolic defect is a deficiency in the activity of the hepatic peroxisomal enzyme alanine glyoxylate aminotransferase (AGT), which utilizes pyridoxine (vitamin B_6) as coenzyme. Massive hyperoxaluria (up to 3 mmol/day or more), associated with a nearly equal glycolate urinary excretion (whereas glycerate excretion is normal), is the hallmark of the disease. Permanent hyperoxaluria results in active, recurrent formation of CaOx monohydrate stones, with a peculiar morphology as mentioned above, associated with nephrocalcinosis. Such an appearance when observed in a child or a young adult with active calcium stone formation is highly suggestive of the disease. Owing to the consequences of both obstructive episodes and parenchymal infiltration with calcium oxalate crystals, progressive renal failure develops, leading to hyperoxalemia and further oxalate accumulation in various tissues (termed oxalosis), including bone marrow, heart, bones, and retina. As renal failure progresses, blood oxalate concentration and oxalosis increase, further reducing renal function in a vicious circle. Diagnosis is based on urinary determination of oxalate and glycolate. Evidence of the enzymatic defect is provided by liver biopsy, although there is not a direct correlation between the type and degree of AGT abnomalities, the level of hyperoxalemia and the clinical expression of the disease.

About one-third of patients respond to pyridoxine supplementation at pharmacologic doses (300-600 mg/day), which enhances the metabolic pathway from glyoxylate to glycine and thus markedly reduces oxalate and glycolate production. Therefore, response to pyridoxine is of primary importance to test in every patient with primary hyperoxaluria type 1. Unfortunately, most patients do not respond to pyridoxine supplementation and develop relentlessly progressive renal failure.

Symptomatic treatment is based on reducing all amendable lithogenic risk factors by maintaining a high urinary flow rate (≥ 2 l per square meter of body surface area), thiazide diuretics to reduce urinary calcium concentration, and magnesium and inorganic phosphate supplementation to inhibit CaOx crystal growth. When end-stage renal failure occurs, even intensive hemodialysis fails to efficiently remove oxalate, and oxalosis still progresses. The optimal treatment is combined hepatic and renal transplantation to restore normal enzyme production.

Primary hyperoxaluria type 2 (PH2), also inherited as an autosomal recessive trait, is due to a defect in D-glycerate dehydrogenase activity that results in hyperoxaluria and increased L-glyceric aciduria. Diagnosis is based on evidence of concomitant hyperoxaluria and glyceraturia while glycolate excretion is normal. The condition is less frequent and also less severe than primary hyperoxaluria type 1, although progressive renal failure may be observed in some cases.

Permanent hyperoxaluria of milder degree (0.5 to 0.9 mmol/day) has been reported in patients with "mild metabolic hyperoxaluria", possibly a variant of the preceding conditions, as well as in a third form of primary hyperoxaluria (PH3) characterized by primary intestinal oxalate hyperabsorption.

Hypocitraturia and renal tubular acidosis

Renal distal tubular acidosis, either complete (with systemic acidosis) or incomplete (plasma bicarbonate level is normal) results in marked hypocitraturia, urinary pH and hypercalciuria, together with potassium loss. Such conditions favor intratubular precipitation of calcium phosphate, mainly carbapatite, resulting in nephrocalcinosis and/or lithiasis. Carbapatite calculi formed in renal distal tubular acidosis patients have a peculiar morphology characterized by a smooth, yellow or light brown glazed appearance.

Congenital renal distal tubular acidosis is transmitted in the autosomal recessive or dominant mode. In the complete form, affected children exhibit from the first year of life hyperchloremic acidosis, which results in bone resorption. Treatment must be prophylactic, based on correction of acidosis by means of sodium bicarbonate and/or potassium citrate in sufficient amounts to normalize plasma bicarbonate levels, together with citrate and calcium excretion. When instituted early, such palliative treatment preserves bone mineralization and statural growth, limits nephrocalcinosis, and preserves renal function.

Treatment of incomplete forms is essentially similar but requires lower doses of alkali.

In adults, renal distal tubular acidosis is more often an acquired condition, secondary to various autoimmune diseases such as Sjögren's syndrome, chronic active hepatitis, and other hypergammaglobulinic states. There is cellular infiltration of the renal interstitium, especially the medulla, thus explaining the preferential alteration of distal parts of the tubules. Treatment of the underlying systemic disease is needed to stop formation of calcium phosphate stones and nephrocalcinosis.

IDIOPATHIC CALCIUM UROLITHIASIS

Taken together, secondary forms represent at best 10% of cases of calcium stone disease which, in the great majority of patients, is idiopathic or primary. However, any secondary cause must be excluded before accepting the diagnosis of primary calcium nephrolithiasis.

Incidence of idiopathic calcium stone disease is almost twice as high in males as in females, and peaks in the fourth or fifth decade of life.

The disease is multifactorial, involving in variable combination increased calcium, oxalate and/or urate urine concentration, decreased citrate or magnesium concentration, and reduced urine volume. Nutritional factors, notably protein and sodium intake as reflected by daily urea and sodium excretion, are of primary concern.

Idiopathic hypercalciuria

Idiopathic hypercalciuria (IH) is defined as a daily calcium excretion in excess of 0.1 mmol/kg body weight/day (4 mg/kg/d) in either gender on spontaneous diet. Based on such a definition, nearly 50% of patients with recurrent CaOx stones exhibit idiopathic hypercalciuria (IH).

The phenotypic classification and causal mechanisms of idiopathic hypercalciuria are still widely debated. The classification proposed by Pak distinguishes two main types. Absorptive idiopathic hypercalciuria is characterized by a normal fasting calcium to creatinine (Ca/Cr) ratio (< 0.12 mg/mg or 0.4 mmol/mmol) and increased post-load increment in Ca/Cr, together with inhibited PTH secretion. Renal hypercalciuria is characterized by a supranormal fasting and post-load Ca/Cr ratio, associated with enhanced, but suppressible, PTH secretion. In fact, elevated PTH level is rarely found even in patients with fasting hypercalciuria, and exaggerated post-load increment in Ca/Cr is not found in every hypercalciuric patient. Finally, there appears to exist a continuum in the values of urinary calcium excretion in stone-former patients, probably reflecting variable combinations between calcium hyperabsorption, defective calcium tubular reabsorption, and bone resorption. In any case, urine calcium concentration is the determinant of crystal formation. We found the incidence of CaOx crystallization to rise sharply when urinary calcium concentration is in excess of 3.8 mmol/l.

It is worthy of note that calcium excretion is increased by a high sodium intake or a high animal protein intake. The relationship between urea excretion (reflecting total protein intake) and natriuresis (reflecting sodium intake), and calcium excretion is more marked in calcium stone-formers than in healthy subjects, and in hypercalciuric than in normocalciuric stone-formers. The mechanisms underlying the increased sensitivity of idiopathic hypercalciuria patients to the hypercalciuric effects of protein and/or sodium load are not fully understood. These findings indicate that environmental factors, such as the nutritional habits now prevalent in affluent societies, add their effects to those of underlying endogenous metabolic disorders, thus increasing the predisposition to stone formation.

The mechanisms that potentially result in excess calcium excretion in idiopathic hypercalciuria are multiple. They possibly involve: (1) primary calcitriol overproduction, or excessive responsiveness of target organs (bones and the kidney itself) to calcitriol; nearly one-third of idiopathic hypercalciuria patients exhibit high-normal calcitriol values, irrespective of PTH concentration; (2) increased number of vitamin D receptors (VRD) in enterocytes, as evidenced in experimental models of idiopathic hypercalciuria rats; (3) vitamin D- independent intestinal calcium hyperabsorption; (4) primary renal tubular leak of calcium; (5) primary renal tubular phosphate leak, resulting in enhanced PTH secretion, calcitriol release, increased calcium absorption and hypercalciuria; (6) primary bone resorption due to monocyte activation and cytokine production; (7) altered transmembrane transport of calcium and/or oxalate ions. Most of the defects are likely to be genetically determined, as familial forms of idiopathic hypercalciuria have been reported. Molecular genetics will certainly improve our knowledge in the near future.

Other lithogenic factors

Moderate hyperoxaluria (0.5-0.9 mmol/day) is often found in idiopathic calcium stone-formers. It was long known and recently rediscovered that an inadequately low dietary calcium intake (<600 mg/day) favors enhanced intestinal oxalate absorption and hyperoxaluria, thus explaining the increased risk of calcium stones in adults whose calcium intake is low. Oxalate excretion is variable and often exhibits large day-to-day variations, with postprandial peaks of CaOx supersaturation. A low urine output is a major factor of increased oxalate concentration. We found that an oxalate concentration >0.3 mmol/l markedly increases CaOx crystal formation.

Hyperuricosuria favors CaOx crystal precipitation. The mechanism involves heterogeneous nucleation of CaOx crystals on uric acid crytals in acidic urine or, more likely, because urate in solution induces the precipitation of CaOx crystals through a salting-out process.

Magnesium ions form soluble complexes with oxalate ions, thus reducing urine supersaturation with respect to CaOx. However, significant hypomagnesuria is very infrequent. A low magnesium output (<1 mmol/day) should alert to the possibility of some enteric disorder.

By contrast, moderate hypocitraturia is frequent in calcium stone-formers, but there are also large day-to-day variations. Hypocitraturia may result in part from high animal protein intake (due to the resulting acid-ash load), high sodium intake, potassium depletion, and/or low net alkali intake – all conditions favored by current western dietary habits. Hypocitraturia in idiopathic hypercalciuria patients is even more significant when related to urine calcium concentration, because citrate acts mainly by binding Ca ions. Thus, a low-normal citrate concentration in the face of a high calcium concentration favors CaOx crystal formation and aggregation. We found a calcium-to-citrate molar ratio > 3 to be associated with enhanced CaOx crystal formation.

Defects in macromolecular polyanions, qualitative rather than quantitative, have been reported. The inhibitory effect of Tamm-Horsfall protein, in particular, is blunted, or even reversed, when polymerization occurs because of high urine sodium or calcium concentration or low pH.

Whatever the daily excretion of lithogenic solutes, a low urine volume is a major factor in stone formation because it increases in the same proportion the concentration of all promoting solutes, whereas the compensatory effect of a higher inhibitor concentration is much less potent. A low daily urine output, especially during the nighttime, is often the only identifiable cause of stone formation.

Treatment

Medical treatment of idiopathic calcium stone disease is aimed at preventing stone recurrence. Prophylactic measures consist mainly in correcting dietary habits. Specific pharmacologic measures are added if hypercalciuria, hyperuricosuria, and/or hypocitraturia persist. Individualized measures are based on careful identification of risk factors present in each patient. They do not depend on any classification of hypercalciuria. The proposed decision algorithm for treatment is presented in Figure 30.2.

The main objective of treatment is, by combining increased diuresis and lowered urinary solute excretion, to reduce the concentration of calcium and oxalate ions.

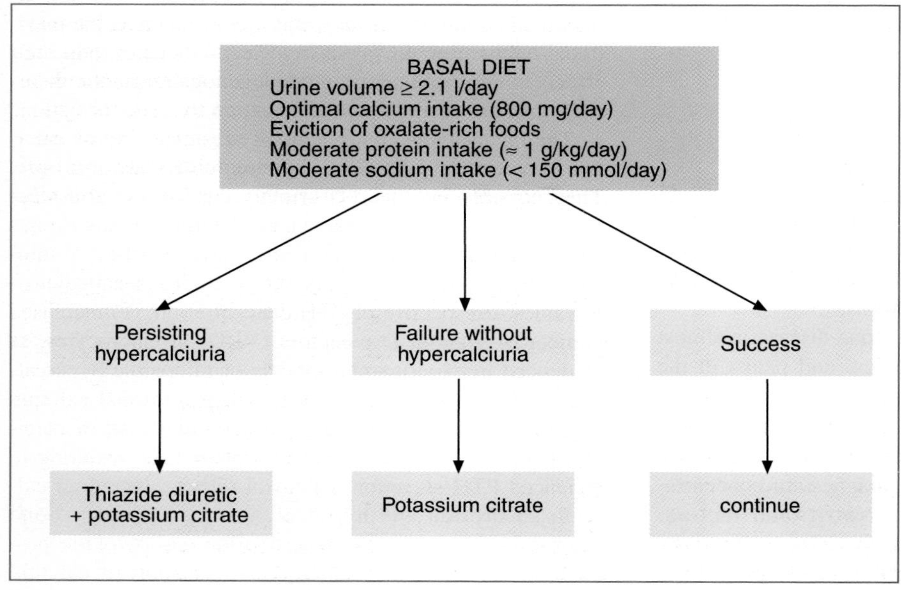

Figure 30.2 Decisional algorithm in calcium stone-formers.

Urine dilution The first measure in any stone-former is to obtain a sufficient urine volume (between 2 and 2.5 l/day) to achieve optimal urine dilution. This value is based on the results of recent epidemiologic studies, which indicate a significantly reduced risk of stone formation in patients with urine output >2 l/day. We recently observed a marked reduction in the incidence of CaOx crystallization when urine specific gravity is below 1012, a value that corresponds to a daily urine volume of 2100 ml. Doubling daily urine volume lessens urinary concentration of both calcium and oxalate by two, thus reducing by nearly four times the CaOx product and CaOx saturation. Increasing urine volume is especially warranted in patients with medullary sponge kidney, in order both to accelerate urine flux in tubular ectatic sections and reduce urinary solute concentration.

Fluid intake should be regularly distributed throughout the nyctohemer. Assessment of specific gravity (SG) in the first morning urine sample is a simple and useful tool to assess dilution of urine formed during the night. In 25% of patients, we observed a high specific gravity (≥ 1025) in early morning urine despite a satisfactory 24-hour urine volume, thus indicating insufficient overnight urine dilution, often in association with persistent crystalluria and stone recurrence. In such cases, the patient should be encouraged to drink a large amount of water at bedtime, and to drink water again when awakened in the night.

Optimal calcium intake Our conception of optimal calcium intake has changed markedly over the recent decades. A reduced intake (≤ 600 mg/day), as traditionally recommended until the 1980s, results in increased intestinal oxalate absorption with augmented oxaluria, and often in negative calcium balance with the risk of decreased bone mineral density. On the other hand, a high dietary intake (>1000 mg/day) increases intestinal absorption and urinary calcium excretion. Therefore, a consensus now exists that a dietary intake of about 800 mg/day should be recommended to all calcium stone-formers, irrespective of the existence or type of idiopathic hypercalciuria.

About half of the calcium intake should be provided in dairy products in order to increase phosphate intake. Patients may choose among milk, yogurt, and cheese with the help of tables that show the calcium content of various products. Calcium content of drinking water (which may vary from 10 to 500 mg/l) should be taken into consideration, with waters of moderate mineralization (about 100-150 mg/l) being preferred. Oxalate-rich foods, such as chocolate and cacao, spinach, rhubarb, sorrel, and berries should be avoided, but the major part of urinary oxalate comes from metabolism, so that urinary oxalate concentration may be reduced essentially by the effect of urine dilution.

Protein and salt moderation Total protein intake, often in excess of 1.3 g/kg/day in affluent countries, should be moderated to about 1 g/kg/day, especially with regard to animal proteins. An average daily intake of 150 g of meat, fish, or poultry appears optimal and is easily acceptable in the long term. Salt intake should be reduced in parallel, as well as consumption of refined sugars. In this respect, fruit juices (rich in rapidly absorbable sugar and oxalate) and regular Coca Cola or equivalent soft drinks (rich in sucrose) should be avoided, as well as excessive beer consumption. There is no evidence for limiting tea consumption, at least briefly infused.

Such "universal" dietary measures are recommended to all calcium stone-formers, either normocalciuric or hypercalciuric. Optimal calcium intake, together with moderation in animal protein and salt intake, is of particular relevance, however, in patients with idiopathic hypercalciuria.

Definition of goals to be achieved The effectiveness of such measures sould be reflected by improvement of urine biochemistry. The proposed goals are given in Table 30.4, expressed in molar concentrations for promoters (calcium, oxalate, and uric acid) and measurable inhibitors (citrate and magnesium). In addition, 24-hour excretion of urea and sodium closely reflects daily protein intake (urea in mmoles multipled by 0.21, or in grams multiplied by 3.5 indicates the corresponding protein intake in grams) and salt intake (a sodium excretion of 150 mmoles corresponds to a salt intake of about 9 grams), respectively.

Regular clinical and laboratory monitoring, performed about every 6 months during the first 2 years, together with yearly X-ray examination, is an important part of the "stone clinic effect". This encourages the patient to comply with diuresis and diet recommendations, and allows the clinician to assess efficacy and tolerance of treatment.

Monitoring of crystalluria, when feasible, is a good index, in addition to laboratory determinations, to evaluate stone disease activity. We found persistent CaOx crystalluria in more than 85% of patients with recurrent stones and in fewer than 30% of those without recurrence.

Pharmacologic treatment If all laboratory parameters return to the optimal zone, the same measures should be maintained in the long term. If hypercalciuria persists, together with exaggerated urea and sodium excretion, a greater effort should be required from the patient to test the benefits of an effective reduction in animal protein and salt intake. If this effort succeeds, the patient should be encouraged to continue the diet on the long term. If hypercalciuria still persists despite effective lowering of urea and sodium excretion, or if moderation in protein intake cannot be achieved, one should consider use of thiazide

Table 30.4 Therapeutic goals to achieve in idiopathic calcium stone-formers (urinary parameters)

Urine volume	> 2 l/day
Calcium	< 3.8 mmol/l
Oxalate	< 0.3 mmol/l
Uric acid	< 2 mmol/l
Citrate	> 1.5 mmol/l
Magnesium	> 1.5 mmol/l
Urea	< 6 mmol/kg/day
Sodium	< 150 mmol/day

diuretics, irrrespective of the absorptive or renal presentation of idiopathic hypercalciuria. Their effect may be blunted if sodium intake (as reflected by natriuresis) remains excessive. Thiazides should be prescribed at moderate dose (25 mg/day of hydrochlorothiazide or chlorthalidone) in order to avoid impotence, fatigue, muscle cramps and hypokalemia.

If significant hypokalemia and/or hypocitraturia occurs, potassium supplementation should be provided in the form of slow-release potassium citrate preparations (30 to 60 mEq/day). If hyperuricosuria persists despite moderation in protein and purine intake, especially if urine pH is <5.5, or if hyperuricemia develops on thiazide therapy, allopurinol (200-300 mg/day) should be added. In the case of persistent hypocitraturia, potassium citrate or magnesium-potassium citrate is indicated. Potassium citrate supplementation may also reduce the risk of recurrence in all calcium stone-formers, whether hypocitraturic or not, by decreasing the amount of free calcium ions available to form calcium-oxalate crystals.

By combining high fluid intake, dietary adjustment and judicious use of potassium citrate and thiazides, stone activity may be stopped in virtually all patients.

URIC ACID UROLITHIASIS

Pure uric acid calculi are totally radiolucent. They can be detected by echography, but they appear only as filling defects in the pelvis or calyces on intravenous pyelogram. They can be differentiated from tumors of the renal pelvis, blood clots, or fragments of papillary necrosis by computerized tomography, since the density of uric acid is clearly higher than that of renal parenchyma.

The solubility of uric acid at body temperature is only 0.6 mmol/l (100 mg/l) at pH 5, whereas the solubility of sodium urate (the predominant form at pH >5.5) is 12 mmol/l (about 2 g/l) at pH 7. Thus, a permanently low urine pH (<5.5) is the main factor of formation of uric acid stones. Other risk factors are a high urate excretion and a low urine output. In fact, formation of uric acid crystals is almost unavoidable whenever urinary pH is consistently lower that 5.5, especially in the presence of hyperuricosuria.

Secondary forms of uric acid lithiasis

The main causes of uric acid urolithiasis are listed in Table 30.5.

Uric acid overproduction occurs as a consequence of rapid cell turnover in myeloproliferative disorders such as polycythemia vera, or from massive nucleolysis following cytotoxic chemotherapy in lymphoproliferative disorders. Hyperuricosuria may provoke intratubular precipitation of uric acid crystals and anuria. Such hyperuricosuria may be prevented by alkaline diuresis and allopurinol, and treated with urate oxydase in the case of sudden, massive uricosuria.

Hereditary deficiency in the enzyme hypoxanthine-guanine-phosphoribosyl transferase (HGPRT), or Lesch-Nyhan's syndrome, a X-linked dominant disorder, manifests in boys as heavy hyperuricemia and uricosuria with severe uric nephrolithiasis and concomitant involvement of the central nervous system. Treatment is based on hyperdiuresis and allopurinol.

Hyperuricosuria without hyperuricemia may result from use of uricosuric drugs, such as tienilic acid, probenecid, or suprofen, especially when used in gouty patients.

Hyperuricosuria with hypouricemia and production of uric acid stones may complicate or reveal a proximal tubulopathy, either congenital (Fanconi's syndrome, either idiopathic or as a consequence of a cystinosis) or acquired (occupational exposure to cadmium, light-chain multiple myeloma, or Sjögren's syndrome). By contrast, familial renal hypouricemia is a benign condition and is not associated with stone production.

Chronic diarrheic states or ileostomy induce fluid and alkali losses, resulting in excretion of acidic, concentrated urine, thus favoring the production of uric acid gravel and stones.

The same factors act in patients with chronic laxative abuse. In addition, because normally functioning kidneys respond to alkali loss by increased ammoniagenesis, stones are typically made of acid ammonium urate. Interestingly, a

Table 30.5 Main causes of uric acid urolithiasis

Metabolic factor	Etiological conditions
Hyperuricosuria with hyperuricemia	Nucleolysis in myelo- or lymphoproliferative disorders Inborn errors of purine metabolism (Lesch-Nyhan's syndrome) Primary uric diathesis with gout
Hyperuricosuria with normo- or hypouricemia	Uricosuric drugs Proximal renal tubular disorders (congenital or acquired Fanconi's syndrome) Purine gluttony
Persistently acidic urine	Chronic diarrheal diseases (enteropathy, ileostomy) Laxative abuse Idiopathic uric acid urolithiasis

similar composition is encountered in endemic bladder stones in young children (mainly boys) in developing countries. At the end of breast-feeding, they receive a diet poor in phosphate and are exposed to infectious diarrheal episodes, thus resulting in enhanced ammoniagenesis (palliating the lack of rise in titratable acidity due to low urine phosphate content) and production of urine with low volume, low pH, and high ammonium content.

Idiopathic uric acid urolithiasis

Such secondary causes account, in fact, for at best 5% of uric acid stones, whereas idiopathic uric acid urolithiasis is largely prevalent. The disorder still accounts for about 10% of stone disease in Europe, occurring in most cases without a personal or family history of gout, but uric urolithiasis is markedly more frequent in gouty patients than in the general population. Idiopathic uric acid urolithiasis is twice as frequent in males as in females and is electively observed in older pateints. In our experience, nearly half the stones seen first in patients over 60 were made of uric acid in males, and about one-quarter in females.

Most often blood and urine concentrations of uric acid are normal, although one must keep in mind that normal values have markedly increased in the general population over the past decades. The main determinant of stone formation is the permanent acidity of urine, with pH often in the range of 4.8 to 5.2 and without diurnal or nocturnal variation. The generally accepted cause of low urinary pH is impaired enzymatic deamination of glutamine in the kidneys, resulting in the production of urine with both low pH and low ammonium content, although the molecular basis for such a disorder has not yet been elucidated. Climatic and genetic factors certainly contribute, as the incidence of uric acid stones is especially high in the Middle East and in tropical countries.

The basis of treatment is urine alkalinization and dilution. Prophylaxis of stone recurrence usually is achieved by means of a moderate alkali intake, such as 4 to 6 g/day of sodium bicarbonate or potassium citrate in divided doses, the goal being to maintain urinary pH between 6 and 6.5. Patients should be instructed to monitor urine pH and dilution by means of dipsticks in order to adjust the dose and timing of alkali supply. Stones present in the kidney may be dissolved by more intensive alkalinization under close supervision. Moderation of purine-rich food is recommended, and if marked hyperuricosuria (>800 mg, or 5 mmol/day) persists, allopurinol (200-300 mg/day) should be added.

Patients with uric acid urolithiasis especially require regular clinical surveillance with frequent ultrasound examination because the abnormally low urine pH is permanent, and rapid recurrence can be observed whenever urine alkalinization and dilution are neglected. The same is true of patients affected with mixed stones containing uric acid and calcium oxalate, who often exibit a particularly severe and recurrent course.

Infrequent purine stones

Errors in purine metabolism also lead to accumulation of rare lithogenic components such as 2,8-DHA and xanthine.

2,8-Dihydroxyadenine (2,8-DHA) nephrolithiasis, an autosomal recessive disease, results from the homozygous defect in adenine phosphoribosyl transferase, leading to increased production of adenine, subsequently oxidized by the enzyme xanthine-oxidase into 2,8-DHA. Owing to poor solubility, crystallization of 2,8-DHA results in the formation of recurrent stones. In addition 2,8-DHA crystals accumulate in the renal parenchyma, leading to progressive renal failure even in the absence of obstruction. 2,8-DHA urolithiasis is frequently underdiagnosed or misdiagnosed, because 2,8-DHA stones are radiolucent and give the same chemical reaction as uric acid on routine testing, so that they are often confused with uric acid stones. This has deleterious consequences because 2,8-DHA, unlike uric acid, is totally insoluble in alkaline urine, the only effective treatment being allopurinol. When left undiagnosed and thus improperly treated, 2,8-DHA lithiasis may lead to end-stage renal failure. Several patients had the disease discovered while already on renal replacement therapy, in some instances by biopsy of the transplanted kidney showing presence of 2,8-DHA crystals.

Xanthinuria is also an infrequent metabolic disease; transmission is autosomal recessive. The defect in the enzyme xanthine-oxidase results in the characteristic association of hypouricemia and hypouricosuria together with increased excretion of xanthine. Xanthine stones may also complicate allopurinol treatment of patients with hypoxanthine-guanine-phosphoribosyl transferase defect and heavy uric acid production.

INFECTION STONES

Infection stones are characterized by the presence of magnesium ammonium phosphate (MAP, or struvite) associated with variable proportions of carbapatite as the major component. Their incidence markedly decreased over the past three decades in all industrialized countries, where they presently represent fewer than 2% of stones. The reason for this decrease is probably the continuous progress in detection and treatment of urinary tract infection. Their incidence is still about three times higher in females than in males, as is the incidence of upper urinary tract infections.

The main lithogenic factor is the precipitation of MAP and carbonate apatite due to the extreme alkalinity of urine (pH ≥8.0). This alkalinity is the consequence of urea splitting by urease producing microorganisms, mainly the *Proteus* group or, less commonly, *Ureaplasma urealyticum* or *Corynebacterium*.

Stones are radiopaque and, if left untreated, may rapidly enlarge, filling the pelvis and calices, leading to the well-known appearance of "staghorn" calculi. The presence of numerous "coffin-lid" struvite crystals in urine is pathognomonic of the presence of a urea-splitting process. Examination of removed stones may allow one to identify a core made of calcium oxalate or uric acid surrounded by struvite, thus indicating that MAP stone occurred as the consequence of the superinfection of a preexisting calculus during an episode of upper urinary tract infection. Therefore, all pyelonephritic episodes due to *Proteus* species should be vigorously treated until complete eradication of infection is achieved.

Recently attention has been given to encrusted pyelitis, a peculiar form of calcium and MAP deposits infiltrating the pelvic wall as a result of urinary tract infection with *Corynebacterium* group D2, a urease-producing strain. Increasing numbers of cases have been reported in the past decade, especially in immunodepressed patients, particularly in renal transplant recipients.

Treatment of infection stones is based on three principles. First, obtain complete removal of the stone, usually by means of percutaneous nephrolithotomy or the combination of percutaneous nephrolithotomy and extracorporeal shock wave lithotripsy, or even by open surgery in the case of very large stones. Second, obtain total and stable eradication of infection by means of adapted and sufficiently prolonged antibiotherapy, using antibacterial agents with a high tissue penetration. Third, search for possible underlying metabolic disorders that may favor stone production and treat them accordingly. Such a policy allows stable cure in the great majority of cases. The use of urease inhibitor drugs such as acetohydroxamic acid, which is only palliative and often results in severe untoward effects such as leukopenia, thromboembolism, or polyneuritis, is of more limited interest.

CYSTINE STONES

Cystine stones are the consequence of cystinuria, an autosomal recessive genetic defect of transepithelial transport of dibasic aminoacids in the kidney and intestine. Cystinuria is the cause of 1-2% of stones observed in adults and about 10% of those occurring in children. There are several variants of cystinuria, but their differentiation does not affect the management of patients.

The only lithogenic factor is the high concentration of cystine in urine, because cystine is very poorly soluble in urine at usual pH. Cystine solubility in urine over the pH range from 5 to 7 is at best 250 mg (≈ 1 mmol) per liter. Homozygotes commonly excrete 800-1200 mg (3.2-4.8 mmoles) per day of cystine, whereas heterozygotes usually excrete values between 50 mg (0.2 mmol) and 300 mg (1.2 mmol) per day (the upper limit in healthy subjects is 20 mg/l).

Clinical findings

The onset of stone episodes is usually in the second or third decade, but may occur before the age of ten or as late as the seventh decade of life. Cystine stones are poorly radiopaque, with a smooth aspect. In severe cases, multiple cystine stones may accumulate in the pelvis and calyces, simulating a staghorn calculus.

Diagnosis is based on evidence of an abnormally high cystine output in urine. The classic cyanide-nitroprusside screening test detects only cystine concentrations > 75 mg (0.3 mmol/l). Microscopic analysis of urine sediment in untreated patients provides immediate diagnosis when showing characteristic large hexagonal crystals of cystine.

Treatment

In the absence of effective therapy, recurrent stone episodes with ureteric obstruction are likely to occur, requiring multiple percutaneous nephrolithotomy, ureteroscopic, or open surgery procedures, because cystine stones are poorly fragmented by extracorporeal shock wave lithotripsy. Ultimately this course can lead to nephrectomy, progressive renal failure, and the need for supportive therapy. Following kidney transplantation the disease does not recur in the grafted kidney.

Prophylactic treatment is crucial to avoid such progression. Medical therapy is aimed at enhancing the capacity of urine to dissolve cystine and at reducing cystine generation and urinary free cystine excretion. The primary measure is to achieve a diuresis of at least 3 liters per day in order to obtain the maximum possible dilution of cystine over the day and night. The patient should ingest water at bedtime and again during the night, taking advantage of the provoked nocturia.

However, this single measure is rarely sufficient, and sustained alkalinization most often is needed to obtain effective cystine solubilization. Approximately 0.2-0.25 g/kg body weight/day of sodium bicarbonate in divided doses must be given to maintain the urine pH at about 7.5, but no more than 8 to avoid precipitation of calcium phosphate that would form a shell around cystine stones, rendering them insoluble. This goal usually is achieved by the administration of 3 to 4 g of sodium bicarbonate four times a day, according to the patient's body weight. Salt intake should be reduced to compensate for this large sodium load. Potassium citrate (60 to 80 mEq/day) appears preferable to sodium bicarbonate (at least when no significant renal failure is present) because high urinary sodium output itself contributes to increased cystine excretion.

Patients should be instructed to monitor urine pH and specific gravity with dipsticks in order to maintain urine pH in the range of 7.5 to 8 and urine density <1010. Disappearance of cystine crystals in first-voided morning urine is an indicator of treatment efficacy. In addition, the patient should moderate the intake of methionine-containing foods, as methionine is the precursor of cystine. Eggs should be avoided, as well as stock fish, caviar, smoked salmon, crayfish, and lobster. Meat or fish intake should be limited at 150 g/day.

The combination of diet, urine dilution, and alkalinization prevents cystine stone formation in the long term in most patients,provided such measures are regularly pursued.

If, despite such measures, there is recurrent stone formation, or if preexisting stones fail to dissolve, dimethylcysteine (D-penicillamine) or alphamercaptopropionylglycine (tiopronin) is indicated. Both compounds are sulfhydryls that cleave cystine into two cysteine molecules to form a mixed disulfide 50 times more soluble than cystine itself . Although 1 gram of D-penicillamine (or tiopronin) is able to solubilize at best 400 mg of cystine, the daily dose usually should be limited to 900 or 1200 mg, because larger doses increase the risk of such side effects as skin rash, leukopenia, thrombocytopenia, proteinuria or full nephrotic syndrome, the last being reversible within several weeks or months after discontinuing the drug. Some patients who developed immunoallergic accidents with D-penicillamine may tolerate tiopronin. Captopril, which is also a sulfhydryl, appears of marginal interest because the maximum authorized dose is 150 mg /day. Therefore, if hypertension occurs, it should be treated with other antihypertensive agent(s), including other angiotensin-converting enzyme inhibitors. Patients have been successfully treated by D-penicillamine for more than 20 years without significant side effects.

However, like others, we prefer to treat, in the first instance, with just diet, dilution, and alkalinization (preferably with potassium citrate) for as long as possible, reserving long-term use of sulfhydryls (associated with alkalinization and hyperdiuresis) for refractory patients. In every case, frequent clinical and echographic surveillance is needed to achieve optimal compliance and to adapt therapy.

OTHER PROBLEMS OF STONE DISEASE

Drug-induced stones

Drug-induced nephrolithiasis accounts for about 1% of stones. The most frequently involved drug in the past decades was triamterene. Its incidence has markedly decreased with better information. Amiloride, which possesses the same properties and is devoid of lithogenic effects, may be used instead of triamterene in stone-forming patients. Sulfadiazine, used at high doses for the treatment of cerebral toxoplasmosis in HIV-positive patients, may result in massive crystalluria and tubular obstruction with anuria, easily preventable by alkaline hydration. Protease inhibitors such as indinavir and ritonavir, recently introduced as combination therapy in HIV-positive patients, induce frequent formation of radiolucent stones and also tubular obstruction with reversible anuria. Indinavir is poorly soluble at urine pH > 5.5, but obtaining lower urinary pH in patients often is unfeasible. The best prevention is ingestion of a large quantity of fluids together with each oral 800 mg dose of indinavir.

Urolithiasis in childhood

Urinary stone disease is five to ten times less frequent in children than in adults, and the distribution of causes is very different. Together, inherited metabolic diseases and morphologic abnormalities of the urinary tract account for nearly one-half of cases. The typical picture of renal colic is infrequent and seen mostly in older children and adolescents. In younger children, urolithiasis most often is revealed by pyuria and/or hematuria.

In children aged less that 5 years, there is a preponderance of stones made of MAP and carbonate apatite, which represent more than half of cases, mainly observed in boys under the age of 2 years, in the context of transient urinary tract infection with a ureolytic strain. There is no recurrence after removal of the stone and appropriate antibacterial therapy. Beyond 5 years of age, CaOx stones become the preponderant type. Malformative uropathies may favor occurrence of urinary tract infection and formation of stones and require proper urologic repair. The most important concern is early identification of inherited metabolic diseases, which, if not properly managed, may impair renal function through parenchymal crystal deposition and obstruction, such as primary hyperoxaluria, severe idiopathic hypercalciuria, distal tubular acidosis or 2,8-DHA nephrolithiasis. Therefore, evaluation of any child with urolithiasis should be carried out by an experienced nephrologist and/or uropediatrician.

Urinary stone disease in pregnancy

Complications of urolithiasis are infrequent during pregnancy (as is urolithiasis in women under 30 years of age) and occur in no more than 1 to 5 of 1000 pregnancies. Pregnancy does not favor stone production, because increased urinary calcium excretion, resulting from enhanced calcitriol synthesis and increased glomerular filtration rate is counterbalanced by an increased production of nephrocalcin. The most frequent problem arises from the ureteral migration of a preexisting kidney stone, favored by hormonally induced dilatation of ureters. It is revealed by renal colic, abdominal pain, frequency, dysuria, hematuria, pyuria or uterine contractions. Indeed, because dilatation affects the upper two-thirds of the ureters, calculus obstruction takes place at the ureteropelvic junction or at the vesicoureteric junction, thus resulting in bladder irritation. Ultrasonography is the first-choice examination; plain X-ray or urography, even restricted to 2 or 3 films, is anxiously accepted by the patient, but should not be performed in the first trimester. Nearly half of stones pass spontaneously. In the case of persistent obstruction, pain or infection there is consensus to propose ureteroscopy for immediate removal of the stone, or placement of a double-J stent until the end of pregnancy under sustained antibacterial therapy. In some cases percutaneous nephrostomy may be performed, but extracorporeal shock wave lithotripsy is contraindicated at any time during pregnancy.

Suggested readings

COE FL, FAVUS MJ, PAK CYC, PARKS JH, PREMINGER GM, eds. Kidney stones: medical and surgical management. Philadelphia: Lippincott-Raven Publishers, 1996.

CONSENSUS CONFERENCE: Prevention and treatment of kidney stones. JAMA 1995;260:978-981.

CURHAN GC, WILLETT WC, RIMM EB, STAMPFER MJ. A prospective study of dietary calcium and other nutrients and the risk of symptomatic kidney stones. N Engl J Med 1993;328:833-8.

DAUDON M, BADER CA, JUNGERS P. Urinary calculi: review of classification methods and correlations with etiology. Scanning Microsc 1993;7:1081-1106.

DAUDON M, HENNEQUIN C, BADER C, JUNGERS P, LACOUR B, DRUEKE T. Inhibitors of crystallization. Adv Nephrol 1995;24:167-216.

DAUDON M, ESTEPA L, VIARD JP, JOLY D, JUNGERS P. Urinary stones in HIV-1 positive patients treated with indinavir. Lancet 1997;349:1294-5.

HOUILLIER P, NORMAND M, FROISSART M, BLANCHARD A, JUNGERS P, PAILLARD M. Calciuric response to an acute acid load in healthy subjects and hypercalciuric stone formers. Kidney Int 1996;50:987-997.

JUNGERS P, DAUDON M, CONORT P. Lithiase rénale: diagnostic et traitement. Paris: Flammarion Médecine-Sciences, 1999.

MONK RD, BUSHINSKY DA. Pathogenesis of idiopathic hypercalciuria. In: Coe Fl, Favus MJ, Pak CYC, Parks JH, Preminger GM, eds. Kidney stones: medical and surgical management. Philadelphia: Lippincott-Raven 1996;759-72.

PAK CYC. Kidney stones. Lancet 1998;351:1797-1801.

PAK CYC. Medical management of nephrolithiasis: a new, simplified approach for general practice. Am J Med Sci 1997;313:215-9.

PREMINGER GM. Is there a need for medical evaluation and treatment of nephrolithiasis in the "age of lithotripsy"? Semin Urol 1994;12:51-64.

SAKHAEE K. Cystinuria: pathogenesis and treatment. Miner Electrolyte Metab 1994;20:414-23.

SUTTON RAL. The medical management of stone disease. In: Oxford Textbook of clinical nephrology. 2nd ed. Oxford: Oxford University Press, 1998;1343-59.

WHITFIELD HN. The surgical management of renal stones. In: Oxford Textbook of clinical nephrology. 2nd ed. Oxford: Oxford University Press, 1998;1361-73.

CHAPTER

31

Urinary tract obstruction

James M. Gloor, Vincente E. Torres

KEY POINTS

- Urinary tract obstruction is a frequent and potentially reversible cause of renal dysfunction.
- The clinical presentation of renal insufficiency due to urinary tract obstruction varies with its acuteness, anatomic location, and the severity of obstruction, and this diagnosis should be considered in all cases of renal failure.
- Prompt alleviation of urinary tract obstruction may allow recovery of renal function. Prolonged obstruction of the urinary tract results in permanent loss of renal function.
- Although dilatation of the urinary tract is seen in many cases of urinary tract obstruction, the absence of dilatation does not eliminate the possibility of high-grade urinary tract obstruction.

Obstructive uropathy may be defined as the impediment of urine flow from the kidney due to anatomic or physiologic factors occurring at any level of the urinary tract. Obstructive uropathy is an important and potentially reversible cause of renal insufficiency. Nevertheless, the degree to which renal functional recovery occurs is directly related to how quickly relief of obstruction is achieved. Prolonged urinary tract obstruction often results in permanent loss of function. It is therefore important that the possibility of obstructive uropathy be considered early in the evaluation of renal insufficiency.

Etiology

The causes of urinary tract obstruction vary with age and sex (Table 31.1). Prenatal ultrasound examinations have resulted in significant numbers of fetuses being identified with greater or lesser degrees of hydronephrosis. Many of these infants remain asymptomatic after birth. Nevertheless, chronic obstruction of the fetal urinary tract may interfere with normal renal growth and development, resulting in postnatal renal insufficiency. Congenital urinary tract malformations resulting in urinary stasis predispose affected infants to urinary tract infections. Urinary tract obstruction may present as infection in pediatric patients, most commonly in infant males or young girls, relating to urinary stasis or such associated urinary tract anomalies as vesicoureteral reflux. Painless macroscopic hematuria may occur in active children and adolescents with ureteropelvic junction obstruction. Urolithiasis is a frequent cause of urinary tract obstruction in young adults. In older women, malignancies such as cervical cancer historically have resulted in urinary tract obstruction, whereas in older men prostatic hypertrophy is common.

Pathogenesis

Determinants of glomerular filtration rate

The glomerular filtration rate is governed by the physical gradients that determine the movement of fluid across membranes in other biologic systems; it is described by the following equation:

$$Jv = K_f\,(\Delta P - \Delta\pi)$$

where Jv = fluid flux across a unit of capillary wall, K_f = the product of the surface area and the permeability coefficient of the capillary, ΔP = the transcapillary hydrostatic pressure gradient, and $\Delta\pi$ = the transcapillary colloid oncotic pressure gradient. In the case of the glomerulus, ΔP, the transcapillary hydrostatic pressure gradient, is the difference between P_{GC}, the intraglomerular, and P_{BS}, the Bowman's space capillary hydrostatic pressures: $\Delta P = P_{GC} - P_{BS}$, the transcapillary oncotic pressure, is the difference between π_{GC}, the glomerular capillary, and π_{BS}, the Bowman's space colloid oncotic pressures:

$$\Delta\pi = (\pi_{GC} - \pi_{BS})$$

Glomerular hydrostatic pressure is related to glomerular blood flow, and thus factors that alter renal afferent or efferent arteriolar tone may change the transglomerular capillary pressure gradient, producing changes in the glomerular filtration rate. In addition, the state of mesangial cell contraction or relaxation, by altering the surface area of the glomerular capillary available for filtration, also may alter glomerular filtration rate. Urinary tract obstruction is associated with profound alterations in the metabolism of multiple vasoactive compounds, which through their effects on determinants of glomerular filtration are capable of producing significant derangements of renal function.

Table 31.1 Causes of obstructive nephropathy

I. Intraluminal	
Calculus, clot, renal papilla, fungus ball	
II. Intrinsic	
Congenital	Calyceal infundibular obstruction
	Ureteropelvic junction obstruction
	Ureteral stricture or valves
	Posterior urethral valves
	Anterior urethral valves
	Urethral stricture
	Meatal stenosis
	Prune-belly syndrome
Neoplastic	Carcinoma of renal pelvis, ureter or bladder polyps
III. Extrinsic	
Congenital (aberrant vessels)	
	Congenital hydrocalycosis
	Ureteropelvic junction obstruction
	Retrocaval ureter
Neoplastic	Benign tumors
	– Benign prostatic hypertrophy
	– Pelvic lipomatosis
	– Cysts
	Primary retroperitoneal tumors
	– Mesodermal origin (e.g., sarcoma)
	– Neurogenic origin (e.g., neurofibroma)
	– Embryonic remnant (e.g., teratoma)
	Retroperitoneal extension of pelvic or abdominal tumor
	– Uterus, cervix
	– Bladder, prostate
	– Rectum, sigmoid colon
	Metastatic tumor
	– Lymphoma
Inflammatory	
	Retroperitoneal fibrosis
	Inflammatory bowel disease
	Diverticulitis
	Infection/abscess
Gynecologic	
	Pregnancy
	Uterine prolapse
	Surgical disruption/ligation
IV. Functional	
Neurogenic bladder	
Drugs (anticholinergics, antidepressants, calcium channel blockers)	

Acute renal hemodynamic response to unilateral or bilateral complete ureteral obstruction

Following acute ureteral obstruction there is a rapid increase in intraluminal pressure to 3-5 times normal values proximal to the obstruction. With persistent obstruction and subsequent dilatation of the ureter proximal to the obstruction, the intrapelvic pressure gradually decreases and becomes normal or only mildly elevated.

Acute obstruction of the urinary tract is associated with marked alterations in renal hemodynamic parameters. In the first 2 hours after unilateral complete ureteral obstruction, there is a reduction in preglomerular vascular resistance and an increase in renal blood flow mediated by increased production of vasodilatory prostaglandins. The increase in renal blood flow and glomerular capillary pressure maintain the glomerular filtration rate at approximately 80% of normal despite an increase in intratubular pressure caused by the obstruction. As the ureteral obstruction persists, activation of the renin angiotensin system and an increased production of thromboxane A2 and endothelin result in progressive vasoconstriction with reductions in renal blood flow and glomerular capillary pressure. The increase in renal vascular resistance associated with the vasoconstrictive effects of these vasoactive substances decreases renal blood flow to 50% of normal values, while glomerular filtration rate drops to approximately 20% of baseline. The decrease in glomerular filtration rate allows the renal intratubular pressure to return to normal levels despite the presence of obstruction.

The hemodynamic changes in the early phase (0-2 hrs) of bilateral ureteral obstruction are similar to those observed after unilateral obstruction. As bilateral obstruction persists, however, there is an accumulation of atrial natriuretic peptide (ANP), which does not occur following unilateral obstruction. The effect of atrial natriuretic peptide on glomerular hemodynamics is to produce preglomerular (arcuate, interlobular, afferent arteriolar) vasodilatation and postglomerular (efferent renal arteriolar) vasoconstriction. The increased ANP levels attenuate the afferent and enhance the efferent vasoconstrictions with maintenance of normal glomerular capillary and elevated tubular pressure.

Despite the differences in observed hemodynamic alterations between unilateral and bilateral ureteral obstruction, the reductions in renal blood flow and glomerular filtration rate 24 hours after obstruction are similar. In unilateral obstruction, increased renal vascular resistance and decreased renal blood flow result from afferent arteriolar constriction, wherease in bilateral ureteral obstruction the increase in renal vascular resistance is predominantly due to efferent arteriolar vasoconstriction.

Renal hemodynamic response to mild partial ureteral obstruction

In mild partial ureteral obstruction, activation of the renin-angiotensin system results in efferent renal arteriolar vasoconstriction and increases efferent renal arteriolar resistance. Angiotensin II- mediated mesangial cell contraction decreases glomerular capillary ultrafiltration coefficient (Kf). A compensatory increase in vasodilatory prostaglandin (PGE_2) synthesis causes afferent renal arteriolar vasodilatation, resulting in decreased afferent arteriolar resistance. These hemodynamic alterations preserve renal blood flow while increasing glomerular capillary hydrostatic pressure (P_{GC}), maintaining glomerular filtration rate at the normal level. Infusion of prostaglandin synthetase inhibitors such as meclofenamate or indomethacin in animals with ureteral obstruction is associated with a rapid decrease in renal blood flow and glomerular filtration rate, indicating that in partial ureteral obstruction renal function is maintained by the interplay between vasoconstrictors and vasodilators. It is likely that other vasoactive factors, such as thromboxane A2, also play a role, particularly in more severe ureteral obstruction accompanied by reductions in renal blood flow and glomerular filtration rate. In animals subjected to unilateral ureteral obstruction, the changes in renal blood flow and glomerular filtration rate are observed only in the ipsilateral kidney. This provides evidence that the hemodynamic alterations provoked by obstruction occur at the level of the kidney rather than due to circulating systemic factors.

Chronic renal hemodynamic response to ureteral obstruction

Chronic complete unilateral ureteral obstruction results in progressively decreased renal blood flow. After 24 hours of obstruction renal blood flow is 40 to 50% of normal. With prolonged obstruction, renal blood flow decreases to 30% at 6 days, 20% at 2 weeks, and 12% at 8 weeks.

Chronic partial ureteral obstruction produces vasoconstriction and results in increased renal vascular resistance. Depending on the duration and severity of obstruction as well as volume status of the individual, variable degrees of relative afferent and efferent arteriolar constriction and changes in ultrafiltration coefficient can be observed, producing variable changes in filtration pressure. This, combined with different levels of renal tubular pressure, produces variable alterations in glomerular filtration rate. Chronic obstruction also may result in loss of nephrons, further decreasing GFR.

Abnormalities of tubular function in obstructive nephropathy

Urinary tract obstruction may result in disturbances in renal tubular function. Several characteristic abnormalities of renal function have been identified in urinary tract obstruction. These abnormalities may have profound physiologic implications when both kidneys are obstructed, or they may be of little clinical significance in cases of unilateral obstruction, because the unobstructed contralateral kidney may provide renal function adequate to prevent significant abnormalities.

Nephrogenic diabetes insipidus occurs in bilateral partial urinary tract obstruction. Polyuria, polydipsia, nocturia, and urinary frequency may result from disordered urinary concentration capacity. Hyperosmolar dehydration and hypernatremia may occur in infants or in older individuals with hypodipsia or inadequate access to water. Several mechanisms have been implicated in the development of urinary concentrating defect in urinary tract obstruction. Sodium chloride reabsorption is decreased in the thick ascending limb of Henle's loop of obstructed kidneys. The resulting impairment of development of the medullary solute gradient decreases effectiveness of antidiuretic hormone-mediated water absorption from the collecting duct. In addition, the cortical collecting duct has been shown to be relatively less responsive to the effects of vasopressin in animal models of ureteral obstruction, further impairing water reabsorption from the distal nephron.

In acute ureteral obstruction, urinary sodium excretion initially decreases. The resultant decrease in fractional excretion of sodium may lead to confusion with prerenal factors in acutely decreased renal function. The mechanism responsible for this decreased fractional excretion of sodium is not clear. In contrast to acute obstruction, in chronic partial urinary tract obstruction renal sodium absorption decreases, resulting in sodium wasting. In unilateral ureteral obstruction the simultaneous decrease in glomerular filtration rate associated with obstruction minimizes the clinical significance of the salt wasting because the unobstructed contralateral kidney retains normal function and is capable of ameliorating the effects produced by the ureteral obstruction on the ipsilateral kidney. Following relief of severe bilateral hydronephrosis, however, marked post-obstructive diuresis may occur. Massive loss of water and electrolytes may on occasion be life-threatening.

The mechanisms involved in post-obstructive diuresis include both appropriate, physiologic factors as well as pathologic phenomena. Excretion of the excess Na and water retained during the period of obstruction correct the expanded extracellular fluid volume. If obstruction has persisted long enough for urea and other osmotically active waste products to accumulate, their excretion may provoke an osmotic diuresis. In addition, if intravenous replacement of large urinary losses is begun before correction of the expanded extracellular fluid volume, a persistent diuresis will ensue, in effect iatrogenically "driving" the polyuria. In addition to these "physiologic" processes, true defects of renal tubular function resulting in large sodium losses also may occur. In cases of rapid recovery of glomerular function following relief of obstruction, there may be massive sodium losses, and these may be associated with serious fluid and electrolyte imbalance.

Interstitial renal injury resulting from urinary tract obstruction may produce a state of relative mineralocorticoid deficiency due to impaired renin production or decreased sensitivity of the distal nephron to aldosterone. This injury may result in type IV renal tubular acidosis with hyperchloremic metabolic acidosis and hyperkalemia. In addition, urinary tract obstruction may cause distal renal tubular sodium wasting, resulting in a voltage-dependent defect in urinary acidification and potassium excretion. This is characterized by an inability to acidify urine maximally, inability to excrete potassium normally, and inability to maintain sodium homeostasis when dietary sodium intake is reduced.

Pathogenesis of tubulointerstitial fibrosis in obstructive nephropathy

The pathogenesis of tubulointerstitial fibrosis in obstructive nephropathy has been extensively studied. Acute ureteral obstruction unleashes chemotactic factors that result in the accumulation of an interstitial infiltrate consisting of macrophages and T-lymphocytes. In conjunction with resident mesangial cells, these infiltrating monocytes produce prostaglandins and thromboxane A2. Concurrent with the production of prostaglandins, the renin-angiotensin system is upregulated. The expression of renin, angiotensinogen, angiotensin-converting enzyme, and the angiotensin II type 1 (AT_1) receptor increases in the affected kidney. Alterations in renal blood flow caused by angiotensin II and thromboxane A2 are partly ameliorated by the effects of vasodilatory prostaglandins. Nevertheless, the net effect of ureteral obstruction is vasoconstriction, decreased renal blood flow, and ischemia. Activation of the renin-angiotensin system is associated with increased fibrogenesis related to increased production of growth factors. The production of TGF-β_1, a cytokine that stimulates extracellular matrix synthesis and inhibits its degradation, is stimulated by angiotensin II. TGF-β_1 increases fibrogenesis by increasing the synthesis of extracellular matrix components such as collagen I and III, fibronectin, and laminin. The pro-fibrogenic effect of TGF-β_1 also results from inhibition of the synthesis and activity of metalloproteinases, enzymes responsible for breakdown and remodeling of extracellular matrix. TGF-β_1 as well as mechanical forces relating to urinary tract obstruction also downregulate production of protective antioxidant factors and increase superoxide and hydrogen peroxide production. The resultant increase in oxidant stress further amplifies the pro-fibrogenic state.

Consequences of urinary tract obstruction on the developing kidney

The effects of urinary tract obstruction on the developing kidney depend on the time of onset, the location, and the degree of obstruction. Urinary tract obstruction during early pregnancy results in disorganization of the renal parenchyma (dysplasia) and a reduction in the number of nephrons. Partial or complete ureteral obstruction in the neonate causes activation of the renin-angiotensin system, with subsequent angiotensin II-mediated vasoconstriction and glomerular hypoperfusion in the affected kidney. In addition to its effects on renal hemodynamics, ureteral obstruction also increases expression of transforming growth factor β_1 (TGF-β_1), which results in interstitial fibrosis. Delayed expression of epidermal growth factor results from obstruction and inhibits normal renal growth. Apoptosis, or programmed cell death, is increased in unilateral ureteral obstruction. Bcl-2, an oncoprotein shown to inhibit apoptosis, is suppressed in unilateral ureteral obstruction.

The degree of impairment of the ipsilateral kidney, in the case of partial unilateral ureteral obstruction, and of compensatory hypertrophy of the contralateral kidney, in the case of partial or complete unilateral ureteral obstruction, is inversely correlated to the age of the animal at the time of obstruction. Clusterin, a large dimeric glycoprotein that inhibits apoptosis in unilateral ureteral obstruction, is expressed to a greater degree in adult kidneys than in immature ones. The older the animal at the time of obstruction, the less the impairment of the ipsilateral kidney and the less is the compensatory growth of the contralateral kidney. In addition, the recovery of renal function after relief of urinary tract obstruction also decreases with the age of the animal.

Clinical findings

The clinical manifestations of urinary tract obstruction vary with its acuteness, location, and severity. Chronic unilateral ureteropelvic junction obstruction may be an asymptomatic incidental finding, with no demonstrable effect on renal function detected in the evaluation of an unrelated condition. Obstructive processes involving both kidneys, as seen in chronic prostatic hypertrophy or pelvic malignancies, may result in the insidious development of uremia and life-threatening electrolyte disturbances. Acute obstruction, as seen in passage of a stone, may cause incapacitating pain from ureteral colic.

In addition to intrinsic abnormalities of the urinary tract itself, obstructive uropathy may be the result of factors extrinsic to the urinary tract. Extrinsic compression, such as that seen in retroperitoneal fibrosis or neoplasia may result in ureteral obstruction. Such systemic disorders as diabetes mellitus or sickle cell anemia may produce renal complications – e.g., papillary necrosis – that can cause urinary tract obstruction; such endocrine disorders as hyperparathyroidism may lead to obstructive urolithiasis.

Bladder and urethra

Individuals with obstruction at the level of the urinary bladder may have acute urinary retention with severe discomfort from bladder distention. Both anatomic and physiologic factors may lead to bladder outlet obstruction with acute urinary retention. Urethral trauma, stone impaction, or obstruction of a bladder catheter may cause obstruction with acute symptoms. In addition, chronic compensated bladder outlet obstruction relating to prostatic hypertrophy or urethral stricture or meatal stenosis may decompensate and result in acute obstructive symptoms.

In chronic urethral or bladder outlet obstruction, irritative symptoms such as nocturia, dysuria, frequency, and urgency may develop. Other symptoms of obstruction such as dribbling, slow urine stream, and hesitancy may predominate. In some individuals the distended bladder may be palpable in the lower abdomen.

Developmental spinal anomalies or diseases of or injuries to the cord may result in abnormal urinary bladder innervation. In the normal urinary bladder, the detrusor, bladder neck, and external urinary sphincter function in a coordinated fashion to permit efficient storage and evacuation of urine. Abnormalities of innervation may produce a "neuropathic" or neurogenic bladder in which proper coordination is deranged, resulting in a functional obstruction of the urinary tract.

Ureteral obstruction

Lesions that can cause ureteral obstruction may be classified as intraluminal or extraluminal, and extraluminal lesions may be characterized as intramural or extramural. The level at which obstruction occurs is important. Most commonly, obstruction from intraluminal factors such as stone, blood clot, or sloughed renal papilla as is seen in acute papillary necrosis occurs at the ureteropelvic or ureterovesicular junction. Intramural or extramural conditions resulting in extrinsic ureteral obstruction may occur at any level of the ureter.

In the normal ureter, peristaltic waves of contraction propel boluses of urine from the renal pelvis to the bladder. During peristalsis the ureteral walls coapt in such a fashion as to prevent retrograde transmission of high pressure to the kidney. Acute ureteral obstruction, as seen in acute ureterolithiasis, is characterized by an initial elevation of intraluminal ureteral pressure. Ureteral dilatation results, and ureteral wall coaptation no longer occurs. High pressure is transmitted in a retrograde manner into the kidney. Elevation of intrarenal and ureteral pressure with subsequent acute distention results in the severe flank pain characteristic of ureteral colic. In chronic ureteral obstruction, ureteral pressure decreases to normal or near-normal levels. Patients may be entirely asymptomatic, especially if the obstruction is unilateral, because contralateral renal function prevents serious metabolic derangement.

Recovery of renal function after relief of complete unilateral ureteral obstruction of variable duration

The recovery of ipsilateral glomerular filtration rate after relief of a unilateral complete ureteral obstruction has been best studied in dogs, and depends on the duration of the obstruction. Complete recovery occurs after 1 week of obstruction. The degree of recovery after 2 or 4 weeks of obstruction is only of 58 and 36%, respectively. No recovery occurs after 6 weeks of obstruction. Rare reports of recovery of renal function in patients with longer periods of unilateral ureteral obstruction may represent high-grade partial obstruction rather than complete obstruction or may reflect differences in lymphatic drainage and renal anatomy between the human and canine kidneys.

Differential diagnosis

Obstruction may be suspected when dilatation of the urinary tract is observed. Nevertheless, in acute high-grade obstruction the rapid increase in renal tubular pressure may abruptly stop urine production, and thus be associated with a normal-appearing nondilated collecting system. Conversely, significant urinary tract dilatation may be associated with normal renal function. Often, a thoughtful evaluation using multiple imaging modalities may be required to define whether urinary tract obstruction is present.

Ultrasonography is an anatomic study that is readily available and noninvasive. The presence and degree of renal pelvic dilatation as well as the degree of associated renal parenchymal atrophy can readily be determined by this method. In addition, the location of an obstructing urinary tract lesion often can be determined with ultrasound, as, for example, in ureteropelvic junction obstruction in a newborn or bladder outlet obstruction from an enlarged prostate in an older man.

Doppler ultrasonography can be used to estimate renal vascular resistance. The resistive index is a calculation based on renal blood flow velocities measured using Doppler ultrasonography during systole and diastole. The renal resistive index (RI) is calculated as:

RI = peak systolic velocity – end diastolic velocity/peak systolic velocity.

Decreased diastolic renal blood flow velocity increases the resistive index, and is associated with conditions in which renal vascular resistance is elevated. Doppler ultrasonographic analysis of resistive index has been used to determine the functional significance of hydronephrosis. In obstructed kidneys the resistive index is higher than in nonobstructed kidneys. This difference can be accentuated with the addition of furosemide with saline infusion. The clinical applicability of this examination remains to be determined, but it may prove to be a simple, noninvasive method of evaluation of hydronephrosis.

Direct observation of the urinary tract with cystoscopy allows evaluation of the lower urinary tract for obstruction at the level of the urethra, bladder, or vesicoureteral junction. In addition, retrograde pyelography performed at the same time permits examination of the ureters for obstruction due to intrinsic or extrinsic lesions. Anatomic detail is revealed better than with ultrasound, and the examination may permit correction of the obstruction. Cystoscopy is invasive and requires urologic consultation; therefore, it often is less readily available than ultrasound.

Ultrasound and cystoscopy provide anatomic, not physiologic information. Obstruction can rarely occur without hydronephrosis, when the ureter and renal pelvis are encased in a fibrotic process and unable to expand, or with high-grade obstruction occurring acutely, as may be seen in cases of ureteral stone impaction. On the other hand, mild dilatation of the collecting system of no functional significance is not unusual. Even hydronephrosis readily seen on ultrasound may in some cases not be associated with functional obstruction. Imaging studies designed to investigate renal function may be required to adequately evaluate an individual suspected of having urinary tract obstruction. Diuresis renography using either standard radiocontrast or radioisotope-labeled and renally excreted agents is helpful when the functional significance of the dilatation of the collecting system is in question. Technetium-99m diuretic renography provides quantifiable information about differential renal function as well as obstruction in cases of upper tract dilatation. In this study, radioisotope-labeled mercaptoacetyl-triglycine (MAG-3) or diethylenetetraaminepentaacetic acid (DTPA) is administered intravenously. The renally excreted agent collects in the dilated collecting system, and cortical activity measured soon after administration permits measurement of differential renal function. At a standardized time after administration of the isotope furosemide is given. The rapidity with which the agent washes out of the collecting system is measured, and the half-life ($t_{1/2}$) of tracer elimination is calculated. Prolongation of $t_{1/2}$ of tracer wash-out corresponds with significant obstruction, whereas prompt elimination following diuretic administration suggests lack of obstruction. A similar study can be performed using standard intravenous radiocontrast agents. Although anatomic detail is better assessed using the standard radiocontrast material, radioisotope diuretic renal scans permit more accurate determination of differential renal function as well as calculation of $t_{1/2}$ of tracer wash-out.

The presence or absence of upper urinary tract obstruction may be assessed using antegrade pressure flow study ("Whitaker test"). In this examination, an antegrade infusion of saline is performed at a standardized rate via a nephrostomy, and the renal pelvic and urinary bladder pressures are measured. The renal pelvic pressure minus bladder pressure equals the relative pressure. Elevation of the relative pressure is seen in obstruction. Although this test has been called the "gold standard" in evaluation of the dilated urinary system, it is invasive and requires expertise. It is most useful in investigating obstruction of the upper urinary tract. When combined with radiocontrast, antegrade ureteropyelography may be useful in determining the etiology and level of obstructions of the urinary tract.

Other techniques such as excretory urography and computed tomography are helpful in determining the cause of urinary tract obstructions. The utility of these examinations is limited in patients with advanced renal insufficiency. Nonfunctioning or poorly functioning kidneys may fail to extract the contrast medium from the circulation and excrete it in urine, resulting in poor visualization of the collecting system. In these cases magnetic resonance urography can provide coronal imaging of the renal collecting systems and ureters that is similar to conventional urography, but without the use of iodinated contrast.

Treatment

The appropriate treatment of urinary tract obstruction is determined by the nature, the location, degree, and acuteness of the obstruction. The degree to which renal function has been affected and the presence of complications such as pain and infection are also of great importance in planning therapy.

The placement of a nephrostomy tube permits rapid decompression of an obstructed kidney. This modality is useful in the setting of complex urinary tract obstructions associated with severe renal insufficiency or sepsis. In critically ill patients, the placement of a nephrostomy may provide rapid improvement of renal function and permit stabilization of the patient's condition before more comprehensive or definitive treatment of the obstruction is undertaken. The procedure may be performed rapidly and safely under ultrasound guidance. Nephrostomy also may provide access to the renal pelvis for stone extraction, antegrade passage of ureteral stents, and endoscopic correction of ureteropelvic junction obstruction. In addition, temporary nephrostomy drainage of a poorly functioning obstructed kidney may allow a period of observation for recovery of renal function. Futile surgery to correct obstruction in irreversibly injured kidneys may thus be avoided.

Ureteral obstruction may be due to intraluminal, intramural, or extramural factors. The most common intraluminal obstructions are due to kidney stones. Stones 4 mm or less in diameter most often pass spontaneously, and appropriate therapy in these cases consists of analgesia, generally requiring narcotics, and vigorous hydration to establish a high urine flow rate. In the absence of urinary tract infection or severe renal insufficiency, patients may be observed for a period of weeks to months to allow an opportunity for the stone to pass. Larger stones, or stones that fail to pass after a period of observation, may be removed. Modalities available for stone extraction include extracorporeal shock wave lithotripsy (ESWL), percutaneous nephrolithotomy and ultrasonic lithotripsy, ureteroscopic extraction, or open or laparoscopic surgery. Certain types of stone (e.g., cystine, uric acid stones) are amenable to chemical dissolution. Intramural obstruction occurring at the ureteropelvic junction may be treated surgically by pyeloplasty. Vesicoureteral junction obstruction can be corrected by resection of the stenotic area and reimplantation of the distal ureter into the bladder. Correction of extramural ureteral obstruction depends on the nature of the obstructing lesion. Placement of ureteral stents, surgical ureteral lysis, and chemotherapy are modalities that may be required to alleviate obstruction. In cases in which the ureters are not amenable to treatment to correct the obstruction, urinary diversion may be necessary.

Urinary bladder dysfunction may result in urinary tract obstruction. The urinary bladder serves two functions: storage and expulsion of urine. Derangement of either of these may result in obstruction to urine flow. In cases in which the bladder is hypotonic or atonic, impaired detrusor contractility results in inadequate expulsion of urine. In such cases, clean intermittent self- catheterization frequently is used periodically to empty the bladder. The frequency of catheterization is variable, depending on the degree of bladder dysfunction, but generally is four to five times daily. Medications possibly useful in improving bladder emptying include cholinergic agents such as bethanechol chloride to increase detrusor contractility and a-adrenergic antagonists such as prazosin hydrochloride or phenoxybenzamine hydrochloride to relax urethral sphincter tone.

In some individuals, bladder dysfunction relates to inadequate urine storage. The function of unstable, low-capacity bladders may be improved with anticholinergic agents such as propantheline hydrochloride or smooth muscle depressants such as oxybutynin hydrochloride, which inhibit detrusor contractility and increase bladder compliance. Clean intermittent catheterization also may be necessary periodically to empty the bladder, preventing urinary stasis and infection.

Urinary tract obstruction at the level of the bladder outlet or urethra may result in renal dysfunction or recurrent urinary tract infection secondary to poor bladder emptying. The obstruction may be alleviated surgically, as in the case of prostatic hypertrophy. Urethral strictures often may be treated by periodic dilatation, although endoscopic urethrotomy may result in long-term improvement of bladder emptying in cases of recurrent urethral obstruction.

Long-term follow-up is necessary to monitor for recurrence of the urethral obstruction.

Prenatal ultrasound examinations have been used increasingly in obstetrics. This has resulted in the identification of hydronephrosis in a significant number of fetuses. Prenatal intervention for fetal hydronephrosis is indicated only in cases of urinary tract obstruction resulting in oligohydramnios, in an attempt to prevent pulmonary hypoplasia and respiratory insufficiency in the newborn. Obstruction occurring at or distal to the level of the bladder outlet is amenable to treatment. Ultrasound-guided placement of vesicoamniotic shunts has the potential to reestablish amniotic fluid volume, permitting more normal pulmonary development to proceed. Fetoscopic endoscopy holds promise for the future. Definitive correction of the urinary malformation resulting in obstruction can then be performed postnatally. Before intervention, an assessment should be made to determine whether irreversible renal dysplasia already has occurred. Serial vesicocenteses allow analysis of fetal urine composition to determine whether irreversible renal insufficiency is present. Fetuses with poor prognoses with respect to renal function are not candidates for prenatal intervention.

RETROPERITONEAL FIBROSIS

Retroperitoneal fibrosis is characterized by the accumulation of inflammatory and fibrotic tissue around the aorta, between the renal hila and the pelvic brim. Most cases are idiopathic.

Retroperitoneal fibrosis has been associated with atherosclerosis of the aorta and an immune response to components of atherosclerotic plaques has been suggested as a possible etiologic factor. Other cases of retroperitoneal fibrosis have been associated with connective tissue disorders, including mediastinal fibrosis, sclerosing cholangitis, Riedel's thyroiditis, and fibrous pseudotumor of the orbit, as well as with such malignancies as lymphoma and retroperitoneal sarcoma. Drugs such as methysergide, hydralazine, and ergot derivatives also have been implicated as causes of retroperitoneal fibrosis.

The clinical presentation of retroperitoneal fibrosis may be nonspecific, resulting in a delay in diagnosis. Patients with idiopathic retroperitoneal fibrosis often exhibit such nonspecific systemic symptoms as malaise, anorexia, and weight loss, and abdominal or flank pain. Encasement of ureters in the fibrotic mass may result in bilateral obstruction and renal insufficiency. Laboratory test results usually demonstrate anemia and an increased sedimentation rate.

Radiographically, the diagnosis of retroperitoneal fibrosis is suggested by the triad of medial deviation of the ureters, unilateral or bilateral hydronephrosis with delayed excretion of radiocontrast, and tapered narrowing of the distal ureters seen on excretory urography. CT scanning is a sensitive diagnostic tool, and permits early diagnosis, as well as determination of the extent of retroperitoneal involvement. In contrast to metastatic disease, retroperitoneal fibrosis rarely displaces vascular structures, and does not cause local bone destruction. Magnetic resonance imaging provides excellent anatomic detail and also permits avoidance of nephrotoxic radiocontrast agents.

In urinary tract obstruction due to retroperitoneal fibrosis, placement of ureteral stents can reestablish renal function. Longer term, administration of corticosteroids is helpful to control the systemic manifestations of the disease and often to reduce the bulk of the tumor and relieve the ureteral obstruction. Administration of corticosteroids, however, should be considered only after malignancy and retroperitoneal infection have been ruled out. As in other chronic renal diseases, administration of corticosteroids should be kept at the minimal level capable of controlling symptoms. Surgical ureterolysis, which consists of freeing the ureters from the fibrotic mass, lateralizing them, and wrapping them in omentum to prevent repeat obstruction, is often necessary. Other immunosuppressive agents have been used rarely when the systemic manifestations of the disease cannot be controlled with safe doses of corticosteroids. In most cases the long-term outcome of idiopathic retroperitoneal fibrosis is satisfactory.

Suggested readings

CHEVALIER RL. Effects of ureteral obstruction on renal growth. Semin Nephrol 1995;15:353-60.

CHEVALIER RL. Growth factors and apoptosis in neonatal ureteral obstruction. J Am Soc Nephrol 1996;7:1098-105.

EL-DAHR SS, GEE J, DIPP S, et al. Upregulation of the renin-angiotensin system and downregulation of kallikrein in obstructive nephropathy. Am J Physiol 1993; 264:F871-4.

GILKESON GS, ALLEN NB. Retroperitoneal fibrosis: a true connective tissue disease. Rheum Dis Clin North Am 1996;22:23-38.

GLOOR JM. Management of prenatally detected fetal hydronephrosis. Mayo Clinic Proc 1995;70:145-52.

ISHIDOYA S, MORRISSEY J, MCCRACKEN R, et al. Angiotensin receptor antagonist ameliorates renal tubulointerstitial fibrosis caused by unilateral ureteral obstruction. Kidney Int 1995;47:1285-94.

KIMURA H, MUJAIS SK. Cortical collecting duct Na-K pump in obstructive uropathy. Am J Physiol 1990;258:F1320.

KLAHR S. New insights into the consequences and mechanisms of renal impairment in obstructive uropathy. Am J Kid Dis 1991;18:689-99.

KLAHR S. Pathophysiology of obstructive nephropathy: a 1991 update. Semin Nephrol 1991;11:156.

KOTTRA JJ, DUNNICK NR. Retroperitoneal fibrosis. Radiol Clin North Am 1996;34:1259-75.

MORRISSEY J, ISHIDOYA S, MCCRACKEN R, KLAHR S. Nitric oxide generation ameliorates the tubulointerstitial fibrosis of obstructive nephropathy. J Am Soc Nephrol 1996;7: 2202-12.

PLATT JF, RUBIN JM, ELLIS HM, DI PIETRO MA. Duplex Doppler US of the kidney: differentiation of obstructive from nonobstructive dilatation. Radiol 1993;150:1192.

QUINTERO RA, JOHNSON MP, ROMERO R, et al. In-utero percutaneous cystoscopy in the management of fetal lower urinary tract uropathy. Lancet 1995;346:537-40.

RICARDO SD, DING G, EUFEMIO M, DIAMOND JR. Antioxidant expression in experimantal hydronephrosis: role of mechanical stretch and growth factors. Am J Physiol 1997;272:F789-98.

SHOKEIR AA, NIJMAN RJM, EL-AZAB M, PROVOOST AP. Partial ureteral obstruction: effect of intravenous normal saline and furosemide on the resistive index. J Urol 1997;157:1074-7.

SECTION 8

Vascular disorders

CHAPTER

32

Essential hypertension and the kidney

José Luño, Soledad Garcia de Vinuesa

KEY POINTS

- The kidney is the most important organ in the regulation of blood pressure.
- The kidney participates in the control of blood pressure through the modulation of sodium excretion and the body balance of sodium and water.
- The kidney also provides an important endocrine function in blood pressure control, secreting renin, which allows the production of the active pressor substance angiotensin II, which is the most important regulator of arterial vasoconstriction and a potent stimulus for secretion of the sodium-retaining hormone, aldosterone.
- The kidney secretes a renomedullary vasodepressor lipid that may participate in blood pressure regulation in some forms of hypertension.
- The kidney plays a central role in the pathogenesis of essential hypertension through a defect in its capacity to excrete excess sodium ingested. Among the theories postulated to explain the renal origin of essential hypertension are: an inherited defect in renal excretion of sodium associated with a resetting of renal pressure – natriuresis. A congenital reduction in the number of nephrons. Heterogeneity in the nephrons, with two functionally abnormal nephron populations – ischemic and nonischemic – which alters the equilibrium between renin secretion and sodium balance.
- Patients with uncontrolled essential hypertension are at risk to develop kidney damage due to malignant or benign nephrosclerosis. Strict blood pressure control with antihypertensive therapy could minimize this risk.

Hypertension and the kidney are closely associated. This relationship between hypertension and the kidney has been known since Richard Bright reported “morbid appearance in 100 cases connected with albuminous urine” in Guy’s Hospital Reports in 1836. In this paper, Bright observed that postmortem examination of those patients who had died from diseases related to “albuminous urine” showed obvious alterations of the kidneys, besides other cardiac abnormalities that consisted of enlargement of the left ventricle with wall hypertrophy that had no intrinsic organic cause that could account for this remarkable cardiac hypertrophy. These observations had been published before human blood pressure could be measured. Although Bright noted that those patients had persistent strong radial pulse, it was not until 60 years later that Riva-Rocci developed the modern sphygmomanometer, which allowed measurement of human blood pressure and a clear definition of the clinical phenomenon of hypertension, demonstrating that patients with renal diseases often had high blood pressure, which produces a chronic cardiac overload leading to progressive left ventricular hypertrophy.

Nevertheless, the relationship between hypertension and the kidney is more complex. Abnormalities of the kidneys can lead to increased blood pressure, but hypertension itself can also produce kidney damage. At present, hypertension is a cause of renal disease in 30% of patients starting on regular dialysis treatment in USA and accounts for 14% of new patients with end-stage renal disease in Europe.

The first description of essential hypertension and its effects on the kidneys was made by Mahomed in 1879, who observed and first described how patients without albuminuria could also have long and persistent pulse associated with other cardiovascular changes that accompany high blood pressure without any clear signs of other organic disease. In his report of Chronic Bright's Disease and its Essential Symptoms, Mahomed concluded that "albuminuria is not a symptom of chronic Bright's disease, but the persistent pulse is, and it is the only pathognomonic one". In postmortem studies, the kidneys of these patients, although sometimes small and contracted, showed a red aspect, unlike the white, pale aspect noted in patients who had died of an albuminuric disease, and Mahomed defined a type of chronic Bright's disease different from the acute albuminuric form: "The symptoms of chronic Bright's disease consist essentially in the signs of high arterial tension or over-fulness of the arteries, taken together with the absence of albuminuria, which subsequently produces hypertrophy of the heart and thickening of the vessels. However, although the cardiovascular phenomena are coexistent with the dropsy and albuminuria in acute disease, in patients with the chronic form of the disease are present alone and are the only signs of the chronic condition".

The cause of hypertension can be identified in about 10% of patients. These primary diseases associated with high blood pressure lead to the concept of secondary hypertension, which has a different etiology (Tab. 32.1). It is not possible, however, to detect any primary condition as a cause of high blood pressure in most patients. The hypertension in this group – about 90% of hypertensive patients – without any known etiology is called essential or primary hypertension, since it is usually related to genetic and environmental factors. Nevertheless, in this group, increasing data also suggest that some documented renal abnormalities could account for the hypertension, at least in part, owing to the inability of the kidneys to excrete adequate quantities of salt. Therefore, both renal hypertension and essential hypertension can have a substrate of some renal abnormalities.

The kidneys play a key role in the regulation of blood pressure by modulating the body's balance of sodium and water by sodium excretion. By secreting renin, the kidneys also act as an endocrine organ for a critical function of maintaining blood pressure. Such secretion allows the generation of the active pressor substance angiotensin II, which apart from its direct vasoconstrictor effect, influences blood pressure control through interactions with the sympathetic nervous system. It is also a potent stimulus for the secretion of aldosterone, the sodium-retaining hormone. The kidney also secretes some vasopressor lipids from the renal medulla.

Epidemiology

Recent epidemiologic studies carried out on a sample of Spanish population aged from 35 to 64 years revealed that in 21.6% of males and 18.1% of females the systolic blood pressure was above 160 mmHg, and/or the diastolic pressure was higher than 95 mmHg, or hypertension already had been diagnosed. These percentages increased by 14.7% when considering those whose blood pressure was above 140/90 mmHg; some data suggest that, in some Spanish regions and in different social groups, the prevalence of hypertension may be even higher. Data obtained in the USA show similar prevalence values, and an often-cited study of prevalence found a prevalence of hypertension of 18% of the population when values above 160/95 mmHg were considered, increasing to 38% when the criterion was

Table 32.1 Causes of secondary hypertension

Renal	Adrenal carcinomas
	Ectopic corticotropin secreting tumors
Renal parenchymal disease	Pheochromocytoma, adrenal medullary chromaffin tumors
Acute glomerulonephritis	
Chronic glomerulonephritis	*Other endocrine causes*
Pyelonephritis	Acromegaly
Polycystic disease	Hyperthyroidism (systolic hypertension)
Diabetic nephropathy	Hypothyroidism
Obstructive nephropathy	Hyperparathyroidism
Hereditary nephritis	Carcinoids
Radiation nephritis	Exogenous hormones
Connective diseases with vasculitis or glomerulitis	Glucocorticoids
Hemolytic uremic syndrome	Mineralocorticoids
Renal insufficiency	Erythropoietin
	Oral contraceptive or estrogens
Renal unilateral parenchymal disease	Toxemia of pregnancy
Reflux nephropathy	
Unilateral pyelonephritis	**Neurologic disorders**
Hydronephrosis	
	Increased intracranial pressure
Renovascular disease	Guillain-Barrè syndrome
Renal artery stenosis	Sleep apnea
Renal artery occlusion, thromboses	Familial dysautonomia
Renal arterial aneurysms	Acute porphyria
Vasculitis	Spinal cord injuries
Coarctation of the aorta	
Renin secreting tumors	**Miscellaneous causes**
Liddle's Syndrome, primary sodium retention	
	Acute stress
Endocrine	Increased intravascular volume
	Aortic valvular insufficiency
Adrenocortical disorders	Arteriovenous fistula
Primary aldosteronism	Licorice ingestion
Bilateral adrenocortical hyperplasia	Sympathomimetics drugs
	Alcohol abuse
Congenital adrenal hyperplasias	Lead poisoning
	Nonsteroidal antinflammatory drugs
Cushing's syndrome	Hypercalcemic status

140/90 mmHg. Likewise, the Third National Health and Nutrition Examination Survey, carried out in the USA has provided important epidemiologic information related to prevalence and control of hypertension in that country. This study consisted of a sample of 9901 people aged over 18 years, and showed a prevalence of hypertension of 24%, as the mean of six evaluations (three taken at home and three at the medical office), the systolic pressure being above 140 mmHg and/or the diastolic above 90 mmHg. The prevalence of hypertension increases with age, being below 10% in males aged between 18 and 29 years and above 50% in those over 60 years; it is higher in black African-Americans than in the white or Mexican-American population. It is higher in men than in women, although cross-sectional studies revealed that this changes in patients aged over 50, when hypertension becomes higher in women, perhaps because of the higher mortality rate in men after this age. The reason why hypertension occurs earlier and more frequently in black persons is unknown. Furthermore, both male and female African-Americans are more liable to exhibit the vascular damage caused by hypertension than are whites; they also show higher rates of cardiovascular complications and higher incidence of chronic renal failure due to hypertension.

Hypertension is about twice as common in those who have at least one parent with hypertension, and epidemiologic studies suggest that genetic factors account for the remarkable variation found in the incidence of hypertension in different populations. A high incidence of hypertension also is associated with environmental factors.

The amount of salt intake has been implicated in the etiology of hypertension; the disease is more common in societies that consume more salt, and it does not usually develop among aboriginal populations whose salt intake is low, although no correlations between salt intake and blood pressure levels have been found. Furthermore, increased salt intake in the normotensive population leads to increased urinary sodium excretion, and no increase in blood pressure is detected. Normotensive subjects reach a new sodium balance with minimal or undetectable increase in blood pressure, whereas hypertensives with increased salt intake need higher blood pressure levels to excrete the salt excess. Their blood pressure constantly rises as a response to the increased salt intake.

Other social and cultural factors and living habits seem to be more clearly associated with increased blood pressure, and, thus, hypertension is more commonly related to obesity, sedentary life, stress, and to an aggressive lifestyle based on economic competition.

Hypertension is the most important cardiovascular risk factor. According to insurance company data, hypertensive patients, considered as a group, have a lower life expectancy than the normotensive population, and this lower life expectancy has been negatively related to high blood pressure. Classic epidemiologic studies, such as the Framingham Study, confirm this fact and prove that increased blood pressure is the principal risk factor in cerebral vascular diseases, heart disease, ischemic coronary disease, and renal failure due to nephrosclerosis.

Several studies report that medical treatment has proved to be the most effective approach to control high blood pressure and to reduce the risk of cardiovascular complications in hypertensive patients. A simple reduction of 5-6 mmHg in the diastolic pressure clearly diminishes the incidence of cardiovascular complications, resulting in a risk reduction of 42% in strokes and 14% in myocardial infarctions. Thus, there are enough data to recommend blood pressure screening programs on a regular basis, with the objective of identifying hypertensive subjects and treating them to reduce their risk of cardiovascular disease and associated morbidity and mortality. Nonetheless, adequate control of blood pressure in the hypertensive population is still far from being achieved. Data from the NHANES-III survey show that although more than 60% of hypertensive patients were aware of it, only about one-half were treated, and only approximately one-fourth of them achieved adequate blood pressure control (140/90 mmHg). Similar data, obtained in the Spanish population, were also disappointing. The analysis of two representative studies, carried out in order to assess blood pressure control in Spanish hypertensive patients treated, showed that the estimated percentage of hypertensive patients achieving blood pressure below 140/90 mmHg accounted for only 16.5% of the hypertensive patients treated.

Different patterns of hypertension

According to the criteria of the Sixth Report of the Joint National Committee on Prevention, Detection, Evaluation and Treatment of High Blood Pressure, hypertension is defined as systolic blood pressure of 140 mmHg or higher, diastolic blood pressure of 90 mmHg or higher, or taking antihypertensive medication. This report also provides a classification of blood pressure for adults 18 years of age and older. Although any classification of blood pressure may be arbitrary, this classification and the definition of several categories according to the different levels of blood pressure are very helpful to clinicians who must make treatment decisions based, among other factors, on blood pressure levels (Tab. 32.2).

During diagnosis, several patterns of hypertension may

Table 32.2 Classification of blood pressure for adults aged 18 years and older

Category	Systolic (mmHg)		Diastolic (mmHg)
Optimal	<120	and	<80
Normal	<130	and	<85
High-normal	130-139	or	85-89
Hypertension			
Stage 1	140-159	or	90-99
Stage 2	160-179	or	100-109
Stage 3	>180	or	>110

(From The Sixth Report of the Joint National Committee on Detection. Evaluation and Treatment of High Blood Pressure. Arch Int Med 1997; 157:2413-46. This definition applies to adults who are not taking antihypertensive drugs and not acutelly ill.)

be seen. First, hypertension may be only systolic or may be accompanied by increased diastolic pressure. Isolated systolic hypertension is common in older people, in whom it is a manifestation of loss of arterial elasticity from atherosclerosis. In these patients, diastolic pressure may be normal or even low. Systolic hypertension may also be a manifestation of an hyperdynamic status resulting from increased beta-adrenergic activity, hyperthyroidism, etc. The Sixth Report of the Joint National Committee concludes that, in older persons, systolic blood pressure is a higher risk factor than diastolic pressure and is a predictor of cardiovascular complications. This report points out that the pulse pressure (systolic blood pressure minus diastolic blood pressure) may be a better marker of cardiovascular risk than the systolic blood pressure itself, and in this group of older patients, the treatment of hypertension is associated with an even greater reduction in cardiovascular risk. *White coat hypertension* is a condition in some patients who have increased blood pressure during office visits that reverts to normal when tested elsewhere. Most patients are anxious when they go to see a physician, and this leads to a remarkable increase in blood pressure not observed at other times. This may occur in 20-30% of patients, and, for a clear diagnosis of hypertension in these patients, ambulatory blood pressure monitoring can be helpful. Labile hypertension is a form of intermittent hypertension that also is referred to as *hyperkinetic syndrome*. This has not been clearly defined, and it is not known whether it represents a pre-hypertensive state that may develop into a sustained form with associated cardiovascular risk. *Borderline hypertension* is the occurrence of occasional readings of blood pressure at the upper limit of normal or slightly higher. Hypertension should be considered resistant or refractory if blood pressure cannot be reduced to below 140/90 mmHg in patients taking a full dose of three appropriate drugs, including a diuretic. Isolated systolic resistant hypertension in older patients is defined as failure to reduce systolic blood pressure below 160 mmHg with a suitable triple drug regimen.

The course of hypertension can be benign or malignant. The benign form of hypertension usually shows no symptoms for years, although prolonged uncontrolled hypertension can cause vascular damage to the arterioles of the eyes, brain, and kidneys, accompanied by left ventricular enlargement. In benign hypertension, the vascular damage is due to a thickening of the arterial walls, leading to progressive narrowing of the lumina of the small arteries and arterioles, but these vascular lesions can remain stable for years, and such a hypertensive patient could eventually die from a cerebrovascular accident or cardiac failure, while renal function remains little affected over time.

Malignant hypertension was first described in 1914 by Volhard and Fahr and is clinically defined by severe hypertension associated with acute retinal changes, with papilledema and renal function deterioration, with rapidly progressive renal failure, and microangiopathic hemolytic anemia. Malignant hypertension can occur as a consequence of essential hypertension and of any form of secondary hypertension. Although malignant hypertension may appear as a first manifestation, it usually occurs as a complication of previously persistent forms of benign hypertension that have not been adequately controlled. Several genetic and environmental factors that lead hypertension to become malignant have been described. These include factors of race (the disease is more common in the black population), presence of determined antigens of the HLA system, poor blood pressure control, smoking, and excessive intake of alcohol and coffee. It also has been reported as associated with the use of contraceptive pills. In malignant hypertension, remarkable increases in plasma renin activity and aldosterone have been described, and the pathologic lesion of the renal vessels in malignant hypertension is characterized by proliferative endarteritis with fibrinoid and necrotizing arteriolitis. Volhard was the first to suggest that malignant hypertension was due to the action of a renal pressor substance released by the renal ischemia caused by reduction of renal blood flow due to severe thickening of the renal arteries, and he suggested that the constriction of the renal arteries caused by this pressor substance could lead to the vicious cycle effect that more vascular damage produces more secretion of the pressor substance, and vice versa.

The first description of this substance was made by Tigerstedt and Bergman, who demonstrated that infusion of extracts of fresh rabbit kidney into normal rabbits produced a prolonged rise in blood pressure, and they called this substance, which is produced by the kidney, renin. The importance of renin in the genesis of hypertension was further documented in 1934 by the landmark experiment of Goldblatt, who demostrated that renal ischemia, induced by constriction of the renal arteries, leads to persistent hypertension in dogs, but more than 20 years passed before the structure of angiotensin II was discovered. Later, in the 1960s, the renin-angiotensin-aldosterone system was clearly defined, and its importance as having a key role in the sodium and potassium balance and blood pressure control was definitively demonstrated.

Etiopathogenesis

A number of factors have been implicated in the pathogenesis of hypertension, and each of these may contribute in a different manner in each individual patient. Genetic factors play an important role, but some environmental factors contribute. For at least three of the latter, salt intake, stress, and obesity, there is good evidence of their significant role in the genesis of hypertension. However, their exact contribution, and the manner in which they may interact to lead to hypertension, is not clearly known. Other factors involved in the pathogenesis of hypertension are: the kidney, the renin-angiotensin system, and the sympathetic nervous system.

Experimental evidence from cross-transplantation studies suggests that the kidney plays a central role in the genesis of hypertension. A defect in the capacity of the kidney to excrete an excess of sodium ingested in the diet has been proposed as the initial mechanism. There are a number of theories to explain how the kidney contributes to the origin of essential hypertension. An inherited defect in renal sodium excretion in relation to a primary resetting of the curve relating blood pressure and urinary sodium excretion – the pressure-natriuresis curve – has been implicated in the origin of hypertension. In hypertensive persons higher blood pressure is needed to maintain a given sodium excretion. Other theories advanced have been:

1. an aberrant response of the tubuloglomerular feedback to salt load;
2. a congenital reduction in the number of nephrons that is associated with low birth weight, with compensatory hypertrophy in existing nephrons that results in glomerular hypertension, progressive glomerular damage, and hypertension;
3. a heterogeneity in the population of nephrons with a minor subgroup of ischemic nephrons with unsuppressible renin secretion and impaired sodium excretion.

Genetics

There is strong evidence confirming that hypertension is more frequent in family members of hypertensive patients. Hypertension is approximately twice as common in those patients who have at least one parent with hypertension, and blood pressure levels are correlated among members of the same family. Several epidemiologic studies also suggest that genetic factors may be responsible for about a 20-40% variation of blood pressure levels in the same population. Hypertension appears to be related to a complex trait that may not be attributable to a single gene locus. Essential hypertension is a polygenic and multifactorial disorder that is a consequence of the interaction of several genes with environmental factors and other lifestyle habits. Recent experimental data have led to the selection of several candidate genes. The human angiotensinogen (Agt) gene has been implicated in some experimental studies, which have demonstrated, with different levels of function of the native angiotensinogen gene, a positive correlation in mice between plasma levels of angiotensinogen, the protein substrate of the renin to generate angiotensin I, and blood pressure values. Increased levels of angiotensinogen have been described in hypertensive patients and in children of hypertensive parents. The other genes that control the renin-angiotensin system – renin, angiotensin-converting enzyme, and angiotensin II-type receptor genes – have not been clearly shown to be associated with hypertension.

Data obtained by cross-transplantation studies in genetic models of hypertension strongly suggest that the inherited defect predisposing to hypertension lies primarily in the kidney, and some investigators have studied the possibility that certain genes may be differentially expressed in the kidneys of animal models of inherited essential hypertension, such as spontaneously hypertensive rats (SHR) and Dahl salt-sensitive rats. One of these genes, the SA gene is expressed in greater amounts in the kidneys of spontaneously hypertensive rats and Dahl salt-sensitive rats compared with other normotensive animals. A higher frequency of the SA genotype also has been found in humans with essential hypertension. Nonetheless, the SA gene product has not yet been defined, and tests must be made to determine whether the SA gene is also found in greater amounts in the kidneys of essential hypertensive patients. Other recent studies on spontaneously hypertensive rats have isolated a region of chromosome 8 that seems to play a major role in hypertension. Transfer of a segment of this region from a normotensive animal resulted in significant reductions of blood pressure.

The genes that encode the membrane-skeleton protein adducin have also been implicated. A mutation in each of the two adducin genes has been demonstrated in genetic hypertensive animal models, and an association of the alpha-adducin locus and salt-sensitive essential hypertension may also be found in humans. This further suggests that the mechanism of hypertension associated with the mutations of the alpha-adducin gene might be, at least in part, due to increased renal tubular sodium transport in the kidney as a consequence of alterations in actin polymerization.

The search for new specific genes continues, and they may be discovered in the near future. Then, physiologic processes regulated by these genes and their contribution to increased blood pressure will be known. At present, there seems to be no doubt that hypertension probably is the consequence of multiple genetic factors acting in conjunction with several environmental influences, and the concept of a "monolithic" single gene defect that causes essential hypertension is extremely unlikely.

Salt intake and blood pressure

The human race is genetically predisposed to eat low quantities of salt. Studies on human nutrition in the Palaeolithic era suggest that Homo sapiens about 40 000 years ago consumed less than 30 mmol of sodium per day. Salt intake rose when human beings discovered its food-preserving properties, and it increased thereafter with the progressively greater consumption of highly-salted preserved food. In fact, only human beings have acquired the habit of consuming salt, and other mammals do not consume excessive salt in their diets. It is likely that increased salt intake is a necessary condition for the development of hypertension, but it is not a sufficient single cause of hypertension. Some epidemiologic studies demonstrated no relationship between blood pressure level and salt intake among individuals living in the same society. Nevertheless, populations with high salt intake appear to have a greater incidence of hypertension compared with people of cultures with very low salt intake, such as the Yanomamo and in Papua New Guinea. In these populations, which eat no salt in their diet, it is well known that hypertension is a rare disorder and that blood pressure does not rise until these people become older. There is a subgroup of essential hypertensive patients who are especially sensitive to the blood pressure effects of high salt intake. These *salt-sensitive* hypertensive patients increase their blood pressure with salt loading and reduce it with sodium restriction. Sodium sensitivity is more frequent in black than in white hypertensive patients, and reduction of blood pressure with sodium restriction depends on the severity of hypertension, being more pronounced in those with higher levels of blood pressure. Although the mechanism of salt sensitivity is not well understood, the pressure action of a high-sodium diet and, conversely, the blunting effect on blood pressure of sodium deprivation suggest that an important role is played by the kidneys through a defect in renal sodium excretion, since the kidneys are the only means to eliminate the sodium consumed in the diet and a deficit in the elimination of the accumulated sodium excess is the main cause of hypertension, which often occurs in chronic renal failure.

Based on the available data, it seems clear that sodium restriction in the diet reduces high blood pressure remarkably in certain salt-sensitive hypertensive subgroups. Although there is no clear evidence to support strict restriction of sodium in all hypertensive patients, moderate sodium restriction appears to be of clear benefit in an overwhelming number of studies. It may prevent the development of hypertension in susceptible people and reduce high levels of blood pressure. However, at present there are no scientific reasons to support the hypothesis that strict salt restriction may prevent the occurrence of hypertension in normal subjects.

RENAL ORIGIN OF ESSENTIAL HYPERTENSION

Cross-transplantation experiments in animal models of genetic hypertension have strongly suggested that the genetic defect causing primary hypertension is a kidney abnormality. These studies were done on different strains of rats: Dahl salt-sensitive rats, spontaneously hypertensive rats, stroke-prone spontaneously hypertensive rats, and Milan hypertensive rats. After bilateral nephrectomy, transplanting a kidney from a hypertensive rat to a normotensive strain of rat produces hypertension in the normotensive rat. In the reverse experiment, transplanting a kidney from a normotensive rat into a young hypertensive strain of rat before hypertension was developed, the rat remains normotensive, and if the normotensive kidney is transplanted to an older rat with sustained hypertension, it lowers the blood pressure significantly. In humans, the study of end-stage renal disease patients who received a kidney transplant suggests that the kidney plays a similar role in the inherited tendency to develop hypertension. Those patients with renal failure who had a kidney transplant from a donor with a hypertensive parent tended to have higher blood pressure and to need more antihypertensive therapy than did those who received a kidney from a donor without a family history of hypertension. In one study done on six African-American hypertensive end-stage renal disease patients suffering from nephrosclerosis and severe refractory hypertension while on dialysis, transplantation of a kidney from young normotensive donors with a negative family history of hypertension led to prolonged normotension with no need for antihypertensive medication.

Resetting of pressure-natriuresis Guyton and co-workers suggested that this primary defect of the kidney is related to the organ's inability to excrete proper quantities of sodium at any given blood pressure level. The relation between sodium excretion and blood pressure is abnormal in all types of experimental and clinical essential hypertension. In cross-transplantation experiments in rats, when the blood pressure increases, there is an incapacity to excrete sodium in relation to the increase of blood pressure, which also suggests that the renal functional defect that produces hypertension could be related to the impaired capacity of the genetically predisposed kidney to excrete sodium. Furthermore, in spontaneously hypertensive rats there is an impaired ability to excrete sodium, in relation to the blood pressure measured at 3 to 7 weeks of age, and this blunted response of renal sodium excretion in relation to increased blood pressure has been associated with increased renal vasoconstriction, due to the thickening of the afferent arterioles.

In healthy normotensive individuals a quantity of ingested sodium normally is excreted in the urine without any change in blood pressure, and if salt ingestion is increased the normotensive subjects will reach a new steady state of extracellular volume and salt balance with minimal elevation of blood pressure, which tends to increase sodium excretion owing to a phenomenon called *pressure natriuresis*. By contrast, in patients with essential hypertension, the same quantities of salt ingested need higher levels of blood pressure for excretion, and the sodium balance – sodium excretion equal to sodium intake – is maintained despite increased blood pressure. Hall, Guyton, and Brands hypothesized that this resetting of the pressure natriuresis effect plays a primary role in causing hypertension and is not an adaptive phenomenon to high blood pressure; they suggest that multiple humoral and intrarenal defects may contribute to this abnormal pressure natriuresis that occurs in essential and other genetic forms of experimental hypertension. These authors have shown two abnormal pressure natriuresis relationships in essential hypertension related to the sensitivity of sodium: a rightward shift of the pressure-natriuresis curve, which may be caused by increased preglomerular vasoconstriction in salt-insensitivity hypertension, and a depressed slope of pressure-natriuresis as a consequence of increased tubule reabsorption of sodium or a decrease in glomerular ultrafiltration coefficient in salt-sensitivity hypertension.

Tubuloglomerular feedback The kidneys receive 1 liter per minute of blood supply, which is the greatest blood supply received by any organ in the body. Blood passes through the glomerular capillaries and produces approximately 100 ml/min of glomerular filtrate. Therefore, about 99% of the amount of glomerular filtrate through glomerular capillaries is reabsorbed along the tubules to produce an amount of 1 ml/min of urine. This very high rate of glomerular filtration, together with the almost 99% tubular reabsorption of the fluid filtered, is needed for the extracellular volume to remain constant throughout a very wide range of changes in fluid and electrolyte intake. In order to maintain the extracellular volume constant despite blood pressure variations, the kidney must keep both the renal blood flow and the glomerular filtration rate constant, and, thus, there is a self-regulation mechanism of renal blood flow by constricting or relaxing the afferent arteriole (myogenic renal response), which allows the renal blood flow to be kept constant. However, glomerular autoregulation also depends on the tubuloglomerular feedback via the juxtaglomerular apparatus.

The tubuloglomerular feedback regulates the contraction or relaxation of the last portion of the afferent arteriole, which does not respond to perfusion pressure changes. This part of the afferent arteriole responds to changes in the delivery rate of chloride to the macula densa. An increase in the glomerular filtration rate produces a higher rate of delivery of tubular fluid to the macula densa, and, thus, the increase in chloride stimulates the cells, which signal the afferent arteriole to constrict, owing to the effects of such vasoactive agents as angiotensin II. It therefore, reduces the glomerular filtration rate and the fluid delivery to the macula densa, resulting in reduced urinary sodium excretion. The tubular feedback activity increases when it is necessary to conserve sodium, as in hypovolemia, and it is reduced in chronic salt loading. An abnormal response of the tubuloglomerular feedback to salt load has been implicated in the pathogenesis of essential hypertension. There are some animal hypertension models, such as the very young spontaneously hypertensive rats, in which there is a paradoxic increase in tubular feedback activity and at the same time there is clear evidence of sodium retention, leading to a rise in blood pressure. This abnormal response of tubuloglomerular feedback returns normal in the twelfth week, by which time blood pressure has increased remarkably.

Because hypertension is rare in human cultures that ingest very little salt, and because high salt intake is a habit that contradicts the function of the kidney, Kurokawa has hypothesised that an abnormal tubuloglomerular feedback response, which may be due to a defective functioning of the juxtaglomerular apparatus, can lead to hypertension only if it is associated with high salt intake. In this case, hypertension is the price we have to pay for the high salt intake of our civilization.

Low birth weight Since 1988 when Gennser and coworkers first described the relationship between low birth weight and hypertension in adults, epidemiologic studies have confirmed that blood pressure could be influenced by the fetal period of life. Low birth weight infants have a higher incidence of hypertension as adults. Furthermore, babies who are small at birth are more likely to have insulin resistance and metabolic abnormalities, such as type II diabetes, hyperlipidemia, and obesity, which are frequently associated with hypertension and coronary disease in later life. Very large epidemiologic studies, such as The Nurses' Health Study which includes 163 940 women and The Health Professionals' Study involving 22 846 men have confirmed this finding.

Brenner and his collaborators advanced the hypothesis of "congenital oligonephropathy", which occurs in low birth weight infants in whom the nephron endowment is reduced because of impaired intrauterine growth, as the cause of hypertension. This hypothesis is that fetal malnutrition causes impairment of nephrogenesis and a congenital nephron deficit. A decreased number of nephrons results in compensatory hypertrophy in the remaining nephrons, associated with intraglomerular hypertension and hyperfiltration, which can lead progressively to proteinuria, segmental glomerular sclerosis of the hyperfiltration type and systemic hypertension after some years.

Experimental data on rodents supporting this hypothesis have been obtained. Maternal protein undernutrition during gestation in rats can cause fetal growth retardation and a reduced number of nephrons in their offspring, both factors associated with hypertension in maturity. These rats develop progressive glomerular lesions. Human infant kidneys with intrauterine growth retardation have been found to be smaller than those of normal infants and to have fewer nephrons than in controls. The association of fetal malnutrition and low birth weight with hypertension in later life could account for the higher prevalence of hypertension in people with low social and economic status, who often have inadequate nutrition. This could also, at least in part, explain the higher prevalence in hypertension among African-Americans in contrast with white Americans. The average socioeconomic status in black Americans is significantly lower than that of other ethnic groups. Women of any ethnic group who have more pregnancies and shorter intervals between them give birth to low-weight infants more often. However, the prevalence of low birth weight is more than double in black women.

The evidence that fetal growth and the number of nephrons at birth is a determinant of blood pressure in adult life may represent an important link between the kidney and the etiology of hypertension. If this is the case, at least in a subgroup of patients with essential hypertension, there will be a preexisting renal disorder characterized by reduced renal mass, which could explain hypertension. These data clearly support the importance of preventing low birth weight. Improvement in maternal nutrition may avoid fetal malnutrition and, consequently, low birth-weight infants, and prevent the later development of hypertension.

Nephron heterogeneity Another hypothesis advanced to explain the role of the kidneys in the genesis of essential hypertension was offered by Sealey on behalf of Laragh's group. They proposed the existence of two groups of functional nephrons in the kidneys of essential hypertensive patients: a smaller population of ischemic hypofiltering nephrons, which chronically hypersecrete renin and have impaired sodium excretion, as well as a larger group of adapting hyperfiltering nephrons, which excrete the sodium excess. The latter exhibit increased glomerular filtration rates and enhance distal sodium supply, and thus chronically suppress renin secretion. The presence of these two nephron populations alters the normal balance between the intake and excretion of sodium in a manner similar to that occurring in the interaction between the two kidneys in the Goldblatt two-kidney one-clip model. In this hypothesis, the normal population of nephrons cannot compensate completely for the sodium retention due to the renin secretion coming from the remaining ischemic nephrons, which attenuates the compensatory natriuresis by causing constriction of the afferent arteriole of the hyperfiltering nephrons and enhancing proximal tubular reabsorption. This discord between the two types of nephrons may result in chronic sodium retention in the face of abnormally high renin levels. This situation provides a basis for observing that treatment with angiotensin-converting enzyme inhibitors in essential hypertension increases renal blood flow and sodium excretion, normalizing blood pressure even in the presence of normal renin levels, because the effect of circulating renin on the hyperfiltrating nephrons stimulates tubular sodium reabsorption and impairs sodium excretion. In addition, this hypothesis could explain why renin secretion is not adequately suppressed in patients with essential hypertension.

RENIN-ANGIOTENSIN SYSTEM

Probably the most important contribution to modern knowledge of hypertension was the discovery of the renin-angiotensin system. Renin was the name given by Tigerstedt and Bergman to a pressure substance obtained from the saline extracts of rabbit kidney. This enzyme is secreted by the renal cells of the juxtaglomerular apparatus, which are localized in the wall of the afferent arteriole next to the area of the macula densa of the same nephron. The renin-angiotensin system has been considered to be the main regulator of intravascular volume and systemic blood pressure. The renin is secreted in response to changes in renal perfusion (e.g., hypovolemia, heart failure, or renal damage) detected by the pressure changes of the afferent arteriole and the sodium content of the macula densa. The renin acts on the renin substrate, angiotensinogen, transforming it into a decapeptide, angiotensin I, on which a converting enzyme, present on the plasma membrane of the endothelial cells, acts hydrolyzing its two terminal aminoacids and forming an octapeptide, angiotensin II (A II). The latter is a powerful vasoconstrictor and acts immediately, producing constriction of the arterioles – and this results in increased blood pressure. At the same time, A II induces the secretion of aldosterone from the adrenal cortex, which also tries to restore the extracellular volume by increasing the tubular reabsorption of sodium. The restoration of the extracellular volume improves the renal blood flow and sodium content of the macula densa and disconnects the releasing signal of renin. Nephrectomized subjects have low plasma renin levels, although components of the renin-angiotensin system have been found in many tissues and its generation and participation have been demonstrated in several local and systemic effects at the level of brain, heart, and other organs.

The A II, final product of the system, is the most important factor, and its activity reflects complex interactions. Two major A II receptors recently have been cloned, AT1 and AT2. Most of the known effects of A II, at least in humans, are AT1-mediated; however, AT2 seems to play a functional role at the renal level. A II acts by binding to its receptors not only in the vascular smooth muscle and the suprarenal cortex, but also in the kidneys, heart, central nervous system, and the adrenergic nerves. Some investigators have suggested that the systemic renin-angiotensin system is important for acute intravascular volume regulation, and the local tissue renin-angiotensin system could be more involved in chronic renal vasculature regulation. In fact, plasma renin activity does not reflect A II renal production. The concentration of A II is more than 1000 times higher in the kidney than in plasma. A II produces vasoconstriction after binding to the vascular AT1 vascular receptors, probably through adenilcyclase inhibition mediated by protein G, causing a sustained increase in blood pressure. Locally in the kidney, A II binds to the receptors of the glomerulus and causes constriction of the mesangial cells and of the afferent and efferent arterioles, altering the glomerular ultrafiltration coefficient. The magnitude of the vasoconstrictive effect induced by A II is higher in the efferent than in the afferent arterioles of the kidney, and this difference is responsible, at least in part, for the renoprotective effects obtained by blocking the renin-angiotensin system with angiotensin-converting enzyme inhibitors acting on glomerular hemodynamics decreasing intraglomerular pressure. The other major effect of A II is related to the stimulation of adrenocortical secretion of aldosterone, which produces a progressive expansion of the extracellular volume due to increase sodium reabsorption and at the cost of potassium loss. These vasoconstrictive and sodium retention effects convert A II into the main defense against volume depletion and add two important hypertensinogenic effects.

A II is also important as a mesangial and vascular growth factor. Several recent findings suggest a key role of A II in the vascular muscle cell growth that can occur as a consequence of hypertension and vascular injury. There is enough evidence to suggest significant participation of A II as a growth factor in cardiac and renal vessels and in the progression of renal damage, increasing the production of matrix proteins by mesangial and epithelial cells and by fibroblasts. Some data have shown that blocking the renin-angiotensin system with angiotensin-converting enzyme inhibitors or AII receptor antagonists has a beneficial effect in experimental models of renal injury and in human studies of diabetic and nondiabetic renal disease and heart hypertrophy, probably reflecting this beneficial effect of the inhibition of the AII effect as a vascular and mesangial growth factor.

Renin hypersecretion is clearly the cause of hypertension in two clinical situations: in patients with renin-secreting tumors; in some patients with end-stage renal disease and hypertension resistant to volume depletion while on dialysis. It has also been experimentally demonstrated that chronic infusion of A II in normal volunteers produces hypertension associated with a positive sodium balance. This effect may be achieved with small doses of A II, and even low doses insufficient to cause an immediate increase in blood pressure in animal models could cause a gradual rise in blood pressure over a period of days. When A II is infused in normal subjects, there is an initial state of A II-induced vasoconstriction, which is gradually replaced by a positive sodium balance because aldosterone secretion increases tubular reabsorption of sodium. As more sodium is retained, the A II pressure effect becomes more important owing to this increasing sensitivity to A II, and the resulted volume expansion can maintain the hypertension with diminished small doses of infused A II.

Predictably, in patients with essential hypertension increased perfusion pressure in the juxtaglomerular cell and the normal or even high extracellular volume usually found in these subjects, there is suppression of renin release and low plasma renin activity (PRA). Some investigators have shown higher levels of plasma renin activity in normal persons compared with those with essential hypertension. Nevertheless, most of these hypertensive patients have normal or increased plasma renin activity levels, and only 30% have low renin values. This fact has led to thorough investigation of the participation of these inadequately increased levels of renin on the pathogenesis of essential hypertension.

Since the early 1970s, Laragh and collaborators have attributed great significance to renin levels in patients with essential hypertension. They divide hypertensive patients into two groups: hypertensive patients with increased renin and hypertensive patients with normal or low renin levels. According to Laragh's hypothesis, in relation to the renin-angiotensin system involvement in hypertension, a continuous spectrum is suggested. At one pole of the spectrum, hypertension is maintained and probably caused by the vasoconstrictive forces of the renin system (high-renin hypertension); at the other pole, hypertension is sustained by sodium retention and volume expansion (low-renin hypertension).

According to this bipolar analysis, the arteriolar vasoconstriction due to A II, accounts for hypertension in hyperreninemic patients, whereas in hyporreninemic patients the responsibility lies in the volume expansion. The existence of these two mechanisms – renin-mediated and sodium-mediated – in the pathogenesis of hypertension is substantiated by Goldblatt's two experimental models of renovascular hypertension. If one kidney is clipped and the other left intact, when renin secretion is stimulated by the low perfused clipped kidney, hypertension results from the renin-induced vasoconstriction, and the sodium-retaining effect is compensated by the increased pressure natriuresis caused by the unclipped kidney. But when the unclipped kidney is removed, or when both kidneys are clipped, the effective filtration rate is compromised. This results in the inability of the kidney to excrete the sodium retained, causing accumulation of fluid and volume expansion, which depresses the renin secretion and leads to a sodium-volume-induced hypertension. However, some researchers have not demonstrated this bipolar relationship in plasma renin levels, and the role of the renin-angiotensin system in renovascular hypertension is not well defined. In a proportion of patients with hypertension due to renal artery stenosis, blood pressure is normalized after correction of renal artery stenosis by surgery in spite of previous preoperative normal levels of plasma renin activity. Furthermore, in other patients with renal artery stenosis and high plasma renin hypertension, corrective renal artery surgery restores the high renin to normal levels, without correcting hypertension. The greatest difficulty found in the analysis of these differences in renin values is perhaps that the studies were carried out at different stages of development of renovascular hypertension. In most cases the hypertension had been established for a long time.

In experimental renovascular hypertension there is a transient increase in plasma renin activity immediately after the clipping of renal artery, showing a normal response to renal ischemia. This increase in renin levels seems to be responsible for the blood pressure elevation, since this hypertension may be prevented by blocking the renin-angiotensin system with angiotensin-converting enzyme inhibitors. However, plasma renin levels begin to decrease after hypertension has been maintained for a variable period, and after 3 to 6 months of hypertension due to experimental renal artery constriction in the rat, plasma renin activity usually is normal.

Bing and co-workers have demonstrated that in rats with Goldblatt two-kidney one-clip hypertension, the infusion of saralasin, a competitive antagonist of A II, in the early phase (36 days after clipping) produced a significant fall in blood pressure. In this phase, plasma renin activity increased remarkably, and the fall in blood pressure correlated significantly with plasma renin activity. Nevertheless, in the chronic phase (151 days after clipping) plasma renin activity was normal, and there was no response to saralasin infusion in this phase. In this study, the removal of the renal artery constriction normalized blood pressure in most animals. Although vascular hypertrophy also has been suggested as the mechanism that maintains hypertension in the chronic phase of renal artery constriction, this does not clearly explain how the release of arterial constriction can correct hypertension.

The implied role of the renin-angiotensin system in the pathogenesis of renovascular hypertension provides the basis for its diagnosis. Renin secretion is increased in the affected kidney owing to ischemia and is suppressed in the contralateral organ, in which the raised systemic blood pressure shuts off the renin secretion in the normal kidney. In unilateral renovascular hypertension, the measurement of renin concentration after the oral administration of an angiotensin-converting enzyme inhibitor, such as captopril (captopril test), could be very useful in the diagnosis. Captopril produces a marked increase in renin secretion from the renal vein of the affected ischemic kidney, and the plasma renin activity could be increased to about 150% of the baseline value in renovascular disease compared with essential hypertension. In bilateral renovascular disease and in the experimental one-kidney Goldblatt model (one kidney is clipped and the other is removed) the inability to excrete the sodium and water excess due to the increased secretion of aldosterone by A II stimulation because of the absence of a functioning contralateral kidney produces a volume expansion that restores the perfusion pressure in the kidneys involved and "shuts off" renin secretion to normal or depressed levels. This normalization of the renin-angiotensin system is achieved at the cost of sodium retention, volume expansion, and sustained hypertension. In this case, sodium dependence hypertension can be demonstrated by the absence of hypertension response to the infusion of A II blocking drugs in animals with the Goldblatt one-clip one-kidney model without sodium restriction. In this model, sodium depletion again increases the renin level, transforming the volume-dependent hypertension into renin-dependent hypertension. The latter can be sensitive to renin-angiotensin system blocking drugs in a continuous equilibrium between renin secretion by the affected kidney and the sodium retention-volume expansion that maintains the hypertension.

Patients with bilateral renovascular disease or with renal artery stenosis in one functioning kidney, e.g., renal transplantation patients, may show a renal function deterioration or even acute renal failure associated with the lowering of blood pressure when drugs that block the renin-angiotensin system are given. This is a consequence of the attenuation of the vasoconstrictor effect of the A II on glomerular vessels, particularly the efferent arteriole. The blockade of the A II effect produces an abrupt dilatation of the constricted glomerular efferent arteriole, which maintains the glomerular filtration rate and produces a dramatic decline in renal function. These patients with bilateral renal artery disease also have difficulty in managing acute sodium and volume loads, and the acute pulmonary edema associated with hypertensive crisis is more common in them than in patients with unilateral disease, particularly when renal function is diminished. The importance of sodium-volume factors in its pathogenesis could be indicated by the higher cardiac output found in these patients.

RENOMEDULLARY ANTIHYPERTENSIVE SYSTEM

The kidney also plays a role in blood pressure control through the secretion of a renomedullary vasodepressing hormone, discovered by Muirhead and collaborators after 40 years of persistent experimental work. The observation of Grollman and associates in 1949 that the hypertension produced by bilateral nephrectomy is not wholly explained by sodium-volume retention (since the same degrees of uremia and volume expansion produced no hypertension in dogs with unilateral nephrectomy and ureterocaval anastomosis) suggests that the presence of the remaining kidney protected the animals from uremia and volume-dependent hypertension. The observations that suggest that this renal substance with hypotensive properties were contained in some renomedullary components came from experiments performed in animals when fragments of tissue culture of murine renal papilla of a healthy animal were subcutaneously or intraperitoneally transplanted in other animals with experimental hypertension of the sodium-volume-dependent type. Even in animals with Goldblatt one-kidney one-clip model, the hypertensive animals showed significantly reduced blood pressure. The antihypertensive effect disappears when the papillary transplant is rejected or removed. Muirhead and co-workers further demonstrated that autotransplantation of the renal medulla also reverses hypertension in bilaterally nephrectomized sodium-loaded hypertensive animals in whom renal cortical transplants produced no effect. This renomedullary substance is secreted by the interstitial cells of the renal papilla and is a lipid named medullipin I, which is conveyed to the liver to be activated into medullipin II. This activation involves the enzymatic system cytocrome P 450, dependent on the liver. Medullipin II is a vasodilator that opposes the actions of A II, suppresses the sympathetic activity, and increases the excretion of sodium: the main factor that stimulates the secretion of medullipin is the increase in renal perfusion pressure. Medullipin had been obtained in great quantities in the renal venous effluent associated with a degranulation of the medullary interstitial cells when the renal perfusion pressure was suddenly increased by unclipping a one-kidney one-clip hypertensive rat model, and it has been shown in numerous experiments in animals that an increase of renal perfusion produces a fall in blood pressure. Further, this provides significant evidence that this vasodepressive lipid may be an important factor responsible for the blood pressure fall occurring about 24 hours after the renal artery deconstriction in the Goldblatt hypertensive model. In another interesting experiment, Gothberg and co-workers showed that when a normal rat is infused with the venous effluent of the ischemic clipped kidney of the two-kidney one-clip hypertensive rat, declipping the kidney produced a profound fall in blood pressure, clearly suggesting that a hypotensive substance released by the suddenly hyperperfused kidney could be responsible for the blood pressure fall that occurs in the extracorporeally perfused normal rat. This hypotensive response depends on the integrity of the renal medulla, and is not modified by renal denervation or by blocking the renin-angiotensin system. This renomedullary antihypertensive system may contribute to the blood pressure fall that occurs after surgical correction of renal artery stenosis in renovascular hypertension.

The secretion of medullipin may be inhibited by A II sympathetic nerve stimulation, by the inhibition of nitric oxide synthase, or by bilateral nephrectomy or chemical medullectomy with injection of a nephrotoxic substance, bromoethylamine hydrobromide, which produces a selective dose-dependent destruction of the renal medulla. The significance of the renomedullary system in blood pressure control in the normal situation is unknown. The granules of the papillary interstitial cells that contain lipids, either intact or disrupted, do not have a hypotensive action when they are injected intravenously. Some forms of experimental hypertension, however, are associated with degenerative changes and a significant decrease in the lipid granules. A syndrome of hyperproduction of medullipin by the interstitial medullary cells, associated with persistent nonorthostatic hypotension also has been described in a patient with advanced renal insufficiency.

SYMPATHETIC NERVOUS SYSTEM AND THE KIDNEY

The sympathetic nervous system is involved in the pathogenesis of essential hypertension. Clinical evidence demonstrates that blood pressure increases with vasomotor alarm reactions, and the beneficial effects of tranquilizers and autonomic blocking drugs are well recognized. This importance of the sympathetic nervous system in the development of hypertension has been confirmed by animal studies, which found severe hypertension in mice subjected to a continuous psychosocial stress, and most authors agree that the sympathetic nervous system makes an important contribution to the onset and maintenance of hypertension. The hypersecretion of catecholamines by the very rare tumors of chromaffin tissue (pheochromocytoma) is a cause of severe hypertension that may be surgically curable.

The sympathetic nervous system plays an important role in circulatory homeostasis through its vascular and cardiac effects, which increase peripheral resistance directly by stimulation of arteriolar vasoconstriction and activation of the renin-angiotensin system. Furthermore, it also increases cardiac output as a result of augmented cardiac contractility and venous return, thus stimulating renal sodium retention. The interactions between the sympathetic nervous system and the kidney in blood pressure control are still not well understood. Adrenergic innervation has been identified in the proximal and distal tubules and in Henle's loop, and sympathetic activity appears to be increased in situations of depletion of effective circulatory volume. In these situations, norepinephrine, a powerful vasoconstrictor, acts to reduce renal blood flow in order to preserve critical coronary and cerebral circulation. Augmented sympathetic activity also increases sodium reabsorption by direct stimulation of proximal and loop sodium transport, mediated by the alpha-1-adrenergic receptors and by activation of the renin-angiotensin system through beta-1-adrenergic receptors and tends to raise the blood pressure. Increased sympathetic activity to the kidney by means of sodium retention could alter the pressure-natriuresis relationship, preventing the perfusion pressure natriuresis, which has a key role in Guyton's theory of hypertension etiology.

It is not possible to confirm whether primary sympathetic hyperactivity plays a central role in the pathogenesis of essential hypertension in humans. However, the sympathetic nervous system has at least a permissive role in the initiation and development of some forms of hypertension. Despite high blood pressure, essential hypertensive patients have been characterized by increased sympathetic nervous system activity and increased peripheral vascular resistance. In a subgroup of essential hypertensive subjects, sympathetic hyperactivity was involved in insulin resistance associated with hypertension. In patients with renovascular hypertension, increased angiotensin II levels have been associated with enhanced muscle sympathetic nervous activity, and this increased sympathetic activity was normalized after the renal artery stenosis was corrected. In patients with chronic renal failure who retain their natural kidneys, hypertension, although largely volume-dependent, also is associated with sympathetic nervous muscular hyperactivity and increased systemic vascular resistance. These augmented responses were normalized after bilateral nephrectomy, suggesting that chronic renal failure is accompanied by sympathetic activation that depends on a signal originating in the diseased kidneys.

The renal sympathetic nerves innervate the preglomerular and postglomerular vasculature, the juxtaglomerular apparatus, and all the segments of the nephron, including the renal tubules. Increased activity of the sympathetic nervous system causes not only renal vasoconstriction but also release of renin and other vasoactive substances promoting renal tubular sodium reabsorption. In spontaneously hypertensive rats, renal denervation delays the onset and slows the increase of blood pressure, and this blood pressure lowering effect of renal denervation has been related to augmented sodium excretion. Conversely, reinnervation was associated with sodium retention in this animal model. Thus, alterations in renal sympathetic activity can produce changes in several renal functions and may facilitate the maintenance of hypertension by shifting the pressure natriuresis curve as a consequence of sodium retention, interfering with the ability of the kidney to compensate for the increase in blood pressure through pressure natriuresis.

ENDOTHELIUM-DERIVED VASOACTIVE FACTORS

The most important vasoactive factors synthezised in the endothelium are: endothelin, which is a vasoconstrictor, and nitric oxide, a vasodilator. Both factors can modulate the renal function, and both have been implicated in the genesis of essential hypertension, although there is still not enough evidence to suggest that these endothelial hormones have an important role in the pathogenesis of essential hypertension.

Endothelin-1 Endothelin-1 (ET-1) is the most potent endogenous vasoconstrictor known. It is produced by most types of renal cells and has a wide range of effects on the kidneys apart from the constriction of renal vessels. These include inhibition of sodium and water reabsorption, which can contribute to the development and maintenance of hypertension associated with its effects on the vasculature. However plasma ET-1 levels usually are normal in essential hypertensive subjects. ET-1 also acts as a renal growth factor and alters the mesangial function, producing mesangial cell contraction and proliferation and extracellular matrix proliferation. Because of this action ET-1 has been implicated in renal disease progression in diabetes mellitus and other chronic renal disorders. Since the kidney is a major site of ET-1 metabolism, renal dysfunction may prolong its half-life. In fact, ET-1 clearance is reduced in patients with renal failure. In patients with renal disease, deranged ET-1 production in the nephron associated with the impaired renal clearance may contribute to hypertension.

Nitric oxide (NO) the endothelium-derived relaxing factor, synthesised in the endothelium by a constitutive nitric oxide synthase, is also produced in the kidney, and plays an important role in the control of some processes that regulate the renal response to changes in blood perfusion pressure. The kidney is particularly sensitive to variations of nitric oxide synthesis. Although no clear role of deficient nitric oxide production in the genesis of essential hypertension has been established, it has been found that certain animal models of hypertension and some types of human hypertension are related to decreased synthesis of nitric oxide, and recent experimental studies seem consistent with this hypothesis. In animal models, the acute blockade of nitric oxide synthesis reduces sodium excretion and increases renal vascular resistance without causing changes in the systemic blood pressure. However, chronic administration of inhibitors of nitric oxide synthesis leads to the development of hypertension, and renal damage occurs when the inhibition of nitric oxide synthesis is prolonged.

Patients with essential hypertension often have endothelial dysfunction, and it has been reported that offspring of parents with essential hypertension have a reduced vasodilator response to acetylcholine, which could be improved by the infusion of L-arginine, a nitric oxide precursor. However, the vasodilator response of the endothelium-independent vasodilator nitroprusside is normal in these offspring. Nevertheless, in patients with established essential hypertension, several studies have found no differences between endothelium-dependent and endothelium-independent vasodilatation responses. These data may support the suggestion that, at least in some patients, an impairment of nitric oxide production could precede the onset of hypertension. Renal production of nitric oxide is involved in the control of renal hemodynamics and tubular reabsorption of sodium, and seems also to be involved in the control of renin release by the macula densa. The vasodilatation induced by insulin appears to be mediated by increased nitric oxide synthesis. This further suggests that decreased production of nitric oxide could contribute to the metabolic syndrome which associates insulin resistance and hypertension. All these observations could explain the role of decreased production of nitric oxide in the development of some forms of hypertension.

ESSENTIAL HYPERTENSION AND KIDNEY DAMAGE

Patients with persistent uncontrolled hypertension may develop chronic renal failure. Malignant hypertension usually produces a rapid deterioration of renal function, and pathologic findings show an association with fibrinoid and necrotizing arteriolitis in renal arterioles and intimal mucoid thickening in small renal arteries.

Nevertheless, most hypertensive patients follow the benign course of essential hypertension. The renal lesion of the benign form of primary hypertension has been termed *benign nephrosclerosis*. Hypertension is associated with frequent vascular lesions in the kidney, which range from small intimal changes in otherwise normal arterioles to severe hyaline degeneration and intimal fibrosis of the arteriolar walls. This leads to a progressive luminal narrowing, which decreases the glomerular blood flow and produces glomerular ischemia and progressive renal damage. Persistent intraglomerular hypertension, due to transmission of high blood pressure to the glomeruli, also has been suggested as an explanation for the progressive renal failure seen in patients with uncontrolled hypertension. As a consequence of systemic hypertension the afferent arterioles become progressively dilated, and this allows a linear transmission of pressure into the glomerular capillaries, leading to glomerular hypertension. Glomerular hypertension plays an important role in the progression of renal damage through the mediation of several growth factors and cytokines; thus causing glomerular injury, progressive glomerulosclerosis, and renal function deterioration. In fact, some experimental studies in animals have found slower progression of renal damage in hypertensive animals treated with drugs that block the renin-angiotensin system, and thereby lower glomerular capillary pressure by their dilating effect, which acts preferentially on the efferent glomerular arteriole.

The risk of chronic renal failure from prolonged uncontrolled hypertension is greater in black people, in whom the incidence of end-stage renal disease due to nephrosclerosis is 10 to 20 times higher than in the white population. Although some authors have found a very high incidence of renal involvement in patients with essential hypertension not given antihypertensive treatment, it must be noted that the percentage of patients with mild or moderate hypertension who have developed chronic renal failure is very small – less than 1% after 15 years – at least when hypertension is adequately treated. It is clear that appropriate blood pressure control prevents the development of renal damage and stabilizes the level of renal function in patients with nephrosclerosis. There are, however, some hypertensive patients who have developed slowly progressive renal failure despite appropriate control of hypertension. The reason why nephrosclerosis can progress in some susceptible subjects and not in others is still unknown. Some authors who do not believe that benign hypertension itself can cause progressive renal damage think that the glomerular changes are evidence of an underlying primary renal disease that led to hypertension and, at the same time, was worsened by hypertension. Some epidemiologic studies have correlated levels of blood pressure with birth weight, suggesting that the renal defect could be a deficit of nephrons at birth in infants with intrauterine growth retardation who also have kidneys smaller than those of controls. This also would result in hypertension and favor renal injury and glomerular lesions due to reduced renal mass and would promote progression of renal failure.

The classic recommendations for controlling blood pressure (140/90 mmHg) may not be enough to prevent nephrosclerosis in susceptible patients, and it is possible that more aggressive control of blood pressure – maintaining a target of 130/85 mmHg or less – could be beneficial in preventing development of renal disease in susceptible hypertensive patients, e.g., black people. Some epidemiologic studies demonstrating that higher blood pressures are associated with more frequent renal damage over the years are compatible with this hypothesis, but rigorous controlled studies are needed. In patients who present with renal damage, however, recent recommendations of the VI Report of the Joint National Committee have suggested more strict control of blood pressure: blood pressure should be kept below 130/85 mmHg in an attempt to slow the progression of renal disease.

Suggested readings

BURT VL, CULTER JA, HIGGINS M, et al. Trends in the prevalence, awareness, treatment and control of hypertension in the adult US population. Data from the health examination surveys, 1960 to 1991. Hypertension 1995;1:60-9.

CONVERSE RL, JACOBSEN TN, TOTO RD, et al. Sympathetic overactivity in patients with chronic renal failure. N Engl J Med 1992;327:1912-8.

DE WARDENER HE, MACGREGOR GA. Blood pressure and the kidney. In: Schrier RW, Gottschalk CW, eds. Diseases of the kidney. Boston: Little, Brown and Company 1996;1303-32.

DIBONA GF. The kidney in the pathogenesis of hypertension: the role of renal nerves. Am J Kidney Dis 1995;5:A27-A31.

GUYTON AC, COLEMAN TG, COWLEY AW, et al. Arterial pressure regulation. Overriding dominance of the kidneys in long-term regulation and in hypertension. Am J Med 1972;52:584-94.

HALL JE, GUYTON AC, BRANDS MW. Pressure-volume regulation in hypertension. Kidney Int 1996;49(suppl 55):s35-s41.

KING AW. Endothelins: multifunctional peptides with potent vasoactive properties. In: Laragh JH, Brenner BM, eds. Hypertension. Pathophysiology. Diagnosis and management. New York: Raven Press 1995;631-72.

LAHERA V, NAVARRO J, CACHOFEIRO V, et al. Nitric oxide, the kidney and hypertension. Am J Hypertens 1997;10:129-40.

LARAGH JH, BLUMENFELD JD. Essential hypertension. In: Brenner BM, ed. The kidney. Philadelphia: WB Saunders 1996;2071-5.

MACKENZIE HS, BRENNER BM. Fewer nephrons at birth: a missing link in the etiology of essential hypertension. Am J Kidney Dis 1995;26:91-8.

MUIRHEAD EE, RIGHTSEL WA, LEACH BE, et al. Reversal of hypertension by transplants and lipid extracts of cultured renomedullary interstitial cells. Lab Invest 1997;36:162-72.

SWALES JD. The kidney and control of blood pressure. In: Davison A. Oxford Textbook of clinical nephrology. Oxford: Oxford University Press 1998;1413-23.

SHEPS SG. In Sixth Report of the Joint National Committee on Prevention, Detection, Evaluation and Treatment of High Blood Pressure. Arch Intern Med 1997;157:2413-46.

WARD R. Familial aggregation and genetic epidemiology of blood pressure. In: Laragh JH, Brenner BM, eds. Hypertension: pathophysiology, diagnosis and management. New York: Raven Press 1995;67-8.

ZUCCHELLI P, ZUCCALA A, Primary hypertension. How does it cause renail failure? Nephrol Dial Transplant 1994;9:223-7.

CHAPTER

33

Renal and renovascular hypertension

Ali Taha Hassan, Fadi G. Lakkis, Manuel Martinez-Maldonado

KEY POINTS

- Renal parenchymal hypertension is caused by either bilateral or unilateral renal disease and is the most common cause of secondary hypertension.
- Blood pressure control in renal parenchymal hypertension may require multiple therapeutic approaches that include dietary sodium restriction, diuretics, and antihypertensive agents that lower total peripheral vascular resistance.
- Renovascular hypertension results from unilateral and bilateral vascular lesions that cause renal ischemia.
- Renal arterial lesions that cause hypertension are classified as atherosclerotic or fibrous. Atherosclerotic lesions predominantly affect men over the age of 40. Fibrous renal lesions are the most common cause of renovascular hypertension in persons under 40, and are much more common in women than in men.
- Management of renovascular hypertension has two therapeutic goals: normalizing blood pressure and preventing ischemic renal damage. The most effective medical management is the use of antihypertensive agents that block components of the renin-angiotensin system. Nonmedical management includes surgical revascularization or percutaneous transluminal renal angioplasty, and vascular stents.

Renal parenchymal and renovascular diseases are the most common causes of secondary hypertension. Novel diagnostic tools, antihypertensive agents, and surgical techniques have enhanced our ability to identify and treat patients with renal and renovascular hypertension. Prompt diagnosis and management of these patients prevent the systemic complications of high blood pressure and, in many cases, preserves renal function.

RENAL PARENCHYMAL HYPERTENSION

Prevalence and etiology

Renal parenchymal hypertension is a form of secondary hypertension caused by intrinsic renal disease. It accounts for 2.5% to 5.0% of all cases of systemic hypertension. Hypertension is both a cause and consequence of renal disease, making it difficult at times to distinguish renal parenchymal hypertension from essential hypertension.

Renal parenchymal hypertension is caused by either unilateral or bilateral renal disease (Tab. 33.1). Causes of unilateral lesions include tumors which secrete renin or lead to increased renin secretion by the surrounding renal parenchyma. Occasionally, renal disorders such as reflux nephropathy or pyelonephritis involving one kidney cause systemic hypertension. Although rodent studies suggest that unilateral nephrectomy leads to hypertension, humans who have been renal transplant donors or those who undergo unilateral nephrectomy for other reasons have not been found to be at increased risk for hypertension. In contrast, patients with unilateral renal agenesis or those who lost more than 50% of their renal mass have increased blood pressure. It is hypothesized that hypertension associated with unilateral renal agenesis is caused by unrecognized congenital disease in the contralateral kidney.

Both acute and chronic bilateral renal parenchymal disorders lead to hypertension (Tab. 33.1). The incidence of hypertension in patients with acute glomerulonephritis or acute vasculitis is greater than that observed in patients with acute tubulointerstitial disorders such as acute tubular necrosis (70% versus 15%). In many of these patients, hypertension persists despite resolution of the acute insult. Patients with chronic renal disease develop hypertension even when the glomerular filtration rate (GFR) is normal. The prevalence of hypertension increases as renal function declines and approaches 90% by the time end-stage renal disease sets in. Epidemiologic studies indicate that hypertension is more common in chronic glomerular than in chronic interstitial disorders. Among the glomerulonephritides, membranoproliferative pathologic change and focal segmental sclerosis are associated with the highest prevalence of hypertension. Diabetic nephropathy is a leading etiology of end-stage renal disease in the United States and is a major cause of renal parenchymal hypertension. Approximately 60% of patients with diabetic nephropathy have elevated blood pressure.

Table 33.1 The causes of renal parenchymal hypertension

Unilateral renal disorders
- Renin-secreting tumors (benign JGA cell tumors)
- Wilms' tumor
- Renal cell carcinoma
- Intrarenal or perinephric hematoma
- Extracorporeal shock wave lithotripsy
- Radiation nephritis
- Reflux nephropathy
- Urinary tract obstruction
- Chronic pyelonephritis
- Unilateral renal agenesis
- Others (simple cysts, renal tuberculosis, renal infarction, segmental hypoplasia)

Bilateral renal disorders
- Acute disorders
  - Glomerulonephritis
  - Systemic and renal vasculitis
  - Interstitial nephritis
  - Microangiopathy (HUS/TTP)
  - Acute tubular necrosis
  - Urinary tract obstruction
- Chronic disorders
  - Diabetic nephropathy
  - Hypertensive nephrosclerosis*
  - Scleroderma
  - Glomerulonephritis, vasculitis, and interstitial nephritis
  - Analgesic nephropathy
  - Polycystic kidney disease
  - Radiation nephritis
  - End-stage renal disease of any cause

*Hypertension causes renal damage, which, in turn, causes more hypertension. Normalizing blood pressure can break this vicious cycle.

Pathophysiology

Renal parenchymal hypertension is mediated by two main pathogenetic mechanisms: increased extracellular fluid (ECF) volume due to sodium retention and increased total peripheral resistance (TPR) due to vasoconstriction. The role of sodium retention in renal parenchymal hypertension is suggested by data demonstrating that: (1) patients with renal insufficiency have increased total exchangeable sodium (compared with control patients with essential hypertension); (2) blood pressure elevation in these patients correlates with total plasma volume; and (3) changes in sodium intake or excretion directly influence blood pressure, especially in patients with advanced renal failure. Despite these observations, not all patients with renal parenchymal hypertension have increased ECF volume, and, in fact, the most consistently observed hemodynamic abnormality in renal parenchymal hypertension is increased TPR. Experimental studies by Guyton and colleagues have underscored the interaction between sodium retention and vasoconstriction in the pathogenesis of hypertension. First, isolated elevations in TPR do not lead to hypertension without concomitant sodium retention. Second, although sodium retention may initiate hypertension, ECF volume and cardiac output return to baseline, and hypertension is then sustained by increased TPR. Renal parenchymal hypertension, therefore, results from the integrated actions of factors that regulate vascular resistance and sodium handling by the kidney. These factors are summarized in Table 33.2.

An important role of the renin-angiotensin system in

Table 33.2 Factors that regulate extracellular fluid volume and total peripheral vascular resistance in renal parenchymal hypertension

Antinatriuretics
- Angiotensin II
- Norepinephrine
- Thromboxane A2*
- Endothelin*

Natriuretics*
- Atrial natriuretic peptide
- Endogenous digitalis-like factor
- Nitric oxide
- Prostaglandin E_2 and prostacyclin
- Kinins

Vasoconstrictors
- Angiotensin II
- Norepinephrine
- Arginine vasopressin (ADH)
- Endogenous digitalis-like factor*
- Endothelin*
- Thromboxane A2*

Vasodilators
- Nitric oxide
- Atrial natriuretic peptide*
- Prostaglandin E_2 and prostacyclin*
- Kinins*

*Data in this context are mostly from experimental animals.

the initiation and maintenance of renal parenchymal hypertension is suggested by several clinical findings. First, plasma renin activity and angiotensin II levels are increased in hypertensive patients with mild to moderate renal insufficiency. Second, plasma renin activity and angiotensin II levels correlate with the severity of hypertension in these patients. Third, blockade of angiotensin II production or action effectively reduces high blood pressure associated with mild to moderate renal insufficiency. The role of the renin-angiotensin levels in hypertensive end-stage renal disease patients, on the other hand, is controversial. Hypertension in the majority of these patients responds to removal of excess ECF volume, suggesting that TPR is normal. High renin and angiotensin levels, however, are present in 20% of hypertensive end-stage renal disease patients who respond to treatment with angiotensin-converting enzyme (ACE) inhibitors.

Diagnosis

Renal parenchymal hypertension is the most common cause of secondary hypertension. Therefore, the possibility of underlying renal disease should be ruled out in someone presenting with new-onset hypertension. In addition to routine blood tests (complete blood count and serum chemistries), a careful examination of the urinary sediment is necessary. Measurement of creatinine clearance and 24-hour protein excretion are indicated in patients with abnormal serum creatinine or active urinary sediment. Renal ultrasound to assess renal size and contour is essential, particularly in patients with a family history of polycystic kidney disease. The decision to perform a renal biopsy (to rule out glomerular or intersititial disease) is based on the overall clinical picture of the individual patient.

Treatment

Controlling blood pressure in patients with renal parenchymal hypertension not only reduces cerebrovascular and cardiovascular complications, but also retards the progression of renal disease. Therapeutic interventions in these patients are aimed at reducing ECF volume and TPR.

Medical treatment

Salt restriction and diuretics

Control of blood pressure in patients with chronic renal disease is extremely difficult without dietary sodium restriction. Therefore, total sodium intake should be restricted to 2 g/day (88 mmol/day), and intensive dietary education may be needed to achieve this. Processed or canned foods, fast foods, and prepackaged seasonings are high in sodium content. Patients with moderate to severe renal insufficiency, however, should be warned against using salt substitutes that contain potassium. Sodium bicarbonate and sodium citrate preparations used for treatment of metabolic acidosis represent a significant sodium load (a typical daily dose provides approximately 1 g of sodium) and may exacerbate hypertension.

Dietary sodium restriction alone rarely controls blood pressure in patients with renal parenchymal hypertension. Thus, diuretic therapy is usually needed. Thiazide diuretics may be effective in mild renal disease, but they do not induce significant natriuresis when the serum creatinine is greater than 2.5 mg/dl or creatinine clearance is below 30 ml/min. Then, loop diuretics such as furosemide and bumetanide become the agents of choice. Loop diuretics reach their target of action, the sodium-potassium/2 chloride cotransporter on the luminal side of the cells of the thick ascending limb of the loop of Henle, after they are filtered by the glomerulus or secreted by the proximal tubule. An increase in dosage is therefore required in patients with advanced renal disease. It is recommended that the dose rather than frequency of administration is raised until the patient reaches the desired level of diuresis. If further diuresis is needed, dose frequency can then be increased. Furosemide generally requires twice-daily dosing, whereas bumetanide is given once daily. The maximum recommended dose of furosemide is approximately 480 mg per day; beyond that level, the risk of ototoxicity becomes significant. In patients resistant to loop diuretics alone, adding a long-acting diuretic such as metolazone could enhance diuresis. Potassium-sparing diuretics should be avoided in patients with renal insufficiency. Finally, the value of achieving dry weight to control hypertension in patients on dialysis cannot be overemphasized.

Nondiuretic antihypertensive agents

In addition to reducing ECF volume, adequate blood pressure control in hypertensive patients with renal parenchymal disease often requires the administration of agents that lower TPR. This underscores the contribution of vasoconstrictive factors to sustaining hypertension in these patients. Although most nondiuretic antihypertensive agents (ACE inhibitors, angiotensin II receptor antagonists, beta-adrenergic receptor antagonists, α_1- and α_2-adrenergic receptor antagonists, calcium channel blockers, and vasodilators) used alone or in combination are effective in controlling blood pressure in these patients, ACE inhibitors and possibly angiotensin II receptor antagonists deserve special consideration. These agents have proved to be reno- and cardioprotective in clinical trials that included patients with diabetic and nondiabetic renal parenchymal disease. In one study, ACE inhibition was found to be five times more effective than a nondihydropiridine long-acting calcium channel blocker in preventing nonfatal cardiovascular events in hypertensive non-insulin-dependent diabetics. The authors, however, emphasize that these results need to be confirmed because cardiovascular events were a secondary and not a primary end-point of the study. The long-term protective effects of calcium channel blockers on cardiovascular and renal sequelae of hypertension are currently being investigated.

Surgical treatment

Renin-secreting juxtaglomerular cell tumors generally are superficial and can be resected surgically without the need for nephrectomy. These tumors do not recur, and hypertension resolves postoperatively. Similarly, surgical excision of renin-producing Wilms' tumors corrects plasma renin activity and normalizes blood pressure. In contrast, unilateral nephrectomy in hypertensive patients with unilateral renal parenchymal disease (for example, chronic pyelonephritis or reflux nephropathy) normalizes blood pressure in only one-fourth of the cases. Surgical cure or improvement in hypertension is limited to patients in whom the ratio of the higher renal venous renin to the contralateral value is greater than or equal to 1.5. It is therefore necessary to measure renal vein renin levels before embarking on a unilateral nephrectomy for the treatment of renal parenchymal hypertension. In general, unilateral nephrectomy should be reserved for those patients with severe hypertension unresponsive to pharmacologic therapy, marked loss of renal function in the affected kidney (less than 8.5 cm kidney on ultrasound and near-absent radionucleide excretion on a MAG-3 scan), *normal* function in the contralateral kidney, and increased renal vein renin levels on the affected side. Bilateral nephrectomy is seldom needed for blood pressure control in patients with end-stage renal disease because of the effectiveness of antihypertensive agents and the safety of ultrafiltration techniques.

RENOVASCULAR HYPERTENSION

Prevalence and etiology

Renovascular hypertension results from unilatral or bilateral vacular lesions that interfere with the renal arterial circulation and cause renal ischemia. Renovascular hypertension is present in approximately 1% of the total hypertensive population, 5% of hospitalized hypertensive patients, and 15 to 40% of patients with suggestive clinical features who are referred for a diagnostic work-up. It is more prevalent among older patients (those over 50 years of age) and among patients with accelerated/malignant hypertension or azotemia. African-Americans are less prone to renovascular hypertension than are Caucasians.

Renal arterial lesions that cause hypertension are traditionally divided into atherosclerotic and fibrous (Tab. 33.3). Atherosclerotic renovascular disease is the underlying cause in most patients (approximately 70% of individuals with renovascular hypertension). It predominantly affects men after the age of 40 and is frequently associated with peripheral and coronary vascular disease. Overall, men are affected twice as often as women, but the gender difference declines with advancing age. Atherosclerotic lesions causing renovascular hypertension are bilateral in 50 to 75% of patients and are located either at the ostium of the renal artery (approximately 80% of all cases) or 1 to 2 cm distal to the ostium (approximately 20% of all cases). Both lesions are characterized histologically by complex plaque formation typical of atherosclerosis with or without the concomitant presence of a luminal thrombus.

Table 33.3 Clinical and anatomic characteristics of renal arterial lesions that cause renovascular hypertension

Lesion	Relative frequency	Sex	Age	Angiographic findings	Natural course
Atherosclerosis	70%	M > F	> 40	Focal stenosis Proximal 2 cm of main renal artery (ostial or nonostial) Bilateral in 50-75%	Progresses in 40-50% Total occlusion in 15%
Fibrous dysplasia Medial (fibromuscular dysplasia)	30% (65-85%)*	F	25-50	Multiple stenoses with intervening aneurysms ("string of beads") Mid to distal main renal artery and branches Bilateral in 60%	Progresses in 30% Complete occlusion is rare
Perimedial	(15%)*	F	15-30	Multiple stenoses without intervening aneurysms Mid to distal main renal artery and branches Bilateral in 30%	Progresses in most Complete occlusion due to dissection or thrombosis is common
Intimal (and medial hyperplasia)	(5%)*	F > M	Children and adolescents	Focal tight stenosis (tubular in appearance) Mid and occasionally proximal main renal artery Rarely bilateral	Progresses in most Complete occlusion due to dissection or thrombosis is common

* Percentage of patients with fibrous dysplasia.

Atherosclerotic renal artery stenosis progresses in 40 to 50% of patients and leads to complete occlusion in 15% of patients. High-degree stenosis (greater than 75% luminal narrowing) at the time of diagnosis is a predictor of progression to complete renal artery occlusion within 2 years.

Fibrous renal artery disease is the most common cause of renovascular hypertension in individuals under the age of 40. It is much more common in women than men, in Caucasians than African-Americans, and is rarely seen in patients aged over 60 years. Three main histologic forms of renal artery fibrous disease have been identified: intimal fibroplasia, medial fibromuscular dysplasia, and perimedial fibroplasia (also referred to as subadventitial fibroplasia). A fourth rare form, referred to as medial hyperplasia, affects children and adolescents and is difficult to differentiate angiographically from intimal fibroplasia. The clinical and anatomic characteristics of these lesions are summarized in Table 33.3. Medial fibromuscular dysplasia is by far the most common form of fibrous renal artery disease. It is bilateral in up to 60% of affected patients. Unlike atherosclerotic lesions, stenosis secondary to medial fibromuscular dysplasia progresses in only one-third of patients and rarely leads to complete occlusion of the renal artery.

Less common renovascular diseases that cause renal ischemia and secondary hypertension include acute arterial embolism, trauma to the renal artery, aortic dissection, aortic or renal artery aneurysm, atheroembolic renal disease (cholesterol emboli), and systemic necrotizing vasculitis involving small arteries in the kidneys (polyarteritis nodosa and Takayasu's arteritis). Large renal cysts or tumors can compress the ipsilateral renal artery and cause renovascular hypertension in a small number of patients.

Pathophysiology

The pathogenesis of renovascular hypertension has been elucidated by renal artery clamping experiments in dogs, sheep, rabbits, and rats. The original experiments were performed by Goldblatt and coworkers in 1934 – thus the term Goldblatt hypertension. Most human renovascular hypertension resembles the two-kidney, one-clip model in which the animal has two functioning kidneys and one renal artery is clipped to induce a 75% or greater stenosis. Lesser luminal narrowing does not trigger hypertension in experimental animals, and the same probably is true in humans. Significant stenosis of the renal artery results in renal ischemia and increases plasma renin activity and angiotensin II levels. Hypertension in the acute period (phase I) of renal artery stenosis (probably the first 3 to 5 years in humans) is characterized by angiotensin II-mediated vasoconstriction and excellent blood pressure control following surgical correction of the arterial lesion. Although the affected kidney retains sodium, pressure natriuresis is observed in the contralateral kidney, and ECF volume is either normal or slightly decreased in this phase. If renal artery stenosis is left uncorrected, renovascular hypertension progresses to phase II, which is characterized by gradual decline in renin and angiotensin II levels and gradual rise in ECF volume. Chronic renovascular hypertension eventually leads to nephrosclerosis in the contralateral kidney (phase III), and elevated blood pressure is then sustained by both increased ECF and increased TPR. Surgical correction of the renal artery stenosis at this point has less than a 25% chance of normalizing the blood pressure. Although renin and angiotensin II levels are normal in phase III, they are inappropriately elevated for the degree of blood pressure. Along with such other vasoconstrictors as norepinephrine and vasopressin, angiotensin II therefore contributes to the increased TPR observed in chronic renovascular hypertension. Recent studies also indicate that intrarenal changes in prostaglandin and nitric oxide production influence urinary sodium excretion and blood pressure levels. These factors play a critical role in sustaining hypertension initiated by the renin-angiotensin axis in renal artery stenosis.

Patients who have renal artery stenosis of a single functioning kidney resemble the one-kidney, one-clip Goldblatt model. The absence of a functioning second kidney capable of pressure natriuresis leads to increased ECF volume. Hypertension in these patients is therefore angiotensin II- and volume-dependent.

Clinical findings

Because definitive diagnosis of renal artery stenosis requires an arteriogram, clinicians tend to rely on certain clinical features of renovascular hypertension to preselect hypertensive patients for further diagnostic work-up. The following clinical features could suggest hemodynamically significant renal artery stenosis:

- age at time of onset of hypertension less than 30 or more than 55 years of age;
- family history of hypertension is absent;
- abrupt onset of hypertension (less than 1 year's duration);
- accelerated hypertension in a previously well-controlled and compliant patient;
- severe or malignant hypertension associated with significant retinopathy;
- hypertension that is refractory to treatment with a three-drug regimen;
- recurrent flash pulmonary edema;
- lateralizing abdominal bruit with systolic and diastolic components;
- evidence of generalized atherosclerotic vascular disease;
- hypokalemia resulting from secondary hyperaldosteronism;
- significant discrepancy in size between the two kidneys;
- gradually worsening renal function in a patient with generalized atherosclerosis and an abrupt rise in creatinine following ACE inhibition suggest the presence of bilateral renal artery stenosis, or unilateral renal artery stenosis in a single functioning kidney.

None of these clinical clues are pathognomic of renal artery stenosis, and most patients with renovascular hypertension cannot be differentiated from those with essential hypertension on simple clinical grounds.

Diagnostic procedures

Definitive diagnosis of renovascular hypertension cannot be made unless the stenotic lesion is visualized and its functional significance proved. Renal arteriography coupled with renin determinations on blood obtained from each renal vein (differential renal vein renin) is the only test capable of providing such information. The invasive nature of angiography, however, precludes its usefulness in screening hypertensive patients. The following is an overview of the various tests employed to diagnose renovascular hypertension.

Conventional renal arteriography and differential renal vein renin determination This test should be performed if clinical suspicion of renovascular hypertension is high and if the patient is a candidate for surgical revascularization or angioplasty. Conventional renal arteriography provides optimal anatomic information about the renal artery and its branches, intrarenal vessels, and collateral circulation. It also provides accurate localization of the stenosis and valuable clues about its nature (atherosclerosis versus fibrodysplasia). Care should be taken to administer saline solutions to minimize the incidence of contrast nephropathy in patients with compromised renal function who are undergoing renal arteriography. Intraarterial digital subtraction arteriography (DSA) has been developed to minimize the load of radiocontrast given. When compared with conventional arteriography, however, DSA has two shortcomings. First, images are often blurred by motion artifact. Second, DSA provides inferior spatial resolution of the renal vasculature.

The functional significance of renal artery stenosis should be established before renovascular hypertension is diagnosed and revascularization is performed. In other words, is the stenosis the cause of hypertension or is it simply an incidental finding? Although less than 50% luminal narrowing does not usually lead to sufficient renal hypoperfusion, the degree of arterial stenosis, presence of poststenotic dilatation, and the presence of collateral circulation are not reliable predictors of renovascular hypertension that responds to surgical or angioplastic intervention. Furthermore, measuring the pressure gradient across a stenotic lesion is highly variable and carries the risk of renal artery dissection or renal embolization. Clinicians have therefore relied on differential renal vein renin determinations to assess the functional significance of renovascular disease. This test is based on the observations of Goldblatt and co-workers that renin production by the kidney with the stenosis is increased while renin production by the contralateral kidney is suppressed. The test requires that plasma renin levels in the inferior vena cava (systemic level), ipsilateral renal vein (ischemic kidney), and contralateral renal vein (nonischemic kidney) be measured. A ratio greater than 1.5 between the ipsilateral and contralateral renal vein renins is considered to be a "lateralizing ratio" and is 90 to 95% predictive of resolution of hypertension when the stenosis is corrected. The major drawback of differential renal vein renin determination, however, is the high degree of false-negatives. Surgical intervention will still ameliorate hypertension in approximately 60% of patients with nonlaterlalizing ratios (less than 1.5). False-negatives are caused by technical errors such as nonsimultaneous sampling from the renal arteries, improper positioning of the catheters leading to admixture of inferior cava blood, and interference by contrast media. False-negatives can also be caused by the presence of bilateral renal artery stenosis, concomitant intake of agents that alter renin secretion (diuretics, beta-blockers, and ACE inhibitors), or the presence of extensive collateral circulation, which can reduce renin production by the previously ischemic kidney. The presence of bilateral renal artery stenosis can be ascertained by determining whether renin release from the nonischemic kidney is suppressed or not. In pure unilateral renal artery stenosis, contralateral (nonischemic) renal vein renin level is equal to that in the inferior vena cava. In bilateral renal artery stenosis, contralateral renal vein renin level is at least 25% greater than that in the inferior vena cava.

In summary, the value of differential renal vein renin determination lies in its high predictive value. The significant false-negative rate, however, has led many to argue against performing renal vein renin measurements. This argument may apply to patients with more than 50 to 75% renal artery stenosis in whom angioplasty rather than vascular surgery is planned or to those in whom surgery is intended to prevent ischemic renal damage.

Renal scan and captopril-enhanced scintigraphy Isotopic scintigraphy of the kidneys (renal scan) is performed using either iodo-hippurate or technicium-DTPA. Hippurate clearance is used as a measure of renal blood flow (effective renal plasma flow) because it is largely excreted by proximal renal tubular cells during a single transit of blood through the kidney. DTPA, on the other hand, is a measure of GFR because it is excreted mainly by glomerular filtration. Technitium-labeled MAG-3 is slowly replacing iodo-hippurate because of its enhanced tubular secretion and ability to provide higher resolution images. Uptake by the kidney of either one of these radiolabeled compounds is measured within 1 to 3 minutes after intravenous injection. Differential delay in isotope uptake between the two kidneys is suggestive of unilateral renal artery stenosis. This test provides about 85% specificity and sensitivity, particularly when hippurate is used. The presence of renal parenchymal disease reduces both specificity and sensitivity of the test. Rapid sequence intravenous pyelography, in which the time it takes the radiocontrast agent to reach the cortex is measured, provides similar specificity and sensitivity. Neither test, however, establishes the diagnosis of renovascular hypertension.

It has been suggested that the sensitivity and specificity of renal scans can be improved by renal scintigraphy after a single dose of captopril. Captopril-mediated ACE inhibition in a patient with unilateral renal artery stenosis causes a significant decline in GFR (reduced DTPA uptake) and a lesser decline in renal blood flow (reduced hippurate uptake) in the ischemic kidney. Uptake of DTPA and hippurate, on the other hand, may increase in the contralateral kidney. Despite the physiologic lure of this test, it has proved to be difficult to standardize and has exhibited immense variability in its specificity and sensitivity (between 40 and 100% among different studies). Its accuracy is also impaired in the presence of renal insufficiency. Moreover, if the patient is receiving ACE inhibitors, these have to be discontinued approximately 2 weeks before captopril-enhanced renal scintigraphy.

Other noninvasive tests Noninvasive anatomic studies used for identifiying renal artery stenosis include duplex ultasonography and magnetic resonance imaging. Duplex ultrasound scanning combines direct visualization of the renal arteries with Doppler measurements, thus providing both anatomic and hemodynamic information. Although this test has been optimized in some medical centers, it is highly operator-dependent, leading to ambiguous results in other centers. Magnetic resonance angiography (MRA) is a safe procedure that does not require injecting nephrotoxic radiocontrast material. Although it is reasonably accurate in detecting main renal artery lesions (80 to 90% sensitivity and specificity), it is less reliable in diagnosing branch stenoses. Technical advances in the field of MRI may eventually make this test an adequate screening tool. Finally, mesurement of plasma renin activity (PRA) at baseline or after captopril provocation as a screening test for renal artery stenosis suffers from low sensitivity and high variability.

Treatment

Adequate management of renovascular hypertension has two therapeutic goals: normalizing blood pressure and preventing ischemic renal damage. Therapeutic options available for patients with renal artery stenosis include surgical revascularization, percutaneous transluminal renal angioplasty (PTRA) with or without stent placement, and medical management.

Medical treatment

Although some studies indicated that surgical or angioplastic treatment of renal artery stenosis is superior to medical therapy, none of these studies were truly randomized or controlled. Generally, young patients with pure renovascular hypertension secondary to fibrodysplastic renal artery disease respond well to surgical or angioplastic intervention. On the other hand, older patients with renovascular atherosclerosis have less favorable outcomes because of coexisting essential hypertension and renal parenchymal hypertension. Medical therapy is therefore indicated in patients with presumed renovascular hypertension who are poor surgical candidates, have inoperable lesions such as diffuse atherosclerosis, have an atrophic kidney distal to the stenosis, or have long-standing hypertension with significant nephrosclerosis.

Beta-blockers and ACE inhibitors are the drugs of choice because the former inhibit renin release while the latter suppress angiotensin II production. Angiotensin II receptor blockers recently have been introduced as alternatives to ACE inhibitors. In patients with long-standing renovascular disease whose hypertension is less angiotensin II-dependent, additional medications may be required to normalize blood pressure. These include diuretics and direct vasodilators such as calcium channel blockers. The most feared side effect of ACE inhibitors is acute renal failure in patients with bilateral renal artery stenosis or high-grade stenosis of an artery to a solitary kidney. Renal function returns to normal in most patients after discontinuing ACE inhibitors. Occasionally, acute tubular necrosis or irreversible acute cortical necrosis occurs. ACE inhibitors can also cause hyperkalemia in patients with renal insufficiency.

All patients receiving medical therapy for renovascular hypertension should be followed up carefully to ensure adequate blood pressure control, stable renal function, and stable renal size on ultrasonography. Evidence for progressive ischemic nephropathy warrants surgical or angioplastic intervention.

Surgical treatment

Surgical revascularization

Several clinical studies have addressed the safety, technical success, and long-term benefits of surgical intervention in patients with renovascular hypertension. Average operative mortality is as low as 0% in younger patients with fibrodysplasia, and as high as 6% in older patients with atherosclerotic renal artery lesions. Technical success is high in both groups, with failure rates due to postoperative thrombosis or restenosis under 10%. The long-term benefits of surgery depend on the underlying cause of renal artery stenosis. Correction of fibrodysplastic lesions normalizes blood pressure in 50 to 60% and improves it in 30 to 40% of patients after revascularization. Hypertension remains unchanged in less than 10% of these patients. On the other hand, failure to achieve long-term reduction of blood pressure in patients with atherosclerotic renal artery disease ranges between 10 and 40%. Higher failure rates are common among patients with diffuse renovascular atheromas. Nevertheless, significant cure rates (20-40%) and improvement in blood pressure control (45%) are achieved. Stabilization or improvement in renal function is attained in approximately 80% of patients in whom ischemic nephropathy is a main concern. These relatively high success rates are attributed to proper patient selection before surgery and to the level of surgical skill at centers conducting clinical studies. In addition to perioperative mortality, elderly patients undergoing revascularization for atherosclerotic renal artery disease are at risk of developing acute renal failure and atheroembolization (cholesterol emboli).

Other measures

Percutaneous transluminal renal angioplasty (PTRA)

PTRA has recently emerged as an alternative to surgical treatment of renal artery stenosis. Success rates equivalent to those seen with surgical revascularization have been achieved in patients with fibrodysplastic lesions, particularly fibromuscular dysplasia. Many patients with fibrodysplastic lesions, however, have branch disease, which is not accessible to PTRA, and surgical treatment remains the optimal choice in this subgroup. The utility of PTRA in the treatment of atherosclerotic renal artery stenosis appears to be largely restricted to patients with nonostial atheromas (these patients comprise only 15 to 25% of all patients with atherosclerotic renovascular disease). Successful balloon dilatation (technical success) is attained in 70 to 90% of nonostial cases and in only 30% of ostial lesions. Meta-analysis of published studies, in which treatment of hypertension was the end-point, indicates that long-term cure, improvement, and failure rates of PRTA performed in patients with atherosclerotic renal artery stenosis is 20, 50, and 30%, respectively. One should keep in mind that these patients were highly preselected and that failure rates in unselected patients may reach 60%. Whether PTRA offers protection against ischemic nephropathy is not entirely clear. Improvement or stabilization of renal function has been reported in 65 to 85% of subjects. The complications of PTRA occur in about 10% of patients, and include contrast nephropathy, atheroembolic renal disease, rupture or dissection of the renal artery, thrombotic occlusion of the renal artery, renal artery spasm, and adverse events at the puncture site (the femoral artery in the majority of cases). Mortality is less than 1%.

Placement of a renal artery stent has been proposed in pateints with ostial atherosclerotic lesions because of difficulty in achieving adequate balloon dilatation and significant incidence of short-term restenosis. A 1-year follow-up study demonstrated renal artery patency in 80% of patients who had a stent placed at the site of an ostial lesion (n = 120). Blood pressure improved in 85%, and renal function stabilized or improved in 70%. Longer follow-up is needed before stent insertion is widely accepted as standard therapy. Placing stents in the distal part of the renal artery may preclude future renal artery bypass surgery.

Suggested readings

Corvol P, Pinet F, Plouin PF, Bruneral P, Menard J. Renin-secreting tumors. Endocrinol Metab Clin North Am 1994;23:255-70.

Dustan HP. Renal arterial disease and hypertension. Med Clin Nort Am 1997;81:1199-1212.

Estacio RO, Barrett JW, Hiatt WR, Biggerstaff SL, Gifford N, Schrier RW. The effect of nisoldipine as compared with enalapril on cardiovascular outcomes in patients with non-insulin-dependent diabetes and hypertension. N Engl J Med 1998;338:645-52.

Giatras I, Lau J, Levey AS. For the angiotensin-converting-enzyme inhibition and progressive renal disease study group. Effect of angiotensin-converting-enzyme inhibitors on the progression of non-diabetic renal disease: a metanalysis of randomized trials. Ann Int Med 1997;127:337-45.

National high blood pressure education program working group. Update of the working group reports on chronic renal failure and renovascular hypertension. Arch Intern Med 1995;156:1938-47.

Kidney DD, Deutsch LS. The indications and results of percutaneous transluminal angioplasty and stenting in renal artery stenosis. Semin Vasc Surg 1996;9:188-97.

Klag MJ, Whelton PK, Randall BL, et al. Blood pressure and end-stage renal disease in men. N Engl J Med 1996;334:13-8.

Lewis EJ, Hunsicker LG, Bain RP, Rohde RD. For the collaborative study group. The effect of angiotensin-converting-enzyme inhibition on diabetic nephropathy. N Engl J Med 1993;329:1456-62.

Ligtenberg G, Blankestijn, PJ, Oey PL, et al. Reduction of sympathetic hyperactivity by enalapril in patients with cronic renal failure. N Engl J Med 1999;17:1321-8.

Luscher TF, Lie JT, Stanson AW, Houser OW, Hollier LH, Sheps SG. Arterial fibromuscular dysplasia. Mayo Clin Proc 1987;62:931-52.

Martinez-Maldonado M. Pathophysiology of renovascular hypertension. Hypertension 1991;17:707-19.

Martinez-Maldonado M. Hypertension in end-stage renal disease. Kidney Int 1998;54:S67-S72.

Saleem S, Lakkis FG, Martinez-Maldonado M. Atheroembolic renal disease. Semin Nephrol 1996;16:309-18.

The joint national commission on prevention, detection, evaluation and treatment of high blood pressure. The sixth report of the joint national committee on prevention, detection, evaluation, and treatment of high blood pressure. Arch Intern Med 1997;157:2413-46.

Wilcox CS. Ischemic nephropathy: noninvasive testing. Semin Nephrol 1996;16:43-52.

CHAPTER

34

Effects of hypertension on the kidney

Pietro C. Zucchelli, Alessandro Zuccalà

KEY POINTS

- Hypertension can induce renal damage through two main mechanisms: those that involve the direct transmission of systemic hypertension to the renal parenchyma and those that act indirectly on the kidney by inducing stenosis or occlusion of preglomerular vessels and in turn ischemia of renal parenchyma.
- The direct transmission of high blood pressure can induce glomerular and tubulointerstitial damage. Glomerular hypertension secondary to the loss of renal autoregulation may be present in diabetes mellitus, in primary renal diseases and when renal mass is reduced. Elevated proteinuria is the clinical hallmark of glomerular hypertension. Moreover, direct transmission of blood pressure to the renal parenchyma can induce tubulointerstitial damage.
- Patients with preglomerular vessel changes, e.g., patients with stenosis of renal arteries or some patients with hypertensive nephrosclerosis present a different clinical picture.
- The correct identification of the pathogenetic pathways may help the practitioner to tailor the best treatment for his/her patients. In patients with glomerular hypertension very strict control of blood pressure is mandatory, preferably with ACE inhibitors.
- In patients with preglomerular vessel changes, hypertension should be treated, but a careful control of serum creatinine is mandatory, particularly when ACE inhibitors are used. Because renal ischemia, not hypertensive stress, is the real problem, excessive reduction in blood pressure can harm the renal parenchyma. In these patients the treatment of choice, when possible, is renal revascularization.

It is well known that there is an ambiguous link between hypertension and kidney disease. This ambivalent connection often has been stressed in lectures and editorials. The debate as to whether the kidney is more the villain or the victim has gone on a long time, and the supporters of either theory can boast eminent ancestors. On the one hand, Bright and Mahomed have stressed the role of hypertension in inducing renal damage; on the other, Volhard and Fahr have underlined the role of primary kidney disease in causing at least some forms of hypertension. Yet nobody can deny that whatever the "primum movens" actually is, a vicious circle is always begun.

Without wishing to join in this debate, we will try to describe the various mechanisms by which systemic high blood pressure can induce renal damage and the clinical pictures that derive from such mechanisms. The clinical aspects of essential hypertension and renal and renovascular hypertension are covered extensively in other chapters of this text.

PATHOGENESIS OF RENAL DAMAGE

Systemic hypertension can induce renal damage by way of different mechanisms, which can be divided into two main groups:

1. mechanisms that involve the direct transmittal of systemic hypertension to the renal perenchyma (i.e., the glomeruli and tubulointerstitium);
2. mechanisms that induce ischemia of the renal parenchyma.

Although systemic hypertension is at the root of both mechanisms, the renal damage derives from completely different, if not opposite, insults, and different clinical pictures occur. Only the correct identification of the basic mechanism behind the clinical picture will allow the best treatment plan for the patient with hypertension and renal damage (Tab. 34.1).

The direct transmittal of hypertension to the renal parenchyma

The first type of mechanism relies on the transmission of systemic hypertension to the glomerular tuft or to the tubulointerstium.

Glomerular damage

Experimental data Since under normal conditions the glomerulus is protected from high blood pressure by preglomerular vessel constriction (autoregulation), a defect in such a mechanism should play a permissive role. There is substantial proof that a defect in autoregulation plays an important role in accelerating glomerular damage in renal parenchymal diseases by permitting the transmission of systemic hypertension to poorly autoregulated glomeruli. A marked decrease in afferent arteriolar resistance resulting in a marked increase in renal plasma flow has been reported in remnant kidney, experimental diabetes, and in experimental glomerulonephritis.

Since the vasodilatory effect on the efferent arteriole is proportionally less pronounced, a rise in glomerular capillary pressure ensues.

In all these experimental models the progressive glomerular sclerosis is anticipated by a net increase in protein excretion. Furthermore, the treatment of experimental animals with antihypertensive drugs, which lower systemic and glomerular hyprtension, reduces proteinuria and ameliorates glomerular structural damage.

Clinical data Direct measurement of glomerular hemodynamics is not available in humans, and therefore it is impossible to establish the role of elevated glomerular pressure in the progression of renal damage. However, many indirect data support the hypothesis that the transmittal of hypertension to the glomerulus plays an important role. Retrospective studies have suggested an important role of antihypertensive therapy in reducing the rate of functional deterioration in patients with primary renal disease and renal insufficiency. The importance of an optimal blood pressure reduction in slowing the rate of progression of renal insufficiency has been confirmed by prospective, randomized studies in patients with nondiabetic renal disease. The positive effects of blood pressure reduction on progression of renal insufficiency also have been demonstrated in patients with diabetic nephropathy in both retrospective and prospective studies. Moreover, patients with elevated proteinuria obtain greater benefits than do those with low to moderate proteinuria when blood pressure is reduced. Finally, treatment with ACE Inhibitors, drugs thought to reduce intraglomerular pressure, is particularly effective in slowing down proteinuria and in slowing the rate of functional deterioration.

For the purposes of clinical practice bear in mind that:

- the available data support the idea that in patients with primary renal disease, diabetes and renal insufficiency, the harmful role of systemic hypertension is the consequence of the direct transmittal of hemodynamic stress to the glomeruli;
- a proteinuria over 1.5 g/day is the clinical hallmark of glomerular hypertension;
- a direct causal link between high blood pressure and renal damage does exist in these patients, meaning that the more you lower blood pressure, the more you lessen renal damage.

Table 34.1 High blood pressure and renal damage: direct causal link

Pathogenesis	Mechanisms of renal damage	Pathologic findings
I Transmission of high blood pressure to glomeruli	Glomerular hypertension Intracapillary hypertension Glomerular capillary wall stress	Focal segmental glomerulosclerosis
II Transmission of high blood pressure to tubuloinsterstitium	Fibroblast and growth factor stimulation Obliteration of post-glomerular capillaries	Interstitial fibrosis Tubular atrophy Mononuclear cell infiltration
III Hypertensive changes of preglomerular vessels	Ischemia of renal parenchyma	Fibroplasia of preglomerular vessels Main renal artery stenosis

Tubulointerstitial damage

The renal interstitium is more than just a passive space in which the glomeruli reside. It is a highly dynamic tissue in which structural support is rendered, fibers and ground substance are produced and degraded, and hormonal functions are conducted.

The notion that tubulointerstitial lesion may be important in hypertension-induced renal damage has recently received some support.

Experimental data The two-kidneys-one-clip (2k1c) model of renovascular hypertension induces a severe form of renal injury in the nonstenotic kidney. By using this model Mai et al. have been able to demonstrate that tubulointerstitial lesions occur much earlier than vascular change and glomerular injuries. They found a perivascular monocytic infiltration, an expansion of interstitial volume, and interstitial accumulation of collagen. Tubular cells showed early evidence of injury and proliferation. In a later paper, using the same model, these authors demonstrated that the development of hypertension resulted in a progressive increase in adhesion molecule (ICAM-1) expression in the perivascular and interstitial areas of the renal cortex and on the proximal tubular brush borders of the unclipped kidney. This increased adhesion molecule was associated with an accumulation of mononuclear cells, and the number of infiltrating cells was significantly correlated with blood pressure values.

Haller et al. confirmed the leukocyte infiltration, the proximal tubular cell proliferation, and the interstitial fibrosis in the unclipped kidney. Very interestingly they found the same lesions in the clipped kidney. This finding suggests that both hypertension and ischemia may induce tubulointerstitial lesions.

Clinical data Patients with essential hypertension do not routinely undergo diagnostic renal biopsy. Therefore our knowledge of the pathology of the hypertensive kidney derives largely from autopsy findings. In one of the few studies where biopsy was used, an increased immunostaining for both type III and type IV collagens was found in the expanded interstitium and damaged tubules, suggesting that an increased accumulation of such types of collagens might play an important role in the tubulointerstitial damage of human hypertensive nephrosclerosis.

The importance of tubulointerstitial lesions also emerges from the study by Ratschek et al., who demonstrated that in hypertensive nephrosclerosis interstitial fibrosis and tubular atrophy are heaviest in the inner cortical layers and are least marked in the outer layers. In these patients the area affected by interstitial fibrosis forms a pyramid with its base at the corticomedullary junction.

Morphometric studies performed on biopsies of hypertensive patients have shown a significant positive correlation between the interstitial volume and the level of serum creatinine. Furthermore, a significant negative correlation between the area of the intertubular capillaries and the serum creatinine concentration was reported, suggesting that the obliteration of the post-glomerular capillary leads to a progressive decrease in the glomerular filtration rate.

The above-cited data suggest that tubulointerstitial damage may be more prevalent than glomerular damage, at least in some groups of hypertensive patients. However, because the tubulointerstitial areas are supplied by postglomerular circulation, we might wonder how the glomeruli, which are upstream, can be spared the hypertensive damage that strikes the tubulo-interstium.

There are three theoretic possibilities. The first relies on the fact that the autoregulation of the outer cortex is more efficient than the autoregulation of the inner layer of the cortex and medulla. Hence, these areas are less protected from hypertensive insults. The data of Ratscheck, showing that hypertensive damage is greater in the deeper layer of the kidney, lends some support to this hypothesis.

The second possibility is that an increased hyperresposiveness of interstitial fibroblasts stimulated by hypertensive stress may be at the root of fibrosis. Dustan has underlined the increased responsiveness of cutaneous fibroblasts of African-Americans and has hypothesized that such a mechanism may also work at the renal site.

The third possibility is that preglomerular vasocostriction aimed to protect the glomeruli from hypertension, if excessive, can induce a relative ischemia of areas supplied by postglomerular vessels (i.e., tubuli and interstitium). In effect, it is well known that the tubular structures are very sensitive to ischemia. In this regard it is interesting to note that African-Americans have a greater reduction in renal blood flow in response to the hypertension than do Caucasian patients.

For the purposes of clinical practice, bear in mind:

- familiarity for renal damage and black race should alert the clinician toward such mechanisms;
- when this mechanism plays a role there is a proteinuria of a lower degree than seen in patients with glomerular involvement;
- even this mechanism indicates a direct causal link between high blood pressure and renal damage; hence, a strict control of blood pressure is important.

Indirect mechanisms of renal damage: ischemic damage

Apart from the transmission of mechanical stress to the parenchyma, hypertension may induce renal damage through the vascular lesion, which in turn provokes ischemic damage. We should distinguish between atherosclerotic lesions of large vessels (abdominal aorta and main renal arteries) and vascular changes that involve intraparenchymal preglomerular vessels.

Involvement of main renal arteries: renovascular disease and ischemic nephropathy

Ischemic damage secondary to atherosclerotic lesions of the main renal artery (ischemic nephropathy) is more frequent than prevously thought. It is likely that some patients considered as having hypertensive nephrosclerosis actually suffer from ischemic nephropathy. One of the reasons for such a misdiagnosis is the inadequacy of the officially accepted classification of diagnoses. In many countries the same code is used for all kidney diseases that are vascular in origin, and the label of hypertensive nephrosclerosis is attached to this heterogeneous group.

Although the exact prevalence of ischemic nephropathy is difficult to determine, many authors believe that such an entity is an important cause of progressive renal damage, especially among older patients. This opinion is based on the results of many autopsy series and arteriography studies. According to these studies, a significant reduction of the diameter of the renal artery(ies) is present in 18 to 42% of older patients, in 10% of diabetic patients with hypertension, in 13 to 28% of patients with coronary disease, and in 14 to 43% of patients with peripheral vascular disease. The prevalence of ischemic nephropathy in patients aged over 50 years who enter regular dialysis treatment has been reported to vary between 14 and 22%.

It is likely that many patients labeled with a clinical diagnosis of hypertensive nephrosclerosis actually suffer from renovascular ischemic nephropathy (Tab. 34.2).

Involvement of parenchymal vessel: pseudorenal artery stenosis syndrome

Some patients with true hypertensive nephrosclerosis show a peculiar behavior in response to the therapy, as reported by Toto et al. In these patients the administration of ACE inhibitors induces a decrease in the glomerular filtration rate, suggesting an important role of the renin angiotensin system in maintaining a normal function. This behavior is reminiscent of bilateral renal artery stenosis where renal hypoperfusion is balanced by the activation of the intrarenal renin angiotensin system. Since a stenosis of the main renal arteries was excluded in these patients by arteriography, it is likely that the hypertensive damage of preglomerular vessels (i.e., the thickening of a fibroelastic type affecting prevalently interlobular arteries) is the cause of ischemia.

Pathophysiology

There are two distinct components in the decrease of the glomerular filtration rate secondary to renal artery stenosis: one reversible and functional, the other irreversible and structural.

The pathogenesis of the first mechanism is obvious: the fall in renal perfusion pressure and/or blood flow due to the stenosis or occlusion of renal arteries. Renal insufficiency in these patients is usually exacerbated by ACE inhibitior administration and is significantly improved by renal revascularization. The genesis of structural damage is more uncertain and is likely to be multifactorial. Al least in humans, it is the consequence of a mixture of hypertensive nephrosclerosis, cholesterol crystal embolization, and chronic or intermittent ischemia.

Effects of chronic ischemia on the kidney

Hypoxia is a potent profibrogenic stimulus for the kidney. Decreased O_2 itself is a potent regulator of gene expression and may play an important role in initiating and maintaining the fibrogenic cascade. Exposure of cells to hypoxia induces the expression of a number of growth factors, in particular TGF-b1, which is central to many scarring processes. Furthermore, hypoxia suppresses matrix metallo proteinase levels (the enzymes that degrade the collagen produced in excess) and induces a fibrogenic phenotype in renal fibroblasts. It is interesting to note that the effects of low O_2 persist after reoxygenation, suggesting that the fibrogenic effect of hypoxia is not reversed even when normal oxygen levels are restored.

This can be relevant to human pathology. In fact it is likely that in patients with renal artery stenosis transient decreases in renal perfusion may occur when blood pressure is lowered by antihypertensive therapy or when ACE inhibitor or prostaglandin inhibitors (NSAIDs, aspirin) are used.

Lastly, alteration of the antigenic profile of the proximal tubule has been reported in the ischemic kidney, suggesting that a coexistent immune mechanism plays a role in renal damage.

For the purposes of clinical practice, bear in mind:

- when the above-described mechanisms are involved the

Table 34.2 The large spectrum of clinical entities clustered under the label of hypertensive nephrosclerosis

Type of lesion	Diagnostic hallmarks	Prophylaxis and therapy
I Glomerular hypertension	Severe proteinuria	Careful blood pressur control Use of ACE inhibitors
II Tubulointerstitial damage	Race, familiarity, young age	Identification of risk families Careful control of blood pressure Antifibrosis drug (?)
III Preglomerular vessel damage	Reversible insufficiency after ACE inhibitors	Do not use ACE inhibitors
IV Renovascular disease	Angiography	Revascularization

correlation between systemic hypertension and renal damage is indirect. This means that:

- renal ischemia, not hypertension, is the cause of renal damage. Hence,
- the antihypertensive therapy may sometimes induce a deterioration of renal function.

SOME ADVICE FOR CLINICAL PRACTICE

Since hypertension may induce renal damage by way of different mechanisms, the efforts of the practitioner should be directed toward the identification of the mechanism that is active in the individual patient. What we are going to say here is intended to help the practitioner in this difficult task by providing some straightforward advice (Fig. 34.1).

When hypertension is associated with important proteinuria (i.e., above 1-1.5 g/day) in a 30- to 50-year-old patient, we should suspect a primary renal disease as a cause of (or coexisting with) hypertension. However, it should be borne in mind that some patients with biopsy-proven hypertensive nephrosclerosis or cholesterol microembolization may have nephrotic-range proteinuria.

Apart from the diagnostic procedure (which often involves the kidney specialist's intervention), the practitioner should realize that *a very strict control of blood pressure must be obtained in such patients*. In fact, it is likely that the direct transmittal of high blood pressure to the glomeruli, with ensuing intraglomerular hypertension, plays an important role in these patients. Many reports have confirmed that patients with elevated proteinuria have major benefits when strict blood pressure control is obtained.The target of blood pressure control in these patients should be fixed at a lower level than in the general population (that is ≤130/80 mmHg).

What drugs should be used with these patients?

There has been a large debate on the respective roles of systemic hypertension and glomerular hypertension in inducing renal damage. Some authors think that only drugs that act on glomerular hypertension (i.e., ACE inhibitors) can lessen or avoid progressive renal damage. Others think that lowering systemic blood pressure is important "per se," irrespective of which drug is used.

Without entering this debate, we suggest that ACE inhibitors should be considered the first-choice drug in patients with elevated proteinuria on the basis of the following considerations:

- ACE inhibitors possess an intrinsic antiproteinuric effect in experimental studies;
- single reports as well as meta-analyses have shown that also in humans ACE inhibitors have a higher antiproteinuric effect than other drugs;
- ACE inhibitors slow down the progression of renal insufficiency more than conventional therapy in patients with elevated proteinuria.

However, we think that a careful control of blood pressure is nevertheless mandatory. If hypertension persists after ACE-inhibitor administration, other drugs should be added. Some experimental data suggest that the association of ACE inhibitors with calcium channel blockers

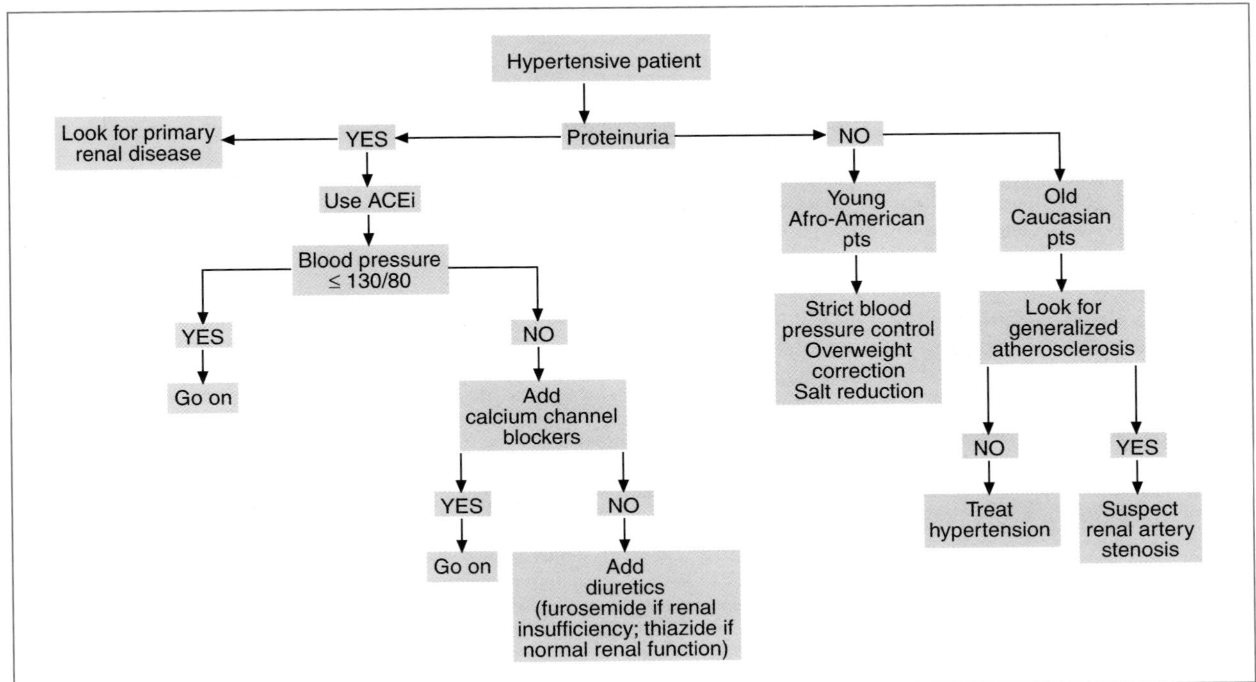

Figure 34.1 Flow chart for a hypertensive patient from a nephrologist's stand-point.

(CCB), particularly non-dihydropyridine CCB, may be effective in this context.

Another clinical picture frequently encountered by the practitioner is that of the 55- to 70-year old Caucasian male with long-standing hypertension, low or absent proteinuria, initial renal insufficiency, signs of generalized atherosclerosis (that is, angina, transitory ischemic attack, claudication, etc.). It is likely that in many of these patients hypertension-related renal damage is mediated by a lesion of the main renal arteries or preglomerular vessels, and that renal ischemia is at the root of renal insufficiency. The practitioner's approach to such a patient should be completely different from that for the previously described patient. Obviously hypertension should be treated, *but a careful control of renal function, particularly if ACE inhibitors are used, is mandatory*. In patients with ischemic nephropathy a rapid or excessive decrease of blood pressure may further impair renal function.

Sometimes, if an association of ACE inhibitors, diuretics, and NSAIDs is used, an irreversible renal failure occurs.

The behavior of renal function just described should direct the practitioner toward a diagnosis of renal artery stenosis. This diagnosis is important because sometimes *only renal revascularization* can prevent end-stage renal failure.

A third clinical picture is that of the African-American patient with hypertension and renal damage. The typical patient is relatively young (40-50 years), often overweight, with severe hypertension, low to moderate proteinuria, and progressive renal insufficiency. There is no conclusive evidence about the pathogenesis of renal damage in such patients, although some data (the absence of elevated proteinuria, familiarity, an inherited hyperresponsiveness of cutaneous fibroblasts) may suggest an important role for the tubulointerstitial lesion in the genesis of renal damage.

Whatever the mechanism involved, strict blood pressure seems useful in slowing the rate of renal insufficency in such patients, so this kind of approach is mandatory. As salt-sensitivity has been reported in such patients, a careful control of dietary habits and suitable advice on salt reduction may be useful.

There is uncertainty over the first choice drug to treat African-Americans. Previous studies suggested that African-American hypertension was volume- dependent. Hence, the drugs acting on the renin-angiotensin system may have been less efficacious in such patients than in Caucasian patients. However, recent studies have demonstrated a good clinical efficacy of ACE inhibitors on renal insufficiency in some series of patients, made up mostly of African-Americans. Moreover, an antifibrotic effect of ACE inhibitors has been experimentally demonstrated. Nonetheless, the ongoing AASK study has been designed, among other things, to answer these questions, and we shall all have to wait for the end of the study to have an evidence-based therapeutic strategy.

In conclusion, hypertension may induce renal damage by different mechanisms. Hence, no one standard therapy exists for the patient with hypertension and renal damage. Only the knowledge of the various mechnisms underpinning renal damage, and the corresponding clinical pictures, may help the practitioner to tailor the best therapy for his/her patient.

Suggested readings

DUSTAN HP. Growth factors and racial differences in severity of hypertension and renal diseases. Lancet 1992;339:1339-40.

FINE LG, ORPHANIDES C, NORMAN JT. Progressive renal disease : The chronic hypoxia hypothesis. Kidney Int 1998;53(Suppl.65):S74-8.

FROHLICH ED. Hemodynamic differences between black patients and white patients with essential hypertension. State of the Art Lecture. Hypertension 1990;15:675-80.

HOSTETTER TH, RENNKE HG, BRENNER BM. The case for intrarenal hypertension in the initiation and progression of diabetic and other glomerulopathies. Am J Med 1982;72:375-80.

KAPLAN NM. Ethnic aspects of hypertension. Lancet 1994;344:450-1.

KLAHR S. The kidney in hypertension: villain and victim. N Engl J Med 1989;320:731-3.

KOOMANS HA, JOLES JA, AND RABELINK TJ. Hypertension and the kidney: culprit and victim. Nephrol Dial Transplant 1996;11:1961-6.

LUFT FC, HALLER H. Hypertension-induced renal injury: is mechanically mediated interstitial inflammation involved? Nephrol Dial Transplant 1995;9:9-11.

MASCHIO G, ALBERTI D, JANIN G, et al. Angiotensin-converting enzyme inhibition in progressive renal insufficiency study group: effect of the angiotensin-converting enzyme inhibitor benazepril on the progression of chronic renal insufficiency. N Engl J Med 1996;334:939-45.

MEYRIER A, HILL GS, SIMON P. Ischemic renal diseases: New insights into old entities. Kidney Int 1998;54:2-13.

RAIJ L, AZAR S, KEANE W. Mesangial immune injury, hypertension, and progressive glomerular damage in Dahl rats. Kidney Int 1984;26:137-43.

RATSCHEK M, RATSCHEK E, BOHLE A. Decompensated benign nephrosclerosisw and secondary malignant nephrosclerosis. Clin Nephrol 1986;25:221-6.

TOTO RD, MITCHELL HC, LEE H-C, MILAM C, PETTINGER WA. Reversible renal insufficiency due to angiotensin converting enzyme inhibitors in hypertensive nephrosclerosis. Ann Intern Med 1991;115:513-9.

ZUCCHELLI P, ZUCCALÀ A, BORGHI M, et al. Long-term comparison between captopril and nifedipine in the progression of renal insufficiency. Kidney Int 1992;42:452-8.

ZUCCHELLI P, ZUCCALÀ A. Ischaemic nephropathy. In: Davison AM, Cameron JS, Grunfeld J-P Kerr DNS, Ritz E, Winearls CG, eds. Oxford Textbook of clinical nephrology, 2nd ed. New York: Oxford University Press, 1998;1445-56.

CHAPTER

35

Thromboembolism and atheroembolic disease of the kidney

Fernando Carrera, João M. Frazão

KEY POINTS

Renal artery thromboembolism

- Renal thromboembolism commonly presents as oliguric or anuric acute renal failure. Pain and tenderness in the abdomen or flank area are the most common symptoms.
- The most common causes are embolic: the endocardium in patients following myocardial infarction and the mitral valve in patients with rheumatic disease. Patients usually have coexisting clinical features of embolism to the brain or extremities or a history of remote embolic phenomena.
- Laboratory findings are nonspecific. The concentrations of lactic dehydrogenase, glutamic-oxaloacetic transaminase, and glutamic-pyruvic transaminase are elevated.
- Isotopic renal flow scan of the kidneys is the best noninvasive diagnostic test. Angiography is indicated if surgery, angioplasty, or thrombolytic therapy are being contemplated.
- Treatment options consist of oral anticoagulation, thrombolytic therapy, angioplasty, and surgical revascularization.

Atheroembolic disease

- Atheroembolism commonly presents with insidious, slowly progressive renal failure. Oliguria may be transient or absent, and a progressive increase in the serum urea and creatinine may be the only abnormality. These may be associated with multisystem features caused by cholesterol emboli: skin (livedo reticularis); brain (transient ischemic attacks or strokes); gastrointestinal tract (abdominal pain or gastrointestinal bleeding); pancreas (pancreatitis); liver (elevated liver enzymes); muscle and eyes (Hollenhorst plaques).
- Usually there is a precipitating event such as angiography, arteriography, cardiac catheterization, any surgical procedure involving manipulation of the aorta, or therapy with anticoagulants or thrombolytics; rarely the disorder occurs spontaneously.
- The patients usually are over 60; the disorder is rare in young patients. Males predominate over females, 3:1; white patients predominate over black patients, 30:1.
- Diagnosis is made by biopsy of skin, muscle, or kidney. Eosinophilia is common; eosinophiluria and hypocomplementemia may occur.
- Therapy is supportive by dialysis, control of blood pressure, and cholesterol-lowering agents. Anticoagulation should be avoided.

Renal artery thromboembolism and atheroembolism to the kidney are two relatively common causes of renal failure. The differences in pathophysiology, clinical presentation, and, most significant, the different treatment approaches make these entities clearly distinct. This chapter will discuss these two syndromes. Thromboembolism usually presents with acute renal failure, and atheroembolism more commonly presents with insidious, slowly progressive renal failure, although rapidly progressive or acute renal failure also can occur. Both syndromes develop more often in older patients with coronary artery disease and generalized arteriosclerosis. These two diseases are commonly underdiagnosed, and a high degree of suspicion is necessary for early diagnosis and the initiation of proper treatment, allowing for a greater chance of recovery.

RENAL ARTERY THROMBOEMBOLISM

Etiopathogenesis

Thromboembolism to the renal artery or arteries commonly presents as oliguric or anuric acute renal failure, although nonoliguric renal failure can occur. The most common causes are embolic: thrombi from the heart of patients with myocardial infarction or left atrial thrombi resulting from mitral valve rheumatic disease are often the source of emboli. Other sources include valvular vegetations in untreated bacterial endocarditis and, rarely, tumor and fat embolism. With better control of cardiac arrhythmias and the use of anticoagulation, atrial fibrillation is now a less common source of emboli. Prosthetic heart valves can generate thrombi that can be the source of small emboli. Rarely, paradoxic renal emboli from the venous system to the arterial system may result when thrombi pass through a patent interatrial or interventricular septal defect. Also, embolism involving the renal artery has occurred as a complication of percutaneous intraarterial catheterization and aortography. Other rarer causes of renal artery occlusion include thrombotic events caused by trauma, arteriosclerosis, hypercoagulable syndromes such as nephrotic syndrome, dissecting aneurysms of the renal artery, and rupture or thrombosis of a renal aneurysm, most often occurring during pregnancy.

Renal infarction may result from acute renal artery occlusion; however, more often the occlusion develops slowly, allowing collateral circulation to develop so that infarction does not occur. Oliguria and azotemia are common after embolism to the kidneys, even if the embolic phenomenon involves only one kidney and the contralateral renal artery remains patent. The mechanism for this impaired contralateral renal function is unknown. In animal experiments, total occlusion of the renal artery for 2 hours or more causes irreversible renal infarction. In contrast, clinical recovery of renal function has occurred many hours or even days following a thromboembolic renal artery occlusion when anticoagulation or fibrinolytic therapy are instituted or when angioplasty or surgical revascularization are performed. This observation suggests that the occlusion occurring in nature is rarely total or that significant collateral circulation exists.

Clinical findings

The clinical features of renal artery occlusion are quite variable, and the laboratory features are nonspecific (Tab. 35.1). With a small segmental infarction, the clinical manifestations can be minimal. Pain and tenderness in the abdomen or flank area are the most common symptoms. The pain can be severe and accompanied by abdominal distention, ileus, and rebound tenderness, leading to an erroneous diagnosis of acute cholecystitis or intestinal obstruction. The flank pain can mimic that of nephrolithiasis or acute pyelonephritis. Fever is a common symptom, and chills may occur. Nausea and/or vomiting can occur and gross hematuria is present in 20 to 25% of the cases. These patients usually have coexisting clinical features of embolism to the brain or extremities, or a history of a remote embolic phenomena. Atrial fibrillation, the presence of rheumatic valvular disease, or a recent myocardial infarction should make the physician suspect the possibility of this diagnosis. In many patients the blood pressure is unchanged, but acute or worsening hypertension may be present. Oliguria and anuria are common.

The laboratory findings (Tab. 35.1) are an increase in serum lactic dehydrogenase, glutamic-oxaloacetic transaminase, and glutamic-pyruvic transaminase. Elevated concentrations persist longer following renal infarction than after myocardial infarction. Creatine phosphokinase is not increased with renal infarction, distinguishing this condition from myocardial infarction. Moderate elevations of alkaline phosphatase may occur in less than 50% of the patients, and this abnormality may

Table 35.1 Clinical and laboratory findings in thromboembolism to the kidney

	Prevalence %
Clinical findings	
Abdominal or flank pain and tenderness	30-80
Nausea and vomiting	50
Gross hematuria	20-25
Acute or worsened hypertension	10-20
Presence of atrial fibrillation, rheumatic valvular disease, or a recent myocardial infarction	90-95
Laboratory findings	
Leukocytosis (11 000-32 000 cells/mm^3)	95
Microscopic hematuria	80
Pyuria	95
Increased serum enzyme levels (lactate dehydrogenase, aspartate aminotransferase and alanine aminotransferase)	50-100
Increased alkaline phosphatase	30-40

persist for up to 10 days. Other laboratory findings include leukocytosis (11 000-32 000 cells/mm^3), microscopic hematuria, and pyuria. The presence of a low urinary sodium concentration has been noted and suggests hypoperfusion of partially functioning nephrons.

Diagnostic procedures

The gold standard diagnostic test is arteriography and/or renal angiography that identify the nature of the occlusion. However, such an invasive procedure is not indicated unless surgery, thrombolytic therapy, or angioplasty is being contemplated. Isotopic renal flow scan is the best noninvasive test, and usually shows absent or markedly reduced flow to the affected kidney or kidneys, a nonspecific finding. Isotopic scans can identify a small infarct due to a segmental embolism. Computed tomography using intravenous contrast may show an area of decreased contrast uptake with an accentuated thin cortical rim. Ultrasound of the kidneys usually is required to exclude other causes of oliguric or anuric renal failure, such as obstruction. Most commonly renal ultrasound studies in these patients are normal, but a focal echogenic area with a triangular shape may suggest an infarction. Intravenous urography will exclude nephrolithiasis or other causes of ureteral obstruction, although a delay in the uptake of dye by the affected kidney with a delay of the appearance of the contrast material in the collecting system may be present.

Treatment

The optimal treatment for renal artery thromboembolism has not been established. Vascular patency can be established with the use of oral anticoagulation, thrombolytic agents, balloon angioplasty, or surgically. If a unilateral segmental embolus is present, oral anticoagulation is effective in many instances. The following algorithm has been proposed for the management of renal artery embolism: (1) with unilateral embolism and an intact contralateral kidney, the initial therapy recommended is intraarterial streptokinase or transluminal angioplasty or both, followed by anticoagulation. In this situation surgical therapy has little benefit, even when medical therapy is not successful; (2) when there is a bilateral embolus or an embolus to a solitary kidney, intraarterial thrombolytic therapy, transluminal angioplasty, or both are recommended. After restoration of renal blood flow occurs, long-term oral anticoagulation is indicated. If restoration of the blood flow does not occur, with prolonged anuria or oliguria, then surgical reconstruction should be considered to establish renal blood flow, even after a period of days to weeks.

Anticoagulation should be life-long after thromboembolism, unless there is a clinical contraindication. Search for the source of embolization should be meticulous, because embolization to other vital organs can lead to death or other dramatic consequences despite the successful treatment of the renal arterial embolization.

ATHEROEMBOLIC RENAL DISEASE

Etiopathogenesis

The clinical presentation of this disease differs significantly from that of renal infarction produced by thromboembolism of the major arteries. This disease occurs in patients with severe ulcerative atheromatous disease. Atheroembolic renal disease arises from the occlusion of multiple small arteries (arcuate and intralobular) and terminal arterioles by cholesterol plaques that are displaced from ulcerative atheromata of the aorta or another great vessel. Because the extent of occlusion of arterioles is scattered and variable, the degree of renal failure varies from mild to severe. The pathology involves cholesterol plaques present as crystals within the lumina of arterioles (Fig. 35.1); there are various degrees of inflammatory reaction with foreign body reaction and multinucleated giant cells. Patchy areas of ischemia and small infarctions occur with tubular and glomerular atrophy and ultimately hyalinization.

One or more previous precipitating factors usually are present: (1) any surgical procedure involving the major vessels or heart; (2) angiography, arteriography, or arterial catheterization of the heart or great vessels; and (3) therapy with anticoagulants or thrombolytic agents. The latter causes atheroembolism by preventing the deposition of fibrin or increasing its removal from the cholesterol plaques, allowing the small cholesterol emboli to break free and enter the circulation. In a minority of the patients no predisposing factor is identified, and this disease can occur spontaneously. With the average age of hospitalized

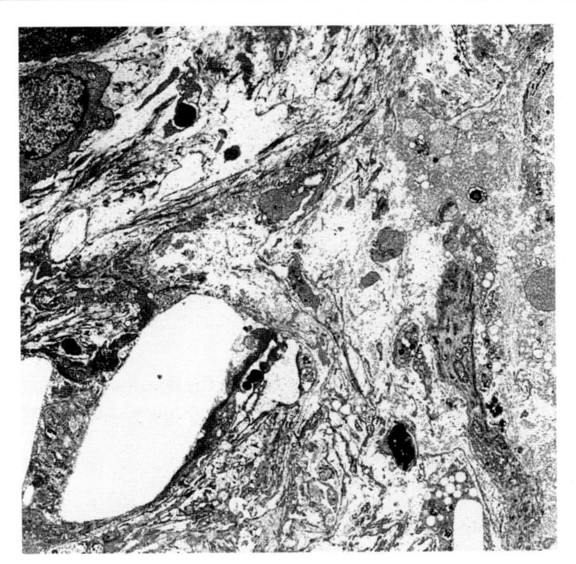

Figure 35.1 Kidney biopsy of a patient with atheroembolic disease. Electron microscopy image showing one to two vascular smooth muscle cells, and parts of three small cholesterol crystal clefts (dissolved away) which loom large under magnification of about 5000 x.

patients increasing, with increasing numbers of cardiac catheterizations and surgeries performed, and with the widespread use of thrombolytic and anticoagulant therapy, the incidence of atheroembolic disease is increasing. Moreover, the diagnosis, understanding, and differential diagnosis between atheroembolism and thromboembolism to the kidney are essential because the therapeutic approach indicated for the latter, based on anticoagulation and thrombolytic therapy, is harmful and therefore absolutely contraindicated for atheroembolic renal disease.

Clinical findings

Atheroembolic renal disease occurs as part of the systemic syndrome of cholesterol crystal embolization. The clinical and laboratory manifestations of this syndrome are summarized in Table 35.2. These result from the occlusion of small arteries – in virtually any organ – and the consequent inflammatory reaction to these crystals. As mentioned above, there usually is a precipitating event, such as cardiac catheterization or any other procedure involving the aorta; more rarely, there is no precipitating event. The patients are over 60; the disorder is rare in young patients. Males predominate over females, 3:1; and white patients predominate over black patients, 30:1. Renal involvement occurs in approximately 50% of the patients with systemic cholesterol embolization, and is usually manifested by subacute (or, less frequently, acute) renal failure that starts abruptly after a precipitating procedure and progresses in a stepwise manner over a period of several weeks. Alternatively, it occurs insidiously up to 4 weeks after the procedure. Oliguria may be transient or even absent, and a progressive increase in the serum urea and creatinine may be the only renal abnormality. Evidence of generalized arteriosclerosis is a common feature. Manifestations of cholesterol embolization to other organs are often present, such as the skin (livedo reticularis and other rashes), brain (transient ischemic attacks or strokes), pancreas (pancreatitis), gastrointestinal tract (abdominal pain or gastrointestinal bleeding), liver (elevated liver enzymes), spleen, and muscle. Another feature is digital cyanosis, the "blue toe syndrome," resulting from ischemic toes or even digital gangrene; the presence of normal pedal pulses helps to differentiate this condition from arterial insufficiency due to peripheral vascular disease. Retinal cholesterol emboli occur in 10% of the patients and can be identified on ophthalmoscopic examination, where they appear as bright copper yellow plaques (Hollenhorst plaques) in the retinal arterioles usually at their bifurcation. Unfortunately, this diagnostic finding is not very common. Some patients develop nonspecific systemic symptoms such as fever, myalgia, headache, and weight loss. Disseminated intravascular coagulation has been reported.

Table 35.2 Clinical and laboratory findings of atheroembolism to the kidney

Clinical findings
- Subacute or less frequently acute renal failure starting after precipitating procedure
- Precipitating procedures: surgery of major vessels, angiography, arteriography, arterial catheterization of the heart or aorta and therapy with anticoagulants or thrombolytics
- Generalized arteriosclerosis
- Evidence of cholesterol embolization to other organs: skin, brain, pancreas, gastrointestinal tract, liver, spleen and muscle
- Digital cyanosis- "Blue Toe Syndrome"
- Retinal cholesterol emboli (Hollenhorst plaques)

Laboratory findings
- Mild proteinuria or more rarely nephrotic range
- Microscopic hematuria with granular and hyaline casts
- *Eosinophiluria* is not uncommon
- Mild leukocytosis with *eosinophilia*
- Reduced serum complement levels
- Rarely antineutrophil cytoplasmic antibodies (ANCA) are present

Diagnostic procedures

The laboratory features of atheroembolic renal disease are nonspecific, and are useful only to exclude other disorders. Increased serum urea and creatinine is the hallmark of renal involvement. A greater than expected serum urea-to-creatinine ratio may occur from decreased glomerular perfusion. Mild proteinuria may be present; less commonly, proteinuria can be in the nephrotic range. The urine sediment can show microscopic hematuria, with granular, hyaline casts, and eosinophiluria is not uncommon. Mild leukocytosis with *eosinophilia* and increased inflammatory markers such as, erythrocyte sedimentation rate, plasma viscosity, and C reactive protein, often are present. Serum complement can be reduced, and, rarely, antineutrophil cytoplasmic antibodies (ANCA) are present. Except in very severe cases, the elevation of enzymes seen in renal thromboembolism is not present.

Differential diagnosis

The diagnosis of renal atheroembolism requires a high degree of suspicion. The multi-system nature of this disease leads to a wide differential diagnosis. It is very important to differentiate this entity from other disorders that can present in a similar fashion, such as renal thromboembolism, acute renal failure due to intravenous contrast material, polyarteritis nodosa, allergic vasculitis, collagen diseases, acute hepatitis, bacterial endocarditis, septicemia, and disseminated intravascular coagulation. One major reason for establishing a specific diagnoses is to avoid unnecessary therapy for other suspected diagnoses with prednisone and immunosuppressive therapy.

The diagnosis of this disease requires histologic visualization of the cholesterol emboli in any affected tissue. A biopsy of affected skin, muscle, or kidney is often diagnostic. Ophthalmologic examination with visualization of Hollenhorst plaques also is diagnostic.

The presence of important clinical clues in the history,

such as a precipitating factor, cutaneous signs, or retinal cholesterol plaques together with laboratory findings, such as eosinophilia, eosinophiluria, and a strong suspicion for this diagnosis usually are clinically adequate, and tissue biopsy is not always necessary.

Treatment

Atheroembolic renal disease is associated with high morbidity and mortality. The most significant morbidity seen with this condition is severe renal insufficiency requiring dialysis, which occurs in approximately 40% of patients, half of whom recover enough renal function to became dialysis-independent. Other morbidities are accelerated hypertension, gangrene of the lower extremities, and gastrointestinal bleeding or perforation. The mortality is greater in dialysis-dependent patients. The causes of death, often related to coexisting generalized arteriosclerosis, are multiple: cardiac, renal, sepsis, malignancies, ruptured aortic aneurysms, cerebrovascular accidents, and gastrointestinal bleeding.

The management of these patients is usually supportive, with adequate control of hypertension, dialytic therapy, a very aggressive cholesterol-lowering diet, and drug therapy. It is essential to withhold anticoagulation unless absolutely necessary. In many situations renal function improves significantly, even after prolonged periods of dialysis, and aggressive supportive care is essential to maximize the chances for a favorable outcome. In patients with repeated embolic episodes the use of transesophageal echocardiography to identify large denuded atherosclerotic areas in the aorta and subsequent surgical "debridement" to remove the source of emboli have been reported to be successful.

Acknowledgments

The authors are grateful to Prof. Barton S. Levine from UCLA and Prof. Alex M. Davison from the University of Leeds for their editorial comments.

We are also thankful to Dr. Thomas M. Stanley and Ms. Katherine A.G. Handelsman from the Department of Pathology, West Los Angeles VA Medical Center, for providing the picture used in this chapter and for their technical collaboration.

Suggested readings

Abuelo J, Gary P. Diagnosing vascular causes of renal failure. Ann Intern Med 1995;123:601-14.

Beraud J-J, Calvet B, Durand A, Mimran A. Reversal of acute renal failure following percutaneous transluminal recanalization of an atherosclerotic renal artery occlusion. J Hypertens 1989;7:909-11.

Bojar RM, Payne DD, Murphy RE, Schwartz SL, Belden JR, Caplan LR, Rastegar H. Surgical treatment of systemic atheroembolism from the thoracic aorta. Ann Thorac Surg 1997;61:1389-93.

Dahlberg PJ, Frecentese DF, Cogbill TH. Cholesterol embolization: experience with 22 histologically proven cases. Surgery 1989;105:737-46.

Fort J, Camps J, Ruiz P, Segarra A, Gomez M, Matas M, Segarra AL, Olmos A, Piera L. Renal artery embolism successfully revascularized by surgery after 5 days anuria. Is it never too late? Nephrol Dial Transplant 1996;11:1843-45.

Kronzon I, Tunick PA. Atheromatous disease of the thoracic aorta: pathologic and clinical implications. Ann Intern Med 1997;126:629-37.

Llach F, Nikakhtar B. Renal thromboembolism, atheroembolism, and renal vein thrombosis. In: Disease of the kidney. Boston, Little, Brown & Co, 1997:1893.

Rhodes JM. Cholesterol crystal embolism: an important "new" diagnosis for the general physician. Lancet 1996;347:1641.

Saleem S, Lakkis FG, Martinez-Maldonado M. Atheroembolic renal disease. Semin Nephrol 1996;16:309-18.

Scholari F, Bracchi M, Valzorio B, Movilli E, Costantino E, Savoldi S, Zorat S, Bonardelli S, Tardanico R, Maiorca R. Cholesterol atheromatous embolism: an increasingly recognized cause of acute renal failure. Nephrol Dial Transplant 1996;11:1607-12.

Takeda M, Katayama Y, Takahashi H, Saito K, Tsutsui T, Komeyama T. Successful fibrinolytic therapy using tissue plasminogen activator in acute renal failure due to acute thrombosis of bilateral renal arteries. Urol Int 1993;51:177-80.

Thadhani RI, Camarco CA Jr, Xavier RJ, Fang LS, Bazari H. Atheroembolic renal failure after invasive procedures. Natural history based on 52 histologically proven cases. Medicine 1995;74:350-8.

Thibault GE. One more hypothesis. N Engl J Med 1993;329:38-42.

Zuccala A, Zucchelli P. A renal disease frequently found at postmortem, but rarely diagnosed in vivo. Nephrol Dial Transplant 1997;12:1762-67.

CHAPTER

36

Hemolytic uremic syndrome and thrombotic thrombocytopenic purpura

Piero Ruggenenti, Giuseppe Remuzzi

KEY POINTS

- Hemolytic uremic syndrome (HUS) and thrombotic thrombocytopenic purpura (TTP) are syndromes of microangiopathic hemolytic anemia and thrombocytopenia in which endothelial dysfunction appears to be important in the sequence of events leading to microvascular thrombosis. The increase in lactate dehydrogenase (LDH) is the most sensitive index of the ongoing microangiopathic hemolysis and is confirmed by detection of fragmented red blood cells in the peripheral smear and a negative Coombs' test. In HUS the microthrombi are confined primarily to the kidneys, and renal failure is the dominant feature. TTP mainly involves the brain; intravascular thrombi apparently form and disperse repeatedly, producing intermittent neurologic signs.
- Typical (epidemic) HUS is due in most cases to *E. coli* O157:H7 gastrointestinal infection, and most often has a good outcome. Antibiotics are not recommended, and antimotility agents are contraindicated. Newer investigative therapies are aimed at preventing target organ exposure to verotoxin; these include orally administered toxin-binding resins.
- Atypical HUS includes forms with severe gastrointestinal prodromes and neurologic involvement (characterized by high mortality), and forms not associated with diarrhea but with progressive deterioration of renal function and neurologic involvement; these may be familial. The former needs only supportive therapy, but the latter, closer to TTP, may require more specific treatment.
- Abrupt onset of neurologic symptoms usually dominates the clinical picture of acute TTP. The infusion or exchange of fresh frozen plasma is the cornerstone of therapy.
- Relapsing episodes of TTP are now reported more often. More patients now recover from the initial acute episode. Plasma infusion has been extensively used for this form of TTP. Occasional patients with HUS or TTP fail to respond to plasma therapy (plasma-resistant HUS/TTP) and invariably have a poor outcome if alternative treatments fail. Bilateral nephrectomy may offer effective rescue therapy for patients who are plasma-resistant or plasma-dependent.
- Familial HUS/TTP has a heterogeneous pattern of inheritance. No markers are available to identify the heterozygous state or for antenatal diagnosis. The outcome is usually poor.
- The outcome of secondary forms of HUS/TTP depends on the underlying conditions. These include pregnancy, HIV, cancer, and chemotherapy, as well as transplant-associated forms. When the condition can be removed or treated, the microangiopathic process subsides, too.

Hemolytic uremic syndrome (HUS) and thrombotic thrombocytopenic purpura (TTP) are syndromes of microangiopathic hemolytic anemia and thrombocytopenia that share the same histologic lesion – widening of the subendothelial space and intraluminal platelet thrombi – and a similar pathophysiologic process of platelet consumption and erythrocyte disruption in the injured microcirculation that leads to thrombocytopenia and hemolytic anemia. Thus, the different clinical manifestations of HUS and TTP are essentially related to the different distribution of the microangiopathic lesions. Although in children glomerular and preglomerular vascular involvement is more frequent and the clinical manifestations of HUS are essentially consequences of renal dysfunction, in adults the microangiopathic process electively affects the brain and causes neurologic symptoms that dominate the clinical picture of TTP.

Etiopathogenesis

Endothelial dysfunction appears to be an important factor in the sequence of events leading to microvascular thrombosis. Consistent with this interpretation are data that most agents associated with the disease, for example bacterial endotoxins, verotoxins, antibodies and immunocomplexes, and certain drugs, are directly toxic to endothelial cells. In addition, verotoxin may bind specific receptors on circulating leukocytes which become active and adhere to the vascular wall. Thus, several mediators released by activated leukocytes may directly induce endothelial cell injury and release of ultralarge vWF multimers in the microcirculation. Endothelial cell injury, in turn, leads to subendothelial expansion and myointimal swelling and proliferation which are followed by narrowing or obliteration of vascular lumina. Vascular narrowing, by increasing resistances, enhances fluid shear stress, and this alters the normal processing of vWF and the interaction of platelets with the endothelium. Actually, in normal conditions, blood flow is laminar and vWF multimers circulate in a coiled form. Upon endothelial cell injury and swelling, blood flow in narrowed vascular lumina becomes turbulent. The consequent increase in shear stress may induce platelet activation and vWF multimers uncoiling. Uncoiled vWF multimers may become exposed to the activity of circulating proteases with consequent abnormal fragmentation. vWF fragments bind activated platelets and contribute to platelet aggregation and thrombi formation. In line with this hypothesis is the evidence that enhanced shear stress in vitro induces a process of vWF fragmentation in normal plasma identical to that seen in vivo in the acute phases of HUS or TTP. Besides vWF, shear stress also influences endothelial nitric oxide (NO) synthesis and release. NO, by inducing tumor necrosis factor (TNF)-α and interleukin (IL)-1 release from inflammatory cells, promotes leukocyte activation and further amplifies the inflammatory damage.

Specific therapies therefore are aimed at preventing or limiting this cascade of events, which ultimately causes intravascular thrombosis and tissue injury. However, the mechanisms accounting for the potentially beneficial effect of certain therapies are poorly understood. Plasma infusion and exchange are usually employed with the rationale of restoring a component that is missing in patient's plasma, possibly an enzyme that by modulating protease(s) activity in vWF handling may prevent abnormal fragmentation of the molecule during the acute phase of the disease. Steroids and immunosuppressants may limit or prevent the formation of autoantibodies or immunocomplexes which could in theory trigger endothelial injury in idiopathic forms of TMA, prostacyclin and antiplatelet agents may reduce the platelet interaction with the vascular wall, thus limiting microvascular thrombi.

Differentiation of the different forms of HUS/TTP may therefore help to predict disease outcome and to establish the most appropriate therapeutic approach (Fig. 36.1). Therefore, we will briefly describe the main clinical features of the different forms of HUS/TTP with emphasis on therapeutic options based on different clinical presentations. To this purpose, the disease is classified as typical (verotoxin-associated) and atypical HUS, acute and chronic/relapsing TTP, plasma-resistant HUS/TTP, familial HUS/TTP, and secondary forms (Tab. 36.1).

Clinical findings and differential diagnosis

Thrombocytopenia and hemolytic anemia are the laboratory hallmarks of HUS/TTP (Fig. 36.1). Thrombocytopenia is caused by platelet aggregation in the microcirculation; hemolytic anemia is likely the consequence of the

Table 36.1 Classification of HUS/TTP

Classification
Hemolytic uremic syndrome
Typical, verotoxin - associated
Atypical
Plasma resistant
Thrombotic thrombocytopenic purpura
Acute
Chronic relapsing
Plasma resistant
Familial forms
Secondary forms
Pregnancy-associated
TTP
Severe preeclampsia/HELLP syndrome
Postpartum HUS
HIV infection-associated
Systemic disease-associated
Systemic lupus erythematosus, scleroderma
Antiphospholipid syndrome
Malignant hypertension
Cancer - and chemiotherapy - associated
Transplant - and cyclosporine - associated

(TTP = thrombotic thrombocytopenic purpura; HUS = hemolytic uremic syndrome.)

mechanical fragmentation of erythrocytes during their passage through narrowed arterioles and capillaries. Thrombocytopenia is usually more severe in TTP than in HUS. At the onset of TTP, platelet count may fall below 20 000/mm^3 whereas values in between 30 000 and 100 000/mm^3 are most commonly reported in HUS. Anemia is usually severe with hemoglobin concentration below 10 g/100 ml. The increase in lactate dehydrogenase (LDH) is the most sensitive index of the ongoing hemolysis, and usually is associated with hyperbilirubinemia (mainly indirect), reticulocytosis, circulating free hemoglobin, and low or undetectable haptoglobin levels. Detection of fragmented red blood cells (schistocytes) with the typical aspect of burr or helmet cells in the peripheral smear (Fig. 36.2, see Color Atlas) together with a negative Coombs test are needed to confirm the microangiopathic nature of the hemolysis. Classic HUS often is associated with leukocytosis with a left shift, whereas white cell count is usually normal in atypical HUS and TTP. Prothrombin time, partial thromboplastin time (PTT), factor V, factor VIII, and fibrinogen are normal in most cases. Occasionally patients may have high levels of fibrin degradation products and prolonged thrombin time. Intravascular platelet aggregation results in reduced platelet survival and determines the thrombotic occlusion of small arterioles and capillaries. In HUS, the microthrombi are confined primarily to the kidneys, and thus renal failure is the dominant feature. TTP mainly involves the brain, and intravascular thrombi apparently form and disperse repeatedly, producing intermittent neurologic signs. In pediatric patients, particularly in children younger than 2 years and in most cases of typical HUS, a pattern of predominant glomerular injury prevails. In older children, as in adults, the renal changes are located predominantly in arteries and arterioles with glomerular ischemia, retraction of the glomerular tuft, and thickening of the capillary wall. Prognosis is good in patients with predominantly glomerular changes, but is much more severe in those with primarily vascular damage.

TYPICAL (VEROTOXIN-ASSOCIATED) HEMOLYTIC UREMIC SYNDROME

Typical (epidemic) HUS – mostly due to *E. coli* O157:H7 infection – is associated with prodromal diarrhea followed by acute renal failure, and is also referred to as D+HUS. D+HUS is usually considered a disease with a good outcome, with complete recovery in about 90% of cases. However, 3 to 5% of patients die during the acute phase, up to 5% are left with severe renal and extrarenal sequelae, and about 40% will still have low GFR at 10-year follow-up. In patients aged under 2 years, severe gastrointestinal prodromes, elevated white cell count, and anuria early in the course of the disease are predictors of the severity of HUS. Anuria for more than 10 days or need for dialysis in the acute phase, as well as proteinuria at 12 months' follow-up have been associated with an increased risk of chronic renal failure in the long term. Patched cortical necrosis or involvement of more than 50% of glomeruli are further predictors of poor outcome.

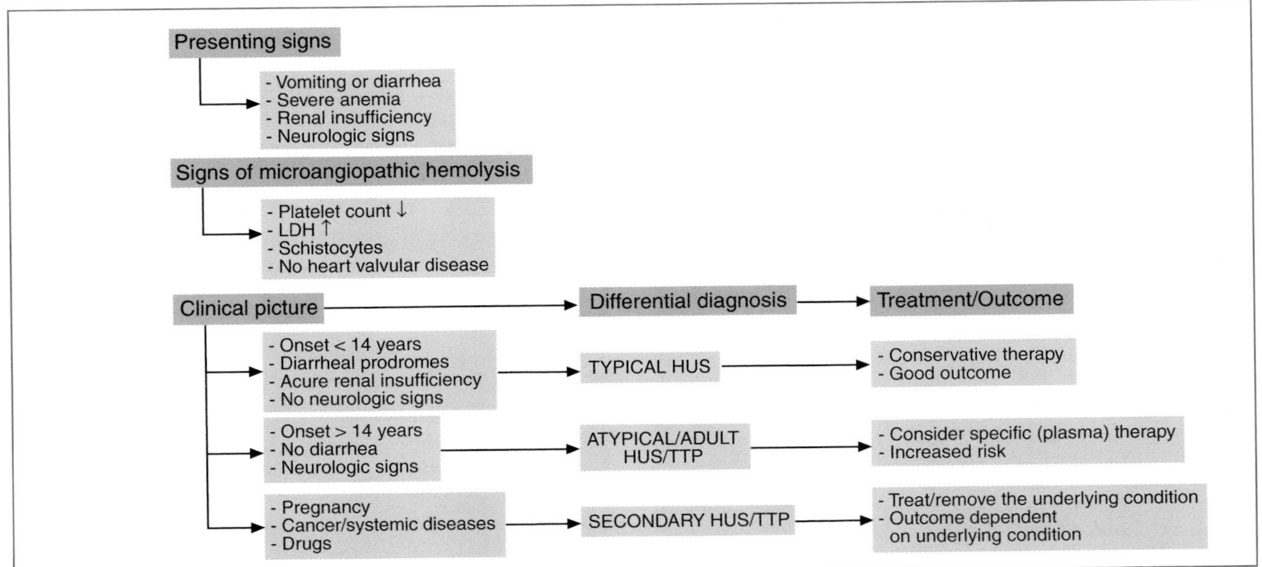

Figure 36.1 A suggested algorithm to help differential diagnosis of thrombotic microangiopathies. Patients with suggestive symptoms should be investigated for the presence of specific signs of microangiopathic hemolysis. Age and presenting symptoms help to differentiate typical from atypical forms. In all adult cases a predisposing condition should be investigated to rule out secondary forms of the disease. A prompt and correct differential diagnosis may help predict disease outcome and establish the most appropriate therapy. A good outcome is predicted and conservative therapy recommended in small children with typical HUS. Specific therapies should be considered only in adults or in atypical forms. In secondary forms, any effort should be aimed to treat or remove the underlying, predisposing condition.

Diagnosis rests on detection of *E. coli* O157:H7 in stool cultures. Serologic tests for antibodies to verotoxin and O157 lipopolysaccharide can be done in research laboratories, and tests are being developed for rapid detection of *E. coli* O157:H7 and shiga-like toxin in stools.

Undercooked ground beef is the commonest source of infection, but ham, turkey, cheese, unpasteurized milk, apple juice and water also have been implicated. Secondary person-to-person contact is an important way of spread in institutional centers, particularly day-care centers and nursing homes. Infected patients should be excluded from day-care centers until two consecutive stool cultures are negative for *E. coli* O157:H7 in order to prevent further transmission. However, the most important preventive measure in child-care centers is supervised hand-washing.

Treatment

Supportive treatment

Bowel rest is important for the enterohemorrhagic colitis associated with D+HUS, together with careful control of fluid balance, to avoid overhydration, particularly in cases with oligo-anuria. Blood transfusions may be required for symptomatic anemia secondary to microangiopathic hemolysis. Dialysis, together with appropriate correction of fluid and electrolyte abnormalities and anemia, has played a major role in the overall reduction in mortality rate over the last 40 years. Antibiotics are not recommended and sulfamethoxazole-trimethoprim may even increase toxin production. Antimotility agents are contraindicated as well, since they enhance the risk of HUS in patients with bloody diarrhea and *E. coli* O157:H7 infection, and increase the severity of neurologic manifestations in patients with overt HUS.

Other treatments

No specific therapy aimed at preventing or limiting the microangiopathic process has been proved to affect the course of D+HUS in children. Plasma therapy may limit short-term renal lesions, but does not affect long-term renal outcome and patients' survival. Heparin and antithrombotic agents may increase the risk of bleeding and should be avoided. Whether tissue-type plasminogen activator (t-PA), discriminating between fibrin and fibrin-bound plasminogen, gives a better risk/benefit profile in the treatment of HUS is worth investigating.

Treatments under investigation

Therapies aimed at preventing target organ exposition to verotoxin including orally administered toxin-binding resins and active or passive immunization, are currently under investigation. A variety of specific oligosaccharides have been attached to inert carrier agents in an effort to bind pathogenic toxins within the lumen of the gastrointestinal tract. Chromosorb is an inert platform molecule – diatomaceous silicon dioxide – that is chemically linked to an oligosaccharide chain specifically tailored to maximize binding of individual enteric toxins. Thus, chromosorb neutralizes the biologic activity of toxin A in stool samples and prevents injury to cultured cells. Its effectiveness in vivo is under investigation in two ongoing clinical trials aimed to test whether chromosorb prevents the occurrence of HUS in children with *E. coli*-associated hemorrhagic colitis or, respectively, may limit the severity of acute renal failure and of extrarenal complications in patients with newly diagnosed HUS (Tab. 36.2).

ATYPICAL HEMOLYTIC UREMIC SYNDROME

Atypical HUS can be covered under two clinical paradigms, one including forms with severe gastrointestinal prodromes, acute onset anuria, and malignant hypertension. These forms have a high mortality rate owing to severe gastrointestinal or neurologic involvement. Renal function fails to recover in about 50% of these cases. The second includes forms without diarrheal prodromes (non-diarrhea-associated HUS) but with progressive renal function deterioration, and neurologic involvement that may resemble TTP. These forms may be familial and mostly follow a relapsing or progressive course to end-stage renal failure or death.

Treatment

The outcome of severe forms of typical HUS (often described after verotoxin producing *E. coli* (VTEC) infection) depends mainly on the quality of supportive therapy and on the possibility (under investigation) of limiting the consequences of infection (see therapy of typical HUS).

Non-diarrhea-associated HUS very likely constitutes a form of the disease that is closer to TTP and may require more specific therapies (Tabs. 36.2 and 36.3) to stop the progression of the microangiopathic process (see therapy of acute TTP). These atypical cases recur more often after kidney transplantation. Plasma infusion and exchange have been found retrospectively to limit residual renal insufficiency or the risk of end-stage renal failure in children with atypical HUS. Uncontrolled studies suggest that plasma infusion or exchange may remarkably lower the mortality rate and risk of end-stage renal failure in adults. However, plasma, either infused or exchanged, is contraindicated in patients with streptococcal pneumonia HUS, since adult plasma contains antibodies against the Thomsen-Friedenreich antigen that may accelerate polyagglutination and hemolysis. These patients should be treated with antibiotics and washed red blood cells. Whole blood or plasma should be avoided. Prostacyclin infusion has been attempted with the aim of correcting the reported deficit and controlling hypertension, but its utility has yet to be proved. Intravenous immunoglobulins have been suggested to limit neurologic involvement in atypical HUS, but their effectiveness too is still unproven.

ACUTE THROMBOTIC THROMBOCYTOGENIC PURPURA

About 90% of patients with TTP present with an abrupt onset of neurologic signs, purpura and fever. Neurologic symptoms usually dominate the clinical picture and may be fleeting and fluctuating, probably because of continuous thrombi formation and dispersion in the brain microcirculation. However, they usually subside within 48 hours of effective therapy. In the early 1960s, acute TTP was almost invariably fatal, but nowadays, thanks to earlier diagnosis, improved intensive care facilities and new techniques such as plasma therapy, survival may reach 90%.

Treatment

Specific treatment

The infusion or exchange of fresh frozen plasma is the

Table 36.2 Treatments most commonly used in HUS/TTP, doses and modalities of administration

Treatment	Administration	Indication-Comment
Treatment of acute renal failure		**HUS**
Peritoneal dialysis	Continuous, 24 hour per day	Well tolerated, may remove plasminogen activator inhibitor I
Verotoxin adsorption		**HUS**
Chromosorb	Oral – 0.5 g/kg body weight, x 7 days	May limit verotoxin absorption and microangiopathic lesions. Under clinical investigation
Antiplatelet agents		**TTP**
Aspirin	Oral – 325-1300 mg/day	Unproven efficacy
Dipyridamole	Oral – 400-600 mg/day	Unproven efficacy
Dextran 70	Intravenous - 500 mg bid	Unproven efficacy
Prostacyclin	Intravenous - 4-20 μg/kg/min	Beneficial in occasional cases. May cause hypotension and worsen diarrhea
Antithrombotic agents		**HUS**
Heparin	Intravenous - 5000 U Intravenous - 750-1000 U/h	Some benefit suggested in postpartum HUS, increased risk of bleeding
Streptokinase	Intravenous - 250 000 U Intravenous - 100 000 U/h	Unproven effectiveness. Should be avoided because of the high risk of hemorrhagic complications
Steroids/vincristine		**TTP**
Prednisone	Oral - 60-200 mg/day, tapered by 5 mg/week	Possibly effective in mild forms
Vincristine	Intravenous - 1 mg/4-7 days x 5	Possibly effective in relapsing forms. Umproven effectiveness in acute and plasma resistant forms Neurologic toxicity
Fresh frozen plasma		**Atypical/adult HUS, TTP**
Infusion	30-40 ml/kg on day 1, then 10-20 ml/kg/day	Probably effective in atypical and adult forms, and in cases associated with neurologic signs
Exchange	1-2 plasma volumes/day	The same indications of plasma infusion. No risk of fluid overload
Cryosupernatant	See plasma infusion/exchange	Occasionally effective in cases resistent to whole plasma
Solvent detergent treated	See plasma infusion/exchange	May limit the risk of viral contamination
Other treatments		
Vitamin E	Oral – 1000 mg/m²/day	**HUS** Safe. Probably effective in typical HUS. To be tested in controlled trials
Gamma globulins	Intravenous – 400 mg/kg/day	**HUS or TTP** Unproven efficacy
Rescue therapies		
Splenectomy		Occasionally effective in relapsing TTP. Umproven efficacy in plasma-resistant TTP
Bilateral nephrectomy		Effective in plasma-resistant HUS

(HUS = hemolytic uremic syndrome; TTP = thrombotic thrombocytopenic purpura.)

cornerstone of therapy in acute TTP (Tabs. 36.2 and 36.3). A randomized trial found an apparent superiority of plasma exchange over plasma infusion in the treatment of TTP. However, patients undergoing the exchange procedure were given three times the amount of plasma given to patients who received infusion alone (21.5 ± 7.81 vs. 6.7 ± 3.3). When equivalent volumes of plasma were given during plasma infusion or exchange, no difference in response rate or survival could be documented. Thus, plasma infusion and exchange may be equally effective in the treatment of acute TTP. However, in situations such as renal insufficiency or heart failure, that limit the amount of plasma that can be provided with infusion alone, plasma exchange should be considered as first-choice therapy. Initial plasma infusion should be considered whenever plasma exchange is not readily available. Plasma infusion also may be considered as maintenance therapy after recovery has been achieved with plasma exchange. Occasional patients appear to require large amounts of plasma and several months of infusion or exchange before achieving remission. Thus, even in those who fail to respond promptly to initial therapy, intensive plasma therapy may eventually succeed in inducing remission of the disease.

Table 36.3 Indication to plasma infusion/exchange in the different forms of HUS/TTP

Disease	Comment
Typical childhood HUS	NO (usually complete spontaneous recovery)
Atypical childhood HUS	Probably YES (to minimize the risk of sequelae)
Adult HUS	YES (to minimize sequelae)
TTP (acute and relapsing forms)	YES (life-saving)
Familial HUS/TTP	Probably YES (but often ineffective)
Secondary TMA	
Pregnancy-associated	
TTP	YES (life saving)
HELLP syndrome	Probably YES (in selected cases and after delivery)
Postpartum HUS	Probably YES (but often ineffective)
HIV-associated	
HIV infection	Probably YES (may be life-saving)
AIDS	Probably NO (usually ineffective)
Cancer-associated	
Mitomycin	Probably YES (with drug withdrawal)
Metastatic disease	Probably NO (usually ineffective)
Transplant-associated	
Cyclosporin	Probably YES (with drug reduction or withdrawal)
Disease recurrency	Probably YES (but often ineffective)

(HUS = hemolytic uremic syndome; TTP = thrombotic thrombocytopenic purpura.)

Other treatments

Treatments given in addition to plasma did not provide any benefit in term of shorter illness duration, lower mortality, or fewer long-term sequelae. Antiplatelet drugs were almost invariably used in combination with steroids, plasma manipulation, and/or splenectomy. In the few studies in which antiplatelets were given alone, the response was less than 15%. The finding that patients treated with steroids and plasma, combined or not with antiplatelet drugs, had the same high survival rate, suggests that these agents are of little help in TTP. The effectiveness of prostacyclin is also unproved. In view of the risk of severe bleeding, antiplatelet agents, are best avoided in the acute phase of TTP. One of these agents, ticlopidine, has even been accused of being a possible trigger of TTP. Antiplatelet agent have sometimes been recommended during the recovery phase, since thrombocytosis may enhance platelet aggregation and the risk of potentially fatal relapses.

Patients with TTP have been given corticosteroids on the assumption that it is an autoimmune disorder, but this is difficult to prove since the steroids were always given in combination with other therapies. Thirty out of 108 patients with either TTP or HUS were recently reported to have recovered after treatment with corticosteroids alone. All of them, however, had mild forms. Anecdotal cases have been reported to respond to vincristine, sometimes when other treatment modalities failed. However, these cases are too few to allow the conclusion that vincristine should be used as first-line therapy in acute TTP. Evidence that immunoglobulins inhibit in vitro platelet-aggregating activity of plasma from patients with acute TTP has led to some recommendations to use them to treat this disease. However, their effectiveness, too, is unproved. Splenectomy was commonly used to treat acute TTP before plasma therapy was available, but it is no longer considered as first-line therapy for acute TTP.

The severe thrombocytopenia in TTP has led many physicians to administer platelet transfusions with the aim of preventing severe bleeding complications. However, reports of sudden death, decreased survival, and delayed recovery after platelet transfusion dramatically document the danger of giving platelets to patients with TTP. Thus, platelet transfusions are contraindicated in acute TTP, with the sole exception of cases of life-threatening bleeding.

RELAPSING THROMBOTIC THROMBOCYTOPENIC PURPURA

Relapsing episodes of TTP are separated by a period of 4 weeks or more of apparent recovery and must be distinguished from recurrences of acute TTP, that are actually flare-ups of the same initial episode, usually the result of stopping treatment too soon.

This once rare form of TTP is being reported increasingly often – in up to 30% of cases in some institutions – as more patients recover from the initial acute episode thanks to improved supportive and specific treatments. Relapses may occur even after symptom-free periods of months or years and some spontaneous remissions have been reported. Although individual attacks usually respond to treatment, long-term prognosis normally is poor. Relapsing forms of thrombotic microangiopathy also have been reported in children, but with the clinical features of HUS.

An extremely rare variant of relapsing TTP is characterized by frequent episodes, recurring after regular symptom-free intervals. This form, also known as "chronic relapsing" or "frequently relapsing" TTP, is associated with persistency of abnormally large vWF multimers in the circulation. The long-term outcome is invariably poor if therapy fails to achieve long-lasting remission.

Treatment

Plasma infusion has been used extensively for relapsing and chronic TTP (Tabs. 36.2 and 36.3). One patient of ours with chronic relapsing TTP provided evidence that at least in these relapsing cases effective treatment depended on infusing a certain amount of normal plasma. This patient, who had more than 100 relapses over 7 years, was given different forms of treatment on different occasions: exchange, plasma infusion alone, or plasma removed and replaced with albumin and saline. Clinical remission and normalization of platelet count within a few days was invariably obtained by plasma exchange or infusion, but plasma removal never raised the platelet count. Thus, plasma infusion is now an established first-line treatment for relapsing episodes of TTP.

Other treatments

Vincristine has been reported to stop cyclic relapses of TTP in isolated cases, but its effectiveness in chronic relapsing TTP has not been proved. Two cases of chronic relapsing TTP were reported to respond to cyclophosphamide and one to azathioprine. Interestingly, the response to azathioprine was associated with the disappearance of the unusually large vWF multimers from the circulation.

Splenectomy might work by removing a major site of synthesis of an autoantibody or a vWF cofactor. Preliminary evidence is available that elective splenectomy during hematologic remission reduces the relapse rate and the need for plasma therapy in patients who have had one or more relapses of TTP. Thus, splenectomy could be considered in patients with disabling disease requiring frequent and prolonged courses of plasma therapy.

PLASMA-RESISTANT HUS/TTP

Occasional patients with HUS or TTP fail to respond to plasma therapy and invariably have a poor outcome if alternative treatments are not effective. Substitution of cryosupernatant fraction (i.e., plasma from which a cryoprecypitate containing the largest plasma vWF multimers, fibrinogen, and fibronectin, has been removed) for fresh frozen plasma has been successful in a small number of patients who did not respond to repeated exchanges or infusions with fresh frozen plasma (Tab. 36.3). The rationale for this approach is that plasma cryosupernatant may provide the same beneficial factor(s) found in whole plasma, but does not contain the potentially harmful factors (including large vWF multimers) that might participate in the formation of intravascular thrombi.

Splenectomy has been attempted in occasional patients who did not respond to corticosteroids and plasma exchange. A deterioration of clinical status with a decrease in hematocrit and platelet count and high serum lactate dehydrogenase was reported in six cases: four became comatose and one died abruptly. The five surviving patients progressively recovered after the reinstitution of plasma exchange. Splenectomy was thus no longer considered for treating TTP refractory to plasma therapy. Although this study was far from conclusive on account of its retrospective design, the role of splenectomy in plasma resistant TTP has to be carefully reconsidered unless new data become available to support its use.

Bilateral nephrectomy may be an effective rescue therapy in rare patients with atypical HUS in imminent danger of death because of severe thrombocytopenia associated with refractory hypertension and/or signs of hypertensive encephalopathy. In such dramatic cases bilateral nephrectomy was followed within 2 weeks by complete hematologic and clinical remission. The rationale of the procedure rests on evidence that removing the kidneys eliminates a major site of vWF fragmentation, which would limit platelet activation and protect patients from the further spreading of microvascular lesions. However, bilateral nephrectomy is irreversible and should be considered only for patients in whom all other approaches have failed. Potential candidates are patients who are plasma-resistant (defined as >20 plasma infusions/exchanges with no improvement of clinical and laboratory findings) or plasma-dependent (patients who have to be continuously infused with plasma to remain in remission, and in whom the platelet count invariably drops, with signs of hemolysis, within a few days after plasma is discontinued).

Nephrectomy should not be considered unless a renal biopsy – taken as soon as the platelet count rises, even transiently, with plasma to a level where the procedure is safe – shows chronic diffuse lesions associated with signs of the disease, meaning arteriolar thrombosis and myointimal proliferation. Finally, nephrectomy should be considered only in the presence of life-threatening signs such as major neurologic dysfunction or coma, or uncontrolled bleeding as a consequence of refractory thrombocytopenia.

FAMILIAL HUS/TTP

This form has a heterogeneous pattern of inheritance (recessive or dominant) and within each family resembles HUS or TTP or, less commonly, one or the other form of the disease. The pathogenesis is unknown. Low C3 complement fraction is occasionally reported in familial HUS or TTP. Genetic counseling is important if further pregnancies are planned. Unfortunately, no markers are available to identify the heterozygous state or for antenatal diagnosis by amniocentesis or chorionic villus biopsy. The outcome is usually poor with death or chronic renal failure being reported in 50 to 100% of cases. No specific therapy is available. Plasma therapy usually is recommended, but its effectiveness is limited.

SECONDARY FORMS OF HUS/TTP

As a general rule, the outcome of secondary forms of HUS/TTP depends on the prognosis of the underlying condition. When this can be removed or treated, the microangiopathic process subsides too. Underlying diseases that do not respond to treatment are almost invariably associated with a poor outcome and HUS/TTP may be the final complication.

Pregnancy-associated

The microangiopathic process in pregnancy may manifest with the clinical features of acute TTP, of the hemolysis, elevated liver enzymes and low platelet (HELLP) syndrome, or of HUS. Differential diagnosis between these conditions may serve to establish the most appropriate therapeutic approach (Fig. 36.3).

Thrombotic thrombocytopenic purpura

Eighty-nine percent of cases ensue in the first 24 weeks of pregnancy; Later in the course of pregnancy, clinical features of TTP and preeclampsia may overlap. Despite limited experience, available series show that the maternal mortality rate has fallen from 68% to almost zero with the institution of plasma therapy (Tab. 36.3).

Measurement of plasma antithrombin (AT) III activity has been suggested as a useful tool to differentiate TTP and preeclampsia. Before gestational week 28 and when AT III plasma activity is normal, TTP is most likely. Plasma therapy could be tried and, if effective, it should be continued until term and/or complete remission of the disease. Delivery can be considered as "rescue" after failure of plasma therapy. The role of other treatments often employed in idiopathic TTP remains elusive.

After week 34 of gestation, preeclampsia is most likely and usually is associated with decreased plasma AT III activity. Delivery is the treatment of choice and usually is followed by complete recovery within 24-48 hours. Persistent disease may be an indication to attempt a course of plasma therapy. Between 28 and 34 weeks, the optimal treatment is controversial. It is sometimes held that delivery should always be considered as first-line therapy, whereas others believe that, if there is no evidence of fetal distress and plasma AT III activity is normal, a course of

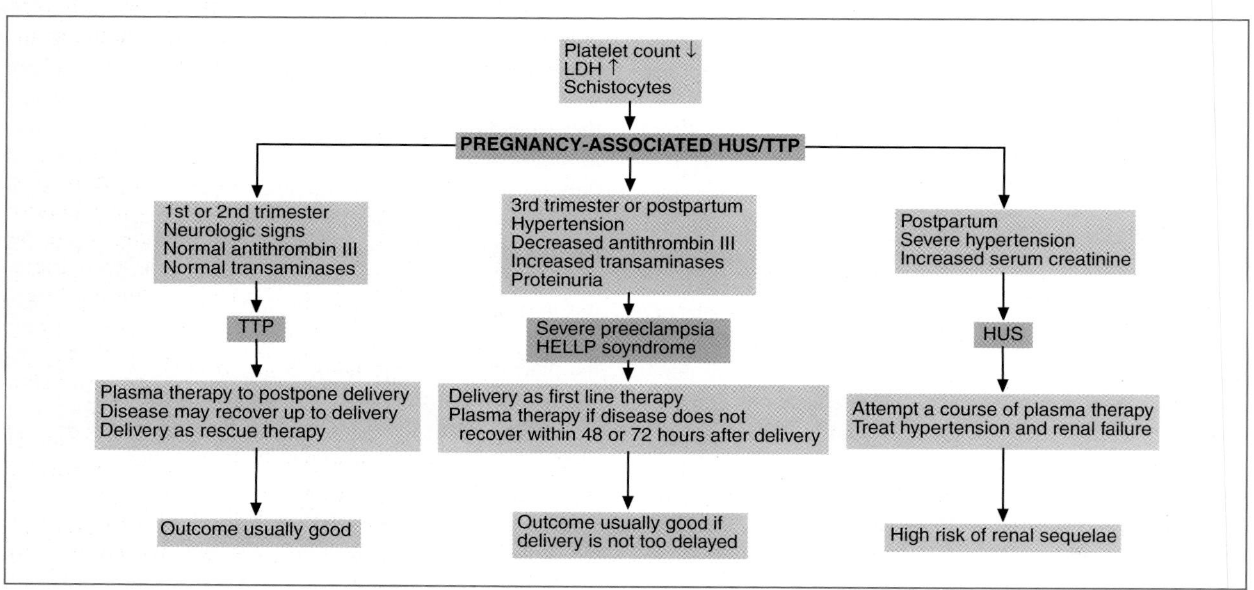

Figure 36.3 A suggested algorithm to help differential diagnosis of pregnancy-associated HUS/TTP. Timing of disease onset, antithrombin III levels, and degree of renal, neurologic and hepatic involvement may help differential diagnosis and may serve to establish the most appropriate therapeutic approach. As a general rule, however, it should always be considered that any delay in inducing delivery may lead to dramatic consequences either for the mother or for the baby.

plasma therapy can be reasonably attempted before inducing delivery.

The HELLP syndrome

The HELLP (an acronym for hemolysis, elevated liver enzymes and low platelet count) syndrome is simply a form of severe preeclampsia in which, besides hypertension and renal dysfunction, there is evidence of microangiopathic hemolysis and liver involvement. The syndrome is most common in white multiparous women with a history of poor pregnancy outcome. It arises in the antepartum period in 70% of cases. Postpartum, symptoms usually arise within 24-48 hours from delivery, occasionally after an uncomplicated pregnancy. Diagnosis is based on: (1) hemolysis (defined as fragmented erythrocytes in the circulation and lactic dehydrogenase ≥ 600 U/l), (2) elevated liver enzymes (serum glutamic oxaloacetic transaminase >70 U/l), and (3) low platelets (platelet count $<100\times103/mm^3$). Overt disseminated intravascular coagulation (DIC) is reported in 25% of cases. Intrahepatic hemorrhage, subcapsular liver hematoma, and liver rupture are rare, life-threatening complications. The maternal and perinatal mortality rates range from 0 to 24% and from 7.7 to 60%, respectively. Most of the perinatal deaths are related to abruptio placentae, intrauterine asphyxia, and extreme prematurity. As many as 44% of the infants are growth-retarded.

Termination of pregnancy is the only definitive therapy. Hydralazyne or dihydralazyne are the first-choice drugs to control pregnancy-induced hypertension, magnesium sulfate to prevent and treat convulsions. Both peritoneal dialysis and hemodialysis have been used to treat acute renal failure. Platelet transfusions are needed only for clinical bleeding or severe thrombocytopenia (platelet count <20 000/μl).

In approximately 5% of patients with HELLP syndrome, symptoms and laboratory abnormalities do not improve after delivery. These are cases with central nervous system abnormalities, associated with renal and cardiopulmonary dysfunction and activation of coagulation. Uncontrolled studies suggest that plasma exchange may help recovery in patients with persistent evidence of disease 72 hours or more after delivery. However, plasma therapy is ineffective during pregnancy and may increase fetal and maternal risk when used to delay delivery. Preliminary evidence suggests that, postpartum, corticosteroids may speed up disease recovery and, antepartum, may postpone delivery of previable fetuses and reduce the mother's need for blood products.

Postpartum HUS

By definition, postpartum HUS follows a normal delivery by no more than six months. The clinical course usually is fulminant. Supportive care including dialysis, transfusions, and careful fluid management remains the most important form of treatment. Whether plasma therapy improves survival or limits renal sequelae has not yet been established. Antiplatelet agents, heparin, and antithrombotic therapy may enhance the risk of bleeding and have no proven efficacy.

HIV-associated

HUS and TTP are both among the complications of AIDS, which may account for as much as 30% of hospitalized HUS/TTP cases. Plasma manipulation appears the only feasible approach (Tab. 36.3). Uncontrolled series provide evidence that the survival rate in HIV patients without AIDS is comparable to that of idiopathic TTP. By contrast, patients with AIDS-associated TTP almost invariably have a poor outcome and do not appear to benefit from plasma therapy.

Cancer- and chemiotherapy-associated

HUS/TTP complicates almost 6% of cases of metastatic carcinoma. The prognosis is extremely poor, and most patients die within a few weeks. A disease with the predominant features of HUS has been described in 2 to 10% of cancer patients treated with mitomycin, particularly among those receiving cumulative doses of 60 mg or higher, or more than one course of therapy. Platinum- and bleomycin-containing combinations have also been reported to induce HUS. The median time to death is about 4 weeks. Patients surviving the acute phase often remain on chronic dialysis, or die later of recurrence of the tumor or metastases.

Therapy is minimally effective (Tab. 36.3). Administration of blood products to correct symptomatic anemia often results in exacerbation of the syndrome, with rapid worsening of hemolysis, deterioration of renal function, and pulmonary edema. The possibility to prevent the syndrome by giving steroids during mitomycin treatment has been suggested and needs to be confirmed in prospective controlled trials. Plasma exchange or perfusion over filters containing staphylococcal protein A have been attempted with the rationale of removing circulating immunocomplexes, but their effectiveness is unproven.

Transplant-associated

Kidney transplantation is the treatment of choice for patients with HUS who develop end-stage renal failure. From an overview of the published literature, it can be estimated that the overall risk of recurrence of HUS after a cadaveric kidney transplant is about 13%, with no differences attributable to cyclosporine. A 30% recurrence rate can instead be reasonably estimated in patients given a living transplant, at least on the basis of the scant available data. The reasons for this difference are not known.

It has been pointed out that the risk of recurrence is higher in patients with recurrent and familial forms of HUS, and negligible in children with the typical form. A recurrence rate of 67% and 17% was reported among 18 children with atypical HUS and six children with typical D+HUS respectively.

The outcome of posttransplant HUS is poor. In 25 children with end-stage renal failure secondary to HUS, 1- and 5- year graft survival was 66 and 37% compared with 80 and 69% in all other pediatric recipients. In this series no recurrence of HUS was reported, and the high graft loss apparently was due to an excess of chronic vascular rejection. The consistency of this evidence is however hard to establish because of the difficulties in differentiating vascular rejection and recurrent HUS.

Early diagnosis and discontinuation of cyclosporine occasionally has led to reversal of the syndrome. However, using the newer immunosuppressive agents derived from fungal peptides, such as FK 506, instead of cyclosporine is not effective. Uncontrolled studies suggest that intravenous immunoglobulin infusion may permit successful management of HUS/TTP without graft loss. These findings however, need confirmation in controlled studies.

CONCLUSIONS

A general consensus has been achieved that therapies (i.e., plasma exchange or infusion) aimed at stopping the microangiopathic process should always be tried in TTP and in adult and/or atypical forms of HUS to minimize the risk of death or long-term sequelae (Tabs. 36.2 and 36.3). By contrast, this approach is seldom effective in secondary forms whose outcome depends mainly on the prognosis of the underlying condition, and it is not risk-effective in typical childhood HUS, which usually recovers spontaneously. Whenever indicated, specific therapy should be started as soon as diagnosis is established in order to speed up disease recovery and minimize the risk of sequelae. Treatment should be continued until complete disease remission is achieved.

Platelet count and serum lactate dehydrogenase are the most sensitive markers for monitoring the response to therapy. In conditions associated with decreased platelet production (cancer- or AIDS-associated HUS/TTP), serum lactate dehydrogenase concentration is a more reliable indicator of disease activity than platelet count. In pregnancy-associated HUS/TTP monitoring serum transaminases may be helpful.

Plasma manipulation is the only therapy of proven efficacy, at least in some forms of HUS/TTP. The infusion of fresh frozen plasma is intended to deliver the equivalent of one plasma volume (about 30 ml/kg of body weight) over the first 24 hours and about 20 ml/kg of body weight daily thereafter. To avoid fluid overload, diuretics or ultrafiltration may be employed. The exchange procedure usually is intended to replace one to two plasma volumes every day. When cryosupernatant fraction is used, during the infusion or exchange procedure patients should be given the same volumes as reported above for whole plasma (Tab. 36.2).

Acknowledgments

The Authors are grateful to Dr. Tullio Bertani and to Gianfranco Marchetti for their invaluable help in preparing the manuscript.

Suggested readings

Bell WR, Braine HG, Ness PM, et al. Improved survival in thrombotic thrombocytopenic purpura-hemolytic uremic syndrome. Clinical experience in 108 patients. N Engl J Med 1991;325:398-403.

Byrnes JJ, Moake JL, Klug P, et al. Effectiveness of the cryosupernatant fraction of plasma in the treatment of refractory thrombotic thrombocytopenic purpura. Am J Hematol 1990; 34:169-74.

Crowther MA, Heddle N, Hayward C, et al. Splenectomy done during hematologic remission to prevent relapse in patients with thrombotic thrombocytopenic purpura. Ann Int Med 1996;125:294-6.

Gianviti A, Perna A, Caringella A, et al. Plasma exchange in children with hemolytic-uremic syndrome at risk of poor outcome. Am J Kidney Dis 1993;22:264-6.

Mannucci PM, Lombardi R, Lattuada A, et al. Enhanced proteolysis of plasma von Willebrand factor in thrombotic thrombocytopenic purpura and the hemolytic uremic syndrome. Blood 1989;74:978-83.

Moake JL, Rudy CK, Troll IH, et al. Unusually large plasma factor VIII: von Willebrand factor multimers in chronic relapsing thrombotic thrombocytopenic purpura. N Engl J Med 1982;307:1432-5.

Noris M, Ruggenenti P, Todeschini M, et al. Increased nitric oxide formation in recurrent thrombotic microangiopathies: a possible mediator of microvascular injury. Am J Kidney Dis 1996;27:790-6.

Remuzzi G, Ruggenenti P. The hemolytic uremic syndrome. Kidney Int 1995;47:2-19.

Remuzzi G, Ruggenenti P, Bertani T. Thrombotic microangiopathies. In Tisher CC, Brenner BM (eds). Renal pathology. 2nd ed, Philadelphia: JP Lippincott, 1994;1154-84.

Remuzzi G, Galbusera M, Salvadori M, et al. Bilateral nephrectomy stopped renal disease progression in plasma-resistant hemolytic uremic syndrome with neurological signs and coma. Kidney Int 1996;49:282-86.

Rizzoni G, Claris-Appiani A, Edefonti A, et al. Plasma infusion for hemolytic uremic syndrome in children: results of a multicenter controlled trial. J Pediatr 1988;112:284-90.

Rock GA, Shumak KH, Buskard NA, et al. Comparison of plasma exchange with plasma infusion in the treatment of thrombotic thrombocytopenic purpura. N Engl J Med 1991; 325:393-7.

Ruggenenti P, Remuzzi G. The pathophysiology and management of thrombotic thrombocytopenic purpura. Eur J Haematol 1996;56:191-207.

Ruggenenti P, Galbusera M, Plata Cornejo R, et al. Thrombotic thrombocytopenic purpura: evidence that infusion rather than removal of plasma induces remission of the disease. Am J Kidney Dis 1993;21:314-8.

Weiner CP. Thrombotic microangiopathy in pregnancy and the postpartum period. Semin Hematol 1987;24:119-29.

CHAPTER

37

Systemic sclerosis

José Miguel Cruz

KEY POINTS

- Systemic sclerosis (SSc) is a generalized connective tissue disorder characterized by vascular lesions, fibrosis, and degenerative changes. The estimated incidence is about 20 new cases per million population per year.
- Involvement of the skin and subcutaneous tissue is the predominant feature, but joints, skeletal muscles, and other multiple organs also are involved.
- A variant of the disease is the CREST syndrome, defined by: calcinosis, Raynaud's phenomenon, esophageal hypomotility, sclerodactyly, and teleangiectasias.
- The most common serologic abnormality is a positive antinuclear antibody response (>1:16) and antibodies to DNA topoisomerase Y.
- Involvement of the kidney manifests as a slowly progressing chronic renal disease or a scleroderma renal crisis (SRC) characterized by malignant hypertension and acute azotemia.
- The most prominent histopathologic changes are subintimal proliferation with luminal narrowing of small and medium-sized arteries in the kidney.
- The pathogenetic hypothesis combines vasospasm, subintimal cellular proliferation, and increased production of collagen.
- Aggressive treatment of hypertension with ACE inhibitors appears to have made a major difference in the prognosis of scleroderma renal crisis.

Systemic sclerosis (SSc) is a generalized connective tissue disorder characterized by vascular lesions, degenerative changes, and fibrosis. It affects the joints, skeletal muscles, skin, and other multiple organs. Involvement of the kidneys commonly presents as a slowly progressing chronic renal disease or as scleroderma renal crisis (SRC) characterized by rapidly progressive renal failure and malignant hypertension. This chapter will present a clinical overview of the disease and will focus on the renal complications of systemic sclerosis.

Epidemiology

Systemic sclerosis is a rare disease. The estimated incidence is about 20 new cases per million population per year in the US. It characteristically affects women between the ages of 30 and 50 years; the actual frequency in women is three times that in men, and the female/male ratio increases to 15:1 during the childbearing years. Children and younger men are rerely affected. Although there is no overall racial predilection, young black women have a tenfold higher frequency of systemic sclerosis than do young white women.

Etiology

The etiology of systemic sclerosis is unknown. Epidemiologic studies, however, have demonstrated association with several environmental factors. An epidemic of chemically induced systemic sclerosis-like syndrome occurred in Spain in 1981 among people who ingested aniline-denatured rapeseed oil. Silicone breast implants, drugs (bleomycin), and silica exposure from gold and coal mining are associated with systemic sclerosis-like illnesses, L-Tryptophan ingestion leads to cutaneous scleroderma changes that usually accompany the other manifestations of the eosinophilia-myalgia syndrome. Systemic sclerosis also has been described in association with chronic graft-versus-host disease. A genetic predisposition to systemic sclerosis is only weakly discernible. Associations with human leukocyte antigens DR3 and DR5 and an increased prevalence of antinuclear antobodies in asymptomatic family members have been reported, and DRB1*11 was associated with antitopoisomerase-I antibody (ATA)-positive patients with a strongest risk factor for pulmonary fibrosis.

Pathophysiology

Autopsy studies demonstrate renal histopathologic changes in the majority of systemic sclerosis patients. Subintimal proliferation with luminal narrowing of small and medium-sized arteries in the kidney is the most prominent finding. The arterial changes coexist with varying degrees of tubule atrophy, interstitial fibrosis, and glomerular obsolescence.

Arterial changes also characterize the scleroderma renal crisis kidney. Small and medium-sized arteries (interlobular and arcuate arteries in the renal cortex) show intimal edema and intimal cell proliferation. Accumulations of a mucoid substance composed of glycoproteins and mucopolysaccharides may separate the endothelium from the internal elastic lamina. Myointimal cells, absent from normal arteries, possibly participate in the intimal thickening seen in systemic sclerosis. The common end-point of these vascular changes is luminal narrowing and subsequent tissue ischemia. The presence of adventitial and periadventitial fibrosis differentiates the renovascular lesions of systemic sclerosis from those of other forms of malignant hypertension. The typical lesion in smaller renal arteries and afferent arterioles in systemic sclerosis is fibrinoid necrosis. Lymphocytes and inflammatory cells are typically absent from the vascular lesions.

Glomerular disease in scleroderma renal crisis is probably ischemic in origin and consists of basement membrane thickening, obliteration of the capillary loops, and glomerulosclerosis. Hyperplasia of the juxtaglomerular apparatus has been observed, but is not specific for scleroderma renal crisis. Tubule epithelial degeneration and scattered interstitial fibrosis also are present. Immunofluorescence findings are generally nonspecific and may reveal immunoglobulin M, complement, and fibrin deposits in small renal arteries. In a few cases, antinuclear antibodies have been eluted from renal biopsy tissue.

One approach to the pathogenesis of systemic sclerosis is to regard the disease as primarily an abnormality of small and medium-sized arteries. A combination of vasospasm, subintimal cellular proliferation, and increased production of collagen in and around the vessel wall leads to luminal narrowing and subsequent tissue ischemia and sclerosis. This hypothesis, however, does not rule out the possibility that autoimmune-mediated events could contribute to the cutaneous and visceral fibrosis that characterizes systemic sclerosis .

Vasospasm

Abnormal vasomotor control is a dominant feature of systemic sclerosis as evidenced by the presence of Raynaud phenomenon in most patients. In addition to vasospasm of the digital arteries, a cold stimulus has been shown to decrease renal, coronary, and pulmonary perfusion. The cause of this abnormal vasomotor control is not known. Renin and angiotensin II levels in systemic sclerosis increase after cold exposure and could possibly contribute to arterial vasospasm. In addition to the juxtaglomerular apparatus, vascular smooth muscle cells produce renin. In a vessel "primed" by renin-angiotensin, severe vasospasm can be precipitated by cold exposure, physical stress, caffeine, or nicotine. More recently, the role of endothelin has been examined. Knock and colleagues demonstrated significantly increased endothelin-binding density in microvessels of skin from patients with systemic sclerosis and primary Raynaud phenomenon compared with that of normal control subjects. The potent vasoconstrictive effects of endothelin suggest that it may play a role in the arterial vasospasm observed in systemic sclerosis.

Increased collagen production

Fibroblast secretion of collagen, the main extracellular matrix component of connective tissue, is markedly increased in systemic sclerosis. Several investigators have provided evidence that transforming growth factor-b could mediate increased collagen production in systemic sclerosis. Gabrielli and co-workers demonstrated increased immunostaining for transforming growth factor-b in the vascular endothelium and dermal fibroblasts of systemic sclerosis patients. Impaired production of interferon-gamma by T lymphocytes isolated from patients with systemic sclerosis and fibrosing alveolitis has been observed. This defect can contribute to fibrosis because interferon-gamma is known to suppress collagen synthesis by fibroblasts. Other investigators have provided evidence for production of abnormal collagen in patients with systemic sclerosis. Douvas demonstrated that Scl-70 (DNA topoisomerase I) binds to collagen genes from scleroderma tissue but not to genes from normal tissues. The pathogenetic significance of this observation is unclear.

Endothelial cell abnormalities

Damage to the endothelial cell has been postulated as a primary event in the pathogenesis of systemic sclerosis. Cytotoxicity of the patient's serum to cultured endothelial cells has been demonstrated. It is possible that platelet aggregation at the site of endothelial denuding could lead to the release of platelet-derived growth factor and transforming growth factor-b. Both cytokines are mitogenic to smooth muscle cells and fibroblasts, in addition to stimulating collagen production. Theoretically, this would account for the subintimal cell proliferation and the fibrosis seen in systemic sclerosis. Increased platelet-derived growth factor levels and circulating platelet aggregates have been demonstrated in patients with systemic sclerosis. Antiplatelet therapy, however, failed to provide any clinical benefit.

Immunologic mediators

Although several antinuclear autoantibodies have been detected in patients with systemic sclerosis, their contribution to the disease process is not established. Indirect evidence of immunologic mechanisms in systemic sclerosis has come to light. Increased gamma-delta T lymphocytes, activated helper T cells, intercellular adhesion molecules, and soluble IL-2 receptor have been demonstrated in patients. Fibroblasts cultured from the skin of patients with systemic sclerosis produce much higher levels of IL-6 than do normal fibroblasts, and may contribute to T cell activation. It is unclear whether these immunologic changes constitute primary events in systemic sclerosis or are epiphenomena.

Clinical findings

Symptoms and signs

Involvement of the skin and subcutaneous tissue is the predominant feature. Systemic sclerosis is classified clinically on the basis of the extent of cutaneous involvement and the presence of features that overlap other connective tissue diseases. In the diffuse cutaneous or classic form of the disease, thickening of the skin is observed on the face, trunk, and distal and proximal extremities. Hardening of the skin usually starts in the hands and manifests initially as swelling and decreased range of motion of fingers. This phase is followed by sclerosis that leads to a taut, shiny appearance of the skin and tapering of the fingertips (sclerodactyly). The skin changes later involve the face (pinched nose and pursed lips), trunk, and lower extremities. Rapid progression of the cutaneous induration with extension into the underlying tendon sheaths and joints is a harbinger of visceral involvement. The limited cutaneous form, on the other hand, is more indolent. The cutaneous thickening usually is confined to the face and fingers, and progression to visceral involvement is delayed. This variant of the disease is also referred to as the CREST syndrome, an acronym identifying the following features: calcinosis, Raynaud phenomenon, esophageal hypomotolity, sclerodactyly, and telangiectasias. Renal and cardiac involvement is rare. Localized scleroderma exclusively involving the skin includes two dermatologic conditions known as morphea (plaquelike) and linear scleroderma. These generally carry a good prognosis, and visceral involvement is extremely rare. Overlap syndrome or mixed connective tissue disease occurs in patients who have diffuse or limited cutaneous sclerosis combined with features of other autoimmune disorders. These include systemic lupus erythematosus, dermatomyositis/polymyositis, Sjögren syndrome, and primary biliary cirrhosis. Some investigators have suggested use of the term "undifferentiated autoimmune connective tissue disorder" because many of these patients later "differentiate" into either systemic sclerosis or systemic lupus erythematosus.

Among the extrarenal manifestations of systemic sclerosis, Raynaud phenomenon is the most prevalent (93-97% of patients) and is usually the first symptom in patients with limited cutaneous disease. It results from increased vasomotor tone and could lead to infarctions of the fingertips. A bedside test, nailfold capillaroscopy, has been suggested for differentiation of systemic sclerosis - associated Raynaud phenomenon from benign Raynaud phenomenon and that associated with autoimmune disorders. Patients with systemic sclerosis have significant capillary dropout in the nail beds. Telangiectasias on the skin of the face and upper torso is common in patients with either diffuse or the limited cutaneous form of the disease (90% of cases). Myopathy presenting as muscle atrophy and fibrosis occurs in approximately 20% of these patients, and usually involves the shoulder and pelvic girdle muscle. Esophageal hypomotility and diminished tone of the lower esophageal sphincter are present in 75% of systemic sclerosis cases. The symptoms include dysphagia and gastroesophageal reflux. Ulcerations and strictures of the distal esophagus have been described. Gastrointestinal involvement can extend to the small and large bowels, resulting in hypomotility, dilatation, malabsorption from bacterial overgrowth, and occasionally volvulus or perforation. Diffuse pulmonary fibrosis occurs in 45% of the patients, causing restrictive lung disease. Intimal proliferation in the small pulmonary arteries can lead to pulmonary hypertension, particularly in the CREST syndrome. Myocardial fibrosis in systemic sclerosis manifests as conduction disturbances and occasionally refractory congestive heart failure. Pericarditis and pericardial effusions have been described. An infrequent finding in systemic sclerosis is fibrosis of the thyroid gland leading to clinical hypothyroidism.

Renal involvement

The association between systemic sclerosis and renal failure was first reported by Auspitz in 1863 and later noted by Osler. A causal relationship between the two was generally accepted after several studies detailed the clinical and renal histologic abnormalities in patients with systemic sclerosis who died of uremia.

Involvement of the kidney in systemic sclerosis manifests as a slowly progressing chronic renal disease or as scleroderma renal crisis characterized by malignant hypertension and acute azotemia. The two presentations are not mutually exclusive. On the basis of autopsy studies, the frequency of renal disease in systemic sclerosis approaches 80%. Clinical indicators of chronic renal involvement in systemic sclerosis include proteinuria, hypertension, and decreased glomerular filtration rate. The proteinuria usually is subnephrotic and occurs in 15 to 36% of the patients.

Hypertension is present in 24%, and elevated blood urea nitrogen in 19%. Estimates of the frequency of chronic renal disease in systemic sclerosis vary, depending on which markers of disease are employed. Renal manifestations rarely antedate the other features of systemic sclerosis.

Scleroderma renal crisis is defined by sudden onset of accelerated or malignant arterial hypertension followed by rapidly progressive oliguric renal failure. The reported frequency of scleroderma renal crisis varies between 5 and 15%. It occurs most commonly during the first 5 years after diagnosis, but in 5 to 10% of cases there is no previous history of systemic sclerosis. Patients with the diffuse cutaneous form are at much higher risk for development of scleroderma renal crisis than are those with limited cutaneous systemic sclerosis. The symptoms are predominantly those of accelerated or malignant hypertension. Presenting complaints include severe and acute left ventricular failure. Grade III or grade IV retinopathy is present in most cases. Oliguria and rapidly rising serum creatinine level follow shortly afterward. Proteinuria is universal but rarely nephrotic. The urinalysis reveals microscopic hematuria and granular casts. Plasma renin activity is markedly elevated during scleroderma renal crisis, but it is unclear whether this is a primary phenomenon or a result of renal ischemia. Scleroderma renal crisis progresses rapidly to severe renal failure requiring dialysis. Before the advent of angiotensin-converting enzyme (ACE) inhibitors, most patients died of hypertensive complications within 1 to 3 months. Other clinical manifestations of scleroderma renal crisis include microangiopathic hemolytic anemia with thrombocytopenia, which also occurs in association with other forms of malignant hypertension HUS has been reported in a patient with mixed connective tissue disease who had combined features of systemic sclerosis and systemic lupus erythematosus.

No reliable predictors of the advent of scleroderma renal crisis exist. The previous presence of proteinuria, renal insufficiency, or hypertension in a patient with diffuse systemic sclerosis does not necessarily portend progression to scleroderma renal crisis. A rise in plasma renin activity does not seem to herald the onset of scleroderma renal crisis, either. A higher frequency of scleroderma renal crisis and hypertension has been noted among African-Americans with systemic sclerosis. It is not clear, however, whether this observation is simply a reflection of the overall increased frequency of essential and malignant hypertension in the African-American population.

In summary, scleroderma renal crisis is a form of malignant arteriolar nephrosclerosis associated with more dramatic worsening of renal function and poorer prognosis than in other forms of malignant hypertension.

Diagnostic procedures

The most common serologic abnormality in systemic sclerosis is a positive antinuclear antibody (ANA) response, which occurs in 86% of the patients. The specificity of the antinuclear antibody test is increased if the immunofluorescence pattern is speckled or nucleolar. Although more specific, antibodies anticentromere are found in a 34%, antitopoisomerase I in a 14%, anti-U1 RNP in 6.5%, antinucleolar total in 16%, anti-Th RNP in 2.2%, and anti-U3 RNP in 3.5%. Anticentromere antibodies are particularly specific for the CREST syndrome. Approximately 30% of the patients have positive test results for rheumatoid factor. Antibodies to double-stranded DNA are rarely noted. Mild lymphopenia and anemia are often present in patients with visceral involvement.

Pulmonary function tests reveal a mixture of restrictive and obstructive changes. The chest radiograph shows a reticular pattern most prominent in the lower two-thirds of the lung fields that can progress to diffuse honeycombing. Hand radiographs may show soft tissue calcifications and occasionally resorption of the terminal phalanges. Pseudodiverticula due to atrophy of the colonic muscularis mucosae can be detected on barium enema examination.

Treatment

The one form of therapy that appears to have made a major difference in the prognosis of scleroderma renal crisis is aggressive treatment of hypertension with ACE inhibitors. In one study, 1-year survival was only 18% for patients treated before the availability of an ACE inhibitor, compared with 76% for those treated with the drug. Progression to severe renal failure requiring dialysis was observed in only half of the patients treated with ACE inhibitors. This suggests that ACE inhibition can forestall progression of scleroderma renal crisis in some but not all of the patients. The management of scleroderma renal crisis with ACE inhibitors does not exclude the concomitant use of other antihypertensive agents. Diuretics are best avoided, however, because of their ability to stimulate more renin release.

In those patients with scleroderma renal crisis who progress to severe renal insufficiency despite antihypertensive treatment, dialysis becomes a necessity. Both peritoneal dialysis and hemodialysis have been employed. The End-Stage Renal Disease Network report on 311 patients with systemic sclerosis-induced end-stage renal disease who underwent dialysis between 1983 and 1985 revealed a 33% survival rate at 3 years. On the bright side, recovery of renal function sufficient to render the patient dialysis-independent occurred in 6.8% of the cases in this series. Other reports have documented reversal of scleroderma renal crisis-induced renal failure with ACE inhibitors even after dialysis had been initiated. Interestingly, Raynaud phenomenon of the hands and Raynaud-type vasospasm of peritoneal blood vessels (manifesting as decreased peritoneal clearance) were observed in SS patients using unheated peritoneal dialysate fluid.

Kidney transplantation for systemic scleroderma renal crisis-induced end-stage renal disease has been performed successfully, and recurrence of systemic sclerosis in the transplanted kidney was documented in one case.

The different agents used for treatment of the nonrenal complications of systemic sclerosis are reviewed elsewhere. Of note is that the use of D-penicillamine can potentiate the toxicity of a sulfhydryl-containing ACE inhibitor such as captopril.

Suggested readings

DONOHOE JF. Scleroderma and the kidney. Kidney Int 1992;41:462-77.

FALANGA V, GERHARDT CO, DASCH JR, et al. Skin distribution and differential expression of transforming growth factor beta 1 and beta 2. J Dermatol Sci 1992;3:131-4.

FANNING GC, WELSH KI, BUNN C, et al. HLA associations in three mutually exclusive autoantibody subgroups in UK systemic sclerosis patients. Br J Rheumatol 1998;37:201-7.

JACOBSEN S, HALBERG P, ULLMAN S, et al. Clinical features and serum antinuclear antibodies in 230 Danish patients with systemic sclerosis. Br J Rheumatol 1998;37:39-45.

KAHALEH MB, YIN TG. Enhanced expression of high-affinity interleukin-2 receptors in scleroderma: Possible role for IL-6. Clin Immunol Immunopathol 1992;62:97-102.

KNOCK GA, TERENGHI G, BUNKER CB, et al. Characterization of endothelin-binding sites in human skin and their regulation in primary Raynaud's phenomenon and systemic sclerosis. J Invest Dermatol 1993;101:73-8.

LONDON RD, DIKMAN SH, SPIERA H. Recovery of renal function in undifferentiated connective tissue disease after treatment with angiotensin-converting enzyme inhibitors. Am J Kidney Dis 1991;18:716-9.

NISSENSON AR, PORT FK. Outcome of end-stage renal disease in patients with rare causes of renal failure. III. Systemic/vascular disorders. Q J Med 1990;273:63-74.

PRIOR C, HASLAM PL. In vivo levels and in vitro production of interferon-gamma in fibrosing interstitial lung diseases. Clin Exp Immunol 1992;88:280-7.

SOLLBERG S, PELTONEN J, UITTO J, JIMENEZ SA. Elevated expression of beta 1 and beta 2 integrins, intercellular adhesion molecule 1 in the skin of patients with systemic sclerosis of recent onset. Arthritis Rheum 1992;35:290-8.

STEEN VD, MEDSGER TA JR. Epidemiology and natural history of systemic sclerosis. Rheum Dis Clin North Am 1990;16:1-8.

STEEN VD, CONSTANTINO JP, SHAPIRO AP, et al. Outcome of renal crisis in systemic sclerosis: relation to availability of angiotensin converting enzyme (ACE) inhibitors. Ann Intern Med 1990;113:352-7.

STONE JH, et al. Management of systemic sclerosis: the art and science. Semin Cutan Med Surg 1998;17:55-9.

TRAUB YM, SHAPIRO AP, RODMAN GP, et al. Hypertension and renal failure (scleroderma renal crisis) in progressive systemic sclerosis. Review of a 25 year experience with 68 cases. Medicine (Baltimore) 1983;62:335-9.

WALSH SJ, et al. Geographical clustering of mortality from systemic sclerosis in the Southeastern United States, 1981-90. J Rheumatol 1997;24:2348-52.

SECTION

9

Diabetic nephropathy

CHAPTER

38

Diabetic nephropathy

Daniel J. Cordonnier

KEY POINTS

- The global incidence and prevalence of diabetic nephropathy is steadily and dramatically increasing in the industrialized world. This is mainly due to noninsulin-dependent diabetes mellitus (NIDDM = Type 2) related nephropathies, since incidence of insulin dependent diabetes mellitus (IDDM = Type 1) nephropathy is slowly decreasing.
- Advanced diabetic nephropathies are associated with major organ complications and handicaps that confer on these diseases the sad title of "major Public Health problem". The high relative mortality among patients with diabetes mellitus results mainly from diabetic nephropathy and its complications.
- Overt diabetic nephropathy cannot be cured, but intensive treatment can delay its evolution and abolish its complications. This is even more true for incipient diabetic nephropathy. At least theoretically, diabetic nephropathy can now be considered as a "preventable disease".
- Independent risk factors for progression have been identified: poor blood glucose control, hypertension, high animal protein intake, dyslipidemia, and smoking. Trials have shown that correction of each of these factors can be beneficial.
- Prevention of diabetic nephropathy is no more a dream. Identification of patients at risk (family history of diabetes or hypertension or nephropathy, smokers), and systematic screening for microalbuminuria in diabetic patients allows very early detection and the introduction of appropriate management.

In an individual patient, incipient diabetic nephropathy can be erroneously considered as a "non-disease" because there are no symptoms. This is particularly true for type 2 patients, who are frequently considered as "normal with a slightly elevated blood glucose" when they are truly diabetic (Fig. 38.1). By contrast, advanced diabetic nephropathy is an awful disease, not particularly because the patient has to face a dialysis-transplantation program, but essentially because of associated neuropathy (cramps, sudden diarrhea, bladder problems, orthostatic hypotension) and retinopathy resulting in visual impairment. Additionally, there is the risk of myocardial infarction and early sudden death. The physician who first faces the situation must think about the next one, take heart to instruct the patient, and be prepared to accompany him/her for a long time. The spouse can help, but also a nutritionist, a podiatrist, and, finally, a network of different medical specialists also will be needed.

Epidemiology

During the last two decades, it has become evident that diabetic nephropathy is increasing as a cause of end-stage renal failure. In the United States, diabetic nephropathy has for more than a decade been the major cause, its prevalence among dialysis patients increasing from 10% in 1986 to 36% in1992. The same has been

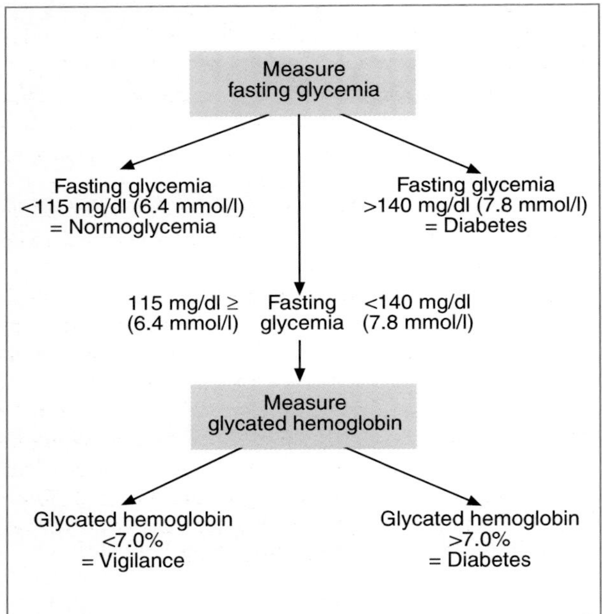

Figure 38.1 New criteria (1997) for the diagnosis of diabetes (according to Peters et al.).

observed in Europe. For example in France, a country with one of the lowest rate of diabetic nephropathy in dialysis patients, prevalence increased from 6.9% in 1989 to 13.1% in 1995; at that time 17.2% of new patients on dialysis (incidence) were diabetic. This is less than seen in some regions where the incidence reaches 42% (52 pat/million population/year in the Neckar region in Germany) or even more than 50% (in the New York area).

This trend is due only to the increased incidence and prevalence of type 2 diabetic nephropathy (probably reflecting the dramatic increase in the prevalence of type 2 diabetes), which frequently reaches or exceeds 80%. By contrast, type 1 diabetic nephropathy in the dialysis population is relatively decreasing.

The prevalence of proteinuria in patients with type 2 diabetes is 12% at 10 years, 20% at 15 years, reaches 30% at 25 years.

Pathogenesis

Diabetic nephropathy is clearly linked to chronic hyperglycemia (Fig. 38.2). Transplantation of normal kidneys to diabetic patients results in recurrence of diabetic glomerulosclerosis in the new kidneys in a time that varies greatly from patient to patient. Conversely, transplantation of a kidney with diabetic changes from a diabetic rat to a non-diabetic animal, results in the progressive disappearance of the diabetic lesions.

In patients, the poorer the glycemic control, the greater the risk of diabetic nephropathy. But, if glucose is necessary, it is not, by itself, a sufficient factor to induce diabetic nephropathy. It is now clear that patients at risk not only have difficulty with glucose control, but also have an inherited ability to retain sodium (tested by the rate of sodium-lithium countertransport), to become hypertensive or to have cardiovascular complications, and finally to activate the renin-angiotensin system. It has been shown, both in experimental animals and in humans, that normalizing blood pressure is beneficial; moreover, inhibiting the renin-angiotensin system is even more effective in lessening the pace of progression or even stopping the evolution of the disease.

Nonenzymatic glycation of proteins is an important pathway; advanced glycosylation end products (AGE), measurable in serum, are more elevated in patients with more severe lesions. They can be demonstrated in glomeruli, arterioles, circulating macrophages, and resident mesangial cells. By way of their receptors, AGEs can induce the production by such cells of different cytokines and an increased synthesis of collagen IV, which accumulates in tissues. High glucose concentrations also inhibit the mesangial ability to degrade some proteins accumulated in the extracellular matrix; this accumulation is facilitated by transforming growth factor beta (TGF-β), which is produced locally by tubular cells.

Parents of type 1 patients with nephropathy have been shown to have much more cardiovascular disease than those without. In the Pima Indians of Arizona, a popula-

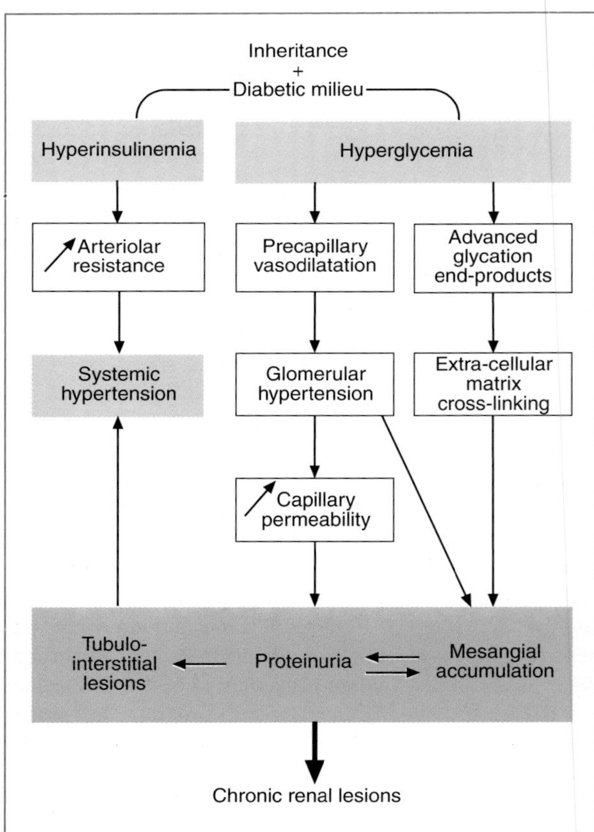

Figure 38.2 Schematic and summarized physiopathology of renal lesions associated with diabetes.

tion at very high risk of type 2 diabetes, 316 families have been studied. Proteinuria occured in 14.3% of the diabetic offspring if neither parent had proteinuria, 22.9% if at least one diabetic parent had proteinuria, and 45.9% if both parents had diabetes and proteinuria. Such familial predisposition to nephropathy is apparently linked to predisposition to hypertension, as suggested by studies of Na^+/Li^+ countertransport or Na^+/H^+ antiport activity measured in red cells or in skin fibroblasts of patients with both types of diabetes. Recently, studies of angiotensin-converting enzyme gene polymorphism have shown conflicting results, suggesting however that the ACE DD genotype is associated not only with an increasd risk of vascular disease in the general population, but also with the presence of diabetic nephropathy in type 1 and type 2 diabetes.

Among other factors, the role of proteinuria as a marker or a factor of progression has been emphasized. Briefly, the greater the amount of proteinuria, the faster the pace of progression. This has been considered as secondary to the limitation of the physiologic reabsorption of albumin and the lesions induced by this disturbed process. It is also possibly related to the cofiltration of albumin and transferrin. Consequently, iron is present in the tubular fluid. This might catalyze a reaction leading to the formation of oxygen free radicals, one of the agents responsible for tubulointerstitial injury and, finally, fibrosis.

Pathophysiology

The typical situation is characterized by diabetic splanchnomegaly; the kidneys are symmetrically enlarged with a nondilated upper tract. This will usually last until renal failure.

The advanced lesions are very characteristic: glomerulosclerosis is either diffuse or nodular, as described by Kimmelstiel and Wilson. The mesangial area is expanded, and involves the capillary loop; some mesangiolysis can occur. Nodules are acellular masses seen in the center of peripheral lobules of the glomeruli. Hyaline capsular "drops" often accompany glomerulosclerosis; these are highly suggestive of diabetes. Arteries are modified: hyaline material takes the place of the normal wall structures. Tubules are also modified, with thickened basement membranes. Interstial tissue is expanded and fibrosed.

Early lesions can be visible, at least with electron microscopy, even before microalbuminuria is detected. Initially there is thickening of the glomerular basement membrane, then expansion of mesangium. Both will progress, grossly paralleling the albumin excretion rate. The expanded mesangial matrix results in a progressive diminution of the filtration surface (which corresponds to the basement membrane not attached to mesangium and which is related to glomerular filtration rate) (Fig. 38.3, see Color Atlas).

Studies using immunofluorescence usually are not helpful. Some slight linear deposits of IgG or IgM can be observed in the earlier stages. Collagen IV and VI, as well as actomyosin have been shown in increased amounts in the mesangial areas. Studies are presently focusing on the interstitium, which is now clearly linked to progression.

The use of repeated biopsies has been limited to clinical research and some unusual individual cases. But such studies have provided interesting information about progression; limited but consistent data are available that show the beneficial effect of tight glycemic control and angiotensin-converting enzyme inhibition on renal structures in diabetic nephropathy.

In unusual situations, (mainly in type 2 diabetic nephropathy), both kidneys can be contracted, and asymmetry of size or irregularities of the cortex, with or without abnormalities of the urinary tract, can be seen.

Microscopically, "nondiabetic" lesions can be observed, alone or superimposed on typical glomerulosclerosis. The most frequent are the consequences of diffuse atheroma (ischemic kidney); then come different types of glomerulonephritis and, less often nowadays, lesions related to urinary tract infections.

Clinical manifestations and laboratory findings

These should not be dissociated. Clinical manifestations occur very late – often "too late" when the diabetic nephropathy usually is irreversible. Therefore, if we want to intervene effectively, we must diagnose the diabetic nephropathy at its preclinical stage. This means that every diabetic patient should be screened systematically and periodically (every year), even if asymptomatic (Tab. 38.1).

Table 38.1 Differential diagnosis. The diagnoses listed below should be checked systematically in every patient with any atypical clinical history, particularly in patients without diabetic retinopathy

Renal artery stenosis
- Patients with severe hypertension
- Patients whose creatininemia and kaliemia increase under ACE-I
- Patients with asymmetric kidneys and clinical signs of atheroma

Nephrosclerosis
- Patients with a long history of hypertension, hypertensive retinopathy, and two symmetric constricted kidneys

Crescentic glomerulonephritis
- Patients with rapidly progressive renal disease

Glomerulonephritis (other)
- Patients with microscopic hematuria, cylindruria, or immunologic disorder

Chronic pyelonephritis
- Patients with a long history of urinary infections and (or) papillary necrosis. Small or dilated kidneys with reflux or urinary obstacle

Preclinical stage

Hyperfiltration or, practically speaking, elevated glomerular filtration rate (GFR) is present very early; it is associated with hyperglycemia, but can continue after its correction by insulin. It is also linked to increased volume of the kidneys. Lack of rapid normalization is probably predictive of an evolution toward diabetic nephropathy; by contrast, its correction might be a benign sign. In type 2 diabetic patients, it is more difficult to demonstrate, since the date of onset of the disease is often unknown.

Microalbuminuria is the hallmark of diabetic nephropathy. In type 1, it occurs usually after 7 to 10 years of diabetes. It signifies (1) that the patient has early significant renal lesions (this stage is termed "incipient nephropathy"); (2) that there will be evolution toward renal insufficiency unless intensive treatment is undertaken, and (3) that the patient is at high risk of adverse cardiovascular events. Besides, it has been shown that blood pressure is slightly more elevated in microalbuminuric patients than in normoalbuminuric patients. Establishing the diagnosis of incipient diabetic nephropathy demands regular monitoring of blood pressure, urinary albumin excretion rate, HbA1c, lipids, creatinine, and testing for retinopathy, neuropathy, coronary heart disease, and peripheral and cerebral vascular disease.

Clinical stage

Proteinuria is detected by a positive dipstick (hence a practical clinical tool) some years after microalbuminuria was noted. Three degrees can be identified: (1) isolated proteinuria with only a modest elevation of blood pressure; (2) abundant proteinuria with the nephrotic syndrome (i.e., edema, hypoalbuminemia, and hyperlipidemia), elevated blood pressure, and modest lessening of the GFR; and (3) proteinuria with hypertension, sometimes diuretic-resistent edema and clear alteration of the GFR. It usually takes 5 to 10 years to evolve from the detection of proteinuria to end-stage renal failure. This evolution is usually linear. However, some aggravating factors can accelerate the pace, and effective treatment can decelerate it (see below). In a diabetic patient, nephropathy is not always due to diabetic glomerulosclerosis.

End-stage renal disease

End-stage renal disease can be considered as reached when GFR is less than 30 ml/min. Indeed, renal replacement therapy is not immediately needed, but it is time to put four questions: (1) is the renal disease certainly irreversible? (2) Is the patient suitable for transplantation(s)? (3) What form of dialysis will be convenient? (4) What is the best use of the time still available before beginning RRT? In other words, how can the patient be optimally prepared?

1. The renal disease can be considered irreversible when the patient, a well-known diabetic patient with specific retinopathy, has been followed for years, when the different evolutionary stages have been recorded, and when the decline in the GFR curve is progressive. In any other situation, another treatable renal or urologic disorder should be looked for, or a transient superimposed aggravating factor should be treated.
2. Acceptability on a transplant waiting list should be discussed for every diabetic patient with uremia (even those who are blind), since preemptive grafts (performed before any dialysis) might be a very good solution. Only patients who have suffered stroke or severe heart attack will most likely be denied. Recurrence of glomerulosclerosis on the grafted kidney has to be expected, but is rarely and belatedly a cause of kidney loss. Only type 1 diabetic patients benefit from pancreatic transplantation.
3. Dialysis remains the only possible renal replacement therapy for the vast majority. The patient should be informed early of the different available possibilities in order to choose, with close relations, the most convenient, keeping clearly in mind that a switch from peritoneal to hemodialysis (or the opposite) could become necessary after some months or years. Life expectancy for diabetic patients on both techniques remains poorer than for nondiabetic dialyzed patients, but it has improved with increased experience of management.
4. The quality of the treatment, as well as the quality of life of the patient (to avoid hospitalizations in intensive care units) requires that the renal replacement therapy period should be carefully prepared. Biguanides (lactic acidosis) and to a lesser degree sulfonamides (hypoglycemic attacks) are contraindicated at this stage and should be replaced by insulin. Vaccinations, particularly against hepatitis B, should be performed early. Calcium carbonate and sometimes vitamin D should be added to the diet. Anemia could be corrected with recombinant erythropoietin. Preparations to access blood should be done carefully to avoid emergency catheters. Finally, one must recall that coronary diseases, very frequent in these patients, often are painless; particularly in transplant candidates, investigations should be systematically discussed. The same is true with foot lesions, which are painless when due to diabetic neuropathy and need systematic care in order to lessen the risk of amputation.

Promoters of progression

It is now universally admitted that elevated blood pressure is a major factor of progression of diabetic nephropathy in both types. Even very modest elevation must be taken into account. Normalization (<140/90 – and, for patients with proteinuria, 120/75 mm Hg) is usually followed by a clear-cut amelioration of the decreasing GFR. The second major progression factor is poor blood glucose control. Intensive control (two to three insulin injections a day or a pump) has clearly been shown to be more effective than "usual" blood control; It is presently considered that a patient with a HbA1c ≤8.1% is protected against progression, at least in the preclinical phase. Other important adverse factors are: significant proteinuria, hyperlipidemia, high animal protein diet, sedentary life-style, and smoking. Combinations of two or more risk factors further accelerate progression.

Diagnosis

Biologic diagnosis of diabetes Commonly accepted diagnostic criteria for diabetes mellitus were developed in 1979 and updated in 1985 by the World Health Organization. They were based on the 75 g oral glucose tolerance test defining diabetes either by a fasting plasma glucose concentration of 7.8 mmol/l or by glucose concentration of ≥ 11.1 mmol/l at 2 hours after the glucose challenge.

In 1997, new criteria were suggested by the American Diabetes Association, one being of major importance both for epidemiology and for clinical practice: an individual with fasting blood glucose of > 7 mmol/l, once confirmed, is diabetic and at risk of developing microangiopathic complications including nephropathy and its consequences (Fig. 38.1).

Screening of microalbuminuria *"Microalbuminuria"* is a term that has nothing to do with the size of albumin, but rather describes the subclinical range of albumin hyperexcretion between 20 and 200 μg/min (30 to 300 mg/24 h). Below that range, one speaks of normoalbuminuria. Above it, one speaks of macroalbuminuria or, better, of proteinuria.

In practice it is usual to check the first morning urine sample. If albumin concentration is > 20 mg/l, one should make sure that the patient has no urinary infection nor cardiac insufficiency and then retest to confirm. If confirmed, one should obtain a 24-hour urine collection. If the albumin excretion rate is more than 300 mg/24 h, a further confirmation 6 weeks later allows the diagnosis of incipient diabetic nephropathy.

Treatment

Since progression toward end-stage renal disease is multifactorial, treament should consequently address step-by-step each of these factors.

Blood pressure control Sufficient data are now available to support the concept that angiotensin-converting enzyme (ACE) inhibitors should be used as first-line agents in patients with diabetes and hypertension. A major advantage of these drugs is their ability to significantly reduce the urinary albumin excretion rate (UAER); as a consequence, albuminemia is increased and cholesterol can be lowered. Usually UAER is reduced by 50% in about 1 month. Precautions should be taken in patients at risk of renal artery or arteriole stenosis (check plasma creatinine levels and for hypo- and hyperkalemia before and after initiating therapy). Only one-third of the patients will completely correct their blood pressure with only one drug. Therapy with two or even three drugs often is needed. The other categories of drugs to be used preferentially are: (1) *Diuretics.* These drugs should be used on a large scale, particularly loop diuretics, because they act directly on the hypervolemia often present in diabetic nephropathy. Additionally, they potentiate ACE-I action. By contrast, thiazides can alter glycemic equilibrium. (2) *Beta-blockers.* For years these have been "the" antihypertensive drug category for diabetic nephropathy. They still are widely used because of their protective effect on coronary vessels. Calcium channel blockers seem to have a nephroprotective effect in diabetic nephropathy when BP is controlled. They have little effect on UAER. Alpha-blockers are potent antihypertensive drugs in diabetic nephropathy, but are neutral in terms of protecting the kidney. Angiotensin II receptor blockers are still under study; they could have effects comparable to ACE-inhibitors.

Blood glucose control Tightened glycemic control is important not only to minimize the progression of renal disease but also to prevent complications in other major organs. This should be compatible with the patient's daily life, avoiding hypoglycemic episodes. Again, when GFR is altered, oral hypoglycemic agents should be changed to insulin.

Dietary protein restriction Probably because they have been instructed to avoid carbohydrates, many diabetic patients eat protein-rich meals. A first therapeutic step should be to educate them about the properties of slow-absorption carbohydrates and try only to "normalize" their protein intake to about 1.2 g/kg/day. A second step is to lower this intake toward 0.9-0.7 g/kg/day and to shift a part of the protein intake from animal to vegetable. The help of a dietician will be required at least for some over-compliant patients who might be at risk for malnutrition.

Lipid control A low-protein diet (also a low-cholesterol diet) sometimes is sufficient to normalize lipid profile. It might be necessary to complement its effects by lipid-lowering drugs, for instance statins or fibrates, depending on how well they are tolerated by the individual patient.

Physical exercise Even moderate exercise helps to improve glycemic and blood pressure control.

Quitting smoking Much evidence has been accumulated showing that smoking is associated in diabetic patients with poorer glycemic control and, consequently, with diverse complications, including diabetic nephropathy. Specific programs should be provided to the patient to achieve smoking cessation.

Prevention

Early detection of diabetes and then nephropathy is unanimously considered to be the best way to diminish mortality, morbidity, and handicaps related to diabetic nephropathy. Early detection must be undertaken in persons at risk – mainly those who have a family history of diabetes and those who are obese or simply overweight, particularly sedentary smokers.

Suggested readings

AMERICAN DIABETES ASSOCIATION. Diabetic nephropathy. Diabetes Care 1998;21:S50-3.

BANGSTADT HJ, OSTERBY R, DAHL-JORGENSEN K, BERG K, HARTMANN A, HANSSEN KF. Improvement of blood glucose control in IDDM patients retards the progression of morphological changes in early diabetic nephropathy. Diabetologia 1994;37:483-90.

COOPER ME. Pathogenesis, prevention and treatment of Diabetic Nephropathy. Lancet 1998;352:213-9.

CORDONNIER D. Glomerular involvement in type 2 diabetes. Is it all diabetic glomerulosclerosis? Nephrol Dial Transplant 1996;11:936-8.

CHATURVEDI N, STEPHENSON JM, FULLER JH. The relationship between smoking and microvascular complications in the Eurodiab IDDM study. Diabetes Care 1995;18:785-92.

GASTER B. The effects of improved glycemic on complications in type 2 diabetes. Arch Int Med 1998;158:134-40.

HANSSON L, ZANCHETTI A, CARRUTHERS G, DAHLOF B, ELMFELDT D, JULIUS S. Effects of intensive blood-pressure lowering and low-dose aspirin in patients with hypertension : principal results of the hypertension optimal treatment (HOT) randomized trial. Lancet 1998;351:1755-62.

KROLEWSKI AS, WARRAM JH, CHRISTLIEB AR. Hypercholesterolemia-a determinant of renal function loss and deaths in IDDM patients with nephropathy. Kidney Int 1994;45:S125-31.

EXPERT COMMITTEE ON THE DIAGNOSIS AND CLASSIFICATION OF DIABETES MELLITUS. Report. Diabetes Care 1997;20:1183-97.

LEWIS EJ, HUNSIKER LG, BAIN RP, RHODE RD. The effect of angiotensin-converting-enzyme inhibition on diabetic nephropathy. N Eng J Med 1993;329:1456-62.

MARRE M, JEUNEMAÎTRE X, GALLOIS Y, et al. Contribution of genetic polymorphism in the renin angiotensin system to the development of renal complications in insulin-dependent diabetes. Génétique de la néphropathie diabétique GENEDIAB study group. J Clin Invest 1997;99:1585-95.

PETTIT DJ, SAAD MF, BENNETT PH, NELSON RG, KNOWLER WC. Familial predisposition to renal disease in two generations of Pima indians with type 2 (non insulin dependent) diabetes mellitus. Diabetologia 1990;33:438-43.

RAVID M, LANG R, RACHMANI R, LISHNER M. Long-term renoprotective effect of angiotensin-converting enzyme inhibition in non insulin dependent diabetes mellitus. A seven year follow-up study. Arch Int Med 1996;156:286-9.

ROSSING P, HOMMEL E, SMIDT UM, PARVING HH. Reduction in albuminuria predicts diminished progression in diabetic nephropathy. Kidney Int 1994;45:S145-9.

TURNER R, HOLMAN R, STRATTON I et al. Tight blood pressure control and risk of macrovascular and microvascular complications in type 2 diabetes: UKPDS 38. BMJ 1998;317:703-13.

COLOR ATLAS

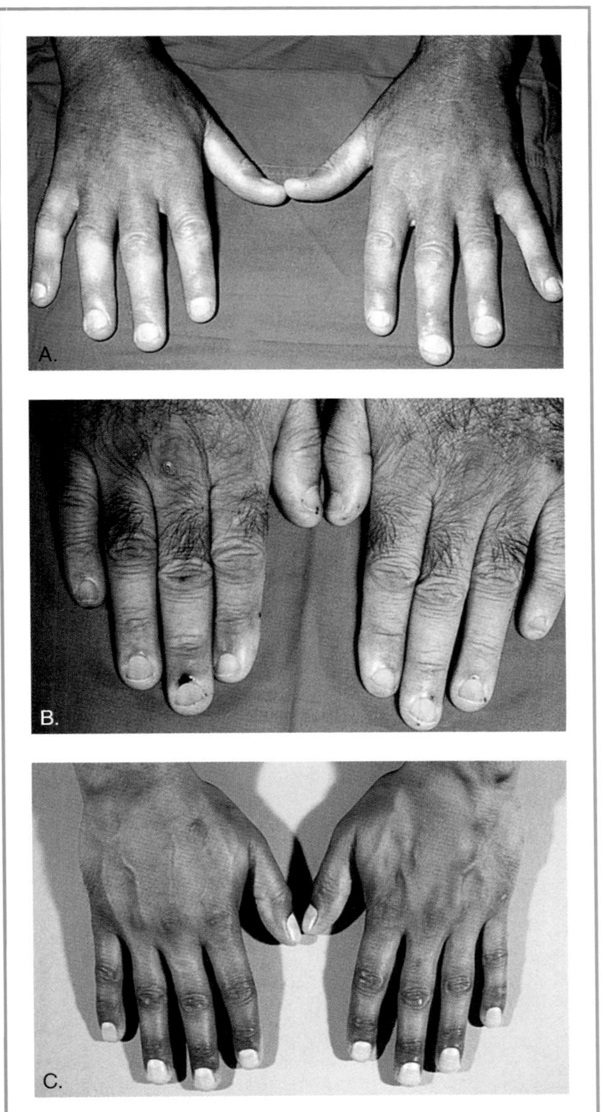

Figure 2.1 Nails. (**A**) Scleroderma showing taught skin over fingers. (**B**) Microscopic polyarteritis showing vasculitis lesions around nails and nail-fold infarcts, (**C**) cyclophosphamide - causing increasing skin pigmentation over distal part of fingers.

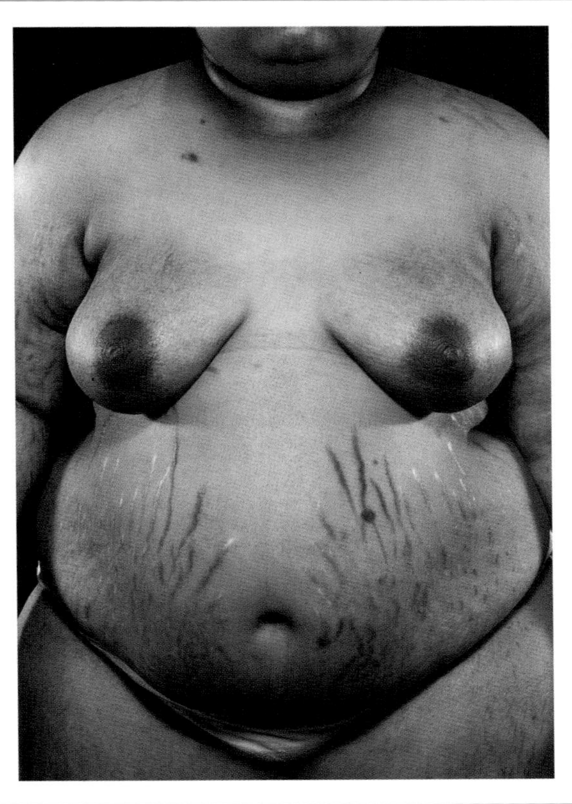

Figure 2.4 Cushingoid appearance. Young girl with systemic lupus erythematosus (SLE) who had been maintained on high doses of oral prednisolone. Note the abdominal striae.

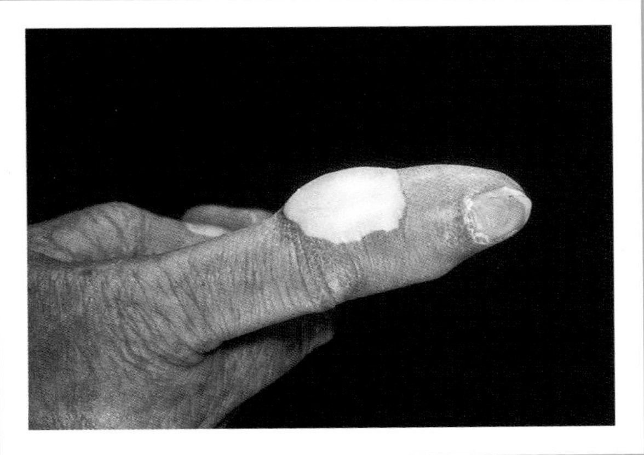

Figure 2.5 Uric acid tophus. Patient with gout and hyper-uricemia.

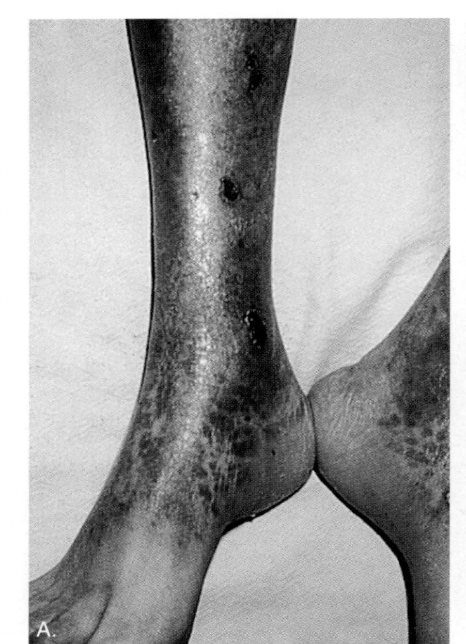

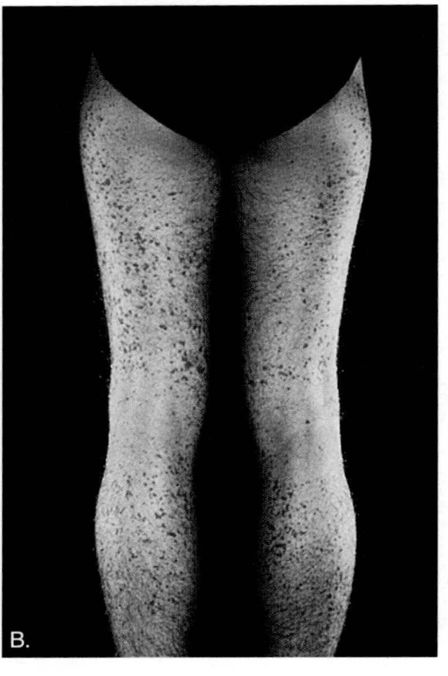

Figure 2.2 Symmetrical skin lesions. (**A**) Cryoglobulinemia: ulceration of skin of medial aspect of legs. Deep pigmentation of skin from multiple previous episodes of vasculitis. (**B**) Henoch-Schönlein purpura: typical distribution of this vasculitic rash.

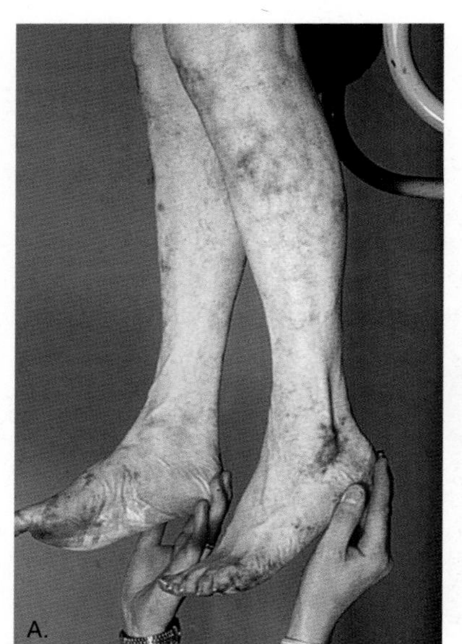

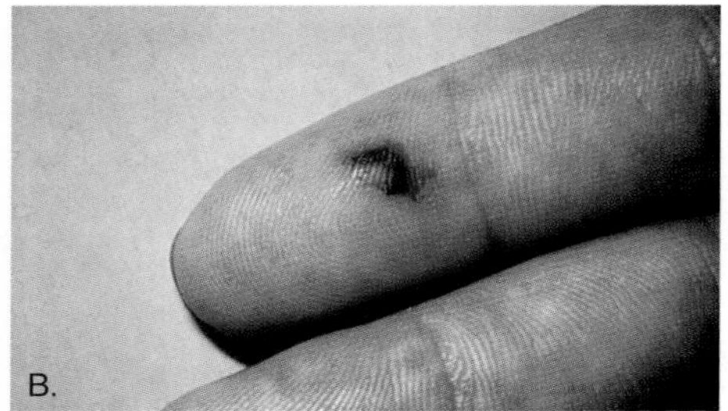

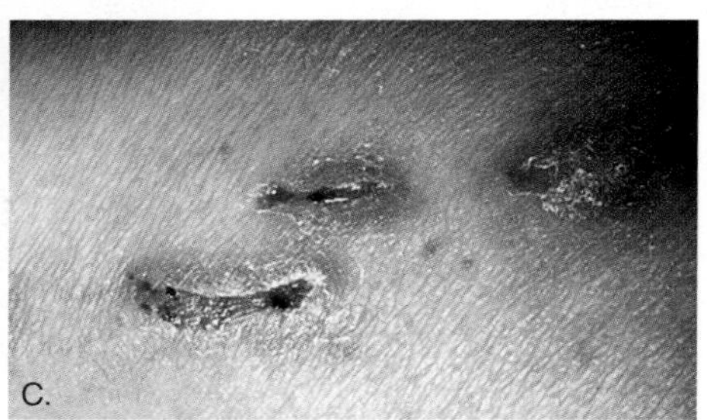

Figure 2.3 Asymmetrical skin lesions. (**A**) "Trash legs": painful, purpura skin lesions over feet, caused by cholesterol emboli but very suggestive of vasculitis. (**B**) *Ecthyma gangrenosa*: this was caused by gonococcal septicemia. (**C**) *Dermatitis artefacta*: self-inflicted scratches in a dialysis patient with severe pruritus.

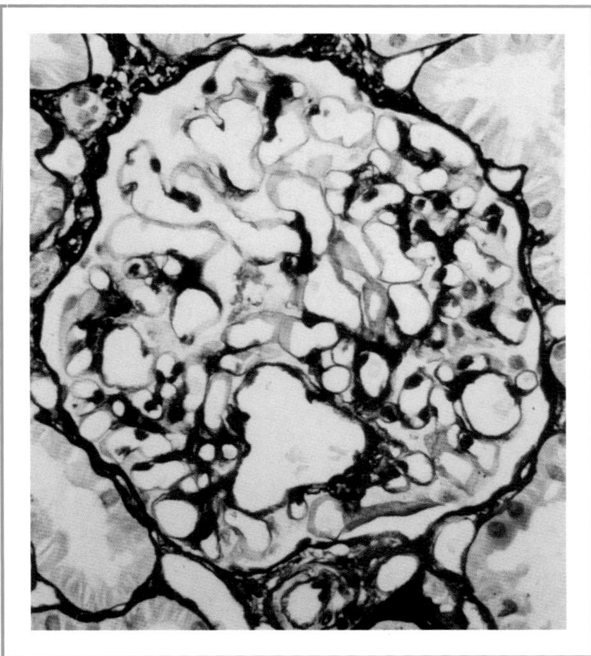

Figure 3.12 Glomerulus in the nephrotic syndrome with normal appearances on periodic acid-methenamine silver staining. This is minimal change nephropathy.

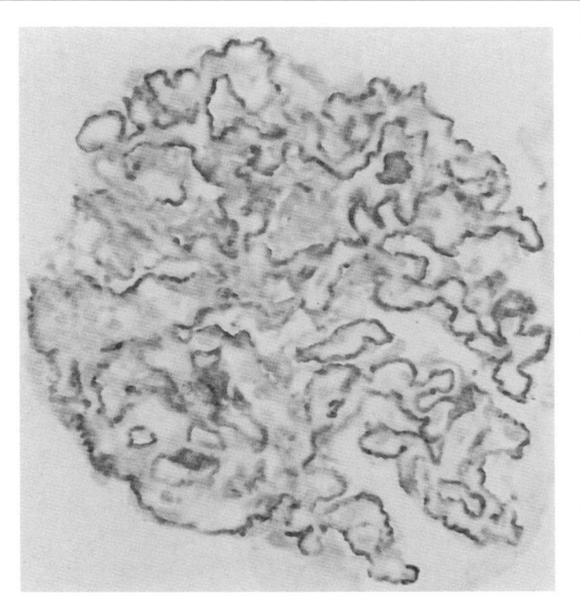

Figure 3.13 Glomerulus with membranous nephropathy, stained by an immunoperoxidase method for IgG. There are regular granular deposits of IgG on the epithelial side of basement membranes.

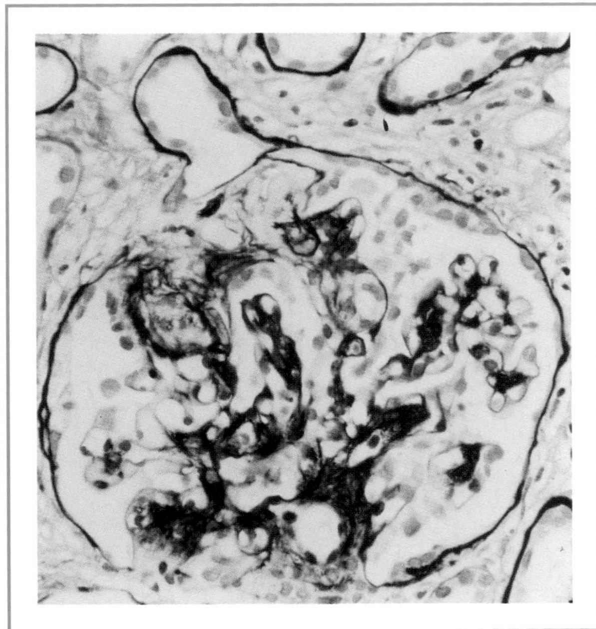

Figure 3.14 Glomerulus at a late stage of a condition often called focal segmental glomerulosclerosis. Periodic acid-methenamine silver staining shows a few erratic areas of sclerosis in the tuft, with adhesions to Bowman's capsule.

Figure 3.15 Glomerulus showing Kimmelstiel-Wilson nodules in diabetic glomerulonephropathy, stained with periodic acid-methenamine silver.

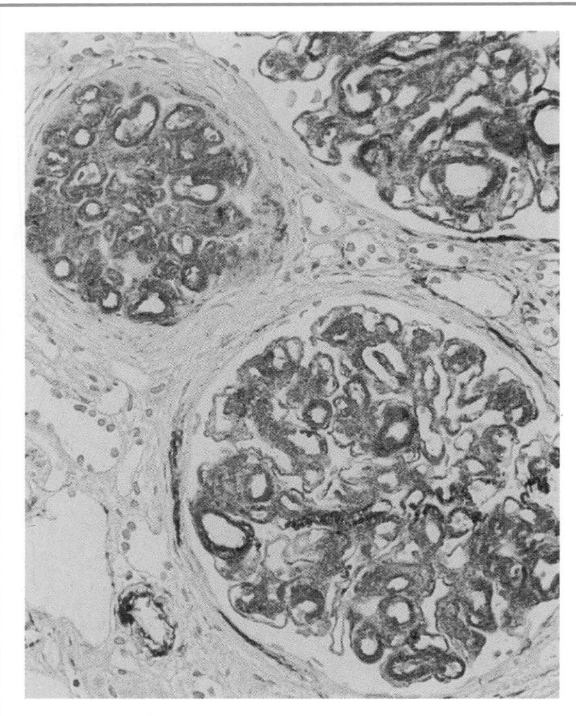

Figure 3.16 Glomeruli containing amyloid, stained by an immunoperoxidase method for amyloid A protein. This is AA amyloid.

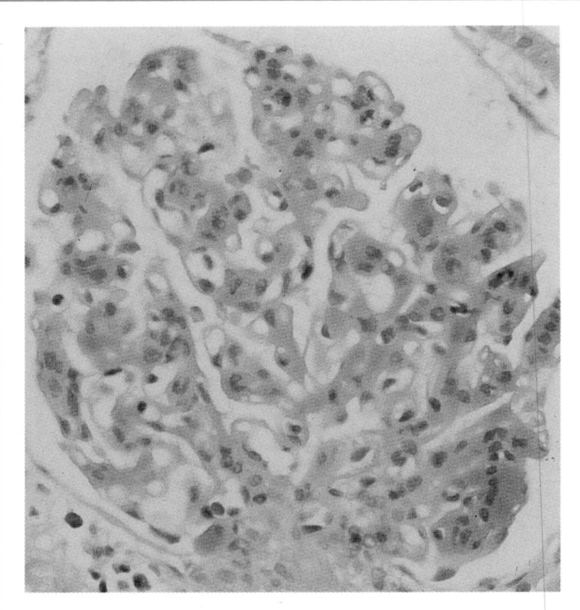

Figure 3.17 Glomerulus stained with hematoxylin and eosin in lupus glomerulonephritis. There is mesangial hypercellularity.

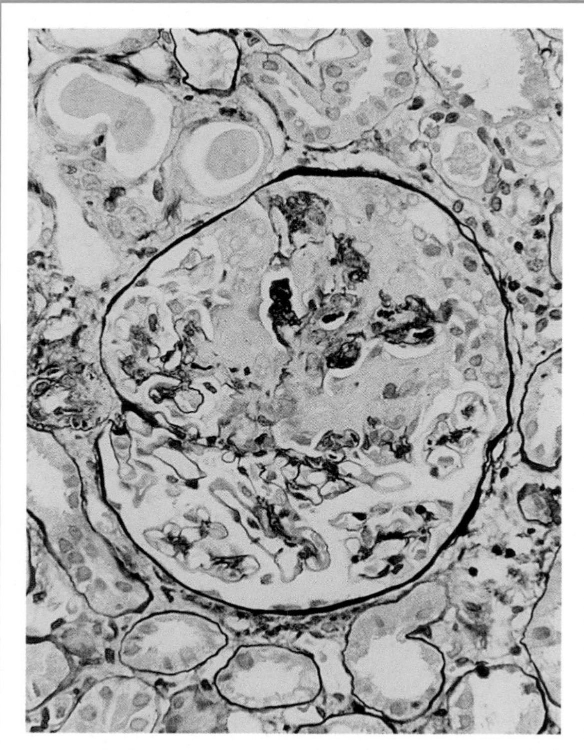

Figure 3.21 Glomerulus stained with periodic acid-methenamine silver, showing acute vasculitic glomerulonephritis. There is a segmental area with disruption of capillary loops and accumulation of fibrin and cells in Bowman's space. Tubules show various amounts of acute damage.

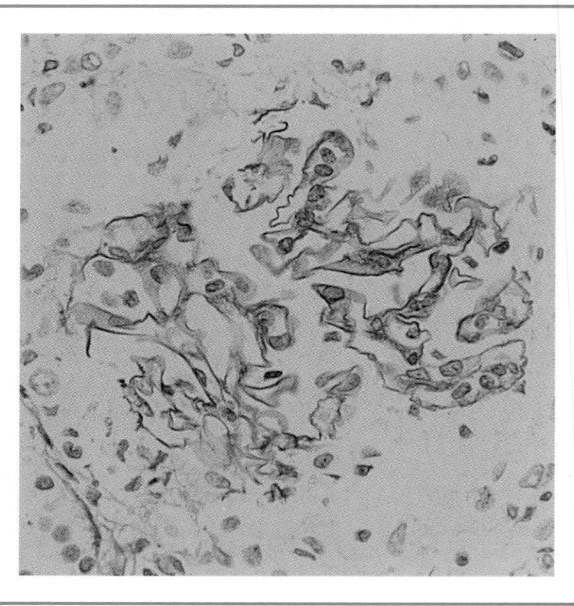

Figure 3.22 Glomerulus in Goodpasture's syndrome, stained by an immunoperoxidase method for IgG which is in a linear pattern in basement membranes.

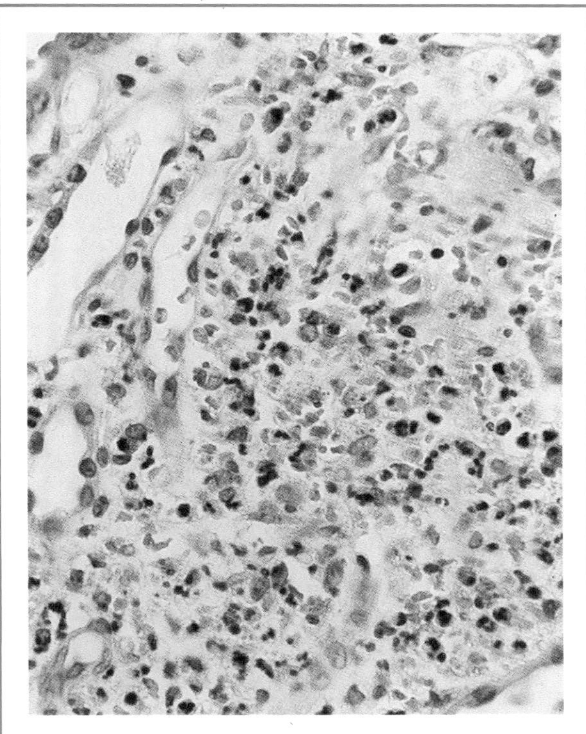

Figure 3.23 Cortex stained with hematoxylin and eosin. There is a heavy interstitial infiltrate of mixed inflammatory cells including many eosinophils. This is acute interstitial nephritis.

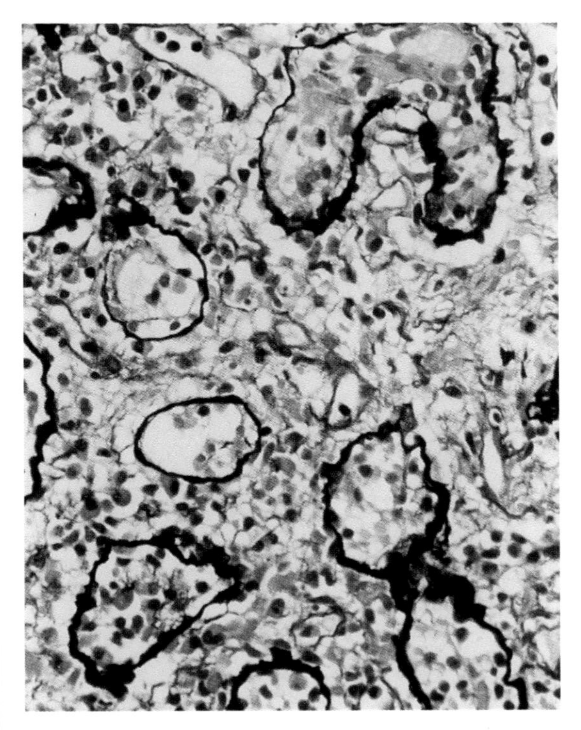

Figure 3.29 Cortex in a renal allograft, stained with periodic acid-methenamine silver. There is a heavy interstitial infiltrate of lymphocytes, many of which are inside tubules. This is significant acute cellular rejection.

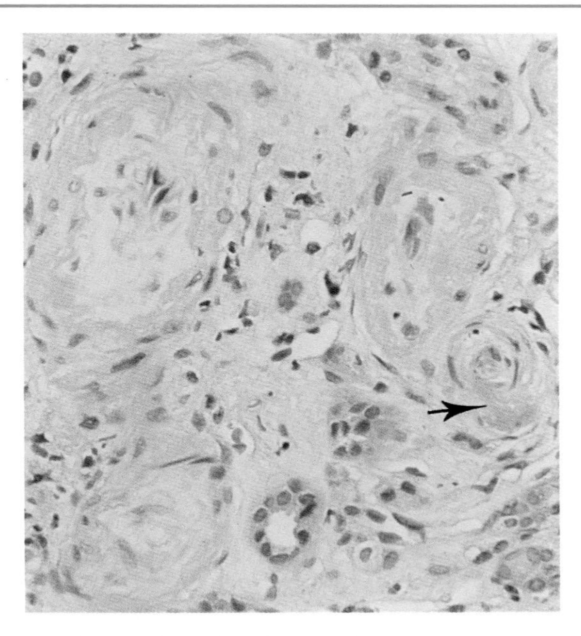

Figure 3.24 Cortex showing small vessel vasculopathy, stained with hematoxylin and eosin. Small arteries have loose intimal thickening and an arteriole, which is arrowed, has fibrinoid necrosis.

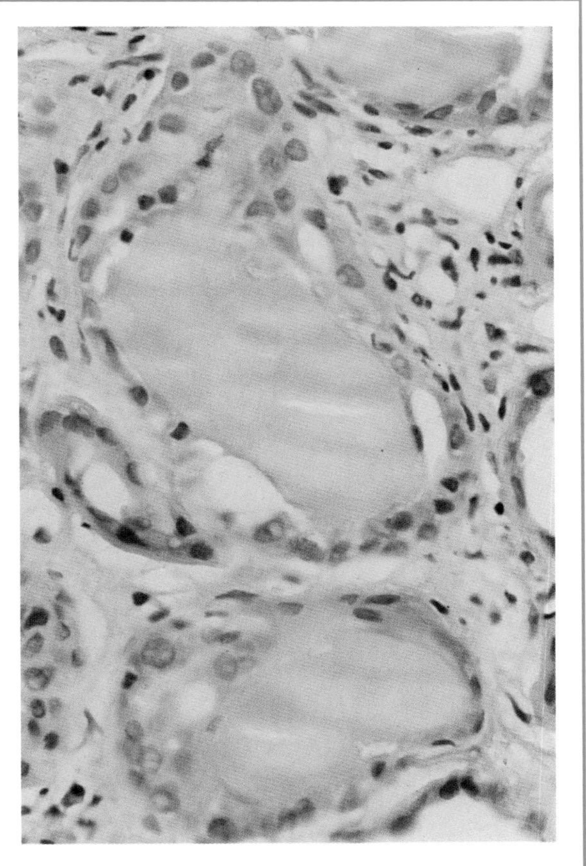

Figure 3.25 Tubules in myeloma kidney, stained with hematoxylin and eosin. There are casts that appear dry and cracked, and are surrounded by giant cells.

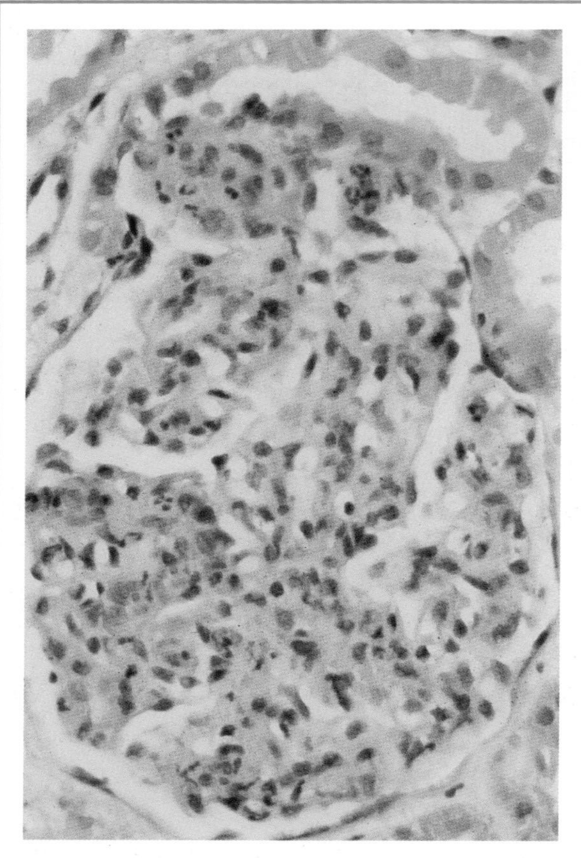

Figure 3.26 Glomerulus in acute post-infective glomerulonephritis, stained with hematoxylin and eosin. The tuft appears solid and infiltrated by polymorphs.

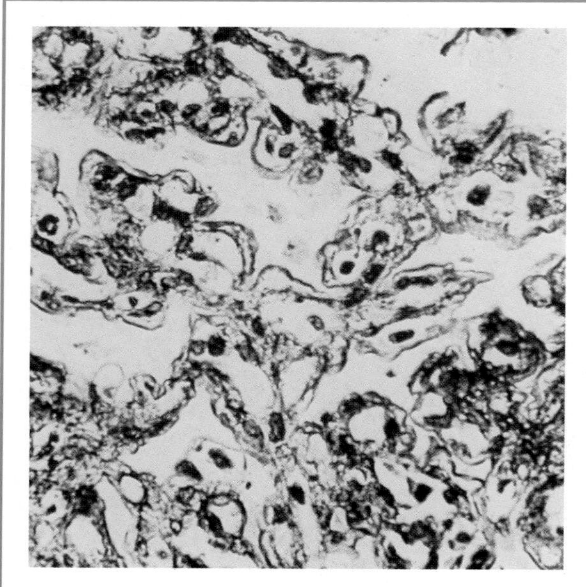

Figure 3.27 Glomerulus in subendothelial type membranoproliferative glomerulonephritis, stained with periodic acid-methenamine silver. Most capillary loops have two basement membranes.

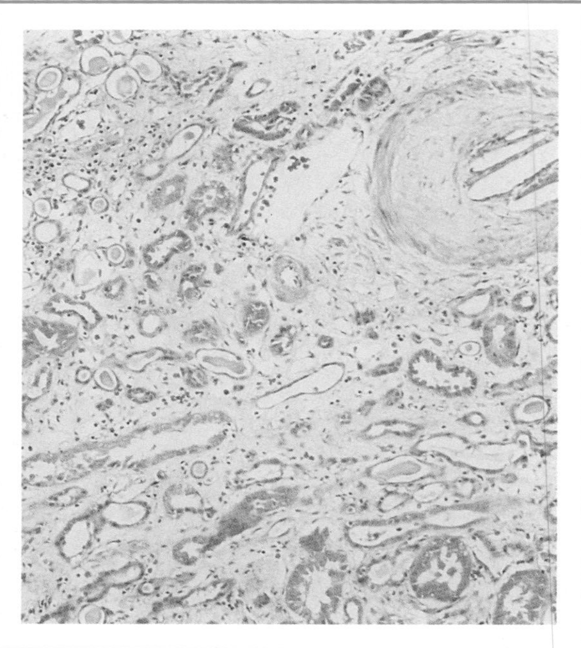

Figure 3.28 Renal biopsy specimen in chronic renal failure due to ischemic damage, stained with hematoxylin and eosin. Tubules are atrophic and an artery is occluded by material including cholesterol clefts, indicating atherosclerotic embolus.

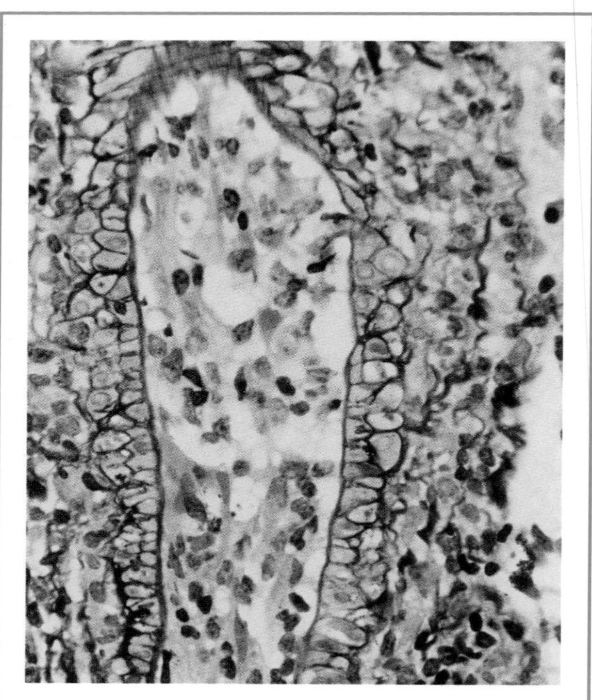

Figure 3.30 Artery in a renal allograft, stained with periodic acid-methenamine silver. The lumen is obscured by an endothelial infiltrate of lymphocytes and other inflammatory cells. This is acute vascular rejection.

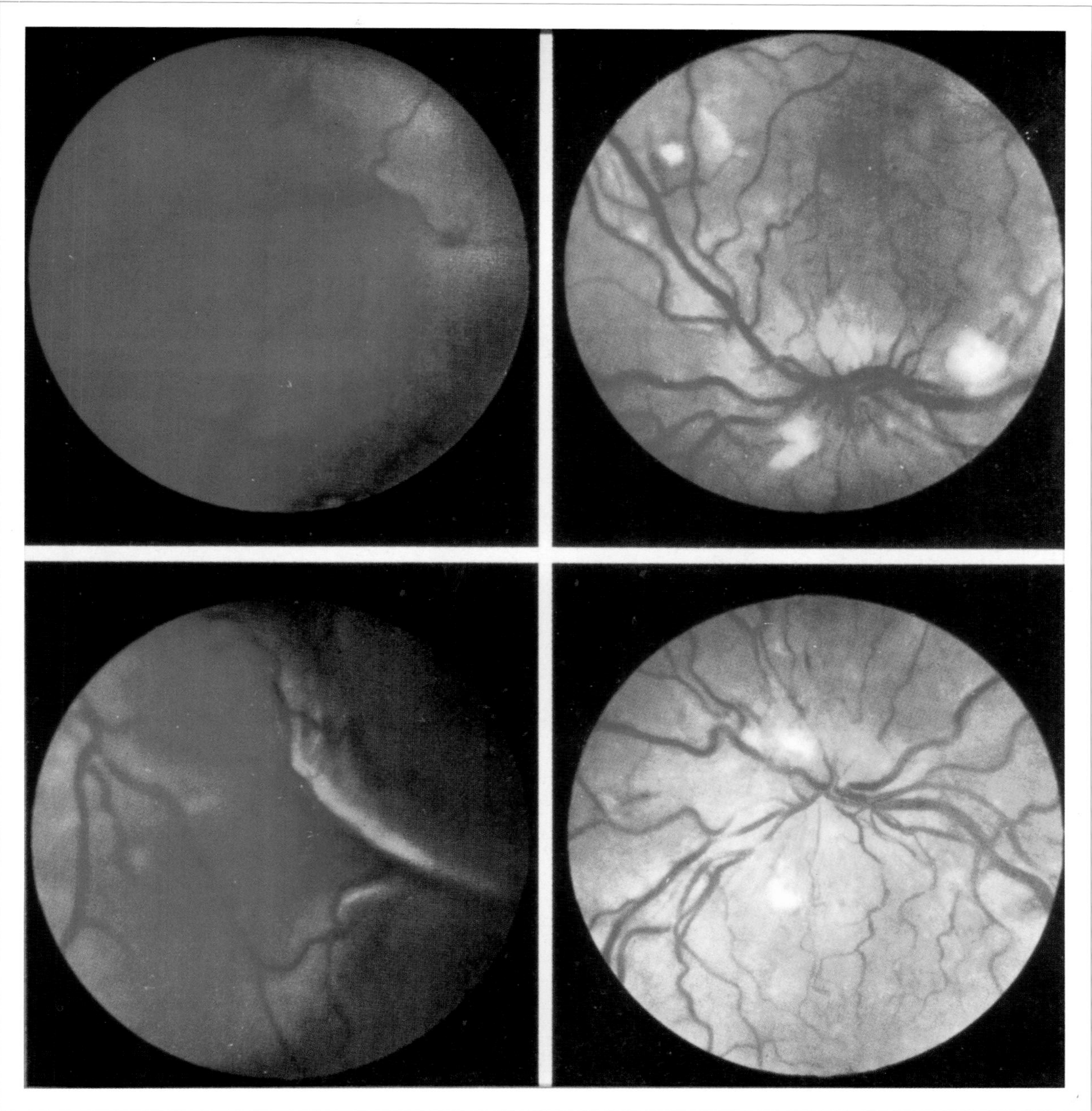

Fig. 8.2 *Upper panel* bilateral retinal detachment in a blind young man with a blood pressure of 300/200 mmHg. *Lower panel*: after blood pressure control, his retinas reattached and his vision returned. However, papilledema and cotton wool exudates (stage IV, see text) are evident. One year later, with normal blood pressure control, his fundi were almost normal.

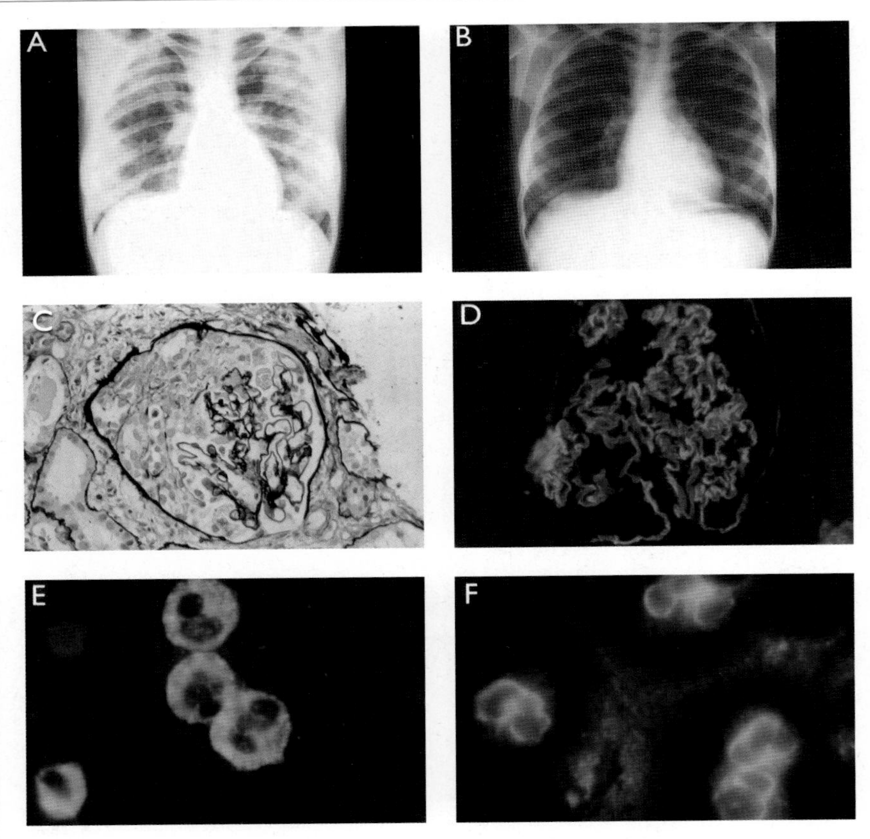

Figure 21.1 Plain chest radiograph of patient with alveolar hemorrhage shows typical diffuse alveolar shadowing with relative sparing of lung bases and normal cardiac silhouette (**A**). This appearance clears rapidly within 5 days (**B**). Silver stain of renal biopsy tissue from a patient with RPGN (basement membranes stain black) shows a large crescent (proliferating epithelial cells and macrophages) occupying Bowman's space and compressing the glomerular tuft (**C**). Immunofluorescence examination of a glomerulus from a patient with anti-GBM disease shows linear deposition of IgG along the glomerular basement membrane (**D**). Antineutrophil cytoplasmic antibody (ANCA) from patients with systemic vasculitis typically gives either a cytoplasmic (**E**) or a perinuclear (**F**) immunofluorescence staining pattern.

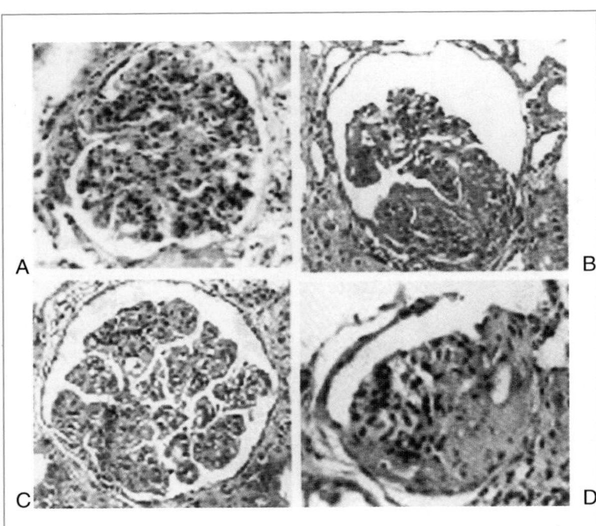

Figure 24.2 Some glomerular lesions associated with infection. (**A**) Acute post-streptococcal glomerulonephritis. Note the panglomerular cellular proliferation and infiltration with neutrophils (H & E x 200). (**B**) Segmental glomerular necrosis in a patient with HIV-associated vasculitis (H & E x 200). (**C**) Type III mesangiocapillary glomerulonephritis in hydatid disease (H & E x 240). **(D)** Focal and segmental glomerulosclerosis in a patient with hepatosplenic schistosomiais (Masson Trichrome stain x 240).

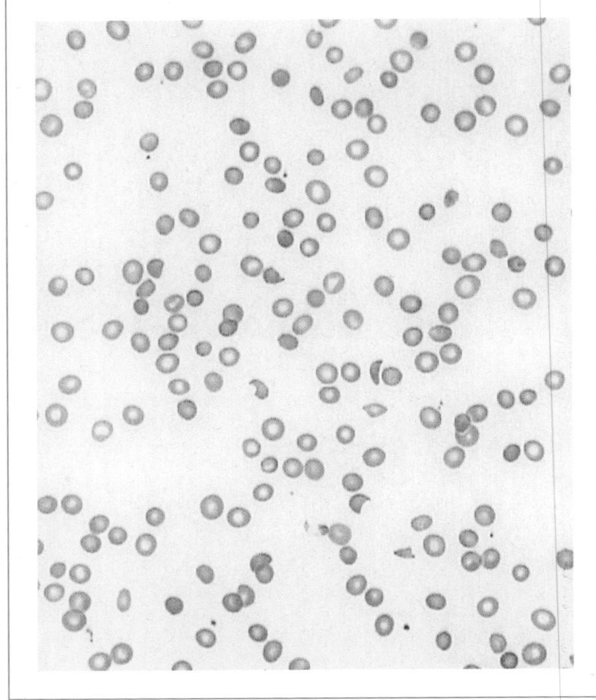

Figure 36.2 Peripheral blood smear of a patient with hemolytic uremic syndrome. The presence of fragmented red blood cells (schistocytes) with the typical aspect of burr or helmet cells in patients with no evidence of heart valvular disease is pathognomonic for microangiopathic hemolysis.

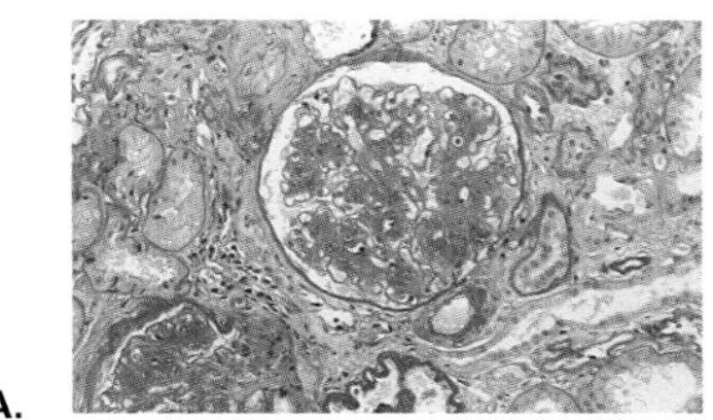

A.

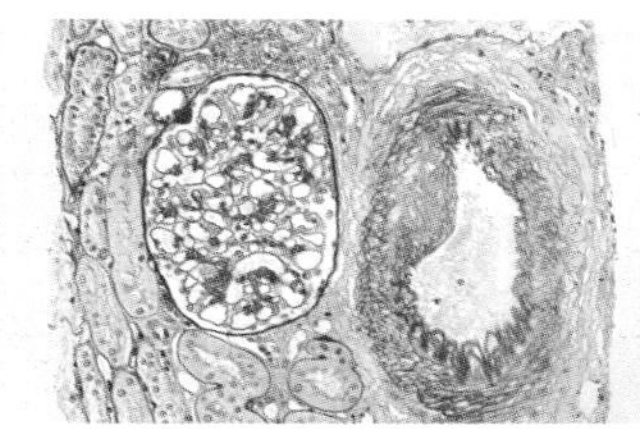

B.

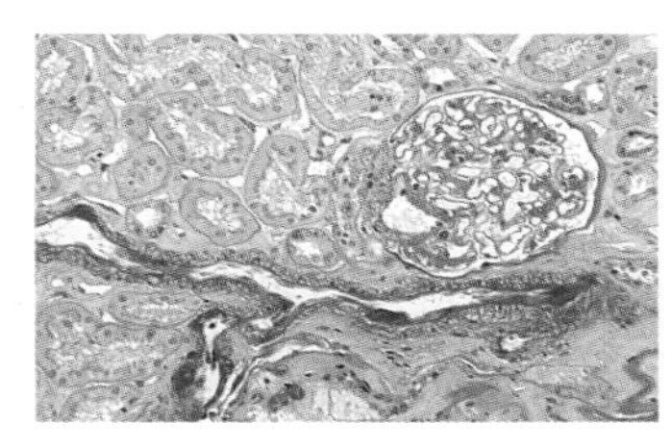

C.

Figure 38.3 Main pathologic aspects of nephropathy in three type 2 diabetic patients (Periodic Acid Schiff Staining, × 264) (Courtesy of Dr Nicole Pinel). (**A**) Patient 1: 61-year-old man; diabetes known for 7 years, insulin treated for 2 years diabetic; diabetic proliferative retinopathy treated with laser; proteinuria 5.2 g/day; creatinine clearance 51 ml/mn; blood pressure 155/85 mmHg with enalapril 20 mg, prazosin 5 mg, and furosemide 20 mg/day. *Typical nodular glomerulosclerosis with reduced filtration surface; thick tubular basement membranes, interstitial tissue expansion and arteriolar hyalinosis.* (**B**) Patient 2: 62-year-old man; smoker: 32 pack/year; diabetes known for 14 years, treated with metformin, hypertensive grade 2 retinopathy, albuminuria 0.45 g/24 h; creatinine clearance 132 ml/mn, blood pressure 140/85 mmHg with atenolol, 100 mg/day, and hydrochlorothiazide 25 mg/day. *Early diffuse glomerulosclerosis with mild mesangial involvement; at 11 hours a capsular hyaline "drop" suggests diabetes. Beside the glomerulus, a interlobular artery is seen, partially modified by a fibrous structure suggestive of atheroma.* (**C**) Patient 3: 59-year-old man; diabetes known for 26 years, treated with glibenclamide; background retinopathy; albuminuria 280 mg/24 h; creatinine clearance 86 ml/mn; blood pressure 140/90 with prazosin 5 mg/day. *Early diffuse glomerulosclerosis. This section allows one to see four hyaline subendothelial deposits, linked to diabetic microvasculopathy.*

SECTION

10

Inherited disorders

CHAPTER

39

Renal cystic diseases

Michael L. Watson

KEY POINTS

- The most common form of cystic kidney disease is autosomal dominant polycystic kidney disease.
- Advances in genetic analysis have made possible a clearer definition of the different subsets of cystic kidney disease.
- About half of affected patients develop end-stage renal failure by the age of 70.
- Hypertension is the most common complication amenable to therapy.
- The increased incidence of cerebral aneurysms causes particular concern.
- Patients need to be fully informed about their condition, the likely prognosis, and the potential impact on other family members.

Cystic kidney diseases, a group of different disorders, when considered together, are among the most common inherited disorders. Their major effects are on the kidney, but multiple other organs in the body also may be involved, causing a variety of systemic features in addition to the formation of kidney cysts. Continuing cyst formation and enlargement, results in progressive renal damage in many affected patients and ultimately in the need for kidney replacement therapy.

Until recently differentiation of the different forms of cystic disease had been based on clinical features. There has, however, been considerable improvement in the understanding of the genetic basis of cystic diseases over the last few years, and this has begun to have an influence on the classification and clinical management of patients – at least insofar as improved accuracy in predicting prognosis, if not yet in treatment.

Epidemiology

The most common form of cystic kidney disease is polycystic kidney disease (PKD), which is inherited as an autosomal dominant trait (ADPKD), affecting approximately 1:800 of the general caucasian population. There is little information on the incidence in other racial groups, but it is probably not significantly different. On average, one in two members of an affected family will inherit the mutation, involving equal numbers of males and females. There are at least three different genetic loci where mutation can result in ADPKD – Types 1, 2, and 3 (Tab. 39.1). Type 1 is the most common, constituting 85% of the affected population. The new mutation rate is relatively low and the penetrance high, and therefore, more often than not, there will be a family history characteristic of the inheritance. Only a very limited number of families have been described with the Type 3 disease.

Autosomal recessive disease (ARPKD) is much less common. Each parent must be a carrier of the mutation, and one in four of offspring will on average be affected. This form often was thought to result in severe and almost invariably fatal disease early in life (infantile polycystic kidney disease). However, as more families have been identified, it has become clearer that a number of affected patients do survive into adult life. It is also the case that a number of patients who previously might have been labeled as having recessive disease, because of presentation in the neonatal period or in infancy, do in fact have the dominant form.

Etiopathogenesis

The macroscopic appearances of cyst formation are due to progressive dilatation of multiple tubular segments with accompanying epithelial cell proliferation and fluid accumulation. The initial changes occur in the embryonic kidney, probably within about 16 weeks' gestation. The exact mechanisms linking the known molecular abnormality with the pathologic process remains unclear, and probably are different in different forms of cystic disease. There does appear to be a fundamental change in processing of certain glycoproteins into the matrix and glycolipids, and also a block on appropriate epithelial cell differentiation.

Different genetic mutations cause the different forms of cystic kidney disease, and this is reflected to some extent in the histologic appearance.

Type 1 ADPKD

Type 1 ADPKD is the most common form and results from a mutation of a gene on the short arm of chromosome 16. This is a large gene encoding for a glycoprotein, polycystin 1, which has an integral role in kidney cell membrane function. It is, however, a complex protein with a long transmembrane domain and both an intracellular component and an extracellular tail that appears to be important in cell-cell and cell-matrix signaling. Normal functioning of the protein also seems to be important during certain periods of kidney development.

Although a number of different mutations have been determined for Type 1, the exact mutations that cause most cases have yet to be clarified – mainly because reduplication of part of the gene on three adjacent sites on the same chromosome has made mutational analysis a very difficult process.

Interruption of the normal function of polycystin results in the formation of cysts, which may affect all parts of the renal tubule and also the glomeruli; initially there may only be a few cysts evident, although microscopically it is possible to detect basement membrane damage very early on. Usually there is a progressive increase in the number of cysts leading to destruction of normal renal parenchyma, interstitial fibrosis, and the development of renal impairment. The mean age of onset of end-stage renal failure is approximately 52 years for men and 58 years for women. There is, however, a wide spectrum of severity of the disorder between different individuals, some being affected only minimally throughout life. Rarely, there may be a very aggressive early form, which leads to massive renal cystic enlargement within the first few months of life. It is important to distinguish this early aggressive dominant form from ARPKD. The genetic basis for this variability remains unclear, but may be a consequence of mutation in both copies of chromosome 16 in the genome – the so-called "two-hit hypothesis." There is therefore a role for both the mutation in the germ line inherited from the parent and a somatic mutation occurring during life in the unaffected chromosome. The "double hit" affecting both chromosomes may then act as the trigger to local cyst formation. Much work remains to be done to clarify this mechanism.

Table 39.1 Different types of inherited forms of kidney disease

Title	Chromosome location	Mendelian inheritance	Estimated occurrences
ADPKD			
Type 1	16	Dominant	1:800-1000
Type 2	4	Dominant	1:6000
Type 3	?	?	?<1:100 000
ARPKD	6	Recessive	1:6000-40 000

As cysts form, they expand in a disparate fashion, resulting in the typical appearance of large kidneys containing cysts of all sizes. Most will be filled with clear fluid, whereas intracystic hemorrhage may cause a dark brown or red appearance in others. These cysts form a dynamic population – relieving pressure by puncturing one cyst may lead to a rapid increase in the size of adjacent cysts.

Secretion of fluid into the cysts seems to be the most important mechanism of fluid accumulation. The fluid is not urine, and the cysts do not communicate with the urinary space.

Other autosomal dominant forms

Although a different mutation is responsible for Type 2 disease, the histologic appearances are the same as in Type 1 disease, although the severity of the damage usually is less. Type 2 ADPKD results from a mutation of a gene on chromosome 4. This codes for a rather smaller protein than polycystin 1, polycystin 2. Polycystin 2 is a protein sharing some homology with polycystin 1, but also some homology with a voltage-activated calcium channel. By complexing with itself or polycystin 1, it would then be in a position to act as a membrane-bound ion channel. The correct function of this system is also required for normal tubulogenesis.

The molecular basis of Type 3 disease is not yet known.

Although the major effects are seen in the kidney, there are a number of extrarenal manifestations (see later). Some of these involve cyst formation in other organs, but the pathologic appearances of some of the other tissues involved is rather different, with no actual cyst formation but with weakness in the basement membrane, resulting in structural weakness of cell walls – for example, in blood vessels. In this case aneurysms may form in the cerebral circulation and indeed in some other parts of the circulation. Certainly polycystin seems to be expressed in a number of different tissues outside the kidney.

Autosomal recessive disease

Despite its rarity, the gene for ARPKD has now been localized to chromosome 6, but the gene has not yet been cloned, and the identity of the relevant protein product remains unknown. Both kidneys are involved and may be massively enlarged – sometimes as much as tenfold more than normal. The vast majority of the cysts are formed from the collecting duct, the extent of involvement being inversely related to the age at presentation. Each cyst may be relatively small, but in contrast to dominant disease, interstitial, vascular, and glomerular changes are not significant features. The liver is invariably involved, with widespread hepatic fibrosis. The consistency of the renal and hepatic abnormalities suggests that maturational arrest in both renal and biliary tubuloepithelial differentiation could act as a common pathologic process.

Other inherited cystic diseases

There are a number of rare forms of inherited cystic kidney disease such as glomerulocystic disease, medullary cystic disease, and possibly medullary sponge kidney, although the inheritance pattern of the latter is not clear.

Two genetic syndromes associated with cystic kidney disease are important:

- *Von-Hippel Lindau*: an autosomal dominant disorder characterized by central nervous system and/or retinal hemangioblastoma and pancreatic cancer. Renal involvement may include simple cysts, hemangiomas, benign adenomas, and malignant hypernephroma. Thirty-five to seventy-five percent of patients can be expected to develop hypernephroma, emphasizing the need for regular follow-up with CT scanning.
- *Tuberous sclerosis*: another autosomal dominant disorder in which the main renal abnormalities are angiomyolipomas, renal cysts, and renal cell carcinoma. Involvement of the kidney is common and may be difficult to separate from ADPKD. Involvement of other organs, including the central nervous system with cortical tubers, skin lesions such as facial angiofibromas, shagreen patches, and involvement of the eyes, heart, and lungs should help guide to the appropriate diagnosis.

Clinical findings

Autosomal dominant disease is usually asymptomatic in childhood and adolescence; symptoms develop and hypertension becomes detectable in early adulthood, followed by a gradual decline in renal function with end-stage renal failure being reached by the mid-50s. There is, however, much variation from this typical pattern, which has become clearer following the introduction of widespread screening of family members of affected cases. In the past, before the availability of ultrasound, many individuals would have reached the age of 70 or more in apparent good health, even though cysts could be present in the kidneys. Indeed we know that approximately one-half of all patients with ADPKD will reach the age of 70 without renal failure. Part of this variability is due to subtle differences in natural history between Types 1 and 2. As a general rule Type 1 patients present earlier and are more severely affected. ARPKD usually presents differently and will be considered separately.

Symptoms and signs

Loin pain

Loin or abdominal pain is a persistent problem for many patients with polycystic kidney disease and may take the form of either chronic low-grade pain over many years, acute exacerbations of pain, or a combination of both. The pain may be unilateral or bilateral and may well require extensive analgesia for relief. The main cause of pain appears to be cyst enlargement, whether by a natural growth of the cyst because of fluid secretion, or sudden expansion because of hemorrhage. Rupture of a cyst may cause acute pain, as may acute infection of a cyst. In severe early forms of the disease, kidney enlargement can be dramatic, but in most instances cysts are evident only on ultrasound scanning, and the kidneys do not become significantly enlarged until early adulthood. Some patients do become aware of a "mass in the side". Large kidneys are a particular problem in childhood (see later).

Chronic, low-grade pain also may be caused by persistent low-grade infection. Approximately 10% of patients may have associated renal calculi, and these can, in turn, give rise to pain. Because of these multiple causes of renal pain, it can be difficult to decide on the exact etiology. Although imaging may help, the diagnosis often is based on clinical suspicion.

Hematuria/dysuria

Macroscopic hematuria is a common presenting symptom and probably most frequently occurs because of a hemorrhage into a cyst. Microscopic hematuria is often present on routine urine testing, with and without the presence of dysuria, and always raises the possibility of a urinary tract infection. Urine from such patients should therefore be cultured intermittently during the course of follow-up. Large polycystic kidneys are particularly vulnerable to trauma, and an episode of hematuria may follow even relatively mild injury.

Headache and cerebral aneurysms

Headache is a very common symptom in the absence of disease, but takes on particular importance in patients with polycystic kidney disease. Cerebral aneurysms may cause headache, particularly if there is sudden enlargement or incipient rupture. CT scanning may identify a subarachnoid hemorrhage, but the availability of the noninvasive technique of magnetic resonance angiography has greatly increased our ability to identify aneurysms before they rupture. This is particularly important when patients complain of persistent severe headache or there is a family history of cerebral aneurysms. The earliest clinical symptom usually is headache, but aneurysms often are asymptomatic, and the patient presents with the features of a subarachnoid hemorrhage. Within the cerebral circulation, the middle cerebral artery is the most likely site for an aneurysm, but they can also occur elsewhere. It is not unusual for there to be more than one aneurysm.

Cerebral aneurysms are most likely to occur if there is a preexisting history of aneurysm formation in the family. Affected members of such families have approximately a 10% incidence of aneurysm formation. These tend to occur earlier in life than in the normal population, even in adolescence. Certainly the presence of persistent headache in an affected individual with a family history of aneurysm formation should prompt a search for aneurysms.

Gastrointestinal tract

A number of other conditions are associated with cystic kidney disease, including hernias, diverticular disease, and pancreatic cysts. The presence of characteristic symptoms or signs also helps in appropriately categorizing these patients, in whom cystic kidney disease is associated with another condition. For example, headache and visual disturbance may accompany Von Hippel Lindau syndrome or complaints of altered facial appearance and/or presence of tubers in tuberous sclerosis.

Hypertension

The onset of hypertension is early in the course of the disease and well before the onset of identifiable renal impairment (Fig. 39.1).

By the age of 18, many patients will have small but significant elevations in blood pressure, which will progressively increase over the years, accelerating in most cases as renal impairment develops. Offspring of parents with hypertension also develop hypertension earlier. Blood pressure tends to rise rather earlier in affected males, also more quickly the larger the kidneys. Left ventricular hypertrophy is more likely by late adolescence, despite the small rise in pressure.

Hypertension is more likely to occur during pregnancy, and although the pressure may return to normal after delivery, further increases are more likely later in life in such patients. Hypertension is also common in severely affected children.

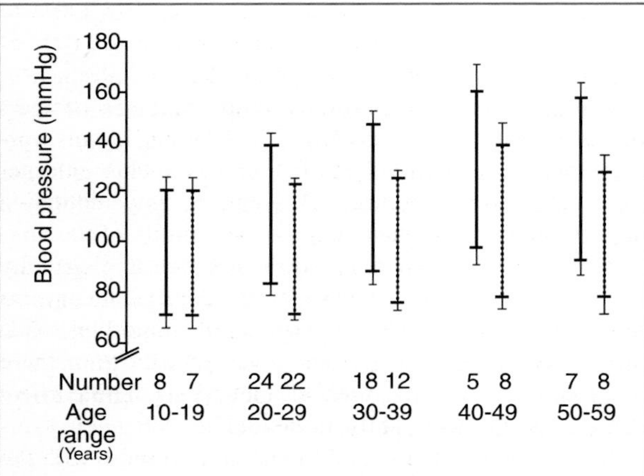

Figure 39.1 The time course of development of hypertension in polycystic kidney disease.

The early detection and treatment of hypertension is of clear benefit to the patient, and constitutes one of the best arguments for screening family members for the condition to allow early intervention to control the small rises in pressure.

Liver cysts and the involvement of other organs

Approximately 40% of patients with Type 1 disease develop liver cysts, the vast majority of which are asymptomatic. Occasionally there may be persistent pain from the cyst, and rarely a liver cyst may become infected. The liver, however, may be grossly enlarged, and this can cause problems, particularly in women. The pancreas and spleen occasionally are involved with cyst formation, but almost invariably are asymptomatic.

Autosomal recessive disease is rather different. Involvement of the liver with hepatic fibrosis is an inevitable association, and indeed the absence of hepatic fibrosis should raise significant doubts about the diagnosis of recessive disease

Heart and circulation

Valvular abnormalities of the heart occur in up to 30% of patients, most commonly mitral valve prolapse. Apart from the possibility of an associated murmur, however, these patients are asymptomatic, and rarely develop hemodynamically significant cardiac disease.

There is a higher incidence of aneurysm formation in the aorta, but much the most common site for aneurysms is in the cerebral circulation.

Diagnostic procedures

Kidney and liver

Abdominal ultrasound is the most effective and cheapest noninvasive investigation for diagnosis. Excellent resolution can be achieved in modern machines, allowing a confident diagnosis to be made early in the course of the disease (Fig. 39.2).

The diagnostic criteria are of some importance because of the confounding factor of simple cyst formation. In patients <30 years old thought to be at risk because of their family history, the presence of at least two cysts > 0.5 cm in diameter in either kidney is required for the diagnosis. However, the incidence of simple cysts increases with age, so more cysts should be present to confidently separate PKD. In the age range 30-59 years at least two cysts should be present in each kidney. From age 60 the recommendation is that there should be at least four cysts in each kidney.

CT scanning can help, but is not usually required to make the diagnosis. Under normal circumstances magnetic resonance imaging is of little extra value, but may help in trying to detect cysts with hemorrhage or infection.

Ultrasound is also the diagnostic method of choice for

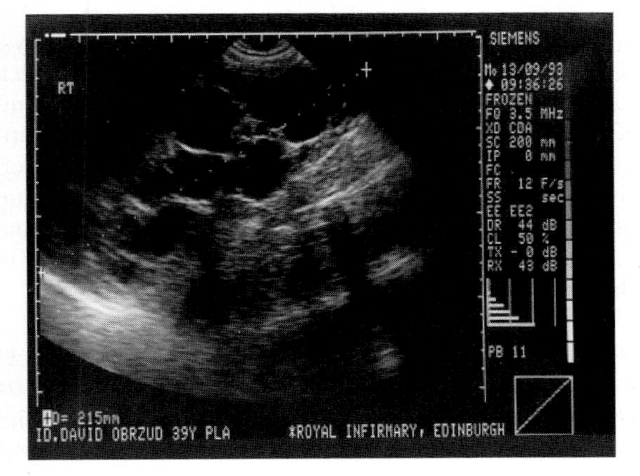

Figure 39.2 Ultrasound appearances of a typically enlarged polycystic kidney. (Courtesy of Dr Paul Allan.)

cysts in the liver and other organs. If more detailed examination is required, for example, before surgery, CT scanning may provide useful information. Liver function tests are not usually altered significantly unless cyst enlargement is particularly severe.

Cardiac abnormalities

Echocardiographic abnormalities are common. Left ventricular hypertrophy detectable on echo occurs early, and significant hypertrophy has been reported in adolescents with only minor elevations of blood pressure. The extent to which this is reversible is unclear.

Cardiac valvular abnormalities, reflecting a systemic connective tissue abnormality, are also common, some series reporting up to a 28% incidence of mitral valve prolapse. Other valves are involved less frequently , and regular echocardiographic examinations are not required.

Increasing lengths of survival of patients on dialysis has highlighted the high overall mortality from cardiovascular disease. Correction of any reversible factors for cardiovascular disease in addition to hypertension is, therefore, important from an early age.

Cerebral aneurysms

Magnetic resonance angiography has transformed imaging of the cerebral circulation and is the best screening method for cerebral aneurysms. Aneurysms as small as 0.5 cm in diameter can be detected, and if required, serial scans can be undertaken at intervals to monitor the rate of enlargement of aneurysms (see below). Evidence suggests that this is very slow.

Genetic methods

Mutation analysis is improving all the time but, unlike conditions such as cystic fibrosis, no one mutation appears to be more frequent than another in either Type 1 or Type 2 disease. Therefore, it is still not possible to identify affected individuals by detection of a specific gene mutation, unless the mutation pattern for that family is already known.

However, it is possible to identify affected individuals with a high degree of probability by linkage analysis. This technique relies on using microsatellite DNA markers closely linked to the PKD gene, whether Type 1, 2, or ARPKD. Using these markers, it is possible to track the passage of the mutated gene through different family members. Provided there are sufficient family members (at least two generations with two affected individuals in one generation, and preferably more) it is possible to predict with a high degree of confidence whether an individual is affected. Clinical use of this technology is limited at present, but it provides a means of antenatal diagnosis (see later) and also a method of deciding whether an individual is Type 1 or Type 2 – which does have prognostic implication. There is little doubt that future advances will allow much better predictive testing of an at-risk individual's status.

Patient management

Making the diagnosis

- *The index case*. These are patients who present with symptoms or signs suggestive of a renal problem – such as loin pain, hypertension with hematuria, or chronic renal failure. The most common age range for such presentation is 30-40 years. The diagnosis almost invariably is made with an ultrasound scan; by this age, all affected patients will have visible cysts on the scan. The diagnosis can be made with more confidence if there is a positive family history. Single isolated cases raise particular issues (see later). As more families are screened, members presenting in this fashion will decrease.
- *Screening the family*. Ultrasound provides an excellent noninvasive method of identifying kidney cysts. Positive information on the presence of appropriate numbers of cysts (see under *Diagnosis*) can confirm the diagnosis in all age groups. The absence of cysts on scanning does not necessarily exclude the diagnosis in childhood and adolescence, since in a proportion of cases cysts have not had time to develop.

The main reasons for screening asymptomatic family members are: (1) to identify the need for genetic counselling in young couples; (2) to help early identification of potential complications such as hypertension or infection; and (3) to set the patient's mind at rest .

This does not raise significant problems in patients over the age of 18, where informed consent can be obtained after appropriate education and counselling. This counselling should include an explanation of the consequences of a positive diagnosis, such as a possible effect on job opportunities and life assurance.

Patients under 18 are less able to provide informed consent. There may be clear clinical indications for confirming or refusing the diagnosis, usually because of the presence of symptoms or development of hypertension, but in many cases the individual is healthy and asymptomatic. Such patients should be regarded as being in an "at-risk category" and subjected to checks on blood pressure and screening for the possibility of urinary tract infection. Whether or not the actual diagnosis is made by ultrasound is an individual issue – but there are real advantages in waiting until the age of 18. Whatever course of action is adopted, it is essential that the patient's family be fully informed of the implications.

- *Counselling and educating the family*. PKD is a complex condition. Patients increasingly expect to be informed about the condition, their prognosis, and the prognosis for other present and future family members. It is very important that these issues be discussed with the patients at an early stage. There also must be recognition that further education will be required as various complications arise and the possibility of renal replacement therapy looms. Good patient education will improve compliance with therapy.
- *Genetic testing*. The need for a significant pedigree in order to undertake linkage analysis limits applicability of genetic testing in Types I and 2 ADPKD. In most cases there is little clinical justification for confirming the genetic status of an individual early in life. Prenatal diagnosis is possible but is rarely undertaken – the most likely indication being where families have had a particularly difficult experience in relation to the disease. This might be because of the early death of a child in the postnatal period, or in families where members have had a particularly traumatic experience of dialysis and transplantation. Detailed counselling is imperative before embarking on such a procedure.

In older patients genetic analysis remains the exception, but because of the more benign natural history of Type 2 disease, there are instances when a clear separation of Types 1 and 2 is clinically useful, especially when making comments about prognosis. Alternatively, it may be important to establish whether or not an individual is affected, when a patient is of reproductive age, and the ultrasound is suggestive but not diagnostic of ADPKD.

ARPKD often affects neonates much more severely than ADPKD, to the extent that some parents would wish to terminate an affected pregnancy. Family screening and antenatal diagnosis have a definite role in such situations, but very few centers are able to provide the necessary services.

- *Isolated case in a family*. Particular difficulties may arise in counselling patients who do not have any family history of PKD and where screening has failed to identify cysts in other family members. New mutations do occur, but the rate is not high. Alternatively, the diagnosis may not be of ADPKD, but of some other cystic kidney disease (including ARPKD) or multiple simple cysts. A further possibility is the presence of "nonpaternity" – where the father is not the individual indicated from the family history. Sensitivity to this possibility is essential in the counselling process.

Monitoring progression of disease

As yet no drugs are available to influence the rate of cyst formation, but there are a number of complications which may accelerate kidney damage and require treatment. Most of these are a standard part of the conservative management of chronic renal failure, such as correction of acidosis, dietary protein restriction, correction of calcium balance, and preparation for dialysis and transplantation. Only those complications that are particularly important in relation to ADPKD will be dealt with in this chapter.

Hypertension Control of hypertension is essential in established renal failure. The target blood pressure to be achieved is probably around 140/90 mmHg, there being little evidence that lowering pressure below this will affect the rate of progression of renal damage, once renal damage is established. It may, however, limit the more general cardiovascular damage.

The choice of drugs for control of blood pressure depends on clinical need. There are, however, some theoretic advantages in using angiotensin-converting enzyme inhibitors, particularly in the early course of the hypertension, before the onset of renal failure. But a number of reported cases in patients with established renal failure exist where the angiotensin-converting enzyme inhibitor has resulted in a further decline of renal function. Renal function therefore needs to be monitored closely. Control of blood pressure nevertheless remains the paramount goal, and other drugs can be employed much as they would in essential hypertension.

Blood pressure does rise well before the onset of renal failure in ADPKD, and the trend at the moment is to advocate particularly tight blood pressure control in this group. A target pressures of 120/80 mmHg has been advocated and probably is a desirable goal – if it can be achieved without significant drug side effects.

Renal failure There are no good predictors of the potential rate of decline of renal function in individual patients. Parameters that have been associated with a more rapid decline of function include the presence of significant hypertension, male gender, and large kidneys (Fig. 39.3).

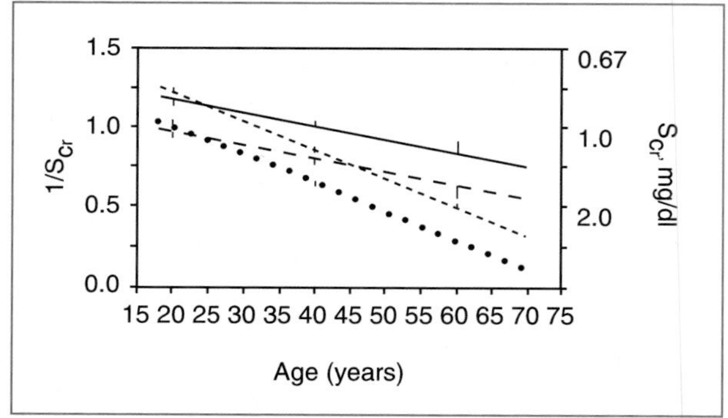

Figure 39.3 Factors affecting the rate of deterioration of renal function. (From Gabow PA, Johnson AM, Kaehny WD. Factors affecting the progression of renal disease in autosomal dominant polycystic kidney disease. Kidney International 1992;41:1311-9.)

Type I disease is associated with more rapid deterioration of kidney function than Type II disease, and as a guide, the mean age of reaching end stage renal failure for males with Type I disease is approximately 52 years and for women 58 years. The age for end-stage renal failure in Type II is significantly later (on average 70 years) and quite a large number of patients will not require renal support therapy at all. Unfortunately there is considerable intrafamily variation in the rate of decline of function, and it therefore is difficult to make a useful conclusion from the family history. Nevertheless it is most important that the patient's renal function be monitored regularly, and one should be particularly aware of the role of reversible factors in any sudden decline in function. There is no established role for regular cyst aspiration as a means of preserving renal function.

Infection Urinary tract infection is common in ADPKD, and patients should be regularly screened for occult infections. Because of the need to avoid cyst infections, early treatment of urinary tract infections with antibiotics is important.

Cyst infection presents a particular clinical challenge. Diagnostic imaging often is not helpful, and confirmation of the diagnosis can be difficult. Although cyst aspiration may help, diagnosis often depends on clinical features. There may be associated bacteremia. Antibiotic penetration into cysts is variable, but there do appear to be some advantages in using the 4-hydroxyquinolone group of drugs.

Cerebral aneurysms The role of screening for cerebral aneurysms has been covered previously. The natural history appears to be for very slow growth of aneurysms, such that screening of individuals from families with a history of intracranial aneurysm need only be undertaken occasionally. Best advice is to screen every 5 years (Fig. 39.4).

This is not to say that sporadic cases will not occur, and this should be borne in mind when counselling patients.

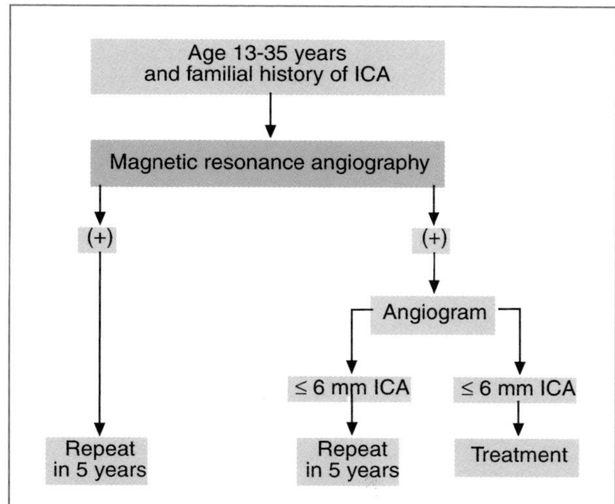

Figure 39.4 Guidelines for the management of cerebral aneurysm. (From Pirson Y. Polycystic kidney disease. Oxford Clinical Nephrology Series 1996:536.)

Further management of detected aneurysms depends on their size. Aneurysms of <0.6 cm in diameter are unlikely to rupture and can be followed up with angiography. Surgical clipping is probably justified for larger aneurysms.

Persistent pain Some patients continue to suffer from loin pain for many years. Therapy can be difficult, and, although it is attractive to advocate needle aspiration of cysts, in the longer term there is little evidence that this significantly limits symptoms – although it may help identify chronic infection. Detailed attention to analgesia is important, but at the same time, analgesics that may lead to decline in renal function should be avoided. Tricyclic antidepressants may have an adjuvant role. In a number of patients the pain is intolerable and, particularly if this is unilateral, consideration should be given to uninephrectomy. Often these kidneys have relatively little remaining function, which can be confirmed on isotope scanning, and therefore there is little to be gained by leaving them in situ. The availability of laparoscopic techniques of nephrectomy has significantly limited the morbidity associated with the operation.

Preparing for dialysis As with other forms of chronic renal failure, the requirement for dialysis can be predicted some considerable time ahead, and the patient and family can be educated about the different methods of dialysis available and be given advice about the appropriate dialysis modality for each individual. The prognosis of patients once on hemodialysis is much the same as the general dialysis population. Hemodialysis is most commonly employed because the patients tend to be younger than average at end-stage renal failure, but there is no specific contradindication to peritoneal dialysis.

Continuing symptoms or other complications from the residual kidneys may necessitate nephrectomy, particularly before transplantation.

Transplantation As a population, patients with PKD do well as transplant recipients. Patient survival at 5 years is approximately 80% and graft survival 70%. There is no risk of the disease recurring in the transplanted kidney, although, for technical reasons, uninephrectomy may be desirable. Malignant transformation has been reported in the residual kidney, but the incidence is probably no greater than that in acquired cystic kidney disease.

Pregnancy Healthy, normotensive affected women with ADPKD, who have fewer than four children before they are 30 are likely to have an uncomplicated pregnancy, producing a normal fetus (Tab. 39.2).

More than four pregnancies increases the likelihood of maternal kidney damage, but the presence of hypertension prepregnancy is by far the most important complication, increasing the risk of both preeclampsia and prematurity (Tab. 39.3). Patients should therefore be closely monitored throughout pregnancy and particular attention paid to the tight control of blood pressure, with appropriate medication.

Children Diagnosis of PKD in utero is difficult. The ultrasound appearances are not characteristic and lack specificity, often merely showing enlarged kidneys. Knowledge of the parental phenotype is therefore essential. At least one-half of patients screened for these reasons are unaware of the presence of cystic kidney disease. The absence of evidence of the disease in the parents also helps to categorize those likely to be at risk of ARPKD.

Children presenting in the first year of life are well recognized to have a poor prognosis with high mortality. The most common presentation in the neonatal period is a palpable abdominal mass. Those surviving the first year develop renal failure early, and also are likely to develop severe hypertension.

Table 39.2 Frequency and type of fetal complications in live births

Complication	ADPKD *N* (%)	NADPKD *N* (%)	*P* Value
Live births	468	200	
Any fetal complication	60 (13)	20 (10)	NS
Intrauterine growth retardation	7 (1.5)	2 (1)	NS
Premature	28 (6)	8 (4)	NS
Premature with clinical problems	9 (2)	8 (4)	NS
Term with clinical problems	11 (2)	2 (1)	NS
Birth defects*	0 (0)	0 (0)	NS
Other	5 (1)	0 (0)	NS

* Two premature infants (and three nonviable fetuses) were also noted as having birth defects.
(NADPKD = non-ADPKD subjects.)

(From Chapman AB, Johnson AM, Gabow PA. Pregnancy outcome and its relationship to progression of renal failure in autosomal dominant polycystic kidney disease. J Am Soc Nephrol 1994;5:1178-85.)

Table 39.3 Frequency and type of maternal complications in pregnancies proceeding beyond 20 weeks

Complication	ADPKD *N* (%)	NADPKD *N* (%)	*P* Value
Pregnancies extending past 20 wk	487	207	
Any maternal complication	170 (35)	38 (19)	<0.001
New HBP	78 (16)	13 (6)	<0.001
Worse HBP	34 (7)	3 (1)	<0.01
Edema	119 (25)	30 (15)	<0.01
Preeclampsia	51 (11)	9 (4)	<0.01
Eclampsia	3 (1)	3 (1)	NS
Other	24 (5)	11 (5)	NS

* A pregnancy may be associated with more than one complication.
(NADPKD = non-ADPKD subjects.)

(From Chapman AB, Johnson AM, Gabow PA. Pregnancy outcome and its relationship to progression of renal failure in autosomal dominant polycystic kidney disease. J Am Soc Nephrol 1994;5:1178-85.)

Older children are usually asymptomatic, and those who develop symptoms tend to have more aggressive disease. Most affected children are detected as a consequence of screening programs and are likely to be asymptomatic, but early detection of any hypertension or asymptomatic urinary infection may prompt treatment that can delay the onset of renal failure.

Children with ARPKD are much more likely to present in the neonatal period. Typically the kidneys are very large at birth and there is oligohydramnios. Respiratory failure occurs in the first few hours, and mortality tends to be very high during this period. Surviving neonates and infants have impaired renal function, but some may not progress to end-stage renal failure until later. Severe hypertension is common in this group, and early aggressive treatment is required.

Patients presenting in adolescence may be very difficult to diagnose, and may well present with portal hypertension and esophageal varices as a consequence of the congenital hepatic fibrosis, rather than with renal failure.

Suggested readings

Baboolal K, Ravine D, Daniels J, et al. Association of the angiotensin 1 converting enzyme gene deletion polymorphism with early onset of ESRF in PKD1 adult polycystic kidney disease. Kidney Int 1997;52:607-13.

Chauveau D, Pirson Y, Verellen-Dumoulin C, et al. Intracranial aneurysms in autosomal dominant polycystic disease. Kidney Int 1994;45:1140-6.

Chapman AB, Johnson AM, Gabow PA. Pregnancy outcome and its relationship to progression of renal failure in autosomal dominant polycystic kidney disease. J Am Soc Nephrol 1994;5:1178-85.

Fick GM, Johnson AM, Hammond WS, Gabow PA. Causes of death in autosomal dominant polycystic kidney disease. J Am Soc Nephrol 1995;5:2048-56.

Gabow PA, Johnson AM, Kaehny WD. Factors affecting the progression of renal disease in autosomal dominant polycystic kidney disease. Kidney Int 1992;41:1311-9.

Griffin MD, Torres VE, Grande JP, Kumar R. Vascular expression of Polycystitin. J Am Soc Nephrol 1997;8:616-26.

Guay-Woodford LM, Muecher G, Hopkins SD, et al. The severe perinatal form of autosomal recessive polycystic kidney disease maps to chromosome 6p21.1-p12: implications for genetic counselling. Am J Human Genet 1995;56:1101-7.

Hughes J, Ward CJ, Peral B, et al. The polycystic kidney disease 1 (PKD1) gene encodes a novel protein with multiple cell recognition domains. Nature Genet 1995;10:151-60.

Klahr S, Breyer JA, Beck GJ, et al. Dietary protein restriction, blood pressure control, and the progression of polycystic kidney disease. J Am Soc Nephrol 1995;5:2037-47.

Mochizuki T, Wa G, Hayashi T, Xenophontos SL, et al. PKD2, a gene for polycystic kidney disease that encodes a "integral membrane protein". Science 1996;272:1339-42.

Qian F, Watnick TJ, Onuchic LF, Germino GG. The molecular basis of focal cyst formation in human autosomal dominant polycystic kidney disease Type 1. Cell 1996;87:979-87.

Ravine D, Gibson RN, Walker RG, et al. Evaluation of ultrasonographic diagnostic criteria for autosomal dominant polycystic kidney disease 1. Lancet. 1994;II:824-7.

Torra R, Badenas C, Darnell A, et al. Linkage, clinical features and prognosis of autosomal dominant polycystic kidney disease Types 1 and 2. J Am Soc Nephrol 1996;7:2142-51.

CHAPTER

40

Inherited glomerular diseases

Jean-Pierre Grünfeld, Dominique Joly

KEY POINTS

- Alport's syndrome is the most prevalent inherited disorder of the glomerulus. It is characterized by progressive hematuric nephritis and sensorineural hearing loss.
- Alport's syndrome is heterogeneous. Different biochemical defects involving type IV collagen chains have been identified. It is also genetically heterogeneous: the X-linked form predominates (85%); autosomal recessive (15%) and dominant (1%) forms are known.
- Genetic counseling rests on correct identification of these various diseases. Rare metabolic or nonmetabolic inherited disorders may include glomerular involvement (e.g., Fabry's disease, nail-patella syndrome etc.)
- Inherited glomerular disorders are not very uncommon. They are readily misdiagnosed and underestimated if systematic investigation of the family history and establishment of the pedigree are not performed.

Epidemiology

Few studies have attempted to answer the question of epidemiology. Between 1970 and 1984, glomerulonephritis was diagnosed in 860 patients in Heidelberg, Germany. Of these, 86 (10%) had at least one first-degree relative with glomerulonephritis. From these 86 index cases, belonging to 45 families, 1674 family members were screened; 172 of them had glomerular diseases that could be classified in 101. Among these, 50% had classic Alport's syndrome; 22% had other forms of hereditary nephritis; 18% had familial IgA nephropathy; and 8% had benign familial hematuria (see below for definitions).

This study was performed in a university reference center and does not provide data about the true prevalence of inherited glomerular disorders in the general population.

Clinical findings

Inherited disorders of the glomerulus may be recognized in adults as well as in children. Routine dipstick urinalysis often shows the only abnormalities: slight or moderate proteinuria associated with microscopic hematuria, or isolated persistent microscopic hematuria. Recurrent macroscopic hematuria often is the presenting symptom in patients under 20 years of age. Gross hematuria may follow febrile upper respiratory tract infection, 1-2 days after onset. Recurrent macroscopic hematuria in children or young adults generally corresponds either to Alport's syndrome and related nephritis, or to IgA nephropathy.

More rarely, the nephrotic syndrome is the first manifestation of an inherited glomerular disease.

In all these cases, hypertension and renal failure may or may not be associated with urinary abnormalities in the early or later course of the disease.

CLASSIFICATION OF INHERITED GLOMERULAR DISORDERS

Progressive hematuric hereditary nephritis

This entity is characterized by micro/macroscopic hematuria and progression to renal failure. Gross hematuria may recur only in the first two decades. Mild nephrotic syndrome develops in 40% of the cases. Sensorineural hearing loss is detected in most families (which defines Alport's syndrome as progressive hereditary nephritis with perceptive hearing defect); it may be profound; it is often slight, detected only by audiometric testing. Ocular changes may be found in approximately 40% of the patients: bilateral anterior lenticonus (altering the normal curving of the lens), perimacular or macular retinal changes that do not affect vision (these perimacular flecks are very suggestive to experienced ophthalmologists), or recurrent corneal erosions.

The primary defect involves the glomerular basement membrane (GBM) – more specifically, the type IV collagen molecules that are a major component of the basement membrane. Study of renal biopsy specimens shows two features: first, by electron microscopy, the GBM is abnormally thick (or sometimes thin), and the lamina densa, its central structure, is split and disorganized. Second, normal antigenicity is lost: anti-GBM antibodies do not bind along Alport's GBMs as normally. These two features are highly specific for hereditary nephritis. Renal biopsy findings may suggest hereditary nephritis even though family history is not positive. However, these findings are observed in only 80% of the cases.

Progressive hereditary nephritis is genetically heterogeneous, i.e., it encompasses different diseases characterized by specific genetic and biochemical defects:

- an X-linked dominant disease, characterized by mutations in the gene encoding for the α5-chain of type IV collagen, located on the long arm of the X-chromosome; this disease is the most common (85% of the families); all affected (hemizygous) males progress to end-stage renal failure, either early in life, before the age of 30 years (homogeneously in families with juvenile-type disease), or later in life, ranging from 30 to 75 years of age (again, homogeneously in families with adult-type disease). In contrast, most (heterozygous) females have slight or intermittent urinary abnormalities, and do not progress to renal failure. However, 10 to 15% of the affected females progress to end-stage renal disease (ESRD), often later than males, unpredictably and at random, without familial clustering. Prevalence of the gene defect is probably 1/5000 individuals;
- an autosomal recessive disease (≅ 15%) characterized by mutations in the genes encoding for the α3 and α4 genes of type IV collagen, located on chromosome 2; homozygous patients have a progressive renal disease, with a similar course in men and women, usually reaching end-stage before the age of 30. Heterozygous subjects may have isolated microscopic hematuria;
- rarely, the disease is transmitted as an autosomal dominant trait; in some families, macrothrombocytopenia is associated with hearing defect and nephritis.

Correct genetic characterization of the disease is required for precise genetic counseling. In X-linked families, affected males do not transmit the defective gene to their sons, whereas all their daughters are affected (often carriers with limited symptoms). Carrier females have a 50% risk of transmitting the mutated gene to their sons and daughters. In contrast, patients with autosomal recessive diseases have virtually no risk of transmission to their offspring. In addition, identification of the mutation may allow to precisely identify carrier females, and to offer if there is a demand prenatal diagnosis in juvenile-type X-linked disease.

Symptomatic management of hypertension and renal failure, and renal replacement therapy are indicated, when needed. Kidney transplantation is an excellent mode of treatment. In very rare cases (fewer than 5%), anti-GBM disease develops after kidney transplantation, more often in patients with large genetic defects (deletions) leading to absent or severely truncated proteins, and thus triggering alloimmunization after kidney grafting.

Familial benign hematuria

The real prevalence of familial benign hematuria is unknown. The disease is transmitted as an autosomal dominant trait, and is characterized by isolated persistent microscopic hematuria, in the absence of gross hematuria, urologic abnormalities, proteinuria, and renal failure in the proband and the family. In patients in whom renal biopsy had been performed (but the indications for biopsy should be carefully discussed in individual cases), thin GBM has been found in most cases, with negative immunofluorescence. Thin GBM represents a lesion, but not a disease: thin GBM also can be found in some families with progressive hereditary nephritis. This underlines the principle that the diagnosis of benign familial hematuria should be accepted in families where males (and not only females) have a benign, nonprogressive course. In some families, subjects with benign familial hematuria have been shown to have heterozygous mutations in α3 or α4 (IV) genes.

Differential diagnoses of progressive hereditary nephritis without deafness and of benign familial hematuria include familial IgA nephropathy. Only renal biopsy can be diagnostic (see Chap. 17).

Metabolic or nonmetabolic inherited disorders with glomerular involvement

Three examples are illustrated in Table 40.1: the congenital nephrotic syndrome of Finnish type, occurring very early in life, and two other disorders in which renal involvement develops in adulthood – Fabry's disease and nail-patella syndrome. The congenital nephrotic syndrome requires aggressive symptomatic management, binephrectomy, chronic peritoneal dialysis, and kidney transplantation. In Fabry's disease, carbamazepine or diphenylhydantoin administration can relieve acroparesthesias; enzyme replacement therapy will be tested in the near future. In Fabry's disease, as in the nail-patella syndrome, renal replacement therapy, including renal transplantation, is indicated in end-stage renal disease patients.

Table 40.1 Three examples of inherited disorders with glomerular involvement

	Prevalence	Renal manifestations	Diagnosis	Mode of transmission	Gene location, identification and product
Congenital nephrotic syndrome of Finnish type	1.2/10 000 in Finland	Early and very severe nephrotic syndrome	No extrarenal abnormality	AR	19q Nephrin
Nail-patella syndrome (osteo-onychodysplasia)		Inconstant (30 to 50% of cases); proteinuria; renal failure; collagen fibrils within the GBM	Nail and osteoarticular changes	AD	9q LMX 1B
Fabry's disease	1/50 000	Males; proteinuria; renal failure; ESRD between 40 and 50 years	Extrarenal abnormalities: acroparesthesias, corneal deposits, skin changes, cardiovascular changes; α galactosidase A deficiency	X-linked	Xq α GAL

Suggested readings

DESNICK RJ, ENG CM. Fabry's disease and the lipidoses. In: Morgan S, Grünfeld JP, eds. Inherited Disorders of the kidney. Oxford: Oxford University Press 1998;355-83.

GRÜNFELD JP, KNEBELMANN B. Alport's syndrome. In: Davison AM, Cameron JS, Grünfeld JP, Kerr DNS, Ritz E, Winearls CG, eds. Oxford Textbook of clinical nephrology. Oxford: Oxford University Press, 1998;2427-37.

KASHTAN C, MICHAEL AF. Alport syndrome. Kidney Int 1996;50:1145-63.

RAMBAUSEK M, HARTZ G, WALDHERR R, et al. Familial glomerulonephritis. Pediatr Nephrol 1987;1:416-8.

CHAPTER

41

Inherited renal tubular disorders

Ruth C. Campbell, Lisa M. Guay-Woodford

KEY POINTS

- Renal tubular transport abnormalities occur as a consequence of systemic diseases, inherited gene defects, or the nephrotoxic effects of drugs or heavy metal exposure.
- Inherited renal tubular transport defects are relatively uncommon.
- The tools of molecular genetics and molecular physiology have begun to elucidate the pathogenesis of these inherited renal tubular disorders, and in the process they have offered insights into the complex molecular mechanisms involved in renal solute transport.
- This chapter will focus on the inherited renal tubular disorders, highlight the molecular defects that have been elucidated, and discuss the implications of these molecular insights for diagnosis and treatment.

DISORDERS OF THE PROXIMAL TUBULE

The proximal tubule is the workhorse of the nephron. This segment is responsible for the iso-osmotic reabsorption of 65-70% of the glomerular filtrate, 80-90% of the filtered bicarbonate, and nearly all of the filtered glucose, amino acids, and phosphate. Two of the most common proximal tubular disorders, cystinuria and X-linked hypophosphatemic rickets, are discussed.

Cystinuria Of the aminoacidurias, cysinuria is the most common and most clinically significant. Cystinuria is characterized by defective transport of cystine and the dibasic amino acids, lysine, arginine, and ornithine in both renal and intestinal epithelia. Three distinct classes of cystinuria have been defined. Type I cystinuria is due to mutations in the gene that encodes the high-affinity, sodium-independent transporter for L-cystine and the L-dibasic amino acids. Type III disease has been mapped to chromosome 19, but the gene has yet to be identified. Type II cystinuria may involve the same gene as Type III, but the data are not yet conclusive.

Diagnosis is often made by direct visualization of cystine crystals in a freshly-voided morning urine specimen. Positive cyanide-nitroprusside test, direct urinary quantification of cystine, and stone analysis are additional diagnostic methods. While screening of all family members is recommended, infants should not be screened before 6 months of age because the functional immaturity of the proximal tubule may cause misleading results.

The clinical manifestations in cystinuria are a direct result of the excessive urinary cysteine excretion (>250 mmol of cystine/g of creatinine per day). Given its poor solubility in urine, cystine precipitates and forms urinary tract calculi. Stone formation can cause urinary tract obstruction and the associated problems of renal colic, infection, and, occasionally, renal failure.

Treatment is aimed at reducing urinary cystine concentration to levels below the solubility threshold. This can be accomplished by aggressive hydration and urinary alkalinization. For patients refractory to conservative management, adjunctive therapy with chelating agents such as D-penicillamine, α-mercaptopropionylglycine, and even captopril should be considered. These agents bind cystine to form soluble salts. Recurrent infection or urinary tract obstruction may necessitate lithotripsy or the surgical removal of stones. These complications increase the risk for long-term renal damage and hypertension. In the occasional patients who progress to end-stage renal disease and undergo renal transplantation, disease recurrence has not been reported.

Hypophosphatemic (vitamin D-resistant) rickets Among the disorders characterized by renal phosphate wasting, X-linked hypophophatemic rickets (HYP) is the most common. The disorder is transmitted as an X-linked dominant trait. Therefore, both males and females are affected. Spontaneous mutations appear to be common, and thus there may be no positive family history.

Several studies suggest that the HYP pathophysiology involves a putative circulating factor, designated *phosphatonin*, which regulates phosphate reabsorption. The disease locus has been mapped to the short arm of the X chromosome, and mutations have been found in a gene designated *PHEX* (*P*hosphate regulating gene with *h*omologies to *e*ndopeptidases on the *X* chromosome). The precise roles of the *PHEX* protein and phosphatonin in the pathogenesis of HYP are not completely understood. Current evidence suggests that PHEX acts at an intracellular site (perhaps in osteoblasts) to regulate phosphatonin release.

HYP patients typically present in the first 2 years of life with lower extremity bowing. Associated abnormalities include dental deformities, with a tendency toward recurrent abscesses, craniosynostosis, and short stature, related to impaired lower extremity growth. Typical laboratory findings include low serum phosphorus, normal serum calcium, and normal serum parathyroid (PTH) levels. Serum 1,25-dihydroxyvitamin D levels are normal, despite defective proximal tubular reabsorption of phosphate. Radiographic findings include rachitic changes, primarily evident in the long bones, with cupping and fraying of the metaphyses.

Combined therapy with phosphate supplementation and calcitriol facilitates bone healing and improves linear growth. Patients must be monitored closely, however, as hypervitaminosis D, hyperparathyroidism, and nephrocalcinosis can develop.

BARTTER-LIKE SYNDROMES

Bartter's syndrome encompasses a set of closely related renal tubular disorders characterized by hypokalemic, hypochloremic, metabolic alkalosis with normal blood pressure despite hyperaldosteronism and hyperplasia of the juxtaglomerular complex. Many cases appear to be sporadic, but family studies suggest an autosomal recessive mode of inheritance.

Bartter's syndromes The antenatal, hypercalciuric variant of Bartter's syndrome presents at birth with dehydration and a history of polyhydramnios, whereas "classic" Bartter's syndrome presents in infants and children, often as failure to thrive. These disorders result from defective transepithelial transport of sodium chloride in the thick ascending loop of Henle (TAL). Under normal physiologic conditions, sodium chloride is transported across the apical membrane via the bumetanide-sensitive, Na^+-K^+-$2Cl^-$ cotransporter (NKCC2) (Fig. 41.1). This transporter is driven by potassium recycling across the apical membrane via the ROMK potassium channel and by the actions of the Na^+-K^+-ATPase pump, the chloride channels, and potassium-chloride cotransporter in the basolateral membrane.

Impaired function of any of these proteins results in increased sodium chloride delivery to more distal nephron segments with associated salt wasting, volume contraction, and stimulation of the renin-angiotensin-aldosterone axis, leading to hypokalemic metabolic alkalosis. In addition, impaired TAL sodium chloride transport reduces the lumen-positive potential that normally drives the paracellular reabsorption of calcium and magnesium. Hypercalciuria is a common feature of Bartter's syndrome, and in antenatal Bartter's syndrome it often leads to nephrocalcinosis. However, for reasons yet to be explained, hypomagnesemia is uncommon in these patients. Loss-of-function mutations in the genes encoding NKCC2 (Bartter type I) and ROMK (Bartter type II) account for most cases of antenatal Bartter's syndrome. Loss-of-function of the CLC-Kb chloride channel (Bartter type III) causes most cases of classic Bartter's syndrome.

The laboratory abnormalities in the Bartter's syndromes mimic those associated with loop diuretic administration; therefore, surreptitious diuretic use should be considered in the differential diagnosis, even in pediatric patients. Bartter's syndromes can be distinguished from other causes of persistent hypokalemic, hypochloremic, metabolic alkalosis, such as chronic vomiting or diarrhea or excessive sweat chloride losses by measurement of urinary chloride excretion, which is low in these disorders and elevated in the Bartter's syndromes.

Treatment is directed toward repleting the electrolyte abnormalities and preventing dehydration. Potassium supplementation, indomethacin (to inhibit prostaglandin synthase), and careful attention to volume status are mainstays of therapy. Severe hypokalemia may necessitate large doses of supplemental potassium, particularly in antenatal Bartter's syndrome patients. Potassium-sparing diuretics may be useful adjuncts.

The long-term prognosis for antenatal Bartter patients is somewhat guarded because these patients tend to have nephrocalcinosis, chronic hypokalemia, and chronic prostaglandin synthase inhibitor therapy, all of which are risk factors for progressive tubulointerstitial disease.

Gitelman's syndrome Loss-of-function mutations in the gene encoding the apical sodium chloride cotransporter (NCCT) have been identified in patients with the hypocalciuric-hypomagnesemic variant known as Gitelman's syndrome (Fig. 41.1). The features of this disorder mimic those associated with chronic thiazide administration. Defective NCCT function increases solute delivery to the collecting duct with resultant solute wasting, mild volume contraction, and an aldosterone-mediated increase in potassium and hydrogen secretion. The NCCT loss-of-function appears to cause hyperpolarization of the distal convoluted tubule cells with consequent activation of apical, voltage-regulated calcium channels and decreased urinary calcium excretion. The mechanism for urinary magnesium losses is not known.

Although Gitelman patients usually have normal serum calcium, chronic alkalosis coupled with hypomagnesemia places them at risk for neuromuscular irritability. Recurrent episodes of muscle spasm and tetany are not uncommon, often precipitated by maneuvers that worsen alkalosis, such as hyperventilation. A few patients develop chondrocalcinosis and arthritis. Treatment of Gitelman's syndrome consists primarily of potassium and magnesium supplementation. Volume resuscitation usually is not necessary because patients rarely become dehydrated.

DISORDERS OF ALDOSTERONE-REGULATED TRANSPORT

The mineralocorticoid, aldosterone, regulates electrolyte transport and intravascular volume via its action in the principal cells of the cortical collecting duct. Four disorders with Mendelian inheritance disrupt the aldosterone-regulated electrolyte transport (Fig. 41.2). Three of these, glucocorticoid remediable aldosteronism (GRA), Liddle's syndrome, and

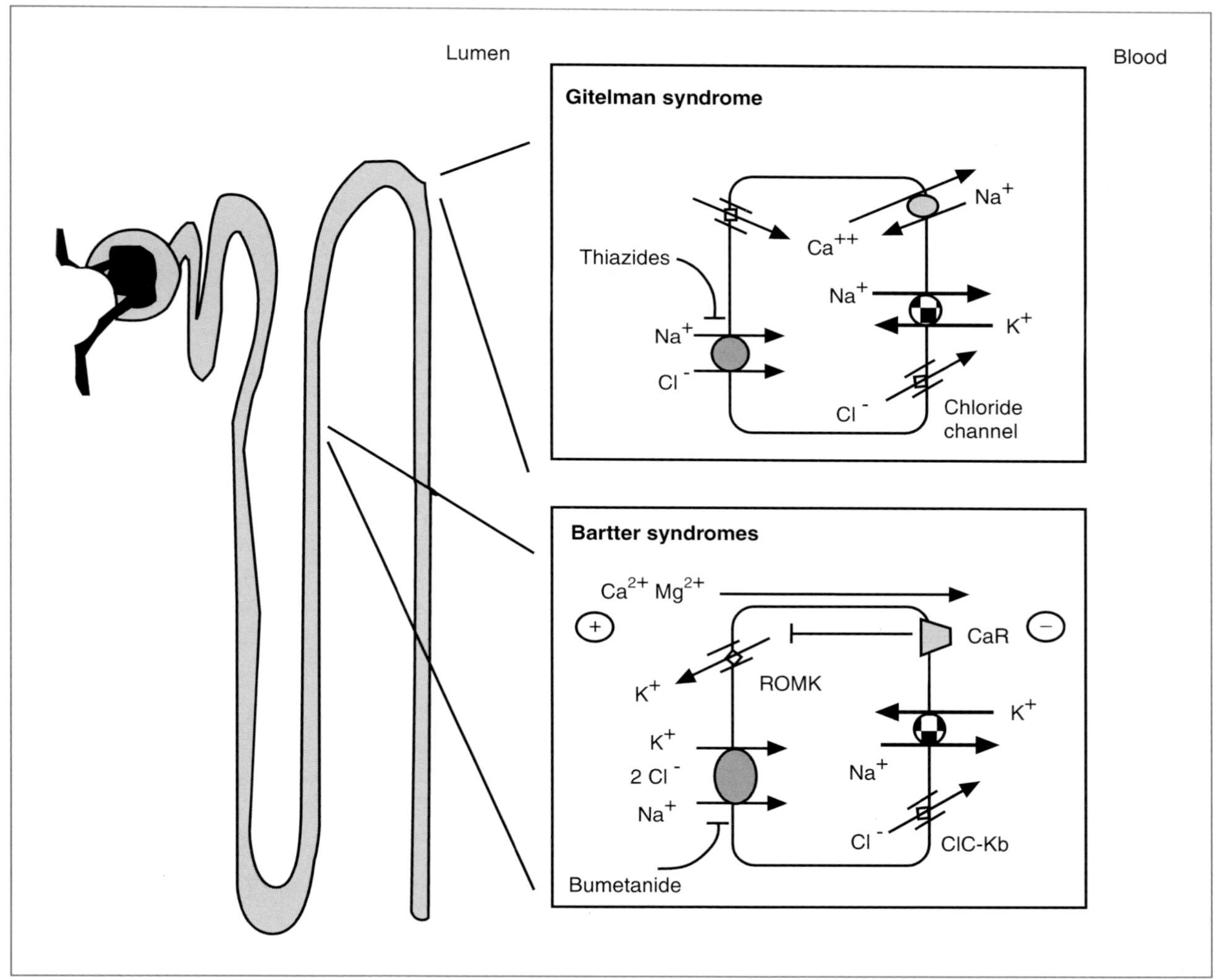

Figure 41.1 Bartter-Gitelman's syndromes. Sodium chloride is reabsorbed in the thick ascending limb by the bumetanide-sensitive, Na^{+}-K^{+}-$2Cl^{-}$ cotransporter (NKCC2). This transporter is driven by the low intracellular sodium and chloride concentrations generated by the sodium-potassium pump (Na^{+}-K^{+}-ATPase) and the basolateral chloride channel (ClC-Kb). In addition, luminal recycling of potassium via the potassium channel (ROMK) ensures the efficient functioning of the Na-K-2Cl cotransporter and generates a lumen-positive transepithelial potential that drives calcium and magnesium reabsorption. Genetic studies have identified putative loss-of-function mutations in NKCC2 or ROMK in antenatal Bartter's syndrome patients, and ClC-Kb mutations in patients with classic Bartter's syndromes. Sodium chloride is reabsorbed by the apical thiazide-sensitive, Na-Cl cotransporter (NCCT) in the distal convoluted tubule. This transporter is driven by the low intracellular sodium and chloride concentrations generated by the sodium-potassium pump (Na^{+}-K^{+}-ATPase) and a basolateral Cl^{-} channel (ClC). In this nephron segment, calcium is reabsorbed via apical calcium channels and exits the cell via a basolateral sodium-coupled exchanger. In Gitelman's syndrome, genetic studies have identified putative loss-of-function mutations in the NCCT. As a result of decreased sodium chloride reabsorption, calcium reabsorption is enhanced.

apparent mineralocorticoid excess (AME), are hypertensive disorders. They share a common clinical presentation that is characterized by severe, early-onset hypertension, normal physical examinations, hypokalemia, and very low plasma renin activity (PRA) and aldosterone levels. The fourth disorder, pseudohypoaldosteronism type 1, is the antithesis of the other three. It is characterized by normal or low blood pressure, severe hyperkalemia, hyponatremia, metabolic acidosis, and elevated plasma renin activity and aldosterone levels.

Low-renin hypertension should be suspected in patients with severe hypertension that is refractory to usual antihypertensive therapy. These patients may present as infants, children, or adolescents. Since glucocorticoid remediable aldosteronism and Liddle's syndrome are autosomal dominant disorders, there may be a similar history of severe hypertension in first-degree relatives. The diagnosis of glucocorticoid remediable aldosteronism may be confirmed by an antihypertensive response to dexamethasone (dexamethasone suppression test). Glucocorticoid remediable aldosteronism, Liddle's syndrome, and apparent mineralocorticoid excess can be distinguished from one another by characteristic urinary steroid profiles. Direct gene-based testing is available and provides the definitive diagnosis.

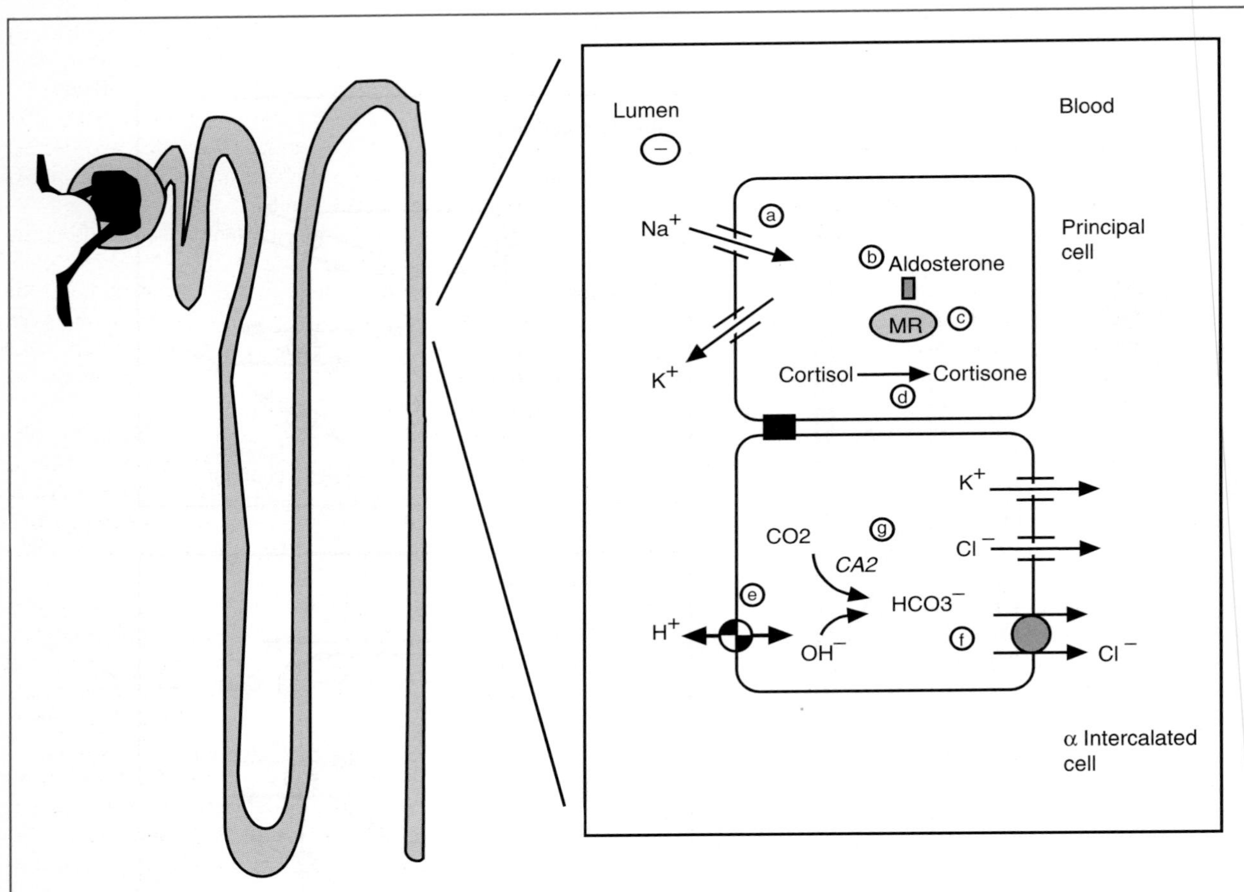

Figure 41.2 Disorders of the distal tubule. Mineralocorticoids regulate sodium reabsorption via the epithelial sodium channel in the principal cells of the cortical collecting duct. The resulting lumen-negative transepithelial voltage drives potassium secretion from the principal cells and proton secretion from the α-intercalated cells. The type I mineralocorticoid receptor (MR) binds both aldosterone and cortisol, but not cortisone. The receptor specificity for aldosterone is mediated by the kidney isoform of 11β-hydroxysteroid dehydrogenase (type II), which converts cortisol to cortisone. Defects in the epithelial sodium channel (*a*) cause either autosomal dominant Liddle's syndrome or autosomal recessive pseudohypoaldosteronism type 1 (PHA1a). Autosomal dominant glucocorticoid remediable aldosteronism results from the abnormal production of aldosterone metabolites (*b*). As a result, sodium reabsorption is regulated by ACTH. Autosomal dominant pseudohypoaldosteronism type 1 (PHA1b) is due to mutations in MR (*c*). Apparent mineralocorticoid excess is a recessive disorder due to loss of function of the 11β-hydroxysteroid dehydrogenase (type II) (*d*). As a result, cortisol rather than aldosterone regulates the function of the mineralocorticoid receptor. The collecting duct is the principal site of distal acidification where the final 5-10% of the filtered bicarbonate load is reabsorbed and the hydrogen ions that were generated from dietary protein catabolism are secreted. Urinary acidification by the α-intercalated cells involves the integrated action of the multi-subunit, proton-translocating ATPase (H^+-ATPase), (*e*) the Cl^-:$HCO3^-$ exchanger (AE1) (*f*) in the basolateral membrane, and the cytosolic carbonic anhydrase II isoenzyme (CA2) which catalyzes the conversion of carbon dioxide and water to hydrogen ions and bicarbonate. Autosomal recessive distal RTA renal tubular acidosis with associated sensorineural deafness is due to loss-of-function mutations in the gene which encodes the B1 subunit of the H^+-ATPase (*e*). Autosomal dominant distal renal tubular acidosis is caused by mutations in the gene encoding basolateral Cl^-:$HCO3^-$ exchanger (*f*). Carbonic anhydrase II deficiency is due to loss-of-function mutations in the enzyme, CA2 (*g*).

Medical management focuses on dietary sodium restriction, blocking the epithelial sodium channel with the potassium-sparing diuretics, e.g., triamterene and amiloride, downregulating the ectopic aldosterone synthesis with glucocorticoids (glucocorticoid remediable aldosteronism), or blocking the type 1 mineralocorticoid receptor using the competitive antagonist spironolactone (glucocorticoid remediable aldosteronism and apparent mineralocorticoid excess).

RENAL TUBULAR ACIDOSIS

Renal tubular acidosis (RTA) is a hyperchloremic, metabolic acidosis due to impairment of one or more acidification mechanisms in the kidney, e.g., proximal tubular reabsorption of bicarbonate, production of ammonia in the proximal tubule, or excretion of H^+ as titratable acids and ammonium ($NH4^+$) in the distal nephron. Isolated proximal renal tubular acidosis (type II) is rare, and most cases of proximal renal tubular acidosis occur in the context of Fanconi's syndrome.

Distal renal tubular acidosis (dRTA) The collecting duct is the principal site of distal tubule acidification where the final 5-10% of the filtered bicarbonate load is reabsorbed and the hydrogen ions that were generated from dietary protein catabolism are secreted. The distal nephron epithelium is composed of two cell types: the principal cells, which transport sodium, potassium, and water; and the intercalated cells, which secrete H^+ and $HCO3^-$. Urinary acidification by the α-intercalated cells involves the integrated action of the multi-subunit, proton-translocating ATPase (H^+-ATPase) in the apical membrane, the chloride/bicarbonate exchanger (Cl^-:$HCO3^-$ exchanger or AE1) in the basolateral membrane, and the cytosolic carbonic anhydrase II isoenzyme which catalyzes the conversion of carbon dioxide and water to hydrogen ions and bicarbonate.

As diagrammed in Figure 41.2, isolated autosomal dominant distal renal tubular acidosis is caused by mutations in the gene encoding basolateral Cl^-:$HCO3^-$exchanger. Autosomal recessive distal renal tubular acidosis with associated sensorineural deafness is due to loss-of-function mutations in the gene that encodes the B1 subunit of the H^+-ATPase. Carbonic anhydrase II deficiency is an autosomal recessive disorder characterized by renal tubular acidosis with both proximal and distal components, osteopetrosis, and cerebral calcification. In carbonic anhydrase type II deficiency, the rise in intracellular pH in the α-intercalated cells impairs the activity of the H^+-ATPase, thus decreasing H^+ secretion.

Patients with distal renal tubular acidosis often present in the newborn period or early infancy with failure to thrive, lethargy, polyuria, vomiting, and dehydration. Hyperchloremic, metabolic acidosis, and a urine pH above 6.0 are characteristic features. Hypokalemia is common and urinary sodium and bicarbonate wasting may occur in infants. Hypercalciuria, with hypocitraturia and a high urine pH, predisposes patients to nephrocalcinosis and renal calculi. The diagnosis of dRTA can be made by demonstrating a positive urine anion gap ($[Na^+] + [K^+] - [Cl^-]$). Early therapeutic intervention with adequate alkali therapy is required to restore linear growth rates, to correct secondary bone disease, and to minimize the risk of nephrocalcinosis. Although hypokalemia usually resolves with alkali therapy, potassium supplementation may be required in infants.

NEPHROGENIC DIABETES INSIPIDUS

Nephrogenic diabetes insipidus (NDI) is characterized by renal tubular unresponsiveness to the antidiuretic hormone, arginine vasopressin (AVP) or its antidiuretic analogue, 1-desamino-8-D-ariginine vasopressin (DDAVP). Both congenital and acquired forms of this disorder are characterized by polyuria, polydipsia, and hyposthenuria despite often elevated AVP levels.

The principal cell of the inner medullary collecting duct is the site where fine tuning of the final urinary composition and volume occurs. In the normal kidney, the antidiuresis involves the binding of AVP to the vasopressin V2 receptor with the consequent insertion of cytoplasmic vesicles carrying water channel proteins, aquaporin-2 (AQP2), into the apical membrane.

A majority of patients (> 90%) inherit nephrogenic diabetes insipidus as an X-linked recessive trait. In these patients, defects in the V2 receptor have been identified. In the remaining cases, the disease is transmitted as either an autosomal recessive or dominant trait involving mutations in the *AQP2* gene.

Patients with congenital nephrogenic diabetes insipidus present in the first weeks of life with dehydration, fever, poor feeding and irritability. The diagnosis is established when urinary osmolality fails to rise in response to administration of the AVP analogue, 1-desamino-8-D-ariginine vasopressin. Direct gene-based testing is recommended for the perinatal assessment of children born to known nephrogenic diabetes insipidus families. Treatment is directed toward maintaining euvolemia and minimizing the episodes of hypernatremic dehydration. Low-solute diets and treatment with thiazide diuretics may help reduce urinary volumes. Since thiazide-induced hypokalemia may further impair urinary concentrating ability in these patients, addition of a potassium-sparing diuretic, e.g., amiloride, may be beneficial in some patients. In patients with refractory polyuria, prostaglandin-synthesis inhibitors such as indomethacin, may be efficacious.

UROLITHIASES (KIDNEY STONES)

Urolithiases are a common urinary tract abnormality. As discussed above, cystinuria is the leading single gene cause of heritable urolithiasis in both children and adults. Three Mendelian disorders, Dent's disease, X-linked recessive nephrolithiasis (XRN), and X-linked recessive hypophosphatemic rickets (XLRH) cause hypercalciuric urolithiasis. The disorders involve a functional loss of the renal chloride channel, ClC-5. It has been proposed that ClC-5 may be involved in other familial disorders associated with calcium-containing kidney stones.

In addition to renal transport deficiencies, defects in metabolic enzymes can also cause urolithiases. Inherited defects in the purine salvage enzymes, hypoxanthine-guanine phosphoribosyltransferase (HPRT) and adenine phosphoribosyltransferase (APRT) or in the catabolic enzyme xanthine dehydrogenase (XDH), can all lead to stone formation. Defective enzymes in the oxalate metabolic pathway result in hyperoxaluria, oxalate stone formation, and a consequent loss of renal function.

Remarkable advances have been made in the understanding of numerous inherited renal tubular disorders. Future research will continue to shed light on the pathophysiology of these genetic diseases, identify new reagents for gene-based diagnostic testing, and provide the platform for developing more targeted therapies. In addition, investigations of these relatively rare disorders may help identify genes and genetic pathways that are involved in more common transport-related disorders, such as idiopathic hypercalciuria, kidney stone formation, diuretic-induced renal potassium wasting, and even some forms of low-renin hypertension.

Acknowledgments

The authors wishes to thank Dr. Rebecca Herink for critically reviewing this manuscript.

Suggested readings

BERGERON M, GOUGOUX A, VINAY P. The renal Fanconi's syndrome. In: Scriver C, Beaudet A, Sly W, Valle D, eds. The metabolic and molecular bases of inherited diseases. Vol. III. New York: McGraw-Hill, 1995;3691-704.

BICHET D, OSCHE A, ROSENTHAL W. Congenital nephrogenic diabetes insipidus. J Am Soc Nephrol 1997;12:1951-8.

BISCEGLIA L, CALONGE MJ, TOTARO A, et al. Localization, by linkage analysis, of the cystinuria type III gene to chromosome 19q13.1. Am J Hum Genet 1997;60:611-6.

BRUCE L, COPE D, JONES G, et al. Familial distal renal tubular acidosis is associated with mutations in the red cell anion exchanger (Band 3, AE1) gene. J Clin Invest 1997;100:1693-1707.

CALONGE MJ, GASPARINI P, CHILLARON J, et al. Cystinuria caused by mutations in rBAT, a gene involved in the transport of cystine. Nat Genet 1994;6:420-5.

CARPENTER T. New perspectives on the biology and treatment of X-linked hypophosphatemic rickets. Pediatr Clin North Am 1997;44:443-66.

CHANG S, GRUNDER S, HANUKOGLU A, et al. Mutations in subunits of the epithelial sodium channel cause salt wasting with hyperkalemic acidosis, pseudohypoaldosteronism type 1. Nature Genet 1996;12:248-53.

DANPURE C, PURDUE P. Primary hyperoxaluria. In: Scriver C, Beaudet A, Sly W, Valle D, eds. The metabolic and molecular basis of inherited diseases vol. II. New York: McGraw-Hill, 1995;2385-424.

DLUHY RG, LIFTON RP. Glucocorticoid-remediable aldosteronism. Endocrinology and Metabolism Clinics of North America 1994;23:285-97.

FRIEDMAN P. Codependence of renal calcium and sodium transport. Ann Rev Physiol 1998;60:179-97.

GELLER DS, RODRIGUEZ-SORIANO J, VALLO BOADO A, et al. Mutations in the mineralocorticoid receptor gene cause autosomal dominant pseudohypoaldosteronism type I. Nature Genet 1998;19:279-81.

KARET F, FINBERG K, NELSON R, et al. Mutations in the gene encoding B1 subunit of H^+-ATPase cause renal tubular acidosis with sensorineural deafness. Nat Genet 1999;21:84-90.

KUMAR R. Phosphatonin-an new phosphaturetic hormone? Lessons from tumor-induced osteomalacia and X-linked hypophophatemia. Nephrol Dial Transplant 1997;12:11-13.

LIPMAN ML, PANDA D, BENNET HP, et al. Cloning of human PEX cDNA. Expression, subcellular localization and endopeptidase activity. J Biol Chem 1998;273:13729-37.

LLOYD S, PEARCE S, FISHER S, et al. A common molecular basis for three inherited kidney stone diseases. Nature 1996;379:445-9.

PAK C. Kidney stones. Lancet 1998;351:1797-1801.

ROWE P. The role of the PHEX gene (PEX) in families with X-linked hypophosphataemic rickets. Curr Opin Nephrol Hyperten 1998;7:367-76.

SCRIVER C, CLOW C, READE T, et al. Ontogeny modifies manifestations of cystinuria genes: implications for counseling. J Pediatr 1985;106:411-16.

SEGAL S, THIER S. Cystinuria. In: Scriver C, Beaudet A, Sly W, Valle D, eds. The metabolic and molecular basis of inherited diseases. Vol. II. New York: McGraw-Hill, 1995;3581-602.

SIMON D, BINDRA R, MANSFIELD T, et al. Mutations in the chloride channel gene, CLCNKB, cause Bartter's syndrome. Nature Genet 1997;17:171-8.

SIMON D, KARET F, HAMDAN J, et al. Bartter's syndrome, hypokalemic alkalosis with hypercalciuria, is caused by mutations in the Na-K-2Cl cotransporter NKCC2. Nature Genet 1996;13:183-8.

SIMON D, KARET F, HAMDAN J, et al. Genetic heterogeneity of Bartter's syndrome revealed by mutations in the K+ channel, ROMK. Nature Genet 1996;14:152-6.

SIMON D, NELSON-WILLIAMS C, BIA M, et al. Gitelman's variant of Bartter's syndrome, inherited hypokalemic alkalosis, is caused by mutations in the thiazide-sensitive Na-Cl cotransporter. Nature Genet 1996;12:24-30.

WARNOCK D. Liddle's syndrome: an autosomal dominant form of human hypertension. Kidney Int 1998;53:18-24.

WHITE P, MUNE T, ROGERSON F, et al. 11-β hydroxysteroid dehydrogenase and its role in the syndrome of apparent mineralocorticoid excess. Pediatr Research 1997;41:25-9.

WILLIAMS GH AND DHULY RG. Glucocorticoid-remediable aldosteronism. J Endocrinol Invest 1995;18:512-7.

YIU V, DLUHY R, LIFTON R, GUAY-WOODFORD L. Low peripheral plasma renin activity as a critical marker in pediatric hypertension. Pediatr Nephrol 1997;11:343-6.

CHAPTER

42 Miscellaneous inherited diseases with renal involvement

Jean-Pierre Grünfeld

CHRONIC RENAL TUBULOINTERSTITIAL DISEASES

The prototype of renal tubulointerstitial diseases is nephronophthisis, which is the most common inherited disorder leading to end-stage renal disease (ESRD) in children. Indeed, the mean age at end-stage renal disease is approximately 13 years. Polyuropolydipsia is the presenting symptom in early childhood. The renal changes include progressive and diffuse interstitial fibrosis, thickening and multilamellation of the tubular basement membrane, and late in the course, medullary cysts. The gene has been located on chromosome 2p and cloned; the corresponding protein has been named nephrocystin; and the mode of transmission is autosomal recessive.

The association of nephronophthisis-like nephropathy with tapetoretinal degeneration is known as *Senior-Loken syndrome*. Retinal changes leading to blindness may be found in various entities with renal involvement (see below).

Familial nephropathy with juvenile gout and/or hyperuricemia is an autosomal dominant disorder. The hallmarks of this disease are hyperuricemia disproportionate to the age, sex, or degree of renal dysfunction; renal hypoexcretion of urate (i.e., low fractional excretion of urate); and progressive renal disease, leading to renal failure between 20 and 40 years of age. Allopurinol treatment is worthwhile, at least for controling hyperuricemia and/or gout, and the dose should be adjusted for renal function.

CYSTINOSIS

Cystinosis is a very rare metabolic disease, inherited as an autosomal recessive trait and characterized by intracellular accumulation of cystine in many organs, including the kidney, due to a complete defect in lysosomal cystine transport. The gene involved has just been identified and cloned.

The presenting manifestations – vomiting, anorexia, polydipsia, rickets, and failure to thrive – do not appear before the age of 3 to 6 months and result from Fanconi's syndrome, i.e., generalized proximal tubular dysfunction due to cystine accumulation in renal tubular cells. The diagnosis is based on increased cystine content of leukocytes. Before the cysteamine era, glomerular filtration rate fell progressively beyond 5 to 6 years of age, and end-stage renal disease was reached at approximately 10 years. Accumulation of cystine in various organs explains the extrarenal signs of cystinosis. The eyes (cornea and retina) are involved early. Then, during the period of renal replacement therapy, other manifestations develop, leading to hypothyroidism, hypogonadism, diabetes mellitus, and liver, spleen, muscle, and central nervous system (CNS) involvement.

Cysteamine, administered early in the disease, i.e., before the first year of age, and continued every day throughout life, represents an effective means of delaying or preventing the complications of the disease. Supportive therapy, including kidney transplantation, is of great importance to patients.

Cystinosis must be distinguished from cystinuria, an inherited defect of cystine reabsorption in the renal proximal tubule leading to stone formation.

MALFORMATION SYNDROMES WITH RENAL AND EXTRARENAL ABNORMALITIES

These syndromes are multiple. Among them, nail-patella and Bardet-Biedl syndromes have been selected.

The nail-patella syndrome, also known as *hereditary osteoonychodysplasia*, is a rare autosomal dominant disorder defined by the association of nail hypoplasia or dysplasia and bone abnormalities, including absent or hypoplastic patellae and iliac horns. Renal involvement occurs in 60% of patients. Progressive renal disease, however, is found in only 15% of patients. The disease is caused by mutations in the *LMX1B* gene, which codes a family of transcription factors implicated in pattern formation during development. This gene is more specifically involved in dorsoventral patterning in the chicken. The study of malformation syndromes in humans contributes to identification of genes involved in normal development.

Renal involvement is a cardinal feature of Bardet-Biedl syndrome, besides obesity, polydactyly, hypogonadism, and pigmentary retinitis. It is inherited as an autosomal dominant fashion. Renal abnormalities include calyceal changes on intravenous pyelogram (IVP) and progressive renal failure in some patients. Five different genetic loci have been found to be linked with Bardet-Biedl syndrome in different families. This is a good example of genetic heterogeneity – similar phenotypic manifestations ascribed to defects in various genes.

Nephrolithiasis due to metabolic diseases

Nephrolithiasis may be related to inherited tubular defects (see Chap. 41). It also may be a major complication of hereditary metabolic diseases.

In primary hyperoxaluria type I, recurrent nephrolithiasis and nephrocalcinosis are the presenting features, often during childhood. Renal stones are formed of calcium oxalate monohydrate, or whewellite. Renal failure develops between the first and third decades in most patients. However, patients with later manifestations have been observed. Concomitant with the progressive impairment of renal function, oxalate accumulates in the body, and calcium oxalate deposition occurs in various organs, not only in the kidney, but also in bones, joints, nerves, artery walls, retinas, etc. (this is called *systemic oxalosis*).

Indeed, the disease is due to an inborn error of metabolism, i.e., a basic defect in glyoxylate metabolism (deficiency of alanine-glyoxalate aminotransferase, which is normally located in peroxisomes of liver cells), resulting in the endogenous overproduction of oxalate and glycolate, which are then excreted by the kidney. The diagnosis therefore is based on increased urinary excretion of these substances. Moreover, the enzyme deficiency can be demonstrated on a liver biopsy specimen.

Pyridoxine-sensitive patients have been described. Thus, pyridoxine sensitivity should be tested in all patients with type I primary hyperoxaluria. Identification of the biochemical defect has generated a new therapeutic approach, combined liver and kidney transplantation, to correct both the enzyme defect and the consequences of oxalate overproduction.

In adenine phosphoriboxyltransferase deficiency, the presenting sign is 2,8-dihydroxyadenine urolithiasis; in very rare cases, intratubular precipitation of this compound may lead to chronic renal damage. The metabolic disturbances are amenable to chronic administration of allopurinol, which represents a highly effective treatment, immediately and in the long term.

PHAKOMATOSES: VON HIPPEL-LINDAU DISEASE AND TUBEROUS SCLEROSIS

Renal cysts and bilateral multifocal renal cell carcinomas are the main clinical features of von Hippel-Lindau disease. Renal carcinoma is discovered at a mean age of 45 years, but it may be found between the ages of 15 and 65 years. It is usually asymptomatic. Kidneys of affected subjects should be screened regularly. Nephron-sparing surgery or nephrectomy is advised according to the size of the tumor(s). Metastatic renal cell carcinoma is one of the main causes of death in von Hippel-Lindau disease because of late detection. The other von Hippel-Lindau lesions are retinal and CNS hemangioblastomas, pheochromocytomas, and pancreatic cysts.

Bilateral renal angiomyolipomas are the most common renal lesions in tuberous sclerosis. Renal cysts also may be found, sometimes mimicking polycystic kidney disease. The incidence of renal cell carcinoma is slightly increased when compared with the general population but is much lower than in von Hippel-Lindau disease. Tuberous sclerosis complex comprises lesions of the skin (facial angiofibromas), retina, CNS (responsible for seizures and/or mental retardation), and heart (rhabdomyoma).

Both diseases are transmitted in an autosomal dominant fashion. Tumor-suppressor genes are involved. These diseases are examples of the "two-hit phenomenon": the first germ-line mutation is, of course, inherited; the second mutation involves the same allele, on the other corresponding chromosome, and occurs only in somatic cells (e.g., in renal carcinoma cells in von Hippel-Lindau patients). In von Hippel-Lindau disease, a single gene is involved. The search for the mutation in an affected family is relevant clinically so as to identify and screen at-risk subjects regularly. In tuberous sclerosis, two genes are involved, *TSC1* and *TSC2*. In both diseases, reduction in renal mass, due to iterative surgery in von Hippel-Lindau and to extension of renal angiomyolipomas or cysts in tuberous sclerosis, may lead to renal failure.

Suggested readings

DAVISON AM, CAMERON JS, GRÜNFELD JP, et al, eds. The patient with inherited disease. Oxford Textbook of clinical nephrology. Oxford: Oxford University Press, 1998: 2375-498.

MORGAN SH, GRÜNFELD JP, eds. Inherited disorders of the kidney. Oxford: Oxford University Press, 1998.

SECTION

11

Therapy

CHAPTER

43

Acute renal failure

Hugh R. Brady, Michael R. Clarkson

KEY POINTS

- Acute renal failure complicates 5% of hospital admissions and is an independent risk factor for increased inpatient morbidity and mortality.
- Most acute renal failure represents a reversible physiologic response to renal hypoperfusion (prerenal acute renal failure) or reflects damage within the renal parenchyma induced by ischemia, nephrotoxins, and / or sepsis.
- In critically ill patients the risk of acute renal failure is reduced by assiduous attention to intravascular volume status, monitoring of circulating drug levels, and adjustment of drug dosing according to body mass and GFR.
- Whereas examination of the urine sediment and urinary biochemical indices may help differentiate acute tubular necrosis from prerenal acute renal failure, definitive diagnosis requires a trial of therapy.
- Management of acute renal failure is supportive, and the routine use of "renal dose dopamine" and other putative renoprotective agents cannot be justified and is potentially deleterious.
- Whereas intermittent hemodialysis plays a central role in the management of acute renal failure, slow continuous forms of renal replacement may be preferable in hemodynamically unstable or highly catabolic patients.

In health, the kidney eliminates nitrogenous waste products, controls extracellular blood volume, maintains acid-base and electrolyte homeostasis, and is the source of important hormones such as erythropoeitin and 1,25- vitamin D. Acute renal failure is characterized by a rapid decline in renal function over hours to days with subsequent retention of waste products and impairment of salt, water, and electrolyte balance. The criteria for the diagnosis of acute renal failure vary, but hinge on an acute increase in the serum urea and creatinine (e.g., an increase of >100 μmol/l or a doubling of serum creatinine over several days). The incidence of acute renal failure varies with the clinical setting. It complicates approximately 5% of nonelective hospital admissions and 30% of admissions to intensive care units. Developments in renal replacement therapy over the past three decades have enabled physicians to effectively manage the metabolic and fluid balance derangements associated with acute renal failure. In spite of this impressive evolution of dialysis technology, overall mortality rates have not changed significantly over this time. The high mortality probably reflects the increasing complexity and comorbidity of patients with acute renal failure. Thus, patients die "with acute renal failure" rather than "from acute renal failure." Patients who do not succumb to comorbid illness usually recover from renal function.

For purposes of classification and differential diagnosis, acute renal failure is conveniently divided into three main sub-types: *prerenal acute renal failure*, the commonest form of acute renal failure, is caused by renal hypoperfusion and is rapidly reversible upon restoration of renal blood flow. *Intrinsic intrarenal acute renal failure* is caused by ischemic, toxic or inflammatory insults to the renal parenchyma. Acute tubular necrosis (ATN) accounts for 90% of all cases of intrinsic acute renal failure and is the term given to the clinical syndrome of acute renal failure induced by ischemic or nephrotoxic insult. It is usually characterized by an identifiable insult, evidence of tubular injury on urinalysis, and a recovery pattern that extends over days to weeks. A minority of intrinsic renal acute renal failure is due to other diseases of the interstitium, the glomeruli, or tubulointerstitium. *Postrenal failure* constitutes a small percentage of cases of acute renal failure and is due to acute obstruction of the renal outflow tracts (acute obstructive uropathy).

In this chapter, we review the etiology, clinical manifestations, pathophysiology, and evaluation of patients with acute renal failure. We focus particularly on prerenal acute renal failure and intrinsic acute renal failure due to acute tubular necrosis. Given that there is no therapy that accelerates recovery from established human acute renal failure, we summarize preventive measures to minimize the incidence of acute tubular necrosis. We discuss the management of the complications of acute tubular necrosis, and highlight promising experimental therapies.

Etiology

Prerenal acute renal failure

Prerenal acute renal failure is, by definition, renal impairment secondary to hypoperfusion that is rapidly (within hours) reversible upon restoration of renal blood flow. Prerenal acute renal failure accounts for 60-70% of acute renal failure and is a significant marker for inpatient morbidity. Prerenal acute renal failure usually is triggered by true hypovolemia or a fall in the "effective" circulatory volume, when systemic hypotension and a reduction in renal blood flow overwhelms the limits of renal blood flow autoregulation. In health, autoregulation of renal blood flow fails once systolic blood pressure falls below 70-80 mm Hg. However, prerenal acute renal failure may manifest at higher arterial pressures in the elderly and in patients with preexisting renal impairment or renovascular disease.

In the outpatient setting prerenal acute renal failure typically complicates gastrointestinal losses (e.g., severe diarrhea or vomiting), diuretic excess or diminished fluid intake due to altered consciousness or neurologic disability. Alternatively, prerenal acute renal failure can complicate severe left ventricular failure when inadequate arterial perfusion pressures result in a fall in the "effective" systemic arterial blood volume. The hepatorenal syndrome (HRS) is a distinct variant of acute renal failure with some features of prerenal acute renal failure. The hepatorenal syndrome typically complicates advanced liver disease and is characterized by intense renal vasoconstriction and failure to respond to volume expansion. It is typically precipitated by a fall in circulating blood volume as a consequence of paracentesis, hemorrhage, diuresis or by prescription drugs that impair intrarenal autoregulatory responses, such as nonsteroidal anti-inflammatory drugs (NSAIDs; see below).

Therapeutic drugs can induce prerenal acute renal failure through several mechanisms (Tab. 43.1). First, any drug that impairs cardiac contractility or causes excessive systemic peripheral vasodilatation can lower blood pressure to levels that compromise renal blood flow and the glomerular filtration rate (GFR). Second, drugs that blunt renal autoregulatory responses to renal hypoperfusion, e.g., angiotensin-converting enzyme (ACE) inhibitors or NSAIDs, can precipitate prerenal acute renal failure in the setting of otherwise compensated renal hypoperfusion. Third, drugs such as cyclosporine and radiocontrast can trigger intrarenal vasoconstriction through direct effects on the renal vasculature. Fourth, ACE inhibitors or

Table 43.1 Major causes of drug-induced acute renal failure

Clinical syndrome	Agent	Mechanism
Prerenal acute renal failure	Angiotensin-converting enzyme inhibitors Angiotensin-II receptor antagonists	Systemic hypotension and fall in intraglomerular pressure due to inhibition of efferent arteriole vasoconstriction
	NSAIDs	Inhibition of prostaglandin-mediated intrarenal vasodilatation
	Antihypertensives	Systemic vasodilatation with hypotension
	Cyclosporine/tacrolimus (FK 506)	Intrarenal vasoconstriction
	Radiocontrast agents	Endothelin release
	Amphotericin B	Intrarenal vasoconstriction
Intrinsic acute renal failure	Aminoglycosides Amphotericin B Cisplatin/ifosfamide NSAIDs	Direct tubular toxicity (acute tubular necrosis)
	Penicillins/cephalosporins Ciprofloxacin/NSAIDs Interferon/furosemide	Allergic interstitial nephritis
	Statins	Rhabdomyolysis
	Cyclosporine/tacrolimus (FK 506)	Hemolytic uremic syndrome
Postrenal failure	Acyclovir	Intratubular precipitation

angiotensin-II receptor antagonists can induce a specific type of acute renal failure in subjects with renal artery stenosis (RAS). In the presence of a hemodynamically significant renal artery stenosis (>60-70% narrowing) blood flow to the affected kidney is reduced and intrarenal renin generation is enhanced as a compensatory response. Renin ultimately drives angiotensin II production, which, in turn, attempts to restore the GFR by raising systemic blood pressure, thereby driving more blood across the stenotic lesion. Angiotensin II also triggers preferential constriction of the efferent arteriole, thereby raising intraglomerular pressure, which also serves to maintain GFR. Acute renal failure may develop in patients with renal artery stenosis following initiation of ACE inhibition, particularly in patients with preexisting hypovolemia due to concomitant use of diuretics.

Intrinsic acute renal failure

Intrinsic acute renal failure implies injury to the renal parenchyma. It is convenient to subclassify intrinsic renal failure into diseases affecting the large and small branches of the renal vasculature and disorders of the glomeruli, tubules and interstitium.

Diseases of the renal arteries and veins rarely cause acute renal failure. Because a single functioning kidney is sufficient to excrete nitrogenous waste, large vessel disease must be either bilateral (or unilateral if there is a solitary functioning kidney) if it is to trigger acute renal failure. Renal artery occlusion or thrombosis can complicate aortic dissection or rupture of an atherosclerotic plaque in the renal artery. Thromboemboli to the renal arteries are uncommon. In contrast, the incidence of acute renal failure due to atheroemboli probably is increasing in frequency with the expansion of endovascular intervention and cardiac surgery. In this setting, emboli are dislodged from atheromatous aortic plaques, become trapped in the renal microvasculature, and excite an inflammatory reaction that impairs renal function.

Acute renal failure due to small vessel injury can complicate an array of diseases, including malignant hypertension, vasculitis, HELLP syndrome, or hemolytic uremic syndrome/thrombotic thrombocytopenic purpura. Severe acute glomerulonephritis can also present with acute renal failure, the latter being a component of the nephritic syndrome. Acute tubulointerstitial nephritis is a major mechanism of drug-induced acute renal failure. This condition is characterized by inflammatory cell infiltration of the tubulointerstitium and generally is an idiosyncratic allergic reaction to antibiotics or analgesics. Uncommon tubulointerstitial causes of acute renal failure include pyelonephritis in a single kidney, allograft rejection and precipitation of uric acid (acute urate nephropathy), or myeloma light chains (myeloma cast nephropathy) in renal tubules. An in-depth review of these disorders is beyond the scope of this chapter, and a more comprehensive discussion is presented elsewhere in this book.

Ischemic acute tubular necrosis

Prerenal acute renal failure and ischemic acute tubular necrosis are part of a spectrum of hypoperfusion injury. In prerenal acute renal failure, the fall in renal blood flow compromises GFR, but does not induce sufficient intrarenal ischemia to cause parenchymal injury. In ischemic acute tubular necrosis, severe renal hypoperfusion leads to microvascular and tubular injury and a decline in glomerular filtration that usually is sustained for 1-3 weeks. Patients with ischemic acute tubular necrosis typically are critically ill, having suffered hypovolemia and hypotension during major surgery or as a consequence of burns, pancreatitis, or major trauma. The resulting ischemic injury often is compounded by the effects of cytokines and endotoxins released during sepsis and by exposure to nephrotoxic agents such as aminoglycosides or radiocontrast.

Nephrotoxic acute tubular necrosis

For several reasons the kidney is relatively sensitive to injury from circulating toxins. It receives one-quarter of cardiac output, and many substances are freely filtered across the glomerular capillary wall into the urinary space. The surface area of the renal vasculature and tubules is very large, thus providing ample opportunity for exposure to toxins. Many circulating compounds are also taken up by transporters into tubule epithelial cells and secreted into the tubule lumen. The concentration of toxins within the kidney may be increased further by the countercurrent exchange system that results from the unique parallel arrangement of tubule and vasculature within the renal medulla. A wide range of structurally diverse endogenous and exogenous compounds are nephrotoxic. The physicochemical properties of the offending agent, its pharmacokinetics, and duration of exposure are important determinants of nephrotoxic injury. In most cases the risk of nephrotoxic acute tubular necrosis is increased by preexisting renal insufficiency, older age, hypovolemia, and coexisting medical conditions such as diabetes mellitus or congestive heart failure. The common causes of nephrotoxic acute tubular necrosis are discussed below.

Exogenous toxins Aminoglycosides are cationic antibiotics used widely for treatment of serious gram-negative infections, and are the most common cause of drug-induced acute tubular necrosis. By virtue of their electrical charge, aminoglycosides bind preferentially to the anionic cell surface protein megalin on the proximal tubule epithelial cell. Following endocytosis, this complex perturbs the function of lysosomes, which become overloaded with recycled cell membrane components and ultimately ruptures, with subsequent intracellular release of cytotoxic enzymes. Acute tubular necrosis characteristically develops during the second week of therapy. The course may be accelerated in the presence of sepsis or ischemia. Acute renal failure complicates 10-20% of courses of aminoglycoside therapy and is common even when drug levels are maintained within the therapeutic range. Acute renal failure is usually nonoliguric and recovery of renal function generally occurs within 2-3 weeks in uncomplicated cases.

Aminoglycosides also interfere with the function of more distal nephron segments, and prolonged therapy may be associated with hypomagnesemia and polyuria, reflecting injury to the thick ascending limb and the medullary collecting duct, respectively. Risk factors for the development of aminoglycoside toxicity include coexisting sepsis, cumulative dose, high peak serum levels (gentamicin levels >10 μg/l), liver disease, and the administration of other nephrotoxins. Consolidated once-daily dosing, as opposed to divided dosing, is potentially less toxic to the renal tubule while maintaining bactericidal efficacy.

Other exogenous nephrotoxins include the chemotherapeutic agents cisplatin and ifosfamide, which mediate their tubular cytotoxicity via mitochondrial injury and free radical release. Amphotericin B, the mainstay of treatment for systemic fungal infections, induces renal vasoconstriction and is also directly tubulotoxic. Because of its effects on other nephron segments amphotericin-induced acute tubular necrosis often is preceded or accompanied by the development of distal renal tubular acidosis, hypokalemia, and hypomagnesemia. Acyclovir can induce renal injury following precipitation in the renal tubules. Nephrotoxicity is most common when acyclovir is administered as a bolus for the treatment of life-threatening herpetic infections.

Endogenous toxins Heme pigment nephropathy occurs in rhabomyolysis or, less commonly, in massive intravascular hemolysis. The development of rhabdomyolysis in previously healthy subjects usually is triggered by trauma, such as a crush injury, or intense physical exercise. The diagnosis should be considered in all cases of acute renal failure following drug overdose and in elderly patients who present following a period of collapse and unconsciousness. Alcoholics are at particular risk of rhabdomyolysis for a variety of reasons, including direct alcohol toxicity, pressure-induced muscle necrosis during periods of unconsciousness, alcohol-induced seizures, and such alcohol-related metabolic abnormalities as hypophosphatemia, hypomagnesemia, and hypokalemia. Drug-induced rhabdomyolysis is well recognized with therapeutic agents such as HMG-CoA reductase inhibitors ("statins") and with such recreational drugs as heroin, amphetamines, and phencyclidine.

The pathophysiology of heme pigment acute renal failure is mediated by several interrelated events. Injury to muscle cells results in leakage of intracellular contents including myoglobin into the bloodstream. When infused into otherwise healthy laboratory animals, myoglobin does not induce acute tubular necrosis; however, in combination with renal hypoperfusion, significant renal injury occurs. These findings corroborate experience in humans, where heme-pigment induced acute tubular necrosis typically occurs in the setting of volume depletion due to third-space losses into damaged muscle or decreased oral intake during periods of unconsciousness. Direct inhibition of nitric oxide, an important vasodilator, by heme pigments further compounds renal ischemia. Precipitation of heme pigments in the tubular lumen also may contribute to the pathophysiology of acute tubular necrosis.

Acute renal failure complicates up to 40% of cases of multiple myeloma and may be the presenting clinical feature. Myeloma light chains are filtered at the glomerulus. Coaggregation of these light chains with Tamm-Horsfall glycoprotein leads to the development of urinary casts, urinary obstruction, and acute renal failure. Many light chains are also directly toxic to the tubule epithelium. These direct effects of light chains on the integrity of the renal parenchyma in myeloma patients may be further compounded by hyperviscosity, hypercalcemia, hyperuricemia, and nephrotoxic antibiotics or chemotherapeutic agents.

Pathophysiology of acute tubular necrosis When discussing the pathophysiology of acute tubular necrosis it is useful to subdivide the clinical course into initiation, maintenance and resolution phases. The initiation phase refers to the period of exposure to ischemia or nephrotoxin during which injury to the renal parenchyma occurs. This period is followed by a maintenance phase during which GFR remains at its nadir, typically 5-10 m/s/min, for 1-2 weeks even after the removal of the initial insult. The maintenance phase is characterised by several key events that contribute to the persistent depression of GFR. First, there is sustained intrarenal vasoconstriction and sludging of red cells in the medullary vessels. Second, there is sloughing of injured or necrotic tubule cells into the tubular lumen. This debris becomes encased in Tamm-Horsfall protein, thereby forming casts that block urine flow, raise intratubular pressure, and compromise GFR. In addition, glomerular filtrate can leak back across the injured epithelium, further limiting clearance of nitrogenous waste. Finally, reperfusion following ischemia is associated with oxidant injury from free radicals generated by resident renal cells or infiltrating leukocytes. The resolution phase of acute tubular necrosis involves clearance of the cellular debris and regeneration of epithelium. This typically takes 10-14 days and is mediated in part by the autocrine and paracrine actions of growth factors produced by resident and infiltrating inflammatory cells.

Postrenal acute renal failure

Although uncommon, postrenal azotemia must be excluded in every case of acute renal failure. Postrenal acute renal failure indicates bilateral ureteric obstruction, unilateral ureteric obstruction in a single functioning kidney, or outflow tract obstruction due to a lesion in the bladder or below. Prostate diseases (hypertrophy or carcinoma) are the most common causes of postrenal acute renal failure. Other less common causes include sloughed papillae, neurogenic bladder, carcinoma of the cervix, inadvertent surgical ligation of the ureters, nephrolithiasis, or blood clots. Diagnosis depends on accurate imaging of the urinary tract, usually by ultrasonography, which has a sensitivity of 80-90%. In its early stages, acute obstruction may not be associated with dilatation of the collecting system, and a retrograde contrast study should be considered if there is a high clinical suspicion of obstruction despite normal ultrasonography. Prompt diagnosis allows early surgical intervention, which is associated with a better functional outcome.

Differential diagnosis

A systematic approach to patients with elevated blood urea and creatinine levels is essential, given the broad differential diagnosis (Tab. 43.2). Initial evaluation should focus on distinguishing between acute renal failure and progression of established chronic renal disease. Discrimination is easy if the results of previous assessments of urea and creatinine are available. If previous reports are not available, then a chronic process is suggested by anemia, marked hypocalcemia or hyperphosphatemia, radiologic evidence of renal osteodystrophy or small kidneys on renal imaging. The sensitivity of these criteria is poor, however, because the laboratory abnormalities described can occur in acute azotemia. In addition, kidney size may be normal or increased in some forms of chronic renal failure, including diabetic nephropathy, amyloidosis, and polycystic kidney disease.

Clinical assessment of patients with acute renal failure should address both the underlying cause and the sequelae of diminished GFR. A review of the patient's daily weights, urine output, baseline blood pressure, and recent drug therapy is essential. During the initial stages, acute renal failure is usually asymptomatic. Oliguria (urinary output <400ml), although commonly associated with acute renal failure, is a relatively poor marker of renal function. Prerenal acute renal failure should be suspected in patients with clinical evidence of volume depletion such as thirst, postural dizziness, diminished jugular venous pressure, orthostatic or absolute hypotension, dry mucous membranes, and reduced skin turgor. Advanced cardiac failure should be obvious from hypotension, a gallop rhythm, lung crackles, elevated jugular venous pressure, and dependent edema. Stigmata of chronic liver disease raise the possibility of hepatorenal syndrome.

Ischemic acute tubular necrosis is the likely diagnosis if a period of serious hemodynamic compromise is followed by sustained renal failure even after the restoration of systemic blood pressure and hemodynamics. It is noteworthy, however, that documented hypotension is absent in up to 30% of cases of otherwise classic ischemic acute tubular necrosis. The diagnosis of nephrotoxic acute tubular necrosis requires a thorough review of the patient's case notes and drug chart. Evidence of exposure to nephrotoxic medications such as aminoglycosides, chemotherapeutic agents, and radiocontrast should be sought. The temporal relationship to drug ingestion is important for diagnosis of iatrogenic acute renal failure. Cumulative exposure to a nephrotoxic agent generally is a prerequisite for the development of acute tubular necrosis, as illustrated by the paradigm of aminoglycoside nephrotoxicity described above. The diagnosis of rhabdomyolysis is relatively straightforward following ischemic muscle injury or excessive muscular activity. A high index of suspicion is required, however, in idiosyncratic drug-related cases because muscle pain or tenderness may not be prominent features. Acute renal failure following chemotherapy for a hematologic malignancy suggests either drug-related toxicity, acute uric acid nephropathy, or hyperphosphatemic nephropathy. Acute interstitial nephritis can result from a single exposure to a nephrotoxin. The onset of acute interstitial nephritis following drug ingestion can occur months after first exposure, but usually is seen within 3-5 days of a second exposure. The presence of a fever, maculopapular rash, and arthralgia support the diagnosis. With regard to rarer causes of acute renal failure, astute clinical assessment is of paramount importance because delay in diagnosis and treatment may have devastating consequences. Livido reticularis and vasculitic skin changes in the extremities may accompany atheroembolic disease. Sinus tenderness, nasal discharge, or ear discomfort suggest Wegener's granulomatosis. Other features of systemic vasculitis include palpable purpura, peripheral neuropathy, arthralgia, and generalized symptoms of malaise and myalgia. Occlusion of a renal artery or vein may be silent or may be associated with flank pain and overt hematuria. Flank pain also has been associated with acute and rapidly progressive glomerulonephritis when the swollen kidney stretches the renal capsule. Malignant hypertension should be obvious, and typically is associated with fundoscopic or neurologic changes. Acute renal failure in an intravenous drug abuser should prompt a meticulous search for infective endocarditis. Acute urinary tract obstruction is accompanied by suprapubic and flank pain due to distention of the bladder and renal pelvis.

Urinalysis

Urinalysis is a cost-effective and invaluable tool in the investigation of patients with acute renal failure. A freshly voided specimen should be examined by dipstick. The sample is then centrifuged and the sediment examined by light microscopy. A "bland" urine sediment with only occasional hyaline casts suggests prerenal acute renal failure. Hyaline casts are formed by precipitation of Tamm-Horsfall protein in a concentrated urine. Pigmented "muddy brown" granular casts suggest acute tubular necrosis due to nephrotoxins or ischemia. Casts are not an absolute requirement for the diagnosis of acute tubular necrosis, being absent in up to one-fifth of cases. Hematuria generally is not prominent in acute tubular necrosis. Clues to the etiology of heme pigment-induced acute tubular necrosis include heme positivity by dipstick but absent or sparse red cells on microscopy. White cells or white cell casts, in otherwise sterile urine, suggest acute interstitial nephritis. Whereas mild proteinuria is common in this setting, proteinuria may be in the nephrotic range in occasional patients with acute interstitial nephritis who suffer concomitant glomerular injury. Hematuria, dysmorphic red cells or red cell casts on microscopy, and moderate to heavy proteinuria on dipstick suggest acute glomerulonephritis or vasculitis. Crystalluria suggests acute urate nephropathy, acyclovir toxicity, or ingestion of ethylene glycol.

Table 43.2 Useful clinical features, urinary findings, and confirmatory tests in the differential diagnosis of major causes of acute renal failure

Cause of acute renal failure	Clinical features	Typical urinalysis*	Confirmatory tests
Prerenal acute renal failure	Evidence of true volume depletion (thirst, postural or absolute hypotension and tachycardia, low jugular vein pressure, dry mucous membranes and axillae, weight loss, fluid output > input) or decreased effective circulatory volume (e.g., heart failure, liver failure), treatment with NSAIDs or ACE inhibitor	Hyaline casts FeNa <1% U_{Na} <10 mEq/l SG >1.018	Occasionally requires invasive hemodynamic monitoring; rapid resolution of acute renal failure on restoration of renal perfusion
Intrinsic acute renal failure			
Diseases involving large renal vessels			
Renal artery thrombosis	History of atrial fibrillation or recent myocardial infarct, nausea, vomiting, flank or abdominal pain	Mild proteinuria; occasionally red blood cells	Elevated lactate dehydrogenase with normal transaminases, renal arteriogram
Atheroembolism	Usually >50 y recent manipulation of aorta, retinal plaques, subcutaneous nodules, palpable purpura, livedo reticularis, vasculopathy, hypertension	Often normal, eosinophiluria, rarely casts	Eosinophilia, hypocomplementemia; skin biopsy, renal biopsy
Renal vein thrombosis	Evidence of nephrotic syndrome or pulmonary embolism, flank pain	Proteinuria, hematuria	Inferior venacavogram and selective renal venogram: Doppler flow studies; MRI
Disease of small vessels and glomeruli			
Glomerulonephritis or vasculitis	Compatible clinical history (e.g., recent infection) sinusitis, lung hemorrhage, rash or skin ulcers, arthralgias, hypertension, edema	Red blood cell or granular casts, red blood cells, white blood cells, mild proteinuria	Low C3, antineutrophil cytopladsmic antibodies, antiglomerular basement membrane antibodies, antinuclear antibodies, anti-streptolysin O, anti-DNase, cryoglobulins, renal biopsy
HUS or TTP	Compatible clinical history (e.g., recent gastrointestinal infection, cyclosporine, anovulants), fever, pallor, ecchymoses, neurologic abnormalities	May be normal, red blood cells, mild proteinuria, rarely red blood cell or granular casts	Anemia, thrombocytopenia, schistocytes on blood smear, increased lactate dehydrogenase, renal biopsy
Malignant hypertension	Severe hypertension with headaches, cardiac failure, retinopathy, neurologic dysfunction, proteinuria, papilledema	Red blood cells, red blood cell casts, proteinuria	LVH by echocardiography or electrocardiography, resolution of acute renal failure with control of blood pressure
Acute renal failure mediated by ischemia or toxins (acute tubular necrosis)			
Ischemia	Recent hemorrhage, hypotension (e.g., cardiac arrest), surgery	Muddy brown granular or tubule epithelial cell casts, FeNa >1%; U_{Na} >20 mEq/l; SG = 1.010	Clinical assessment and urinalysis usually sufficient for diagnosis
Exogenous toxins	Recent radiocontrast study, nephrotoxic antibiotic or anticancer agents often coexistent with volume depletion, sepsis, or chronic renal insufficiency	Muddy brown granular or tubul epithelial cell casts. FeNa >1%; U_{Na} >20 mEq/l; SG = 1.010	Clinical assessment and urinalysis usually sufficient for diagnosis
Endogenous toxins	History suggestive of rhabdomyolysis (seizures, coma, ethanol abuse, trauma)	Urine supernatant tests positive for heme	Hyperkalemia, hyperphosphatemia, hypocalcemia; increased circulating myoglobin, creatine kinase MM, uric acid
	History suggestive of hemolysis (blood transfusion)	Urine supernatant pink and positive for heme	Hyperkalemia, hyperphosphatemia, hypocalcemia, hyperuricemia, pink plasma positive for hemoglobin
	History suggestive of tumor lysis (recent chemotherapy), myeloma (bone pain), or ethylene glycol ingestion	Urate crystals, dipstick-negative proteinuria, oxalate crystals, respectively	Hyperuricemia, hyperkalemia, hyperphosphatemia (for tumor lysis): circulating or urinary monoclonal spike (for myeloma): toxicology screen, acidosis, osmolal gap (for ethylene glycol)
Acute diseases of the tubulo-interstitium			
Allergic interstitial nephritis	Recent ingestion of drug and fever, rash, or arthralgias	White blood cell casts, white blood cells (frequently eosinophiluria), red blood cells, rarely red blood cell casts, proteinuria (occasionally nephrotic)	Systemic eosinophilia, skin biopsy of rash area (leukocytoclastic vasculitis), renal biopsy
Acute bilateral pyelonephritis	Flank pain and tenderness, toxic state, febrile	Leukocytes, proteinuria, red blood cells, bacteria	Urine and blood cultures
Postrenal azotemia	Abdominal or flank pain, palpable bladder	Frequently normal, hematuria if stones, hemorrhage, malignancy or prostatic hypertrophy	Plain film, renal ultrasonography, intravenous pyelography, retrograde or anterograde pyelography, computed tomography

* FeNa = fractional excretion of sodium; U_{Na} = urine Na^+ concentration; SG = specific gravity.

(From Brady HR, Brenner BM, Liberthal W. Acute renal faiture. In: Brenner BM, Rector FC, eds. The kidney. 5th ed. Philadelphia: W.B. Saunders, 1996.)

Urine biochemistry indices

Urinary biochemistry is useful for differentiating prerenal acute renal failure from acute tubular necrosis. Prerenal acute renal failure is characterized by avid sodium and water reabsorption by tubular epithelium in an attempt to restore circulating blood volume. This appropriate compensatory response lowers urinary sodium concentration (<10 mmol/l) and increases urinary osmolality (>500 mosm/l). In acute tubular necrosis, salt and water conservation is impaired owing to tubule cell damage. As a result, the urinary sodium concentration is typically > 20 mmol/l, and the urine is isosmolar with plasma (>300 mosm) even if patients are hypotensive. The fractional excretion of sodium (FeNa) is a more sensitive indicator of tubular function. The FeNa relates sodium clearance to creatinine clearance.

$$\text{FeNa}\ (\%) = \frac{U_{Na} \times P_{Cr}}{P_{Na} \times U_{Cr}} \times 100$$

U_{Na} = Urinary sodium
P_{Cr} = Plasma creatinine
U_{Cr} = Urinary creatinine
P_{Na} = Plasma sodium

Patients with prerenal acute renal failure typically have a FeNa < 1%, whereas the FeNa is usually >1% in acute tubular necrosis. The discriminatory value of these "renal failure indices" is not absolute, and low sodium excretion rates may be seen in milder forms of nephrotoxic acute renal failure and during the early stages of ischemic acute renal failure. On the other hand, patients using diuretics, and those with chronic renal, adrenal insufficiency, or metabolic alkalosis may have inappropriately high rates of sodium excretion concurrent with volume depletion.

Laboratory findings

The typical biochemical abnormalities associated with acute renal failure include elevation in the serum urea and creatinine, hyperkalemia, hyperphosphatemia, and a wide anion gap metabolic acidosis. A proportionally greater rise in serum urea than serum creatinine is typical of prerenal acute renal failure. Here, clearance of urea is reduced as a consequence of impaired GFR. Urea is also reabsorbed from the tubule lumen with sodium and water in response to hemodynamic and hormonal stimuli. In contrast, whereas clearance of creatinine is also reduced due to impairment of GFR, there is compensatory secretion of creatinine by epithelial cells into the tubule lumen. Rhabdomyolysis, on the other hand, is characterized by a rise in serum creatinine that is proportionally greater than the increment in urea.

The time course of changes in serum creatinine may also aid differential diagnosis. In ischemic acute tubular necrosis, serum creatinine typically starts to rise within 2-3 days of the period of hypotension, plateaus between days 7-10, and then returns within days 10-14 to premorbid levels. As alluded to above, the rise in serum creatinine typically is delayed until 5-10 days after initiation of nephrotoxic drugs such as aminoglycosides, cisplatin, and amphotericin B. In radiocontrast nephropathy serum creatinine rises within 24-48 hours of administration of contrast, plateaus within 3-5 days, and subsequently falls to baseline values within 7-10 days. The profile is similar during the initial phase of atheroembolic injury; however, the recovery usually is slower and incomplete.

Serum potassium typically rises at a rate of 0.5 mmol/24 h in nonoliguric (urine output >400 ml/day) and 1 mmol/24 h in oliguric acute tubular necrosis. Hyperkalemia may develop at a faster rate in catabolic patients and following rhabdomyolysis or tumor lysis. The metabolic acidosis of acute renal failure usually is associated with a wide anion gap and reflects the failure of the kidney to excrete the acid load generated by daily protein metabolism. Patients with circulatory collapse or sepsis will have an additional contribution from lactic acid generation. Hyponatremia is common in prerenal acute renal failure and may be a clue to the presence of a fall in true or "effective" circulating volume. In this setting, antidiuretic hormone is secreted by the posterior pituitary in response to baroreceptor activation by hypotension. ADH is a potent vasopressor but also causes water retention and a fall in serum sodium concentration and osmolality. In acute tubular necrosis, the serum sodium concentration may be normal or reduced if excessive water (including dextrose solutions) is administered to patients with severely compromised GFR. Serum calcium is usually normal in acute tubular necrosis, in contrast to the typical hypocalcemia of chronic renal failure, but may be reduced if calcium is sequestered by injured tissues following rhabdomyolysis or pancreatitis. Serum phosphate rises gradually in patients with acute tubular necrosis, and hyperphosphatemia may be severe in highly catabolic patients with sepsis, rhabdomyolysis, or tumor lysis.

Treatment

Treatment of prerenal acute renal failure focuses on the restoration of euvolemia, cardiac contractility, and vascular tone, depending on the cause of circulatory collapse. Physicians are hampered in their efforts to treat established acute tubular necrosis by a complete lack of therapies to accelerate renal recovery. Thus, management of acute tubular necrosis focuses on the prevention of further injury, on the prevention and treatment of uremic complications, and the dose adjustment of drugs that normally are excreted by the kidney (Fig. 43.1).

Prevention

The incidence of acute renal failure in high-risk subjects can be reduced greatly by simple interventions that require little more than close attention to clinical detail and protocol. The close monitoring and support of intravascular volume may prevent acute tubular necrosis in individuals undergoing major surgery or nephrotoxic studies. Prevention of further systemic hypotension is very important in patients with established acute tubular necrosis because renal blood flow autoregulation is impaired, and small fluctuations in perfusion pressure can exacerbate ischemic injury. Invasive hemodynamic monitoring may be required in critically ill patients when clinical signs are equivocal or conflicting. There is no compelling evidence to support the administration of either mannitol, loop diuretics or "renal dose" dopamine for prevention of acute tubular necrosis. Adjustment of drug dosing guided by body mass and estimated GFR lowers, but does not eliminate, the risk of nephrotoxic acute renal failure. The use of nephrotoxic agents such as aminoglycosides and radiocontrast should be minimized in patients with preexisting renal insufficiency. Several interventions are known to reduce the incidence of rarer causes of acute renal failure. Forced mannitol-alkaline diuresis, for example, may prevent or attenuate acute renal failure in patients with rhabdomyolysis. A typical regimen involves infusion of 10 g of mannitol together with 40 mmol of sodium bicarbonate in 1 liter of 0.45% normal saline. The target urinary output is 300 ml/h; the infusion should be discontinued if this is not achieved. Alkalization of the urine (pH >6.5) may reduce the incidence of acute urate nephropathy in patients undergoing the treatment of malignancy and should be combined with xanthine oxidase inhibition. Removal of a serum paraprotein by plasmapheresis may prevent or limit myeloma cast nephropathy in patients with very high circulating light chain levels; however, chemotherapy remains the primary intervention. Ethylene glycol toxicity may be prevented by early administration of ethanol, which competitively inhibits the generation of the toxic metabolite oxalic acid by alcohol dehydrogenase. Contrast nephropathy can be prevented by prior hydration. High-risk patients (e.g., diabetics or those with chronic renal insufficiency) should receive 1 ml/kg 0.45% normal saline for 12 hours before and after the administration of radiocontrast.

Complications

As alluded to above, the kidney plays a key role in the excretion of salt and water, potassium, hydrogen ions, phosphate, and nitrogenous waste. It is also an important source of vitamin D and erythropoeitin. Consequently, acute renal failure may be complicated by hypervolemia, hyperkalemia, acidosis, hyperphosphatemia, hypocalcemia, anemia, and the uremic syndrome. The latter refers to the clinical consequences of retention of nitrogenous waste products and includes neuromuscular hyperexcitability, altered consciousness, nausea and vomiting, and pericarditis – among other manifestations.

In the following section, we shall discuss the general principles of management of the complications of acute renal failure. Many of the complications of acute renal failure are life-threatening and demand prompt intervention.

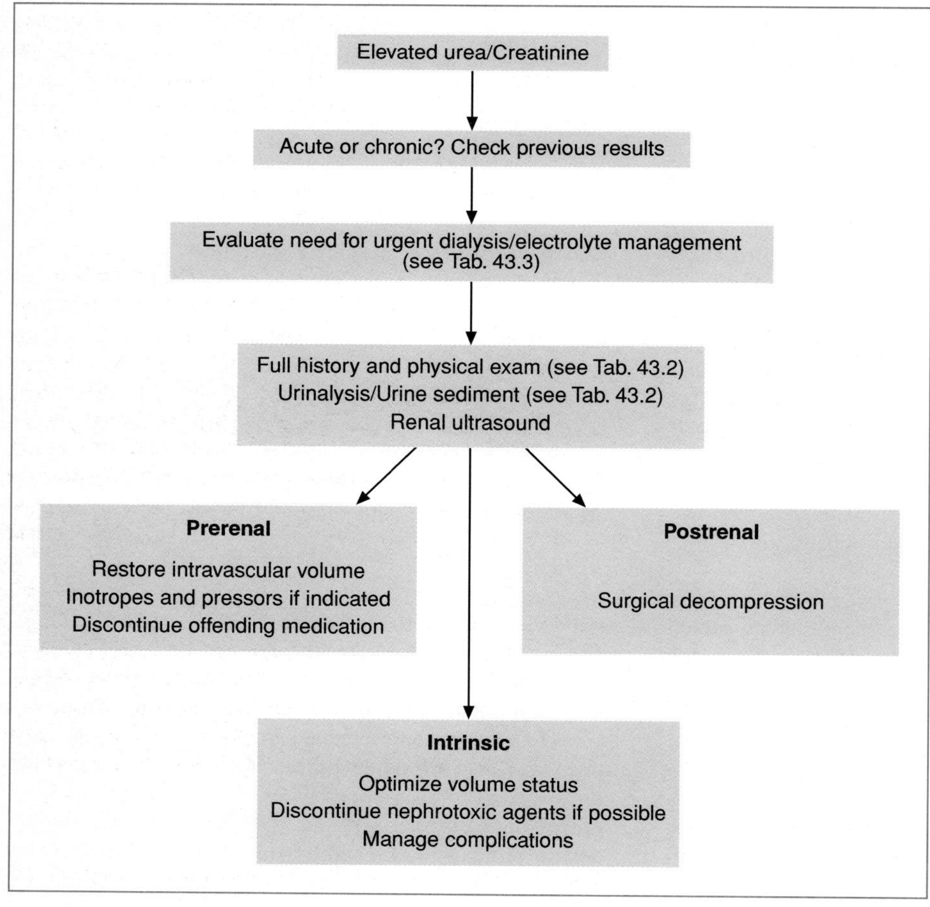

Figure 43.1 Management algorithm for acute renal failure.

Disturbance of intravascular volume Hypervolemia is a common complication of oliguric acute renal failure and is managed by salt and fluid restriction, diuretics, and dialysis. The need for the latter modalities is guided by the patient's daily weight, physical examination (e.g., elevated jugular venous pressure, lung crackles, dependent edema), chest X-ray (e.g., pulmonary edema), and pulmonary gas exchange (e.g., hypoxemia). If diuretics are necessary, higher doses than average usually are required (e.g., furosemide 100-200 mg as a bolus or by continuous infusion of 10-40 mg/h iv). Failure to respond promptly should lead to discontinuation of diuretic treatment to avoid ototoxicity. If conservative measures fail to control hypervolemia, ultrafiltration, usually in combination with hemodialysis, is often needed. The recovery phase of acute tubular necrosis may be complicated by a diuretic phase. The latter usually reflects appropriate excretion of salt and water accumulated during the maintenance phase of acute tubular necrosis. In some patients, however, the diuresis may be inappropriately robust and lead to hypovolemia. Under these circumstances, the polyuria is driven by multiple factors: excretion of retained salt and water, osmotic diuresis accompanying the excretion of nitrogenous waste, and delayed recovery of the function of the tubule epithelium following recovery of glomerular filtration. Intravenous fluid replacement with hypotonic solutions such as 0.45% saline may be required if the patient is unable to drink freely during the diuretic phase.

Electrolyte disturbances Modest hyperkalemia can be controlled by dietary restriction and discontinuation of potassium-sparing diuretics or oral supplements. Further increments may be ameliorated with anion exchange resins such as calcium resonium, 15-30 g every 4-6 hours. In nonoliguric patients kaliuresis may be augmented with intravenous loop diuretics. Severe hyperkalemia (K^+ >6.5 or lower values accompanied by electrocardiographic changes) is a medical emergency. Intravenous calcium gluconate (bolus of 10 mls of a 10% solutions over min) is administered to stabilize electrical activity in the myocardium and neuromuscular system while measures are taken to lower the extracellular potassium concentration. In the latter regard, temporizing measures include intravenous infusion of insulin-dextrose (e.g., 10-15 units of short-acting insulin in 50 mls of 50% dextrose over 30 min) and/or sodium bicarbonate (100 mls of 8.4% of $NaHCO_3$), which cause a transient intracellular shift of potassium. Failure to control hyperkalemia with these measures is an indication for emergency dialysis. Hypo- and hypernatremia usually are mild in acute renal failure and are managed by the restriction of free water and the administration of hypotonic solutions, respectively. Hypocalcemia, if present, usually is mild, and treatment rarely is necessary. Phosphate retention is often marked and should be controlled with dietary restriction and oral phosphate binders such as calcium carbonate taken with meals. A calcium-phosphate product > 5.65 (>70 when expressed in mg/dl) can trigger deposition of calcium-phosphate within soft tissues.

Acidosis Acidosis does not require correction unless the serum bicarbonate falls below 15mmol/l or the pH drops below 7.2 (some authorities argue <12 mmol/l and 7.1, respectively). Oral or intravenous bicarbonate can be administered, the dose being calculated from estimates of the patient's bicarbonate deficit. Assiduous attention must be paid to the possible complications of bicarbonate administration, including fluid overload, hypernatremia, hypocalcemia, hypokalemia, and "overshoot" alkalosis.

Anemia and bleeding Anemia is common in acute renal failure, although generally not marked in the absence of overt bleeding. Recombinant erythropoeitin has a slow onset of action, and resistance to its effects is usual during acute illness. Therefore, blood transfusion remains the mainstay in the management of symptomatic anemia in acute renal failure. Prolongation of the bleeding time complicates both acute and chronic renal failure. This diathesis rarely requires intervention unless there is active bleeding or an invasive procedure is planned. In the latter settings desmopressin or dialysis generally are effective in restoring adequate hemostasis.

Malnutrition The combination of decreased nutritional intake and catabolism results in significant malnutrition in most patients with acute renal failure. This complication requires a multidisciplinary approach involving physicians, nursing staff, and clinical nutritionists. The goal is to provide adequate caloric intake while minimizing the generation of nitrogenous waste products. This equates with a restriction of dietary protein intake to 0.5-0.7 g/kg daily and a calorie intake of 30-50 kcal/kg/day. Enteral feeding is the preferred route of nutrition, and routine parenteral alimentation is not recommended in patients with a functional gastrointestinal tract.

Infection The frequent need for invasive procedures in critically ill patients combined with impaired host responses in acute renal failure results in a high incidence of fatal infections. Aseptic management of intravenous lines and urethral catheters is essential. Prevention and management hinges on a low threshold for microbiologic investigation and prompt treatment of infection with culture-directed dose-adjusted antimicrobial agents. Prophylactic antibiotics do not improve survival, and are potentially deleterious by promoting the growth of resistant organisms.

Uremic syndrome The development of the uremic syndrome is a medical emergency and is an absolute indication for dialysis. The clinical manifestations of this syndrome that typically prompt initiation of dialysis are altered consciousness, neuromuscular excitability (asterixis, hyperreflexia or seizure), nausea and vomiting, and pericarditis or tamponade.

Dialysis

The absolute indications for dialysis in acute renal failure are clinical evidence of the uremic syndrome, life-threatening hypervolemia, hyperkalemia, or acidosis that cannot be controlled by other maneuvers (Tab. 43.3). There is no absolute level of serum urea or creatinine that warrants dialysis; however, many physicians initiate dialysis at urea concentrations >35-40 μmol/l and creatinine 600-700> μmol/l in oliguric patients if there is no sign of renal recovery on the basis that the onset of the uremic syndrome and metabolic complications is inevitable. The dialysis options are conventional intermittent hemodialysis, slow continuous hemodialytic techniques such as continuous venovenous hemodialysis (CVVHD) or continuous venovenous hemodiafiltration (CVVHDF), and acute peritoneal dialysis. Regardless of the modality chosen, it is important to note that dialysis does not accelerate recovery in acute renal failure. Indeed further ischemic or inflammatory renal injury can occur during dialysis as a consequence of systemic intradialytic hypotension or renal injury by circulating leukocytes activated by the dialysis membrane. The more "biocompatible" dialysis membranes, although more expensive, may afford a better outcome, probably because they cause less leukocyte activation.

The choice of dialysis modality and the dialysis prescription should be tailored to the specific needs of the individual patient. Conventional intermittent hemodialysis for 3-4 hours daily or on alternate days affords effective clearance and ultrafiltration in most cases. Intermittent hemodialysis may not be tolerated or may not provide adequate clearance in hemodynamically unstable or highly catabolic patients. In the latter, continuous hemodialytic therapies offer more gradual control of metabolic and electrolyte disturbance and fluid removal with less hemodynamic compromise. Drawbacks of continuous hemodialysis include the need for continuous anticoagulation and prolonged exposure of blood to the dialysis membrane. To date, no adequate prospective data confirm any survival advantage of the continuous therapies over conventional hemodialysis. Peritoneal dialysis is less commonly used now, owing to difficulties with access and the potential for respiratory compromise. It remains a valuable tool, however, particularly in regions where access to the more sophisticated and expensive dialytic techniques is limited.

Table 43.3 Indications for dialysis in acute renal failure

Uremic syndrome
- Altered consciousness
- Neuromuscular excitability
- Asterixis
- Uremic pericarditis
- Nausea and vomiting

Failure of medical management to control the following
- Volume overload
- Hyperkalemia
- Acidosis

Future directions in the management of acute renal failure

Recent advances in our understanding of the pathophysiology of acute tubular necrosis have suggested novel strategies for treating established acute tubular necrosis (Tab. 43.4). In animal studies, agents that augment renal blood flow, prevent tubular obstruction, and stimulate epithelial regeneration have all shown promise. As yet, none have proved effective in randomized studies in humans when used as monotherapy. It is likely that further dissection of the molecular events that underpin acute tubular necrosis will yield effective therapies for this common and problematic syndrome. It is also likely that a multidrug approach will be required that targets several key pathophysiologic events simultaneously (e.g., restore blood flow and promote repair).

Prognosis

The mortality among patients with acute tubular necrosis has not changed over the past decades despite the introduction of more sophisticated renal replacement therapies. This probably reflects the fact that aggressive medical and surgical interventions are bringing ever greater numbers of older and more complex critically ill patients with acute tubular necrosis to the attention of nephrologists. The gross mortality for patients requiring acute dialysis averages 50%. Poor prognostic features include oliguria, older age, and such comorbid conditions as diabetes mellitus or heart disease. The highest mortality is seen in critically ill patients with multi-organ failure, in whom mortality exceeds 90%. It should be stressed again that patients die from comorbid conditions and not from uremia, which can be adequately controlled by dialysis. Indeed, almost 90% of survivors achieve complete renal recovery. Approximately 5% of patients fail to recover renal function following acute renal failure, presumably because of cortical necrosis, and a further 5% develop progressive renal impairment in the years following the initial insult. Because such patients with acute tubular necrosis do not recover and will require long-term maintenance hemodial-

Table 43.4 Experimental therapies for acute renal failure

Target	Agent
Renal vasoconstriction	Atrial natriuretic peptide Endothelin receptor antagonists Prostaglandins
Intratubular obstruction	RGD peptides
Leucocyte recruitment	Anti-adhesion strategies
Cellular ATP depletion	Glycine $MgATPCl_2$
Epithelial regeneration	Epidermal growth factor Hepatocyte growth factor Insulin-like growth factor

ysis, measures to preserve venous access in the nondominant upper limb should be instituted in order to facilitate arteriovenous fistula formation if required at a later stage.

Suggested readings

BLASER J, KONIG C. Once daily aminoglycosides. Eur J Clin Microbiol 1995;14:1029-35.

BRADY HR, BRENNER BM, LIBERTHAL W. Acute renal failure. In: Brenner BM, Rector FC, eds. The kidney. 5th ed. Philadelphia: WB Saunders, 1996;1200-52.

BRADY HR, SINGER GG. Acute renal failure. Lancet 1995;346:1533-40.

CONGER JD. Interventions in clinical acute renal failure: What are the data? Am J Kid Dis 1995;26:565-76.

CONGER JD. Does hemodialysis delay recovery from acute renal failure? Semin Nephrol 1990;3:146-8.

DENTON MD, CHERTOW GM, BRADY HR. "Renal-dose" dopamine for the treatment of acute renal failure: Scientific rationale, experimental studies and clinical trials. Kidney Int 1996;49:4-14.

FORNI LG, HILTON PJ. Continuous hemofiltration in the treatment of acute renal failure. N Eng J Med 1997;336:1303-9.

HAKIM RM, WINGARD RL, PARKER RA. Effect of dialysis membrane in the treatment of patients with acute renal failure. N Eng J Med 1994;334:1338-42.

HOU SH, BUSHINSKY DA, WISH JB, et al. Hospital acquired renal insufficiency: a prospective study. Am J Med 1983;74:243-8.

HUMES HD. Acute renal failure: prevailing challenges and prospects for the future. Kidney Int 1995;50:S26-32.

SHUSTERMAN N, STROM B, MURRAY T, et al. Risk factors and outcome of hospital acquired acute renal failure. Am J Med 1987;83:65-71.

SOLOMON R. Contrast medium induced acute renal failure. Kidney Int 1998;53:230-42.

SPONSEL H, CONGER JD. Is parenteral nutrition therapy of value in acute renal failure patients? Am J Kid Dis 1995;25:96-102.

THADANI R, PASCUAL M, BONAVENTRE JV. Acute renal failure. N Eng J Med 1996;334:1448-60.

CHAPTER

44

Management of the patient with declining renal function

Eberhard Ritz, Michael W. Schömig, Giulio Odoni

KEY POINTS

- In many renal diseases, loss of renal function continues (progression) even if the kidney is no longer exposed to the primary insult. Main factors mediating progression are high blood pressure and high protein intake.
- The main causes of end-stage renal failure are glomerulonephritis and diabetic nephropathy.
- An adequate clinical indicator of renal function is the serum creatinine concentration. It is valid only if muscle mass is not changed. Otherwise measurement of endogenous creatinine clearance is recommended.
- The risk of progression can be predicted by the rate of urinary protein excretion, which should be monitored at regular intervals.

Diagnosis of reversible causes of renal failure

In a patient who presents with renal failure of unknown origin, particularly if there is a uremic emergency, it is important to assess which of the following disorders is present: (1) *acute renal failure*; (2) *acute on chronic renal failure*; or (3) *chronic progressive renal failure*. A distinction usually can be made on the basis of history, renal ultrasonography, and other findings that suggest chronicity (Tab. 44.1).

It is particularly important to exclude reversible causes of deterioration of renal function in patients with preexisting chronic renal failure (CRF), i.e., "acute on chronic renal failure". The major causes to be considered are summarized in Table 44.2.

Reversible *prerenal azotemia* from fluid or electrolyte depletion may occur as a consequence of vomiting, overzealous use of diuretics (including concealed diuretic abuse), sweating in hot climates, diarrhea, or inadequate fluid intake, particularly in patients with impaired mentation, nausea, etc. Some renal diseases are known to particularly predispose to renal electrolyte loss, e.g., analgesic nephropathy, polycystic kidney disease, renal tubular acidosis. The diagnosis of volume depletion in the presence of renal insufficiency must be made clinically by looking for the following signs: orthostatic circulatory dysregulation (blood pressure and pulse rate change in excess of 15% upon standing after lying supine); decreased central venous filling pressure (invisibility of pulse wave from internal jugular vein when patient's head is supine or slightly raised; central venous pressure <5 mmHg, pulmonary wedge pressure <7 mmHg). Less reliable signs are: reduced skin turgor, softness of the eyeballs, absence of sweat from the axillae, dryness of mucous membranes. If necessary fluid should be administered intravenously until adequate urine output (> 40 ml/h) is restored or a total of 3000 ml has been given. At this time reevaluation of plasma electrolyte parameters and exclusion of fluid overload is indicated because of the limited ability of the kidney to excrete excess free water and electrolytes in chronic renal failure.

Uncomplicated *urinary tract infection* is not a common cause of renal failure, but urinary tract infection may cause renal damage in the presence of urodynamic abnormalities, renal stones, postrenal obstruction or neurogenic bladder dysfunction. Renal failure is usually associated with bacteremia, intrarenal microabscesses or papillary necrosis. Diagnosis is then helped by imaging techniques (ultrasound, CT or gallium scan). Management includes recognition and correction of urologic problems and administration of antibiotics (considering impaired renal excretion).

Subvesical and supravesical *obstruction* frequently occur in papillary necrosis due to phenacetin abuse, renal stone disease, prostatic hyperplasia, urethral narrowing (often history of indwelling bladder catheter). Retention of bladder urine also is seen in patients with mental obtundation and patients on tricyclic antidepressants. The diagnosis is made by ultrasonography.

Congestive heart failure is a frequent cause of deterioration of kidney function in chronic renal failure patients. If symptoms and signs of circulatory congestion are present, i.e., dyspnea on exertion, orthopnea, pleural effusion, distended neck veins, hepatomegaly with hepatojugular reflux, dependent edema, pulmonary congestion, etc., extracardiac circulatory congestion must be distinguished from cardiac pump failure. Echocardiography to monitor ejection fraction and other indices of contractility may be helpful. Painless myocardial infarction is an important consideration when left heart failure supervenes, particularly in diabetic patients. To treat extracardiac circulatory congestion, high-ceiling diuretics (loop diuretics, e.g., furosemide), lowering of arterial blood pressure and negative fluid balance are advisable.

Rapid deterioration of renal function in chronic renal failure patients with severe hypertension may be due to *malignant hypertension*. The diagnosis is made by fundoscopy (striated hemorrhage, cotton wool exsudates, papillary swelling).

Potentially reversible deterioration of renal function may have *iatrogenic causes*, e.g., volume contraction from diuretics, administration of cyclooxygenase inhibitors (particularly in patients with a nephrotic syndrome or systemic lupus erythematosus), administration of nephrotoxic antibiotics, e.g., aminoglycosides or amphotericin. Drugs may also cause interstitial nephritis, particularly thiazides (in patients with nephrotic syndrome), nonsteroidal antiinflammatory agents, or rifampicin.

Administration of contrast media is hazardous in patients with chronic renal failure, particularly in proteinuric diabetic patients. It can be prevented to a large extent by careful hydration of the patient, temporal interruption of treatment with diuretics and ACE inhibitors, and reduction of the radiocontrast dose.

Monitoring and treating progressive decline in glomerular filtration rate

Once a major loss of renal function has occurred, renal function often will subsequently deteriorate progressively. This is due primarily to the maladaptive features of a compensatory increase of "work" by residual nephrons. Effective strategies have been developed to interfere with such progressive decline in renal function.

Glomerular filtration rate (GFR) Progressive loss of chronic renal failure can be monitored by (1) measuring the time course of *plasma creatinine* or *creatinine clearance* and (2) evaluating *protein excretion*. Proteinuria is the single most powerful predictor of the renal risk. The efficacy of therapeutic interventions (see below) is best reflected by a decrease in proteinuria. In very early stages of renal disease, particularly in diabetic renal disease, specific measurement of urinary albumin is advisable. In nondiabetic renal disease, measurement of total urinary protein (Biuret method) is sufficient (24-hour urine or protein/creatinine ratio in spot urine).

Table 44.1 Features pointing to chronic renal failure in a patient presenting with uremia

Presence of symptoms at least for months
Long-standing history of nycturia
Absence of acute illness potentially causing acute renal failure
Anemia (in the absence of acute blood loss or hemolysis)
Bone disease
Sexual dysfunction
Skin disorders (xeroderma, nail changes, pruritus)
Small kidneys on renal imaging

Table 44.2 Potential causes of acute on chronic renal failure

Dehydration
Hypotension, often iatrogenic due to overuse of antihypertensives, particularly ACE inhibitors/angiotensin receptor blockers
Accelerated hypertension (malignant HT), cardiac failure
Nephrotoxic drugs (e.g., NSAIDs aminoglycosides), contrast media
Other causes of acute tubular necrosis
Acute interstitial nephritis (e.g., drugs: rifampicin, nonsteroidal antiinflammatory agents, thiazides, etc.)
Use of analgesics (papillary necrosis)
Infection (e.g., urinary tract infection, septicemia, bacterial endocarditis)
Urinary tract obstruction
Atheroembolic disease
Renal vein thrombosis
Superimposition of crescentic glomerulonephritis on standard chronic GN
Flare of primary systemic disease
Hypercalcemia
Acute hyperuricemia

Table 44.3 lists measures that have been shown to prevent progression (or are suspected to do so).

Blood pressure In patients with renal disease, even when chronic renal failure is still normal, blood pressure increases, first within the range of normotension according to WHO or JNC VI; subsequently blood pressure is in the frankly hypertensive range. On the one hand, hypertension is caused by the impairment in renal function. On the other hand, elevated blood pressure injures the kidney and promotes progressive loss of renal function. This occurs because preglomerular vessels are dilated and autoregulation is lost. As a consequence, a higher proportion of systemic blood pressure is transmitted into the glomerular microcirculation, thus aggravating glomerular injury. The causes for the rise in blood pressure include: (1) the tendency of salt retention (abnormal salt/blood pressure relationship); (2) inappropriate activity of the renin system; and (3) sympathetic overactivity as a consequence of afferent signals from the diseased kidney that stimulate the sympathetic nerve system. These considerations of pathogenesis are important for a rational selection of antihypertensive agents. It has become increasingly clear that, at least in patients with glomerular disease, as indicated by protein excretion > 1 g/24 h, target blood pressure should be further lowered within the range of normotension, according to the recommendations of the National Kidney Foundation to approximately 125/75 mmHg. Because a night/time increase of blood pressure is particularly injurious, it is advisable to monitor ambulatory blood pressure and to give an effective dose of antihypertensive medication at bedtime.

There are good arguments that angiotensin II (ANG II) is injurious to the kidney and promotes progression through hemodynamic and nonhemodynamic mechanisms. Conversely, *ACE inhibitors and angiotensin II receptor blockers* (AT-1-subtype) provide particular benefit (renoprotective action) by attenuating progression more than can be explained by lowering of blood pressure alone. In patients with chronic renal failure ACE inhibitors may cause side effects, including: (1) acute aggravation of chronic renal failure (which is explained by decreased glomerular pressure); (2) hyperkalemia (which is rare if diuretics are coadministered); and (3) anemia. After administration of ACE inhibitors in chronic renal failure patients, particularly in advanced chronic renal failure and in patients on intensive diuretic treatment, plasma creatinine may rise by up to 70%. It is therefore no longer advisable to administer ACE inhibitors as first-line treatment once plasma creatinine is above approximately 6 mg/dl. The therapeutic success of administration of ACE inhibitors is predicted by a decrease in proteinuria. Protein excretion should be monitored after ACE inhibitor treatment has been instituted. The action of ACE inhibitors to lower blood pressure and to retard progression is promoted by coadministration of diuretics and/or by dietary sodium restriction. In patients with impaired renal function, the more effective loop diuretics must be administered, but natriuresis is potentiated if they are given in combination with thiazides. Potassium-sparing diuretics are strictly contraindicated. Angiotensin II receptor blockers are as effective as ACE inhibitors to acutely reduce proteinuria, but whether they are similarly effective in the long term to halt progression is currently unknown.

The renoprotective action of *calcium channel blockers* (CCB) is less consistent. Part of the explanation is that they cause preferential afferent vasodilatation. Thus, they cause glomerular hypertension unless systemic blood pressure is substantially lowered. Short-acting dihydropyridine calcium channel blockers which activate the sympathetic system are not advisable. At least in diabetic nephropathy, calcium channel blockers are more effective than beta-blockers in reducing proteinuria and preventing the progressive loss of creatinine clearance. There are strong reasons to combine ACE inhibitors and calcium channel blockers, i.e., to interfere with the synthesis of angiotensin II and to block some calcium-mediated effects of angiotensin II on target organs.

Diet For decades protein restriction has been advocated in patients with chronic renal failure, but only recently has prevention of progression been clearly established as a rationale for this measure. Its efficacy has been documented in animal experiments, but the clinical evidence is still controversial. In western societies, daily intake of protein is approximately 1.4 g/kg/day, while the recommended dietary intake is 0.8 g/kg/day. Although definite epidemiologic information is not yet in, dietary intakes of protein above the recommended range presumably increase the risk of progression in patients with renal disease, at least in early stages of diabetic nephropathy. In animal experiments, protein of animal origin is particularly injurious, and this is plausible because ingestion of protein of animal, but not of plant origin, acutely alters renal hemodynamics in humans. It is sensible to advise patients with renal disease to stick to the recommended dietary protein intake (0.8 g/kg/d) and to reduce protein of animal origin. In advanced renal failure, the effect of a low-protein diet is modest at best and definitely inferior to that of blood pressure control. On the other hand it may cause catabolism, particularly during intercurrent disease. In our opinion it should be considered, in advanced renal failure if at all, only in stable patients with a chronic, slowly progressive course of proteinuric renal disease.

Table 44.3 Measures to prevent progression

Lowering of blood pressure (administration of ACE inhibitors/angiotensin receptor blockers)
Dietary protein restriction
Cessation of smoking
Dietary salt restriction?
High water intake (3 l/d)?
Correction of dyslipidemia?
Other (correction of morbid obesity, cessation of analgesic abuse, etc.)

Smoking cessation There are many good reasons to stop smoking, but in both diabetic and non-diabetic renal disease smoking also accelerates the progression of kidney disease. This appears plausible because smoking (1) acutely increases blood pressure and heart rate, presumably by activating the sympathetic nerve system, (2) increases renal vascular resistance, and (3) acutely increases protein excretion.

Dietary sodium restriction Habitual dietary sodium intake, e.g., approximately 15 g/day in western societies, aggravates renal hypertension. At least in animal experiments, dietary salt also amplifies glomerular injury independent of blood pressure and increases angiotensin II responsiveness. It is therefore sensible to recommend a dietary intake of no more than approximately 6 g/day (which can be monitored by measuring urinary sodium excretion). Since many patients are unable to achieve this goal, diuretic treatment is required (see above). This must be supervised to avoid hypovolemia, which may cause acute on chronic renal failure.

High water intake When the patient is on a normal diet an obligatory osmotic load of around 600 mosml./day must be excreted via the kidneys. In chronic renal failure renal concentrating ability is reduced (isothenuria of 300-500 mosm/kg H_2O). Therefore fluid intake of 1.5-2 l/day is necessary to maintain external fluid balance. This is crucial for two reasons: (1) on the one hand deficient fluid intake may cause dehydration, volume contraction, and a further decline of renal function; (2) on the other based, excessive fluid intake (> 3-5 l/24 h) exposes the patient to the risk of symptomatic hyponatremia. The ability to excrete large quantities of osmotically free water is impaired in chronic renal failure, particularly if patients are on diuretics. If patients are unable to drink, intravenous administration of fluid (saline: 5% glucose 1:1) may be necessary. Body weight and urine output must be monitored during iv administration.

Based on recent animal experiments, it is possible that water restriction accelerates progression by increasing glomerular filtration pressure. This provides an additional rationale to maintain higher than usual water intakes in patients with chronic renal failure.

The reduced ability of the kidneys to excrete salt and water reduces the tolerated maximal and minimal intake of salt and water respectively, as schematically shown in Figure 44.1.

Correction of dyslipidemia Dyslipidemia should be treated in the patient with chronic renal failure because of its role as a cardiovascular risk factor. At least in animal experiments, dyslipidemia also accelerates progression of renal injury. Whether this is also true in humans is unknown.

Preventing late complications of chronic renal failure

It has become obvious that many of the complications that interfere with medical rehabilitation and reduce life expectancy in end-stage renal failure actually begin in very early stages of chronic renal failure. Although little controlled information is available, it is plausible that by early intervention late sequelae, e.g., coronary heart disease, left ventricular hypertrophy, secondary hyperparathyroidism, etc., can be mitigated or prevented.

Cardiac risk factors In patients with renal disease, cardiac remodeling and left ventricular hypertrophy (LVH) are demonstrable even when renal function is still normal. This is mainly the result of higher blood pressure. The prevalence of left ventricular hypertrophy increases progressively with decreasing renal function, so that approximately 70% of patients entering renal replacement therapy have echocardiographic evidence of left ventricular hypertrophy. Independent of blood pressure, left ventricular hypertrophy is a predictor of overall mortality and cardiac death. Apart from elevated blood pressure (increased afterload), important pathogenetic factors include hypervolemia (increased preload), anemia, and abnormal left ventricular loading because of reduced aortic elasticity. There is a consensus that blood pressure should be lowered into the low normal range and that hypervolemia should be avoided. Preliminary data indicate that prevention of anemia by early administration of rhEPO mitigates the development of left ventricular hypertrophy.

In patients with chronic renal failure, cardiac mortality is higher by a factor of 4-20 compared with the general population. A major cause of excess mortality is the high frequency of myocardial infarction. Coronary artery disease is more frequent and presumably also more progressive. Documented risk factors include dyslipidemia (not adequately reflected by total cholesterol and total triglyceride concentrations, risk is best related to Lp(a) concentrations and abnormal apo-A/apo-E lipoprotein ratio), but this does not fully explain the increased risk. In our view because of the high coronary risk, it is justified to admin-

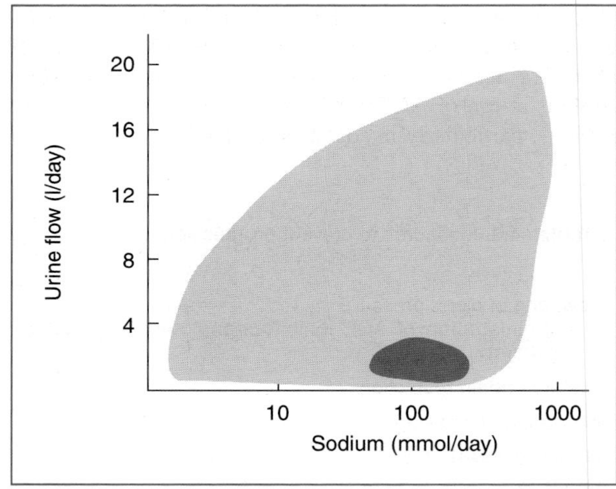

Figure 44.1 Scheme describing maximal and minimal excretion rates of water and sodium in the healthy individual (outer curve) and a hypothetical patient with chronic renal failure (inner curve). The graph illustrates the restricted ability of the diseased kidney to adapt to extremes of fluid and water intake.

ister statines to all patients with chronic renal failure irrespective of cholesterol concentrations, since statines reduce the cardiac risk irrespective of baseline cholesterol concentration.

A novel risk factor is homocystein. Plasma homocystein concentrations are elevated in very early stages of renal failure and are lowered by administration of folate, but whether this reduces cardiac mortality is currently unknown. At any given plasma folate concentration, plasma homocystein concentrations are higher in chronic renal failure patients than in nonrenal individuals, presumably reflecting relative folate resistance. Plasma folate concentrations are also determined by a genetic polymorphism in the methylenetetrahydrofolate reductase gene. It is important to exclude B_{12} deficiency before administering folate because otherwise neurologic lesions may be provoked.

A novel cardiac risk factor is hyperphosphatemia, which causes excessive and progressive calcification of plaques, but also influences cardiac remodeling. Furthermore, hyperphosphatemia causes aortic valve and annular calcification. These considerations further argue for strict control of plasma phosphate concentrations apart from the role of this measure in preventing hyperparathyroidism.

Dyslipidemia In chronic renal failure, an abnormal lipoprotein subfraction pattern can be noted very early on with an increase of incompletely catabolized highly atherogenic particles (IDL, i.e., intermediate density lipoproteins and chylomicrons). In end-stage renal disease, type IV hyperlipoproteinemia with hypertriglyceridemia is the prevailing pattern, while in patients with nephrotic proteinuria, type II hyperlipoproteinemia is commonly present. Although hypertriglyceridemia of renal failure can be corrected by dietary manipulation (carbohydrate restriction; high polyunsaturated/saturated fatty acid ratio) or by fibrates, these measures are not widely used. Dietary restrictions are poorly adhered to by anorectic patients, and fibrates are associated with the risk of rhabdomyolysis. HMG-CoA-reductase inhibitors (statines) are not excreted via the kidney, and their safety has been well documented in patients with nephrotic syndrome and chronic renal failure. Consequently they are currently widely used. Whether lipid lowering with statines reduces cardiac mortality is currently under investigation.

Calcium and phosphorous metabolism The disturbance of calcium metabolism in chronic renal failure is mainly caused by a combination of two factors – *phosphate retention* (as a reflection of the failing exocrine function of the kidney) and *deficiency of active vitamin D*, i.e., $1{,}25(OH)_2D_3$, (as a consequence of the failing endocrine function of the kidney). Both disturbances lead to activation of the parathyroid gland and secondary hyperparathyroidism.

In renal failure, the intestine is unable to adapt to a low calcium diet, while, on the other hand, low-calcium diets are commonly self-selected by anorectic uremic patients. This exposes the patient to the risk of hypocalcemia, and a negative *calcium balance* is frequently seen. If low plasma calcium is found in the presence of normal total protein, oral calcium salts should be administered (e.g., 1 g elemental calcium as calcium carbonate per day), but this requires regular monitoring of plasma and urinary calcium.

Hyperphosphatemia is usually observed when GFR has decreased to approximately 30 ml/min. Hyperphosphatemia must be prevented. It promotes secondary hyperparathyroidism (1) via reduced synthesis of active vitamin D and possibly (2) via direct stimulation of the parathyroid gland. Furthermore, hyperphosphatemia causes extraosseous calcifications, i.e., vascular, periarticular, and visceral calcifications (aortic valves!). Use of phosphate-rich dairy products should be discouraged, but otherwise low-phosphorous diets expose the chronic renal failure patient to the risk of malnutrition. Consequently, administration of phosphate binders is necessary. These trap phosphate in the intestinal lumen by precipitating insoluble phosphate salts. Administration of calcium carbonate has the double advantage of simultaneously normalizing plasma calcium and reducing intestinal absorption of phosphate. If calcium carbonate alone is ineffective, nephrologists used to resort to aluminium-containing phosphate binders. Today these should be avoided because of the risk of aluminium intoxication. Several novel oral phosphate binders that do not contain calcium or aluminium are currently under active investigation. Noncompliance with oral phosphate binders is a common problem. It is advisable to find the most accepted preparation (tablets, gels, cookies, etc.) by trial and error. It is important to instruct the patients that these must be ingested *with* meals and with snacks.

Although low $25(OH)D_3$ concentrations are not a feature of uremia per se, low $25(OH)D_3$ concentrations are frequent because of insufficient sun exposure, melanosis cutis (and thereby resistance to UV light), and loss of vitamin D metabolites bound to vitamin D binding protein in proteinuric patients. $25(OH)D_3$ is the substrate for $1{,}25(OH)_2D_3$. In chronic renal failure this interconversion is substrate-dependent. Consequently, it is wise to correct vitamin D deficiency by administering 1000 U/d cholecalciferol to chronic renal failure patients whose $25(OH)D_3$ is low (< 50 nmol/l).

Because of impaired renal synthesis of $1{,}25(OH)_2D_3$ it appears logical to substitute for the failing kidney's role by administering exogenous $1{,}25(OH)_2D_3$ or $1\text{-}alpha(OH)D_3$. Low doses of active vitamin D (0.125-0.25 µg $1{,}25(OH)_2D_3$/d) prevent the rise in PTH concentration. Whether they also interfere with the development of parathyroid hyperplasia is currently under investigation.

As a practical approach one should first normalize plasma phosphate and exclude 25(OH)D deficiency. If then elevation of PTH concentration persists, one should administer low doses of active vitamin D.

Anemia Anemia of renal failure is multifactorial in origin (Tab. 44.4). Normal or low plasma erythropoietin levels that are inappropriate for the prevailing hemoglobin concentration, and possibly also accumulation of inhibitors of erythropoiesis and, to a minor extent, obligatory gastrointestinal blood loss and reduced erythrocyte life span play a role in its genesis. Because adaptive mechanisms such as resetting the oxygen affinity of hemoglobulin occur, patients usually tolerate anemia without major symptoms. Furthermore, even in terminal renal failure, hemoglobin levels usually do not decrease below 7 g/dl. If anemia is present in early renal failure (GFR 30-40 ml/min), or if it is excessive (Hb < 7 g/dl), complicating factors should be excluded, e.g., iron deficiency (reflected by low plasma ferritin concentrations, except in hepatic disease or infection), gastrointestinal blood loss (common), malnutrition (common), folic acid deficiency (rare), or associated disease, e.g., myeloma, systemic lupus erythematosus , microangiopathic hemolytic anemia (HUS or malignant hypertension).

Even if no remediable form of anemia is found, administration of iron orally or as short intravenous iron infusions may succeed to some extent. There is an increasing tendency to prevent at least higher grades of anemia in chronic renal failure patients by early administration of rhEPO. Because of the relation between mortality and Hb in patients on renal replacement therapy and because of the partial dependence of left ventricular hypertrophy on anemia, this approach appears sensible, although it is currently not supported by controlled evidence and is plagued by the problem of high cost.

Metabolic acidosis Chronic renal failure is characterized by impaired renal excretion of protons, so that acid equivalents generated in the metabolism of proteins, and to a lesser extent, of phospholipids, can no longer be adequately excreted. Another factor is renal wasting of bicarbonate.

Metabolic acidosis decreases bone mineral content and renal generation of $1,25(OH)_2D_3$, but whether this is relevant in the genesis of uremic osteodystrophy is controversial. Other long-term hazards of metabolic acidosis have not been clearly documented in chronic renal failure patients, but in experimental studies metabolic acidosis has been identified as an important factor in the genesis of catabolism.

Metabolic acidosis of renal failure usually is quite well tolerated unless the plasma bicarbonate concentration is below 15-17 mmol/l. At this point, dyspnea and circulatory disturbances resulting from catecholamine unresponsiveness, may be observed.

Reduced dietary protein intake reduces the generation of acid equivalents, but carries the risk of protein malnutrition unless properly supervised. In symptomatic patients, oral sodium bicarbonate should be administered in amounts sufficient to raise the bicarbonate concentration until the patient is asymptomatic. Acid-base chemistry and plasma calcium levels should be monitored, and the patient should be watched for signs of tetany if acidosis is rapidly corrected. During long-term administration of sodium bicarbonate, patients must be examined to detect signs of fluid overload (hypertension, dilutional anemia, edema). The risk of sodium retention is considerably less, however, for sodium bicarbonate than for sodium chloride.

Hyperuricemia Hyperuricemia is common in renal failure. Fractional excretion of urate increases to a variable extent so that no constant relationship is observed between GFR and plasma uric acid levels. In the past patients with untreated gout often developed chronic renal failure, but there is little evidence that this was due to hyperuricemia per se. In our opinion, allopurinol should be administered when plasma uric acid levels constantly exceed approximately 10 mg/dl or if a history of gout is present. The rationale is then to prevent gout (and not to prevent progression). Because allopurinol metabolites accumulate, low doses (100-150 mg/day) usually are adequate.

Special problems in diabetics For several reasons, glycemic control is more difficult in the diabetic patient with chronic renal failure. On the one hand, patients are more susceptible to hyperglycemia, particularly after administration of thiazides, and this may even lead to hyperosmolar coma. This is due to insulin resistance and reduced glucose loss via the kidney if hyperglycemia supervenes. On the other hand, and for several reasons, patients are prone to develop hypoglycemic episodes. First, the half-life of insulin is prolonged. Second, most oral hypoglycemic agents (or their active metabolites) are excreted via the kidney, except for gliquidon and glimepirid. Patients are also often anorectic and skip meals. In patients with polyneuritis, gastroparesis may cause dissociation of the timing between insulin administration and intestinal absorption of glucose. Because the net effect of these factors is variable, glycemia should be monitored frequently in the diabetic patient with chronic renal failure. Because of the risk of lactic acidosis metformin is strictly contraindicated in diabetic patients with chronic renal failure.

Drug dosage in renal failure In chronic renal failure the handling of drugs (pharmacokinetics) may be altered because of impaired renal elimination, altered protein

Table 44.4 Differential diagnosis of anemia in patients with renal insufficiency

Defective erythropoiesis (inappropriate EPO concentration)

Gastrointestinal bleeding and iron deficiency:
- Mallory-Weiss syndrome from vomiting
- erosions from uremic gastritis
- angiodysplasia
- uremic colitis

Autoimmune hemolysis (in systemic lupus erythematosus)

Microangiopathic hemolytic uremia:
- malignant hypertension
- hemolytic uremic syndrome

Folic acid deficiency in malnourished patients

Bone marrow infiltration (e.g., myeloma)

Splenomegaly

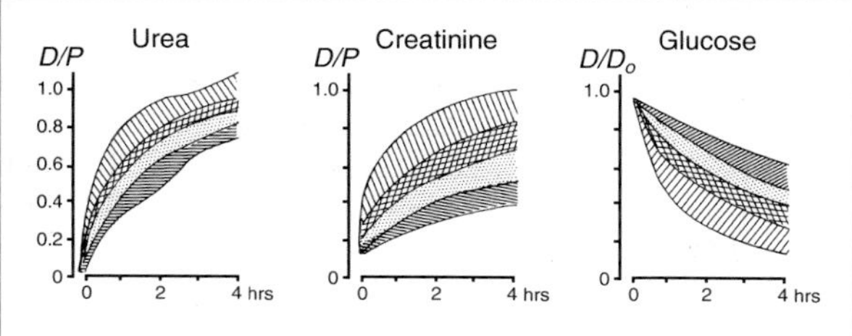

Figure 45.1 The results of 103 peritoneal equilibration tests using 2.5% glucose dialysate. The upper zones of *D/P* ratios of urea and creatinine represent high transporters (greater than mean+SD); the adjacent zones, high-average transporters (between mean and mean+SD); the following zone, the low average transporters (between mean and mean–SD); and the lowest zone, the low transporters (less than mean–SD). The same symbols, but in a mirror view, indicate the same transport categories for D/D_0 glucose. (Redrawn with permission from Twardowski ZJ, Nolph KD, Khanna R, et al. Peritoneal equilibration test. Perit Dial Bull 1987; 7:138.)

Both the *D/P* ratio and the *MTAC* provide information on the peritoneal membrane and can be used as a guidance for the dialysis prescription. For instance, a patient with a large surface area will have a high absorption rate of glucose, which leads to a rapid disappearance of the crystalloid osmotic gradient and therefore impaired ultrafiltration, especially during long dwells. Consequently, such a patient might benefit from a shorter exchange with a high glucose concentration. Measurement of fluid kinetics also should be done using a standardized 4-hour dwell, preferably with 3.86% glucose dialysate. This has two advantages: (1) the drained amount of dialysate is larger, so the results are less subject to confounding factors, and (2) it allows examination of the sieving of sodium. Sodium sieving is a phenomenon in which the Na^+ concentration of the dialysate decreases during the initial phase of a hypertonic dwell. This decrease, which occurs when ultrafiltration is at its maximum value, is caused by dilution due to channel-mediated water transport without transport of Na^+ through these channels. The *D/P* ratio of Na^+ measured at 60 minutes therefore can be used as a parameter of water transport through the endothelial water channels. For separate measurements of transcapillary ultrafiltration and lymphatic absorption, a macromolecular marker has to be given intraperitoneally, but this is not necessary in routine clinical practice.

When the effect of the applied dialysis prescription on total solute removal must be analyzed, the peritoneal equilibration test or the mass transfer area coefficient cannot be used. Twenty-four-hour dialysate and urine should be collected for measurement of the total amount of a solute removed from the body during a day. These collections can be used to calculate clearances of urea and creatinine. For urea, it is normally expressed as Kt/V, where K is the clearance, t is the time, and V is the volume of distribution of urea, which equals total-body water, and for creatinine, it is expressed as creatinine clearance, mostly depicted as liters per week per 1.73 m^2. Kt/V_{urea} is also expressed per week. V cannot be measured easily and therefore is estimated. This can be done as a percentage of body weight (e.g., 60%) or by Watson's formula. The Watson's formula for men is:

$$V\text{ (liters)} = 2.447 + 0.3362\text{ weight (kg)} + 0.1074\text{ height (cm)} - 0.09516\text{ age (years)}$$

The Watson's formula for women is

$$V = -2.097 + 0.2466\text{ weight (kg)} + 0.1069\text{ height (cm)}$$

Both Kt/V_{urea} and weekly creatinine clearances provide information on the adequacy of peritoneal dialysis as far as solute removal is concerned. Peritoneal Kt/V_{urea} is almost exclusively determined by the drained dialysate volume because of the presence of near equilibrium between plasma and dialysate concentrations. Peritoneal creatinine clearance is determined not only by the drained volume but also by the vascular peritoneal surface area.

In every peritoneal dialysis patient, 24-hour urine and dialysate collections should be done every 6 months to assess Kt/V_{urea}, creatinine clearance, and residual glomerular filtration rate (GFR). The latter is most easily measured as the mean of residual urea and creatinine clearance. At least once a year, but more frequently when loss of ultrafiltration is suspected, a peritoneal equilibration test-like test should be done using 3.86% glucose with determination of the *D/P* ratio for Na^+ after 60 minutes.

INDICATIONS AND CONTRAINDICATIONS FOR PERITONEAL DIALYSIS

The personal preference of the patient often determines the choice between hemodialysis and peritoneal dialysis. Patients may prefer continuous ambulatory peritoneal dialysis because of the greater freedom this mode of self-dialysis offers when compared with hemodialysis. The most important advantage of continuous ambulatory peritoneal dialysis is the steady state of the patient with regard to the fluid and solute composition of the extracellular space. This is especially important in patients with cardiovascular instability. Moreover, anticoagulants are not necessary, which may be important in patients with bleeding disorders. Various studies have shown that residual renal function is better preserved in peritoneal dialysis than in hemodialysis patients. The cause for this is not known, but it may relate to the steady state of the fluid balance.

Contraindications for peritoneal dialysis are mainly determined by local factors, such as multiple abdominal surgeries with the risk of adhesions, obesity, poor abdominal wall tone, uncorrected hernias, chronic respiratory insufficiency, and inflammatory bowel disease. Polycystic kidney disease is not a contraindication in itself. However, large polycystic kidneys are a risk for the complications of elevated intraperitoneal pressure, such as hernias, leakage of dialysate, and increased lymphatic absorption. A history of diverticulitis is also a contraindication; isolated diverticulosis without signs of inflammation is not. Continuous ambulatory peritoneal dialysis in the presence of a diaphragmatic hernia can increase the severity of the complaints.

PERITONEAL ACCESS AND DELIVERY SYSTEMS

The presence of a permanent catheter in the peritoneal cavity is required for chronic peritoneal dialysis. Such a catheter, made from silicone-rubber, was first developed by Tenckhoff. It consists of an intraperitoneal part with an opening at the end and a number of side holes, a subcutaneous part, and an outer part with an opening at the end on which a connecting device is placed. It has Dacron cuffs at both ends of the subcutaneous part to allow ingrowth of fibroblasts. The inner cuff is placed on the peritoneum, and the outer cuff is placed subcutaneously. A single-cuff catheter with only an internal cuff is also available. Several modifications have been developed. To eliminate the resilience force that tends to extrude the external cuff when a straight catheter is forced into an arcuate tunnel, the Swan-neck catheter has been designed. It has a permanent bend between the cuffs and therefore can be placed in an unstressed condition with both the internal and external parts of the catheter directed downward. The coil catheter reduces patients discomfort by minimizing the "jet effect" caused by the high flow rate of the dialysis solution during instillation. The Toronto Western Hospital catheter has a flange and a bend at the deep cuff, combined with two disks at the intraperitoneal segment. Most catheters can be inserted blindly, under laparoscopic guidance, or during laparotomy. Implantation in the midline is more often complicated by early dialysate leakage than the paramedian insertion technique, where the inner cuff rests on the rectus muscle. The subcutaneous cuff should be near the skin and not less than 2 cm from the exit site. The exit site should face downward or laterally, and the intraabdominal segment of the catheter should be placed between the visceral and parietal peritoneum toward Douglas's pouch.

Peritoneal dialysis fluids are most commonly delivered in plastic bags. Via a transfer set, consisting of a line and connectors, the dialysate is administered to the peritoneal cavity by gravity. Using the classic nondisconnect system, the line and the empty bag are worn by the patient on his/her body. At the end of the dwell time, the peritoneal cavity is drained into the same bag, again by gravity. After drainage, the bag is disconnected from the transfer set, followed by connection of a new bag. This procedure has a high risk of bacterial contamination, especially during the bag exchanges, when the system is open. Nondisconnect systems have to a large extent been replaced by disconnect systems. These systems use the "flush-before-fill" technique. In its original form, a Y-piece is connected to the peritoneal catheter. One arm of the Y is used for drainage; the other is used to administer fresh dialysate. Before the fresh dialysate is allowed to enter the peritoneal cavity, a small volume is permitted to flow into the bag along with the drained dialysate, taking with it any bacterial contamination that may have occurred during the connection. Integrated disconnect systems are the most simple, safe, and effective administration systems. They consist of a fresh dialysate container, a drainage container, and a Y-shaped line (Fig. 45.2). The sets are used in conjunction with a catheter extension line, which is closed during dwell time by a cap. The O-flush-disconnect system is a modification of the Y-piece system in which the ends of the connector are joined to each other and form a closed circuit between exchanges. The introduction of the "flush-before-fill" systems has reduced the incidence of peritonitis from 1 episode every 9 to 10 patient-months to 1 every 28 to 43 patient-months. This reduction has been especially impressive for episodes of Staphylococcus epidermidis infection.

DIALYSIS TECHNIQUES

Intermittent peritoneal dialysis (IPD) in its original form consists of two 20-hour treatments per week using hourly exchanges. This regimen is inadequate for solute removal when compared with daily treatments. It was rapidly replaced by continuous ambulatory peritoneal dialysis when this technique became available in the late 1970s. Most patients on peritoneal dialysis are treated with continuous ambulatory peritoneal dialysis because the procedure is easy to learn, does not require complicated machinery, and has the advantage of producing a steady state situation with regard to composition of the extracellular fluid. Daily ambulatory peritoneal dialysis (DAPD) is a modification of continuous ambulatory peritoneal dialysis characterized by four exchanges of 4 hours during the day and an empty peritoneal cavity at night. Daily ambulatory peritoneal dialysis has been used in patients with impaired ultrafiltration during long exchanges due to high glucose absorption rates. However, daily ambulatory peritoneal dialysis is less effective for the removal of low-molecular-weight solutes than continuous ambulatory peritoneal dialysis

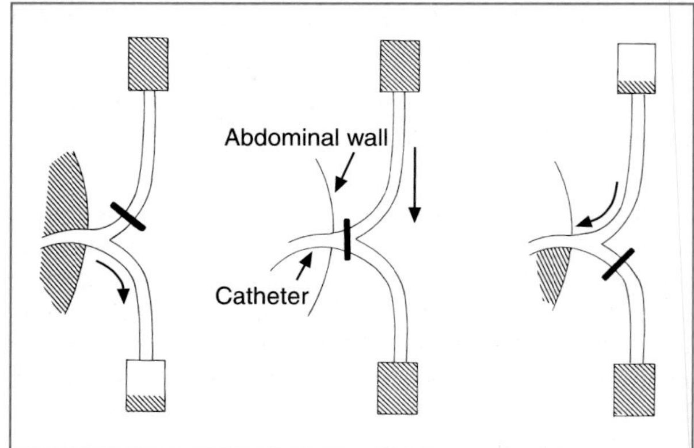

Figure 45.2 A schematic representation of the "flush-before-fill" system. (*Left*) The peritoneal cavity is drained into the empty bag. The bag with fresh dialysis fluid is closed. (*Center*) The first few milliliters from the fresh dialysate bag are drained directly into the drainage bag. The connection to the peritoneal catheter is closed. (*Right*) The fresh dialysate is instilled into the peritoneal cavity. The connection to the drainage bag is closed. The arrows indicate the direction of dialysate flow.

and is markedly inferior in the clearance of larger molecules.

Continuous ambulatory peritoneal dialysis and daily ambulatory peritoneal dialysis are dialysis techniques that are done manually. Automated peritoneal dialysis (APD) requires the use of a cycler. This machine can be programmed with regard to the number of exchanges, their duration, and the glucose concentration used. All automated peritoneal dialysis techniques are based on daily treatment regimens, mostly done at night when the patient is in the supine position. Automated peritoneal dialysis can be done as an intermittent treatment with an empty peritoneal cavity during the day or as a continuous technique with the long exchange during daytime. Cyclic peritoneal dialysis (CCPD) and tidal peritoneal dialysis (TPD) are the continuous forms of automated peritoneal dialysis. Cyclic peritoneal dialysis consists of four short exchanges during the night followed by a long exchange during the day. In this original form, cyclic peritoneal dialysis is less effective in the removal of uremic toxins than continuous ambulatory peritoneal dialysis. Therefore, modifications have been applied, such as increasing the number of short exchanges and/or adding one or more manual exchanges during the day. During tidal peritoneal dialysis, the peritoneal cavity is not drained completely in order to avoid the inefficiency of the dialysis during the inflow and outflow period of the short exchanges. The tidal peritoneal volume is usually 50% of the instilled volume. Nightly intermittent peritoneal dialysis (NIPD) and tidal intermittent peritoneal dialysis (TIPD) are modifications that are inferior to the continuous dialysis prescriptions with regard to solute removal.

Medical reasons for automated peritoneal dialysis instead of continuous ambulatory peritoneal dialysis are (1) insufficient low-molecular-weight solute clearance during continuous ambulatory peritoneal dialysis, (2) impaired ultrafiltration during continuous ambulatory peritoneal dialysis, (3) complications from a high intraperitoneal pressure (such as hernias), (4) low back pain, and (5) loss of appetite. Freedom from the dialysis procedure during the day is the most important nonmedical indication. These advantages are counterbalanced by the higher costs of automated peritoneal dialysis and the fact that it is more difficult to learn.

DIALYSIS SOLUTIONS

Peritoneal dialysis fluids are sterile solutions of electrolytes, a buffer, and an osmotic agent. The electrolyte concentrations are Na^+, 132 to 134 mmol/l; Ca^{2+}, 1.25 to 1.75 mmol/l; Mg2+, 0.25 to 0.75 mmol/l, and Cl^-, 100 to 104 mmol/l. The most commonly used buffer is lactate (35-40 mmol/l). Glucose is added to remove fluid from the circulation by crystalloid osmosis. The usual concentrations are 1.36% (70 mmol/l), 2.27% (120 mmol/l), and 3.86% (200 mmol/l). These dialysis fluids have a low pH (5.5) and are hypertonic; their osmolarity ranges from 334 mosmol/l (1.36% glucose) to 486 mosmol/l (3.86% glucose). During heat sterilization, glucose degradation products, mainly aldehydes, are formed. The low pH is required to prevent caramelization of glucose during the sterilizing procedure. In vitro studies have shown that fresh dialysate fluid is toxic to cells normally present in the peritoneal cavity, such as mesothelial cells and macrophages. The combination of lactate and a low pH induces a decrease in the intracellular pH. In addition, glucose inhibits various cell functions. This bioincompatibility of peritoneal dialysis solutions has stimulated research for other buffers and osmotic agents. Bicarbonate and bicarbonate-lactate combinations are under investigation. These bicarbonate-based solutions are prepared in a double-chamber system in which the bicarbonate-containing chamber is separated from that containing glucose, calcium, and magnesium. A connection between the two chambers is made immediately before inflow into the peritoneal cavity. Another application of the double-chamber system is in the reduction of glucose degradation products. This can be achieved by separate sterilization of a concentrated glucose solution at very low pH in one chamber and mixing it with the other dialysate constituents that are present in the other chamber just before inflow.

Alternatives for glucose as osmotic agents are amino acids and the glucose polymer icodextrin. Amino acids (MW 100-200 Da) have found particular use in continuous ambulatory peritoneal dialysis patients with malnutrition. These solutions cannot be used for all exchanges because of the nitrogen load and the occurrence of metabolic acidosis. Because of their low molecular weights, amino acids are less effective as an osmotic agent than glucose. Dextrin 20 or icodextrin is a glucose polymer with an average molecular weight of 16 000 to 20 000 Da. The glucose molecules are mainly linked at the 1,4 positions. An isoosmotic 7.5% solution of this high-molecular-weight osmotic agent induces ultrafiltration by colloid osmosis, similar to albumin. It generates water transport through the small pore system, while that through the water channels is neglectable because the resistance to transport through the small pores is much less than that through the water channels. Because of the high molecular weight of icodextrin, its disappearance from the peritoneal cavity is mainly into the lymphatic system. Therefore, it is especially effective during long dwells and in patients with impaired ultrafiltration due to the presence of a large vascular surface area. In the latter condition, a large number of pores is available for water transport, but this advantage is counteracted by a rapid dissipation of the crystalloid osmotic gradient using glucose-based solutions due to diffusion out of the peritoneal cavity. Since the disappearance of icodextrin is not by diffusion, this osmotic agent is especially effective in inducing ultrafiltration in such patients. The time course of the in situ intraperitoneal volume with glucose- and icodextrin-based dialysates is shown in Figure 45.3. The absorbed icodextrin is degraded to maltose by amylase. Consequently, the plasma concentration of maltose rises 20 to 30 times above normal in uremic plasma. It remains stable, however, when only one

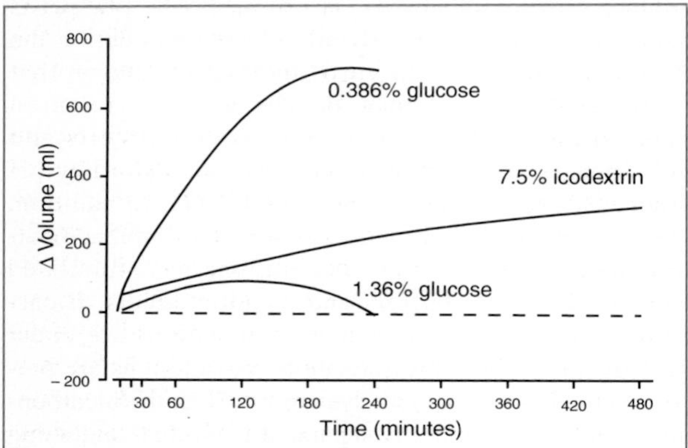

Figure 45.3 The time courses of the changes in the in situ intraperitoneal volume obtained with 1.36% glucose, 3.86% glucose, and 7.5% icodextrin-based dialysate. For each dialysis solution, the median values of 10 patients were used.

exchange per day is used and declines within 1 week to baseline after discontinuation. Signs of toxicity have not been seen. The fact that 7.5% icodextrin can only be used once daily and amino acids one to two times daily means that no single osmotic agents can fully replace glucose and the development of combinations is necessary.

SURGICAL AND CATHETER-RELATED COMPLICATIONS

Postoperative shoulder pain, interpreted as reference pain from the diaphragm, is present in about 25% of patients after implantation of the peritoneal catheter. It disappears spontaneously within a few days. During the first few months of peritoneal dialysis, half the patients have complaints of abdominal pain, usually localized in Douglas's pouch. This pain is most prominent when the peritoneal cavity is empty and during rapid inflow. The most likely causes are pressure of the catheter tip on an internal organ and/or a "jet effect" during inflow. The pain usually disappears within a few months after the start of peritoneal dialysis.

Leakage of dialysate through the catheter exit site is a complication that usually occurs in the immediate postoperative period in 7 to 24% of the patients. It is promoted by insufficient wound healing and an elevated intraperitoneal pressure. This complication often can be prevented by delaying the start of peritoneal dialysis for 10 to 14 days after implantation of the catheter to allow sufficient time for wound healing and for fibrous tissue to anchor the Dacron cuffs of the catheter. Dialysate leaks also may occur as a late complication. They are usually provoked by a sudden increase in intraperitoneal pressure, e.g., during severe coughing, or by mechanical trauma. Leakage can be treated by cessation of peritoneal dialysis for about 2 weeks. Dialysate can leak not only through the exit site but also into the soft tissues of the anterior abdominal wall. This may occur along the catheter insertion site or through defects in the peritoneum. It can lead to edema of the anterior abdominal wall and genital swelling. Patients with this complication may complain of decreased dialysate returns together with an increase in abdominal girth. The diagnosis can be made by nuclear medicine imaging using intraperitoneally administered ^{99m}Tc or by computed tomographic (CT) scanning after the addition of diatrizoate sodium to the dialysis fluid. To facilitate movement of dialysate and marker, it is important that the patient is ambulatory for some hours after instillation, until the images are made. Before considering an operation, the effect of temporary discontinuation for about 2 weeks should be awaited. Hydrothorax secondary to leakage of dialysate is a complication that occurs in 2 to 10% of patients. It is caused by anatomic defects of the diaphragm in the presence of increased intraabdominal pressure. The diagnosis can be made easily by determination of the glucose and lactate concentrations in the effusion. Treatment with temporary discontinuation, reducing the dialysate volume, or chemical pleurodesis is often not successful. When transfer to hemodialysis is not possible, surgical closure of the diaphragmatic defects can be considered.

Dislocation of the peritoneal catheter should be suspected when one-way obstruction occurs: inflow is easy, but outflow is absent or impaired. It is usually an early complication, and it occurs in 1 to 28% of the patients. Malposition can be diagnosed easily with a plain straight abdominal x-ray when radiopaque catheters are used. The problem often can be solved by mobilization of the patient and administration of enemas to stimulate peristaltic forces. When these measures are not successful, catheter manipulation with a guidewire or under peritoneoscopy can be tried. Removal and reinsertion of a new catheter eventually may be required. A bidirectional obstruction of the catheter can develop as a result of fibrin deposition, cellular debris, or blood clots. Forcing 20 to 50 ml of dialysate into the catheter lumen with a syringe may relieve the obstruction. This should be followed by intraperitoneal administration of heparin, up to 2000 IU/liter. Finally, the fibrinolytic agents streptokinase and urokinase can be used to dissolve the clot. For this purpose, 250 000 IU is dissolved in 100 ml of normal saline and infused into the peritoneal catheter in 1 hour. This is followed by peritoneal lavage with 1.36% glucose dialysate containing 500 to 1000 IU/liter of heparin. "Capture" of the catheter by omentum also may cause bidirectional obstruction. This occurs most frequently in thin young patients. In such cases, replacement of the catheter with omentectomy may be necessary.

Herniations of the abdominal wall occur in 9 to 24% of peritoneal dialysis patients. Umbilical, inguinal, and incisional hernias are the most common types. Predisposing factors are a weak anterior abdominal wall (multiparity), congenital defects of the abdominal wall, and polycystic kidney disease. Small hernias have a risk for bowel incarceration and strangulation. Large hernias are no great risk but may be troublesome for the patient. Hernias should be repaired surgically. Peritoneal dialysis usually can be restarted 2 to 4 weeks after the operation.

Peritonitis is the major infectious complication of peritoneal dialysis. The diagnosis is made when two of the following three criteria are present: (1) abdominal symptoms, (2) turbid peritoneal effluent caused by greater than 100 leukocytes/mm3 with predominantly polymorphonuclear cells, and (3) the presence of microorganisms on Gram's stain or culture of the effluent. In addition, fever and nausea may be present. Ultrafiltration frequently is impaired owing to inflammation-induced hyperemia of the peritoneum (see also "Long-term results", below). Microorganisms can enter the peritoneal cavity along the inside or outside of the catheter, from the bowel, or as a result of hematogenous spread. The inner-catheter route is most likely when touch contamination with skin flora has occurred during bag exchange. *S. epidermidis* and *S. aureus* are the most common organisms. Migration along the external catheter surface is the route when peritonitis is preceded by an exit-site or tunnel infection. *S. aureus* and *Pseudomonas* spp. often are the causative microorganisms in this situation. Penetration of bacteria through the intestinal wall is possible, and this may be the route of contamination in peritonitis episodes caused by Enterobacteriaceae. When this penetration is great, e.g., in the presence of a perforated diverticulum, fecal peritonitis with a mixture of gram-negative rods and anaerobes may develop. Many bacteria, especially streptococci, also can be spread by the hematogenous route. About 70% of all peritonitis episodes are caused by gram-positive bacteria. These consisted mainly of *S. epidermidis* when the old nondisconnect systems were used, but *S. aureus* has become relatively more important with the disconnect systems. Gram-negative rods are found in 20% of the episodes, and the remaining 10% are either caused by fungi or remain culture-negative.

Antibiotic treatment should be started immediately on the clinical diagnosis of peritonitis, even before the culture results are known. Gram's stain is positive in about 30% of cases. The antibiotics should be given intraperitoneally. Systemic or oral administration is only effective for antibiotics with a low molecular weight and almost no protein binding, such as cephradine. The recommended initial treatment should consist of a combination of a first-generation cephalosporin and an aminoglycoside. These antibiotics are added to every dialysate bag. Continuous ambulatory peritoneal dialysis should be continued. Often this can be done on an outpatient basis. The use of a peritoneal lavage with many short exchanges will relieve abdominal pain but impairs the local host defense mechanisms. Recommended dosages of some of the more frequently used antibiotics are given in Table 45.1. Oral treatment with cephradine (250 mg at every exchange) is possible when microorganisms are sensitive to this antibiotic. Resistance to cephradine is usual when methicillin resistance is present. It occurs in 30 to 50% of the *S. epidermidis* strains. To avoid this problem, vancomycin has been advocated as first-line treatment, but this has now been abolished because of the risk of the development of vancomycin resistance. Aminoglycosides generally have been administered continuously. This may increase the risk of ototoxicity and vestibulotoxicity, especially in patients

Table 45.1 Dosages of some frequently used antibiotics in peritonitis

Antibiotic	Starting dose	Maintenance dose	Adequate serum level
Cephradine, IP	250 mg/l	125 mg/l	10-50 μg/ml
Cephradine, orally	500 mg	250 mg with every exchange	
Gentamicin/ tobramycin, IP continuously	8 mg/l	4 mg/l	2-5 μg/ml
Gentamicin/ tobramycin, IP intermittently	0.6 mg/kg/l in one bag/day	0.6 mg/kg/l in one bag/day	
Vancomycin, IP	1000 mg/l	25 mg/l	15-25 μg/ml
Clindamycin, IP	300 mg/l	150 mg/l	0.8-3 μg/ml
Ciprofloxacin, IP	50 mg/l	25 mg/l	0.5-8 μg/ml
Amoxicillin, IP	250 mg/l	50 mg/l	10-50 μg/ml
Flucloxacillin, IP	250 mg/l	125 mg/l	7-15 μg/ml
Ticarcillin, IP	1000 mg/l	250 mg/l	150-200 μg/ml
Rifampicin, orally	450-600 mg/24 h	450-600 mg/24 h	8 μg/ml
Cotrimoxazole, IP	320/1600 mg/l	80/400 mg/l	10-50 g/ml
Cefotaxime, IP	500 mg/l	250 mg/l	10-10 μg/ml
Ceftazidime, IP	250 mg/l	125 mg/l	No range
Amphotericin B, IP	1.5 mg/l	1.5 mg/l	0.5-1.5 μg/ml
Flucytosine, IP	100 mg/l for 72 h	50 mg/l	50 μg/ml

(IP = intraperitoneal.)

who have been exposed to large cumulative doses. Since intermittent high systemic dosing of aminoglycosides is advantageous in patients with normal renal function, intermittent intraperitoneal dosing (gentamicin 0.6 mg/kg/l in one bag per day) has been advocated, but the experience with this approach is very limited in continuous ambulatory peritoneal dialysis patients. Since serum concentrations of gentamicin are variable, depending, for instance, on residual renal function, regular measurement of serum levels is necessary. When the reaction to antibiotic treatment is favorable, the cell count in the peritoneal effluent should have decreased by 48 hours after the initiation of treatment. In this situation, the antibiotics should be continued for at least 1 week after the effluent cell count has decreased to less than 100/mm3 and the culture is negative. Removal of the peritoneal catheter should be considered when (1) clinical symptoms worsen despite adequate antibiotic treatment; (2) cultures remain positive despite prolonged treatment with appropriate antibiotics; and (3) fecal peritonitis is present. Literature data report catheter removal in 5 to 20% of peritonitis episodes.

Fecal and fungal peritonitis episodes often require removal of the catheter. Fecal peritonitis should be suspected when more than one gram-negative rod is cultured and is certain when anaerobes are also present. This is an absolute indication for catheter removal and termination of peritoneal dialysis. When a perforation is suspected or present, a laparotomy with resection of the affected part of the bowel should be considered. Fungal peritonitis mostly is caused by *Candida* spp. Most authors recommend immediate removal of the catheter in combination with antifungal treatment. However, in a number of patients, the combination of intraperitoneally administered amphotericin B and flucytosine for 3 weeks is effective without requiring catheter removal. Intraperitoneal administration of amphotericin B may irritate the peritoneum, resulting in persistently elevated cell counts in the effluent.

Besides peritonitis, exit-site and tunnel infections are other important infectious complications of chronic peritoneal dialysis. Exit-site infection can be defined as the presence of marked redness around the exit site accompanied by one of the other signs of inflammation such as pain, irritation, liquid drainage, and exuberant granulation tissue. Finding a microorganism in the culture of the exit supports the diagnosis. A positive culture of the exit site in the absence of inflammation should be interpreted as colonization. A tunnel infection is present when erythema, edema, and/or tenderness of the subcutaneous catheter pathway are present. *S. aureus* is responsible for the majority of exit-site infections. Nasal carriage of the microorganism is associated with a fourfold increased risk of exit-site infection. Prophylactic treatment of persistent nasal carriers with intranasal mupirocin reduced the incidence of *S. aureus* exit-site infections by 70%. Exit-site infections caused by *Pseudomonas* spp. often lead to loss of the peritoneal catheter. Little data are available on the therapeutic effectiveness of the various treatments for exit-site and tunnel infections. Erythema in the absence of purulent drainage can be treated with topical chlorhexidine, mupirocin, or diluted hydrogen peroxide. Excessive granulation tissue around the exit site can be cauterized with silver nitrate. Gram-positive bacteria can be treated with oral antibiotics such as flucloxacillin, cephradine, or cotrimoxazole. Rifampicin can be added for persistent *S. aureus* infection. Clindamycin is also effective in tunnel infections, especially when administered intraperitoneally. The recommended duration of antibiotic treatment is 10 to 14 days, but a longer duration may be considered in case of a chronic exit-site infection. The tunnel should be explored when the exit-site infection persists. Excision of the subcutaneous cuff (shaving) should be considered when the infection persists for more than 2 to 3 weeks despite proper antibiotic treatment. Tunnel infections often are difficult to treat and may require catheter removal.

ADEQUACY OF PERITONEAL DIALYSIS

Adequate means "proportionate to the requirements or sufficient." *Adequate dialysis* therefore should be defined as a situation where the mode and degree of blood purification is such that patients have no uremic symptoms, a well-regulated blood pressure and volume status, a good nutritional state, little or no side effects of the treatment, and an acceptable quality of life and rehabilitation. Unfortunately, this adequacy concept has narrowed during the last few years to defining minimal targets of urea and creatinine removal, thereby neglecting other targets, especially with regard to blood pressure regulation and fluid status. The removal of low-molecular-weight solutes is usually expressed as Kt/V_{urea} and weekly creatinine clearance normalized for body surface area (see section on "Measurements of peritoneal transport kinetics", above). In addition to Kt/V_{urea}, the normalized protein catabolic rate (nPCR) often is calculated as a parameter of protein intake. Various equations have been used to calculate normalized protein catabolic rate, but they all depend on the quantity of urea in the dialysate and urine. A number of studies has shown a correlation between Kt/V_{urea} and normalized protein catabolic rate. Now, however, it has become evident that a mathematical coupling is present between Kt/V_{urea} and normalized protein catabolic rate: both have the dialysate and urine concentrations of urea in the numerator of the equations and body weight in the denominator. This makes interpretation of the normalized protein catabolic rate very difficult in terms of pathophysiology. The correlation between Kt/V_{urea} and normalized protein catabolic rate clearly cannot be used to prove that more peritoneal dialysis, e.g., by employing larger dialysate volumes, makes patients eat better.

A large prospective cohort study done in new peritoneal dialysis patients taken into treatment in Canada and the United States (CANUSA) has shown that both a higher Kt/V_{urea} and a higher creatinine clearance were associated with a reduced relative risk of death. However, no distinction was made between the contributions of residual renal function to solute removal and the peritoneal membrane.

Based on these statistical associations derived from multivariate analysis, the Dialysis Outcome Quality Initiative (DOQI) instituted in the United States defined minimum targets for peritoneal dialysis. These are a minimum total (renal + peritoneal) Kt/V_{urea} of 2.0 per week and a creatinine clearance of 60 l/1.73 m^2 per week for continuous ambulatory peritoneal dialysis. The value of these targets has not been investigated in prospective, randomized trials. As a consequence of the relatively short follow-up in the CANUSA study (the average follow-up per patient was 15 months), an important part of the relationship between higher Kt/V_{urea} and reduced mortality risk may have been caused by differences in residual renal function and not by the dialysis dose delivered. The Dialysis Outcome Quality Initiative recommendations are very hard to achieve in patients without residual renal function, especially when they have a large body mass. In continuous ambulatory peritoneal dialysis it often requires the use of five exchanges with 2.5 liters per day. Because of this, and because of the doubts on the validity of the Dialysis Outcome Quality Initiative recommendations, others have proposed lower targets that also may be adequate based on clinical experience: a Kt/V_{urea} of 1.7 per week and a creatinine clearance of 50 to 55 l/1.73 m^2 per week. The adequacy goals have not taken into account the effects of clinical judgment, especially with regard to control of blood pressure and hydration status.

LONG-TERM RESULTS

The majority of retrospective studies comparing peritoneal dialysis with hemodialysis found no difference in patient survival between the two modalities, especially not after correction of case mix. However, the technique survival is less than in hemodialysis. Discontinuation of peritoneal dialysis is mainly due to death, transplantation, and technique failure. All account for approximately one-third of the dropout. Consequently, the number of patients continuing on peritoneal dialysis averages 50% after 2 years, 35% after 4 years, and 2% after 8 years. Reasons for transfer to hemodialysis are infectious complications and inadequate dialysis due to either insufficient control of uremia or ultrafiltration failure. Loss of ultrafiltration is the main reason for withdrawal of peritoneal dialysis in long-term patients.

A clinical definition of ultrafiltration failure is the inability to achieve fluid balance despite the use of three or more 3.86% glucose exchanges combined with a restriction of fluid intake. It should be distinguished from apparent loss of peritoneal ultrafiltration capacity such as fluid overload caused by (1) decreased residual urine production, (2) excessive fluid intake, (3) noncompliance with the dialysis schedule, and (4) subcutaneous and pleural leaks. A better definition is net ultrafiltration less than 400 ml during a standardized 4-hour dwell with 3.86% glucose. Causes of impaired ultrafiltration are (1) the presence of a large vascular surface area leading to a rapid dissipation of the osmotic gradient, (2) a high lymphatic absorption rate, and (3) impaired channel-mediated water transport. Temporary ultrafiltration failure on glucose-based solutions is present during peritonitis because the hyperemia of the inflamed peritoneum leads to enlargement of the vascular surface area with high solute transport rates. In this situation, ultrafiltration on icodextrin-based fluids is increased because of the larger number of pores available for transport. Persistent loss of ultrafiltration is mainly a problem of long-term peritoneal dialysis and is especially marked in patients with peritoneal sclerosis. The prevalence of ultrafiltration failure is 3% after 1 year on continuous ambulatory peritoneal dialysis but increases to 31% after 6 years of treatment. Two prospective studies in which more than 10 patients were followed for more than 3 years and in which standardized dwells were used reported a decrease in ultrafiltration with time on continuous ambulatory peritoneal dialysis, sometimes accelerated by peritonitis, but also occurring in patients with a low peritonitis incidence. It was mainly associated with increased transport kinetics of low-molecular-weight solutes. It has become evident recently that long-term peritoneal dialysis patients and especially those with peritoneal sclerosis have neoangiogenesis in their peritoneal interstitial tissue. Impaired channel-mediated water transport can contribute to ultrafiltration loss. This can be measured as the decrease in the *D/P* ration of Na^+ after 60 minutes of a hypertonic (3.86% glucose) dialysis dwell (see "Measurements of peritoneal transport kinetics", above). Some patients have impaired fluid removal due to a high lymphatic absorption rate. An effect of time on this cause has never been reported. Once ultrafiltration failure has been established, treatment can be either by automated peritoneal dialysis using short exchanges and/or using icodextrin-based dialysis fluids for the long exchange. These measures are especially effective when a large vascular surface area is present. When a high lymphatic absorption rate is the most important cause, large dialysate volumes should be avoided.

Peritoneal sclerosis is a serious complication of long-term peritoneal dialysis that develops in a number of patients with ultrafiltration failure. Its overall prevalence is 0.7% of all patients but almost 20% in patients treated for 8 years. The incidence of peritoneal sclerosis in the 1980s was 1.5 to 1.9 per 1000 patient-years, but it increased to 3.5 to 4.2 in the 1990s. In contrast, the incidence of infectious peritonitis markedly decreased during these two decades. These figures point to an increase in peritoneal sclerosis related to the duration of peritoneal dialysis. At operation or autopsy, the bowel walls are thickened, and the mesothelium and/or the parietal peritoneum and adherent bowel loops are covered by thick fibrous tissue. Sclerotic encapsulation of bowel loops can be present. Light microscopy shows replacement of the mesothelium by a thick collagenous rind, under which extensive fibrosis is present with many microvessels. These microvessels have a thick wall, with deposition of collagen IV in the extracellular matrix. The capillaries are dilated. Some etiologic factors have been defined, such as the use of acetate as a dialysate buffer and chlorhexidine when used as a disinfectant for the bag exchanges. A relationship with the incidence of infectious peritonitis has not been found, although severe or nonresolving peritonitis often preceded the clinical manifestations of bowel obstruction. Moreover, peritoneal sclerosis also can develop in patients who never suffered episodes of infectious peritonitis. Evidence has accumulated that continuous exposure to the extremely high glucose concentrations present in peritoneal effluent is important in the pathogenesis of the peritoneal membrane alterations. This includes the results of in vitro studies on cultured mesothelial cells, the neoangiogenesis with deposition of collagen IV as in diabetic microangiopathy, and the deposition of advanced glycosylation end products in the peritoneal tissues of continuous ambulatory peritoneal dialysis patients.

The clinical manifestations are bowel obstruction, sometimes with blood-stained effluent, and the formation of ascites in patients in whom peritoneal dialysis had been discontinued. All patients have severe ultrafiltration failure. CT scanning of the peritoneal cavity may show abnormalities but is not very sensitive. It should be done with a dialysate-filled peritoneal cavity and with contrast material in the bowel. At laparotomy it is often impossible to separate the bowel loops. Treatment should consist of discontinuation of peritoneal dialysis, nasogastric suction, and often prolonged parenteral nutrition. A few studies suggested a beneficial effect of steroids, but others have not been able to confirm this. In some patients, the bowel passage improves spontaneously. Despite this, mortality rates of more than 50% have been reported. Prevention of peritoneal sclerosis should be aimed at reducing the glucose exposure of the peritoneum. This can be done by replacing 3.86% glucose by 7.5% icodextrin for the long dwell. A few reports have shown a beneficial effect of temporary discontinuation of continuous ambulatory peritoneal dialysis (peritoneal rest for 4 weeks) in patients with impaired ultrafiltration, but the results will have to be confirmed. The development of more biocompatible peritoneal dialysis solutions is likely to be most important in making chronic peritoneal dialysis a mode of renal replacement therapy that has not only good short- and midterm results but also can be extended to periods of more than 5 to 10 years in all patients who need it.

Suggested readings

CHURCHILL DN, TAYLOR DW, KESHAVIAH PR. Adequacy of dialysis and nutrition in continuous peritoneal dialysis: association with clinical outcomes. J Am Soc Nephrol 1996;7:198-207.

CHURCHILL DN, TAYLOR DW, VAS SI, OREOPOULOS DG. Peritonitis in continuous ambulatory peritoneal dialysis (CAPD): a multi-centre randomized clinical trial comparing the Y connector disinfectant system to standard systems. Perit Dial Int 1989;9:159-63.

DAVIES SJ, BRYAN J, PHILLIPS L, RUSSELL GI. Longitudinal changes in peritoneal kinetics: the effects of peritoneal dialysis and peritonitis. Nephrol Dial Transplant 1996;11:498-506.

GOLPER T, CHURCHILL D, BURKART J, et al. NKF-DOQI clinical practice guidelines for peritoneal dialysis adequacy. National Kidney Foundation. Am J Kidney Dis 1997;30:S67-136.

HEIMBURGER O, WANIEWSKI J, WERYNSKI A, ET AL. Peritoneal transport in CAPD patients with permanent loss of ultrafiltration capacity. Kidney Int 1990;38:495-506.

HENDRIKS PMEM, HO-DAC-PANNEKEET MM, VAN GULIK TM, et al. Peritoneal sclerosis in chronic peritoneal dialysis patients: analysis of clinical presentation, and peritoneal transport kinetics. Perit Dial Int 1997;17:136-43.

HO-DAC-PANNEKEET MM, KREDIET RT. Water channels in the peritoneum. Perit Dial Int 1996;16:255-9.

HO-DAC-PANNEKEET MM, SCHOUTEN N, LANGEDIJK MJ, et al. Peritoneal transport characteristics with glucose polymer based dialysate. Kidney Int 1996;50:979-86.

IMHOLZ ALT, KOOMEN GCM, STRUIJK DG, et al. Effect of dialysate osmolarity on the transport of low-molecular weight solutes and proteins during CAPD. Kidney Int 1993;43:1339-46.

KEANE WF, ALEXANDER SR, BAILIE G, et al. Peritoneal dialysis-related peritonitis treatment recommendations: 1996 update. Perit Dial Int 1996;16:557-73.

MISTRY CD, GOKAL R, PEERS E. A randomized multicenter clinical trial comparing isosmolar icodextrin with hyperosmolar glucose solutions in CAPD. Kidney Int 1994;46:496-503.

NAKAYAMA M, KAWAGUCHI Y, YAMADA K, et al. Immunohistochemical detection of advanced glycosylation end products in the peritoneum and its possible pathophysiological role in CAPD. Kidney Int 1997;51:182-6.

PANNEKEET MM, IMHOLZ ALT, STRUIJK DG, et al. The standard peritoneal permeability analysis: a tool for the assessment of peritoneal permeability characteristics in CAPD patients. Kidney Int 1995;48:866-75.

RIPPE B, STELIN G. Simulations of peritoneal solute transport during CAPD: application of two-pore formalism. Kidney Int 1989;35:1234-44.

SELGAS R, FERNANDEZ-REYES M-J, BOSQUE E, et al. Functional longevity of the human peritoneum: how long is continuous peritoneal dialysis possible? Results of a prospective medium long-term study. Am J Kidney Dis 1994;23:644-73.

CHAPTER

46 Hemodialysis

Thomas A. Depner

KEY POINTS

- Hemodialysis is the most common form of renal replacement therapy.
- Currently, throughout the world, life is sustained by hemodialysis in more than 1 million people.
- Although transplantation is preferred, the supply of organs is limited, so hemodialysis is and will continue to be the predominant form of renal replacement in the foreseeable future.
- Mortality rates are high and rise steeply with age, but indefinite survival is possible. The most common causes of mortality are cardiovascular disease and infections.
- Mortality is highly correlated with patient characteristics such as age and diabetes and with dialysis methods such as the amount of dialysis.
- Improved quality of life and reduced risk from hemodialysis have resulted from developments in membrane chemistry, water preparation, and dialysate delivery systems and from reversal of severe anemia with recombinant erythropoietin.
- The vascular access device continues to be a source of expense and hospitalization.
- Psychological adjustments to end-stage renal disease and to dialysis are major hurdles for the patient.

Dialysis was introduced in 1854 by Thomas Graham, a noted Scottish chemist, who demonstrated a method for separating solutes in solution based on their capacity to diffuse across a semipermeable membrane. When water was placed on one side of the membrane and a mixture of solutes on the other, small, permeable solutes moved across, whereas the larger, impermeable solutes remained behind. Although the permeability of the membrane that Graham devised from treated parchment was modest at best, he was able to demonstrate the principles of osmosis and diffusion on which all modern therapeutic dialysis is based.

Hemodialysis is a medical application of this process that removes unwanted solutes from the body by continuous treatment of the blood at a location outside the body. Blood is routed from a blood vessel that has a high blood flow rate to an external device where the blood equilibrates across a semipermeable membrane with a buffered physiologic salt solution, called the *dialysate*. The hemodialysis circuit diverts a small fraction of cardiac output to the dialysis membrane, where equilibration takes place, and then returns it back to the patient. The returning dialyzed blood then equilibrates with tissues throughout the body, effectively reducing tissue concentrations of solutes that are not contained in the dialysate. Although it is usually designed to remove solutes from the blood, hemodialysis also can be applied in reverse, to add solutes to the blood or to exchange heat. Most of the standard dialysate solutes are added to prevent their removal, but the concentrations can be adjusted to cause a net gain as well as a loss from the patient.

Origin of hemodialysis

Attempts to apply hemodialysis to humans met with only minimum success until 1943 when Wilhelm Kolff introduced therapeutic hemodialysis for the treatment of acute renal failure. He used a metal or wooden drum wound with sausage tubing through which the blood flowed while both the drum and tubing were partially immersed and rotated in the dialysate salt solution. Taking advantage of the availability of heparin to prevent clotting in his apparatus, he was able to reduce the body and blood concentration of toxins that accumulated in patients with acute renal failure. The treatment not only reversed uremic symptoms, often during a single treatment, but also prolonged life for many days, allowing time for renal recovery.

In 1960, Belding Scribner first applied this treatment to patients with irreversible renal failure and succeeded in prolonging life indefinitely. His success is attributed to a blood access device that he developed in collaboration with his associates Wayne Quinton and David Dillard at the University of Washington in Seattle. This device, which has since been replaced by subcutaneous fistulas and grafts, as well as central venous catheters, allowed repeated access to the blood indefinitely and eventually came to be known as the *Scribner shunt*.

The success of hemodialysis as a treatment for renal failure was so self-evident that no controlled trials to demonstrate its efficacy were required. The demand quickly overran the supply of dialysis equipment and trained personnel, so committees were established to decide who would be treated and who would die. These "death committees" proved to be an overwhelming burden and thankfully were eliminated in the United States when the federal government agreed in 1973 to fund hemodialysis for all who needed it, regardless of age, as part of the Medicare public health insurance program. At present, hemodialysis is the only entitlement in the Medicare program for patients younger than 65 years.

Comparison with other treatments

Hemodialysis can be distinguished from peritoneal dialysis, an equally effective treatment for renal failure, by its extracorporeal location, i.e., outside the patient's body. The peritoneal method also dialyzes the patient's blood, but the exchange of solutes occurs within the patient's peritoneal cavity, a form of intracorporeal dialysis. The success of hemodialysis spawned other extracorporeal treatments, including hemofiltration, hemoperfusion, plasmapheresis, and plasma exchange, for a variety of disorders such as acute renal failure, poisonings, and drug intoxication. Hemofiltration, which is used primarily as a substitute for hemodialysis, also moves solutes across a semipermeable membrane but by convection driven by hydraulic pressure instead of a chemical gradient. The removed filtrate is replenished with intravenous saline or a physiologic salt solution that is devoid of the offending solutes. The net effect is similar to hemodialysis, lowering toxic solute levels within the patient. Hemoperfusion also removes substances from the blood, but instead of passing solutes across a semipermeable membrane, solutes are adsorbed to a scaffolding of insoluble material with a large surface area (e.g., activated charcoal) through which the blood percolates. This technology is used primarily in emergency settings to remove drugs and ingested toxins. Plasmapheresis is similar to hemofiltration, but the membrane is much more permeable, allowing removal of plasma proteins such as immunoglobulins in patients with autoimmune disease. The removed plasma is usually replaced with albumin or banked plasma. Plasma also may be removed selectively by centrifuging the blood using a device that continuously separates and concentrates cellular formed elements, returning them to the patient without the plasma.

Scope of maintenance hemodialysis

As awareness increased and clinical tolerance of hemodialysis improved over the past 25 years, the criteria for acceptance gradually relaxed, and increasing numbers of patients have been enrolled. Today in the United States over 300 000 people, approximately 1 in every 1000, survive without benefit of their native kidneys. These patients have end-stage renal disease (ESRD), a disease that did not exist prior to 1960. Approximately 60% of these patients are supported by hemodialysis, whereas the remainder are maintained by peritoneal dialysis or a transplanted kidney. The most common single cause of ESRD is diabetic glomerulosclerosis, which accounts for an increasing percentage of patients, currently totaling approximately 33%, as shown in Table 46.1. It is estimated that over 1 million people throughout the world currently benefit from regular maintenance hemodialysis, without which nearly all would die within a few weeks. Many live relatively normal lives compromised only by their regular hemodialysis treatments. Most have no urine output, and some are anephric following surgical removal of their native kidneys. Many anticipate renal transplantation, but most are not candidates for transplant because of lack of a suitable donor organ, advanced age, personal choice, or insurmountable impediments to transplantation such as persistent humoral or cellular histocompatibility antibodies.

Prognosis of ESRD managed with hemodialysis

Mortality rates vary widely from country to country, ranging from 7% per year in Japan to over 20% per year in the

Table 46.1 Causes of end-stage renal disease in the United States

Cause	%
Diabetes mellitus	32.5%
Hypertension	24.5%
Glomerulonephritis	17.7%
Cystic disease	4.7%
Interstitial and obstructive nephropathy	2.0%
Other	11.4%
Unknown	5.0%
Cause not listed	2.3%
Total	100.0%

(From U.S. Renal Data System Annual Report of Point Prevalence, December 31, 1996: 283 932 patients.)

United States. Reasons for the relatively high mortality rate in the United States are not entirely clear, but more liberal selection of patients and the use of dialysis techniques and reimbursement strategies that foster shortened dialysis may contribute.

Despite the alarming overall mortality rate, individual patients in the United States have survived for more than 25 years with little or no native kidney function. These long-term survivors were among the first dialysis patients, starting their treatments shortly after dialysis first became available to substantial numbers of patients, so it appears that indefinite survival is possible.

Mortality is highly correlated with patient age and with the dose of dialysis expressed in terms of fractional solute clearance or K_t/V. Other mortality associated risks differ strikingly in these patients compared with the general population, as shown in Table 46.2. Patients with lower blood pressure have higher mortality, probably reflecting cardiac disease with poor cardiac contractility. The lower survival rates noted in thinner patients, in those with less weight gain between dialysis treatments, and in those with lower blood urea nitrogen (BUN), serum cholesterol, and serum creatinine concentrations probably relate to malnutrition, in many cases caused by the coexistence of other life-threatening diseases (e.g., heart disease or infection). Since uremia, the symptomatic phase of renal failure, also can cause malnutrition, excess mortality due to malnutrition may result in some instances from inadequate dialysis (see "Adequacy of Dialysis," below). Population statistics show higher mortality rates at both extremes of serum urea concentration, probably due to poor nutrition at one extreme and to inadequate dialysis at the other.

Hemodialysis membranes

The most vital component of a hemodialyzers is its semipermeable membrane. Dialysis membranes used for industrial, chemical, and pharmaceutical purposes prior to the turn of the century were commonly derived from animal gut or collodion. By the time therapeutic hemodialysis was introduced in 1943, these had been replaced by cellophane, a thinner membrane material manufactured from regenerated cellulose. Improvements in the manufacturing process during the first half of this century produced stronger and thinner cellulose-derived membranes that were more permeable to larger solutes. However, because cellulose is derived from wood and cotton, it is treated as a foreign substance by the body, which mounts a subtle yet biochemically profound inflammatory reaction to it. The magnitude of this inflammatory reaction is considered a measure of the membrane's biocompatibility. More recent refinements to the cellulosic membrane manufacturing process include the addition of acetate (cellulose acetate and triacetate) and other moieties to the cellulosic backbone to improve biocompatibility and to further increase permeability.

Table 46.2 Predictors of mortality in hemodialysis patients

Factors that correlate positively with survival in the United States
- Young age
- Male gender
- African-American race
- Body size
- Body mass index
- Serum albumin concentration
- Serum creatinine concentration
- Serum cholesterol concentration
- Normalized urea clearance (K_t/V)

Factors with a bimodal relationship to mortality
- Blood pressure
- Serum urea concentration
- Serum bicarbonate concentration

Over the past 10 years, these natural carbohydrate-derived membranes have been replaced gradually with synthetic polymers, products of the petroleum-derived plastics industry. These synthetic membranes have significantly improved permeability and biocompatibility and have a sharper cutoff at the high end of the molecular size spectrum, which prevents losses of vital plasma proteins and peptides. The geometry of membranes has evolved from sausage tubing, to multiple parallel flat plates, to the current hollow-fiber configuration used in most dialysis centers.

Biocompatibility is a measure of the membrane's capacity to activate inflammatory and immunologic responses in the patient. These adverse reactions are mediated by blood leukocytes, serum complement, cytokines, and growth factors, which, when activated, can be harmful to the patient, either immediately or as a cumulative phenomenon from repeated exposure of the patient's blood to the membrane over a prolonged time. Within the first 10 minutes after exposure to a cellulosic dialysis membrane, activated leukocytes are removed from the peripheral circulation by the lungs and perhaps other organs, causing a sharp fall in neutrophil and monocyte counts in the peripheral blood to less than 20% of predialysis levels. This complement-mediated leukopenic response to dialysis was one of the earliest tests of biocompatibility. More recently activation of cytokines such as interleukin-1 and tumor necrosis factor in the patient has been used as a more sensitive test of biocompatibility.

Solutes removed by hemodialysis: reversal of uremia

Hemodialysis is an empirical treatment, the success of which helped to define the uremic syndrome. Despite many decades of research dating back to the last century, the precise cause of the multiple symptoms and signs of uremia have not been defined. Many solutes are known to accumulate in patients with renal failure, but the blood concentration of each solute is below the toxic range even in patients with overt manifestations such as pericarditis, uremic stupor, or even coma. Since dialysis reverses all these signs of uremic toxicity, usually within a single treatment, accumulation of small-molecular-weight dialyzable solutes must be fundamental to the underlying pathophysiology of uremia. The success of dialysis demonstrates that the uremic syndrome is due to the cumulative effect of retained toxic solutes.

The solutes targeted for removal during hemodialysis generally are small-molecular-weight compounds of less than 1000 Da. The most abundant organic solute removed is urea (MW = 60 Da), an end-product of protein metabolism that normally is excreted almost entirely by the native kidneys. Several hundred small solutes removed by dialysis have been identified, most of which are also removed by the native kidneys and are found in normal urine. Many of these are organic acid anions, both metabolizable and nonmetabolizable, that accumulate as products of normal oxidative metabolism. The excess hydrogen ion that accompanies these and other anions produced from normal metabolism is neutralized during dialysis by basic anions added to the dialysate side of the membrane. The anion is either bicarbonate or a bicarbonate precursor such as acetate that diffuses in the reverse direction through the membrane, effectively neutralizing the accumulated acid.

Dialysate

The dialysate acts as a sink for small solutes that diffuse out of the blood along their respective concentration gradients. Vital nontoxic compounds, including sodium, potassium, magnesium, calcium, chloride, and glucose, are added to the dialysate to prevent net removal. Bicarbonate is added in excess, as explained earlier, to neutralize accumulated acid.

Earlier dialyzers, such as the Kolff rotating drum kidney and its immediate successors, used a vat of stirred dialysate into which the dialyzer was immersed. Modern dialysate delivery systems provide a constant single pass of fresh dialysate through the dialyzer, countercurrent to the blood flow to maximize solute clearance.

The final dialysate solution usually is prepared by diluting a concentrated solution containing the essential electrolytes (acid concentrate) and a concentrated solution of sodium bicarbonate (bicarbonate concentrate) with purified water just before exposure to the membrane. This three-component mixing and dilution of concentrates is monitored with redundant conductivity meters to eliminate any chance of dilution error. The pH is adjusted at the time of dilution by including a small amount of acetic acid in the concentrated solution of electrolytes (usually 4 mmol/liter after dilution), which also confers the name *acid concentrate*. When mixed with the bicarbonate concentrate and diluted to an isotonic concentration, the final pH is approximately 7.40. The acetic acid also facilitates storage and handling of the concentrate by providing a deterrent to bacterial growth. In contrast, the bicarbonate concentrate is an excellent bacterial growth medium that must be mixed fresh in a clean environment within 24 hours of use. Neither the two concentrates nor the water for dilution must be sterile because organisms, including viruses, cannot penetrate the dialysis membrane. However, as mentioned earlier, pyrogens can cross the membrane, causing a febrile response and perhaps other adverse reactions in the patient exposed to contaminated dialysate. For this reason, efforts must be made to minimize contamination of both the dialysate and the source water. The final dialysate should be examined on a regular basis for pyrogens; current standards call for fewer than 2000 organisms per milliliter of final dialysate, fewer than 200 organisms per milliliter of supply water, and an endotoxin content of less than 1 ng/ml.

In the past, acetate was added to the dialysate in much higher concentrations as a nonvolatile substitute for bicarbonate to simplify the storage and preparation of a single concentrate instead of two. The acetate diffused across the dialyzer into the bloodstream where it was transported to the liver and quickly metabolized to bicarbonate, so the net effect was equivalent to dialyzing against bicarbonate. This practice has been all but abandoned because of the toxic effects noted sporadically in the early years of dialysis but recognized more consistently when high-efficiency dialyzers began to appear. The improved clearance afforded by these dialyzers increased acetate influx beyond the limit of the patient's capacity to metabolize it.

Because lower temperatures are associated with fewer episodes of hypotension, dialysate temperature is often maintained below body core temperature to improve hemodynamic stability during treatment. The vasoconstrictive effect of the lower temperature allows faster fluid removal but causes patient discomfort if the dialysate is too cool. Dialysate temperatures of 36 °C usually are well tolerated, provided the patient uses a blanket or other warming device. Because the dialyzer and blood lines are exposed to ambient temperature, blood that leaves the dialyzer at 36 °C generally will drop one more degree before returning to the patient. As an alternative to cooling the patient, extending the time on dialysis allows more time for vascular refilling but also adds expense to the procedure if paid supervision is required.

Preparation of the dialysate also includes deaeration to prevent heat-induced air accumulation in the dialysate compartment, which reduces the effective surface area for diffusion.

Vascular access

The blood access device is a necessary and vital component of hemodialysis that must deliver blood flow rates as high as 400 to 500 ml/min through the dialyzer. Two general types are available: catheters placed in a central vein, often used for patients with acute renal failure, and more permanent arteriovenous shunts placed peripherally, usually in the forearm or upper arm and occasionally in the leg or rarely on the chest.

Catheter access

The hemodialysis catheter is long (20-50 cm) with single or double lumens, a wide bore (inside diameter 1.7-2.5 mm), and multiple sideholes at the tip to enhance blood flow, especially inflow. The length is necessary to reach the vena cava, and the bore must be wide enough to permit an adequate flow rate. When blood is pumped through these catheters, typical postpump pressures rise to 50 to 300 mmHg, and prepump pressures fall to approximately -50 to -400 mmHg.

If it is to be used for an extended time, the catheter should have a felt cuff. The cuff is placed near the site of exit from the skin, where it serves both to anchor the catheter and to prevent bacterial tracking along the catheter. Strict aseptic technique is required during insertion and both before and after exposure of the lumen to the atmosphere. Periodic cleansing of the exit site is required to prevent exit-site infections. Antiseptic scrubbing of the connection usually with povidone-iodine before disconnecting is designed to prevent life-threatening catheter-induced sepsis.

Catheters usually are selected for patients who require temporary access for treatment of acute renal failure or for patients with end-stage renal failure while their permanent access is healing (see below). Cuffed catheters may be used for a longer duration than uncuffed catheters, but are more prone to infection and thrombosis than peripheral arteriovenous shunts. In most centers, use of hemodialysis catheters for other purposes, e.g., use for blood sampling or infusion of medications is prohibited to minimize the risk of infection from repeated entry and improper decontamination.

Peripheral arteriovenous shunts

The original Scribner shunt consisted of two pieces of plastic tubing inserted percutaneously and sewn into the artery and vein of the forearm and connected externally with a piece of Silastic tubing. These shunts subsequently were replaced by two types of subcutaneous arteriovenous shunting devices: (1) arteriovenous (A-V) fistulas created surgically, usually in the forearm between the radial artery and cephalic vein, and (2) bridging A-V grafts, also preferentially placed in the forearm but often in a loop configuration between the brachial artery and the cephalic or basilic vein. The most common material for grafting is expanded polytetrafluoroethylene, a highly biocompatible polymer that is currently the most popular synthetic material for general surgical replacement of blood vessels. Native fistulas are preferred because of decreased clotting and increased longevity, but the patient must have a large superficial vein for puncturing and adequate flow rates during dialysis. In general, older patients, females, and patients who have had multiple venipunctures or intravenous injections are more likely to require a graft. The longevity of a fistula or graft depends on the age of the patient, the underlying setting in which it is placed, the skill of the surgeon, and the care taken subsequently both by the patient and by the patient's caregivers who place the needles for hemodialysis. On average, grafts function for 2 to 3 years before failure, whereas fistulas survive for 3 to 5 years; in older patients, the difference in survival between fistulas and grafts is less, but the complication rate is lower for fistulas. Much longer survivals for both fistulas and grafts, some over 20 years, have been documented, suggesting that unknown factors may help to preserve some of these devices. Longevity may be extended by routine monitoring of access blood flow coupled with angiography and angioplasty when the flow falls below 600 ml/min.

Anticoagulation

Exposure of fresh blood to an artificial surface initiates the cascade of events involved in the intrinsic clotting pathway. If unchecked, this process normally leads to clotting in the dialyzer and tubing within a few minutes after starting the blood pump. For nearly all extracorporeal devices, a method for inhibiting this clotting process is required.

Ideally, clotting is inhibited within the dialysis apparatus but not in the patient, who often has a bleeding risk that may prohibit use of a systemic anticoagulant. Because techniques for limiting anticoagulation to the dialyzer part of the circuit (regional anticoagulation) are complicated and expensive, and because dialyzers have become less thrombogenic in more recent years, most centers inhibit clotting both in the patient and in the dialyzer temporarily by injecting heparin intravenously in small to moderate doses during dialysis. In some centers, a low dose of heparin is also infused continuously directly into the dialyzer to enhance the effect locally. In patients with peripheral A-V access devices, the heparin treatment usually is stopped $^1/_2$ to 1 hour before the end of dialysis to allow recovery of normal clotting and control of bleeding when the needles are removed.

For patients who are at high risk for bleeding, more complicated regional anticoagulation schemes have been devised using protamine infused into the dialyzer blood outflow line to neutralize the heparin. Regional anticoagulation with citrate infused into the inflow line and calcium infused into the outflow line also has been used successfully. In high-risk patients, simple bolus infusions of normal saline into the dialyzer periodically during the treatment have been shown to reduce the potential for clotting and may eliminate the need for heparin. If the patient requires long-acting oral anticoagulants such as sodium warfarin (Coumadin) for another reason, e.g., access patency, deep venous thrombosis, or cardiac prophylaxis, often no additional anticoagulation is required during the dialysis. For patients who develop heparin sensitivity (e.g., heparin-induced thrombocytopenia), other short-acting anticoagulants such as prostaglandin E, hirudin, nafamostat, danaparoid, or citrate have been infused during the treatment to prevent clotting (see "Hemodialysis for acute renal failure," below).

Water preparation

The water and chemicals used for preparation of dialysate must be ultrapure because the patient usually is exposed to 100 liters or more during each treatment. Impurities such as aluminum, chlorine, chloramines, copper, silicone, calcium, and bacterial pyrogens may cause life-threatening toxicity in the patient. Water treatment should include deionization and charcoal filtration to remove ionic and organic materials, followed by reverse osmosis to render the water ultrapure. Purified water is more reactive and susceptible to bacterial contamination, so it must not be exposed to bare metal or other potentially dissolvable substances, and care must be taken to avoid exposure to potential sources of bacteria. Bacterial products collectively known as *pyrogens* may incite an inflammatory reaction in the patient even in the absence of viable bacteria. Some of these substances are capable of crossing the dialysis membrane. Prolonged storage of the treated water for dialysis is ill-advised because of the greater potential for bacterial growth in a stagnant pool. If storage tanks are required, they must be monitored for bacterial growth and mechanically cleaned periodically. Some bacteria and algae generate a biofilm in stagnant solutions that increases their resistance to cleaning agents and disinfectants.

Hemodialysis for acute renal failure

The procedure for dialyzing patients with acute renal failure (ARF) in a hospital setting, usually in an intensive care unit, is similar to the treatment of end-stage renal failure with a few exceptions. Special needs of these patients are listed in Table 46.3.

Many patients with ARF have a bleeding diathesis that prohibits the use of heparin. A frequently used alternative to heparin is the infusion of saline boluses into the dialyzer on a regular basis, as mentioned earlier under "Anticoagulation." Infusion of saline has two purposes: (1) to visualize the dialyzer hollow fibers for existing clots and (2) to reduce the potential for clotting. As the saline bolus travels through the dialyzer, clotted fibers appear as dark linear streaks. Only the peripheral fibers can be seen, but presumably they are representative of the whole dialyzer. The saline bolus inhibits clotting by periodically reducing the concentration of plasma proteins at the membrane surface. This interrupts the molecular cascade of events that ultimately causes polymerization of fibrinogen on the membrane surface. The extra saline administered to the patient during this heparin-free dialysis is easily removed by stepping up the dialyzer ultrafiltration rate.

Citrate infusion is currently the best choice if regional anticoagulation is considered necessary. Indications include heparin sensitivity or active bleeding in the patient. Regional anticoagulation also has been used successfully for continuous hemodialysis and hemofiltration. Frequent monitoring of the serum sodium, bicarbonate, and calcium levels is necessary because the infused sodium citrate is hypertonic and is metabolized quickly to sodium bicarbonate. Regional heparin anticoagulation, by infusing protamine to neutralize the heparin after it passes through the dialyzer, is less popular primarily because the titration of heparin with protamine is not precise and protamine in large doses has anticoagulant properties.

Maintaining fluid balance may be more difficult and is often more critical in patients with ARF. Obligatory fluid intake from parenteral nutrition, blood products, saline for blood pressure support, and medications may add up to several liters per day. For patients dialyzed every other day or three times per week, it may not be possible to remove 2 or 3 days of accumulated fluid in a single 3- or 4-hour treatment. The hypotensive patient is particularly difficult to manage because of the large volumes of fluids required to support the blood pressure and intolerance of fluid removal during hemodialysis. These concerns recently have popularized use of continuous treatments such as continuous hemofiltration and peritoneal dialysis for ARF. Daily hemodialysis administered either as routine short treatments or as slow and prolonged treatments is also increasing in popularity for these patients. Evidence is increasing for benefits from avoidance of fluid overload and avoidance of hypotension that frequently accompanies high ultrafiltration rates during dialysis.

Solute kinetics during hemodialysis in patients with ARF also deserve special attention. The patients are often catabolic due to infection or trauma, causing the concentration of urea and presumably other uremic toxins to rise rapidly between dialyses as labile body proteins are consumed. In addition to maintaining life, dialysis in these patients should be designed to promote recovery by providing an optimal environment for wound healing, inflammatory responses, and immunologic responses, all of which are known to be impaired by uremia. Whether increasing the weekly dose of hemodialysis will improve these host functions remains to be demonstrated, but at a minimum, the standards set for stable outpatients should be applied. One advantage with respect to solute removal afforded by catheter access is the elimination of cardiopulmonary recirculation, a cause of reduced dialysis efficiency due to rapid recirculation of dialyzed blood through the heart and lungs in patients with peripheral A-V shunts. Elimination of cardiopulmonary recirculation has the potential to improve the efficiency of dialysis by about 5 to 10%. However, disequilibrium due to hypotension and poor perfusion of muscle and other large vascular beds may counteract this benefit. At the present time, because of the potential for increased disequilibrium, no compensation for cardiopulmonary recirculation is recommended for catheter access in patients with ARF (Tab. 46.3).

Complications of hemodialysis

Hemodialysis intolerance

Disequilibrium syndrome The dialysis disequilibrium syndrome is a threat to patients who are new to hemodialysis. The syndrome begins with headache, blurred vision, nausea, and vomiting but may progress to seizures and death. It is experienced more often by patients with slowly progressive renal failure than by patients with ARF and can be prevented in these patients by starting slowly with daily increments in dialysis intensity and duration. The ultimate cause of the syndrome is unknown, but the symptoms suggest brain swelling, originally thought due to solute disequilibrium within the patient. Urea and other solutes are

Table 46.3 Hemodialysis for patients with acute renal failure

• Bleeding risk is increased, so consideration should be given to reducing or omitting heparin
• Alternatives to heparin: 1. Saline bolus infusions into the dialyzer inflow (arterial) line (100 ml every 15-60 min) to inhibit clotting in the dialyzer and lines 2. Regional citrate anticoagulation (infuse calcium into the return line) 3. Regional heparin (infuse protamine into the return line) 4. Other anticoagulants: hirudin, nafamostat, danaparoid, urokinase
• Infection: antibiotic dosages must be adjusted for little or no renal function (see Chap. 48)
• Solute disequilibrium: Enhanced by low cardiac output (e.g., patients with heart failure or shock) Diminished by venovenous catheter access
• Protein catabolism may be higher, increased by parenteral nutrition. Protein catabolism causes a rapid rise in BUN between dialyses. Generation rate of other toxins is speculative but may be increased
• Consider daily hemodialysis
• Consider continuous hemofiltration or continuous hemofiltration with dialysis (e.g., CVVH or CVVHD)
• Catheter access (see above) eliminates cardiopulmonary recirculation (see solute kinetics, below)
• Fluid balance may be more critical, to prevent pulmonary edema. Parenteral nutrition adds an extra burden of fluid
• Consider monitoring cardiac filling pressures
• Consider daily dialysis or continuous hemofiltration
• Maintain hematocrit higher than 30% with transfusions if necessary. The effectiveness of erythropoietin may be reduced because of concomitant infection and other inflammatory conditions that inhibit the bone marrow response

removed faster from the extracellular compartment than from the intracellular compartment, causing osmotic movement of water in the opposite direction and consequent swelling of the brain. Brain swelling has been observed both in animals and in humans during hemodialysis, but the osmotic gradient that develops is small and unlikely to be responsible for the swelling. Whether the symptoms are due to swelling and what causes the swelling are both subjects of controversy and investigation.

Most patients managed with intermittent hemodialysis experience, to varying degrees, feelings of lethargy and somnolence following their treatments that often are described as a "washed-out feeling." The cause of this postdialysis syndrome, which does not occur in continuously dialyzed patients, is not completely understood, but a major component is the removal of several liters of fluid over a relatively short time period. Patients who gain less weight between dialyses usually tolerate the treatment better. The postdialysis syndrome is probably also enhanced by the relatively rapid change in concentration of several solutes, including urea, potassium, phosphate, and H^+ ion. Others have speculated that both the disequilibrium syndrome and the postdialysis syndrome result in part from removal of compounds with CNS activity, causing a CNS withdrawal syndrome.

Acetate intolerance

Acetate intolerance, which was well described in the past years, included peripheral vasodilation and a negative inotropic effect that led to feelings of malaise, nausea, vomiting, and hypotension during and shortly after completion of a single dialysis treatment. As mentioned earlier under "Dialysate," these adverse effects of hemodialysis are disappearing due to the near-universal switch to bicarbonate-containing dialysate. The latter provides a more physiologic resolution of uremic acidosis, avoiding the infusion of large amounts of acetate. At the current time, the small amount of acetate contained in the acid concentrate (see "Dialysate," above) is not enough to overwhelm the metabolic pathways for acetate disposal and is well tolerated even during high-efficiency dialysis.

Hemodynamic stress due to fluid removal

The requirement for fluid removal during intermittent hemodialysis treatments often leads to hypotension, requiring treatment with higher dialysate sodium concentrations or hypertonic saline infusions that stimulate thirst and fluid gain between dialyses. In addition, if the fluid gain exacerbates hypertension and/or causes heart failure, removal may be even less well tolerated due to compromises in cardiac contractility. These potentially vicious cycles can be interrupted if fluid balance is managed by other means such as dietary control, prolonging each dialysis treatment, or increasing the frequency of dialysis. Careful control of the rate of ultrafiltration during dialysis using a modeling approach is also helpful. The ultimate solution is continuous dialysis, which eliminates the variability in the patient's weight and body fluid compartments. For outpatients, this approach is available only in the form of peritoneal dialysis, but ongoing research designed to increase the frequency of hemodialysis may provide an alternative in the future.

Hypotension

For patients dialyzed according to the usual schedule of three treatments per week, hypotension must be anticipated and a treatment plan prepared in advance. When first encountered, mild declines in blood pressure may respond to slowing or temporarily stopping ultrafiltration. More profound drops usually require slowing the blood pump temporarily and intravenous infusion of normal saline. In patients with recurrent or persistent hypotension, infusion of albumin or blood (in anemic patients) is very effective, although expensive, and carries the risk of infection. Recurrent hypotension or anticipated hypotension in a patient with a large interdialysis weight gain may be treated prophylactically with hypertonic saline, with hypertonic glucose, or by increasing the dialysate sodium concentration.

Development of pulmonary edema from excessive fluid gain between dialyses is a common reason for hospitalization of ESRD patients. Typically, the patient is admitted on Sunday, Monday, or Tuesday following the 3-day interval between dialyses (three times per week schedule). To prevent such occurrences, the patient should focus more on limiting salt intake than water intake, although both must be emphasized in some patients. In patients with diabetes, control of the blood glucose concentration is crucial to prevent extracellular volume expansion and excessive thirst. Treatment of pulmonary edema requires dialysis, but standard therapies such as high-dose loop diuretics in patients with significant residual function, as well as morphine and nitrates, are appropriate as temporizing measures before dialysis is begun.

Other complications

Many problems described during the early days of dialysis are infrequent or nonexistent now, although their threat remains. These include hemorrhage from separation of blood lines, air emboli, overheating of dialysate, hemolysis due to improper mixing of dialysate, and contamination of the dialysate with bacteria, copper, and aluminum. Because the blood pressure often drops especially after short-duration hemodialysis, patients may become dizzy or faint immediately following the treatment and fall, suffering head injury or fractures. Special precautions must be taken to support the blood pressure before allowing the patient to stand or to leave the dialysis center. Driving an automobile immediately after dialysis should be discouraged.

A common source of complications that is better recognized today is inadequate dialysis. Thanks to programs initiated by the Renal Physicians Association (APA), the National Institutes of Health (NIH) and recently highlighted by the National Kidney Foundation's Dialysis Outcomes Quality Initiative (DOQI), minimum standards for dialysis adequacy and other aspects of dialysis treatment have been established in the United States. The minimum dose of hemodialysis is a normalized fractional urea clearance per dialysis (K_t/V) of 1.2 or a urea reduction ratio of 65% for patients dialyzed three times weekly. These efforts have significantly improved the delivery of dialysis in the United States, and coincident with the improvement, the mortality rate has fallen significantly.

Treatment of the patient receiving hemodialysis

The hemodialysis treatment alone is not enough to ensure good health and quality of life for patients with ESRD. Optimal management requires treatment of hypertension and replacement of hormones as prophylactic treatment of anemia and bone disease. One of the most important requirements by nearly all patients as well as the families of patients with ESRD is support for psychosocial needs as the patient struggles to adapt to reliance on hemodialysis.

Hypertension

Hypertension in ESRD patients is usually caused or exacerbated by fluid overload. Elimination of excess fluid after initiating hemodialysis often allows reduction and sometimes discontinuation of antihypertensive medications. Hypertension is apparently cured sometimes in patients treated for many years with antihypertensive therapy prior to end stage. Many patients, however, have non-volume-dependent hypertension requiring continuous treatment with medications. Diuretics are rarely appropriate at this stage and should be discontinued. Angiotensin-converting enzyme (ACE) inhibitors or angiotensin II receptor blockers are encouraged because of their potential to reverse left ventricular hypertrophy and to reduce interdialytic thirst, but the serum potassium concentration may require monitoring for a short time after starting these agents in patients with substantial residual renal function. In addition, caution should be exercised when ACE inhibitors are given to patients dialyzed with polyacrylonitrile membranes because of reported anaphylactic reactions. Beta blockers, calcium channel blockers, clonidine, alpha blockers, and minoxidil have all been used successfully in ESRD patients. Older agents such as hydralazine, guanethidine, and alpha methyl dopa are discouraged because of excessive side effects.

Anemia and erythropoietin

When erythropoietin was first used to treat anemia in patients with ESRD, improvements were reported in exercise tolerance, but patients also reported improvements in mental alertness, sexual function, and appetite that previously were considered symptoms of uremia, i.e., caused directly by accumulated uremic toxins. Reversal of severe anemia constitutes the single most important advance in dialysis therapy since the introduction of dialysis itself over three decades ago. The current targeted hematocrit for hemodialyzed patients is 33 to 36% at midweek predialysis. This is the nadir in these patients, whose hematocrit rises during dialysis often by 5 to 10 percentage points, rebounds to a slightly lower hematocrit within 30 minutes after dialysis, and then falls more slowly as fluid accumulates between dialyses. Iron levels also must be watched closely, especially when starting erythropoietin, because the increase in red cell mass consumes large amounts of iron (~1 mg/ml of packed cells), usually much larger than body stores. Often, iron supplements must be given intravenously (50-100 mg per dialysis) to compensate for losses of blood during each dialysis. In iron-replete patients, the dose of erythropoietin required to achieve the target hematocrit has diagnostic as well as therapeutic benefits. Uncomplicated adult patients usually respond to 2000 to 4000 units given intravenously per dialysis or 5000 to 10 000 units given subcutaneously per week. Inflammatory blockade of the bone marrow response and other causes of resistant anemia such as a vitamin deficiency or hemoglobinopathy may be uncovered if the response to erythropoietin is incomplete.

Bone disease

Children with growing bones are most susceptible to the effects of uremia on bone metabolism, but renal osteodystrophy also may occur in adults, in whom it may be equally life-threatening. The most important contributing factor is deficiency of the renal hormone calcitriol, the trihydroxylated active metabolite of vitamin D. Lack of this hormone causes calcium malabsorption and a clinical syndrome in children resembling vitamin D deficiency known as *renal rickets*. Stunting of growth and enlargement of the epiphyseal ends of long bones are seen characteristically in children, whereas bone decalcification and fractures occur in adults. In adults, the major effect of calcitriol deficiency is mediated by hypocalcemia and hyperphosphatemia that stimulate production of parathyroid hormone and hypertrophy of the parathyroid glands. Deficiency of calcitriol, which normally has a suppressive effect on parathyroid hormone production, also plays a role. The resulting high parathyroid hormone level causes a pattern of bone disease resembling osteitis fibrosa cystica, seen in adults with primary hyperparathyroidism.

At the current time, nearly all patients with ESRD as well as those approaching end stage are supplemented with oral or intravenous calcitriol. The dose is adjusted by monitoring serum parathyroid hormone concentrations, targeting a level just above the upper range of normal. The powerful suppressive effect of calcitriol on the parathyroid glands can be excessive, suppressing bone turnover too much and causing an adynamic or aplastic bone lesion that weakens the bone and leads to fractures. In recent years, the latter lesion has replaced osteitis fibrosa cystica as the most common bone lesion observed in bone biopsies from dialysis patients.

Persistent efforts also must be made to control hyperphosphatemia to prevent soft tissue calcification, worsening hypocalcemia, and further stimulation of the parathyroid glands. Phosphate accumulates due to failure of normal renal excretion, to poor removal by the dialyzer, and to parathyroid hormone that releases phosphate from bone. Failure of removal is related more to disequilibrium in the patient than to failure of dialyzer clearance, so other steps must be taken to limit intestinal absorption of phosphate following meals. Most patients require treatment with oral calcium carbonate or calcium acetate taken with each meal to bind phosphate and prevent its absorption. Magnesium and aluminum hydroxides are also effective phosphate binders but are relatively contraindicated in dialysis patients because of the potential for magnesium and aluminum intoxication.

Another form of bone disease that has been recognized within the past decade is caused by dialysis amyloidosis. Accumulation of the polypeptide β_2-microglobulin in the serum of dialysis patients eventually leads to its polymerization to an insoluble b-pleated substance with other characteristics of amyloid. The amyloid preferentially accumulates in bone and joints especially along the wrist tendons, causing synovitis, and in the hips and lower legs, leading to arthritis and bone fractures. Although the disease is insidious and may take years to develop and progress, there is increasing evidence that dialysis with high-flux membranes may prevent its progression.

Psychological support

Advances in dialysis technology have leapt far ahead of understanding of the human psychological reaction to dialysis. Only in the past decade have caregivers come to grips with the tremendous upheaval in psychosocial adjustments caused by dialysis. Discovery of renal failure in oneself is akin to discovery of cancer and all its implications. People react to these discoveries with visions of distorted body image, anger, denial, depression, and rebellion, the latter especially in younger people, so it is not surprising that compliance with prescribed treatments, no matter how carefully laid out, is often poor. On the other hand, many patients manage to survive and to thrive, some continuing to work full time, despite the absence of native kidney function. The secret to success is support and understanding both by the patient and by the patient's caregivers. As renal failure progresses, support must intensify when the time to initiate dialysis approaches. It is not unusual for a previously compliant patient to miss an appointment for vascular access evaluation or fail to appear for access surgery. Despite clear indications and instructions to the contrary, patients cling to the concept that their kidneys will improve and dialysis will be avoided. To appear for vascular access surgery is to dash that hope. Even after the treatments have begun, many often anticipate regaining native kidney function. In patients who continue to show such signs of hope, it is reasonable for caregivers to avoid this issue and focus on other aspects of the therapy, allowing time to bring the patient into better focus with reality. Although it should not be presented as such, the patient may consider control of fluid, phosphorus, potassium, and blood pressure as temporary measures until kidney function returns.

In the patient who is a candidate for transplantation, the expectation that renal function will be restored is comforting and helps the patient to focus on his/her health care while less burdened by concerns about interminable dependence on dialysis. Compliance may be improved in such patients by emphasis on maintaining health to prepare for the transplant.

In patients who are not candidates for transplant, the task may be more difficult. Maintenance of a positive attitude cannot be overemphasized. The patient who views dialysis as an obstruction to his/her life will fare much more poorly than the patient who views dialysis as an opportunity to extend life beyond natural limits. Group therapy is often successful with this aspect of dialysis, allowing patients to compare notes among themselves rather than with others who have less interest in dialysis and serve as a constant reminder of the patient's limitations.

The dialysis center

The dialysis center is a highly specialized clinic designed to provide replacement of renal function for a large number of patients. The majority of centers are located outside the hospital in outpatient clinics, where they cater to as few as 10 and to as many as 200 patients with ESRD (average 50 in the United States). These centers are steeply integrated workplaces with a highly diversified staff whose tasks are divided and specialized to deliver treatment more efficiently. Required personnel include one or more administrators; bookkeepers; social workers, nurses, clerks, and technicians specializing in patient care; dialysis machinery; computer and communications support; dialyzer reuse, research, janitorial services; and security. Multiple shifts of patients are accommodated each day, often with more than one shift of staff, so scheduling both patients and staff is a major task that often requires more than one scheduler. Tension and stress take their toll in such a setting, where mistakes can be costly to the patient, patient deaths are relatively frequent, and vacations from dialysis are not allowed. Stress management for both patients and staff is vital to maintain a reasonable working environment for the staff who are then in a better position to reduce the pressure on the patients. Stress also comes from the patient's own psychosocial environment, typically from sources such as marriage and personal finances, that are usually complicated by the intrusion of dialysis itself.

Cost of hemodialysis

Cost is a concern for the dialysis administrator and for the patient whose life depends on dialysis but who often views the government's or society's promise of support as shaky at best. A stable and prosperous economy is vital to ensure continued provision of dialysis services by the taxpayer. Fortunately, the cost of dialysis per treatment has fallen during the past two decades on both a relative (inflation-adjusted) and an absolute scale, largely because the number of patients has increased, creating economy of scale. However, the increase in volume caused the total cost to increase in most countries. In the United States, where reimbursements per patients are lower than the average, the public entitlement program for dialysis costs the taxpayers approximately $10 billion per year to maintain approximately 200 000 hemodialysis patients or approximately $ 50 000 per year per patient. Approximately half this cost is devoted to hospital care. In countries with limited budgets, selection of patients can reduce this cost considerably, but selection is difficult to control. The mortality rate is high in the United States, yet the prevalence rate is increasing, reflecting a high incidence rate. Anticipated improvements in mortality will add to the prevalence, and as a consequence, the total cost may escalate in the future even if the entry rate of new patients declines.

Reuse of dialyzers

The reuse issue is basically a question of cost. Reuse of dialyzers was promoted previously as a method to improve dialyzer biocompatibility because the older cellulosic membranes became coated with plasma proteins, preventing exposure of the membrane to the inflammatory components of blood. The newer synthetic membranes and substituted cellulose membranes, including polysulfone, polyacrylonitrile, and cellulose triacetate, are much less prone to cause such reactions. Many centers in the United States have been forced to reuse dialyzers to avoid financial losses, but many justify it as an environmentally sound practice, a cost savings for the taxpayer, and an incentive for investment in dialysis corporations. Procedures for reuse have been automated, further enhancing both the safety and cost savings.

Comparison with other renal replacement therapies

Peritoneal dialysis has potential for reducing the cost of renal replacement therapy, but concerns about its safety and adequacy recently have prompted most nephrologists to increase the dose, which has increased the cost to a level comparable with that of hemodialysis. Bedside generation of sterile peritoneal dialysate, similar to the generation of hemodialysate, is a potential method of reducing cost that has not yet been realized. Transplantation has proven to be the most cost-efficient method to maintain ESRD patients, but unfortunately, the supply of donor organs is limited, with no relief in sight. Many patients are not candidates for transplantation, so hemodialysis likely will remain the most common replacement modality for ESRD patients in the foreseeable future.

When to start dialysis

In patients with progressive renal disease, it is important to recognize the impending need for dialysis as early as possible and to take steps to prepare them. First, the patient should be advised to protect the forearm veins to allow placement of an A-V fistula. The fistula surgery should be scheduled early, when the urea clearance is approximately 10 ml/min in the average adult. This corresponds to a creatinine clearance of approximately 15 ml/min and a serum creatinine concentration of approximately 6 mg/dl in a male or 4 mg/dl in a female. These are average numbers and can be modified depending on the rate of progression of renal failure.

To match the minimum K_t/V for urea in patients dialyzed continuously, the minimum equivalent of continuous native kidney clearance should be 2.0 per week, which corresponds to a urea clearance of 8 ml/min in a 40-liter patient or a creatinine clearance of approximately 12 to 13 ml/min. Arguments have been made to begin dialysis incrementally by varying the frequency and volume of peritoneal dialysate exchanges or by varying the frequency and duration of hemodialysis. Although logical, this approach has a psychologically depressing effect on the patient, who often views each increment in dialysis intensity as a defeat.

Equally important as the vascular access is preparing the patient for anticipated long-term dialysis. This requires considerable information exchange and psychological support, taking advantage of orientation programs and visits to the dialysis center and preferably including the patient's family.

Selection of modality

Within the limits of availability, patients should be given a choice of modalities provided they and their families are well informed about the relative merits and risks of each. Hemodialysis is often the default, the first modality chosen because it requires no training or work by the patient, who typically is subject to stages of denial, depression, anger, and noncompliance as dialysis options are presented. It is difficult in this changing setting of psychological stress to initiate a training program for either peritoneal dialysis or home hemodialysis, but it can be done in selected patients.

The choice of modality also may vary from country to country depending on the availability of resources and funding.

Frequently asked questions about hemodialysis

- *Is it painful or uncomfortable?*
  The large-bore needles required for hemodialysis usually are inserted into the A-V fistula or graft under local anesthesia. If catheter access is used, there is no pain with initiation of dialysis. Occasional muscle cramps during the treatment can be prevented by control of fluid intake by the patient between treatments and by hypertonic saline injections during the treatment.

- *How long does each treatment take, and how often?*
  The standard is three dialyses per week for 3 to 5 hours per treatment depending on patient size, residual renal function, and access blood flow.

- *How much risk is entailed?*
  The procedure itself is very safe, having been administered in many centers over a million times each without serious complications. See potential problems listed above in the section "Complications of hemodialysis."

- *How long can one survive with no kidney function?*
  Young people with no associated systemic diseases have survived for over 25 years on dialysis, so no limit to survival can be identified. Average mortality rates vary greatly with patient age and other comorbid conditions. See "Prognosis of ESRD managed with hemodialysis," above.

- *What does it cost?*
  The cost depends primarily on services provided by the technical staff and can be sharply reduced if the procedure is done by the patient at home. In-center dialysis costs approximately $ 25 000 to 30 000 per year in the United States. This does not include the cost of hospitalization. The cost of transplantation is less in the long run.

- *What are the alternatives?*
  As noted earlier under "Comparison with other treatments," the alternatives to hemodialysis are hemofiltration, peritoneal dialysis, transplantation, and nothing. The latter is usually not recommended because eventually it will lead to death. However, it is important to note that a patient may choose this alternative without violating legal or moral codes. Approximately 17% of deaths in U.S. dialysis patients occur after regular dialysis is discontinued voluntarily.

- *How does survival compare with transplantation? with peritoneal dialysis?*
  On average, survival of transplanted patients is better, although patient selection plays a role, and there is an initial risk from the surgery and immunosuppression.

- *What medications are required?*
  All patients require some medications, and some require many. The average number per outpatient has been estimated at 6 to 10. Routine medications include vitamins B and C, folic acid, calcium carbonate, a stool softener, calcitriol, iron, and erythropoietin. Most patients require one or more antihypertensive medications.

- *What dietary restrictions are required?*
  One of the advantages to the patient who initiates hemodialysis treatments is a relaxation of dietary restrictions, and this is one of the reasons for the recent recommendations that dialysis be started earlier to avoid malnutrition. Limits on salt intake for hypertensive patients and moderate limitations on both potassium and phosphate usually are required once dialysis is started.

Suggested readings

AGODOA LYC, HELD PJ, WOLFE RA, PORT FK. U.S. Renal data system. 1998 Annual Data Report. 10th ed. Springfield, VA: National Technical Information Service, 1998.

DAUGIRDAS JT, ING TS. Handbook of dialysis. 2nd ed. Boston: Little, Brown, 1993.

CRADDOCK PR, FEHR J, DALMASSO AP, et al. Hemodialysis leukopenia. Pulmonary vascular leukostasis resulting from complement activation by dialyzer cellophane membranes. J Clin Invest 1977;59:879-88.

DEPNER TA. Prescribing hemodialysis: a guide to urea modeling. Boston: Kluwer Academic Publishers, 1991.

ESCHBACH JW, EGRIE JC, DOWNING MR, et al. Correction of the anemia of end-stage renal disease with recombinant human erythropoietin: results of a combined phase I and II clinical trial. N Engl J Med 1987;316:73-8.

GOTCH FA. Kinetic modeling in hemodialysis. In: Nissenson AR, Fine RN, Gentile DE, eds. Clinical dialysis. 3rd ed. Norwalk, CT: Appleton and Lange, 1995:156-88.

HENRICH WL. Principles and practice of dialysis. 2nd ed. Baltimore: Williams & Wilkins, 1999.

KOLFF WJ, BERK HTJ, TER WELLE M, et al. The artificial kidney, a dialyzer with a great area. Acta Med Scand 1944;117:121-8.

Lowrie EG, Lew NL. Death risk in hemodialysis patients: the predictive value of commonly measured variables and an evaluation of death rate differences between facilities. Am J Kidney Dis 1990;15:458-82.

Maher JF. Replacement of renal function by dialysis. Dordrecht: Kluwer Academic Publishers, 1989.

National Kidney Foundation. Dialysis outcomes quality initiative: clinical practice guidelines for hemodialysis adequacy. Am J Kidney Dis 1997;30:22-63.

Scribner BH, Caner JEZ, Buri R, Quinton WE. The technique of continuous hemodialysis. Trans Am Soc Artif Intern Organs 1960;6:88-93.

CHAPTER

47 Kidney transplantation

Fokko J. van der Woude

KEY POINTS

- Transplantation of kidneys, either from living or post-mortal donor, has become an established clinical procedure worldwide.
- Transplantability of patients with renal disease can be screened with pre-transplantation check-lists.
- The HLA-system is important in kidney transplantation for two reasons: anti-donor HLA antibodies may lead to hyperacute rejection and better matching for donor/recipient HLA leads to better results post-transplantation. This is true for both post-mortal and living donor kidney transplantation.
- Immunosuppression is a necessity after kidney transplantation and can never be stopped completely. Most transplant centers start with a combination of corticosteroids and a calcineurin inhibitor (like cyclosporine A or FK 506). Other immunosuppressive agents can be added.
- The most frequent infection after kidney transplantation is cytomegalovirus. For optimal treatment of transplanted patients, transplant physicians with special knowledge of opportunistic infections and immunosuppressive drugs have to be part of the therapeutic team.
- Chronic graft loss is still the major problem after kidney transplantation.

Renal transplantation is now accepted all over the world as the treatment for patients in end-stage renal failure that not only restores life, but also gives an acceptable quality of life to such patients. Although the first human kidney transplant was probably carried out by Ullmann in 1902 in Vienna, it was not until the 1950s that Murray (recipient of the Nobel prize in 1992) performed the first operations resulting in long-term patient and graft survival, transplanting kidneys between identical twins in Boston. The technique of transplanting the kidney in the iliac fossa had also been developed in the early fifties. This site is now commonly used, because it is simple, easily observed and accessible for biopsy.

The modern era of organ transplantation began in the early sixties with the introduction of azathioprine and corticosteroids as maintenance immunosuppressive therapy. Tissue-typing and organ-allocation programs based on organ preservation, human leucocyte antigen (HLA) typing and cross-matching, as well as the introduction of newer immunosuppressive agents such as cyclosporine A are developments of the last 30 years and have established kidney transplantation as a successful clinical procedure.

Donor and recipient selection

Since most normal persons have two kidneys, with a reserve capacity that is more than 4 to 5 times the required minimal function, living donors can be used to enable kidney transplantation. Nowadays we therefor have to distinguish between cadaver, living-related and unrelated donors; the use of nonhuman donors (xenografts) for kidney transplantation has not yet been established clinically.

The use of *living kidney donors*, although started more than 40 years ago, has frequently been the subject of debate. Originally started within monozygotic twins to maximize biological compatibility between graft and recipient, the procedure was later extended to siblings, parents and children where it led to a significant better graft and patient survival compared to post-mortal kidneys, even after cyclosporine and monoclonal antibody immunosuppression had become available. The results with intrafamilial donors are directly related to the degree of histocompatibility as well as to the opportunity to provide pretransplant recipient preparation such as donor-specific transfusions (see Transplant immunology, below). More recently, it has become clear that living-donor grafts from living unrelated donors such as spouses have also a superior graft survival (81-85% after 3 years) as compared to post-mortal kidneys (70% after 3 years). The superior survival rate of grafts from unrelated donors could not be attributed to better HLA matching, white race, younger donor age, or shorter cold-ischemia times, but might be explained by damage due to shock before removal in 10% of the post-mortal kidneys. Although the advantages for the recipient such as a better graft survival and life expectancy (especially for diabetic patients), limited waiting time on dialysis and avoidance of the fast-growing waiting lists for post-mortal kidneys are clear, there is always the disadvantage of exposing a healthy donor to the significant risk of morbidity and mortality associated with the donor nephrectomy. Some groups have therefore organized the transplant team in such a manner, that the (potential) organ donors and recipients are never seen by the same doctors, nurses or social workers to make certain that the representation of the interests of donor and recipient are separated. It is generally accepted that potential donors should be well informed about possible risks and benefits, not be under emotional or financial pressure and emotionally stable. For genetically unrelated donors most hospitals in the Western world require a stable emotional relationship between donor and recipient. Donation for profit is generally condemned, but most unfortunately practised in some developing countries.

After screening of the emotional feasibility of donor and recipient, major blood group testing is usually the first medical step to be taken. Thereafter, the procedure should make certain that the donor is in excellent health and has bilateral renal function. Donor renal function is especially relevant when the living-related recipient has developed renal insufficiency caused by a hereditary problem, e.g., polycystic disease, diabetes mellitus, hypertension or if the donor is over 60 years of age. After tissue typing and leucocyte crossmatching an aortogram or digital subtraction angiogram is usually the final diagnostic study scheduled.

In most countries a living donor will not be available for the vast majority of patients with renal insufficiency, so that most patients will have to be considered for a kidney transplant from a *post-mortal donor*. It is clear that only after the development of the concept of brain death the use of post-mortal donors for organ retrieval became possible. Organ preservation up to 40 hours and longer with more sophisticated organ preservation fluids and more sophisticated tissue typing methods have led to organ exchange and allocation organizations like UNOS in the USA and Eurotransplant in Europe. These organizations have enabled transplant surgeons and physicians to establish a fair and evidence-based policy of organ allocation, allowing patients with rare tissue antigens or with a high degree of sensitization to be transplanted relatively safely while avoiding excessively long waiting periods. The ideal donor is a young male, previously healthy, who died after a head injury. Although results with kidneys from female donors, or from selected donors in their seventh or eighth decade of life tend to be less good, success can also be achieved with such organs. Kidneys from children can also be used successfully, but technical difficulties are much greater. In Table 47.1 criteria to test the suitability of potential cadaver donors are listed.

The percentage of patients on renal replacement therapy accepted as *kidney transplant recipients* varies from country to country. This variation is probably influenced by differences in patient demography such as age and epidemiology of underlying diseases and cardiovascular complications, as well as by the number of available organs, cultural influences and (lack of) financial incentive for transplantation as compared to hemodialysis in some countries. In general, a tendency to be less stringent in accepting patients on the waiting list exists. A nice review on this topic with a practical checklist has been published by Kasiske et al. The liberalization of criteria for acceptance is illustrated by the broadening of the age limits for transplant recipients; children as young as 6 months can now successfully be transplanted in specialized centers on the one hand, while on the other hand no well-defined cut-off point for senior citizens has been set. Patients over 70 years of age, if in good shape, can do very well after transplantation. Another change in this direction is that extensive urologic investigations such as cystoscopy or voiding cystoureterography are being performed only when there is clinical evidence of a bladder or ureteral abnormality. However, among the basic information required for all potential transplant recipients, remains a precise diagnosis of the cause of the renal failure, any history of repeated urinary infections and a current report of urine cultures. The presence of vesicoureteral reflux is only an indication for pretransplant

Table 47.1 Criteria for screening potential cadaver donors

1. Age: cave: too young (<1 yr) or too old (>70 yrs)
2. History (do not accept donors with malignancies other than treated nonmelanoma skin cancer or brain tumor)
3. No evidence of:
   - primary renal disease
   - generalized viral or bacterial infection
   - iv drug abuse
4. Only minor abnormalities in urine analysis
5. Normal initial blood urea nitrogen and creatinine
6. Total warm ischemia < 60 minutes
7. Negative serology for hepatitis B and human immunodeficiency; serology for hepatitis C, Epstein-Barr, and cytomegalovirus should be known

nephroureterectomy when the ureters are extremely dilated or in the presence of infections. If there are anatomic bladder abnormalities a good surgical reconstruction should be attempted; in patients with neurologic bladder abnormalities without urinary incontinence self-catheterization is an option. When the recipient's bladder cannot be used, the donor ureter can be connected to an ileal or colonconduit.

Important in the general assessment of the patient are the presence or absence of *hypertension, cardiac and vascular disease, peptic ulcer disease* or *infection*. Bilateral nephrectomy has been advocated as a means to control high renin hypertension in dialysis patients in whom blood pressure is hard to manage. The necessity for this procedure has declined now that better antihypertensive agents have become available. Since the age of the patients on renal replacement therapy has increased as has the percentage of diabetic patients, premature vascular disease leading to stroke, myocardial infarction and lower limb ischemia is becoming more important for the pretransplant workup of the patients. Apart from the normal clinical indications for coronary arteriography, most centers investigate this potential in all diabetic patients with end-stage renal disease being considered for transplantation, irrespective of the presence of evidence for ischemic heart disease on clinical examination or with other diagnostic methods. Coronary artery bypass grafting should be considered before transplantation in the presence of clinically significant vessel disease. Peptic ulcers and infections should be cured before transplantation. Infections that are easily overlooked are tropical parasites; even 20 years after leaving (sub)tropical areas patients can contract a life-threatening *Strongyloides stercoralis* infection after receiving a graft. Appropriate stool and serologic examinations should therefor always be performed in such patients to enable pre-emptive eradication of remaining parasites.

Malignancies represent a special problem, most transplantations are delayed 1 to 2 years. Exceptions are: nonmelanotic skin cancers (no contraindication); colon and breast carcinoma patients usually wait 4 additional years.

A special problem are those kidney diseases that may lead to *recurrent disease* after kidney transplantation. These diseases are listed in Table 47.2. Alport's syndrome is listed, but transplanted patients do not suffer from a real recurrence; in Alport's syndrome the Goodpasture antigen is lacking and anti-GBM antibodies may develop after transplantation as a response to the antigen in the donor kidney.

Many transplant centers work with pre-transplantation check-lists to facilitate the pretransplant workup of the patients in the dialysis centers. As an example, the checklist of the transplant center in Mannheim is shown in Table 47.3.

Transplant immunology

In concert with the progress observed in the field of clinical organ transplantation, the development of the understanding of the mechanisms underlying organ rejection has been quite striking in the last 40 years. In this paragraph we will point out some of the mechanisms involved in the allograft response that are relevant to understand the clinical manifestations of the rejection process and the clinical possibilities to prevent or treat rejection.

A simplified scheme of the response to a renal allograft is given in Figure 47.1. The key event triggering the alloimmune response is the interaction between processed antigen presented by an antigen-presenting cell (dendritic cell or macrophage) in association with *major histocompatibility complex* (MHC) Class II antigens to the T-helper

Table 47.2 Recurrence of the original disease in renal allografts

Disease	Recurrence (%)	Remarks
Diabetic nephropathy	100	Proteinuria may occur, seldom renal insufficiency
Alport's syndrome	10-20	Anti-GBM disease; symptoms after 6-8 months; renal failure may occur rapidly
Hyperoxaluria	Variable	Combined liver and kidney transplantation is recommended
Amyloidosis	20	Seldom renal failure
Hemolytic uremic syndrome	Children <5 Adults 25	Unfavorable outcome; cyclosporine may cause recurrence
Focal glomerulosclerosis	30	Subgroup* 70% recurrence rate
Membranous glomerulopathy	10	Recurrence more unfavorable course; de novo 1% of cases, more benign
IgA nephropathy and purpura Henoch-Schönlein	50	Mild hematuria and proteinuria, renal failure uncommon
Mesangiocapillary glomerulonephritis:		Renal failure in 30%, usually asymptomatic nephrotic syndrome or renal failure may occur
– subendothelial form	15	
– dense deposits	90	
Anti-GBM nephritis	Rare	Wait until 5 months after disappearance of anti-GBM antibodies
ANCA-associated disease	Rare	Clinical symptoms more important than ANCA titers
SLE	Rare	

* Subgroup defined by a short interval between the onset of the nephrotic syndrome and the development of renal failure in the native kidneys. If a first graft is lost due to recurrence, 80% chance of recurrence for a subsequent graft.

Table 47.3 Pretransplant checklist for possible kidney recipients

History and physical examination

General
- Cause of renal failure, duration of disease, duration of hypertension
- Urinary tract infections, other infectious foci
- Previous transplantations

Other diseases
- Cardiovascular, respiratory, gastrointestinal
- Diabetes mellitus/tuberculosis

Previous operations
- Nephrectomy, splenectomy, parathyroidectomy, other

Family history

Current clinical data and treatment
- Mode and duration of dialysis
- Blood pressure
- Urine production
- Signs or symptoms of neuropathy
- Previous blood transfusions, pregnancies
- Diet, drugs

Laboratory examination
- Hematocrit
- Leukocyte and thrombocyte count
- Calcium, phosphorus, alkaline phosphatase
- Alanine aminotransferase, aspartate aminotransferase
- Albumin, Kt/V
- CMV antibodies, HBs antigen, Hbs antibodies, HIV antibodies
- HC antibodies
- Urine cultures (3 times)

Radiologic examinations
- Chest radiograph

Miscellaneous investigations
- Electrocardiogram, fundoscopy
- Urological examination (optional), tuberculosis skin test
- Stool and serologic tests for *Strongyloides stercoralis* (optional)

Immunologic investigations
- Blood group typing
- Tissue typing, family typing
- Antibody screening

lymphocyte. The major histocompatibility complex in man is called *HLA* (Human Leucocyte Antigen) system and plays a pivotal role in the induction of the allograft response. Histocompatibility antigens are glycoproteins present on the cell membrane; they can be divided into two broad categories: Class I (HLA A, B and C in man) are expressed on the cell surface of virtually all nucleated cells and comprise a heavy chain (molecular weight 45 kD) which is polymorphic, and a non-polymorphic invariable light chain which is β_2-microglobulin (molecular weight 12 kDa), Class II (HLA DR, DQ and DP in man) have a limited tissue distribution, being expressed on B lymphocytes, dendritic cells, macrophages and some endothelial cells. During preservation injury or inflammation gamma-interferon may induce Class II expression on other cell types as well; in the kidney this is frequently observed on tubular cells. Class II antigens have two chains, a heavy or α chain (molecular weight 35 kDa), and a light or β chain (molecular weight 28 kDa), both of which are polymorphic. The structure of the major histocompatibility complex antigens has been elucidated by x-ray crystallography. It has been shown that a cleft is formed between two alpha helices that lie across a beta pleated sheet. Small peptide fragments of antigens are displayed in this cleft for recognition by T-cells. Major histocompatibility complex molecules display specificity for peptide fragments dependent upon amino acid residues at specific sites within the fragment; thereby it is possible to predict from the protein sequence of an antigen, which peptides will be recognized in the context of different major histocompatibility complex antigens. This phenomenon has led to speculations that the extensive polymorphism of the major histocompatibility complex has evolved to provide efficient immune defence mechanisms against infections in a population. In other words, our capacity to survive as an outbred population in different geographical biotopes full of a great variety of infectious agents has lead to the fact that organ transplantation between unrelated persons is hardly ever possible without immunosuppressive therapy.

The immunogenicity of major histocompatibility complex molecules may vary and depend upon the type of tissue, and the site of transplantation. Major histocompatibility complex antigens themselves are not strong immunogens and need to be presented on the surface of viable cells together with adhesion molecules and co-stimulatory molecules such as CD80 (B7-1), CD86 (B7-2), CD40, Fas or Fas-ligand to initiate an immune response. Interactions between T-cells without the appropriate co-stimulatory molecules may give rise to the induction of antigen-specific suppressor cells. Co-stimulatory molecules are abundantly present on dendritic cells (Fig. 47.1), and these cells are known to be very efficient initiators of the immune response. Fragments of donor antigens can be presented to T-cells either by donor (direct presentation) or recipient (indirect presentation) dendritic cells. The indirect pathway is thought to be of importance later after transplantation and to be less suppressible by immunosuppressive agents. Recently, it has become clear that graft parenchymal cells like tubular cells and endothelial cells may become effective antigen presenting cells in the presence of cytokines like gamma-interferon. T-cells reacting to donor major histocompatibility complex plus tissue specific peptides have been cloned from rejecting human kidneys by several groups.

The term "major histocompatibility complex" was defined based upon data generated with transplantation experiments in inbred mouse strains. In the mouse at least 30 other, so called *minor histocompatibilty antigens*, have been identified. Relatively little is known about minor histocompatibility antigens in man, although the relevance of a few systems such as the endothelial-monocyte (EM) alloantigen system, has now been established (see for review van der Woude et al, 1994).

After initiation of the immune response the destruction of the graft will be mediated by the *efferent limb of the*

remove unwanted and inadvertent toxicity from crossreacting antibodies. Although these commercially available preparations are highly effective for steroid-resistant rejection, the major disadvantage of these preparations is the lack of standardization between different preparations or even from batch to batch. Administration is exclusively by intravenous injection (the substances may cause a severe local thrombophlebitis), and many centers adapt the dosage based upon daily counts of circulating lymphocytes or CD3+ cells. Most side effects such as fever and dyspnea are observed after the first dosage and can be treated by stopping the infusion temporarily and giving antihistamines or opiates. It is very important to rule out overfilling before the first dose is given. The symptoms are caused by cytokines released from affected lymphocytes. Another known complication is serum sickness, due to the production of antibodies against the injected immunoglobulins. The hybridoma technique has given the opportunity to produce *monoclonal anti-T-cell antibody preparations*, that show less cross-reactivity and can be better standardized. Such a preparation is monoclonal anti CD3 (or OKT3), that is commercially available and widely used. OKT3 binds to the CD3 antigen (T-cell receptor) on the surface of T-lymphocytes. Although the treatment does not result in lymphopenia like that seen in ATG-treated patients, CD3+ lymphocytes disappear from the circulation after OKT3-infusion. However, CD3+ cells can be found in renal biopsies taken from OKT3-treated patients, so that the mode of action is not entirely clear. Side effects after OKT3 treatment are generally more severe compared to ATG treatment: up to 90% get a syndrome of fever, chills, rigor and general malaise. This response is probably also caused by cytokines released from activated lymphocytes and usually lasts several days. As with ATG, it is crucial to rule out any fluid overloading before initiating the treatment. OKT3 should only be given in specialized units; many side effects like aseptic meningitis, may occur. *New developments* are the production of humanized monoclonal antibodies, where only the antigen binding part of the genetically engineered molecule, binding to cytokine receptors on the cell surface of lymphocytes, is not human. These agents look very promising, in terms of efficacy and favourable side effect profile.

Clinical course and management in transplanted patients

The immediate post-operative course is influenced to a great extent by the pre- and perioperative management. Adequate preoperative dialysis and a relatively dehydrated state will allow the use of crystalloids and blood products during surgery without the necessity for immediate postoperative dialysis, with its associated risks of heparinization, if the allograft fails to function direct after transplantation. A single dose of a broad spectrum antibiotic (usually a second-generation cephalosporin) given at the induction of anasthesia diminishes the incidence of postoperative wound infections significantly. Chances of immediate graft function can be increased by monitoring central venous pressure. Mannitol is given in many centers during revascularization of the donor kidney, because it may

reduce the incidence of acute tubular necrosis. Perioperative calcium channel blockers have been described to decrease the incidence and severity of early graft dysfunction in recipients of cadaver renal transplants and increase 1-year graft survival. In the first hours after transplantation, urine production may vary between poly- and oliguria. Care should be taken that the urine output is replaced by saline or 5% dextrose in half-normal saline infusions (e.g., last hour's output). With sufficient diuresis potassium problems usually do not occur.

Early graft dysfunction is a frequent and challenging diagnostic problem. Mechanical leak, ureteral stenosis, vascular complications or a postoperative lymphocele should be investigated; nonmechanical factors responsible for early graft dysfunction can be hypovolemia, acute tubular necrosis, rejection and cyclosporine toxicity. The first step in the evaluation of early graft dysfunction is to ascertain the permeability and positioning of the urinary bladder catheter and to rule out hypovolemia. The next diagnostic tool is an ultrasound investigation. Urinary tract obstruction may be suggested by dilation of the collecting system or ureter. Perinephric fluid collections can be caused by a ureterovesical leak, hematoma or lymphocele. Decreased or absent flow in the renal vein and artery suggests critical kinking, thrombosis or rejection. During a prolonged period of post-transplant anuria, repeated renal scintigraphy with orthoiodohippurate or ^{99m}Tc-DTPA is useful to monitor graft dysfunction and anatomy. Bleeding, leakage and obstruction can be diagnosed by this methodology. A deteriorating graft perfusion demonstrated by scintigraphy is an indication for renal biopsy. Renal transplant biopsy remains the gold standard to distinguish rejection from cyclosporine A toxicity (see Transplant immunology). Many patients with delayed graft function, however, do not have histologic signs of rejection, cyclosporine A toxicity or tubular necrosis in the biopsy. In patients with contraindications against biopsy, the renal scintigram can be used to rule out the presence of a nonviable graft or to evaluate the effect of anti-rejection treatment of altered dosages of cyclosporine A. The impact of delayed graft function on long-term allograft survival is controversial. Most series have found a relationship between serum creatinine at discharge and graft survival; the severity of initial dysfunctioning does not necessarily affect long-term functioning.

Although the incidence of *infection* after kidney transplantation has decreased considerably over the last 30 years, it is still a major problem. Not only immunosuppressive therapy causes opportunistic infections, major surgery involving vascular and urologic procedures, and immunosuppression caused by uremia predispose to infection. A classic scheme, depicting the timetable of infections after renal transplantation, is shown in Figure 47.3. *Bacterial infections* are most common during the first month after transplantation and are mostly related to wound problems to indwelling catheters.

The infection that causes most morbidity after transplantation is without doubt *cytomegalovirus* (CMV). It

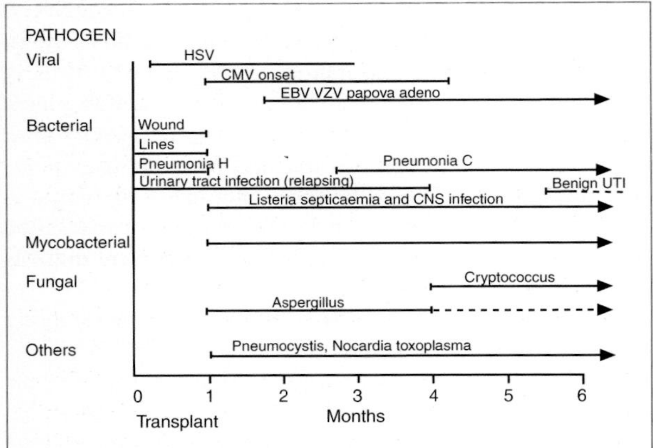

Figure 47.3 The timetable of infections occurring after renal transplantation which has been drawn up by Rubin et al (1981). (From Rubin RH. Transplantation Proceedings 1988;29:12-8.)

usually occurs during the second to fourth month after transplantation and may be either asymptomatic or cause illness of varying severity. Two factors are important for the occurrence of CMV infection and its severity: the serostatus of donor and recipient and the use of poly- or monoclonal anti-T-cell agents. Infection will occur in about 70 to 80% of seronegative patients who receive a kidney from a seropositive donor, and symptomatic illness will develop in 90% of those infected. A typical symptomatic infection begins as a spiking or constant fever with leukopenia, thrombocytopenia and atypical lymphocytes. A rise in serum aspartate aminotransferase levels and development of respiratory symptoms, dyspnea with abnormal blood gases, begin several days after the fever. Less common features are arthralgia, overt hepatitis, splenomegaly, myalgia, gastrointestinal ulceration with bleeding and encephalitis. CMV predisposes the patient to other opportunistic infections. In experimental animals it also may induce rejection, although this has never convincingly been documented in humans. In the diagnosis of CMV, it is important to distinguish between carriage, active infection (as indicated by a serologic response and/or excretion of the virus) and disease. Early diagnosis of CMV disease is essential because early treatment is crucial. CMV can be cultured (results take 5-28 days), but more rapid methods are DNA hybridization, polymerase chain reaction or direct CMV-antigen detection in peripheral blood leukocytes. The last method has a high degree of correlation with clinical disease. Ganciclovir has strongly influenced the course of CMV infections after renal transplantation. The drug is a guanine analogue that is phosphorylated by cellular enzymes to the active triphosphate form, and it inhibits replication of all human herpes virus including CMV in vitro. The normal dosage is 5 mg/kg intravenously twice a day, but may have to be reduced in patients with impaired renal function. The drug is highly effective in established infections, and may be given prophylactically in patients at high risk for disease during antilymphocytic rejection therapy. Although it is customary to reduce immunosuppression during treatment for clinical significant CMV infection, rejection can be successfully treated concurrently with ganciclovir therapy.

Pulmonary infections are an important cause of morbidity and death after renal transplantation. A practical rather than an exhaustive list of possibilities is given in Table 47.7. Opportunistic infection is most common between 1 and 6 months posttransplantation. Before and after this time, especially when there is good renal function accompanied by low-dose immunosuppression, bacterial pneumonias are more common. If an opportunistic lung infection is suspected, bronchial-alveolar lavage or even lung biopsy may be indicated to enable diagnosis and treatment.

Urinary tract infections are very common, especially during the first 3 months after transplantation, and they are important because they may cause bacteremia and pyelonephritis. Some groups have reported excellent results with prophylactic treatment with sulfonamides but this approach is certainly not absolutely necessary. *Central nervous system* (CNS) *infections* occur not earlier than after 1 month and are characterized by a subacute onset and the frequent lack of systemic signs. Fever and a mild headache are common. Frank meningism and focal neurologic abnormalities are generally absent, but these infections have a high mortality. The slightest suspicion should lead to an extensive neurologic work up, including lumbar punction and CT scan. The most common micro-organisms found are Listeria, Cryptococcus and Aspergillus. Some viral infections have a peculiar course after kidney transplantation. *Hepatitis B* will lead to progressive liver disease in the majority of patients carrying the virus. For *Hepatitis C* this has not so clearly been shown. Epstein-Barr virus may induce Burkitt-type B cell lymphomas in patients receiving anti-T-cell agents combined with cyclosporine A.

Table 47.7 Causes of pulmonary infection after renal transplantation

Bacteria
Pneumococcus
Staphylococcus
Gram-negatives
Legionella
Nocardia
Mycobacteria

Viruses
Herpes viruses (especially cytomegalovirus)

Fungi
Aspergillus
Candida

Parasites
Pneumocystis carinii

Long term complications after kidney transplantation After kidney transplantation there is about a three fold increased risk to develop a *malignancy* as compared to a control population. Squamous cell *skin carcinoma* is by far the most common type of malignancy and in Australia 50% of patients has developed this cancer type 15 years after transplantation; in areas with less exposure to ultraviolet light skin cancers tend to appear later. Other factors such as HLA type and mismatches and the presence of skin warts contribute to the risk. During cyclosporine A therapy the incidence seems to be lower that on azathioprine. In contrast to skin cancer, *lymphomas* represent a greater proportion of the tumours observed in cyclosporine A-treated patients than on azathioprine. Epstein-Barr virus plays a role in the induction of poly- and monoclonal B cell tumors; the polyclonal variety may react favorably to antiviral therapy and withdrawal of immunosuppression. The risk to develop Kaposi sarcoma is 200 to 1000-fold higher after kidney transplantation. Other frequently observed tumors are renal carcinoma and carcinomas of cervix and vagina. The relative risks for the various tumors is dependent on the genetic background and the geographic area where the patient is living. For example, in Japan the overall excess risk to develop cancer after kidney transplantation is similarly increased compared to Western countries, where the distribution of tumors is however different. The main cause of death after kidney transplantation is however not cancer, but cardiovascular. The increase in absolute incidence of cardiovascular mortality after kidney transplantation in the last decade is an inevitable sequel to the increased transplantation rate of older patients and of patients with diabetic nephropathy as underlying disease. Risk factors are hyperlipidemia, hyperglycemia, hypertension, weight gain, rising hematocrit and smoking. Many of these risk factors are unfavorable influenced by the current standard of maintenance immunosuppressive therapy consisting of corticosteroids and cyclosporine A. It is absolutely mandatory to treat hyperlipemia, newly developed diabetes mellitus and hypertension rigorously, council patients to prevent obesity and stop or avoid smoking after transplantation.

Bone disease is usually favorably influenced by kidney transplantation. With good renal function phosphate excretion, $1,25(OH)_2D_3$ synthesis and aluminium excretion are rapidly normalized. Marked hyperplasia of the parathyroid glands may not completely regress and a biochemical state comparable to primary hyperparathyroidism may appear. The decision to perform a parathyroidectomy is usually best postponed until at least 1 year posttransplant. One of the worst long-term complications of renal transplantation is aseptic necrosis of bone leading to joint destruction. The most common site is the femoral head. Most lesions develop within 3 years after transplantation, but the incidence seems to be declining, probably due to lower oral steroid dosages. A well functioning graft produces a sufficient amount of erythropoietin leading to increasing hemoglobulin values after transplantation. *Polycythemia* occurs in 8 to 17% of patients with satisfactory graft function and is usually related to autonomous production of erythropoietin in the native kidney. ACE-inhibitors are quite often successful in treating this condition, otherwise regular blood-letting is advised to keep the hematocrit under 50% and prevent thromboembolic complications. Quality of life improves after a successful kidney transplantation. The majority of patients rehabilitates to a normal life-style and *reproduction* is part of this normal process. There is generalized agreement that women should avoid pregnancy for 12 to 24 months post-transplantation and should be in good metabolic control preconception. During this period it should be discussed which birth-control method is most suitable and acceptable. Each method of contraception has its inherent problems; oral contraceptive agents may exacerbate cyclosporine A-induced hypertension and cause thromboembolism. Intrauterine devices can increase the risk of infection and are therefore not recommended. It appears that the barrier methods of contraception (including condoms, diaphragms, sponges, and foam) may be the safest alternatives. Maternal drug-treated hypertension, diabetes mellitus and elevated serum creatinine may be predictors for loss of graft in pregnant kidney recipients. Risks to the offsprings are a high rate of prematurity, low birth-weight, and intrauterine growth retardation. In conclusion, it is generally safe for women after transplantation to become pregnant, but the risks to the infant and the mother should be fully discussed before conception. Mothers on cyclosporine A should not breast feed their infants, since the drug will appear in the colostrum.

Long-term results

The long-term results in terms of patient and graft survival have considerably improved over the last 3 decades. Important factors causing these improvements were improved surgical techniques, improved tissue typing and cross-match methodology, the application of pre-operative blood transfusions and more effective immune suppression. Patient mortality is now less than 5% during the first year after transplantation. Actuarial graft survival curves from patients transplanted in the Eurotransplant area are shown in Figure 47.4. It is clear that grafts from HLA identical living-related donors have the best long-term

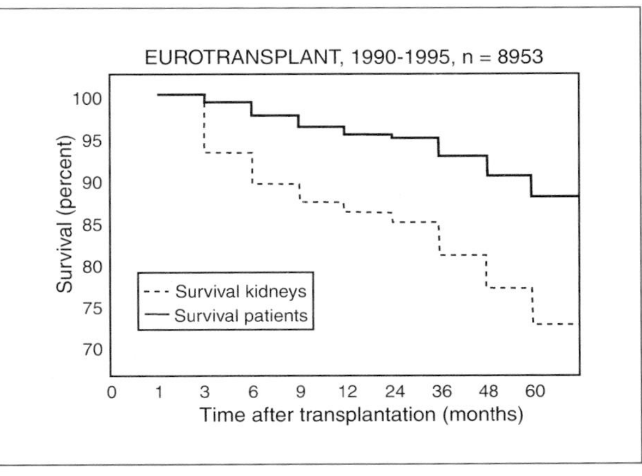

Figure 47.4 Actuarial survival of patients and kidneys after cadaveric kidney transplantation.

prognosis; however, HLA matching is also of importance both in grafts from living and from post-mortal donors.

Another factor with a positive impact on long-term survival is female sex of the recipient; this probably can be explained by size matching – women tend to have less body mass, and male kidneys are larger. Characteristics with a negative impact on long-term outcome are:

- recipient received a previous kidney transplant (around 10% lower graft survival);
- recipient has diabetes or a systemic disease;
- recipient is black;
- recipient needs dialysis within the first week post-transplant (especially important when rejection occurs concomitantly);
- recipient experiences rejection episodes within 3 months posttransplant (especially true for vascular rejection);
- donor was black.

The striking improvement in graft survival since the early days of post-mortal renal transplantation has been observed in the graft survival rates after 1 year; beyond 1 year the graphs for survival remain roughly parallel. It remains a major challenge for the years to come to improve the outlook 1 year after kidney transplantation in post-mortal graft recipients. Since no immunosuppressive drug has yet been shown to have a major impact on late graft loss, all we can do for the moment is to seek close HLA matching without excessive prolonging of the cold ischemia periods. Rapid diagnosis and treatment of early rejection is also important to achieve maximal renal function; grafts with a creatinine clearance under 30 ml/min after 1 year have poor long-term prognosis.

Appropriate treatment of high blood pressure and proteinuria with ACE inhibitors or other antihypertensive drugs during long-term follow-up is likely to reduce and postpone late graft loss.

Suggested readings

Bouwes Bavinck JN, Vermeer BJ, van der Woude FJ, et al. Relation between skin cancer and HLA antigens in renal-transplant recipients. N Engl J Med 1991;325:843-8.

Hoshida Y, Tsukuma H, Yasunaga Y, et al. Cancer risk after renal transplantation in Japan. Int J Cancer 1997;16:517-20.

Kasiske BL, Ramos EL, Gaston RS, et al. The evaluation of renal transplant candidates: clinical practice guidelines. Patient Care and Education Committee of the American Society of Transplant Physicians. J Am Soc Nephrol 1995;6:1-34.

De Koning J, van Dorp WT, van Es LA, et al. Ganciclovir effectively treats cytomegalovirus disease after solid-organ transplantation, even during rejection treatment. Nephrol Dial Transplant 1992;7:350-6.

Opelz G, Scherer S, Mytilineos J. Analysis of HLA-DR-split-specificity matching in cadaver kidney transplantation: a report of the Collaborative Transplant Study. Transplantation 1997;63:57-9.

Opelz G, Vanrenterghem Y, Kirste G, et al. Prospective evaluation of pretransplant blood transfusions in cadaver kidney recipients. Transplantation 1997;63:964-7.

Pallis C. Brainstem death: The evolution of a concept. In: Morris, ed. Kidney transplantation. Principles and practice. Philadelphia: WB Saunders 1994;71-85.

Solez K, et al. International standardisation of nomenclature for the histologic diagnosis of renal allograft rejection: the Banff working classification of kidney transplant pathology. Kidney Int 1993;44:415-22.

Terasaki PI, Cecka JM, Gjertson DW, Takemoto S. High survival rates of kidney transplants from spousal and living unrelated donors. N Engl J Med 1995;329:333-6.

van Saase JL, van der Woude FJ, Thorogood J, et al. The relation between acute vascular and interstitial renal allograft rejection. Transplantation 1995;59:1280-5.

van der Woude FJ, Kager PA, van der Jagt EJ, et al. Strongyloides stercoralis hyperinfection as a consequence of immunosuppressive treatment. Neth J Med 1985;28:315-7.

van der Woude FJ, Schrama E, van Es LA, et al. The role of unconventional alloantigens in interstitial and vascular rejection after transplantation. Transplant Immunol 1994;2:271-7.

CHAPTER

48

Use of drugs in patients with renal function impairment

Gerjan Navis, Paul E. de Jong, Dick de Zeeuw

KEY POINTS

- The kidney plays a leading role in the excretion and metabolism of drugs.
- In renal disease pharmacokinetics as well as pharmacodynamics can be altered, leading to an increased risk for renal and extrarenal drug toxicity in renal patients.
- Asymptomatic renal function impairment is common in elderly patients, even in the absence of overt renal disease.
- Patients with renal function impairment often require multiple drugs, and thus are at increased risk for drug interactions.
- Adjustment of drug treatment to impaired renal function can be obtained by dose reduction and/or increasing dose interval, depending on the specifics of the drug involved. The exceptions to this rule are the diuretics; to be effective in patients with renal function impairment, the diuretic dose must be increased.
- Volume depletion potentiates the toxicity of nephrotoxic drugs; thus, volume repletion should be pursued when such drugs are indicated.

The kidney is a major route of excretion and metabolism, not only of endogenous substances, but also of such exogenous compounds as drugs. As a result, renal functional impairment can lead to accumulation of drugs and their metabolites. Renal disease can also alter distribution volume of drugs and affect renal and nonrenal drug metabolism. Not only pharmacokinetics but also pharmacodynamics may be altered in renal patients, i.e., the response to therapy can be different, irrespective of the drug levels obtained. Therefore, pharmacotherapy in renal patients requires special caution with respect to dosing as well as monitoring of therapeutic effects and adverse effects. Renal patients are not only at risk for extrarenal adverse effects – related to altered pharmacokinetics and pharmacodynamics – but also tend to have an enhanced susceptibility to drug-induced renal damage. Finally, it is important to realize that most renal patients are older persons who require multiple drugs for multiple conditions. This requires special caution to avoid adverse effects due to interactions.

Pharmacokinetics in patients with renal disease

A general outline of drug distribution and metabolism is given in Figure 48.1. Renal disease not only affects renal metabolism and renal excretion of drugs; it also can affect almost any pharmacokinetic parameter, as summarized in Table 48.1. In renal patients several parameters are often affected simultaneously; moreover, the disposition of inactive and active metabolites also can be altered. The net effects of renal function impairment on drug action depend on patient factors, i.e., the severity of renal function impairment, the presence of other features of the renal condition such as hypoalbuminemia in nephrotic syndrome, and comorbidity – as well as on the physicochemical properties of the drug and its metabolites. These multiple interactions make it impossible to predict the effects of renal function impairment from theoretic considerations only. Drug treatment in renal patients therefore should always be based on empiric evidence in the renal popula-

Table 48.1 Alterations in pharmacokinetics in renal failure

	Mechanism	Effect
Gastrointestinal absorption/ Bioavailability	Vomiting/diarrhea/constipation	Bioavailability: ↓/↓/↑
	Altered gastric pH	↓
	Intestinal edema	↓
	Cotreatment (phosphate-binding antacids)	↓
	Decreased first-pass effect	↑
Distribution volume	Reduced protein binding due to: – hypoproteinemia – accumulated uremic toxins	Distribution volume: ↑
	Increased/decreased tissue binding	↑/↓
	Expansion of extracellular volume	↑
Metabolism	Renal/hepatic cytochrome P450 activity	Metabolism: ↓
Elimination	Reduced glomerular filtration	Excretion: ↓
	Reduced tubular secretion	↓

tion and should be accompanied by careful monitoring of the effects of therapy by clinical parameters and, if necessary, by laboratory parameters and monitoring of drug levels as well. The clinical effects of changes in drug disposition depend not only on the magnitude of these changes but also on the therapeutic range of the particular drug. Obviously, for drugs with a narrow therapeutic-to-toxic window (e.g., digoxin), relatively modest changes in kinetics will more easily result in either subtherapeutic or toxic effects, requiring dose adjustment. For drugs with a large therapeutic window, on the other hand, even relatively large changes in disposition can be tolerated without the need for dose adjustment.

Absorption

Uremia as such presumably does not directly affect gastrointestinal absorption of drugs. However, in severe renal function impairment and end-stage renal failure, gastrointestinal complaints are common and may interfere with absorption. Vomiting or diarrhea may reduce gastrointestinal absorption. Constipation – which also is common - may enhance absorption. The use of aluminium- or calcium-containing phosphate binding antacids may interfere with drug absorption by increasing gastric pH, hampering absorption of drugs more easily absorbed at a low pH, and by formation of insoluble complexes. In severely nephrotic patients, edema of the bowel wall may impair intestinal absorption. The latter is considered one of the causes of diuretic resistance in severely nephrotic patients with excessive edema, and may be circumvented by parenteral administration of the diuretic. Finally, impairment of hepatic drug metabolism in uremia can increase bioavailability of drugs with a large first-pass effect. Clinical consequences of such an increased bioavailability were reported only for the analgesics dextropropoxyphene and dihydrocodeine.

Distribution, protein binding

Renal disease can profoundly affect distribution volume (V_d) of many drugs. For drugs eliminated by glomerular

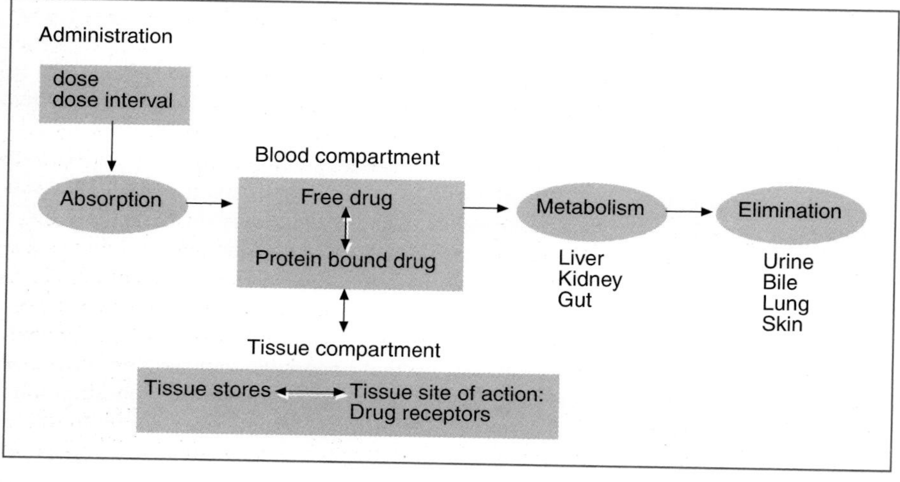

Figure 48.1 A general model of pharmacokinetics. In renal disease absorption, distribution and protein binding, metabolism and elimination can all be altered. Drug response is determined by the concentration of the drug at its tissue receptor site. To adjust treatment to the altered pharmacokinetics, the physician can adjust dose, dose interval or both.

filtration, a rise in distribution volume results in a net reduction of renal elimination, because a smaller proportion is available for filtration. A rise in distribution volume can result from decreased protein binding, increased tissue binding, and alterations in body fluid composition. In chronic renal failure protein binding of acidic drugs is reduced by altered protein conformation, accumulation of uremic substances competing for binding sites, and hypoproteinemia. The latter is relevant mainly in patients with nephrotic syndrome and/or malnutrition. Reduced protein binding not only increases distribution volume but also alters the ratio of free to bound drug. Altered protein binding may hamper the interpretation of measured plasma drug levels, because these usually entail total drug concentration, whereas biologic activity correlates more closely with the free fraction. Thus, a "safe" drug level may be associated with unexpected toxicity. This bears clinical consequences mainly for drugs with extensive protein binding and a narrow therapeutic range, and for which large fluctuations in free to bound ratio occur. For some of these, like warfarin, close monitoring of biologic activity is possible. For others, like phenytoin, monitoring of free drug levels is recommended. Renal function impairment can also be associated with decrease in distribution volume, owing to decreased tissue binding. This occurs, for instance, with digoxin. Thus, a given dosage results in higher than expected plasma drug levels.

Metabolism

The kidney, in particular the proximal tubule, is involved in metabolism of endogenous and exogenous substances by various pathways. These include conjugation (glucuronidation and sulfation) and cytochrome P450 oxidases. Moreover, the proximal tubule metabolizes many low-molecular weight proteins like insulin. Decreased tubular insulin breakdown, for instance, accounts for the reduced insulin requirement in advanced renal failure. For most endogenous and exogenous substances the impact of impaired renal metabolism on drug disposition in renal failure is poorly quantified. Of note, in chronic renal failure nonrenal drug metabolism also may be affected. Reduced hepatic cytochrome P450 activity – attributed to accumulation of uremic toxins – has been described, accounting for a decreased nonrenal clearance of several drugs. For other drugs, however, an increased nonrenal clearance is present in patients with renal failure. The clinical impact of altered metabolism depends not only on the specific alteration in metabolism but also on the biologic activity of the metabolites. Inactive metabolites may compete with the active drug for drug receptors, and toxic metabolites may accumulate without being detected by drug level monitoring. Knowledge of the fate of metabolites is therefore important in the pharmacologic management of renal patients.

Elimination

The routes of renal handling of drugs are essentially similar to those of endogenous substances, that is, glomerular filtration, active tubular secretion and tubular reabsorption. In chronic renal failure, with ongoing loss of functioning nephrons, glomerular filtration and tubular secretion usually fall proportionately.

Glomerular filtration accounts for the renal excretion of non-protein-bound drugs. The glomerular filtration barrier allows the filtration of substances up to a molecular weight of approximately 65 000 daltons – that is, solutes and small molecules are freely filtered, but albumin and other large serum proteins do not pass the filtration barrier. The molecular weight of most drugs is considerably lower. The main restriction to glomerular filtration of drugs is therefore the extent of protein binding, as only the unbound fraction is available for filtration. The rate of elimination of unbound drugs by filtration depends not only on filtration rate but also on distribution volume: when distribution volume is large because of tissue binding, only a small proportion is available for filtration. Unlike tubular secretion, there is no transport maximum for glomerular filtration – that is, with increasing drug levels the amount of filtered drug increases linearly.

Tubular elimination of drugs results from the combined effects of tubular secretion and reabsorption. Active secretion by the proximal tubules is an important and rapid excretion route for many endogenous and exogenous organic anions and cations. Moreover, active secretion by the proximal tubulus is a highly efficient route of excretion for many protein bound drugs. The rapid renal elimination of penicillin by tubular secretion with a consequent need for frequent administration, for instance, was an important problem during the early days of penicillin use, when supplies were still very limited. In those days probenecid, a competitive inhibitor of tubular secretion, was often used as an adjunct treatment to slow down the renal elimination of penicillin.

Pharmacologic treatment in the renal patient

Application of pharmacokinetic and pharmacodynamic principles is necessary, but not sufficient for safe and effective drug treatment in patients with renal function impairment. General guidelines for drug treatment in renal patients are summarized in Table 48.2.

First, it is important for the clinician to use only a limited number of drugs in order to become thoroughly familiar with their use. This general principle applies to all drug-prescribing, but it is all the more important in populations susceptible to unwanted side effects and/or altered efficacy, like the renal population. Next, it is crucial to be alert to the possibility of renal function impairment, even in patients without a diagnosis of renal disease. Considerable renal function impairment is common in older subjects and may be completely asymptomatic. In patients with known renal impairment, the risk for renal and extrarenal drug toxicity may be enhanced by concomitant volume depletion – further compromising renal drug handling – and by comorbidity that affects alternative routes of drug disposition, e.g., hepatic dysfunction. Recognition and correction of reversible risk factors for drug toxicity – such as volume depletion – before administration often makes it possible to reduce drug toxicity. Dosing of drugs in renal patients should be based on knowledge of the alterations in drug action induced by the renal disorders, allowing one to make a proper dose adjustment. Therefore, as a general rule, one should refrain from using drugs not tested in renal patients – unless a grave clinical condition overshadows this safety issue. The final and perhaps most important guideline is to monitor closely the effects of therapy from clinical parameters and, if necessary, from laboratory parameters and/or drug levels as well in order to be able to make a proper adjustment of therapy if the efficacy safety do not meet expectations. In this respect it is important to realize that sudden changes in renal function, e.g., intercurrent volume depletion or urinary tract infection, can occur in patients with otherwise stable renal function impairment that can exacerbate renal and extrarenal drug toxicity despite an unchanged therapeutic regimen.

Detection of renal function impairment

To adjust drug dosage properly for renal function, the first thing is to suspect the possibility of renal function impairment. Creatinine clearance, calculated from serum creatinine and 24-hour urinary excretion of creatinine, theoretically provides a reasonable estimate of renal function, but considerable errors can be expected from inaccurate collection of 24-hour urine. Estimation of renal function from serum creatinine provides a feasible alternative, but should account for the fact that serum creatinine level not only reflects the rate of elimination by the kidneys but also creatinine supply, i.e., the turnover of body muscle mass. Moreover, the relationship between serum creatinine and glomerular filtration rate is not linear, but exponential. When renal function deteriorates, a rise in serum creatinine does not occur until glomerular filtration rate is reduced by some 50%. Accordingly, patients with a low muscle mass, e.g., women, older persons, and the chronically ill or immobilized, may have a serum creatinine well within normal range in spite of considerable renal function impairment. An estimate of creatinine clearance from serum creatinine that takes into account muscle mass can be made by the empirically determined Cockroft-Gault formula:

$$\text{GFR (ml / min)} = \frac{(140 - \text{age}) \times \text{ideal body weight (kg)}}{\text{serum creatinine (mg/dl)} \times 72}$$

For women the outcome should be multiplied by 0.85. This calculation assumes steady state and thus is invalid when renal function changes rapidly, such as in acute renal failure.

Table 48.2 General guidelines for pharmacologic treatment in renal patients

Use only a limited number of drugs and get thoroughly familiar with these
Be alert on possible renal function impairment before prescribing, particularly in the elderly
Be alert on additional risk factors for drug toxicity
Do not use drugs not tested in renal patients
Adjust dosage according to prevailing guidelines
Monitor therapeutic effects and toxicity and modify therapy if required

Dose adjustment in renal failure

Loading dose A loading dose can be useful in clinical conditions when one wants to attain steady-state therapeutic drug levels quickly. The decision to use a loading dose depends on the clinical condition of the patient and the time required to obtain therapeutic levels without a loading dose. The latter can be estimated as approximately four to five times the half-life of the drug. Thus, a loading dose provides a benefit mainly for drugs with a long half-life, e.g., digoxin, where it takes approximately a week to obtain steady state levels without a loading dose. The loading dose depends on the desired drug level and the distribution volume; adjustment is required mainly for drugs with a narrow therapeutic range. The main clinical condition applicable to renal patients where adjustment of the loading dose deserves consideration is atrial fibrillation requiring digoxin therapy. Distribution volume for digoxin may be reduced in renal patients – especially when extracellular volume depletion is present. Thus, in the latter condition it would be prudent to reduce the usual loading dose by 10 to 25%. For other drugs with altered distribution volume in renal failure, a prompt onset of drug action often is not as crucial, and there is thus no need for a loading dose.

Maintenance dose The maintenance dose is the main determinant of steady state drug levels – and thus the main determinant of therapeutic efficacy as well as renal and extrarenal toxicity. Maintenance dose can be adjusted for renal function impairment in two ways. First, the absolute amount of drug administered at each dosing interval can be reduced in proportion to the severity of renal function impairment with unchanged dosing interval. This results in relatively stable drug levels. Second, dosing interval can be increased. This results in increased fluctuations in drug levels. The latter can be a desired effect when therapeutic efficacy depends on high peak levels, but, on the other hand, it is not wanted for drugs where the difference in therapeutic and toxic drug levels is small. Thus, the most desirable approach – which also may be a combination of the two – depends on the particular properties of the drug. Many drugs normally excreted or metabolized by the kidney require a reduction of maintenance dose in renal patients, in proportion to the severity of renal function impairment. The required adjustments are given for individual drugs in the Appendix.

Specific pharmacologic issues in the renal patient

Most patients known to have chronically impaired renal function require multiple drugs for the management of their renal condition. Diuretics and antihypertensives are required by most renal patients for the management of volume status and blood pressure. Hyperuricemia requires allopurinol treatment in many patients. Supplementation of an active form of vitamin D is required for the prevention of secondary hyperparathyroidism, together with phosphate-binding antacids when renal function impairment becomes more severe. Knowledge of the use of these classes of drugs in renal failure, their mutual interactions, and their possible interaction with drugs needed for comorbidity provides a practical framework for pharmacologic treatment of renal patients.

Diuretics

Impairment of sodium excretion is common in renal patients, especially when renal function loss is moderate to severe. Therefore, many renal patients require diuretic treatment for the control of volume status and blood pressure. When considering diuretic efficacy it is important to realize that excess sodium intake can completely annihilate the therapeutic effect, in spite of appropriate pharmacologic action. Thus, diuretic therapy and dietary sodium restriction should be considered as adjunct therapeutic modalities rather than as each other's substitute.

With the sole exception of spironolactone, diuretics exert their effect on the luminal side of the tubule. Thus, to exert their effect on the kidney, diuretics need to be excreted first. Their renal excretion occurs mainly by active tubular secretion. Accordingly, in renal function impairment a decreased intratubular delivery of diuretics blunts their efficacy. Thus, unlike all other classes of drugs, for diuretics dose adjustment for renal failure requires increased dosage. When creatinine clearance falls below approximately 30 ml/min, loop diuretics are the agents of choice, because – as a monotherapy – thiazides tend to be less effective with severe renal function impairment, and potassium-sparing diuretics are contraindicated because of the risk for hyperkalemia.

Renal sodium retention can be pronounced in renal patients, particularly in patients with nephrotic syndrome or severe renal function impairment. With diuretic monotherapy – i.e., inhibition of tubular sodium reabsorption at a single tubule site – avid sodium reabsorption at other tubule sites may underly resistance to therapy. In such conditions, the combination of diuretics with a different tubular site of action – together with dietary sodium restriction – can restore diuretic efficacy. Thus, in a patient resistant to a loop diuretic, addition of a thiazide can be useful even if, as monotherapy, it would exert no effect.

Antihypertensives

Hypertension is a hallmark of renal disease and most renal patients require some form of antihypertensive treatment. Most classes of antihypertensive drugs are effective in renal patients. In patients with diabetic nephropathy and in nondiabetic proteinuric patients, ACE inhibitors retard the rate of long-term loss of function more effectively than other classes of drugs that exert a similar effect on blood pressure. Therefore, in these patients ACE inhibitors are considered a first line of therapy. For other renal patients a specific renal advantage of ACE inhibitors, in addition to their effect on blood pressure, has not been demonstrated convincingly thus far, but nevertheless their antihypertensive efficacy renders them useful as a first step of therapy in these patients as well. Specific renal effects of ACE inhibitors – while providing the basis for their long-term renoprotective effect – can, under certain circumstances, also lead to adverse effects on the kidney. When renal perfusion is impaired, as in volume depletion, or in a kidney behind a renal artery stenosis, filtration pressure is critically dependent on angiotensin-II-mediated postglomerular vascular tone. Under such circumstances inhibition of angiotensin II formation by ACE inhibition can result in a sharp decrease in glomerular filtration rate. Such an ACE inhibitor-induced acute impairment of renal function is usually reversible – by virtue of its hemodynamic mechanism – by withdrawal of the ACE inhibitor and restoration of renal perfusion. In cases where volume deficit is the factor predisposing to ACE inihibitor nephrotoxicity, ACE inhibition usually can be resumed safely after volume repletion, but it would be prudent to choose a lower dose for reinstitution. In this respect it is relevant that most ACE inhibitors are excreted renally. Thus, when volume depletion leads to prerenal failure superimposed on chronically impaired renal function, the previously appropriate dose becomes too high.

Because ACE inhibitors reduce aldosterone levels they lower renal potassium excretion, which may elicit hyperkalemia in patients with impaired renal function. Patients with diabetic nephropathy appear to be particularly at risk for this adverse effect, presumably because of the relatively common occurrence of hyporeninemic hypoaldosteronism in this population. Hyperkalemia can be elicited even in patients with normal renal function by the combination of ACE inhibitors with potassium-sparing diuretics or wtih NSAIDs. Thus, these combinations are best avoided. If the clinical condition requires the use of such a combination, careful monitoring of serum potassium is necessary.

Phosphate-binding antacids

Aluminium- or calcium-containing phosphate-binding antacids may interfere with drug absorption by increasing gastric pH, hampering absorption of drugs more easily absorbed at a low pH, and by formation of insoluble complexes (Tab. 48.3). Moreover, antacids can exert unpredictable effects on reabsorption of all "enteric coated" administration forms. To prevent such interaction, phosphate binders and the concomitant medication should be taken at different times. As phosphate binders need to be taken concomitantly with food to bind food-borne phosphate effectively, this suggests that other drugs should be taken between meals. It should be noted here that aluminium-containing phosphate binders should be used only as a last resort to avoid the toxicity of aluminium accumulation. Accordingly, the use of aluminium- containing agents for other indications such as gastrointestinal complaints should be avoided altogether.

Nonsteroidal antiinflammatory drugs (NSAIDs)

Nonsteroidal antiinflammatory drugs (NSAIDs) are among the most commonly used drugs, both on physicians' prescriptions and as over-the-counter preparations. NSAIDs, however, can have pronounced renal effects in patients with renal function impairment and/or volume depletion. During depletion of circulating volume, glomerular filtration pressure becomes critically dependent on intrarenal formation of vasodilator prostaglandins, even in healthy subjects. Thus, in volume-depleted subjects inhibition of prostaglandin synthesis by NSAIDs may elicit a sharp fall in renal function, even to the extent that oliguric acute renal failure occurs. Fortunately, such hemodynamically-mediated acute renal failure is readily reversible upon discontinuation of the NSAID and restoration of extracellular volume.

NSAIDs induce tubular retention of sodium and potassium that may go unnoticed in otherwise healthy persons. The sodium retention blunts the effect of diuretics, which may adversely affect the clinical symptoms in patients critically dependent on diuretics, such as heart failure patients. The impairment of potassium excretion may elicit severe hyperkalemia in patients with compromised renal potassium excretion, i.e., patients with moderate to severe renal function impairment, or patients using potassium-sparing drugs, such as potassium-sparing diuretics or ACE inhibitors. Hyperkalemia may be particularly pronounced when a concomitant fall in glomerular filtration rate occurs.

Antibiotics

Many antibiotics are excreted by the kidney, and thus require dose adjustment in renal function impairment, as presented in detail in the Appendix 1. Among the commonly used classes of antibiotics, tetracyclines are best avoided in patients with severe renal function impairment, because of the formation of toxic metabolites. Sulfonamides may exert renal toxicity in renal patients due to intratubular crystal formation. The latter may be elicited by a low urine flow, e.g., in dehydrated patients. Conversely, volume repletion and maintaining a large diuresis limit tubular crystal formation. Co-trimoxazole selectively inhibits tubular creatinine secretion, which may mimic a reduction in renal function.

For treatment of urinary tract infections, antibiotics need to be excreted into the urinary tract. Thus, renal function impairment as well as dose reduction to limit extrarenal toxicity may blunt their therapeutic effects. Urinary tract infections in renal patients are therefore best treated with drugs with a renal route of excretion and little systemic toxicity in order to obtain a therapeutic concentration in the urine without systemic toxicity.

Table 48.3 Selected drugs with impaired absorption by phosphate-binding antacids

Tetracyclines	Kinidine
Quinolone antibiotics	Atropine
Cloxacillin	Aspirin
Isoniazid	Ferrous sulfate
H_2-receptor blockers	Folic acid
Digoxin	Chlorpropamide

Prevention of renal and nonrenal toxicity in renal patients

Preventive measures can substantially reduce the risk of renal toxicity of the most common nephrotoxic agents. To this purpose recognition of high-risk conditions is important. The risk for renal toxicity depends on patient factors as well as on the properties of the required drug. Patient-related risk factors for renal toxicity tend to be the same for various nephrotoxic agents and include: prior renal function impairment; compromised renal perfusion with consequently low urine output (due to either volume depletion or forward failure); and concomitant hepatic morbidity. The use of multiple medications also predisposes to unwanted toxicity. In patients with diabetic nephropathy or myeloma, the kidney may be particularly susceptible to nephrotoxicity.

High-risk therapies include, notably, aminoglycosides and radiographic contrast media. Among the drugs commonly used in outpatient populations, ACE inhibitors and NSAIDs can be considered high-risk therapies as well.

The main preventive measures to ameliorate renal toxicity are to avoid combinations that may potentiate toxicity and to correct any volume depletion before starting therapy. Volume repletion helps prevent both hemodynamically-mediated renal function loss (as with ACE inhibitors and NSAIDs) and tubular toxicity. Tubular toxicity (as seen with radiographic contrast media and with crystal-forming agents like sulfonamides) is directly related to the intratubular concentration of the incriminated substance. Accordingly, toxicity is reduced in dilute urine, and maintenance of a high urine flow is warranted. Diuretics may be useful for this purpose in patients in whom generous fluid supply does not result in the required diuresis, because of either renal function impairment or cardiac failure.

Suggested readings

BESSEGHIR K, ROCH-RAMEL F. Renal excretion of drugs and other xenobiotics. Renal Physiol 1987;10:221-41.

COCKROFT DW, GAULT MH. Prediction of creatinine clearance from serum creatinine. Nephron 1976;16:31-41.

MATZKE GR, FRYE RF. Drug adminstration in patients with renal insufficiency. Minimizing renal and extrarenal toxicity. Drug Safety 1997;16:205-31.

NAVIS GJ, FABER HJ, DE ZEEUW D, DE JONG PE. ACE-inhibitors and the kidney: a risk-benefit assessment. Drug Safety 1996;15:200-11.

SCHLONDORFF D. Renal complications of nonsteroidal antiinflammatory drugs. Kidney Int 1993;44:643-53.

SECTION

12

Renal disorders in particular settings

CHAPTER

49

Renal disorders in particular settings: pregnancy

John M. Davison

KEY POINTS

Urinary tract infection

- The most frequent complication during otherwise normal pregnancy.
- It is mostly asymptomatic or covert bacteriuria uncovered by routine screening.
- Cystitis, acute pyelonephritis and rarely peripheric abscess may also develop.
- Most would screen all gravidas and treat with the appropriate antibiotic: covert bacteriuria for 7-10 days and pyelonephritis for 14 days.
- Prolonged nonresponsiveness of infection should prompt exclusion of acute hydronephrosis.

Pregnancy in women with chronic renal disease

- Provided prepregnancy kidney dysfunction minimal and hypertension absent, pregnancy is not contraindicated and successful obstetric outcome is attained.
- Mostly, pregnancy does not adversely affect the course of the renal disease but with moderate or severe dysfunction further loss of function occurs in up to 50% of women of whom at least 10% progress post-delivery to end-stage failure.

Obstetric acute renal failure

- Occurs in pregnancy in situations similar to those in nonpregnant patients but pathology peculiar to pregnancy must always be considered.
- Acute fatty liver can be complicated by renal failure and its early recognition with prompt treatment reduces fetal and maternal mortality rates.
- Hemolytic-uremic syndrome is associated with a high morbidity and mortality.
- Treatment aims at preventing uremic symptomatology as well as acid-base, electrolyte and volume disturbances.
- Method of dialysis (peritoneal or hemodialysis) is dictated by facilities available and by clinical circumstances.
- Peritoneal dialysis is effective and safe and may minimize rapid metabolic changes.

Pregnancy in women on long-term dialysis

- Patients usually infertile but contraception should not be neglected.
- On balance, pregnancy probably contraindicated, as it is invariably complicated with major risks for mother and a live birth outcome of 40-50%, even when therapeutic terminations are excluded.

Pregnancy in women with renal allografts

- Suitable prepregnancy guidelines should be fulfilled if pregnancy is to be advised.
- Overall complications rate is about 50% but chances of success are 95%.
- If complications (usually hypertension, renal deterioration, and/or rejection) occur before 28 weeks then successful obstetric outcome is reduced by 20%.
- Pregnancy does not compromise long-term renal prognosis.

NORMAL PREGNANCY

The kidneys enlarge during pregnancy because of both vascular volume and interstitial space increase. There is a 70% overall increase in renal volume by the third trimester. The calyces, renal pelves, and ureters dilate markedly, invariably more prominently on the right side, and are evident in 90% of women by the third trimester.

Renal plasma flow and glomerular filtration rate (GFR) increase 50 to 70% above pre-pregnancy values. GFR, as 24-hour creatinine clearance, increases in early pregnancy; thereafter, serum levels of creatinine (S_{cr}) and urea, which average 73 μmol/l (0.82 mg/dl) and 4.3 mmol/l (25 mg/dl), respectively, in nonpregnant women, decrease to mean values of 51 μmol/l (0.58 mg/dl) and 3.3 mmol (20 mg/dl) in pregnancy. Thus, values for serum creatinine of 75 μmol/l (0.85 mg/dl) and urea of 4.5 mmol/l (27 mg/dl), which are acceptable in nonpregnant women, are suspect in pregnancy. It also should be remembered that caution is necessary when serially assessing renal function on the basis of serum creatinine alone (especially if there is renal disease), because even with loss of renal function of up to 50% S_{cr} can still be less than 130 μmol/l (145 mg/dl).

URINARY TRACT INFECTIONS

These infections are common in both pregnant and nonpregnant women. Susceptibility relates to basic immunologic differences, structural/functional abnormalities and socioeconomic factors, and may be further increased in pregnancy owing to ureteropelvic dilatation and increased urinary nutrient content (glucose and amino acids). Diagnosis can be difficult because normal pregnancy symptoms include urinary frequency, dysuria, nocturia, and urgency; therefore, laboratory evidence is needed.

A standard definition of infection is a colony count greater than 100 000 bacteria per ml of urine, although counts as low as 20 000 may represent active infection in pregnancy. Urinary white cell count tends to increase in pregnancy, and moderate pyuria thus may be normal. *Escherichia coli* is the predominant infecting organism (75-90% of cases); *Klebsiella, Proteus,* and *Enterobacter* account for most of the remainder.

Asymptomatic bacteriuria

A covert asymptomatic urinary infection is present in 5% of pregnant women, 30% of whom will develop a symptomatic infection if not treated. Urinary infection increases the risk of pregnancy complications, including premature labor, fetal growth retardation and preeclampsia. Most obstetricians advocate routine screening at antenatal booking, with additional screening (monthly) in women with a history of urinary infections and/or renal disorders – a policy that would predict 70% of those destined to have symptomatic infections. Treatment should be governed by organism sensitivity and continued for at least 7-10 days for initial infections and 21 days for recurrences. Regardless of the antimicrobial agent used or duration of treatment, 30% of women will relapse. Some authorities advocate prophylactic therapy following re-infections.

There is no evidence that asymptomatic infections cause permanent renal damage in adults with normal urinary tracts. Radiologic abnormalities of the urinary tract are present in 20% of pregnant women with asymptomatic bacteriuria, although the association in some is incidental.

Cystitis

Acute cystitis occurs in 2% of pregnancies, often in women who initially had negative screening in early pregnancy. It probably has a pathogenesis different from asymptomatic bacteriuria or acute pyelonephritis postdelivery. Infection may be related to bladder catheterization, a procedure commonly employed during labor, and with Caesarean section. Treatment of cystitis reduces the risk of ascending infections.

Acute pyelonephritis

Ureteric dilatation may increase susceptibility to gestational pyelonephritis, which despite routine screening still complicates 1% of pregnancies (3% in unscreened populations). High fever (often fluctuating), vomiting, rigors, and severe loin pain are common findings, but may be absent in the early stages. Diagnosis should be supported by urine microscopy and culture. Severe infections can have serious sequelae, including septic shock, adult respiratory distress syndrome, and perinephric abscess formation.

The differential diagnosis in pregnancy is similar to that in nonpregnant subjects, but, in addition, loin pain may be referred from the lumbosacral vertebrae or sacroiliac joints (due to increased lumbar lordosis and softening of pelvic ligaments) or as a result of acute hydrourertero-/hydronephrosis, which might require ureteric catheterization (stenting). Abdominal pain may also be due to placental abruption, degenerating fibroids, chorioamnionitis, or acute appendicitis, the latter having an atypical presentation in late pregnancy when the uterus is maximally enlarged.

Management needs to be aggressive and undertaken in a hospital. Fluid and electrolyte balance should be monitored and intravenous fluids given to correct hypovolemia. Fetal tachycardia is common, making fetal heart monitoring difficult to interpret. There is a risk of premature labor, and the use of beta sympathomimetics may exacerbate endotoxin-induced cardiovascular effects and increase the risk of respiratory complications. Initially, a penicillin or cephalosporin should be administered intravenously pending conformation of organism sensitivity. Oral therapy should be continued for 2 weeks. Failure to respond to treatment may indicate an underlying pelvic-ureteric or ureteric obstruction or the presence of calculi; it warrants further investigation.

When gram-negative sepsis is suspected, blood cultures should be taken and an aminoglycoside (gentamicin or tobramycin) added to the regimen, although the new penicillins (e.g., piperacillin) appear to be equally effective with less risk to the fetus. Blood levels of an aminoglycoside should be monitored, since its clearance is altered in pregnancy.

UROLITHIASIS (RENAL TRACT CALCULI)

Although factors associated with renal stone formation are known to increase in pregnancy – namely, urinary stasis, ascending infections, and excretion of stone-forming salts (e.g., calcium, urate and cystine) – the incidence of renal calculi is low (1 in 2000 pregnancies). Furthermore, pregnancy does not appear to increase symptomatic calculi in known "stone formers." Enhanced excretion of inhibitors of calcium stone formation such as magnesium, citrate, and nephrocalcin as well as increased alkalinity of the urine may afford some protection.

The presentation of renal calculi is similar to that in nonpregnant subjects. Most ureteric colic occurs in the second or third trimester when ureteric dilatation is greatest and perhaps previously asymptomatic stones pass into the ureter, only to become stuck at the pelvic brim. The mainstay of diagnosis of calculi is ultrasound. Interpretation of findings and visualization of the ureter can be difficult, but may be enhanced with color flow Doppler scanning. Renal function should be assessed and infection excluded, but any in-depth analysis of urine and plasma biochemistry to determine the cause of stone formation should be delayed until 4 months postdelivery when non-pregnant "norms" can be applied. Conservative management usually is successful, or delivery can be effected before undertaking surgical or minimally invasive intervention. Any definitive surgery should be delayed until at least 4 months post-delivery. Lithotripsy is not advisable in pregnancy. Drugs used to treat "stone formers" (thiazides, xanthine oxidase inhibitors, D-penicillamine) are best avoided.

PREGNANCY IN WOMEN WITH CHRONIC RENAL DISEASE

Fertility and the ability to sustain an uncomplicated pregnancy generally relate to the degree of functional impairment and the presence or absence of hypertension rather than to the nature of the underlying disorder. Women can be arbitrarily considered in three categories: those with (1) preserved or only mildly impaired renal function [serum creatinine ≤125 μmol/l (1.4 mg/dl)] and no hypertension; (2) moderate renal insufficiency [serum creatinine ≤125-250 μmol/l (1.4-2.8 mg/dl) (some use 220 μmol/l or 2.5 mg/dl as the cut-off)]; and (3) severe renal insufficiency (serum creatinine ≥250 μmol/l or 2.8 mg/dl) (Tab. 49.1).

Women in the first category usually have successful obstetric outcomes, and pregnancy does not appear to affect the underlying disease adversely; perinatal mortality in this group is now less than 3%, and evidence of irreversible renal functional loss in the mother is even lower. This generalization, however, may not hold true for certain kidney diseases (Tab. 49.2). For instance, patients with scleroderma and periarteritis nodosa, disorders often associated with hypertension, do poorly, and conception in such women is best discouraged. Women with lupus nephritis do not do as well as patients with glomerulopathies, especially if the disease has flared within 6 months of conception, and some believe that pregnancy adversely affects the natural history of IgA nephritis, focal glomerular sclerosis, membranoproliferative nephritis, and reflux nephropathy, a view for which there is little supporting evidence.

Table 49.1 Severity of renal disease and prospects for pregnancy

Prospects	Category		
	Mild (%)	Moderate (%)	Severe (%)
Pregnancy complications	26	47	86
Successful obstetric outcome	96 (85)	*90 (59)	*25 (71)
Long-term sequelae	<3 (9)	25 (80)	53 (92)

Estimates are based on 2370 women/3495 pregnancies (1973-1995) and do not include collagen diseases. Numbers in parentheses refer to prospects when complication(s) develop before 28 weeks' gestation.

*In recent years obstetric outcome has improved enormously. The infant survival rate was over 90% in 82 pregnancies in 67 women with moderate and severe disease from 6 tertiary referral centers, presumably reflecting the specialist obstetric and neonatal care at those centers. Maternal complications were still inevitable (70%) and pregnancy-related loss of renal function occurred in almost 50%, of whom 10% progressed rapidly to end-stage failure. In another study of 43 pregnancies in 30 women spanning 20 years, obstetric success was achieved in 82% (84% in 1985-1994 and 55% in 1975-84) but acceleration toward end-stage failure was evident in 7 women (23%), all of whom had severe hypertension and heavy proteinuria pre-pregnancy.

The various problems specifically associated with particular diseases are summarized in Table 49.2. The following guidelines apply to all clinical situations.

Renal function

If renal function deteriorates significantly at any stage of pregnancy, then reversible causes, such as urinary tract infection, subtle dehydration, or electrolyte imbalance (occasionally precipitated by inadvertent diuretic therapy) should be sought. Near term, as in normal pregnancy, a decrease in function of 15 to 20%, which affects serum creatinine minimally, is permissible. Failure to detect a reversible cause of a significant decrement is grounds to end the pregnancy by elective delivery. When proteinuria occurs and persists, but blood pressure is normal and renal function preserved, pregnancy can be allowed to continue.

Blood pressure

Most of the specific risks of hypertension in pregnancy appear to be related to superimposed preeclampsia. The true incidence of superimposed preeclampsia in women with preexisting renal disease is uncertain because the diagnosis cannot be made with certainty on clinical grounds alone; hypertension and proteinuria may be manifestations of the underlying renal disease. Treatment of mild hypertension (diastolic blood pressure ≥ 95 mmHg in the second trimester or ≥ 100 mmHg in the third) is not necessary during normal pregnancy, but many would treat women with underlying renal disease more aggressively, believing that this preserves kidney function.

Fetal surveillance and timing of delivery

Serial assessment of fetal well-being is essential because renal disease can be associated with intrauterine growth retardation, and, when complications do arise, the judicious moment for intervention can be assessed by changes in fetal status. Current technology should minimize the incidence of intrauterine fetal death as well as neonatal morbidity and mortality. Regardless of gestational age, most babies weighing 1500 g or more survive better in a special care nursery than in a hostile intrauterine environment. Planned preterm delivery may be necessary if there are signs of impending intrauterine fetal death, if renal function deteriorates substantially, if uncontrollable hypertension supervenes, or if eclampsia occurs.

OBSTETRIC ACUTE RENAL FAILURE

Obstetric complications used to be a common cause of acute renal failure (ARF), but these are now rare, except in third-world countries. Improved obstetric management, particularly of preeclampsia and acute hemorrhage, as well as liberalization of abortion laws, preventing the need for illegal procedures that can lead to sepsis, have dramatically reduced the incidence of acute renal failure. Most cases are now related to preeclampsia (PE) and its complications, although any cause of acute renal failure may arise in pregnancy (Tab. 49.3).

Table 49.2 Specific kidney diseases and pregnancy

Renal disease	Effects and outcomes
Chronic glomerulonephritis	Usually no adverse effect in the absence of hypertension. One view is that glomerulonephritis is adversely affected by the coagulation changes of pregnancy. Urinary tract infections may occur more frequently
IgA nephropathy	Risks of uncontrolled and/or sudden escalating hypertension and worsening of renal function
Pyelonephritis	Bacteriuria in pregnancy can lead to exacerbation. Multiple organ system derangements may ensue including adult respiratory distress syndrome
Reflux nephropathy	Risks of sudden escalating hypertension and worsening of renal function
Urolithiasis	Infections can be more frequent, but ureteral dilatation and stasis do not seem to affect natural history. Limited data on lithotripsy; thus it is best avoided
Polycystic disease	Functional impairment and hypertension usually minimal in childbearing years
Diabetic nephropathy	Usually no adverse effect on the renal lesion, but there is increased frequency of infection, edema, and/or preeclampsia
Systemic lupus erythematosus (SLE)	Controversial; prognosis most favorable if disease in remission >6 months prior to conception. Steroid dosage should be increased postpartum
Periarteritis nodosa	Fetal prognosis is dismal, and maternal death often occurs
Scleroderma (SS)	If onset during pregnancy then can be rapid overall deterioration. Reactivation of quiescent scleroderma may occur postpartum
Previous urinary tract surgery	Might be associated with other malformations of the urogenital tract. Urinary tract infection common during pregnancy. Renal function may undergo reversible decrease. No significant obstructive problem but Caesarean section often needed for abnormal presentation and/or to avoid disruption of the continence mechanism if artificial sphincter present
After nephrectomy, solitary kidney and pelvic kidney	Might be associated with other malformations of urogenital tract. Pregnancy well tolerated. Dystocia rarely occurs with pelvic kidney
Wegener's granulomatosis	Limited information. Proteinuria (± hypertension) is common from early in pregnancy. Immunosuppressives are safe, but cytotoxic drugs are best avoided
Renal artery stenosis	May present as chronic hypertension or as recurrent isolated preeclampsia. If diagnosed then, transluminal angioplasty can be undertaken in pregnancy if appropriate

Acute tubular necrosis usually is the underlying lesion, but a higher proportion are due to renal cortical necrosis than in nonpregnant subjects. Nevertheless, when acute renal failure is associated with pregnancy-specific conditions such as preeclampsia and the Hemolysis, Elevated Liver enzymes, and Low Platelets (HELLP) syndrome, spontaneous recovery can be surprisingly rapid following delivery. Occasionally there is no hemolysis and the syndrome is termed ELLP.

Invariably pregnancy has advanced far enough for the fetus to be viable, and coordination with the neonatal team allows optimal timing of delivery. In the obstetric setting, however, the current pregnancy may represent the best chance of perinatal success so, with the exclusion of preeclampsia, many would advocate early and frequent dialysis to prolong the pregnancy.

Preeclampsia

This condition is characterized by generalized vasoconstriction, often associated with minor renal dysfunction. Acute renal failure is rare unless there are other complications such as HELLP syndrome and/or placental abruption.

Uterine sepsis and pyelonephritis

Serious postabortion and postpartum sepsis is now rare. Improved supportive therapy and evacuation of retained products of conception usually prevent serious sequelae. Clostridial infection can rapidly supervene, resulting in acute renal failure, hemolysis, coagulopathy, and hypocalcemia, although death usually is due to overwhelming sepsis rather than renal failure. Surgical removal of the uterus is a management option, but some prefer conservative management, stating that complications make surgery too risky.

Acute pyelonephritis is rarely associated with renal dysfunction or acute renal failure in non-pregnant women. In pregnancy, however, transient functional deterioration is common and the risk of acute renal failure appears to be greater, perhaps because of increased sensitivity of renal vasculature to bacterial endotoxins.

Acute fatty liver of pregnancy (AFLP)

Occurring in late pregnancy or early puerperium, this condition is associated with severe hepatic dysfunction and coagulopathy. Renal dysfunction may be mild, although acute renal failure is not uncommon. Despite its rarity, awareness of acute renal failure is essential because its initial presentation may be subtle (nausea, vomiting, mild jaundice) or it may be complicated by other conditions such as preeclampsia, in which case there may be rapid progress to severe maternal and fetal compromise. Mortality rates for both mother and baby have been quoted as greater than 70%, although, nowadays, earlier recognition has led to earlier intervention that has reduced mortality rates to less than 20%. As well as excluding other causes of hepatic dysfunction, delivery must be effected immediately, followed by maximal supportive care.

Idiopathic postpartum renal failure

Idiopathic postpartum renal failure is rare but is a recognized cause of acute renal failure in the first few weeks following delivery. Its etiology is obscure, but there are histologic similarities with hemolytic uremic syndrome (HUS) and malignant nephrosclerosis. Outcome is poor, and few women make a complete recovery.

PREGNANCY IN WOMEN ON LONG-TERM DIALYSIS

Reduced libido and relative infertility are common in women on hemodialysis and peritoneal dialysis, but they can still conceive and must therefore use contraception if they wish to avoid pregnancy. Although conception is not common (an incidence of 1 in 150 patients has been quoted), its true frequency is unknown because most pregnancies in dialyzed patients probably end in early spontaneous abortion and there is a high therapeutic abortion rate in this group of patients.

Table 49.3 Obstetric acute renal failure

Volume contraction/hypotension	Antepartum hemorrhage due to placenta previa. Postpartum hemorrhage from uterus or extensive soft tissue trauma. Abortion. Hyperemesis gravidarum. Adrenocortical failure/usually failure to augment steroids on long-term therapy
Volume contraction/hypotension and coagulopathy	Antepartum hemorrhage due to abruptio placentae. Preeclampsia/eclampsia. Amniotic fluid embolism. Incompatible blood transfusion. Drug reaction(s). Acute fatty liver of pregnancy. Hemolytic uremic syndrome
Volume contraction/hypotension, coagulopathy and infection	Septic abortion. Chorioamnionitis. Pyelonephritis. Puerperal sepsis
Urinary tract obstruction	Polyhydramnios. Damage to ureters during Cesarean section or repair of cervical/vaginal lacerations. Pelvic hematoma. Broad ligament hematoma. Calculus or clot in ureter(s) primarily in a single kidney

Some women do achieve delivery of a viable infant, but most authorities do not advise attempts at pregnancy or its continuation if present when the woman has severe renal insufficiency. These women are prone to volume overload, severe exacerbations of their hypertension, and/or superimposed preeclampsia and polyhydramnios. They also have high fetal wastage at all stages of pregnancy. Even when therapeutic terminations are excluded, the live birth outcome at the very best is 40 to 50%. Fetal growth retardation and prematurity are common. As the debate continues, more and more women are choosing to take the chance.

Women frequently present in advanced pregnancy because pregnancy was not suspected. Irregular menstruation is common in dialysis patients, and missed periods usually are ignored. Urine pregnancy tests are unreliable (even if there is any urine available). Ultrasound is needed to confirm and to date the pregnancy.

There appear to be no specific advantages to any particular dialysis modality, but, whatever the route, the dialysis strategy involves a 50% increase in hours and frequency and several aims:

- maintain serum urea ≤ 20 mmol/l (120 mg/dl); some would argue ≤ 15 mmol/l (90 mg/dl), because intrauterine death is more likely if levels are much in excess of 20 mmol/l. Success occasionally has been achieved despite levels of 25 mmol/l (150 mg/dl) for many weeks;
- avoid hypotension during dialysis, which could be damaging to the fetus. In late pregnancy the uterus and the supine posture may aggravate this by decreasing venous return;
- ensure rigid control of blood pressure;
- avoid rapid fluctuations in intravascular volume, by limiting interdialysis weight gain to about 1 kg until late pregnancy;
- scrutinize carefully for preterm labour, because dialysis and uterine contractions are associated;
- watch calcium levels closely to avoid hypercalcemia.

Dialysis patients usually are anemic, and this invariably is aggravated in pregnancy. Blood transfusion may be needed, especially before delivery. Caution is necessary because transfusion may exacerbate hypertension and impair the ability to control circulatory overload, even with extra dialysis. Low-dose synthetic erythropoietin (rHuEpo) can be used to treat anemia in pregnancy without ill-effect, and the need to increase the dose in an otherwise stable patient may be an indication that she is pregnant.

PREGNANCY IN WOMEN WITH RENAL ALLOGRAFTS

Post-transplantation, renal, endocrine and sexual functions return rapidly. About 1 in 50 women of childbearing age with a functioning transplant becomes pregnant. Of the conceptions, 30% do not go beyond the first trimester because of spontaneous or therapeutic abortion. However, well over 90% of pregnancies that do continue past the first trimester end successfully (Tab. 49.4).

A woman should be counselled about the various treatments for renal failure and the potential for optimal rehabilitation. Couples who want a child should be encouraged to discuss all the implications, including the harsh realities of maternal survival prospects (Tab. 49.4). In most, a wait of 18 months to 2 years post-transplant is advised. By then, the patient will have recovered from surgery, graft function will have stabilized and immunosuppression will be at maintenance levels. Also, if function is well maintained at 2 years, there is a high probability of allograft survival at 5 years. A set of guidelines is given here, but the criteria are only relative:

- good general health for about 2 years post-transplant;
- status compatible with good obstetric outcome;
- no or minimal proteinuria;
- no hypertension. Due to the high incidence of hypertension in women on cyclosporine "well-controlled hypertension" may be more appropriate than "no hypertension";
- no evidence of graft rejection;
- no pelvicalyceal distention on a recent ultrasound assessment;
- stable renal function with serum creatinine ≤ 180 μmol/l (2 mg/dl) (preferably ≤ 125 μmol/l [1.4 mg/dl]);
- drug therapy reduced to maintenance levels: prednisone 15 mg per day or less, azathioprine 2 mg/kg per day or less, and cyclosporine 5 mg/kg per day or less.

In most women, renal function is augmented during pregnancy, but permanent impairment occurs in 15% of pregnancies. In others there may be transient deterioration in late pregnancy (with or without proteinuria). There is a 30% chance of developing hypertension, preeclampsia, or both. Preterm delivery occurs in 46 to 60%, and intrauterine growth retardation in 20 to 40% of pregnancies. Despite its pelvic location, the transplanted kidney rarely produces dystocia and is not injured during vaginal delivery. Caesarean section should be reserved for obstetric reasons only. Neonatal complications include respiratory distress syndrome, leukopenia, thrombocytopenia, adrenocortical insufficiency, and infection. More information is needed about the intrauterine effects and neonatal aftermath of immunosuppression, which, at maintenance levels, appears to be harmless. From the limited data available it seems that pregnancy does not necessarily compromise long-term renal outlook, but it must be remembered

Table 49.4 Pregnancy implications for renal allograft recipients

Problems in pregnancy	Successful obstetric outcome	Long-term problems
49%	95% (75%)	12% (25%)

Estimates based on 4220 women in 5370 pregnancies which attained at least 28 weeks' gestation (1961-1998). Figures in brackets refer to implications when complication(s) developed prior to 28 weeks' gestation.

that these patients have a malignancy rate many times greater than normal, and the female genital tract is no exception.

Suggested readings

ARMENTI VT, MORITZ MJ, DAVISON JM. Medical management of the pregnant transplant recipient. Adv Renal Rep Therapy 1998;5:14-23.

BAYLIS C, DAVISON JM. The normal renal physiological changes which occur during pregnancy. In: Davison JM, Cameron JS, Grunfeld J-P, Kerr DNS, Ritz E, eds. Oxford Textbook of clinical nephrology. 2nd ed. Oxford: Oxford University Press, 1998;2297-15.

CUNNINGHAM FG, LUCAS MJ. Urinary tract infections complicating pregnancy. Clinics in Obstetrics and Gynaecology (Baillière) 1994;8:353-73.

DANTAL J, HORUMANT M, CANTAROVICH D, et al. Effect of long-term immunosuppression in kidney graft recipients on cancer incidence: randomised comparison of two cyclosporin regimens. Lancet 1998;351:623-8.

DAVISON JM, LIND T, ULDALL PR. Planned pregnancy in renal transplant recipient. Br J Obstet Gynecol 1976;83:518-27.

DAVISON JM, BAYLIS C. Pregnancy in patients with underlying renal disease. In: Davison JM, Cameron JC, Grunfeld J-P, Kerr DNS, Ritz E, Winearls CG, eds. Oxford Textbook of nephrology. 2nd ed. Oxford: Oxford University Press, 1998;2327.

JONES DC, HAYSLETT JP. Outcome of pregnancy in women with moderate or severe renal insufficiency. N Engl J Med 1997;335:226-2.

JUNGERS P, CHAUVEAU D. Pregnancy in renal disease. Kidney Int 1997;52:871-85

OKUNDAYE IB, ABRINKO P, HOU SH. Registry of pregnancy in dialysis patients. Am J Kidney Dis 1998;31:766-73.

PETUISET N, GRÜNFELD JP. Acute renal failure in pregnancy. Clinics in Obstetrics and Gynaecology (Baillière) 1994;8:333-51.

STURGISS SN, DAVISON JM. Effect of pregnancy on long-term function of renal allografts. Am J Kidney Dis 1995;26:54-6.

CHAPTER

50

Renal disorders in neonates and the young child

KEY POINTS

- The clinical practice of neonatal nephrology differs in several aspects from renal medicine in other ages of childhood owing to the interactions among inherited, congenital and acquired pathologic mechanisms with the physiology of the developing kidney.
- Most renal functions require a maturation during the first year of life, and the consideration of this evolutionary process has important therapeutic and diagnostic implications.
- Hematuria can derive from tumors, malformative uropathies, cystic, vascular and interstitial diseases, or from microlithiasis. Proteinuria is more infrequent and can be an expression of a rare glomerular diseases with neonatal onset, such as the congenital nephrotic syndrome, or of glomerular or tubulointerstitial diseases sustained by metabolic abnormalities or of hereditary nephropaties.
- The neonate, because of still immature renal adaptation mechanisms, is particularly susceptible to renal failure, particularly when renal hypoperfusion, even temporary, occurs. Vascular interstitial and toxic causes, together with obstructive uropathies also may account for a large number of cases of acute renal failure.

PHYSIOLOGY OF RENAL FUNCTION

Rosanna Coppo

Neonatal nephrology differs from renal medicine in other ages of childhood because of the effects of inherited, congenital, and acquired pathogenetic mechanisms that affect the developing kidney. At 34 weeks' gestation the full complement of nephrons is attained; however, fully expressed glomerular and tubular function is reached only at the end of the first year of life.

The first micturition generally occurs during the first 24 hours of life (Tab. 50.1). If no diuresis occurs by the seventy-second hour of life, severe nephrourologic disease should be considered. Oliguria is defined as urine <1 ml/kg/hour.

The glomerular filtration rate (GFR) is extremely low at birth, particularly in premature infants. Adult values (corrected for body surface area) are reached between the first and the second years of life (Tab. 50.2).

Plasma creatinine at birth is equal to that of the mother (1-1.2 mg/dl), falling to 0.4-0.5 mg/dl within the first 5 to 7 days after delivery. Creatinine can be used in the neonate to estimate GFR by using the following formula:

for prematures: $GFR = (0.4 \times \text{length in cm}) / \text{plasma creatinine}$;

for full-term: $GFR = (0.45 \times \text{length in cm}) / \text{plasma creatinine}$.

The concentrating capacity, particularly in premature children, is low, owing to a reduced ADH response. The full concentrating capacity of 1200 mOsm/l is attained after the second year of life.

In neonates the renin-aldosterone system is very active: plasma renin activity in neonates has values of 10-12 ng/ml/h and reaches adult levels at 6 years of age. In premature newborns there is instead a major risk of hyponatremia, owing to a limited tubular aldosteron response, to an immature reabsorbing system, and to a decreased Na^+-ATPase activity.

Neonates have a physiologic metabolic acidosis, expecially when preterm, because of a reduced urine acidification capacity. The net acid excretion reaches adult values within 2 months (Tab. 50.3).

Neonates and preterm infants have a physiologic hypercalciuria (calciuria/creatininuria ratio = 0.4 – 0.6 in preterm, 0.3 until 6 months of life, 0.2 in adult) due to lower tubular calcium reabsorption and a high-calcium diet. Therapy with loop diuretics, vitamin D supplements, and the total parenteral nutrition often required in premature infants enhances the risk of renal calcification.

Table 50.1 Urine flow in children from birth to adulthood

Age	Diuresis volume (ml)
Day 1-2	30-60
Day 3-10	100-300
Day 10-2 months	250-450
2 months - 1 year	400-500
1-3 years	500-600
3-5 years	600-700
5-8 years	650-1000
8-14 years	800-1400

Table 50.2 GRF in children

Age	GFR ml/min/1.73 m²
<34 weeks gestational age	8
34-40 weeks gestational age	13-15
Full term	20-45
2 weeks	40-60
8 weeks	60-80
1 year	120

Table 50.3 Plasma bicarbonate levels in children

Age	HCO_3^- mEq/l
Premature	14-16
Full term	20
2 weeks	21.5
1 year	24

Clinical findings

Finding oligohydramnios suggests a severe renal malformation, such as agenesia, hypodysplasia, or urinary tract obstruction – mostly urethral valves. The lack of amniotic fluid leads to the "fetal compression" (Potter's) syndrome with altered facies, pulmonary hypoplasia, and growth deficiency. The less frequent polyhydramnios suggests nephrogenic diabetes insipidus or congenital Bartter's syndrome. Hypertrophied placenta is typical in congenital nephrotic syndrome (see below).

Macroscopic hematuria

Gross hematuria can be caused by various renal malformations or cystic disorders or by acquired vascular disorders (Tab. 50.4).

Proteinuria

During the first 5 days of life a transient proteinuria of 0.5 g/l can be observed; then it does not exceed 0.15 mg/kg/h (50 mg/l). Table 50.5 lists the renal disorders most often associated with proteinuria in the neonate.

Acute renal failure

Acute renal failure in the newborn infant can be secondary to acute circulatory insufficiency, to severe renal parenchymal damage, or to urinary tract obstructions (Tab. 50.6). Oliguria < 1 ml/kg/h usually is present; however,

Table 50.4 Causes of hematuria in neonates

Tumors
Renal tumors (nephroblastoma, mesoblastic nephroma, fetal hamartomas)
Vesical tumors (rhabdomyosarcoma)

Malformative uropathies
Obstructive: uretropelvic junction stenosis, posterior urethral valves, ureterocele
Dysplasia: hypodysplasia, cystic dysplasia

Cystic diseases
Polycystic kidney disease (infant or adult type)
Multicystic kidney

Vascular diseases
Renal vein thrombosis
Acute tubular necrosis (on a vasomotor base)
Corticomedullary necrosis
Microemboli
Hemolytic uremic syndrome

Interstitial nephropathies
Acute pyelonephritis
Urinary tract infection
Sepsis
Drugs (penicillins syndrome, aminoglucosides, anticonvulsivants, diuretics)

Urolithiasis
Microscopic lithiasis (hypercalciuria, hyperoxaluria)

the urine volume can be maintained. Plasma urea increases >50 mg/dl, with a daily increase >10 mg/dl. Plasma creatinine >1 mg/dl defines acute renal failure in the newborn. Its daily increase is about 0.2 mg/dl. The physiologic variations of plasma creatinine during the first weeks of life should be taken into account (see above).

NEPHROTIC SYDROME IN THE FIRST YEAR OF LIFE

Licia Peruzzi, Gabriella Porcellini

The nephrotic syndrome with onset before the third month of life is defined "congenital nephrotic syndrome" and includes renal diseases characterized by peculiar genetic, clinical, and pathologic aspects that differ from infantile idiopatic nephrotic syndrome.

Congenital nephrotic syndrome of Finnish type

Epidemiology

In Finland this autosomal recessive disease has an incidence of 1 per 8000 births, much more frequent than seen in other ethnic groups.

Physiopathology

At first there are no specific lesions, with mild mesangial changes. Irregular microcystic dilatation of proximal tubules, considered specific for congenital nephrotic syndrome of Finnish type, are detected after the third month; then interstitial fibrosis, cell infiltration, tubular atrophy, and periglomerular fibrosis develop in parallel with glomerular sclerosis.

Etiopathogenesis

An inherited error in the structure of the glomerular capillary filter has been proposed that involves loss of charge selectivity of the basement membrane. However, neither modifications in the laminin, type IV collagen, fibronectin content, or vascular endothelial growth factor activity have been proved. The gene involved in congenital nephrotic syndrome of Finnish type has been localized to the long arm of chromosome 19 (q13.1), in linkage disequilibrium with other markers, allowing the identification in the Finnish population of 8 aplotypes. The prenatal diagnosis can now be carried out on chorionic villi samples, even in families having no affected offspring, whereas the previously used a-fetoprotein detection is far less specific.

Clinical findings

The placenta is enlarged, being more than 20-30% of the total birth weight, favoring facial and limb deformities. Edema is often present at birth. Within the third month of life severe nephrotic syndrome develops, bringing poor nutritional status, with failure to thrive, high susceptibility to infections, and thromboembolic complications. End-stage renal failure invariably occurs at 3-8 years of age. Owing to the absolute resistance to steroids and immunosuppressive drugs and the difficulty of renal transplantation at this age, there is a high mortality rate in the first year of life, and achieving a prolonged sur-

Table 50.5 Renal disorders presenting with proteinuria in the neonate

Physiologic proteinuria

Vascular diseases
- Renal vein thrombosis
- Corticomedullary necrosis

Glomerular diseases
- Neonatal nephrotic syndrome (hereditary Finnish type, secondary to infections)
- Nail patella syndrome
- Hereditary metabolic diseases (sialidosis, glycogenosis)

Tubulointerstitial diseases
- Hereditary interstitial nephropathies
- Fanconi's syndrome (Loewe's syndrome, cystinosis, galactosemia)

Table 50.6 Etiology of acute renal failure in the neonate

Prerenal factors: renal hypoperfusion	
Hypotension	
Hypovolemia	
Hypoxia/asphyxia	
Cardiac failure	
Renal factors	
Arterial	Thromboembolism Hemolytic uremic syndrome
Venous	Renal vein thrombosis
Parenchymal	Hypoplasia/dysplasia Agenesis Bilateral cystic dysplasia Polycystic kidney disease of neonatal type
Tubular	Acute tubular necrosis ischemic or toxic tubular obstruction: myglobinuria, hemoglobinuria, urates or phosphates precipitation
Interstitial	Acute interstitial nephritis Pyelonephritis
Postrenal factors: obstructive nephropathy	
Urologic malformations	Posterior urethral valves, other urethral obstructions, bilateral ureteral obstruction

vival is made possible only by adopting strict supportive therapy. This includes continuous albumin infusion to maintain levels at >1.5 g/dl, limiting protein malnutrition and edema, and hypercaloric (110 kcal/kg/bw), slightly hyperproteic diet (2-3 g/kg/bw), gamma globulin replacement, vitamins and thyroxine substitution, and prevention of infections and thrombotic complications. Some patients may require bilateral nephrectomy before the development of renal failure to prevent continued massive protein losses. The disease does not recur after renal transplantation.

Diffuse mesangial sclerosis

The second main cause of congenital nephrotic syndrome is diffuse mesangial sclerosis, distinguished from congenital nephrotic syndrome of Finnish type by the rapid evolution to end-stage renal failure and by a characteristic histologic appearance. Diffuse mesangial sclerosis is seen exclusively in infants and displays an autosomal recessive inheritance, but the responsible gene is still unidentified.

Physiopathology

Glomerular basement membrane thickening and massive enlargement of mesangial areas, leading to reduction of the capillary lumina are present. Hypertrophic mesangial cells are surrounded by abundant mesangial matrix. Tubular damage often is severe.

Etiopathogenesis

The pathogenesis of the isolated form of diffuse mesangial sclerosis is unknown. A primary defect of the epithelial cells or of the glomerular extracellular matrix has been hypothesized.

Clinical findings

Affected children appear normal at birth with no placental enlargement. Proteinuria develops after birth, increasing during the first or the second year of life. The mortality due to nephrotic syndrome complications is rare, while the decline in renal function is rapid – within a few months after diagnosis – in the first years of life.

Treatment

Diffuse mesangial sclerosis is resistant to corticosteroids and immunosuppressive drugs. Proteinuria is less severe than in congenital nephrotic syndrome of Finnish type, and supplemental therapy is not required.

Diffuse mesangial sclerosis with Drash syndrome

Epidemiology and pathophysiology

The Drash Syndrome is usually sporadic. Constitutional mutations in the Wilms' tumor predisposing gene, WT1 (11p13), which determines the loss of tumor suppressor genes have been described.

Clinical findings

Diffuse mesangial sclerosis is a constant feature of Drash syndrome, and the clinical course is analogous. The first clinical symptoms may be due to Wilms' tumor. Male pseudohermaphroditism, characterized by ambiguous genitalia or female phenotype with dysgenetic testis is observed in 46 XY patients, while 46 XX children have a normal female phenotype.

Idiopathic nephrotic syndrome

Idiopathic nephrotic syndrome is rarely diagnosed at birth, but the diagnosis is not so infrequent during the first year of life. The morphologic lesions include minimal change, diffuse mesangial proliferation, and focal and segmental glomerular sclerosis. Some patients are steroid-responsive with a favorable course, even though most cases, often familial, are resistant to therapy and progress to end-stage renal disease.

Others

Congenital or infantile nephrotic syndrome has been reported in association with congenital syphylis, toxoplasmosis, and severe viral infections, including cytomegalovirus, rubeola, and human immunodeficiency virus.

PRIMARY HYPEROXALURIA AND OXALOSIS

Alessandro Amore, Giovanni Conti

The systemic deposition of calcium oxalate, or oxalosis, is the advanced phase of a rare autosomal recessive metabolic disorder, primary hyperoxaluria, characterized by an increased synthesis of oxalate from glyoxalate possibly due to two enzyme defects. The most frequent, characteristic of primary hyperoxaluria type 1 (PH1), is caused by mutations of the hepatic peroxysomal enzyme alanine:glyoxalate aminotransferase (alanine: glyoxalate aminotransferase), catalyzing the synthesis of alanine from glyoxalate, using pyridoxalphosphate (derived from vitamin B_6) as cofactor. The other, far less frequent, is characteristic of primary hyperoxaluria type 2 (PH2), and is due to the lack of the cytosolic enzyme glyoxalate reductase/D-glycerate dehydrogenase, localized both in liver and leukocytes. Subjects presenting with this defect have increased amounts of L-glyceric acid as well as oxalate (Fig. 50.1).

Epidemiology

Primary hyperoxaluria type 1 accounts for more than 90% of the cases, particularly in the pediatric age group. This disease is responsible for 1-2% of end-stage renal failure in children, with an incidence of 0.5-1.5 new cases/millions children/year.

Etiopathogenesis

A complex phenotype has been identified:

- absence of both immunoreactive alanine: glyoxalate aminotransferase protein and alanine: glyoxalate aminotransferase catalytic activity;
- presence of immunoreactive alanine: glyoxalate aminotransferase protein without alanine: glyoxalate aminotransferase catalytic activity;
- presence of both immunoreactive alanine: glyoxalate aminotransferase protein and alanine: glyoxalate aminotransferase catalytic activity. In this last case the enzyme is present and potentially active, but is mislocalized in mitochondria instead of peroxisomes, where is scarcely active because glyoxalate cannot be translocated across the mithocondrial membrane.

Genetics The alanine: glyoxalate aminotransferase gene maps to chromosome 2q36-37. Two alleles, major and minor, which differ by only a few amino acids have been identified. Most of the mutations are on the minor allele. One of the most frequent mutations is G630A, which is responsible for mistargeting to the mitochondria of the enzyme.

The increased amount of oxalate produced by these enzyme defects is cleared by the kidney, causing hyperoxaluria, with crystal aggregates in the urinary tract or parenchymal deposition. Oxalate plasma levels are kept within the normal range until glomerular filtration values are around 40 ml/min. Below this threshold a rapid increase occurs with progressive tissue deposition of oxalate, particularly in bone and kidney.

Clinical findings

Fifty percent of the cases of primary hyperoxaluria type 1 display clinical symptoms, mainly urinary, before 5 years of age, and 15% in the first year of life. The infantile form of chronic renal failure occurs after massive renal oxalosis. Older children present with symptoms of urolithiasis of calcium oxalate stones, which are bilateral and radiopaque on X-ray.

Systemic oxalosis is rapidly progressive when the glomerular filtration rate is <25 ml/min/1.73 m^2, when the combination of oxalate overproduction and reduced urinary oxalate excretion results in systemic deposition in heart, blood vessels, joints, bone, and retina.

Symptoms include cardiac conduction defects and even arrest, vessel occlusion, and distal gangrene.

Bone disease is extremely severe in children in chronic renal failure, with precipitation in the metaphyses of long and trabecular bones, eventually leading to pathologic fractures.

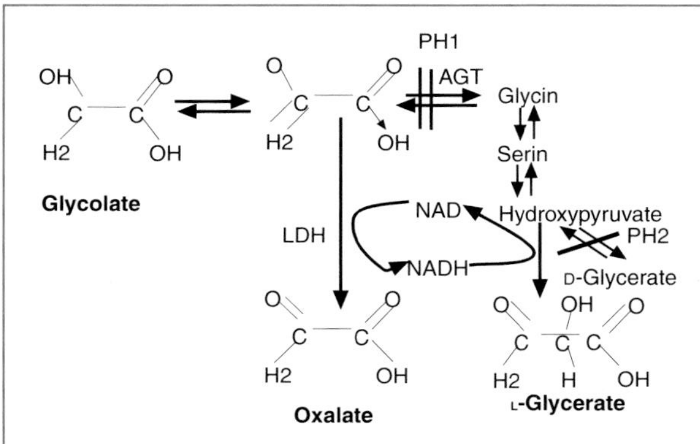

Figure 50.1 Metabolic pathways of oxalate.

Diagnostic procedures

Diagnosis is mainly clinical, and primary hyperoxaluria should be suspected in children with recurrent bilateral calcium stones and marked hyperoxaluria in the absence of gastrointestinal disease or the ingestion of megadoses of vitamin C.

Normal urinary oxalate excretion per 1.73 m^2 is less than 45 mg/day or 0.5 mmol/day; values as high as 135 to 270 mg/day (1.5 to 3 mmol/day) can occur in primary hyperoxaluria type 1. Primary hyperoxaluria type 2 is associated with increased urinary L-glycerate excretion.

The presence of alanine: glyoxalate aminotransferase deficiency should be confirmed by liver biopsy with quantification of the enzymatic activity and immunoelectronic detection of the site of alanine: glyoxalate aminotransferase. Alanine: glyoxalate aminotransferase activity is less than 2% of normal in one-third of cases.

Prenatal diagnosis Prenatal diagnosis can be made by evaluating alanine: glyoxalate aminotransferase activity on hepatic biopsy. When the family is helpful, DNA analysis on a chorionic villi sample can be diagnostic.

Treatment

The efficacy of treatment depends on early diagnosis. The keystone of therapy is an aggressive treatment that aims to minimize renal oxalate deposition. The means are: (1) a high urine output (above 3 l/day/1.73 m^2); (2) low oxalate diet; (3) high-dose pyridoxine (3.0 to 3.5 mg/kg), which is a coenzyme of alanine: glyoxalate aminotransferase that promotes the conversion of glyoxalate to glycine, rather than to oxalate; (4) crystal inhibitors: orthophosphate (30 to 40 mg/kg), potassium citrate (0.15 g/kg), and/or magnesium oxide (500 mg/day per m^2). This therapy is effective if begun when renal function is still relatively normal. At a glomerular filtration rate of 30-40 ml/min/1.73 m^2, some centers in Europe propose an isolated liver transplant, with the aim to correct the enzyme defect, thus avoiding renal failure. However, ethical questions arise, particularly considering the risk of a liver transplant at the time of good general condition. Once end-stage renal failure has developed, oxalosis is progressively rapid owing to the low efficiency in depurating oxalate by standard dialysis procedures. Intensive hemodiafiltration on a daily basis may provide a better clearance of oxalates, but can be proposed only if transplantation is imminent. After isolated renal transplantation, oxalosis leading to loss of the graft occurs in many patients. Data from the EDTA Registry have shown a 3-year graft survival rate of only 23% for living related donor kidneys and 17% for cadaver kidneys. In the US good results have been obtained by daily aggressive dialysis to deplete the oxalate pool followed by transplantation. Combined liver-kidney transplantation represents the treatment of choice for children with primary hyperoxaluria type 1 with renal insufficiency. The outcome may be best if transplantation is performed when the GFR falls to 25 ml/min per 1.73 m^2 at the beginning of marked tissue oxalate deposition. Actuarial graft survival is 88% at 1 year and patient survival is 80% at 5 years.

It is conceivable that in a few years gene therapy, transfecting a high percentage of hepatocytes, will become available and will replace the transplantation of a functioning liver for a malfunctioning one.

RENAL TUBULAR ACIDOSIS (RTA)

Gabriella Porcellini, Licia Peruzzi

Grouped under this definition is a series of hereditary tubule diseases that manifest in the neonatal period or in early childhood and involve derangement of bicarbonate reabsorption or hydrogen ion secretion, causing hyperchloremic metabolic acidosis with normal plasma anion gap.

Renal tubular acidoses are classified in proximal (type II), distal (type I), mixed (type III) and hyperkaliemic (type IV).

Proximal (type II) renal tubular acidosis

The defect in bicarbonate reabsorption is rarely isolated, being more frequently associated with other defects of the proximal tubule function, such as reabsorption of amino acids, glucose, and phosphate, leading to the full Fanconi's syndrome.

Type II renal tubular acidosis can present as primary, sporadic or familial, or secondary to genetic diseases (cystinosis, galactosemia, Loewe syndrome, tyrosinemia, glycogenosis) or to acquired diseases (paraproteinemias, amyloidosis, Sjögren's syndrome, renal vein thrombosis, graft rejection, and tubulotoxic drug assumption).

In the proximal tubule 80-90% of the filtered bicarbonate is resorbed; in proximal renal tubular acidosis there is a reduced bicarbonate threshold, leading to bicarbonate waste. A reduction of plasma bicarbonate occurs: then the tubule is able to completely resorb the filtered bicarbonate, and a new "steady state" for lower threshold (around 15 mEq/l) is created. At this new equilibrium no bicarbonate reaches the distal tubule and the distal acidification system is not altered. Defects of the luminal antiporter Na^+/H^+, of the Na^+/K^+ATPase on the basolateral membrane have been identified.

The reduced threshold for bicarbonate determines a metabolic hyperchloremic acidosis, which is not severe, because a new equilibrium is reached for lower bicarbonate plasma concentrations. In the forms associated with Fanconi's syndrome, the clinical picture frequently is dominated by rickets due to massive phosphate loss combined with a defective 25-OH-Vit.D_3 hydroxylation within the tubule. Moreover, the chronic fluid depletion induces activation of the renin-angiotensin aldosterone axis leading to hypokalemia.

Distal (type I) renal tubular acidosis

This is sustained by a defective H^+ excretion in the distal and collecting tubule. It can be primary or associated to chronic interstitial nephropathies, drug assumption, or genetic diseases (Marfan's syndrome, Wilson's syndrome, Fabry's disease).

At least four pathogenetic mechanisms have been proposed in distal renal tubular acidosis: (1) absence/malfunction of the H^+-ATPase, responsible for the active H^+ secretion; (2) diminished distal Na^+ reabsorption, inducing a slower H^+ secretion due to an unfavorable electric gradient; (3) backdiffusion, due to a membrane permeability defect with loss of bicarbonates and back influx of H^+; (4) reduced distal NH_3 flux (acceptor of the H^+ ions) determining a block of H^+ secretion. A defective H^+ secretion deranges the urinary acidification system and blocks the bicarbonate rescue, electrically associated with H^+ secretion. The progressive bicarbonate depletion – since the bicarbonates to buffer the daily acidic production (1-3 mEq/day in children) are not regenerated – causes a severe metabolic acidosis.

Urine is persistently alkaline in the presence of acidosis, and this aspect represents the hallmark of type I renal tubular acidosis. Hypovolemia, due to reduced distal Na^+ reabsorption, exchanged with H^+, and reduced proximal Na-HCO_3 load, is frequently observed, aggravated by renin-angiotensin activation and secondary hypokalemia. Persistent acidosis mobilizes calcium and phosphates from bony structures with consequent hypercalciuria and PTH activation and induces a higher mitochondrial citrate uptake and subsequent hypocitraturia. The association of alkaline urines, hypercalciuria and hypocitraturia facilitates intratubular and parenchymal calcium precipitation until overt nephrocalcinosis. Failure to thrive and growth retardation are frequent, owing to the negative effect of acidosis on bones, the possible hyperparathyroidism, and to the altered growth hormone and insulin growth factor 1 (IGF-1) secretion which are induced by chronic acidosis.

Type III renal tubular acidosis

This is characterized by an altered distal H^+ secretion, analogous to distal renal tubular acidosis, with an associated lower proximal threshold for bicarbonates. The proximal defect is usually transient and typical of small children who will later develop a distal renal tubular acidosis.

Type IV renal tubular acidosis

This is more frequent in adults and usually is associated with aldosterone deficiency or with the use of aldosterone antagonists. The defect seems to be due to a reduced mineralocorticoid stimulation of the H^+-ATPase pump and to the reduced synthesis of NH_3, aggravated by hyperkalemia. There is a reduced NH_4^+ and K^+ secretion. In children, type IV renal tubular acidosis is observed in cases of pseudohypoaldosteronism due to obstructive uropathies.

Diagnosis

The diagnosis of renal tubular acidosis usually is clinical in secondary forms; in primary forms, diagnosis depends strongly on a series of urinary and serum analyses and on provocative tests.

Urinary pH, when persistently alkaline in the presence of metabolic acidosis, is an extremely specific index of distal renal tubular acidosis, once urinary infection, severe hypokalemia (which stimulates ammoniagenesis) or severe dehydration with sodium retention have been excluded. Urinary pH by itself, however, cannot distinguish between an initial proximal renal tubular acidosis with bicarbonaturia or different forms of distal renal tubular acidosis.

Net acid excretion [(titratable acid excretion + NH_4^+ excretion) – urinary bicarbonate)] expresses the kidney potential to modify urinary acid excretion through the modulation of NH_3 synthesis. It identifies the forms of renal tubular acidosis due to lack of NH_4^+. A net positive charge anion gap (urinary $Na^+ + K^+ - Cl^-$) suggests an inadequate ammonium excretion as well.

Urinary acidification tests are indicated in incomplete forms. The urinary acidification capacity in the next 6-8 hours and after 3 days following ammonium chloride loading is evaluated.

Fractional bicarbonate excretion is the only specific and reliable test for the diagnosis of proximal renal tubular acidosis, evaluating urinary bicarbonate excretion at increasing levels of plasma bicarbonate. In proximal renal tubular acidosis the fractional excretion of bicarbonates is higher than 15%, while in distal forms it is 3-5%. In distal renal tubular acidosis the diagnosis is supported by the finding of hypocitraturia and hypercalciuria.

Treatment

The cornerstone of treatment of renal tubular acidosis is the administration of alkali in amounts necessary to correct acidosis. On initial presentation, with severe acidosis, a large amount of bicarbonate is required, as high as 5-15 mEq/kg/day in four divided doses. Once acidosis is corrected, patients can be maintained with 1-2 mEq/kg/day, which equals the endogenous daily acid production in children. The most-used alkali is bicarbonate; however, potassium or sodium (Shohl's solution) citrate also may be used, in particular when potassium or citrate supplements are indicated.

In proximal renal tubular acidosis associated with Fanconi's syndrome, the specific treatment is available only in a few cases (such as oral cysteamine therapy in cystinosis); in the others, potassium, alkali, and water supplements are required as well as additional phosphate and vitamin D to prevent rickets.

In type IV renal tubular acidosis, mineralocorticoids sometimes are required, along with dietary potassium restriction.

Suggested readings

BATLLE D, FLORES G. Underlying defects in distal renal tubular acidosis: new understandings. Am J Kidney Dis 1996;27: 896-915.

BROYER M, JOUVET P, DAUDON M, REVILLON Y. Management of oxalosis. Kidney Int 1996;49(suppl 53):93-8.

DANPURE CJ. Advances in the enzymology and molecular genetics of primary hyperoxaluria type 1. Prospects for gene therapy. Nephrol Dial Transplant 1995;10(suppl 8):24-9.

HABIB R. Nephrotic syndrome in the first year of life. Pediatr Nephrol 1993;7:347-53.

HABIB R, GUBLER MC, ANTIGNAC C, GAGNADOUX MF. Diffuse mesangial sclerosis: A congenital glomerulopathy with nephrotic syndrome. In: Grunfeld JP, ed. Advances in Nephrology, Chicago: Year Book. 1993;43-56.

HOLMBERG C, JALANKO H, KOSKIMIES O, et al. Renal transplantation in small children with congenital nephrotic syndrome of the Finnish type. Transplant Proc 1991;23:1378-9.

JADRESIC L, LEAKE J, GORDON I, et al. Clinicopathologic review of twelve children with nephropathy, Wilms' tumor and genital abnormalities (Drash syndrome). J Pediatr 1990;117:717-25.

JAMIESON NV. The European Primary Hyperoxaluria Type 1 Transplant Registry report on the results of combined liver/kidney transplantation for primary hyperoxaluria 1984-1992. Transplant Proc. 1995;27:1234-6.

MANNIKKO M, KESTILA M, LENKKERI U, et al. Improved prenatal diagnosis of the congenital nephrotic syndrome of the Finnish type based on DNA analysis. Kidney Int 1997;51:868-72.

MANZ F, KALHOFF H, RENER T. Renal acid excretion in early infancy. Pediatr Nephrol 1997;11:231-43.

RUMSBY G, MANDEL H, AVEY C, GERAERTS A. Polymorphisms in the alanine:glyoxylate aminotransferase gene and their application to the prenatal diagnosis of primary hyperoxaluria type 1. Nephrol Dial Transplant 1995;10(suppl 8):30-2.

SMULDERS YM, FRISSEN PHJ, SLAATS EH SILBERBUSCH J. Renal tubular acidosis. Pathophysiology and diagnosis. Arch Int Med 1997;156:1629-36.

WATTS RW. The clinical spectrum of primary hyperoxalurias and their treatment. J Nephrol 1998;(suppl 1)11:4-7.

CHAPTER

51

Renal disorders in particular settings: the elderly

Francisco J. Gómez-Campderà

KEY POINTS

- Because of the structural and functional changes that occur with age, elderly patients are at greater risk of developing acute renal failure and require important pharmacologic modifications.
- Glomerulonephritis is not a rare disease in the elderly.
- Evaluation of the nephrotic syndrome must include a renal biopsy.
- The diagnostic approach to renal failure in elderly individuals, which has multiple causes, usually requires a renal biopsy.
- Many chronic nephropathies in the elderly have an insidious and slow course and, because of this, are diagnosed in the advanced stage of the disease.
- Old age itself is no longer an exclusion criterion for chronic dialysis treatment, and even renal transplantation is a good choice for selected elderly patients.

The aging of the population in western countries makes it imperative to reconsider the physiologic modifications associated to aging. From adolescence to maturity, renal function remains relatively stable, but as age advances, there is a slow deterioration in many of the renal functions.

MORPHOLOGIC CHANGES WITH AGE

The process of involution inevitably leads to loss of renal mass. This loss is mainly vascular, affecting the cortical region and conserving the medullar region. The changes are heterogeneous, with different degrees of atrophy, sclerosis, hypertrophy, and hyperplasia, affecting all the renal structures.

Blood vessels

Variable sclerotic changes take place in the larger vessel walls, narrowing of the lumen. The endothelium loses its uniformity, and blood flow can become less laminated. Depositions of collagen between the intima and the internal elastica lamina replace muscle cells, diminishing elasticity. There is hyalinization in the arterioles. All these changes begin to become evident after age 40.

Glomerules

At birth, human beings have approximately 1 million glomeruli; this remains constant until the fourth decade of life, when the number begins to decrease gradually. The number of sclerotic glomeruli increases from 1 to 4% during the fourth decade to 4 to 8% during the eighth decade. The proportion is greater in patients with severe arteriosclerosis, particularly in the external cortex. There is a progressive collapse and hyalinization of the glomerular tufts and sharp termination of the arterioles in the external cortex that gives rise to a reduction in cortical flow. On the other hand, a shunt develops between the afferent and efferent arterioles in the rudimentary juxtamedullar glomeruli by which blood flow reaches the medulla through straight descending vessels.

Interstitium

In the elderly kidney, tubular length and volume diminish progressively, replaced by conjunctive tissue with almost no inflammatory response as a result of ischemia (apoptosis). Viable nephrons may show signs of hypertrophy, hyperplasia, and luminal dilatation. The cortical interstitium shows little increase in conjunctive tissue, which is significant in the medulla. After age 50, the cell content of the medulla is replaced by intercellular material, and calcium deposits may be observed. The vascular structure is preserved.

FUNCTIONAL CHANGES WITH AGE

Renal blood flow

Renal blood flow (RBF) diminishes with age. This is a consequence of an increase in vascular resistance as a result of the anatomic changes that affect both the afferent and efferent arterioles. The functional vascular response to vasodilating agents also diminishes with age.

Glomerular filtration rate

Glomerular filtration rate (GFR) diminishes with age, whether measured by creatinine (C_{Cr}) or insulin clearance (C_{In}), at the rate of 1 ml/min per year between the ages of 40 and 80 and seems to be more rapid in males. Despite this reduction in C_{Cr} with age, values do not rise proportionally because they depend on muscular mass, which in turn diminishes with aging. Therefore, increase in serum creatinine in elderly patients is more significant than in younger patients when evaluating renal function. The analytic evaluation of C_{Cr} can be done using anthropometric formulas, the most commonly used of which is Cockroft and Gault's, based on age and body weight, when difficulties exist in proper and precise collection of 24-hour urine samples.

$$C_{cr} = \frac{(140 - \text{age}) \times [\text{lean body weight (kg)}]}{72 \times \text{serum creatinine} \left(\text{mg/dl}\right)}$$

This uses a correction factor of 0.85 for females.

Tubular function

Maximum tubular secretion of para-aminohippurate (PAH) and maximum reabsorption of glucose lower with age, parallel to the descent in C_{In}.

Sodium and potassium balance

Renal conservation of sodium (Na) is lost with age. The elderly show a poorer response to deprivation or overload of salinity than do younger patients.

Concentration-dilution

Maximum urinary concentration capacity diminishes with age. This decrease is not due to the decrease in GFR, osmotic diuresis by intact nephrons, or decreased release of vasopressin. It seems to be a consequence of lower medullar tone, secondary to a defect in the transport of solutes through the ascending handle. This alteration in urinary concentration, together with the loss of Na, makes the elderly susceptible to volume depletion and hypernatremia. Renal capacity for urinary dilution, as well as free-water clearance, also diminishes with age. The responsible factors are the decrease in GFR, alterations in the transport of solutes in the ascending loop of Henle, and inadequate suppression of the release of vasopressin. This increased release of vasopressin in response to osmotic stimuli, together with a lower sensitivity to osmoreceptors, may lead to water retention and hyponatremia.

Renal acid excretion

Despite the decrease in renal function, under basal conditions, the acid-base status of the elderly patient is similar to that of young adults. In cases of acid overload, net acid excretion (ammonia + titratable acid) is less in older patients. This reduction is due to a decrease in ammonia excretion, parallel to the decrease in GFR. This decrease may contribute to the development of and slow recuperation from metabolic acidosis.

DISORDERS IN ELECTROLYTE AND ACID-BASE METABOLISM

The most frequent and clinically significant of these are as follows.

HYPONATREMIA

Hyponatremia is found frequently in the elderly, often induced by medical measures and based on the functional alterations previously mentioned.

Etiology

The causes are similar to those in younger patients. In elderly patients, the most common form is euvolemic hyponatremia, followed by the hypo- and hypervolemic forms.

1. *Euvolemic hyponatremia.* The inadequate secretion of antidiuretic hormone (ADH) syndrome is responsible for the majority of hyponatremias seen in hospitalized elderly patients and is usually related to the central nervous system, generally vascular, diseases. Other causes include intrathoracic tumors and drugs such as chloropropamide and carbamazepine. Idiopathic cases follow months after malignant diseases. Hyponatremia induced by diuretics affects the elderly, in whom, above all, thiazides, furosemide, and more rarely, triamterene or

amiloride, together with strict low-salt diets and a high ingestion of water, are responsible for more than 70% of the hyponatremias seen in hospitals. Although the reasons are not clear, females seem to be affected more than males. In males, the most common cause is the postoperative period after transurethral prostate resections, while undergoing electrolyte-poor irrigation, in which the preceding factors, together with reabsorption of these solutions through prostate vessels, usually occur.

2. *Hypovolemic hyponatremia.* This is typical of elderly patients hospitalized for congestive heart failure (CHF) and on diuretics and low-sodium diets. Maintaining aggressive diuretic regimens despite clinical improvement leads to volume depletion, thirst, and inappropriate water ingestion with volume retention. In this situation, reversible prerenal azotemia is usually observed.
3. *Hypervolemic hyponatremia.* A contraction of volume creates the stimulus for the release of vasopressin, which leads to water retention and gives rise to volume overload and dilutional hyponatremia. CHF, cirrhosis, and nephrotic syndrome (NS), in which one must rule out pseudohyponatremia secondary to hyperlipidemia, are other causes. Acute renal failure (ARF) or chronic renal failure (CRF) may be accompanied by hypervolemic hyponatremia, partly due to the excessive ingestion of free water together with the renal incapacity for its elimination.

Clinical manifestations and diagnosis generally are similar to those observed in younger patients.

Treatment

The norms are similar to those for younger patients, taking into account that in the elderly, body water is less, representing only 40 to 50% of body weight.

HYPERNATREMIA

The incidence of hypernatremia is higher in the elderly. Alterations in urinary concentration capacity and saline loss, together with a diminished thirst associated with cerebrovascular diseases, with sensory alterations or hypothalamic-pituitary dysfunction, are the causes of this higher risk.

Diagnosis

Diagnosis requires an evaluation of extracellular volume. Most cases are due to volume losses of gastrointestinal or urinary origin. Clinical manifestations depend on the underlying disease and are associated with dementia, sepsis, CHF, coma, etc. In the absence of CRF, Na elimination is less than 20 mEq/liter, and metabolic alkalosis is usually present. It is usually a marker of poor prognosis of the underlying disease, and mortality depends on other associated problems, such as CRF, CHF, multiorgan failure, etc.

Treatment

Treatment does not differ from that for younger patients, with the exception that the water deficit should be calculated on 40 to 50% of body weight.

HYPERKALEMIA

The incidence of hyperkalemia increases with age, probably in relation to the decrease in GFR, as well as the frequent use, in these patients, of drugs that alter the metabolism of potassium. Pathogenesis, clinical findings, and treatment do not differ from those in younger patients.

Calcium metabolism Although serum calcium does not change with age, PTH secretion and vitamin D metabolism do. The fall in GFR is again the cause, with an inverse correlation between serum Cr and PTH, which after age 65 can double its previous value. Plasma levels of 25-OHD$_3$ usually are lower in older patients, and factors such as exposure to the sun and ingestion and quality of lactates may be influential. Low levels of 1,25(OH)$_2$D$_3$ can be observed in elderly patients and are a consequence of reduced synthesis in relation to lower GFR or an increase in catabolism.

HYPERCALCEMIA

This is observed in 2 to 3% of older hospitalized patients; more than half are female. The principal causes, responsible for more than 80% of hypercalcemias, are hyperparathyroidism, tumors, and drug toxicity (thiazides and vitamin D metabolites in patients with CRF). Hyperparathyroidism is more frequent in females and may be caused by the postmenopausal state. Clinical manifestations are similar to those in younger patients, although in older patients neuromuscular effects include asthenia, fatigue, and neuropsychiatric dysfunction. Treatment does not differ from that given to younger patients, including parathyroidectomy, which, in experienced hands, is curative and of low risk.

Phosphorus metabolism Serum phosphorus levels fall with age in both sexes. The high levels of PTH and defects in tubular reabsorption of phosphorus may be the cause. The incidence, etiology, pathogenesis, clinical presentation, and treatment of hypo- and hyperphosphatemia are not different from those in younger patients.

PHARMACOLOGIC CONSIDERATIONS IN THE ELDERLY

The elderly population suffers a number of chronic diseases that are treated, many times indefinitely, with a variety of drugs. The therapeutic and adverse effects of these depend on the serum and tissue levels reached. The pharmacokinetics of these medicines depend on factors such as absorption, volume of distribution, metabolism, and excretion, which are altered in the elderly owing to the morphologic changes already described. While hepatic metabolic changes are difficult to predict, renal modifications are easily quantified.

Before prescribing medication to an elderly patient, it is essential to study all the principal functions of the organism (hepatic, renal, and cardiac); to evaluate associated pathologies; and to be aware of the pharmacokinetics of the drug. Treatment should be started with lower doses than those indicated for younger patients, increasing progressively. It is important to look for any signs or symptoms considered unusual, which could indicate intolerance. Treatment should not be prolonged unnecessarily, and care should be taken with associated pathologies to avoid any potentially dangerous interactions.

PRIMARY GLOMERULONEPHRITIS

The generalized use of renal biopsies and more complete studies of their results have allowed us to recognize primary glomerulonephritis as occurring not infrequently in the elderly, contrary to earlier opinions. However, the renal manifestations of systemic diseases (e.g., diabetes, vasculitis, amyloidosis, etc.), as well as the structural and functional changes caused by age in the kidney, often mask primary glomerular nephropathies that slip by undiagnosed.

Recent studies suggest that clinical presentation, histologic appearance, and prognosis of these glomerulonephritides (GNs) in the elderly do not significantly differ from those observed in young adults. Therefore, clinical evaluation should not be different in function for the different age groups.

Epidemiology

This is difficult to specify. Most groups selected for study do not share indication criteria for biopsy, especially elderly patients. On the other hand, a high degree of suspicion must exist to attribute and histologically diagnose GN, since the signs and symptoms can be easily attributed to extrarenal pathology. Two facts seem to differentiate the frequency of the different morphologic variants between the elderly patient population and younger patients: on the one hand, the higher incidence of membranous and extracapillary GN and, on the other, the lower frequency of immunoglobulin A (IgA) GN, probably due to the more restrictive policy on renal biopsies in the older patient.

Clinical findings

In elderly patients, the manifestations of GN can be masked by the extrarenal pathology, which frequently initially orients the diagnosis erroneously. The clinical manifestations of primary GN in older patients can be included in the same syndromes as in younger patients. The most frequent syndromes and pathologic glomerular diseases in this population are as follows.

Acute nephritic syndrome, acute and/or rapidly progressive renal failure

Acute postinfectious GN The prototype is acute poststreptococcal GN. Nevertheless, other infectious bacterial diseases (e.g., pneumococcal, staphylococcal, salmonellosis, etc.) can complicate infectious GN. Diabetes mellitus can act as a predisposing factor. In the elderly, the incidence is 4% of all primary GNs. Clinically, patients are typified by the appearance of a nephritic syndrome following between 1 and 3 weeks after the infectious episode. Basic analytical data confirm the diagnosis: a decrease in serum complement in the initial phase (from the second to the eighth weeks) and an increase in antistriptolysine or another specific serologic marker, based on the etiologic agent. Circulating immune complexes and cryoglobulins (generally IgG/C3 or IgG/IgM/C3) also can be observed in the initial phase. The histologic findings, to which the characteristics of the senile kidney are added, are typical. With regard to prognosis and evolution, although formerly there tended to be a negative prognosis for elderly patients, more recent and more clinically and histologically documented studies have shown a disease course and prognosis similar to those in younger patients. Treatment is symptomatic, including treatment of hypertension, edema (diet and diuretics), and ARF support (dialysis), if necessary.

Rapidly progressive GN Based on the immunohistologic findings in renal biopsies, this entity can be divided into three varieties or types: type I, mediated by antimembrane basal glomerular antibodies (antiMBG); type II, with granulous deposition of immune complexes (ICs) on the glomerulus, generally of IgG and C3; and type III, with negative immunofluorescence. This disease usually appears in adult males of middle or advanced age, but it is a frequent and almost exclusive type in the elderly and represents approximately 12% of primary GN. I will concentrate on this type. Its etiopathogenesis is not clear, although various groups consider it an exclusively renal vasculitis. The beginning of the medical pattern can be rapid, with microscopic hematuria and edema, but more frequently its presentation is insidious, with signs of volume overload or uremic syndrome. Renal biopsy provides the diagnosis, many times unsuspected. Differential diagnosis should include other causes of ARF. Prognosis is poor and is somewhat worse than in younger adults. The natural history of the untreated disease is difficult to know, since most published patients have received some type of treatment. Without treatment, the course toward end-stage renal disease (ESRD) is inevitable in days or months, although a rare case of spontaneous recuperation has been described. Although there is a general consensus that prognosis of the disease without treatment is poor, there is

Table 51.1 Causes of acute renal failure

Prerenal failure	Intrinsic renal failure
Decrease cardiac output Myocardial infarction Cardiac arrythmia Descompensated congestive heart failure Cardiac tamponade Pulmonary embolsim Positive-pressure mechanical ventilation	**Glomerular diseases** Acute postinfective glomerulonephritis Goodpasture's syndrome Rapidly progressive glomerulonephritis Lupus nephritis IgA nephropathy Interstitial nephritis
Hypovolemia with or without hypotension Decreased intake External losses of extracellular fluid Renal losses Gastrointestinal losses Dermal losses	**Tubulointerstitial nephritis** Infectious causes *Staphyloccocus*, gram-negative bacteria, leptospirosis, brucellosis, viruses, fungi, acid-fast bacilli Infiltrative causes Leukemia, lymphoma, sarcoidosis, other granulomas Related to drugs Penicillins, cephalosporins, NSAIDs, allupurinol, thiazide diuretics, cimetidine, phenytoin, furosemide, analgesics, rifampicin Ciprofloxacin Idiopathic
Internal losses, redistribution, or third spacing Hypoalbulinemia Cirrhosis of the liver Nephrotic syndrome Pancreatitis Traumatized tissues Periotonitis Intestinal obstruction Burns	**Acute tubular necrosis** Ischemics Ischemic injury Prolonged prerenal azotemia Shock, postoperative Crush syndrome, major trauma Nephrotoxic Nephrotoxic injury Antibodies, radiographic contrast media, anesthetic agents, chemotherapeutic agents, immunosuppressive agents, amphotericin B, large doses of mannitol, organic solvents, pesticides, heavy metals
Peripheral vasodilatation Sepsis Shock Liver failure Antihypertensive agents Drug overdose	**Vascular diseases** Malignant hypertension Vasculitis Hemolytic-uremic syndrome Thrombotic thrombocytopenic purpura Preeclampsia Postpartum nephrosclerosis Cholesterol emboli Renal cortical necrosis
Renal vascular occlusion or severe constriction Atherosclerosis Embolism Thrombosis Vasculitis Renal pedicle compression Dissection of abdominal aortic aneurysm Endotoxin Cyclosporin A	**Pigment injury** Myoglobinuria Hemoglobinuria
Disruption in renal autoregulation Prostaglandin inhibitors ACE inhibitors Postrenal failure (obstruction)	**Crystal-induced injury** Uric acid nephropathy Oxalate nephropathy Sulfadiazine Acyclovir Methotrexate
Intraureteral obstruction Blood clots Stones Papillary necrosis Fungus balls	**Metabolic causes** Hypercalcemia Myeloma proteins Light-chan nephropathy
Extraureteral obstruction Aberrant vessels Ligation Malignancy Endometriosis Retroperitoneal fibrosis, tumors	
Lower urinary tract obstruction Urethral stricture Prostatic hypertrophy or cancer Bladder cancer Cervical cancer Neurogenic bladder	

rect the risk factors as much as possible, and proper hydration or even a slight volume overload by adding furosemide or mannitol in the pre- and postcontrast hours is recommended. All medications with a possible nephrotoxic effect should be stopped before the use of a contrast agent. At present, the new low-osmolarity contrast agents have not yet been proven to have a lesser nephrotoxic effect. Thus radiologic studies using contrast agents should be restricted in such patients.

Acute interstitial nephritis (AIN) The most frequent AIN in the elderly is secondary to the use of certain medications. Clinical manifestations are common to all patients: usually nonoliguric ARF, high Na excretion fraction, fever, rash, eosinophilia, eosinophils in urine, and less frequently microhematuria, slight proteinuria, arthralgias, pain in the side, and adenopathy. AIN usually appears 7 days or more after starting treatment, independent of the dose administered, and renal function usually is recovered on suspension of the causal medication. Improvement may be faster with the help of corticoids. NSAIDs are the most frequent cause of AIN secondary to medication in the elderly, after aminoglycosides. Their wide use in this patient group should make physicians reconsider the risks involved before prescribing NSAIDs in the elderly. In AIN caused by NSAIDs, there is usually proteinuria in the nephrotic range that also reverts on restoration of renal function. Beta-lactamic acid derivatives are the second most important agents causing AIN secondary to medication. Other less frequent causes of AIN in this patient group are particular infections and immunologic diseases such as SLE, cryoglobulinemia, etc.

Vascular diseases The incidence of atheromatous vascular disease is higher in the elderly due to bilateral renal arteriosclerosis, which causes secondary renal ischemia (ischemic nephropathy). This should be suspected in patients showing a progressive loss of renal function, often with decreased kidney size not due to abuse of analgesics, obstruction, or primary glomerulopathy. Such patients often have hypertension not necessarily refractive to treatment with hypotensors and frequently show arteriosclerosis in other areas. Proteinuria typically is lower than 1 g/day. Other more acute forms of renal artery occlusion are also more frequent in the elderly, such as acute thrombosis of the renal artery secondary to arteriosclerosis, angiography of the aorta or of the renal artery, etc., as well as spontaneous renal atheroembolism, secondary to surgery or vascular manipulation, or after fibrinolytic treatment for myocardial infarction. Clinically, the sudden obstruction of the renal arteries (thrombosis or embolism) is usually accompanied by anuric ARF, fever, nausea, vomiting, pain in the side, hematuria, pyuria, proteinuria, leukocytosis, elevation of lactate dehydrogenase, SGOT, SGPT, and alkaline phosphate. The manifestation may be more insidious when the obstruction is unilateral or is caused by various episodes of microembolism, with progressive deterioration of the renal function and secondary renal atrophy. Aortic artery aneurysm affecting the renal arteries is another, more remote cause of vascular ARF in the elderly.

Postrenal ARF

Obstructive ARF is extremely important in the elderly patient because of its high incidence and prevalence and because it is usually treatable once diagnosed. Prostate hypertrophy and prostate cancer in the male and cervical cancer in the female are the most frequent causes of bilateral or partial uretheral obstruction. In males, the obstructive process at the prostate level causes an increase in residual urine volume in the bladder, giving rise to a higher number of urinary infections. If a urinary infection is present when ARF appears, prognosis is worse, since there is a higher risk of sepsis.

Diagnosis and treatment

Requires management in specialized centers.

Prognosis

Mortality from ARF is between 50 and 80%. In elderly patients with ARF, the most frequent causes of death are infections (especially pneumonia), acute myocardial infarction, CHF, and gastric hemorrhage.

Although ARF in the elderly is usually multifactorial in cause, many of these causes can be corrected or avoided, giving the physician an important role in the prevention of this high-mortality disorder. The physician should be especially careful to ensure that the patient maintains proper hydration and to control analytical observations in those elderly patients who will undergo surgery, radiologic diagnostic testing with contrast agents, and treatment with potentially nephrotoxic drugs such as some chemotherapy antineoplastics, antibiotics, aminoglycosides, etc. Aminoglycosides and other medications should be adjusted according to C_{Cr} and not according to serum Cr. Special precautions must be taken when prescribing NSAIDs and ACE inhibitors in older patients with arteriosclerosis or altered renal function.

CHRONIC RENAL FAILURE

Epidemiology and etiology

The etiology of CRF is probably multifactorial in elderly patients. There are few epidemiologic studies on this subject, and some of the existing ones are imprecise. The insidious course of chronic nephropathies means that renal failure is often discovered in the terminal phase, if diagnostic methods are not used fully or are inconclusive. On the one hand, the generalization of replacement techniques in the last few years has allowed the inclusion of older patients who just a few years ago were rejected for this type of treatment. This has provoked specific changes in the causes of CRF. The spectrum of clinical and pathologic diseases is different in the elderly than in younger patients, and nearly a third of the pathologic lesions are diagnosed incorrectly clinically. On the other hand, more than 20% of patients diagnosed with CRF had a treatable lesion at the time biopsy was performed (ATN, renal vascular disease, immunoallergic IN, etc.). In studies based only on patients diagnosed with CRF on renal biopsy in the United States (Virginia), 65% of cases were secondary to diabetes mellitus and/or hypertension. Without renal biopsy, many small terminal kidneys are called chronic GN, nephroangiosclerosis, cause unknown, or others.

Clinical findings

CRF in the elderly is a multifactorial disorder secondary to systemic diseases that dominate the clinical state in the early stages, making the course of the chronic nephropathies insidious and frequently resulting in diagnosis of CRF in its later stages. At this point, the clinical situation is dominated by uremic symptoms that, in the older patient, will be complex and will add to the generalized physical deterioration of the patient. Therefore, the clinical state is rarely an isolated renal problem but rather affects all the organs and body systems to a greater or lesser degree. In the elderly uremic patient, there will be clinical manifestations as consequence of the base disease (diabetes mellitus, amyloidosis, hypertension, etc.), of the CRF itself (osteodystrophy, polyneuritis, etc.), or independent but aggravated by the same (ischemic cardiomyopathy, peripheral vasculopathy, etc.).

Diagnosis

Determination of the cause of CRF in the elderly should be approached as in any other age group. As mentioned earlier, it is not unusual to find that older patients with CRF are studied for the first time when the deterioration of the renal function is very advanced. The most valuable analytical data in measuring renal function in the elderly, as in younger patients, is the serum Cr, and especially its clearance (C_{Cr}). However, Cr is not the ideal parameter for measurement of GFR, since it is eliminated by proximal tubular secretion. Therefore, C_{Cr}, and a valid method for its calculation, knowing serum Cr and using anthropometric values that can evaluate the nutritional state, is the method proposed by Cockcroft and Gault, as already mentioned. Mitch and colleagues suggested that most, although not all, patients with progressive CRF tended to decline, given their C_{Cr}. This deterioration varied from one patient to another, but in the same patient could be foreseen by a simple evaluation method, the inverse of serum Cr (1/serum Cr). In this way, 1/serum Cr may be used to represent C_{Cr}; its representation over time can be a sure method of following the patient's renal function. When a sufficient number of measurements are available, a slope of serum Cr reciprocates may be made, from which some interesting considerations may be reached: first, the time within which the patient will need dialysis can be predicted. Dialysis will be needed when 1/serum Cr has fallen to 0.1 to 0.15. However, some older patients may need dialysis sooner because of overestimation of GFR. Second, modifications in the slope can suggest intercurrent problems and efficient therapeutic management. A slope with no modifications implies that nothing interferes with the natural course of the disease.

There are three vital aspects in the diagnosis and later treatment of these patients:

1. *Diagnosis of the cause of CRF.* In those patients for whom previous evolutive data are unknown, it can be difficult to differentiate diagnosis between CRF and a chronic process. Clinical history and meticulous physical examination may establish the difference in a high number patients. In doubtful cases, the following are helpful: the size of renal silhouette through nephrotomography or ultrasound, since this will be small in the majority of cases of CRF, with the exception of polycystosis, diabetes mellitus, and amyloidosis; the existence of signs of renal osteodystrophy; the presence of anemia; and disproportionately good clinical tolerance to other metabolic disorders of the uremic syndrome such as acidosis and hypocalcemia. Apart from these situations, the use of other, more aggressive explorations should be considered with caution. It is preferable to avoid those which will not substantially modify treatment or life expectancy and entail even a minimum of risk. It is better to individualize the study in each case and not fall into routine diagnosis, the result of which many times is the deterioration of the patient's general state.
2. *Exclusion of factors that make CRF acute.* Possible acute reversible complications, added to a base CRF, always should be taken into account. The most frequent etiologies of these in the elderly are (a) volume depletion (vomiting, diarrhea, hemorrhage, salt-free diets, and incorrect use of diuretics are the most frequent causes), (b) use of medication (the abusive use of medication is typical in this patient population, and there are many medications that can result in deterioration of intact or previously altered renal function through a diversity of mechanisms), (c) obstructive uropathy, many times with few symptoms, even maintaining diuresis (this should be taken into account in the face of sudden, inexplicable deterioration, and it is easy to diagnose through physical examination, palpating the vesicular globe or use of a rectal probe and ultrasound), and (d) infections (these are more frequent in patients with CRF and may be accompanied by a reversible deterioration of renal function).
3. Once the CRF is confirmed as established and nonreversible, the first priority is *an evaluation of the visceral effects of the same*, with a view toward therapeutic pos-

sibilities. It is better to refer the patient to a nephrologist because delay is a prognostic factor in the morbidity and mortality of this patient group.

Treatment

The therapeutic focus in the elderly patient with CRF should take into account the same considerations as diagnosis. Finally, if, paraphrasing Henriksen, our objective is to "add life to the years of the elderly patient, not only add years to their lives," we must continue working with this patient population without regard to their age.

Suggested readings

CAMERON JS, MACIAS NUÑEZ JF. Renal function in the elderly. In: Davison AM, Cameron JS, Grúnfeld J-P, et al, eds. Oxford textbook of clinical nephrology. Vol 1. 2nd ed. Oxford, England: Oxford Medical Publishers, 1998;77-91.

GÓMEZ CAMPDERÁ FJ. Nefrología geriátrica. Nefrología 1997; 17(suppl 3):1-72; 1998;18(suppl 4):1-68.

GÓMEZ CAMPDERÁ FJ, RENGEL MA. Diálisis y trasplante renal en el anciano. In: Llach F, Valderrábano F eds. Insuficiencia renal crónica. Vol 2. 2nd ed. Madrid: Ediciones Norma, 1997:1775-810.

LUSVARGHI E, VANDELLI L, DAVISON AM. Renal disease and ageing. Nephrol Dial Transplant 1996;11(suppl 9):1-112.

MACIAS-NUÑEZ JF, CAMERON JS eds. Renal function and disease in the elderly. London: Butterworths, 1987.

MARTINEZ MALDONADO M. Renal disease in the elderly. Semin Nephrol 1996;16:263-362.

MICHELIS MF, DAVIS BB, PREUSS HG, eds. Geriatric nephrology. New York: Field, Rich and Associates, 1986.

MIGNON F. Nephrologie prospective: le 3 age. Nephrologie 1990;11:273-364.

OREOPOULOS DG, MICHELIS MF, HERSCHORN S, eds. Nephrology and urology in the aged patient. Dordrecht: Kluwer Academic Publishers, 1993.

PORUSH JG, FAUBERT PF. Renal disease in the aged. Boston: Little, Brown, 1991.

PROCEEDINGS OF AN INTERNATIONAL CONFERENCE. Geriatric nephrology and urology: Interdisciplinary perspectives. Am J Kidney Dis 1990;16:273-395.

CHAPTER

52 Renal disorders occurring in particular geographic settings

Carlos Chiurchiu, Pablo U. Massari

KEY POINTS

- Geographic factors can influence the type of renal disease seen, its clinical presentation, and its prevalence.
- From the perspective of global health studies, the interrelations of geography and disease are seen most often in the tropics.
- Infectious diseases are prevalent in the tropical belt, as are the renal diseases and syndromes they can induce.
- An understanding of the geoepidemiologic background, correct diagnosis, and appropriate and timely referrals will contribute to better patient care and proper epidemiologic alerts.
- Tropical acute renal failure almost always is severe and hypercatabolic; it has a high mortality rate.
- Tropical nephrotic syndrome is due to glomerular lesions that frequently progress to end-stage renal failure.

Geography is a strong conditioning factor in the presentation and prevalence of a disease. Local environmental factors (climate, altitude, forestation, etc.) are known to influence the prevalence and type of infectious diseases in various regions of the world. Socioeconomic factors associated with geographic areas (demography, degree of development, nutrition, culture, etc.) also contribute to our understanding of current epidemiologic indices.

In the so-called tropical belt there is a particularly close association between these factors and disease type and prevalence. More than half of the world's population lives in this region, which also is characterized by the fastest rate of population growth, underdevelopment, poverty, low educational level, malnutrition, and cultural conflicts.

Recent trends in world climate have made this situation even worse. The picture is further complicated by recent population movements toward urban enclaves with poor sanitation and a shortage of drinking water. Moreover, it is well known that the sort of development associated with Western culture tends to be heralded by its more painful and undesirable effects, whereas the wave of benefits and well-being lags behind.

Internists and general practitioners worldwide must be acquainted with the diseases commonly suffered by the inhabitants of the tropical belt. Migrant workers, businessmen, and tourists are likely to appear in any medical office or hospital in the developed world suffering from diseases they have acquired in the tropics.

A high prevalence of renal diseases and syndromes caused by infectious agents is seen in the tropical belt. Of the several entities with high prevalence in the tropics we have chosen here to summarize the characteristics of the tropical nephrotic syndrome and tropical acute renal failure.

TROPICAL NEPHROTIC SYNDROME

Proteinuria and the nephrotic syndrome are frequent in the tropics. Nephrotic syndrome is an important cause of hospital admissions in the region. Preliminary data indicate that chronic glomerular diseases are the main etiologic factor of chronic renal failure in many countries of the African continent, Asia, and Latin America. Unlike the syndrome seen in the developed countries, tropical nephrotic syndrome occurs most often in older children and young adults. Edema and hypoalbuminemia are aggravated by poor nutritional status. Ascites is frequent. Proteinuria usually is poorly selective, and serum complement levels may be decreased, but these are not consistent findings.

The pathophysiology of tropical nephrotic syndrome is best explained by chronic exposure to bacterial and parasitic antigens. Table 52.1 lists the most common infectious diseases that cause nephrotic syndrome in the tropics.

Malaria

Malaria is the leading cause of nephrotic syndrome in children, teenagers, and young adults in subSaharan Africa. Malaria nephrotic syndrome is also seen in some tropical Asian countries. The recent increment in malaria prevalence in tropical South America has not been accompanied by this syndrome because the recent reemergence of malaria has been due mostly to *Plasmodium falciparum*. Malarial nephrotic syndrome is due to an immune complex-mediated membranous nephritis that is associated with infection by *Plasmodium malaria*.

The syndrome can be seen a few weeks after the first clinical manifestation of the infection, and it progresses to chronic renal failure in 3 to 5 years. High blood pressure appears only in very late stages of the disease. Complement levels usually are normal. Diagnosis is made by appropriate microscopic examination of peripheral blood and identification of the parasite inside the red blood cells. Serologic diagnosis is not useful. Treatments with steroids or any other immune suppressant have failed whenever tried. Antiparasitic regimens based on chloroquine or its derivatives usually are successful in eradicating the infection, but once the renal lesion has been established, progression to renal failure seems to be the rule. No information is available thus far about the use of drugs or diet to stop the progression of the disease.

Schistosomiasis

Chronic schistosomal infection (*S. hematobium* in Africa and Asia, *S. mansoni* in Latin America and Africa, and *S. japonium* in China, the Philippines, and Japan) is one of the most important public health problems in the tropical belt. According to recent World Health Organization estimates, the incidence of the disease is approximately 50% among the 700 million people at risk.

The importance of considering this etiology in patients with nephrotic syndrome and positive geoepidemiologic antecedents stems from the fact that between 15 and 20% of patients with schistosomiasis eventually develop a chronic renal insufficiency usually associated with other organic involvement. Chronic renal failure appears after 4 to 6 years of evolution, and is associated with other urinary tract disorders and infections in one-half of the patients. It is an important cause of end-stage renal failure in the Brazilian Amazonia, central and northern Africa, and in the Indian subcontinent. The finding of liver and spleen enlargement in a patient with nephrotic syndrome suggests a lymphoma as the underlying disease to nearly every first-world physician, but schistosomiasis is first on the list for a physician in the tropical belt. High peripheral eosinophil counts are the rule. It is also a renal disease mediated by immune complexes. IgA deposition in the glomeruli seems to be the earlier pathophysiologic finding in these patients. Definitive diagnosis of schistosomiasis is done by identification of the parasite eggs in feces or urine. Parasite removal by treatment based on praziquantel usually is successful, but the chronic lesions caused by deposition of eggs in the liver and lungs – and those, like the renal disease, induced by immune-mediated mechanisms – rarely are responsive.

It has been clearly shown that adding immune suppressants, like steroids and/or cyclosporine, to the antiparasitic treatment results in a negligible response rate and does not alter the progression of the renal disease. Appropriate control of hypertension and of the associated urinary tract abnormalities eventually may delay such progression. It is also noteworthy that amyloidosis has been seen in association with chronic schistosomal infections and that preliminary information would favor the use of colchicine in this condition. The possibility of amyloid in the kidney of schistosomiasis patients adds a new indication for performing renal biopsies.

The histopathologic spectrum of schistosomal nephropathies ranges from minimal proliferative lesions to severe glomerular sclerosis, but the most common finding is the mesangial proliferative type.

Table 52.1 Infectious diseases associated with tropical nephrotic syndrome

Malaria
Schistosomiasis
Hepatitis B and C
Leprosy
Filariasis

Viral hepatitis

Information coming from Asian countries – where between 5 and 7% of the population show serologic evidence of hepatitis C infection, and 10 to 15% of hepatitis B – has clearly shown the relationship between chronic infection with the viruses of hepatitis B and C and the occurrence of nephrotic syndrome. Noteworthy is the fact that a huge proportion of patients with nephrotic syndrome, especially children, have biopsy findings compatible with membranous nephropathy, whereas this diagnosis is seldom seen in pediatric nephrotic syndrome in the developed world. However, worldwide reports attest now to the association of chronic viral hepatitis and nephrotic syndrome in adults. Clinical manifestations of active liver disease usually are absent, but viral antigens are detected in serum. Hepatitis B has been shown to be associated with membranous nephropathy and with membranoproliferative glomerulonephritis.

Hepatitis C virus also has been implicated in the genesis of a membranous lesion and with membranoproliferative changes in conjunction with mixed type II cryoglobulinemia, which usually presents with arthralgia, palpable purpura, moderate renal failure, nephrotic syndrome, hypocomplementemia, positive rheumatoid factor, and anicteric hepatitis. Immunopathogenic studies indicate the presence of hepatitis virus antigens in the immune complexes and the presence of viral nucleic acids in every form of glomerulopathy associated with these agents.

Serologic testing for hepatitis B and C antigens and antibodies is now mandatory in every patient with nephrotic syndrome. This information is very important from the therapeutic point of view. It has been shown that the use of corticosteroids, although inducing temporary remission of the liver and renal disease, has not proved to be of real benefit, and there is evidence that after discontinuation of therapy there is an increase in viral replication, with reactivation of liver and renal disease.

Recent reports have also shown that benefits from interferon therapy are temporary. More promising are reports of a combination of interferon alpha with lamivudine or ribavirin. Establishing the real benefit of these therapeutic maneuvers awaits further investigation.

Other diseases

Tropical nephrotic syndrome also has been reported in association with other chronic bacterial and parasitic diseases. Filariasis, African trypanosomiasis, and leprosy are known causes of tropical nephrotic syndrome. The real significance of these entities in causing renal disease and chronic renal failure is still unknown.

TROPICAL ACUTE RENAL FAILURE

Community-acquired acute renal failure occurs quite frequently in the tropics, and it is a frequent cause of hospital admissions. It is almost always originated by an infectious agent and in some cases and places by insect or animal bites; it is then mostly work-related. From an etiologic point of view, tropical acute renal failure could be divided into four categories (Tab. 52.2).

Table 52.2 Acute renal failure in the tropics

Diarrheal bacterial syndromes (water- and foodborne)
Cholera
Typhoid
Salmonellosis
E. coli
Systemic parasitic infections (vector-borne)
Falciparum malaria
Hemorrhagic fevers (vector-borne)
Dengue
Leptospirosis
Animal and insect bites
Snakes
Bees
Spiders

Acute renal failure associated with diarrheal syndromes

V. cholera, *Salmonella*, *E. coli*, and *Shigella* are bacterial agents that cause acute diarrheal syndromes that frequently complicate with acute renal failure. The clinical picture and the renal and metabolic disturbances are quite similar in all of them, cholera being the prototype of the group.

After many years of uncontrolled, stable, endemic indices in some parts of Africa and Asia, cholera appeared again as a devastating epidemic along the Pacific coasts of South America, in 1991, starting in Peru. It rapidly spread to inner country areas following people and water trails.

The epidemic was controlled in less than 2 years, but permanent endemicity has continued during the last 7 years. Several examples of cholera appearing in distant places in the world after traveling by ship and airplane were shown. During the first 2 years, 300 000 people were affected in Latin America with a fatality count of 3000. Incidence of acute renal failure requiring dialysis was less than 1%, but prerenal azotemia was as presenting manifestation in more than 70% of 4300 admissions in one center.

The pathogenesis of acute renal failure in these acute diarrhea syndromes is consistent with a state of severe volume depletion and the hormonal and sympathetic responses that ensue, causing acute tubular necrosis.

Clinical presentation is usually an acute diarrhea syndrome with fever and vomiting, with rapid deterioration, severe hypotension, and shock. Definitive diagnosis should be made only by culturing the *V. cholera* from feces. Recently, rapid diagnosis has been made easier with tests that investigate the presence of the toxin or bacterial antigens in a small sample of diarrheal fluid, utilizing ELISA essays. Rapid therapeutic intervention is needed to improve survival and to abort the development of further electrolyte disturbances and acute renal failure. In patients with severe hypotension, a rapid intravenous infusion of normal saline solution, of up to 4 to 6 liters in the first 2 hours, has been the most successful therapeutic maneuver. Infusion of Ringer's lactate solution also has been employed, but shows no advantages over normal saline. After hemodynamic stabilization and after obtaining a urine output of at least 40 ml per hour, fluid and salt replenishment could be continued, using oral rehydration solutions constituted mainly of chloride salts of sodium and potassium and glucose. Milder cases are managed only by oral rehydration. In every case, administration of an antibiotic with anticholera activity seems advisable. Monodoses of demeclocycline and/or full doses of norfloxacin have been used with success.

When the syndrome is caused by salmonella, *E. coli*, and/or shigella species, diarrhea is less dramatic and severe hypotension and shock are seldom seen; however, they may complicate with a hemolytic uremic syndrome, causing acute renal failure. Small, limited outbreaks of acute diarrhea and hemolytic uremic syndrome following *E. coli* infection, type OH 157, are regularly reported from many countries. We do not have appropriate information about the real incidence of *E. coli*-induced diarrhea syndrome in the tropical belt, although everybody agrees that the incidence must be an order of magnitude higher than that currently reported.

Several electrolyte disturbances also have been reported during the recent cholera epidemic. Hyponatremia due to inappropriate replacement of fluid losses with hypotonic solutions is still seen. Metabolic acidosis almost always complicates the picture in patients with severe hypotension. It is frequently of the high anion gap type due to hypotension-induced poor tissue perfusion and lactic acidosis. In milder cases a normal anion gap type metabolic acidosis could be seen due to base losses through the stools. This metabolic acidosis seldom requires bicarbonate supplementation and is easily handled by fluid replacement and hemodialysis when the patient develops acute renal failure. Hypocalcemia and hypophosphatemia also can be seen after several days of uncontrolled diarrhea.

Systemic parasitic infection

Falciparum malaria is also on the rise. Epidemiologic reports show a striking increase in cases of *falciparum* malaria worldwide; this also is due to the ease of modern travel.

Many cases are seen on arrival in developed nontropical countries.

Just in the United States about 1000 new cases are diagnosed every year, almost all of them in immigrants and travelers.

In Latin America, there were 1 187 316 new cases reported in 1992. Worldwide, current estimates indicate that, in 1998, 200 million new cases will occur and 2 million will die of malaria.

Parasite drug-resistant and vector insecticide-resistant organisms are contributing factors to these megapandemics.

Acute renal failure in *falciparum* malaria occurs with an incidence of 1 to 4% of all cases, but may be as high as 60% in cases of so-called malignant malaria. Mortality from the syndrome varies between 15 and 30% and usually is associated with multi-organ failure, especially cerebral malaria.

Diagnosis is readily made in the febrile patient by examination of a thick drop of blood stained by Giemsa. More recently, fluorescenin stained with acrydin orange on peripheral blood has shown to have better sensitivity.

The pathophysiology of acute renal failure in *falciparum* malaria is due to a combination of factors set in motion by both host- and parasite-related mechanisms. The magnitude of parasitemia (parasite counts) maintains a close positive correlation with the severity of the syndrome, organ involvement, and mortality.

Plasmodium falciparum infection is characterized by heavy parasitemia, massive infection of red blood cells during the erythrocytic phase and, as a consequence, disturbances in the microcirculation that affect the function of the kidney and other organs. The host response is characterized by activation of cellular immunity and cytokine production. As a result of these mechanisms hypovolemia, hemolysis, rhabdomyolysis, hyperviscosity, jaundice, and intravascular coagulation develop, becoming determining factors for acute renal failure with an anatomic substrate of acute tubular necrosis and acute tubular interstitial nephritis; glomerular hypercellularity and infiltrative lesions also can be seen.

Falciparum malaria-induced acute renal failure is almost always hypercatabolic and is best managed by daily hemodialysis, along with specific antiparasitic treatment with chloroqine or derivatives.

TROPICAL ACUTE RENAL FAILURE ASSOCIATED TO HEMORRHAGIC FEVERS

Dengue

Dengue, a reemerging infectious disease, is caused by the four types of dengue viruses. Its prevalence has been increasing recently in many countries of the tropical belt, leading to several recent epidemic outbreaks in Latin America. Clinically, dengue is an acute febrile illness characterized by severe frontal and retro-orbital headache, excruciating muscle and joint pain, and an incubation period of 1 to 2 weeks. The most severe form of the disease, dengue hemorrhagic fever, is characterized by spontaneous bleeding associated with thrombocytopenia. Hypovolemia, due to a generalized capillary leaking of fluid and hemoconcentration, leads repidly to acute renal failure. Intravascular coagulation and rhabdomyolysis also can occur and contribute to the development of acute renal failure.

Diagnosis is made by an ELISA assay that detects IgM antibodies.

Leptospirosis

Leptospirosis, caused by a spirochete, is a disease that affects wild animals; it has a high prevalence in the tropics. Humans become infected after contact with water contaminated by the urine of infected rodents. Prevalence of the human disease is rapidly increasing in association with recent floods in Central America and southeast Asia. About 10% of patients infected by *Leptospira icterohemorragica* eventually develop renal failure due to a combination of hypovolemia and intravascular coagulation. Polyuric forms are common in association to hypokalemia, but usually it has a hypercatabolic state that requires daily dialysis. Diagnosis is made by a microscopic agglutination test that detects *leptospiras* antibodies. *Leptospiras* DNA sequences can also be detected rapidly in serum or urine by PCR.

Suggested readings

BARSOUM RS. Schistosomal glomerulopathies. Kidney Int 1993;44:1-12.

BARSOUM RS. Malarial nephropathies. Nephrol Dial Transplant 1998;13:1588-97.

CERULLI M, DE ANGELIS S, SEBASTIANI A. Tropical renal and urological diseases. Milano: Wichtig Ed., 1997.

CIEZA J, GAMARRA G, TORRES C, et al. Evolucion de los electrolitos sericos durante el tratamiento de rehidratacion de pacientes con diarrea aguda coleriforme. Rev Med Hered (Lima) 1993;4:3-11.

CIEZA J, GAMARRA G, TORRES C. Letalidad y riesgo de IRA por colera en el Hospital Cayetano Heredia de Lima - Perú. Rev Med Hered (Lima) 1993;4:75-8.

CHUGH KS. Snake-bite-induced acute renal failure in India. Kidney Int 1989;35:891-907.

EIAM-ONG S, SITPRIJA V. Falciparum malaria in the kidney: a model of inflammation. Am J Kidney Dis 1998;32:361-75.

EKNOYAN G. Glomerular abnormalities in liver disease. In: Epstein M, ed. The kidney in liver disease. 4th ed. Philadelphia: Hanley and Belfus, 1996.

GUBLER DJ. Resurgent vector-borne diseases as a global health problem. Emerging Infectious Diseases 1998;4:1-7.

MIYAHIRA J, ACOSTA R, ZURITA S Y TORRES C. Insuficiencia renal aguda en el Hospital Cayetano Heredia durante la epidemia del colera. Rev Med Hered (Lima) 1993;4:64-74.

PAN AMERICAN HEALTH ORGANIZATION. Las condiciones de la salud en las Americas. Washington, 1994.

RASHID HR. South asian renal disease. Bangladesh: Asian Coler Printing, 1997.

SITPRIJA V. Nephropathy in falciparum malaria. Kidney Int 1998;34:867-77.

SECTION 13

Emergency in nephrology

CHAPTER

53

Emergencies in nephrology

Michel Jadoul

This chapter reviews the initial diagnostic workup and management of major nephrologic emergencies: electrolyte or acid-base disturbances, hypertensive emergencies, exogenous intoxications requiring urgent hemodialysis, and finally, complications in patients on renal replacement therapy.

ELECTROLYTE AND ACID-BASE EMERGENCIES

SEVERE HYPERKALEMIA

The detection of severe (>6.5 mmol/l) hyperkalemia requires immediate attention.

Etiopathogenesis

The possibility of spurious hyperkalemia should be borne in mind and excluded by contact with the laboratory (hemolysis, marked thrombocytosis, etc.) and/or repeated testing, especially in the absence of the main risk factors for hyperkalemia. The development of actual severe hyperkalemia indeed usually results from reduced renal excretion of potassium in the face of a normal or increased intake with or without redistribution of body potassium (acidosis).

Drugs are frequent contributing factors: angiotensin-converting enzyme (ACE) inhibitors and angiotensin II receptor antagonists, nonsteroidal anti-inflammatory drugs (NSAIDs), potassium-sparing diuretics (e.g., spironolactone, triamterene, amiloride), high-dose trimethoprim, and cyclosporine.

Clinical findings

The clinical picture may be absent or include a flaccid paralysis resembling Guillain-Barré syndrome with or without signs of cardiac toxicity. The changes of the electrocardiogram (ECG) generally parallel the degree of hyperkalemia, with initial tenting of the T wave progressing to P-wave flattening, widening of the QRS complex, and development of a deep S wave. Ultimately, ventricular fibrillation leads to death. An ECG thus should be recorded immediately in any patient with severe hyperkalemia.

Treatment

In the presence of such clinical or ECG signs, intravenous calcium should be given immediately to counteract the cardiotoxicity of hyperkalemia. The second step is to shift potassium into the intracellular compartment, using the emergency regimen detailed in Table 53.1, and to stop all the above-mentioned drugs. The third step is to reduce the potassium body burden. Patients with severe renal failure and/or treated with multiple drugs should be referred urgently to the nephrologist for hemodialysis, whereas patients with mild renal failure on a single drug (e.g., ACE inhibitor only) usually can be treated conservatively, with the preceding regimen, coupled with sodium polystyrene sulfonate and monitoring of potassium plasma level until normalized.

SEVERE HYPONATREMIA

Severe hyponatremia may be defined as a sodium plasma level below 120 mmol/liter.

Diagnosis

Pseudohyponatremia should be ruled out by the measurement of plasma osmolality (normal in pseudohyponatremia due to severe hyperlipidemia, hyperproteinemia, hyperglycemia, or mannitol treatment). The differential diagnosis should then start with a careful physical examination: are there signs of dehydration or edema (Fig. 53.1)? In addition, urine osmolality should be measured (low in primary polydipsia, high in other causes), as well as urine sodium concentration (Fig. 53.1).

Clinical findings

When the natremia falls below 125 mmol/l, the patient

Table 53.1 Emergency treatment of hyperkalemia

Urgency	Treatment	Dose	Time for effect
Emergent	Calcium	20 ml 10% Ca gluconate iv (5'), repeat q15-20 min as needed	5 min
Urgent	Insulin + glucose	50 ml 50% dextrose + 5-10 U insulin, then 10% dextrose plus 20 U regular insulin per liter at 50 to 100 ml/h	15 min
Urgent	Bicarbonate	50-100 mEq $NaHCO_3$ iv (5')	15 min
Urgent	Albuterol	10 mg by nebulized inhalation (15')	15-30 min
Urgent	Hemodialysis	0 mEq/l K dialysate	30 min
Less urgent	Exchange resins	Sodium polystyrene sulfonate 30 g po in 100 ml 20% sorbitol or 60 g rectally in 200 ml water	2 h
Less urgent	Loop diuretic	Furosemide 250 mg iv	2-4 h

may complain of nausea and malaise. Below 120 mmol/liter, headache and obtundation may appear, with eventual seizures, and coma appears below 110 mmol/l, especially if the hyponatremia has developed rapidly. There is, however, substantial interpatient variability in symptoms of hyponatremia, with premenopausal women at much higher risk of severe symptoms and irreversible neurologic damage than men.

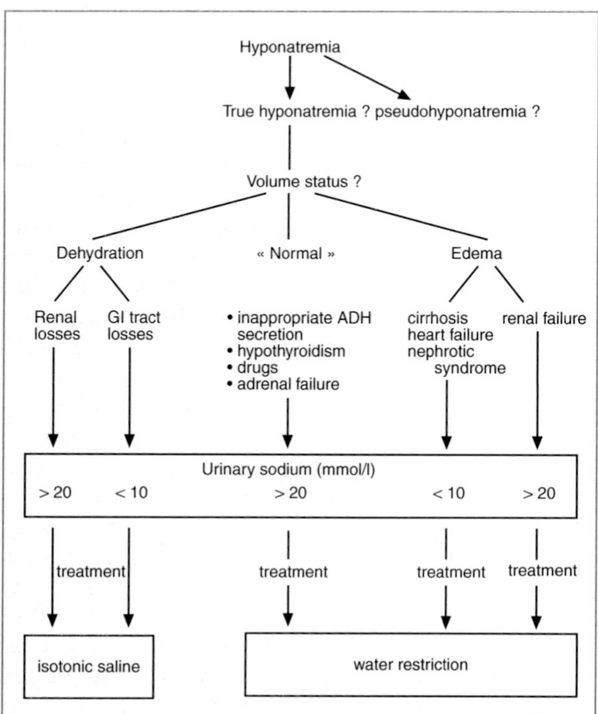

Figure 53.1 Differential diagnosis and management of hyponatremia.

Treatment

The oral intake and intravenous administration of hypoosmolar fluids should be stopped. In severe hyponatremia of demonstrated recent onset (<24 hours) with neurologic symptoms or signs, the plasma sodium concentration should be increased urgently. If dehydration is present, isotonic saline should be provided generously intravenously. In the absence of dehydration, 3% saline (containing 500 mmol Na per liter) should be administered intravenously, if necessary with a loop diuretic to control the extracellular fluid volume status. Plasma sodium level should be increased by no more than 5 mmol/l over the first 4 hours and by no more than 8 mmol/l (and to no more than 120 mmol/l) over the first 24 hours of treatment. It should be checked frequently (every 4-12 hours initially), and aggressive therapy should be withdrawn progressively as symptoms improve. The amount of sodium required to raise the plasma sodium level to 120 mmol/liter can be estimated from the following formula:

$$\text{sodium deficit} = 0.5 \times \text{lean body weight (kg)} \times \times (120 - \text{plasma sodium level})$$

By contrast, in chronic hyponatremia with mild symptoms (the most frequent occurrence), the attitude should be less aggressive to avoid pontine myelinolysis. Water restriction alone is recommended.

SEVERE METABOLIC ACIDOSIS

Diagnosis

Metabolic acidosis is characterized by a low arterial pH (thus a high H^+ plasma concentration) and a reduced plasma bicarbonate concentration leading to compensatory hyperventilation (Kussmaul's respiration) and thus to a decreased P_{CO_2}. It should be differentiated from the compensation of chronic respiratory alkalosis by measurement of the arterial pH (low in metabolic acidosis with acidemia, normal or high in chronic respiratory alkalosis).

In clinical practice, the detection of a markedly reduced plasma bicarbonate concentration (below 12 mmol/l) should prompt the measurement of P_{CO_2} and pH of arterial blood to confirm the suspected acidosis and assess the extent of respiratory compensation.

The diagnostic workup should include, in addition to arterial blood gas measurement, the measurement of plasma electrolytes, creatinine, glucose, and lactate.

Calculation of the plasma anion gap is the next diagnostic step: plasma anion gap = Na – HCO_3 – Cl = normally 8 to 12 mmol/l. The anion gap is increased in renal failure, diabetic ketoacidosis, lactic acidosis, and some exogenous intoxications (e.g., methanol, ethylene glycol, etc.). It is, by contrast, normal in diarrhea, ureterosigmoidostomy, tubular acidosis, etc. (Tab. 53.2).

Clinical findings

The clinical picture specific to severe metabolic acidosis is limited to Kussmaul's respiration (deeper, regular respiration). Much more frequently, the clinical picture will be dominated by the signs of the underlying disease (e.g., sepsis, diabetes, etc.).

Treatment

Treatment of the underlying cause may prove lifesaving (e.g., treatment of sepsis or ketoacidosis, emergency hemodialysis for methanol intoxication, withdrawal of biguanides, etc.). In addition, severe metabolic acidosis usually warrants initial intravenous correction with sodium bicarbonate, either isotonic or, less frequently, hypertonic (in case of severe associated hyponatremia), together with etiologic treatment. The initial aim is to increase plasma bicarbonate level to 16 to 18 mmol/l.

Table 53.2 Differential diagnosis of metabolic acidosis

Anion gap = Na - HCO_3 - Cl (mmol/l)	
≤ 12	**> 12**
Diarrhea	Ketoacidosis (diabetes, alcohol)
Ureterosigmoïdostomy	Intoxication: methanol, ethylene glycol
Renal tubular acidosis	Lactic acidosis
Acetazolamide	Renal failure

HYPERTENSIVE EMERGENCIES

ACCELERATED HYPERTENSION

A diastolic blood pressure repeatedly greater than 120 mmHg in adults should raise the suspicion of accelerated hypertension. One should remember, however, that an elevated blood pressure alone, in the absence of symptoms or new or progressive target-organ damage, rarely requires emergency therapy.

Diagnosis

Creatinine, electrolytes, and lactate dehydrogenase (LDH) serum levels should be measured and a full blood count done. Funduscopy should be performed urgently, with grade III (hemorrhages and exudates) or grade IV (edema) retinopathy diagnostic of accelerated hypertension.

Clinical findings

Headache is a common but nonspecific symptom in such patients. Impairment of vision frequently develops, sometimes with focal neurologic signs. Additional symptoms and signs may include generalized weakness, weight loss, and signs of heart failure and/or acute renal failure.

Treatment

All such patients should be managed in the hospital. Hypertensive emergencies are situations that require immediate blood pressure reduction (not necessarily to the normal range) to prevent or limit target-organ damage (e.g., hypertensive encephalopathy, intracranial hemorrhage, acute myocardial infarction, acute left ventricular failure with pulmonary edema, dissecting aortic aneurysm). Most hypertensive emergencies are treated initially with a parenteral drug, e.g., sodium nitroprusside (initially 1 μg/kg per minute, preferably in an intensive care unit with an indwelling arterial line), labetalol or nicardipine. The initial goal of therapy is to reduce mean arterial blood pressure by no more than 25% (within minutes to 2 hours) and then towards 160/100 mmHg within 2 to 6 hours, avoiding excessive falls in pressure that may precipitate renal, cerebral, or coronary ischemia. Hypertensive urgencies are those situations in which it is desirable to reduce blood pressure within a few hours (e.g., hypertension with stage IV retinopathy, severe perioperative hypertension). They can be managed with oral doses of drugs of relatively fast onset of action, with ACE inhibitors particularly effective.

SEVERE HYPERTENSION IN PREGNANCY

Severe hypertension may be defined, in a pregnant patient, as a diastolic blood pressure greater than 105 mmHg.

Diagnosis

The first question is: is the hypertension of recent onset (presumably pregnancy-induced hypertension or preeclampsia), or is it a worsening of preexisting chronic hypertension? The former is absent during the first 20 weeks of pregnancy and may follow a fulminant course. It requires prompt attention. The second question is: are there signs of severity? The coexistence of headaches and/or epigastric pain, proteinuria, liver dysfunction, thrombocytopenia, and/or grade III/IV retinopathy should prompt hospitalization.

The severity of the disease must be monitored: blood pressure profile, quantification of proteinuria, full blood count, electrolytes, plasma urate and creatinine, liver function, and hemostasis tests. The fetus should be assessed using methods appropriate for gestational age and the clinical problem (e.g., ultrasonographic assessment of growth, cardiotoxography, Doppler assessment of umbilical artery flow velocity waveform).

Treatment

The aim is to protect the mother and fetus from the consequences of hypertension and to prolong the pregnancy to avoid the problems of prematurity. Thus a constant evaluation of the respective risks for mother and fetus of continuing the pregnancy versus delivery is required. Severe preeclampsia, pulmonary edema, gross hepatic dysfunction, coagulopathy, and renal compromise usually are indications for immediate delivery. Hypertension should be treated with methyldopa (0.5-2 g/day) and/or labetalol or nifedipine. Seizures should be treated with intravenous diazepam, followed by phenytoin or magnesium sulphate.

EXOGENOUS INTOXICATIONS REQUIRING EMERGENCY HEMODIALYSIS

The place of extracorporeal techniques in the treatment of exogenous intoxication is limited. Withdrawal of the offending agent, administration of antidotes, and use of supportive nonspecific therapy remain the mainstay of the treatment of the poisoned patient. However, the outcome of a few not uncommon intoxications may be improved dramatically by emergency hemodialysis. The causal poisons share a low apparent volume of distribution and low molecular weight, a low plasma protein binding, and limited tissue-binding properties.

METHYL-ALCOHOL (METHANOL) INTOXICATION

Clinical findings

Methanol causes central nervous system effects similar to those caused by ethanol. In addition, 6 to 24 hours after ingestion, subjective visual changes are accompanied by peripapillary edema and severe metabolic acidosis with a high anion gap.

Treatment

The toxicity of methanol mainly results from the formation of formaldehyde and then formic acid (which raises the anion gap) under the action of alcohol dehydrogenase. Therapy consists of the administration of ethanol to delay the metabolism of methanol and of hemodialysis to remove methanol from the circulation. Hemodialysis may be indicated whenever the methanol plasma level exceeds 50 mg/dl. The sooner hemodialysis is started, the better the prognosis. A plasma level of ethanol of 100 mg/dl should be maintained concurrently.

LITHIUM INTOXICATION

Clinical findings

Acute toxicity of lithium is often superimposed on chronic accumulation. The clinical picture includes neuromuscular excitability, confusion, fever subsequently leading to coma, vomiting, and cardiac complications. Any unexplained neuromuscular symptom or sign in a patient under lithium should thus prompt urgent plasma lithium measurement, especially if risk factors for intoxication are present (e.g., renal failure, fever, vomiting, or diarrhea).

Treatment

Since acute lithium poisoning is a severe complication with a 10% mortality rate and an additional 10% rate of permanent neurologic damage, hemodialysis should be started whenever the plasma lithium level exceeds 2.5 mmol/liter and/or symptoms of intoxication are severe and/or renal insufficiency makes the standard treatment (i.e., discontinuation of lithium and intravenous hydration) problematic.

EMERGENCIES IN THE PATIENT ON RENAL REPLACEMENT THERAPY

HEMODIALYSIS PATIENTS

Fever

Etiology

In addition to common causes of fever, fulminant infection

originating in the vascular access is frequent and should be always considered in a febrile hemodialysis patient. The etiologic agent is usually *Staphylococcus aureus*. The main risk factors include the type of access (higher risk with prosthetic grafts or central venous catheters than with arteriovenous fistulas) and diabetes.

Diagnosis

The clinical picture may be limited initially to fever and chills, with subsequent evidence for metastatic bacterial foci (e.g., septic arthritis, focal neurologic signs, endocarditis). Multiple blood cultures should be obtained together with culture of any discharge from the access site, if present. The absence of local level of inflammatory signs (graft or catheter) does not exclude infection, however.

Treatment

Unexplained fever and/or chills in a hemodialysis patient *a priori* should be considered as suspicious for staphylococcal origin, and empirical antibiotics should be considered seriously (e.g., cefazoline 1 g iv every 48 hours).

Other complications related to the vascular access

Hemorrhage Bleeding from an arteriovenous fistula or prosthetic graft occasionally may occur at a distance from the last hemodialysis session and be rather abundant because of the high pressure in an arterialized vascular access. The attitude should be to exert gentle compression to ensure hemostasis. The effectiveness of compression may be checked by direct vision. It also should be checked from time to time that compression is not too strong, to avoid the risk of access thrombosis. This may be checked by auscultation (presence of a systolodiastolic murmur) and/or palpation (detection of a thrill). When bleeding has stopped, the puncture sites should be dressed like any minor wound after appropriate disinfection.

Thrombosis If one observes between two hemodialysis sessions that the thrill characteristic of the patency of the arteriovenous fistula or prosthetic graft is no longer detectable, acute thrombosis of the access is likely. Such a patient should be referred urgently to the hemodialysis unit to confirm the diagnosis and plan emergency interventional radiologic or surgical therapy of thrombosis. The earlier the intervention, the higher are the chances of success.

Hyperkalemia and acute pulmonary edema

Hemodialysis patients poorly compliant to dietary and fluid restriction may present, usually at the end of the longest interdialytic interval, with signs of hyperkalemia and/or pulmonary edema. Both complications require emergency hemodialysis.

PERITONEAL DIALYSIS PATIENTS

Peritonitis

Clinical findings

The peritoneal dialysis (PD) effluent becomes turbid, and the patient experiences abdominal pain, with or without fever, and occasionally with vomiting. The diagnosis is confirmed by the presence of more than 100 cells/mm^3 of dialysate and eventually by PD fluid culture.

Treatment

The earlier the diagnosis of peritonitis, the better is the chance for cure with antibiotics. The preceding clinical picture thus should prompt immediate drawing of 20 ml of effluent dialysate to be cultured under both aerobic and anaerobic conditions. Empirical antibiotic therapy should be started immediately, without waiting for the results of PD fluid culture.

Leaks of peritoneal fluid

Clinical findings

PD fluid may leak through many anatomic routes. This may lead to edema of the labia or scrotum and penis, of the soft tissue planes from the catheter insertion site, or through a hernia. Finally, hydrothorax resulting from pleural accumulation of PD fluid is a rare but sometimes life-threatening complication. Thus the development in a PD patient of sudden, unexplained accumulation of fluid in a trunkal body compartment always should raise the suspicion of a leak.

Treatment

Peritoneal dialysis should be stopped immediately and the patient referred to the nephrologic team for further diagnostic workup (computed tomography and scintigraphy) and management.

RENAL TRANSPLANT RECIPIENT

Two main emergencies with specific characteristics may develop in the renal transplant recipient: acute graft dysfunction and fever.

Acute renal failure

Chimical findings

The development of (hyper)acute renal failure will present

as oligoanuria with or without associated signs such as fever, hematuria, etc. Usually the graft will not be painful, irrespectively of inflammation, due to the absence of graft innervation.

Diagnosis

Ultrasonography as well as duplex Doppler scanning of the renal graft artery and vein should be obtained, together with blood chemistries and measurement of immunosuppressants levels. This will help identify a pre- or postrenal cause of the renal failure (i.e., acute renal artery or vein thrombosis, obstructive uropathy). An intrinsic renal cause (i.e., acute rejection or drug-induced dysfunction) is the most common cause of acute renal failure after transplantation, however.

Treatment

The patient with acute severe graft dysfunction should be referred urgently to the transplantation team. After exclusion of both nonparenchymal causes of renal failure and drug nephrotoxicity, empirical treatment of rejection usually is started, awaiting the results of graft biopsy.

Fever

Clinical findings

The signs and symptoms accompanying the fever may give important clues to the origin of the fever: cough, dyspnea, urinary complaints, headaches, diarrhea, abdominal pain, etc.

Diagnosis

Routine blood tests, blood and urine cultures, and a chest x-ray and a cytomegalovirus antigen test should be obtained initially.

Empirical treatment

The most likely diagnosis usually will deserve empirical treatment, awaiting diagnostic confirmation. In the early posttransplant period (<6 months), all such patients should be referred back urgently to their transplant team.

In the initial posttransplant period (<1 month), bacterial infection is the most common cause. Broad-spectrum antibiotics should be started (e.g., a third-generation cephalosporin plus an aminoglycoside) after appropriate workup, including blood, urine, sputum cultures.

From the second to the sixth month posttransplantation, the most common causes of fever are infections due to impaired cellular immunity, especially cytomegalovirus infection and, less frequently, pneumocystic or fungal infection. This possibility will be even more likely shortly after an intensification of the immunosuppressive treatment, e.g., a course of antilymphocyte antibodies for graft rejection. Empirical ganciclovir should be considered, awaiting the results of the diagnostic tests, including cultures of bronchoalveolar fluid in patients with respiratory signs.

Suggested readings

ADROGUE HJ, MADIAS NE. Hyponatremia. N Engl J Med 2000; 342:1581-9.

ADROGUE HJ, MADIAS NE. Management of life-threatening acid-base disorders. N Engl J Med 1998;338:26-34.

BARGMAN JM. Noninfectious complications of peritoneal dialysis. In: Gokal R, Nolph KD, eds. The textbook of peritoneal dialysis. Dordrecht: Kluwer Academic Publishers, 1994;555-90.

COLLEE GG, HANSON GC. The management of acute poisoning. Br J Anaesthesiol 1993;70:562-73.

DADELSZEN P. Management of hypertension in pregnancy. Br Med J 1999;318:1332-6.

DOHERTY CC. Graft dysfunction and its differential diagnosis. In: McGeown MG, ed. Clinical management of renal transplantation. Dordrecht: Kluwer Academic Publishers, 1992;243-62.

GARELLA S. Extracorporeal techniques in the treatment of exogenous intoxications. Kidney Int 1988;33:735-54.

GOKAL R, MALLICK NP. Peritoneal dialysis. Lancet 1999;353:823-8.

GREENBERG A. Hyperkalemia: treatment options. Semin Nephrol 1998;18:46-57.

HALPERIN ML, KAMEL KS. Potassium. Lancet 1998;352:135-40.

IFUDU O. Care of patients undergoing hemodialysis. N Engl J Med 1998;339:1054-62.

THE SIXTH REPORT OF THE JOINT NATIONAL COMMITTEE ON PREVENTION, DETECTION, EVALUATION AND TREATMENT OF HIGH BLOOD PRESSURE. Arch Intern Med 1997;157:2413-46.

WALKER JJ. Pre-eclampsia. Lancet 2000;356:1260-65.

SECTION

14

Principles of drug therapy

CHAPTER

54

Principles of drug therapy

Michael Trimble

This chapter considers the pharmacology of drugs used in the treatment of renal disease and hypertension. Care is always needed when prescribing in renal impairment. Certain drugs are best avoided, and others may require adjustment of the dose. While the dosages of certain agents are given herein, readers should consult the appropriate product literature and also should read Chapter 48 in this volume for guidance. For treatment of specific diseases, the relevant chapters should be consulted. Some of these therapies, such as erythropoietin and the immunosuppressive agents, should only be used in specialist centers.

DIURETICS

In order to understand the mode of action of diuretic agents, it is necessary to first discuss the normal processes of filtration, excretion, and reabsorption in the kidney. The basic function of the kidney is to clear the plasma of unwanted substances. The basic structural unit of the kidney is the nephron. A nephron consists of the glomerulus, the proximal convoluted tubule, the loop of Henle, the distal convoluted tubule, and the collecting ducts. The rate of blood flow through the kidneys of an average 70-kg man is 1200 ml/min; this represents about 20% of the cardiac output. The plasma is filtered at the glomeruli, and the total volume of filtrate produced by both kidneys is around 120 ml/min; this is the glomerular filtration rate (GFR). Water is freely filtered at the glomerulus, but the permeability of its basement membrane for different solutes is related to their molecular weight. Small molecules such as insulin (M_r = 5200) are freely filtered, but larger molecules such as albumin (M_r = 69 000) cannot pass through. Molecular weight is not the only determinant of permeability; electric charge also plays a part – strongly negatively charged molecules are less able to cross. This means that osmotically important molecules such as plasma proteins are not filtered (nor are drugs bound to them). Around 180 liters of filtrate will be produced each day, and all but 1000 to 1500 ml will be reabsorbed as it passes along the nephron.

In the proximal convoluted tubule, there is active reabsorption of sodium bicarbonate and sodium chloride. Sodium enters the cell as hydrogen ions leave via a sodium-hydrogen ion exchanger on the apical (luminal) membrane of the tubular epithelial cell. The process is driven by the working of a Na,K-ATPase pump on the basal membrane of the cell; this keeps the intracellular sodium concentration low, encouraging entry of sodium down the concentration gradient. The process depends on the combination of secreted hydrogen ions and filtered bicarbonate forming carbonic acid in the tubular lumen and then being dehydrated to water and carbon dioxide, a reaction catalyzed by the enzyme carbonic anhydrase. The CO_2 passes back into the cell and forms carbonic acid. This again dissociates to bicarbonate and hydrogen ion, the hydrogen being excreted as above and the bicarbonate passing into the bloodstream. Chloride is passively absorbed and combines with sodium ions removed from the cell at the basal Na,K-ATPase pump. Water follows the reabsorbed solutes by passive diffusion. About 65% of water and solute are reabsorbed in the proximal tubule.

The next section is the loop of Henle. The first segment of the loop is the thin descending limb. Here the tubule passes through a region of renal medulla that is hypertonic, and further water is reabsorbed by passive diffusion. After the thin ascending limb there is the thick ascending limb. Here, at the luminal membrane of the epithelial cells, there exist sodium/potassium-chloride cotransporter molecules that allow these ions to enter. Again, the driving force for this process is the entry of sodium down the concentration gradient maintained by the basal membrane Na,K-ATPase pump sodium. The thick ascending limb is responsible for the reabsorption of approximately 35% of the filtered sodium load.

In the next segment, the distal convoluted tubule, about 10% of the filtered sodium is reabsorbed. This time a specific sodium-chloride cotransporter is involved, and again, the process depends on the entry of sodium down a concentration gradient created by the Na,K-ATPase molecule on the basal membrane of the tubular cell.

Two specific cell types are found in the wall of the collecting tubule. First are the principal cells; these cells have specific channels in the luminal membrane where sodium ions can enter and potassium ions leave, each traveling down the concentration gradient maintained, as always, by the Na,K-ATPase pump. The activity of these channels is regulated by the hormone aldosterone, which increases the activity of these channels. In addition, water channels that depend on antidiuretic hormone (ADH) are found. In the absence of ADH, the collecting tubules are impermeable to water. The other cell in the collecting duct is the intercalated cell. These cells are the main site of hydrogen ion secretion by means of an ATP-dependent pump.

Acetazolamide

This weakly diuretic drug inhibits the enzyme carbonic anhydrase, which is critical for the reabsorption of bicarbonate in the proximal tubule. At maximal dosage, up to 85% of the enzyme's activity is inhibited, although bicarbonate will be reabsorbed at later stages in the nephron, so the effect on total bicarbonate excretion is much less marked. An alkaline diuresis ensues. The bicarbonate depletion leads to a metabolic acidosis. For most indications this drug has been superseded by more modern compounds, but it still has a role in treatment of glaucoma and as prophylaxis against acute mountain sickness.

Loop diuretics

These agents are specific inhibitors of the sodium/potassium-chloride cotransporter found in the luminal membrane of the thick ascending limb of the loop of Henle. They are filtered at the glomerulus and excreted as organic acids.

Approximately 25% of filtered sodium is reabsorbed in the thick ascending limb, and more distal parts of the nephron cannot compensate for the loss at this site; hence loop diuretics are the most potent diuretic agents available. Their duration of action is between 2 and 6 hours, so the kidney can attempt to increase sodium reabsorption after this period.

They are effective in treating pulmonary edema and congestive heart failure, and they may be used for treatment of fluid retention in oliguric renal failure. An attempt may be made to convert oliguric renal failure to nonoliguric renal failure. They are the diuretics most likely to be effective in patients with impaired renal function, but high doses may be necessary. Other indications include treatment of hypercalcemia because they increase excretion of this ion. Care must be taken in patients with liver cirrhosis because overdiuresis can precipitate encephalopathy. Other adverse effects include hyponatremia, hypokalemia, gout, metabolic alkalosis, hypocalcemia, tinnitus and deafness in high doses intravenously.

Thiazide diuretics

These drugs inhibit the sodium-chloride cotransporter, and therefore, their effect is seen predominantly in the distal convoluted tubule. They also enhance calcium reabsorption in this segment, although the mechanism is uncertain.

Thiazides are absorbed orally and compete with other organic acids (such as uric acid) for secretion at the kidney. Unlike the loop diuretics, they are ineffective an if the GFR falls below 30 to 40 ml/min. Since only 5% of the total filtered sodium load reaches the distal convoluted tubule, the diuretic effect of the thiazides is modest. The duration of action of these drugs is long enough to permit once-daily dosing. On their own, thiazides are effective an therapy for hypertension; their antihypertensive effect is seen at low doses (e.g., bendroflumethiazide 2.5 mg daily) and does not increase with increasing dose. They may be used in mild heart failure, although loop diuretics are preferred.

These drugs can act synergistically with the loop diuretics. By preventing the usual distal tubular compensatory increase in sodium reabsorption induced by the loop diuretics, a profound diuresis may be obtained. Metolazone is the drug of choice in this setting. Potential adverse effects of thiazides include electrolyte imbalance (hypokalemia, hyponatremia, hypomagnesemia, hypercalcemia), metabolic alkalosis, hyperuricemia and gout, impaired glucose tolerance, dyslipidemia, and impotence in men.

Potassium-sparing diuretics

There are two groups of agents in this class. Spironolactone is a synthetic steroid that blocks the action of aldosterone in the cortical collecting tubules and hence inhibits the activation of the sodium and potassium channels in this segment. Triamterene and amiloride act to block the sodium channels present in the principal cells, so inhibiting sodium reabsorption. These agents are weak diuretics, since only a small amount of sodium remains to be absorbed at this stage. They are a useful adjunct to loop or thiazide diuretics, countering the hypokalemic tendency of these drugs. Spironolactone is particularly useful in edema due to hyperaldosteronemic states such as hepatic cirrhosis, although, if used alone, it may take several days for full therapeutic effect to be seen. The obvious potential adverse effects for these agents will be hyperkalemia and hyponatremia. Care needs to be taken especially in patients with renal impairment and those on angiotensin-converting enzyme (ACE) inhibitors.

Osmotic diuretics

Mannitol is an osmotically active agent filtered at the glomerulus and neither secreted nor absorbed. Its osmotic pressure limits the reabsorption of water from the tubular fluid. It may be used to reduce intracranial hypertension, and occasionally it is used in rhabdomyolysis to attempt to flush debris through the kidney.

Doses of diuretics

See Table 54.1.

Diuretics

See preceding Section.

Adrenergic blocking drugs

The sympathetic nervous system is important in regulating cardiovascular function, particularly in response to stress – the "fight or flight" response. Its effects are mediated by the release of norepinephrine from the nerve terminals in the peripheral sympathetic system and epinephrine from the adrenal medulla. Several different subtypes of receptor exist within the sympathetic system, and these mediate many different effects in different tissues. The receptors can be divided broadly into alpha (α) and beta (β) and dopamine (D) responsive subtypes.

Further subdivisions exist:

- α_1: stimulation of these receptors results in vascular smooth muscle constriction, papillary dilatation, pilomotor erection, and increased myocardial contraction;
- α_2: stimulation of these receptors has many CNS effects and also causes platelet aggregation, inhibition of lipolysis, and some degree of vascular smooth muscle contraction;
- β_1: stimulation of these receptors results in an increase in heart rate and force of contraction;
- β_2: stimulation here produces vascular smooth muscle relaxation, bronchial relaxation, and uterine relaxation. In addition, there is increased hepatic glycogenolysis and uptake of potassium into myocytes;
- β_3: these receptors mediate lypolysis in adipose tissue;
- D_1: renal vasodilatation results.

Other dopamine receptor subtypes exist, but their effects are predominantly within the CNS and therefore will not be discussed further. Both alpha and beta adrenoceptor blocking drugs are used in the management of hypertension.

Alpha blockers

Mechanism of action The drugs used in the management of hypertension are selective α_1-receptor blocking agents. Nonselective alpha blocking drugs such as phentolamine and phenoxybenzamine are available, but their use is restricted to the diagnosis and treatment of hypertensive episodes due to pheochromocytoma. Blockade of the postsynaptic alpha$_1$ adrenoceptor results in a decrease in arteriolar resistance and venous capacitance and therefore a drop in blood pressure. Initially, there is a reflex sympathetic response with an increase in heart rate and plasma renin activity. With long-term administration, the heart rate, cardiac output, and plasma renin activity return to normal; however, salt and water retention occur in many patients if a diuretic is not prescribed concomitantly. No adverse effect on renal blood flow has been observed. The

Table 54.1 Doses of diuretics

Thiazides		
Bendroflumethiazide	Hypertension Edema	2.5 mg daily po 5-10 mg daily po
Metolazone	Hypertension Edema	5 mg alternate days po 5-10 mg daily, 20 mg in resistant edema
Loop diuretics		
Furosemide	Edema Acute pulmonary edema Oliguria	40 mg po initially; maintenance 20-80 mg daily 50 mg iv 250 mg daily po, larger doses may be required
Bumetanide	Edema/oliguria	1-2 mg daily po; maximum 5 mg iv, 1-2 mg repeated after 20 min if required
Ethacrynic acid	Edema requiring urgent diuresis	50-100 mg slow iv infusion
Potassium-sparing diuretics		
Spironolactone	Edema, ascites, congestive heart failure	100-200 mg daily, increased to 400 mg if required
Amiloride	Edema, potassium conservation with loop or thiazide diuretics	5-10 mg daily
Triamterene	Edema, potassium conservation with loop or thiazide diuretics	150-250 mg daily; reduce to alternate days after 1 week

effect on blood pressure is more marked in the upright than the supine position. A rapid response may occur, with the first dose producing postural hypotension, thus it should be low and taken as the patient retires to bed. Side effects include dizziness, nausea, vertigo, headache, fatigue, and rhinitis, but generally these drugs are well tolerated. A beneficial effect on plasma lipids may be observed with a reduction in triglycerides, total cholesterol, and the low-density lipoprotein fraction and an increase in high-density lipoprotein cholesterol. Alpha receptor blocking drugs may not provide adequate control of hypertension when used as monotherapy and so are not often used as first-line therapy. These drugs are also used in the treatment of benign prostatic hyperplasia.

Doses See Table 54.2.

Beta blockers

Beta adrenoceptor blocking drugs block the effect of beta adrenergic stimulation in many tissues: heart, peripheral vasculature, bronchi, liver, and pancreas. They are effective antihypertensive agents and also have important antianginal and antiarrhythmic effects. They have been shown to reduce mortality when given after acute myocardial infarction and are now being demonstrated to be of use in the management of heart failure. This account will restrict discussion to their use in the management of hypertension.

Mechanism of action Beta adrenoceptor blockers competitively inhibit the action of catecholamines at β_1 and β_2 receptor subtypes. Within this class of drugs, some have approximately equal affinity for both β_1 and β_2 receptors (e.g., propranolol), whereas others exhibit greater affinity for β_1 receptors (e.g., atenolol, bisoprolol, and metoprolol) and therefore are termed *cardioselective beta blockers*. Those with greatest β_1 selectivity should have fewer unwanted β_2-mediated effects, although no drug is completely β_1-specific, and so these drugs should be avoided in asthma. Other differences between these drugs relate to whether they are pure antagonists or whether they have partial agonist properties, i.e., intrinsic sympathomimetic activity (ISA). When sympathetic tone is high, these drugs will act as antagonists, but when sympathetic tone is low, they cause increased heart rate and contractility. Beta blockers with ISA include acebutolol, esmolol, and pindolol. A further difference in side-effect profile may be observed between those drugs which are lipid-soluble and those which are water-soluble (e.g., atenolol, bisoprolol, and metoprolol). The water-soluble drugs are less likely to enter the CNS and should have a lower incidence of adverse events such as sleep disturbance and nightmares. In addition to their beta-blocking properties, labetolol and carvedilol have alpha adrenoceptor blocking effects.

Beta adrenoceptor drugs reduce blood pressure by several mechanisms. There is a reduction in heart rate and cardiac output. There is a reduction in circulating levels of renin and therefore also angiotensin II. This in turn means a reduction in the aldosterone-mediated conservation of sodium and water. Other postulated mechanisms include alteration of central sympathetic control, change in baroreceptor sensitivity, and alteration in peripheral adrenergic neuronal function.

Advantages Beta-blocking drugs are effective antihypertensive agents and are suitable as first-line therapy. They have additional beneficial effects in those with angina, after myocardial infarction, and in some tachyarrhythmic conditions.

Disadvantages Commonly reported side effects include fatigue and cold peripheries and less commonly bronchoconstriction and wheeze, sleep disturbance, dry eyes, psoriasis, and sexual dysfunction in males. Metabolic complications may include minor adverse effects on blood lipid profile and impaired glucose tolerance. Loss of awareness of hypoglycemia in treated diabetics has deterred many from using beta blockers in these patients, but the risk is probably overstated, and diabetics benefit from the cardioprotective effects of these drugs.

Contraindications Beta blockers should not be prescribed in asthmatic patients and must be used with caution in those with peripheral vascular disease. They are contraindicated in those with bradyarrhythmias, sick sinus syndrome, second- or third-degree atrioventricular (AV) block, hypotension, or uncontrolled heart failure. Owing to potential proar-

Table 54.2 Doses of alpha blockers

Doxazosin	Hypertension	1 mg daily, increased to 2 mg after 1-2 weeks and then to 4 mg daily according to response; maximum daily dose 16 mg
Prazosin	Hypertension	500 μg 2-3 times daily, increasing to 1 mg 2-3 times daily after 3-7 days if required; maximum total daily dose 20 mg
Indoramin	Hypertension	25 mg twice daily, increasing by 25 mg daily at 2-week intervals; maximum daily dose 200 mg in 2-3 divided doses

rhythmogenic effects this drug, sotolol is no longer indicated for the treatment of hypertension, and its use should be limited to treatment of life-threatening arrhythmias.

Doses Dosages given are for the treatment of hypertension (for other indications, please consult product literature). In general, a low dose of beta blocker (e.g., atenolol 50 mg daily) will have as great an effect on blood pressure as a higher dose but with a reduced incidence of side effects. If additional antihypertensive effect is required, a drug of a different class, such as a thiazide diuretic, should be added, also at a low dose (e.g., bendroflumethiazide 2.5 mg daily).

Noncardioselective beta blockers

Without ISA Propranolol: initially 80 mg bid; increase at weekly intervals as required. Usual maintenance dose is 160 to 320 mg daily.

With ISA Oxprenolol: 80 to 160 mg daily in two or three divided doses, increasing at 1- to 2-week intervals to maximum total daily dose of 320 mg. Pindolol: 5 mg two to three times daily or 15 mg once daily, increased at weekly intervals as required to a maintenance dose of 15 to 30 mg daily.

Cardioselective beta blockers

Without ISA Atenolol: 50 mg once daily. Bisoprolol: 5 to 10 mg once daily. Maximum dose 20 mg daily. Metoprolol: 100 mg daily; may be increased to 200 mg daily.

With ISA Acebutolol: 400 mg once daily, increased to 400 mg bid after 2 weeks if required.

Angiotensin-converting enzyme (ACE) inhibitors

Mechanism of action In the normal kidney, renin is released from the juxtaglomerular apparatus of the renal cortex in response to several stimuli: reduction in renal arterial pressure, increased sympathetic activity, decreased sodium delivery to the apparatus, or increased sodium concentration in the distal tubule. Renin acts on angiotensinogen, an α_2-globulin, to produce angiotensin I. This inactive decapeptide is the substrate for angiotensin-converting enzyme producing the active substance angiotensin II. Angiotensin II has many actions: it is a potent vasoconstrictor both systemically and in the renal vascular bed; it stimulates release of aldosterone, which promotes renal conservation of sodium and water; and it is also involved in tropic changes in tissues such as the heart. It can be seen that the vasoconstriction and sodium retention are important factors in blood pressure control. There are two receptor subtypes for angiotensin II. The angiotensin type 1 receptor (AT1) is involved in vasoconstriction of arteriolar smooth muscle, aldosterone release, and possibly a direct antinatriuretic effect on the kidney. The role of angiotensin type 2 (AT2) is less well understood. ACE inhibitors are competitive inhibitors of angiotensin-converting enzyme.

Their effect therefore is to produce systemic and renal vasodilation, reduction in sodium and water retention, and therefore a drop in blood pressure. Serum angiotensin-converting enzyme also has a role in the inactivation of bradykinin, and therefore, ACE inhibition will lead to increased levels of this vasodilatory peptide. The consequences of this are uncertain.

The effects on renal hemodynamics have been studied extensively. There is a drop in systemic blood pressure and an increase in renal blood flow. There is a greater degree of vasodilation produced in the efferent arteriole than in the afferent arteriole; thus, filtration pressure is decreased. Angiotensin II produces a contraction of mesangial cells and therefore a decrease in filtration area; when angiotensin-converting enzyme is inhibited, this is reversed. Thus, while glomerular filtration pressure is reduced, renal blood flow and filtration area are increased. The net effect on GFR may be an increase, a decrease, or no change. In addition to the hemodynamic effects, there are postulated effects on mesangial cell proliferation and endothelial cell function. In proteinuric renal failure, control of blood pressure can slow the rate of deterioration of renal function and reduce the degree of proteinuria. ACE inhibitors have been found to reduce the degree of proteinuria to a greater extent than other antihypertensive medications, producing a similar degree of blood pressure lowering. In diabetic nephropathy, ACE inhibitors have been found to retard the progression of microalbuminuria to overt proteinuria and to slow the rate of deterioration of renal function. However, the recent U.K. Prospective Diabetes Study (UKPDS) found no significant difference between hypertensive diabetics treated with ACE inhibitors and those treated with beta blockers. The effects of ACE inhibition on nondiabetic proteinuric renal disease with low-grade proteinuria remains to be determined by prospective controlled studies.

In patients with impaired systolic function and symptomatic heart failure, ACE inhibition will improve cardiac systolic function and reduce both symptoms and mortality. The effect is believed to be a combination of hemodynamic effects, i.e., reduction in preload (reduced sodium and water retention) and afterload (vasodilation), and also modulation of myocyte growth. ACE inhibitors have been found to have an important role in modulating cardiac remodeling after myocardial infarction, reducing the incidence of left ventricular dysfunction and overt cardiac failure.

Indications Hypertension, heart failure, after myocardial infarction, diabetic nephropathy (microalbuminuria > 30 mg/day).

Contraindications/cautions Previous hypersensitivity to ACE inhibitors, pregnancy, aortic stenosis or outflow tract obstruction, renovascular disease.

In patients with severe bilateral renal artery stenosis or

renal artery stenosis in a single functioning kidney, where glomerular blood flow depends on high efferent arteriolar tone, ACE inhibitors may greatly reduce GFR and may cause severe renal failure. A similar effect may be seen in patients with low renal perfusion due to hypovolemia or heart failure. These effects are exacerbated by sodium depletion. In cases of renal artery stenosis with a contralateral normal functioning kidney, the overall renal function is not likely to be greatly diminished, but the GFR of the affected kidney will be greatly reduced or even abolished. Generalized atheromatous disease, in particular, peripheral vascular disease, may warn of an increased risk of renovascular disease. Renal function (urea and electrolytes) should be checked prior to initiation of therapy and then monitored periodically. For those at high risk – hyponatremia (Na < 130 mmol/liter), hypotension (systolic BP < 90 mm Hg), renal impairment (plasma creatinine > 150 mmol/liter) – or on high-dose diuretic therapy, hospital initiation may be appropriate.

Side effects Profound hypotension may occur on initiation of therapy. It is more common in patients who are volume-depleted, e.g., heart failure patients treated with diuretic, and withdrawal of diuretic for a few days prior to commencing the ACE inhibitor may help. A chronic daily dry cough is seen in up to 20% of patients. Hyperkalemia may occur particularly in those taking potassium-sparing diuretics. In addition, a maculopapular rash, neutropenia, proteinuria, and angioedema have been reported.

Interactions Loss of effect and risk of renal impairment with nonsteroidal anti-inflammatory drugs (NSAIDs). Hyperkalemia with potassium supplements or potassium-sparing diuretics. Lithium excretion is reduced.

Doses See Table 54.3.

Angiotensin II receptor antagonists

These drugs are specific inhibitors of angiotensin II. They have a high affinity for the AT1 receptor subtype and compete with angiotensin II for binding at this site. As with ACE inhibitors, systemic and renal vasodilation and inhibition of aldosterone secretion result. AT2 receptors are unaffected, and there is no effect on bradykinin.

Indications At present, these drugs are licensed only for the treatment of hypertension. There are ongoing studies to investigate their role in the management of heart failure and renal disease. It is anticipated that they will have similar benefits as ACE inhibitors.

Contraindications/cautions Avoid in pregnancy and during breast-feeding. Avoid in hepatic failure and aortic stenosis. Caution if risk of renal artery stenosis or renal impairment is present. Monitoring of renal function and electrolytes is advised.

Side effects Possible side effects include symptomatic hypotension, especially in those with intravascular volume depletion, hyperkalemia and angioedema.

Doses Candesartan cilexetil: initially 4 mg (2 mg in renal impairment or the elderly); increase according to blood pressure. Usual maintenance dose, 8 mg; maximum, 16 mg daily. Irbesartan: 150 mg once daily, increasing to 300 mg daily. In those over 75 years of age or hemodialysis patients, 75 mg may be appropriate. Losartan potassium: 50 mg once daily, increasing after several weeks if required to 100 mg daily. In the elderly or in moderate to severe renal impairment, 25 mg daily. Valsartan: 80 mg once daily, increasing after at least 4 weeks to 160 mg daily. In mild to moderate hepatic impairment or moderate

Table 54.3 Doses of ACE inhibitors

Captopril	Hypertension	12.5 mg bid
	Heart failure	6.25 mg initially, increasing to a maintenance dose of 25 mg tid
	Diabetic nephropathy	75-100 mg daily in divided doses
Enalapril	Hypertension	5 mg daily initially (2.5 mg in elderly or in renal impairment); usual maintenance dose 10-20 mg daily; maximum dose 40 mg daily
Lisinopril	Hypertension	2.5 mg, increasing to a maintenance dose of 10-20 mg daily (40 mg maximum)
	Heart failure	2.5 mg initially, increasing to a maintenance dose of 5-20 mg daily
	Diabetic nephropathy	2.5 mg initially, increasing to achieve a diastolic blood pressure of <75 mmHg in normotensive diabetics and < 90 mmHg in hypertensive diabetics
Trandolopril	Hypertension	500 μg once daily, increasing at 2- to 4-week intervals to maintenance dose of 1-2 mg daily (maximum 4 mg daily)

to severe renal impairment and in the elderly (>75 years of age), 40 mg may be sufficient.

Calcium channel blockers

This is an umbrella term for three groups of compounds: phenylalkylamines (such as verapamil), benzothiazepines (such as diltiazem), and dihydropyridines (such as nifedipine).

Mechanism of action An influx of calcium is necessary for myocyte contraction. The calcium enters the cell by specific voltage-activated channels. Several subtypes of calcium channel exist, but in cardiac and smooth muscle, the L-type predominates. Nifedipine and other dihydropyridines bind to one type of receptor; verapamil and diltiazem bind to other related but not identical sites. When bound, the drugs reduce the frequency of opening of the calcium channels, resulting in a decrease in transmembrane calcium flux. The effect in the smooth muscle of the vascular wall is relaxation and resulting decrease in resting tone. In the heart, there is a decrease in cardiac muscle contractility and also a slowing of sinus node pacemaker rate and a decrease in conduction velocity at the AV node. The degree to which the heart or peripheral circulation is affected varies with the different types of calcium channel blockers used.

Dihydropyridines

These act predominantly on the vasculature, with less effect on the heart. A reflex tachycardia may be seen in response to treatment with these drugs when short-acting preparations are used, and these may result in adverse cardiac events. Long-acting or sustained-release preparations are preferred.

Indications Hypertension, prophylaxis of angina.

Contraindications Cardiogenic shock, advanced aortic stenosis, within 1 month of acute myocardial infarction, unstable angina, porphyria.

Cautions Poor cardiac reserve, hypotension, pregnancy, breast feeding, hepatic impairment.

Interactions Grapefruit juice increases concentrations; see product literature for further details of individual drugs.

Side effects Headache, flushing, dizziness, ankle edema, and rash.

Doses Nifedipine, sustained release: 30 to 60 mg daily. Amlodipine: 5 to 10 mg daily. Felodipine: 5 to 10 mg daily.

Verapamil

Indications Verapamil relaxes vascular smooth muscle and is negatively inotropic and negatively chronotropic. It has the greatest effect on the heart, being used for treatment of tachyarrhythmias in addition to hypertension and angina.

Contraindications Hypotension, bradycardia, second- or third-degree AV block, heart failure or impaired left ventricular function, and atrial flutter or fibrillation in those with Wolff-Parkinson-White syndrome.

Side effects Constipation, nausea, vomiting, fatigue, headache, flushing, and ankle edema.

Interactions With beta-blockers, there is a risk of hypotension, bradycardia and asystole; grapefruit juice also interacts.

Doses In hypertension, 240 to 480 mg daily in two to three divided doses.

Diltiazem

Indications Diltiazem is between verapamil and the dihydropyridines in its effects. It is a peripheral vasodilator useful in hypertension and angina. It is weakly negatively inotropic, less so than verapamil. Its antiarrhythmic effects are useful in treating supraventricular tachyarrhythmias.

Contraindications Bradycardia, left ventricular failure, sick sinus syndrome, second- or third-degree AV block, pregnancy, and lactation.

Side effects Bradycardia, heart block, hypotension, ankle edema.

Interactions With beta blockers, there is a risk of severe bradycardia and AV block.

Doses 60 to 120 mg tid. Note that many different sustained-release preparations of diltiazem are available, and prescribers should specify which brand is to be dispensed.

Centrally acting antihypertensive drugs

These agents reduce sympathetic vasomotor tone by reducing sympathetic drive from the rostral ventrolateral medulla. Clonidine exerts its effect by stimulating central alpha-adrenergic receptors (predominantly α_2) in this site. Clonine also binds to a nonadrenoreceptor, the imidazoline receptor, which also produces a reduction in blood pressure. Methyldopa stimulates the central alpha-adrenergic receptors but does not act at the imidazoline receptor sites. Moxonidine is a novel drug that is a selective imidazoline receptor agonist. Side effects of these drugs include dry mouth, nausea, and sedation and are centrally mediated. There is development of a positive Coombs test in 10 to 20% of patients treated with methyldopa, which may make crossmatching for blood transfusion difficult. Withdrawal of clonidine can provoke a life-threatening hypertensive crisis. These agents may be used when more conventional drugs such as diuretics and beta blockers are not appropriate. Methyldopa is a safe choice in pregnant patients.

Doses Methyldopa: 250 mg bid to tid, increased at intervals of 2 or more days to maximum total daily dose of 3 g. In the elderly, a starting dose of 125 mg and a total daily dose of 2 g are appropriate. Clonidine: 50 to 100 μg tid, increased if necessary every second or third day to a maximum of 1.2 mg daily. Moxonidine: 200 μg daily, increased if required after 3 weeks to 400 μg daily (maximum daily dose 600 mg)

LIPID-LOWERING THERAPY

Renal disease can cause many abnormalities of lipid metabolism with elevated plasma cholesterol and triglyceride levels. Much of the excess mortality in the chronic renal failure population is due to ischemic heart disease. The severity of hypercholesterolemia often reflects the degree of proteinuria. Hypertriglyceridemia is a feature of declining glomerular filtration rate. Both chronic renal failure and proteinuria are associated with reduced high-density-lipoprotein (HDL) cholesterol.

Anion exchange resins

Cholestyramine and cholestipol

Mechanism of action These drugs bind bile acids in the intestinal lumen and prevent their reabsorption. Bile acids are metabolites of cholesterol and normally are reabsorbed from the gut with about 95% efficiency. Their removal from the enterohepatic circulation results in the synthesis of more bile acids from cholesterol in the liver. There is upregulation of hepatic low-density lipoprotein (LDL) receptors and hence increased removal of circulating LDL from plasma. In patients without functioning LDL receptors, e.g., as in homozygous familial hypercholesterolemia, they will be ineffective.

Indications Hyperlipidemias, especially type IIa, where diet has not been effective. They are also of use in primary biliary cirrhosis to treat pruritus associated with biliary obstruction.

Contraindications They are ineffective in complete biliary obstruction.

Side effects Nausea, vomiting, gastrointestinal discomfort, constipation, diarrhea, hyperchloremic acidosis with prolonged use, interference with absorption of fat-soluble vitamins (A, D, K); increased bleeding tendency has been reported due to vitamin K deficiency. Many patients find the side effects troublesome, and the medicine difficult to take; therefore, long-term compliance may be poor.

Fibrates

Mechanism of action The precise mode of action of this class of drug remains unclear. They have many effects on serum lipids. The most marked effect is reduction in triglyceride-rich lipoproteins such as very low-density lipoprotein. There is also a reduction in LDL cholesterol and a rise in HDL cholesterol. All the agents in this class can cause a myositis syndrome. Patients with renal impairment seem to be particularly at risk, and so these drugs should be prescribed with care in this population. In mild to moderate renal impairment, the dose should be reduced by half, and in severe renal impairment, these agents should be avoided completely. Myositis is also more common when fibrates are prescribed in conjunction with a statin.

Indications Hyperlipidemia, especially hypertriglyceridemia.

Contraindications Severe renal or hepatic dysfunction, gallbladder disease, pregnancy, breast-feeding. Dose reductions are necessary in children.

Doses Bezafibrate: 200 mg tid with food, or sustained-release preparation, 400 mg at night. Ciprofibrate: 100 mg daily. Clofibrate: in patients with 50 to 65 kg of body weight, 1.5 g daily in two to three divided doses. In patients with over 65 kg of body weight, 2 g daily in divided doses. Fenofibrate: 67 mg two to three times daily or 200 mg once daily. Gemfibrozil: 0.9 to 1.2 g daily in two divided doses.

HMG-CoA reductase inhibitors (statins)

These drugs competitively inhibit 3-hydroxy-3-methylgltaryl-coenzyme A (HMG-CoA) reductase. This enzyme is a rate-limiting step in cholesterol synthesis, especially in the liver. Statins are principally effective in lowering LDL cholesterol, although atorvastatin also has appreciable effects on plasma triglyceride levels. They are generally well tolerated in those with renal impairment, although there is interaction with cyclosporine. Experimental work suggests that statins may have additional benefits other than their effects on lipids and that they may cause regression of mesangial cell proliferation.

Indication Hypercholesterolemia.

Contraindications Active liver disease, pregnancy, and lactation.

Cautions Care must be taken in patients with hepatic disease or high alcohol intake. In all patients, liver function tests should be performed before commencing therapy, again after 3 months of treatment, and then at intervals of 6 months for a year. Treatment should be discontinued if serum transaminases rise to and persist at three times the upper limit of normal. There is potential for drug interaction in patients being treated with cyclosporine, and increased levels of statin may result in risk of muscle toxicity.

Doses Simvastatin: initially 10 mg at night, increasing to 40 mg maximum if required. Pravaststin: 10 to 40 mg at night. Atorvastatin: usually 10 to 40 mg daily; may be increased to 80 mg if required. Fluvastatin: 20 to 40 mg at night. Cerivastatin: 100 to 300 μg at night.

Other lipid-lowering drugs

These have largely been superseded by the introduction of statins. Ispaghula husk is a form of soluble fiber that may be used as an adjunct to diet in patients with mild hypercholesterolemia. Nicotinic acid derivatives are suitable for type IIa, IIb, and IV hyperlipidemias. Use is limited by side effects of flushing, headache, and urticaria.

DRUGS USED IN RENAL OSTEODYSTROPHY

Pathophysiology Vitamin D is necessary for absorption of dietary calcium from the gastrointestinal tract. Vitamin D is a cholesterol-derived steroid hormone and as such acts within the target cell nucleus to stimulate mRNA production. The most important of the naturally occurring vitamin D compounds, vitamin D3 (cholecalciferol) is synthesized in the skin.

Other similar compounds are obtained from the diet. Before they become biologically active, they must undergo hydroxylation first in the liver and then in the kidney, the active form being 1,25-dihydroxycholecalciferol. In severe chronic renal disease, this final step in activation is impaired. The regulation of vitamin D metabolism is complex. In renal disease, loss of the active form results in hypocalcemia. This stimulates increased parathyroid hormone (secondary hyperparathyroidism) in an attempt to raise calcium levels, and this, in turn, causes phosphate retention. The resulting bone disease is a spectrum involving osteomalacia, adynamic bone disease, and osteitis fibrosa.

In an attempt to rectify these metabolic abnormalities, calcium carbonate may be given. In addition to supplying calcium, this acts as a phosphate binder, reducing the availability of dietary phosphate. Aluminum-containing phosphate binders are no longer favored because of the occurrence of cognitive impairment with these agents.

Biologically active vitamin D preparations should be used. These include calcitriol (1,25-dihydroxycholecalciferol) and alfacalcidol (1α-hydroxycholecalciferol). The dose is adjusted to correct plasma calcium levels and to suppress parathyroid hormone levels.

Cautions Careful monitoring of plasma calcium, initially on a weekly basis, is important when using these drugs, and they must be discontinued if hypercalcemia occurs.

Side effects Symptoms of overdosage may be anorexia, nausea, vomiting, weight loss, and polyuria.

Doses In adults, the dose of alfacalcidol is initially 1 μg daily po or slow intravenous injection, maintenance dose being 0.25 to 1 μg daily. With calcitriol, the dosage regime depends on the commercial preparation.

IMMUNOSUPPRESSANTS

These drugs are used in both immune-mediated renal disease such as the vasculitides and in the prevention of rejection of renal transplants. Readers are advised to consult the relevant chapters regarding management of specific conditions because the dosing regimes will vary greatly.

Corticosteroids

Examples listed in order of decreasing anti-inflammatory effect: dexamethazone, methylprednisolone, prednisolone, hydrocortisone, cortisone.

Mechanism of action These drugs all have a combination of glucocorticoid and mineralocorticoid effects. For example, the mineralocorticoid effects of cortisone or hydrocortisone are too great for their long-term use as immunosuppressive agents. The immunosuppressive action of corticosteroids is mediated by inhibition of production of inflammatory mediators such as platelet-activating factor, leukotrienes, prostaglandins, histamine, and bradykinin. Glucocorticoids are toxic to certain T-cell subsets and may interfere with the cell cycle of activated lymphoid cells. They reduce chemotaxis and bactericidal properties of neutrophils and monocytes. Cellular immunity is affected to a greater extent than humoral immunity. An increase in neutrophil count is often seen on the blood count with an accompanying reduction in circulating lymphocytes.

Indications Corticosteroids are used to treat many immune-mediated renal diseases, and readers are advised to consult the appropriate chapters regarding management. They are also a cornerstone in the prevention of rejection of renal transplant.

Contraindications Systemic infection unless appropriate therapy is instituted.

Side effects Mineralocorticoid effects: hypertension, sodium and water retention, and hypokalemia. Glucocorticoid effects: diabetes, osteoporosis, avascular necrosis of the femoral head in high-dose administration, mental disturbances including euphoria and paranoid ideation (steroid psychosis), muscle wasting, peptic ulceration is a weak association. Prolonged high doses may cause Cushing's syndrome. In children, growth suppression may occur, and if corticosteroids are given during pregnancy, adrenal development of the child may be affected. There is increased susceptibility to infection, which may be of increased severity and atypical presentation. Patients who have not had chickenpox and who are receiving steroids are at high risk of severe varicella-zoster infection, which may result in pneumonia, hepatitis, and disseminated intravascular coagulation. Nonimmune patients require passive immunization with varicella-zoster immunoglobulin if exposed to chickenpox during or within 3 months of receiving steroids. The corticosteroids should not be discontinued. Adrenal suppression will occur with prolonged therapy, and abrupt withdrawal in this setting may precipitate an addisonian crisis that could be fatal.

Interactions Antagonism of effect of diuretics and antihypertensive agents; cyclosporine levels increased with high-dose methylprednisolone.

Cyclosporine

Mechanism of action Cyclosporine has selective inhibitory effects on T-lymphocyte function with suppression of the early cellular response to antigenic stimuli. It is a cyclic peptide derived from the fungus *Tolypocladium inflatum Gams*. The molecule binds to cyclophilin, and this drug-receptor complex inhibits the enzyme calcineurin, which is necessary for T-cell activation. There is decreased production of interleukin 2 (IL-2), IL-3, and interferon-γ. Introduced in 1983, there were initial problems with variable absorption, but the development of a microemulsion formulation has resulted in improved and more predictable bioavailability. Cyclosporine has little adverse effect on bone marrow.

Indications Cyclosporine is used mainly in the prevention of rejection in organ transplantation; however, it is now also being used in the management of autoimmune disease such as rheumatoid arthritis and inflammatory bowel disease.

Cautions Cyclosporine may produce hypertension in 20 to 50% of recipients. An adverse effect on lipid profile is also seen. More worrying is the development of irreversible renal injury with tubular atrophy, interstitial fibrosis, and arteriolar changes. The minimum effective dose should be used. Hypertrichosis, gingival hypertrophy, and hepatic dysfunction are also observed.

Interactions An interaction with HMG-CoA reductase inhibitors will result in increased risk of myopathy with these drugs. Grapefruit juice will increase plasma cyclosporine concentrations.

Doses In organ transplantation, initially 10 to 15 mg/kg po 4 to 12 hours before transplantation and then 10 to 15 mg/kg daily for 1 to 2 weeks, reducing then to 2 to 6 mg/kg daily as a maintenance dose. Dose should be adjusted according to blood levels. If other immunosuppressive agents are being used, the dose should be reduced.

Tacrolimus

This drug is a macrolide antibiotic. It is not chemically related to cyclosporine, but its mechanism of action and effects on T-cell function are similar, as is its side-effect profile.

Doses In renal transplantation in adults, 150 to 300 mg/kg daily in two divided doses orally commencing within 24 hours of transplantation or 50 to 100 mg/kg by intravenous infusion over 24 hours. Maintenance dose is adjusted according to response.

Cytotoxic immunosuppressants

Cyclophosphamide

Mechanism of action This drug belongs to the nitrogen mustard class of alkylating agents and exerts its effects by alkylating DNA, especially in proliferating cells. B- and T-lymphocytes are both affected, although the effect on B cells is more pronounced. Hence there is greater suppression of humoral immunity. When cyclophosphamide is given in large doses synchronous with a new antigenic insult, specific tolerance to the antigen may result. Effects on T-cell-mediated immune responses are more variable.

Indications In small doses, cyclophosphamide is used for the treatment of autoimmune disorders such as Wegener's granulomatosis and systemic lupus erythematosus. In large doses, cyclophosphamide may be used in the treatment of hematologic malignancy and the prevention of rejection of solid-organ and bone marrow transplants.

Adverse effects Bone marrow suppression with pancytopenia. Peripheral blood count must be checked prior to commencing therapy and monitored during treatment. Fever in a neutropenic patient is an indication for urgent intravenous therapy with broad-spectrum antibiotics. All cytotoxic agents are teratogenic, and contraceptive precautions must be observed in women of childbearing age. Hemorrhagic cystitis is due to the effects of acrolein, a urinary metabolite of cyclophosphamide, on the bladder. A high fluid intake may help to prevent this. If high-dose intravenous cyclophosphamide is to be given, then intravenous MESNA, a sulfhydryl compound that reacts with acrolein in the bladder, may prevent this rare but serious complication.

Doses Protocols for management of specific conditions should be consulted.

Mechanism of action This drug is a derivative of mercaptopurine and, like cyclophosphamide, is a cytotoxic immunosuppressant. It acts as an antimetabolite or structural analogue, disrupting purine synthesis and therefore DNA replication. Its immunosuppressive effects are due to interference with lymphocyte proliferation in response to antigenic stimuli.

Indications Azothiaprine has been a key component of antirejection therapy in organ transplantation for many years. It is also used as therapy for autoimmune conditions such as rheumatoid arthritis when corticosteroid therapy alone has been ineffective or as a "steroid-sparing agent" in an attempt to reduce steroid dose.

Adverse effects Bone marrow suppression. Patients should be warned to report any unexpected bleeding, bruising, or infection. Blood counts should be carried out weekly during the initial 2 months of therapy and then every 3 months during the course of therapy. Other adverse effects include hypersensitivity reactions, cholestatic jaundice, hepatic dysfunction, and interstitial nephritis.

Interactions Azothioprine is metabolized to mercaptopurine, which is in turn metabolized by the enzyme xanthine oxidase. This enzyme is inhibited by allopurinol, and therefore, coadministration of allopurinol with azothioprine or mercaptopurine will result in increased effects and potential for toxicity.

Doses Suppression of transplant rejection: initially 5 mg/kg daily orally or intravenously, reducing to a maintenance dose of 1 to 4 mg/kg daily. Immunologic disease: 3 mg/kg daily, reducing to a maintenance dose of 1 to 3 mg/kg daily. Withdraw if no response is seen within 3 months.

Mycophenolate mofetil

Mechanism of action This drug blocks the *de novo* synthesis of purine nucleotides – a pathway critical for lymphocytes. There is suppression of lymphocyte proliferation and of antibody production by B cells.

Indications Suppression of acute rejection of organ transplant.

Cautions As with the other cytotoxic immunosuppressants, marrow suppression may occur, and close monitoring of the blood count is required.

Doses Starting within 72 hours of transplantation, 1 g bid.

Antilymphocyte and antithymocyte antibodies

Antithymocyte globulin (polyclonal antilymphocyte antibodies) may be used to limit T-cell proliferation in order to prevent acute reject of renal allografts. The purified immunoglobulin is prepared from hyperimmune serum of sheep, horse, rabbit, or goat. It binds to the surface of circulating T-lymphocytes, producing lymphopenia. Since it is a foreign protein, it may produce chills, fever, serum sickness, nephritis, and occasionally, anaphylaxis. Specific monoclonal antibodies to prevent T-cell response are also used. Murine monoclonal antibody (Murmonoab, OKT3) has been raised against the CD3 glycoprotein on T-lymphocytes. When the antibody is bound to this site, it blocks the adjacent antigen-recognition complex, preventing the binding of circulating antigen and hence diminishing the immune response. The antibody also activates some T cells, causing release of cytokines, further limiting the immune response. The release of cytokines may cause adverse reactions ranging from flulike illness to life-threatening shock. The use of these agents should be restricted to specialist centers.

Basiliximab

Indications Prevention of acute rejection following allogeneic renal transplantation.

Contraindications Pregnancy, breast-feeding.

Side effects No specific effects reported.

Doses 20 mg by intravenous infusion 2 hours before transplantation and a further 20 mg 4 days after the operation.

Erythropoetin

Epoetin/EPO

Recombinant human erythropoetin (rHuEpo or epoetin) is produced in a mammalian cell expression system using recombinant DNA technology. Two different preparations are available, epoetin alpha and epoetin beta. The clinical efficacy of both preparations is similar. They are particularly suitable for treatment of anemia associated with chronic renal failure, where the normal synthesis of erythropetin in the peritubular cortex of the kidney is decreased. Erythropoetin is a glycosylated protein that stimulates proliferation and differentiation of red cell precursors in the bone marrow. An increase in reticulocyte count is usually seen within 10 days of starting treatment and an increase in hemoglobin concentration in 2 to 6 weeks. Response rate should be aiming for an increase in hemoglobin concentration 2 g/100 ml per month, with a target hemoglobin level of 10 to 12 g/100 ml in adults.

Indications Anemia associated with chronic renal failure.

Cautions Other factors contributing to the anemia such as

iron, vitamin B_{12}, or folate deficiency should be screened for and corrected before therapy. Parenteral iron supplements may be required. Control of blood pressure before commencing therapy is necessary, and uncontrolled hypertension is a contraindication.

Side effects A dose-dependent rise in blood pressure may be observed. If hypertension develops during epoetin therapy, the treatment must be discontinued until the blood pressure is controlled. Occasionally, hypertensive crisis with encephalopathy and seizures may occur-this may be heralded by a sudden stabbing migraine – like headache. A rapid rise in hematocrit may occur. Thrombocytosis and thrombotic complications may arise, including thrombosis of arteriovenous fistulas. Other reported complications include hyperkalemia, hyperphosphatemia, convulsions, and anaphylaxis.

Doses Many protocols currently are in use, and local guidelines should be consulted. Erythropoetin may be administered intravenously or subcutaneously. The usual starting dose for adults is around 50 to 100 units per kilogram three times weekly. The maintenance dose is determined by response.

Suggested readings

DE MATTOS AM, OLYAEI AJ, BENNETT WM. Pharmacology of immunosuppressive medications used in renal diseases and transplantation. Am J Kidney Dis 1996;28:631-67.

DUNN CJ, MARKHAM A. Epoetin beta: a review of its pharmacological properties and clinical use in the management of anemia associated with chronic renal failure Drugs 1996;51:299-318.

FIRST MR. Clinical application of immunosuppressive agents in renal transplantation. Surg Clin North Am 1998;78:61-76.

HANSSON L, ZANCHETTI A, CARRUTHERS SG, et al. Effects of intensive blood pressure lowering and low-dose aspirin in patients with hypertension: principal results of the Hypertension Optimal Treatment (HOT) randomised trial. Lancet 1998;351:1755-62.

HARDMAN JG, LIMBARD LE, MOLINOFF PB, et al, eds. Goodman & Gilman's The pharmacological basis of therapeutics, 9th ed. New York: McGraw-Hill, 1996.

HRUSKA KA. Renal osteodystrophy. Baillières Clin Endocrinol Metab 1997;11:165-94.

KATZUNG BG ed. Basic and clinical pharmacology. 7th ed. Stamford, CT: Appleton & Lange, 1998.

LANGFORD CA, KLIPPEL JH, BALOW JE, et al. Use of cytotoxic agents and cyclosporin in the treatment of autoimmune disease: 1. Rheumatologic and renal disease. Ann Intern Med 1998;128:1021-8.

SALVETTI A, MATTEI P, SUDANO I. Renal protection and antihypertensive drugs. Drugs 1999; 57:665-93.

U.K. PROSPECTIVE DIABETES STUDY GROUP. Tight blood pressure control and risk of macrovascular and microvascular complications in type 2 diabetes: UKPDS 38. Br Med J 1998; 317:703-13.

U.K. PROSPECTIVE DIABETES STUDY GROUP. Efficacy of atenolol and captopril in reducing risk of macrovascular and microvascular complications in type 2 diabetes: UKPDS 39. Br Med J 1998;317:713-20.

WHEELER DC. Statins and the kidney. Curr Opin Nephrol Hypertens 1998;7:579-84.

Appendix

APPENDIX

Use of drugs in patients with renal function impairment: dose adjustment

Gerjan Navis

INTRODUCTION: HOW TO USE THESE TABLES

Principles underlying dose adjustment in renal functional impairment are discussed in Chapter 39. Dose adjustment may be needed because of altered pharmacokinetics or an altered drug sensitivity despite unchanged kinetics. The tables herein provide a guideline for maintenance doses in relation to the severity of renal functional impairment and should be considered a global indication of a typical dosing regimen. However, it is important to realize that drug response may display considerable interindividual differences both for therapeutic efficacy and for unwanted side effects. Thus drug response should be monitored closely in renal patients, and treatment should be adjusted on an individual basis if necessary. Adjustment may be achieved by dose reduction and/or increasing dosing interval; in most cases below, one preferred method of adjustment is indicated. For an individual dosing regimen the two approaches may be combined.

Abbreviations

D = dose-reduction method; the percentage of the dose for patients with normal renal function is given.
I = interval extension method; recommended dosing interval is given.
NA = no sufficient data available.

Table A.1 Antimicrobial agents

Drug	Method	Adjustment in renal functional impairment			Remarks
		GFR < 10 ml/min	10-50 ml/min	> 50 ml/min	
ANTIBACTERIAL DRUGS					For urinary tract infections (see Chap. 39), urinary drug levels determine therapeutic efficacy
Aminoglycosides					All aminoglycosides are nephrotoxic and ototoxic. Loop diuretics may potentiate ototoxicity. Monitoring of drug levels is recommended
Amikacin	D and I	25% per 24-48 h	30-70% per 12 h	70-100% per 8-12 h	
Gentamycin	D and I	25% per 24-48 h	30-70% per 12 h	70-100% per 8-12 h	
Netilmycin	D and I	25% per 24-48 h	30-70% per 12 h	70-100% per 8-12 h	
Tobramycin	D and I	25% per 24-48 h	30-70% per 12 h	70-100% per 8-12 h	
Cephalosporin antibiotics					
Cefaclor	D	50%	50%	100%	
Cefalexin	I	8-12 h	6 h	6 h	Usual dose required for urinary tract infection
Cefamandole	I	12 h	6-8 h	4-8 h	
Cefotaxim	I	24 h	8-12 h	6 h	Active metabolite
Cefotetan	D	25%	50%	100%	
Cefoxitin	I	24-48 h	8-12 h	6-8 h	
Ceftazidime	I	48-72 h	24-48 h	8-12 h	
Ceftriaxone	D	100%	100%	100%	
Cefuroxime	I	24 h	8-12 h	8 h	
Cephalotin	I	12 h	6-8 h	6 h	
Macrolides					
Clindamycin	–	100%	100%	100%	
Erythromycin	D	50-75%	100%	100%	
Lincomycin	I	12-24 h	6-12 h	6 h	
Penicillins					High doses may induce seizures in renal patients. High doses may induce coagulopathy. Most penicillins provide a signifcant sodium or potassium load. Penicillins may inactivate concurrently administered aminoglycosides
Amoxicillin	I	12 h	8-12 h	8 h	Usual dose for urinary tract infection in renal patients
Ampicillin	I	12 h	6-12 h	6 h	Usual dose for urinary tract infection in renal patients
Benzathine-benzylpenicillin	–	100%	100%	100%	
Benzylpenicillin	D	25-50%	75%	100%	Upper dose limit in patients with renal function impairment: 4-6: MU/day
Carbenicillin	I	24-48 h	12-24 h	8-12 h	May induce hypokalemic alkalosis
Cloxacillin	–	100%	100%	100%	
Dicloxacillin	–	100%	100%	100%	

(*continued*)

Table A.1 Continued

Drug	Method	Adjustment in renal functional impairment GFR < 10 ml/min	10-50 ml/min	> 50 ml/min	Remarks
Flucloxacillin	D	50% 100%	100%		
Methicillin	D	8-12 h 6-8 h	4-6 h		
Mezlocillin	I	8 h	6-8 h	4-6 h	
Nafcillin	D	100%	100%	100%	Reduce dose in combined liver and renal function impairment
Oxacillin	D	100%	100%	100%	
Piperacillin	I	8 h	6-8 h	4-6 h	
Procaine	–				
Benzylpenicillin	–	100%	100%	100%	
Ticarcillin	D and I	30% per 12 h	30-60% per 8 h	60-100% per 4 h	May induce hypokalemic alkalosis; inactivates aminoglycosides
Quinolones					Absorption impaired by
antacids/phosphate binders					
Ciprofloxacin	D	33%	50%	100%	
Norfloxacin	I	Avoid	12-24 h	12 h	
Ofloxacin	D	25-50%	50%	100%	
Tetracyclin antibiotics					In renal function impair ment, tetracyclines potentiate acidosis and uremia. Avoid in renal patients if other option is available
Doxycycline	–	100%	100%	100%	Drug of choice of this group for renal patients if a tetracycline is required. Dosing interval 24 h
Minocycline	–	100%	100%	100%	
Tetracycline	I	Avoid	12-24 h	6-8 h	
Tuberculostatics					
Ethambutol	I	48 h	24-36 h	24 h	May induce peripheral neuropathy and ocular toxicity
Isoniazid	D	50%	75-100%	100%	
p-Aminosalicylic-acid	I	Avoid	12 h	8 h	Worsens acidosis; active metabolites acid
Pyrazinamide	I	Avoid	Avoid	24 h	Impairs uric acid excretion; can elicit gout
Rifampicin	D	50	50-100%	100%	Active metabolites accumulate; tubulotoxic
Streptomycin	I	96-72 h	24-72 h	24 h	
Miscellaneous					Sulfonamides have group toxicity, accumulation of acetylated metabolites (nausea, skin reactions), and crystalluria
Aztreonam	D	25%	50-75%	100%	
Chloramphenicol	–	100%	100%	100%	Adjust dose in combined liver and renal dysfunction
Clavulanic acid	D	75-50%	100%	100%	
Clindamycin	–	100%	100%	100%	
Imipenem	D	25%	50%	100%	
Imipenem +cilastatin	D	Avoid	50%	100%	Combination of imipenem and cilastatin is not rational in renal functional impairment
Moxalactam	I	24-48 h	12-24 h	8 h	May induce coagulopathy

(*continued*)

Table A.1 Continued

Drug	Method	Adjustment in renal functional impairment			Remarks
		GFR < 10 ml/min	10-50 ml/min	> 50 ml/min	
Nalidixic acid	–	Avoid	Avoid	100%	Not effective in severe renal function impairment; accumulation of toxic metabolites
Nitrofurantoin	–	Avoid	Avoid	100%	Not effective in renal function impairment; accumulation of metabolites; may induce neuropathy
Trimethoprim	I	24 h	18 h	8-12 h	
Sulfamethoxazole+trimethoprim	D or I	50% or 24 h	100% or 12-24 h	100% or 12 h	
Sulfisoxazole	I	12-24 h	8-12 h	6 h	Use normal dose for urinary tract infection
Vancomycin	I	7-10 days	2-7 days	12-24 h	Ototoxic at high serum levels
ANTIFUNGAL DRUGS					
Amphotericin B	–	100%	100%	100%	Nephrotoxic: tubular acidosis, hypokalemia, diabetes insipidus. Monitor plasma levels, renal function, and electrolytes
Flucytosine	I	48-24 h	12-24 h	6-8 h	Susceptibility to bone marrow toxicity in renal patients
Griseofulvin	–	100%	100%	100%	
Ketoconazole	–	100%	100%	100%	
Miconazole	–	100%	100%	100%	
Nystatin	–	100%	100%	100%	
ANTIHELMINTHIC DRUGS					
Mebendazole	–	100%	100%	100%	
Praziquantel	–	100%	100%	100%	
Thiabendazol	D	Avoid	50-100%	100%	
ANTIPROTOZOAL DRUGS					
Chloroquine	–	100%	100%	100%	
Mefloquine	–	100%	100%	100%	
Metronidazole	D	50%	100%	100%	
Pentamidine	I	48 h	24-36 h	24 h	
Proguanil	D	50%	100%	100%	
Quinine	I	24 h	8-12 h	8 h	Tissue accumulation
Pyrimethamine	–	100%	100%	100%	Tissue accumulation
ANTIVIRAL DRUGS					
Acyclovir	D and I	50% per 24 h	100% per 12-24 h	100% per 8-12 h	Neurotoxic in renal patients; nephrotoxic at rapid iv administration
Amantadine	I	168 h	48-72 h	12-24 h	
Foscarnet	D	25%	50%	75%	Nephrotoxic; may induce seizures
Ganciclovir	I	48-96 h	24 h	8-12 h	

Table A.2 Cardiovascular drugs

Drug	Method	Adjustment in renal functional impairment			Remarks
		GFR < 10 ml/min	10-50 ml/min	> 50 ml/min	
ANTIANGINAL DRUGS					
Glyceryl trinitrate	–	100%	100%	100%	
Isosorbide dinitrate	–	100%	100%	100%	
ANTIARRYTHMICS					Drug level monitoring is recommended
Amiodarone	–	100%	100%	100%	Increases plasma digoxin levels
Bretylium	D	Avoid	25-50%	100%	
Disopyramide	I	24-48 h	12-24 h	6-8 h	May induce urinary retention
Flecainide	D	75%	100%	100%	Accumulation of metabolites in CRF
Lidocaine	–	100%	100%	100%	Metabolites may accumulate, depending on hepatic blood flow
Mexiletine	–	100%	100%	100%	
Procainamide	I	12-24 h	6-12 h	3-4 h	Active metabolite accumulates
Acetyl-procainamide	D and I	25% per 12 h	50% per 8-12 h	100% per 6-8 h	
Quinidine	D	75%	100%	100%	Active metabolite
Tocainide	D	50%	100%	100%	
ANTIHYPERTENSIVES					Use blood pressure response to guide dosing; hypotension should prompt dose reduction (see also Chap. 39)
ACE inhibitors					ACE inhibitors may induce reversible GFR reduction in renal patients, especially during volume depletion, and may exacerbate hyperkalemia. Volume depletion potentiates (and volume overload blunts) the pharmacologic effects of ACE inhibitors
Captopril	D and I	50% per 24 h	75% per 12 h	100%	
Enalapril	D	50%	75-100%	100%	
Fosinopril	–	100%	100%	100%	Avoid in combined liver and renal functional impairment
Lisinopril	D	25-50%	50-75%	100%	
Ramipril	D	25-50%	50-75%	100%	
AT1 receptor blockers					Pharmacologic effects and adverse effects the same as ACE inhibitors. Main route of excretion hepatic. Hyperkalemia or hypotension should prompt dose reduction in renal failure, even in the absence of drug accumulation. Data on severe renal functional impairment are still limited
Candesartan	D	NA	25-50%	100%	
Irbesartan	D	50%	100%	100%	

(*continued*)

Table A.2 Continued

Drug	Method	Adjustment in renal functional impairment			Remarks
		GFR < 10 ml/min	10-50 ml/min	> 50 ml/min	
Losartan	D	50%	100%	100%	Active metabolite; combined hepatic/renal elimination
Valsartan	–	NA	100%	100%	
Beta blockers					
Acebutolol	D	30-50%	50%	100%	Accumulation of active metabolite in renal functional impairment
Atenolol	D	25%	50%	100%	Accumulation in renal functional impairment
Carvedilol	D	75%	100%	100%	
Labetolol	–	100%	100%	100%	
Metoprolol	–	100%	100%	100%	
Nadolol	D	25%	50%	100%	Accumulation in renal functional impairment
Pindolol	–	100%	100%	100%	
Propranolol	–	100%	100%	100%	Accumulation of active metabolite in renal functional impairment
Sotalol	D	15-30%	30%	100%	
Timolol	–	100%	100%	100%	
Calcium channel blockers					Calcium channel blockers can induce sodium retention and edema
Amlodipine	–	100%	100%	100%	
Diltiazem	–	100%	100%	100%	
Isradipine	–	100%	100%	100%	
Nicardipine	–	100%	100%	100%	
Nifedipine	–	100%	100%	100%	
Nitrendipine	–	100%	100%	100%	
Verapamil	–	100%	100%	100%	
Miscellaneous					
Clonidine	–	100%	100%	100%	Rebound hypertension on abrupt withdrawal; may give excessive sedation
Doxazosin	–	100%	100%	100%	Renal patients may be particularly susceptible to hypotensive action
Hydralazine	I	12 h	8 h	8 h	
Methyldopa	I	12-24 h	8-12 h	8 h	Accumulation of active metabolites in renal functional impairment
Minoxidil	–	100%	100%	100%	Sodium retention
Monoxidine	D	Avoid	50-75%	100%	
Prasozin	–	100%	100%	100%	Renal patients may be particularly susceptible to hypotensive action
Reserpine	–	100%	100%	100%	May cause excessive sedation in renal patients
Terasozin	–	100%	100%	100%	
CARDIAC GLYCOSIDES					Narrow therapeutic window. Toxicity potentiated by hypokalemia and hypomagnesemia
Digoxin	D and I	10-25% per 48 h	25-75% per 24 h	100%	Reduce loading dose 10-25% in renal patients when volume depleted (see Chap. 39)
Digitoxin	–	100%	100%	100%	

Table A.3 Diuretics

Drug	Method	Adjustment in renal functional impairment			Remarks
		GFR < 10 ml/min	10-50 ml/min	> 50 ml/min	
Diuretics					Avoid potassium-sparing diuretics in renal functional impairment. Thiazide monotherapy is ineffective in moderate to severe renal functional impairment (GFR < 30 ml/min). Higher than usual doses of loop diuretics can circumvent therapy resistance in moderate to severe renal functional impairment
Acetazolamide	I	Avoid	12 h	6-12 h	May potentiate acidosis and urolithiasis. Ineffective when GFR below 30 ml/min
Amiloride	D	Avoid	50%	100%	Exacerbates hyperkalemia and acidosis in renal functional impairment
Bumetanide	–	100%	100%	100%	Higher than usual dose may be useful renal functional impairment
Chlorthalidone	–	Avoid	24 h	24 h	Monotherapy ineffective when GFR below 30 ml/min
Ethacrynic acid	I	Avoid	6 h	6 h	Ototoxic in high doses, in particular when combined with aminoglycosides
Furosemide	–	100%	100%	100%	Higher than usual dose may be useful in renal functional impairment
Hydrochlorothiazide		Avoid	100%	100%	Monotherapy ineffective when GFR below 30 ml/min
Indapamide	–	100%	100%	100%	
Metolazone	–	100%	100%	100%	Monotherapy ineffective when GFR below 30 ml/min
Spironolactone	I	Avoid	12-24 h	8 h	Active metabolite may exacerbate hyperkalemia and metabolic acidosis
Triamterene	D	Avoid	100%	8 h	May exacerbate hyperkalemia in renal function impairment

Table A.4 Drugs used in neurology and psychiatry

Drug	Method	Adjustment in renal functional impairment			Remarks
		GFR < 10 ml/min	10-50 ml/min	> 50 ml/min	
ANTIDEPRESSANT AGENTS					Renal patients may have enhanced susceptibility to neurologic side effects
Tricyclic antidepressants					Anticholinergic action may elicit urinary retention, excessive sedation
Amitryptiline	–	100%	100%	100%	
Desipramine	–	100%	100%	100%	
Doxepin	–	100%	100%	100%	
Imipramine	–	100%	100%	100%	
Nortryptiline	–	100%	100%	100%	
Protryptiline	–	100%	100%	100%	
MISCELLANEOUS					
Fluoxetine	–	100%	100%	100%	
Maprotiline	D	50-75%	100%	100%	
Anticonvulsants					
Carbamazepine	D	75%	100%	100%	Active metabolites may induce inappropriate ADH secretion
Ethosuximide	D	50%	75-100%	100%	
Phenytoin	–	100%	100%	100%	V_d increased and protein binding decreased in moderate to severe renal functional impairment; monitoring of free drug level recommended
Primidone	I	12-24 h	8-12 h	8 h	May induce excessive sedation
Valproic acid	–	100%	100%	100%	
Antipsychotics					
Chlorpromazine	–	100%	100%	100%	Excessive sedation
Haloperidol	–	100%	100%	100%	Excessive sedation, hypotension
Antiparkinson agents					
Bromocriptine	–	100%	100%	100%	
Levodopa	–	100%	100%	100%	Active metabolites
Carbidopa	–	100%	100%	100%	
Trihexphenidyl	–	100%	100%	100%	May induce urinary retention
Barbiturates					
Phenobarbital	D and I	50% per 12 h	100% per 8-12 h	100%	
Secobarbital	–	100%	100%	100%	
Benzodiazepines					May cause excessive sedation in renal patients
Alprazolam	–	100%	100%	100%	
Chlordiazepoxide	D	50%	100%	100%	Active metabolites accumulate
Diazepam	–	100%	100%	100%	Active metabolite accumulates
Flurazepam	–	100%	100%	100%	Active metabolite accumulates
Lorazepam	–	100%	100%	100%	
Oxazepam	–	100%	100%	100%	Metabolite accumulates
Temazepam	–	100%	100%	100%	
Miscellaneous					
Chloral hydrate	–	Avoid	Avoid	100%	
Lithium	D	25-50%	50-75%	100%	Nephrotoxic: nephrogenic diabetes insipidus; interstitial fibrosis on prolonged use; volume depletion (diuretics!) may elicit lithium accumulation/toxicity
Meprobamate	D and I	50% per 12 h	8-12 h	6 h	

Table A.5 Analgesics, antipyretics, and anti-inflammatory drugs

Drug	Method	Adjustment in renal functional impairment			Remarks
		GFR < 10 ml/min	10-50 ml/min	> 50 ml/min	
Acetaminophen	I	8 h	6 h	4 h	Hepato- and nephrotoxic at overdose; metabolites may accumulate in renal functional impairment; drug of choice for simple analgesic use in renal patients
Aspirin	I	Avoid	4 h	4–6 h	May reduce renal function, especially during volume depletion; salicylate, nephrotoxic at overdose
OPIOIDS					Increased sensitivity to sedative effects in renal functional impairment
Codeine	D	50%	75%	100%	
Dextopropoxyphene	D	25%	100%	100%	Active metabolite accumulates
Methadone	D	50-75%	100%	100%	
Morphine	D	50%	75%	100%	Renal metabolism decreased in CRF
Pentazocine	D	50%	75%	100%	
Pethidine (meperidine)	D	50-75%	100%	100%	Active metabolite accumulates and may induce seizures, excessive sedation, and respiratory depression
Tramadol	D	50%	100%	100%	
NSAIDS					(See also Chap. 39) May reduce GFR, especially during volume depletion. May elicit hyperkalemia in renal functional impairment, especially when combined with ACE inhibitor or potassium-sparing diuretics (monitor creatinine and potassium concentrations). May blunt efficacy of diuretics
Diclofenac	–	100%	100%	100%	
Fenoprofen	–	100%	100%	100%	
Ibuprofen	–	100%	100%	100%	
Indomethacin	–	100%	100%	100%	
Mefenamic acid	–	100%	100%	100%	
Naproxen	–	100%	100%	100%	
Piroxicam	–	100%	100%	100%	
Sulindac	–	100%	100%	100%	
Tolectin	–	100%	100%	100%	

Table A.6 Gastrointestinal drugs

Drug	Method	Adjustment in renal functional impairment			Remarks
		GFR < 10 ml/min	10-50 ml/min	> 50 ml/min	
Antacids	–	(see text)			In renal functional impairment, absorption of the cation constituents of antacids, Ca, Mg, or Al, can lead to hypercalcemia, hypermagnesemia, or aluminium toxicity. Monitor serum levels
Bismuth compounds	–	Avoid	Avoid	See text	Bismuth is neuro- and nephrotoxic at high doses and with prolonged use. Elimination of absorbed bismuth is by the renal route. Duration of treatment should not exceed 2 months and should be followed by a bismuth-free period of at least 2 months
Cisapride	–	100%	100%	100%	
Metoclopramide	D	50%	75%	75-100%	
Misoprostol	–	100%	100%	100%	
Odansetron	–	100%	100%	100%	
Prochlorperazine	–	100%	100%	100%	
Sucralfate	D	Avoid	Avoid	50-100%	Contains aluminium, which may accumulate in CRF
Cimetidine	D	25-50%	50-75%	75-100%	
Famotidine	D	10%	25-50%	50-100%	
Ranitidine	D	25%	50%	50-100%	
Roxatidine	D	25%	50%	50-100%	
Omeprazole	–	100%	100%	100%	

Table A.7 Antidiabetics and lipid lowering agents

Drug	Method	Adjustment in renal functional impairment			Remarks
		GFR < 10 ml/min	10-50 ml/min	> 50 ml/min	
ANTIDIABETICS					
Acarbose	–	N A	100%	100%	
Sulfonylurea derivatives					Mainly hepatic metabolism to active or inactive metabolites with renal elimination. Active metabolites may elicit prolonged hypoglycemia in renal functional impairment
Acetohexamide	–	Avoid	Avoid	100%	May induce prolonged hypoglycemia in renal functional impairment
Chlorpropamide	–	Avoid	Avoid	100%	May induce prolonged hypoglycemia in renal functional impairment
Gliclazide	–	100%	100%	100%	
Glipizide	–	100%	100%	100%	
Glyburide (glibencamide)	–	Avoid	Avoid	100%	May induce prolonged hypoglycemia in renal functional impairment
Metformin	–	Avoid	Avoid	100%	May elicit lactic acidosis in renal functional impairment

(continued)

Table A.7 Continued

Drug	Method	Adjustment in renal functional impairment			Remarks
		GFR < 10 ml/min	10-50 ml/min	> 50 ml/min	
Tolazamide	–	Avoid	100%	100%	May induce prolonged hypoglycemia in renal functional impairment
Tolbutamide	–	100%	100%	100%	May impair renal water excretion
LIPID-LOWERING DRUGS					Multiple lipid abnormalities are present in renal patients, with mainly hypertriglyceridemia in renal functional impairment and mainly hypercholesterolemia in proteinuria. Improvement of lipid profile often requires combination therapy. The safety of combination regimens has been insufficiently tested in renal patients
Fibrates					Effective for the hypertriglyceridemia of chronic renal functional impairment. Associated with toxic myopathy; monitor muscle enzymes. Few safety data in renal patients
Bezafibrate	D	25%	50%	100%	
Clofibrate	I	Avoid	12-24 h	12 h	May cause hyperkalemia and toxic myopathy. Highly protein bound; reduce dose in hypoproteinemia (nephrosis). Impairs renal water excretion. Other fibrates are preferred
Fenofibrate	D	Avoid	25-50%	100%	
Gemfibrozil	–	100%	100%	100%	
Statins					Effective for hypercholes terolemia in renal functional impairment and proteinuria. Associated with toxic myopathy and liver toxicity. Monitor liver and muscle enzymes
Atorvastatin	–	100%	100%	100%	
Lovastatin	–	100%	100%	100%	
Pravastatin	–	100%	100%	100%	
Simvastatin	–	100%	100%	100%	
Miscellaneous					
Colestyramine	–	See text	100%	100%	May induce hyperchloremic acidosis in renal patients. Use with caution
Colestipol	–	See text	100%	100%	May induce hyperchloremic acidosis in renal patients. Use with caution
Nicotinic acid	D	25%	50%	100%	
Probucol	–	100%	100%	100%	

Table A.8 Bronchodilators, antihistaminics, and antiallergics

Drug	Method	Adjustment in renal functional impairment			Remarks
		GFR < 10 ml/min	10-50 ml/min	> 50 ml/min	
BRONCHODILATORS					
Albuterol (salbutamol)	D	50%	75%	100%	
Bitolterol	–	100%	100%	100%	
Ipratropium	–	100%	100%	100%	
Dyphylline	D	25%	50%	100%	
Terbutaline	D	Avoid	50%	100%	
Theophylline	–	100%	100%	100%	Great interindividual variability in kinetics
ANTIHISTAMINICS					May cause excessive sedation
Astemizole	–	100%	100%	100%	
Flunarizine	–	100%	100%	100%	
Orphenadrine	–	100%	100%	100%	
Promethazine	–	100%	100%	100%	
Terfenadrine	–	100%	100%	100%	

Table A.9 Drugs affecting coagulation

Drug	Method	Adjustment in renal functional impairment			Remarks
		GFR < 10 ml/min	10-50 ml/min	> 50 ml/min	
Dipyridamole	–	100%	100%	100%	
Heparin	–	100%	100%	100%	
Streptokinase	–	100%	100%	100%	
Sulfinpyrazon	D	Avoid	100%	100%	
Ticlopidine	–	100%	100%	100%	
Warfarin	–	100%	100%	100%	Adjust dose by titrating for effect on coagulation

Table A.10 Antineoplastic and immunosuppressive agents

Drug	Method	Adjustment in renal functional impairment			Remarks
		GFR < 10 ml/min	10-50 ml/min	> 50 ml/min	
Azathioprine	I	24-36 h	24 h	24 h	
Bleomycin	D	50%	100%	100%	Pulmonary toxicity enhanced in uremia
Cisplatin	D	50%	75%	100%	Nephrotoxic, renal Mg wasting
Cyclophosphamide	I	18-24 h	12 h	12 h	May induce hemorrhagic cystitis and bladder carcinoma
Cyclosporin A	–	100%	100%	100%	Nephrotoxic and hypertensinogenic; may induce hyperkalemia; multiple drug interactions
Doxorubicin	D	75%	100%	100%	Cardiotoxic; rarely, nephrotic syndrome
Fluorouracil	–	100%	100%	100%	
Melphalan	D	50-75%	100%	100%	
Methotrexate	D	Avoid	50%	100%	High doses are nephrotoxic by tubular precipitation of metabolite
Tamoxifen	–	100%	100%	100%	
Vinblastine	–	100%	100%	100%	May induce inappropriate ADH secretion

Table A.11 Miscellaneous agents

Drug	Method	Adjustment in renal functional impairment			Remarks
		GFR < 10 ml/min	10-50 ml/min	> 50 ml/min	
Allopurinol	D	25%	50%	100%	Accumulation of metabolites may elicit skin symptoms
Colchicine	D	25%	50%	100%	Enhanced risk for myopathy or neuropathy in renal patients
Naloxone	–	100%	100%	100%	
Pentoxifylline	I	24 h	8-12 h	8 h	
Probenicid	D	Avoid	Avoid	100%	
Penicillamine	D	Avoid	Avoid	100%	
Thyroxine	–	100%	100%	100%	
Methimazole	–	100%	100%	100%	
Propylthiouracil	–	100%	100%	100%	
Cortisone	–	100%	100%	100%	
Dexamethasone	–	100%	100%	100%	
Prednisone/ prednisolone	–	100%	100%	100%	

Suggested readings

In the preparation of the dose recommendations provided above we owe much to the following publications:

BENNETT WM. Guide to drug dosage in renal failure. In: Speight TM, Holford NHG, eds. Avery's Drug treatment. 4th ed. Aukland: Adis, 1997;1725-56.

MOLINOFF PB, RUDDON RW, eds. Goodman & Gilman's The pharmacological basis of therapeutics. 9th ed. New York: McGraw-Hill, 1996.

MATZKE GR, FRYE RF. Drug therapy individualization for patients with renal insufficiency. In: Dipiro JT, ed. Pharmacotherapy: a pathophysiological approach, 3d ed. Stanford: Appleton and Lange, 1997;1083-103.

MATZKE GR, FRYE RF. Drug administration in patients with renal insufficiency: minimizing renal and extrarenal toxicity. Drug Safety 1997;16:205-31.

SWAN SK, BENNETT WM. Use of drugs in patients with renal failure. In: Schrier RW, Gottschalk CW, eds. Diseases of the Kidney. Vol. 3. 6th ed. Boston: Little, Brown, 1977; 2965-3017.

INDEX

Page numbers followed by t and f indicate tables and figures respectively.

I

P

V